INTRODUCTION TO

JAVA™

PROGRAMMING

COMPREHENSIVE VERSION

Sixth Edition

Y. Daniel Liang

Armstrong Atlantic State University

PEARSON

Prentice
Hall

Upper Saddle River, NJ 07458

Library of Congress Cataloging-in-Publication Data

Liang, Y. Daniel.
  Introduction to Java programming: comprehensive version/Y. Daniel Liang.--6 th ed.
    p.   cm.
  Includes index.
  ISBN 0-13-222158-6
  QA76.73.J38L523 2004
  005.2¢762—dc22

                                                    2003065629

Vice President and Editorial Director, ECS: *Marcia J. Horton*
Executive Editor: *Tracy Dunkelberger*
Associate Editor: *Carole Snyder*
Editorial Assistant: *Christianna Lee*
Executive Managing Editor: *Vince O'Brien*
Managing Editor: *Camille Trentacoste*
Production Editor: *Craig Little*
Director of Creative Services: *Paul Belfanti*
Creative Director: *Juan Lopez*
Art Director and Cover Manager: *Maureen Eide*
Cover and Interior Designer: *Dina Curro*
Managing Editor, AV Management and Production: *Patricia Burns*
Art Editor: *Xiaohong Zhu*
Director, Image Resource Center: *Melinda Reo*
Manager, Rights and Permissions: *Zina Arabia*
Manager, Visual Research: *Beth Brenzel*
Manager, Cover Visual Research and Permissions: *Karen Sanatar*
Manufacturing Manager, ESM: *Alexis Heydt-Long*
Manufacturing Buyer: *Lisa McDowell*
Executive Marketing Manager: *Robin O'Brien*
Marketing Assistant: *Mack Patterson*
Photo Credits:
  Cover: The Pyramid of the Niches, El Tajin, Mexico. Photographer: Adalberto Rios Szalay/Sexto Sol. Courtesy Getty Images.
  Part Opener: The Goddess Chalchihuitlicue, found in the Valley of Mexico, 1300-1500 AD (stone), Aztec / Musée de l'Homme, Paris, France / Bridgeman Art Library.
  Chapter Opener: Mayan God Shel, Mexico. Photographer: Philip Coblentz. Courtesy Brand X Pictures.

© 2007, 2004, 2002, 2001 Pearson Education, Inc.
Pearson Prentice Hall
Pearson Education, Inc.
Upper Saddle River, NJ 07458

Pearson Prentice Hall™ is a trademark of Pearson Education, Inc.
All other tradmarks or product names are the property of their respective owners.

The author and publisher of this book have used their best efforts in preparing this book. These efforts include the development, research, and testing of the theories and programs to determine their effectiveness. The author and publisher make no warranty of any kind, expressed or implied, with regard to these programs or the documentation contained in this book. The author and publisher shall not be liable in any event for incidental or consequential damages in connection with, or arising out of, the furnishing, performance, or use of these programs.

Printed in the United States of America

10 9 8 7 6 5 4 3 2 1

ISBN: 0-13-222158-6

Pearson Education Ltd., *London*
Pearson Education Australia Pty. Ltd., *Sydney*
Pearson Education Singapore, Pte. Ltd.
Pearson Education North Asia Ltd., *Hong Kong*
Pearson Education Canada, Inc., *Toronto*
Pearson Educación de Mexico, S.A. de C.V.
Pearson Education—Japan, *Tokyo*
Pearson Education Malaysia, Pte. Ltd.
Pearson Education, Inc., *Upper Saddle River, New Jersey*

To Samantha, Michael, and Michelle

PREFACE

Welcome to *Introduction to Java Programming, Sixth Edition*. This edition is a substantial improvement on the previous edition in respect to clarity, content, presentation, code listings, and exercises, thanks to comments and suggestions by instructors and students. Overall, it is a great leap forward. We invite you to take a close look and be the judge.

Versions

The book is available in two versions:

- The fundamentals first version (Chapters 1–19).
- The comprehensive version (Chapters 1–36).

The following diagram summarizes the contents of the comprehensive version:

Introduction to Java Programming, Sixth Edition, Comprehensive Version

Part 1 Fundamentals of Programming
  Chapter 1 Introduction to Computers, Programs, and Java
  Chapter 2 Primitive Data Types and Operations
  Chapter 3 Selection Statements
  Chapter 4 Loops
  Chapter 5 Methods
  Chapter 6 Arrays

Part 2 Object-Oriented Programming
  Chapter 7 Objects and Classes
  Chapter 8 Strings and Text I/O
  Chapter 9 Inheritance and Polymorphism
  Chapter 10 Abstract Classes and Interfaces
  Chapter 11 Object-Oriented Design

Part 3 GUI Programming
  Chapter 12 Getting Started with GUI Programming
  Chapter 13 Graphics
  Chapter 14 Event-Driven Programming
  Chapter 15 Creating User Interfaces
  Chapter 16 Applets and Multimedia

Part 4 Exception Handling, I/O, and Recursion
  Chapter 17 Exceptions and Assertions
  Chapter 18 Binary I/O
  Chapter 19 Recursion

Part 5 Data Structures
  Chapter 20 Lists, Stacks, Queues, Trees, and Heaps
  Chapter 21 Generics
  Chapter 22 Java Collections Framework
  Chapter 23 Algorithm Efficiency and Sorting

Part 6 Concurrency, Networking, and Internationalization
  Chapter 24 Multithreading
  Chapter 25 Networking
  Chapter 26 Internationalization

Part 7 Advanced GUI Programming
  Chapter 27 JavaBeans and Bean Events
  Chapter 28 Containers, Layout Managers, and Borders
  Chapter 29 Menus, Toolbars, Dialogs, and Internal Frames
  Chapter 30 MVC and Swing Models
  Chapter 31 JTable and JTree

Part 8 Web Programming
  Chapter 32 Java Database Programming
  Chapter 33 Advanced Java Database Programming
  Chapter 34 Servlets
  Chapter 35 JavaServer Pages
  Chapter 36 Remote Method Invocations

---

fundamentals first

Fundamentals First introduces the fundamentals of programming, problem-solving, object-oriented programming, and GUI programming. This version is suitable for an introductory course on problem-solving and object-oriented programming.

comprehensive version

The *Comprehensive Version* contains all the chapters in the fundamentals first version. Additionally, it covers data structures, networking, internationalization, advanced GUI programming, and Web programming.

Teaching Strategies

Both imperative and OOP are important programming paradigms with distinct advantages for certain applications. Some programs should be developed using the imperative approach and others are better developed using the object-oriented approach. Today's students need to know both paradigms and use them effectively. This book introduces both imperative and OOP paradigms. Students will learn when and how to apply these two paradigms effectively.

imperative and OOP

There are several strategies in teaching Java. This book adopts the *fundamentals-first* strategy, proceeding at a steady pace through all the necessary and important basic concepts, then moving to object-oriented programming, and then to the use of the object-oriented approach to build interesting GUI applications and applets with exception handling, and advanced features.

fundamentals first

My own experience, confirmed by the experience of many colleagues, demonstrates that learning basic logic and *fundamental programming techniques* like loops and step-wise refinement is essential for new programmers to succeed. Students who cannot write code in procedural programming are not able to learn object-oriented programming. A good introduction on primitive data types, control statements, methods, and arrays prepares students to learn object-oriented programming.

fundamental programming techniques

The fundamentals-first approach reinforces object-oriented programming by first presenting the procedural solutions and demonstrating how they can be improved using the object-oriented approach. Students can learn when and how to apply OOP effectively.

using OOP effectively

At every SIGCSE (Computer Science Education) conference prior to 2005, the object-early approach was trumpeted and the voice for the fundamentals-first approach was muted. This changed when some former proponents of object-early began to air their frustrations and declared that object-early was a failure. This book is fundamentals-first and *object-right*. OOP is introduced right after fundamental programming techniques are covered. Many instructors of this book, from research universities to community colleges, have embraced the approach and have succeeded.

object-early failed?
object-right

Programming isn't just syntax, classes, or objects. It is really *problem solving*. Loops, methods, and arrays are fundamental techniques for problem solving. From fundamental programming techniques to object-oriented programming, there are many layers of abstraction. Classes are simply a layer of abstraction. Applying the concept of abstraction in the design and implementation of software projects is the key to developing software. The overriding objective of the book, therefore, is to teach students to use many layers of abstraction in solving problems and to see problems in small and in large. The examples and exercises throughout the book center on problem solving and foster the concept of developing reusable methods and classes and using them to create practical projects.

problem solving

Learning Strategies

A programming course is quite different from other courses. In a programming course, you learn from examples, from *practice*, and from mistakes. You need to devote a lot of time to writing programs, testing them, and fixing errors.

practice

For first-time programmers, learning Java is like learning any high-level programming language. The fundamental point in learning programming is to develop the critical skills of formulating *programmatic solutions* for real problems and translating them into programs using selection statements, loops, and methods.

programmatic solution

Once you acquire the basic skills of writing programs using loops, methods, and arrays, you can begin to learn *object-oriented programming*. You will learn how to develop object-oriented software using class encapsulation and class inheritance.

object-oriented programming

Once you understand the concept of object-oriented programming, learning Java becomes a matter of learning the *Java API*. The Java API establishes a framework for programmers to develop applications using Java. You have to use the classes and interfaces in the API and follow their conventions and rules to create applications. The best way to learn the Java API is to imitate examples and do exercises. The following diagram highlights the API covered in the book.

Java API

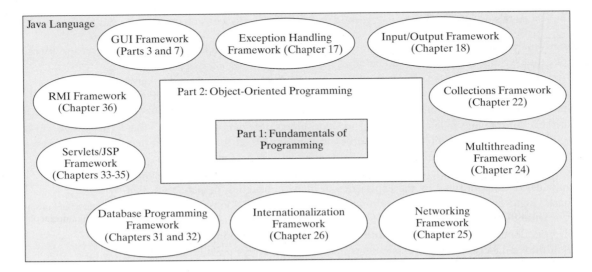

What's New in This Edition?

This edition substantially enhances *Introduction to Java Programming, Fifth Edition.* The major changes are as follows:

syntax coloring
■ All the Java code in the book now uses syntax coloring for keywords, literals, and comments. This makes the code more readable and understandable.

full Java 5 update
■ The Java 5 features are fully integrated in this edition. (Note: the fifth edition treats Java 5 features in separate optional sections.)

complete revision
■ The book is completely revised in every detail to enhance clarity, content, presentation, and exercises. All code samples and listings have been shortened and revised to be more compelling and to keep students even more engaged.

GUI options in Part 2
■ Optional GUI sections are provided at the end of Chapters 7–10 in Part 2, "Object-Oriented Programming," while a complete introduction of GUI programming is presented in Part 3, "GUI Programming," GUI components are excellent examples to demonstrate OOP. The optional GUI sections can be used as additional examples for OOP.

early interesting programs
■ Students can now write short, interesting, graphical game programs starting from Chapter 2.

JOptionPane or **Scanner**
■ Chapter 2, "Primitive Data Types and Operations," introduces the use of `JOptionPane` and `Scanner` to receive input. Students can use either `JOpationPane` or `Scanner` for obtaining input.

new recursion chapter
■ The discussion of recursion is expanded to form Chapter 19, "Recursion," a brand-new chapter. It can be covered after Chapter 5, "Methods."

early text I/O
■ High-level text I/O using the `Scanner` and `PrintWriter` classes is introduced in Chapter 8 along with strings. Binary I/O is covered in Chapter 18 "Binary I/O."

early **ArrayList**
■ `ArrayList` is introduced early in Chapter 9, "Inheritance and Polymorphism."

UML exercises
■ New exercises are provided in Part 2, "Object-Oriented Programming," for achieving three objectives: (1) design and draw UML for classes; (2) implement classes from the UML; (3) use classes to develop applications.

extensive supplements
■ Extensive supplements (e.g., installing and configuring JDK, IDE tutorials, design patterns, rapid GUI development, database design, SQL) are provided for instructors to customize a course.

- Part 1, "Fundamentals of Programming," is expanded into six chapters to focus on problem-solving and basic programming techniques with many new illustrations and practical examples, such as math tutor. New organization reinforces the teaching of fundamental problem-solving techniques.

Part 1 enhancement

- Part 2, "Object-Oriented Programming," is expanded into five chapters to give a comprehensive introduction on OOP and how to use it to design programs. New organization enhances the presentation of object-oriented programming and enables GUI programming to be covered earlier.

Part 2 enhancement

- Part 3, "GUI Programming," is expanded into five chapters to introduce GUI programming, graphics painting, event-driven programming, creating user interfaces, and applets.

Part 3 enhancement

- Part 4, "Exception Handling, I/O, and Recursion," contains a brand new chapter on recursion. New short and simple examples are used to introduce the concept of exception handling. Since the text I/O has moved to Chapter 8, "Strings and Text I/O," the I/O chapter covers only the binary I/O.

Part 4 enhancements

- Part 5, "Data Structures," is expanded to cover data structure design and implementation (array list, linked list, stack, queue, heap, priority queue, and binary tree), generics, Java Collections Framework, and algorithm efficiencies and sorting.

Part 5 enhancement

- Part 6, "Concurrency, Networking, and Internationalization," is updated to cover Java 5 thread pooling, locks, and semaphores.

Part 6 enhancement

- Part 7, "Advanced GUI Programming," is expanded into five chapters with short, simple new examples to teach complex subjects. For example, a new example is used to demonstrate how to develop source components. The MVC architecture is introduced along with the Swing models.

Part 7 enhancement

- Part 8, "Web Programming," is expanded into five chapters. Advanced database programming is in a separate chapter and may be skipped. Several new examples are presented to introduce the JSP.

Part 8 enhancement

Pedagogical Features

The philosophy of the Liang Java Series is *teaching by example and learning by doing*. Basic features are explained by example so that you can learn by doing. The book uses the following elements to get the most from the material:

teaching by example
learning by doing

- **Objectives** list what students should have learned from the chapter. This will help them to determine whether they have met the objectives after completing the chapter.

- **Introduction** opens the discussion with a brief overview of what to expect from the chapter.

- **Code Listings** are used to teach programming concepts. Syntax coloring makes the code easier to follow.

- **Chapter Summary** reviews the important subjects that students should understand and remember. It helps them to reinforce the key concepts they have learned in the chapter.

- **Optional Sections** cover nonessential but valuable features. Instructors may choose to include or skip an optional section, or cover it later. The section headers of optional sections are marked by ❖ .

- **Review Questions** are grouped by sections to help students track their progress and evaluate their learning.

- **Margin Notes** are featured throughout the book to emphasize key terms and important concepts.

■ **Programming Exercises** are grouped by sections to provide students with opportunities to apply on their own the new skills they have learned. The level of difficulty is rated as easy (no asterisk), moderate (*), hard (**), or challenging (***). The trick of learning programming is practice, practice, and practice. To that end, the book provides a great many exercises.

■ **Interactive Self-Test** lets students test their knowledge interactively online. The Self-Test is accessible from the Companion Website. It provides more than one thousand multiple-choice questions organized by sections in each chapter. The Instructor Resource Website contains the quiz generator with additional multiple-choice questions.

■ **Notes**, **Tips**, and **Cautions** are inserted throughout the text to offer valuable advice and insight on important aspects of program development.

Note
Provides additional information on the subject and reinforces important concepts.

Tip
Teaches good programming style and practice.

Caution
Helps students steer away from the pitfalls of programming errors.

Flexible Chapter Orderings

The book provides flexible chapter orderings to enable GUI, exception handling, generics, and the Java Collections Framework to be covered earlier. Three common alternative orderings are shown as follows:

GUI Early

Chapter 9	Inheritance and Polymorphism
Chapter 12	GUI Basics
Chapter 13	Graphics
Chapter 10	Abstract Classes and Interfaces
Chapter 14	Event-Driven Programming
Chapter 15	Creating User Interfaces
Chapter 16	Applets and Multimedia

Exception Early

| Chapter 9 | Inheritance and Polymorphism |
| Chapter 17 | Exceptions and Assertions |

Data Structures Early

Chapter 9	Inheritance and Polymorphism
Chapter 10	Abstract Classes and Interfaces
Chapter 20	Lists, Stacks, Queues, Trees, and Heaps
Chapter 21	Generics
Chapter 22	Java Collections Framework

Many of the chapters after Chapter 16 can be covered in any order. The following diagram shows the chapter dependencies.

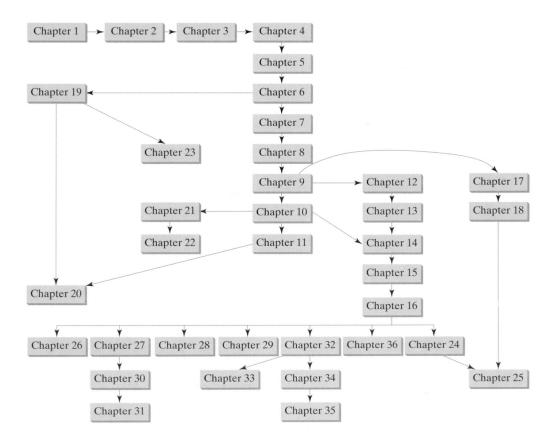

 Note
Some of the optional examples and exercises in later chapters may be dependent on earlier chapters. In such cases the examples and exercises can be omitted. For example, Chapter 17 has an example that uses GUI components from Chapter 15. If you have not covered Chapter 15, these examples and exercises can be skipped.

Java Development Tools

You can use a text editor, such as the Windows Notepad or WordPad, to create Java programs, and compile and run the programs from the command window. You can also use a Java development tool, such as TextPad, JBuilder, NetBeans, or Eclipse. These tools support an integrated development environment (IDE) for rapidly developing Java programs. Editing, compiling, building, executing, and debugging programs are integrated in one graphical user interface. Using these tools effectively will greatly increase your programming productivity. TextPad is a primitive IDE tool. JBuilder, NetBeans, and Eclipse are more sophisticated, but they are easy to use if you follow the tutorials. Tutorials on TextPad, JBuilder, NetBeans, and Eclipse will be found in the supplements on the Companion Website.

Companion Website

The Companion Website at www.prenhall.com/liang features a host of resources for students and instructors, including the following:

■ Answers to review questions

■ Solutions to programming exercises

■ Source code for the code listings in the book

- Links to software and Web resources

- The **Online Quiz Generator** enables instructors to generate quizzes as well as assign students to take quizzes online with the results emailed to the instructor. This can be done in a closed lab or at home. Instructors may assign a set of 10, 15, or 20 questions and specify that the questions to be randomly generated. Go to www.prenhall.com/liang to access the Online Quiz.

Supplements

The text covers the essential subjects. The supplements extend the text to introduce additional topics that might be of interest to readers. The supplements that are available from the Companion Website are listed in this table.

Supplements for Introduction to Java Programming, 6E

Part I General Supplements
- A Glossary
- B Installing and Configuring JDK
- C Compiling and Running Java from the Command Window
- D Java Coding Style Guidelines
- E Creating Desktop Shortcuts for Java Applications on Windows

Part II IDE Supplements
- A TextPad Tutorial
- B JBuilder Tutorial
- C Learning Java Effectively with JBuilder
- D NetBeans Tutorial
- E Learning Java Effectively with NetBeans
- F Eclipse Tutorial
- G Learning Java Effectively with Eclipse

Part III Data Structures Supplements
- A Hashing
- B B-Tree
- C Graph Algorithms

Part IV Database Supplements
- A SQL Statements for Creating and Initializing Tables Used in the Book
- B MySQL Tutorial
- C Oracle Tutorial
- D Microsoft Access Tutorial
- E Introduction to Database Systems
- F Relational Database Concept
- G Database Design
- H SQL Basics
- I Advanced SQL

Part V Java Supplements
- A More on Regular Expressions
- B Enumerated Types (Java 5)
- C Java 2D

- D Security
- E Java Media Framework
- F Java Sound
- G Java Mail
- H Design Patterns

Part VI Obsolete Java Features
- A StringTokenizer
- B Text I/O using Reader and Writer

Part VII Web Programming Supplements
- A HTML and XHTML Tutorial
- B CSS Tutorial
- C XML
- D Java and XML
- E Tomcat Tutorial

Part VIII Visual GUI Development Using NetBeans
- A Getting Started with NetBeans
- B Visual Design Using NetBeans
- C Rapid Component Development Using NetBeans
- D Customizing Property Editors in NetBeans

Part IX Visual GUI Development Using JBuilder
- A Getting Started with JBuilder
- B Basic UI Design Using JBuilder
- C Rapid Component Development Using JBuilder
- D Customizing Property Editors in JBuilder

Part X Visual GUI Development Using Eclipse
- A Getting Started with Eclipse
- B Basic UI Design Using Eclipse
- C Rapid Component Development Using Eclipse
- D Customizing Property Editors in Eclipse

Instructor Resource Center

The Instructor Resource Center, accessible from www.prenhall.com/liang, contains the following resources:

- Over 2000 Microsoft PowerPoint lecture slides. They bring the illustrations from the text to life in the classroom. Featuring full-color, syntax-highlighted source code and the ability to run programs live without leaving the slides and trace program execution using animation.

- Sample exams. In general, each exam has four parts:
    1. Multiple-choice questions or short-answer questions (most of these are different from the questions in the self-test on the Companion Website)
    2. Correct programming errors
    3. Trace programs
    4. Write programs

- Solutions to all the exercises (available to instructors only). Students will have access to the solutions of even-numbered exercises.

- UML Diagram Solutions to all the UML exercises (for instructors only). Students are provided solutions to even-numbered exercises.

- TestGen, a test bank of over 2000 programming questions.

- Online quiz. (Students can take the online quiz for each chapter and a quiz report will be sent to the instructor.)

- Ten sample exams, each with multiple choice or short-answer questions. They test how students correct programming errors, test programs, and write their own programs.

- Online Homework and Assessment. GOAL (Gradiance Online Accelerated Learning) is a sophisticated online homework tool that can be purchased and used alongside the textbook. Multiple choice problems based on the concept of a "root question" and challenging programming labs are designed to save instructors time grading programming assignments and to deliver meaningful feedback to students immediately. All code is tested against a real data set. Contact your local Pearson Prentice Hall sales representative to learn more about GOAL.

Some readers have requested the materials from the Instructor Resource Website. Please understand that these are for instructors only. Such requests will not be answered.

Acknowledgments

I would like to thank Ray Greenlaw and my colleagues at Armstrong Atlantic State University for enabling me to teach what I write and for supporting me in writing what I teach. Teaching is the source of inspiration for continuing to improve the book. I am grateful to the instructors and students who have offered comments, suggestions, bug reports, and praise.

This book was greatly enhanced thanks to outstanding reviews. The reviewers for the previous editions were:

Yang Ang	University of Wollongong (Australia)
David Champion	DeVry Institute
James Chegwidden	Tarrant County College
Harold Grossman	Clemson University
Ron Hofman	Red River College (Canada)
Hong Lin	DeVry Institute
Dan Lipsa	Armstrong Atlantic State University
Vladan Jovanovic	Georgia Southern University

Larry King	University of Texas at Dallas
Nana Kofi	Langara College (Canada)
Roger Kraft	Purdue University at Calumet
Debbie Masada	Sun Microsystems
Blayne Mayfield	Oklahoma State University
Michel Mitri	James Madison University
Kenrick Mock	University of Alaska Anchorage
Jun Ni	University of Iowa
Gavin Osborne	University of Sakatchewan
Kevin Parker	Idaho State University
Mary Ann Pumphrey	De Anza Junior College
Ronald F. Taylor	Wright State University
Carolyn Schauble	Colorado State University
David Scuse	University of Manitoba
Ashraf Shirani	San Jose State University
Daniel Spiegel	Kutztown University
Lixin Tao	Pace University
Russ Tront	Simon Fraser University
Deborah Trytten	University of Oklahoma
Kent Vidrine	George Washington University
Bahram Zartoshty	California State University at Northridge

The reviewers for this edition are:

Kevin Bierre	Rochester Institute of Technology
James Chegwidden	Tarrant County College
Charles Dierbach	Towson University
Deena Engel	New York University
Vladan Jovanovic	Georgia Southern University
Frank Malinowski	Aelera Corporation
John McGrath	J.P. McGrath Consulting
Shyamal Mitra	University of Texas at Austin
Benjamin Nystuen	University of Colorado at Colorado
Roger Priebe	University of Texas at Austin

It is a great pleasure, honor, and privilege to work with Prentice Hall. I would like to thank Marcia Horton, Tracy Dunkelberger, Robin O'Brien, Christianna Lee, Jennifer Cappello, Vince O'Brien, Camille Trentacoste, Craig Little, Xiaohong Zhu, and their colleagues for organizing, producing, and promoting this project, and Robert Milch for copy editing.

As always, I am indebted to my wife, Samantha, for her love, support, and encouragement.

Y. Daniel Liang
liang@armstrong.edu
www.cs.armstrong.edu/liang/intro6e

BRIEF CONTENTS

CONTENTS

PART 2 ■ OBJECT-ORIENTED PROGRAMMING 211

Chapter 7 Objects and Classes 213

Chapter 8 Strings and Text I/O 261

Chapter 9 Inheritance and Polymorphism 301

Chapter 10 Abstract Classes and Interfaces

Chapter 11 Object-Oriented Design

PART 3 ▪ GUI PROGRAMMING

Chapter 12 Getting Started with GUI Programming

PART 1

FUNDAMENTALS OF PROGRAMMING

By now you have heard a lot about Java and are anxious to start writing Java programs. The first part of the book is a stepping stone that will prepare you to embark on the journey of learning Java. You will begin to know Java and will develop fundamental programming skills. Specifically, you will learn how to write simple Java programs with primitive data types, control statements, methods, and arrays.

Prerequisites for Part I

This book does not require any prior programming experience, nor any mathematics, other than elementary high school algebra and *basic computer skills* such as using Windows, Internet Explorer, and Microsoft Word.

basic computer skills

You may cover the concept and simple examples of recursive programming in §§19.1–19.3 in Chapter 19, *"Recursion,"* after Chapter 5, "Methods."

recursion

You may cover Chapter 23, "Algorithm Efficiency and Sorting," after Chapter 6, "Arrays." Two simple *sorting algorithms* are introduced in Chapter 6. Chapter 23 introduces several advanced sorting algorithms.

sorting algorithms

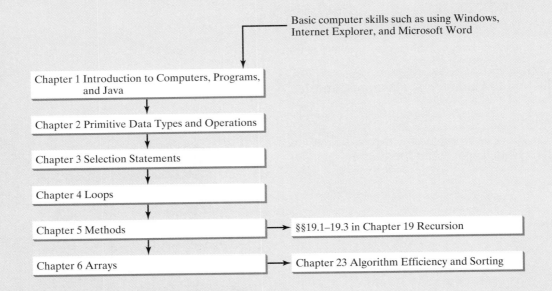

Basic computer skills such as using Windows, Internet Explorer, and Microsoft Word

Chapter 1 Introduction to Computers, Programs, and Java

Chapter 2 Primitive Data Types and Operations

Chapter 3 Selection Statements

Chapter 4 Loops

Chapter 5 Methods → §§19.1–19.3 in Chapter 19 Recursion

Chapter 6 Arrays → Chapter 23 Algorithm Efficiency and Sorting

CHAPTER 1

INTRODUCTION TO COMPUTERS, PROGRAMS, AND JAVA

Objectives

- To review computer basics, programs, and operating systems (§§1.2–1.4).
- (Optional) To represent numbers in binary, decimal, and hexadecimal (§1.5).
- To understand the relationship between Java and the World Wide Web (§1.6).
- To distinguish the terms API, IDE, and JDK (§1.7).
- To write a simple Java program (§1.8).
- To create, compile, and run Java programs (§1.9).
- To know the basic syntax of a Java program (§1.10).
- To display output in a dialog box (§1.11).

1.1 Introduction

You use word processors to write documents, Web browsers to explore the Internet, and email programs to send email over the Internet. Word processors, browsers, and email programs are all examples of software that runs on computers. Software is developed using programming languages. There are many programming languages. So why Java? The answer is that Java enables users to develop and deploy applications on the Internet for servers, desktop computers, and small hand-held devices. The future of computing is being profoundly influenced by the Internet, and Java promises to remain a big part of that future. Java is *the* Internet programming language.

You are about to begin an exciting journey, learning a powerful programming language. Before the journey, it is helpful to review computer basics, programs, and operating systems, and to become familiar with number systems. You may skip the review in §§1.2–1.4 if you are familiar with such terms as CPU, memory, disks, operating systems, and programming languages. You may also skip §1.5 and use it as reference when you have questions regarding binary and hexadecimal numbers.

1.2 What Is a Computer?

A computer is an electronic device that stores and processes data. A computer includes both *hardware* and *software*. In general, hardware is the physical aspect of the computer that can be seen, and software is the invisible instructions that control the hardware and make it perform specific tasks. Computer programming consists of writing instructions for computers to perform. You can learn a programming language without knowing computer hardware, but you will be better able to understand the effect of the instructions in the program if you do. This section gives a brief introduction to computer hardware components and their functionality.

hardware
software

A computer consists of the following major hardware components, as shown in Figure 1.1.

- Central Processing Unit (CPU)

- Memory (main memory)

- Storage Devices (disks, CDs, tapes)

- Input and Output Devices (monitors, keyboards, mice, printers)

- Communication Devices (modems and network interface cards (NICs))

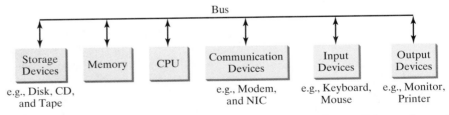

FIGURE 1.1 A computer consists of a CPU, memory, hard disk, floppy disk, monitor, printer, and communication devices.

The components are connected through a subsystem called a *bus* that transfers data or power between the components.

1.2.1 Central Processing Unit

CPU

The *central processing unit (CPU)* is the brain of a computer. It retrieves instructions from memory and executes them. The CPU usually has two components: a *control unit* and an *arithmetic/logic unit*. The control unit controls and coordinates the actions of the other components. The arithmetic and logic unit performs numeric operations (addition, subtraction, multiplication, division) and logical operations (comparisons).

Today's CPU is built on a small silicon semiconductor chip with millions of transistors. The *speed* of the CPU is mainly determined by clock speed. Every computer has an internal clock. The faster the clock speed, the more instructions are executed in a given period of time. The clock emits electronic pulses at a constant rate, and these are used to control and synchronize the pace of operations. The unit of measurement is called a *hertz* (Hz), with 1 hertz equaling 1 pulse per second. The clock speed of computers is usually measured in *megahertz* (MHz) (1 MHz is 1 million Hz). The speed of the CPU has been improved continuously. If you buy a PC now, you can get an Intel Pentium 4 Processor at 3 *gigahertz* (GHz) (1 GHz is 1000 MHz).

speed

hertz
megahertz

gigahertz

1.2.2 Memory

Computers use zeros and ones because digital devices have two stable states, referred to as *zero* and *one* by convention. Data of various kinds, such as numbers, characters, and strings, are encoded as a series of *bits* (*b*inary dig*its*: zeros and ones). *Memory* stores data and program instructions for the CPU to execute. A memory unit is an ordered sequence of *bytes*, each holding eight bits, as shown in Figure 1.2.

bit
byte

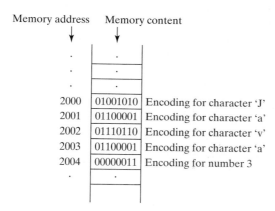

FIGURE 1.2   Memory stores data and program instructions.

The programmer need not be concerned about the encoding and decoding of data, which is performed automatically by the system based on the encoding scheme. The encoding scheme varies. For example, character 'J' is represented by 01001010 in one byte in the popular ASCII encoding. A small number such as 3 can be stored in a single byte. If a computer needs to store a large number that cannot fit into a single byte, it uses several adjacent bytes. No two data items can share or split the same byte. A byte is the minimum storage unit.

A program and its data must be brought to memory before they can be executed. A memory byte is never empty, but its initial content may be meaningless to your program. The current content of a memory byte is lost whenever new information is placed in it.

Every byte has a unique address. The address is used to locate the byte for storing and retrieving data. Since the bytes can be accessed in any order, the memory is also referred to as *RAM* (random-access memory). Today's personal computers usually have at least 128 megabytes of RAM. A *megabyte* (abbreviated MB) is about 1 million bytes. For a precise definition of megabyte, please see http://en.wikipedia.org/wiki/Megabyte. Like the CPU, memory is built on silicon semiconductor chips containing thousands of transistors embedded on their surface. Compared to the CPU chips, memory chips are less complicated, slower, and less expensive.

RAM

megabyte
megabyte URL

1.2.3 Storage Devices

Memory is volatile, because information is lost when the power is turned off. Programs and data are permanently stored on storage devices and are moved to memory when the computer actually uses them. The reason for this is that memory is much faster than storage devices. There are four main types of storage devices:

- Disk drives (hard disks and floppy disks)
- CD drives (CD-R, CD-RW, and DVD)
- Tape drives
- USB flash drives

drive

Drives are devices for operating a medium, such as disks, CDs, and tapes.

Disks

hard disk
floppy disk

There are two kinds of disks: *hard disks* and *floppy disks*. Personal computers usually have a 3.5-inch floppy disk drive and a hard drive. A floppy disk has a fixed capacity of about 1.44 MB. Hard disk capacities vary. The capacity of the hard disks of the latest PCs is in the range of 30 gigabytes to 160 gigabytes. Hard disks provide much faster performance and larger capacity than floppy disks. Both disk drives are often encased inside the computer. A floppy disk is removable. A hard disk is mounted inside the case of the computer. Removable hard disks are also available. Floppy disks will eventually be replaced by CD-RW and flash drives.

CDs and DVDs

CD-R

CD-RW

CD stands for compact disc. There are two types of CD drives: CD-R and CD-RW. A *CD-R* is for read-only permanent storage, and the user cannot modify its contents once they are recorded. A *CD-RW* can be used like a floppy disk, and thus can be read and rewritten. A single CD can hold up to 700 MB. Most software is distributed through CD-ROMs. Most new PCs are equipped with a CD-RW drive that can work with both CD-R and CD-RW.

DVD stands for digital versatile disc. DVDs and CDs look alike. You can store data using a CD or DVD. A DVD can hold more information than a CD. A standard DVD storage is 4.7 GB in capacity.

Tapes

Tapes are mainly used for backup of data and programs. Unlike disks and CDs, tapes store information sequentially. The computer must retrieve information in the order it was stored. Tapes are very slow. It would take one to two hours to back up a 1-gigabyte hard disk.

USB Flash Drives

USB flash drives are popular new devices for storing and transporting data. They are small—about the size of a package of gum. They act like a portable hard disk that can be plugged into the USB port of your computer. USB flash drives are currently available with up to 2 GB storage capacity.

1.2.4 Input and Output Devices

Input and output devices let the user communicate with the computer. The common input devices are *keyboards* and *mice*. The common output devices are *monitors* and *printers*.

The Keyboard

A computer *keyboard* resembles a typewriter keyboard except that it has extra keys for certain special functions.

Function keys are located at the top of the keyboard with prefix F. Their use depends on the software.

A *modifier key* is special key (e.g., Shift, Alt, Ctrl) that modifies the normal action of another key when the two are pressed in combination.

The *numeric keypad,* located on the right-hand corner of the keyboard, is a separate set of number keys for quick input of numbers.

Arrow keys, located between the main keypad and the numeric keypad, are used to move the cursor up, down, left, and right.

The *insert, delete, page up,* and *page down keys*, located above the arrow keys, are used in word processing for performing insert, delete, page up, and page down.

The Mouse

A *mouse* is a pointing device. It is used to move an electronic pointer called a cursor around the screen or to click on an object on the screen to trigger it to respond.

The Monitor

The *monitor* displays information (text and graphics). The resolution and dot pitch determine the quality of the display.

The *resolution* specifies the number of pixels per square inch. Pixels (short for "picture elements") are tiny dots that form an image on the screen. A common resolution for a 17-inch screen, for example, is 1024 pixels wide and 768 pixels high. The resolution can be set manually. The higher the resolution, the sharper and clearer the image is.   *screen resolution*

The *dot pitch* is the amount of space between pixels. Typically, it has a range from 0.21 to 0.81 millimeters. The smaller the dot pitch, the better the display.   *dot pitch*

1.2.5   Communication Devices

Computers can be networked through communication devices. Commonly used communication devices are the dialup *modem*, *DSL*, cable modem, and network interface card. A dialup   *modem*
modem uses a phone line and can transfer data at a speed up to 56,000 bps (bits per second).   *DSL*
A DSL (digital subscriber line) also uses a phone line and can transfer data at a speed 20 times faster than a dialup modem. A cable modem uses the TV cable line maintained by the cable company. A cable modem is as fast as DSL. A network interface card (*NIC*) is a device that   *NIC*
connects a computer to a local area network (*LAN*). The LAN is commonly used in business,   *LAN*
universities, and government organizations. A typical NIC called *10BaseT* can transfer data at 10 *mbps* (million bits per second).   *mbps*

1.3 Programs

Computer *programs*, known as *software*, are instructions to the computer. You tell a computer what to do through programs. Without programs, a computer is an empty machine. Computers do not understand human languages, so you need to use computer languages to communicate with them.   *software*

The language a computer speaks is the computer's native language or machine language. The *machine language* is a set of primitive instructions built into every computer. Machine   *machine language*
languages are different for different type of computers. The instructions are in the form of binary code, so you have to enter binary codes for various instructions. Programming using

a native machine language is a tedious process. Moreover, the programs are highly difficult to read and modify. For example, to add two numbers, you might have to write an instruction in binary like this:

1101101010011010

assembly language

Assembly language is a low-level programming language in which a mnemonic is used to represent each of the machine-language instructions. For example, to add two numbers, you might write an instruction in assembly code like this:

ADDF3 R1, R2, R3

assembler

Assembly languages were developed to make programming easy. Since the computer cannot understand assembly language, however, a program called *assembler* is used to convert assembly language programs into machine code, as shown in Figure 1.3.

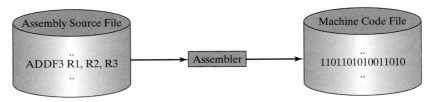

FIGURE 1.3 Assembler translates assembly language instructions to machine code.

Since assembly language is machine-dependent, an assembly program can only be executed on a particular machine. Assembly programs are written in terms of machine instructions with easy-to-remember mnemonic names. The high-level languages were developed in order to overcome the platform-specific problem and make programming easier.

high-level language

The *high-level languages* are English-like and easy to learn and program. Here, for example, is a high-level language statement that computes the area of a circle with radius 5:

area = 5 * 5 * 3.1415;

There are over one hundred high-level languages. The popular languages used today are:

- COBOL (COmmon Business Oriented Language)
- FORTRAN (FORmula TRANslation)
- BASIC (Beginner All-purpose Symbolic Instructional Code)
- Pascal (named for Blaise Pascal)
- Ada (named for Ada Lovelace)
- C (whose developer designed B first)
- Visual Basic (Basic-like visual language developed by Microsoft)
- Delphi (Pascal-like visual language developed by Borland)
- C++ (an object-oriented language, based on C)
- C# (a Java-like language developed by Microsoft)
- Java

Each of these languages was designed for a specific purpose. COBOL was designed for business applications and now is used primarily for business data processing. FORTRAN was designed for mathematical computations and is used mainly for numeric computations. BASIC, as its name suggests, was designed to be learned and used easily. Ada was developed for the Department of Defense and is mainly used in defense projects. C combines the power of an assembly language with the ease of use and portability of a high-level language. Visual Basic and Delphi are used in developing graphical user interfaces and in rapid application development. C++ is popular for system software projects like writing compilers and operating systems. The Microsoft Windows operating system was coded using C++.

A program written in a high-level language is called a *source program*. Since a computer cannot understand a source program, a program called a *compiler* is used to translate the source program into a machine-language program. The machine-language program is often then linked with other supporting library code to form an executable file. The executable file can be executed on the machine, as shown in Figure 1.4. On Windows, executable files have extension .exe.

source program
compiler

Figure 1.4   A source program is compiled into a machine-language file, which is then linked with the system library to form an executable file.

You can port (i.e., move) a source program to any machine with appropriate compilers. The source program must be recompiled, however, because the machine-language program can only run on a specific machine. Nowadays computers are networked to work together. Java was designed to run on any platform. With Java, you write the program once and compile the source program into a special type of machine-language code known as *bytecode*. The bytecode can then run on any computer with a Java Virtual Machine (*JVM*), as shown in Figure 1.5. The Java Virtual Machine is software that interprets Java bytecode.

bytecode
JVM

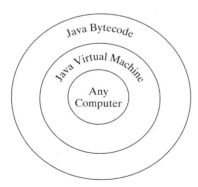

Figure 1.5   Java bytecode can be executed on any computer with a Java Virtual Machine.

 Note

Java bytecode is interpreted. The difference between compiling and interpreting is as follows. Compiling translates the high-level code into a target language code as a single unit. Interpreting translates the individual steps in a high-level program one at a time rather than the whole program as a single unit. Each step is executed immediately after it is translated.

compiling vs. interpreting

1.4 Operating Systems

OS

The *operating system (OS)* is the most important program that runs on a computer to manage and control its activities. You are probably using Windows (98, NT, 2000, XP, or ME), Mac OS, or Linux. Windows is currently the most popular PC operating system. Application programs, such as a Web browser or a word processor, cannot run without an operating system. The interrelationship of hardware, operating system, application software, and the user is shown in Figure 1.6.

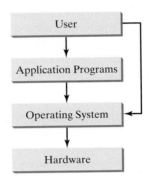

FIGURE 1.6   The operating system is the software that controls and manages the system.

The major tasks of the operating systems are:

- Controlling and monitoring system activities

- Allocating and assigning system resources

- Scheduling operations

1.4.1   Controlling and Monitoring System Activities

Operating systems are responsible for security, ensuring that unauthorized users do not access the system. Operating systems perform basic tasks, such as recognizing input from the keyboard, sending output to the monitor, keeping track of files and directories on the disk, and controlling peripheral devices, such as disk drives and printers. Operating systems also make sure that different programs and users running at the same time do not interfere with one other.

1.4.2   Allocating and Assigning System Resources

The OS is responsible for determining what computer resources a program needs (e.g., CPU, memory, disks, input and output devices) and for allocating and assigning them to run the program.

1.4.3   Scheduling Operations

The OS is responsible for scheduling programs to use the system resources efficiently. Many of today's operating systems support such techniques as *multiprogramming*, *multithreading*, or *multiprocessing* to increase system performance.

multiprogramming

Multiprogramming allows multiple programs to run simultaneously by sharing the CPU. The CPU is much faster than the other components. As a result, it is idle most of the time; for example, while waiting for data to be transferred from the disk or from other sources. A multiprogramming OS takes advantage of this by allowing multiple programs to use the CPU when it would otherwise be idle. For example, you may use a word processor to edit a file while the Web browser is downloading a file at the same time.

Multithreading allows concurrency within a program, so that its subunits can run at the same time. For example, a word-processing program allows users to simultaneously edit text and save it to a file. In this example, editing and saving are two tasks within the same application. These two tasks may run on separate threads concurrently.

multithreading

Multiprocessing, or parallel processing, uses two or more processors together to perform a task. It is like a surgical operation where several doctors work together on one patient.

multiprocessing

1.5 (Optional) Number Systems

Note
You can skip this section and use it as reference when you have questions regarding binary and hexadecimal numbers.

Computers use *binary numbers* internally because storage devices like memory and disk are made to store 0s and 1s. A number or a character inside a computer is stored as a sequence of 0s and 1s. Each 0 or 1 is called a *bit*. The binary number system has two digits, 0 and 1.

binary number

Since we use *decimal numbers* in our daily life, binary numbers are not intuitive. When you write a number like 20 in a program, it is assumed to be a decimal number. Internally, computer software is used to convert decimal numbers into binary numbers, and vice versa.

decimal number

You write programs using decimal number systems. However, if you write programs to deal with a system like an operating system, you need to use binary numbers to reach down to the "machine-level." Binary numbers tend to be very long and cumbersome. *Hexadecimal numbers* are often used to abbreviate binary numbers, with each hexadecimal digit representing exactly four binary digits. The hexadecimal number system has sixteen digits: 0, 1, 2, 3, 4, 5, 6, 7, 8, 9, A, B, C, D, E, and F. The letters A, B, C, D, E, and F correspond to the decimal numbers 10, 11, 12, 13, 14, and 15.

hexadecimal number

The digits in the decimal number system are 0, 1, 2, 3, 4, 5, 6, 7, 8, and 9. A decimal number is represented using a sequence of one or more of these digits. The value that each digit in the sequence represents depends on its position. A position in a sequence has a value that is an integral power of 10. For example, the digits 7, 4, 2, and 3 in decimal number 7423 represent 7000, 400, 20, and 3, respectively, as shown below:

$$\boxed{7\ |\ 4\ |\ 2\ |\ 3} = 7 \times 10^3 + 4 \times 10^2 + 2 \times 10^1 + 3 \times 10^0$$
$$10^3\ 10^2\ 10^1\ 10^0\ = 7000 + 400 + 20 + 3 = 7423$$

The decimal number system has ten digits, and the position values are integral powers of 10. We say that 10 is the *base* or *radix* of the decimal number system. Similarly, the base of the binary number system is 2 since the binary number system has two digits, and the base of the hex number system is 16 since the hex number system has sixteen digits.

base
radix

1.5.1 Conversions Between Binary Numbers and Decimal Numbers

Given a binary number $b_n b_{n-1} b_{n-2} \cdots b_2 b_1 b_0$, the equivalent decimal value is

$$b_n \times 2^n + b_{n-1} \times 2^{n-1} + b_{n-2} \times 2^{n-2} + \cdots + b_2 \times 2^2 + b_1 \times 2^1 + b_0 \times 2^0$$

The following are examples of converting binary numbers to decimals:

binary to decimal

Binary	Conversion Formula	Decimal
10	$1 \times 2^1 + 0 \times 2^0$	2
1000	$1 \times 2^3 + 0 \times 2^2 + 0 \times 2^1 + 0 \times 2^0$	8
10101011	$1 \times 2^7 + 0 \times 2^6 + 1 \times 2^5 + 0 \times 2^4 + 1 \times 2^3 + 0 \times 2^2 +$ $1 \times 2^1 + 1 \times 2^0$	171

decimal to binary

To convert a decimal number d to a binary number is to find the bits $b_n, b_{n-1}, b_{n-2}, \ldots, b_2, b_1$, and b_0 such that

$$d = b_n \times 2^n + b_{n-1} \times 2^{n-1} + b_{n-2} \times 2^{n-2} + \cdots + b_2 \times 2^2 + b_1 \times 2^1 + b_0 \times 2^0$$

These bits can be found by successively dividing d by 2 until the quotient is 0. The remainders are $b_0, b_1, b_2, \ldots, b_{n-2}, b_{n-1}$, and b_n.

For example, the decimal number 123 is 1111011 in binary. The conversion is done as follows:

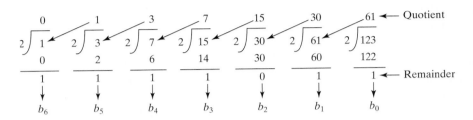

Tip

The Windows Calculator, as shown in Figure 1.7, is a useful tool for performing number conversions. To run it, choose *Programs*, *Accessories*, and *Calculator* from the Start button.

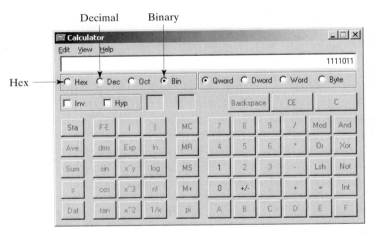

FIGURE 1.7 You can perform number conversions using the Windows Calculator.

1.5.2 Conversions Between Hexadecimal Numbers and Decimal Numbers

Given a hexadecimal number $h_n h_{n-1} h_{n-2} \cdots h_2 h_1 h_0$, the equivalent decimal value is

$$h_n \times 16^n + h_{n-1} \times 16^{n-1} + h_{n-2} \times 16^{n-2} + \cdots + h_2 \times 16^2 + h_1 \times 16^1 + h_0 \times 16^0$$

hex to decimal

The following are examples of converting hexadecimal numbers to decimals:

Hexadecimal	Conversion Formula	Decimal
7F	$7 \times 16^1 + 15 \times 16^0$	127
FFFF	$15 \times 16^3 + 15 \times 16^2 + 15 \times 16^1 + 15 \times 16^0$	65535
431	$4 \times 16^2 + 3 \times 16^1 + 1 \times 16^0$	1073

To convert a decimal number d to a hexadecimal number is to find the hexadecimal digits   decimal to hex
$h_n, h_{n-1}, h_{n-2}, \ldots, h_2, h_1,$ and h_0 such that

$$d = h_n \times 16^n + h_{n-1} \times 16^{n-1} + h_{n-2} \times 16^{n-2} + \cdots + h_2 \times 16^2$$
$$+ h_1 \times 16^1 + h_0 \times 16^0$$

These numbers can be found by successively dividing d by 16 until the quotient is 0. The remainders are $h_0, h_1, h_2, \ldots, h_{n-2}, h_{n-1},$ and h_n.

For example, the decimal number 123 is 7B in hexadecimal. The conversion is done as follows:

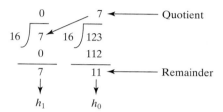

1.5.3   Conversions Between Binary Numbers and Hexadecimal Numbers

To convert a hexadecimal number to a binary number, simply convert each digit in the hexa-   hex to binary
decimal number into a four-digit binary number using Table 1.1.

TABLE 1.1   Converting Hexadecimal to Binary

Hexadecimal	Binary	Decimal
0	0	0
1	1	1
2	10	2
3	11	3
4	100	4
5	101	5
6	110	6
7	111	7
8	1000	8
9	1001	9
A	1010	10
B	1011	11
C	1100	12
D	1101	13
E	1110	14
F	1111	15

For example, the hexadecimal number 7B is 1111011, where 7 is 111 in binary, and B is 1011 in binary.

binary to hex

To convert a binary number to a hexadecimal, convert every four binary digits from right to left in the binary number into a hexadecimal number.

For example, the binary number 1110001101 is 38D, since 1101 is D, 1000 is 8, and 11 is 3, as shown below.

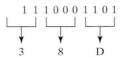

Note
Octal numbers are also useful. The octal number system has eight digits, 0 to 7. A decimal number 8 is represented as 10 in the octal system.

1.6 Java, the World Wide Web, and Beyond

This book introduces Java programming. Java was developed by a team led by James Gosling at Sun Microsystems. Originally called *Oak*, it was designed in 1991 for use in embedded consumer electronic appliances. In 1995, renamed *Java*, it was redesigned for developing Internet applications. For the history of Java, see java.sun.com/features/1998/05/birthday.html.

Java history URL

Java has become enormously popular. Java's rapid rise and wide acceptance can be traced to its design characteristics, particularly its promise that you can write a program once and run it anywhere. As stated in the Java language white paper by Sun, Java is *simple, object-oriented, distributed, interpreted, robust, secure, architecture-neutral, portable, high-performance, multi-threaded*, and *dynamic*. For the anatomy of Java characteristics, see www.cs.armstrong.edu/liang/intro6e/JavaCharacteristics.pdf.

Java characteristics URL
Java's versatility

Java is a full-featured, general-purpose programming language that is capable of developing robust mission-critical applications. Today, it is used not only for Web programming, but also for developing standalone applications across platforms on servers, desktops, and mobile devices. It was used to develop the code to communicate with and control the robotic rover that rolled on Mars. Many companies that once considered Java to be more hype than substance are now using it to create distributed applications accessed by customers and partners across the Internet. For every new project being developed today, companies are asking how they can use Java to make their work easier.

The World Wide Web is an electronic information repository that can be accessed on the Internet from anywhere in the world. You can use the Web to book a hotel room, buy an airline ticket, register for a college course, download the *New York Times*, chat with friends, or listen to live radio. There are countless activities you can do on the Internet. Many people spend a good part of their computer time surfing the Web for fun and profit.

The Internet is the infrastructure of the Web. The Internet has been around for more than thirty years, but has only recently become popular. The colorful World Wide Web and sophisticated Web browsers are the major reason for its popularity.

The primary authoring language for the Web is the Hypertext Markup Language (HTML). HTML is a markup language: a simple language for laying out documents, linking documents on the Internet, and bringing images, sound, and video alive on the Web. However, it cannot interact with the user except through simple forms. Web pages in HTML are essentially static and flat.

applet

Java initially became attractive because Java programs can be run from a Web browser. Java programs that run from a Web browser are called *applets*. Applets use a modern graphical user interface with buttons, text fields, text areas, radio buttons, and so on, to interact with users on the Web and process their requests. Applets make the Web responsive, interactive, and fun to use. Figure 1.8 shows an applet running from a Web browser.

Enter this URL from a
Web browser

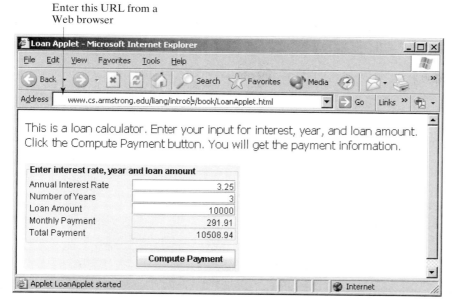

FIGURE 1.8 A Java applet for computing loan payments is embedded in an HTML page. The user can use the applet to compute the loan payments.

 Tip

For a demonstration of Java applets, visit java.sun.com/applets. This site provides a rich Java resource as well as links to other cool applet demo sites. java.sun.com is the official Sun Java website.

Java can also be used to develop applications on the server side. These applications, called *Java servlets* or *JavaServer Pages (JSP)*, can be run from a Web server to generate dynamic Web pages. The Self-Test website for this book, as shown in Figure 1.9, was developed using Java servlets. The Web pages for the questions and answers are dynamically generated by the servlets.

servlet
JSP

Enter this URL from a
Web browser

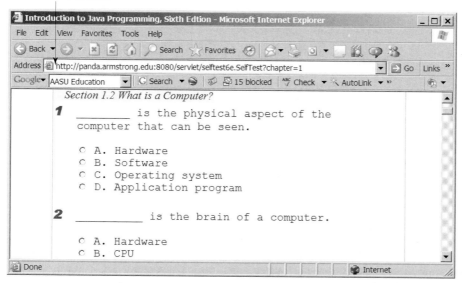

FIGURE 1.9 Java was used to develop the self-test in the Companion Website for this book.

Java is a versatile programming language. You can use it to develop applications on your desktop and on the server. You can also use it to develop applications for small hand-held devices, such as personal digital assistants and cell phones. Figure 1.10 shows a Java program that displays the calendar on a BlackBerry® and on a cell phone.

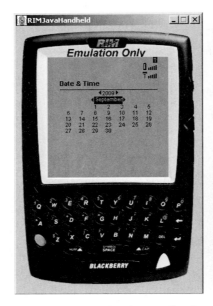 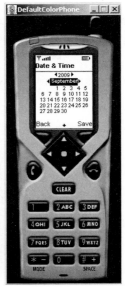

FIGURE 1.10   Java can be used to develop applications for hand-held and wireless devices, such as a BlackBerry (left) and a cell phone (right).

1.7 The Java Language Specification, API, JDK, and IDE

Computer languages have strict rules of usage. If you do not follow the rules when writing a program, the computer will be unable to understand it. Sun Microsystems, the originator of Java, intends to retain control of this important new computer language—and for a very good reason: to prevent it from losing its unified standards. The Java language specification and Java API define the Java standard.

The Java language specification is a technical definition of the language that includes the syntax and semantics of the Java programming language. The complete Java language specification can be found at java.sun.com/docs/books/jls.

API

The *application program interface* (*API*) contains predefined classes and interfaces for developing Java programs. The Java language specification is stable, but the API is still expanding. At the Sun Java website (java.sun.com), you can view and download the latest version of the Java API.

Java was introduced in 1995. Sun announced the Java 2 platform in December 1998. Java 2 is the overarching brand that applies to current Java technology. There are three editions of the Java API: *Java 2 Standard Edition (J2SE)*, *Java 2 Enterprise Edition (J2EE)*, and *Java 2 Micro Edition (J2ME)*. Java is a full-fledged and powerful language that can be used in many ways. J2SE can be used to develop client-side standalone applications or applets. J2EE can be used to develop server-side applications, such as Java servlets and JavaServer Pages. J2ME can be used to develop applications for mobile devices, such as cell phones. This book uses J2SE to introduce Java programming.

There are many versions of J2SE. The latest version is J2SE 5.0, which will be used in this book. Sun releases each version of J2SE with a *Java Development Toolkit* (JDK). For J2SE 5.0, the Java Development Toolkit is called JDK 5.0. JDK 5.0 was formerly known as JDK 1.5.

Since most Java programmers are familiar with the name JDK 1.5, this book uses the names JDK 5.0 and JDK 1.5 interchangeably.

JDK 1.5 = JDK 5.0

JDK consists of a set of separate programs for developing and testing Java programs, each of which is invoked from a command line. Besides JDK, there are more than a dozen Java development tools on the market today. Three major development tools are:

- JBuilder by Borland (www.borland.com)
- NetBeans Open Source by Sun (www.netbeans.org)
- Eclipse Open Source by IBM (www.eclipse.org)

Other useful tools are:

- Code Warrior by Metrowerks (www.metrowerks.com)
- TextPad Editor (www.textpad.com)
- JCreator LE (www.jcreator.com)
- JEdit (www.jedit.org)
- JGrasp (www.jgrasp.org)
- BlueJ (www.bluej.org)
- DrJava (http://drjava.sourceforge.net)

A Java development tool is software that provides an *integrated development environment* (*IDE*) for rapidly developing Java programs. Editing, compiling, building, debugging, and online help are integrated in one graphical user interface. Just enter source code in one window or open an existing file in a window, then click a button, menu item, or function key to compile and run the program.

Java IDE

1.8 A Simple Java Program

A Java program can be written in many ways. This book introduces Java *applications*, applets, and servlets. Applications are standalone programs that can be executed from any computer with a JVM. *Applets* are special kinds of Java programs that run from a Web browser. Servlets are special kinds of Java programs that run from a Web server to generate dynamic Web contents. Applets will be introduced in Chapter 16, and servlets will be introduced in Chapter 34.

application

applet

Let us begin with a simple Java program that displays the message "Welcome to Java!" on the console. The program is shown in Listing 1.1.

LISTING 1.1   Welcome.java

Comments ⟶ `// This application program prints Welcome to Java!`

Class heading ⟶
Main method signature

```
public class Welcome {    Class Name
  public static void main(String[] args) {

    System.out.println("Welcome to Java!");    String
  }
}
```

Every Java program must have at least one class. A class is a construct that defines data and methods. Each class has a name. By convention, *class names* start with an uppercase letter. In this example, the class name is `Welcome`.

class name

In order to run a class, the class must contain a method named `main`. The JVM executes the program by invoking the `main` method.

main method

A method is a construct that contains statements. The `main` method in this program contains the `System.out.println` statement. This statement prints a message "Welcome to Java!" to the console.

console output

Note

You are probably wondering about such points as why the `main` method is declared this way and why `System.out.println(...)` is used to display a message to the console. Your questions cannot be fully answered yet. For the time being, you will just have to accept that this is how things are done. You will find the answers in the coming chapters.

 Note

syntax rules

Like any other programming language, Java has its own syntax, and you need to write code that obeys the *syntax rules*. The Java compiler will report syntax errors if your program violates the syntax rules.

1.9 Creating, Compiling, and Executing a Java Program

You have to create your program and compile it before it can be executed. This process is repetitive, as shown in Figure 1.11. If your program has compilation errors, you have to fix them by modifying the program, then recompile it. If your program has runtime errors or does not produce the correct result, you have to modify the program, recompile it, and execute it again.

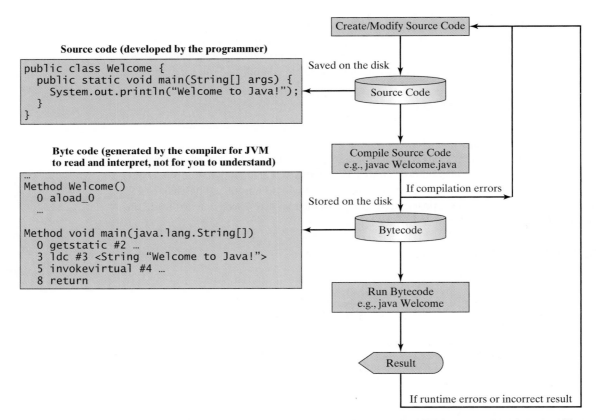

FIGURE 1.11 The Java programming-development process consists of creating/modifying source code, compiling, and executing programs.

editor

You can use any text *editor* to create and edit a Java source code file, or you can use an IDE like Eclipse, JBuilder or NetBeans. Figure 1.12 shows how to use NotePad to create and edit the source code file.

FIGURE 1.12   You can create the Java source file using Windows NotePad.

This file must end with the extension .java and must have the exact same name as the public class name. For example, the file for the source code in Listing 1.1 should be named Welcome.java, since the public class name is `Welcome`.

A Java compiler translates a *Java source file* into a Java bytecode file. The following command *compiles* Welcome.java:

.java source file

compile

```
javac Welcome.java
```

 Note

You must first install and configure JDK before compiling and running programs. See *Supplement I.B,* "Installing and Configuring JDK 5.0," on how to install JDK and how to set up the environment to compile and run Java programs. If you have trouble compiling and running programs, please see *Supplement I.C,* "Compiling and Running Java from the Command Window." This supplement also explains how to use basic DOS commands and how to use Windows NotePad and WordPad to create and edit files. All the supplements are accessible from the Companion Website.

Supplement I.B

Supplement I.C

Caution

Java source programs are *case-sensitive*. It would be wrong, for example, to replace `main` in the program with `Main`. Program filenames are case-sensitive on UNIX but generally not on Windows; JDK treats filenames as case-sensitive on any platform. If you try to compile the program using `javac welcome.java`, you will get a file-not-found error.

case-sensitive

If there are no syntax errors, the *compiler* generates a bytecode file with a .class extension. So the preceding command generates a file named **Welcome.class**. The bytecode is similar to machine instructions but is architecture-neutral and can run on any platform that has a JVM. This is one of Java's primary advantages: *Java bytecode can run on a variety of hardware platforms and operating systems.*

.class bytecode file

To execute a Java program is to *run* the program's bytecode. You can execute the bytecode on any platform with a JVM. The following command runs the bytecode:

run

```
java Welcome
```

Figure 1.13 shows the **javac** command for compiling Welcome.java. The compiler generated the Welcome.class file. This file is executed using the **java** command.

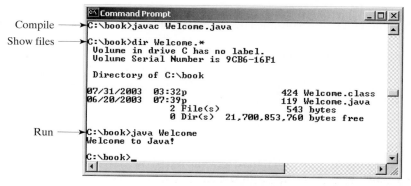

FIGURE 1.13   The output of Listing 1.1 displays the message Welcome to Java!

Caution

Do not use the extension .class in the command line when executing the program. The JVM assumes that the first argument in the command is the filename and then fetches **filename.class** to execute. It would attempt to fetch **filename.class.class** if you used **java filename.class** in the command line.

NoClassDefFoundError

NoSuchMethodError

Tip

If you execute a class file that does not exist, a **NoClassDefFoundError** exception will occur. If you execute a class file that does not have a **main** method or you mistype the **main** method (e.g., by typing **Main** instead of **main**), a **NoSuchMethodError** will occur.

class loader

bytecode verifier

Note

When executing a Java program, the JVM first loads the bytecode of the class to memory using a program called the *class loader*. If your program uses other classes, the class loader dynamically loads them just before they are needed. After a class is loaded, the JVM uses a program called *bytecode verifier* to check the validity of the bytecode and ensure that the bytecode does not violate Java's security restrictions. Java enforces strict security to make sure that Java programs arriving from the network do not harm your computer.

1.10 Anatomy of a Java Program

The application program in Listing 1.1 has the following components:

- Comments
- Reserved words
- Modifiers
- Statements
- Blocks
- Classes
- Methods
- The **main** method

To build a program, you need to understand these basic elements. They are explained in the sections that follow.

1.10.1 Comments

The first line in Welcome.java in Listing 1.1 is a *comment* that documents what the program is and how the program is constructed. Comments help programmers to communicate and understand the program. Comments are not programming statements and thus are ignored by the compiler. In Java, comments are preceded by two slashes (//) on a line, called a *line comment*, or enclosed between /* and */ on one or several lines, called a *paragraph comment*. When the compiler sees //, it ignores all text after // on the same line. When it sees /*, it scans for the next */ and ignores any text between /* and */.

line comment
paragraph comment

Here are examples of the two types of comments:

```
// This application program prints Welcome to Java!
/* This application program prints Welcome to Java! */
/* This application program
   prints Welcome to Java! */
```

Note

In addition to the two comment styles, `//` and `/*`, Java supports comments of a special type, referred to as *javadoc comments*. javadoc comments begin with `/**` and end with `*/`. They are used for documenting classes, data, and methods. They can be extracted into an HTML file using JDK's **javadoc** command. For more information, see java.sun.com/j2se/javadoc.

javadoc comment

1.10.2 Reserved Words

Reserved words, or *keywords*, are words that have a specific meaning to the compiler and cannot be used for other purposes in the program. For example, when the compiler sees the word **class**, it understands that the word after **class** is the name for the class. Other reserved words in Listing 1.1 are **public**, **static**, and **void**. Their use will be introduced later in the book.

reserved word

Tip

Because Java is *case-sensitive*, **public** is a reserved word, but **Public** is not. Nonetheless, for clarity and readability, it would be best to avoid using reserved words in other forms. (See Appendix A, "Java Keywords.")

case-sensitive

1.10.3 Modifiers

Java uses certain reserved words called *modifiers* that specify the properties of the data, methods, and classes and how they can be used. Examples of modifiers are **public** and **static**. Other modifiers are **private**, **final**, **abstract**, and **protected**. A **public** datum, method, or class can be accessed by other classes. A **private** datum or method cannot be accessed by other classes.

modifier

1.10.4 Statements

A *statement* represents an action or a sequence of actions. The statement **System.out. println("Welcome to Java!");** in the program in Listing 1.1 is a statement to display the greeting "Welcome to Java!" Every statement in Java ends with a *semicolon (;)*.

statement

semicolon

1.10.5 Blocks

The braces in the program form a *block* that groups the components of the program. In Java, each block begins with an opening brace (`{`) and ends with a closing brace (`}`). Every class has a *class block* that groups the data and methods of the class. Every method has a *method block* that groups the statements in the method. Blocks can be *nested*, meaning that one block can be placed within another, as shown in the following code.

block

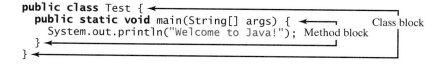

1.10.6 Classes

The *class* is the essential Java construct. To program in Java, you must understand classes and be able to write and use them. The mystery of classes will be unveiled throughout the book. For now, though, it is enough to know that a program is defined by using one or more classes.

class

1.10.7 Methods

method

What is **System.out.println**? **System.out** is known as the *standard output object*. **println** is a *method* in the object, which consists of a collection of statements that perform a sequence of operations to display a message to the standard output device. If you run the program from the command window, the output from the **System.out.println** is displayed in the command window. The method can be used even without fully understanding the details of how it works. It is used by invoking a statement with a string argument. The string argument is enclosed in parentheses. In this case, the argument is **"Welcome to Java!"** You can call the same **println** method with a different argument to print a different message.

1.10.8 The **main** Method

main method

Every Java application must have a user-declared **main** method that defines where the program execution begins. The JVM executes the application by invoking the **main** method. The **main** method looks like this:

```
public static void main(String[] args) {
  // Statements;
}
```

1.11 Displaying Text in a Message Dialog Box

The program in Listing 1.1 displays the text on the console, as shown in Figure 1.13. You can rewrite the program to display the text in a message dialog box. To do so, you need to use the **showMessageDialog** method in the **JOptionPane** class. **JOptionPane** is one of the many predefined classes in the Java system that you can reuse rather than "reinventing the wheel." You can use the **showMessageDialog** method to display any text in a message dialog box, as shown in Figure 1.14. The new program is given in Listing 1.2.

JOptionPane

showMessageDialog

FIGURE 1.14 "Welcome to Java!" is displayed in a message box.

LISTING 1.2 WelcomeInMessageDialogBox.java

paragraph comment

import

main method

display message

```
 1  /** This application program displays Welcome to Java!
 2   *  in a message dialog box.
 3   */
 4  import javax.swing.JOptionPane;
 5
 6  public class WelcomeInMessageDialogBox {
 7    public static void main(String[] args) {
 8      // Display Welcome to Java! in a message dialog box
 9      JOptionPane.showMessageDialog(null, "Welcome to Java!",
10        "Display Message", JOptionPane.INFORMATION_MESSAGE);
11    }
12  }
```

The line numbers are not part of the program, but are displayed for reference purposes.

This program uses a Java class **JOptionPane** (line 9). Java's predefined classes are grouped into packages. **JOptionPane** is in the **javax.swing** package. **JOptionPane** is imported to the program using the **import** statement in line 4 so that the compiler can locate the class. Recall that you have used the **System** class in the statement *System.out. println("Welcome to Java");* in Listing 1.1. The **System** class is not imported because it is in the **java.lang** package. All the classes in the **java.lang** package are implicitly imported in every Java program.

 Note

If you replace **JOptionPane** on line 9 with **javax.swing.JOptionPane**, you don't need to import it in line 4. **javax.swing.JOptionPane** is the full name for the **JOptionPane** class.

The **showMessageDialog** method is a *static* method. Such a method should be invoked by using the class name followed by a dot operator (.) and the method name with arguments. Static methods will be introduced in Chapter 5, "Methods." The **showMessageDialog** method can be invoked with four arguments, as in lines 9–10.

The first argument can always be **null**. **null** is a Java keyword that will be fully introduced in Part II, "Object-Oriented Programming." The second argument can be a string for text to be displayed. The third argument is the title of the message box. The fourth argument can be **JOptionPane.INFORMATION_MESSAGE**, which causes the icon ( ) to be displayed in the message box.

 Note

There are several ways to use the **showMessageDialog** method. For the time being, all you need to know are two ways to invoke it. One is to use a statement, as shown in the example:

```
JOptionPane.showMessageDialog(null, x,
    y, JOptionPane.INFORMATION_MESSAGE);
```

where **x** is a string for the text to be displayed, and **y** is a string for the title of the message box. The other is to use a statement like this one:

```
JOptionPane.showMessageDialog(null, x);
```

where **x** is a string for the text to be displayed.

KEY TERMS

.class file   19
.java file   19
assembly language   8
binary numbers   11
bit   5
block   20
byte   5
bytecode   9
bytecode verifier   20

cable modem   7
central processing unit (CPU)   4
class loader   20
comment   20
compiler   9
dot pitch   7
DSL (digital subscriber line)   7
hardware   4
hexadecimal numbers   11

high-level language   8

Integrated Development Environment
(IDE)   17

java command   19

javac command   19

Java Development Toolkit (JDK)   16

Java Virtual Machine (JVM)   9

keyword (or reserved word)   21

machine language   7

`main` method   17

memory   4

modem   7

network interface card (NIC)   7

operating system (OS)   10

pixel   7

resolution   7

software   4

source code/program   9, 18

source file   9, 18

storage devices   6

statement   21

Note

The above terms are defined in this chapter. *Supplement I.A*, "Glossary," lists all the key terms and descriptions in the book, organized by chapters.

Supplement I.A

CHAPTER SUMMARY

■   A computer is an electronic device that stores and processes data. A computer includes both *hardware* and *software*. In general, hardware is the physical aspect of the computer that can be seen, and software is the invisible instructions that control the hardware and make it perform tasks.

■   Computer *programs*, known as *software*, are instructions to the computer. You tell a computer what to do through programs. Computer programming consists of writing instructions for computers to perform.

■   The *machine language* is a set of primitive instructions built into every computer. *Assembly language* is a low-level programming language in which a mnemonic is used to represent each of the machine-language instructions.

■   *High-level languages* are English-like and easy to learn and program. There are over one hundred high-level languages. A program written in a high-level language is called a s*ource program*. Since a computer cannot understand a source program, a program called a *compiler* is used to translate the source program into a machine language program, which is then linked with other supporting library code to form an executable file.

■   The *operating system* (OS) is a program that manages and controls a computer's activities. Application programs, such as Web browsers and word processors, cannot run without an operating system.

■   Java was developed by a team led by James Gosling at Sun Microsystems. It is an Internet programming language. Since its inception in 1995, it has quickly become a premier language for building software.

■   Java is platform-independent, meaning that you can write a program once and run it anywhere.

■ Java programs can be embedded in HTML pages and downloaded by Web browsers to bring live animation and interaction to Web clients.

■ Java source files end with the .java extension. Every class is compiled into a separate file bytecode that has the same name as the class and ends with the .class extension.

■ To compile a Java source code file, use the **javac** command. To run a Java class, use the **java** command.

■ Every Java program is a set of class definitions. The keyword `class` introduces a class definition. The contents of the class are included in a block. A block begins with an opening brace ({) and ends with a closing brace (}). Methods are contained in a class.

■ A Java application must have a `main` method. The `main` method is the entry point where the application program starts when it is executed.

REVIEW QUESTIONS

 Note
Answers to review questions are on the Companion Website.

Sections 1.2–1.4

1.1   Define hardware and software.

1.2   Define machine language, assembly language, and high-level programming language.

1.3   What is an operating system?

Section 1.5

1.4   Convert the following decimal numbers into hexadecimal and binary numbers.

100; 4340; 2000

1.5   Convert the following binary numbers into hexadecimal numbers and decimal numbers.

1000011001; 100000000; 100111

1.6   Convert the following hexdecimal numbers into binary and decimal numbers.

FEFA9; 93; 2000

Sections 1.6–1.8

1.7   Describe the history of Java. Can Java run on any machine? What is needed to run Java on a computer?

1.8   What are the input and output of a Java compiler?

1.9   List some Java development tools. Are tools like Eclipse, NetBeans, and JBuilder different languages from Java, or are they dialects or extensions of Java?

1.10   What is the relationship between Java and HTML?

Sections 1.9–1.11

1.11 Explain the Java keywords. List some Java keywords you learned in this chapter.

1.12 Is Java case-sensitive? What is the case for Java keywords?

1.13 What is the Java source filename extension, and what is the Java bytecode filename extension?

1.14 What is a comment? What is the syntax for a comment in Java? Is the comment ignored by the compiler?

1.15 What is the statement to display a string on the console? What is the statement to display the message "Hello world" in a message dialog box?

1.16 Identify and fix the errors in the following code:

```
1 public class Welcome {
2   public void Main(String[] args) {
3     System.out.println('Welcome to Java!);
4   }
5 }
```

1.17 What is the command to compile a Java program? What is the command to run a Java application?

1.18 If the exception NoClassFoundError is raised when you run a program, what is the cause of the error?

1.19 If the exception "NoSuchMethodError: main" is raised when you run a program, what is the cause of the error?

PROGRAMMING EXERCISES

1.1 (*Creating, compiling, and running a Java program*) Create a source file containing a Java program. Perform the following steps to compile the program and run it (see §1.9, "Creating, Compiling, and Executing a Java Program"):

1. Create a file named **Welcome.java** for Listing 1.1. You can use any editor that will save your file in text format.
2. Compile the source file.
3. Run the bytecode.
4. Replace "Welcome to Java" with "My first program" in the program; save, compile, and run the program. You will see the message "My first program" displayed.
5. Replace main with Main, and recompile the source code. The compiler returns an error message because the Java program is case-sensitive.
6. Change it back, and compile the program again.
7. Instead of the command javac Welcome.java, use javac welcome.java. What happens?
8. Instead of the command java Welcome, use java Welcome.class. What happens?

CHAPTER 2

PRIMITIVE DATA TYPES AND OPERATIONS

Objectives

- To write Java programs to perform simple calculations (§2.2).
- To use identifiers to name variables, constants, methods, and classes (§2.3).
- To use variables to store data (§§2.4–2.5).
- To program with assignment statements and assignment expressions (§2.5).
- To use constants to store permanent data (§2.6).
- To declare Java primitive data types: `byte`, `short`, `int`, `long`, `float`, `double`, and `char` (§§2.7–2.9).
- To use Java operators to write numeric expressions (§§2.7–2.8).
- To represent characters using the `char` type (§2.9).
- To represent a string using the `String` type (§2.10).
- To obtain input using the `JOptionPane` input dialog boxes (§2.11).
- To obtain input from the console using the `Scanner` class (§2.13).
- To become familiar with Java documentation, programming style, and naming conventions (§2.14).
- To distinguish syntax errors, runtime errors, and logic errors (§2.15).
- To debug logic errors (§2.16).

2.1   Introduction

In the preceding chapter, you learned how to create, compile, and run a Java program. In this chapter, you will be introduced to Java primitive data types and related subjects, such as variables, constants, data types, operators, and expressions. You will learn how to write programs using primitive data types, input and output, and simple calculations.

2.2   Writing Simple Programs

To begin, let's look at a simple program that computes the area of a circle. The program reads in the radius of a circle and displays its area. The program will use variables to store the radius and the area, and will use an expression to compute the area.

algorithm

Writing this program involves designing simple program and data structures, as well as translating algorithms into programming code. An *algorithm* describes how a problem is solved in terms of the actions to be executed, and it specifies the order in which the actions should be executed. Algorithms can help the programmer plan a program before writing it in a programming language. The algorithm for this program can be described as follows:

1. Read in the radius.

2. Compute the area using the following formula:

$$\text{area} = \text{radius} \times \text{radius} \times \pi$$

3. Display the area.

Many of the problems you will meet when taking an introductory course in programming using this text can be described with simple, straightforward algorithms. As your education progresses, and you take courses on data structures or on algorithm design and analysis, you will encounter complex problems that require sophisticated solutions. You will need to design accurate, efficient algorithms with appropriate data structures in order to solve such problems.

primitive data types

Data structures involve data representation and manipulation. Java provides data types for representing integers, floating-point numbers (i.e., numbers with a decimal point), characters, and Boolean types. These types are known as *primitive data types*. Java also supports array and string types as objects. Some advanced data structures, such as stacks, sets, and lists, have built-in implementation in Java.

To novice programmers, coding is a daunting task. When you *code*, you translate an algorithm into a programming language understood by the computer. You already know that every Java program begins with a class declaration in which the keyword **class** is followed by the class name. Assume that you have chosen **ComputeArea** as the class name. The outline of the program would look like this:

```
public class ComputeArea {
  // Data and methods to be given later
}
```

As you know, every application must have a **main** method where program execution begins. So the program is expanded as follows:

```
public class ComputeArea {
  public static void main(String[] args) {
    // Step 1: Read in radius

    // Step 2: Compute area

    // Step 3: Display the area
  }
}
```

The program needs to read the radius entered by the user from the keyboard. This raises two important issues:

- Reading the radius.

- Storing the radius in the program.

Let's address the second issue first. In order to store the radius, the program needs to declare a symbol called a *variable* that will represent the radius. Variables are used to store data and computational results in the program.

variable

Rather than using **x** and **y**, choose *descriptive names*: in this case, **radius** for radius, and **area** for area. Specify their data types to let the compiler know what **radius** and **area** are, indicating whether they are integer, float, or something else. Declare **radius** and **area** as double-precision floating-point numbers. The program can be expanded as follows:

descriptive names

```java
public class ComputeArea {
  public static void main(String[] args) {
    double radius;
    double area;

    // Step 1: Read in radius

    // Step 2: Compute area

    // Step 3: Display the area
  }
}
```

The program declares **radius** and **area** as variables. The reserved word **double** indicates that **radius** and **area** are double-precision floating-point values stored in the computer.

The first step is to read in **radius**. Reading a number is not a simple matter. For the time being, let us assign a fixed number to **radius** in the program. In §2.11, "Getting Input from Input Dialogs," and §2.13, "Getting Input from the Console," you will learn how to obtain a numeric value from an input dialog and from the console.

The second step is to compute **area** by assigning the expression **radius * radius * 3.14159** to **area**.

In the final step, print **area** on the console by using the **System.out.println** method.

The complete program is shown in Listing 2.1. A sample run of the program is shown in Figure 2.1.

LISTING 2.1 ComputeArea.java

```java
1 public class ComputeArea {
2   /** Main method */
3   public static void main(String[] args) {
4     double radius; // Declare radius          radius  [no value]
5     double area; // Declare area              area    [no value]
6
7     // Assign a radius
8     radius = 20; // New value is radius        radius  [20]
9
10    // Compute area
11    area = radius * radius * 3.14159;          area    [1256.636]
12
```

```
13      // Display results
14      System.out.println("The area for the circle of radius " +
15        radius + " is " + area);
16    }
17  }
```

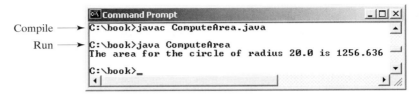

Compile
Run

FIGURE 2.1   The program displays the area of a circle.

declaring variable

assign value

Variables such as **radius** and **area** correspond to memory locations. Every variable has a name, a type, a size, and a value. Line 4 declares that **radius** can store a **double** value. The value is not defined until you assign a value. Line 8 assigns 20 into **radius**. Similarly, line 5 declares variable **area**, and line 11 assigns a value into **area**.

concatenating strings

concatenating strings with numbers

The plus sign (+) has two meanings: one for addition and the other for *concatenating strings*. The plus sign (+) in lines 14–15 is called a *string concatenation operator*. The string concatenation operator connects two strings if two operands are strings. If one of the operands is a non-string (e.g., a number), the non-string value is converted into a string and concatenated with the other string. So the plus signs (+) in lines 14–15 concatenate strings into a longer string, which is then displayed in the output. More on strings and string concatenation will be discussed in §2.10, "The **String** Type."

 Caution

A string constant cannot cross lines in the source code. Thus the following statement would result in a compilation error:

```
System.out.println("Introduction to Java Programming,
  by Y. Daniel Liang");
```

breaking a long string

To fix the error, break the string into substrings, and use the concatenation operator (+) to combine them:

```
System.out.println("Introduction to Java Programming, " +
  "by Y. Daniel Liang");
```

 Tip

incremental development and testing

This example consists of three steps. It is a good approach to develop and test these steps incrementally by adding one step at a time. You should apply this approach to all the programs, although the problem-solving steps are not explicitly stated in many programs in this book.

2.3 Identifiers

identifier

Just as every entity in the real world has a name, so you need to choose names for the things you will refer to in your programs. Programming languages use special symbols called *identifiers* to name such programming entities as variables, constants, methods, classes, and packages. Here are the rules for naming identifiers:

- An identifier is a sequence of characters that consists of letters, digits, underscores (_), and dollar signs ($).

- An identifier must start with a letter, an underscore (_), or a dollar sign ($). It cannot start with a digit.

- An identifier cannot be a reserved word. (See Appendix A, "Java Keywords," for a list of reserved words.)

- An identifier cannot be **true**, **false**, or **null**.

- An identifier can be of any length.

For example, **$2**, **ComputeArea**, **area**, **radius**, and **showMessageDialog** are legal identifiers, whereas **2A** and **d+4** are illegal identifiers because they do not follow the rules. The Java compiler detects illegal identifiers and reports syntax errors.

Note

Since Java is *case-sensitive*, **X** and **x** are different identifiers.

case-sensitive

Tip

Identifiers are used for naming variables, constants, methods, classes, and packages. Descriptive identifiers make programs easy to read. Besides choosing *descriptive names* for identifiers, there are naming conventions for different kinds of identifiers. Naming conventions are summarized in §2.14, "Programming Style and Documentation."

descriptive names

Tip

Do not name identifiers with *the $ character*. By convention, the $ character should be used only in mechanically generated source code.

the $ character

2.4 Variables

Variables are used to store data in a program. In the program in Listing 2.1, **radius** and **area** are variables of double-precision, floating-point type. You can assign any numerical value to **radius** and **area**, and the values of **radius** and **area** can be reassigned. For example, you can write the code shown below to compute the area for different radii:

```
// Compute the first area
radius = 1.0;
area = radius * radius * 3.14159;
System.out.println("The area is " + area + " for radius " + radius);

// Compute the second area
radius = 2.0;
area = radius * radius * 3.14159;
System.out.println("The area is " + area + " for radius " + radius);
```

2.4.1 Declaring Variables

Variables are for representing data of a certain type. To use a variable, you declare it by telling the compiler the name of the variable as well as what type of data it represents. This is called a *variable declaration*. Declaring a variable tells the compiler to allocate appropriate memory space for the variable based on its data type. The syntax for declaring a variable is:

```
datatype variableName;
```

Here are some examples of variable declarations:

declaring variable

```
int x;              // Declare x to be an integer variable;
double radius;      // Declare radius to be a double variable;
double interestRate; // Declare interestRate to be a double variable;
char a;             // Declare a to be a character variable;
```

The examples use the data types **int**, **double**, and **char**. Later you will be introduced to additional data types, such as **byte**, **short**, **long**, **float**, and **boolean**.

If variables are of the same type, they can be declared together, as follows:

```
datatype variable1, variable2, ..., variablen;
```

The variables are separated by commas. For example,

```
int i, j, k; // Declare i, j, and k as int variables
```

 Note

naming variables

By convention, variable names are in lowercase. If a name consists of several words, concatenate all of them and capitalize the first letter of each word except the first. Examples of variables are **radius** and **interestRate**.

2.5 Assignment Statements and Assignment Expressions

assignment statement
assignment operator

After a variable is declared, you can assign a value to it by using an *assignment statement*. In Java, the equal sign (=) is used as the *assignment operator*. The syntax for assignment statements is as follows:

```
variable = expression;
```

expression

An *expression* represents a computation involving values, variables, and operators that together evaluates to a value. For example, consider the following code:

```
int x = 1;                    // Assign 1 to variable x;
double radius = 1.0;          // Assign 1.0 to variable radius;
x = 5 * (3 / 2) + 3 * 2;      // Assign the value of the expression to x;
x = y + 1;                    // Assign the addition of y and 1 to x;
area = radius * radius * 3.14159; // Compute area
```

A variable can also be used in an expression. For example,

```
x = x + 1;
```

In this assignment statement, the result of **x + 1** is assigned to **x**. If **x** is **1** before the statement is executed, then it becomes **2** after the statement is executed.

To assign a value to a variable, the variable name must be on the left of the assignment operator. Thus, **1 = x** would be wrong.

In Java, an assignment statement can also be treated as an expression that evaluates to the value being assigned to the variable on the left-hand side of the assignment operator. For this reason, an assignment statement is also known as an *assignment expression*. For example, the following statement is correct:

assignment expression

```
System.out.println(x = 1);
```

which is equivalent to

```
x = 1;
System.out.println(x);
```

The following statement is also correct:

```
i = j = k = 1;
```

which is equivalent to

```
k = 1;
j = k;
i = j;
```

Note

In an assignment statement, the data type of the variable on the left must be compatible with the data type of the value on the right. For example, `int x = 1.0` would be illegal because the data type of `x` is `int`. You cannot assign a `double` value (`1.0`) to an `int` variable without using type casting. Type casting is introduced in §2.8, "Numeric Type Conversions."

2.5.1   Declaring and Initializing Variables in One Step

Variables often have initial values. You can declare a variable and initialize it in one step. Consider, for instance, the following code:

```
int x = 1;
```

This is equivalent to the next two statements:

```
int x;
x = 1;
```

You can also use a shorthand form to declare and initialize variables of the same type together. For example,

```
int i = 1, j = 2;
```

Tip

A variable must be declared before it can be assigned a value. A variable declared in a method must be assigned a value before it can be used. Whenever possible, declare a variable and assign its initial value in one step. This will make the program easy to read and avoid programming errors.

2.6 Constants

The value of a variable may change during the execution of the program, but a *constant* represents permanent data that never changes. In our **ComputeArea** program, π is a constant. If you use it frequently, you don't want to keep typing `3.14159`; instead, you can define a constant for π. Here is the syntax for declaring a constant:

constant

```
final datatype CONSTANTNAME = VALUE;
```

A constant must be declared and initialized in the same statement. The word `final` is a Java keyword which means that the constant cannot be changed. For example, in the **ComputeArea** program, you could define π as a constant and rewrite the program as follows:

```java
// ComputeArea.java: Compute the area of a circle
public class ComputeArea {
  /** Main method */
  public static void main(String[] args) {
    final double PI = 3.14159; // Declare a constant

    // Assign a radius
    double radius = 20;
```

```
    // Compute area
    double area = radius * radius * PI;

    // Display results
    System.out.println("The area for the circle of radius " +
      radius + " is " + area);
  }
}
```

Caution

naming constants

By convention, constants are named in uppercase: PI, not pi or Pi.

Note

benefits of constants

There are three benefits of using constants: (1) you don't have to repeatedly type the same value; (2) the value can be changed in a single location if necessary; (3) a descriptive name for a constant makes the program easy to read.

2.7 Numeric Data Types and Operations

Every data type has a range of values. The compiler allocates memory space to store each variable or constant according to its data type. Java provides eight primitive data types for numeric values, characters, and Boolean values. In this section, numeric data types are introduced.

Table 2.1 lists the six numeric data types, their ranges, and their storage sizes.

TABLE 2.1 Numeric Data Types

Name	Range	Storage Size
byte	-2^7 (-128) to $2^7 - 1$ (127)	8-bit signed
short	-2^{15} (-32768) to $2^{15} - 1$ (32767)	16-bit signed
int	-2^{31} (-2147483648) to $2^{31} - 1$ (2147483647)	32-bit signed
long	-2^{63} to $2^{63} - 1$ (i.e., -9223372036854775808 to 9223372036854775807)	64-bit signed
float	Negative range: $-3.4028235E+38$ to $-1.4E-45$ Positive range: $1.4E-45$ to $3.4028235E+38$	32-bit IEEE 754
double	Negative range: $-1.7976931348623157E+308$ to $-4.9E-324$ Positive range: $4.9E-324$ to $1.7976931348623157E+308$	64-bit IEEE 754

Note

IEEE 754 is a standard approved by the Institute of Electrical and Electronics Engineers for representing floating-point numbers on computers. The standard has been widely adopted. Java has adopted the 32-bit **IEEE 754** for the float type and the 64-bit **IEEE 754** for the double type. The **IEEE 754** standard also defines special values and operations in Appendix F, "Special Floating-Point Values."

integer

Java uses four types for integers: byte, short, int, and long. Choose the type that is most appropriate for your variable. For example, if you know an integer stored in a variable is within a range of byte, declare the variable as a byte.

floating-point

Java uses two types for *floating-point* numbers: float and double. The double type is twice as big as float. So, the double is known as *double precision*, while float is known as *single precision*. Normally, you should use the double type because it is more accurate than the float type.

2.7.1 Numeric Operators

The operators for numeric data types include the standard arithmetic operators: addition (+), subtraction (−), multiplication (*), division (/), and remainder (%), as shown in Table 2.2.

operators +, −, *, /, %

TABLE 2.2 Numeric Operators

Name	Meaning	Example	Result
+	Addition	34 + 1	35
−	Subtraction	34.0 − 0.1	33.9
*	Multiplication	300 * 30	9000
/	Division	1.0 / 2.0	0.5
%	Remainder	20 % 3	2

The result of *integer division* is an integer. The fractional part is truncated. For example, **5/2** yields **2**, not **2.5**, and **−5 / 2** yields **−2**, not **−2.5**.

integer division

The **%** operator yields the remainder after division. The left-hand operand is the dividend, and the right-hand operand is the divisor. Therefore, **7 % 3** yields **1**, **12 % 4** yields **0**, **26 % 8** yields **2**, and **20 % 13** yields **7**.

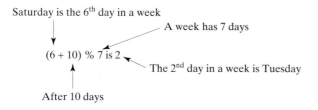

The **%** operator is often used for positive integers but also can be used with negative integers and floating-point values. The remainder is negative only if the dividend is negative. For example, **−7 % 3** yields **−1**, **−12 % 4** yields **0**, **−26 % −8** yields **−2**, and **20 % −13** yields **7**.

Remainder is very useful in programming. For example, an even number **% 2** is always **0**, and an odd number **% 2** is always **1**. So you can use this property to determine whether a number is even or odd. Suppose today is Saturday, you and your friend are going to meet in **10** days. What day is in **10** days? You can find that day is Tuesday using the following expression:

Saturday is the 6ᵗʰ day in a week
A week has 7 days
(6 + 10) % 7 is 2
The 2ⁿᵈ day in a week is Tuesday
After 10 days

Listing 2.2 gives a program that obtains minutes and remaining seconds from an amount of time in seconds. For example, **500** seconds contains **8** minutes and **20** seconds.

LISTING 2.2 DisplayTime.java

```java
1 import javax.swing.JOptionPane;
2
3 public class DisplayTime {
4   public static void main(String[] args) {
5     int seconds = 500;
```

```
 6     int minutes = seconds / 60;
 7     int remainingSeconds = seconds % 60;
 8     JOptionPane.showMessageDialog(null,
 9       seconds + " seconds is " + minutes +
10       " minutes and " + remainingSeconds
11       + " seconds");
12   }
13 }
```

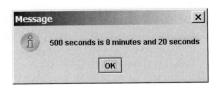

Line 6 obtains the minutes using **seconds / 60**. Line 7 (**seconds % 60**) obtains the remaining seconds after taking away the minutes.

unary operator
binary operator

The + and − operators can be both unary and binary. A *unary* operator only one operand; a *binary* operator has two operands. For example, the − operator in −**5** can be considered a unary operator to negate number **5**, whereas the − operator in **4 − 5** is a binary operator for subtracting **5** from **4**.

approximation

Note

Calculations involving floating-point numbers are approximated because these numbers are not stored with complete accuracy. For example,

```
System.out.println(1.0 - 0.1 - 0.1 - 0.1 - 0.1 - 0.1);
```

displays **0.5000000000000001**, not **0.5**, and

```
System.out.println(1.0 - 0.9);
```

displays **0.09999999999999998**, not **0.1**. Integers are stored precisely. Therefore, calculations with integers yield a precise integer result.

2.7.2 Numeric Literals

literal

A *literal* is a constant value that appears directly in a program. For example, **34**, **1000000**, and **5.0** are literals in the following statements:

```
int i = 34;
long k = 1000000;
double d = 5.0;
```

Integer Literals

An integer literal can be assigned to an integer variable as long as it can fit into the variable. A compilation error would occur if the literal were too large for the variable to hold. The statement **byte b = 128**, for example, would cause a compilation error, because **128** cannot be stored in a variable of the **byte** type. (Note that the range for a byte value is from −**128** to **127**.)

An integer literal is assumed to be of the **int** type, whose value is between −2^{31} (−**2147483648**) and 2^{31}−1 (**2147483647**). The statement **System.out.println (2147483648)**, for example, would cause a compilation error, because **2147483648** is too long as an **int** value.

To denote an integer literal of the **long** type, append the letter **L** or **l** to it (e.g., 2147483648L). **L** is preferred because **l** (lowercase L) can easily be confused with 1 (the digit one). Since **2147483648** exceeds the range for the **int** type, it must be denoted as 2147483648L.

long literal

Note

By default, an integer literal is a decimal number. To denote an octal integer literal, use a leading *0* (zero), and to denote a hexadecimal integer literal, use a leading *0x* or *0X* (zero x). For example, the following code displays the decimal value **65535** for hexadecimal number **FFFF**.

octal and hex literals

```
System.out.println(0xFFFF);
```

Hexadecimal numbers, binary numbers, and octal numbers were introduced in §1.5, "Number Systems."

Floating-Point Literals

Floating-point literals are written with a decimal point. By default, a floating-point literal is treated as a **double** type value. For example, **5.0** is considered a **double** value, not a **float** value. You can make a number a **float** by appending the letter **f** or **F**, and you can make a number a **double** by appending the letter **d** or **D**. For example, you can use **100.2f** or **100.2F** for a **float** number, and **100.2d** or **100.2D** for a **double** number.

suffix **f** or **F**
suffix **d** or **D**

Note

The **double** type values are more accurate than the **float** type values. For example,

double vs. **float**

```
System.out.println("1.0 / 3.0 is " + 1.0 / 3.0);
```

displays **1.0 / 3.0 is 0.3333333333333333**.

```
System.out.println("1.0F / 3.0F is " + 1.0F / 3.0F);
```

displays **1.0F / 3.0F is 0.33333334**.

Scientific Notations

Floating-point literals can also be specified in scientific notation; for example, **1.23456e+2**, the same as **1.23456e2**, is equivalent to $1.23456 \times 10^2 = 123.456$ and **1.23456e-2** is equivalent to $1.23456 \times 10^{-2} = 0.0123456$. E (or **e**) represents an exponent and can be either in lowercase or uppercase.

Note

The **float** and **double** types are used to represent numbers with a decimal point. Why are they called *floating-point numbers*? These numbers are stored into scientific notation. When a number such as **50.534** is converted into scientific notation such as **5.053e1**, its decimal point is moved (i.e., floated) to a new position.

why called floating-point?

2.7.3 Arithmetic Expressions

Writing numeric expressions in Java involves a straightforward translation of an arithmetic expression using Java operators. For example, the arithmetic expression

$$\frac{3 + 4x}{5} - \frac{10(y - 5)(a + b + c)}{x} + 9\left(\frac{4}{x} + \frac{9 + x}{y}\right)$$

can be translated into a Java expression as:

```
(3 + 4 * x) / 5 - 10 * (y - 5) * (a + b + c) / x +
9 * (4 / x + (9 + x) / y)
```

The numeric operators in a Java expression are applied the same way as in an arithmetic expression. Operators contained within pairs of parentheses are evaluated first. Parentheses can be nested, in which case the expression in the inner parentheses is evaluated first. Multiplication, division, and remainder operators are applied next. If an expression contains several multiplication, division, and remainder operators, they are applied from left to right. Addition and subtraction operators are applied last. If an expression contains several addition and subtraction operators, they are applied from left to right.

Listing 2.3 gives a program that converts a Fahrenheit degree to Celsius using the formula $celsius = \left(\frac{5}{9}\right)(fahrenheit - 32)$.

LISTING 2.3 FahrenheitToCelsius.java

```
1 public class FahrenheitToCelsius {
2   public static void main(String[] args) {
3     double fahrenheit = 100; // Say 100;
4     double celsius = (5.0 / 9) * (fahrenheit - 32);
5     System.out.println("Fahrenheit " + fahrenheit + " is " +
6       celsius + " in Celsius");
7   }
8 }
```

integer vs. decimal division

Be careful when applying division. Division of two integers yields an integer in Java. $\frac{5}{9}$ is translated to **5.0 / 9** instead of **5 / 9** in line 4, because **5 / 9** yields **0** in Java.

2.7.4 Shorthand Operators

Very often the current value of a variable is used, modified, and then reassigned back to the same variable. For example, the following statement adds the current value of **i** with **8** and assigns the result back to **i**.

```
i = i + 8;
```

shorthand operator

Java allows you to combine assignment and addition operators using a *shorthand operator*. For example, the preceding statement can be written as:

```
i += 8;
```

shorthand operator

The += is called the *addition assignment operator*. Other *shorthand operators* are shown in Table 2.3.

TABLE 2.3 Shorthand Operators

Operator	Name	Example	Equivalent
+=	Addition assignment	i += 8	i = i + 8
-=	Subtraction assignment	f -= 8.0	f = f - 8.0
*=	Multiplication assignment	i *= 8	i = i * 8
/=	Division assignment	i /= 8	i = i / 8
%=	Remainder assignment	i %= 8	i = i % 8

++ and --

There are two more shorthand operators for incrementing and decrementing a variable by 1. This is handy because that is often how much the value needs to be changed. These two operators are ++ and --. They can be used in prefix or suffix notation, as shown in Table 2.4.

TABLE 2.4 Increment and Decrement Operators

Operator	Name	Description
++var	preincrement	The expression (++var) increments var by 1 and evaluates to the *new* value in var *after* the increment.
var++	postincrement	The expression (var++) evaluates to the *original* value in var and increments var by 1.
−−var	predecrement	The expression (−−var) decrements var by 1 and evaluates to the *new* value in var *after* the decrement.
var−−	postdecrement	The expression (var−−) evaluates to the *original* value in var and decrements var by 1.

If the operator is *before* (prefixed to) the variable, the variable is incremented or decremented by 1, then the *new* value of the variable is returned. If the operator is *after* (suffixed to) the variable, the original *old* value of the variable is returned, then the variable is incremented or decremented by 1. Therefore, the prefixes ++x and −−x are referred to, respectively, as the *preincrement operator* and the *predecrement operator*; and the suffixes x++ and x−− are referred to, respectively, as the *postincrement operator* and the *postdecrement operator*. The prefix form of ++ (or −−) and the suffix form of ++ (or −−) are the same if they are used in isolation, but they cause different effects when used in an expression. The following code illustrates this:

preincrement, predecrement
postincrement, postdecrement

```
int i = 10;
int newNum = 10 * i++;
```
Same effect as →
```
int newNum = 10 * i;
i = i + 1;
```

In this case, i is incremented by 1, then the *old* value of i is returned and used in the multiplication. So newNum becomes 100. If i++ is replaced by ++i as follows,

```
int i = 10;
int newNum = 10 * (++i);
```
Same effect as →
```
i = i + 1;
int newNum = 10 * i;
```

i is incremented by 1, and the new value of i is returned and used in the multiplication. Thus newNum becomes 110.

Here is another example:

```
double x = 1.0;
double y = 5.0;
double z = x-- + (++y);
```

After all three lines are executed, y becomes 6.0, z becomes 7.0, and x becomes 0.0.

The increment operator ++ and the decrement operator −− can be applied to all integer and floating-point types. These operators are often used in loop statements. A *loop statement* is a structure that controls how many times an operation or a sequence of operations is performed in succession. This structure, and the subject of loop statements, is introduced in Chapter 4, "Loops."

 Tip
Using increment and decrement operators makes expressions short, but it also makes them complex and difficult to read. Avoid using these operators in expressions that modify multiple variables or the same variable multiple times, such as this one: int k = ++i + i.

Note

Like the assignment operator (=), the operators (+=, -=, *=, /=, %=, ++, and --) can be used to form an assignment statement as well as an expression. For example, in the following code, `x = 2` is a statement in the first line and is an expression in the second line.

```
x = 2; // statement
System.out.println(x = 2); // expression
```

expression statement

If a statement is used as an expression, it is called an *expression statement*.

Caution

There are no spaces in the shorthand operators. For example, + = should be +=.

2.8 Numeric Type Conversions

Sometimes it is necessary to mix numeric values of different types in a computation. Consider the following statements:

```
byte i = 100;
long k = i * 3 + 4;
double d = i * 3.1 + k / 2;
```

Are these statements correct? Java allows binary operations on values of different types. When performing a binary operation involving two operands of different types, Java automatically converts the operand based on the following rules:

converting operands

1. If one of the operands is **double**, the other is converted into **double**.

2. Otherwise, if one of the operands is **float**, the other is converted into **float**.

3. Otherwise, if one of the operands is **long**, the other is converted into **long**.

4. Otherwise, both operands are converted into **int**.

For example, the result of `1 / 2` is `0`, because both operands **int** values. The result of `1.0 / 2` is `0.5`, because `1.0` is **double** and `2` is converted to `2.0`.

The range of numeric types increases in this order:

range increases

→

byte, short, int, long, float, double

You can always assign a value to a numeric variable whose type supports a larger range of values; thus, for instance, you can assign a **long** value to a **float** variable. You cannot, however, assign a value to a variable of a type with smaller range unless you use *type casting*. Casting is an operation that converts a value of one data type into a value of another data type. Casting a variable of a type with a small range to a variable of a type with a larger range is known as *widening a type*. Casting a variable of a type with a large range to a variable of a type with a smaller range is known as *narrowing a type*. Widening a type can be performed automatically without explicit casting. Narrowing a type must be performed explicitly.

type casting

widening a type
narrowing a type

The syntax for casting gives the target type in parentheses, followed by the variable's name or the value to be cast. For example:

```
float f = (float)10.1;
int i = (int)f;
```

In the first line, the **double** value **10.1** is cast into **float**. In the second line, **i** has a value of **10**; the fractional part in **f** is truncated.

Caution

Casting is necessary if you are assigning a value to a variable of a smaller type range, such as assigning a **double** value to an **int** variable. A compilation error will occur if casting is not used in situations of this kind. Be careful when using casting. Lost information might lead to inaccurate results.

possible loss of precision

Note

Casting does not change the variable being cast. For example, **d** is not changed after casting in the following code:

```
double d = 4.5;
int i = (int)d;   // d is not changed
```

Note

To assign a variable of the **int** type to a variable of the **short** or **byte** type, explicit casting must be used. For example, the following statements have a syntax error:

```
int i = 1;
byte b = i; // Error because explicit casting is required
```

However, so long as the integer literal is within the permissible range of the target variable, explicit casting is not needed to assign an integer literal to a variable of the **short** or **byte** type. Please refer to §2.7.2, "Numeric Literals."

Listing 2.4 gives a program that displays the sales tax with two digits after the decimal point.

LISTING 2.4 SalesTax.java

```
1 public class SalesTax {
2   public static void main(String[] args) {
3     double purchaseAmount = 197.55;
4     double tax = purchaseAmount * 0.06;
5     System.out.println((int)(tax * 100) / 100.0);
6   }
7 }
```

Variable **purchaseAmount** is **197.55** (line 3). The sales tax is 6% of the purchase, so the **tax** is evaluated as **11.853** (line 4). The statement in line 5 displays the tax **11.85** with two digits after the decimal point. Note that **(int)(tax * 100)** is **1185**, so **(int)(tax * 100) / 100.0** is **11.85**.

formatting numbers

2.9 Character Data Type and Operations

The character data type, **char**, is used to represent a single character. A character literal is enclosed in single quotation marks. Consider the following code:

char type

```
char letter = 'A';
char numChar = '4';
```

The first statement assigns character **A** to the **char** variable **letter**. The second statement assigns the digit character **4** to the **char** variable **numChar**.

Caution

A string literal must be enclosed in quotation marks. A character literal is a single character enclosed in single quotation marks. So **"A"** is a string, and **'A'** is a character.

char literal

2.9.1 Unicode and ASCII Code

character encoding

Computers use binary numbers internally. A character is stored as a sequence of 0s and 1s in a computer. The process of converting a character to its binary representation is called *encoding*. There are different ways to encode a character. How characters are encoded is defined by an *encoding scheme*.

Unicode

original Unicode

Java supports *Unicode*, an encoding scheme established by the Unicode Consortium to support the interchange, processing, and display of written texts in the world's diverse languages. Unicode was originally designed as a 16-bit character encoding. The primitive data type `char` was intended to take advantage of this design by providing a simple data type that could hold any character. However, it turned out that the 65,536 characters possible in a 16-bit encoding are not sufficient to represent all the characters in the world. The Unicode standard therefore has been extended to allow up to 1,112,064 characters. Those characters that go beyond the original 16-bit limit are called *supplementary characters*. JDK 1.5 supports supplementary characters. Processing and representing supplementary characters are beyond the scope of this book. For simplicity, this book considers only the original 16-bit Unicode characters. These characters can be stored in a `char` type variable.

supplementary Unicode

A 16-bit Unicode takes two bytes, preceded by `\u`, expressed in four hexadecimal digits that run from `'\u0000'` to `'\uFFFF'`. For example, the word "welcome" is translated into Chinese using two characters, 欢迎. The Unicodes of these two characters are `"\u6B22\u8FCE"`. Listing 2.5 gives a program that displays two Chinese characters and three Greek letters.

LISTING 2.5 DisplayUnicode.java

```java
import javax.swing.JOptionPane;

public class DisplayUnicode {
  public static void main(String[] args) {
    JOptionPane.showMessageDialog(null,
      "\u6B22\u8FCE \u03b1 \u03b2 \u03b3",
      "\u6B22\u8FCE Welcome",
      JOptionPane.INFORMATION_MESSAGE);
  }
}
```

If no Chinese font is installed on your system, you will not be able to see the Chinese characters. The Unicodes for the Greek letters α β γ are `\u03b1 \u03b2 \u03b3`.

ASCII

Most computers use *ASCII* (*American Standard Code for Information Interchange*), a 7-bit encoding scheme for representing all uppercase and lowercase letters, digits, punctuation marks, and control characters. Unicode includes ASCII code, with `'\u0000'` to `'\u007F'` corresponding to the 128 ASCII characters. (See Appendix B, "The ASCII Character Set," for a list of ASCII characters and their decimal and hexadecimal codes.) You can use ASCII characters like `'X'`, `'1'`, and `'$'` in a Java program as well as Unicodes. Thus, for example, the following statements are equivalent:

```java
char letter = 'A';
char letter = '\u0041'; // Character A's Unicode is 0041
```

Both statements assign character `A` to `char` variable `letter`.

Note

char increment and decrement

The increment and decrement operators can also be used on `char` variables to get the next or preceding Unicode character. For example, the following statements display character `b`.

```java
char ch = 'a';
System.out.println(++ch);
```

2.9.2   Escape Sequences for Special Characters

Java allows you to use escape sequences to represent special characters, as shown in Table 2.5. An escape sequence begins with the backslash character (\) followed by a character that has a special meaning to the compiler.

TABLE 2.5   Java Escape Sequences

Character Escape Sequence	Name	Unicode Code
\b	Backspace	\u0008
\t	Tab	\u0009
\n	Linefeed	\u000A
\f	Formfeed	\u000C
\r	Carriage Return	\u000D
\\	Backslash	\u005C
\'	Single Quote	\u0027
\"	Double Quote	\u0022

Suppose you want to print the quoted message shown below:

```
He said "Java is fun"
```

The statement to print it should be

```
System.out.println("He said \"Java is fun\"");
```

2.9.3   Casting Between char and Numeric Types

A char can be cast into any numeric type, and vice versa. When an integer is cast into a char, only its lower sixteen bits of data are used; the other part is ignored.

For example, see the following code:

```
char c = (char)0XAB0041; // the lower 16 bits hex code 0041 is
                         // assigned to c
System.out.println(c);   // c is character A
```

When a floating-point value is cast into a char, the integral part of the floating-point value is cast into a char.

```
char c = (char)65.25;    // decimal 65 is assigned to t
System.out.println(c);   // c is character A
```

When a char is cast into a numeric type, the character's Unicode is cast into the specified numeric type.

```
int i = (int)'A';        // the Unicode of character A is assigned to i
System.out.println(i);   // i is 65
```

Implicit casting can be used if the result of a casting fits into the target variable. Otherwise, explicit casting must be used. For example, since the Unicode of 'a' is 97, which is within the range of a byte, these implicit castings are fine:

```
byte b = 'a';
int i = 'a';
```

But the following casting is incorrect, because the Unicode \uFFF4 cannot fit into a byte:

```
byte b = '\uFFF4';
```

To force assignment, use explicit casting, as follows:

```
byte b = (byte)'\uFFF4';
```

Any positive integer between 0 and FFFF in hexadecimal can be cast into a character implicitly. Any number not in this range must be cast into a **char** explicitly.

Note

numeric operators
on characters

All numeric operators can be applied to **char** operands. A **char** operand is automatically cast into a number if the other operand is a number or a character. If the other operand is a string, the character is concatenated with the string. For example, the following statements

```
int i = '2' + '3'; // (int)'2' is 50 and (int)'3' is 51
System.out.println("i is " + i);

int j = 2 + 'a'; // (int)'a' is 97
System.out.println("j is " + j);
System.out.println(j + " is the Unicode for character " + (char)j);

System.out.println("Chapter " + '2');
```

display

```
i is 101
j is 99
99 is the Unicode for character c
Chapter 2
```

Note

The Unicodes for lowercase letters are consecutive integers starting from the Unicode for 'a', then for 'b', 'c', ..., and 'z'. The same is true for the uppercase letters. Furthermore, the Unicode for 'a' is greater than the Unicode for 'A'. So 'a' – 'A' is the same as 'b' – 'B'. For a lowercase letter *ch*, its corresponding uppercase letter is (char)('A' + (ch – 'a')).

2.10 The **String** Type

The **char** type only represents one character. To represent a string of characters, use the data type called **String**. For example, the following code declares the message to be a string that has an initial value of "Welcome to Java".

```
String message = "Welcome to Java";
```

String is actually a predefined class in the Java library just like the **System** class and **JOptionPane** class. The **String** type is not a primitive type. It is known as a *reference type*. Any Java class can be used as a reference type for a variable. Reference data types will be thoroughly discussed in Chapter 7, "Classes and Objects." For the time being, you only need to know how to declare a **String** variable, how to assign a string to the variable, and how to concatenate strings.

As first shown in Listing 2.1, two strings can be concatenated. The plus sign (+) is the concatenation operator if one of the operands is a string. If one of the operands is a non-string (e.g., a number), the non-string value is converted into a string and concatenated with the other string. Here are some examples:

concatenating strings
and numbers

```
// Three strings are concatenated
String message = "Welcome " + "to " + "Java";

// String Chapter is concatenated with number 2
String s = "Chapter" + 2; // s becomes Chapter2
```

```
// String Supplement is concatenated with character B
String s1 = "Supplement" + 'B'; // s becomes SupplementB
```

If neither of the operands is a string, the plus sign (+) is the addition operator that adds two numbers.

The shorthand += operator can also be used for string concatenation. For example, the following code appends the string "and Java is fun" with the string "Welcome to Java" in message.

```
message += " and Java is fun";
```

So the new message is "Welcome to Java and Java is fun".

Suppose that i = 1 and j = 2, what is the output of the following statement?

```
System.out.println("i + j is " + i + j);
```

The output is "i + j is 12" because "i + j is " is concatenated with the value of i first. To force i + j to be executed first, enclose i + j in the parentheses, as follows:

```
System.out.println("i + j is " + (i + j));
```

2.11 Getting Input from Input Dialogs

In Listing 2.1, the radius is fixed in the source code. To use a different radius, you have to modify the source code and recompile it. Obviously, this is not convenient. You can use the showInputDialog method in the JOptionPane class to get input at runtime. When this method is executed, a dialog is displayed to enable you to enter an input value, as shown in Figure 2.2.

JOptionPane class

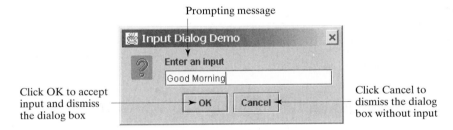

FIGURE 2.2 The input dialog box enables the user to enter a string.

After entering a string, click OK to accept the input and dismiss the dialog box. The input is returned from the method as a string. You can invoke the method with four arguments, as follows:

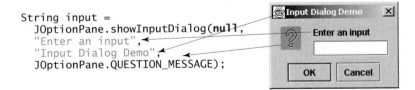

The first argument can always be null. The second argument is a string that prompts the user. The third argument is the title of the input box. The fourth argument can be JOptionPane.QUESTION_MESSAGE, which causes the icon ( ) to be displayed in the input box.

Note

There are several ways to use the showInputDialog method. For the time being, you only need to know two ways to invoke it.

showInputDialog method

One is to use a statement as shown in the example:

```
String string = JOptionPane.showInputDialog(null, x,
    y, JOptionPane.QUESTION_MESSAGE));
```

where x is a string for the prompting message, and y is a string for the title of the input dialog box.

The other is to use a statement like this one:

```
JOptionPane.showInputDialog(x);
```

where x is a string for the prompting message.

2.11.1 Converting Strings to Numbers

The input returned from the input dialog box is a string. If you enter a numeric value such as **123**, it returns **"123"**. You have to convert a string into a number to obtain the input as a number.

Integer.parseInt method

To convert a string into an **int** value, use the **parseInt** method in the **Integer** class, as follows:

```
int intValue = Integer.parseInt(intString);
```

where **intString** is a numeric string such as **"123"**.

Double.parseDouble method

To convert a string into a **double** value, use the **parseDouble** method in the **Double** class, as follows:

```
double doubleValue = Double.parseDouble(doubleString);
```

where **doubleString** is a numeric string such as **"123.45"**.

The **Integer** and **Double** classes are both included in the **java.lang** package, and thus are automatically imported.

2.12 Case Studies

In the preceding sections, you learned about variables, constants, primitive data types, operators, and expressions. You are now ready to use them to write interesting programs. This section presents three examples: computing loan payments, breaking a sum of money down into smaller units, and displaying the current time.

2.12.1 Example: Computing Loan Payments

This example shows you how to write a program that computes loan payments. The loan can be a car loan, a student loan, or a home mortgage loan. The program lets the user enter the interest rate, number of years, and loan amount, and then computes the monthly payment and the total payment. It concludes by displaying the monthly and total payments.

The formula to compute the monthly payment is as follows:

$$\frac{loanAmount \times monthlyInterestRate}{1 - \dfrac{1}{(1 + monthlyInterestRate)^{numberOfYears \times 12}}}$$

You don't have to know how this formula is derived. Nonetheless, given the monthly interest rate, number of years, and loan amount, you can use it to compute the monthly payment. Here are the steps in developing the program:

1. Prompt the user to enter the annual interest rate, number of years, and loan amount.

2. Obtain the monthly interest rate from the annual interest rate.

3. Compute the monthly payment using the preceding formula.

4. Compute the total payment, which is the monthly payment multiplied by 12 and multiplied by the number of years.

5. Display the monthly payment and total payment in a message dialog.

In the formula, you have to compute $(1 + monthlyInterestRate)^{number\ Of\ Years \times 12}$. The **pow(a, b)** method in the **Math** class can be used to compute a^b. The **Math** class, which comes with the Java API, is available to all Java programs. Other useful methods in the **Math** class will be introduced in Chapter 5, "Methods."   **pow(a, b)** method

Listing 2.6 gives the complete program. Figure 2.3 shows a sample run of the program.

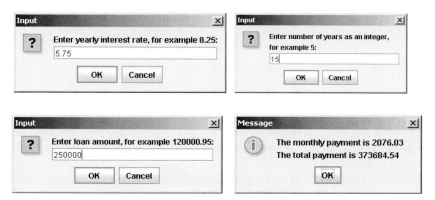

FIGURE 2.3   The program accepts the annual interest rate, number of years, and loan amount, then displays the monthly payment and total payment.

LISTING 2.6   ComputeLoan.java

```
 1 import javax.swing.JOptionPane;
 2
 3 public class ComputeLoan {
 4   /** Main method */
 5   public static void main(String[] args) {
 6     // Enter yearly interest rate
 7     String annualInterestRateString = JOptionPane.showInputDialog(
 8       "Enter yearly interest rate, for example 8.25:");
 9
10     // Convert string to double
11     double annualInterestRate =
12       Double.parseDouble(annualInterestRateString);
13
14     // Obtain monthly interest rate
15     double monthlyInterestRate = annualInterestRate / 1200;
16
17     // Enter number of years
18     String numberOfYearsString = JOptionPane.showInputDialog(
19       "Enter number of years as an integer, \nfor example 5:");
20
21     // Convert string to int
22     int numberOfYears = Integer.parseInt(numberOfYearsString);
23
24     // Enter loan amount
25     String loanString = JOptionPane.showInputDialog(
26       "Enter loan amount, for example 120000.95:");
27
```

enter interest rate

convert string
to double

monthlyPayment

totalPayment

preparing output

```
28      // Convert string to double
29      double loanAmount = Double.parseDouble(loanString);
30
31      // Calculate payment
32      double monthlyPayment = loanAmount * monthlyInterestRate / (1
33        - 1 / Math.pow(1 + monthlyInterestRate, numberOfYears * 12));
34      double totalPayment = monthlyPayment * numberOfYears * 12;
35
36      // Format to keep two digits after the decimal point
37      monthlyPayment = (int)(monthlyPayment * 100) / 100.0;
38      totalPayment = (int)(totalPayment * 100) / 100.0;
39
40      // Display results
41      String output = "The monthly payment is " + monthlyPayment +
42        "\nThe total payment is " + totalPayment;
43      JOptionPane.showMessageDialog(null, output);
44    }
45  }
```

The `showInputDialog` method in lines 7–8 displays an input dialog. Enter the interest rate as a double value and click OK to accept the input. The value is returned as a string that is assigned to the `String` variable `annualInterestRateString`. The `Double.parseDouble(annualInterestRateString)` (line 12) is used to convert the string into a `double` value. If you entered an input other than a numeric value, a runtime error would occur. In Chapter 17, "Exceptions and Assertions," you will learn how to handle the exception so that the program can continue to run.

Each new variable in a method must be declared once and only once. Choose the most appropriate data type for the variable. For example, `numberOfYears` is best declared as an `int` (line 22), although it could be declared as a `long`, `float`, or `double`. Note that `byte` might be the most appropriate for `numberOfYears`. For simplicity, however, the examples in this book will use `int` for integer and `double` for floating-point values.

The formula for computing the monthly payment is translated into Java code in lines 32–33.

formatting numbers

The statements in lines 37–38 are for formatting the number to keep two digits after the decimal point. For example, if `monthlyPayment` is `2076.0252175`, `(int)(monthlyPayment * 100)` is `207602`. Therefore, `(int)(monthlyPayment * 100) / 100.0` yields `2076.02`.

The strings are concatenated into `output` in lines 11–25. The linefeed escape character `'\n'` is in the string to display the text after `'\n'` in the next line.

Note

If you click *Cancel* in the input dialog box, no string is returned. A runtime error would occur.

2.12.2 Example: Counting Monetary Units

This section presents a program that classifies a given amount of money into smaller monetary units. The program lets the user enter an amount as a `double` value representing a total in dollars and cents, and outputs a report listing the monetary equivalent in dollars, quarters, dimes, nickels, and pennies, as shown in Figure 2.4.

Your program should report the maximum number of dollars, then the maximum number of quarters, and so on, in this order.

Here are the steps in developing the program:

1. Prompt the user to enter the amount as a decimal number such as `11.56`.

2. Convert the amount (e.g., `11.56`) into cents (`1156`).

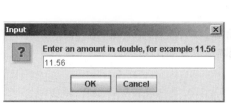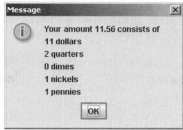

FIGURE 2.4 The program receives an amount in decimals and breaks it into dollars, quarters, dimes, nickels, and pennies.

3. Divide the cents by **100** to find the number of dollars. Obtain the remaining cents using the cents remainder **100**.

4. Divide the remaining cents by **25** to find the number of quarters. Obtain the remaining cents using the remaining cents remainder **25**.

5. Divide the remaining cents by **10** to find the number of dimes. Obtain the remaining cents using the remaining cents remainder **10**.

6. Divide the remaining cents by **5** to find the number of nickels. Obtain the remaining cents using the remaining cents remainder **5**.

7. The remaining cents are the pennies.

8. Display the result.

The complete program is given in Listing 2.7.

LISTING 2.7 ComputeChange.java

```
1  import javax.swing.JOptionPane;
2
3  public class ComputeChange {
4    /** Main method */
5    public static void main(String[] args) {
6      // Receive the amount
7      String amountString = JOptionPane.showInputDialog(
8        "Enter an amount in double, for example 11.56");
9
10     // Convert string to double
11     double amount = Double.parseDouble(amountString);
12
13     int remainingAmount = (int)(amount * 100);
14
15     // Find the number of one dollars
16     int numberOfOneDollars = remainingAmount / 100;           dollars
17     remainingAmount = remainingAmount % 100;
18
19     // Find the number of quarters in the remaining amount
20     int numberOfQuarters = remainingAmount / 25;              quarters
21     remainingAmount = remainingAmount % 25;
22
23     // Find the number of dimes in the remaining amount
24     int numberOfDimes = remainingAmount / 10;                 dimes
25     remainingAmount = remainingAmount % 10;
26
```

nickels

pennies

```
27      // Find the number of nickels in the remaining amount
28      int numberOfNickels = remainingAmount / 5;
29      remainingAmount = remainingAmount % 5;
30
31      // Find the number of pennies in the remaining amount
32      int numberOfPennies = remainingAmount;
33
34      // Display results
35      String output = "Your amount " + amount + " consists of \n" +
36        numberOfOneDollars + " dollars\n" +
37        numberOfQuarters + " quarters\n" +
38        numberOfDimes + " dimes\n" +
39        numberOfNickels + " nickels\n" +
40        numberOfPennies + " pennies";
41      JOptionPane.showMessageDialog(null, output);
42    }
43 }
```

The variable `amount` stores the amount entered from the input dialog box (lines 7–11). This variable is not changed because the amount has to be used at the end of the program to display the results. The program introduces the variable `remainingAmount` (line 13) to store the changing `remainingAmount`.

The variable `amount` is a `double` decimal representing dollars and cents. It is converted to an `int` variable `remainingAmount`, which represents all the cents. For instance, if `amount` is `11.56`, then the initial `remainingAmount` is `1156`. The division operator yields the integer part of the division. So `1156 / 100` is `11`. The remainder operator obtains the remainder of the division. So `1156 % 100` is `56`.

The program extracts the maximum number of singles from the total amount and obtains the remaining amount in the variable `remainingAmount` (lines 16–17). It then extracts the maximum number of quarters from `remainingAmount` and obtains a new `remainingAmount` (lines 20–21). Continuing the same process, the program finds the maximum number of dimes, nickels, and pennies in the remaining amount.

loss of precision

One serious problem with this example is the possible *loss of precision* when casting a `double` amount to an `int remainingAmount`. This could lead to an inaccurate result. If you try to enter the amount `10.03`, `10.03 * 100` becomes `1002.9999999999999`. You will find that the program displays `10` dollars and `2` pennies. To fix the problem, enter the amount as an integer value representing cents (see Exercise 2.10).

As shown in Figure 2.4, `0` dimes, `1` nickels, and `1` pennies are displayed in the result. It would be better not to display `0` dimes, and to display `1` nickel and `1` penny using the singular forms of the words. You will learn how to use selection statements to modify this program in the next chapter (see Exercise 3.7).

2.12.3 Example: Displaying the Current Time

This section presents a program that displays the current time in GMT (Greenwich Mean Time) in the format hour:minute:second, such as `13:19:8`, as shown in Figure 2.5.

FIGURE 2.5 The program displays the current GMT.

currentTimeMillis

The `currentTimeMillis` method in the `System` class returns the current time in milliseconds elapsed since the time `00:00:00` on January 1, 1970 GMT, as shown in Figure 2.6.

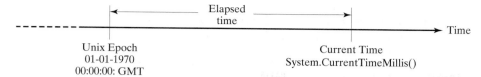

Figure 2.6 The `System.currentTimeMillis()` returns the number of milliseconds since the Unix epoch.

This time is known as the *Unix epoch* because 1970 was the year when the Unix operating system was formally introduced.

Unix epoch

You can use this method to obtain the current time, and then compute the current second, minute, and hour as follows.

1. Obtain the total milliseconds since midnight, Jan 1, 1970 in `totalMilliseconds` by invoking `System.currentTimeMillis()` (e.g., 1103203148368 milliseconds).

2. Obtain the total seconds `totalSeconds` by dividing `totalMilliseconds` by 1000 (e.g., 1103203148368 milliseconds / 1000 = 1103203148 seconds).

3. Compute the current second from `totalSeconds % 60` (e.g., 1103203148 seconds % 60 = 8, which is the current second).

4. Obtain the total minutes `totalMinutes` by dividing `totalSeconds` by 60 (e.g., 1103203148 seconds / 60 = 18386719 minutes).

5. Compute the current minute from `totalMinutes % 60` (e.g., 18386719 minutes % 60 = 19, which is the current minute).

6. Obtain the total hours `totalHours` by dividing `totalMinutes` by 60 (e.g., 18386719 minutes / 60 = 306445 hours).

7. Compute the current hour from `totalHours % 24` (e.g., 306445 hours % 24 = 19, which is the current hour).

The program follows, and the output is shown in Figure 2.5.

Listing 2.8 ShowCurrentTime.java

```
1  import javax.swing.JOptionPane;
2
3  public class ShowCurrentTime {
4    public static void main(String[] args) {
5      // Obtain the total milliseconds since the midnight, Jan 1, 1970
6      long totalMilliseconds = System.currentTimeMillis();
7
8      // Obtain the total seconds since the midnight, Jan 1, 1970
9      long totalSeconds = totalMilliseconds / 1000;
10
11     // Compute the current second in the minute in the hour
12     int currentSecond = (int)(totalSeconds % 60);
13
14     // Obtain the total minutes
15     long totalMinutes = totalSeconds / 60;
16
17     // Compute the current minute in the hour
18     int currentMinute = (int)(totalMinutes % 60);
19
20     // Obtain the total hours
21     long totalHours = totalMinutes / 60;
22
```

totalSeconds

currentSecond

totalMinutes

currentMinute

totalHours

currentHour

preparing output

```
23      // Compute the current hour
24      int currentHour = (int)(totalHours % 24);
25
26      // Display results
27      String output = "Current time is " + currentHour + ":"
28        + currentMinute + ":" + currentSecond + " GMT";
29
30      JOptionPane.showMessageDialog(null, output);
31    }
32 }
```

When `System.currentTimeMillis()` (line 6) is invoked, it returns the difference, measured in milliseconds, between the current GMT and midnight, January 1, 1970 GMT. This method returns the milliseconds as a `long` value.

2.13 Getting Input from the Console

You can obtain input from an input dialog box using the `JOptionPane.showInputDialog` method. Alternatively, you may obtain input from the console.

Java uses `System.out` to refer to the standard output device, and `System.in` to the standard input device. By default the output device is the console, and the input device is the keyboard. To perform console output, you simply use the `println` method to display a primitive value or a string to the console. Console input is not directly supported in Java, but you can use the `Scanner` class to create an object to read input from `System.in`, as follows:

```
Scanner scanner = new Scanner(System.in);
```

`Scanner` is a new class in JDK 1.5. The syntax *new Scanner(System.in)* creates an object of the `Scanner` type. The syntax *Scanner scanner* declares that `scanner` is a variable whose type is `Scanner`. The whole line *Scanner scanner = new Scanner(System.in)* creates a `Scanner` object and assigns its reference to the variable `scanner`. An object may contain methods. Invoking a method on an object is to ask the object to perform a task. A `Scanner` object contains the following methods for reading an input:

- `next()`: reading a string. A string is delimited by spaces.

- `nextByte()`: reading an integer of the `byte` type.

- `nextShort()`: reading an integer of the `short` type.

- `nextInt()`: reading an integer of the `int` type.

- `nextLong()`: reading an integer of the `long` type.

- `nextFloat()`: reading a number of the `float` type.

- `nextDouble()`: reading a number of the `double` type.

For example, the following statements prompt the user to enter a double value from the console.

```
System.out.print("Enter a double value: ");
Scanner scanner = new Scanner(System.in);
double d = scanner.nextDouble();
```

 Note

More details on classes and objects will be introduced in Chapter 7, "Classes and Objects." For the time being, you will just have to accept that this is how to obtain input from the console.

Note

The **print** method is identical to the **println** method except that **println** moves the cursor to the next line after displaying the string, but **print** does not advance the cursor to the next line when completed.

print vs. **println**

Listing 2.9 gives an example that reads various types of data from the console using the **Scanner** class. A sample run of this program is shown in Figure 2.7.

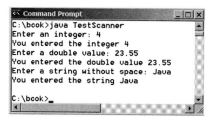

FIGURE 2.7   You can enter input from a command window.

LISTING 2.9   TestScanner.java

```java
 1 import java.util.Scanner; // Scanner is in java.util
 2
 3 public class TestScanner {
 4   public static void main(String args[]) {
 5     // Create a Scanner
 6     Scanner scanner = new Scanner(System.in);
 7
 8     // Prompt the user to enter an integer
 9     System.out.print("Enter an integer: ");
10     int intValue = scanner.nextInt();
11     System.out.println("You entered the integer " + intValue);
12
13     // Prompt the user to enter a double value
14     System.out.print("Enter a double value: ");
15     double doubleValue = scanner.nextDouble();
16     System.out.println("You entered the double value "
17       + doubleValue);
18
19     // Prompt the user to enter a string
20     System.out.print("Enter a string without space: ");
21     String string = scanner.next();
22     System.out.println("You entered the string " + string);
23   }
24 }
```

Tip

One benefit of using the console input is that you can store the input values in a text file and pass the file from the command line using the following command:

```
java TestScanner < input.txt
```

where input.txt is a text file that contains the data, as shown in Figure 2.8(a). The output of **java TestScanner < input.txt** is shown in Figure 2.8(b).

You can also save the output into a file using the following command:

```
java TestScanner < input.txt > out.txt
```

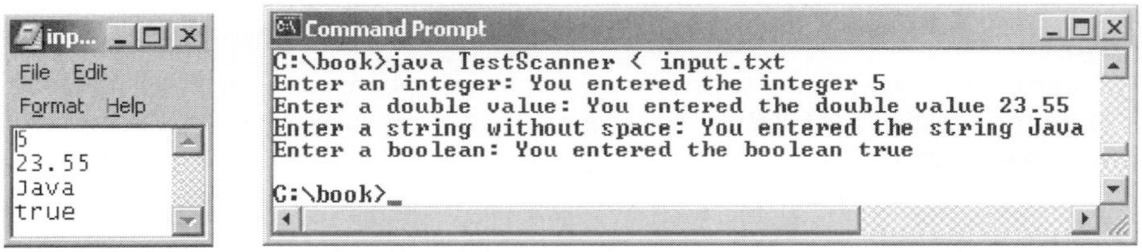

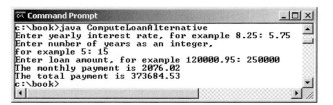

FIGURE 2.8 (a) You can create a text file using NotePad. (b) The data in the text file is passed to the program.

Caution

whitespace

By default, a **Scanner** object reads a string separated by *whitespaces* (i.e., ' ', '\t', '\f', '\r', and '\n'). To read a string with embedded spaces, see §8.8.2, "Reading Data Using **Scanner**."

Pedagogical NOTE

JOptionPane or **Scanner**?

You can use **JOptionPane** or **Scanner** for obtaining input, whichever is convenient. The examples in the book use **JOptionPane** for getting input for consistency. You can easily revise the examples using **Scanner** for getting input.

Listing 2.6 uses input dialog boxes to obtain input. Alternatively, you can read input from the console in Listing 2.10. A sample run of the new program is shown in Figure 2.9.

FIGURE 2.9 The program receives input from the console.

LISTING 2.10 ComputeLoanAlternative.java

```java
 1 import java.util.Scanner;
 2
 3 public class ComputeLoanAlternative {
 4   /** Main method */
 5   public static void main(String[] args) {
 6     // Create a scanner for input
 7     Scanner input = new Scanner(System.in);
 8
 9     // Enter yearly interest rate
10     System.out.print("Enter yearly interest rate, for example 8.25: ");
11     double annualInterestRate = input.nextDouble();
12
13     // Obtain monthly interest rate
14     double monthlyInterestRate = annualInterestRate / 1200;
15
16     // Enter number of years
17     System.out.print(
18       "Enter number of years as an integer, \nfor example 5: ");
19     int numberOfYears = input.nextInt();
20
21     // Enter loan amount
22     System.out.print("Enter loan amount, for example 120000.95: ");
```

create a scanner (line 7)

annualInterestRate (line 11)

monthlyInterestRate (line 14)

numberOfYears (line 19)

```
23    double loanAmount = input.nextDouble();                              loanAmount
24
25    // Calculate payment
26    double monthlyPayment = loanAmount * monthlyInterestRate / (1         monthlyPayment
27      - 1 / Math.pow(1 + monthlyInterestRate, numberOfYears * 12));
28    double totalPayment = monthlyPayment * numberOfYears * 12;            totalPayment
29
30    // Format to keep two digits after the decimal point
31    monthlyPayment = (int)(monthlyPayment * 100) / 100.0;                 formatting output
32    totalPayment = (int)(totalPayment * 100) / 100.0;
33
34    // Display results
35    System.out.println("The monthly payment is " + monthlyPayment);
36    System.out.println("The total payment is " + totalPayment);
37  }
38 }
```

2.14 Programming Style and Documentation

Programming style deals with what programs look like. A program can compile and run properly even if written on only one line, but writing it all on one line would be bad programming style because it would be hard to read. *Documentation* is the body of explanatory remarks and comments pertaining to a program. Programming style and documentation are as important as coding. Good programming style and appropriate documentation reduce the chance of errors and make programs easy to read. So far you have learned some good programming styles. This section summarizes them and gives several guidelines. More detailed guidelines on programming style and documentation can be found in Supplement I.D, "Java Coding Style Guidelines," on the Companion Website.

programming style

2.14.1 Appropriate Comments and Comment Styles

Include a summary at the beginning of the program to explain what the program does, its key features, its supporting data structures, and any unique techniques it uses. In a long program, you should also include comments that introduce each major step and explain anything that is difficult to read. It is important to make comments concise so that they do not crowd the program or make it difficult to read.

Use *javadoc comments* (/** ... */) for commenting on an entire class or an entire method. These comments must precede the class or the method header, and can be extracted in a javadoc HTML file. For commenting on steps inside a method, use line comments (//).

javadoc comments

2.14.2 Naming Conventions

Make sure that you choose descriptive names with straightforward meanings for the variables, constants, classes, and methods in your program. Names are case-sensitive. Listed below are the conventions for naming variables, methods, and classes.

- Use lowercase for variables and methods. If a name consists of several words, concatenate them into one, making the first word lowercase and capitalizing the first letter of each subsequent word; for example, the variables **radius** and **area** and the method **showInputDialog**.

  naming variables and methods

- Capitalize the first letter of each word in a class name; for example, the class names **ComputeArea**, **Math**, and **JOptionPane**.

  naming classes

- Capitalize every letter in a constant, and use underscores between words; for example, the constants **PI** and **MAX_VALUE**.

  naming constants

naming conventions

Tip

It is important to become familiar with the *naming conventions*. Understanding them will help you to understand Java programs. If you stick with the naming conventions, other programmers will be more willing to accept your program.

naming classes

Caution

Do not choose class names that are already used in the Java library. For example, since the `Math` class is defined in Java, you should not name your class `Math`.

using full descriptive names

Tip

Avoid using abbreviation for identifiers. Using complete words is more descriptive. For example, `numberOfStudents` is better than `numStuds`, `numOfStuds`, or `numOfStudents`.

2.14.3 Proper Indentation and Spacing

indent code

A consistent indentation style makes programs clear and easy to read. *Indentation* is used to illustrate the structural relationships between a program's components or statements. Java can read the program even if all of the statements are in a straight line, but it is easier to read and maintain code that is aligned properly. Indent each subcomponent or statement *two* spaces more than the structure within which it is nested.

A single space should be added on both sides of a binary operator, as shown in the following statement:

```
int i= 3+4 * 4;
```
— Bad style

```
int i = 3 + 4 * 4;
```
— Good style

A single space line should be used to separate segments of the code to make the program easier to read.

2.14.4 Block Styles

A block is a group of statements surrounded by braces. There are two popular styles, *next-line* style and *end-of-line* style, as shown in Figure 2.10. The next-line style aligns braces vertically and makes programs easy to read, whereas the end-of-line style saves space and may help avoid some subtle programming errors. Both are acceptable block styles. The choice

Next-line style

```
public class Test
{
  public static void main(String[] args)
  {
    System.out.println("Block Styles");
  }
}
```

End-of-line style

```
public class Test {
  public static void main(String[] args) {
    System.out.println("Block Styles");
  }
}
```

FIGURE 2.10 The opening brace is placed at the beginning of a new line for next-line style and at the end of the line for end-of-line style.

depends on personal or organizational preference. You should use a style consistently. Mixing styles is not recommended. This book uses the *end-of-line* style to be consistent with the Java API source code.

2.15 Programming Errors

Programming errors are unavoidable, even for experienced programmers. Errors can be categorized into three types: syntax errors, runtime errors, and logic errors.

2.15.1 Syntax Errors

Errors that occur during compilation are called *syntax errors* or *compilation errors*. Syntax errors result from errors in code construction, such as mistyping a keyword, omitting some necessary punctuation, or using an opening brace without a corresponding closing brace. These errors are usually easy to detect, because the compiler tells you where they are and what caused them. For example, compiling the following program results in a syntax error, as shown in Figure 2.11.

syntax errors

```java
// ShowSyntaxErrors.java: The program contains syntax errors
public class ShowSyntaxErrors {
  public static void main(String[] args) {
    i = 30;
    System.out.println(i + 4);
  }
}
```

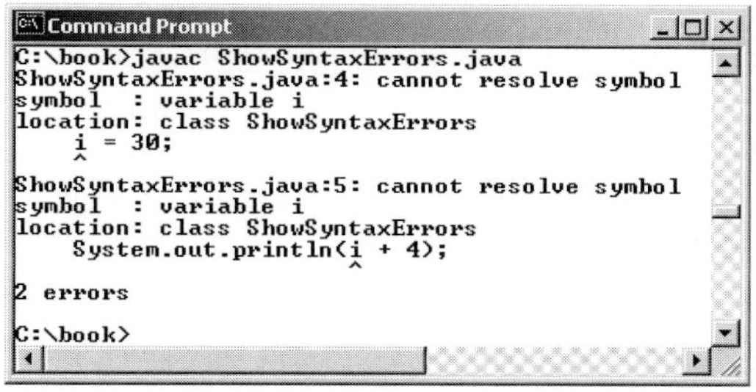

syntax error

FIGURE 2.11 The compiler reports syntax errors.

Two errors are detected. Both are the result of not declaring variable i. Since a single error will often display many lines of compilation errors, it is a good practice to start debugging from the top line and work downward. Fixing errors that occur earlier in the program may also fix additional errors that occur later.

2.15.2 Runtime Errors

Runtime errors are errors that cause a program to terminate abnormally. Runtime errors occur while an application is running if the environment detects an operation that is impossible to carry out. Input errors are typical runtime errors.

runtime errors

An *input error* occurs when the user enters an unexpected input value that the program cannot handle. For instance, if the program expects to read in a number, but instead the user enters a string, this causes data-type errors to occur in the program. To prevent input errors, the program should prompt the user to enter the correct type of values. It may display a message like **"Please enter an integer"** before reading an integer from the keyboard.

Another common source of runtime errors is division by zero. This happens when the divisor is zero for integer divisions. For instance, the following program would cause a runtime error, as shown in Figure 2.12.

runtime error

```
// ShowRuntimeErrors.java: Program contains runtime errors
public class ShowRuntimeErrors {
  public static void main(String[] args) {
    int i = 1 / 0 ;
  }
}
```

```
Command Prompt                                            _ □ ×
C:\book>java ShowRuntimeErrors
Exception in thread "main" java.lang.ArithmeticException: / by zero
        at ShowRuntimeErrors.main(ShowRuntimeErrors.java:4)

C:\book>
```

FIGURE 2.12 The runtime error causes the program to terminate abnormally.

2.15.3 Logic Errors

Logic errors occur when a program does not perform the way it was intended to. Errors of this kind occur for many different reasons. For example, suppose you wrote the following program to add **number1** to **number2**.

```
// ShowLogicErrors.java: The program contains a logic error
public class ShowLogicErrors {
  public static void main(String[] args) {
    // Add number1 to number2
    int number1 = 3;
    int number2 = 3;
    number2 += number1 + number2;
    System.out.println("number2 is " + number2);
  }
}
```

The program does not have syntax errors or runtime errors, but it does not print the correct result for **number2**. See if you can find the error.

2.16 Debugging

In general, syntax errors are easy to find and easy to correct, because the compiler gives indications as to where the errors came from and why they are there. Runtime errors are not difficult to find either, since the Java interpreter displays them on the console when the program aborts. Finding logic errors, on the other hand, can be very challenging.

bugs
debugging
hand-traces

Logic errors are called *bugs*. The process of finding and correcting errors is called *debugging*. A common approach to debugging is to use a combination of methods to narrow down to the part of the program where the bug is located. You can *hand-trace* the program (i.e., catch errors by reading the program), or you can insert print statements in order to show the values of the variables or the execution flow of the program. This approach might work for a short, simple program. But for a large, complex program, the most effective approach for debugging is to use a debugger utility.

JDK includes a command-line debugger (jdb), which is invoked with a class name. jdb is itself a Java program, running its own copy of Java interpreter. All the Java IDE tools, such as JBuilder, NetBeans, and Eclipse, include integrated debuggers. The debugger utilities let you follow the execution of a program. They vary from one system to another, but they all support most of the following helpful features:

■ **Executing a single statement at a time:** The debugger allows you to execute one statement at a time so that you can see the effect of each statement.

■ **Tracing into or stepping over a method:** If a method is being executed, you can ask the debugger to enter the method and execute one statement at a time in the method, or you can ask it to step over the entire method. You should step over the entire method if you know that the method works. For example, always step over system-supplied methods, such as `System.out.println`.

- **Setting breakpoints:** You can also set a breakpoint at a specific statement. Your program pauses when it reaches a breakpoint and displays the line with the breakpoint. You can set as many breakpoints as you want. Breakpoints are particularly useful when you know where your programming error starts. You can set a breakpoint at that line and have the program execute until it reaches the breakpoint.

- **Displaying variables:** The debugger lets you select several variables and display their values. As you trace through a program, the content of a variable is continuously updated.

- **Displaying call stacks:** The debugger lets you trace all of the method calls and lists all pending methods. This feature is helpful when you need to see a large picture of the program-execution flow.

- **Modifying variables:** Some debuggers enable you to modify the value of a variable when debugging. This is convenient when you want to test a program with different samples but do not want to leave the debugger.

 Tip

If you use an IDE such as JBuilder, NetBeans, or Eclipse, please refer to *Learning Java Effectively with JBuilder/NetBeans/Eclipse* in the supplement on the Companion Website. The supplement shows you how to use a debugger to trace programs and how debugging can help in learning Java effectively.

debugging in IDE

KEY TERMS

algorithm   28
assignment operator (=)   32
assignment statement   32
backslash (\)   43
`byte` type   34
casting   40
`char` type   41
constant   33
data type   28
debugger   58
debugging   58
declaration   31
decrement operator (--)   39
`double` type   34
encoding   42
`final`   33
`float` type   34
floating-point number   28
expression   32
expression statement   40

identifier   30
increment operator (++)   39
incremental development and testing   30
indentation   56
`int` type   34
literal   36
logic error   58
`long` type   34
narrowing (of types)   40
operator   32
primitive data type   28
runtime error   57
`short` type   34
syntax error   57
supplementary Unicode   42
Unicode   42
Unix epoch   51
variable   29
widening (of types)   54
whitespace   54

CHAPTER SUMMARY

- Java provides four integer types (`byte`, `short`, `int`, `long`) that represent integers of four different sizes, and two floating-point types (`float`, `double`) that represent floating-point numbers of two different precisions. Character type (`char`) represents a single character. These are called primitive data types. Java's primitive types are portable across all computer platforms. They have exactly the same values on all platforms. When they are declared, the variables of these types are created and assigned memory space.

- Java provides operators that perform numeric operations: + (addition), – (subtraction), * (multiplication), / (division), and % (remainder). Integer division (/) yields an integer result. The remainder operator (%) yields the remainder of the division.

- The increment operator (++) and the decrement operator (−−) increment or decrement a variable by 1. If the operator is prefixed to the variable, the variable is first incremented or decremented by 1, then used in the expression. If the operator is a suffix to the variable, the variable is incremented or decremented by 1, but then the original old value is used in the expression.

- All the numeric operators can be applied to characters. When an operand is a character, the character's Unicode value is used in the operation.

- You can use casting to convert a value of one type into another type. Casting a variable of a type with a small range to a variable of a type with a larger range is known as *widening a type*. Casting variable of a type with a large range to a variable of a type with a smaller range is known as *narrowing a type*. Widening a type can be performed automatically without explicit casting. Narrowing a type must be performed explicitly.

- Programming errors can be categorized into three types: syntax errors, runtime errors, and logic errors. Errors that occur during compilation are called *syntax errors* or *compilation errors*. *Runtime errors* are errors that cause a program to terminate abnormally. *Logic errors* occur when a program does not perform the way it was intended to.

REVIEW QUESTIONS

Sections 2.2–2.6

2.1 Which of the following identifiers are valid?

`applet`, `Applet`, `a++`, `−−a`, `4#R`, `$4`, `#44`, `apps`

2.2 Which of the following are Java keywords?

`class`, `public`, `int`, `x`, `y`, `radius`

2.3 Translate the following pseudocode into Java code:

- Step 1: Declare a `double` variable named `miles` with initial value `100`;
- Step 2: Declare a `double` constant named `MILE_TO_KILOMETER` with value `1.609`;
- Step 3: Declare a `double` variable named `kilometer`, multiply miles and `MILE_TO_KILOMETER` and assign the result to `kilometer`;
- Step 4: Display `kilometer` to the console.

What is `kilometer` after Step 4?

2.4 What are the benefits of using constants? Declare an `int` constant `SIZE` with value `20`.

Section 2.7 Numeric Data Types and Operations

2.5 Assume that `int a = 1` and `double d = 1.0`, and that each expression is independent. What are the results of the following expressions?

```
a = 46 / 9;
a = 46 % 9 + 4 * 4 - 2;
a = 45 + 43 % 5 * (23 * 3 % 2);
```

```
a %= 3 / a + 3;
d = 4 + d * d + 4;
d += 1.5 * 3 + (++a);
d -= 1.5 * 3 + a++;
```

2.6   Show the result of the following remainders.

```
56 % 6
78 % -4
-34 % 5
-34 % -5
5 % 1
1 % 5
```

2.7   Find the largest and smallest `byte`, `short`, `int`, `long`, `float`, and `double`. Which of these data types requires the least amount of memory?

2.8   What is the result of `25 / 4`? How would you rewrite the expression if you wished the result to be a floating-point number?

2.9   Are the following statements correct? If so, show the output.

```
System.out.println("the output for 25 / 4 is " + 25 / 4);
System.out.println("the output for 25 / 4.0 is " + 25 / 4.0);
```

2.10   How would you write the following arithmetic expression in Java?

$$\frac{4}{3(r + 34)} - 9(a + bc) + \frac{3 + d(2 + a)}{a + bd}$$

2.11   Which of these statements are true?

(a)   Any expression can be used as a statement.
(b)   The expression `x++` can be used as a statement.
(c)   The statement `x = x + 5` is also an expression.
(d)   The statement `x = y = x = 0` is illegal.

2.12   Which of the following are correct literals for floating-point numbers?

`12.3, 12.3e+2, 23.4e-2, -334.4, 20, 39F, 40D`

2.13   Identify and fix the errors in the following code:

```
1 public class Test {
2   public void main(string[] args) {
3     int i;
4     int k = 100.0;
5     int j = i + 1;
6
7     System.out.println("j is " + j + " and
8       k is " + k);
9   }
10 }
```

Section 2.8 Numeric Type Conversions

2.14   Can different types of numeric values be used together in a computation?

2.15   What does an explicit conversion from a `double` to an `int` do with the fractional part of the *double* value? Does casting change the variable being cast?

2.16   Show the following output:

```
float f = 12.5F;
int i = (int)f;
System.out.println("f is " + f);
System.out.println("i is " + i);
```

Section 2.9 Character Data Type and Operations

2.17   Use print statements to find out the ASCII code for `'1'`, `'A'`, `'B'`, `'a'`, `'b'`. Use print statements to find out the character for the decimal code 40, 59, 79, 85, 90. Use print statements to find out the character for the hexadecimal code 40, 5A, 71, 72, 7A.

2.18   Which of the following are correct literals for characters?

`'1'`, `'\u345dE'`, `'\u3fFa'`, `'\b'`, `\t`

2.19   How do you display characters \ and "?

2.20   Evaluate the following:

```
int i = '1';
int j = '1' + '2';
int k = 'a';
char c = 90;
```

2.21   Can the following conversions involving casting be allowed? If so, find the converted result.

```
char c = 'A';
i = (int)c;

float f = 1000.34f;
int i = (int)f;

double d = 1000.34;
int i = (int)d;

int i = 97;
char c = (char)i;
```

Section 2.10 The `String` Type

2.22   Show the output of the following statements:

```
System.out.println("1" + 1);
System.out.println('1' + 1);
System.out.println("1" + 1 + 1);
System.out.println("1" + (1 + 1));
System.out.println('1' + 1 + 1);
```

2.23   Evaluate the following expressions:

```
1 + "Welcome " + 1 + 1
1 + "Welcome " + (1 + 1)
1 + "Welcome " + ('\u0001' + 1)
1 + "Welcome " + 'a' + 1
```

Sections 2.11–2.12

2.24   How do you convert a decimal string into a `double` value? How do you convert an integer string into an `int` value?

2.25   How do you obtain the current minute using the `System.currentTimeMillis()` method?

Sections 2.14–2.15

2.26   How do you denote a comment line and a comment paragraph?

2.27   What are the naming conventions for class names, method names, constants, and variables? Which of the following items can be a constant, a method, a variable, or a class according to the Java naming conventions?

```
MAX_VALUE, Test, read, readInt
```

2.28 Reformat the following program according to the programming style and documentation guidelines. Use the next-line brace style.

```java
public class Test
{
    // Main method
    public static void main(String[] args) {
    /** Print a line */
    System.out.println("2 % 3 = "+2%3);
    }
}
```

2.29 Describe syntax errors, runtime errors, and logic errors.

PROGRAMMING EXERCISES

Note

Solutions to even-numbered exercises are on the Companion website. Solutions to all exercises are on the Instructor Resource website. The *level of difficulty* is rated as easy (no star), moderate (*), hard (**), or challenging (***).

level of difficulty

Pedagogical Note

Students may first write a program with a *fixed input* value and later modify it using an input dialog box or using the console input.

fixed input

Debugging Tip

The compiler usually gives a reason for a syntax error. If you don't know how to correct it, compare your program closely with similar examples in the text character by character.

learn from examples

Sections 2.2–2.8

2.1 (*Converting Fahrenheit to Celsius*) Write a program that reads a Fahrenheit degree in double from an input dialog box, then converts it to Celsius and displays the result in a message dialog box. The formula for the conversion is as follows:

$$\text{celsius} = (5/9) * (\text{fahrenheit} - 32)$$

Hint

In Java, **5 / 9** is 0, so you need to write **5.0 / 9** in the program to obtain the correct result.

2.2 (*Computing the volume of a cylinder*) Write a program that reads in the radius and length of a cylinder and computes its volume using the following formulas:

$$\text{area} = \text{radius} * \text{radius} * \pi$$
$$\text{volume} = \text{area} * \text{length}$$

2.3 (*Converting feet into meters*) Write a program that reads a number in feet, converts it to meters, and displays the result. One foot is **0.305** meters.

2.4 (*Converting pounds into kilograms*) Write a program that converts pounds into kilograms. The program prompts the user to enter a number in pounds, converts it to kilograms, and displays the result. One pound is **0.454** kilograms.

2.5* (*Calculating tips*) Write a program that reads the subtotal and the gratuity rate, and computes the gratuity and total. For example, if the user enters **10** for subtotal and **15%** for gratuity rate, the program displays **$1.5** as gratuity and **$11.5** as total.

2.6** (*Summing the digits in an integer*) Write a program that reads an integer between 0 and 1000 and adds all the digits in the integer. For example, if an integer is 932, the sum of all its digits is 14.

Hint

Use the % operator to extract digits, and use the / operator to remove the extracted digit. For instance, 932 % 10 = 2 and 932 / 10 = 93

Section 2.9 Character Data Type and Operations

2.7* (*Converting an uppercase letter to lowercase*) Write a program that converts an uppercase letter to a lowercase letter. The character is typed in the source code as a literal value. In Chapter 8, "Strings and Text I/O," you will learn how to enter a character from an input dialog box.

Hint

In the ASCII table (see Appendix B), uppercase letters appear before lowercase letters. The offset between any uppercase letter and its corresponding lowercase letter is the same. So you can find a lowercase letter from its corresponding uppercase letter, as follows:

```
int offset = (int)'a' - (int)'A';
char lowercase = (char)((int)uppercase + offset);
```

2.8* (*Finding the character of an ASCII code*) Write a program that receives an ASCII code (an integer between 0 and 127) and displays its character. For example, if the user enters 97, the program displays character a.

Sections 2.10–2.12

2.9* (*Calculating the future investment value*) Write a program that reads in investment amount, annual interest rate, and number of years, and displays the future investment value using the following formula:

```
futureInvestmentValue =
    investmentAmount x (1 + monthlyInterestRate)numberOfYears*12
```

For example, if you entered amount 1000, annual interest rate 3.25%, and number of years 1, the future investment value is 1032.98.

Hint

Use the Math.pow(a, b) method to compute a raised to the power of b.

2.10* (*Monetary units*) Rewrite Listing 2.7, ComputeChange.java, to fix the possible loss of accuracy when converting a double value to an int value. Enter the input as an integer whose last two digits represent the cents. For example, the input 1156 represents 11 dollars and 56 cents.

Section 2.13 Getting Input from the Console

2.11* (*Using the console input*) Rewrite Listing 2.7, ComputeChange.java, using the console input and output.

2.12* (*Payroll*) Write a program that reads the following information and prints a payroll statement:

- Employee's name (e.g., Smith)
- Number of hours worked in a week (e.g., 10)
- Hourly pay rate (e.g., 6.75)

- Federal tax withholding rate (e.g., 20%)
- State tax withholding rate (e.g., 9%)

Write this program in two versions: (a) Use dialog boxes to obtain input and display output; (b) Use console input and output. A sample run of the console input and output is shown in Figure 2.13.

Obtain input ———→
Display output ———→

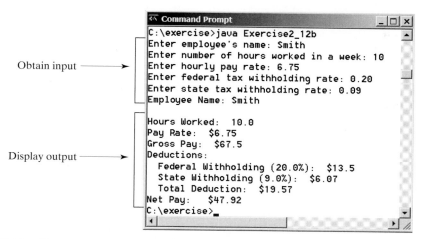

FIGURE 2.13 The program prints a payroll statement.

2.13* (*Calculating interest*) If you know the balance and the annual percentage interest rate, you can compute the interest on the next monthly payment using the following formula:

$$interest = balance \times (annualInterestRate\ /\ 1200)$$

Write a program that reads the balance and the annual percentage interest rate and displays the interest for the next month in two versions: (a) Use dialog boxes to obtain input and display output; (b) Use console input and output. A sample run of the console input and output is shown in Figure 2.14.

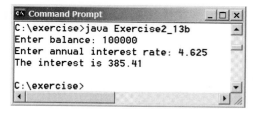

FIGURE 2.14 The program prints interest.

CHAPTER 3

SELECTION STATEMENTS

Objectives

- To declare `boolean` type and write Boolean expressions (§3.2).

- To distinguish between conditional and unconditional `&&` and `||` operators (§3.2.1).

- To use Boolean expressions to control selection statements (§§3.3–3.5).

- To implement selection control using `if` and nested `if` statements (§3.3).

- To implement selection control using `switch` statements (§3.4).

- To write expressions using the conditional operator (§3.5).

- To display formatted output using the `System.out.printf` method and to format strings using the `String.format` method (§3.6).

- To know the rules governing operand evaluation order, operator precedence, and operator associativity (§§3.7–3.8).

3.1 Introduction

why selection?
pseudocode

In Chapter 2, "Primitive Data Types and Operations," if you assigned a negative value for `radius` in Listing 2.1, ComputeArea.java, the program would print an invalid result. If the radius is negative, you don't want the program to compute the area. Like all high-level programming languages, Java provides selection statements that let you choose actions with two or more alternative courses. You can use selection statements in the following *pseudocode* (i.e., natural language mixed with programming code) to rewrite Listing 2.1:

```
if the radius is negative
    the program displays a message indicating a wrong input;
else
    the program computes the area and displays the result;
```

Selection statements use conditions. Conditions are Boolean expressions. This chapter first introduces Boolean types, values, operators, and expressions.

3.2 **boolean** Data Type and Operations

Often in a program you need to compare two values, such as whether i is greater than j. Java provides six *comparison operators* (also known as *relational operators*), shown in Table 3.1, which can be used to compare two values. The result of the comparison is a Boolean value: `true` or `false`. For example, the following statement displays `true`:

comparison operators

```
System.out.println(1 < 2);
```

TABLE 3.1 Comparison Operators

Operator	Name	Example	Answer
<	less than	1 < 2	true
<=	less than or equal to	1 <= 2	true
>	greater than	1 > 2	false
>=	greater than or equal to	1 >= 2	false
==	equal to	1 == 2	false
!=	not equal to	1 != 2	true

compare characters

Note
You can also *compare characters*. Comparing characters is the same as comparing the Unicodes of the characters. For example, 'a' is larger than 'A' because the Unicode of 'a' is larger than the Unicode of 'A.'

== vs. =

Caution
The equality comparison operator is two equal signs (==), not a single equal sign (=). The latter symbol is for assignment.

Boolean variable

A variable that holds a Boolean value is known as a *Boolean variable*. The `boolean` data type is used to declare Boolean variables. The domain of the `boolean` type consists of two literal values: `true` and `false`. For example, the following statement assigns `true` to the variable `lightsOn`:

```
boolean lightsOn = true;
```

Boolean operators, also known as *logical operators*, operate on Boolean values to create a new Boolean value. Table 3.2 contains a list of Boolean operators. Table 3.3 defines the not (!) operator. The not (!) operator negates **true** to **false** and **false** to **true**. Table 3.4 defines the and (&&) operator. The and (&&) of two Boolean operands is **true** if and only if both operands are **true**. Table 3.5 defines the or (||) operator. The or (||) of two Boolean operands is **true** if at least one of the operands is **true**. Table 3.6 defines the exclusive or (∧) operator. The exclusive or (∧) of two Boolean operands is **true** if and only if the two operands have different Boolean values.

Boolean operators

TABLE 3.2   Boolean Operators

Operator	Name	Description
!	not	logical negation
&&	and	logical conjunction
||	or	logical disjunction
∧	exclusive or	logical exclusion

TABLE 3.3   Truth Table for Operator !

p	!p	Example
true	false	!(1 > 2) is **true**, because (1 > 2) is **false**.
false	true	!(1 > 0) is **false**, because (1 > 0) is **true**.

TABLE 3.4   Truth Table for Operator &&

p1	p2	p1 && p2	Example
false	false	false	(2 > 3) && (5 > 5) is **false**, because
false	true	false	either (2 > 3) or (5 > 5) is **false**.
true	false	false	(3 > 2) && (5 > 5) is **false**, because (5 > 5) is **false**.
true	true	true	(3 > 2) && (5 >= 5) is **true**, because (3 > 2) and (5 >= 5) are both **true**.

TABLE 3.5   Truth Table for Operator ||

p1	p2	p1 || p2	Example
false	false	false	(2 > 3) || (5 > 5) is **false**, because (2 > 3)
false	true	true	and (5 > 5) are both **false**.
true	false	true	(3 > 2) || (5 > 5) is **true**, because (3 > 2)
true	true	true	is **true**.

TABLE 3.6   Truth Table for Operator ∧

p1	p2	p1 ∧ p2	Example
false	false	false	(2 > 3)∧(5 > 5) is **true**, because (2 > 3)
false	true	true	is **false** and (5 > 1) is **true**.
true	false	true	(3 > 2)∧(5 > 1) is **false**, because both
true	true	false	(3 > 2) and (5 > 1) are **true**.

Listing 3.1 gives a program that checks whether a number is divisible by **2** and **3**, whether a number is divisible by **2** or **3**, and whether a number is divisible by **2** or **3** but not both:

LISTING 3.1 TestBoolean.java

```
 1 import javax.swin ptionPane;
 2
 3 public class TestBoolean {
 4   public static void main(String[] args) {
 5     int number = 18;
 6
 7     JOptionPane.showMessageDialog(null,
 8       "Is " + number +
 9       "\n divisible by 2 and 3? " +
10       (number % 2 == 0 && number % 3 == 0)
11       + "\ndivisible by 2 or 3? " +
12       (number % 2 == 0 || number % 3 == 0) +
13       "\ndivisible by 2 or 3, but not both? "
14       + (number % 2 == 0 ∧ number % 3 == 0));
15   }
16 }
```

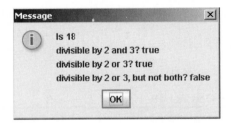

A long string is formed by concatenating the substrings in lines 8–14. The three \n characters display the string in four lines. **(number % 2 == 0 && number % 3 == 0)** (line 10) checks whether the number is divisible by 2 and 3. **(number % 2 == 0 || number %** **3 == 0)** (line 12) checks whether the number is divisible by 2 or 3. **(number % 2 == 0 ∧** **number % 3 == 0)** (line 14) checks whether the number is divisible by **2** or **3**, but not both.

3.2.1 Unconditional vs. Conditional Boolean Operators

If one of the operands of an **&&** operator is **false**, the expression is **false**; if one of the operands of an **||** operand is **true**, the expression is **true**. Java uses these properties to improve the performance of these operators.

When evaluating **p1 && p2**, Java first evaluates **p1** and then evaluates **p2** if **p1** is **true**; if **p1** is **false**, it does not evaluate **p2**. When evaluating **p1 || p2**, Java first evaluates **p1** and then evaluates **p2** if **p1** is **false**; if **p1** is **true**, it does not evaluate **p2**. Therefore, **&&** is referred to as the *conditional* or *short-circuit AND* operator, and **||** is referred to as the *conditional* or *short-circuit OR* operator.

conditional operator
short-circuit operator

Java also provides the **&** and **|** operators. The **&** operator works exactly the same as the **&&** operator, and the **|** operator works exactly the same as the **||** operator with one exception: the **&** and **|** operators always evaluate both operands. Therefore, **&** is referred to as the *unconditional AND* operator, and **|** is referred to as the *unconditional OR* operator. In some rare situations when needed, you can use the **&** and **|** operators to guarantee that the right-hand operand is evaluated regardless of whether the left-hand operand is **true** or **false**. For example, the expression **(width < 2) & (height-- < 2)** guarantees that **(height--** **< 2)** is evaluated. Thus the variable **height** will be decremented regardless of whether **width** is less than 2 or not.

unconditional operator

Tip

Avoid using the & and | operators. The benefits of the & and | operators are marginal. Using them will make the program difficult to read and could cause errors. For example, the expression **(x != 0) & (100 / x)** results in a runtime error if x is 0. However, **(x != 0) && (100 / x)** is fine. If **x** is **0**, **(x != 0)** is false. Since **&&** is a short-circuit operator, Java does not evaluate **(100 / x)** and returns the result as false for the entire expression **(x != 0) && (100 / x)**.

 Note

The & and | operators can also apply to *bitwise operations*. See Appendix G, "Bit Manipulations," for details.

bitwise operations

 Note

As shown in the preceding chapter, a **char** value can be cast into an **int** value, and vice versa. A Boolean value, however, cannot be cast into a value of other types, nor can a value of other types be cast into a Boolean value.

 Note

true and **false** are literals, just like a number such as **10**, so they are not keywords, but you cannot use them as identifiers, just as you cannot use **10** as an identifier.

Boolean literals

3.2.2   Example: Determining Leap Year

This section presents a program that lets the user enter a year in a dialog box and checks whether it is a leap year.

A year is a *leap year* if it is divisible by **4** but not by **100** or if it is divisible by **400**. So you can use the following Boolean expression to check whether a year is a leap year:

leap year

```
(year % 4 == 0 && year % 100 != 0) || (year % 400 == 0)
```

Listing 3.2 gives the program. Two sample runs of the program are shown in Figure 3.1.

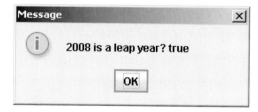

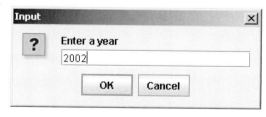

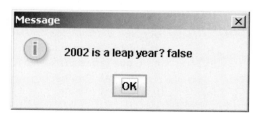

FIGURE 3.1   The program determines whether a year is a leap year.

LISTING 3.2   LeapYear.java

```java
1 import javax.swing.JOptionPane;
2
3 public class LeapYear {
4   public static void main(String args[]) {
5     // Prompt the user to enter a year
```

show input dialog

```
 6    String yearString = JOptionPane.showInputDialog("Enter a year");
 7
 8    // Convert the string into an int value
```
convert to **int**
```
 9    int year = Integer.parseInt(yearString);
10
11    // Check if the year is a leap year
```
leap year?
```
12    boolean isLeapYear =
13      (year % 4 == 0 && year % 100 != 0) || (year % 400 == 0);
14
15    // Display the result in a message dialog box
```
show message dialog
```
16    JOptionPane.showMessageDialog(null,
17      year + " is a leap year? " + isLeapYear);
18  }
19 }
```

3.2.3 Example: A Simple Math Learning Tool

This example creates a program to let a first grader practice addition. The program random-ly generates two single-digit integers **number1** and **number2** and displays a question such as **"What is 7 + 9?"** to the student, as shown in Figure 3.2(a). After the student types the answer in the input dialog box, the program displays a message dialog box to indicate whether the answer is true or false, as shown in Figure 3.2(b).

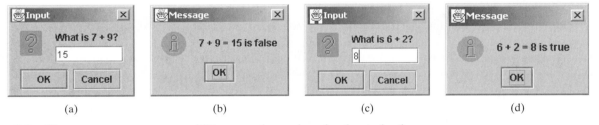

(a) (b) (c) (d)

FIGURE 3.2 The program generates an addition question and grades the student's answer.

There are many good ways to generate random numbers. For now, generate the first integer using **System.currentTimeMillis() % 10** and the second using **System.current-TimeMillis() * 7 % 10**. Listing 3.3 gives the program. Lines 5–6 generate two numbers, **number1** and **number2**. Line 11 displays a dialog box and obtains an answer from the user. The answer is graded in line 15 using a Boolean expression **number1 + number2 == answer**.

LISTING 3.3 AdditionTutor.java

```
 1 import javax.swing.*;
 2
 3 public class AdditionTutor {
 4   public static void main(String[] args) {
```
generate **number1**
generate **number2**
```
 5     int number1 = (int)(System.currentTimeMillis() % 10);
 6     int number2 = (int)(System.currentTimeMillis() * 7 % 10);
 7
```
show question
```
 8     String answerString = JOptionPane.showInputDialog
 9       ("What is " + number1 + " + " + number2 + "?");
10
11     int answer = Integer.parseInt(answerString);
12
```
display result
```
13     JOptionPane.showMessageDialog(null,
14       number1 + " + " + number2 + " = " + answer + " is " +
15       (number1 + number2 == answer));
16   }
17 }
```

3.3 **if** Statements

The example in Listing 3.3 displays a message such as "6 + 2 = 7 is false." If you wish the message to be "6 + 2 = 7 is incorrect," you have to use a selection statement.

This section introduces selection statements. Java has several types of selection statements: simple **if** statements, **if ... else** statements, nested **if** statements, **switch** statements, and conditional expressions.

3.3.1 Simple **if** Statements

A simple **if** statement executes an action if and only if the condition is **true**. The syntax for a simple **if** statement is shown below:

```
if (booleanExpression) {
    statement(s);
}
```

if statement

The execution flow chart is shown in Figure 3.3(a).

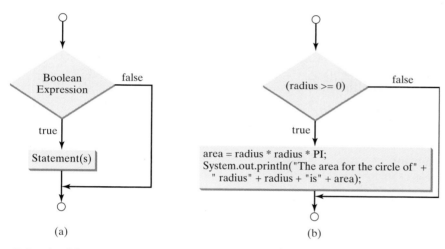

(a)	(b)

FIGURE 3.3 An **if** statement executes statements if the **booleanExpression** evaluates to **true**.

If the **booleanExpression** evaluates to **true**, the statements in the block are executed. As an example, see the following code:

```
if (radius >= 0) {
    area = radius * radius * PI;
    System.out.println("The area for the circle of radius " +
        radius + " is " + area);
}
```

The flow chart of the preceding statement is shown in Figure 3.3(b). If the value of **radius** is greater than or equal to 0, then the **area** is computed and the result is displayed; otherwise, the two statements in the block will not be executed.

Note

The **booleanExpression** is enclosed in parentheses for all forms of the **if** statement. Thus, for example, the outer parentheses in the following **if** statements are required.

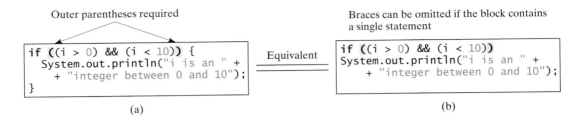

Outer parentheses required

```
if ((i > 0) && (i < 10)) {
  System.out.println("i is an " +
    + "integer between 0 and 10");
}
```
(a)

Equivalent

Braces can be omitted if the block contains
a single statement

```
if ((i > 0) && (i < 10))
  System.out.println("i is an " +
    + "integer between 0 and 10");
```
(b)

The braces can be omitted if they enclose a single statement.

Caution

Forgetting the braces when they are needed for grouping multiple statements is a common programming error. If you modify the code by adding new statements in an `if` statement without braces, you will have to insert the braces if they are not already in place.

The following statement determines whether a number is even or odd:

```
// Prompt the user to enter an integer
String intString = JOptionPane.showInputDialog(
  "Enter an integer:");

// Convert string into int
int number = Integer.parseInt(intString);

if (number % 2 == 0)
  System.out.println(number + " is even.");

if (number % 2 != 0)
  System.out.println(number + " is odd.");
```

Caution

Adding a semicolon at the end of an `if` clause, as shown in (a) in the following code, is a common mistake.

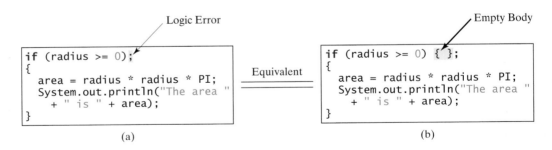

Logic Error

```
if (radius >= 0);
{
  area = radius * radius * PI;
  System.out.println("The area "
    + " is " + area);
}
```
(a)

Equivalent

Empty Body

```
if (radius >= 0) { };
{
  area = radius * radius * PI;
  System.out.println("The area "
    + " is " + area);
}
```
(b)

This mistake is hard to find because it is neither a compilation error nor a runtime error, it is a logic error. The code in (a) is equivalent to (b) with an empty body.

This error often occurs when you use the next-line block style. Using the end-of-line block style will prevent this error.

3.3.2 `if ... else` Statements

A simple `if` statement takes an action if the specified condition is **true**. If the condition is **false**, nothing is done. But what if you want to take alternative actions when the condition is **false**? You can use an `if ... else` statement. The actions that an `if ... else` statement specifies differ based on whether the condition is **true** or **false**.

Here is the syntax for this type of statement:

```java
if (booleanExpression) {
   statement(s)-for-the-true-case;
}
else {
   statement(s)-for-the-false-case;
}
```

The flow chart of the statement is shown in Figure 3.4.

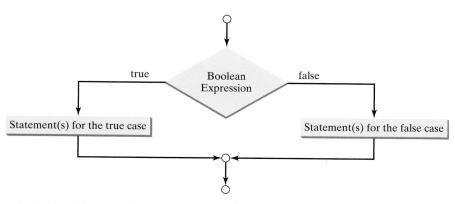

FIGURE 3.4 An **if ... else** statement executes statements for the **true** case if the **boolean** expression evaluates to **true**; otherwise, statements for the **false** case are executed.

If the **booleanExpression** evaluates to **true**, the **statement(s)** for the true case is executed; otherwise, the **statement(s)** for the false case is executed. For example, consider the following code:

```java
if (radius >= 0) {
   area = radius * radius * PI;
   System.out.println("The area for the circle of radius " +
      radius + " is " + area);
}
else {
   System.out.println("Negative input");
}
```

    if-else statement

If **radius >= 0** is **true**, **area** is computed and displayed; if it is **false**, the message **"Negative input"** is printed.

As usual, the braces can be omitted if there is only one statement within them. The braces enclosing the **System.out.println("Negative input")** statement can therefore be omitted in the preceding example.

Using the **if ... else** statement, you can rewrite the code for determining whether a number is even or odd in the preceding section, as follows:

```java
if (number % 2 == 0)
   System.out.println(number + " is even.");
else
   System.out.println(number + " is odd.");
```

This is more efficient because whether **number % 2** is **0** is tested only once.

3.3.3 Nested `if` Statements

The statement in an `if` or `if ... else` statement can be any legal Java statement, including another `if` or `if ... else` statement. The inner `if` statement is said to be *nested* inside the outer `if` statement. The inner `if` statement can contain another `if` statement; in fact, there is no limit to the depth of the nesting. For example, the following is a nested `if` statement:

nested `if` statement

```java
if (i > k) {
  if (j > k)
    System.out.println("i and j are greater than k");
}
else
  System.out.println("i is less than or equal to k");
```

The `if (j > k)` statement is nested inside the `if (i > k)` statement.

The nested `if` statement can be used to implement multiple alternatives. The statement given in Figure 3.5(a), for instance, assigns a letter grade to the variable `grade` according to the score, with multiple alternatives.

```java
if (score >= 90.0)
  grade = 'A';
else
  if (score >= 80.0)
    grade = 'B';
  else
    if (score >= 70.0)
      grade = 'C';
    else
      if (score >= 60.0)
        grade = 'D';
      else
        grade = 'F';
```

(a)

Equivalent

This is better

```java
if (score >= 90.0)
  grade = 'A';
else if (score >= 80.0)
  grade = 'B';
else if (score >= 70.0)
  grade = 'C';
else if (score >= 60.0)
  grade = 'D';
else
  grade = 'F';
```

(b)

FIGURE 3.5 A preferred format for multiple alternative `if` statements is shown in (b).

The execution of this `if` statement proceeds as follows. The first condition (`score >= 90.0`) is tested. If it is `true`, the grade becomes `'A'`. If it is `false`, the second condition (`score >= 80.0`) is tested. If the second condition is `true`, the grade becomes `'B'`. If that condition is `false`, the third condition and the rest of the conditions (if necessary) continue to be tested until a condition is met or all of the conditions prove to be `false`. If all of the conditions are `false`, the grade becomes `'F'`. Note that a condition is tested only when all of the conditions that come before it are `false`.

The `if` statement in Figure 3.5(a) is equivalent to the `if` statement in Figure 3.5(b). In fact, Figure 3.5(b) is the preferred writing style for multiple alternative `if` statements. This style avoids deep indentation and makes the program easy to read.

 Note

matching `else` with `if`

The `else` clause matches the most recent unmatched `if` clause in the same block. For example, the following statement in (a) is equivalent to the statement in (b).

The compiler ignores indentation. Nothing is printed from the statements in (a) and (b). To force the `else` clause to match the first `if` clause, you must add a pair of braces:

```java
int i = 1; int j = 2; int k = 3;
if (i > j) {
```

```
int i = 1;
int j = 2;
int k = 3;

if (i > j)
  if (i > k)
    System.out.println("A");
else
    System.out.println("B");
```
(a)

Equivalent

This is better
with correct
indentation

```
int i = 1;
int j = 2;
int k = 3;

if (i > j)
  if (i > k)
    System.out.println("A");
  else
    System.out.println("B");
```
(b)

```
  if (i > k)
    System.out.println("A");
}
else
  System.out.println("B");
```

This statement prints **B**.

Tip

Often new programmers write the code that assigns a test condition to a **boolean** variable like
the code in (a):

assign boolean variable

```
if (number % 2 == 0)
  even = true;
else
  even = false;
```
(a)

Equivalent

This is better

```
boolean even
  = number % 2 == 0;
```
(b)

The code can be simplified by assigning the test value directly to the variable, as shown in (b).

Caution

To test whether a **boolean** variable is **true** or **false** in a test condition, it is redundant to use
the equality comparison operator like the code in (a):

test boolean value

```
if (even == true)
  System.out.println(
    "It is even.");
```
(a)

Equivalent

This is better

```
if (even)
  System.out.println(
    "It is even.");
```
(b)

Instead, it is better to use the **boolean** variable directly, as shown in (b). Another good reason
to use the **boolean** variable directly is to avoid errors that are difficult to detect. Using the =
operator instead of the == operator to compare equality of two items in a test condition is a common error. It could lead to the following erroneous statement:

```
if (even = true)
  System.out.println("It is even.");
```

This statement does not have syntax errors. It assigns **true** to **even** so that **even** is always
true.

Tip
If you use an IDE such as JBuilder, NetBeans, or Eclipse, please refer to *Learning Java Effectively with JBuilder/NetBeans/Eclipse* in the supplements. This supplement shows you how to use a debugger to trace a simple `if-else` statement.

3.3.4 Example: Computing Taxes

This section uses nested `if` statements to write a program to compute personal income tax. The United States federal personal income tax is calculated based on filing status and taxable income. There are four filing statuses: single filers, married filing jointly, married filing separately, and head of household. The tax rates for 2002 are shown in Table 3.7. If you are, say, single with a taxable income of $10,000, the first $6,000 is taxed at 10% and the other $4,000 is taxed at 15%. So your tax is $1,200.

TABLE 3.7 2002 U.S. Federal Personal Tax Rates

Tax rate	Single filers	Married filing jointly or qualifying widow/widower	Married filing separately	Head of household
10%	Up to $6,000	Up to $12,000	Up to $6,000	Up to $10,000
15%	$6,001–$27,950	$12,001–$46,700	$6,001–$23,350	$10,001–$37,450
27%	$27,951–$67,700	$46,701–$112,850	$23,351–$56,425	$37,451–$96,700
30%	$67,701–$141,250	$112,851–$171,950	$56,426–$85,975	$96,701–$156,600
35%	$141,251–$307,050	$171,951–$307,050	$85,976–$153,525	$156,601–$307,050
38.6%	$307,051 or more	$307,051 or more	$153,526 or more	$307,051 or more

Your program should prompt the user to enter the filing status and taxable income and computes the tax for the year 2002. Enter 0 for single filers, 1 for married filing jointly, 2 for married filing separately, and 3 for head of household. A sample run of the program is shown in Figure 3.6.

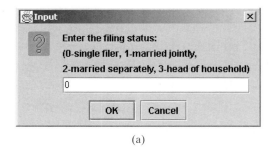
(a)

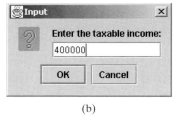
(b)

(c)

FIGURE 3.6 The program computes the tax using `if` statements.

Your program computes the tax for the taxable income based on the filing status. The filing status can be determined using `if` statements outlined as follows:

```
if (status == 0) {
  // Compute tax for single filers
}
else if (status == 1) {
  // Compute tax for married file jointly
}
else if (status == 2) {
  // Compute tax for married file separately
}
```

```
else if (status == 3) {
  // Compute tax for head of household
}
else {
  // Display wrong status
}
```

For each filing status, there are six tax rates. Each rate is applied to a certain amount of taxable income. For example, of a taxable income of $400,000 for single filers, $6,000 is taxed at 10%, (27950 – 6000) at 15%, (67700 – 27950) at 27%, (141250 – 67700) at 35%, and (400000 – 307050) at 38.6%.

Listing 3.4 gives the solution to compute taxes for single filers. The complete solution is left as an exercise.

LISTING 3.4 ComputeTaxWithSelectionStatement.java

```
 1  import javax.swing.JOptionPane;                                    import class
 2
 3  public class ComputeTaxWithSelectionStatement {
 4    public static void main(String[] args) {
 5      // Prompt the user to enter filing status
 6      String statusString = JOptionPane.showInputDialog(             input dialog
 7        "Enter the filing status:\n" +
 8        "(0-single filer, 1-married jointly,\n" +
 9        "2-married separately, 3-head of household)");
10      int status = Integer.parseInt(statusString);                   convert string
11                                                                     to int
12      // Prompt the user to enter taxable income
13      String incomeString = JOptionPane.showInputDialog(             input dialog
14        "Enter the taxable income:");
15      double income = Double.parseDouble(incomeString);              convert string
16                                                                     to double
17      // Compute tax
18      double tax = 0;                                                compute tax
19
20      if (status == 0) { // Compute tax for single filers
21        if (income <= 6000)
22          tax = income * 0.10;
23        else if (income <= 27950)
24          tax = 6000 * 0.10 + (income - 6000) * 0.15;
25        else if (income <= 67700)
26          tax = 6000 * 0.10 + (27950 - 6000) * 0.15 +
27            (income - 27950) * 0.27;
28        else if (income <= 141250)
29          tax = 6000 * 0.10 + (27950 - 6000) * 0.15 +
30            (67700 - 27950) * 0.27 + (income - 67700) * 0.30;
31        else if (income <= 307050)
32          tax = 6000 * 0.10 + (27950 - 6000) * 0.15 +
33            (67700 - 27950) * 0.27 + (141250 - 67700) * 0.30 +
34            (income - 141250) * 0.35;
35        else
36          tax = 6000 * 0.10 + (27950 - 6000) * 0.15 +
37            (67700 - 27950) * 0.27 + (141250 - 67700) * 0.30 +
38            (307050 - 141250) * 0.35 + (income - 307050) * 0.386;
39      }
40      else if (status == 1) { // Compute tax for married file jointly
41        // Left as exercise
42      }
```

```
43    else if (status == 2) { // Compute tax for married separately
44       // Left as exercise
45    }
46    else if (status == 3) { // Compute tax for head of household
47       // Left as exercise
48    }
49    else {
50       System.out.println("Error: invalid status");
51       System.exit(0);
52    }
53
54    // Display the result
55    JOptionPane.showMessageDialog(null, "Tax is " +
56       (int)(tax * 100) / 100.0);
57  }
58 }
```

exit program

message dialog

The **import** statement (line 1) makes the class **javax.swing.JOptionPane** available for use in this example.

The program receives the filing status and taxable income. The multiple alternative **if** statements (lines 22, 42, 45, 48, 51) check the filing status and compute the tax based on the filing status.

exit method

Like the **showMessageDialog** method, **System.exit(0)** (line 53) is also a static method. This method is defined in the **System** class. Invoking this method terminates the program. The argument **0** indicates that the program is terminated normally.

Note

An initial value of **0** is assigned to **tax** (line 20). A syntax error would occur if it had no initial value because all of the other statements that assign values to **tax** are within the **if** statement. The compiler thinks that these statements may not be executed and therefore reports a syntax error.

3.3.5 Example: An Improved Math Learning Tool

This example creates a program for a first grader to practice subtraction. The program randomly generates two single-digit integers **number1** and **number2** with **number1 > number2** and displays a question such as "**What is 9–2?**" to the student, as shown in Figure 3.7(a). After the student types the answer in the input dialog box, the program displays a message dialog box to indicate whether the answer is correct, as shown in Figure 3.7(b).

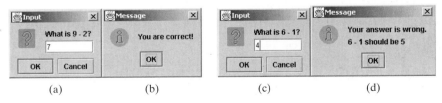

(a)   (b)   (c)   (d)

FIGURE 3.7 The program generates a subtraction question and grades the student's answer.

random() method

To generate a random number, use the **random()** method in the **Math** class. Invoking this method returns a random double value **d** such that $0.0 \leq d < 1.0$ So **(int)(Math.random() * 10)** returns a random single-digit integer (i.e., a number between **0** and **9**).

The program may work as follows:

■ Generate two single-digit integers into **number1** and **number2**.

■ If **number1 < number2**, swap **number1** with **number2**.

- Prompt the student to answer `"what is number1 - number2?"`
- Check the student's answer and display whether the answer is correct.

The complete program is shown in Listing 3.5.

Listing 3.5   SubtractionTutor.java

```
1  import javax.swing.JOptionPane;
2
3  public class SubtractionTutor {
4    public static void main(String[] args) {
5      // 1. Generate two random single-digit integers
6      int number1 = (int)(Math.random() * 10);
7      int number2 = (int)(Math.random() * 10);
8
9      // 2. If number1 < number2, swap number1 with number2
10     if (number1 < number2) {
11       int temp = number1;
12       number1 = number2;
13       number2 = temp;
14     }
15
16     // 3. Prompt the student to answer "what is number1 - number2?"
17     String answerString = JOptionPane.showInputDialog
18       ("What is " + number1 + " - " + number2 + "?");
19     int answer = Integer.parseInt(answerString);
20
21     // 4. Grade the answer and display the result
22     String replyString;
23     if (number1 - number2 == answer)
24       replyString = "You are correct!";
25     else
26       replyString = "Your answer is wrong.\n" + number1 + " - "
27         + number2 + " should be " + (number1 - number2);
28     JOptionPane.showMessageDialog(null, replyString);
29   }
30 }
```

import class

random numbers

input dialog

message dialog

To swap two variables `number1` and `number2`, a temporary variable `temp` (line 11) is used to first hold the value in `number1`. The value in `number2` is assigned to `number1` (line 12), and the value in `temp` is assigned to `number2`.

3.4 **switch** Statements

The `if` statement in Listing 3.4 makes selections based on a single `true` or `false` condition. There are four cases for computing taxes, which depend on the value of `status`. To fully account for all the cases, nested `if` statements were used. Overuse of nested `if` statements makes a program difficult to read. Java provides a `switch` statement to handle multiple conditions efficiently. You could write the following `switch` statement to replace the nested `if` statement in Listing 3.4:

```
switch (status) {
  case 0:  compute taxes for single filers;
           break;
  case 1:  compute taxes for married file jointly;
           break;
```

```
case 2:   compute taxes for married file separately;
          break;
case 3:   compute taxes for head of household;
          break;
default:  System.out.println("Errors: invalid status");
          System.exit(0);
}
```

The flow chart of the preceding `switch` statement is shown in Figure 3.8.

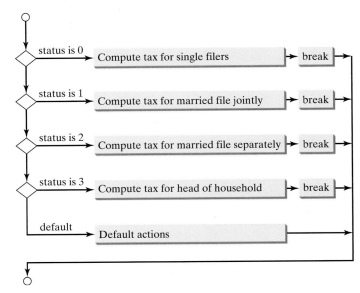

FIGURE 3.8 The `switch` statement checks all cases and executes the statements in the matched case.

This statement checks to see whether the status matches the value 0, 1, 2, or 3, in that order. If matched, the corresponding tax is computed; if not matched, a message is displayed. Here is the full syntax for the `switch` statement:

`switch` statement

```
switch (switch-expression) {
  case value1: statement(s)1;
               break;
  case value2: statement(s)2;
               break;
  ...
  case valueN: statement(s)N;
               break;
  default:     statement(s)-for-default;
}
```

The `switch` statement observes the following rules:

■ The `switch-expression` must yield a value of `char`, `byte`, `short`, or `int` type and must always be enclosed in parentheses.

■ The `value1`, ..., and `valueN` must have the same data type as the value of the `switch-expression`. Note that `value1`, ..., and `valueN` are constant expressions, meaning that they cannot contain variables in the expression, such as 1 + x.

- When the value in a `case` statement matches the value of the `switch-expression`, the statements *starting from this case* are executed until either a `break` statement or the end of the switch statement is reached.

- The keyword `break` is optional. The `break` statement immediately ends the `switch` statement.

- The `default` case, which is optional, can be used to perform actions when none of the specified cases matches the `switch-expression`.

- The `case` statements are checked in sequential order, but the order of the cases (including the default case) does not matter. However, it is good programming style to follow the logical sequence of the cases and place the default case at the end.

Caution

Do not forget to use a `break` statement when one is needed. Once a case is matched, the statements starting from the matched case are executed until a `break` statement or the end of the `switch` statement is reached. This phenomenon is referred to as the *fall-through* behavior. For example, the following code prints character a three times if `ch` is `'a'`:

without **break**

fall-through behavior

```java
switch (ch) {
  case 'a': System.out.println(ch);
  case 'b': System.out.println(ch);
  case 'c': System.out.println(ch);
}
```

ch is 'c' —true→ System.out.println(ch)
false ↓
ch is 'b' —true→ System.out.println(ch)
false ↓
ch is 'c' —true→ System.out.println(ch)
false ↓

Tip

To avoid programming errors and improve code maintainability, it is a good idea to put a comment in a case clause if `break` is purposely omitted.

3.5 Conditional Expressions

You might want to assign a value to a variable that is restricted by certain conditions. For example, the following statement assigns 1 to y if x is greater than 0, and −1 to y if x is less than or equal to 0.

```java
if (x > 0)
  y = 1
else
  y = -1;
```

Alternatively, as in this example, you can use a conditional expression to achieve the same result.

```java
y = (x > 0) ? 1 : -1;
```

Conditional expressions are in a completely different style, with no explicit `if` in the statement. The syntax is shown below:

```
booleanExpression ? expression1 : expression2;
```

conditional
expression

The result of this conditional expression is `expression1` if `booleanExpression` is `true`; otherwise the result is `expression2`.

Suppose you want to assign the larger number between variable `num1` and `num2` to `max`. You can simply write a statement using the conditional expression:

```
max = (num1 > num2) ? num1 : num2;
```

For another example, the following statement displays the message `"num is even"` if `num` is even, and otherwise displays `"num is odd."`

```
System.out.println((num % 2 == 0) ? "num is even" : "num is odd");
```

> **Note**
> The symbols `?` and `:` appear together in a conditional expression. They form a conditional operator. This operator is called a *ternary operator* because it uses three operands. It is the only ternary operator in Java.

3.6 Formatting Console Output and Strings

You already know how to display console output using the `println` method. JDK 1.5 introduced a new `printf` method that enables you to format output. The syntax to invoke this method is

printf

```
System.out.printf(format, item1, item2, ..., itemk)
```

specifier

where `format` is a string that may consist of substrings and format specifiers. A format specifier specifies how an item should be displayed. An item may be a numeric value, a character, a boolean value, or a string. Each specifier begins with a percent sign. Table 3.8 lists some frequently used specifiers.

TABLE 3.8 Frequently Used Specifiers

Specifier	Output	Example
%b	a boolean value	`true` or `false`
%c	a character	`'a'`
%d	a decimal integer	200
%f	a floating-point number	45.460000
%e	a number in standard scientific notation	4.556000e+01
%s	a string	`"Java is cool"`

Here is an example:

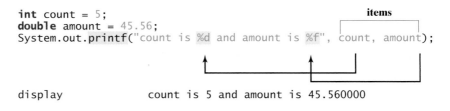

```
int count = 5;
double amount = 45.56;
System.out.printf("count is %d and amount is %f", count, amount);
```

display   count is 5 and amount is 45.560000

Items must match the specifiers in order, in number, and in exact type. For example, the specifier for `count` is `%d` and for `amount` is `%f`. By default, a floating-point value is displayed with six digits after the decimal point. You can specify the width and precision in a specifier, as shown in the examples in Table 3.9.

TABLE 3.9 Examples of Specifying Width and Precision

Example	Output
`%5c`	Output the character and add four spaces before the character item.
`%6b`	Output the boolean value and add one space before the false value and two spaces before the true value.
`%5d`	Output the integer item with width at least 5. If the number of digits in the item is <5, add spaces before the number. If the number of digits in the item is >5, the width is automatically increased.
`%10.2f`	Output the floating-point item with width at least 10 including a decimal point and two digits after the point. Thus there are 7 digits allocated before the decimal point. If the number of digits before the decimal in the item is <7, add spaces before the number. If the number of digits before the decimal in the item is >7, the width is automatically increased.
`%10.2e`	Output the floating-point item with width at least 10 including a decimal point, two digits after the point and the exponent part. If the displayed number in scientific notation has width less than 10, add spaces before the number.
`%12s`	Output the string with width at least 12 characters. If the string item has less than 12 characters, add spaces before the string. If the string item has more than 12 characters, the width is automatically increased.

You can put the minus sign (–) in the specifier to specify that the item is left-justified in the output within the specified field. For example, the following statement

left justify

```
System.out.printf("%8d%-8s\n", 1234, "Java");
System.out.printf("%-8d%-8s\n", 1234, "Java");
```

displays

```
    1234Java
1234    Java
```

Caution

The items must match the specifiers in exact type. The item for the specifier `%f` or `%e` must be a floating-point type value such as `40.0`, not `40`. Thus an `int` variable cannot match `%f` or `%e`.

Tip

The `%` sign denotes a specifier. To output a literal `%` in the format string, use `%%`.

You can print formatted output to the console using the `printf` method. Can you display formatted output in a message dialog box? To accomplish this, use the static `format` method in the `String` class to create a formatted string. The syntax to invoke this method is

formatting strings

```
String.format(format, item1, item2, ..., itemk)
```

This method is similar to the `printf` method except that the `format` method returns a formatted string, whereas the `printf` method displays a formatted string. For example,

```
String s = String.format("count is %d and amount is %f", 5, 45.56));
```

creates a formatted string `"count is 5 and amount is 45.560000"`.

The following statement displays a formatted string in a message dialog box:

```
JOptionPane.showMessageDialog(null,
    String.format("Sales tax is %1.2f",
    24.3454));
```

3.7 Operator Precedence and Associativity

Operator precedence and associativity determine the order in which operators are evaluated. Suppose that you have this expression:

```
3 + 4 * 4 > 5 * (4 + 3) - 1
```

precedence

What is its value? How does the compiler know the execution order of the operators? The expression in the parentheses is evaluated first. (Parentheses can be nested, in which case the expression in the inner parentheses is executed first.) When evaluating an expression without parentheses, the operators are applied according to the precedence rule and the associativity rule. The precedence rule defines precedence for operators, as shown in Table 3.10, which contains the operators you have learned so far. Operators are listed in decreasing order of precedence from top to bottom. Operators with the same precedence appear in the same group. (See Appendix C, "Operator Precedence Chart," for a complete list of Java operators and their precedence.)

TABLE 3.10 Operator Precedence Chart

Precedence	Operator
Highest Order	**var++** and **var--** (Postfix)
	+, - (Unary plus and minus), **++var** and **--var** (Prefix)
	(type) (Casting)
	! (Not)
	*, /, % (Multiplication, division, and remainder)
	+, - (Binary addition and subtraction)
	<, <=, >, >= (Comparison)
	==, != (Equality)
	& (Unconditional AND)
	^ (Exclusive OR)
	| (Unconditional OR)
	&& (Conditional AND)
	|| (Conditional OR)
Lowest Order	=, +=, -=, *=, /=, %= (Assignment operator)

associativity

If operators with the same precedence are next to each other, their *associativity* determines the order of evaluation. All binary operators except assignment operators are *left-associative*. For example, since + and − are of the same precedence and are left-associative, the expression

$$a - b + c - d \quad \underset{\text{equivalent}}{\underline{\hspace{3cm}}} \quad ((a - b) + c) - d$$

Assignment operators are *right-associative*. Therefore, the expression

$$a = b \ \text{+=} \ c = 5 \quad \underline{\text{equivalent}} \quad a = (b \ \text{+=} \ (c = 5))$$

Suppose **a**, **b**, and **c** are **1** before the assignment; after the whole expression is evaluated, **a** becomes **6**, **b** becomes **6**, and **c** becomes **5**. Note that left associativity for the assignment operator would not make sense.

Applying the operator precedence and associativity rule, the expression **3 + 4 * 4 > 5 * (4 + 3) - 1** is evaluated as follows:

```
3 + 4 * 4 > 5 * (4 + 3) - 1
                    |_____ (1) inside parentheses first
3 + 4 * 4 > 5 * 7 - 1
    |_____ (2) multiplication
3 + 16 > 5 * 7 - 1
         |_____ (3) multiplication
3 + 16 > 35 - 1
  |_____ (4) addition
19 > 35 - 1
       |_____ (5) subtraction
19 > 34
  |_____ (6) greater than
false
```

Tip

You can use parentheses to force an evaluation order as well as to make a program easy to read. Use of redundant parentheses does not slow down the execution of the expression.

3.8 Operand Evaluation Order

The precedence and associativity rules specify the order of the operators but not the order in which the operands of a binary operator are evaluated. Operands are evaluated strictly *from left to right* in Java. *The left-hand operand of a binary operator is evaluated before any part of the right-hand operand is evaluated.* This rule takes precedence over any other rules that govern expressions. Consider this expression:

from left to right

```
a + b * (c + 10 * d) / e
```

a, **b**, **c**, **d**, and **e** are evaluated in this order. *If no operands have side effects that change the value of a variable, the order of operand evaluation is irrelevant.* Interesting cases arise when operands do have a side effect. For example, **x** becomes 1 in the following code because **a** is evaluated to 0 before **++a** is evaluated to **1**.

```
int a = 0;
int x = a + (++a);
```

But **x** becomes **2** in the following code because **++a** is evaluated to **1**, and then **a** is evaluated to **1**.

```
int a = 0;
int x = ++a + a;
```

The order for evaluating operands takes precedence over the operator precedence rule. In the former case, **(++a)** has higher precedence than addition (**+**), but since **a** is a left-hand operand of the addition (+), it is evaluated before any part of its right-hand operand (e.g., **++a** in this case).

In summary, the rule of evaluating an expression is:

evaluation rule

- Rule 1: Evaluate whatever subexpressions you can possibly evaluate from left to right.

- Rule 2: The operators are applied according to their precedence, as shown in Table 3.10.

- Rule 3: The associativity rule applies for two operators next to each other with the same precedence.

Applying the rule, the expression **3 + 4 * 4 > 5 * (4 + 3) - 1** is evaluated as follows:

```
3 + 4 * 4 > 5 * (4 + 3) - 1
```
(1) 4 * 4 is the first subexpression that can be evaluated from the left.

```
3 + 16 > 5 * (4 + 3) - 1
```
(2) 3 + 16 is evaluated now.

```
19 > 5 * (4 + 3) - 1
```
(3) 4 + 3 is now the leftmost subexpression that should be evaluated.

```
19 > 5 * 7 - 1
```
(4) 5 * 7 is evaluated now.

```
19 > 35 - 1
```
(5) 35 - 1 is evaluated now.

```
19 > 34
```
(6) 19 > 34 is evaluated now.

false

The result happens to be the same as applying Rule 2 and Rule 3 without applying Rule 1. In fact, Rule 1 is not necessary if no operands have side effects that change the value of a variable in an expression.

KEY TERMS

boolean expression   68
boolean value   68
boolean type   68
break statement   81, 101
conditional operator   84
fall-through behavior   83

operand evaluation order   87
operator associativity   86
operator precedence   86
selection statement   73
short-circuit evaluation   70

CHAPTER SUMMARY

- Java has eight primitive data types. The preceding chapter introduced **byte**, **short**, **int**, **long**, **float**, **double**, and **char**. This chapter introduced the **boolean** type that represents a **true** or **false** value.

- The Boolean operators **&&, &, ||, |, !**, and **∧** operate with Boolean values and variables. The relational operators (**<, <=, ==, !=, >, >=**) work with numbers and characters, and yield a Boolean value.

- When evaluating **p1 && p2**, Java first evaluates **p1** and then evaluates **p2** if **p1** is **true**; if **p1** is **false**, it does not evaluate **p2**. When evaluating **p1 || p2**, Java first evaluates **p1** and then evaluates **p2** if **p1** is **false**; if **p1** is **true**, it does not evaluate p2. Therefore, && is referred to as the *conditional* or *short-circuit AND* operator, and || is referred to as the *conditional* or *short-circuit OR* operator.

■ Java also provides the & and | operators. The & operator works exactly the same as the && operator, and the | operator works exactly the same as the || operator with one exception: the & and | operators always evaluate both operands. Therefore, & is referred to as the *unconditional AND* operator, and | is referred to as the *unconditional OR* operator.

■ Selection statements are used for building selection steps into programs. There are several types of selection statements: if statements, if ... else statements, nested if statements, switch statements, and conditional expressions.

■ The various if statements all make control decisions based on a Boolean expression. Based on the true or false evaluation of the expression, these statements take one of two possible courses.

■ The switch statement makes control decisions based on a switch expression of type char, byte, short, int, or boolean.

■ The keyword break is optional in a switch statement, but it is normally used at the end of each case in order to terminate the remainder of the switch statement. If the break statement is not present, the next case statement will be executed.

■ The operands of a binary operator are evaluated from left to right. No part of the right-hand operand is evaluated until all the operands before the binary operator are evaluated.

■ The operators in arithmetic expressions are evaluated in the order determined by the rules of parentheses, operator precedence, and associativity.

■ Parentheses can be used to force the order of evaluation to occur in any sequence. Operators with higher precedence are evaluated earlier. The associativity of the operators determines the order of evaluation for operators of the same precedence.

■ All binary operators except assignment operators are left-associative, and assignment operators are right-associative.

REVIEW QUESTIONS

Section 3.2 boolean Data Type and Operations

3.1 List six comparison operators.

3.2 Assume that x is 1, show the result of the following Boolean expressions:

```
(true) && (3 > 4)
!(x > 0) && (x > 0)
(x > 0) || (x < 0)
(x != 0) || (x == 0)
(x >= 0) || (x < 0)
(x != 1) == !(x == 1)
```

3.3 Write a Boolean expression that evaluates to true if a number stored in variable num is between 1 and 100.

3.4   Write a Boolean expression that evaluates to `true` if a number stored in variable `num` is between `1` and `100` or the number is negative.

3.5   Assume that `x` and `y` are `int` type. Which of the following are correct Java expressions?

```
x > y > 0
x = y && y
x /= y
x or y
x and y
(x != 0) || (x = 0)
```

3.6   Can the following conversions involving casting be allowed? If so, find the converted result.

```
boolean b = true;
i = (int)b;
int i = 1;
boolean b = (boolean)i;
```

3.7   Suppose that `x` is 1. What is `x` after the evaluation of the following expression?

```
(x > 1) & (x++ > 1)
```

3.8   Suppose that `x` is 1. What is `x` after the evaluation of the following expression?

```
(x > 1) && (x++ > 1)
```

3.9   Show the output of the following program:

```java
public class Test {
  public static void main(String[] args) {
    char x = 'a';
    char y = 'c';

    System.out.println(++y);
    System.out.println(y++);
    System.out.println(x > y);
    System.out.println(x - y);
  }
}
```

Section 3.3 if Statements

3.10   Suppose `x = 3` and `y = 2`, show the output, if any, of the following code. What is the output if `x = 3` and `y = 4`? What is the output if `x = 2` and `y = 2`? Draw a flowchart of the following code:

```java
if (x > 2) {
  if (y > 2) {
    int z = x + y;
    System.out.println("z is " + z);
  }
}
else
  System.out.println("x is " + x);
```

3.11   Which of the following statements are equivalent? Which ones are correctly indented?

```
if (i > 0) if
(j > 0)
x = 0; else
if (k > 0) y = 0;
else z = 0;
```

(a)

```
if (i > 0) {
  if (j > 0)
    x = 0;
  else if (k > 0)
    y = 0;
}
else
  z = 0;
```

(b)

```
if (i > 0)
  if (j > 0)
    x = 0;
  else if (k > 0)
    y = 0;
  else
    z = 0;
```

(c)

```
if (i > 0)
  if (j > 0)
    x = 0;
  else if (k > 0)
    y = 0;
else
  z = 0;
```

(d)

3.12 Suppose $x = 2$ and $y = 3$, show the output, if any, of the following code. What is the output if $x = 3$ and $y = 2$? What is the output if $x = 3$ and $y = 3$? (Hint: please indent the statement correctly first.)

```
if (x > 2)
  if (y > 2) {
    int z = x + y;
    System.out.println("z is " + z);
  }
else
  System.out.println("x is " + x);
```

3.13 Are the following two statements equivalent?

```
if (income <= 10000)
  tax = income * 0.1;
else if (income <= 20000)
  tax = 1000 +
    (income - 10000) * 0.15;
```

```
if (income <= 10000)
  tax = income * 0.1;
else if (income > 10000 &&
         income <= 20000)
  tax = 1000 +
    (income - 10000) * 0.15;
```

3.14 Which of the following is a possible output from invoking `Math.random()`?

`323.4, 0.5, 34, 1.0, 0.0, 0.234`

3.15 How do you generate a random integer i such that $0 \le i < 20$?

How do you generate a random integer i such that $10 \le i < 20$?

How do you generate a random integer i such that $10 \le i \le 50$?

Section 3.4 `switch` Statements

3.16 What data types are required for a `switch` variable? If the keyword `break` is not used after a case is processed, what is the next statement to be executed? Can you convert a `switch` statement to an equivalent `if` statement, or vice versa? What are the advantages of using a `switch` statement?

3.17 What is `y` after the following `switch` statement is executed?

```
x = 3; y = 3;
switch (x + 3) {
  case 6:  y = 1;
  default: y += 1;
}
```

3.18 Use a `switch` statement to rewrite the following `if` statement and draw the flowchart for the `switch` statement:

```
if (a == 1)
  x += 5;
else if (a == 2)
  x += 10;
else if (a == 3)
  x += 16;
else if (a == 4)
  x += 34;
```

Section 3.5 Conditional Expressions

3.19 Rewrite the following `if` statement using the conditional operator:

```
if (count % 10 == 0)
  System.out.print(count + "\n");
else
  System.out.print(count + " ");
```

Section 3.6 Formatting Console Output and Strings

3.20 What are the specifiers for outputting a boolean value, a character, a decimal integer, a floating-point number, and a string?

3.21 What is wrong in the following statements?

```
(a) System.out.printf("%5d %d", 1, 2, 3);
(b) System.out.printf("%5d %f", 1);
(c) System.out.printf("%5d %f", 1, 2);
```

3.22 Show the output of the following statements.

```
(a) System.out.printf("amount is %f %e\n", 32.32, 32.32);
(b) System.out.printf("amount is %5.4f %5.4e\n", 32.32, 32.32);
(c) System.out.printf("%6b\n", (1 > 2));
(d) System.out.printf("%6s\n", "Java");
(e) System.out.printf("%-6b%s\n", (1 > 2), "Java");
(f) System.out.printf("%6b%-s\n", (1 > 2), "Java");
```

3.23 How do you create a formatted string?

Sections 3.7–3.8

3.24 List the precedence order of the Boolean operators. Evaluate the following expressions:

```
true | true && false
true || true && false
true | true & false
```

3.25 Show and explain the output of the following code:

```
(a)      int i = 0;
         System.out.println(--i + i + i++);
         System.out.println(i + ++i);
```

```
(b)      int i = 0;
         i = i + (i = 1);
         System.out.println(i);
```

(c)   ```
           int i = 0;
           i = (i = 1) + i;
           System.out.println(i);
           ```

**3.26**  Assume that `int a = 1` and `double d = 1.0`, and that each expression is independent. What are the results of the following expressions?

```
a = (a = 3) + a;
a = a + (a = 3);
a += a + (a = 3);
a = 5 + 5 * 2 % a--;
a = 4 + 1 + 4 * 5 % (++a + 1);
d += 1.5 * 3 + (++d);
d -= 1.5 * 3 + d++;
```

PROGRAMMING EXERCISES

Section 3.2 `boolean` Data Type and Operations

Pedagogical Note

For each exercise, students should carefully analyze the problem requirements and the design strategies for solving the problem before coding.

think before coding

Pedagogical Note

Instructors may ask students to *document analysis and design* for selected exercises. Students should use their own words to analyze the problem, including the input, output, and what needs to be computed and describe how to solve the problem using pseudocode. This has two benefits: (1) it mandates students to think before typing code; (2) it fosters writing skills.

document analysis and design

Debugging Tip

Before you ask for help, read and explain the program to yourself, and trace it using several representative inputs by hand or using an IDE debugger. You learn how to program by debugging your own mistakes.

learn from mistakes

Note

Do not use selection statements for Exercises 3.1–3.6.

3.1* (*Validating triangles*) Write a program that reads three edges for a triangle and determines whether the input is valid. The input is valid if the sum of any two edges is greater than the third edge. For example, if your input for three edges is 1, 2, 1, the output should be:

```
Can edges 1, 2, and 1 form a triangle? false
```

If your input for three edges is 2, 2, 1, the output should be:

```
Can edges 2, 2, and 1 form a triangle? true
```

3.2 (*Checking whether a number is even*) Write a program that reads an integer and checks whether it is even. For example, if your input is 25, the output should be:

```
Is 25 an even number? false
```

If your input is 2000, the output should be:

```
Is 2000 an even number? true
```
```

3.3* (*Using the &&, || and ^ operators*) Write a program that prompts the user to enter an integer and determines whether it is divisible by **5** and **6**, whether it is divisible by **5** or **6**, and whether it is divisible by **5** or **6**, but not both. For example, if your input is **10**, the output should be

```
Is 10 divisible by 5 and 6? false
Is 10 divisible by 5 or 6? true
Is 10 divisible by 5 or 6, but not both? true
```

3.4** (*Learning addition*) Write a program that generates two integers under **100** and prompts the user to enter the addition of these two integers. The program then reports **true** if the answer is correct, **false** otherwise. The program is similar to Listing 3.3.

3.5** (*Addition for three numbers*) The program in Listing 3.3 generates two integers and prompts the user to enter the addition of these two integers. Revise the program to generate three single-digit integers and prompt the user to enter the addition of these three integers.

3.6* (*Using the console input*) Rewrite Listing 3.2, LeapYear.java, using the console input.

Section 3.3 Selection Statements

3.7 (*Monetary units*) Modify Listing 2.4 to display the non-zero denominations only, using singular words for single units like **1** dollar and **1** penny, and plural words for more than one unit like **2** dollars and **3** pennies. (Use **23.67** to test your program.)

3.8* (*Sorting three integers*) Write a program that sorts three integers. The integers are entered from the input dialogs and stored in variables **num1**, **num2**, and **num3**, respectively. The program sorts the numbers so that *num1 ≤ num2 ≤ num3*.

3.9 (*Computing the perimeter of a triangle*) Write a program that reads three edges for a triangle and computes the perimeter if the input is valid. Otherwise, display that the input is invalid. The input is valid if the sum of any two edges is greater than the third edge (also see Exercise 3.1).

3.10 (*Computing taxes*) Listing 3.4 gives the source code to compute taxes for single filers. Complete Listing 3.4 to give the complete source code.

3.11* (*Finding the number of days in a month*) Write a program that prompts the user to enter the month and year, and displays the number of days in the month. For example, if the user entered month 2 and year 2000, the program should display that February 2000 has 29 days. If the user entered month 3 and year 2005, the program should display that March 2005 has 31 days.

3.12 (*Checking a number*) Write a program that prompts the user to enter an integer and checks whether the number is divisible by both **5** and **6**, neither, or just one of them. Here are some sample outputs for inputs **10**, **30**, and **23**.

```
10 is divisible by 5 or 6, but not both
30 is divisible by both 5 and 6
23 is not divisible by either 5 or 6
```

3.13 (*An addition learning tool*) Listing 3.5, SubtractionTutor.java, randomly generates a subtraction question. Revise the program to randomly generate an addition question with two integers less than **100**.

LOOPS

Objectives

- To use `while`, `do-while`, and `for` loop statements to control the repetition of statements (§§4.2–4.4).

- To understand the flow of control in loop statements (§§4.2–4.4).

- To use Boolean expressions to control loop statements (§§4.2–4.4).

- To know the similarities and differences between three types of loops (§4.5).

- To write nested loops (§4.6).

- To implement program control with `break` and `continue` (§4.9).

4.1 Introduction

Suppose that you need to print a string (e.g., `"Welcome to Java!"`) a hundred times. It would be tedious to have to write the following statement a hundred times:

```
System.out.println("Welcome to Java!");
```

why loop?

Java provides a powerful control structure called a *loop* that controls how many times an operation or a sequence of operations is performed in succession. Using a loop statement, you simply tell the computer to print a string a hundred times without having to code the print statement a hundred times.

Loops are structures that control repeated executions of a block of statements. The concept of looping is fundamental to programming. Java provides three types of loop statements: `while` loops, `do-while` loops, and `for` loops.

4.2 The `while` Loop

The syntax for the `while` loop is as follows:

`while` loop

```
while (loop-continuation-condition) {
    // Loop body
    Statement(s);
}
```

loop body
iteration

The `while` loop flow chart is shown in Figure 4.1(a). The part of the loop that contains the statements to be repeated is called the *loop body*. A one-time execution of a loop body is referred to as an *iteration of the loop*. Each loop contains a loop-continuation condition, a Boolean expression that controls the execution of the body. It is always evaluated before the loop body is executed. If its evaluation is true, the loop body is executed; if its evaluation is false, the entire loop terminates and the program control turns to the statement that follows the `while` loop. For example, the following `while` loop prints `"Welcome to Java!"` a hundred times.

```
int count = 0;
while (count < 100) {
    System.out.println("Welcome to Java!");
    count++;
}
```

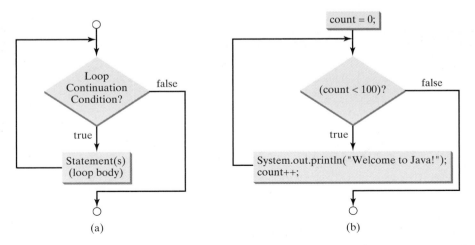

(a) (b)

FIGURE 4.1 The `while` loop repeatedly executes the statements in the loop body when the `loop-continuation-condition` evaluates to `true`.

The flow chart of the preceding statement is shown in Figure 4.1(b). The variable `count` is initially 0. The loop checks whether (`count < 100`) is true. If so, it executes the loop body to print the message `"Welcome to Java!"` and increments count by 1. It repeatedly executes the loop body until (`count < 100`) becomes `false`. When (`count < 100`) is `false` (i.e., when `count` reaches 100), the loop terminates and the next statement after the loop statement is executed.

Note

The `loop-continuation-condition` must always appear inside the parentheses. The braces enclosing the loop body can be omitted only if the loop body contains one or no statement.

Caution

Make sure that the `loop-continuation-condition` eventually becomes `false` so that the program will terminate. A common programming error involves infinite loops. That is, the program cannot terminate because of a mistake in the `loop-continuation-condition`. For instance, if you forgot to increase `count` (`count++`) in the code, the program would not stop. To terminate the program, press CTRL+C.

infinite loop

Tip

If you use an IDE such as JBuilder, NetBeans, or Eclipse, please refer to *Learning Java Effectively with JBuilder/NetBeans/Eclipse* in the supplements. This supplement shows you how to use a debugger to trace a simple loop statement.

debugging in IDE

4.2.1   Example: An Advanced Math Learning Tool

The Math subtraction learning tool program in Listing 3.5, SubtractionTutor.java, generates just one question for each run. You can use a loop to generate questions repeatedly. Listing 4.1 gives a program that generates ten questions and reports the number of correct answers after a student answers all ten questions. The program also displays the time spent on the test and lists all the questions, as shown in Figure 4.2.

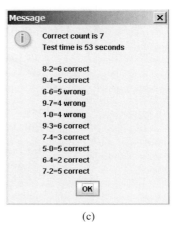

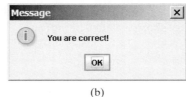

(a)   (b)   (c)

FIGURE 4.2   (a) The program prompts the user to answer the first question. (b) The program grades the answer. (c) The program displays a summary of the answers.

LISTING 4.1   SubtractionTutorLoop.java

```java
1 import javax.swing.JOptionPane;
2
3 public class SubtractionTutorLoop {
4   public static void main(String[] args) {
```

get start time

loop

display a question

grade an answer

increase correct count

increase control variable

prepare output

get end time

test time

display result

```
5      int correctCount = 0; // Count the number of correct answers
6      int count = 0; // Count the number of questions
7      long startTime = System.currentTimeMillis();
8      String output = "";
9
10     while (count < 10) {
11       // 1. Generate two random single-digit integers
12       int number1 = (int)(Math.random() * 10);
13       int number2 = (int)(Math.random() * 10);
14
15       // 2. If number1 < number2, swap number1 with number2
16       if (number1 < number2) {
17         int temp = number1;
18         number1 = number2;
19         number2 = temp;
20       }
21
22       // 3. Prompt the student to answer "what is number1 - number2?"
23       String answerString = JOptionPane.showInputDialog
24         ("What is " + number1 + " - " + number2 + "?");
25       int answer = Integer.parseInt(answerString);
26
27       // 4. Grade the answer and display the result
28       String replyString;
29       if (number1 - number2 == answer) {
30         replyString = "You are correct!";
31         correctCount++;
32       }
33       else
34         replyString = "Your answer is wrong.\n" + number1 + " - "
35           + number2 + " should be " + (number1 - number2);
36       JOptionPane.showMessageDialog(null, replyString);
37
38       // Increase the count
39       count++;
40
41       output += "\n" + number1 + "-" + number2 + "=" + answerString +
42         ((number1 - number2 == answer) ? " correct" : " wrong");
43     }
44
45     long endTime = System.currentTimeMillis();
46     long testTime = endTime - startTime;
47
48     JOptionPane.showMessageDialog(null,
49       "Correct count is " + correctCount + "\nTest time is " +
50       testTime / 1000 + " seconds\n" + output);
51   }
52 }
```

The program uses the control variable count to control the execution of the loop. **count** is initially **0** (line 6) and is increased by **1** in each iteration (line 39). A subtraction question is displayed and processed in each iteration. The program obtains the time before the test starts in line 7 and the time after the test ends in line 45, and computes the test time in line 46. The test time is in milliseconds and is converted to seconds in line 50.

4.2.2 Controlling a Loop with a Confirmation Dialog

confirmation dialog

The preceding example executes the loop ten times. If you want the user to decide whether to take another question, you can use a confirmation dialog to control the loop. A confirmation dialog can be created using the following statement:

```
int option =
   JOptionPane.showConfirmDialog
      (null, "Continue");
```

When a button is clicked, the method returns an option value. The value is JOptionPane.YES_OPTION (0) for the Yes button, JOptionPane.NO_OPTION (1) for the No button, and JOptionPane.CANCEL_OPTION (2) for the Cancel button. For example, the following loop continues to execute until the user clicks the No or Cancel button.

```
int option = 0;
while (option == JOptionPane.YES_OPTION) {
   System.out.println("continue loop");
   option = JOptionPane.showConfirmDialog(null, "Continue?");
}
```

You can rewrite Listing 4.1 using a confirmation dialog to let the user decide whether to continue the next question.

4.2.3   Controlling a Loop with a Sentinel Value

Another common technique for controlling a loop is to designate a special value when reading and processing a set of values. This special input value, known as a *sentinel value*, signifies the end of the loop.

sentinel value

Listing 4.2 writes a program that reads and calculates the sum of an unspecified number of integers. The input 0 signifies the end of the input. Do you need to declare a new variable for each input value? No. Just use one variable named data (line 9) to store the input value and use a variable named sum (line 12) to store the total. Whenever a value is read, assign it to data and added to sum (line 14) if it is not zero.

LISTING 4.2   SentinelValue.java

```
1  import javax.swing.JOptionPane;
2
3  public class SentinelValue {
4    /** Main method */
5    public static void main(String[] args) {
6      // Read an initial data
7      String dataString = JOptionPane.showInputDialog(
8        "Enter an int value:\n(the program exits if the input is 0)");
9      int data = Integer.parseInt(dataString);
10
11     // Keep reading data until the input is 0
12     int sum = 0;
13     while (data != 0) {
14       sum += data;
15
16       // Read the next data
17       dataString = JOptionPane.showInputDialog(
18         "Enter an int value:\n(the program exits if the input is 0)");
19       data = Integer.parseInt(dataString);
20     }
21
22     JOptionPane.showMessageDialog(null, "The sum is " + sum);
23   }
24 }
```

input dialog

convert string
to **int**

loop

message dialog

A sample run of the program is shown in Figure 4.3. If data is not 0, it is added to the `sum` (line 14) and the next items of input data are read (lines 12–19). If `data` is 0, the loop body is no longer executed and the `while` loop terminates. The input value 0 is the sentinel value for this loop. Note that if the first input read is 0, the loop body never executes, and the resulting `sum` is 0.

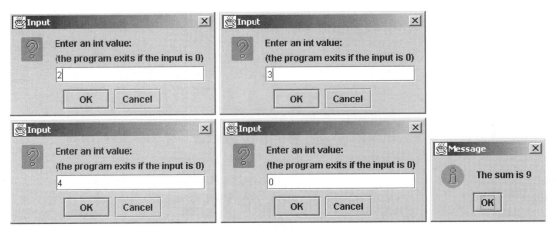

FIGURE 4.3 The program uses a `while` loop to add an unspecified number of integers.

Caution

Don't use floating-point values for equality checking in a loop control. Since floating-point values are approximations for some values, using them could result in imprecise counter values and inaccurate results. This example uses `int` value for `data`. If a floating-point type value is used for `data`, `(data != 0)` may be `true` even though `data` is exactly 0.

Here is a good example provided by a reviewer of this book:

```
// data should be zero
double data = Math.pow(Math.sqrt(2), 2) - 2;

if (data == 0)
  System.out.println("data is zero");
else
  System.out.println("data is not zero");
```

numeric error

Like `pow`, `sqrt` is a method in the `Math` class for computing the square root of a number. The variable `data` in the above code should be zero, but it is not, because of rounding-off errors.

4.3 The **do-while** Loop

The `do-while` loop is a variation of the `while` loop. Its syntax is given below:

do-while loop

```
do {
  // Loop body;
  Statement(s);
} while (loop-continuation-condition);
```

Its execution flow chart is shown in Figure 4.4.

The loop body is executed first. Then the `loop-continuation-condition` is evaluated. If the evaluation is `true`, the loop body is executed again; if it is `false`, the `do-while` loop terminates. The major difference between a `while` loop and a `do-while` loop is the order in which the `loop-continuation-condition` is evaluated and the loop body executed.

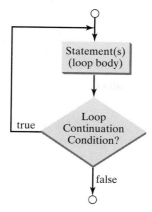

FIGURE 4.4   The **do-while** loop executes the loop body first, and then checks the **loop-continuation-condition** to determine whether to continue or terminate the loop.

The **while** loop and the **do-while** loop have equal expressive power. Sometimes one is a more convenient choice than the other. For example, you can rewrite the **while** loop in Listing 4.2 using a **do-while** loop, as shown in Listing 4.3.

LISTING 4.3   TestDo.java

```java
1 import javax.swing.JOptionPane;
2
3 public class TestDoWhile {
4   /** Main method */
5   public static void main(String[] args) {
6     int data;
7     int sum = 0;
8
9     // Keep reading data until the input is 0
10    do {
11      // Read the next data
12      String dataString = JOptionPane.showInputDialog(null,
13        "Enter an int value:\n(the program exits if the input is 0)",
14        "TestDo", JOptionPane.QUESTION_MESSAGE);
15
16      data = Integer.parseInt(dataString);
17
18      sum += data;
19    } while (data != 0);
20
21    JOptionPane.showMessageDialog(null, "The sum is " + sum,
22      "TestDo", JOptionPane.INFORMATION_MESSAGE);
23  }
24 }
```

loop

Tip
Use the **do-while** loop if you have statements inside the loop that must be executed at least once, as in the case of the **do-while** loop in the preceding **TestDoWhile** program. These statements must appear before the loop as well as inside the loop if you use a **while** loop.

4.4 The **for** Loop

Often you write a loop in the following common form:

```
i = initialValue;  // Initialize loop control variable
while (i < endValue) {
  // Loop body
  ...
  i++; // Adjust loop control variable
}
```

A **for** loop can be used to simplify the preceding loop:

```
for (i = initialValue; i < endValue; i++) {
  // Loop body
  ...
}
```

In general, the syntax of a **for** loop is as shown below:

for loop

```
for (initial-action; loop-continuation-condition;
      action-after-each-iteration) {
  // Loop body;
  Statement(s);
}
```

The flow chart of the **for** loop is shown in Figure 4.5(a).

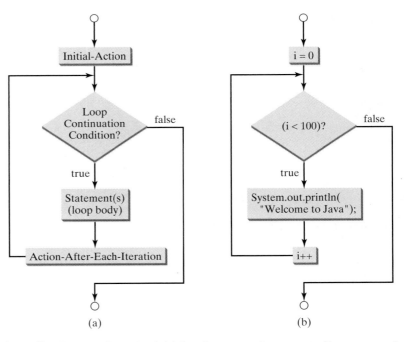

(a)   (b)

FIGURE 4.5 A **for** loop performs an initial action once, then repeatedly executes the statements in the loop body, and performs an action after an iteration when the **loop-continuation-condition** evaluates to **true**.

The **for** loop statement starts with the keyword **for**, followed by a pair of parentheses enclosing **initial-action**, **loop-continuation-condition**, and **action-after-each-iteration**, and followed by the loop body enclosed inside braces. **initial-action**, loop-continuation-condition, and `action-after-each-iteration` are separated by semicolons.

A `for` loop generally uses a variable to control how many times the loop body is executed and when the loop terminates. This variable is referred to as a *control variable*. The `initial-action` often initializes a control variable, the `action-after-each-iteration` usually increments or decrements the control variable, and the `loop-continuation-condition` tests whether the control variable has reached a termination value. For example, the following `for` loop prints `"Welcome to Java!"` a hundred times:

control variable

```java
int i;
for (i = 0; i < 100; i++) {
   System.out.println("Welcome to Java!");
}
```

The flow chart of the statement is shown in Figure 4.5(b). The `for` loop initializes `i` to `0`, then repeatedly executes the `println` statement and evaluates `i++` while `i` is less than `100`.

The `initial-action`, i = 0, initializes the control variable, `i`. The `loop-continuation-condition`, i < 100 is a Boolean expression. The expression is evaluated at the beginning of each iteration. If this condition is `true`, execute the loop body. If it is `false`, the loop terminates and the program control turns to the line following the loop.

The `action-after-each-iteration`, i++, is a statement that adjusts the control variable. This statement is executed after each iteration. It increments the control variable. Eventually, the value of the control variable should force the `loop-continuation-condition` to become false. Otherwise the loop is infinite.

```java
for (int i = 0; i < 100; i++) {
   System.out.println("Welcome to Java!");
}
```

If there is only one statement in the loop body, as in this example, the braces can be omitted.

Tip

The control variable must always be declared inside the control structure of the loop or before the loop. If the loop control variable is used only in the loop, and not elsewhere, it is good programming practice to declare it in the `initial-action` of the `for` loop. If the variable is declared inside the loop control structure, it cannot be referenced outside the loop. For example, you cannot reference `i` outside the `for` loop in the preceding code, because it is declared inside the `for` loop.

Note

The `initial-action` in a `for` loop can be a list of zero or more comma-separated variable declaration statements or assignment expressions. For example,

```java
for (int i = 0, j = 0; (i + j < 10); i++, j++) {
   // Do something
}
```

The `action-after-each-iteration` in a `for` loop can be a list of zero or more comma-separated statements. For example,

```java
for (int i = 1; i < 100; System.out.println(i), i++);
```

This example is correct, but it is not a good example, because it makes the code difficult to read. Normally, you declare and initialize a control variable as initial action, and increment or decrement the control variable as an action after each iteration.

Note

If the `loop-continuation-condition` in a `for` loop is omitted, it is implicitly `true`. Thus the statement given below in (a), which is an infinite loop, is correct. Nevertheless, it is better to use the equivalent loop in (b) to avoid confusion:

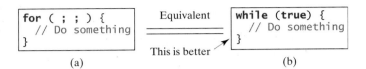

```
for ( ; ; ) {
    // Do something
}
```
(a)

Equivalent

This is better

```
while (true) {
    // Do something
}
```
(b)

4.5 Which Loop to Use?

pre-test loop
post-test loop

The `while` loop and `for` loop are called *pre-test loops* because the continuation condition is checked before the loop body is executed. The `do-while` loop is called a *post-test loop* because the condition is checked after the loop body is executed. The three forms of loop statements, `while`, `do-while`, and `for`, are expressively equivalent; that is, you can write a loop in any of these three forms. For example, a `while` loop in (a) in the following figure can always be converted into the `for` loop in (b):

```
while (loop-continuation-condition) {
    // Loop body
}
```
(a)

Equivalent

```
for ( ; loop-continuation-condition; ) {
    // Loop body
}
```
(b)

A `for` loop in (a) in the next figure can generally be converted into the `while` loop in (b) except in certain special cases (see Review Question 4.12 for such a case):

```
for (initial-action;
     loop-continuation-condition;
     action-after-each-iteration) {
    // Loop body;
}
```
(a)

Equivalent

```
initial-action;
while (loop-continuation-condition) {
    // Loop body;
    action-after-each-iteration;
}
```
(b)

Use the loop statement that is most intuitive and comfortable for you. In general, a `for` loop may be used if the number of repetitions is known, as, for example, when you need to print a message a hundred times. A `while` loop may be used if the number of repetitions is not known, as in the case of reading the numbers until the input is `0`. A `do-while` loop can be used to replace a `while` loop if the loop body has to be executed before the continuation condition is tested.

 Caution

Adding a semicolon at the end of the `for` clause before the loop body is a common mistake, as shown below in (a). In (a), the semicolon signifies the end of the loop prematurely. The loop body is actually empty, as shown in (b). (a) and (b) are equivalent.

Error

```
for (int i = 0; i < 10; i++);
{
  System.out.println("i is " + i);
}
```

(a)

Empty Body

```
for (int i = 0; i < 10; i++)  { };
{
  System.out.println("i is " + i);
}
```

(b)

Similarly, the loop in (c) is also wrong. (c) is equivalent to (d).

Error

```
int i = 0;
while (i < 10);
{
  System.out.println("i is " + i);
  i++;
}
```

(c)

Empty Body

```
int i = 0;
while (i < 10) { };
{
  System.out.println("i is " + i);
  i++;
}
```

(d)

These errors often occur when you use the next-line block style.

In the case of the **do-while** loop, the semicolon is needed to end the loop.

```
int i = 0;
do {
  System.out.println("i is " + i);
  i++;
} while (i < 10);  ◄——— Correct
```

4.6 Nested Loops

Nested loops consist of an outer loop and one or more inner loops. Each time the outer loop is repeated, the inner loops are reentered, and started anew.

Listing 4.4 presents a program that uses nested **for** loops to print a multiplication table, as shown in Figure 4.6.

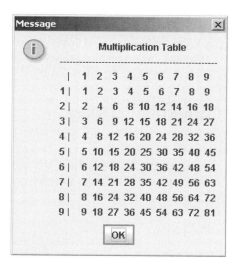

FIGURE 4.6 The program uses nested **for** loops to print a multiplication table.

LISTING 4.4 `MultiplicationTable.java`

```
1 import javax.swing.JOptionPane;
2
3 public class MultiplicationTable {
4   /** Main method */
5   public static void main(String[] args) {
6     // Display the table heading
7     String output = "                    Multiplication Table\n";
8     output += "-------------------------------------------------\n";
9
10    // Display the number title
11    output += "    | ";
12    for (int j = 1; j <= 9; j++)
13      output += "    " + j;
14
15    output += "\n";
16
17    // Print table body
18    for (int i = 1; i <= 9; i++) {
19      output += i + " | ";
20      for (int j = 1; j <= 9; j++) {
21        // Display the product and align properly
22        if (i * j < 10)
23          output += "    " + i * j;
24        else
25          output += "   " + i * j;
26      }
27      output += "\n";
28    }
29
30    // Display result
31    JOptionPane.showMessageDialog(null, output);
32  }
33 }
```

table title — (line 7)

table body — (line 18)

nested loop — (line 20)

The program displays a title (line 7) on the first line and dashes (–) (line 8) on the second line. The first **for** loop (lines 12–13) displays the numbers **1** through **9** on the third line.

The next loop (lines 18–28) is a nested **for** loop with the control variable **i** in the outer loop and **j** in the inner loop. For each **i**, the product **i * j** is displayed on a line in the inner loop, with **j** being **1, 2, 3, ... , 9**. The **if** statement in the inner loop (lines 22–25) is used so that the product will be aligned properly. If the product is a single digit, it is displayed with an extra space before it.

4.7 Minimizing Numerical Errors

Numeric errors involving floating-point numbers are inevitable. This section discusses how to minimize such errors through an example.

Listing 4.5 presents an example that sums a series that starts with **0.01** and ends with **1.0**. The numbers in the series will increment by **0.01**, as follows: **0.01 + 0.02 + 0.03** and so on. The output of the program appears in Figure 4.7.

LISTING 4.5 `TestSum.java`

```
1 import javax.swing.JOptionPane;
2
3 public class TestSum {
4   public static void main(String[] args) {
```

```
 5    // Initialize sum
 6    float sum = 0;
 7
 8    // Add 0.01, 0.02, ..., 0.99, 1 to sum
 9    for (float i = 0.01f; i <= 1.0f; i = i + 0.01f)          loop
10      sum += i;
11
12    // Display result
13    JOptionPane.showMessageDialog(null, "The sum is " + sum);
14  }
15 }
```

FIGURE 4.7   The program uses a `for` loop to sum a series from `0.01` to `1.0` in increments of `0.01`.

The `for` loop (lines 9–10) repeatedly adds the control variable `i` to the sum. This variable, which begins with `0.01`, is incremented by `0.01` after each iteration. The loop terminates when `i` exceeds `1.0`.

The `for` loop initial action can be any statement, but it is often used to initialize a control variable. From this example, you can see that a control variable can be a `float` type. In fact, it can be any data type.

The exact `sum` should be `50.50`, but the answer is `50.499985`. The result is not precise because computers use a fixed number of bits to represent floating-point numbers, and thus cannot represent some floating-point numbers exactly. If you change `float` in the program to `double` as follows, you should see a slight improvement in precision because a `double` variable takes sixty-four bits, whereas a `float` variable takes thirty-two bits.   double precision

```
// Initialize sum
double sum = 0;

// Add 0.01, 0.02, ..., 0.99, 1 to sum
for (double i = 0.01; i <= 1.0; i = i + 0.01)
  sum += i;
```

However, you will be stunned to see that the result is actually `49.50000000000003`. What went wrong? If you print out `i` for each iteration in the loop, you will see that the last `i` is slightly larger than `1` (not exactly `1`). This causes the last `i` not to be added into `sum`. The fundamental problem is that the floating-point numbers are represented by approximation. Errors commonly occur. There are two ways to fix the problem:

- Minimizing errors by processing large numbers first.   numeric error

- Using an integer count to ensure that all the numbers are processed.

- To minimize errors, add numbers from `1.0`, `0.99`, down to `0.1`, as follows:

```
// Add 1, 0.99, ..., 0.01 to sum
for (double i = 1.0; i >= 0.01; i = i - 0.01)
  sum += i;
```

To ensure that all the items are added to **sum**, use an integer variable to count the items. Here is the new loop:

```java
double currentValue = 0.01;

for (int count = 0; count < 100; count++) {
  sum += currentValue;
  currentValue += 0.01;
}
```

After this loop, **sum** is 50.50000000000003.

4.8 Case Studies

Control statements are fundamental in programming. The ability to write control statements is essential in learning Java programming. *If you can write programs using loops, you know how to program!* For this reason, this section presents three additional examples of how to solve problems using loops.

4.8.1 Example: Finding the Greatest Common Divisor

This section presents a program that prompts the user to enter two positive integers and finds their greatest common divisor.

GCD

The greatest common divisor of two integers 4 and 2 is 2. The greatest common divisor of two integers 16 and 24 is 8. How do you find the greatest common divisor? Let the two input integers be **n1** and **n2**. You know that number 1 is a common divisor, but it may not be the greatest common divisor. So you can check whether **k** (for **k** = 2, 3, 4 and so on) is a common divisor for **n1** and **n2**, until **k** is greater than **n1** or **n2**. Store the common divisor in a variable named **gcd**. Initially, **gcd** is 1. Whenever a new common divisor is found, it becomes the new **gcd**. When you have checked all the possible common divisors from 2 up to **n1** or **n2**, the value in variable **gcd** is the greatest common divisor. The idea can be translated into the following loop:

```java
int gcd = 1;
int k = 1;

while (k <= n1 && k <= n2) {
  if (n1 % k == 0 && n2 % k == 0)
    gcd = k;
  k++;
}

// After the loop, gcd is the greatest common divisor for n1 and n2
```

The complete program is given in Listing 4.6, and a sample run of the program is shown in Figure 4.8.

LISTING 4.6 GreatestCommonDivisor.java

```java
1  import javax.swing.JOptionPane;
2
3  public class GreatestCommonDivisor {
4    /** Main method */
5    public static void main(String[] args) {
6      // Prompt the user to enter two integers
7      String s1 = JOptionPane.showInputDialog("Enter first integer");
8      int n1 = Integer.parseInt(s1);
9
10     String s2 = JOptionPane.showInputDialog("Enter second integer");
11     int n2 = Integer.parseInt(s2);
12
13     int gcd = 1;
```

input

input

```
14        int k = 1;
15        while (k <= n1 && k <= n2) {
16          if (n1 % k == 0 && n2 % k == 0)
17            gcd = k;                                            gcd
18          k++;
19        }
20
21        String output = "The greatest common divisor for " + n1 + " and "
22          + n2 + " is " + gcd;
23        JOptionPane.showMessageDialog(null, output);            output
24      }
25 }
```

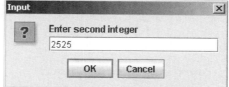

FIGURE 4.8   The program finds the greatest common divisor for two integers.

How did you write this program? Did you immediately begin to write the code? No. It is
important to *think before you type*. Thinking enables you to generate a logical solution for the
problem without concern about how to write the code. Once you have a logical solution, type
the code to translate the solution into a Java program. The translation is not unique. For example, you could use a `for` loop to rewrite the code as follows:

think before you type

```
for (int k = 1; k <= n1 && k <= n2; k++) {
  if (n1 % k == 0 && n2 % k == 0)
    gcd = k;
}
```

A problem often has multiple solutions. The GCD problem can be solved in many ways. Exercise
4.15 suggests another solution. A more efficient solution is to use the classic Euclidean algorithm. See http://www.cut-the-knot.org/blue/Euclid.shtml for more information.

multiple solutions

You might think that a divisor for a number `n1` cannot be greater than `n1 / 2`. So you
would attempt to improve the program using the following loop:

erroneous solutions

```
for (int k = 1; k <= n1 / 2 && k <= n2 / 2; k++) {
  if (n1 % k == 0 && n2 % k == 0)
    gcd = k;
}
```

This revision is wrong. Can you find the reason? See Review Question 4.9 for the answer.

4.8.2   Example: Finding the Sales Amount

You have just started a sales job in a department store. Your pay consists of a base salary and
a commission. The base salary is $5,000. The scheme shown below is used to determine the
commission rate.

Sales Amount	Commission Rate
$0.01–$5,000	8 percent
$5,000.01–$10,000	10 percent
$10,000.01 and above	12 percent

Your goal is to earn $30,000 a year. This section writes a program that finds the minimum amount of sales you have to generate in order to make $30,000.

Since your base salary is $5,000, you have to make $25,000 in commissions to earn $30,000 a year. What is the sales amount for a $25,000 commission? If you know the sales amount, the commission can be computed as follows:

```
if (salesAmount >= 10000.01)
  commission =
    5000 * 0.08 + 5000 * 0.1 + (salesAmount - 10000) * 0.12;
else if (salesAmount >= 5000.01)
  commission = 5000 * 0.08 + (salesAmount - 5000) * 0.10;
else
  commission = salesAmount * 0.08;
```

This suggests that you can try to find the **salesAmount** to match a given commission through incremental approximation. For a **salesAmount** of $0.01 (1 cent), find **commission**. If **commission** is less than $25,000, increment **salesAmount** by 0.01 and find **commission** again. If **commission** is still less than $25,000, repeat the process until it is greater than or equal to $25,000. This is a tedious job for humans, but it is exactly what a computer is good for. You can write a loop and let a computer execute it painlessly. The idea can be translated into the following loop:

```
Set COMMISSION_SOUGHT as a constant;
Set an initial salesAmount;

do {
  Increase salesAmount by 1 cent;
  Compute the commission from the current salesAmount;
} while (commission < COMMISSION_SOUGHT);
```

The complete program is given in Listing 4.7, and a sample run of the program is shown in Figure 4.9.

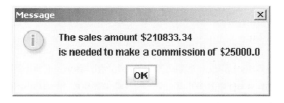

FIGURE 4.9   The program finds the sales amount for the given commission.

LISTING 4.7   FindSalesAmount.java

```
1  import javax.swing.JOptionPane;
2
3  public class FindSalesAmount {
4    /** Main method */
5    public static void main(String[] args) {
6      // The commission sought
7      final double COMMISSION_SOUGHT = 25000;
8      final double INITIAL_SALES_AMOUNT = 0.01;
```

constants

```
 9       double commission = 0;
10       double salesAmount = INITIAL_SALES_AMOUNT;
11
12       do {                                                            loop
13         // Increase salesAmount by 1 cent
14         salesAmount += 0.01;
15
16         // Compute the commission from the current salesAmount;
17         if (salesAmount >= 10000.01)
18           commission =
19             5000 * 0.08 + 5000 * 0.1 + (salesAmount - 10000) * 0.12;
20         else if (salesAmount >= 5000.01)
21           commission = 5000 * 0.08 + (salesAmount - 5000) * 0.10;
22         else
23           commission = salesAmount * 0.08;
24       } while (commission < COMMISSION_SOUGHT);
25
26       // Display the sales amount
27       String output =                                                 prepare output
28         "The sales amount $" + (int)(salesAmount * 100) / 100.0 +
29         "\nis needed to make a commission of $" + COMMISSION_SOUGHT;
30       JOptionPane.showMessageDialog(null, output);                    output
31     }
32 }
```

The **do-while** loop (lines 12–24) is used to repeatedly compute **commission** for an incremental **salesAmount**. The loop terminates when **commission** is greater than or equal to a constant COMMISSION_SOUGHT.

In Exercise 4.17, you will rewrite this program to let the user enter COMMISSION_SOUGHT dynamically from an input dialog.

You can improve the performance of this program by estimating a higher INITIAL_SALES_AMOUNT (e.g., **25000**).

What is wrong if **saleAmount** is incremented after the commission is computed, as follows?

```
do {
  // Compute the commission from the current salesAmount;
  if (salesAmount >= 10000.01)
    commission =
      5000 * 0.08 + 5000 * 0.1 + (salesAmount - 10000) * 0.12;
  else if (salesAmount >= 5000.01)
    commission = 5000 * 0.08 + (salesAmount - 5000) * 0.10;
  else
    commission = salesAmount * 0.08;

  // Increase salesAmount by 1 cent
  salesAmount += 0.01;
} while (commission < COMMISSION_SOUGHT);
```

The change is erroneous because **saleAmount** is 1 cent more than is needed for the commission when the loop ends. This is a common error in loops, known as the *off-by-one* error.   off-by-one error

Tip

This example uses *constants* COMMISSION_SOUGHT and INITIAL_SALES_AMOUNT. Using   constants
constants makes programs easy to read and maintain.

4.8.3   Example: Displaying a Pyramid of Numbers

This section presents a program that prompts the user to enter an integer from **1** to **15** and displays a pyramid. If the input integer is **12**, for example, the output is shown in Figure 4.10.

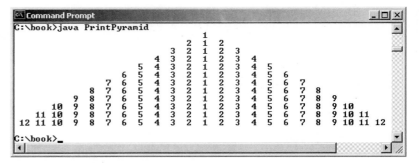

FIGURE 4.10 The program uses nested loops to print numbers in a triangular pattern.

Your program receives the input for an integer (`numberOfLines`) that represents the total number of lines. It displays all the lines one by one. Each line has three parts. The first part comprises the spaces before the numbers; the second part, the leading numbers, such as 3 2 1 in line 3; and the last part, the ending numbers, such as 2 3 in line 3.

Each number occupies three spaces. Display an empty space before a double-digit number, and display two empty spaces before a single-digit number.

You can use an outer loop to control the lines. At the nth row, there are (`numberOfLines` − n) * 3 leading spaces, the leading numbers are n, n-1, ..., 1, and the ending numbers are 2, ..., n. You can use three separate inner loops to print each part.

Here is the algorithm for the problem:

```
Input numberOfLines;

for (int row = 1; row <= numberOfLines; row++) {
  Print (numberOfLines - row) * 3 leading spaces;
  Print leading numbers row, row - 1, ..., 1;
  Print ending numbers 2, 3, ..., row - 1, row;
  Start a new line;
}
```

The complete program is given in Listing 4.8.

LISTING 4.8 PrintPyramid.java

```
1  import javax.swing.JOptionPane;
2
3  public class PrintPyramid {
4    /** Main method */
5    public static void main(String[] args) {
6      // Prompt the user to enter the number of lines
7      String input = JOptionPane.showInputDialog(
8        "Enter the number of lines:");
9      int numberOfLines = Integer.parseInt(input);
10
11     if (numberOfLines < 1 || numberOfLines > 15) {
12       System.out.println("You must enter a number from 1 to 15");
13       System.exit(0);
14     }
15
16     // Print lines
17     for (int row = 1; row <= numberOfLines; row++) {
18       // Print NUMBER OF LINES - row) leading spaces
19       for (int column = 1; column <= numberOfLines - row; column++)
20         System.out.print("   ");
21
```

print lines

print spaces

```
22        // Print leading numbers row, row - 1, ..., 1
23        for (int num = row; num >= 1; num-)                        print leading
24          System.out.print((num >= 10) ? " " + num : "  " + num);      numbers
25
26        // Print ending numbers 2, 3, ..., row - 1, row
27        for (int num = 2; num <= row; num++)                       print ending
28          System.out.print((num >= 10) ? " " + num : "  " + num);      numbers
29
30        // Start a new line
31        System.out.println();                                      a new line
32      }
33    }
34 }
```

The program uses the print method (lines 20, 24, and 28) to display a string to the console. The conditional expression `(num >= 10) ? " " + num : "  " + num` in lines 24 and 28 returns a string with a single empty space before the number if the number is greater than or equal to `10`, and otherwise returns a string with two empty spaces before the number.

Printing patterns like this one and the ones in Exercises 4.18 and 4.19 is a good exercise for practicing loop control statements. The key is to understand the pattern and to describe it using loop control variables.

The last line in the outer loop (line 31), `System.out.println()`, does not have any argument in the method. This call moves the cursor to the next line.

4.9 Keywords **break** and `continue`

Two statements, `break` and `continue`, can be used in loop statements to provide the loop with additional control.

- `break` immediately ends the innermost loop that contains it. It is generally used with an `if` statement. \
  break

- `continue` only ends the current iteration. Program control goes to the end of the loop body. This keyword is generally used with an `if` statement. \
  continue

You have already used the keyword `break` in a `switch` statement. You can also use `break` and `continue` in a loop. Listings 4.9 and 4.10 present two programs to demonstrate the effect of the `break` and `continue` keywords in a loop.

The program in Listing 4.9 adds the integers from `1` to `20` in this order to `sum` until `sum` is greater than or equal to `100`. Without the `if` statement (line 10), the program calculates the sum of the numbers from `1` to `20`. But with the `if` statement, the loop terminates when the sum becomes greater than or equal to `100`. The output of the program is shown in Figure 4.11(a).

(a)   (b)

FIGURE 4.11   (a) The `break` statement in the `TestBreak` program forces the `while` loop to exit when `sum` is greater than or equal to `100`. (b) The `break` statement is not executed in the modified `TestBreak` program because `sum == 100` cannot be `true`.

If you changed the `if` statement as shown below, the output would resemble that in Figure 4.11(b).

```
if (sum == 100) break;
```

In this case, the `if` condition will never be true. Therefore, the `break` statement will never be executed.

LISTING 4.9 TestBreak.java

```
1 public class TestBreak {
2   /** Main method */
3   public static void main(String[] args) {
4     int sum = 0;
5     int number = 0;
6
7     while (number < 20) {
8       number++;
9       sum += number;
10      if (sum >= 100) break;
11    }
12
13    System.out.println("The number is " + number);
14    System.out.println("The sum is " + sum);
15  }
16 }
```

break

The program in Listing 4.10 adds all the integers from 1 to 20 except 10 and 11 to `sum`. With the `if` statement in the program (line 9), the `continue` statement is executed when number becomes 10 or 11. The `continue` statement ends the current iteration so that the rest of the statement in the loop body is not executed; therefore, number is not added to `sum` when it is 10 or 11. The output of the program is shown in Figure 4.12(a).

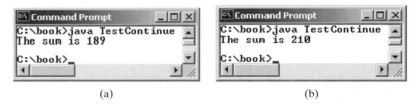

(a)   (b)

FIGURE 4.12   (a) The `continue` statement in the `TestContinue` program forces the current iteration to end when `number` equals 10 or 11. (b) Since the modified `TestContinue` program has no `continue` statement, every number is added to `sum`.

Without the `if` statement in the program, the output would look like Figure 4.12(b). In this case, all of the numbers are added to `sum`, even when `number` is 10 or 11. Therefore, the result is 210, which is 21 more than it was with the `if` statement.

LISTING 4.10 TestContinue.java

```
1 public class TestContinue {
2   /** Main method */
3   public static void main(String[] args) {
4     int sum = 0;
5     int number = 0;
6
```

```
 7      while (number < 20) {
 8        number++;
 9        if (number == 10 || number == 11) continue;
10        sum += number;
11      }
12
13      System.out.println("The sum is " + sum);
14    }
15 }
```

continue

Note

The continue statement is always inside a loop. In the while and do-while loops, the loop-continuation-condition is evaluated immediately after the continue statement. In the for loop, the action-after-each-iteration is performed, then the loop-continuation-condition is evaluated immediately after the continue statement.

Tip

You can always write a program without using break or continue in a loop. See Review Question 4.13. In general, it is appropriate to use break and continue if their use simplifies coding and makes programs easier to read.

4.9.1 (Optional) Statement Labels and Breaking with Labels

Every statement in Java can have an optional label as an identifier. Labels are often associated with loops. You can use a break statement with a label to break out of the labeled loop, and a continue statement with a label to break out of the current iteration of the labeled loop.

The break statement given below, for example, breaks out of the outer loop if (i * j > 50) and transfers control to the statement immediately following the outer loop.

```
outer:
  for (int i = 1; i < 10; i++) {
  inner:
    for (int j = 1; j < 10; j++) {
      if (i * j > 50)
        break outer;

      System.out.println(i * j);
    }
  }
```

If you replace breakouter with break in the preceding statement, the break statement would break out of the inner loop and continue to stay inside the outer loop.

The following continue statement breaks out of the inner loop if (i * j > 50) and starts a new iteration of the outer loop if i < 10 is true after i is incremented by 1.

```
outer:
  for (int i = 1; i < 10; i++) {
  inner:
    for (int j = 1; j < 10; j++) {
      if (i * j > 50)
        continue outer;

      System.out.println(i * j);
    }
  }
```

If you replace `continue outer` with `continue` in the preceding statement, the `continue` statement would break out of the current iteration of the inner loop and continue the next iteration of the inner loop if `j < 10` is true after `j` is incremented by `1`.

> **Note**
> Some programming languages have a `goto` statement, but labeled `break` statements and labeled `continue` statements in Java are completely different from `goto` statements. The `goto label` statement would indiscriminately transfer the control to any labeled statement in the program and execute it. The `break label` statement breaks out of the labeled loop, and the `continue label` statement breaks out of the current iteration in the labeled loop.

goto

 ### 4.9.2 (Optional) Example: Displaying Prime Numbers

This section presents a program that displays the first fifty prime numbers in five lines, each of which contains ten numbers, as shown in Figure 4.13. An integer greater than 1 is *prime* if its only positive divisor is 1 or itself. For example, 2, 3, 5, and 7 are prime numbers, but 4, 6, 8, and 9 are not.

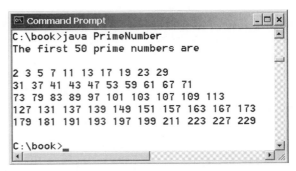

FIGURE 4.13 The program displays the first fifty prime numbers.

The problem can be broken into the following tasks:

- Determine whether a given number is prime.
- For `number = 2, 3, 4, 5, 6, . . .`, test whether it is prime.
- Count the prime numbers.
- Print each prime number, and print ten numbers per line.

Obviously, you need to write a loop and repeatedly test whether a new `number` is prime. If the `number` is prime, increase the count by 1. The `count` is `0` initially. When it reaches `50`, the loop terminates.

Here is the algorithm for the problem:

```
Set the number of prime numbers to be printed as
  a constant NUMBER_OF_PRIMES;
Use count to track the number of prime numbers and
  set an initial count to 0;
Set an initial number to 2;

while (count < NUMBER_OF_PRIMES) {
  Test if number is prime;

  if number is prime {
    Print the prime number and increase the count;
  }

  Increment number by 1;
}
```

To test whether a number is prime, check whether it is divisible by 2, 3, 4, up to number/2. If a divisor is found, the number is not a prime. The algorithm can be described as follows:

```
Use a boolean variable isPrime to denote whether
  the number is prime; Set isPrime to true initially;
for (int divisor = 2; divisor <= number / 2; divisor++) {
  if (number % divisor == 0) {
    Set isPrime to false
    Exit the loop;
  }
}
```

The complete program is given in Listing 4.11.

LISTING 4.11   PrimeNumber.java

```java
 1 public class PrimeNumber {
 2   /** Main method */
 3   public static void main(String[] args) {
 4     final int NUMBER_OF_PRIMES = 50; // Number of primes to display
 5     final int NUMBER_OF_PRIMES_PER_LINE = 10; // Display 10 per line
 6     int count = 0; // Count the number of prime numbers
 7     int number = 2; // A number to be tested for primeness
 8
 9     System.out.println("The first 50 prime numbers are \n");
10
11     // Repeatedly find prime numbers
12     while (count < NUMBER_OF_PRIMES) {
13       // Assume the number is prime
14       boolean isPrime = true; // Is the current number prime?
15
16       // Test if number is prime
17       for (int divisor = 2; divisor <= number / 2; divisor++) {
18         if (number % divisor == 0) { // the number is not prime
19           isPrime = false; // Set isPrime to false
20           break; // Exit the for loop
21         }
22       }
23
24       // Print the prime number and increase the count
25       if (isPrime) {
26         count++; // Increase the count
27
28         if (count % NUMBER_OF_PRIMES_PER_LINE == 0) {
29           // Print the number and advance to the new line
30           System.out.println(number);
31         }
32         else
33           System.out.print(number + " ");
34       }
35
36       // Check if the next number is prime
37       number++;
38     }
39   }
40 }
```

count prime numbers
subproblem

check primeness

exit loop

print if prime

This is a complex example for novice programmers. The key to developing a programmatic solution to this problem, and to many other problems, is to break it into subproblems and develop solutions for each of them in turn. Do not attempt to develop a complete solution in the first trial. Instead, begin by writing the code to determine whether a given number is prime, then expand the program to test whether other numbers are prime in a loop.

To determine whether a number is prime, check whether it is divisible by a number between 2 and `number/2` inclusive. If so, it is not a prime number; otherwise, it is a prime number. For a prime number, display it. If the count is divisible by 10, advance to a new line. The program ends when the count reaches 50.

 Note

The program uses the **break** statement in line 23 to exit the **for** loop as soon as the number is found to be a nonprime. You can rewrite the loop (lines 17–22) without using the **break** statement, as follows:

```
for (int divisor = 2; divisor <= number / 2 && isPrime;
    divisor++) {
  // If true, the number is not prime
  if (number % divisor == 0) {
    // Set isPrime to false, if the number is not prime
    isPrime = false;
  }
}
```

However, using the **break** statement makes the program simpler and easier to read in this case.

KEY TERMS

break statement 89, 113
continue statement 113
infinite loop 97
iteration 96
labeled break statement 115
labled continue statement 115

loop 96
loop-continuation-condition 96
loop body 96
nested loop 105
off-by-one error 111
sentinel value 99

CHAPTER SUMMARY

■ Program control specifies the order in which statements are executed in a program. There are three types of control statements: sequence, selection, and repetition. The preceding chapters introduced sequence and selection statements. This chapter introduced repetition statements.

■ There are three types of repetition statements: the **while** loop, the **do-while** loop, and the **for** loop. In designing loops, you need to consider both the loop control structure and the loop body.

■ The **while** loop checks the **loop-continuation-condition** first. If the condition is **true**, the loop body is executed; if it is **false**, the loop terminates. The **do-while** loop is similar to the **while** loop, except that the **do-while** loop executes the loop body first and then checks the **loop-continuation-condition** to decide whether to continue or to terminate.

■ Since the **while** loop and the **do-while** loop contain the **loop-continuation-condition**, which is dependent on the loop body, the number of repetitions is determined by the loop body. The **while** loop and the **do-while** loop are often used when the number of repetitions is unspecified.

■ The **for** loop is generally used to execute a loop body a predictable number of times; this number is not determined by the loop body. The loop control has three parts. The first part is an initial action that often initializes a control variable. The second part, the **loop-continuation-condition**, determines whether the loop body is to be executed. The third part is executed after each iteration and is often used to adjust the control variable. Usually, the loop control variables are initialized and changed in the control structure.

■ Two keywords, **break** and **continue**, can be used in a loop. The keyword **break** immediately ends the innermost loop, which contains the break. The keyword **continue** only ends the current iteration.

REVIEW QUESTIONS

Sections 4.2–4.8

4.1   How many times is the following loop body repeated? What is the printout of the loop?

```
int i = 1;
while (i > 10)
  if ((i++) % 2 == 0)
    System.out.println(i);
```
(a)

```
int i = 1;
while (i < 10)
  if ((i++) % 2 == 0)
    System.out.println(i);
```
(b)

4.2   What are the differences between a **while** loop and a **do-while** loop?

4.3   Do the following two loops result in the same value in **sum**?

```
for (int i = 0; i < 10; ++i) {
  sum += i;
}
```
(a)

```
for (int i = 0; i < 10; i++ ) {
  sum += i;
}
```
(b)

4.4   What are the three parts of a **for** loop control? Write a **for** loop that prints the numbers from **1** to **100**.

4.5   What does the following statement do?

```
for ( ; ; ) {
  do something;
}
```

4.6   If a variable is declared in the **for** loop control, can it be used after the loop exits?

4.7   Can you convert a **for** loop to a **while** loop? List the advantages of using **for** loops.

4.8   Convert the following **for** loop statement to a **while** loop and to a **do-while** loop:

```
long sum = 0;
for (int i = 0; i <= 1000; i++)
  sum = sum + i;
```

4.9   Will the program work if **n1** and **n2** are replaced by **n1 / 2** and **n2 / 2** in line 15 in Listing 4.6?

Section 4.9 Keywords **break** and **continue**

4.10 What is the keyword break for? What is the keyword continue for? Will the following program terminate? If so, give the output.

```
int balance = 1000;
while (true) {
  if (balance < 9)
    break;
  balance = balance - 9;
}
System.out.println("Balance is "
  + balance);
int balance = 1000;
```

(a)

```
while (true) {
  if (balance < 9)
    continue;
  balance = balance - 9;
}
System.out.println("Balance is "
  + balance);
```

(b)

4.11 Can you always convert a while loop into a for loop? Convert the following while loop into a for loop.

```
int i = 1;
int sum = 0;
while (sum < 10000) {
  sum = sum + i;
  i++;
}
```

4.12 The for loop on the left is converted into the while loop on the right. What is wrong? Correct it.

```
for (int i = 0; i < 4; i++) {
  if (i % 3 == 0) continue;
  sum += i;
}
```

Converted

Wrong
Conversion

```
int i = 0;
while (i < 4) {
  if (i % 3 == 0) continue;
  sum += i;
  i++;
}
```

4.13 Rewrite the programs TestBreak and TestContinue in Listings 4.9 and 4.10 without using break and continue.

4.14 After the break outer statement is executed in the following loop, which statement is executed?

```
outer:
  for (int i = 1; i < 10; i++) {
  inner:
    for (int j = 1; j < 10; j++) {
      if (i * j > 50)
        break outer;

      System.out.println(i * j);
    }
  }

next:
```

4.15 After the continue outer statement is executed in the following loop, which statement is executed?

```
outer:
  for (int i = 1; i < 10; i++) {
```

```
      inner:
        for (int j = 1; j < 10; j++) {
          if (i * j > 50)
            continue outer;
          System.out.println(i * j);
        }
      }

    next:
```

Comprehensive

4.16   Identify and fix the errors in the following code:

```
1 public class Test {
2   public void main(String[] args) {
3     for (int i = 0; i < 10; i++);
4       sum += i;
5
6     if (i < j);
7       System.out.println(i)
8     else
9       System.out.println(j);
10
11    while (j < 10);
12    {
13      j++;
14    };
15
16    do {
17      j++;
18    } while (j < 10)
19   }
20 }
```

4.17   What is wrong with the following program?

```
1 public class ShowErrors {
2   public static void main(String[] args) {
3     int i;
4     int j = 5;
5
6     if (j > 3)
7       System.out.println(i + 4);
8   }
9 }
```
(a)

```
1 public class ShowErrors {
2   public static void main(String[] args) {
3     for (int i = 0; i < 10; i++);
4       System.out.println(i + 4);
5   }
6 }
```
(b)

4.18   Show the output of the following programs:

```
public class Test {
  /** Main method */
  public static void main(String[] args) {
    for (int i = 1; i < 5; i++) {
      int j = 0;
      while (j < i) {
        System.out.print(j + " ");
        j++;
      }
    }
  }
}
```
(a)

```
public class Test {
  /** Main method */
  public static void main(String[] args) {
    int i = 0;
    while (i < 5) {
      for (int j = i; j > 1; j--)
        System.out.print(j + " ");
      System.out.println("****");
      i++;
    }
  }
}
```
(b)

```java
public class Test {
  public static void main(String[] args) {
    int i = 5;
    while (i >= 1) {
      int num = 1;
      for (int j = 1; j <= i; j++) {
        System.out.print(num + "xxx");
        num *= 2;
      }

      System.out.println();
      i--;
    }
  }
}
```
(c)

```java
public class Test {
  public static void main(String[] args) {
    int i = 1;
    do {
      int num = 1;
      for (int j = 1; j <= i; j++) {
        System.out.print(num + "G");
        num += 2;
      }

      System.out.println();
      i++;
    } while (i <= 5);
  }
}
```
(d)

4.19 Reformat the following programs according to the programming style and documentation guidelines proposed in §2.14. Use the next-line brace style.

```java
public class Test {
  public static void main(String[] args) {
    int i = 0;
    if (i>0)
    i++;
    else
    i--;

    char grade;

    if (i >= 90)
     grade = 'A';
    else
      if (i >= 80)
        grade = 'B';

  }
}
```
(a)

```java
public class Test {
  public static void main(String[] args) {
    for (int i = 0; i<10; i++)
      if (i>0)
        i++;
      else
        i--;
  }
}
```
(b)

Programming Exercises

 Pedagogical Note

A problem often can be solved in many different ways. Students are encouraged to explore various solutions.

explore solutions

Sections 4.2–4.7

4.1* (*Repeating additions*) Listing 4.1, SubtractionTutorLoop.java, generates ten random subtraction questions. Revise the program to generate ten random addition questions for two integers between 1 and 15. Display the number of correct answers and test time.

4.2* (*Counting positive and negative numbers and computing the average of numbers*) Write a program that reads an unspecified number of integers, determines how many positive and negative values have been read, and computes the total and average of the input values, not counting zeros. Your program ends with the input 0. Display the average as a floating-point number. (For example, if you entered 1, 2, and 0, the average should be 1.5.)

4.3 (*Conversion from kilograms to pounds*) Write a program that displays the following table (note that 1 kilogram is 2.2 pounds):

```
Kilograms    Pounds

1            2.2
3            6.6
...
197          433.4
199          437.8
```

4.4 (*Conversion from miles to kilometers*) Write a program that displays the following table (note that 1 mile is 1.609 kilometers):

```
Miles       Kilometers

1           1.609
2           3.218
...
9           14.481
10          16.09
```

4.5 (*Conversion from kilograms to pounds*) Write a program that displays the following two tables side-by-side (note that 1 kilogram is 2.2 pounds):

```
Kilograms    Pounds      Pounds      Kilograms

1            2.2         20          9.09
3            6.6         25          11.36
...
197          433.4       510         231.82
199          437.8       515         234.09
```

4.6 (*Conversion from miles to kilometers*) Write a program that displays the following two tables side-by-side (note that 1 mile is 1.609 kilometers):

```
Miles       Kilometers   Kilometers   Miles

1           1.609        20           12.430
2           3.218        25           15.538
...
9           14.481       60           37.290
10          16.09        65           40.398
```

4.7** (*Computing future tuition*) Suppose that the tuition for a university is $10,000 this year and increases 5% every year. Write a program that uses a loop to compute the tuition in ten years. Write another program that computes the total cost of four years' worth of tuition starting ten years from now.

4.8 (*Finding the highest score*) Write a program that prompts the user to enter the number of students and each student's name and score, and finally displays the student with the highest score.

4.9* (*Finding the two highest scores*) Write a program that prompts the user to enter the number of students and each student's name and score, and finally displays the student with the highest score and the student with the second-highest score.

4.10 (*Finding numbers divisible by 5 and 6*) Write a program that displays all the numbers from 100 to 1000, ten per line, that are divisible by 5 and 6.

4.11 (*Finding numbers divisible by 5 or 6, but not both*) Write a program that displays all the numbers from 100 to 200, ten per line, that are divisible by 5 or 6, but not both.

4.12 (*Finding the smallest n such that $n^2 > 12000$*) Use a `while` loop to find the smallest integer n such that n is greater than 12,000.

4.13 (*Finding the largest n such that* $n^3 < 12000$) Use a `while` loop to find the largest integer **n** such that n^3 is less than `12,000`.

4.14* (*Displaying the ACSII character table*) Write a program that prints the characters in the ASCII character table from '!' to '~'. Print ten characters per line.

Section 4.8 Case Studies

4.15* (*Computing the greatest common divisor*) Another solution for Listing 4.6 to find the greatest common divisor of two integers **n1** and **n2** is as follows: First find **d** to be the minimum of **n1** and **n2**, then check whether **d**, **d-1**, **d-2**, ..., **2**, or **1** is a divisor for both **n1** and **n2** in this order. The first such common divisor is the greatest common divisor for **n1** and **n2**.

4.16** (*Finding the factors of an integer*) Write a program that reads an integer and displays all its smallest factors. For example, if the input integer is `120`, the output should be as follows: `2, 2, 2, 3, 5`.

4.17* (*Finding the sales amount*) Rewrite Listing 4.7, FindSalesAmount.java, as follows:

- Use a `for` loop instead of a `do-while` loop.
- Let the user enter `COMMISSION_SOUGHT` instead of fixing it as a constant.

4.18* (*Printing four patterns using loops*) Use nested loops that print the following patterns in four separate programs:

```
Pattern I          Pattern II        Pattern III        Pattern IV
1                  1 2 3 4 5 6                 1         1 2 3 4 5 6
1 2                1 2 3 4 5                 2 1           1 2 3 4 5
1 2 3              1 2 3 4                 3 2 1             1 2 3 4
1 2 3 4            1 2 3                 4 3 2 1               1 2 3
1 2 3 4 5          1 2                 5 4 3 2 1                 1 2
1 2 3 4 5 6        1                 6 5 4 3 2 1                   1
```

4.19** (*Printing numbers in a pyramid pattern*) Write a nested `for` loop that prints the following output:

```
                              1
                        1     2     1
                  1     2     4     2     1
            1     2     4     8     4     2     1
      1     2     4     8    16     8     4     2     1
   1  2     4     8    16    32    16     8     4     2     1
 1  2     4     8    16    32    64    32    16     8     4     2     1
1   2     4     8    16    32    64   128    64    32    16     8     4     2     1
```

Hint

Here is the pseudocode solution:

```
for the row from 0 to 7 {
  Pad leading blanks in a row using a loop like this:
  for the column from 1 to 7-row
    System.out.print("    ");

  Print left half of the row for numbers 1, 2, 4, up to
     2^row using a look like this:
  for the column from 0 to row
    System.out.print("    " + (int)Math.pow(2, column));

  Print the right half of the row for numbers
     2^(row-1), 2^(row-2), ..., 1 using a loop like this:
```

```
for (int column = row - 1; column >= 0; col--)
  System.out.print("    " + (int)Math.pow(2, column));

Start a new line
System.out.println();
}
```

You need to figure out how many spaces to print before the number. This is dependent on the number. If a number is a single digit, print four spaces. If a number has two digits, print three spaces. If a number has three digits, print two spaces.

The `Math.pow()` method was introduced in §2.12.1, "Example: Computing Loan Payments." Can you write this program without using it?

4.20* (*Printing prime numbers between 2 and 1000*) Modify Listing 4.11 to print all the prime numbers between 2 and 1000, inclusively. Display eight prime numbers per line.

Comprehensive

4.21**(*Comparing loans with various interest rates*) Write a program that lets the user enter the loan amount and loan period in number of years and displays the monthly and total payments for each interest rate starting from 5% to 8%, with an increment of 1/8. Suppose you enter the loan amount 10,000 for five years; display a table as follows:

```
Loan Amount: 10000
Number of Years: 5
Interest Rate      Monthly Payment      Total Payment

5%                 188.71               11322.74
5.125%             189.28               11357.13
5.25%              189.85               11391.59
...
7.85%              202.16               12129.97
8.0%               202.76               12165.83
```

4.22** (*Displaying the loan amortization schedule*) The monthly payment for a given loan pays the principal and the interest. The monthly interest is computed by multiplying the monthly interest rate and the balance (the remaining principal). The principal paid for the month is therefore the monthly payment minus the monthly interest. Write a program that lets the user enter the loan amount, number of years, and interest rate, and displays the amortization schedule for the loan. Suppose you enter the loan amount 10,000 for one year with an interest rate of 7%; display a table as follows:

```
Loan Amount: 10000
Number of Years: 1
Annual Interest Rate: 7%

Monthly Payment: 865.26
Total Payment: 10383.21

Payment#     Interest     Principal     Balance

1            58.33        806.93        9193.07
2            53.62        811.64        8381.43
...
11           10.0         855.26        860.27
12           5.01         860.25        0.01
```

Note

The balance after the last payment may not be zero. If so, the last payment should be the normal monthly payment plus the final balance.

Hint

Write a loop to print the table. Since monthly payment is the same for each month, it should be computed before the loop. The balance is initially the loan amount. For each iteration in the loop, compute the interest and principal, and update the balance. The loop may look like this:

```
for (i = 1; i <= numberOfYears * 12; i++) {
  interest = monthlyInterestRate * balance;
  principal = monthlyPayment - interest;
  balance = balance - principal;
  System.out.println(i + "\t\t" + interest
    + "\t\t" + principal + "\t\t" + balance);
}
```

4.23* (*Demonstrating cancellation errors*) A cancellation error occurs when you are manipulating a very large number with a very small number. The large number may cancel out the smaller number. For example, the result of `100000000.0 + 0.000000001` is equal to `100000000.0`. To avoid cancellation errors and obtain more accurate results, carefully select the order of computation. For example, in computing the following series, you will obtain more accurate results by computing from right to left rather than from left to right:

$$1 + \frac{1}{2} + \frac{1}{3} + \cdots + \frac{1}{n}$$

Write a program that compares the results of the summation of the preceding series, computing from left to right and from right to left with `n = 50000`.

4.24* (*Summing a series*) Write a program to sum the following series:

$$\frac{1}{3} + \frac{3}{5} + \frac{5}{7} + \frac{7}{9} + \frac{9}{11} + \frac{11}{13} + \cdots + \frac{95}{97} + \frac{97}{99}$$

4.25**(*Computing* π) You can approximate π by using the following series:

$$\pi = 4\left(1 - \frac{1}{3} + \frac{1}{5} - \frac{1}{7} + \frac{1}{9} - \frac{1}{11} + \frac{1}{13} - \cdots - \frac{1}{2i-1} + \frac{1}{2i+1}\right)$$

Write a program that displays the π value for `i = 10000, 20000, ...,` and `100000`.

4.26**(*Computing e*) You can approximate **e** by using the following series:

$$e = 1 + \frac{1}{1!} + \frac{1}{2!} + \frac{1}{3!} + \frac{1}{4!} + \cdots + \frac{1}{i!}$$

Write a program that displays the **e** value for `i = 10000, 20000, ...,` and `100000`.

Hint

Since $i! = i \times (i-1) \times \cdots \times 2 \times 1$, $\frac{1}{i!}$ is $\frac{1}{i(i-1)!}$. Initialize **e** and **item** to be 1 and keep adding a new **item** to **e**. The new item is the previous item divided by **i** for $i = 2, 3, 4, \ldots$.

4.27**(*Displaying leap years*) Write a program that displays all the leap years, ten per line, in the twenty-first century (from **2001** to **2100**).

4.28**(*Displaying the first days of each month*) Write a program that prompts the user to enter the year and first day of the year, and displays the first day of each month in the year on the console. For example, if the user entered the year 2005, and 6 for Saturday, January 1, 2005, your program should display the following output:

```
January 1, 2005 is Saturday
...
December 1, 2005 is Thursday
```

4.29** (*Displaying calendars*) Write a program that prompts the user to enter the year and first day of the year, and displays the calendar table for the year on the console. For example, if the user entered the year 2005, and 6 for Saturday, January 1, 2005, your program should display the calendar for each month in the year, as follows:

January 2005

Sun	Mon	Tue	Wed	Thu	Fri	Sat
						1
2	3	4	5	6	7	8
9	10	11	12	13	14	15
16	17	18	19	20	21	22
23	24	25	26	27	28	29
30	31					

...

December 2005

Sun	Mon	Tue	Wed	Thu	Fri	Sat
				1	2	3
4	5	6	7	8	9	10
11	12	13	14	15	16	17
18	19	20	21	22	23	24
25	26	27	28	29	30	31

METHODS

Objectives

- To create methods, invoke methods, and pass arguments to a method (§§5.2–5.5).
- To use method overloading and understand ambiguous overloading (§5.6).
- To determine the scope of variables (§5.8).
- To know how to use the methods in the `Math` class (§5.9).
- To learn the concept of method abstraction (§5.11).
- To design and implement methods using stepwise refinement (§5.11).
- (Optional) To group classes into packages (§5.12).

5.1 Introduction

In the preceding chapters, you learned about such methods as `System.out.println`, `JOptionPane.showMessageDialog`, `JOptionPane.showInputDialog`, `Integer.parseInt`, `Double.parseDouble`, `System.exit`, `Math.pow`, and `Math.random()`. A method is a collection of statements that are grouped together to perform an operation. When you call the `System.out.println` method, for example, the system actually executes several statements in order to display a message on the console.

This chapter introduces methods. You will learn how to create your own methods with or without return values, invoke a method with or without parameters, overload methods using the same names, and apply method abstraction in the program design.

5.2 Creating a Method

In general, a method has the following syntax:

```
modifier returnValueType methodName(list of parameters) {
   // Method body;
}
```

Let's take a look at a method created to find which of two integers is bigger. This method, named `max`, has two `int` parameters, `num1` and `num2`, the larger of which is returned by the method. Figure 5.1 illustrates the components of this method.

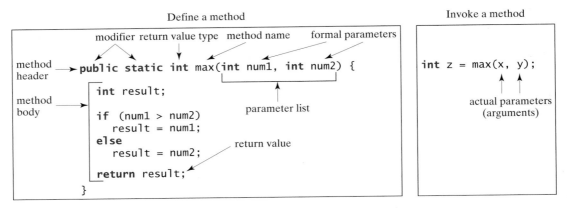

FIGURE 5.1 A method declaration consists of a method header and a method body.

The method header specifies the *modifiers*, *return value type*, *method name*, and *parameters* of the method. The modifier, which is optional, tells the compiler how to call the method. The static modifier is used for all the methods in this chapter. The reason for using it will be discussed in Chapter 7, "Objects and Classes."

A method may return a value. The `returnValueType` is the data type of the value the method returns. Some methods perform the desired operations without returning a value. In this case, the `returnValueType` is the keyword `void`. For example, the `returnValueType` in the `main` method is `void`, as well as in `System.exit`, `System.out.println`, and `JOptionPane.showMessageDialog`. The method that returns a value is called a *nonvoid method*, and the method that does not return a value is called a *void method*.

nonvoid method

void method

parameter

argument

parameter list

The variables defined in the method header are known as *formal parameters* or simply *parameters*. A parameter is like a placeholder. When a method is invoked, you pass a value to the parameter. This value is referred to as *actual parameter or argument*. The *parameter list* refers to the type, order, and number of the parameters of a method. The method name and the parameter list together constitute the *method signature*. Parameters are optional; that is, a method may contain no parameters.

method signature

The method body contains a collection of statements that define what the method does. The method body of the `max` method uses an `if` statement to determine which number is larger and return the value of that number. A return statement using the keyword `return` is *required* for a nonvoid method to return a result. The method terminates when a return statement is executed.

Note

In certain other languages, methods are referred to as *procedures* and *functions*. A method with a nonvoid return value type is called a *function*; a method with a `void` return value type is called a *procedure*.

Caution

You need to declare a separate data type for each parameter. For instance, `int num1, num2` should be replaced by `int num1, int num2`.

5.3 Calling a Method

In creating a method, you give a definition of what the method is to do. To use a method, you have to *call* or *invoke* it. There are two ways to call a method; the choice is based on whether the method returns a value or not.

If the method returns a value, a call to the method is usually treated as a value. For example,

```
int larger = max(3, 4);
```

calls `max(3, 4)` and assigns the result of the method to the variable `larger`. Another example of a call that is treated as a value is

```
System.out.println(max(3, 4));
```

which prints the return value of the method call `max(3, 4)`.

If the method returns `void`, a call to the method must be a statement. For example, the method `println` returns `void`. The following call is a statement:

```
System.out.println("Welcome to Java!");
```

Note

A method with a nonvoid return value type can also be invoked as a statement in Java. In this case, the caller simply ignores the return value. This is rare, but permissible if the caller is not interested in the return value.

When a program calls a method, program control is transferred to the called method. A called method returns control to the caller when its return statement is executed or when its method-ending closing brace is reached.

Listing 5.1 shows a complete program that is used to test the `max` method. The output of the program is shown in Figure 5.2.

FIGURE 5.2   The program invokes `max(i, j)` in order to get the maximum value between `i` and `j`.

LISTING 5.1   TestMax.java

<table>
<tr><td>main method</td><td>

```
 1  public class TestMax {
 2    /** Main method */
 3    public static void main(String[] args) {
 4      int i = 5;
 5      int j = 2;
```
</td></tr>
</table>

```
 1  public class TestMax {
 2    /** Main method */
 3    public static void main(String[] args) {
 4      int i = 5;
 5      int j = 2;
 6      int k = max(i, j);
 7      System.out.println("The maximum between " + i +
 8        " and " + j + " is " + k);
 9    }
10
11    /** Return the max between two numbers */
12    public static int max(int num1, int num2) {
13      int result;
14
15      if (num1 > num2)
16        result = num1;
17      else
18        result = num2;
19
20      return result;
21    }
22  }
```

invoke max (line 6)

declare method (line 12)

This program contains the `main` method and the `max` method. The `main` method is just like any other method except that it is invoked by the JVM.

The `main` method's header is always the same, like the one in this example, with the modifiers `public` and `static`, return value type `void`, method name `main`, and a parameter of the `String[]` type. `String[]` indicates that the parameter is an array of `String`, a subject addressed in Chapter 6, "Arrays."

The statements in `main` may invoke other methods that are defined in the class that contains the `main` method or in other classes. In this example, the `main` method invokes `max(i, j)`, which is defined in the same class with the `main` method.

When the `max` method is invoked (line 6), variable `i`'s value 5 is passed to `num1`, and variable `j`'s value 2 is passed to `num2` in the `max` method. The flow of control transfers to the `max` method. The `max` method is executed. When the `return` statement in the `max` method is executed, the `max` method returns the control to its caller (in this case the caller is the `main` method). This process is illustrated in Figure 5.3.

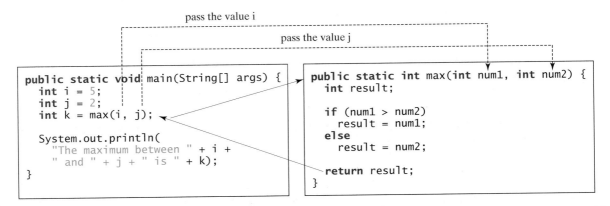

FIGURE 5.3   When the `max` method is invoked, the flow of control transfers to the `max` method. Once the `max` method is finished, it returns the control back to the caller.

Caution

A `return` statement is required for a nonvoid method. The method shown below in (a) is logically correct, but it has a compilation error because the Java compiler thinks it possible that this method does not return any value.

```
public static int sign(int n) {
   if (n > 0) return 1;
   else if (n == 0) return 0;
   else if (n < 0) return -1;
}
```
(a)

Should be →

```
public static int sign(int n) {
   if (n > 0) return 1;
   else if (n == 0) return 0;
   else return -1;
}
```
(b)

To fix this problem, delete `if (n < 0)` in (a), so that the compiler will see a `return` statement to be reached regardless of how the `if` statement is evaluated.

Note

One of the benefits of methods is for reuse. The `max` method can be invoked from any class besides `TestMax`. If you create a new class, `Test`, you can invoke the `max` method using `ClassName.methodName` (i.e., `TestMax.max`).

reusing method

5.3.1 Call Stacks

Each time a method is invoked, the system stores parameters and variables in an area of memory, known as a *stack*, which stores elements in last-in first-out fashion. When a method calls another method, the caller's stack space is kept intact, and new space is created to handle the new method call. When a method finishes its work and returns to its caller, its associated space is released.

stack

Understanding call stacks helps you to comprehend how methods are invoked. The variables defined in the `main` method are `i`, `j`, and `k`. The variables defined in the `max` method are `num1`, `num2`, and `result`. The variables `num1` and `num2` are defined in the method signature and are parameters of the method. Their values are passed through method invocation. Figure 5.4 illustrates the variables in the stack.

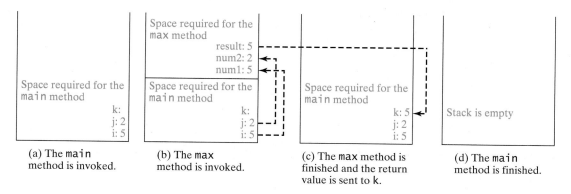

FIGURE 5.4 When the `max` method is invoked, the flow of control transfers to the `max` method. Once the `max` method is finished, it returns the control back to the caller.

Tip

If you use an IDE such as JBuilder, NetBeans, or Eclipse, please refer to *Learning Java Effectively with JBuilder/NetBeans/Eclipse* in the supplements. This supplement shows you how to use a debugger to trace method invocations.

debugging in IDE

5.4 void Method Example

The preceding section gives an example of a nonvoid method. This section shows how to declare and invoke a void method. Listing 5.2 gives a program that declares a method named printGrade and invokes it to print the grade for a given score.

LISTING 5.2   TestVoidMethod.java

main method
invoke **printGrade**

printGrade method

```
 1  public class TestVoidMethod {
 2    public static void main(String[] args) {
 3      printGrade(78.5);
 4    }
 5
 6    public static void printGrade(double score) {
 7      if (score >= 90.0) {
 8        System.out.println('A');
 9      }
10      else if (score >= 80.0) {
11        System.out.println('B');
12      }
13      else if (score >= 70.0) {
14        System.out.println('C');
15      }
16      else if (score >= 60.0) {
17        System.out.println('D');
18      }
19      else {
20        System.out.println('F');
21      }
22    }
23  }
```

invoke **void** method

The printGrade method is a void method. It does not return any value. A call to a void method must be a statement. So, it is invoked as a statement in line 3 in the main method. This statement is like any Java statement terminated with a semicolon.

 Note

return in **void** method

A return statement is not needed for a void method, but it can be used for terminating the method and returning to the method's caller. The syntax is simply

```
return;
```

This is rare, but sometimes useful for circumventing the normal flow of control in a void function. For example, the following code has a return statement to terminate the function when the score is invalid.

```
public static void printGrade(double score) {
  if (score < 0 || score > 100)
    System.out.println("Invalid score");
    return;
  }

  if (score >= 90.0) {
    System.out.println('A');
  }
  else if (score >= 80.0) {
    System.out.println('B');
  }
  else if (score >= 70.0) {
```

```
        System.out.println('C');
    }
    else if (score >= 60.0) {
        System.out.println('D');
    }
    else {
        System.out.println('F');
    }
}
```

5.5 Passing Parameters by Values

The power of a method is its ability to work with parameters. You can use `println` to print any string and `max` to find the maximum between any two `int` values. When calling a method, you need to provide arguments, which must be given in the same order as their respective parameters in the method specification. This is known as *parameter order association*. For example, the following method prints a message `n` times:

parameter order association

```
public static void nPrintln(String message, int n) {
    for (int i = 0; i < n; i++)
        System.out.println(message);
}
```

You can use `nPrintln("Hello", 3)` to print "Hello" three times. The `nPrintln("Hello", 3)` statement passes the actual string parameter, `"Hello"`, to the parameter, `message`; passes `3` to `n`; and prints `"Hello"` three times. However, the statement `nPrintln(3, "Hello")` would be wrong. The data type of `3` does not match the data type for the first parameter, `message`, nor does the second parameter, `"Hello"`, match the second parameter, `n`.

Caution

The arguments must match the parameters in *order*, *number*, and *compatible type*, as defined in the method signature. Compatible type means that you can pass an argument to a parameter without explicit casting, such as passing an `int` value argument to a `double` value parameter.

parameter matching

When you invoke a method with a parameter, the value of the argument is passed to the parameter. This is referred to as *pass-by-value*. If the argument is a variable rather than a literal value, the value of the variable is passed to the parameter. The variable is not affected, regardless of the changes made to the parameter inside the method. We will examine an interesting scenario in the following example, in which the parameters are changed in the method but the arguments are not affected.

pass-by-value

Listing 5.3 is a program that demonstrates the effect of passing by value. The program creates a method for swapping two variables. The `swap` method is invoked by passing two arguments. Interestingly, the values of the arguments are not changed after the method is invoked. The output of the program is shown in Figure 5.5.

```
Command Prompt                                      _ □ ×
C:\book>java TestPassByValue
Before invoking the swap method, num1 is 1 and num2 is 2
        Inside the swap method
                Before swapping n1 is 1 n2 is 2
                After swapping n1 is 2 n2 is 1
After invoking the swap method, num1 is 1 and num2 is 2

C:\book>_
```

FIGURE 5.5 The contents of the arguments are not swapped after the `swap` method is invoked.

LISTING 5.3 TestPassByValue.java

```java
 1  public class TestPassByValue {
 2    /** Main method */
 3    public static void main(String[] args) {
 4      // Declare and initialize variables
 5      int num1 = 1;
 6      int num2 = 2;
 7
 8      System.out.println("Before invoking the swap method, num1 is " +
 9        num1 + " and num2 is " + num2);
10
11      // Invoke the swap method to attempt to swap two variables
12      swap(num1, num2);
13
14      System.out.println("After invoking the swap method, num1 is " +
15        num1 + " and num2 is " + num2);
16    }
17
18    /** Swap two variables */
19    public static void swap(int n1, int n2) {
20      System.out.println("\tInside the swap method");
21      System.out.println("\t\tBefore swapping n1 is " + n1
22        + " n2 is " + n2);
23
24      // Swap n1 with n2
25      int temp = n1;
26      n1 = n2;
27      n2 = temp;
28
29      System.out.println("\t\tAfter swapping n1 is " + n1
30        + " n2 is " + n2);
31    }
32  }
```

false swap

Before the swap method is invoked (line 12), num1 is 1 and num2 is 2. After the swap method is invoked, num1 is still 1 and num2 is still 2. Their values are not swapped after the swap method is invoked. As shown in Figure 5.6, the values of the arguments num1 and num2 are passed to n1 and n2, but n1 and n2 have their own memory locations independent of num1 and num2. Therefore, changes in n1 and n2 do not affect the contents of num1 and num2.

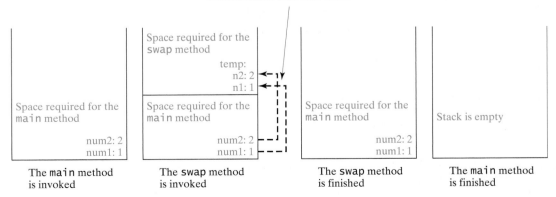

FIGURE 5.6   The values of the variables are passed to the parameters of the method.

Another twist is to change the parameter name n1 in swap to num1. What effect does this have? No change occurs because it makes no difference whether the parameter and the argument have the same name. The parameter is a variable in the method with its own memory space. The variable is allocated when the method is invoked, and it disappears when the method is returned to its caller.

Note

For simplicity, Java programmers often say *passing an argument* x *to a parameter* y, which actually means *passing the value of* x *to* y.

5.6 Overloading Methods

The max method that was used earlier works only with the int data type. But what if you need to find which of two floating-point numbers has the maximum value? The solution is to create another method with the same name but different parameters, as shown in the following code:

```
public static double max(double num1, double num2) {
  if (num1 > num2)
    return num1;
  else
    return num2;
}
```

If you call max with int parameters, the max method that expects int parameters will be invoked; if you call max with double parameters, the max method that expects double parameters will be invoked. This is referred to as *method overloading*; that is, two methods have the same name but different parameter lists within one class. The Java compiler determines which method is used based on the method signature.

method overloading

Listing 5.4 is a program that creates three methods. The first finds the maximum integer, the second finds the maximum double, and the third finds the maximum among three double values. All three methods are named max. The output of the program is shown in Figure 5.7.

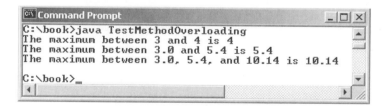

FIGURE 5.7 The program invokes three different max methods that all have the same name: max(3, 4), max(3.0, 5.4), and max(3.0, 5.4, 10.14).

LISTING 5.4 TestMethodOverloading.java

```
1  public class TestMethodOverloading {
2    /** Main method */
3    public static void main(String[] args) {
4      // Invoke the max method with int parameters
5      System.out.println("The maximum between 3 and 4 is "
6        + max(3, 4));
7
```

```
8     // Invoke the max method with the double parameters
9     System.out.println("The maximum between 3.0 and 5.4 is "
10       + max(3.0, 5.4) );
11
12    // Invoke the max method with three double parameters
13    System.out.println("The maximum between 3.0, 5.4, and 10.14 is "
14       + max(3.0, 5.4, 10.14) );
15  }
16
17  /** Return the max between two int values */
18  public static int max(int num1, int num2) {
19    if (num1 > num2)
20      return num1;
21    else
22      return num2;
23  }
24
25  /** Find the max between two double values */
26  public static double max(double num1, double num2) {
27    if (num1 > num2)
28      return num1;
29    else
30      return num2;
31  }
32
33  /** Return the max among three double values */
34  public static double max(double num1, double num2, double num3) {
35    return max(max(num1, num2), num3);
36  }
37 }
```

When calling `max(3, 4)` (line 6), the `max` method for finding the maximum of two integers is invoked. When calling `max(3.0, 5.4)` (line 10), the `max` method for finding the maximum of two doubles is invoked. When calling `max(3.0, 5.4, 10.14)` (line 14), the `max` method for finding the maximum of three double values is invoked.

Can you invoke the `max` method with an `int` value and a `double` value, such as `max(2, 2.5)`? If so, which of the `max` methods is invoked? The answer to the first question is yes. The answer to the second is that the `max` method for finding the maximum of two `double` values is invoked. The argument value `2` is automatically converted into a `double` value and passed to this method.

You may be wondering why the method `max(double, double)` is not invoked for the call `max(3, 4)`. Both `max(double, double)` and `max(int, int)` are possible matches for `max(3, 4)`. The Java compiler finds the most specific method for a method invocation. Since the method `max(int, int)` is more specific than `max(double, double)`, `max(int, int)` is used to invoke `max(3, 4)`.

Tip

Overloading methods can make programs clearer and more readable. Methods that perform closely related tasks should be given the same name.

Note

Overloaded methods must have different parameter lists. You cannot overload methods based on different modifiers or return types.

Note

Sometimes there are two or more possible matches for an invocation of a method, but the compiler cannot determine the most specific match. This is referred to as *ambiguous invocation*. Ambiguous invocation causes a compilation error. Consider the following code:

ambiguous invocation

```java
public class AmbiguousOverloading {
  public static void main(String[] args) {
    System.out.println(max(1, 2));
  }

  public static double max(int num1, double num2) {
    if (num1 > num2)
      return num1;
    else
      return num2;
  }

  public static double max(double num1, int num2) {
    if (num1 > num2)
      return num1;
    else
      return num2;
  }
}
```

Both `max(int, double)` and `max(double, int)` are possible candidates to match `max(1, 2)`. Since neither of them is more specific than the other, the invocation is ambiguous, resulting in a compilation error.

5.7 Case Study: Computing Taxes with Methods

The program in Listing 3.4 uses `if` statements to check the filing status and computes the tax based on the filing status. This example uses methods to simplify Listing 3.4.

Each filing status has six brackets. The code for computing taxes is nearly the same regardless of filing status except that each filing status has different bracket ranges. For example, the brackets of the single-filer status are [0, 6000], (6000, 27950], (27950, 67700], (67700, 141250], (141250, 307050], (307050, ∞), and the six brackets of the married–file jointly status are [0, 12000], (12000, 46700], (46700, 112850], (112850, 171950], (171950, 307050], (307050, ∞). The first bracket of each filing status is taxed at 10%, the second at 15%, the third at 27%, the fourth at 30%, the fifth at 35%, and the sixth at 38.6%. So you can write a method with the brackets as arguments to compute the tax for the filing status. The header of the method is:

```java
public static double computeTax(double income, ←──────── 400000
    int r1, int r2, int r3, int r4, int r5)
```

[0, 6000], [6000, 27950], [27950, 67700], [67700, 141250], [141250, 307050], (307050, ∞)

For example, you can invoke `computeTax(400000, 6000, 27950, 67700, 141250, 307050)` to compute the tax for single filers with $400,000 of taxable income.

Listing 5.5 gives the solution to the problem. The output of the program is similar to Figure 3.3.

LISTING 5.5   ComputeTaxWithMethod.java

<table>
<tr><td></td><td>1</td><td>

```
import javax.swing.JOptionPane;
```

</td></tr>
<tr><td></td><td>2</td><td></td></tr>
<tr><td></td><td>3</td><td>

```
public class ComputeTaxWithMethod {
```

</td></tr>
<tr><td></td><td>4</td><td>

```
  public static void main(String[] args) {
```

</td></tr>
<tr><td></td><td>5</td><td>

```
    // Prompt the user to enter filing status
```

</td></tr>
<tr><td>input status</td><td>6</td><td>

```
    String statusString = JOptionPane.showInputDialog(
```

</td></tr>
<tr><td></td><td>7</td><td>

```
      "Enter the filing status:");
```

</td></tr>
<tr><td>input income</td><td>8</td><td>

```
    int status = Integer.parseInt(statusString);
```

</td></tr>
<tr><td></td><td>9</td><td></td></tr>
<tr><td></td><td>10</td><td>

```
    // Prompt the user to enter taxable income
```

</td></tr>
<tr><td></td><td>11</td><td>

```
    String incomeString = JOptionPane.showInputDialog(
```

</td></tr>
<tr><td></td><td>12</td><td>

```
      "Enter the taxable income:");
```

</td></tr>
<tr><td></td><td>13</td><td>

```
    double income = Double.parseDouble(incomeString);
```

</td></tr>
<tr><td></td><td>14</td><td></td></tr>
<tr><td></td><td>15</td><td>

```
    // Display the result
```

</td></tr>
<tr><td></td><td>16</td><td>

```
    JOptionPane.showMessageDialog(null, "Tax is " +
```

</td></tr>
<tr><td>compute tax</td><td>17</td><td>

```
      (int)(computeTax(status, income) * 100) / 100.0);
```

</td></tr>
<tr><td></td><td>18</td><td>

```
  }
```

</td></tr>
<tr><td></td><td>19</td><td></td></tr>
<tr><td></td><td>20</td><td>

```
  public static double computeTax(double income,
```

</td></tr>
<tr><td></td><td>21</td><td>

```
    int r1, int r2, int r3, int r4, int r5) {
```

</td></tr>
<tr><td>computeTax</td><td>22</td><td>

```
    double tax = 0;
```

</td></tr>
<tr><td></td><td>23</td><td></td></tr>
<tr><td></td><td>24</td><td>

```
    if (income <= r1)
```

</td></tr>
<tr><td></td><td>25</td><td>

```
      tax = income * 0.10;
```

</td></tr>
<tr><td></td><td>26</td><td>

```
    else if (income <= r2)
```

</td></tr>
<tr><td></td><td>27</td><td>

```
      tax = r1 * 0.10 + (income - r1) * 0.15;
```

</td></tr>
<tr><td></td><td>28</td><td>

```
    else if (income <= r3)
```

</td></tr>
<tr><td></td><td>29</td><td>

```
      tax = r1 * 0.10 + (r2 - r1) * 0.15 + (income - r2) * 0.27;
```

</td></tr>
<tr><td></td><td>30</td><td>

```
    else if (income <= r4)
```

</td></tr>
<tr><td></td><td>31</td><td>

```
      tax = r1 * 0.10 + (r2 - r1) * 0.15 +
```

</td></tr>
<tr><td></td><td>32</td><td>

```
        (r3 - r2) * 0.27 + (income - r3) * 0.30;
```

</td></tr>
<tr><td></td><td>33</td><td>

```
    else if (income <= r5)
```

</td></tr>
<tr><td></td><td>34</td><td>

```
      tax = r1 * 0.10 + (r2 - r1) * 0.15 + (r3 - r2) * 0.27 +
```

</td></tr>
<tr><td></td><td>35</td><td>

```
        (r4 - r3) * 0.30 + (income - r4) * 0.35;
```

</td></tr>
<tr><td></td><td>36</td><td>

```
    else
```

</td></tr>
<tr><td></td><td>37</td><td>

```
      tax = r1 * 0.10 + (r2 - r1) * 0.15 + (r3 - r2) * 0.27 +
```

</td></tr>
<tr><td></td><td>38</td><td>

```
        (r4 - r3) * 0.30 + (r5 - r4) * 0.35 + (income - r5) * 0.386;
```

</td></tr>
<tr><td></td><td>39</td><td></td></tr>
<tr><td></td><td>40</td><td>

```
    return tax;
```

</td></tr>
<tr><td></td><td>41</td><td>

```
  }
```

</td></tr>
<tr><td></td><td>42</td><td></td></tr>
<tr><td>overloaded</td><td>43</td><td>

```
  public static double computeTax(int status, double income) {
```

</td></tr>
<tr><td>computeTax</td><td>44</td><td>

```
    switch (status) {
```

</td></tr>
<tr><td></td><td>45</td><td>

```
      case 0: return
```

</td></tr>
<tr><td></td><td>46</td><td>

```
        computeTax(income, 6000, 27950, 67700, 141250, 307050);
```

</td></tr>
<tr><td></td><td>47</td><td>

```
      case 1: return
```

</td></tr>
<tr><td></td><td>48</td><td>

```
        computeTax(income, 12000, 46700, 112850, 171950, 307050);
```

</td></tr>
<tr><td></td><td>49</td><td>

```
      case 2: return
```

</td></tr>
<tr><td></td><td>50</td><td>

```
        computeTax(income, 6000, 23350, 56425, 85975, 153525);
```

</td></tr>
<tr><td></td><td>51</td><td>

```
      case 3: return
```

</td></tr>
<tr><td></td><td>52</td><td>

```
        computeTax(income, 10000, 37450, 96700, 156600, 307050);
```

</td></tr>
<tr><td></td><td>53</td><td>

```
      default: return 0;
```

</td></tr>
<tr><td></td><td>54</td><td>

```
    }
```

</td></tr>
<tr><td></td><td>55</td><td>

```
  }
```

</td></tr>
<tr><td></td><td>56</td><td>

```
}
```

</td></tr>
</table>

This program does the same thing as the one in Listing 3.4. Instead of writing the same code for computing taxes for different filing statuses, the new program uses a method for computing taxes. Using the method not only shortens the program, it also makes the program simpler, easy to read, and easy to maintain.

The program uses two overloaded computeTax methods (lines 20, 43). The first computeTax method in line 20 computes the tax for the specified brackets and taxable income. The second computeTax method in line 43 computes the tax for the specified status and taxable income.

5.8 The Scope of Variables

The *scope of a variable* is the part of the program where the variable can be referenced. A variable defined inside a method is referred to as a *local variable*.

scope
local variable

The scope of a local variable starts from its declaration and continues to the end of the block that contains the variable. A local variable must be declared before it can be used.

A *parameter* is actually a local variable. The scope of a method parameter covers the entire method.

parameter

A variable declared in the initial action part of a **for** loop header has its scope in the entire loop. But a variable declared inside a **for** loop body has its scope limited in the loop body from its declaration to the end of the block that contains the variable, as shown in Figure 5.8.

for loop control variable

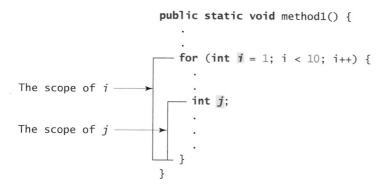

FIGURE 5.8   A variable declared in the initial action part of a **for** loop header has its scope in the entire loop.

You can declare a local variable with the same name multiple times in different non-nesting blocks in a method, but you cannot declare a local variable twice in nested blocks, as shown in Figure 5.9.

multiple declarations

Caution

Do not declare a variable inside a block and then attempt to use it outside the block. Here is an example of a common mistake:

```
for (int i = 0; i < 10; i++) {
}

System.out.println(i);
```

The last statement would cause a syntax error because variable i is not defined outside of the for loop.

It is fine to declare *i* in two non-nesting blocks

It is wrong to declare *i* in two nesting blocks

```
public static void method1() {
    int x = 1;
    int y = 1;

    for (int i = 1; i < 10; i++) {
        x += i;
    }

    for (int i = 1; i < 10; i++) {
        y += i;
    }
}
```

```
public static void method2() {

    int i = 1;
    int sum = 0;

    for (int i = 1; i < 10; i++)
        sum += i;

}
```

FIGURE 5.9 A variable can be declared multiple times in non-nested blocks, but can be declared only once in nested blocks.

5.9 The Math Class

The **Math** class contains the methods needed to perform basic mathematical functions. You have already used the **pow(a, b)** method to compute a^b in Listing 2.6, ComputeLoan.java, and the Math.random() in Listing 3.5, SubtractionTutor.java. This section introduces other useful methods in the **Math** class. They can be categorized as *trigonometric methods*, *exponent methods*, and *service methods*. Besides methods, the **Math** class provides two useful **double** constants, **PI** and **E** (the base of natural logarithms). You can use these constants as **Math.PI** and **Math.E** in any program.

5.9.1 Trigonometric Methods

The **Math** class contains the following trigonometric methods:

```
public static double sin(double radians)
public static double cos(double radians)
public static double tan(double radians)
public static double asin(double radians)
public static double acos(double radians)
public static double atan(double radians)
public static double toRadians(double degree)
public static double toDegrees(double radians)
```

Each method has a single **double** parameter, and its return type is **double**. The parameter represents an angle in radians. One degree is equal to $\pi/180$ in radians. For example, **Math.sin(Math.PI)** returns the trigonometric sine of π. Since JDK 1.2, the **Math** class has also provided the method **toRadians(double angdeg)** for converting an angle in degrees to radians, and the method **toDegrees(double angrad)** for converting an angle in radians to degrees.

For example,

```
Math.sin(0) returns 0.0
Math.sin(Math.toRadians(270)) returns -1.0
Math.sin(Math.PI / 6) returns 0.5
Math.sin(Math.PI / 2) returns 1.0
Math.cos(0) returns 1.0
Math.cos(Math.PI / 6) returns 0.866
Math.cos(Math.PI / 2) returns 0
```

5.9.2   Exponent Methods

There are five methods related to exponents in the `Math` class:

```
/** Return e raised to the power of x (ex) */
public static double exp(double x)

/** Return the natural logarithm of x (ln(x) = loge(x)) */
public static double log(double x)

/** Return the base 10 logarithm of x (log10(x)) */
public static double log10(double x)

/** Return a raised to the power of b (xb) */
public static double pow(double x, double b)

/** Return the square root of a (√x̄) */
public static double sqrt(double x)
```

Note that the parameter in the `sqrt` method must not be negative.
For example,

```
Math.exp(1) returns 2.71828
Math.log(Math.E) returns 1.0
Math.log10(10) returns 1.0
Math.pow(2, 3) returns 8.0
Math.pow(3, 2) returns 9.0
Math.pow(3.5, 2.5) returns 22.91765
Math.sqrt(4) returns 2.0
Math.sqrt(10.5) returns 3.24
```

5.9.3   The Rounding Methods

The `Math` class contains five rounding methods:

```
/** x rounded up to its nearest integer. This integer is
  * returned as a double value. */
public static double ceil(double x)

/** x is rounded down to its nearest integer. This integer is
  * returned as a double value. */
public static double floor(double x)

/** x is rounded to its nearest integer. If x is equally close
  * to two integers, the even one is returned as a double. */
public static double rint(double x)

/** Return (int)Math.floor(x + 0.5). */
public static int round(float x)

/** Return (long)Math.floor(x + 0.5). */
public static long round(double x)
```

For example,

```
Math.ceil(2.1) returns 3.0
Math.ceil(2.0) returns 2.0
Math.ceil(-2.0) returns -2.0
Math.ceil(-2.1) returns -2.0
Math.floor(2.1) returns 2.0
Math.floor(2.0) returns 2.0
```

```
Math.floor(-2.0) returns -2.0
Math.floor(-2.1) returns -3.0
Math.rint(2.1) returns 2.0
Math.rint(2.0) returns 2.0
Math.rint(-2.0) returns -2.0
Math.rint(-2.1) returns -2.0
Math.rint(2.5) returns 2.0
Math.rint(-2.5) returns -2.0
Math.round(2.6f) returns 3 // Returns int
Math.round(2.0) returns 2  // Returns long
Math.round(-2.0f) returns -2
Math.round(-2.6) returns -3
```

5.9.4 The `min`, `max`, and `abs` Methods

The `min` and `max` methods are overloaded to return the minimum and maximum numbers between two numbers (`int`, `long`, `float`, or `double`). For example, `max(3.4, 5.0)` returns `5.0`, and `min(3, 2)` returns `2`.

The `abs` method is overloaded to return the absolute value of the number (`int`, `long`, `float`, and `double`). For example,

```
Math.max(2, 3) returns 3
Math.max(2.5, 3) returns 3.0
Math.min(2.5, 3.6) returns 2.5
Math.abs(-2) returns 2
Math.abs(-2.1) returns 2.1
```

5.9.5 The `random` Method

The `Math` class also has a powerful method, `random`, which generates a random `double` value greater than or equal to 0.0 and less than 1.0 (`0.0 <= Math.random() < 1.0`). This method is very useful. Listing 3.5, SubtractionTutor.java, uses this method to generate a single-digit integer. You can use it to write a simple expression to generate random numbers in any range. For example,

$$(\textbf{int})(\text{Math. random}() * 10) \longrightarrow \text{Returns a random integer between } 0 \text{ and } 9.$$

$$50 + (\textbf{int})(\text{Math. random}() * 50) \longrightarrow \text{Returns a random integer between } 50 \text{ and } 99.$$

In general,

$$a + \text{Math. random}() * b \longrightarrow \text{Returns a random number between } a \text{ and } a + b, \text{ excluding } a + b.$$

Tip
You can view the complete documentation for the `Math` class online at http://java.sun.com/ j2se/1.5.0/docs/api/index.html, as shown in Figure 5.10. You can also download `jdk-1_5_0-doc.zip` from the same website and install it on your PC so that you can browse the documents locally.

Note
Not all classes need a `main` method. The `Math` class and `JOptionPane` class do not have `main` methods. These classes contain methods for other classes to use.

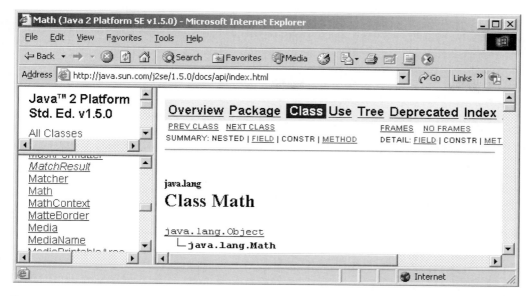

FIGURE 5.10   You can view the documentation for Java API online.

5.10 Case Study: Generating Random Characters

Computer programs process numerical data and characters. You have seen many examples that involve numerical data. It is also important to understand characters and how to process them. This section presents an example for generating random characters.

As introduced in §2.9, every character has a unique Unicode between 0 and FFFF in hexadecimal (65535 in decimal). To generate a random character is to generate a random integer between 0 and 65535 using the following expression (note that since 0.0 <= Math.random() < 1.0, you have to add 1 to 65535):

```
(int)(Math.random() * (65535 + 1))
```

Now let us consider how to generate a random lowercase letter. The Unicodes for lowercase letters are consecutive integers starting from the Unicode for 'a,' then for 'b', 'c', ..., and 'z.' The Unicode for 'a' is

```
(int)'a'
```

So a random integer between (int)'a' and (int)'z' is

```
(int)((int)'a' + Math.random() * ((int)'z' - (int)'a' + 1)
```

As discussed in §2.9.4, all numeric operators can be applied to the char operands. The char operand is cast into a number if the other operand is a number or a character. Thus the preceding expression can be simplified as follows:

```
'a' + Math.random() * ('z' - 'a' + 1)
```

and a random lowercase letter is

```
(char)('a' + Math.random() * ('z' - 'a' + 1))
```

To generalize the foregoing discussion, a random character between any two characters ch1 and ch2 with ch1 < ch2 can be generated as follows:

```
(char)(ch1 + Math.random() * (ch2 - ch1 + 1))
```

This is a simple but useful discovery. Let us create a class named **RandomCharacter** in Listing 5.6 with five methods to get a certain type of character randomly. You can use these methods in your future projects.

LISTING 5.6 RandomCharacter.java

```java
 1  public class RandomCharacter {
 2    /** Generate a random character between ch1 and ch2 */
 3    public static char getRandomCharacter(char ch1, char ch2) {
 4      return (char)(ch1 + Math.random() * (ch2 - ch1 + 1));
 5    }
 6
 7    /** Generate a random lowercase letter */
 8    public static char getRandomLowerCaseLetter() {
 9      return getRandomCharacter('a', 'z');
10    }
11
12    /** Generate a random uppercase letter */
13    public static char getRandomUpperCaseLetter() {
14      return getRandomCharacter('A', 'Z');
15    }
16
17    /** Generate a random digit character */
18    public static char getRandomDigitCharacter() {
19      return getRandomCharacter('0', '9');
20    }
21
22    /** Generate a random character */
23    public static char getRandomCharacter()  {
24      return getRandomCharacter('\u0000', '\uFFFF');
25    }
26  }
```

Listing 5.7 gives a test program that displays one hundred lowercase letters.

LISTING 5.7 TestRandomCharacter.java

```java
 1  public class TestRandomCharacter {
 2    /** Main method */
 3    public static void main(String args[]) {
 4      final int NUMBER_OF_CHARS = 175;
 5      final int CHARS_PER_LINE = 25;
 6
 7      // Print random characters between '!' and '~', 25 chars per line
 8      for (int i = 0; i < NUMBER_OF_CHARS; i++) {
 9        char ch = RandomCharacter.getRandomLowerCaseLetter() ;
10        if ((i + 1) % CHARS_PER_LINE == 0)
11          System.out.println(ch);
12        else
13          System.out.print(ch);
14      }
15    }
16  }
```

constants

lowercase letter

5.11 Method Abstraction and Stepwise Refinement

method abstraction

The key to developing software is to apply the concept of abstraction. You will learn many levels of abstraction from this book. *Method abstraction* is achieved by separating the use of a method from its implementation. The client can use a method without knowing how it is implemented.

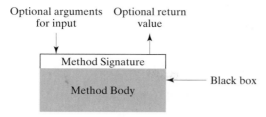

FIGURE 5.11   The method body can be thought of as a black box that contains the detailed implementation for the method.

The details of the implementation are encapsulated in the method and hidden from the client who invokes the method. This is known as *information hiding* or *encapsulation*. If you decide to change the implementation, the client program will not be affected, provided that you do not change the method signature. The implementation of the method is hidden from the client in a "black box," as shown in Figure 5.11.

information hiding

You have already used the `System.out.print` method to display a string, the `JOptionPane.showInputDialog` method to read a string from a dialog box, and the `max` method to find the maximum number. You know how to write the code to invoke these methods in your program, but as a user of these methods, you are not required to know how they are implemented.

The concept of method abstraction can be applied to the process of developing programs. When writing a large program, you can use the "divide and conquer" strategy, also known as *stepwise refinement*, to decompose it into subproblems. The subproblems can be further decomposed into smaller, more manageable problems.

divide and conquer

stepwise refinement

Suppose you write a program that displays the calendar for a given month of the year. The program prompts the user to enter the year and the month, and then displays the entire calendar for the month, as shown in Figure 5.12.

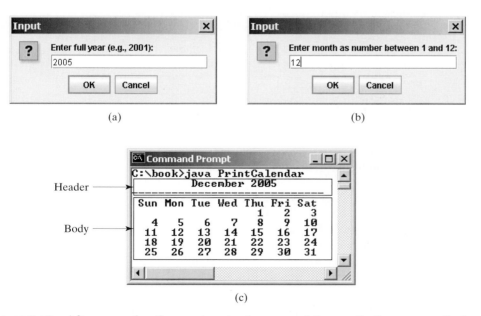

FIGURE 5.12   After prompting the user to enter the year and the month, the program displays the calendar for that month.

Let us use this example to demonstrate the divide-and-conquer approach.

5.11.1 Top-Down Design

How would you get started on such a program? Would you immediately start coding? Beginning programmers often start by trying to work out the solution to every detail. Although details are important in the final program, concern for detail in the early stages may block the problem-solving process. To make problem-solving flow as smoothly as possible, this example begins by using method abstraction to isolate details from design and only later implements the details.

For this example, the problem is first broken into two subproblems: get input from the user, and print the calendar for the month. At this stage, the creator of the program should be concerned with what the subproblems will achieve, not with how to get input and print the calendar for the month. You can draw a structure chart to help visualize the decomposition of the problem (see Figure 5.13(a)).

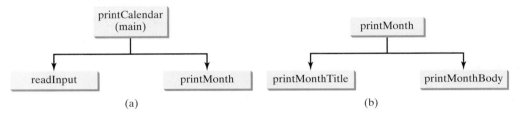

FIGURE 5.13 The structure chart shows that the `printCalendar` problem is divided into two subproblems, `readInput` and `printMonth`, and that `printMonth` is divided into two smaller subproblems, `printMonthTitle` and `printMonthBody`.

Use the `JOptionPane.showInputDialog` method to display input dialog boxes that prompt the user to enter the year and the month.

The problem of printing the calendar for a given month can be broken into two subproblems: print the month title, and print the month body, as shown in Figure 5.13(b). The month title consists of three lines: month and year, a dash line, and the names of the seven days of the week. You need to get the month name (e.g., January) from the numeric month (e.g., 1). This is accomplished in `getMonthName` (see Figure 5.14(a)).

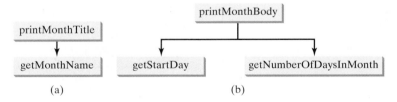

FIGURE 5.14 (a) To `printMonthTitle`, you need `getMonthName`. (b) The `printMonthBody` problem is refined into several smaller problems.

In order to print the month body, you need to know which day of the week is the first day of the month (`getStartDay`) and how many days the month has (`getNumberOfDaysInMonth`), as shown in Figure 5.14(b). For example, December 2005 has thirty-one days, and the first of the month is Thursday, as shown in Figure 5.12.

How would you get the start day for the first date in a month? There are several ways to find the start day. The simplest approach is to use the `Calendar` class in §9.3, "The `Calendar` and `GregorianCalendar` Classes." For now, an alternative approach is used. Assume that you know that the start day (`startDay1800 = 3`) for January 1, 1800 was Wednesday. You could compute the total number of days (`totalNumberOfDays`) between January 1, 1800 and the first date of the calendar month. The start day for the calendar month is `(totalNumberOfDays + startDay1800) % 7`, since every week has seven days. So the `getStartDay` problem can be further refined as `getTotalNumberOfDays`, as shown in Figure 5.15(a).

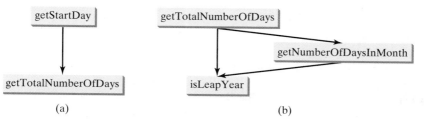

FIGURE 5.15   (a) To `getStartDay`, you need `getTotalNumberOfDays`. (b) The `getTotalNumberOfDays` problem is refined into two smaller problems.

To get the total number of days, you need to know whether the year is a leap year and the number of days in each month. So `getTotalNumberOfDays` is further refined into two subproblems: `isLeapYear` and `getNumberOfDaysInMonth`, as shown in Figure 5.15(b). The complete structure chart is shown in Figure 5.16.

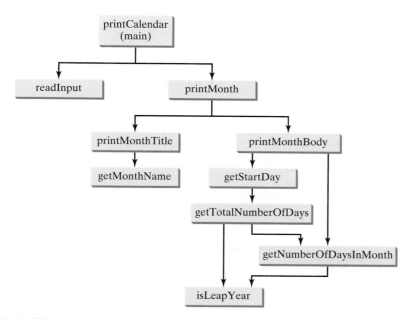

FIGURE 5.16   The structure chart shows the hierarchical relationship of the subproblems in the program.

5.11.2   Top-Down or Bottom-Up Implementation

Now we turn our attention to implementation. In general, a subproblem corresponds to a method in the implementation, although some are so simple that this is unnecessary. You would need to decide which modules to implement as methods and which to combine in other methods. Decisions of this kind should be based on whether the overall program will be easier to read as a result of your choice. In this example, the subproblem `readInput` can be simply implemented in the `main` method.

You can use either a "top-down" approach or a "bottom-up" approach. The "top-down" approach implements one method in the structure chart at a time from the top to the bottom. Stubs can be used for the methods waiting to be implemented. A *stub* is a simple but incomplete version of a method. The use of stubs enables you to test invoking the method from a caller. Implement the `main` method first, and then use a stub for the `printMonth` method. For example, let `printMonth` display the year and the month in the stub. Thus, your program may begin like this:

top-down approach

stub

```java
public class PrintCalendar {
  /** Main method */
  public static void main(String[] args) {
    // Prompt the user to enter year
    String yearString = JOptionPane.showInputDialog(
      "Enter full year (e.g., 2001):");

    // Convert string into integer
    int year = Integer.parseInt(yearString);

    // Prompt the user to enter month
    String monthString = JOptionPane.showInputDialog(
      "Enter month as number between 1 and 12:");

    // Convert string into integer
    int month = Integer.parseInt(monthString);

    // Print calendar for the month of the year
    printMonth(year, month);
  }

  /** A stub for printMonth may look like this */
  public static void printMonth(int year, int month) {
    System.out.print(month + " " + year);
  }

  /** A stub for printMonthTitle may look like this */
  public static void printMonthTitle(int year, int month) {
  }

  /** A stub for getMonthName may look like this */
  public static String getMonthName(int month) {
    return "January"; // a dummy value
  }

  /** A stub for getMonthNmae may look like this */
  public static int getStartDay(int year, int month) {
    return 1; // a dummy value
  }

  /** A stub for getNumberOfDaysInMonth may look like this */
  public static int getNumberOfDaysInMonth(int year, int month) {
    return 31; // a dummy value
  }

  /** A stub for getTotalNumberOfDays may look like this */
  public static int getTotalNumberOfDays(int year, int month) {
    return 10000; // a dummy value
  }

  /** A stub for getTotalNumberOfDays may look like this */
  public static boolean isLeapYear(int year) {
    return true; // a dummy value
  }
}
```

Compile and test the program, and fix any errors. You can now implement the `printMonth` method. For methods invoked from the `printMonth` method, you can again use stubs.

The bottom-up approach implements one method in the structure chart at a time from the bottom to the top. For each method implemented, write a test program to test it. The top-down and bottom-up approaches are both fine. Both approaches implement methods incrementally, help to isolate programming errors, and make debugging easy. Sometimes they can be used together.

5.11.3 Implementation Details

The `isLeapYear(int year)` method can be implemented using the following code:

```
return (year % 400 == 0 || (year % 4 == 0 && year % 100 != 0));
```

Use the following facts to implement `getTotalNumberOfDaysInMonth(int year, int month)`:

- January, March, May, July, August, October, and December have thirty-one days.

- April, June, September, and November have thirty days.

- February has twenty-eight days during a regular year and twenty-nine days during a leap year. A regular year, therefore, has 365 days, whereas a leap year has 366 days.

To implement `getTotalNumberOfDays(int year, int month)`, you need to compute the total number of days (`totalNumberOfDays`) between January 1, 1800 and the first day of the calendar month. You could find the total number of days between the year 1800 and the calendar year and then figure out the total number of days prior to the calendar month in the calendar year. The sum of these two totals is `totalNumberOfDays`.

To print a body, first pad some space before the start day and then print the lines for every week, as shown for December 2005 (see Figure 5.12).

The complete program is given in Listing 5.8.

LISTING 5.8 PrintCalendar.java

```
1   import javax.swing.JOptionPane;
2
3   public class PrintCalendar {
4     /** Main method */
5     public static void main(String[] args) {
6       // Prompt the user to enter year
7       String yearString = JOptionPane.showInputDialog(
8         "Enter full year (e.g., 2001):");
9
10      // Convert string into integer
11      int year = Integer.parseInt(yearString);
12
13      // Prompt the user to enter month
14      String monthString = JOptionPane.showInputDialog(
15        "Enter month in number between 1 and 12:");
16
17      // Convert string into integer
18      int month = Integer.parseInt(monthString);
19
20      // Print calendar for the month of the year
21      printMonth(year, month);
22    }
23
24    /** Print the calendar for a month in a year */
25    static void printMonth(int year, int month) {
26      // Print the headings of the calendar
27      printMonthTitle(year, month);
28
```

```
29        // Print the body of the calendar
30        printMonthBody(year, month);
31    }
32
33    /** Print the month title, e.g., May, 1999 */
34    static void printMonthTitle(int year, int month) {
35      System.out.println("              " + getMonthName(month)
36        + " " + year);
37      System.out.println("----------------------------");
38      System.out.println(" Sun Mon Tue Wed Thu Fri Sat");
39    }
40
41    /** Get the English name for the month */
42    static String getMonthName(int month) {
43      String monthName = null;
44      switch (month) {
45        case 1: monthName = "January"; break;
46        case 2: monthName = "February"; break;
47        case 3: monthName = "March"; break;
48        case 4: monthName = "April"; break;
49        case 5: monthName = "May"; break;
50        case 6: monthName = "June"; break;
51        case 7: monthName = "July"; break;
52        case 8: monthName = "August"; break;
53        case 9: monthName = "September"; break;
54        case 10: monthName = "October"; break;
55        case 11: monthName = "November"; break;
56        case 12: monthName = "December";
57      }
58
59      return monthName;
60    }
61
62    /** Print month body */
63    static void printMonthBody(int year, int month) {
64      // Get start day of the week for the first date in the month
65      int startDay = getStartDay(year, month);
66
67      // Get number of days in the month
68      int numberOfDaysInMonth = getNumberOfDaysInMonth(year, month);
69
70      // Pad space before the first day of the month
71      int i = 0;
72      for (i = 0; i < startDay; i++)
73        System.out.print("    ");
74
75      for (i = 1; i <= numberOfDaysInMonth; i++) {
76        if (i < 10)
77          System.out.print("   " + i);
78        else
79          System.out.print("  " + i);
80
81        if ((i + startDay) % 7 == 0)
82          System.out.println();
83      }
84
85      System.out.println();
86    }
87
88    /** Get the start day of the first day in a month */
89    static int getStartDay(int year, int month) {
```

```
 90        // Get total number of days since 1/1/1800
 91        int startDay1800 = 3;
 92        int totalNumberOfDays = getTotalNumberOfDays(year, month);
 93
 94        // Return the start day
 95        return (totalNumberOfDays + startDay1800) % 7;
 96      }
 97
 98      /** Get the total number of days since January 1, 1800 */
 99      static int getTotalNumberOfDays(int year, int month) {
100        int total = 0;
101
102        // Get the total days from 1800 to year - 1
103        for (int i = 1800; i < year; i++)
104          if (isLeapYear(i))
105            total = total + 366;
106          else
107            total = total + 365;
108
109        // Add days from January to the month prior to the calendar month
110        for (int i = 1; i < month; i++)
111          total = total + getNumberOfDaysInMonth(year, i);
112
113        return total;
114      }
115
116      /** Get the number of days in a month */
117      static int getNumberOfDaysInMonth(int year, int month) {
118        if (month == 1 || month == 3 || month == 5 || month == 7 ||
119          month == 8 || month == 10 || month == 12)
120          return 31;
121
122        if (month == 4 || month == 6 || month == 9 || month == 11)
123          return 30;
124
125        if (month == 2) return isLeapYear(year) ? 29 : 28;
126
127        return 0; // If month is incorrect
128      }
129
130      /** Determine if it is a leap year */
131      static boolean isLeapYear(int year) {
132        return year % 400 == 0 || (year % 4 == 0 && year % 100 != 0);
133      }
134    }
```

The program does not validate user input. For instance, if the user enters either a month not in the range between 1 and 12 or a year before 1800, the program would display an erroneous calendar. To avoid this error, add an if statement to check the input before printing the calendar.

This program prints calendars for a month but could easily be modified to print calendars for a whole year. Although it can only print months after January 1800, it could be modified to trace the day of a month before 1800.

Note

Method abstraction modularizes programs in a neat, hierarchical manner. Programs written as collections of concise methods are easier to write, debug, maintain, and modify than would otherwise be the case. This writing style also promotes method reusability.

Tip
When implementing a large program, use the top-down or bottom-up approach. Do not write the entire program at once. This approach seems to take more time for coding (because you are repeatedly compiling and running the program), but it actually saves time and makes debugging easier.

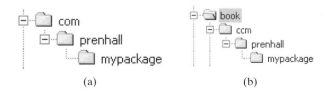 5.12 (Optional) Packages

Packages are used to group classes. So far, all the classes in this book are grouped into a default package. You can explicitly specify a package for each class. There are four reasons for using packages.

why package

- **To locate classes.** Classes with similar functions can be placed in the same package to make them easy to locate.

- **To avoid naming conflicts.** When you develop reusable classes to be shared by other programmers, naming conflicts often occur, i.e., two classes with the same name. To prevent this, put your classes into packages so that they can be referenced through package names.

- **To distribute software conveniently.** Packages group related classes so that they can be easily distributed.

- **To protect classes.** Packages provide protection so that the protected members of the classes are accessible to the classes in the same package, but not to the external classes.

5.12.1 Package-Naming Conventions

Packages are hierarchical, and you can have packages within packages. For example, `java.lang.Math` indicates that `Math` is a class in the package `lang` and that `lang` is a package in the package `java`. Levels of nesting can be used to ensure the uniqueness of package names.

Choosing a unique name is important because your package may be used on the Internet by other programs. Java designers recommend that you use your Internet domain name in reverse order as a package prefix. Since Internet domain names are unique, this prevents naming conflicts. Suppose you want to create a package named `mypackage` on a host machine with the Internet domain name `prenhall.com`. To follow the naming convention, you would name the entire package `com.prenhall.mypackage`. By convention, package names are all in lowercase.

5.12.2 Package Directories

Java expects one-to-one mapping of the package name and the file system directory structure. For the package named `com.prenhall.mypackage`, you must create a directory, as shown in Figure 5.17(a). In other words, a package is actually a directory that contains the bytecode of the classes.

(a)   (b)

FIGURE 5.17 The package `com.prenhall.mypackage` is mapped to a directory structure in the file system.

The `com` directory does not have to be the root directory. In order for Java to know where your package is in the file system, you must modify the environment variable `classpath` so that it points to the directory in which your package resides. Such a directory is known as the *classpath* for the class. Suppose the `com` directory is under `c:\book`, as shown in Figure 5.17(b). The following line adds `c:\book` into the `classpath`:

classpath

```
set classpath=.;c:\book;
```

The period (.) indicating the current directory is always in `classpath`. The directory `c:\book` is in `classpath` so that you can use the package `com.prenhall.mypackage` in the program.

current directory

You can add as many directories as necessary in `classpath`. The order in which the directories are specified is the order in which the classes are searched. If you have two classes of the same name in different directories, Java uses the first one it finds.

The `classpath` variable is set differently in Windows and Unix, as outlined below.

classpath

- Windows 98: Edit autoexec.bat using a text editor, such as Microsoft Notepad.

- Windows NT/2000/XP: Go to the start button and choose control panel, select the system icon, then modify `classpath` in the Environment Variables.

- UNIX: Use the `setenv` command to set `classpath`, such as

```
setenv classpath .:/home/book
```

If you insert this line into the .cshrc file, the `classpath` variable will be set automatically when you log on.

Note

On Windows 95 and Window 98, you must restart the system in order for the `classpath` variable to take effect. On Windows NT/2000/ME/XP, however, the settings are effective immediately. They affect any new command windows, but not the existing command windows.

5.12.3 Putting Classes into Packages

Every class in Java belongs to a package. The class is added to a package when it is compiled. All the classes that you have used so far in this book were placed in the current directory (a default package) when the Java source programs were compiled. To put a class in a specific package, you need to add the following line as the first noncomment and nonblank statement in the program:

```
package packagename;
```

Let us create a class named `Format` and place it in the package `com.prenhall.mypackage`. The `Format` class contains the `format(number, numberOfDecimalDigits)` method, which returns a new number with the specified number of digits after the decimal point. For example, `format(10.3422345, 2)` returns `10.34`, and format `(-0.343434, 3)` returns `-0.343`.

1. Create Format.java in Listing 5.9 and save it into `c:\book\com\prenhall\mypackage`.

LISTING 5.9 Format.java

```
1  package com.prenhall.mypackage;
2
3  public class Format {
4    public static double format(
5        double number, int numberOfDecimalDigits) {
```

specify a package

```
6      return Math.round(number * Math.pow(10, numberOfDecimalDigits)) /
7        Math.pow(10, numberOfDecimalDigits);
8    }
9 }
```

2. Compile Format.java and place it in `c:\book\com\prenhall\mypackage`.

A class must be defined as public in order to be accessed by other programs. If you want to put several classes into the package, you have to create separate source files for them, because each file can have only one public class.

Format.java can be placed under `anyDir\com\prenhall\mypackage`, Format.class in `anyOtherDir\com\prenhall\mypackage`, and `anyDir` and `anyOtherDir` may be the same or different. To make the class available, add `anyOtherDir` in the classpath, using the command:

`set classpath=%classpath%;anyOtherDir`

 Note
Class files can be archived into a single file for convenience. For instance, you may compress all the class files in the folder mypackage into a single zip file named mypackage.zip with subfolder information kept as shown in Figure 5.18. To make the classes in the zip file available for use, add the zip file to the classpath like this:

`classpath=%classpath%;c:\mypackage.zip`

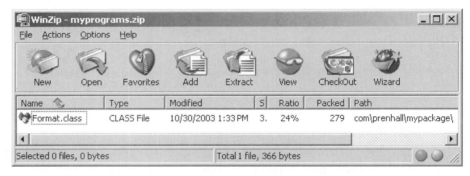

FIGURE 5.18   Class files can be archived into a single compressed file.

IDE source path
IDE class path

 Note
An IDE such as JBuilder uses the *source directory path* to specify where the source files are stored and uses the *class directory path* to specify where the compiled class files are stored.

A source file must be stored in a package directory under the source directory path. For example, if the source directory is `c:\mysource`, and the package statement in the source code is `package com.prenhall.mypackage`, then the source code file is automatically stored in `c:\mysource\com\prenhall\mypackage`.

A class file must be stored in a package directory under the class directory path. For example, if the class directory is `c:\myclass`, and the package statement in the source code is `package com.prenhall.mypackage`, then the class file is automatically stored in `c:\myclass\com\prenhall\mypackage`.

5.12.4   Using Classes from Packages

There are two ways to use classes from a package. One way is to use the fully qualified name of the class. For example, the fully qualified name for `JOptionPane` is `javax.swing.JOptionPane`. For `Format` in the preceding example, it is `com.prenhall.`

`mypackage.Format`. This is convenient if the class is used only a few times in the program. The other way is to use the `import` statement. For example, to import all the classes in the `javax.swing` package, you can use

```
import javax.swing.*;
```

An import that uses an * is called *an import on demand* declaration. You can also import a specific class. For example, this statement imports `javax.swing.JOptionPane`:

```
import javax.swing.JOptionPane;
```

The information for the classes in an imported package is not read in at compile time or runtime unless the class is used in the program. The import statement simply tells the compiler where to locate the classes. There is no performance difference between an import on demand declaration and a specific class import declaration.

Let us write a program that uses the `Format` class in the `com.prenhall.mypackage.mypackage` package.

1. Create TestFormatClass.java in Listing 5.10 and save it into `c:\book`.

LISTING 5.10 TestFormatClass.java

```
1   import com.prenhall.mypackage.Format;                          import class
2
3   public class TestFormatClass {
4     /** Main method */
5     public static void main(String[] args) {
6       System.out.println(Format.format(10.3422345, 2));
7       System.out.println(Format.format(-0.343434, 3));
8     }
9   }
```

2. Run TestFormatClass, as shown in Figure 5.19.

```
Command Prompt                                          _ □ X
C:\book\com\prenhall\mypackage>javac Format.java

C:\book\com\prenhall\mypackage>cd c:\book

C:\book>javac TestFormatClass.java

C:\book>java TestFormatClass
10.34
-0.343

C:\book>
```

FIGURE 5.19 `TestFormatClass` uses `Format` defined in `com.prenhall.mypackage`.

TestFormatClass.java can be placed anywhere as long as `c:\book` is in the classpath so that the `Format` class can be found. Please note that `Format` is defined as public so that it can be used by classes in other packages.

The program uses an `import` statement to get the class `Format`. You cannot import entire packages, such as `com.prenhall.*.*`. Only one asterisk (*) can be used in an `import` statement.

Note

The `format` method can be invoked from any class. If you create a new class in the same package with `Format`, you can invoke the `format` method using `ClassName.methodName` (e.g., `Format.format`). If you create a new class in a different package, you can invoke the `format` method using **packagename.ClassName.methodName** (e.g., **com.prenhall. mypackage.Format.format**).

KEY TERMS

actual parameter   131
argument   131
ambiguous invocation   139
divide and conquer   147
formal parameter (i.e., parameter)   130
information hiding   147
method   130
method abstraction   146
method overloading   137
method signature   131

modifier   130
package   154
pass-by-value   135
parameter   130
return type   130
return value   130
scope of variable   141
stepwise refinement   146
stub   149

CHAPTER SUMMARY

■ Making programs modular and reusable is one of the central goals in software engineering. Java provides many powerful constructs that help to achieve this goal. Methods are one such construct.

■ The method header specifies the *modifiers*, *return value type*, *method name*, and *parameters* of the method. The modifier, which is optional, tells the compiler how to call the method. The static modifier is used for all the methods in this chapter.

■ A method may return a value. The `returnValueType` is the data type of the value the method returns. If the method does not return a value, the `returnValueType` is the keyword `void`.

■ The *parameter list* refers to the type, order, and number of the parameters of a method. The method name and the parameter list together constitute the *method signature*. Parameters are optional; that is, a method may contain no parameters.

■ A return statement can also be used in a `void` method for terminating the method and returning to the method's caller. This is useful occasionally for circumventing the normal flow of control in a method.

■ The arguments that are passed to a method should have the same number, type, and order as the parameters in the method definition.

■ When a program calls a method, program control is transferred to the called method. A called method returns control to the caller when its return statement is executed or when its method-ending closing brace is reached.

■ A method with a nonvoid return value type can also be invoked as a statement in Java. In this case, the caller simply ignores the return value. In the majority of cases, a call to a method with return value is treated as a value. In some cases, however, the caller is not interested in the return value.

■ Each time a method is invoked, the system stores parameters, local variables, and system registers in a space known as a *stack*. When a method calls another method, the caller's stack space is kept intact, and new space is created to handle the new method call. When a method finishes its work and returns to its caller, its associated space is released.

■ A method can be overloaded. This means that two methods can have the same name as long as their method parameter lists differ.

■ The scope of a local variable is limited locally to a method. The scope of a local variable starts from its declaration and continues to the end of the block that contains the variable. A local variable must be declared before it can be used, and it must be initialized before it is referenced.

■ *Method abstraction* is achieved by separating the use of a method from its implementation. The client can use a method without knowing how it is implemented. The details of the implementation are encapsulated in the method and hidden from the client who invokes the method. This is known as *information hiding* or *encapsulation*.

■ Method abstraction modularizes programs in a neat, hierarchical manner. Programs written as collections of concise methods are easier to write, debug, maintain, and modify than would otherwise be the case. This writing style also promotes method reusability.

■ When implementing a large program, use the top-down or bottom-up coding approach. Do not write the entire program at once. This approach seems to take more time for coding (because you are repeatedly compiling and running the program), but it actually saves time and makes debugging easier.

REVIEW QUESTIONS

Sections 5.2–5.3

5.1   What are the benefits of using a method? How do you declare a method? How do you invoke a method?

5.2   What is the `return` type of a `main` method?

5.3   Can you simplify the `max` method in Listing 5.1 using the conditional operator?

5.4   True of false? A call to a method with a `void` return type is always a statement itself, but a call to a method with a nonvoid return type is always a component of an expression.

5.5   What would be wrong with not writing a `return` statement in a nonvoid method? Can you have a `return` statement in a `void` method, such as the following?

```java
public static void main(String[] args) {
  int i;
  while (true) {
    // Prompt the user to enter an integer
    String intString = JOptionPane.showInputDialog(
      "Enter an integer:");

    // Convert a string into int
    int i = Integer.parseInt(intString);
```

```
        if (i == 0)
          return;
        System.out.println("i = " + i);
      }
    }
```

Does the `return` statement in the following method cause syntax errors?

```
public static void xMethod(double x, double y) {
  System.out.println(x + y);
  return x + y;
}
```

5.6 Define the terms parameter, argument, method signature.

5.7 Write method headers for the following methods:

- Computing a sales commission, given the sales amount and the commission rate.
- Printing the calendar for a month, given the month and year.
- Computing a square root.
- Testing whether a number is even, and returning `true` if it is.
- Printing a message a specified number of times.
- Computing the monthly payment, given the loan amount, number of years, and annual interest rate.
- Finding the corresponding uppercase letter, given a lowercase letter.

5.8 Identify and correct the errors in the following program:

```
1  public class Test {
2    public static method1(int n, m) {
3      n += m;
4      xMethod(3.4);
5    }
6
7    public static int xMethod(int n) {
8      if (n > 0) return 1;
9      else if (n == 0) return 0;
10     else if (n < 0) return -1;
11   }
12 }
```

5.9 Reformat the following program according to the programming style and documentation guidelines proposed in §2.14, "Programming Style and Documentation." Use the next-line brace style.

```
public class Test {
  public static double xMethod(double i,double j)
  {
  while (i<j) {
    j--;
  }
  return j;
  }
}
```

Section 5.5 Passing Parameters

5.10 How is an argument passed to a method? Can the argument have the same name as its parameter?

5.11 What is pass-by-value? Show the result of the following programs:

```java
public class Test {
  public static void main(String[] args) {
    int max = 0;
    max(1, 2, max);
    System.out.println(max);
  }

  public static void max(
      int value1, int value2, int max) {
    if (value1 > value2)
      max = value1;
    else
      max = value2;
  }
}
```

(a)

```java
public class Test {
  public static void main(String[] args) {
    // Initialize times
    int times = 3;
    System.out.println("Before the call,"
      + " variable times is " + times);

    // Invoke nPrintln and display times
    nPrintln("Welcome to Java!", times);
    System.out.println("After the call,"
      + "variable times is " + times);
  }

  // Print the message n times
  public static void nPrintln(
      String message, int n) {
    while (n > 0) {
      System.out.println("n = " + n);
      System.out.println(message);
      n--;
    }
  }
}
```

(b)

```java
public class Test {
  public static void main(String[] args) {
    int i = 1;
    while (i <= 6) {
      xMethod(i, 2);
      i++;
    }
  }

  public static void xMethod(
      int i, int num) {
    for (int j = 1; j <= i; j++) {
      System.out.print(num + " ");
      num *= 2;
    }

    System.out.println();
  }
}
```

(c)

```java
public class Test {
  public static void main(String[] args) {
    int i = 0;
    while (i <= 4) {
      xMethod(i);
      i++;
    }

    System.out.println("i is " + i);
  }

  public static void xMethod(int i) {
    do {
      if (i % 3 != 0)
        System.out.print(i + " ");
      i--;
    }
    while (i >= 1);

    System.out.println();
  }
}
```

(d)

5.12 For (a) in the preceding question, show the contents of the stack just before the method **max** is invoked, just entering **max**, just before **max** is returned, and right after **max** is returned.

Section 5.6 Overloading Methods

5.13 What is method overloading? Is it possible to define two methods that have the same name but different parameter types? Is it possible to define two methods in a class that have identical method names and parameter lists but with different return value types or different modifiers?

5.14   What is wrong in the following program?

```
public class Test {
  public static void method(int x) {
  }

  public static int method(int y) {
    return y;
  }
}
```

Section 5.8 The Scope of Local Variables

5.15   Identify and correct the errors in the following program:

```
1 public class Test {
2   public static void main(String[] args) {
3     nPrintln("Welcome to Java!", 5);
4   }
5
6   public static void nPrintln(String message, int n) {
7     int n = 1;
8     for (int i = 0; i < n; i++)
9       System.out.println(message);
10  }
11 }
```

Section 5.9 The Math Class

5.16   True or false? The argument for trigonometric methods represents an angle in radians.

5.17   Write an expression that returns a random integer between 34 and 55. Write an expression that returns a random integer between 0 and 999. Write an expression that returns a random number between 5.5 and 55.5. Write an expression that returns a random lowercase letter.

5.18   Evaluate the following method calls:
A. Math.sqrt(4)
B. Math.sin(2 * Math.PI)
C. Math.cos(2 * Math.PI)
D. Math.pow(2, 2)
E. Math.log(Math.E)
F. Math.exp(1)
G. Math.max(2, Math.min(3, 4))
H. Math.rint(-2.5)
I. Math.ceil(-2.5)
J. Math.floor(-2.5)
K. Math.round(-2.5f)
L. Math.round(-2.5)
M. Math.rint(2.5)
N. Math.ceil(2.5)
O. Math.floor(2.5)
P. Math.round(2.5f)
Q. Math.round(2.5)
R. Math.round(Math.abs(-2.5))

Section 5.12 (Optional) Packages

5.19   What are the benefits of using packages?

5.20   If a class uses the package statement "package java.chapter5", where should the source code be stored, and where should the .class files be stored? How do you make the class available for use by other programs?

5.21   Why do you have to import JOptionPane but not the Math class?

PROGRAMMING EXERCISES

Sections 5.2–5.7

5.1 (*Converting an uppercase letter to lowercase*) Write a method that converts an uppercase letter to a lowercase letter. Use the following method header:

```
public static char upperCaseToLowerCase(char ch)
```

For example, upperCaseToLowerCase('B') returns b. See Exercise 2.7 on how to convert an uppercase letter to lowercase.

5.2* (*Summing the digits in an integer*) Write a method that computes the sum of the digits in an integer. Use the following method header:

```
public static int sumDigits(long n)
```

For example, sumDigits(234) returns 2 + 3 + 4 = 9.

Hint

Use the % operator to extract digits, and the / operator to remove the extracted digit. For instance, to extract 4 from 234, use 234 % 10 (= 4). To remove 4 from 234, use 234 / 10 (= 23) Use a loop to repeatedly extract and remove the digit until all the digits are extracted.

5.3* (*Displaying an integer reversed*) Write the following method to display an integer in reverse order:

```
public static void reverse(int number)
```

For example, reverse(3456) displays 6543.

5.4** (*Returning an integer reversed*) Write the following method to return an integer reversed:

```
public static int reverse(int number)
```

For example, reverse(3456) returns 6543.

5.5* (*Sorting three numbers*) Write the following method to display three numbers in increasing order:

```
public static void sort(double num1, double num2, double num3)
```

5.6* (*Displaying patterns*) Write a method to display a pattern as follows:

```
        1
      2 1
    3 2 1
...
n n-1 ... 3 2 1
```

The method header is

```
public static void displayPattern(int n)
```

5.7* (*Computing the future investment value*) Write a method that computes future investment value at a given interest rate for a specified number of years. The future investment is determined using the formula in Exercise 2.9.

Use the following method header:

```
public static double futureInvestmentValue(
    double investmentAmount, double monthlyInterestRate, int years)
```

For example, `futureInvestmentValue(10000, 0.05/12, 5)` returns `12833.59`.

Write a test program that prompts the user to enter the investment amount (e.g., 1000) and the interest rate (e.g., 9%), and print a table that displays future value for the years from 1 to 30, as shown below:

```
The amount invested: 1000
Annual interest rate: 9%
Years        Future Value
  1             1093.8
  2             1196.41
...
  29            13467.25
  30            14730.57
```

5.8 (*Conversions between Celsius and Fahrenheit*) Write a class that contains the following two methods:

```
/** Converts from Celsius to Fahrenheit */
public static double celsiusToFahrenheit(double celsius)

/** Converts from Fahrenheit to Celsius */
public static double fahrenheitToCelsius(double fahrenheit)
```

The formula for the conversion is:

```
fahrenheit = (9.0 / 5) * celsius + 32
```

Write a test program that invokes these methods to display the following tables:

Celsius	Fahrenheit	Fahrenheit	Celsius
40.0	105.0	120.0	48.89
39.0	102.2	110.0	43.33
...			
32.0	89.6	40.0	5.44
31.0	87.8	30.0	−1.11

5.9 (*Conversions between feet and meters*) Write a class that contains the following two methods:

```
/** Converts from feet to meters */
public static double footToMeter(double foot)

/** Converts from meters to feet */
public static double meterToFoot(double meter)
```

The formula for the conversion is:

```
meter = 0.305 * foot
```

Write a test program that invokes these methods to display the following tables:

Feet	Meters	Meters	Feet
1.0	0.305	20.0	65.574
2.0	0.61	25.0	81.967
...			
9.0	2.745	60.0	195.721
10.0	3.05	65.0	213.115

5.10   (*Computing GCD*) Write a method that returns the greatest common divisor between two positive integers, using the following header:

```
public static int gcd(int m, int n)
```

Write a test program that computes gcd(24, 16) and gcd(255, 25).

5.11   (*Computing commissions*) Write a method that computes the commission, using the scheme in §4.8.2 "Example: Finding the Sales Amount." The header of the method is:

```
public static double computeCommission(double salesAmount)
```

Write a test program that displays the following table:

SalesAmount	Commission
10000	900.0
15000	1500.0
...	
95000	11100.0
100000	11700.0

5.12   (*Displaying characters*) Write a method that prints characters using the following header:

```
public static void printChars(char ch1, char ch2,
    int numberPerLine)
```

This method prints the characters between ch1 and ch2 with the specified numbers per line. Write a test program that prints ten characters per line from '1' and 'Z.'

5.13*   (*Summing series*) Write a method to compute the following series:

$$m(i) = \frac{1}{2} + \frac{2}{3} + \cdots + \frac{i}{i+1}$$

Write a test program that displays the following table:

i	m(i)
2	0.5
3	1.1667
...	
19	15.4523
20	16.4023

5.14*   (*Computing series*) Write a method to compute the following series:

$$m(i) = 4\left(1 - \frac{1}{3} + \frac{1}{5} - \frac{1}{7} + \frac{1}{9} - \frac{1}{11} + \frac{1}{13} - \cdots - \frac{1}{2i-1} + \frac{1}{2i+1}\right)$$

5.15*   (*Printing a tax table*) Use the computeTax methods in Listing 5.5, ComputeTaxWithMethod.java, to write a program that prints a 2002 tax table for taxable income from $50,000 to $60,000 with intervals of $50 for all four statuses, as follows:

Taxable Income	Single	Married Joint	Married Separate	Head of a House
50000	9846	7296	10398	8506
50050	9859	7309	10411	8519
...				
59950	12532	9982	13190	11192
60000	12546	9996	13205	11206

5.16* (*Revising Listing 4.11, PrimeNumber.java*) Write a program that meets the following requirements:

■ Declare a method to determine whether an integer is a prime number. Use the following method header:

```
public static boolean isPrime(int num)
```

An integer greater than 1 is a *prime number* if its only divisor is 1 or itself. For example, isPrime(11) returns true, and isPrime(9) returns false.

■ Use the isPrime method to find the first thousand prime numbers and display every ten prime numbers in a row, as follows:

```
2    3    5    7    11   13   17   19   23   29
31   37   41   43   47   53   59   61   67   71
73   79   83   89   97   ...
...
```

Section 5.9 The Math Class

5.17* (*Displaying matrix of 0s and 1s*) Write a method that displays an n by n matrix using the following header:

```
public static void printMatrix(int n)
```

Each element is 0 or 1, which is generated randomly. Write a test program that prints a 3 by 3 matrix that may look like this:

```
0 1 0
0 0 0
1 1 1
```

5.18 (*Using the Math.sqrt method*) Write a program that prints the following table using the sqrt method in the Math class.

Number	SquareRoot
0	0.0000
2	1.4142
...	
18	5.2426
20	5.4721

5.19* (*The MyTriangle class*) Create a class named MyTriangle that contains the following two methods:

```
/** Returns true if the sum of any two sides is
 *  greater than the third side. */
public static boolean isValid(
  double side1, double side2, double side3)

/** Returns the area of the triangle. */
public static double area(
  double side1, double side2, double side3)
```

The formula for computing the area is

$$s = (side1 + side2 + side3)/2;$$

$$area = \sqrt{s(s - side1)(s - side2)(s - side3)}$$

Write a test program that reads three sides for a triangle and computes the area if the input is valid. Otherwise, it displays that the input is invalid.

5.20 (*Using trigonometric methods*) Print the following table to display the `sin` value and `cos` value of degrees from 0 to 360 with increments of 10 degrees. Round the value to keep four digits after the decimal point.

Degree	Sin	Cos
0	0.0	1.0
10	0.1736	0.9848
...		
350	−0.1736	0.9848
360	0.0	1.0

5.21**(*Computing mean and standard deviation*) In business applications, you are often asked to compute the mean and standard deviation of data. The mean is simply the average of the numbers. The standard deviation is a statistic that tells you how tightly all the various data are clustered around the mean in a set of data. For example, what is the average age of the students in a class? How close are the ages? If all the students are the same age, the deviation is 0. Write a program that generates ten random numbers between 0 and 1000, and computes the mean and standard deviations of these numbers using the following formula:

$$mean = \frac{\sum\limits_{i=1}^{n} x_i}{n} = \frac{x_1 + x_2 + \cdots + x_n}{n} \qquad deviation = \sqrt{\frac{\sum\limits_{i=1}^{n} x_i^2 - \frac{\left(\sum\limits_{i=1}^{n} x_i\right)^2}{n}}{n-1}}$$

5.22**(*Approximating the square root*) Implement the `sqrt` method. The square root of a number, `num`, can be approximated by repeatedly performing a calculation using the following formula:

```
nextGuess = (lastGuess + (num / lastGuess)) / 2
```

When `nextGuess` and `lastGuess` are almost identical, `nextGuess` is the approximated square root.

The initial guess will be the starting value of `lastGuess`. If the difference between `nextGuess` and `lastGuess` is less than a very small number, such as 0.0001, you can claim that `nextGuess` is the approximated square root of `num`.

Sections 5.10–5.11

5.23* (*Generating random characters*) Use the methods in `RandomCharacter` in Listing 5.6 to print one hundred uppercase letters and then one hundred single digits, and print ten per line.

5.24**(*Displaying current date and time*) Listing 2.8, ShowCurrentTime.java, displays the current time. Improve this example to display the current date and time. The calendar example in §5.11, "Method Abstraction and Stepwise Refinement," should give you some ideas on how to find year, month, and day.

5.25**(*Converting milliseconds to hours, minutes, and seconds*) Write a method that converts milliseconds to hours, minutes, and seconds using the following header:

public static String convertMillis(**long** millis)

The method returns a string as `hours:minutes:seconds`. For example, `convertMillis(5500)` returns a string `0:0:5`, `convertMillis(100000)` returns a string `0:1:40`, and `convertMillis(555550000)` returns a string `154:19:10`.

ARRAYS

Objectives

- To describe why arrays are necessary in programming (§6.1).
- To learn the steps involved in using arrays: declaring array reference variables and creating arrays (§§6.2.1–6.2.2).
- To initialize the values in an array (§6.2.3).
- To access array elements using indexed variables (§6.2.4).
- To simplify programming using the JDK 1.5 foreach loops (§6.2.5).
- To declare, create, and initialize an array using an array initializer (§6.2.6).
- To copy contents from one array to another (§6.3).
- To develop and invoke methods with array arguments and return values (§§6.4–6.5).
- (Optional) To declare a method with variable-length argument list (§6.6).
- To search elements using the linear (§6.7.1) or binary (§6.7.2) search algorithm.
- To sort an array using the selection sort (§6.8.1).
- (Optional) To sort an array using the insertion sort algorithms (§6.8.2).
- To use the methods in the Arrays class (§6.9).
- To declare and create two-dimensional arrays (§6.10).
- (Optional) To declare and create multidimensional arrays (§6.11).

6.1 Introduction

Often you will have to store a large number of values during the execution of a program. Suppose, for instance, that you want to read one hundred numbers, compute their average, and find out how many numbers are above the average. Your program first reads the numbers and computes their average, and then compares each number with the average to determine whether it is above the average. The numbers must all be stored in variables in order to accomplish this task. You have to declare one hundred variables and repeatedly write almost identical code one hundred times. From the standpoint of practicality, it is impossible to write a program this way. An efficient, organized approach is needed. Java and all other high-level languages provide a data structure, the *array*, which stores a fixed-size sequential collection of elements of the same type.

6.2 Array Basics

An array is used to store a collection of data, but it is often more useful to think of an array as a collection of variables of the same type. Instead of declaring individual variables, such as `number0`, `number1`, ..., and `number99`, you declare one array variable such as `numbers` and use `numbers[0]`, `numbers[1]`, ..., and `numbers[99]` to represent individual variables. This section introduces how to declare array variables, create arrays, and process arrays using indexed variables.

6.2.1 Declaring Array Variables

To use an array in a program, you must declare a variable to reference the array, and you must specify the type of array the variable can reference. Here is the syntax for declaring an array variable:

```
dataType[] arrayRefVar;
```

or

```
dataType arrayRefVar[]; // This style is allowed, but not preferred
```

The following code snippets are examples of this syntax:

```
double[] myList;
```

or

```
double myList[]; // This style is allowed, but not preferred
```

Note
The style `dataType[] arrayRefVar` is preferred. The style `dataType arrayRefVar[]` comes from the C/C++ language and was adopted in Java to accommodate C/C++ programmers.

6.2.2 Creating Arrays

Unlike declarations for primitive data type variables, the declaration of an array variable does not allocate any space in memory for the array. Only a storage location for the reference to an array is created. If a variable does not reference to an array, the value of the variable is `null`. You cannot assign elements to an array unless it has already been created. After an array variable is declared, you can create an array by using the `new` operator with the following syntax:

```
arrayRefVar = new dataType[arraySize];
```

This statement does two things: (1) it creates an array using `new dataType[arraySize]`; (2) it assigns the reference of the newly created array to the variable `arrayRefVar`.

Declaring an array variable, creating an array, and assigning the reference of the array to the variable can be combined in one statement, as shown below:

```
dataType[] arrayRefVar = new dataType[arraySize];
```

or

```
dataType arrayRefVar[] = new dataType[arraySize];
```

Here is an example of such a statement:

```
double[] myList = new double[10];
```

This statement declares an array variable, `myList`, creates an array of ten elements of `double` type, and assigns its reference to `myList`. Figure 6.1 illustrates an array with sample element values.

double[] myList = **new double**[10];

myList[0]	5.6
myList[1]	4.5
myList[2]	3.3
myList[3]	13.2
myList[4]	4.0
myList[5]	34.33
myList[6]	34.0
myList[7]	45.45
myList[8]	99.993
myList[9]	11123

myList `reference`

Array reference variable

Array element at index 5

Element value

FIGURE 6.1   The array `myList` has ten elements of `double` type and `int` indices from 0 to 9.

Note

An array variable that appears to hold an array actually contains a reference to that array. Strictly speaking, an array variable and an array are different, but most of the time the distinction between them can be ignored. Thus it is all right to say, for simplicity, that `myList` is an array, instead of stating, at greater length, that `myList` is a variable that contains a reference to an array of ten double elements. When the distinction makes a subtle difference, the longer phrase should be used.

array vs. array variable

6.2.3   Array Size and Default Values

When space for an array is allocated, the array size must be given, to specify the number of elements that can be stored in it. The size of an array cannot be changed after the array is created. Size can be obtained using `arrayRefVar.length`. For example, `myList.length` is 10.

array length

When an array is created, its elements are assigned the *default value* of 0 for the numeric primitive data types, `'\u0000'` for `char` types, and `false` for `boolean` types.

default values

6.2.4   Array Indexed Variables

The array elements are accessed through the index. Array indices are 0-*based*; that is, they start from 0 to `arrayRefVar.length-1`. In the example in Figure 6.1, `myList` holds ten `double` values and the indices are from 0 to 9.

array index
0-based

Each element in the array is represented using the following syntax, known as an *indexed variable*:

indexed variables

```
arrayRefVar[index];
```

For example, `myList[9]` represents the last element in the array `myList`.

Caution

Some languages use parentheses to reference an array element, as in `myList(9)`. But Java uses brackets, as in `myList[9]`.

After an array is created, an indexed variable can be used in the same way as a regular variable. For example, the following code adds the values in `myList[0]` and `myList[1]` to `myList[2]`:

```
myList[2] = myList[0] + myList[1];
```

The following loop assigns 0 to `myList[0]`, 1 to `myList[1]`, ..., and 9 to `myList[9]`:

```
for (int i = 0; i < myList.length; i++) {
  myList[i] = i;
}
```

6.2.5 Array Initializers

array initializer

Java has a shorthand notation, known as the *array initializer*, which combines declaring an array, creating an array, and initializing in one statement using the following syntax:

```
dataType[] arrayRefVar = {value0, value1, ..., valuek};
```

For example,

```
double[] myList = {1.9, 2.9, 3.4, 3.5};
```

This statement declares, creates, and initializes the array `myList` with four elements, which is equivalent to the statements shown below:

```
double[] myList = new double[4];
myList[0] = 1.9;
myList[1] = 2.9;
myList[2] = 3.4;
myList[3] = 3.5;
```

Caution

The new operator is not used in the array initializer syntax. Using an array initializer, you have to declare, create, and initialize the array all in one statement. Splitting it would cause a syntax error. Thus the next statement is wrong:

```
double[] myList;
myList = {1.9, 2.9, 3.4, 3.5};
```

6.2.6 Processing Arrays

When processing array elements, you will often use a `for` loop. Here are the reasons why:

■ All of the elements in an array are of the same type. They are evenly processed in the same fashion by repeatedly using a loop.

■ Since the size of the array is known, it is natural to use a `for` loop.

Here are some examples of processing arrays:

1. (*Initializing arrays with random values*) The following loop initializes the array `myList` with random values between `0.0` and `99.0`:

```java
for (int i = 0; i < myList.length; i++) {
  myList[i] = Math.random() * 100;
}
```

2. (*Printing arrays*) To print an array, you have to print each element in the array using a loop like the one shown below.

```java
for (int i = 0; i < myList.length; i++) {
  System.out.print(myList[i] + " ");
}
```

Tip

For an array of the `char[]` type, it can be printed using one print statement. For example, the fol-   print character array
lowing code displays `Dallas`:

```java
char[] city = {'D', 'a', 'l', 'l', 'a', 's'};
System.out.println(city);
```

3. (*Summing all elements*) Use a variable named `total` to store the sum. Initially `total` is `0`. Add each element in the array to `total`, using a loop like this:

```java
double total = 0;
for (int i = 0; i < myList.length; i++) {
  total += myList[i];
}
```

4. (*Finding the largest element*) Use a variable named `max` to store the largest element. Initially `max` is `myList[0]`. To find the largest element in the array `myList`, compare each element in `myList` with `max`, and update `max` if the element is greater than `max`.

```java
double max = myList[0];
for (int i = 1; i < myList.length; i++) {
  if (myList[i] > max) max = myList[i];
}
```

5. (*Finding the smallest index of the largest element*) Often you need to locate the largest element in an array. If an array has more than one largest element, find the smallest index of such an element. Suppose the array `myList` is {1, 5, 3, 4, 5, 5}. The largest element is `5`, and the smallest index for `5` is `1`. Use a variable named `max` to store the largest element and a variable named `indexOfMax` to denote the index of the largest element. Initially `max` is `myList[0]`, and `indexOfMax` is `0`. Compare each element in `myList` with `max`, and update `max` and `indexOfMax` if the element is greater than `max`.

```java
double max = myList[0];
int indexOfMax = 0;
for (int i = 1; i < myList.length; i++) {
  if (myList[i] > max) {
    max = myList[i];
    indexOfMax = i;
  }
}
```

What is the consequence if `(myList[i] > max)` is replaced by `(myList[i] >= max)`?

6.2.7 `foreach` Loops

JDK 1.5 introduced a new **for** loop, known as **foreach** *loop* or *enhanced* **for** *loop*, which enables you to traverse the complete array sequentially without using an index variable. For example, the following code displays all the elements in the array `myList`:

```
for (double element: myList) {
  System.out.println(element);
}
```

You can read the code as "for each element in `myList` do the following." Note that the variable, `element`, must be declared the same type as the elements in `myList`.

In general, the syntax for a **foreach** loop is

```
for (elementType element: arrayRefVar) {
  // Process the element
}
```

You still have to use an index variable if you wish to traverse the array in a different order or change the elements in the array.

6.2.8 Example: Testing Arrays

This section presents a program that reads six integers, finds the largest of them, and counts its occurrences. Suppose that you entered 3, 5, 2, 5, 5, 5, as shown in Figure 6.2; the program finds that the largest is 5 and that the occurrence count for 5 is 4.

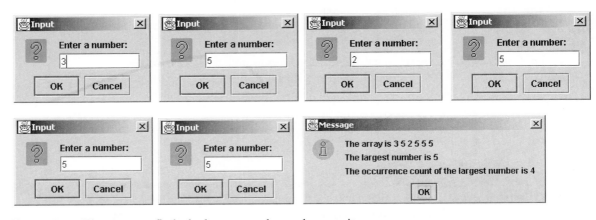

FIGURE 6.2 The program finds the largest number and counts its occurrences.

An intuitive solution is to first read the numbers and store them in an array, then find the largest number in the array, and finally count the occurrences of the largest number in the array. The program is given in Listing 6.1.

LISTING 6.1 TestArray.java

```
1 import javax.swing.JOptionPane;
2
3 public class TestArray {
4   /** Main method */
5   public static void main(String[] args) {
6     final int TOTAL NUMBERS = 6;
7     int[] numbers = new int[TOTAL NUMBERS];
8
```

create array

```
9       // Read all numbers
10      for (int i = 0; i < numbers.length;  i++) {          store numbers
11        String numString = JOptionPane.showInputDialog(
12          "Enter a number:");
13
14        // Convert string into integer
15        numbers[i] = Integer.parseInt(numString);
16      }
17
18      // Find the largest
19      int max = numbers[0];
20      for (int i = 1; i < numbers.length; i++) {
21        if (max < numbers[i] )
22          max = numbers[i];                                update max
23      }
24
25      // Find the occurrence of the largest number
26      int count = 0;
27      for (int i = 0; i < numbers.length;  i++) {
28        if (numbers[i] == max ) count++;                   count occurrence
29      }
30
31      // Prepare the result
32      String output = "The array is ";
33      for (int i = 0; i < numbers.length;  i++) {
34        output += numbers[i] + " ";
35      }
36
37      output += "\nThe largest number is " + max;          prepare output
38      output += "\nThe occurrence count of the largest number "
39        + "is " + count;
40
41      // Display the result
42      JOptionPane.showMessageDialog(null, output);         output
43    }
44  }
```

The program declares and creates an array of six integers (line 7). It finds the largest number in the array (lines 19–23), counts its occurrences (lines 26–29), and displays the result (lines 32–42). To display the array, you need to display each element in the array using a loop.

Without using the **numbers** array, you would have to declare a variable for each number entered, because all the numbers are compared to the largest number to count its occurrences after it is found.

Caution

Accessing an array out of bounds is a common programming error that throws a runtime **ArrayIndexOutOfBoundsException**. To avoid it, make sure that you do not use an index beyond **arrayRefVar.length – 1**.

    Programmers often mistakenly reference the first element in an array with index 1, so that the index of the tenth element becomes 10. This is called the *off-by-one error*.

ArrayIndexOutOfBounds
Exception

off-by-one error

Tip

If you use an IDE such as JBuilder, NetBeans, or Eclipse, please refer to *Learning Java Effectively with JBuilder/NetBeans/Eclipse* in the supplements. It will show you how to use a debugger to inspect arrays.

debugging in IDE

6.2.9 Example: Assigning Grades

This example writes a program that reads student scores, gets the best score, and then assigns grades based on the following scheme:

Grade is A if score is $>=$ best $-$ 10;

Grade is B if score is $>=$ best $-$ 20;

Grade is C if score is $>=$ best $-$ 30;

Grade is D if score is $>=$ best $-$ 40;

Grade is F otherwise.

The program prompts the user to enter the total number of students, then prompts the user to enter all of the scores, and concludes by displaying the grades.

The program reads the scores, then finds the best score, and finally assigns grades to the students based on the preceding scheme. Listing 6.2 gives the solution to the problem. The output of a sample run of the program is shown in Figure 6.3.

LISTING **6.2** AssignGrade.java

```java
 1 import javax.swing.JOptionPane;
 2
 3 public class AssignGrade {
 4   /** Main method */
 5   public static void main(String[] args) {
 6     // Get number of students
 7     String numberOfStudentsString = JOptionPane.showInputDialog(
 8       "Please enter number of students:");
 9
10     // Convert string into integer
11     int numberOfStudents = Integer.parseInt(numberOfStudentsString);
12
13     int[] scores = new int[numberOfStudents]; // Array scores
14     int best = 0; // The best score
15     char grade; // The grade
16
17     // Read scores and find the best score
18     for (int i = 0; i < scores.length ; i++) {
19       String scoreString = JOptionPane.showInputDialog(
20         "Please enter a score:");
21
22       // Convert string into integer
23       scores[i] = Integer.parseInt(scoreString);
24       if (scores[i] > best)
25         best = scores[i];
26     }
27
28     // Declare and initialize output string
29     String output = "";
30
31     // Assign and display grades
32     for (int i = 0; i < scores.length ; i++) {
33       if (scores[i] >= best - 10)
34         grade = 'A';
35       else if (scores[i] >= best - 20)
36         grade = 'B';
```

number of students

create array

get a score

update best

assign grade

```
37          else if (scores[i] >= best - 30)
38            grade = 'C';
39          else if (scores[i] >= best - 40)
40            grade = 'D';
41          else
42            grade = 'F';
43
44          output += "Student " + i + " score is " +
45            scores[i] + " and grade is " + grade + "\n";
46        }
47
48        // Display the result
49        JOptionPane.showMessageDialog(null, output);
50      }
51 }
```

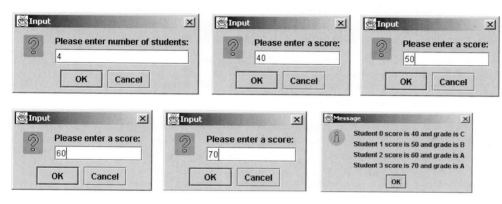

Figure 6.3   The program receives the number of students and their scores, and then assigns grades.

The program declares and creates scores as an array of int type in order to store the students' scores (line 13) after the user enters the number of students into numberOfStudents in lines 7–11. The size of the array is set at runtime; it cannot be changed once the array is created.

The array is not needed to find the best score, but it is needed to keep all of the scores so that grades can be assigned later on, and it is needed when scores are printed along with the students' grades.

6.3 Copying Arrays

Often, in a program, you need to duplicate an array or a part of an array. In such cases you could attempt to use the assignment statement (=), as follows:

```
list2 = list1;
```

This statement does not copy the contents of the array referenced by list1 to list2, but merely copies the reference value from list1 to list2. After this statement, list1 and list2 reference to the same array, as shown in Figure 6.4. The array previously referenced by list2 is no longer referenced; it becomes garbage, which will be automatically collected by the Java Virtual Machine.

In Java, you can use assignment statements to copy primitive data type variables, but not arrays. Assigning one array variable to another array variable actually copies one reference to another and makes both variables point to the same memory location.

copy reference

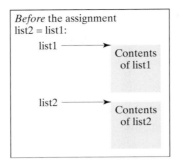
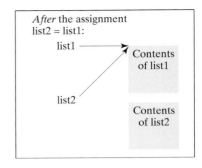

FIGURE 6.4 Before the assignment statement, `list1` and `list2` point to separate memory locations. After the assignment, the reference of the `list1` array is passed to `list2`.

There are three ways to copy arrays:

- Use a loop to copy individual elements one by one.

- Use the static `arraycopy` method in the `System` class.

- Use the `clone` method to copy arrays; this will be introduced in Chapter 9, "Inheritance and Polymorphism."

You can write a loop to copy every element from the source array to the corresponding element in the target array. The following code, for instance, copies `sourceArray` to `targetArray` using a `for` loop:

```java
int[] sourceArray = {2, 3, 1, 5, 10};
int[] targetArray = new int[sourceArray.length];
for (int i = 0; i < sourceArray.length; i++) {
  targetArray[i] = sourceArray[i];
}
```

Another approach is to use the `arraycopy` method in the `java.lang.System` class to copy arrays instead of using a loop. The syntax for `arraycopy` is shown below:

```java
arraycopy(sourceArray, srcPos, targetArray, tarPos, length);
```

The parameters `srcPos` and `tarPos` indicate the starting positions in `sourceArray` and `targetArray`, respectively. The number of elements copied from `sourceArray` to `targetArray` is indicated by `length`. For example, you can rewrite the loop using the following statement:

```java
System.arraycopy(sourceArray, 0, targetArray, 0, sourceArray.length);
```

arraycopy method

The `arraycopy` *method* does not allocate memory space for the target array. The target array must have already been created with its memory space allocated. After the copying takes place, `targetArray` and `sourceArray` have the same content but independent memory locations.

Note

The `arraycopy` method violates the Java naming convention. By convention, this method should be named `arrayCopy` (i.e., with an uppercase C).

6.4 Passing Arrays to Methods

Just as you can pass primitive type values to methods, you can also pass arrays to methods. For example, the following method displays the elements in an `int` array:

```java
public static void printArray(int[] array) {
  for (int i = 0; i < array.length; i++) {
    System.out.print(array[i] + " ");
  }
}
```

You can invoke it by passing an array. For example, the following statement invokes the `printArray` method to display 3, 1, 2, 6, 4, and 2:

```java
printArray(new int[]{3, 1, 2, 6, 4, 2});
```

Note

The preceding statement creates an array using the following syntax:

```java
new dataType[]{value0, value1, ..., valuek};
```

There is no explicit reference variable for the array. Such an array is called an *anonymous array*.

anonymous arrays

Java uses *pass-by-value* to pass arguments to a method. There are important differences between passing the values of variables of primitive data types and passing arrays.

pass-by-value

- For an argument of a primitive type, the argument's value is passed.

- For an argument of an array type, the value of the argument contains a reference to an array; this reference is passed to the method.

Take the following code, for example:

```java
public class Test {
  public static void main(String[] args) {
    int x = 1; // x represents an int value
    int[] y = new int[10]; // y represents an array of int values

    m(x, y); // Invoke m with arguments x and y
    System.out.println("x is " + x);
    System.out.println("y[0] is " + y[0]);
  }

  public static void m(int number, int[] numbers) {
    number = 1001; // Assign a new value to number
    numbers[0] = 5555; // Assign a new value to numbers[0]
  }
}
```

You will see that after `m` is invoked, `x` remains 1, but `y[0]` is 5555. This is because `y` and `numbers` reference to the same array, although `y` and `numbers` are independent variables, as illustrated in Figure 6.5. When invoking `m(x, y)`, the values of `x` and `y` are passed to `number` and `numbers`. Since `y` contains the reference value to the array, `numbers` now contains the same reference value to the same array.

Note

The JVM stores the array in an area of memory called the *heap*, which is used for dynamic memory allocation where blocks of memory are allocated and freed in an arbitrary order.

heap

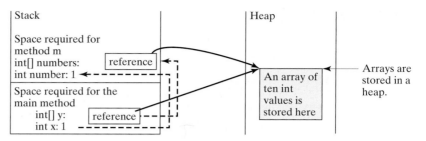

FIGURE 6.5   The primitive type value in x is passed to `number`, and the reference value in y is passed to `numbers`.

6.4.1   Example: Passing Array Arguments

Listing 6.3 gives another example that shows the difference between passing a primitive data type value and an array reference variable to a method.

The example contains two methods for swapping elements in an array. The first method, named `swap`, fails to swap two `int` arguments. The second method, named `swapFirst-TwoInArray`, successfully swaps the first two elements in the array argument. Figure 6.6 shows a sample run of the program.

LISTING 6.3   `TestPassArray.java`

false swap

swap array elements

```
 1  public class TestPassArray {
 2    /** Main method */
 3    public static void main(String[] args) {
 4      int[] a = {1, 2};
 5
 6      // Swap elements using the swap method
 7      System.out.println("Before invoking swap");
 8      System.out.println("array is {" + a[0] + ", " + a[1] + "}");
 9      swap(a[0], a[1]);
10      System.out.println("After invoking swap");
11      System.out.println("array is {" + a[0] + ", " + a[1] + "}");
12
13      // Swap elements using the swapFirstTwoInArray method
14      System.out.println("Before invoking swapFirstTwoInArray");
15      System.out.println("array is {" + a[0] + ", " + a[1] + "}");
16      swapFirstTwoInArray(a);
17      System.out.println("After invoking swapFirstTwoInArray");
18      System.out.println("array is {" + a[0] + ", " + a[1] + "}");
19    }
20
21    /** Swap two variables */
22    public static void swap(int n1, int n2) {
23      int temp = n1;
24      n1 = n2;
25      n2 = temp;
26    }
27
28    /** Swap the first two elements in the array */
29    public static void swapFirstTwoInArray(int[] array) {
30      int temp = array[0];
```

```
31      array[0] = array[1];
32      array[1] = temp;
33    }
34  }
```

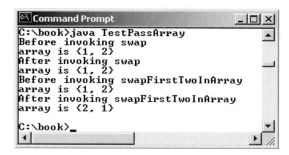

FIGURE 6.6 The program attempts to swap two elements using the `swap` method and the `swapFirstTwoInArray` method.

As shown in Figure 6.6, the two elements are not swapped using the `swap` method. However, they are swapped using the `swapFirstTwoInArray` method. Since the parameters in the `swap` method are primitive type, the values of `a[0]` and `a[1]` are passed to `n1` and `n2` inside the method when invoking `swap(a[0], a[1])`. The memory locations for `n1` and `n2` are independent of the ones for `a[0]` and `a[1]`. The contents of the array are not affected by this call. This is pictured in Figure 6.7.

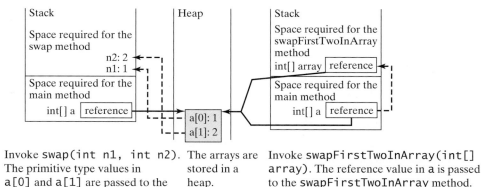

Invoke `swap(int n1, int n2)`. The primitive type values in `a[0]` and `a[1]` are passed to the `swap` method.

The arrays are stored in a heap.

Invoke `swapFirstTwoInArray(int[] array)`. The reference value in `a` is passed to the `swapFirstTwoInArray` method.

FIGURE 6.7 When passing an array to a method, the reference of the array is passed to the method.

The parameter in the `swapFirstTwoInArray` method is an array. As shown in Figure 6.7, the reference of the array is passed to the method. Thus the variables `a` (outside the method) and `array` (inside the method) both refer to the same array in the same memory location. Therefore, swapping `array[0]` with `array[1]` inside the method `swapFirstTwoInArray` is the same as swapping `a[0]` with `a[1]` outside of the method.

6.5 Returning an Array from a Method

You can pass arrays when invoking a method. A method may also return an array. For example, the method shown below returns an array that is the reversal of another array:

```
 1 public static int[] reverse(int[] list) {
 2   int[] result = new int[list.length];
 3
 4   for (int i = 0, j = result.length - 1;
 5        i < list.length; i++, j--) {
 6     result[j] = list[i];
 7   }
 8
 9   return result;
10 }
```

return array

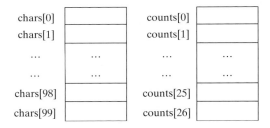

Line 2 creates a new array `result`. Lines 4–7 copies elements from array `list` to array `result`. Line 9 returns the array. For example, the following statement returns a new array `list2` with elements 6, 5, 4, 3, 2, 1:

```
int[] list1 = {1, 2, 3, 4, 5, 6};
int[] list2 = reverse(list1);
```

6.5.1 Example: Counting the Occurrences of Each Letter

Listing 6.4 presents a program to count the occurrences of each letter in an array of characters. The program does the following:

1. Generate one hundred lowercase letters randomly and assign them to an array of characters, as shown in Figure 6.8. You can obtain a random letter by using the `getRandomLowerCaseLetter()` method in the `RandomCharacter` class in Listing 5.6.

chars[0]		counts[0]	
chars[1]		counts[1]	
...	...	...	...
...	...	...	...
chars[98]		counts[25]	
chars[99]		counts[26]	

FIGURE 6.8 The `chars` array stores 100 characters, and the `counts` array stores 26 counts, each of which counts the occurrences of a letter.

2. Count the occurrences of each letter in the array. To count the occurrences of each letter in the array, create an array, say `counts`, of twenty-six `int` values, each of which counts the occurrences of a letter, as shown in Figure 6.8. That is, `counts[0]` counts the number of `a`'s, `counts[1]` counts the number of `b`'s, and so on. Figure 6.9 shows a sample run of the program.

LISTING 6.4 CountLettersInArray.java

```
1 public class CountLettersInArray {
2   /** Main method */
3   public static void main(String args[]) {
4     // Declare and create an array
5     char[] chars = createArray();
6
7     // Display the array
8     System.out.println("The lowercase letters are:");
9     displayArray(chars);
```

create array

pass array

```
10
11     // Count the occurrences of each letter
12     int[] counts = countLetters(chars);                                          return array
13
14     // Display counts
15     System.out.println();
16     System.out.println("The occurrences of each letter are:");
17      displayCounts(counts);                                                       pass array
18   }
19
20   /** Create an array of characters */
21   public static char[] createArray() {
22     // Declare an array of characters and create it
23     char[] chars = new char[100];
24
25     // Create lowercase letters randomly and assign
26     // them to the array
27     for (int i = 0; i < chars.length; i++)
28       chars[i] = RandomCharacter.getRandomLowerCaseLetter();
29
30     // Return the array
31     return chars;
32   }
33
34   /** Display the array of characters */
35   public static void displayArray(char[] chars) {
36     // Display the characters in the array 20 on each line
37     for (int i = 0; i < chars.length; i++) {
38       if ((i + 1) % 20 == 0)
39         System.out.println(chars[i] + " ");
40       else
41         System.out.print(chars[i] + " ");
42     }
43   }
44
45   /** Count the occurrences of each letter */
46   public static int[] countLetters(char[] chars) {
47     // Declare and create an array of 26 int
48     int[] counts = new int[26];
49
50     // For each lowercase letter in the array, count it
51     for (int i = 0; i < chars.length; i++)
52       counts[chars[i] - 'a']++;                                                   count
53
54     return counts;
55   }
56
57   /** Display counts */
58   public static void displayCounts(int[] counts) {
59     for (int i = 0; i < counts.length; i++) {
60       if ((i + 1) % 10 == 0)
61         System.out.println(counts[i] + " " + (char)(i + 'a'));
62       else
63         System.out.print(counts[i] + " " + (char)(i + 'a') + " ");
64     }
65   }
66 }
```

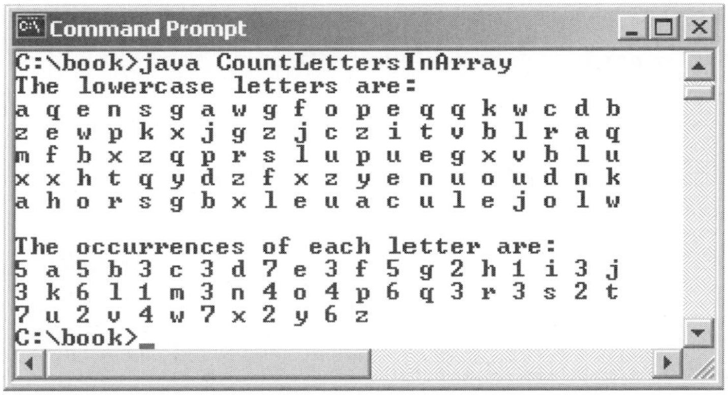

Figure 6.9 The program generates one hundred lowercase letters randomly and counts the occurrences of each letter.

The `createArray` method (lines 21–32) generates an array of one hundred random lower-case letters. Line 5 invokes the method and assigns the array to `chars`. What would be wrong if you rewrote the code as follows?

```java
char[] chars = new char[100];
chars = createArray();
```

You would be creating two arrays. The first line would create an array by using `new char[100]`. The second line would create an array by invoking `createArray()` and assign the reference of the array to `chars`. The array created in the first line would be garbage because it is no longer referenced. Java automatically collects garbage behind the scenes. Your program would compile and run correctly, but it would create an array unnecessarily.

Invoking `getRandomLowerCaseLetter()` (line 28) returns a random lowercase letter. This method is defined in the `RandomCharacter` class in Listing 5.6.

The `countLetters` method (lines 46–55) returns an array of twenty-six `int` values, each of which stores the number of occurrences of a letter. The method processes each letter in the array and increases its count by one. A brute-force approach to count the occurrences of each letter might be as follows:

```java
for (int i = 0; i < chars.length; i++)
  if (counts[chars[i] == 'a')
    count[0]++;
  else if (counts[chars[i] == 'b')
    count[1]++;
  ...
```

But a better solution is given in lines 51–52.

```java
for (int i = 0; i < chars.length; i++)
  counts[chars[i] - 'a']++;
```

If the letter (`chars[i]`) is `'a'`, the corresponding count is `counts['a' - 'a']` (i.e., `counts[0]`). If the letter is `'b'`, the corresponding count is `counts['b' - 'a']` (i.e., `counts[1]`), since the Unicode of `'b'` is one more than that of `'a'`. If the letter is `'z'`, the corresponding count is `counts['z' - 'a']` (i.e., `counts[25]`), since the Unicode of `'z'` is `25` more than that of `'a'`.

Figure 6.10 shows the call stack and heap *during* and *after* executing `createArray`. See Review Question 6.14 to show the call stack and heap for other methods in the program.

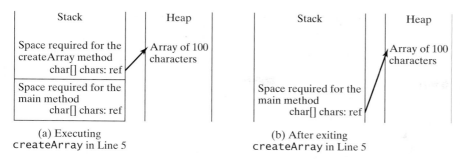

FIGURE 6.10 (a) An array of one hundred characters is created when executing `createArray`. (b) This array is returned and assigned to the variable `chars` in the `main` method.

6.6 (Optional) Variable-Length Argument Lists

JDK 1.5 enables you to pass a variable number of arguments of the same type to a method. The parameter in the method is declared as follows:

```
typeName... parameterName
```

In the method declaration, you specify the type followed by an ellipsis (. . .) Only one variable-length parameter may be specified in a method, and this parameter must be the last parameter. Any regular parameters must precede it.

Java treats a variable-length parameter as an array. You can pass an array or a variable number of arguments to a variable-length parameter. When invoking a method with a variable number of arguments, Java creates an array and passes the arguments to it. Listing 6.5 contains a method that prints the maximum value in a list of an unspecified number of values.

LISTING 6.5 `VarargsDemo.java`

```java
1  public class VarargsDemo {
2    public static void main(String args[]) {
3      printMax(34, 3, 3, 2, 56.5);
4      printMax(new double[]{1, 2, 3});
5    }
6
7    public static void printMax( double... numbers) {
8      if (numbers.length == 0) {
9        System.out.println("No argument passed");
10       return;
11     }
12
13     double result = numbers[0];
14
15     for (int i = 1; i < numbers.length; i++)
16       if (numbers[i] > result)
17         result = numbers[i];
18
19     System.out.println("The max value is " + result);
20   }
21 }
```

pass variable-length **arg** list

pass an array **arg**

a variable-length **arg** parameter

Line 3 invokes the `printMax` method with a variable-length argument list passed to the array `numbers`. If no arguments are passed, the length of the array is 0 (line 7).

Line 4 invokes the `printMax` method with an array.

linear search
binary search

6.7 Searching Arrays

Searching is the process of looking for a specific element in an array; for example, discovering whether a certain score is included in a list of scores. Searching is a common task in computer programming. There are many algorithms and data structures devoted to searching. In this section, two commonly used approaches are discussed, *linear search* and *binary search*.

6.7.1 The Linear Search Approach

The linear search approach compares the key element **key** sequentially with each element in the array. The method continues to do so until the key matches an element in the array or the array is exhausted without a match being found. If a match is made, the linear search returns the index of the element in the array that matches the key. If no match is found, the search returns –1. The **linearSearch** method in Listing 6.6 gives the solution.

LISTING 6.6 LinearSearch.java

```
 1 public class LinearSearch {
 2   /** The method for finding a key in the list */
 3   public static int linearSearch(int[] list, int key) {
 4     for (int i = 0; i < list.length; i++) {
 5       if (key == list[i])
 6         return i;
 7     }
 8
 9     return -1;
10   }
11 }
```

```
            [0] [1] [2] ...
list   [ | | |         | | ]

key  Compare key with list[i] for i = 0, 1, ...
```

Please trace the method using the following statements:

```
int[] list = {1, 4, 4, 2, 5, -3, 6, 2};
int i = linearSearch(list, 4);   // returns 1
int j = linearSearch(list, -4);  // returns -1
int k = linearSearch(list, -3);  // returns 5
```

The linear search method compares the key with each element in the array. The elements in the array can be in any order. On average, the algorithm will have to compare half of the elements in an array before finding the key if it exists. Since the execution time of a linear search increases linearly as the number of array elements increases, linear search is inefficient for a large array.

6.7.2 The Binary Search Approach

Binary search is the other common search approach for a list of values. For binary search to work, the elements in the array must already be ordered. Without loss of generality, assume that the array is in ascending order. The binary search first compares the key with the element in the middle of the array. Consider the following three cases:

- If the key is less than the middle element, you only need to continue to search for the key in the first half of the array.

- If the key is equal to the middle element, the search ends with a match.

- If the key is greater than the middle element, you only need to continue to search for the key in the second half of the array.

Clearly, the binary search method eliminates half of the array after each comparison. Suppose that the array has *n* elements. For convenience, let **n** be a power of 2. After the first comparison, there are **n/2** elements left for further search; after the second comparison, there are **(n/2)/2** elements left for further search. After the kth comparison, there are $n/2^k$ elements left for further search. When $k = \log_2 n$, only one element is left in the array, and you only need one more comparison. Therefore, in the worst case, you need $\log_2 n + 1$ comparisons to find an element in the sorted array when using the binary search approach. For a list of **1024**

(2^{10}) elements, binary search requires only eleven comparisons in the worst case, whereas a linear search would take **1024** comparisons in the worst case.

The portion of the array being searched shrinks by half after each comparison. Let `low` and `high` denote, respectively, the first index and last index of the array that is currently being searched. Initially, `low` is **0** and `high` is `list.length-1`. Let `mid` denote the index of the middle element. So `mid` is `(low + high)/2`. Figure 6.11 shows how to find key **11** in the list {2, 4, 7, 10, 11, 45, 50, 59, 60, 66, 69, 70, 79} using binary search.

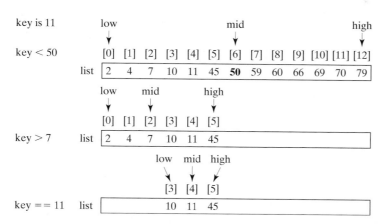

FIGURE 6.11   Binary search eliminates half of the list from further consideration after each comparison.

The binary search returns the index of the search key if it is contained in the list. Otherwise, it returns $-(\text{insertion point} + 1)$. The insertion point is the point at which the key would be inserted into the list. For example, the insertion point for key **5** is **2**, so the binary search returns -3; the insertion point for key **51** is **7**, so the binary search returns -8.

You now know how the binary approach works. The next task is to implement it in Java, as shown in Listing 6.7.

LISTING 6.7   BinarySearch.java

```
1 public class BinarySearch {
2    /** Use binary search to find the key in the list */
3    public static int binarySearch(int[] list, int key) {
4       int low = 0;
5       int high = list.length - 1;
6
7       while (high >= low) {
8          int mid = (low + high) / 2;
9          if (key < list[mid])
10            high = mid - 1;
11         else if (key == list[mid])
12            return mid;
13         else
14            low = mid + 1;
15      }
16
17      return -low - 1;
18   }
19 }
```

You start by comparing the key with the middle element in the list whose low index is **0** and high index is `list.length-1`. If `key < list[mid]`, set the high index to `mid-1`; if key == list[mid], a match is found and return mid; if key > list[mid], set the low index to mid+1. Continue the search until low > high or a match is found. If low > high, return -1 - low, where low is the insertion point.

What happens if (high >= low) in line 7 is replaced by (high > low)? The search would miss a possible matching element. Consider a list with just one element. The search would miss the element.

Does the method still work if there are duplicate elements in the list? Yes, as long as the elements are sorted in increasing order in the list. The method returns the index of one of the matching elements if the element is in the list.

Please trace the program using the following statements:

```
int[] list = {2, 4, 7, 10, 11, 45, 50, 59, 60, 66, 69, 70, 79};
int i = binarySearch(list, 2);   // returns 0
int j = binarySearch(list, 11);  // returns 4
int k = binarySearch(list, 12);  // returns -6
```

 Note

Linear search is useful for finding an element in a small array or an unsorted array, but it is inefficient for large arrays. Binary search is more efficient, but requires that the array be pre-sorted.

6.8 Sorting Arrays

Sorting, like searching, is a common task in computer programming. It would be used, for instance, if you wanted to display the grades from Listing 6.2 in alphabetical order. Many different algorithms have been developed for sorting. This section introduces two simple, intuitive sorting algorithms: selection sort and insertion sort.

6.8.1 Selection Sort

Suppose that you want to sort a list in ascending order. Selection sort finds the largest number in the list and places it last. It then finds the largest number remaining and places it next to last, and so on until the list contains only a single number. Figure 6.12 shows how to sort a list {2, 9, 5, 4, 8, 1, 6} using selection sort.

You know how the selection sort approach works. The task now is to implement it in Java. Beginners find it difficult to develop a complete solution on the first attempt. Start by writing the code for the first iteration to find the largest element in the list and swap it with the last element, and then observe what would be different for the second iteration, the third, and so on. The insight this gives will enable you to write a loop that generalizes all the iterations.

The solution can be described as follows:

```
for (int i = list.length - 1; i >= 1; i--) {
  select the largest element in list[0..i];
  swap the largest with list[i], if necessary;
  // list[i] is in its correct position
  // The next iteration apply on list[0..i-1]
}
```

Listing 6.8 implements the solution.

LISTING 6.8 SelectionSort.java

```
1 public class SelectionSort {
2   /** The method for sorting the numbers */
3   public static void selectionSort(double[] list) {
4     for (int i = list.length - 1; i >= 1; i--) {
5       // Find the maximum in the list[0..i]
6       double currentMax = list[0];
7       int currentMaxIndex = 0;
```

```
8
9       for (int j = 1; j <= i; j++) {
10        if (currentMax < list[j]) {
11          currentMax = list[j];
12          currentMaxIndex = j;
13        }
14      }
15
16      // Swap list[i] with list[currentMaxIndex] if necessary;
17      if (currentMaxIndex != i) {
18        list[currentMaxIndex] = list[i];
19        list[i] = currentMax;
20      }
21    }
22  }
23 }
```

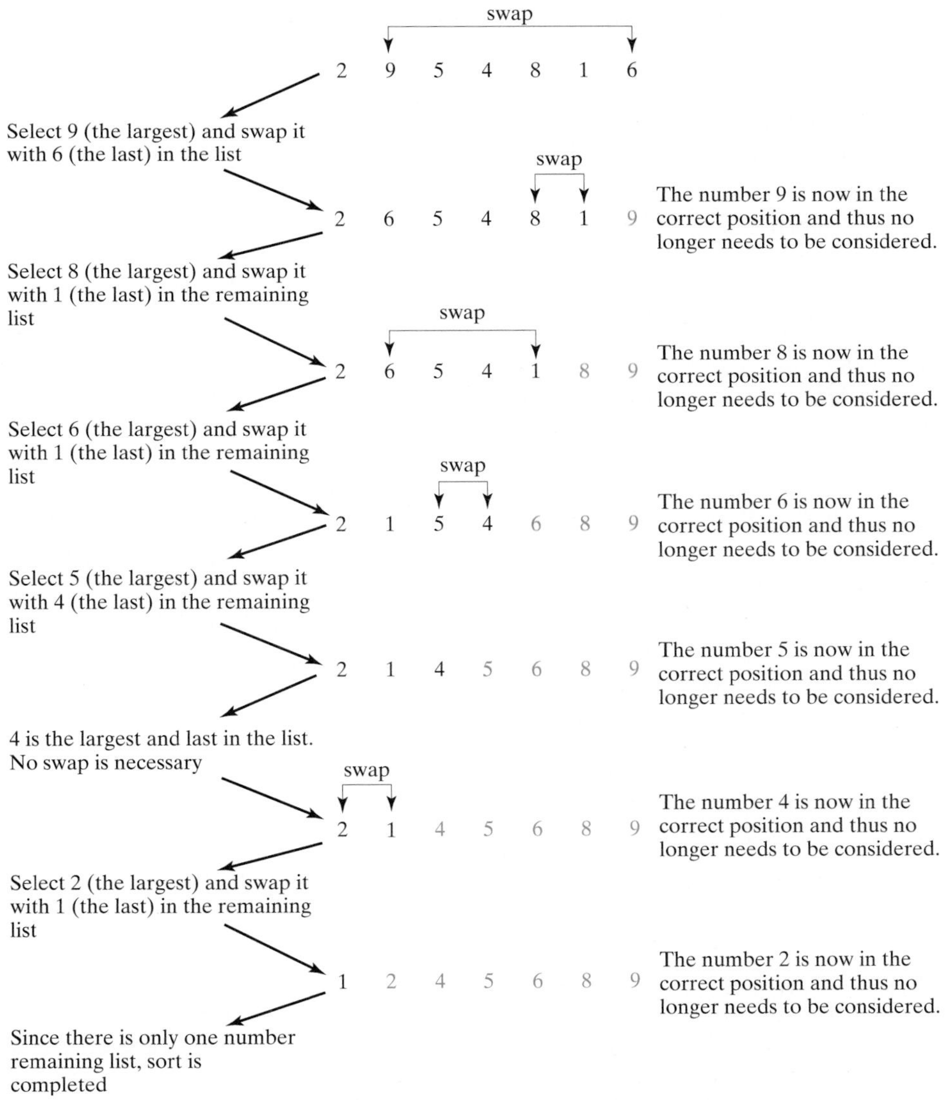

FIGURE 6.12 Selection sort repeatedly selects the largest number and swaps it with the last number in the list.

The `selectionSort(double[] list)` method sorts any array of double elements. The method is implemented with a nested **for** loop. The outer loop (with the loop control variable i) (line 4) is iterated in order to find the largest element in the list, which ranges from `list[0]` to `list[i]`, and exchange it with the current last element, `list[i]`.

The variable i is initially `list.length-1`. After each iteration of the outer loop, `list[i]` is in the right place. Eventually, all the elements are put in the right place; therefore, the whole list is sorted.

Please trace the method with the following statements:

```
selectionSort(new double[]{2, 1});
selectionSort(new double[]{2, 3, 1});
selectionSort(new double[]{1, 2, 1});
```

6.8.2 (Optional) Insertion Sort

Suppose that you want to sort a list in ascending order. The insertion-sort algorithm sorts a list of values by repeatedly inserting a new element into a sorted sublist until the whole list is sorted. Figure 6.13 shows how to sort a list {2, 9, 5, 4, 8, 1, 6} using insertion sort.

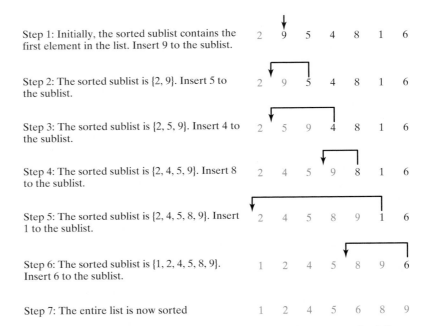

FIGURE 6.13 Insertion sort repeatedly inserts a new element into a sorted sublist.

The algorithm can be described as follows:

```
for (int i = 1; i < list.length; i++) {
    insert list[i] into a sorted sublist list[0..i-1] so that
    list[0..i] is sorted.
}
```

To insert `list[i]` into `list[0..i-1]`, save `list[i]` into a temporary variable, say `currentElement`. Move `list[i-1]` to `list[i]` if `list[i-1] > currentElement`, move `list[i-2]` to `list[i-1]` if `list[i-2] > currentElement`, and so on, until `list[i-k] <= currentElement`. Assign `currentElement` to `list[i-k+1]`. For example, to insert 4 into {2, 5, 9} in Step 3 in Figure 6.13, move `list[2]` (9) to `list[3]` since 9 > 4, move `list[1]` (5) to `list[2]` since 5 > 4. Finally, move `currentElement` (4) to `list[1]`, as shown in Figure 6.14.

The algorithm can be expanded and implemented in Listing 6.9.

LISTING 6.9 InsertionSort.java

```java
 1 public class InsertionSort {
 2   /** The method for sorting the numbers */
 3   public static void insertionSort(double[] list) {
 4     for (int i = 1; i < list.length; i++) {
 5       /** insert list[i] into a sorted sublist list[0..i-1] so that
 6           list[0..i] is sorted. */
 7       double currentElement = list[i];
 8       int k;
 9       for (k = i - 1; k >= 0 && list[k] > currentElement; k--) {
10         list[k + 1] = list[k];
11       }
12
13       // Insert the current element into list[k+1]
14       list[k + 1] = currentElement;
15     }
16   }
17 }
```

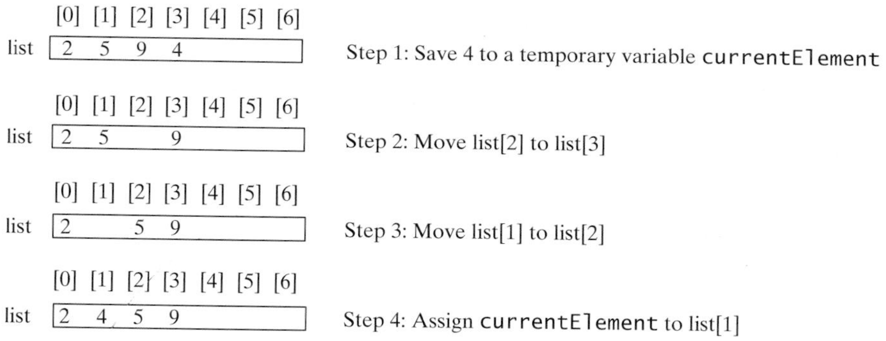

FIGURE 6.14   A new element is inserted into a sorted sublist.

The `insertionSort(double[] list)` method sorts any array of double elements. The method is implemented with a nested `for` loop. The outer loop (with the loop control variable `i`) (line 4) is iterated in order to obtain a sorted sublist, which ranges from `list[0]` to `list[i]`. The inner loop (with the loop control variable `k`) inserts `list[i]` into the sublist from `list[0]` to `list[i-1]`.

Please trace the method with the following statements:

```java
insertionSort(new double[]{2, 1});
insertionSort(new double[]{2, 3, 1});
insertionSort(new double[]{1, 2, 1});
```

6.9 The **Arrays** Class

The `java.util.Arrays` class contains various static methods for sorting and searching arrays, comparing arrays, and filling array elements. These methods are overloaded for all primitive types.

You can use the **sort** method to sort a whole array or a partial array. For example, the following code sorts an array of numbers and an array of characters:

```
double[] numbers = {6.0, 4.4, 1.9, 2.9, 3.4, 3.5};
java.util.Arrays.sort(numbers); // Sort the whole array

char[] chars = {'a', 'A', '4', 'F', 'D', 'P'};
java.util.Arrays.sort(chars, 1, 3); // Sort part of the array
```

Invoking **sort(numbers)** sorts the whole array **numbers**. Invoking **sort(chars, 1, 3)** sorts a partial array from **chars[1]** to **chars[3-1]**.

You can use the **binarySearch** method to search for a key in an array. The array must be pre-sorted in increasing order. If the key is not in the array, the method returns −(*insertion point* + *1*). For example, the following code searches the keys in an array of integers and an array of characters:

```
int[] list = {2, 4, 7, 10, 11, 45, 50, 59, 60, 66, 69, 70, 79};
System.out.println("(1) Index is " +
  java.util.Arrays.binarySearch(list, 11));
System.out.println("(2) Index is " +
  java.util.Arrays.binarySearch(list, 12));

char[] chars = {'a', 'c', 'g', 'x', 'y', 'z'};
System.out.println("(3) Index is " +
  java.util.Arrays.binarySearch(chars, 'a'));
System.out.println("(4) Index is " +
  java.util.Arrays.binarySearch(chars, 't'));
```

The output of the preceding code is

(1) Index is 4

(2) Index is −6

(3) Index is 0

(4) Index is −4

You can use the **equals** method to check whether two arrays are equal. Two arrays are equal if they have the same contents. In the following code, **list1** and **list2** are equal, but **list2** and **list3** are not:

```
int[] list1 = {2, 4, 7, 10};
int[] list2 = {2, 4, 7, 10};
int[] list3 = {4, 2, 7, 10};
System.out.println(java.util.Arrays.equals(list1, list2) ); // true
System.out.println(java.util.Arrays.equals(list2, list3) ); // false
```

You can use the **fill** method to fill in the whole array or part of the array. For example, the following code fills **list1** with 5 and fills 8 into elements **list2[1]** and **list2[3-1]**:

```
int[] list1 = {2, 4, 7, 10};
int[] list2 = {2, 4, 7, 10};
java.util.Arrays.fill(list1, 5); // fill 5 to the whole array
java.util.Arrays.fill(list2, 1, 3, 8); // fill 8 to a partial array
```

6.10 Two-Dimensional Arrays

Thus far, you have used one-dimensional arrays to model linear collections of elements. You can use a two-dimensional array to represent a matrix or a table.

6.10.1 Declaring Variables of Two-Dimensional Arrays and Creating Two-Dimensional Arrays

Here is the syntax for declaring a two-dimensional array:

```
dataType[][] arrayRefVar;
```

or

```
dataType arrayRefVar[][]; // This style is allowed, but not preferred
```

As an example, here is how you would declare a two-dimensional array variable matrix of int values:

```
int[][] matrix;
```

or

```
int matrix[][]; // This style is allowed, but not preferred
```

You can create a two-dimensional array of 5 by 5 int values and assign it to matrix using this syntax:

```
matrix = new int[5][5];
```

Two subscripts are used in a two-dimensional array, one for the row, and the other for the column. As in a one-dimensional array, the index for each subscript is of the int type and starts from 0, as shown in Figure 6.15(a).

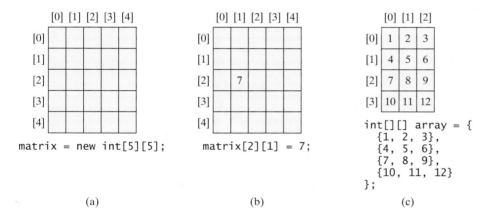

FIGURE 6.15 The index of each subscript of a two-dimensional array is an int value starting from 0.

To assign the value 7 to a specific element at row 2 and column 1, as shown in Figure 6.15(b), you can use the following:

```
matrix[2][1] = 7;
```

Caution

It is a common mistake to use matrix[2, 1] to access the element at row 2 and column 1. In Java, each subscript must be enclosed in a pair of square brackets.

You can also use an array initializer to declare, create, and initialize a two-dimensional array. For example, the following code in (a) creates an array with the specified initial values, as shown in Figure 6.15(c). This is equivalent to the code in (b).

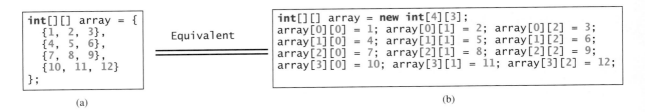

(a)   (b)

6.10.2. Obtaining the Lengths of Two-Dimensional Arrays

A two-dimensional array is actually an array in which each element is a one-dimensional array. The length of an array `x` is the number of elements in the array, which can be obtained using `x.length`. `x[0]`, `x[1]`, ..., and `x[x.length-1]` are arrays. Their lengths can be obtained using `x[0].length`, `x[1].length`, ..., and `x[x.length-1].length`.

For example, suppose `x = new int[3][4]`, `x[0]`, `x[1]`, and `x[2]` are one-dimensional arrays and each contains four elements, as shown in Figure 6.16. `x.length` is 3, and `x[0].length`, `x[1].length`, and `x[2].length` are 4.

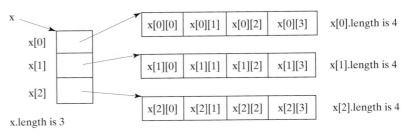

Figure 6.16 A two-dimensional array is a one-dimensional array in which each element is another one-dimensional array.

6.10.3 Ragged Arrays

ragged array

Each row in a two-dimensional array is itself an array. Thus the rows can have different lengths. An array of this kind is known as a *ragged array*. Here is an example of creating a ragged array:

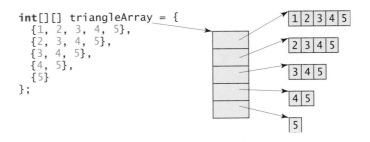

As can be seen, `triangleArray[0].length` is 5, `triangleArray[1].length` is 4, `triangleArray[2].length` is 3, `triangleArray[3].length` is 2, and `triangleArray[4].length` is 1.

If you don't know the values in a ragged array in advance, but you know the sizes, say the same as before, you can create a ragged array using the syntax that follows:

```java
int[][] triangleArray = new int[5][];
triangleArray[0] = new int[5];
triangleArray[1] = new int[4];
triangleArray[2] = new int[3];
triangleArray[3] = new int[2];
triangleArray[4] = new int[1];
```

You can now assign values to the array. For example,

```java
triangleArray[0][3] = 50;
triangleArray[4][0] = 45;
```

Note

The syntax `new int[5][]` for creating an array requires the first index to be specified. The syntax `new int[][]` would be wrong.

6.10.4. Processing Two-Dimensional Arrays

Suppose an array `matrix` is declared as follows:

```java
int[][] matrix = new int[10][10];
```

Here are some examples of processing two-dimensional arrays:

1. (*Initializing arrays with random values*) The following loop initializes the array with random values between 0 and 99:

```java
for (int row = 0; row < matrix.length; row++) {
  for (int column = 0; column < matrix[row].length; column++) {
    matrix[row][column] = (int)(Math.random() * 100);
  }
}
```

2. (*Printing arrays*) To print a two-dimensional array, you have to print each element in the array using a loop like the following:

```java
for (int row = 0; row < matrix.length; row++) {
  for (int column = 0; column < matrix[row].length; column++) {
    System.out.print(matrix[row][column] + " ");
  }

  System.out.println();
}
```

3. (*Summing all elements*) Use a variable named `total` to store the sum. Initially `total` is 0. Add each element in the array to `total` using a loop like this:

```java
int total = 0;
for (int row = 0; row < matrix.length; row++) {
  for (int column = 0; column < matrix[row].length; column++) {
    total += matrix[row][column];
  }
}
```

4. (*Summing elements by column*) For each column, use a variable named `total` to store its sum. Add each element in the column to `total` using a loop like this:

```java
for (int column = 0; column < matrix[0].length; column++) {
  int total = 0;
  for (int row = 0; row < matrix.length; row++)
```

```
        total += matrix[row][column];
      System.out.println("Sum for column " + column + " is " + total);
   }
```

5. (*Which row has the largest sum?*) Use variables `maxRow` and `indexOfMaxRow` to track the largest sum and index of the row. For each row, compute its sum, and update `maxRow` and `indexOfMaxRow` if the new sum is greater.

```
int maxRow = 0;
int indexOfMaxRow = 0;

// Get sum of the first row in maxRow
for (int column = 0; column < matrix[0].length; column++) {
  maxRow += matrix[0][column];
}

for (int row = 1; row < matrix.length; row++) {
  int totalOfThisRow = 0;
  for (int column = 0; column < matrix[row].length; column++) {
    totalOfThisRow += matrix[row][column];
    if (totalOfThisRow > maxRow) {
      maxRow = totalOfThisRow;
      indexOfMaxRow = row;
    }
  }
}

System.out.println("Row " + indexOfMaxRow
    + " has the maximum sum" + " of " + maxRow);
```

6.10.5 Example: Grading a Multiple-Choice Test

This example presents a program that grades multiple-choice tests. Suppose there are eight students and ten questions, and the answers are stored in a two-dimensional array. Each row records a student's answers to the questions. For example, the array shown below stores the test.

```
            Students' Answers to the Questions:
            0 1 2 3 4 5 6 7 8 9

Student 0   A B A C C D E E A D
Student 1   D B A B C A E E A D
Student 2   E D D A C B E E A D
Student 3   C B A E D C E E A D
Student 4   A B D C C D E E A D
Student 5   B B E C C D E E A D
Student 6   B B A C C D E E A D
Student 7   E B E C C D E E A D
```

The key is stored in a one-dimensional array:

```
            Key to the Questions:
            0 1 2 3 4 5 6 7 8 9

     Key    D B D C C D A E A D
```

Your program grades the test and displays the result, as shown in Figure 6.17.

The program compares each student's answers with the key, counts the number of correct answers, and displays it. Listing 6.10 gives the program.

LISTING 6.10 GradeExam.java

```java
 1 public class GradeExam {
 2   /** Main method */
 3   public static void main(String args[]) {
 4     // Students' answers to the questions
 5     char[][] answers = {
 6       {'A', 'B', 'A', 'C', 'C', 'D', 'E', 'E', 'A', 'D'},
 7       {'D', 'B', 'A', 'B', 'C', 'A', 'E', 'E', 'A', 'D'},
 8       {'E', 'D', 'D', 'A', 'C', 'B', 'E', 'E', 'A', 'D'},
 9       {'C', 'B', 'A', 'E', 'D', 'C', 'E', 'E', 'A', 'D'},
10       {'A', 'B', 'D', 'C', 'C', 'D', 'E', 'E', 'A', 'D'},
11       {'B', 'B', 'E', 'C', 'C', 'D', 'E', 'E', 'A', 'D'},
12       {'B', 'B', 'A', 'C', 'C', 'D', 'E', 'E', 'A', 'D'},
13       {'E', 'B', 'E', 'C', 'C', 'D', 'E', 'E', 'A', 'D'}};
14
15     // Key to the questions
16     char[] keys = {'D', 'B', 'D', 'C', 'C', 'D', 'A', 'E', 'A', 'D'};
17
18     // Grade all answers
19     for (int i = 0; i < answers.length ; i++) {
20       // Grade one student
21       int correctCount = 0;
22       for (int j = 0; j < answers[i].length ; j++) {
23         if (answers[i][j] == keys[j] )
24           correctCount++;
25       }
26
27       System.out.println("Student " + i + "'s correct count is " +
28         correctCount);
29     }
30   }
31 }
```

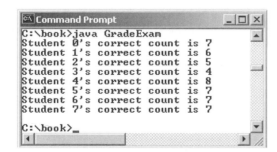

FIGURE 6.17   The program grades students' answers to the multiple-choice questions.

The statement in lines 5–13 declares, creates, and initializes a two-dimensional array of characters and assigns the reference to **answers** of the **char[][]** type.

The statement in line 16 declares, creates, and initializes an array of **char** values and assigns the reference to **keys** of the **char[][]** type.

Each row in the array **answers** stores a student's answer, which is graded by comparing it with the key in the array **keys**. The result is displayed immediately after a student's answer is graded.

✿ 6.10.6 (Optional) Example: Computing Taxes

Listing 5.5, ComputeTaxWithMethod.java, simplified Listing 3.4, ComputeTaxWithSelection-Statement.java. Listing 5.5 can be further improved using arrays. For each filing status, there are six tax rates. Each rate is applied to a certain amount of taxable income. For example, from the taxable income of $400,000 for a single filer, $6,000 is taxed at 10%, $(27950 - 6000)$ at 15%, $(67700 - 27950)$ at 27%, $(141250 - 67700)$ at 30%, $(307050 - 141250)$ at 35%, and $(400000 - 307050)$ at 38.6%. The six rates are the same for all filing statuses, which can be represented in the following array:

```java
double[] rates = {0.10, 0.15, 0.27, 0.30, 0.35, 0.386};
```

The brackets for each rate for all the filing statuses can be represented in a two-dimensional array as follows:

```java
int[][] brackets = {
  {6000, 27950, 67700, 141250, 307050}, // Single filer
  {12000, 46700, 112850, 171950, 307050}, // Married jointly
  {6000, 23350, 56425, 85975, 153525}, // Married separately
  {10000, 37450, 96700, 156600, 307050} // Head of household
};
```

Suppose the taxable income is $400,000 for single filers, the tax can be computed as follows:

```java
brackets[0][0] * rates[0] +
(brackets[0][1] - brackets[0][0]) * rates[1] +
(brackets[0][2] - brackets[0][1]) * rates[2] +
(brackets[0][3] - brackets[0][2]) * rates[3] +
(brackets[0][4] - brackets[0][3]) * rates[4] +
(400000 - brackets[0][4]) * rates[5]
```

Listing 6.11 gives the solution to the program.

LISTING 6.11 ComputeTax.java

```java
 1 import javax.swing.JOptionPane;
 2
 3 public class ComputeTax {
 4   public static void main(String[] args) {
 5     // Prompt the user to enter filing status
 6     String statusString = JOptionPane.showInputDialog(
 7       "Enter the filing status:\n" +
 8       "(0-single filer, 1-married jointly,\n" +
 9       "2-married separately, 3-head of household)");
10     int status = Integer.parseInt(statusString);
11
12     // Prompt the user to enter taxable income
13     String incomeString = JOptionPane.showInputDialog(
14       "Enter the taxable income:");
15     double income = Double.parseDouble(incomeString);
16
17     // Compute and display the result
18     JOptionPane.showMessageDialog(null, "Tax is " +
19       (int)(computeTax(status, income) * 100) / 100.0);
20   }
21
22   public static double computeTax(int status, double income) {
23     double[] rates = {0.10, 0.15, 0.27, 0.30, 0.35, 0.386};
24
```

```
25      int[][] brackets = {
26        {6000, 27950, 67700, 141250, 307050}, // Single filer
27        {12000, 46700, 112850, 171950, 307050}, // Married jointly
28        {6000, 23350, 56425, 85975, 153525}, // Married separately
29        {10000, 37450, 96700, 156600, 307050} // Head of household
30      };
31
32      double tax = 0; // Tax to be computed
33
34      // Compute tax in the first bracket
35      if (income <= brackets[status][0])
36        return tax = income * rates[0]; //Done
37      else
38        tax = brackets[status][0] * rates[0];
39
40      // Compute tax in the 2nd, 3rd, 4th, and 5th brackets, if needed
41      for (int i = 1; i < brackets[0].length; i++) {
42        if (income > brackets[status][i])
43          tax += (brackets[status][i] - brackets[status][i - 1]) *
44            rates[i];
45        else {
46          tax += (income - brackets[status][i - 1]) * rates[i];
47          return tax; // Done
48        }
49      }
50
51      // Compute tax in the last (i.e., 6th) bracket
52      return  tax += (income - brackets[status][4]) * rates[5];
53    }
54 }
```

The `computeTax` method computes the tax for the taxable income of a given filing status. The tax for the first bracket (`0` to `brackets[status][0]`) is computed in lines 35–38. The taxes for the second, third, fourth, and fifth brackets are computed in the loop in lines 41–49. The tax for the last bracket is computed in line 52.

6.11 (Optional) Multidimensional Arrays

In the preceding section, you used a two-dimensional array to represent a matrix or a table. Occasionally, you will need to represent *n*-dimensional data structures. In Java, you can create *n*-dimensional arrays for any integer *n*.

The way to declare two-dimensional array variables and create two-dimensional arrays can be generalized to declare *n*-dimensional array variables and create *n*-dimensional arrays for *n* >= 3. For example, the following syntax declares a three-dimensional array variable `scores`, creates an array, and assigns its reference to `scores`:

```
double[][][] scores = new double[10][5][2];
```

A multidimensional array is actually an array in which each element is another array. A three-dimensional array consists of an array of two-dimensional arrays, each of which is an array of one-dimensional arrays. For example, suppose `x = new int[2][2][6]`, `x[0]`, and `x[1]` are two-dimensional arrays. `X[0][0]`, `x[0][1]`, `x[1][0]`, and `x[1][1]` are one-dimensional arrays and each contains five elements. `x.length` is `2`, `x[0].length` and `x[1].length` are `2`, and `X[0][0].length`, `x[0][1].length`, `x[1][0].length`, and `x[1][1].length` are `6`.

6.11.1 Example: Computing Student Scores

Listing 6.12 gives a program that calculates the total score for the students in a class. Suppose the scores are stored in a three-dimensional array named `scores`. The first index in `scores` refers to a student, the second refers to an exam, and the third refers to a part of the exam. Suppose there are seven students, five exams, and each exam has two parts: a multiple-choice part and a programming part. `scores[i][j][0]` represents the score on the multiple-choice part for the `i`'s student on the `j`'s exam. `scores[i][j][1]` represents the score on the programming part for the `i`'s student on the `j`'s exam. The program processes the `scores` array for all the students. For each student, it adds the two scores from all exams to `totalScore` and displays `totalScore`. Your program displays the total score for each student, as shown in Figure 6.18.

LISTING 6.12 TotalScore.java

```java
 1 public class TotalScore {
 2   /** Main method */
 3   public static void main(String args[]) {
 4     double[][][] scores = {
 5       {{7.5, 20.5}, {9.0, 22.5}, {15, 33.5}, {13, 21.5}, {15, 2.5}},
 6       {{4.5, 21.5}, {9.0, 22.5}, {15, 34.5}, {12, 20.5}, {14, 9.5}},
 7       {{6.5, 30.5}, {9.4, 10.5}, {11, 33.5}, {11, 23.5}, {10, 2.5}},
 8       {{6.5, 23.5}, {9.4, 32.5}, {13, 34.5}, {11, 20.5}, {16, 7.5}},
 9       {{8.5, 26.5}, {9.4, 52.5}, {13, 36.5}, {13, 24.5}, {16, 2.5}},
10       {{9.5, 20.5}, {9.4, 42.5}, {13, 31.5}, {12, 20.5}, {16, 6.5}},
11       {{1.5, 29.5}, {6.4, 22.5}, {14, 30.5}, {10, 30.5}, {16, 6.0}}};
12
13     // Calculate and display total score for each student
14     for (int i = 0; i < scores.length; i++) {
15       double totalScore = 0;
16       for (int j = 0; j < scores[i].length; j++)
17         for (int k = 0; k < scores[i][j].length; k++)
18           totalScore += scores[i][j][k] ;
19
20       System.out.println("Student " + i + "'s score is " +
21         totalScore);
22     }
23   }
24 }
```

`scores[0][3][0]`

`scores[0][3][1]`

`scores[[4][1`

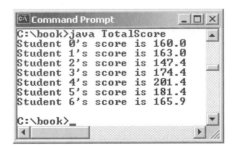

FIGURE 6.18 The program displays the total score for each student.

To understand this example, it is essential to know how data in the three-dimensional array are interpreted. `scores[0]` is a two-dimensional array that stores all the exam scores for the first student. `scores[0][0]` is {7.5, 20.5}, a one-dimensional array, which stores two scores for the two parts of the first student's first exam. `scores[0][0][0]` is 7.5, which is the score for the first part of the first student's first exam. `scores[5]` is a two-dimensional array that stores all the exam scores for the sixth student. `scores[5][4]` is `{16, 6.5}`, a one-dimensional array, which stores two scores for the two parts of the sixth student's fifth exam. `scores[5][4][1]` is 6.5, which is the score for the second part of the sixth student's fifth exam.

The statement in lines 4–11 declares, creates, and initializes a three-dimensional array of `double` values and assigns the reference to `scores` of the `double[][][]` type.

The scores for each student are added in lines 16–18, and the result is displayed in lines 20–21. The `for` loop in line 14 process the scores for all the students.

KEY TERMS

anonymous array 179	indexed variable 174
array 172	insertion sort 188
array initializer 172	linear search 188
binary search 185	multidimensional array 199
garbage collection 177	ragged array 194
index 171	selection sort 188

CHAPTER SUMMARY

- A variable is declared as an array type using the syntax `dataType[] arrayRefVar` or `dataType arrayRefVar[]`. The style `dataType[] arrayRefVar` is preferred, although `dataType arrayRefVar[]` is legal.

- Unlike declarations for primitive data type variables, the declaration of an array variable does not allocate any space in memory for the array. An array variable is not a primitive data type variable. An array variable contains a reference to an array.

- You cannot assign elements to an array unless it has already been created. You can create an array by using the `new` operator with the following syntax: `new dataType [arraySize]`.

- Each element in the array is represented using the syntax `arrayRefVar[index]`. An index must be an integer or an integer expression.

- After an array is created, its size becomes permanent and can be obtained using `arrayRefVar.length`. Since the index of an array always begins with 0, the last index is always `arrayRefVar.length - 1`. An out-of-bounds error will occur if you attempt to reference elements beyond the bounds of an array.

- Programmers often mistakenly reference the first element in an array with index 1, so that the index of the tenth element becomes 10. This is called the *index off-by-one error*.

- Java has a shorthand notation, known as the *array initializer*, which combines declaring an array, creating an array, and initializing in one statement using the syntax: `dataType[] arrayRefVar = {value0, value1, ..., valuek}`.

- When you pass an array argument to a method, you are actually passing the reference of the array; that is, the called method can modify the elements in the caller's original array.

- You can use arrays of arrays to form multidimensional arrays. For example, a two-dimensional array is declared as an array of arrays using the syntax `dataType[][] arrayRefVar` or `dataType arrayRefVar[][]`.

REVIEW QUESTIONS

Section 6.2 Array Basics

6.1 How do you declare and create an array?

6.2 How do you access elements of an array?

6.3 Is memory allocated when an array is declared? When is the memory allocated for an array? What is the printout of the following code?

```
int x = 30;
int[] numbers = new int[x];
x = 60;
System.out.println("x is " + x);
System.out.println("The size of numbers is " + numbers.length);
```

6.4 Indicate true or false for the following statements:
- Every element in an array has the same type.
- The array size is fixed after it is declared.
- The array size is fixed after it is created.
- The elements in an array must be of primitive data type.

6.5 Which of the following statements are valid array declarations?

```
int i = new int(30);
double d[] = new double[30];
char[] r = new char(1..30);
int i[] = (3, 4, 3, 2);
float f[] = {2.3, 4.5, 6.6};
char[] c = new char();
```

6.6 What is the array index type? What is the lowest index?

6.7 What is the representation of the third element in an array named a?

6.8 What happens when your program attempts to access an array element with an invalid index?

6.9 Identify and fix the errors in the following code:

```
1 public class Test {
2   public static void main(String[] args) {
3     double[100] r;
4
5     for (int i = 0; i < r.length(); i++);
6       r(i) = Math.random * 100;
7   }
8 }
```

Section 6.3 Copying Arrays

6.10 Use the arraycopy() method to copy the following array to a target array t:

```
int[] source = {3, 4, 5};
```

6.11 Once an array is created, its size cannot be changed. Does the following code resize the array?

```
int[] myList;
myList = new int[10];
// Some time later you want to assign a new array to myList
myList = new int[20];
```

Sections 6.4–6.5

6.12   When an array is passed to a method, a new array is created and passed to the method. Is this true?

6.13   Show the output of the following two programs:

```java
public class Test {
  public static void main(String[] args) {
    int number = 0;
    int[] numbers = new int[1];

    m(number, numbers);

    System.out.println("number is " + number
      + " and numbers[0] is " + numbers[0]);
  }

  public static void m(int x, int[] y) {
    x = 3;
    y[0] = 3;
  }
}
```

(a)

```java
public class Test {
  public static void main(String[] args) {
    int[] list = {1, 2, 3, 4, 5};
    reverse(list);
    for (int i = 0; i < list.length; i++)
      System.out.print(list[i] + " ");
  }

  public static void reverse(int[] list) {
    int[] newList = new int[list.length];

    for (int i = 0; i < list.length; i++)
      newList[i] = list[list.length - 1 - i];

    list = newList;
  }
}
```

(b)

6.14   Where are the arrays stored during execution? Show the contents of the stack and heap during and after executing `createArray`, `displayArray`, `countLetters`, `displayCounts` in Listing 6.4,

Section 6.6 Variable-Length Argument Lists

6.15   What is wrong in the following method declaration?

```java
public static void print(String... strings, double... numbers)
public static void print(double... numbers, String name)
public static double... print(double d1, double d2)
```

6.16   Can you invoke the `printMax` method in Listing 6.5 using the following statements?

```java
printMax(1, 2, 2, 1, 4);
printMax(new double[]{1, 2, 3});
printMax(new int[]{1, 2, 3});
```

Sections 6.7–6.8

6.17   Use Figure 6.11 as an example to show how to apply the binary search approach to a search for key 10 and key 12 in list {2, 4, 7, 10, 11, 45, 50, 59, 60, 66, 69, 70, 79}.

6.18   Use Figure 6.12 as an example to show how to apply the selection sort approach to sort {3.4, 5, 3, 3.5, 2.2, 1.9, 2}.

6.19   Use Figure 6.13 as an example to show how to apply the insertion sort approach to sort {3.4, 5, 3, 3.5, 2.2, 1.9, 2}.

6.20   How do you modify the `selectionSort` method in Listing 6.8 to sort numbers in decreasing order?

6.21   How do you modify the `insertionSort` method in Listing 6.9 to sort numbers in decreasing order?

Section 6.9 The **Arrays** Class

6.22 What types of array can be sorted using the `java.util.Arrays.sort` method? Does this `sort` method create a new array?

6.23 To apply `java.util.Arrays.binarySearch(array, key)`, should the array be sorted in increasing order, in decreasing order, or either?

6.24 Show the contents of the array after the execution of each line.

```java
int[] list = {2, 4, 7, 10};
java.util.Arrays.fill(list, 7);
java.util.Arrays.fill(list, 1, 3, 8);
System.out.print(java.util.Arrays.equals(list, list));
```

Section 6.10 Two-Dimensional Arrays

6.25 Declare and create a 4 × 5 `int` matrix.

6.26 Can the rows in a two-dimensional array have different lengths?

6.27 What is the output of the following code?

```java
int[][] array = new int[5][6];
int[] x = {1, 2};
array[0] = x;
System.out.println("array[0][1] is " + array[0][1]);
```

6.28 Which of the following statements are valid array declarations?

```java
int[][] r = new int[2];
int[] x = new int[];
int[][] y = new int[3][];
```

PROGRAMMING EXERCISES

Section 6.2 Array Basics

6.1 (*Analyzing input*) Write a program that reads ten numbers, computes their average, and finds out how many numbers are above the average.

6.2 (*Alternative solution to Listing 6.1, TestArray.java*) The solution of Listing 6.1 counts the occurrences of the largest number by comparing *each number* with the largest. So you have to use an array to store all the numbers. Another way to solve the problem is to maintain two variables, `max` and `count`. `max` stores the current max number, and `count` stores its occurrences. Initially, assign the first number to `max` and 1 to `count`. Compare each subsequent number with `max`. If the number is greater than `max`, assign it to `max` and reset `count` to 1. If the number is equal to `max`, increment `count` by 1. Use this approach to rewrite Listing 6.1.

6.3 (*Reversing the numbers entered*) Write a program that reads ten integers and displays them in the reverse of the order in which they were read.

6.4 (*Analyzing scores*) Write a program that reads an unspecified number of scores and determines how many scores are above or equal to the average and how many scores are below the average. Enter a negative number to signify the end of the input. Assume that the maximum number of scores is 100.

6.5** (*Printing distinct numbers*) Write a program that reads in ten numbers and displays distinct numbers (i.e., if a number appears multiple times, it is displayed only once). Hint: Read a number and store it to an array if it is new. If the number is already in the array, discard it. After the input, the array contains the distinct numbers.

6.6* (*Revising Listing 4.11, PrimeNumber.java*) Listing 4.11 determines whether a number n is prime by checking whether 2, 3, 4, 5, 6, ..., n/2 is a divisor. If a divisor is found, n is not prime. A more efficient approach to determine whether n is prime is to check whether any of the prime numbers less than or equal to $\sqrt{n}$ can divide n evenly. If not, n is prime. Rewrite Listing 4.11 to display the first fifty prime numbers using this approach. You need to use an array to store the prime numbers and later use them to check whether they are possible divisors for n.

6.7* (*Counting single digits*) Write a program that generates one hundred random integers between 0 and 9 and displays the count for each number. Hint: Use `(int)(Math.random() * 10)` to generate a random integer between 0 and 9. Use an array of ten integers, say `counts`, to store the counts for the number of 0's, 1's, ..., 9's.

Sections 6.4–6.5

6.8 (*Averaging an array*) Write two overloaded methods that return the average of an array with the following headers:

```
public static int average(int[] array);
public static double average(double[] array);
```

Use {1, 2, 3, 4, 5, 6} and {6.0, 4.4, 1.9, 2.9, 3.4, 3.5} to test the methods.

6.9 (*Finding the smallest element*) Write a method that finds the smallest element in an array of integers. Use {1, 2, 4, 5, 10, 100, 2, –22} to test the method.

6.10 (*Finding the index of the smallest element*) Write a method that returns the index of the smallest element in an array of integers. If there are more than one such elements, return the smallest index. Use {1, 2, 4, 5, 10, 100, 2, –22} to test the method.

6.11* (*Computing deviation*) Exercise 5.21 computes the standard deviation of numbers. This exercise uses a different but equivalent formula to compute the standard deviation of n numbers.

$$mean = \frac{\sum\limits_{i=1}^{n} x_i}{n} = \frac{x_1 + x_2 + \cdots + x_n}{n} \qquad deviation = \sqrt{\frac{\sum\limits_{i=1}^{n} (x_i - mean)^2}{n - 1}}$$

To compute deviation with this formula, you have to store the individual numbers using an array, so that they can be used after the mean is obtained. Use {1, 2, 3, 4, 5, 6, 7, 8, 9, 10} to test the method.

6.12* (*Reversing an array*) The **reverse** method in §6.5 reverses an array by copying it to a new array. Rewrite the method without creating new arrays.

6.13* (*Increasing array size*) Once an array is created, its size is fixed. Occasionally, you need to add more values to an array, but it is full. In such cases, you can create a new, larger array to replace the existing array. Write a method with the following header:

```
public static int[] doubleCapacity(int[] list)
```

The method returns a new array that doubles the size of the parameter `list`.

Section 6.6 Variable-Length Argument Lists

6.14 (*Computing average*) Write a method that returns the average of an unspecified number of numeric arguments.

Sections 6.7–6.9

6.15 (*Finding the sales amount*) Rewrite Listing 4.7, FindSalesAmount.java, using the binary search approach. Since the sales amount is between `1` and `COMMISSION_SOUGHT/0.08`, you can use a binary search to improve Listing 4.7.

6.16 (*Timing execution*) Write a program that randomly generates an array of `100000` integers and a key. Estimate the execution time of invoking the `linearSearch` method in Listing 6.6. Sort the array and estimate the execution time of invoking the `binarySearch` method in Listing 6.7. You can use the following code template to obtain the execution time:

```
long startTime = System.currentTimeMillis();
perform the task;
long endTime = System.currentTimeMillis();
long executionTime = endTime - startTime;
```

6.17* (*Revising selection sort*) In §6.8, you used selection sort to sort an array. The selection sort method repeatedly finds the largest number in the current array and swaps it with the last number in the array. Rewrite this example by finding the smallest number and swapping it with the first number in the array.

6.18** (*Bubble sort*) Write a sort method that uses the bubble-sort algorithm. The bubble-sort algorithm makes several passes through the array. On each pass, successive neighboring pairs are compared. If a pair is in decreasing order, its values are swapped; otherwise, the values remain unchanged. The technique is called a *bubble sort* or *sinking sort* because the smaller values gradually "bubble" their way to the top and the larger values sink to the bottom.

The algorithm can be described as follows:

```
boolean changed = true;
do {
  changed = false;
  for (int j = 0; j < list.length - 1; j++)
    if (list[j] > list[j + 1]) {
      swap list[j] with list[j + 1];
      changed = true;
    }
} while (changed);
```

Clearly, the list is in increasing order when the loop terminates. It is easy to show that the do loop executes at most `list.length` −1 times.

Use {6.0, 4.4, 1.9, 2.9, 3.4, 2.9, 3.5} to test the method.

6.19** (*Sorting students*) Write a program that prompts the user to enter the number of students, and student names and their scores, and prints the student names in decreasing order of their scores.

Section 6.10 Two–Dimensional Arrays

6.20* (*Summing all the numbers in a matrix*) Write a method that sums all the integers in a matrix of integers. Use {{1, 2, 4, 5}, {6, 7, 8, 9}, {10, 11, 12, 13}, {14, 15, 16, 17}} to test the method.

6.21* (*Summing the major diagonal in a matrix*) Write a method that sums all the integers in the major diagonal in a matrix of integers. Use {{1, 2, 4, 5}, {6, 7, 8, 9}, {10, 11, 12, 13}, {14, 15, 16, 17}} to test the method.

6.22* (*Sorting students on grades*) Rewrite Listing 6.10, GradeExam.java, to display the students in increasing order of the number of correct answers.

6.23* (*Computing the weekly hours for each employee*) Suppose the weekly hours for all employees are stored in a two-dimensional array. Each row records an employee's seven-day work hours with seven columns. For example, the following array stores the work hours for eight employees. Write a program that displays employees and their total hours in decreasing order of the total hours.

	Su	M	T	W	H	F	Sa
Employee 0	2	4	3	4	5	8	8
Employee 1	7	3	4	3	3	4	4
Employee 2	3	3	4	3	3	2	2
Employee 3	9	3	4	7	3	4	1
Employee 4	3	5	4	3	6	3	8
Employee 5	3	4	4	6	3	4	4
Employee 6	3	7	4	8	3	8	4
Employee 7	6	3	5	9	2	7	9

6.24 (*Adding two matrices*) Write a method to add two matrices. The header of the method is as follows:

```
public static int[][] addMatrix(int[][] a, int[][] b)
```

In order to be added, the two matrices must have the same dimensions and the same or compatible types of elements. As shown below, two matrices are added by adding the two elements of the arrays with the same index:

$$
\begin{pmatrix}
a_{11} & a_{12} & a_{13} & a_{14} & a_{15} \\
a_{21} & a_{22} & a_{23} & a_{24} & a_{25} \\
a_{31} & a_{32} & a_{33} & a_{34} & a_{35} \\
a_{41} & a_{42} & a_{43} & a_{44} & a_{45} \\
a_{51} & a_{52} & a_{53} & a_{54} & a_{55}
\end{pmatrix}
+
\begin{pmatrix}
b_{11} & b_{12} & b_{13} & b_{14} & b_{15} \\
b_{21} & b_{22} & b_{23} & b_{24} & b_{25} \\
b_{31} & b_{32} & b_{33} & b_{34} & b_{35} \\
b_{41} & b_{42} & b_{43} & b_{44} & b_{45} \\
b_{51} & b_{52} & b_{53} & b_{54} & b_{55}
\end{pmatrix}
$$

$$
=
\begin{pmatrix}
a_{11} + b_{11} & a_{12} + b_{12} & a_{13} + b_{13} & a_{14} + b_{14} & a_{15} + b_{15} \\
a_{21} + b_{21} & a_{22} + b_{22} & a_{23} + b_{23} & a_{24} + b_{24} & a_{25} + b_{25} \\
a_{31} + b_{31} & a_{32} + b_{32} & a_{33} + b_{33} & a_{34} + b_{34} & a_{35} + b_{35} \\
a_{41} + b_{41} & a_{42} + b_{42} & a_{43} + b_{43} & a_{44} + b_{44} & a_{45} + b_{45} \\
a_{51} + b_{51} & a_{52} + b_{52} & a_{53} + b_{53} & a_{54} + b_{54} & a_{55} + b_{55}
\end{pmatrix}
$$

6.25** (*Multiplying two matrices*) Write a method to multiply two matrices. The header of the method is as follows:

```
public static int[][] multiplyMatrix(int[][] a, int[][] b)
```

To multiply matrix **a** by matrix **b**, the number of columns in **a** must be the same as the number of rows in **b**, and the two matrices must have elements of the same or compatible types. Let **c** be the result of the multiplication, and **a**, **b**, and **c** are denoted as follows:

$$\begin{pmatrix} a_{11} & a_{12} & a_{13} & a_{14} & a_{15} \\ a_{21} & a_{22} & a_{23} & a_{24} & a_{25} \\ a_{31} & a_{32} & a_{33} & a_{34} & a_{35} \\ a_{41} & a_{42} & a_{43} & a_{44} & a_{45} \\ a_{51} & a_{52} & a_{53} & a_{54} & a_{55} \end{pmatrix} \times \begin{pmatrix} b_{11} & b_{12} & b_{13} & b_{14} & b_{15} \\ b_{21} & b_{22} & b_{23} & b_{24} & b_{25} \\ b_{31} & b_{32} & b_{33} & b_{34} & b_{34} \\ b_{41} & b_{42} & b_{43} & b_{44} & b_{44} \\ b_{51} & b_{52} & b_{53} & b_{54} & b_{54} \end{pmatrix} =$$

$$\begin{pmatrix} c_{11} & c_{12} & c_{13} & c_{14} & c_{15} \\ c_{21} & c_{22} & c_{23} & c_{24} & c_{25} \\ c_{31} & c_{32} & c_{33} & c_{34} & c_{35} \\ c_{41} & c_{42} & c_{43} & c_{44} & c_{45} \\ c_{51} & c_{52} & c_{53} & c_{54} & c_{55} \end{pmatrix}$$

where $c_{ij} = a_{i1} \times b_{1j} + a_{i2} \times b_{2j} + a_{i3} \times b_{3j} + a_{i4} \times b_{4j} + a_{i5} \times b_{5j}$.

6.26* (*TicTacToe board*) Write a program that randomly fills in 0s and 1s into a Tic-TacToe board, prints the board, and finds the rows, columns, or diagonals with all 0s or 1s. Use a two-dimensional array to represent a TicTacToe board. Here is a sample run of the program:

```
001
001
111
All 0's on row 0
All 1's on row 2
All 1's on column 2
```

6.27** (*Checker board*) Write a program that randomly fills in 0s and 1s into an 8 × 8 checker board, prints the board, and finds the rows, columns, or diagonals with all 0s or 1s. Use a two-dimensional array to represent a checker board. Here is a sample run of the program:

```
10101000
10100001
11100011
10100001
11100111
10000001
10100111
00100001
All 0's on subdiagonal
```

6.28*** (*Playing a TicTacToe game*) In a game of TicTacToe, two players take turns marking an available cell in a 3 × 3 grid with their respective tokens (either X or O). When one player has placed three tokens in a horizontal, vertical, or diagonal row on the grid, the game is over and that player has won. A draw (no winner) occurs when all the cells on the grid have been filled with tokens and neither player has achieved a win. Create a program for playing TicTacToe, as follows:

1. The program prompts the first player to enter an X token, and then prompts the second player to enter an O token. Whenever a token is entered,

the program refreshes the board and determines the status of the game (win, draw, or unfinished).

2. To place a token, display two dialog boxes to prompt the user to enter the row and the column for the token.

6.29*** (*Least common multiple*) Write a program that prompts the user to enter two integers and finds their least common multiple (LCM). The LCM of two numbers is the smallest number that is a multiple of both. For example, the LCM for 8 and 12 is 24, for 15 and 25 it is 75, and for 120 and 150 it is 600. There are many ways to find the LCM. In this exercise, you will use the approach described as follows:

To find the LCM of two numbers, first create a prime factor table for each number. The first column of the table consists of all the prime factors, and the second column tracks the occurrence of the corresponding prime factor in the number. For example, the prime factors for 120 are 2, 2, 2, 3, 5, so the prime factor table for number 120 is shown as follows:

prime factors for 120	# of occurrence		
2	3	table[0][0] = 2	table[0][1] = 3
3	1	table[1][0] = 3	table[1][1] = 1
5	1	table[2][0] = 5	table[2][1] = 1

The prime factors for 150 are 2, 3, 5, 5, so the prime factor table for number 150 is shown as follows:

prime factors for 120	# of occurrence		
2	1	table[0][0] = 2	table[0][1] = 1
3	1	table[1][0] = 3	table[1][1] = 1
5	2	table[2][0] = 5	table[2][1] = 2

The LCM of the two numbers consists of the factors with the most frequent occurrence in the two numbers. So the LCM for 120 and 150 is $2 \times 2 \times 2 \times 3 \times 5 \times 5$, where 2 appears three times in 120, 3 one time in 120, and 5 two times in 150.

Hint

The prime factor table can be represented using a two-dimensional array. Write a method named `getPrimeFactors(int number)` that returns a two-dimensional array for the prime factor table.

PART 2

OBJECT-ORIENTED PROGRAMMING

In Part 1, "Fundamentals of Programming," you learned how to write simple Java applications using primitive data types, control statements, methods, and arrays, all of which are features commonly available in procedural programming languages. Java, however, is an object-oriented programming language that uses abstraction, encapsulation, inheritance, and polymorphism to provide great flexibility, modularity, and reusability for developing software. In this part of the book you will learn how to define, extend, and work with classes and their objects.

Chapter 7
Objects and Classes

Chapter 8
Strings and Text I/O

Chapter 9
Inheritance and Polymorphism

Chapter 10
Abstract Classes and Interfaces

Chapter 11
Object-Oriented Design

Prerequisites for Part 2

optional GUI sections

Optional GUI sections are provided at the end of Chapters 7–10 in Part 2, while a complete introduction to GUI programming is presented in Part 3. This serves two purposes: (1) GUI can be covered early to stimulate student interest in programming; (2) GUI components are excellent examples to demonstrate object-oriented programming. The optional GUI sections can be used as additional examples to teach OOP.

text I/O

The *text I/O* in Chapter 8, "Strings and Text I/O," can be covered whenever text I/O is needed.

exception

Exception handling and binary I/O can be covered after Chapter 9, "Inheritance and Polymorphism."

Part 3, "GUI Programming," may be intertwined with Part 2. You can cover GUI programming in Chapters 12 and 13, "GUI Basics" and "Graphics," after you have covered

abstract classes

abstract classes in Chapter 10, "Abstract Classes and Interfaces."

interfaces

Interfaces in Chapter 10, "Abstract Classes and Interfaces," can be covered just before introducing Chapter 14, "Event-Driven Programming."

Chapter 11

The sections in *Chapter 11*, "Object-Oriented Design," can be covered selectively. For example, if you want to use sequence diagrams to model dynamic behaviors, you can cover sequence diagrams at that time.

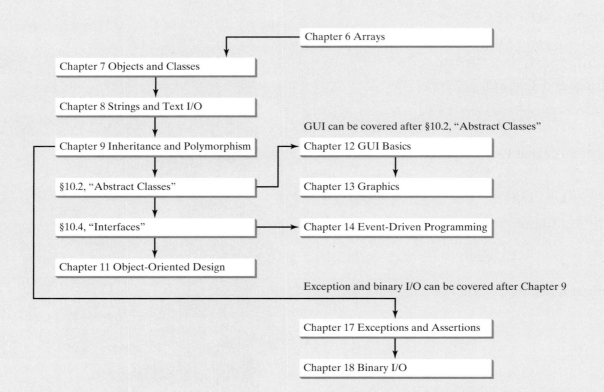

OBJECTS AND CLASSES

Objectives

- To understand objects and classes, and use classes to model objects (§7.2).

- To use UML graphical notations to describe classes and objects (§7.2).

- To learn how to declare a class and how to create an object of a class (§7.3).

- To understand the role of constructors when creating objects (§7.3).

- To distinguish between object reference variables and primitive data type variables (§7.4).

- To use classes in the Java library (§7.5).

- To understand the difference between instance and static variables and methods (§7.6).

- To declare private data fields with appropriate `get` and `set` methods for data field encapsulation to make classes easy to maintain (§§7.7–7.8).

- To create immutable objects from immutable classes (§7.9).

- To develop methods with object arguments (§7.10).

- To determine the scope of variables in the context of a class (§7.11).

- To use the keyword `this` to refer to the calling object (§7.12).

- To store and process objects in arrays (§7.13).

- To apply class abstraction to develop software (§§7.14–7.17).

- (Optional GUI) To create windows using `JFrame` (§7.18).

7.1 Introduction

Programming in procedural languages like C, Pascal, BASIC, Ada, and COBOL involves choosing data structures, designing algorithms, and translating algorithms into code. An object-oriented language like Java combines the power of procedural languages with an added dimension that provides more flexibility, modularity, clarity, and reusability through abstraction, encapsulation, inheritance, and polymorphism.

In procedural programming, data and operations on the data are separate, and this methodology requires sending data to methods. Object-oriented programming places data and the operations that pertain to them within a single entity called an *object*; this approach solves many of the problems inherent in procedural programming. The object-oriented programming approach organizes programs in a way that mirrors the real world, in which all objects are associated with both attributes and activities. Using objects improves software reusability and makes programs easier to develop and easier to maintain. Programming in Java involves thinking in terms of objects; a Java program can be viewed as a collection of cooperating objects.

This chapter introduces declaring classes, creating objects, manipulating objects, and making objects work together.

7.2 Defining Classes for Objects

object-oriented programming

Object-oriented programming (OOP) involves programming using objects. An *object* represents an entity in the real world that can be distinctly identified. For example, a student, a desk, a circle, a button, and even a loan can all be viewed as objects. An object has a unique identity, state, and behaviors.

state

- The *state* of an object is represented by *data fields* (also known as *properties*) with their current values.

behavior

- The *behavior* of an object is defined by a set of methods. Invoking a method on an object means that you ask the object to perform a task.

A circle object, for example, has a data field, `radius`, which is the property that characterizes a circle. One behavior of a circle is that its area can be computed using the method `getArea()`.

Objects of the same type are defined using a common class. A class is a template or blueprint that defines what an object's data and methods will be. An object is an instance of a class. You can create many instances of a class. Creating an instance is referred to as *instantiation*. The terms *object* and *instance* are often interchangeable. The relationship between classes and objects is analogous to the relationship between apple pie recipes and apple pies. You can make as many apple pies as you want from a single recipe. Figure 7.1 shows a class named `Circle` and its three objects.

instantiation
object
instance

class
data field
method
constructor

A Java *class* uses variables to define *data fields* and *methods* to define behaviors. Additionally, a class provides methods of a special type, known as *constructors*, which are invoked when

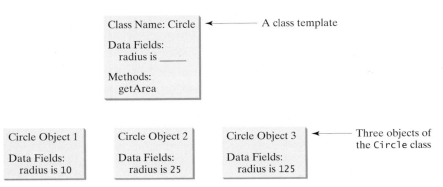

FIGURE 7.1 A class is a template for creating objects.

a new object is created. A constructor is a special kind of method. A constructor can perform any action, but constructors are designed to perform initializing actions, such as initializing the data fields of objects. Figure 7.2 shows an example of the class for `Circle` objects.

```
class Circle {
    /** The radius of this circle */
    double radius = 1.0;  ◄──────────────── Data field

    /** Construct a circle object */
    Circle() {
    }
                                          ◄──── Constructors
    /** Construct a circle object */
    Circle(double newRadius) {
        radius = newRadius;
    }

    /** Return the area of this circle */
    double getArea() {  ◄──────────────── Method
        return radius * radius * Math.PI;
    }
}
```

FIGURE 7.2   A class is a construct that defines objects of the same type.

The `Circle` class is different from all of the other classes you have seen thus far. It does not have a `main` method and therefore cannot be run; it is merely a definition used to declare and create `Circle` objects. For convenience, the class that contains the `main` method will be referred to as the *main class* in this book.

main class

The illustration of class templates and objects in Figure 7.1 can be standardized using UML (Unified Modeling Language) notations. This notation, as shown in Figure 7.3, is called a *UML class diagram*, or simply a *class diagram*. For more information on UML, see www.rational.com/uml/.

UML class diagram

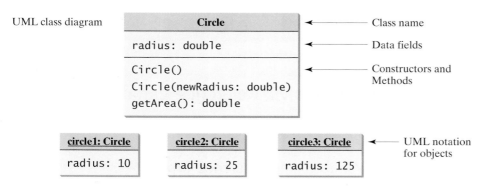

FIGURE 7.3   Classes and objects can be represented using UML notations.

In the class diagram, the data field is denoted as

```
dataFieldName: dataFieldType
```

The constructor is denoted as

```
ClassName(parameterName: parameterType)
```

The method is denoted as

```
methodName(parameterName: parameterType): returnType
```

7.3 Constructors

The constructor has exactly the same name as the defining class. Like regular methods, con-

overloading constructors

structors can be overloaded (i.e., multiple constructors with the same name but different signatures), making it easy to construct objects with different initial data values.

To construct an object from a class, invoke a constructor of the class using the **new** operator, as
follows:

```
new ClassName(arguments);
```

For example, **new Circle()** creates an object of the **Circle** class using the first constructor
defined in the **Circle** class, and **new Circle(5)** creates an object using the second constructor defined in the **Circle** class.

A class normally provides a constructor without arguments (e.g., **Circle()**). Such a con-

no-arg constructor

structor is called a *no-arg* or *no-argument constructor*.

A class may be declared without constructors. In this case, a no-arg constructor with an

default constructor

empty body is implicitly declared in the class. This constructor, called *a default constructor*, is
provided automatically *only if no constructors are explicitly declared in the class.*

Note

Constructors are a special kind of method, with three differences:

constructor's name

■ Constructors must have the same name as the class itself.

no return type

■ Constructors do not have a return type—not even **void**.

new operator

■ Constructors are invoked using the **new** operator when an object is created. Constructors play
the role of initializing objects.

Caution

It is a common mistake to put the **void** keyword in front of a constructor. For example,

```
public void Circle() {
}
```

In this case, **Circle()** is a method, not a constructor.

7.4 Accessing Objects via Reference Variables

Newly created objects are allocated in the memory. How can they be accessed? The answer is
given in this section.

7.4.1 Reference Variables and Reference Types

reference variable

Objects are accessed via object *reference variables*, which contain references to the objects.
Such variables are declared using the following syntax:

```
ClassName objectRefVar;
```

reference type

A class defines a type, known as a *reference type*. Any variable of the class type can reference
to an instance of the class. The following statement declares the variable **myCircle** to be of the
Circle type:

```
Circle myCircle;
```

The variable `myCircle` can reference a `Circle` object. The next statement creates an object and assigns its reference to `myCircle`.

```
myCircle = new Circle();
```

Using the syntax shown below, you can write one statement that combines the declaration of an object reference variable, the creation of an object, and the assigning of an object reference to the variable.

```
ClassName objectRefVar = new ClassName();
```

Here is an example:

```
Circle myCircle = new Circle();
```

The variable `myCircle` holds a reference to a `Circle` object.

Note

An object reference variable that appears to hold an object actually contains a reference to that object. Strictly speaking, an object reference variable and an object are different, but most of the time the distinction between them can be ignored. So it is fine, for simplicity, to say that `myCircle` is a `Circle` object rather than a more long-winded phrase stating that `myCircle` is a variable that contains a reference to a `Circle` object. When the distinction makes a subtle difference, the long phrase should be used.

object vs. object reference variable

Note

Arrays are treated as objects in Java. Arrays are created using the **new** operator. An array variable is actually a variable that contains a reference to an array.

array object

7.4.2 Accessing an Object's Data and Methods

After an object is created, its data can be accessed and its methods invoked using the *dot operator* (.), also known as the *object member access operator*:

dot operator

- `objectRefVar.dataField` references a data field in the object.
- `objectRefVar.method(arguments)` invokes a method on the object.

For example, `myCircle.radius` references the radius in `myCircle`, and `myCircle.getArea()` invokes the `getArea` method on `myCircle`. Methods are invoked as operations on objects.

The data field `radius` is referred to as an *instance variable* because it is dependent on a specific instance. For the same reason, the method `getArea` is referred to as an *instance method*, because you can only invoke it on a specific instance. The object on which an instance method is invoked is referred to as a *calling object*.

instance variable
instance method

calling object

Note

Most of the time, you create an object and assign it to a variable. Later you can use the variable to reference the object. Occasionally, an object does not need to be referenced later. In this case, you can create an object without explicitly assigning it to a variable, as shown below:

```
new Circle();
```

or

```
System.out.println("Area is " + new Circle(5).getArea());
```

The former statement creates a `Circle` object. The latter statement creates a `Circle` object and invokes its `getArea` method to return its area. An object created in this way is known as an *anonymous object.*

anonymous object

7.4.3 Example: Declaring Classes and Creating Objects

Listing 7.1 is a program that declares a circle class. To avoid a naming conflict with several improved versions of the `Circle` class introduced later in this book, the `Circle` class in this example is named `Circle1`.

The program constructs a circle object with radius 5 and an object with radius 1 and displays the radius and area of each of the two circles. Change the radius of the second object to 100 and display its new radius and area, as shown in Figure 7.4.

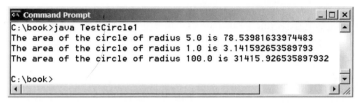

FIGURE 7.4 The program constructs two circles with radii of 5 and 1, and displays their radii and areas.

LISTING 7.1 `TestCircle1.java`

```java
 1 public class TestCircle1 {
 2   /** Main method */
 3   public static void main(String[] args) {
 4     // Create a circle with radius 5.0
 5     Circle1 myCircle = new Circle1(5.0);
 6     System.out.println("The area of the circle of radius "
 7       + myCircle.radius + " is " + myCircle.getArea());
 8
 9     // Create a circle with radius 1
10     Circle1 yourCircle = new Circle1();
11     System.out.println("The area of the circle of radius "
12       + yourCircle.radius + " is " + yourCircle.getArea());
13
14     // Modify circle radius
15     yourCircle.radius = 100;
16     System.out.println("The area of the circle of radius "
17       + yourCircle.radius + " is " + yourCircle.getArea());
18   }
19 }
20
21 // Define the circle class with two constructors
22 class Circle1 {
23   double radius;
24
25   /** Construct a circle with radius 1 */
26   Circle1() {
27     radius = 1.0;
28   }
29
30   /** Construct a circle with a specified radius */
31   Circle1(double newRadius) {
32     radius = newRadius;
33   }
```

no-arg constructor

second constructor

```
34
35    /** Return the area of this circle */
36    double getArea() {
37      return radius * radius * Math.PI;
38    }
39 }
```

The program contains two classes. The first class, TestCircle1, is the main class. Its sole purpose is to test the second class, Circle1. Every time you run the program, the JVM invokes the main method in the main class.

You can put the two classes into one file, but only one class in the file can be a public class. Furthermore, the public class must have the same name as the file name and the main method must be in a public class. Therefore, the file name is TestCircle1.java if the TestCircle1 and Circle1 classes are both in the same file.

The main class contains the main method (line 3) that creates two objects. The constructor Circle1(5.0) was used to create myCircle with a radius of 5.0 (line 5), and the constructor Circle1() was used to create yourCircle with a radius of 1.0 (line 10).

These two objects (referenced by myCircle and yourCircle) have different data but share the same methods. Therefore, you can compute their respective areas by using the getArea() method.

To write the getArea method in a procedural programming language like Pascal, you would pass radius as an argument to the method. But in object-oriented programming, radius and getArea are defined in the object. The radius is a data member in the object, which is accessible by the getArea method. In procedural programming languages, data and methods are separated, but in an object-oriented programming language, data and methods are grouped together.

The getArea method is an instance method that is always invoked by an instance in which the radius is specified.

There are many ways to write Java programs. For instance, you can combine the two classes in the example into one, as shown in Listing 7.2.

LISTING 7.2 Circle1.java

```
 1 public class Circle1 {
 2    /** Main method */
 3    public static void main(String[] args) {          main method
 4      // Create a circle with radius 5.0
 5      Circle1 myCircle = new Circle1(5.0);
 6      System.out.println("The area of the circle of radius "
 7        + myCircle.radius + " is " + myCircle.getArea());
 8
 9      // Create a circle with radius 1
10      Circle1 yourCircle = new Circle1();
11      System.out.println("The area of the circle of radius "
12        + yourCircle.radius + " is " + yourCircle.getArea());
13
14      // Modify circle radius
15      yourCircle.radius = 100;
16      System.out.println("The area of the circle of radius "
17        + yourCircle.radius + " is " + yourCircle.getArea());
18    }
19
20    double radius;
21
22    /** Construct a circle with radius 1 */
23    Circle1() {                                        no-arg constructor
```

```
24      radius = 1.0;
25    }
26
27    /** Construct a circle with a specified radius */
28    Circle1(double newRadius) {
29      radius = newRadius;
30    }
31
32    /** Return the area of this circle */
33    double getArea() {
34      return radius * radius * Math.PI;
35    }
36 }
```

second constructor is marked at line 28.

Since the combined class has a `main` method, it can be executed by the Java interpreter. The `main` method creates `myCircle` as a `Circle1` object and then displays radius and finds area in `myCircle`. This demonstrates that you can test a class by simply adding a `main` method in the same class.

Caution

Recall that you use `Math.methodName(arguments)` (e.g., `Math.pow(3, 2.5)`) to invoke a method in the `Math` class. Can you invoke `getArea()` using `Circle1.getArea()`? The answer is no. All the methods in the `Math` class are static methods, which are defined using the `static` keyword. However, `getArea()` is an instance method, and thus non-static. It must be invoked from an object using `objectRefVar.methodName(arguments)` (e.g., `myCircle.getArea()`). More explanations will follow in §7.6, "Static Variables, Constants, and Methods."

Tip

If you use an IDE such as JBuilder, NetBeans, or Eclipse, please refer to *Learning Java Effectively with JBuilder/NetBeans/Eclipse* in the supplements. This supplement shows you how to use a debugger to inspect objects.

7.4.4 Reference Data Fields and the `null` Value

The data fields can be of reference types. For example, the following `Student` class contains a data field `name` of the `String` type. `String` is a predefined Java class.

```
class Student {
  String name; // name has default value null
  int age; // age has default value 0
  boolean isScienceMajor; // isScienceMajor has default value false
  char gender; // c has default value '\u0000'
}
```

If a data field of a reference type does not reference any object, the data field holds a special Java value, `null`. `null` is a literal just like `true` and `false`. While `true` and `false` are Boolean literals, `null` is a literal for a reference type.

The default value of a data field is `null` for a reference type, `0` for a numeric type, `false` for a `boolean` type, and `'\u0000'` for a `char` type. However, Java assigns no default value to a local variable inside a method. The following code displays the default values of data fields `name`, `age`, `isScienceMajor`, and `gender` for a `Student` object:

```
class Test {
  public static void main(String[] args) {
    Student student = new Student();
```

Margin notes:
- invoking methods
- debugging in IDE
- reference data fields
- null value
- default field values

```
      System.out.println("name? " + student.name);
      System.out.println("age? " + student.age);
      System.out.println("isScienceMajor? " + student.isScienceMajor);
      System.out.println("gender? " + student.gender);
   }
}
```

The following code has a compilation error because local variables x and y are not initialized:

```
class Test {
  public static void main(String[] args) {
    int x; // x has no default value
    String y; // y has no default value
    System.out.println("x is " + x);
    System.out.println("y is " + y);
  }
}
```

Caution

NullPointerException is a common runtime error. It happens when you invoke a method on a reference variable with **null** value. Make sure you assign an object reference to the variable before invoking the method through the reference variable.

NullPointerException

7.4.5 Differences Between Variables of Primitive Types and Reference Types

Every variable represents a memory location that holds a value. When you declare a variable, you are telling the compiler what type of value the variable can hold. For a variable of a primitive type, the value is of the primitive type. For a variable of a reference type, the value is a reference to where an object is located. For example, as shown in Figure 7.5, the value of **int** variable i is **int** value 1, and the value of **Circle** object c holds a reference to where the contents of the **Circle** object are stored in the memory.

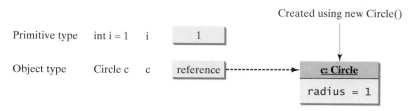

FIGURE 7.5 A variable of a primitive type holds a value of the primitive type, and a variable of a reference type holds a reference to where an object is stored in the memory.

When you assign one variable to another, the other variable is set to the same value. For a variable of a primitive type, the real value of one variable is assigned to the other variable. For a variable of a reference type, the reference of one variable is assigned to the other variable. As shown in Figure 7.6, the assignment statement i = j copies the contents of j into i for primitive variables. As shown in Figure 7.7, the assignment statement c1 = c2 copies the reference of c2 into c1 for reference variables. After the assignment, variables c1 and c2 refer to the same object.

Primitive type assignment i = j

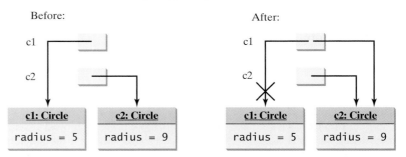

FIGURE 7.6 Primitive variable j is copied to variable i.

Object type assignment c1 = c2

FIGURE 7.7 Reference variable c2 is copied to variable c1.

Note

As shown in Figure 7.7, after the assignment statement c1 = c2, c1 points to the same object referenced by c2. The object previously referenced by c1 is no longer useful and therefore is now known as *garbage*. Garbage occupies memory space. The JVM detects garbage and automatically reclaims the space it occupies. This process is called *garbage collection*.

garbage
garbage collection

Tip

If you know that an object is no longer needed, you can explicitly assign null to a reference variable for the object. The JVM will automatically collect the space if the object is not referenced by any reference variable.

7.5 Using Classes from the Java Library

Listing 7.1 declared the `Circle1` class and created objects from the class. You will frequently use the classes in the Java library to develop programs. This section gives some examples of the classes in the Java library.

7.5.1 The `Date` Class

In Listing 2.5, ShowCurrentTime.java, you learned how to obtain the current time using `System.currentTimeMillis()`. You used the division and remainder operators to extract the current second, minute, and hour. Java provides a system-independent encapsulation of date and time in the `java.util.Date` class, as shown in Figure 7.8.

`java.util.Date` class

You can use the no-arg constructor in the `Date` class to create an instance for the current date and time, its `getTime()` method to return the elapsed time since January 1, 1970, GMT, and its `toString` method to return the date and time as a string. For example, the following code

The + sign indicates public modifer →

java.util.Date	
+Date()	Constructs a **Date** object for the current time.
+Date(elapseTime: long)	Constructs a **Date** object for a given time in milliseconds elapsed since January 1, 1970, GMT.
+toString(): String	Returns a string representing the date and time.
+getTime(): long	Returns the number of milliseconds since January 1, 1970, GMT.
+setTime(elapseTime: long): void	Sets a new elapse time in the object.

FIGURE 7.8 A Date object represents a specific date and time.

```
java.util.Date date = new java.util.Date();                         create object
System.out.println("The elapsed time since Jan 1, 1970 is " +
   date.getTime() + " milliseconds");                                get elapsed time
System.out.println(date.toString());                                 invoke toString
```

displays the output like this:

```
The elapse time since Jan 1, 1970 is 1100547210284 milliseconds
Mon Nov 15 14:33:30 EST 2004
```

The Date class has another constructor, Date(long elapseTime), which can be used to construct a Date object for a given time in milliseconds elapsed since January 1, 1970, GMT.

7.5.2 The Random Class

You have used Math.random() to obtain a random double value between 0.0 and 1.0 (excluding 1.0). A more useful random number generator is provided in the java.util.Random class, as shown in Figure 7.9.

java.util.Random	
+Random()	Constructs a **Random** object with the current time as its seed.
+Random(seed: long)	Constructs a **Random** object with a specified seed.
+nextInt(): int	Returns a random **int** value.
+nextInt(n: int): int	Returns a random **int** value between 0 and n (exclusive).
+nextLong(): long	Returns a random **long** value.
+nextDouble(): double	Returns a random double value between 0.0 and 1.0 (exclusive).
+nextFloat(): float	Returns a random float value between 0.0F and 1.0F (exclusive).
+nextBoolean(): boolean	Returns a random boolean value.

FIGURE 7.9 A Random object can be used to generate random values.

You can create a Random object for generating random values using its no-arg constructor with the current elapse time as its seed. You can also create a Random object using new Random(seed) with a specified seed. If two Random objects have the same seed, they will generate identical sequences of numbers. For example, the following code creates two Random objects with the same seed, 3:

```
Random random1 = new Random(3);
System.out.print("From random1: ");
for (int i = 0; i < 10; i++)
  System.out.print(random1.nextInt(1000) + " ");
```

```
Random random2 = new Random(3);
System.out.print("\nFrom random2: ");
for (int i = 0; i < 10; i++)
    System.out.print(random2.nextInt(1000) + " ");
```

The code generates the same sequence of random `int` values:

```
From random1: 734 660 210 581 128 202 549 564 459 961
From random2: 734 660 210 581 128 202 549 564 459 961
```

7.6 Static Variables, Constants, and Methods

instance variable

The data field `radius` in the circle class in Listing 7.1 is known as an *instance variable*. An instance variable is tied to a specific instance of the class; it is not shared among objects of the same class. For example, suppose that you create the following objects:

```
Circle circle1 = new Circle();
Circle circle2 = new Circle(5);
```

The `radius` in `circle1` is independent of the `radius` in `circle2`, and is stored in a different memory location. Changes made to `circle1`'s `radius` do not affect `circle2`'s `radius`, and vice versa.

static variable

If you want all the instances of a class to share data, use *static variables*. Static variables store values for the variables in a common memory location. Because of this common location, all objects of the same class are affected if one object changes the value of a static variable. Java supports static methods as well as static variables. *Static methods* can be called without creating an instance of the class.

static method

Let us modify the `Circle` class by adding a static variable `numberOfObjects` to count the number of circle objects created. When the first object of this class is created, `numberOfObjects` is 1. When the second object is created, `numberOfObjects` becomes 2. The UML of the new circle class is shown in Figure 7.10. The `Circle` class defines the instance variable `radius` and the static variable `numberOfObjects`, the instance methods `getRadius`, `setRadius`, and `getArea`, and the static method `getNumberOfObjects`. (Note that static variables and functions are *underlined* in the UML class diagram.)

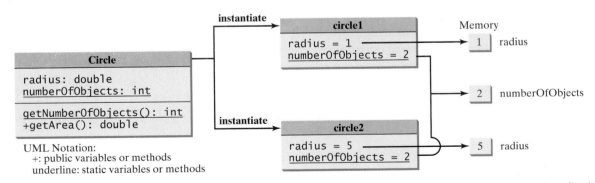

FIGURE 7.10 Instance variables belong to the instances and have memory storage independent of one another. Static variables are shared by all the instances of the same class.

To declare a static variable or a static method, put the modifier `static` in the variable or method declaration. The static variable `numberOfObjects` and the static method `getNumberOfObjects()` can be declared as follows:

```
static int numberOfObjects;
static int getNumberObjects() {
  return numberOfObjects;
}
```

declare **static**
variable
declare **static**
method

Constants in a class are shared by all objects of the class. Thus, constants should be declared `final static`. For example, the constant `PI` in the `Math` class is defined as:

```
final static double PI = 3.14159265358979323846;
```

The new circle class, named `Circle2`, is declared in Listing 7.3.

declare constant

LISTING 7.3   Circle2.java

```
 1 public class Circle2 {
 2   /** The radius of the circle */
 3   double radius;
 4
 5   /** The number of the objects created */
 6   static int numberOfObjects = 0;
 7
 8   /** Construct a circle with radius 1 */
 9   Circle2() {
10     radius = 1.0;
11     numberOfObjects++;
12   }
13
14   /** Construct a circle with a specified radius */
15   Circle2(double newRadius) {
16     radius = newRadius;
17     numberOfObjects++;
18   }
19
20   /** Return numberOfObjects */
21   static int getNumberOfObjects() {
22     return numberOfObjects;
23   }
24
25   /** Return the area of this circle */
26   double getArea() {
27     return radius * radius * Math.PI;
28   }
29 }
```

static variable

increase by 1

increase by 1

static method

Method `getNumberOfObjects()` in `Circle2` is a static method. Other examples of static methods are `showMessageDialog` and `showInputDialog` in the `JOptionPane` class, and all the methods in the `Math` class. In fact, so are all the methods used in Part 1 of this book, including the `main` method.

Instance methods (e.g., `getArea()`) and instance data (e.g., `radius`) belong to instances and can only be used after the instances are created. They are accessed via a reference variable. Static methods (e.g., `getNumberOfObjects()`) and static data (e.g., `numberOfObjects`) can be accessed from a reference variable or from their class name.

The program in Listing 7.4 demonstrates how to use instance and static variables and methods, and illustrates the effects of using them. Its output is shown in Figure 7.11.

LISTING 7.4 TestCircle2.java

```
1 public class TestCircle2 {
2   /** Main method */
3   public static void main(String[] args) {
4     // Create c1
5     Circle2 c1 = new Circle2();
6
7     // Display c1 BEFORE c2 is created
8     System.out.println("Before creating c2");
9     System.out.println("c1 is : radius (" + c1.radius +
10      ") and number of Circle objects (" +
11      c1.numberOfObjects + ")");
12
13    // Create c2
14    Circle2 c2 = new Circle2(5);
15
16    // Change the radius in c1
17    c1.radius = 9;
18
19    // Display c1 and c2 AFTER c2 was created
20    System.out.println("\nAfter creating c2 and modifying " +
21      "c1's radius to 9");
22    System.out.println("c1 is : radius (" + c1.radius +
23      ") and number of Circle objects (" +
24      c1.numberOfObjects + ")");
25    System.out.println("c2 is : radius (" + c2.radius +
26      ") and number of Circle objects (" +
27      c2.numberOfObjects +")");
28  }
29 }
```

```
Command Prompt                                    _ □ ×
C:\book>java TestCircle2
Before creating c2
c1 is : radius (1.0) and number of Circle objects (1)

After creating c2 and modifying c1's radius to 9
c1 is : radius (9.0) and number of Circle objects (2)
c2 is : radius (5.0) and number of Circle objects (2)

C:\book>_
```

FIGURE 7.11 The program uses the instance variable radius as well as the static variable numberOfObjects. All of the objects share the same numberOfObjects.

The main method creates two circles, c1 and c2 (lines 5, 14). The instance variable radius in c1 is modified to become 9 (line 17). This change does not affect the instance variable radius in c2, since these two instance variables are independent. The static variable numberOfObjects becomes 1 after c1 is created (line 5), and it becomes 2 after c2 is created (line 14).

Note that PI is a constant defined in Math and Math.PI access the constant. c1.numberOfObjects and c2.numberOfObjects could be replaced by Circle2.numberOfObjects. This improves readability. You can also replace Circle2.numberOfObjects by Circle2.getNumberOfObjects().

Tip

Use `ClassName.methodName(arguments)` to invoke a static method and `ClassName.staticVariable`. This improves readability because the user can easily recognize the static method and data in the class.

use class name

Note

You can use a new JDK 1.5 feature to directly import static variables and methods from a class. The imported data and methods can be referenced or called without specifying a class. For example, you can use `PI` (instead of `Math.PI`), and `random()` (instead of `Math.random()`), if you have the following import statement in the class:

static import

```
import static java.lang.Math.*;
```

Caution

Static variables and methods can be used from instance or static methods in the class. However, instance variables and methods can only be used from instance methods, not from static methods, since static variables and methods belong to the class as a whole and not to particular objects. Thus the code given below would be wrong.

```java
public class Foo {
  int i = 5;
  static int k = 2;

  public static void main(String[] args) {
    int j = i; // Wrong because i is an instance variable
    m1(); // Wrong because m1() is an instance method
  }

  public void m1() {
    // Correct since instance and static variables and methods
    // can be used in an instance method
    i = i + k + m2(i, k);
  }

  public static int m2(int i, int j) {
    return (int)(Math.pow(i, j));
  }
}
```

Tip

How do you decide whether a variable or method should be an instance one or a static one? A variable or method that is dependent on a specific instance of the class should be an instance variable or method. A variable or method that is not dependent on a specific instance of the class should be a static variable or method. For example, every circle has its own radius. Radius is dependent on a specific circle. Therefore, `radius` is an instance variable of the `Circle` class. Since the `getArea` method is dependent on a specific circle, it is an instance method. None of the methods in the `Math` class, such as `random`, `pow`, `sin`, and `cos`, is dependent on a specific instance. Therefore, these methods are static methods. The `main` method is static, and can be invoked directly from a class.

instance or static?

Caution

It is a *common design error* to declare an instance method that should have been declared static. For example, the following method `factorial(int n)` should be declared static, because it is independent of any specific instance.

common design error

```
public class Test {
  public int factorial(int n) {
    int result = 1;
    for (int i = 1; i <= n; i++)
      result *= i;

    return result;
  }
}
```

(a) Wrong design

```
public class Test {
  public static int factorial(int n) {
    int result = 1;
    for (int i = 1; i <= n; i++)
      result *= i;

    return result;
  }
}
```

(b) Correct design

7.7 Visibility Modifiers

Java provides several modifiers that control access to data fields, methods, and classes. This section introduces the `public`, `private`, and default modifiers.

public

- `public` makes classes, methods, and data fields accessible from any class.

private

- `private` makes methods and data fields accessible only from within its own class.

package-private

- If `public` or `private` is not used, then by default the classes, methods, and data fields are accessible by any class in the same package. This is known as *package-private* or *package-access*.

Figure 7.12 illustrates how a public, default, and private data field or method in class **C1** can be accessed from a class **C2** in the same package, and from a class **C3** in a different package.

```
package p1;

public class C1 {
  public int x;
  int y;
  private int z;

  public void m1() {
  }
  void m2() {
  }
  private void m3() {
  }
}
```

```
public class C2 {
  void aMethod() {
    C1 o = new C1();
    can access o.x;
    can access o.y;
    cannot access o.z;

    can invoke o.m1();
    can invoke o.m2();
    cannot invoke o.m3();
  }
}
```

```
package p2;

public class C3 {
  void aMethod() {
    C1 o = new C1();
    can access o.x;
    cannot access o.y;
    cannot access o.z;

    can invoke o.m1();
    cannot invoke o.m2();
    cannot invoke o.m3();
  }
}
```

FIGURE 7.12 The private modifier restricts access to its defining a class, the default modifier restricts access to a package, and the public modifier enables unrestricted access.

If a class is not declared public, it can only be accessed within the same package, as shown in Figure 7.13.

A visibility modifier specifies how data fields and methods in a class can be accessed from the outside of the class. There is no restriction on accessing data fields and methods from inside

inside access

the class. As shown in Figure 7.14(b), an object **foo** of the **Foo** class cannot access its private members, because **foo** is in the **Test** class. As shown in Figure 7.14(a), an object **foo** of the **Foo** class can access its private members, because **foo** is declared inside its own class.

Note

private data field
private method

The `private` modifier applies solely to the members of a class (e.g., data fields or methods). The various Java modifiers are summarized in the table in Appendix D, "Java Modifiers."

```
package p1;
    class C1 {      public class C2 {
        ...             can access C1
    }               }
```

```
package p2;
    public class C3 {
        cannot access C1;
        can access C2;
    }
```

FIGURE 7.13   A non-public class has package-access.

```
public class Foo {
  private boolean x;

  public static void main(String[] args) {
    Foo foo = new Foo();
    System.out.println(foo.x);
    System.out.println(foo.convert());
  }

  private int convert() {
    return x ? 1 : -1;
  }
}
```

```
public class Test {
  public static void main(String[] args) {
    Foo foo = new Foo();
    System.out.println(foo.x);
    System.out.println(foo.convert());
  }
}
```

(a) This is OK because object **foo** is used inside the **Foo** class   (b) This is wrong because **x** and **convert** are private in **Foo**.

FIGURE 7.14   An object can access its private members if it is declared in its own class.

Note

Visibility modifiers are used for the members of the class, not local variables inside the methods. Using a visibility modifier on local variables would cause a compilation error.

Note

In most cases, the constructor should be public. However, if you want to prohibit the user from creating an instance of a class, you can use a *private constructor*. For example, there is no reason to create an instance from the **Math** class because all of the data fields and methods are static. One solution is to define a dummy private constructor in the class. The **Math** class cannot be instantiated because it has a private constructor, as follows:

private constructor

```
private Math() {
}
```

The **Math** class that comes with the Java system was introduced in §5.8, "The **Math** Class."

7.8 Data Field Encapsulation

The data fields **radius** and **numberOfObjects** in the **Circle2** class in Listing 7.2 can be modified directly (e.g., **myCircle.radius = 5** or **Circle2.numberOfObjects = 10**). This is not a good practice for two reasons:

- First, data may be tampered. For example, **numberOfObjects** is to count the number of objects created, but it may be set to an arbitrary value (e.g., **Circle2.numberOfObjects = 10**).

- Second, it makes the class difficult to maintain and vulnerable to bugs. Suppose you want to modify the **Circle2** class to ensure that the radius is non-negative after other programs have already used the class. You have to change not only the **Circle2** class, but also the programs that use the **Circle2** class. Such programs

client

are often referred to as *clients*. This is because the clients may have modified the radius directly (e.g., `myCircle.radius = -5`).

data field encapsulation

To prevent direct modifications of properties, you should declare the field private, using the `private` modifier. This is known as *data field encapsulation*.

A private data field cannot be accessed by an object through a direct reference outside the class that defines the private field. But often a client needs to retrieve and modify a data field. To make a private data field accessible, provide a *get* method to return the value of the data field. To enable a private data field to be updated, provide a *set* method to set a new value.

 Note

accessor

mutator

Colloquially, a `get` method is referred to as a *getter* (or *accessor*), and a `set` method is referred to as a *setter* (or *mutator*).

A `get` method has the following signature:

public returnType get*PropertyName*()

boolean accessor

If the `returnType` is `boolean`, the `get` method should be defined as follows by convention:

public boolean is*PropertyName*()

A set method has the following signature:

public void set*PropertyName*(*dataType propertyValue*)

Let us create a new circle class with a private data field radius and its associated accessor and mutator methods. The class diagram is shown in Figure 7.15. The new circle class, named `Circle3`, is declared in Listing 7.5.

The - sign indicates private modifier ⟶

Circle
-radius: double
-numberOfObjects: int
+Circle()
+Circle(radius: double)
+getRadius(): double
+setRadius(radius: double): void
+getNumberOfObject(): int
+getArea(): double

The radius of this circle (default: 1.0).
The number of circle objects created.

Constructs a default circle object.
Constructs a circle object with the specified radius.
Returns the radius of this circle.
Sets a new radius for this circle.
Returns the number of circle objects created.
Returns the area of this circle.

FIGURE 7.15   The `Circle` class encapsulates circle properties and provides get/set and other methods.

LISTING 7.5   Circle3.java

encapsulate radius

encapsulate **numberOfObjects**

```
1 public class Circle3 {
2   /** The radius of the circle */
3   private double radius = 1;
4
5   /** The number of the objects created */
6   private static int numberOfObjects = 0;
7
8   /** Construct a circle with radius 1 */
9   public Circle3() {
10    numberOfObjects++;
11  }
```

```
12
13    /** Construct a circle with a specified radius */
14    public Circle3(double newRadius) {
15      radius = newRadius;
16      numberOfObjects++;
17    }
18
19    /** Return radius */
20    public double getRadius() {                              access method
21      return radius;
22    }
23
24    /** Set a new radius */
25    public void setRadius(double newRadius) {                mutator method
26      radius = (newRadius >= 0) ? newRadius : 0;
27    }
28
29    /** Return numberOfObjects */
30    public static int getNumberOfObjects() {                 access method
31      return numberOfObjects;
32    }
33
34    /** Return the area of this circle */
35    public double getArea() {
36      return radius * radius * Math.PI;
37    }
38 }
```

The `getRadius()` method (lines 20–22) returns the radius, and the `setRadius(newRadius)` method (lines 25–27) sets a new radius into the object. If the new radius is negative, `0` is set to the radius in the object. Since these methods are the only ways to read and modify radius, you have total control over how the `radius` property is accessed. If you have to change the implementation of these methods, you need not change the client programs. This makes the class easy to maintain.

Here is a client program that uses the `Circle3` class to create a `Circle3` object and modifies the radius using the `setRadius` method.

```
1  // TestCircle3.java: Demonstrate private modifier
2  public class TestCircle3 {
3    /** Main method */
4    public static void main(String[] args) {
5      // Create a Circle with radius 5.0
6      Circle myCircle = new Circle(5.0);
7      System.out.println("The area of the circle of radius "
8        + myCircle.getRadius() + " is " + myCircle.getArea());
9
10     // Increase myCircle's radius by 10%
11     myCircle.setRadius(myCircle.getRadius() * 1.1);
12     System.out.println("The area of the circle of radius "
13       + myCircle.getRadius() + " is " + myCircle.getArea());
14   }
15 }
```

The data field `radius` is declared private. Private data can only be accessed within their defining class. You cannot use `myCircle.radius` in the client program. A compilation error would occur if you attempted to access private data from a client.

Since `numberOfObjects` is private, it cannot be modified. This prevents tampering. For example, the user cannot set `numberOfObjects` to 100. The only way to make it 100 is to create one hundred objects of the `Circle3` class.

Suppose you combined `TestCircle3` and `Circle3` into one class by moving the `main` method in `TestCircle3` into `Circle3`. Could you use `myCircle.radius` in the `main` method? See Review Question 7.15 for the answer.

Note

When you compile `TestCircle3.java`, the Java compiler automatically compiles `Circle3.java` if it has not been compiled since the last change.

Tip

To prevent data from being tampered with and to make the class easy to maintain, most of the data fields in this book will be private.

7.9 Immutable Objects and Classes

immutable object
immutable class

If the contents of an object cannot be changed once the object is created, the object is called an *immutable object* and its class is called an *immutable class*. If you delete the `set` method in the `Circle3` class in the preceding example, the class would be immutable because radius is private and cannot be changed without a `set` method.

A class with all private data fields and no mutators is not necessarily immutable. For example, the following class `Student` has all private data fields and no mutators, but it is mutable.

Student class

```java
public class Student {
  private int id;
  private BirthDate birthDate;

  public Student(int ssn, int year, int month, int day) {
    id = ssn;
    birthDate = new BirthDate(year, month, day);
  }

  public int getId() {
    return id;
  }

  public BirthDate getBirthDate() {
    return birthDate;
  }
}
```

BirthDate class

```java
public class BirthDate {
  private int year;
  private int month;
  private int day;

  public BirthDate(int newYear, int newMonth, int newDay) {
    year = newYear;
    month = newMonth;
    day = newDay;
  }

  public void setYear(int newYear) {
    year = newYear;
  }
}
```

As shown in the following code, the data field `birthDate` is returned using the `getBirthDate()` method. This is a reference to a `BirthDate` object. Through this reference, the year of the birth date is changed, which effectively changes the contents of the `Student` object.

```java
public class Test {
  public static void main(String[] args) {
    Student student = new Student(111223333, 1970, 5, 3);
    BirthDate date = student.getBirthDate();
    date.setYear(2010); //Now the student birth year is changed!
  }
}
```

For a class to be immutable, it must mark all data fields private and provide no mutator methods and no accessor methods that would return a reference to a mutable data field object.

7.10 Passing Objects to Methods

So far, you have learned how to pass arguments of primitive types and array types to methods. You can also pass objects to methods. Like passing an array, passing an object is actually passing the reference of the object. The following code passes the `myCircle` object as an argument to the `printCircle` method:

```java
public class TestPassObject {
  public static void main(String[] args) {
    Circle3 myCircle = new Circle3(5.0);
    printCircle(myCircle);
  }

  public static void printCircle(Circle3 c) {
    System.out.println("The area of the circle of radius "
      + c.getRadius() + " is " + c.getArea());
  }
}
```

Java uses exactly one mode of passing arguments: *pass-by-value*. In the preceding code, the value of `myCircle` is passed to the `printCircle` method. This value is a reference to a `Circle3` object.

pass-by-value

Let us demonstrate the difference between passing a primitive type value and passing a reference value with the program in Listing 7.6.

LISTING 7.6 TestPassObject.java

```java
 1 public class TestPassObject {
 2   /** Main method */
 3   public static void main(String[] args) {
 4     // Create a Circle object with radius 1
 5     Circle3 myCircle = new Circle3(1);
 6
 7     // Print areas for radius 1, 2, 3, 4, and 5.
 8     int n = 5;
 9     printAreas(myCircle, n);
10
11     // See myCircle.radius and times
12     System.out.println("\n" + "Radius is " + myCircle.getRadius());
13     System.out.println("n is " + n);
14   }
15
```

```
16   /** Print a table of areas for radius */
17   public static void printAreas(Circle3 c, int times) {
18     System.out.println("Radius \t\tArea");
19     while (times >= 1) {
20       System.out.println(c.getRadius() + "\t\t" + c.getArea());
21       c.setRadius(c.getRadius() + 1);
22       times--;
23     }
24   }
25 }
```

The program passes a `Circle3` object `myCircle` and an integer value from `n` to invoke `printAreas(myCircle, n)` (line 19), which prints a table of areas for radii 1, 2, 3, 4, and 5, as shown in Figure 7.16.

FIGURE 7.16 The program passes a `Circle` object `myCircle` and an integer value `n` as arguments to the `printAreas` method, which displays a table of the areas for radii 1, 2, 3, 4, and 5.

Figure 7.17 shows the call stack for executing the methods in the program. Note that the objects are stored in a heap.

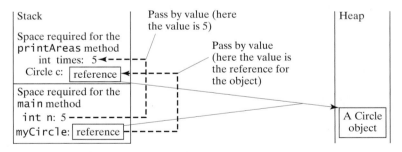

FIGURE 7.17 The value of `n` is passed to `times`, and the reference of `myCircle` is passed to `c` in the `printAreas` method.

When passing an argument of a primitive data type, the value of the argument is passed. In this case, the value of `n` (5) is passed to `times`. Inside the `printAreas` method, the content of `times` is changed; this does not affect the content of `n`. When passing an argument of a reference type, the reference of the object is passed. In this case, `c` contains a reference for the object that is also referenced via `myCircle`. Therefore, changing the properties of the object through `c` inside the `printAreas` method has the same effect as doing so outside the method through the variable `myCircle`.

7.11 The Scope of Variables

Chapter 5, "Methods," discussed local variables and their scope rules. Local variables are declared and used inside a method locally. This section discusses the scope rules of all the variables in the context of a class.

Instance and static variables in a class are referred to as the *class's variables* or *data fields*. A variable defined inside a method is referred to as a local variable. The scope of a class's variables is the entire class, regardless of where the variables are declared. A class's variables and methods can be declared in any order in the class, as shown in Figure 7.18(a). The exception is when a data field is initialized based on a reference to another data field. In such cases, the other data field must be declared first, as shown in Figure 7.18(b).

```
public class Circle {
  public double find getArea() {
    return radius * radius * Math.PI;
  }

  private double radius = 1;
}
```

```
public class Foo {
  private int i;
  private int j = i + 1;
}
```

(a) variable radius and method getArea() can be declared in any order

(b) i has to be declared before j because j's initial value is dependent on i.

FIGURE 7.18 Members of a class can be declared in any order, with one exception.

You can declare a class's variable only once, but you can declare the same variable name in a method many times in different non-nesting blocks.

If a local variable has the same name as a class's variable, the local variable takes precedence and the class's variable with the same name is hidden. For example, in the following program, x is defined as an instance variable and as a local variable in the method.

```
class Foo {
  int x = 0; // instance variable
  int y = 0;

  Foo() {
  }

  void p() {
    int x = 1; // local variable
    System.out.println("x = " + x);
    System.out.println("y = " + y);
  }
}
```

What is the printout for `f.p()`, where f is an instance of Foo? The printout for `f.p()` is 1 for x and 0 for y. Here is why:

■ x is declared as a data field with the initial value of 0 in the class, but is also defined in the method `p()` with an initial value of 1. The latter x is referenced in the `System.out.println` statement.

■ y is declared outside the method `p()`, but is accessible inside it.

Tip
As demonstrated in the example, it is easy to make mistakes. To avoid confusion, do not declare the same variable name twice in a class, except for method parameters.

7.12 The **this** Keyword

hidden variable

Sometimes you need to reference a class's *hidden variable* in a method. For example, a property name is often used as the parameter name in a **set** method for the property. In this case, you need to reference the hidden property name in the method in order to set a new value to it. A hidden static variable can be accessed simply by using the `ClassName.StaticVariable` reference. A hidden instance variable can be accessed by using the keyword `this`, as shown in Figure 7.19(a).

```
class Foo {
  int i = 5;
  static double k = 0;

  void setI(int i) {
    this.i = i;
  }

  static void setK(double k) {
    Foo.k = k;
  }
}
```

Suppose that f1 and f2 are two objects of Foo.

Invoking f1.setI(10) is to execute
►f1.i = 10, where *this* is replaced by f1

Invoking f2.setI(45) is to execute
►f2.i = 45, where *this* is replaced by f2

(a)   (b)

FIGURE 7.19 The keyword `this` serves as the proxy for the object that invokes the method.

The line `this.i = i` means "assign the value of parameter `i` to the data field `i` of the calling object." The keyword `this` serves as a proxy for the object that invokes the instance method `setI`, as shown in Figure 7.19(b). The line `Foo.k = k` means that the value in parameter `k` is assigned to the static data field `k` of the class, which is shared by all the objects of the class.

call another constructor

The keyword `this` can also be used inside a constructor to invoke another constructor of the same class. For example, you can redefine the `Circle` class as follows:

```
public class Circle {
  private double radius;

  public Circle(double radius) {
    this.radius = radius;
  }

  public Circle() {
    this(1.0);
  }

  public double getArea() {
    return this.radius * this.radius * Math.PI;
  }
}
```

This must be explicitly used to reference the data field radius of the object being constructed

this is used to invoke another constructor

Every instance variable belongs to an instance represented by **this**, which is normally omitted

The line `this(1.0)` invokes the constructor with a **double** value argument in the class.

Tip

If a class has multiple constructors, it is better to implement them using `this(arg-list)` as much as possible. In general, a constructor with no or fewer arguments can invoke the constructor with more arguments using `this(arg-list)`. This often simplifies coding and makes the class easier to read and to maintain.

Note
Java requires that the `this(arg-list)` statement appear first in the constructor before any other statements.

7.13 Array of Objects

In Chapter 6, "Arrays," arrays of primitive type elements were created. You can also create arrays of objects. For example, the following statement declares and creates an array of ten `Circle` objects:

```
Circle[] circleArray = new Circle[10];
```

To initialize the `circleArray`, you can use a `for` loop like this one:

```
for (int i = 0; i < circleArray.length; i++) {
  circleArray[i] = new Circle();
}
```

An array of objects is actually an *array of reference variables*. So invoking `circleArray[1].getArea()` involves two levels of referencing, as shown in Figure 7.20. `circleArray` references the entire array. `circleArray[1]` references a `Circle` object.

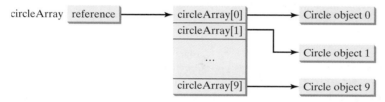

FIGURE 7.20 In an array of objects, an element of the array contains a reference to an object.

Note
When an array of objects is created using the **new** operator, each element is a reference variable with a default value of `null`.

Listing 7.7 gives an example that demonstrates how to use an array of objects. The program summarizes the areas of an array of circles. The program creates `circleArray`, an array composed of ten `Circle3` objects; it then initializes circle radii with random values, and displays the total area of the circles in the array. The output of a sample run of the program is shown in Figure 7.21.

LISTING 7.7 `TotalArea.java`

```
 1 public class TotalArea {
 2   /** Main method */
 3   public static void main(String[] args) {
 4     // Declare circleArray
 5     Circle3[] circleArray;
 6
 7     // Create circleArray
 8     circleArray = createCircleArray();
 9
10     // Print circleArray and total areas of the circles
11     printCircleArray(circleArray);
12   }
13
```

```
14   /** Create an array of Circle objects */
15   public static Circle3[] createCircleArray() {
16     Circle3[] circleArray = new Circle3[10];
17
18     for (int i = 0; i < circleArray.length; i++) {
19       circleArray[i] = new Circle3(Math.random() * 100);
20     }
21
22     // Return Circle array
23     return circleArray;
24   }
25
26   /** Print an array of circles and their total area */
27   public static void printCircleArray
28       (Circle3[] circleArray) {
29     System.out.println("Radius\t\t\t\t" + "Area");
30     for (int i = 0; i < circleArray.length; i++) {
31       System.out.print(circleArray[i].getRadius() + "\t\t" +
32         circleArray[i].getArea() + '\n');
33     }
34
35     System.out.println("--------------");
36
37     // Compute and display the result
38     System.out.println("The total areas of circles is \t" +
39       sum(circleArray));
40   }
41
42   /** Add circle areas */
43   public static double sum(Circle3[] circleArray) {
44     // Initialize sum
45     double sum = 0;
46
47     // Add areas to sum
48     for (int i = 0; i < circleArray.length; i++)
49       sum += circleArray[i].getArea();
50
51     return sum;
52   }
53 }
```

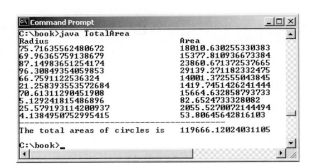

FIGURE 7.21 The program creates an array of `Circle3` objects, then displays their total area.

The program invokes `createCircleArray()` (line 8) to create an array of ten `Circle3` objects. Several `Circle` classes were introduced in this chapter. This example uses the `Circle3` class introduced in §7.8, "Data Field Encapsulation."

The circle radii are randomly generated using the `Math.random()` method (line 19). The `createCircleArray` method returns an array of `Circle3` objects (line 23). The array is passed to the `printCircleArray` method, which displays the radii of the total area of the circles.

The sum of the areas of the circle is computed using the `sum` method (line 39), which takes the array of `Circle3` objects as the argument and returns a `double` value for the total area.

7.14 Class Abstraction and Encapsulation

In Chapter 5, "Methods," you learned about method abstraction and used it in program development. Java provides many levels of abstraction. *Class abstraction* is the separation of class implementation from the use of a class. The creator of a class provides a description of the class and lets the user know how the class can be used. The collection of methods and fields that are accessible from outside the class, together with the description of how these members are expected to behave, serves as the *class's contract*. As shown in Figure 7.22, the user of the class does not need to know how the class is implemented. The details of implementation are encapsulated and hidden from the user. This is known as *class encapsulation*. For example, you can create a `Circle` object and find the area of the circle without knowing how the area is computed.

class abstraction

class encapsulation

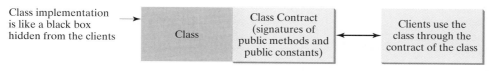

FIGURE 7.22   Class abstraction separates class implementation from the use of the class.

Class abstraction and encapsulation are two sides of the same coin. There are many real-life examples that illustrate the concept of class abstraction. Consider building a computer system, for instance. Your personal computer is made up of many components, such as a CPU, CD-ROM, floppy disk, motherboard, fan, and so on. Each component can be viewed as an object that has properties and methods. To get the components to work together, all you need to know is how each component is used and how it interacts with the others. You don't need to know how it works internally. The internal implementation is encapsulated and hidden from you. You can build a computer without knowing how a component is implemented.

The computer-system analogy precisely mirrors the object-oriented approach. Each component can be viewed as an object of the class for the component. For example, you might have a class that models all kinds of fans for use in a computer, with properties like fan size and speed, and methods like start, stop, and so on. A specific fan is an instance of this class with specific property values.

Consider getting a loan, for another example. A specific loan can be viewed as an object of a `Loan` class. Interest rate, loan amount, and loan period are its data properties, and computing monthly payment and total payment are its methods. When you buy a car, a loan object is created by instantiating the class with your loan interest rate, loan amount, and loan period. You can then use the methods to find the monthly payment and total payment of your loan. As a user of the `Loan` class, you don't need to know how these methods are implemented.

7.15 Case Study: The **Loan** Class

Let us use the `Loan` class as an example to demonstrate the creation and use of classes. `Loan` has the data fields: `annualInterestRate`, `numberOfYears`, `loanAmount`, and `loanDate`, and the methods `getAnnualInterestRate`, `getNumberOfYears`, `getLoanAmount`, `getLoanDate`, `setAnnualInterestRate`, `setNumberOfYears`, `setLoanAmount`, `getMonthlyPayment`, and `getTotalPayment`, as shown in Figure 7.23.

Loan
-annualInterestRate: double
-numberOfYears: int
-loanAmount: double
-loanDate: Date
+Loan()
+Loan(annualInterestRate: double, numberOfYears: int, loanAmount: double)
+getAnnualInterestRate(): double
+getNumberOfYears(): int
+getLoanAmount(): double
+getLoanDate(): Date
+setAnnualInterestRate(annualInterestRate: double): void
+setNumberOfYears(numberOfYears: int): void
+setLoanAmount(loanAmount: double): void
+getMonthlyPayment(): double
+getTotalPayment(): double

The annual interest rate of the loan (default: 2.5).
The number of years for the loan (default: 1).
The loan amount (default: 1000).
The date this loan was created.

Constructs a default Loan object.
Constructs a loan with specified interest rate, years, and loan amount.

Returns the annual interest rate of this loan.
Returns the number of the years of this loan.
Returns the amount of this loan.
Returns the date of the creation of this loan.
Sets a new annual interest rate for this loan.

Sets a new number of years for this loan.

Sets a new amount for this loan.

Returns the monthly payment of this loan.
Returns the total payment of this loan.

FIGURE 7.23   The Loan class models the properties and behaviors of loans.

composition

Note

An object can contain another object. The relationship between the two is called *composition*. In this example, a Loan object contains a Date object.

The UML diagram in Figure 7.23 serves as the contract for the Loan class. Throughout the book, you will play the role of both class user and class writer. The user can use the class without knowing how the class is implemented. Assume that the Loan class is available. Let us begin by writing a test program that uses the Loan class in Listing 7.8.

LISTING 7.8 TestLoanClass.java

```java
1 import javax.swing.JOptionPane;
2
3 public class TestLoanClass {
4   /** Main method */
5   public static void main(String[] args) {
6     // Enter yearly interest rate
7     String annualInterestRateString = JOptionPane.showInputDialog(
8       "Enter yearly interest rate, for example 8.25:");
9
10     // Convert string to double
11     double annualInterestRate =
12       Double.parseDouble(annualInterestRateString);
13
14     // Enter number of years
15     String numberOfYearsString = JOptionPane.showInputDialog(
16       "Enter number of years as an integer, \nfor example 5:");
17
18     // Convert string to int
19     int numberOfYears = Integer.parseInt(numberOfYearsString);
```

```
20
21    // Enter loan amount
22    String loanString = JOptionPane.showInputDialog(
23      "Enter loan amount, for example 120000.95:");
24
25    // Convert string to double
26    double loanAmount =  Double.parseDouble(loanString);
27
28    // Create Loan object
29    Loan loan =
30      new Loan(annualInterestRate, numberOfYears, loanAmount);
31
32    // Format to keep two digits after the decimal point
33    double monthlyPayment =
34      (int)(loan.getMonthlyPayment() * 100) / 100.0;
35    double totalPayment =
36      (int)(loan.getTotalPayment() * 100) / 100.0;
37
38    // Display results
39    String output = "The loan was created on " +
40      loan.getLoanDate().toString() + "\nThe monthly payment is " +
41      monthlyPayment + "\nThe total payment is " + totalPayment;
42    JOptionPane.showMessageDialog(null, output);
43  }
44 }
```

The **main** method reads interest rate, payment period (in years), and loan amount; creates a **Loan** object; and then obtains the monthly payment (lines 33–34) and total payment (lines 35–36) using the instance methods in the **Loan** class. Figure 7.24 shows the output of a sample run of the program.

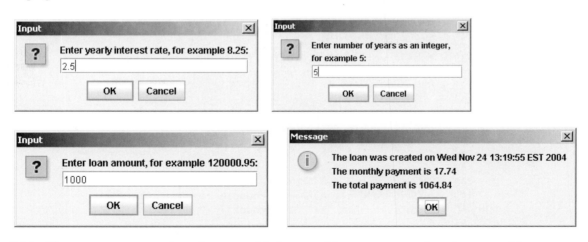

FIGURE 7.24 The program creates a **Loan** instance with the annual interest rate, number of years, and loan amount, and displays the loan date, monthly payment, and total payment by invoking the methods of the instance.

The **Loan** class can be implemented in Listing 7.9.

LISTING 7.9 Loan.java

```
1 public class Loan {
2    private double annualInterestRate;
3    private int numberOfYears;
4    private double loanAmount;
```

```
 5    private java.util.Date loanDate;
 6
 7    /** Default constructor */
 8    public Loan() {
 9      this(7.5, 30, 100000);
10    }
11
12    /** Construct a loan with specified annual interest rate,
13        number of years and loan amount
14     */
15    public Loan(double annualInterestRate, int numberOfYears,
16        double loanAmount) {
17      this.annualInterestRate = annualInterestRate;
18      this.numberOfYears = numberOfYears;
19      this.loanAmount = loanAmount;
20      loanDate = new java.util.Date();
21    }
22
23    /** Return annualInterestRate */
24    public double getAnnualInterestRate() {
25      return annualInterestRate;
26    }
27
28    /** Set a new annualInterestRate */
29    public void setAnnualInterestRate(double annualInterestRate) {
30      this.annualInterestRate = annualInterestRate;
31    }
32
33    /** Return numberOfYears */
34    public int getNumberOfYears() {
35      return numberOfYears;
36    }
37
38    /** Set a new numberOfYears */
39    public void setNumberOfYears(int numberOfYears) {
40      this.numberOfYears = numberOfYears;
41    }
42
43    /** Return loanAmount */
44    public double getLoanAmount() {
45      return loanAmount;
46    }
47
48    /** Set a newloanAmount */
49    public void setLoanAmount(double loanAmount) {
50      this.loanAmount = loanAmount;
51    }
52
53    /** Find monthly payment */
54    public double getMonthlyPayment() {
55      double monthlyInterestRate = annualInterestRate / 1200;
56      return loanAmount * monthlyInterestRate / (1 -
57        (Math.pow(1 / (1 + monthlyInterestRate), numberOfYears * 12)));
58    }
59
60    /** Find total payment */
61    public double getTotalPayment() {
62      return getMonthlyPayment() * numberOfYears * 12;
63    }
```

no-arg constructor

constructor

```
64
65    /** Return loan date */
66    public java.util.Date getLoanDate() {
67      return loanDate;
68    }
69 }
```

From a class developer's perspective, a class is designed for use by many different customers. In order to be useful in a wide range of applications, a class should provide a variety of ways for customization through constructors, properties, and methods.

The Loan class contains two constructors, four get methods, three set methods, and the methods for finding monthly payment and total payment. You can construct a Loan object by using the no-arg constructor or the one with three parameters: annual interest rate, number of years, and loan amount. When a loan object is created, its date is stored in the loanDate field. The getLoanDate method returns the date. The three get methods, getAnnualInterest, getNumberOfYears, and getLoanAmount, return annual interest rate, payment years, and loan amount, respectively. All the data properties and methods in this class are tied to a specific instance of the Loan class. Therefore, they are instance variables or methods.

Recall that the java.util.Date can be used to create an instance to represent current date and time in §7.5.1, "The Date Class." The Loan class contains the accessor method for loanDate, but no mutator method for it. Does this mean that the contents of loanDate cannot be changed? See Review Question 7.24.

 Important Pedagogical Tip

The UML diagram for the Loan class is shown in Figure 7.23. Students should begin by writing a test program that uses the Loan class even though they don't know how the Loan class is implemented. This has three benefits:

- It demonstrates that developing a class and using a class are two separate tasks.

- It makes it possible to skip the complex implementation of certain classes without interrupting the sequence of the book.

- It is easier to learn how to implement a class if you are familiar with the class through using it.

For all the examples from now on, you may first create an object from the class and try to use its methods and then turn your attention to its implementation.

7.16 Case Study: The **Course** Class

This section uses the Course class to demonstrate the creation and use of classes. The UML diagram for the class is shown in Figure 7.25.

Course
-name: String
-students: String[]
-numberOfStudents: int
+Course(name: String)
+getName(): String
+addStudent(student: String): void
+getStudents(): String[]
+getNumberOfStudents(): int

The name of the course.
The students who take the course.
The number of students (default: 0).
Creates a course with the specified name.
Returns the course name.
Adds a new student to the course list.
Returns the students for the course.
Returns the number of students for the course.

FIGURE 7.25   The Course class models the courses.

A **Course** object can be created using the constructor **Course(String name)** by passing a course name. You can add students to the course using the **addStudent (String student)** method and return all the students for the course using the **getStudents()** method. Suppose the class is available, Listing 7.10 gives a test class that creates two courses and adds students to the courses.

LISTING 7.10 TestCourse.java

```
1 public class TestCourse {
2   public static void main(String[] args) {
3     Course course1 = new Course("Data Structures");
4     Course course2 = new Course("Database Systems");
5
6     course1.addStudent("Peter Jones");
7     course1.addStudent("Brian Smith");
8     course1.addStudent("Anne Kennedy");
9
10    course2.addStudent("Peter Jones");
11    course2.addStudent("Steve Smith");
12
13    System.out.println("Number of students in course1: "
14      + course1.getNumberOfStudents());
15    String[] students = course1.getStudents();
16    for (int i = 0; i < course1.getNumberOfStudents(); i++)
17      System.out.print(students[i] + ", ");
18
19    System.out.println();
20    System.out.print("Number of students in course2: "
21      + course2.getNumberOfStudents());
22  }
23 }
```

create a course *(lines 3–4)*

add a student *(lines 6–10)*

number of students
return students *(lines 14–15)*

The **Course** class is implemented in Listing 7.11. The **Course** class uses an array to store the students for the course. For simplicity, assume that the maximum course enrollment is **100**. The array is created using **new String[100]** in line 3. The **addStudent** method (line 10) adds a student to the array. Whenever a new student is added to the course, **numberOfStudents** is increased (line 11). The **getStudents** method returns the array.

LISTING 7.11 Course.java

```
1 public class Course {
2   private String name;
3   private String[] students = new String[100];
4   private int numberOfStudents;
5
6   public Course(String name) {
7     this.name = name;
8   }
9
10  public void addStudent(String student) {
11    students[numberOfStudents] = student;
12    numberOfStudents++;
13  }
14
15  public String[] getStudents() {
16    return students;
17  }
18
```

create students *(line 3)*

add a course *(line 6)*

return students *(line 15)*

```
19   public int getNumberOfStudents() {
20     return numberOfStudents;
21   }
22
23   public String getName() {
24     return name;
25   }
26 }
```

number of students

The array size is fixed in Listing 7.11. You can improve it to automatically increase the array size in Exercise 7.8.

Note

When you create a **Course** object, an array object is created. A **Course** object contains a reference to the array. For simplicity, you can say that the **Course** object contains the array.

Note

The user can create a **Course** and manipulate it through the public methods **addStudent**, **getNumberOfStudents**, and **getStudents**. However, the user doesn't need to know how these methods are implemented. The **Course** class encapsulates the internal implementation. This example uses an array to store students. You may use a different data structure to store students. The program that uses **Course** does not need to change as long as the contract of the public methods remains unchanged.

7.17 (Optional) Case Study:
The **StackOfIntegers** Class

This section gives another example to demonstrate the creation and use of classes. Let us create a class for stacks.

A *stack* is a data structure that holds objects in a last-in first-out fashion. It has many applications. For example, the compiler uses a stack to process method invocations. When a method is invoked, its parameters and local variables are pushed into a stack. When a method calls another method, the new method's parameters and local variables are pushed into the stack. When a method finishes its work and returns to its caller, its associated space is released from the stack.

stack

For simplicity, assume the stack holds the **int** values and name the stack class **StackOfIntegers**. The UML diagram for the class is shown in Figure 7.26.

StackOfIntegers	
-elements: int[] -size: int	An array to store integers in the stack. The number of integers in the stack.
+StackOfIntegers() +StackOfIntegers(capacity: int) +empty(): boolean +peek(): int +push(value: int): int +pop(): int +getSize(): int	Constructs an empty stack with a default capacity of 16. Constructs an empty stack with a specified capacity. Returns true if the stack is empty. Returns the integer at the top of the stack without 　removing it from the stack. Stores an integer in the top of the stack. Removes the integer at the top of the stack and returns it. Returns the number of elements in the stack.

FIGURE 7.26 The **StackOfIntegers** class encapsulates the stack storage and provides the operations for manipulating the stack.

Suppose that the class is available. Let us write a test program in Listing 7.12 that uses the class to create a stack (line 3), stores ten integers 0, 1, 2, ..., and 9 (line 6), and displays them in reverse order (line 9).

LISTING 7.12 TestStackOfIntegers.java

```java
 1 public class TestStackOfIntegers {
 2   public static void main(String[] args) {
 3     StackOfIntegers stack = new StackOfIntegers();
 4
 5     for (int i = 0; i < 10; i++)
 6       stack.push(i);
 7
 8     while (!stack.empty())
 9       System.out.print(stack.pop() + " ");
10   }
11 }
```

create a stack

push to stack

pop from stack

How do you implement the **StackOfIntegers** class? The elements in the stack are stored in an array named **elements**. When you create a stack, the array is also created. The no-arg constructor creates an array with the default capacity of 16. The variable **size** counts the number of elements in the stack, and **size – 1** is the index of the element at the top of the stack, as shown in Figure 7.27. For an empty stack, **size** is 0.

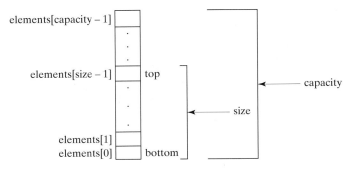

FIGURE 7.27 The **StackOfIntegers** class encapsulates the stack storage and provides the operations for manipulating the stack.

The **StackOfIntegers** class is implemented in Listing 7.13. The methods **empty()**, **peek()**, **pop()**, and **getSize()** are easy to implement. To implement **push(int value)**, assign **value** to **elements[size]** if **size < capacity** (line 24). If the stack is full (i.e., **size >= capacity**), create a new array of twice the current capacity (line 19), copy the contents of the current array to the new array (line 19), and assign the reference of the new array to the current array in the stack (line 20). Now you can add the new value to the array (line 24).

LISTING 7.13 StackOfIntegers.java

max capacity 16

```java
 1 public class StackOfIntegers {
 2   private int[] elements;
 3   private int size;
 4   public static final int DEFAULT_CAPACITY = 16;
 5
 6   /** Construct a stack with the default capacity 16 */
 7   public StackOfIntegers() {
 8     this(DEFAULT_CAPACITY);
 9   }
```

```
10
11    /** Construct a stack with the specified maximum capacity */
12    public StackOfIntegers(int capacity) {
13      elements = new int[capacity];
14    }
15
16    /** Push a new integer into the top of the stack */
17    public int push(int value) {
18      if (size >= elements.length) {
19        int[] temp = new int[elements.length * 2];            double the capacity
20        System.arraycopy(elements, 0, temp, 0, elements.length);
21        elements = temp;
22      }
23
24      return elements[size++] = value;                         add to stack
25    }
26
27    /** Return and remove the top element from the stack */
28    public int pop() {
29      return elements[--size];
30    }
31
32    /** Return the top element from the stack */
33    public int peek() {
34      return elements[size - 1];
35    }
36
37    /** Test whether the stack is empty */
38    public boolean empty() {
39      return size == 0;
40    }
41
42    /** Return the number of elements in the stack */
43    public int getSize() {
44      return size;
45    }
46 }
```

Note

Stacks are frequently used in programming. Java provides the **Stack** class in the **java.util** package, which will be introduced in Chapter 22, "Java Collections Framework."

7.18 (Optional GUI) Creating Windows

When you develop programs to create graphical user interfaces, you will use Java classes such as **JFrame**, **JButton**, **JRadioButton**, **JComboBox**, and **JList** to create frames, buttons, radio buttons, combo boxes, lists, and so on. Listing 7.14 is an example that creates two windows using the **JFrame** class. The output of the program is shown in Figure 7.28.

LISTING 7.14   TestFrame.java (Using Java API Classes)

```
1 import javax.swing.JFrame;
2
3 public class TestFrame {
4   public static void main(String[] args) {
5     JFrame frame1 = new JFrame();                    create an object
6     frame1.setTitle("Window 1");                     invoke a method
```

create an object
invoke a method

```
 7       frame1.setSize(200, 150);
 8       frame1.setLocation(200, 100);
 9       frame1.setDefaultCloseOperation(JFrame.EXIT_ON_CLOSE);
10       frame1.setVisible(true);
11
12       JFrame frame2 = new JFrame();
13       frame2.setTitle("Window 2");
14       frame2.setSize(200, 150);
15       frame2.setLocation(410, 100);
16       frame2.setDefaultCloseOperation(JFrame.EXIT_ON_CLOSE);
17       frame2.setVisible(true);
18     }
19 }
```

FIGURE 7.28   The program creates two windows using the JFrame class.

This program creates two objects of the JFrame class (lines 5, 12) and then uses the methods setTitle, setSize, setLocation, setDefaultCloseOperation, and setVisible to set the properties of the objects. The setTitle method sets a title for the window (lines 6, 13). The setSize method sets the window's width and height (lines 7, 14). The setLocation method specifies the location of the window's upper-left corner (lines 8, 15). The setDefaultCloseOperation method terminates the program when the frame is closed (lines 9, 16). The setVisible method displays the window. You can add graphical user interface components, such as buttons, labels, text fields, combo boxes, lists, and menus, to the window. The components are defined using classes. GUI programming will be introduced in Part 3, "GUI Programming."

KEY TERMS

accessor method (getter)   230
class   214
class abstraction   239
class encapsulation   239
class's contract   239
composition   240
constant   224
constructor   216
data field encapsulation   229
default constructor   216
dot operator (.)   217
immutable class   232
instance   214
instance method   217
instance variable   217
instantiation   214
mutator method (setter)   230

null   220
no-arg constructor   216
object-oriented programming
    (OOP)   214
Unified Modeling Language
    (UML)   215
package-private
    (or package-access)   228
private   228
public   228
reference variable   237
reference type   216
stack   234
static method   224
static variable   224
this keyword   236

CHAPTER SUMMARY

■ A class is a template for objects. It defines the generic properties of objects, and provides constructors for creating objects and methods for manipulating them.

■ A class is also a data type. You can use it to declare object reference variables. An object reference variable that appears to hold an object actually contains a reference to that object. Strictly speaking, an object reference variable and an object are different, but most of the time the distinction between them can be ignored.

■ An object is an instance of a class. You use the `new` operator to create an object, and the dot (`.`) operator to access members of that object through its reference variable.

■ An instance variable or method belongs to an instance of a class. Its use is associated with individual instances. A static variable is a variable shared by all instances of the same class. A static method is a method that can be invoked without using instances.

■ Every instance of a class can access the class's static variables and methods. However, it is better to invoke static variables and methods using `ClassName.variable` and `ClassName.method` for clarity.

■ Modifiers specify how the class, method, and data are accessed. A `public` class, method, or data is accessible to all clients. A `private` method or data is only accessible inside the class.

■ You can provide a `get` method or a `set` method to enable clients to see or modify the data. Colloquially, a `get` method is referred to as a *getter* (or *accessor*), and a `set` method is referred to as a *setter* (or *mutator*).

■ A `get` method has the signature `public returnType getPropertyName()`. If the `returnType` is `boolean`, the `get` method should be defined as `public boolean isPropertyName()`. A `set` method has the signature `public void setPropertyName(dataType propertyValue)`.

■ All parameters are passed to methods using pass-by-value. For a parameter of a primitive type, the actual value is passed; for a parameter of a reference type, the reference for the object is passed.

■ The scope of instance and static variables is the entire class, regardless of where the variables are declared. Instance and static variables can be declared anywhere in the class.

■ The keyword `this` can be used to refer to the calling object. It can also be used inside a constructor to invoke another constructor of the same class.

■ A Java array is an object that can contain primitive type values or object type values. When an array is created, its elements are assigned the default value of `0` for the numeric primitive data types, `'\u0000'` for `char` types, `false` for `boolean` types, and `null` for object types.

REVIEW QUESTIONS

Sections 7.2–7.4

7.1 Describe the relationship between an object and its defining class. How do you declare a class? How do you declare an object reference variable? How do you create an object? How do you declare and create an object in one statement?

7.2 What are the differences between constructors and methods?

7.3 Is an array an object or a primitive type value? Can an array contain elements of an object type as well as a primitive type? Describe the default value for the elements of an array.

7.4 What is wrong with the following program?

```java
public class ShowErrors {
  public static void main(String[] args) {
    ShowErrors t = new ShowErrors(5);
  }
}
```

(a)

```java
public class ShowErrors {
  public static void main(String[] args) {
    ShowErrors t = new ShowErrors();
    t.x();
  }
}
```

(b)

```java
public class ShowErrors {
  public void method1() {
    Circle c;
    System.out.println("What is radius "
      + c.getRadius());
    c = new Circle();
  }
}
```

(c)

```java
public class ShowErrors {
  public static void main(String[] args) {
    C c = new C(5.0);
    System.out.println(c.value);
  }
}

class C {
  int value = 2;
}
```

(d)

7.5 What is wrong in the following code?

```java
1 class Test {
2   public static void main(String[] args) {
3     A a = new A();
4     a.print();
5   }
6 }
7
8 class A {
9   String s;
10
11   A(String s) {
12     this.s = s;
13   }
14
15   public void print() {
16     System.out.print(s);
17   }
18 }
```

7.6   What is the printout of the following code?

```java
public class Foo {
  private boolean x;

  public static void main(String[] args) {
    Foo foo = new Foo();
    System.out.println(foo.x);
  }
}
```

Sections 7.5 Using Classes from the Java Library

7.7   How do you create a Date for the current time? How do you display the current time?

7.8   How do you create a Random object and obtain a random int value, double value, and boolean value?

7.9   Which packages contain the classes Date, Random, JOptionPane, System, and Math?

Section 7.6 Static Variables, Constants, and Methods

7.10   Suppose that the class Foo is defined in (a). Let f be an instance of Foo. Which of the statements in (b) are correct?

```java
public class Foo {
  int i;
  static String s;

  void imethod() {
  }

  static void smethod() {
  }
}
```

```java
System.out.println(f.i);
System.out.println(f.s);
f.imethod();
f.smethod();
System.out.println(Foo.i);
System.out.println(Foo.s);
Foo.imethod();
Foo.smethod();
```

(a)   (b)

7.11   Add the static keyword in the place of ? if appropriate.

```java
public class Test {
  private int count;

  public ? void main(String[] args) {
    ...
  }

  public ? int getCount() {
    return count;
  }

  public ? int factorial(int n) {
    int result = 1;
    for (int i = 1; i <= n; i++)
      result *= i;

    return result;
  }
}
```

7.12 Can you invoke an instance method or reference an instance variable from a static method? Can you invoke a static method or reference a static variable from an instance method? What is wrong in the following code?

```
 1 public class Foo {
 2   public static void main(String[] args) {
 3     method1();
 4   }
 5
 6   public void method1() {
 7     method2();
 8   }
 9
10   public static void method2() {
11     System.out.println("What is radius " + c.getRadius());
12   }
13
14   Circle c = new Circle();
15 }
```

Sections 7.7–7.9

7.13 What is an accessor method? What is a mutator method? What are the naming conventions for accessor methods and mutator methods?

7.14 What are the benefits of data field encapsulation?

7.15 In the following code, **radius** is private in the **Circle** class, and **myCircle** is an object of the **Circle** class. Does the following highlighted code cause any problems? Explain why.

```
public class Circle {
  private double radius = 1.0;

  /** Find the area of this circle */
  double getArea() {
    return radius * radius * Math.PI;
  }

  public static void main(String[] args) {
    Circle myCircle = new Circle();
    System.out.println("Radius is " + myCircle.radius);
  }
}
```

7.16 If a class contains only private data fields and no set methods, is the class immutable?

7.17 If all the data fields in a class are private and primitive type, and the class contains no set methods, is the class immutable?

Section 7.10 Passing Objects to Methods

7.18 Describe the difference between passing a parameter of a primitive type and passing a parameter of a reference type. Show the output of the following program:

```java
public class Test {
  public static void main(String[] args) {
    Count myCount = new Count();
    int times = 0;

    for (int i = 0; i < 100; i++)
      increment(myCount, times);

    System.out.println("count is " + myCount.count);
    System.out.println("times is " + times);
  }

  public static void increment(Count c, int times) {
    c.count++;
    times++;
  }
}
```

```java
public class Count {
  public int count;

  Count(int c) {
    count = c;
  }

  Count() {
    count = 1;
  }
}
```

7.19   Show the output of the following program:

```java
public class Test {
  public static void main(String[] args) {
    Circle circle1 = new Circle(1);
    Circle circle2 = new Circle(2);

    swap1(circle1, circle2);
    System.out.println("After swap1: circle1 = " +
      circle1.radius + " circle2 = " + circle2.radius);

    swap2(circle1, circle2);
    System.out.println("After swap2: circle1 = " +
      circle1.radius + " circle2 = " + circle2.radius);
  }

  public static void swap1(Circle x, Circle y) {
    Circle temp = x;
    x = y;
    y = temp;
  }

  public static void swap2(Circle x, Circle y) {
    double temp = x.radius;
    x.radius = y.radius;
    y.radius = temp;
  }
}

class Circle {
  double radius;

  Circle(double newRadius) {
    radius = newRadius;
  }
}
```

7.20 Show the printout of the following code:

```
public class Test {
  public static void main(String[] args) {
    int[] a = {1, 2};
    swap(a[0], a[1]);
    System.out.println("a[0] = " + a[0]
      + " a[1] = " + a[1]);
  }

  public static void swap(int n1, int n2) {
    int temp = n1;
    n1 = n2;
    n2 = temp;
  }
}
```

(a)

```
public class Test {
  public static void main(String[] args) {
    int[] a = {1, 2};
    swap(a);
    System.out.println("a[0] = " + a[0]
      + " a[1] = " + a[1]);
  }

  public static void swap(int[] a) {
    int temp = a[0];
    a[0] = a[1];
    a[1] = temp;
  }
}
```

(b)

```
public class Test {
  public static void main(String[] args) {
    T t = new T();
    swap(t);
    System.out.println("e1 = " + t.e1
      + " e2 = " + t.e2);
  }

  public static void swap(T t) {
    int temp = t.e1;
    t.e1 = t.e2;
    t.e2 = temp;
  }
}

class T {
  int e1 = 1;
  int e2 = 2;
}
```

(c)

```
public class Test {
  public static void main(String[] args) {
    T t1 = new T();
    T t2 = new T();
    System.out.println("t1's i = " +
      t1.i + " and j = " + t1.j);
    System.out.println("t2's i = " +
      t2.i + " and j = " + t2.j);
  }
}

class T {
  static int i = 0;
  int j = 0;

  T() {
    i++;
    j = 1;
  }
}
```

(d)

Sections 7.11–7.12

7.21 What is the output of the following program?

```
public class Foo {
  static int i = 0;
  static int j = 0;

  public static void main(String[] args) {
    int i = 2;
    int k = 3;

    {
      int j = 3;
      System.out.println("i + j is " + i + j);
    }
```

```
        k = i + j;
        System.out.println("k is " + k);
        System.out.println("j is " + j);
    }
}
```

7.22 Describe the role of the `this` keyword. What is wrong in the following code?

```
1 public class C {
2     int p;
3
4     public void setP(int p) {
5         p = p;
6     }
7 }
```

Sections 7.13–7.17

7.23 What is wrong in the following code?

```
1 public class Test {
2     public static void main(String[] args) {
3         java.util.Date[] dates = new java.util.Date[10];
4         System.out.println(dates[0]);
5         System.out.println(dates[0].toString());
6     }
7 }
```

7.24 If you redefine the `Loan` class without set methods, is the class immutable?

7.25 Is the `StackOfIntegers` class immutable?

PROGRAMMING EXERCISES

Pedagogical Note

The exercises in Part 2 achieve *three objectives*:

> three objectives

1. Design and draw UML for classes.
2. Implement classes from the UML.
3. Use classes to develop applications.

Solutions for the UML diagrams for the even-numbered exercises can be downloaded from the Student Web Site and all others can be downloaded from the Instructor Web Site.

Sections 7.2–7.11

7.1 (*The Rectangle class*) Design a class named `Rectangle` to represent a rectangle. The class contains:

- Two `double` data fields named `width` and `height` that specify the width and height of the rectangle. The default values are `1` for both `width` and `height`.
- A string data field named `color` that specifies the color of a rectangle. Hypothetically, assume that all rectangles have the same color. The default color is white.
- A no-arg constructor that creates a default rectangle.
- A constructor that creates a rectangle with the specified `width` and `height`.
- The accessor and mutator methods for all three data fields.
- A method named `getArea()` that returns the area of this rectangle.
- A method named `getPerimeter()` that returns the perimeter.

Draw the UML diagram for the class. Implement the class. Write a test program that creates two `Rectangle` objects. Assign width `4` and height `40` to the first object and width `3.5` and height `35.9` to the second object. Assign color red to all `Rectangle` objects. Display the ~~properties~~ of both objects and find their areas and perimeters *in this order. width, height*

7.2 (*The Fan class*) Design a class named `Fan` to represent a fan. The class contains:

- Three constants named `SLOW`, `MEDIUM`, and `FAST` with values `1`, `2`, and `3` to denote the fan speed.
- An `int` data field named `speed` that specifies the speed of the fan (default `SLOW`).
- A `boolean` data field named `on` that specifies whether the fan is on (default `false`).
- A `double` data field named `radius` that specifies the radius of the fan (default `5`).
- A string data field named `color` that specifies the color of the fan (default `blue`).
- A no-arg constructor that creates a default fan.
- The accessor and mutator methods for all four data fields.
- A method named `toString()` that returns a string description for the fan. If the fan is on, the method returns the fan speed, color, and radius in one combined string. If the fan is not on, the method returns fan color and radius along with the string `"fan is off"` in one combined string.

Draw the UML diagram for the class. Implement the class. Write a test program that creates two `Fan` objects. Assign maximum speed, radius `10`, color `yellow`, and turn it on to the first object. Assign medium speed, radius `5`, color `blue`, and turn it off to the second object. Display the objects by invoking their `toString` method.

7.3 (*The Account class*) Design a class named `Account` that contains:

- An `int` data field named `id` for the account (default `0`).
- A `double` data field named `balance` for the account (default `0`).
- A `double` data field named `annualInterestRate` that stores the current interest rate (default `0`).
- A `Date` data field named `dateCreated` that stores the date when the account was created.
- A no-arg constructor that creates a default account.
- The accessor and mutator methods for `id`, `balance`, and `annualInterest-Rate`.
- The accessor method for `dateCreated`.
- A method named `getMonthlyInterestRate()` that returns the monthly interest rate.
- A method named `withDraw` that withdraws a specified amount from the account.
- A method named `deposit` that deposits a specified amount to the account.

Draw the UML diagram for the class. Implement the class. Write a test program that creates an `Account` object with an account ID of `1122`, a balance of `20000`, and an annual interest rate of `4.5%`. Use the `withdraw` method to withdraw $2500, use the `deposit` method to deposit $3000, and print the balance, the monthly interest, and the date when this account was created.

7.4 (*The Stock class*) Design a class named `Stock` that contains:

- A string data field named `symbol` for the stock's symbol.
- A string data field named `name` for the stock's name.
- A `double` data field named `previousClosingPrice` that stores the stock price for the previous day.
- A `double` data field named `currentPrice` that stores the stock price for the current time.
- A constructor that creates a stock with specified symbol and name.
- The accessor methods for all data fields.
- The mutator methods for `previousClosingPrice` and `currentPrice`.
- A method named `changePercent()` that returns the percentage changed from `previousClosingPrice` to `currentPrice`.

Draw the UML diagram for the class. Implement the class. Write a test program that creates a `Stock` object with the stock symbol SUNW, the name Sun Microsystems Inc, and the previous closing price of 100. Set a new current price to 90 and display the price-change percentage.

7.5* (*Using the GregorianCalendar class*) Java API has the `GregorianCalendar` class in the `java.util` package that can be used to obtain the year, month, and day of a date. The no-arg constructor constructs an instance for the current date, and the methods `get(GregorianCalendar.YEAR)`, `get(GregorianCalendar.MONTH)`, and `get(GregorianCalendar.DAY_OF_MONTH)` return the year, month, and day. Write a program to test this class to display the current year, month, and day.

7.6** (*Displaying calendars*) Rewrite the `PrintCalendar` class in §5.11, "Method Abstraction and Stepwise Refinement," to display calendars in a message dialog box. Since the output is generated from several static methods in the class, you may define a static `String` variable `output` for storing the output and display it in a message dialog box.

7.7* (*The Time class*) Design a class named `Time`. The class contains:

- Data fields `hour`, `minute`, and `second` that represents a time.
- A no-arg constructor that creates a `Time` object for the current time. (The data fields value will represent the current time)
- A constructor that constructs a `Time` object with a specified elapse time since the middle night, January 1, 1970 in milliseconds. (The data fields value will represent this time.)
- Three get methods for the data fields `hour`, `minute`, and `second`, respectively.

Draw the UML diagram for the class. Implement the class. Write a test program that creates two `Time` objects (using `new Time()` and `new Time(555550000)`) and display their hour, minute, and second.

Hint

The No-arg constructor uses the current time. The current time can be obtained using `System.currentTimeMillis()`, as shown in Listing 2.8, ShowCurrentTime.java. The other constructor sets the hour, minute, and second for the specified elapse time. For example, if the elapse time is 555550000 milliseconds, the hour is 10, the minute is 19, and the second is 10.

7.8* (*The Course class*) The array size is fixed in Listing 7.11. Improve it to automatically increase the array size by creating a new larger array and copying the contents of the current array to it.

Sections 7.12–7.16

7.9 (*The* `MyInteger` *class*) Design a class named `MyInteger`. The class contains:

- An `int` data field named `value` that stores the `int` value represented by this object.
- A constructor that creates a `MyInteger` object for the specified `int` value.
- A get method that returns the `int` value.
- Methods `isEven()`, `isOdd()`, and `isPrime()` that return `true` if the value is even, odd, or prime, respectively.
- Static methods `isEven(int)`, `isOdd(int)`, and `isPrime(int)` that return `true` if the specified value is even, odd, or prime, respectively.
- Static methods `isEven(MyInteger)`, `isOdd(MyInteger)`, and `isPrime (MyInteger)` that return `true` if the specified value is even, odd, or prime, respectively.
- Methods `equals(int)` and `equals(MyInteger)` that return `true` if the value in the object is equal to the specified value.
- A static method `parseInt(int)` that converts a string to an `int` value.

Draw the UML diagram for the class. Implement the class. Write a client program that tests all methods in the class.

7.10 (*Modifying the* `Loan` *class*) Rewrite the `Loan` class to add two static methods for computing monthly payment and total payment, as follows:

```
public static double monthlyPayment(double annualInterestRate,
    int numOfYears, double loanAmount)
```

```
public static double totalPayment(double annualInterestRate,
    int numOfYears, double loanAmount)
```

Write a client program to test these two methods.

7.11 (*The* `MyPoint` *class*) Design a class named `MyPoint` to represent a point with x and y-coordinates. The class contains:

- Two data fields `x` and `y` that represent the coordinates.
- A no-arg constructor that creates a point (`0`, `0`).
- A constructor that constructs a point with specified coordinates.
- Two get methods for data fields `x` and `y`, respectively.
- A method named `distance` that returns the distance from this point to another point of the `MyPoint` type.
- A method named `distance` that returns the distance from this point to another point with specified x and y-coordinates.

Draw the UML diagram for the class. Implement the class. Write a test program that creates two points (`0`, `0`) and (`10`, `30.5`) and displays the distance between them.

7.12* (*Displaying the prime factors*) Write a program that receives a positive integer and displays all its smallest factors in decreasing order. For example, if the integer is `120`, the smallest factors are displayed as `5`, `3`, `2`, `2`, `2`. Use the `StackOfIntegers` class to store the factors (e.g., `2`, `2`, `2`, `3`, `5`) and retrieve and display them in reverse order.

7.13** (*Displaying the prime numbers*) Write a program that displays all the prime numbers less than 120 in decreasing order. Use the `StackOfIntegers` class to store the prime numbers (e.g., `2`, `3`, `5`, …) and retrieve and display them in reverse order.

7.14*** (*The Tax class*) Design a class named `Tax` to contain the following instance data fields:

- `int filingStatus`: One of the four tax filing statuses: `0` — single filer, `1` — married filing jointly, `2` — married filing separately, and `3` — head of household. Use the public static constants `SINGLE_FILER` (`0`), `MARRIED_JOINTLY` (`1`), `MARRIED_SEPARATELY` (`2`), `HEAD_OF_HOUSEHOLD` (`3`) to represent the status.
- `int[][] brackets`: Stores the tax brackets for each filing status (see Listing 6.11, ComputeTax.java).
- `double[] rates`: Stores tax rates for each bracket (see Listing 6.11).
- `double taxableIncome`: Stores the taxable income.

Provide the get and set methods for each data field and the `getTax()` method that returns the tax. Also provide a no-arg constructor and the constructor `Tax(filingStatus, brackets, rates, taxableIncome)`.

Draw the UML diagram for the class. Implement the class. Write a test program that uses the `Tax` class to print the 2001 and 2002 tax tables for taxable income from $50,000 to $60,000 with intervals of $1,000 for all four statuses. The tax rates for the year 2002 were given in Table 3.7. The tax rates for 2001 are shown in Table 7.1.

TABLE 7.1   2001 United States Federal Personal Tax Rates

Tax rate	Single filers	Married filing jointly or qualifying widow(er)	Married filing separately	Head of household
15%	Up to $27,050	Up to $45,200	Up to $22,600	Up to $36,250
27.5%	$27,051–$65,550	$45,201–$109,250	$22,601–$54,625	$36,251–$93,650
30.5%	$65,551–$136,750	$109,251–$166,500	$54,626–$83,250	$93,651–$151,650
35.5%	$136,751–$297,350	$166,501–$297,350	$83,251–$148,675	$151,651–$297,350
39.1%	$297,351 or more	$297,351 or more	$148,676 or more	$297,351 or more

STRINGS AND TEXT I/O

Objectives

- To use the `String` class to process fixed strings (§8.2).

- To use the `Character` class to process a single character (§8.3).

- To use the `StringBuilder`/`StringBuffer` class to process flexible strings (§8.4).

- To know the differences between the `String`, `StringBuilder`, and `StringBuffer` classes (§§8.2–8.4).

- To learn how to pass strings to the `main` method from the command line (§8.5).

- (Optional) To use the regular expressions to represent patterns for matching, replacing, and splitting strings (§8.6).

- To discover file properties, delete and rename files using the `File` class (§8.7).

- To write data to a file using the `PrintWriter` class (§8.8.1).

- To read data from a file using the `Scanner` class (§8.8.2).

- (Optional GUI) To add components to a frame (§8.9).

8.1 Introduction

Strings are used often in programming. A *string* is a sequence of characters. In many languages, strings are treated as arrays of characters, but in Java a string is an object. Java provides the `String`, `StringBuilder`, and `StringBuffer` classes for storing and processing strings.

In most cases, you use the `String` class to create strings. The `String` class is efficient for storing and processing strings, but strings created with the `String` class cannot be modified. The `StringBuilder` and `StringBuffer` classes enable you to create flexible strings that can be modified.

This chapter also introduces how to process command-line arguments to the `main` method and how to perform simple text input and output using the `Scanner` class and the `PrintWriter` class.

8.2 The `String` Class

The `java.lang.String` class models a sequence of characters as a string. You have already used string literals, such as the parameter in the `println(String s)` method. The Java compiler converts the string literal into a string object and passes it to `println`.

The `String` class has eleven constructors and more than forty methods for examining individual characters in a sequence, comparing strings, searching substrings, obtaining substrings, and creating a copy of a string with all the characters translated to uppercase or lowercase. The most frequently used methods are listed in Figure 8.1.

8.2.1 Constructing a String

You can create a string object from a string value or from an array of characters. To create a string from a string literal, use a syntax like this one:

```
String newString = new String(stringLiteral);
```

The argument `stringLiteral` is a sequence of characters enclosed inside double quotes. The following statement creates a `String` object `message` for the string literal `"Welcome to Java"`:

```
String message = new String("Welcome to Java");
```

string literal object

Since strings are used frequently, Java treats a string literal as a `String` object. So the following statement is valid:

```
String message = "Welcome to Java";
```

You can also create a string from an array of characters. For example, the following statements create the string "Good Day".

```
char[] charArray = {'G', 'o', 'o', 'd', ' ', 'D', 'a', 'y'};
String message = new String(charArray);
```

Note

string, string variable,
string value

A `String` variable holds a reference to a `String` object that stores a string value. Strictly speaking, the terms `String` *variable*, `String` *object*, and *string value* are different, but the distinctions between them can be ignored most of the time. For simplicity, the term *string* will often be used to refer to `String` variable, `String` object, and string value.

java.lang.String	
+String()	Constructs an empty string.
+String(value: String)	Constructs a string with the specified string literal value.
+String(value: char[])	Constructs a string with the specified character array.
+charAt(index: int): char	Returns the character at the specified index from this string.
+compareTo(anotherString: String): int	Compares this string with another string.
+compareToIgnoreCase(anotherString: String): int	Compares this string with another string ignoring case.
+concat(anotherString: String): String	Concatenate this string with another string.
+endsWith(suffix: String): boolean	Returns true if this string ends with the specified suffix.
+equals(anotherString: String): boolean	Returns true if this string is equal to another string.
+equalsIgnoreCase(anotherString: String): boolean	Checks whether this string equals another string ignoring case.
+getChars(srcBegin: int, srcEnd: int, dst: char[] dstBegin: int): void	Copies characters from this string into the destination character array.
+indexOf(ch: int): int	Returns the index of the first occurrence of ch.
+indexOf(ch: int, fromIndex: int): int	Returns the index of the first occurrence of ch after fromIndex.
+indexOf(str: String): int	Returns the index of the first occurrence of str.
+indexOf(str: String, fromIndex: int): int	Returns the index of the first occurrence of str after fromIndex.
+lastIndexOf(ch: int): int	Returns the index of the last occurrence of ch.
+lastIndexOf(ch: int, fromIndex: int): int	Returns the index of the last occurrence of ch before fromIndex.
+lastIndexOf(str: String): int	Returns the index of the last occurrence of str.
+lastIndexOf(str: String, fromIndex: int): int	Returns the index of the last occurrence of str before fromIndex.
+regionMatches(toffset: int, other: String, offset: int, len: int): boolean	Returns true if the specified subregion of this string exactly matches the specified subregion of the string argument.
+length(): int	Returns the number of characters in this string.
+replace(oldChar: char, newChar: char): String	Returns a new string with oldChar replaced by newChar.
+replaceFirst(oldString: String, newString: String): String	Replace the first matching substring in this string with the new substring.
+replaceAll(oldString: String, newString: String): String	Replace all matching substrings in this string with the new substring.
+startsWith(prefix: String): boolean	Returns true if this string starts with the specified prefix.
+subString(beginIndex: int): String	Returns the substring from beginIndex.
+subString(beginIndex: int, endIndex: int): String	Returns the substring from beginIndex to endIndex –1.
+toCharArray(): char[]	Returns a char array consisting of characters from this string.
+toLowerCase(): String	Returns a new string with all characters converted to lowercase.
+toString(): String	Returns a new string with itself.
+toUpperCase(): String	Returns a new string with all characters converted to uppercase.
+trim(): String	Returns a string with blank characters trimmed on both sides.
+copyValueOf(data: char[]): String	Returns a new string consisting of the char array data.
+valueOf(c: char): String	Returns a string consisting of the character c.
+valueOf(data: char[]): String	Same as copyValueOf(data: char[]): String.
+valueOf(d: double): String	Returns a string representing the double value.
+valueOf(f: float): String	Returns a string representing the float value.
+valueOf(i: int): String	Returns a string representing the int value.
+valueOf(l: long): String	Returns a string representing the long value.

FIGURE 8.1   The **String** class provides the methods for processing a string.

8.2.2 Immutable Strings and Interned Strings

A **String** *object is immutable; its contents cannot be changed.* Does the following code   immutable
change the contents of the string?

```
String s = "Java";
s = "HTML";
```

The answer is no. The first statement creates a **String** object with the content "Java" and
assigns its reference to **s**. The second statement creates a new **String** object with the content "HTML" and assigns its reference to **s**. The first **String** object still exists after the
assignment, but it can no longer be accessed because variable **s** now points to the new object,
as shown in Figure 8.2.

Since strings are immutable and are frequently used, the JVM improves efficiency and
saves memory, by using a unique instance for string literals with the same character sequence.

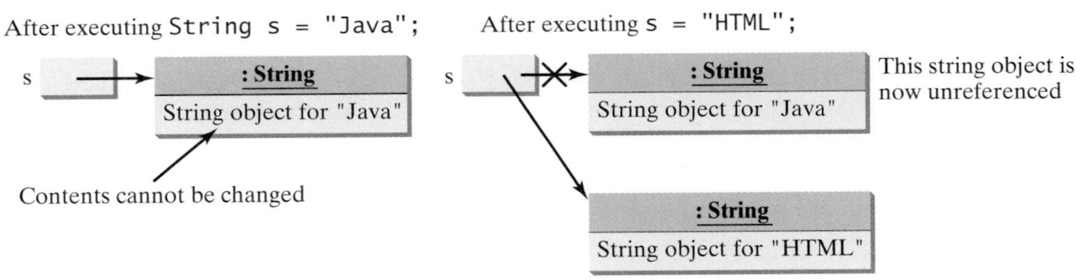

After executing `String s = "Java";`   After executing `s = "HTML";`

FIGURE 8.2 Strings are immutable; their contents cannot be changed once created.

Such an instance is called *interned*. You can also use a `String` object's `intern` method to return an *interned string*. For example, the following statements:

interned string

```
String s = "Welcome to Java";
String s1 = new String("Welcome to Java");
String s2 = s1.intern();
String s3 = "Welcome to Java";
System.out.println("s1 == s is " + (s1 == s));
System.out.println("s2 == s is " + (s2 == s));
System.out.println("s == s3 is " + (s == s3));
```

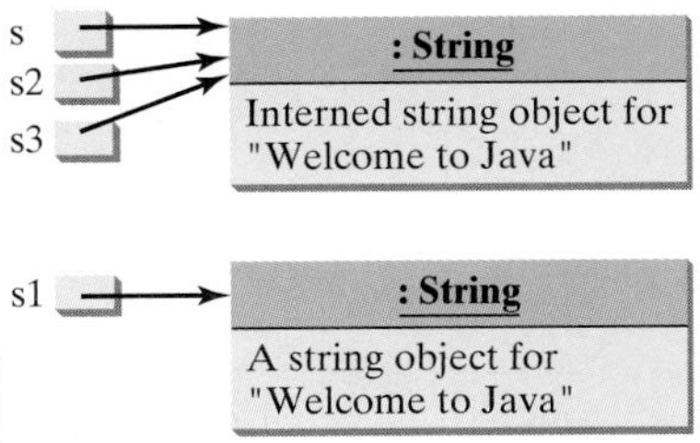

display

```
s1 == s is false
s2 == s is true
s == s3 is true
```

In the preceding statements, `s`, `s2`, and `s3` refer to the same interned string `"Welcome to Java"`, therefore `s2 == s` and `s == s3` are `true`. However, `s1 == s` is `false`, because `s` and `s1` are two different string objects even though they have the same contents.

8.2.3 String Comparisons

Often, in a program, you need to compare the contents of two strings. You might attempt to use the `==` operator, as follows:

==

```
if (string1 == string2)
    System.out.println("string1 and string2 are the same object");
else
    System.out.println("string1 and string2 are different objects");
```

However, the `==` operator only checks whether `string1` and `string2` refer to the same object; it does not tell you whether `string1` and `string2` contain the same contents. Therefore, you cannot use the `==` operator to find out whether two string variables have the same contents. Instead, you should use the `equals` method for an equality comparison of the contents of objects. The code given below, for instance, can be used to compare two strings.

s1.equals(s2)

```
if (string1.equals(string2))
    System.out.println("string1 and string2 have the same contents");
else
    System.out.println("string1 and string2 are not equal");
```

Note

Strings with the same contents do not always share the same object. For example, the following two variables, s1 and s2, are different even though their contents are identical:

```
String s1 = new String("Welcome to Java");
String s2 = "Welcome to Java";

System.out.println("s1 == s2 is " + (s1 == s2));
System.out.println("s1.equals(s2) is " + (s1.equals(s2)));
```

In this case, s1 == s2 is false since they point to two different objects, but *s1.equals(s2)* is true since the objects have the same contents. For safety and clarity, you should always use the equals method to test whether two strings have the same contents, and the == operator to test whether the two strings have the same references (i.e., point to the same memory location).

Note

For two strings x and y, x.equals(y) if and only if x.intern() == y.intern().

The compareTo method can also be used to compare two strings. For example, consider the following code:

```
s1.compareTo(s2)
```

The method returns the value 0 if s1 is equal to s2, a value less than 0 if s1 is lexicographically less than s2, and a value greater than 0 if s1 is lexicographically greater than s2.

The actual value returned from the compareTo method depends on the offset of the first two distinct characters in s1 and s2 from left to right. For example, suppose s1 is "abc" and s2 is "abg", and s1.compareTo(s2) returns -4. The first two characters (a vs. a) from s1 and s2 are compared. Because they are equal, the second two characters (b vs. b) are compared. Because they are also equal, the third two characters (c vs. g) are compared. Since the character c is 4 less than g, the comparison returns -4.

s1.compareTo(s2)

Caution

Syntax errors will occur if you compare strings by using comparison operators, such as >, >=, <, or <=. Instead, you have to use s1.compareTo(s2).

Note

The equals method returns true if two strings are equal, and false if they are not equal. The compareTo method returns 0, a positive integer, or a negative integer, depending on whether one string is equal to, greater than, or less than the other string.

The String class also provides equalsIgnoreCase and regionMatches methods for comparing strings. The equalsIgnoreCase method ignores the case of the letters when determining whether two strings are equal. The regionMatches method compares portions of two strings for equality. You can also use str.startsWith(prefix) to check whether string str starts with a specified prefix, and str.endsWith(suffix) to check whether string str ends with a specified suffix.

8.2.4   String Length and Retrieving Individual Characters

You can get the length of a string by invoking its length() method. For example, message.length() returns the length of the string message.

The s.charAt(index) method can be used to retrieve a specific character in a string s, where the index is between 0 and s.length() - 1. For example, message.charAt(0) returns the character W, as shown in Figure 8.3.

length()
charAt(index)

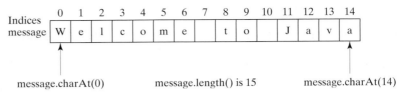

message.charAt(0) message.length() is 15 message.charAt(14)

FIGURE 8.3 A `String` object is represented using an array internally.

Note

string literal

When you use a string, you often know its literal value. For convenience, Java allows you to use the *string literal* to refer directly to strings without creating new variables. Thus, `"Welcome to Java".charAt(0)` is correct and returns `W`.

Note

encapsulating string

A string value is represented using a private array variable internally. The array cannot be accessed outside of the `String` class. The `String` class provides many public methods, such as `length()` and `charAt(index)`, to retrieve the array information. This is a good example of encapsulation: the detailed data structure of the class is hidden from the user through the private modifier, and thus the user cannot directly manipulate the internal data structure. If the array were not private, the user would be able to change the string content by modifying the array. This would violate the tenet that the `String` class is immutable.

Caution

string index range

Accessing characters in a string `s` out of bounds is a common programming error. To avoid it, make sure that you do not use an index beyond `s.length()` – 1. For example, `s.charAt(s.length())` would cause a `StringIndexOutOfBoundsException`.

Caution

length()

`length` is a method in the `String` class but is a property of an array object. So you have to use `s.length()` to get the number of characters in string `s`, and `a.length` to get the number of elements in array `a`.

8.2.5 String Concatenation

You can use the `concat` method to concatenate two strings. The statement shown below, for example, concatenates strings `s1` and `s2` into `s3`:

```
String s3 = s1.concat(s2);
```

Since string concatenation is heavily used in programming, Java provides a convenient way to concatenate strings. You can use the plus (+) sign to concatenate two or more strings. So the above statement is equivalent to

s1 + s2

```
String s3 = s1 + s2;
```

The following code combines the strings `message`, `" and "`, and `"HTML"` into one string:

```
String myString = message + " and " + "HTML";
```

Recall that the + sign can also concatenate a number with a string. In this case, the number is converted into a string and then concatenated. Note that at least one of the operands must be a string in order for concatenation to take place.

8.2.6   Obtaining Substrings

You can obtain a single character from a string using the charAt method. You can also obtain a substring from a string using the substring method in the String class. The substring method has two versions:

■ **public String substring(int beginIndex, int endIndex)**
Returns a new string that is a substring of the string. The substring begins at the specified beginIndex and extends to the character at index endIndex - 1, as shown in Figure 8.4. Thus the length of the substring is endIndex-beginIndex.

substring(int, int)

■ **public String substring(int beginIndex)**
Returns a new string that is a substring of the string. The substring begins with the character at the specified index and extends to the end of the string, as shown in Figure 8.4.

substring(int)

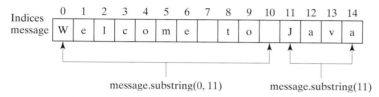

FIGURE 8.4   The substring method obtains a substring from a string.

For example,

```
String message = "Welcome to Java".substring(0, 11) + "HTML";
```

The string message now becomes "Welcome to HTML".

8.2.7   String Conversions

The contents of a string cannot be changed once the string is created. But you can obtain a new string using the toLowerCase, toUpperCase, trim, and replace methods. The toLowerCase and toUpperCase methods return a new string by converting all the characters in the string to lowercase or uppercase. The trim method returns a new string by eliminating blank characters from both ends of the string. The replace(oldChar, newChar) method can be used to replace all occurrences of a character in the string with a new character.
For example,

```
"Welcome".toLowerCase()  returns a new string, welcome.
"Welcome".toUpperCase()  returns a new string, WELCOME.
"  Welcome".trim()  returns a new string, Welcome.
"Welcome".replace('e', 'A')  returns a new string, WAlcomA.
"Welcome".replaceFirst("e", "A")  returns a new string, WAlcome.
"Welcome".replaceAll("e", "A")  returns a new string, WAlcomA.
```

toLowerCase()
toUpperCase()
trim()
replace

8.2.8   Finding a Character or a Substring in a String

You can use the indexOf and lastIndexOf methods to find a character or a substring in a string. Four overloaded indexOf methods and four overloaded lastIndexOf methods are defined in the String class.

■ **public int indexOf(int ch)**
   (***public int lastIndexOf(int ch)***)

Returns the index of the first (*last*) character in the string that matches the specified character ch. Returns −1 if the specified character is not in the string. When you pass a character to ch (e.g., indexOf('a')), the character's Unicode value is passed to the parameter ch (e.g., the Unicode value for 'a' is 97 in decimal).

- **public int** indexOf(**int** ch, **int** fromIndex)
  (**public int** lastIndexOf(**int** ch, **int** endIndex))

  Returns the index of the first (*last*) character in the string starting from (*ending at*) the specified fromIndex (endIndex) that matches the specified character ch. Returns −1 if the specified character is not in the substring beginning at position fromIndex (*ending at position* endIndex).

- **public int** indexOf(String str)
  (**public int** lastIndexOf(String str))

  Returns the index of the first character of the (*last*) substring in the string that matches the specified string str. Returns −1 if the str argument is not in the string.

- **public int** indexOf(String str, **int** fromIndex)
  (**public int** lastIndexOf(String str, int endIndex))

  Returns the index of the first character of the (*last*) substring in the string starting from (*ending at*) the specified fromIndex (endIndex) that matches the specified string str. Returns −1 if the str argument is not in the substring.

For example,

indexOf
```
"Welcome to Java".indexOf('W') returns 0.
"Welcome to Java".indexOf('o') returns 4.
"Welcome to Java".indexOf('o', 5) returns 9.
"Welcome to Java".indexOf("come") returns 3.
"Welcome to Java".indexOf("Java", 5) returns 11.
"Welcome to Java".indexOf("java", 5) returns -1.
```

lastIndexOf
```
"Welcome to Java".lastIndexOf('W') returns 0.
"Welcome to Java".lastIndexOf('o') returns 9.
"Welcome to Java".lastIndexOf('o', 5) returns 4.
"Welcome to Java".lastIndexOf("come") returns 3.
"Welcome to Java".lastIndexOf("Java", 5) returns -1.
"Welcome to Java".lastIndexOf("java", 5) returns -1.
```

8.2.9 Conversion Between Strings and Arrays

Strings are not arrays, but a string can be converted into an array, and vice versa. To convert a string to an array of characters, use the toCharArray method. For example, the following statement converts the string "Java" to an array:

toCharArray
```
char[] chars = "Java".toCharArray();
```

So chars[0] is 'J', chars[1] is 'a', chars[2] is 'v', and chars[3] is 'a'.

You can also use the getChars(int srcBegin, int srcEnd, char[] dst, int dstBegin) method to copy a substring of the string from index srcBegin to index srcEnd-1 into a character array dst starting from index dstBegin. For example, the following code copies a substring "3720" in "CS3720" from index 2 to index 6 − 1 into the character array dst starting from index 4:

getChars
```
char[] dst = {'J', 'A', 'V', 'A', '1', '3', '0', '1'};
"CS3720".getChars(2, 6, dst, 4);
```

Thus dst becomes {'J', 'A', 'V', 'A', '3', '7', '2', '0'}.

To convert an array of characters into a string, use the `String(char[])` constructor or the `valueOf(char[])` method. For example, the following statement constructs a string from an array using the `String` constructor:

```
String str = new String(new char[]{'J', 'a', 'v', 'a'});
```

The next statement constructs a string from an array using the `valueOf` method.

```
String str = String.valueOf(new char[]{'J', 'a', 'v', 'a'});
```

valueOf

8.2.10 Converting Characters and Numeric Values to Strings

The `valueOf` method can be used to convert an array of characters into a string. There are several overloaded versions of the `valueOf` method that can be used to convert a character and numeric values to strings with different parameter types, `char`, `double`, `long`, `int`, and `float`. For example, to convert a double value `5.44` to a string, use `String.valueOf(5.44)`. The return value is a string consisting of the characters `'5'`, `'.'`, `'4'`, and `'4'`.

overloaded **valueOf**

Note

Use `Double.parseDouble(str)` or `Integer.parseInt(str)` to convert a string to a `double` value or an `int` value.

Tip

You can use *regular expressions* to parse and validate strings. For more information, see §8.6, "Regular Expressions."

regular expression

8.2.11 Example: Checking Palindromes

This example writes a program that prompts the user to enter a string and reports whether the string is a palindrome, as shown in Figure 8.5. A string is a palindrome if it reads the same forward and backward. The words "mom," "dad," and "noon," for instance, are all palindromes.

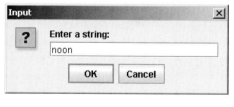

FIGURE 8.5 The program checks whether a string is a palindrome.

One solution is to check whether the first character in the string is the same as the last character. If so, check whether the second character is the same as the second-last character. This process continues until a mismatch is found or all the characters in the string are checked, except for the middle character if the string has an odd number of characters.

To implement this idea, use two variables, say `low` and `high`, to denote the position of two characters at the beginning and the end in a string `s`, as shown in Listing 8.1 (lines 24, 27). Initially, `low` is 0 and `high` is `s.length() - 1`. If the two characters at these positions match, increment `low` by 1 and decrement `high` by 1 (lines 33–34). This process continues until (`low >= high`) or a mismatch is found.

Listing 8.1 CheckPalindrome.java

```
 1 import javax.swing.JOptionPane;
 2
 3 public class CheckPalindrome {
 4   /** Main method */
 5   public static void main(String[] args) {
 6     // Prompt the user to enter a string
 7     String s = JOptionPane.showInputDialog("Enter a string:");
 8
 9     // Declare and initialize output string
10     String output = "";
11
12     if (isPalindrome(s))
13       output = s + " is a palindrome";
14     else
15       output = s + " is not a palindrome";
16
17     // Display the result
18     JOptionPane.showMessageDialog(null, output);
19   }
20
21   /** Check if a string is a palindrome */
22   public static boolean isPalindrome(String s) {
23     // The index of the first character in the string
24     int low = 0;
25
26     // The index of the last character in the string
27     int high = s.length ()- 1;
28
29     while (low < high) {
30       if (s.charAt(low) != s.charAt(high))
31         return false; // Not a palindrome
32
33       low++;
34       high--;
35     }
36
37     return true; // The string is a palindrome
38   }
39 }
```

input string — line 7
low index — line 24
high index — line 27
update indices — line 33

8.3 The **Character** Class

Java provides a wrapper class for every primitive data type. These classes are `Character`, `Boolean`, `Byte`, `Short`, `Integer`, `Long`, `Float`, and `Double` for `char`, `boolean`, `byte`, `short`, `int`, `long`, `float`, and `double`. All these classes are in the `java.lang` package. They enable the primitive data values to be treated as objects. They also contain useful methods for processing primitive values. This section introduces the `Character` class. The other wrapper classes will be introduced in Chapter 10, "Abstract Classes and Interfaces."

The `Character` class has a constructor and several methods for determining a character's category (uppercase, lowercase, digit, etc.) and for converting characters from uppercase to lowercase, and vice versa, as shown in Figure 8.6.

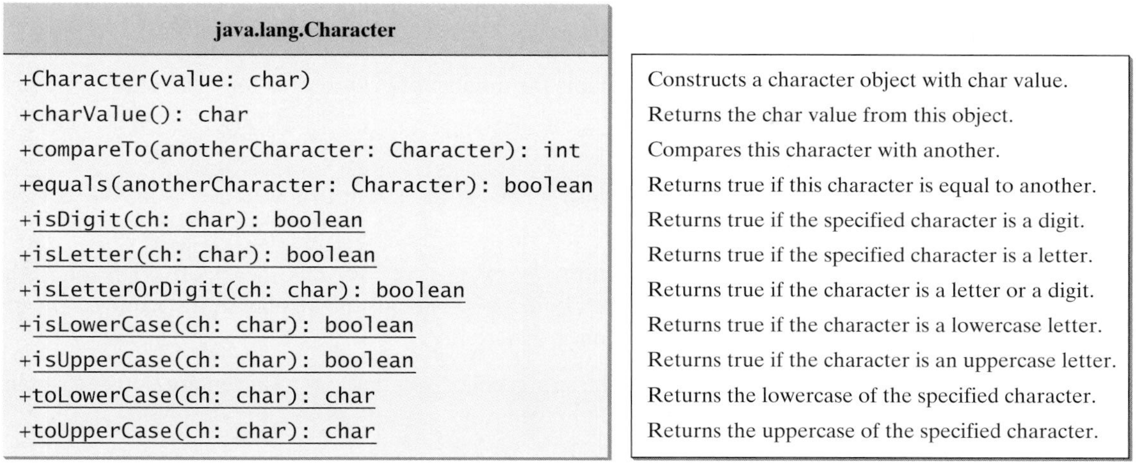

java.lang.Character	
+Character(value: char)	Constructs a character object with char value.
+charValue(): char	Returns the char value from this object.
+compareTo(anotherCharacter: Character): int	Compares this character with another.
+equals(anotherCharacter: Character): boolean	Returns true if this character is equal to another.
+isDigit(ch: char): boolean	Returns true if the specified character is a digit.
+isLetter(ch: char): boolean	Returns true if the specified character is a letter.
+isLetterOrDigit(ch: char): boolean	Returns true if the character is a letter or a digit.
+isLowerCase(ch: char): boolean	Returns true if the character is a lowercase letter.
+isUpperCase(ch: char): boolean	Returns true if the character is an uppercase letter.
+toLowerCase(ch: char): char	Returns the lowercase of the specified character.
+toUpperCase(ch: char): char	Returns the uppercase of the specified character.

FIGURE 8.6   The `Character` class provides the methods for manipulating a character.

You can create a `Character` object from a `char` value. For example, the following statement creates a `Character` object for the character `'a'`.

```
Character character = new Character('a');
```

The `charValue` method returns the character value wrapped in the `Character` object. The `compareTo` method compares this character with another character and returns an integer that is the difference between the Unicodes of this character and the other character. The `equals` method returns `true` if and only if the two characters are the same. For example, suppose `charObject` is `new Character('b')`:

```
charObject.compareTo(new Character('a')) returns 1
charObject.compareTo(new Character('b')) returns 0
charObject.compareTo(new Character('c')) returns -1
charObject.compareTo(new Character('d') returns -2
charObject.equals(new Character('b')) returns true
charObject.equals(new Character('d')) returns false
```

Most of the methods in the `Character` class are static methods. The `isDigit(char ch)` method returns `true` if the character is a digit. The `isLetter(char ch)` method returns `true` if the character is a letter. The `isLetterOrDigit(char ch)` method is `true` if the character is a letter or a digit. The `isLowerCase(char ch)` method is `true` if the character is a lowercase letter. The `isUpperCase(char ch)` method is `true` if the character is an uppercase letter. The `toLowerCase(char ch)` method returns the lowercase letter for the character, and the `toUpperCase(char ch)` method returns the uppercase letter for the character.

8.3.1   Example: Counting Each Letter in a String

This example presents a program that prompts the user to enter a string and counts the number of occurrences of each letter in the string regardless of case, as shown in Figure 8.7.

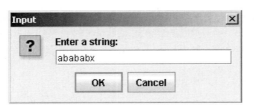 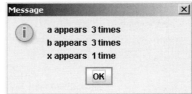

FIGURE 8.7 The program counts the number of occurrences for each letter in the string.

Here are the steps to solve this problem:

1. Convert all the uppercase letters in the string to lowercase using the `toLowerCase` method in the `String` class.

2. Create an array, say `counts` of twenty-six `int` values, each of which counts the occurrences of a letter. That is, `counts[0]` counts the number of `a`'s, `counts[1]` counts the number of `b`'s, and so on.

3. For each character in the string, check whether it is a (lowercase) letter. If so, increment the corresponding count in the array.

LISTING 8.2 CountEachLetter.java

```java
 1 import javax.swing.JOptionPane;
 2
 3 public class CountEachLetter {
 4   /** Main method */
 5   public static void main(String[] args) {
 6     // Prompt the user to enter a string
 7     String s = JOptionPane.showInputDialog("Enter a string:");
 8
 9     // Invoke the countLetters method to count each letter
10     int[] counts = countLetters(s.toLowerCase());
11
12     // Declare and initialize output string
13     String output = "";
14
15     // Display results
16     for (int i = 0; i < counts.length; i++) {
17       if (counts[i] != 0)
18         output += (char)('a' + i) + " appears  " +
19           counts[i] + ((counts[i] == 1) ? " time\n" : " times\n");
20     }
21
22     // Display the result
23     JOptionPane.showMessageDialog(null, output);
24   }
25
26   // Count each letter in the string
27   public static int[] countLetters(String s) {
28     int[] counts = new int[26];
29
30     for (int i = 0; i < s.length(); i++) {
31       if (Character.isLetter(s.charAt(i)))
32         counts[s.charAt(i) - 'a']++;
33     }
34
35     return counts;
36   }
37 }
```

input string (line 7)

count letters (line 10)

count a letter (line 32)

The `main` method reads a string (line 7) and counts the number of occurrences of each letter in the string by invoking the `countLetters` method (line 10). Since the case of the letters is ignored, the program uses the `toLowerCase` method to convert the string into all lowercase and pass the new string to the `countLetters` method.

The `countLetters` method (lines 27–36) returns an array of twenty-six elements. Each element counts the number of occurrences of a letter in the string `s`. The method processes each character in the string. If the character is a letter, its corresponding count is increased by 1. For example, if the character (`s.charAr(i)`) is `'a'`, the corresponding count is `counts['a' - 'a']` (i.e., `counts[0]`). If the character is `'b'`, the corresponding count is `counts['b' - 'a']` (i.e., `counts[1]`) since the Unicode of `'b'` is 1 more than that of `'a'`. If the character is `'z'`, the corresponding count is `counts['z' - 'a']` (i.e., `counts[25]`) since the Unicode of `'z'` is 25 more than that of `'a'`.

8.4 The **StringBuilder/StringBuffer** Class

The `StringBuilder`/`StringBuffer` class is an alternative to the `String` class. In general, a `StringBuilder`/`StringBuffer` can be used wherever a string is used. `StringBuilder`/`StringBuffer` is more flexible than `String`. You can add, insert, or append new contents into a string buffer, whereas the value of a `String` object is fixed once the string is created.

`StringBuilder`

The `StringBuilder` class, introduced in JDK 1.5, is similar to `StringBuffer` except that the `update` methods in `StringBuffer` are synchronized. Use `StringBuffer` if it may be accessed by multiple tasks concurrently. Using `StringBuilder` is more efficient if it is accessed by a single task. The constructors and methods in `StringBuffer` and `StringBuilder` are almost the same. This section covers `StringBuffer`. You may replace `StringBuffer` by `StringBuilder`. The program can compile and run without any other changes.

The `StringBuffer` class has three constructors and more than thirty methods for managing the buffer and modifying strings in the buffer. You can create an empty string buffer or a string buffer from a string. The most frequently used methods are listed in Figure 8.8.

java.lang.StringBuffer	
+StringBuffer()	Constructs an empty string buffer with capacity 16.
+StringBuffer(capacity: int)	Constructs a string buffer with the specified capacity.
+StringBuffer(str: String)	Constructs a string buffer with the specified string.
+append(data: char[]): StringBuffer	Appends a char array into this string buffer.
+append(data: char[], offset: int, len: int): StringBuffer	Appends a subarray in data into this string buffer.
+append(v: aPrimitiveType): StringBuffer	Appends a primitive type value as a string to this buffer.
+append(str: String): StringBuffer	Appends a string to this string buffer.
+capacity(): int	Returns the capacity of this string buffer.
+charAt(index: int): char	Returns the character at the specified index.
+delete(startIndex: int, endIndex: int): StringBuffer	Deletes characters from startIndex to endIndex-1.
+deleteCharAt(index: int): StringBuffer	Deletes a character at the specified index.
+insert(index: int, data: char[], offset: int, len: int): StringBuffer	Inserts a subarray of the data in the array to the buffer at the specified index.
+insert(offset: int, data: char[]): StringBuffer	Inserts data into this buffer at the position offset.
+insert(offset: int, b: aPrimitiveType): StringBuffer	Inserts a value converted to a string into this buffer.
+insert(offset: int, str: String): StringBuffer	Inserts a string into this buffer at the position offset.
+length(): int	Returns the number of characters in this buffer.
+replace(int startIndex, int endIndex, String str): StringBuffer	Replaces the characters in this buffer from startIndex to endIndex-1 with the specified string.
+reverse(): StringBuffer	Reverses the characters in the buffer.
+setCharAt(index: int, ch: char): void	Sets a new character at the specified index in this buffer.
+setLength(newLength: int): void	Sets a new length in this buffer.
+substring(startIndex: int): String	Returns a substring starting at startIndex.
+substring(startIndex: int, endIndex: int): String	Returns a substring from startIndex to endIndex-1.

FIGURE 8.8 The `StringBuffer` class provides the methods for processing a string buffer.

8.4.1 Modifying Strings in the Buffer

You can append new contents at the end of a string buffer, insert new contents at a specified position in a string buffer, and delete or replace characters in a string buffer.

The `StringBuffer` class provides several overloaded methods to append `boolean`, `char`, `char array`, `double`, `float`, `int`, `long`, and `String` into a string buffer. For example, the following code appends strings and characters into `strBuf` to form a new string, `"Welcome to Java"`.

```
StringBuffer strBuf = new StringBuffer();
```

append
```
strBuf.append("Welcome");
strBuf.append(' ');
strBuf.append("to");
strBuf.append(' ');
strBuf.append("Java");
```

The `StringBuffer` class also contains overloaded methods to insert `boolean`, `char`, `char array`, `double`, `float`, `int`, `long`, and `String` into a string buffer. Consider the following code:

insert
```
strBuf.insert(11, "HTML and ");
```

Suppose `strBuf` contains `"Welcome to Java"` before the `insert` method is applied. This code inserts `"HTML and "` at position 11 in `strBuf` (just before J). The new `strBuf` is `"Welcome to HTML and Java"`.

You can also delete characters from a string in the buffer using the two `delete` methods, reverse the string using the `reverse` method, replace characters using the `replace` method, or set a new character in a string using the `setCharAt` method.

For example, suppose `strBuf` contains `"Welcome to Java"` before each of the following methods is applied:

delete
reverse
replace
setCharAt
```
strBuf.delete(8, 11)  changes the buffer to Welcome Java.
strBuf.deleteCharAt(8)  changes the buffer to Welcome o Java.
strBuf.reverse()  changes the buffer to avaJ ot emocleW.
strBuf.replace(11, 15, "HTML")  changes the buffer to Welcome to HTML.
strBuf.setCharAt(0, 'w')  sets the buffer to welcome to Java.
```

Note

All these modification methods except `setCharAt` do two things: (1) change the contents of the string buffer, (2) return the reference of the string buffer. For example, the following statement

```
StringBuffer strBuf1 = strBuf.reverse();
```

reverses the string in the buffer and assigns the reference of the buffer to `strBuf1`. Thus `strBuf` and `strBuf1` both point to the same `StringBuffer` object. Recall that a method with nonvoid return value type may be invoked as a statement if you are not interested in the return value of the method. In this case, the return value is simply ignored. For example, in the following statement

```
strBuf.reverse();
```

the return value is ignored.

Tip

If a string does not require any change, use `String` rather than `StringBuffer`. Java can perform some optimizations for `String`, such as sharing interned strings.

8.4.2 The `toString`, `capacity`, `length`, `setLength`, and `charAt` Methods

The `StringBuffer` class provides many other methods for manipulating string buffers.

- The `toString()` method returns the string from the string buffer.

  `toString()`

- The `capacity()` method returns the current capacity of the string buffer. The capacity is the number of characters it is able to store without having to increase its size.

  `capacity()`

- The `length()` method returns the number of characters actually stored in the string buffer.

  `length()`

- The `setLength(newLength)` method sets the length of the string buffer. If the `newLength` argument is less than the current length of the string buffer, the string buffer is truncated to contain exactly the number of characters given by the `newLength` argument. If the `newLength` argument is greater than or equal to the current length, sufficient `null` characters (`'\u0000'`) are appended to the string buffer so that `length` becomes the `newLength` argument. The `newLength` argument must be greater than or equal to `0`.

  `setLength(int)`

- The `charAt(index)` method returns the character at a specific `index` in the string buffer. The first character of a string buffer is at index `0`, the next at index `1`, and so on. The `index` argument must be greater than or equal to `0`, and less than the length of the string buffer.

  `charAt(int)`

Note

The length of the string is always less than or equal to the capacity of the buffer. The length is the actual size of the string stored in the buffer, and the capacity is the current size of the buffer. The buffer's capacity is automatically increased if more characters are added to exceed its capacity. Internally, a string buffer is an array of characters, so the buffer's capacity is the size of the array. If the buffer's capacity is exceeded, the array is replaced by a new array. The new array size is `2 * (the previous array size + 1)`.

length and capacity

Tip

You can use `new StringBuffer(initialCapacity)` to create a `StringBuffer` with a specified *initial capacity*. By carefully choosing the initial capacity, you can make your program more efficient. If the capacity is always larger than the actual length of the buffer, the JVM will never need to reallocate memory for the buffer. On the other hand, if the capacity is too large, you will waste memory space.

initial capacity

8.4.3 Example: Ignoring Nonalphanumeric Characters When Checking Palindromes

Listing 8.1, CheckPalindrome.java, considered all the characters in a string to check whether it was a palindrome. Write a new program that ignores nonalphanumeric characters in checking whether a string is a palindrome. A sample run of the program is shown in Figure 8.9.

Here are the steps to solve the problem:

1. Filter the string by removing the nonalphanumeric characters. This can be done by creating an empty string buffer, adding each alphanumeric character in the string to a string buffer, and returning the string from the string buffer. You can use the `isLetterOrDigit(ch)` method in the `Character` class to check whether character `ch` is a letter or a digit.

2. Obtain a new string that is the reversal of the filtered string. Compare the reversed string with the filtered string using the `equals` method.

The complete program is shown in Listing 8.3.

LISTING 8.3 PalindromeIgnoreNonAlphanumeric.java

```
 1 import javax.swing.JOptionPane;
 2
 3 public class PalindromeIgnoreNonAlphanumeric {
 4   /** Main method */
 5   public static void main(String[] args) {
 6     // Prompt the user to enter a string
 7     String s = JOptionPane.showInputDialog("Enter a string:");
 8
 9     // Declare and initialize output string
10     String output = "Ignoring nonalphanumeric characters, \nis "
11       + s + " a palindrome? " + isPalindrome(s);
12
13     // Display the result
14     JOptionPane.showMessageDialog(null, output);
15   }
16
17   /** Return true if a string is a palindrome */
18   public static boolean isPalindrome(String s) {
19     // Create a new string by eliminating nonalphanumeric chars
20     String s1 = filter(s);
21
22     // Create a new string that is the reversal of s1
23     String s2 = reverse(s1);
24
25     // Compare if the reversal is the same as the original string
26     return s2.equals(s1);
27   }
28
29   /** Create a new string by eliminating nonalphanumeric chars */
30   public static String filter(String s) {
31     // Create a string buffer
32     StringBuffer strBuf = new StringBuffer();
33
34     // Examine each char in the string to skip alphanumeric char
35     for (int i = 0; i < s.length(); i++) {
36       if (Character.isLetterOrDigit(s.charAt(i))) {
37         strBuf.append(s.charAt(i));
38       }
39     }
40
41     // Return a new filtered string
42     return strBuf.toString();
43   }
44
45   /** Create a new string by reversing a specified string */
46   public static String reverse(String s) {
47     StringBuffer strBuf = new StringBuffer(s);
48     strBuf.reverse(); // Use the reverse method for StringBuffer object
49     return strBuf.toString();
50   }
51 }
```

check palindrome (line 18)

add letter or digit (line 37)

The `filter(String s)` method (lines 30–43) examines each character in string `s` and copies it to a string buffer if the character is a letter or a numeric character. The `filter` method returns the string in the buffer. The `reverse(String s)` method (lines 46–50)

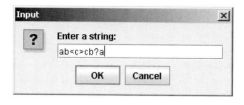
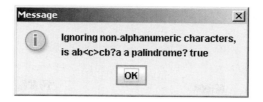

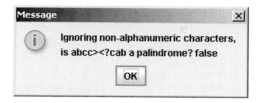

FIGURE 8.9   The program checks whether a string is a palindrome, ignoring nonalphanumeric characters.

creates a new string that reverses the specified string s. The `filter` and `reverse` methods both return a new string. The original string is not changed.

The program in Listing 8.1 checks whether a string is a palindrome by comparing pairs of characters from both ends of the string. Listing 8.3 uses the `reverse` method in the `StringBuffer` class to reverse the string, then compares whether the two strings are equal to determine whether the original string is a palindrome.

8.5 Command-Line Arguments

Perhaps you have already noticed the unusual declarations for the `main` method, which has parameter `args` of `String[]` type. It is clear that `args` is an array of strings. The `main` method is just like a regular method with a parameter. You can call a regular method by passing actual parameters. Can you pass arguments to `main`? Of course, yes. For example, the `main` method in class `B` is invoked by a method in `A`, as shown below.

A `main` method is just a regular method. Furthermore, you can pass arguments from the command line.

```
public class A {
  public static void main(String[] args) {
    String[] strings = {"New York",
      "Boston", "Atlanta"};
    B.main(strings);
  }
}
```

```
class B {
  public static void main(String[] args) {
    for (int i = 0; i < args.length; i++)
      System.out.println(args[i]);
  }
}
```

8.5.1   Passing Strings to the `main` Method

You can pass strings to a `main` method from the command line when you run the program. The following command line, for example, starts the program `TestMain` with three strings: `arg0`, `arg1`, and `arg2`:

```
java TestMain arg0 arg1 arg2
```

`arg0`, `arg1`, and `arg2` are strings, but they don't have to appear in double quotes on the command line. The strings are separated by a space. A string that contains a space must be enclosed in double quotes. Consider the following command line:

```
java TestMain "First num" alpha 53
```

It starts the program with three strings: `"First num"` and `alpha`, and `53`, a numeric string. Note that `53` is actually treated as a string. You can use `"53"` instead of `53` in the command line.

When the `main` method is invoked, the JVM creates an array to hold the command-line arguments and pass the array reference to `args`. For example, if you invoke a program with `n` arguments, the Java interpreter creates an array like this one:

```
args = new String[n];
```

The Java interpreter then passes `args` to invoke the `main` method.

Note

If you run the program with no strings passed, the array is created with `new String[0]`. In this case, the array is empty with length `0`. `args` references to this empty array. Therefore, `args` is not `null`, but `args.length` is `0`.

8.5.2 Example: Processing Command-Line Arguments

The strings passed to the main program are stored in `args`, which is an array of strings. The first string is stored in `args[0]`, and `args.length` is the number of strings passed.

This example presents a program that performs binary operations on integers. The program receives three arguments: an integer followed by an operator and another integer. For example, to add two integers, use this command:

```
java Calculator 2 + 3
```

The program will display the following output:

```
2 + 3 = 5
```

Figure 8.10 shows sample runs of the program.

```
Command Prompt                                          _ □ ×
c:\book>java Calculator
Usage: java Calculator operand1 operator operand2

c:\book>java Calculator 63 + 40
63 + 40 = 103

c:\book>java Calculator 63 - 40
63 - 40 = 23

c:\book>java Calculator 63 "*" 40
63 * 40 = 2520

c:\book>java Calculator 63 / 40
63 / 40 = 1

c:\book>
```

FIGURE 8.10 The program takes three arguments (operand1 operator operand2) from the command line and displays the expression and the result of the arithmetic operation.

Here are the steps in the program:

1. Use `args.length` to determine whether three arguments have been provided in the command line. If not, terminate the program using `System.exit(0)`.

2. Perform a binary arithmetic operation on the operands `args[0]` and `args[2]` using the operator specified in `args[1]`.

The program is shown in Listing 8.4.

Listing 8.4 Calculator.java

```
 1 public class Calculator {
 2   /** Main method */
 3   public static void main(String[] args) {
 4     // Check number of strings passed
 5     if (args.length != 3) {
 6       System.out.println(
 7         "Usage: java Calculator operand1 operator operand2");
 8       System.exit(0);
 9     }
10
11     // The result of the operation
12     int result = 0;
13
14     // Determine the operator
15     switch (args[1].charAt(0)) {                          check operator
16       case '+': result = Integer.parseInt(args[0]) +
17                          Integer.parseInt(args[2]);
18               break;
19       case '-': result = Integer.parseInt(args[0]) -
20                          Integer.parseInt(args[2]);
21               break;
22       case '*': result = Integer.parseInt(args[0]) *
23                          Integer.parseInt(args[2]);
24               break;
25       case '/': result = Integer.parseInt(args[0]) /
26                          Integer.parseInt(args[2]);
27     }
28
29     // Display result
30     System.out.println(args[0] + ' ' + args[1] + ' ' + args[2]
31       + " = " + result);
32   }
33 }
```

`Integer.parseInt(args[0])` (line 16) converts a digital string into an integer. The string must consist of digits. If not, the program will terminate abnormally.

In the sample run, `"*"` had to be used instead of `*` for the command

```
java Calculator 63 "*" 40
```

In JDK 1.1 and above, the `*` symbol refers to all the files in the current directory when it is used on a command line. Therefore, in order to specify the multiplication operator, the `*` must be enclosed in quote marks in the command line. The following program displays all the files in the current directory when issuing the command `java Test *`:

```
public class Test {
  public static void main(String[] args) {
    for (int i = 0; i < args.length; i++)
      System.out.println(args[i]);
  }
}
```

8.6 (Optional) Regular Expressions

A *regular expression* (abbreviated *regex*) is a string that describes a pattern for matching a   regular expression
set of strings. Regular expression is a powerful tool for string manipulations. You can use reg-   regex
ular expressions for matching, replacing, and splitting strings.

Pedagogical Note

The previous edition of this book introduced the `StringTokenizer` class for extracting tokens from a string. Using regular expressions is more powerful and flexible than `StringTokenizer` for splitting strings. Therefore, `StringTokenizer` is obsolete.

StringTokenizer
obsolete

8.6.1 Matching Strings

Let us begin with the `matches` method in the `String` class. At first glance, the `matches` method is very similar to the `equals` method. For example, the following two statements both evaluate to `true`:

matches(regex)

```
"Java".matches("Java");
"Java".equals("Java");
```

However, the `matches` method is more powerful. It can match not only a fixed string, but also a set of strings that follow a pattern. For example, the following statements all evaluate to `true`:

```
"Java is fun".matches("Java.*")
"Java is cool".matches("Java.*")
"Java is powerful".matches("Java.*")
```

`"Java.*"` in the preceding statements is a regular expression. It describes a string pattern that begins with Java followed by any zero or more characters. Here, the substring `.*` matches any zero or more characters.

8.6.2 Regular Expression Syntax

A regular expression consists of literal characters and special symbols. Table 8.1 lists some frequently used syntax for regular expressions.

Note

backslash (\)

Backslash is a special character that starts an escape sequence in a string. So you need to use `"\\d"` in Java to represent `\d`.

Note

whitespace

Recall that a *whitespace* (or a *whitespace character*) is any character which does not display itself but does take up space. The characters `' '`, `'\t'`, `'\n'`, `'\r'`, `'\f'` are whitespace characters. So `\s` is the same as `[ \t\n\r\f]`, and `\S` is the same as `[^ \t\n\r\f\v]`.

Note

word characters

A *word character* is any letter, digit, or the underscore character. So `\w` is the same as `[a-z[A-Z][0-9]_]` or simply `[a-zA-Z0-9_]`, and `\W` is the same as `[^a-zA-Z0-9_]`.

Note

quantifiers

The last six entries `*`, `+`, `?`, `{n}`, `{n,}`, and `{n, m}` in Table 8.1 are called *quantifiers* that specify how many times the pattern before a quantifier may repeat. For example, `A*` matches zero or more A's, `A+` matches one or more A's, `A?` matches zero or one A's, `A{3}` matches exactly AAA, `A{3,}` matches at least three A's, and `A{3,6}` matches between 3 and 6 A's. `*` is the same as `{0,}`, `+` is the same as `{1,}`, and `?` is the same as `{0,1}`.

Caution

no spaces

Do not use spaces in the repeat quantifiers. For example, `A{3,6}` cannot be written as `A{3, 6}` with a space after the comma.

Note

grouping pattern

You may use parentheses to group patterns. For example, `(ab){3}` matches `ababab`, but `ab{3}` matches `abbb`.

TABLE 8.1   Frequently Used Regular Expressions

Regular Expression	Matches	Example
x	a specified character x	Java matches Java
.	any single character	Java matches J . . a
(ab|cd)	ab or cd	ten matches t(en|im)
[abc]	a, b, or c	Java matches Ja[uvwx]a
[^abc]	any character except a, b, or c	Java matches Ja[^ars]a
[a-z]	a through z	Java matches [A-M]av[a-d]
[^a-z]	any character except a through z	Java matches Jav[^b-d]
[a-e[m-p]]	a through e or m through p	Java matches [A-G[I-M]]av[a-d]
[a-e&&[c-p]]	intersection of a-e with c-p	Java matches [A-P&&[I-M]]av[a-d]
\d	a digit, same as [1-9]	Java2 matches "Java[\\d]"
\D	a non-digit	$Java matches "[\\D][\\D]ava"
\w	a word character	Java matches "[\\w]ava"
\W	a non-word character	$Java matches "[\\W][\\w]ava"
\s	a whitespace character	"Java 2" matches "Java\\s2"
\S	a non-whitespace char	Java matches "[\\S]ava"
*p**	zero or more occurrences of pattern *p*	Java matches "[\w]*"
p+	one or more occurrences of pattern *p*	Java matches "[\ \w]+"
p?	zero or one occurrence of pattern *p*	Java matches "[\\w]?Java" Java matches "[\\w]?ava"
p{n}	exactly n occurrences of pattern *p*	Java matches "[\ \w]{4}"
p{n,}	at least n occurrences of pattern *p*	Java matches "[\ \w]{3,}"
p{n, m}	between n and m occurrences (inclusive)	Java matches "[\ \w]{1, 9}"

Let us use several examples to demonstrate how to construct regular expressions.

Example 1

The pattern for social security numbers is xxx-xx-xxxx, where x is a digit. A regular expression for social security numbers can be described as

    [\\d]{3}-[\\d]{2}-[\\d]{4}

Example 2

An even number ends with digits 0, 2, 4, 6, or 8. The pattern for even numbers can be described as

    [\\d]*[02468]

Example 3

The pattern for telephone numbers is (xxx) xxx-xxxx, where x is a digit and the first digit cannot be zero. A regular expression for telephone numbers can be described as

```
\\([1-9][\\d]{2}\\) [\\d]{3}-[\\d]{4}
```

Note that the parentheses symbols (and) are special characters in a regular expression for grouping patterns. To represent a literal (or) in a regular expression, you have to use \\(and \\).

Example 4

Suppose the last name consists of at most twenty five letters and the first letter is in upper-case. The pattern for a last name can be described as

```
[A-Z][a-zA-Z]{1,24}
```

Note that you cannot have arbitrary whitespace in a regular expression. For example, [A-Z][\\a-zA-Z]{1, 24} would be wrong.

Example 5

Java identifiers are defined in §2.3, "Identifiers."

- An identifier must start with a letter, an underscore (_), or a dollar sign ($). It cannot start with a digit.

- An identifier is a sequence of characters that consists of letters, digits, underscores (_), and dollar signs ($).

  The pattern for identifiers can be described as

```
[a-zA-Z_$][\\w$]*
```

Example 6

What strings are matched by the regular expression "Welcome to (Java|HTML)"? The answer is Welcome to Java or Welcome to HTML.

Example 7

What strings are matched by the regular expression ".*"? The answer is any string.

8.6.3 Replacing and Splitting Strings

The matches method in the String class returns true if the string matches the regular expression. The String class also contains the replaceAll, replaceFirst, and split methods for replacing and splitting strings, as shown in Figure 8.11.

The replaceAll method replaces all matching substring and the replaceFirst method replaces the first matching substring. For example, the following code

replaceAll(regex, string)

```
System.out.println("Java Java Java".replaceAll("v\\w", "wi"));
```

displays

```
Jawi Jawi Jawi
```

java.lang.String	
+matches(regex: String): boolean	Returns true if this string matches the pattern.
+replaceAll(regex: String, replacement: String): String	Returns a new string that replaces all matching substrings with the replacement.
+replaceFirst(regex: String, replacement: String): String	Returns a new string that replaces the first matching substring with the replacement.
+split(regex: String): String[]	Returns an array of strings consisting of the substrings split by the matches.
+split(regex: String, limit: int): String[]	Same as the preceding split method except that the limit parameter controls the number of times the pattern is applied.

FIGURE 8.11 The `String` class contains the methods for matching, replacing, and splitting strings using regular expressions.

The following code

```
System.out.println("Java Java Java".replaceFirst("v\\w", "wi"));
```
`replaceFirst(regex, string)`

displays

```
Jawi Java Java
```

There are two overloaded `split` methods. The `split(regex)` method splits a string into substrings delimited by the matches. For example, the following statement

```
String[] tokens = "Java1HTML2Perl".split("\\d");
```
`split(regex)`

splits string `"Java1HTML2Perl"` into `Java`, `HTML`, and `Perl` and saved in `tokens[0]`, `tokens[1]`, and `tokens[2]`.

In the `split(regex, limit)` method, the `limit` parameter determines how many times the pattern is matched. If `limit <= 0`, `split(regex, limit)` is the same as `split(regex)`. If `limit > 0`, the pattern is matched at most `limit - 1` times. Here are some examples:

```
"Java1HTML2Perl".split("\\d", 0); splits into Java, HTML, Perl
"Java1HTML2Perl".split("\\d", 1); splits into Java1HTML2Perl
"Java1HTML2Perl".split("\\d", 2); splits into Java, HTML2Perl
"Java1HTML2Perl".split("\\d", 3); splits into Java, HTML, Perl
"Java1HTML2Perl".split("\\d", 4); splits into Java, HTML, Perl
"Java1HTML2Perl".split("\\d", 5); splits into Java, HTML, Perl
```
`split(regex, limit)`

Note

By default, all the quantifiers are *greedy*. This means that they will match as many occurrences as possible. For example, the following statement displays JRvaa, since the first match is **aaa**:

`greedy match`

```
System.out.println("Jaaavaa".replaceFirst("a+",   "R"));
```

You can change a quantifier's default behavior by appending a question mark (?) after it. The quantifier becomes *reluctant*, which means that it will match as few occurrences as possible. For example, the following statement displays JRaavaa, since the first match is **a**:

`reluctant match`

```
System.out.println("Jaaavaa".replaceFirst("a+?", "R"));
```

8.7 The **File** Class

Data stored in variables, arrays, and objects is temporary and is lost when the program terminates. To permanently store the data created in a program, you need to save them in a file on a disk or a CD. The file can be transported and can be read later by other programs. Since data are stored in files, this section introduces how to use the `File` class to obtain file properties and to delete and rename files. The next section introduces how to read/write data from/to text files.

absolute file name

Every file is placed in a directory in the file system. An *absolute file* name contains a file name with its complete path and drive letter. For example, `c:\book\Welcome.java` is the absolute file name for the file `Welcome.java` on the Windows operating system. Here

directory path

`c:\book` is referred to as the *directory path* for the file. Absolute file names are machine-dependent. On Unix, the absolute file name may be `/home/liang/book/Welcome.java`, where `/home/liang/book` is the directory path for the file `Welcome.java`.

The `File` class is intended to provide an abstraction that deals with most of the machine-dependent complexities of files and path names in a machine-independent fashion. The `File` class contains the methods for obtaining file properties and for renaming and deleting files, as shown in Figure 8.12. However, the `File` class does not contain the methods for reading and writing file contents.

java.io.File	
+File(pathname: String)	Creates a File object for the specified pathname. The pathname may be a directory or a file.
+File(parent: String, child: String)	Creates a File object for the child under the directory parent. The child may be a filename or a subdirectory.
+File(parent: File, child: String)	Creates a File object for the child under the directory parent. The parent is a File object. In the preceding constructor, the parent is a string.
+exists(): boolean	Returns true if the file or the directory represented by the File object exists.
+canRead(): boolean	Returns true if the file represented by the File object exists and can be read.
+canWrite(): boolean	Returns true if the file represented by the File object exists and can be written.
+isDirectory(): boolean	Returns true if the File object represents a directory.
+isFile(): boolean	Returns true if the File object represents a file.
+isAbsolute(): boolean	Returns true if the File object is created using an absolute path name.
+isHidden(): boolean	Returns true if the file represented in the File object is hidden. The exact definition of *hidden* is system-dependent. On Windows, you can mark a file hidden in the File Properties dialog box. On Unix systems, a file is hidden if its name begins with a period character '.'.
+getAbsolutePath(): String	Returns the complete absolute file or directory name represented by the File object.
+getCanonicalPath(): String	Returns the same as getAbsolutePath() except that it removes redundant names, such as "." and "..", from the pathname, resolves symbolic links (on Unix platforms), and converts drive letters to standard uppercase (on Win32 platforms).
+getName(): String	Returns the last name of the complete directory and file name represented by the File object. For example, newFile("c:\\book\\test.dat").getName() returns test.dat.
+getPath(): String	Returns the complete directory and file name represented by the File object. For example, new File("c:\\book\\test.dat").getPath() returns c:\book\test.dat.
+getParent(): String	Returns the complete parent directory of the current directory or the file represented by the File object. For example, new File("c:\\book\\test.dat").getParent() returns c:\book.
+lastModified(): long	Returns the time that the file was last modified.
+delete(): boolean	Deletes this file. The method returns true if the deletion succeeds.
+renameTo(dest: File): boolean	Renames this file. The method returns true if the operation succeeds.

FIGURE 8.12 The `File` class can be used to obtain file and directory properties and to delete and rename files.

The filename is a string. The File class is a wrapper class for the file name and its directory path. For example, new File("c:\\book") creates a File object for the directory c:\book, and new File("c:\\book\\test.dat") creates a File object for the file c:\\book\\test.dat, both on Windows. You can use the File class's isDirectory() method to check whether the object represents a directory, and the isFile() method to check whether the object represents a file name.

Caution

The directory separator for Windows is a backslash (\). The backslash is a special character in Java and should be written as \\ in a string literal (see Table 2.5).

\ in file names

Note

Constructing a File instance does not create a file on the machine. You can create a File instance for any filename regardless of whether it exists or not. You can invoke the exists() method on a File instance to check whether the file exists.

Do not use absolute file names in your program. If you use a file name such as "c:\\book\\Welcome.java", it will work on Windows but not on other platforms. You should use a file name relative to the current directory. For example, you may create a File object using new File("Welcome.java") for the file Welcome.java in the current directory. You may create a File object using new File("image/us.gif") for the file us.gif under the image directory in the current directory. The forward slash (/) is the Java directory separator, which is the same as on Unix. The statement new File("image/us.gif") works on Windows, Unix, or any other platform.

relative file name

Java directory separator (/)

Listing 8.5 demonstrates how to create a File object and use the methods in the File class to obtain its properties. The program creates a File object for the file us.gif. This file is stored under the image directory in the current directory.

LISTING 8.5   TestFileClass.java

```
 1  public class TestFileClass {
 2    public static void main(String[] args) {
 3      java.io.File file = new java.io.File("image/us.gif");
 4      System.out.println("Does it exist? " + file.exists());
 5      System.out.println("Can it be read? " + file.canRead());
 6      System.out.println("Can it be written? " + file.canWrite());
 7      System.out.println("Is it a directory? " + file.isDirectory());
 8      System.out.println("Is it a file? " + file.isFile());
 9      System.out.println("Is it absolute? " + file.isAbsolute());
10      System.out.println("Is it hidden? " + file.isHidden());
11      System.out.println("Absolute path is " +
12        file.getAbsolutePath());
13      System.out.println("Last modified on " +
14        new java.util.Date(file.lastModified()));
15    }
16  }
```

create a **File**
file exist?
can read?
can write?
is directory?
is file?
is absolute name?
is hidden?

The lastModified() method returns the date and time when the file was last modified, measured in milliseconds since the Unix time (00:00:00 GMT, January 1, 1970). The Date class is used to display it in a readable format in lines 13–14.

Figure 8.13(a) shows a sample run of the program on Windows, and Figure 8.13(b), a sample run on Unix. As shown in the figures, the path-naming conventions on Windows are different from those on Unix.

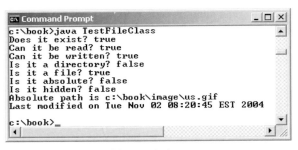

(a) On Windows   (b) On Unix

FIGURE 8.13   The program creates a `File` object and displays file properties.

8.8 Text I/O

A `File` object encapsulates the properties of a file or a path, but does not contain the methods for reading/writing data from/to a file. In order to perform I/O, you need to create objects using appropriate Java I/O classes. The objects contain the methods for reading/writing data from/to a file. This section introduces how to read/write strings and numeric values from/to a text file using the `Scanner` and `PrintWriter` classes.

8.8.1   Writing Data Using `PrintWriter`

The `java.io.PrintWriter` class can be used to write data to a text file. First, you have to create a `PrintWriter` object for a text file as follows:

```
PrintWriter output = new PrintWriter(filename);
```

Then, you can invoke the `print`, `println`, and `printf` methods on the `PrintWriter` object to write data to a file. Figure 8.14 summarizes frequently used methods in `PrintWriter`.

Listing 8.6 gives an example that creates an instance of `PrintWriter` and writes two lines to the file "scores.txt". Each line consists of first name (a string), middle name initial (a character), last name (a string), and score (an integer).

java.io.PrintWriter	
+PrintWriter(filename: String)	Creates a PrintWriter object for the specified file.
+print(s: String): void	Writes a string.
+print(c: char): void	Writes a character.
+print(cArray: char[]): void	Writes an array of character.
+print(i: int): void	Writes an int value.
+print(l: long): void	Writes a long value.
+print(f: float): void	Writes a float value.
+print(d: double): void	Writes a double value.
+print(b: boolean): void	Writes a boolean value.
Also contains the overloaded println methods.	A println method acts like a print method; additionally it prints a line separator. The line separator string is defined by the system. It is \r\n on Windows and \n on Unix.
Also contains the overloaded printf methods.	The printf method was introduced in §3.6, "Formatting Console Output and Strings."

FIGURE 8.14   The `PrintWriter` class contains the methods for writing data to a text file.

LISTING 8.6   WriteData.java

```
1 public class WriteData {
2   public static void main(String[] args) throws Exception {
3     java.io.File file = new java.io.File("scores.txt");
```

throws an exception

create `File` object

```
 4        if (file.exists()) {
 5          System.out.println("File already exists");
 6          System.exit(0);
 7        }
 8
 9        // Create a file
10        java.io.PrintWriter output = new java.io.PrintWriter(file);
11
12        // Write formatted output to the file
13        output.print("John T Smith ");
14        output.println(90);
15        output.print("Eric K Jones ");
16        output.println(85);
17
18        // Close the file
19        output.close();
20      }
21 }
```

file exist?

create **PrintWriter**

John T Smith 90 | scores.txt
Eric K Jones 85

print data
close file

Lines 3–7 check whether the file scores.txt exists. If so, exit the program (line 6).

Invoking the constructor `new PrintWriter(String filename)` will create a new file if   create a file
the file does not exist. If the file already exists, the current content in the file will be discarded.

Invoking the constructor `new PrintWriter(String filename)` may throw an I/O
exception. Java forces you to write the code to deal with this type of exception. You will learn
how to handle it in Chapter 17, "Exceptions and Assertions." For now, simply declare `throws`   throws Exception
`Exception` in the method declaration (line 2).

You have used the `System.out.print` and `System.out.println` methods to write   **print** method
text to the console. `System.out` is a standard Java object for the console. You can create
objects for writing text to any file using `print`, `println`, and `printf` (lines 13–16).

The `close()` method must be used to close the file. If this method is not invoked, the data   close file
may not be saved properly in the file.

8.8.2 Reading Data Using Scanner

The `java.util.Scanner` class was used to read strings and primitive values from the console in §2.13, "Console Input using the **Scanner** Class." A **Scanner** breaks its input into
tokens delimited by whitespace characters. To read from the keyboard, you create a **Scanner**
for `System.in`, as follows:

```
Scanner input = new Scanner(System.in);
```

To read from a file, create a **Scanner** for a file, as follows:

```
Scanner input = new Scanner(new File(filename));
```

Figure 8.15 summarizes frequently used methods in **Scanner**.

Listing 8.7 gives an example that creates an instance of **Scanner** and reads data from the
file "scores.txt".

LISTING 8.7 ReadData.java

```
1 public class ReadData {
2    public static void main(String[] args) throws Exception {
3      // Create a File instance
4      java.io.File file = new java.io.File("scores.txt");
5
6      // Create a Scanner for the file
7      java.util.Scanner input = new java.util.Scanner(file);
8
```

create a **File**

create a **Scanner**

has next?
read items

```
 9      // Read data from a file
10      while (input.hasNext()) {
11        String firstName = input.next();
12        String mi = input.next();
13        String lastName = input.next();
14        int score = input.nextInt();
15        System.out.println(
16          firstName + " " + mi + " " + lastName + " " + score);
17      }
18
19      // Close the file
20      input.close();
21    }
22  }
```

```
John  T  Smith  90
Eric  K  Jones  85
```

close file

java.util.Scanner	
+Scanner(source: File)	Creates a Scanner that produces values scanned from the specified file.
+Scanner(source: String)	Creates a Scanner that produces values scanned from the specified string.
+close()	Closes this scanner.
+hasNext(): boolean	Returns true if this scanner has another token in its input.
+next(): String	Returns next token as a string.
+nextByte(): byte	Returns next token as a byte.
+nextShort(): short	Returns next token as a short.
+nextInt(): int	Returns next token as an int.
+nextLong(): long	Returns next token as a long.
+nextFloat(): float	Returns next token as a float.
+nextDouble(): double	Returns next token as a double.
+useDelimiter(pattern: String): Scanner	Sets this scanner's delimiting pattern.

FIGURE 8.15 The Scanner class contains the methods for scanning data.

File class

Note that new Scanner(String) creates a Scanner for a given string. To create a Scanner to read data from a file, you have to use the java.io.File class to create an instance of the File using the constructor new File(filename) (line 4), and use new Scanner(File) to create a Scanner for the file (line 7).

throws **Exception**

Invoking the constructor new Scanner(File) may throw an I/O exception. So the main method declares throws Exception in line 2.

Each iteration in the while loop reads first name, mi, last name, and score from the text file (lines 10–17). The file is closed in line 20.

close file

It is not necessary to close the input file (line 20), but it is a good practice to do so to release the resources occupied by the file.

Note

set delimiter

By default, the delimiters for separating tokens in a Scanner are whitespace. You can use the useDelimiter(String regex) method to set a new pattern for delimiters.

8.8.3 Example: Replacing Text

Write a class named ReplaceText that replaces a string in a text file with a new string. The filename and strings are passed as command-line arguments as follows:

```
java ReplaceText sourceFile targetFile oldString newString
```

For example, invoking

```
java ReplaceText FormatString.java t.txt StringBuilder StringBuffer
```

replaces all the occurrences of `StringBuilder` by `StringBuffer` in `FormatString.java` and saves the new file in `t.txt`.

Listing 8.8 gives the solution to the problem. The program checks the number of arguments passed to the `main` method (lines 7–11), checks whether the source and target files exist (lines 14–25), creates a `Scanner` for the source file (line 28), creates a `PrintWriter` for the target file, and repeatedly reads a line from the source file (line 32), replaces the text (line 33), and writes a new line to the target file (line 34). You must close the output file (line 38) to ensure that data is saved to the file properly.

LISTING 8.8 ReplaceText.java

```java
 1 import java.io.*;
 2 import java.util.*;
 3
 4 public class ReplaceText {
 5   public static void main(String[] args) throws Exception {
 6     // Check command line parameter usage
 7     if (args.length != 4) {
 8       System.out.println(
 9         "Usage: java ReplaceText sourceFile targetFile oldStr newStr");
10       System.exit(0);
11     }
12
13     // Check if source file exists
14     File sourceFile = new File(args[0]);
15     if (!sourceFile.exists()) {
16       System.out.println("Source file " + args[0] + " does not exist");
17       System.exit(0);
18     }
19
20     // Check if target file exists
21     File targetFile = new File(args[1]);
22     if (targetFile.exists()) {
23       System.out.println("Target file " + args[1] + " already exists");
24       System.exit(0);
25     }
26
27     // Create input and output files
28     Scanner input = new Scanner(sourceFile);
29     PrintWriter output = new PrintWriter(targetFile);
30
31     while (input.hasNext()) {
32       String s1 = input.nextLine();
33       String s2 = s1.replaceAll(args[2], args[3]);
34       output.println(s2);
35     }
36
37     input.close();
38     output.close();
39   }
40 }
```

check command usage

source file exists?

target file exists?

*create a **Scanner***
*create a **PrintWriter***

has next?
read a line

close file

Pedagogical Note

The previous edition of this book introduced text I/O using many subclasses of `java.io.Writer` and `java.io.Reader`. These classes are lower-level and difficult to learn. The new features in `java.io.PrinterWriter` and `java.util.Scanner` classes are sufficient for all text I/O needs. For this reason, the old-style text I/O is now moved to Supplement VI.B, "Text I/O Using `Reader` and `Writer`."

simplifying text I/O

8.9 (Optional GUI) Containers and Layout Managers

container

JFrame is a *container* that can hold other components. You can add GUI components such as labels, buttons, checkboxes, radio buttons, and combo boxes to a GUI container. Listing 8.9 gives an example that adds a button to a **JFrame**, as shown in Figure 8.16(a).

LISTING 8.9 HoldComponents.java

```
1 import javax.swing.*;
2
3 public class HoldComponents {
4   public static void main(String[] args) {
5     JFrame frame = new JFrame();
6
7     // Add a button to frame
8     JButton jbtOK = new JButton("OK");
9     frame.add(jbtOK);
10
11    frame.setTitle("Window 1");
12    frame.setSize(200, 150);
13    frame.setLocation(200, 100);
14    frame.setDefaultCloseOperation(JFrame.EXIT_ON_CLOSE);
15    frame.setVisible(true);
16  }
17 }
```

create a frame

create a button
add button

display frame

Using default layout manager

Using default FlowLayout manager

(a)   (b)

FIGURE 8.16 The frame holds a button using a default layout manager in (a) and using a **FlowLayout** manager in (b).

layout manager

The program creates a **JFrame** in line 5 and a **JButton** in line 8. The button is added to the frame in line 9. Line 14 displays the frame. Each container uses a *layout manager* object to automatically arrange the components in a container. If you don't specify a layout manager, the default layout manager is used. In this case, the button is placed in the center of the frame and occupies the whole frame, as shown in Figure 8.16(a). To display a button in its preferred size as shown in Figure 8.16(b), use a **FlowLayout** manager as shown in Listing 8.10.

FlowLayout manager

LISTING 8.10 UseFlowLayout.java

```
1 import javax.swing.*;
2 import java.awt.*;
3
4 public class UseFlowLayout {
5   public static void main(String[] args) {
6     JFrame frame = new JFrame();
7
8     // Set FlowLayout for the frame
9     FlowLayout layout = new FlowLayout();
10    frame.setLayout(layout);
11
12    // Add a button to frame
13    JButton jbtOK = new JButton("OK");
14    frame.add(jbtOK);
15
```

import package

create a frame

create **FlowLayout**
set layout

```
16        frame.setTitle("Window 1");
17        frame.setSize(200, 150);
18        frame.setLocation(200, 100);
19        frame.setDefaultCloseOperation(JFrame.EXIT_ON_CLOSE);
20        frame.setVisible(true);                                            display frame
21    }
22  }
```

The FlowLayout class is in the java.awt package, which is imported in line 2. A FlowLayout manager is created in line 9 and is set to the frame in line 10. The frame will use the FlowLayout to place the components. Listing 8.11 gives another example that adds two buttons in a frame of FlowLayout, as shown in Figure 8.17.

LISTING 8.11   TwoButtons.java

```
1  import javax.swing.*;
2  import java.awt.*;
3
4  public class TwoButtons {
5    public static void main(String[] args) {
6      JFrame frame = new JFrame();                                       create a frame
7
8      // Set FlowLayout for the frame
9      FlowLayout layout = new FlowLayout();                              create FlowLayout
10     frame.setLayout(layout);                                           set layout
11
12     // Add two buttons to frame
13     JButton jbtOK = new JButton("OK");                                 OK button
14     JButton jbtCancel = new JButton("Cancel");                         Cancel button
15     frame.add(jbtOK);                                                  add button
16     frame.add(jbtCancel);                                              add button
17
18     frame.setTitle("Window 1");
19     frame.setSize(200, 150);
20     frame.setLocation(200, 100);
21     frame.setDefaultCloseOperation(JFrame.EXIT_ON_CLOSE);
22     frame.setVisible(true);                                            display frame
23   }
24 }
```

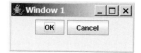

FIGURE 8.17   The frame holds two buttons using a FlowLayout manager.

KEY TERMS

CHAPTER SUMMARY

■ Strings are objects encapsulated in the String class. A string can be constructed using one of the eleven constructors or using a string literal shorthand initializer.

■ A String object is immutable; its contents cannot be changed. To improve efficiency and save memory, the JVM stores string literals in a unique object if two literal strings have the same character sequence. This unique object is called an interned string object.

■ You can get the length of a string by invoking its `length()` method, and retrieve a character at the specified `index` in the string using the `charAt(index)` method.

■ You can use the `concat` method to concatenate two strings, or the plus (+) sign to concatenate two or more strings.

■ You can use the `substring` method to obtain a substring from the string.

■ You can use the `equals` and `compareTo` methods to compare strings. The `equals` method returns `true` if two strings are equal, and `false` if they are not equal. The `compareTo` method returns `0`, a positive integer, or a negative integer, depending on whether one string is equal to, greater than, or less than the other string.

■ The `Character` class is a wrapper class for a single character. The `Character` class provides useful static methods to determine whether a character is a letter (`isLetter(char)`), a digit (`isDigit(char)`), uppercase (`isUpperCase(char)`), or lowercase (`isLowerCase(char)`).

■ The `StringBuilder`/`StringBuffer` class can be used to replace the `String` class. The `String` object is immutable, but you can add, insert, or append new contents into a `StringBuilder`/`StringBuffer` object. Use `String` if the string contents do not require any change, and use `StringBuilder`/`StringBuffer` if they change.

■ You can pass strings to the `main` method from the command line. Strings passed to the `main` program are stored in `args`, which is an array of strings. The first string is represented by `args[0]`, and `args.length` is the number of strings passed.

■ The `File` class is used to obtain file properties and manipulate files. It does not contain the methods for reading/writing data from/to a file.

■ You can use `Scanner` to read string and primitive data value from a text file and use `PrintWriter` to write data to a text file.

■ You can use the regular expressions to represent patterns for matching, replacing, and splitting strings.

REVIEW QUESTIONS

Section 8.2 The `String` Class

8.1 Suppose that `s1`, `s2`, `s3`, and `s4` are four strings, given as follows:

```java
String s1 = "Welcome to Java";
String s2 = s1;
String s3 = new String("Welcome to Java");
String s4 = s3.intern();
```

What are the results of the following expressions?

(1) s1 == s2   (3) s1.equals(s2)
(2) s1 == s3   (4) s2.equals(s3)

(5) `s1.compareTo(s2)`
(6) `s2.compareTo(s3)`
(7) `s1 == s4`
(8) `s1.charAt(0)`
(9) `s1.indexOf('j')`
(10) `s1.indexOf("to")`
(11) `s1.lastIndexOf('a')`
(12) `s1.lastIndexOf("o", 15)`
(13) `s1.length()`
(14) `s1.substring(5)`

(15) `s1.substring(5, 11)`
(16) `s1.startsWith("Wel")`
(17) `s1.endsWith("Java")`
(18) `s1.toLowerCase()`
(19) `s1.toUpperCase()`
(20) `"  Welcome ".trim()`
(21) `s1.replace('o', 'T')`
(22) `s1.replaceAll("o", "T")`
(23) `s1.replaceFirst("o", "T")`
(24) `s1.toCharArray()`

8.2 Suppose that `s1` and `s2` are two strings. Which of the following statements or expressions are incorrect?

```java
String s = new String("new string");
String s3 = s1 + s2;
String s3 = s1 - s2;
s1 == s2;
s1 >= s2;
s1.compareTo(s2);
int i = s1.length();
char c = s1(0);
char c = s1.charAt(s1.length());
```

8.3 What is the printout of the following code?

```java
String s1 = "Welcome to Java";
String s2 = "Welcome to Java";
System.out.println("s1 == s2 is " + s1 == s2);
System.out.println("s1 == s2 is " + (s1 == s2));
```

8.4 How do you compare whether two strings are equal without considering cases? How do you convert all the letters in a string to uppercase? How do you convert all the letters in a string to lowercase? Do the conversion methods (`toLowerCase`, `toUpperCase`, `trim`, `replace`) change the contents of the string that invokes them?

8.5 Suppose string `s` is created using `new String()`; what is `s.length()`?

8.6 How do you convert a `char`, an array of characters, or a number to a string?

8.7 Why does the following code cause a `NullPointerException`?

```java
1 public class Test {
2   private String text;
3
4   public Test(String s) {
5     String text  = s;
6   }
7
8   public static void main(String[] args) {
9     Test test = new Test("ABC");
10    System.out.println(test.text.toLowerCase());
11  }
12 }
```

8.8 What is wrong in the following program?

```java
1 public class Test {
2   String text;
3
```

```
4    public void Test(String s) {
5      this.text  = s;
6    }
7
8    public static void main(String[] args) {
9      Test test = new Test("ABC");
10      System.out.println(test);
11    }
12 }
```

Section 8.3 The **Character** Class

8.9   How do you determine whether a character is in lowercase or uppercase?

8.10   How do you determine whether a character is alphanumeric?

Section 8.4 The **StringBuilder/StringBuffer** Class

8.11   What is the difference between **StringBuilder** and **StringBuffer**?

8.12   How do you create a string buffer for a string? How do you get the string from a string buffer?

8.13   Write three statements to reverse a string s using the **reverse** method in the **StringBuffer** class.

8.14   Write three statements to delete a substring from a string s of twenty characters, starting at index 4 and ending with index 10. Use the **delete** method in the **StringBuffer** class.

8.15   What is the internal structure of a string and a string buffer?

8.16   Suppose that s1 and s2 are given as follows:

```
StringBuffer s1 = new StringBuffer("Java");
StringBuffer s2 = new StringBuffer("HTML");
```

Show the results of the following expressions of s1 after each statement. Assume that the expressions are independent.

```
(1) s1.append(" is fun");     (7)  s1.deleteCharAt(3);
(2) s1.append(s2);            (8)  s1.delete(1, 3);
(3) s1.insert(2, "is fun");   (9)  s1.reverse();
(4) s1.insert(1, s2);         (10) s1.replace(1, 3, "Computer");
(5) s1.charAt(2);             (11) s1.substring(1, 3);
(6) s1.length();             (12) s1.substring(2);
```

8.17   Show the output of the following program:

```
public class Test {
  public static void main(String[] args) {
    String s = "Java";
    StringBuffer buffer = new StringBuffer(s);
    change(s, buffer);

    System.out.println(s);
    System.out.println(buffer);
  }

  private static void change(String s, StringBuffer buffer) {
    s = s + " and HTML";
    buffer.append(" and HTML");
  }
}
```

Section 8.5 Command-Line Arguments

8.18   This book declares the `main` method as

```
public static void main(String[] args)
```

Can it be replaced by one of the following lines?

```
public static void main(String args[])
public static void main(String[] x)
public static void main(String x[])
static void main(String x[])
```

8.19   Show the output of the following program when invoked using

(1)   java Test I have a dream
(2)   java Test "1 2 3"
(3)   java Test
(4)   java Test "*"
(5)   java Test *

```java
public class Test {
  public static void main(String[] args) {
    System.out.println("Number of strings is " + args.length);
    for (int i = 0; i < args.length; i++)
      System.out.println(args[i]);
  }
}
```

Section 8.6 Regular Expressions

8.20   Describe whitespace characters, word characters, quantifiers, and grouping patterns in regular expressions.

8.21   Show the output of the following statements:

```java
System.out.println("abc".matches("a[\\w]c"));
System.out.println("12Java".matches("[\\d]{2}[\\w]{4}"));
System.out.println("12Java".matches("[\\w]*"));
System.out.println("12Java".matches("[\\W]*"));
System.out.println("12Java".matches("[\\d]*"));
System.out.println("12Java".matches("[\\d]{2}[\\w]"));
System.out.println("12Java".matches("[\\d]{2}[\\W]*"));
System.out.println("12Java".matches("[\\D]{2}[\\w]+"));
System.out.println("12Java".matches("[\\d]{1}[\\w]"));
System.out.println("12Java".matches("[\\d]{1}[\\w]*"));
System.out.println("12_Java".matches("[\\d]{2}[\\w]{5}"));
System.out.println("12Java".matches("[\\d]{2}[\\w]{1,15}"));
System.out.println("12#Java".matches("[\\d]{2}[\\w]{1,15}"));
```

8.22   Show the output of the following statements:

```java
System.out.println("Java".replaceAll("[av]", "RX"));
System.out.println("Java".replaceAll("av", "RX"));
System.out.println("Java".replaceAll("[a][v]", "RX"));
System.out.println("Java".replaceFirst("\\w", "RX"));
System.out.println("Java".replaceFirst("\\w*", "RX"));
System.out.println("Java12".replaceAll("\\d", "RX"));
System.out.println("Java".replaceAll("\\d", "RX"));
System.out.println("Java".replaceAll("\\W", "RX"));
System.out.println("Java".replaceAll("\\D", "RX"));
System.out.println("Java".replaceAll("\\w*", "RX"));
```

```
System.out.println("Java".replaceAll("\\w+", "RX"));
System.out.println("Java".replaceAll("\\w+?", "RX"));
System.out.println("Java".replaceFirst("\\w+?", "RX"));
```

8.23 The following methods split a string into substrings. Show the substrings for each method.

```
"Java".split("[a]")
"Java".split("[av]")
"Java#HTML#PHP".split("#")
"JavaTOHTMLToPHP".split("TO|To")
"JavaTOHTMLToPHP".split("TH")
"JavaTOHTMLToPHP".split("T|H")
"JavaTOHTMLToPHP".split("J")
```

8.24 How do you check whether a string contains all numeric digits?

Section 8.7 The File Class

8.25 What is wrong about creating a File object using the following statement?

```
new File("c:\book\test.dat");
```

8.26 How do you check whether a file already exists? How do you delete a file? How do you rename a file? Can you find the file size (the number of bytes) using the File class?

8.27 Can you use the File class for I/O?

Section 8.8 Text I/O

8.28 How do you create a PrintWriter to write data to a file? What is the reason to declare throws Exception in the main method in Listing 8.6, WriteData.java. What would happen if the close() method is not invoked in Listing 8.6.

8.29 Show the contents of the file temp.txt after the following program is executed:

```
public class Test {
  public static void main(String[] args) throws Exception {
    java.io.PrintWriter output = new java.io.PrintWriter("temp.txt");
    output.printf("amount is %f %e\r\n", 32.32, 32.32);
    output.printf("amount is %5.4f %5.4e\r\n", 32.32, 32.32);
    output.printf("%6b\r\n", (1 > 2));
    output.printf("%6s\r\n", "Java");
    output.close();
  }
}
```

8.30 How do you create a Scanner to read data from a file? What is the reason to declare throws Exception in the main method in Listing 8.7, ReadData.java. What would happen if the close() method is not invoked in Listing 8.7.

8.31 What will happen if you attempt to create a Scanner for a nonexistent file? What will happen if you attempt to create a PrintWriter for an existing file?

PROGRAMMING EXERCISES

Section 8.2 The **String** Class

8.1* (*Revising Listing 8.1 CheckPalindrome.java*) Rewrite Listing 8.1 by creating a new string that is a reversal of the string and compare the two to determine whether the string is a palindrome. Write your own `reverse` method using the following header:

```
public static String reverse(String s)
```

8.2* (*Revising Listing 8.1 CheckPalindrome.java*) Rewrite Listing 8.1 to ignore cases.

8.3** (*Checking substrings*) You can check whether a string is a substring of another string by using the `indexOf` method in the `String` class. Write your own method for this function. Write a program that prompts the user to enter two strings, and check whether the first string is a substring of the second.

8.4* (*Occurrences of a specified character*) Write a method that finds the number of occurrences of a specified character in the string using the following header:

```
public static int count(String str, char a)
```

For example, `count("Welcome", 'e')` returns `2`.

Section 8.3 The **Character** Class

8.5** (*Occurrences of each digit in a string*) Write a method that counts the occurrences of each digit in a string using the following header:

```
public static int[] count(String s)
```

The method counts how many times a digit appears in the string. The return value is an array of ten elements, each of which holds the count for a digit. For example, after executing `int[] counts = count("12203AB3")`, `counts[0]` is `1`, `counts[1]` is `1`, `counts[2]` is `2`, `counts[3]` is `2`.

Write a `main` method to display the count for `"SSN is 343 32 4545 and ID is 434 34 4323"`.

8.6* (*Counting the letters in a string*) Write a method that counts the number of letters in the string using the following header:

```
public static int countLetters(String s)
```

Write a `main` method to invoke `countLetters("Java in 2008")` and display its return value.

8.7* (*Hex to decimal*) Write a method that parses a hex number as a string into a decimal integer. The method header is as follows:

```
public static int parseHex(String hexString)
```

For example, `hexString` A5 is `165` ($10 \times 16 + 5 = 165$) and FAA is `4129` ($15 \times 16^2 + 10 \times 16 + 10 = 4129$). So   `parseHex("A5")` returns `165`, and parseHex("FAA") returns 4129. Use hex strings ABC and 10A to test the method. Note that Integer.parseInt("FAA", 16) parses a hex string to a decimal value. Do not use this method in this exercise.

8.8* (*Binary to decimal*) Write a method that parses a binary number as a string into a decimal integer. The method header is as follows:

```
public static int parseBinary(String binaryString)
```

For example, binaryString 10001 is 17 ($1 \times 2^4 + 0 \times 2^3 + 0 \times 2^2 + 0 \times 2 + 1 = 17$) So, parseBinary("10001") returns 17. Use binary string 11111111 to test the method. Note that Integer.parseInt("10001", 2) parses a binary string to a decimal value. Do not use this method in this exercise.

Section 8.4 The `StringBuilder/StringBuffer` Class

8.9** (*Decimal to hex*) Write a method that parses a decimal number into a hex number as a string. The method header is as follows:

```
public static String convertDecimalToHex(int value)
```

See §1.5, "Number Systems," for converting a decimal into a hex. Use decimal 298 and 9123 to test the method.

8.10** (*Decimal to binary*) Write a method that parses a decimal number into a binary number as a string. The method header is as follows:

```
public static String convertDecimalToBinary(int value)
```

See §1.5, "Number Systems," for converting a decimal into a binary. Use decimal 298 and 9123 to test the method.

8.11** (*Sorting characters in a string*) Write a method that returns a sorted string using the following header:

```
public static String sort(String s)
```

For example, sort("acb") returns abc.

8.12** (*Anagrams*) Write a method that checks whether two words are anagrams. Two words are anagrams if they contain the same letters in any order. For example, "silent" and "listen" are anagrams. The header of the method is as follows:

```
public static boolean isAnagram(String s1, String s2)
```

Write a main method to invoke isAnagram("silent", "listen"), isAnagram("garden", "ranged"), and isAnagram("split", "lisp").

Section 8.5 Command-Line Arguments

8.13* (*Passing a string to check palindromes*) Rewrite Example 8.1, "Checking Palindromes," by passing the string as a command-line argument.

8.14* (*Summing integers*) Write two programs. The first program passes an unspecified number of integers as separate strings to the main method and displays their total. The second program passes an unspecified number of integers in one string to the main method and displays their total. Name the two programs Exercise8_14a and Exercise8_14b, as shown in Figure 8.18.

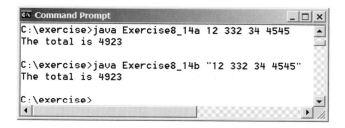

FIGURE 8.18

The program adds all the numbers passed from the command line.

8.15* (*Finding the number of uppercase letters in a string*) Write a program that passes a string to the `main` method and displays the number of uppercase letters in a string.

Section 8.6 Regular Expressions

8.16* (*Monetary units*) Rewrite Listing 2.7, ComputeChange.java, to receive the input as a string, and extract the dollars and cents using the split method in the `String` class.

8.17* (*Extracting words*) Write a program that extracts words from a string using the spaces and punctuation marks as delimiters. Enter the string from an input dialog box.

8.18* (*Summing values*) Write a program that reads a string from an input dialog box. The string consists of double values separated by spaces. Display the sum of the values.

Sections 8.7–8.8

8.19**(*Reformatting Java source code*) Write a program that converts the Java source code from the next-line brace style to the end-of-line brace style. For example, the following Java source in (a) uses the next-line brace style. Your program converts it to the end-of-line brace style in (b).

```
public class Test
{
  public static void main(String[] args)
  {
    // Some statements
  }
}
```

(a) Next-line brace style

```
public class Test {
  public static void main(String[] args) {
    // Some statements
  }
}
```

(b) End-of-line brace style

Your program can be invoked from the command line with the Java source code file as the argument. It converts the Java source code to a new format. For example, the following command converts the Java source code file Test.java to the end-of-line brace style.

```
java Exercise8_19 Test.java
```

8.20* (*Counting characters, words, and lines in a file*) Write a program that will count the number of characters (excluding control characters `'\r'` and `'\n'`), words, and lines, in a file. Words are separated by spaces, tabs, carriage-returns, or line-feed characters. The filename should be passed as a command-line argument, as shown in Figure 8.19.

FIGURE 8.19 The program displays the number of characters, words, and lines in a given file.

8.21* (*Processing scores in a text file*) Suppose that a text file named `Exercise8_21.txt` contains an unspecified number of scores. Write a program that reads the scores from the file and displays their total and average. Scores are separated by blanks.

8.22* (*Writing/Reading data*) Write a program to create a file named `Exercise8_22.txt` if it does not exist. Write one hundred integers created randomly into the file using text I/O. Integers are separated by spaces in the file. Read the data back from the file and display the sorted data.

8.23**(*Replacing text*) Listing 8.8, ReplaceText.java, gives a program that replaces text in a source file and saves the change into a new file. Revise the program to save the change into the original file. For example, invoking

    java Exercise8_23 file oldString newString

replaces `oldString` in the source file with `newString`.

Hint

Read each line from the file, replace all the occurrences of `oldString` with `newString`, and append it into a string builder. Finally write the string builder to the original file.

8.24**(*Removing text*) Write a program that removes all the occurrences of a specified string from a text file. For example, invoking

    java Exercise8_24 John filename

removes string `John` from the specified file.

Hint

Read each line from the file, remove all the occurrences of the text in the line, and append the line into a string builder. Finally write the string builder to the source file.

INHERITANCE AND POLYMORPHISM

Objectives

- To develop a subclass from a superclass through inheritance (§9.2).

- To invoke the superclass's constructors and methods using the `super` keyword (§9.3).

- To override methods in the subclass (§9.4).

- To distinguish differences between overriding and overloading (§9.5).

- To explore the useful methods (`equals(Object)`, `hashCode()`, `toString()`, `finalize()`, `clone()`, and `getClass()`) in the `Object` class (§9.6, §9.13 Optional).

- To comprehend polymorphism, dynamic binding, and generic programming (§9.7).

- To describe casting and explain why explicit downcasting is necessary (§9.8).

- To store, retrieve, and manipulate objects in an `ArrayList` (§9.9).

- To implement a `Stack` class using `ArrayList` (§9.10).

- To restrict access to data and methods using the `protected` visibility modifier (§9.11).

- To declare constants, unmodifiable methods, and nonextendable classes using the `final` modifier (§9.12).

- (Optional) To understand the effect of hiding data fields and static methods (§9.14).

- (Optional) To initialize data using initialization blocks and to distinguish between instance initialization and static initialization blocks (§9.15).

- (Optional GUI) To use inheritance in GUI programming (§9.16).

9.1 Introduction

Object-oriented programming allows you to derive new classes from existing classes. This is called *inheritance*. Inheritance is an important and powerful concept in Java. In fact, every class you define in Java is inherited from an existing class, either explicitly or implicitly. The classes you created in the preceding chapters were all extended implicitly from the `java.lang.Object` class.

This chapter introduces the concept of inheritance. Specifically, it discusses superclasses and subclasses, the use of the keyword `super`, and the `Object` class, explores polymorphism and dynamic binding, generic programming, and casting objects, and introduces the modifiers `protected` and `final`.

9.2 Superclasses and Subclasses

In Java terminology, a class `C1` extended from another class `C2` is called a *subclass*, and `C2` is called a *superclass*. A superclass is also referred to as a *supertype*, a *parent class,* or a *base class*, and a subclass as a *subtype*, a *child class*, an *extended class*, or a *derived class*. A subclass inherits accessible data fields and methods from its superclass, and may also add new data fields and methods.

Consider geometric objects. Suppose you want to design the classes to model geometric objects like circles and rectangles. Geometric objects have many common properties and behaviors. They can be drawn in a certain color, filled or unfilled. Thus a general class `GeometricObject` can be used to model all geometric objects. This class contains the properties `color` and `filled` and their appropriate get and set methods. Assume that this class also contains the `dateCreated` property and the `getDateCreated()` and `toString()` methods. The `toString()` method returns a string representation for the object. Since a circle is a special type of geometric object, it shares common properties and methods with other geometric objects. Thus it makes sense to define the `Circle` class that extends the `GeometricObject` class. Likewise, `Rectangle` can also be declared as a subclass of `GeometricObject`. Figure 9.1 shows the relationship among these classes. An arrow pointing to the superclass is used to denote the inheritance relationship between the two classes involved.

The `Circle` class inherits all accessible data fields and methods from the `GeometricObject` class. In addition, it has a new data field, `radius`, and its associated get and set methods. It also contains the `getArea()`, `getPerimeter()`, and `getDiameter()` methods for returning the area, perimeter, and diameter of the circle.

The `Rectangle` class inherits all accessible data fields and methods from the `GeometricObject` class. In addition, it has the data fields `width` and `height`, and the associated get and set methods. It also contains the `getArea()` and `getPerimeter()` methods for returning the area and perimeter of the rectangle.

 Note

To avoid naming conflict with improved versions of the `GeometricObject`, `Circle`, and `Rectangle` classes introduced in the next chapter, put classes `GeometricObject`, `Circle`, and `Rectangle` into a package named `chapter9`. The package name must be mapped to the file system directory structure, so, place the files `GeometricObject.java`, `Circle.java`, and `Rectangle.java` into `c:\book\chapter9`.

The `GeometricObject`, `Circle`, and `Rectangle` classes are shown in Listings 9.1, 9.2, and 9.3.

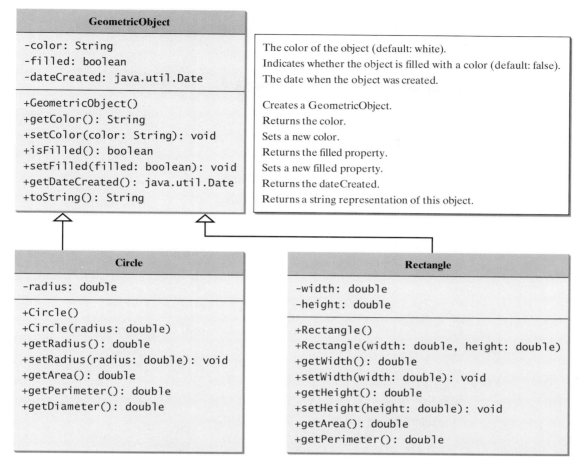

FIGURE 9.1 The `GeometricObject` class is the superclass for `Circle` and `Rectangle`.

LISTING 9.1   GeometricObject.java

```java
1 package chapter9;                                              package
2
3 public class GeometricObject {
4   private String color = "white";                             data fields
5   private boolean filled;
6   private java.util.Date dateCreated;
7
8   /** Construct a default geometric object */
9   public GeometricObject() {                                  constructor
10     dateCreated = new java.util.Date();                      date constructed
11   }
12
13   /** Return color */
14   public String getColor() {                                 methods
15     return color;
16   }
17
```

```
18    /** Set a new color */
19    public void setColor(String color) {
20      this.color = color;
21    }
22
23    /** Return filled. Since filled is boolean,
24      so, the get method name is isFilled */
25    public boolean isFilled() {
26      return filled;
27    }
28
29    /** Set a new filled */
30    public void setFilled(boolean filled) {
31      this.filled = filled;
32    }
33
34    /** Get dateCreated */
35    public java.util.Date getDateCreated() {
36      return dateCreated;
37    }
38
39    /** Return a string representation of this object */
40    public String toString() {
41      return "created on " + dateCreated + "\ncolor: " + color +
42        " and filled: " + filled;
43    }
44  }
```

LISTING 9.2 Circle.java

package

```
1 package chapter9;
2
3 public class Circle extends GeometricObject {
```

data fields

```
4    private double radius;
5
```

constructor

```
6    public Circle() {
7    }
8
9    public Circle(double radius) {
10     this.radius = radius;
11   }
12
```

methods

```
13    /** Return radius */
14    public double getRadius() {
15      return radius;
16    }
17
18    /** Set a new radius */
19    public void setRadius(double radius) {
20      this.radius = radius;
21    }
22
23    /** Return area */
24    public double getArea() {
25      return radius * radius * Math.PI;
26    }
27
28    /** Return diameter */
29    public double getDiameter() {
30      return 2 * radius;
31    }
32
```

```
33    /** Return perimeter */
34    public double getPerimeter() {
35      return 2 * radius * Math.PI;
36    }
37
38    /* Print the circle info */
39    public void printCircle() {
40      System.out.println("The circle is created " + getDateCreated() +
41        " and the radius is " + radius);
42    }
43  }
```

LISTING 9.3   Rectangle.java

```
1  package chapter9;                                                   package
2
3  public class Rectangle extends GeometricObject {
4    private double width;                                             data fields
5    private double height;
6
7    public Rectangle() {                                             constructor
8    }
9
10   public Rectangle(double width, double height) {
11     this.width = width;
12     this.height = height;
13   }
14
15   /** Return width */                                              methods
16   public double getWidth() {
17     return width;
18   }
19
20   /** Set a new width */
21   public void setWidth(double width) {
22     this.width = width;
23   }
24
25   /** Return height */
26   public double getHeight() {
27     return height;
28   }
29
30   /** Set a new height */
31   public void setHeight(double height) {
32     this.height = height;
33   }
34
35   /** Return area */
36   public double getArea() {
37     return width * height;
38   }
39
40   /** Return perimeter */
41   public double getPerimeter() {
42     return 2 * (width + height);
43   }
44 }
```

The classes `Circle` and `Rectangle` extend the `GeometricObject` class. The reserved word `extends` tells the compiler that these classes extend the `GeometricObject` class, thus inheriting the methods `getColor`, `setColor`, `isFilled`, `setFilled`, and `toString`.

The following code in Listing 9.4 creates objects of `Circle` and `Rectangle`, and invokes the methods on these objects.

LISTING 9.4 TestCircleRectangle.java

package

```
 1 package chapter9;
 2
 3 public class TestCircleRectangle {
 4   public static void main(String[] args) {
 5     Circle circle = new Circle(1);
 6     System.out.println("A circle " + circle.toString());
 7     System.out.println(circle.getRadius());
 8     System.out.println("The radius is " + circle.getRadius());
 9     System.out.println("The area is " + circle.getArea());
10     System.out.println("The diameter is " + circle.getDiameter());
11
12     Rectangle rectangle = new Rectangle(2, 4);
13     System.out.println("\nA rectanlge " + rectangle.toString());
14     System.out.println("The area is " + rectangle.getArea());
15     System.out.println("The perimeter is " +
16       rectangle.getPerimeter());
17   }
18 }
```

Circle object
invoke **toString**

Rectangle object
invoke **toString**

```
Command Prompt                                    _ □ ×
C:\book>java chapter9.TestCircleRectangle
A circle created on Thu Sep 01 12:24:24 EDT 2005
color: white and filled: false
1.0
The radius is 1.0
The area is 3.141592653589793
The diameter is 2.0

A rectanlge created on Thu Sep 01 12:24:24 EDT 2005
color: white and filled: false
The area is 8.0
The perimeter is 12.0

C:\book>
```

FIGURE 9.2 The methods in `GeometricObject` are inherited in `Circle` and `Rectangle`.

Since `radius` is 1, `color` is `white`, and `filled` is `false` by default, the output is as shown in Figure 9.2. Note that `TestCircleRectangle.java` is stored in `c:\book\chapter9` and the `TestCircleRectangle` class is in package `chapter9`. Thus you have to run it from `c:\book` using the command **java chapter9.TestCircleRectangle** with the complete class name.

Note

more in subclass

Contrary to the conventional interpretation, a subclass is not a subset of its superclass. In fact, a subclass usually contains more information and functions than its superclass.

Caution

no blind extension

Inheritance is used to model the *is-a* relationship. Do not blindly extend a class just for the sake of reusing methods. For example, it makes no sense for a `Tree` class to extend a `Person` class. A subclass and its superclass must have the is-a relationship.

9.3 Using the **super** Keyword

A subclass inherits accessible data fields and methods from its superclass. Does it inherit constructors? Can superclass constructors be invoked from subclasses? This section addresses these questions and their ramification.

The discussion in §7.12, "The `this` Keyword," introduced the use of the keyword `this` as a surrogate to refer to the calling object. The keyword `super` refers to the superclass of the class in which `super` appears. It can be used in two ways:

- To call a superclass constructor.
- To call a superclass method.

9.3.1 Calling Superclass Constructors

The syntax to call a superclass constructor is:

```
super(), or super(parameters);
```

The statement `super()` invokes the no-arg constructor of its superclass, and the statement `super(arguments)` invokes the superclass constructor that matches the `arguments`. The statement `super()` or `super(arguments)` must appear in the first line of the subclass constructor and is the only way to invoke a superclass constructor.

Caution

You must use the keyword `super` to call the superclass constructor, and the call must be the first statement in the constructor. Invoking a superclass constructor's name in a subclass causes a syntax error.

Note

A constructor is used to construct an instance of a class. Unlike properties and methods, the constructors of a superclass are not inherited in the subclass. They can only be invoked from the constructors of the subclasses, using the keyword `super`.

9.3.2 Constructor Chaining

A constructor may invoke an overloaded constructor or its superclass's constructor. If neither of them is invoked explicitly, the compiler puts `super()` as the first statement in the constructor. For example,

```
public A() {
}
```
is equivalent to
```
public A() {
    super();
}
```

```
public A(double d) {
    // some statements
}
```
is equivalent to
```
public A(double d) {
    super();
    // some statements
}
```

In any case, constructing an instance of a class invokes the constructors of all the superclasses along the inheritance chain. A superclass's constructor is called before the subclass's constructor. This is called *constructor chaining*. Consider the following code:

constructor chaining

```
1  public class Faculty extends Employee {
2    public static void main(String[] args) {
3      new Faculty();
4    }
```

```
 5
 6    public Faculty() {
 7      System.out.println("(4) Faculty's no-arg constructor is invoked");
 8    }
 9 }
10
11 class Employee extends Person {
12    public Employee() {
13      this("(2) Invoke Employee's overloaded constructor");
14      System.out.println("(3) Employee's no-arg constructor is invoked");
15    }
16
17    public Employee(String s) {
18      System.out.println(s);
19    }
20 }
21
22 class Person {
23    public Person() {
24      System.out.println("(1) Person's no-arg constructor is invoked");
25    }
26 }
```

invoke overloaded
constructor

In line 3, `new Faculty()` invokes `Faculty`'s no-arg constructor. Since `Faculty` is a sub-class of `Employee`, `Employee`'s no-arg constructor is invoked before any statements in `Faculty`'s constructor are executed. `Employee`'s no-arg constructor invokes `Employee`'s second constructor (line 12). Since `Employee` is a subclass of `Person`, `Person`'s no-arg constructor is invoked before any statements in `Employee`'s second constructor are execut-ed. Therefore, the output of creating an instance of `Faculty` is:

```
(1) Person's no-arg constructor is invoked
(2) Invoke Employee's overloaded constructor
(3) Employee's no-arg constructor is invoked
(4) Faculty's no-arg constructor is invoked
```

 Caution

no-arg constructor

If a class is designed to be extended, it is better to provide a no-arg constructor to avoid pro-gramming errors. Consider the following code:

```
1 public class Apple extends Fruit {
2 }
3
4 class Fruit {
5    public Fruit(String name) {
6      System.out.println("Fruit's constructor is invoked");
7    }
8 }
```

Since no constructor is explicitly defined in `Apple`, `Apple`'s default no-arg constructor is declared implicitly. Since `Apple` is a subclass of `Fruit`, `Apple`'s default constructor automati-cally invokes `Fruit`'s no-arg constructor. However, `Fruit` does not have a no-arg constructor because `Fruit` has an explicit constructor defined. Therefore, the program cannot be compiled.

9.3.3 Calling Superclass Methods

The keyword **super** can also be used to reference a method other than the constructor in the superclass. The syntax is like this:

```
super.method(parameters);
```

You could rewrite the `printCircle()` method in the `Circle` class as follows:

```
public void printCircle() {
  System.out.println("The circle is created " +
    super.getDateCreated() + " and the radius is " + radius);
}
```

It is not necessary to put `super` before `getDateCreated()` in this case, however, because `getDateCreated` is a method in the `GeometricObject` class and is inherited by the `Circle` class. Nevertheless, in some cases, as shown in the next section, the keyword `super` is needed.

Caution

You can use `super.p()` to invoke the method `p()` defined in the superclass. Suppose A extends B, and B extends C, and a method `p()` is defined in C. Can you invoke `super.super.p()` from A? The answer is no. It is illegal to have such a chain of `super`s in Java.

no multiple **super**s

9.4 Overriding Methods

A subclass inherits methods from a superclass. Sometimes it is necessary for the subclass to modify the implementation of a method defined in the superclass. This is referred to as *method overriding*.

method overriding

The `toString` method in the `GeometricObject` class returns the string representation for a geometric object. This method can be overridden to return the string representation for a circle. To override it, add the following new method in Listing 9.2, Circle.java:

```
public class Circle extends GeometricObject {
  // Other methods are omitted

  /** Override the toString method defined in GeometricObject */
  public String toString() {
    return super.toString() + "\nradius is " + radius;
  }
}
```

The `toString()` method is defined in the `GeometricObeject` class and modified in the `Circle` class. Both methods can be used in the `Circle` class. To invoke the `toString` method defined in the `GeometricObject` class, use `super.toString()`. Can a subclass of `Circle` access the `toString` method defined in the `GeometricObject` class using a syntax such as `super.super.toString()`? No. This is a syntax error. Can an instance of `Circle` invoke the `toString` method defined in the `GeometricObject` class? No, not any more, since `toString()` in `GeometricObject` has been overridden in `Circle`.

Note

Private data fields and methods in a superclass are not accessible outside of the class. Therefore, they are not inherited in a subclass.

private members

Note

An instance method can be overridden only if it is accessible. Thus a private method cannot be overridden, because it is not accessible outside its own class. If a method defined in a subclass is private in its superclass, the two methods are completely unrelated.

override accessible instance method

Note

Like an instance method, a static method can be inherited. However, a static method cannot be overridden. If a static method defined in the superclass is redefined in a subclass, the method defined in the superclass is hidden. Hiding static methods will be further discussed in §9.14, "Hiding Data Fields and Static Methods."

cannot override static method

9.5 Overriding vs. Overloading

You have learned about overloading methods in §5.6, "Overloading Methods." Overloading a method is a way to provide more than one method with the same name but with different signatures to distinguish them. To override a method, the method must be defined in the subclass using the same signature and same return type as in its superclass.

same signature
same return type

Let us use an example to show the differences between overriding and overloading. In (a), the method `p(int i)` in class `A` overrides the same method defined in class `B`. However, in (b), the method `p(double i)` in class `A` and the method `p(int i)` in class `B` are two overloaded methods. The method `p(int i)` in class `B` is inherited in `A`.

```java
public class Test {
  public static void main(String[] args) {
    A a = new A();
    a.p(10);
  }
}

class B {
  public void p(int i) {
  }
}

class A extends B {
  // This method overrides the method in B
  public void p(int i) {
    System.out.println(i);
  }
}
```

(a)

```java
public class Test {
  public static void main(String[] args) {
    A a = new A();
    a.p(10);
  }
}

class B {
  public void p(int i) {
  }
}

class A extends B {
  // This method overloads the method in B
  public void p(double i) {
    System.out.println(i);
  }
}
```

(b)

When you run the `Test` class in (a), `a.p(10)` invokes the `p(int i)` method defined in class `A`, so the program displays 10. When you run the `Test` class in (b), `a.p(10)` invokes the `p(int i)` method defined in class `B`, so nothing is printed.

9.6 The `Object` Class and Its `toString()` Method

Every class in Java is descended from the `java.lang.Object` class. If no inheritance is specified when a class is defined, the superclass of the class is `Object` by default. For example, the following two class declarations are the same:

```java
public class Circle {
  ...
}
```

Equivalent

```java
public class Circle extends Object {
  ...
}
```

Classes like `String`, `StringBuffer`, `Loan`, and `GeometricObject` are implicitly subclasses of `Object` (as are all the main classes you have seen in this book so far). It is important to be familiar with the methods provided by the `Object` class so that you can use them in your classes. This section introduces the `toString()` method. Other methods will be introduced in §9.13.

The signature of the `toString()` method is

```java
public String toString()
```

Invoking `toString()` on an object returns a string that represents the object. By default, it returns a string consisting of a class name of which the object is an instance, an at sign (@), and the object's hash code in hexadecimal. For example, consider the following code for the `Loan` class defined in Listing 7.9:

string representation

```
Loan loan = new Loan();
System.out.println(loan.toString());
```

The code displays something like `Loan@15037e5`. This message is not very helpful or informative. Usually you should override the `toString` method so that it returns a descriptive string representation of the object. For example, the `toString` method in the `GeometricObject` class in Listing 9.1 was overridden as follows:

```
public String toString() {
  return "color: " + color + "and is filled: " + filled;
}
```

 Note
You can also pass an object to invoke `System.out.println(object)` or `System.out.print(object)`. This is equivalent to invoking `System.out.println(object.toString())` or `System.out.print(object.toString())`. So you could replace `System.out.println(loan.toString())` with `System.out.println(loan)`.

print object

9.7 Polymorphism, Dynamic Binding, and Generic Programming

The inheritance relationship enables a subclass to inherit features from its superclass with additional new features. A subclass is a specialization of its superclass; every instance of a subclass is an instance of its superclass, but not vice versa. For example, every circle is an object, but not every object is a circle. Therefore, you can always pass an instance of a subclass to a parameter of its superclass type. Consider the code in Listing 9.5.

LISTING 9.5 PolymorphismDemo.java

```
1 package chapter9;
2
3 public class PolymorphismDemo {
4   public static void main(String[] args) {
5     m(new GraduateStudent());
6     m(new Student());
7     m(new Person());
8     m(new Object());
9   }
10
11  public static void m(Object x) {
12    System.out.println(x.toString());
13  }
14 }
15
16 class GraduateStudent extends Student {
17 }
18
19 class Student extends Person {
20   public String toString() {
21     return "Student";
22   }
23 }
24
```

package

polymorphic call

dynamic binding

*override **toString()***

override **toString()**

```
25 class Person extends Object {
26   public String toString() {
27     return "Person";
28   }
29 }
```

It produces the output shown in Figure 9.3. Why? Let us discuss the reason. Method m (line 11) takes a parameter of the **Object** type. You can invoke m with any object (e.g., **new GraduateStudent()**, **new Student()**, **new Person()**, and **new Object()**) in lines 5–8). An object of a subtype can be used wherever its supertype value is required.

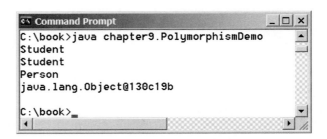

FIGURE 9.3 An instance of a subclass is also an instance of its superclass.

When the method **m(Object x)** is executed, the argument **x**'s **toString** method is invoked. **x** may be an instance of **GraduateStudent**, **Student**, **Person**, or **Object**. Classes **GraduateStudent**, **Student**, **Person**, and **Object** have their own implementations of the **toString** method. Which implementation is used will be determined dynamically by the Java Virtual Machine at runtime. This capability is known as *dynamic binding*. It is also known as *polymorphism* (from a Greek word meaning "many forms") because one method has many implementations.

dynamic binding
polymorphism

Dynamic binding works as follows: Suppose an object **o** is an instance of classes C_1, C_2, ..., C_{n-1}, and C_n, where C_1 is a subclass of C_2, C_2 is a subclass of C_3, ..., and C_{n-1} is a subclass of C_n, as shown in Figure 9.4. That is, C_n is the most general class, and C_1 is the most specific class. In Java, C_n is the **Object** class. If **o** invokes a method **p**, the JVM searches the implementation for the method **p** in C_1, C_2, ..., C_{n-1}, and C_n, in this order, until it is found. Once an implementation is found, the search stops and the first-found implementation is invoked. For example, when **m(new GraduateStudent())** is invoked in line 5, the **toString** method defined in the **Student** class is used.

If **o** is an instance of C_1, **o** is also an instance of C_2, C_3, ..., C_{n-1}, and C_n

java.lang.Object

FIGURE 9.4 The method to be invoked is dynamically bound at runtime.

Note

matching vs. binding

Matching a method signature and binding a method implementation are two separate issues. The *declared type* of the reference variable decides which method to match at compile time. The compiler finds a matching method according to parameter type, number of parameters, and order of the parameters at compile time. A method may be implemented in several subclasses. The Java Virtual Machine dynamically binds the implementation of the method at runtime, decided by the *actual class* of the object referenced by the variable.

Note

Dynamic binding enables new classes to be loaded on the fly without recompilation. There is no need for developers to create, and for users to install, major new software versions. New features can be incorporated transparently as needed. For example, suppose you have placed the classes `Test`, `GraduateStudent`, `Student`, `Person` in four separate files. If you change `Graduate-Student` as follows:

benefits of dynamic binding

```
class GraduateStudent extends Student {
  public String toString() {
    return "Graduate Student";
  }
}
```

You have a new version of `GraduateStudent` with a new `toString` method, but you don't have to recompile the classes `Test`, `Student`, and `Person`. When you run `Test`, the JVM dynamically binds the new `toString` method for the object of `GraduateStudent` when executing `m(new GraduateStudent())`.

Polymorphism allows methods to be used generically for a wide range of object arguments. This is known as *generic programming*. If a method's parameter type is a superclass (e.g., `Object`), you may pass an object to this method of any of the parameter's subclasses (e.g., `Student` or `String`). When an object (e.g., a `Student` object or a `String` object) is used in the method, the particular implementation of the method of the object invoked (e.g., `toString`) is determined dynamically.

generic programming

9.8 Casting Objects and the **instanceof** Operator

You have already used the casting operator to convert variables of one primitive type to another. Casting can also be used to convert an object of one class type to another within an inheritance hierarchy. In the preceding section, the statement

```
m(new Student());
```

assigns the object `new Student()` to a parameter of the `Object` type. This statement is equivalent to

```
Object o = new Student(); // Implicit casting
m(o);
```

The statement `Object o = new Student()`, known as *implicit casting*, is legal because an instance of `Student` is automatically an instance of `Object`.

implicit casting

Suppose you want to assign the object reference `o` to a variable of the `Student` type using the following statement:

```
Student b = o;
```

A compilation error would occur. Why does the statement `Object o = new Student()` work and the statement `Student b = o` doesn't? Because a `Student` object is always an instance of `Object`, but an `Object` is not necessarily an instance of `Student`. Even though you can see that `o` is really a `Student` object, the compiler is not clever enough to know it. To tell the compiler that `o` is a `Student` object, use an *explicit casting*. The syntax is similar to the one used for casting among primitive data types. Enclose the target object type in parentheses and place it before the object to be cast, as follows:

explicit casting

```
Student b = (Student)o; // Explicit casting
```

It is always possible to cast an instance of a subclass to a variable of a superclass (known as *upcasting*), because an instance of a subclass is *always* an instance of its superclass. When

upcasting

downcasting

casting an instance of a superclass to a variable of its subclass (known as *downcasting*), explicit casting must be used to confirm your intention to the compiler with the (**SubclassName**) cast notation. For the casting to be successful, you must make sure that the object to be cast is an instance of the subclass. If the superclass object is not an instance of the subclass, a runtime

ClassCastException

ClassCastException occurs. For example, if an object is not an instance of **Student**, it cannot be cast into a variable of **Student**. It is a good practice, therefore, to ensure that the object is an instance of another object before attempting a casting. This can be accomplished

instanceof

by using the **instanceof** operator. Consider the following code:

```
Object myObject = new Circle();
... // Some lines of code
/** Perform casting if myObject is an instance of Circle */
if (myObject instanceof Circle) {
  System.out.println("The circle diameter is " +
    ((Circle)myObject).getDiameter());
  ...
}
```

You may be wondering why casting is necessary. Variable **myObject** is declared **Object**. The *declared type* decides which method to match at compile time. Using **myObject.getDiameter()** would cause a compilation error because the **Object** class does not have the **getDiameter** method. The compiler cannot find a match for **myObject.getDiameter()**. It is necessary to cast **myObject** into the **Circle** type to tell the compiler that **myObject** is also an instance of **Circle**.

Why not declare **myObject** as a **Circle** type in the first place? To enable generic programming, it is a good practice to declare a variable with a supertype, which can accept a value of any subtype.

Note

lowercase keywords

instanceof is a Java keyword. Every letter in a Java keyword is in lowercase.

Tip

casting analogy

To help understand casting, you may also consider the analogy of fruit, apple, and orange, with the **Fruit** class as the superclass for **Apple** and **Orange**. An apple is a fruit, so you can always safely assign an instance of **Apple** to a variable for **Fruit**. However, a fruit is not necessarily an apple, so you have to use explicit casting to assign an instance of **Fruit** to a variable of **Apple**.

9.8.1 Example: Demonstrating Polymorphism and Casting

Listing 9.6 is an example that demonstrates polymorphism and casting. The program creates two objects (lines 7–8), a circle and a rectangle, and invokes the **displayObject** method to display them (lines 11–12). The **displayObject** method displays the area and diameter if the object is a circle (line 17), and the area if the object is a rectangle (line 23). Figure 9.5 shows the output of the program.

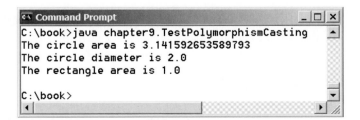

FIGURE 9.5 The program demonstrates polymorphism and casting.

LISTING 9.6   TestPolymorphismCasting.java

```
 1 package chapter9;
 2
 3 public class TestPolymorphismCasting {
 4   /** Main method */
 5   public static void main(String[] args) {
 6     // Declare and initialize two objects
 7     Object object1 = new Circle(1);
 8     Object object2 = new Rectangle(1, 1);
 9
10     // Display circle and rectangle
11     displayObject(object1);
12     displayObject(object2);
13   }
14
15   /** A method for displaying an object */
16   public static void displayObject(Object object) {
17     if (object instanceof Circle) {
18       System.out.println("The circle area is " +
19         ((Circle)object).getArea());
20       System.out.println("The circle diameter is " +
21         ((Circle)object).getDiameter());
22     }
23     else if (object instanceof Rectangle) {
24       System.out.println("The rectangle area is " +
25         ((Rectangle)object).getArea());
26     }
27   }
28 }
```

package chapter9

The `displayObject(Object object)` method is an example of generic programming. It can be invoked by passing any instance of `Object`.

The program uses implicit casting to assign a `Circle` object to `object1` and a `Rectangle` object to `object2` (lines 7–8), and then invokes the `displayObject` method to display the information on these objects (lines 11–12).

In the `displayObject` method (lines 16–27), explicit casting is used to cast the object to `Circle` if the object is an instance of `Circle`, and the methods `getArea` and `getDiameter` are used to display the area and diameter of the circle.

Casting can only be done when the source object is an instance of the target class. The program uses the `instanceof` operator to ensure that the source object is an instance of the target class before performing a casting (line 17).

Explicit casting to `Circle` (lines 19, 21) and to `Rectangle` (line 25) is necessary because the `getArea` and `getDiameter` methods are not available in the `Object` class.

 Caution

The object member access operator (.) precedes the casting operator. Use parentheses to ensure that casting is done before the . operator, as in

. precedes casting

```
((Circle)object).getArea();
```

9.9 The **ArrayList** Class

You can create an array to store objects. But the array's size is fixed once the array is created. Java provides the `ArrayList` class that can be used to store an unlimited number of objects. Figure 9.6 shows some methods in `ArrayList`.

java.util.ArrayList	
+ArrayList()	Creates an empty list.
+add(o: Object): void	Appends a new element o at the end of this list.
+add(index: int, o: Object): void	Adds a new element o at the specified index in this list.
+clear(): void	Removes all the elements from this list.
+contains(o: Object): boolean	Returns true if this list contains the element o.
+get(index: int): Object	Returns the element from this list at the specified index.
+indexOf(o: Object):int	Returns the index of the first matching element in this list.
+isEmpty(): boolean	Returns true if this list contains no elements.
+lastIndexOf(o: Object): int	Returns the index of the last matching element in this list.
+remove(o: Object): boolean	Removes the element o from this list.
+size(): int	Returns the number of elements in this list.
+remove(index: int): boolean	Removes the element at the specified index.
+set(index: int, o: Object): Object	Sets the element at the specified index.

FIGURE 9.6 An `ArrayList` stores an unlimited number of objects.

Listing 9.7 is an example of using `ArrayList`. The program creates an `ArrayList` using its no-arg constructor (line 4). The **add** method adds any instance of **Object** into the list. Since **String** is a subclass of **Object**, strings can be added to the list in lines 7–17. The **add** method (lines 7–17) adds an object to the end of list. So, after `cityList.add("London")` (line 7), the list contains

```
[London]
```

After `cityList.add("New York")` (line 9), the list contains

```
[London, New York]
```

After adding Paris, Toronto, Hong Kong, and Singapore (lines 11–17), the list would contain

```
[London, New York, Paris, Toronto, Hong Kong, Singapore]
```

Invoking `size()` (line 21) returns the size of the list, which is currently 6. Invoking `contains("Toronto")` (line 23) checks whether the object is in the list. In this case, it returns `true`, since `Toronto` is in the list. Invoking `indexOf("New York")` (line 25) returns the index of the object in the list, which is 1 in this case. If the object is not in the list, it returns −1. The `isEmpty()` method (line 27) checks whether the list is empty. It returns `false`, since the list is not empty.

The statement `cityList.add(2, "Beijing")` (line 30) inserts an object to the list at the specified index. After this statement, the list becomes

```
[London, New York, Beijing, Paris, Toronto, Hong Kong, Singapore]
```

The statement `cityList.remove("Toronto")` (line 35) removes the object from the list. After this statement, the list becomes

```
[London, New York, Beijing, Paris, Hong Kong, Singapore]
```

The statement `cityList.remove(1)` (line 40) removes the object at the specified index from the list. After this statement, the list becomes

```
[London, Beijing, Paris, Hong Kong, Singapore]
```

The `get(index)` method (line 45) returns the object at the specified index. Figure 9.7 shows the output of the program.

FIGURE 9.7 The program demonstrates how to use `ArrayList`.

LISTING 9.7 TestArrayList.java

```
1  public class TestArrayList {
2    public static void main(String[] args) {
3      // Create a list to store cities
4      java.util.ArrayList cityList = new java.util.ArrayList();          create ArrayList
5
6      // Add some cities in the list
7      cityList.add("London");                                           add element
8      // cityList now contains [London]
9      cityList.add("New York");
10     // cityList now contains [London, New York]
11     cityList.add("Paris");
12     // cityList now contains [London, New York, Paris]
13     cityList.add("Toronto");
14     // cityList now contains [London, New York, Paris, Toronto]
15     cityList.add("Hong Kong");
16     // contains [London, New York, Paris, Toronto, Hong Kong]
17     cityList.add("Singapore");
18     // contains [London, New York, Paris, Toronto,
19     //           Hong Kong, Singapore]
20
21     System.out.println("List size? " + cityList.size());              list size
22     System.out.println("Is Toronto in the list? " +
23       cityList.contains("Toronto"));                                  contains element?
24     System.out.println("The location of New York in the list? "
25       + cityList.indexOf("New York"));                                element index
26     System.out.println("Is the list empty? " +
27       cityList.isEmpty()); // Print false                             is empty?
28
29     // Insert a new city at index 2
30     cityList.add(2, "Beijing");
31     // contains [London, New York, Beijing, Paris, Toronto,
32     //           Hong Kong, Singapore]
33
34     // Remove a city from the list
35     cityList.remove("Toronto");                                       remove element
36     // contains [London, New York, Beijing, Paris,
37     //           Hong Kong, Singapore]
38
39     // Remove a city at index 1
40     cityList.remove(1);                                               remove element
41     // contains [London, Beijing, Paris, Hong Kong, Singapore]
42
```

get element

create `ArrayList`

```
43      // Display London Beijing Paris Hong Kong Singapore
44      for (int i = 0; i < cityList.size(); i++)
45        System.out.print(cityList.get(i) + " ");
46      System.out.println();
47
48      // Create a list to store two circles
49      java.util.ArrayList list = new java.util.ArrayList();
50
51      // Add two circles
52      list.add(new Circle(2));
53      list.add(new Circle(3));
54
55      // Display the area of the first circle in the list
56      System.out.println("The area of the circle? " +
57        ((Circle)list.get(0)).getArea());
58    }
59  }
```

Note

compile with –X1int opiton

You will get a compilation warning "unchecked operation" in JDK 1.5 when compiling this program. Ignore it and recompile it with the –X1int option, as shown in Figure 9.5. This warning can be fixed using generic types in Chapter 21, "Generics."

array vs. `ArrayList`

`ArrayList` objects can be used like arrays, but there are many differences. Table 9.1 lists their similarities and differences.

TABLE 9.1 Differences and Similarity between Arrays and `ArrayList`

	Array	ArrayList
Creating an array/ArrayList	`Object[] a = new Object[10]`	`ArrayList list = new ArrayList()`
Accessing an element	`a [index]`	`list.get(index)`
Updating an element	`a [index] = "London";`	`list.set(index, "London");`
Returning size	`a.length`	`list.size()`
Adding a new element		`list.add("London")`
Inserting a new element		`list.add(index, "London")`
Removing an element		`list.remove(index)`
Removing an element		`list.remove(Object)`
Removing all elements		`list.clear()`

Once an array is created, its size is fixed. You can access an array element using the square bracket notation (e.g., `a[index]`). When an `ArrayList` is created, its size is 0. You cannot use the `get` and `set` method if the element is not in the list. It is easy to add, insert, and remove elements in a list, but it is rather complex to add, insert, and remove elements in an array. You have to write the code to manipulate the array in order to perform these operations.

Note

`Vector` class

`java.util.Vector` is also a class for storing objects, which is very similar to the `ArrayList` class. All the methods in `ArrayList` are also available in `Vector`. The `Vector` class was introduced in JDK 1.1. The `ArrayList` class introduced in JDK 1.2 was intended to replace the `Vector` class.

9.10 A Custom Stack Class

"Case Study: The StackOfIntegers Class," in §7.17, presented a stack class for storing int values. This section introduces a stack class to store objects. Recall that a stack is a data structure that holds objects in a last-in first-out fashion. You can use an ArrayList to implement Stack, as shown in Listing 9.8. The UML diagram for the class is shown in Figure 9.8.

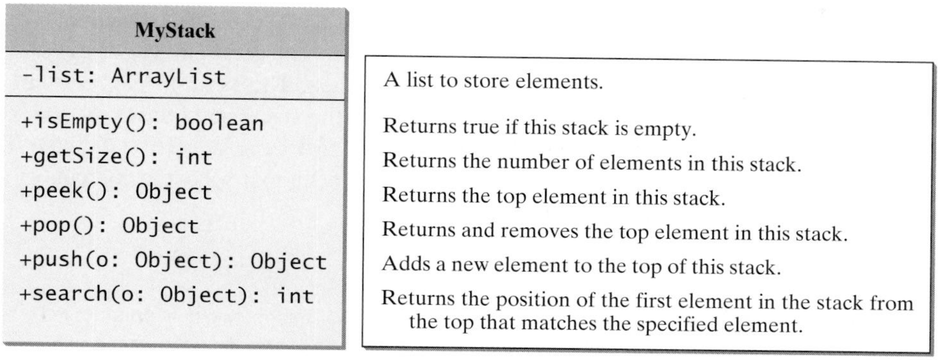

MyStack	
-list: ArrayList	A list to store elements.
+isEmpty(): boolean	Returns true if this stack is empty.
+getSize(): int	Returns the number of elements in this stack.
+peek(): Object	Returns the top element in this stack.
+pop(): Object	Returns and removes the top element in this stack.
+push(o: Object): Object	Adds a new element to the top of this stack.
+search(o: Object): int	Returns the position of the first element in the stack from the top that matches the specified element.

FIGURE 9.8 The MyStack class encapsulates the stack storage and provides the operations for manipulating the stack.

LISTING 9.8 MyStack.java

```
1  public class MyStack {
2    private java.util.ArrayList list = new java.util.ArrayList();    array list
3
4    public boolean isEmpty() {                                        stack empty?
5      return list.isEmpty();
6    }
7
8    public int getSize() {                                           get stack size
9      return list.size();
10   }
11
12   public Object peek() {                                            peek stack
13     return list.get(getSize() - 1);
14   }
15
16   public Object pop() {                                             remove
17     Object o = list.get(getSize() - 1);
18     list.remove(getSize() - 1);
19     return o;
20   }
21
22   public Object push(Object o) {                                    add
23     list.add(o);
24     return o;
25   }
26
27   public int search(Object o) {                                     search
28     return list.lastIndexOf(o);
29   }
30
```

```
31   /** Override the toString in the Object class */
32   public String toString() {
33     return "stack: " + list.toString();
34   }
35 }
```

An array list is created to store the elements in the stack (line 2). The `isEmpty()` method (lines 4–6) returns `list.isEmpty()`. The `getSize()` method (lines 8–10) returns `list.size()`. The `peek()` method (lines 12–14) looks at the element at the top of the stack without removing it. The end of the list is the top of the stack. The `pop()` method (lines 16–20) removes the top element from the stack and returns it. The `push(Object element)` method (lines 22–25) adds the specified element to the stack. The `search(Object element)` method checks whether the specified element is in the stack, and returns the index of first-matching element in the stack from the top by invoking `list.lastIndexOf(o)`. The `toString()` method defined in the `Object` class is overridden to display the contents of the stack by invoking `list.toString()`.

Note

In Listing 9.8, `MyStack` contains `ArrayList`. The relationship between `MyStack` and `ArrayList` is called *composition*. While inheritance models an *is-a* relationship, composition models a *has-a* relationship. You may also implement `MyStack` as a subclass of `ArrayList`. Relationships will be discussed in detail in Chapter 11, "Object-Oriented Design."

composition
is-a
has-a

9.11 The **protected** Data and Methods

The modifier `protected` can be applied to data and methods in a class. A protected datum or a protected method in a public class can be accessed *by any class in the same package or its subclasses*, even if the subclasses are in different packages.

The modifiers `private`, `protected`, and `public` are known as *visibility* or *accessibility modifiers* because they specify how class and class members are accessed. The visibility of these modifiers increases in this order:

Visibility increases
───→
private, none (if no modifier is used), protected, public

Table 9.2 summarizes the accessibility of the members in a class. Figure 9.9 illustrates how a public, protected, default, and private datum or method in class `C1` can be accessed from a class `C2` in the same package, from a subclass `C3` in the same package, from a subclass `C4` in a different package, and from a class `C5` in a different package.

Use the `private` modifier to hide the members of the class completely so that they cannot be accessed directly from outside the class. Use no modifiers to allow the members of the

TABLE 9.2 Data and Methods Visibility

Modifier on members in a class	Accessed from the same class	Accessed from the same package	Accessed from a subclass	Accessed from a different package
public	✓	✓	✓	✓
protected	✓	✓	✓	–
(default)	✓	✓	–	–
private	✓	–	–	–

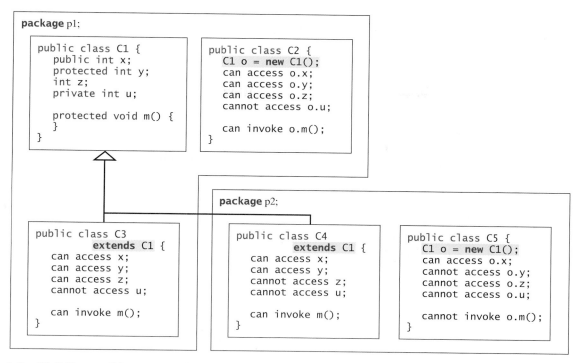

FIGURE 9.9 Visibility modifiers are used to control how data and methods are accessed.

class to be accessed directly from any class within the same package but not from other packages. Use the `protected` modifier to enable the members of the class to be accessed by the subclasses in any package or classes in the same package. Use the `public` modifier to enable the members of the class to be accessed by any class.

Your class can be used in two ways: for creating instances of the class, and for creating subclasses by extending the class. Make the members `private` if they are not intended for use from outside the class. Make the members `public` if they are intended for the users of the class. Make the fields or methods `protected` if they are intended for the extenders of the class but not the users of the class.

The `private` and `protected` modifiers can only be used for members of the class. The `public` modifier and the default modifier (i.e., no modifier) can be used on members of the class as well on the class. A class with no modifier (i.e., not a public class) is not accessible by classes from other packages.

 Note

A subclass may override a protected method in its superclass and change its visibility to public. However, a subclass cannot weaken the accessibility of a method defined in the superclass. For example, if a method is defined as public in the superclass, it must be defined as public in the subclass.

9.12 The **final** Classes, Methods, and Variables

You have already seen the `final` modifier used in declaring constants. You may occasionally want to prevent classes from being extended. In such cases, use the `final` modifier to indicate that a class is final and cannot be a parent class. The `Math` class, introduced in Chapter 5, "Methods," is a final class. The `String` and `StringBuffer` classes, introduced in Chapter 8, "Strings," are also final classes.

You also can define a method to be final; a final method cannot be overridden by its subclasses.

final local variable

Note
The modifiers are used on classes and class members (data and methods), except that the `final` modifier can also be used on local variables in a method. A final local variable is a constant inside a method.

9.13 (Optional) Methods in the **Object** Class

The discussion in §9.6 introduced the `toString` method in the `Object` class. Other useful methods are as follows:

- **public boolean** equals(Object object)
- **public int** hashCode()
- **protected void** finalize() **throws** Throwable
- **protected native** Object clone() **throws** CloneNotSupportedException
- **public final native** Class getClass()

native method

Note
A `native` method is implemented using a programming language other than Java. Some methods, such as `clone`, need to access hardware using the native machine language or the C language. These methods are marked `native`. A native method can be `final`, `public`, `private`, `protected`, overloaded, or overridden.

Note
A `finalize` method may throw **Throwable**, and the `clone` method may throw **CloneNotSupportedException**. Exception handling will be introduced in Chapter 17, "Exceptions and Assertions." (*Chapter 17 can be covered after this chapter.*) For now, you need to know that **throws Throwable** and **throws CloneNotSupportedException** are part of the method declarations for the `finalize` and `clone` methods.

9.13.1 The `equals` Method

The `equals` method tests whether two objects are equal. The syntax for invoking it is:

```
object1.equals(object2);
```

The default implementation of the `equals` method in the `Object` class is:

```
public boolean equals(Object obj) {
  return (this == obj);
}
```

Thus, using the `equals` method is equivalent to the == operator in the `Object` class, but it is really intended for the subclasses of the `Object` class to modify the `equals` method to test whether two distinct objects have the same content.

You have already used the `equals` method to compare two strings in §8.2, "The `String` Class." The `equals` method in the `String` class is inherited from the `Object` class and is modified in the `String` class to test whether two strings are identical in content. You can override the `equals` method in the `Circle` class to compare whether two circles are equal based on their radius, as follows:

```
public boolean equals(Object o) {
  if (o instanceof Circle) {
```

```
      return radius == ((Circle)o).radius;
    }
    else
      return false;
  }
```

Note

The == comparison operator is used for comparing two primitive data type values or for determining whether two objects have the same references. The **equals** method is intended to test
whether two objects have the same contents, provided that the method is modified in the defining class of the objects. The == operator is stronger than the **equals** method, in that the ==
operator checks whether the two reference variables refer to the same object.

== vs. **equals**

Caution

Using the signature **equals(SomeClassName obj)** (e.g., **equals(Circle c)**) to override the **equals** method in a subclass is a common mistake. You should use **equals(Object
obj)**). See Review Question 9.16.

equals(Object)

9.13.2   The hashCode Method

Invoking **hashCode()** on an object returns the object's hash code. *Hash code* is an integer that
can be used to store the object in a hash set so that it can be located quickly. Hash sets will be
introduced in Chapter 22, "Java Collections Framework." The **hashCode** implemented in the
Object class returns the internal memory address of the object in hexadecimal. Your class
should override the **hashCode** method whenever the **equals** method is overridden. By contract, if two objects are equal, their hash codes must be same. Two unequal objects may have
the same hash code, but you should implement the **hashCode** method to avoid too many such
cases. Additionally, invoking the **hashCode** method multiple times must return the same integer during one execution of the program. The integer need not be the same in different executions. For example, the **hashCode** method is overridden in the **String** class by returning
$s_0*31^{(n-1)} + s_1*31^{(n-2)} + \cdots + s_{n-1}$ as the hash code, where s_i is **s.charAt(i)**.

hash code

If you override the **equals** method in a class, you should also override the **hashCode**
method in the same class to ensure that two equal **Circle** objects have the same **hashCode**.
For example, you may override the **hashCode** method in the **Circle** class as follows:

```
public int hashCode() {
    return (int)(radius * 1999711);
}
```

9.13.3   The finalize Method

The **finalize** method is invoked on an object by the garbage collector when the object
becomes garbage. An object becomes garbage if it is no longer accessed. By default, the
finalize method does nothing. A subclass should override the **finalize** method to dis-
pose of system resources or to perform other cleanup, if necessary.

Note

The **finalize** method is invoked by the JVM. You should never write the code to invoke it in
your program. For this reason, the protected modifier is appropriate.

Listing 9.9 demonstrates the effect of overriding the **finalize()** method.

LISTING 9.9   FinalizationDemo.java

```
1 public class FinalizationDemo {
2   public static void main(String[] args) {
3     Cake a1 = new Cake(1);
```

```
 4        Cake a2 = new Cake(2);
 5        Cake a3 = new Cake(3);
 6
 7        // To dispose the objects a2 and a3
 8        a2 = a3 = null;
 9        System.gc(); // Invoke the Java garbage collector
10      }
11  }
12
13  class Cake extends Object {
14      private int id;
15
16      public Cake(int id) {
17          this.id = id;
18          System.out.println("Cake object " + id + " is created");
19      }
20
21      protected void finalize() throws java.lang.Throwable {
22          super.finalize();
23          System.out.println("Cake object " + id + " is disposed");
24      }
25  }
```

garbage collecting (margin, line 9)

override finalize (margin, line 21)

The following is the output of this program:

```
Cake object 1 is created
Cake object 2 is created
Cake object 3 is created
Cake object 2 is disposed
Cake object 3 is disposed
```

Line 8 assigns `null` to `a2` and `a3`. The objects previously referenced by `a2` and `a3` are no longer accessible. Therefore, they are garbage. `System.gc()` in line 9 requests the garbage collector to be invoked to reclaim space from all discarded objects. Normally you don't need to invoke this method explicitly, because the JVM automatically invokes it whenever necessary. The `finalize` method on the objects `a2` and `a3` are invoked by the garbage collector. When the program terminates, `a1` also becomes garbage, and `a1`'s `finalize` method is then invoked. Since the program has already exited, no message is displayed on the console.

Line 22 invokes the `finalize()` method in the superclass. This is a good practice to ensure that the finalization operations defined in the superclass are carried out.

9.13.4 The `clone` Method

Sometimes you need to make a copy of an object. Mistakenly, you might use the assignment statement, as follows:

```
newObject = someObject;
```

This statement does not create a duplicate object. It simply assigns the reference of `someObject` to `newObject`. To create a new object with separate memory space, use the `clone()` method:

```
newObject = someObject.clone();
```

This statement copies `someObject` to a new memory location and assigns the reference of the new object to `newObject`. For example,

```
java.util.Date date = new java.util.Date();
java.util.Date date1 = (java.util.Date)(date.clone());
```

creates a new **Date** object, **date**, and its clone **date1**. Note that **date.equals(date1)** is **true**, but **date == date1** is **false**.

Note

Not all objects can be cloned. For an object to be cloneable, its class must implement the **java.lang.Cloneable** interface, which is introduced in §10.4.4, "The **Cloneable** Interface."

Tip

An array is treated as an object in Java and is an instance of the **Object** class. The **clone** method can also be used to copy arrays. The following statement uses the **clone** method to copy the **sourceArray** of the **int[]** type to the **targetArray**:

```
int[] targetArray = (int[])sourceArray.clone();
```

Since the return type of the **clone** method is **Object**, **(int[])** is used to cast it to the **int[]** type.

9.13.5 The **getClass** Method

A class must be loaded in order to be used. When the JVM loads the class, it creates an object that contains the information about the class, such as class name, constructors, and methods. This object is an instance of **java.lang.Class**. It is referred to as a *meta-object* in this book, because it describes the information about the class.

meta-object

Through the meta-object, you can discover the information about the class at runtime. Every object can use the **getClass()** method to return its meta-object. For example, the following code

```
Object obj = new Object();
Class metaObject = obj.getClass();
System.out.println("Object obj's class is "
   + metaObject.getName());
```

displays

```
Object obj's class is java.lang.Object
```

Note

There is only one meta-object for a class. Every object has a meta-object. If two objects were created from the same class, their meta-objects are the same.

9.14 (Optional) Hiding Data Fields and Static Methods

This section is marked optional because hidden instance/static data fields and static methods are rarely useful, and they should not be used, for the sake of simplicity and clarity. You may skip this section now and consult it for reference in the future.

You can override an instance method, but you cannot override a data field (instance or static) or a static method. If you declare a data field or a static method in a subclass with the same name as one in the superclass, the one in the superclass is hidden, but it still exists. The two data fields or static methods are independent. You can reference the hidden data field or static method using the keyword **super** in the subclass. The hidden field or method can also be accessed via a reference variable of the superclass's type.

When invoking an instance method from a reference variable, the *actual class of the object* referenced by the variable decides which implementation of the method is used *at runtime*. When accessing a data field or a static method, the *declared type* of the reference variable decides which field or static method is used *at compile time*. This is the key difference between invoking an instance method and accessing a data field or a static method.

Listing 9.10 demonstrates the effect of hiding data fields and static methods.

LISTING 9.10 HidingDemo.java

```
1 public class HidingDemo {
2   public static void main(String[] args) {
3     A x = new B();
4
5     // Access instance data field i
6     System.out.println("(1) x.i is " + x.i);
7     System.out.println("(2) (B)x.i is " + ((B)x).i);
8
9     // Access static data field j
10    System.out.println("(3) x.j is " + x.j);
11    System.out.println("(4) ((B)x).j is " + ((B)x).j);
12
13    // Invoke static method m1
14    System.out.println("(5) x.m1() is " + x.m1());
15    System.out.println("(6) ((B)x).m1() is " + ((B)x).m1());
16
17    // Invoke instance method m2
18    System.out.println("(7) x.m2() is " + x.m2());
19    System.out.println("(8) x.m3() is " + x.m3());
20  }
21 }
22
23 class A {
24   public int i = 1;
25   public static int j = 11;
26
27   public static String m1() {
28     return "A's static m1";
29   }
30
31   public String m2() {
32     return "A's instance m2";
33   }
34
35   public String m3() {
36     return "A's instance m3";
37   }
38 }
39
40 class B extends A {
41   public int i = 2;
42   public static int j = 12;
43
44   public static String m1() {
45     return "B's static m1";
46   }
47
48   public String m2() {
49     return "B's instance m2";
50   }
51 }
```

Annotations (left margin):

- (line 10) same as **A.j**
- (line 11) same as **B.j**
- (line 14) same as **A.m1()**
- (line 15) same as **B.m1()**
- (line 18) dynamic binding
- (line 19) dynamic binding
- (line 41) hiding data field
- (line 42) hiding data field
- (line 44) hiding static method
- (line 48) override instance method

The printout of the program is:

```
(1) x.i is 1
(2) (B)x.i is 2
(3) x.j is 11
```

(4) ((B)x).j is 12
(5) x.m1() is A's static m1
(6) ((B)x).m1() is B's static m1
(7) x.m2() is B's instance m2
(8) x.m3() is A's instance m3

Here are the explanations:

1. x.i is 1 because x's declared type is class A.

2. To use i in class B, you need to cast x to B using ((B)x).i.

3. x.j is 11 because x's declared type is class A. x.j is better written as A.j.

4. To use j in class B, you need to cast x to B using ((B)x).j. ((B)x).j is better written as B.j.

5. x.m1() invokes the static m1 method in A because x's declared type is A. x.m1() is better written as A.m1().

6. ((B)x).m1() invokes the static m1 method in B because the type for (B)x is B. ((B)x).m1() is better written as B.m1().

7. x.m2() invokes the m2 method in B at runtime because x actually references to the object of class B.

8. x.m3() invokes the m3 method in A at runtime because m3 is implemented in A.

Note

A static method or a static field can always be accessed using its declared class name, regardless of whether it is hidden or not.

 # 9.15 (Optional) Initialization Blocks

Initialization blocks can be used to initialize objects along with the constructors. An *initialization block* is a block of statements enclosed inside a pair of braces. An initialization block appears within the class declaration, but not inside methods or constructors. It is executed as if it were placed at the beginning of every constructor in the class.

Initialization blocks can simplify the classes if you have multiple constructors sharing a common code and none of them can invoke other constructors. The common code can be placed in an initialization block, as shown in the example in Figure 9.10(a). In this example, none of the constructors can invoke any of the others using the syntax this(...). When an instance is created using a constructor of the Book class, the initialization block is executed to increase the object count by 1. The program is equivalent to Figure 9.10(b).

Note

A class may have multiple initialization blocks. In such cases, the blocks are executed in the order they appear in the class.

The initialization block in Figure 9.10(a) is referred to as an *instance initialization block* because it is executed whenever an instance of the class is created. A *static initialization block* is much like an instance initialization block except that it is declared static, can only refer to static members of the class, and is executed when the class is loaded. The JVM loads the class dynamically when it is needed. A superclass is loaded before its subclasses. The order of the execution can be summarized as follows:

instance initialization block
static initialization block

loading a class

1. When a class is used for the first time, it needs to be loaded. Loading involves two phases:

   1.1. Load superclasses. Before loading any class, its superclass must be loaded if it is not already loaded. This is a recursive process until a superclass along the inheritance chain is already loaded.

```
public class Book {
  private static int numOfObjects;
  private String title
  private int id;

  public Book(String title) {
    this.title = title;
  }

  public Book(int id) {
    this.id = id;
  }

  {
    numOfObjects++;
  }
}
```

Equivalent

```
public class Book {
  private static int numOfObjects;
  private String title;
  private int id;

  public Book(String title) {
    numOfObjects++;
    this.title = title;
  }

  public Book(int id) {
    numOfObjects++;
    this.id = id;
  }
}
```

(a) A class with initialization blocks   (b) An equivalent class

FIGURE 9.10   An initialization block can simplify coding for constructors.

1.2. After a class is loaded to the memory, its static data fields and static initialization block are executed in the order they appear in the class.

2. Invoking a constructor of the class involves three phases:

2.1. Invoke a constructor of the superclass. This is a recursive process until the superclass is `java.lang.Object`.

2.2. Initialize instance data fields and execute initialization blocks in the order they appear in the class.

2.3. Execute the body of the constructor.

Listing 9.11 demonstrates the execution order of initialization blocks.

LISTING 9.11   InitializationDemo.java

instance initialization block

static initialization block

```
 1 public class InitializationDemo {
 2   public static void main(String[] args) {
 3     new InitializationDemo();
 4   }
 5
 6   public InitializationDemo() {
 7     new M();
 8   }
 9
10   {
11     System.out.println("(2) InitializationDemo's instance block");
12   }
13
14   static {
15     System.out.println("(1) InitializationDemo's static block");
16   }
17 }
18
19 class M extends N {
20   M() {
```

```
21      System.out.println("(8) M's constructor body");
22   }
23
24   {
25      System.out.println("(7) M's instance initialization block");
26   }
27
28   static {
29      System.out.println("(4) M's static initialization block");
30   }
31 }
32
33 class N {
34   N() {
35      System.out.println("(6) N's constructor body");
36   }
37
38   {
39      System.out.println("(5) N's instance initialization block");
40   }
41
42   static {
43      System.out.println("(3) N's static initialization block");
44   }
45 }
```

instance initialization block *(line 24–26)*

static initialization block *(line 28–30)*

instance initialization block *(line 38–40)*

static initialization block *(line 42–44)*

The output of this program is:

```
(1) InitializationDemo's static block
(2) InitializationDemo's instance block
(3) N's static initialization block
(4) M's static initialization block
(5) N's instance initialization block
(6) N's constructor body
(7) M's instance initialization block
(8) M's constructor body
```

The program is executed in the following order:

1. The superclass of `InitializationDemo`, `java.lang.Object` is loaded first. Then class `InitializationDemo` is loaded, so `InitializationDemo`'s static initialization block is executed.

2. `InitializationDemo`'s constructor is invoked (line 3), so `InitializationDemo`'s instance initialization block is executed.

3. When executing `new M()` (line 7), class `M` needs to be loaded, which causes class `M`'s superclass (i.e., `N`) to be loaded first. So `N`'s static initialization block is executed. (Note that `N`'s superclass `java.lang.Object` has already been loaded in (1)).

4. Class `M` is now loaded. So `M`'s static initialization block is executed.

5. When invoking `M`'s constructor, the no-arg constructor of `M`'s superclass is invoked first; therefore, `N`'s instance initialization block is executed.

6. The regular code in `N`'s no-arg constructor is invoked after `N`'s instance initialization block is executed.

7. After N's no-arg constructor is invoked, M's no-arg constructor is invoked, which causes M's instance initialization block to be executed first.

8. The regular code in M's no-arg constructor is invoked after M's instance initialization block is executed.

Note

instance variable

static variable

If an *instance variable* is declared with an initial value (e.g., **double radius = 5**), the variable is initialized just as in an initialization block. That is, it is initialized when the constructor of the class is executed. If a *static variable* is declared with an initial value (e.g., **static double radius = 5**), the variable is initialized just as in a static initialization block. That is, it is initialized when the class is loaded.

9.16 (Optional GUI) Inheriting GUI Components

You learned how to create frames in the optional GUI sections in the preceding two chapters. The frames were created in the **main** method. A frame created in this way cannot be reused. It is better to declare a custom frame class by extending the **JFrame** class. To demonstrate, let us rewrite Listing 8.11, TwoButtons.java, using a custom frame class, as shown in Listing 9.12.

LISTING 9.12 CustomFrame.java

custom frame class
frame constructor

set layout

create a button

add button
display frame

```java
 1  import javax.swing.*;
 2  import java.awt.*;
 3
 4  public class CustomFrame extends JFrame {
 5    public CustomFrame() {
 6      // Set FlowLayout for the frame
 7      FlowLayout layout = new FlowLayout();
 8      setLayout(layout);
 9
10      // Add two buttons to frame
11      JButton jbtOK = new JButton("OK");
12      JButton jbtCancel = new JButton("Cancel");
13      add(jbtOK);
14      add(jbtCancel);
15    }
16
17    public static void main(String[] args) {
18      JFrame frame = new CustomFrame();
19      frame.setTitle("Window 1");
20      frame.setSize(200, 150);
21      frame.setLocation(200, 100);
22      frame.setDefaultCloseOperation(JFrame.EXIT_ON_CLOSE);
23      frame.setVisible(true);
24    }
25  }
```

The CustomFrame class extends JFrame to inherit all accessible methods from JFrame. Invoking **new CustomFrame()** in line 18 creates an instance of CustomFrame, which is also an instance of JFrame. The constructor of CustomFrame sets a FlowLayout for the frame in line 8 and adds two buttons in lines 13–14. The CustomFrame class can now be reused, as shown in Listing 9.13.

LISTING 9.13 UseCustomFrame.java

```java
 1  import javax.swing.*;
 2
 3  public class UseCustomFrame {
```

```
4   public static void main(String[] args) {
5     JFrame frame = new CustomFrame();                          create a frame
6     frame.setTitle("Use CustomFrame");
7     frame.setSize(200, 150);
8     frame.setLocation(200, 100);
9     frame.setDefaultCloseOperation(JFrame.EXIT_ON_CLOSE);
10    frame.setVisible(true);                                    display frame
11  }
12 }
```

KEY TERMS

array list 315	is-a relationship 320
casting objects 313	meta-object 325
constructor chaining 307	override 309
dynamic binding 311	polymorphism 311
final 301	protected 320
generic programming 313	subclass 302
has-a relationship 320	subtype 302
inheritance 302	superclass 302
initialization block 327	supertype 302
instanceof 314	

CHAPTER SUMMARY

■ You can derive a new class from an existing class. This is known as *class inheritance*. The new class is called a *subclass*, *child class*, or *extended class*. The existing class is called a *superclass*, *parent class*, or *base class*.

■ A constructor is used to construct an instance of a class. Unlike properties and methods, the constructors of a superclass are not inherited in the subclass. They can only be invoked from the constructors of the subclasses, using the keyword **super**.

■ A constructor may invoke an overloaded constructor or its superclass's constructor. If none of them is invoked explicitly, the compiler puts **super()** as the first statement in the constructor.

■ To override a method, the method must be defined in the subclass using the same signature as in its superclass.

■ An instance method can be overridden only if it is accessible. Thus a private method cannot be overridden, because it is not accessible outside its own class. If a method defined in a subclass is private in its superclass, the two methods are completely unrelated.

■ Like an instance method, a static method can be inherited. However, a static method cannot be overridden. If a static method defined in the superclass is redefined in a subclass, the method defined in the superclass is hidden.

■ Every class in Java is descended from the `java.lang.Object` class. If no inheritance is specified when a class is defined, the superclass of the class is `Object`.

■ If a method's parameter type is a superclass (e.g., `Object`), you may pass an object to this method of any of the parameter's subclasses (e.g., `Circle` or `String`). When an object (e.g., a `Circle` object or a `String` object) is used in the method, the particular implementation of the method of the object that is invoked (e.g., `toString`) is determined dynamically.

■ It is always possible to cast an instance of a subclass to a variable of a superclass, because an instance of a subclass is *always* an instance of its superclass. When casting an instance of a superclass to a variable of its subclass, explicit casting must be used to confirm your intention to the compiler with the (`SubclassName`) cast notation.

■ You can override an instance method, but you cannot override a field (instance or static) or a static method. If you declare a field or a static method in a subclass with the same name as one in the superclass, the one in the superclass is hidden, but it still exists. The two fields or static methods are independent. You can reference the hidden field or static method using the `super` keyword in the subclass. The hidden field or method can also be accessed via a reference variable of the superclass's type.

■ When invoking an instance method from a reference variable, the *actual class of the object* referenced by the variable decides which implementation of the method is used *at runtime*. When accessing a field or a static method, the *declared type* of the reference variable decides which method is used *at compile time*.

■ You can use `obj instanceof AClass` to check whether an object is an instance of a class.

■ You can use the `protected` modifier to prevent the data and methods from being accessed by non-subclasses from a different package.

■ You can use the `final` modifier to indicate that a class is final and cannot be a parent class.

REVIEW QUESTIONS

Sections 9.2–9.5

9.1 What is the printout of running the class `C` in (a)? What problem arises in compiling the program in (b)?

```
class A {
  public A() {
    System.out.println(
      "A's no-arg constructor is invoked");
  }
}

class B extends A {
}

public class C {
  public static void main(String[] args) {
    B b = new B();
  }
}
```

(a)

```
class A {
  public A(int x) {
  }
}

class B extends A {
  public B() {
  }
}

public class C {
  public static void main(String[] args) {
    B b = new B();
  }
}
```

(b)

9.2 True or false? (1) A subclass is a subset of a superclass. (2) When invoking a constructor from a subclass, its superclass's no-arg constructor is always invoked. (3) You can override a private method defined in a superclass. (4) You can override a static method defined in a superclass.

9.3 Identify the problems in the following classes:

```java
 1 public class Circle {
 2   private double radius;
 3
 4   public Circle (double radius) {
 5     radius = radius;
 6   }
 7
 8   public double getRadius() {
 9     return radius;
10   }
11
12   public double getArea() {
13     return radius * radius * Math.PI;
14   }
15 }
16
17 class B extends Circle {
18   private double length;
19
20   B(double radius, double length) {
21     Circle(radius);
22     length = length;
23   }
24
25   /** Override getArea() */
26   public double getArea() {
27     return getArea() * length;
28   }
29 }
```

9.4 Explain the difference between method overloading and method overriding.

Section 9.6 The `Object` class and Its `toString()` Method

9.5 Does every class have a `toString` method? Where does it come from? How is it used? Is it appropriate to override this method?

9.6 Show the output of following program:

```java
 1 public class Test {
 2   public static void main(String[] args) {
 3     A a = new A(3);
 4   }
 5 }
 6
 7 class A extends B {
 8   public A(int t) {
 9     System.out.println("A's constructor is invoked");
10   }
11 }
12
```

```
13 class B {
14   public B() {
15     System.out.println("B's constructor is invoked");
16   }
17 }
```

Is the no-arg constructor of `Object` invoked when `new A(3)` is invoked?

Sections 9.6–9.7

9.7 For the `GeometricObject` and `Circle` classes in Listings 9.1 and 9.2, answer the following questions:

(a) Assume that `circle` is a `Circle object` and `object1` is a `Geometric-Object`, are the following Boolean expressions true or false?

```
(circle instanceof GeometricObject)
(object1 instanceof GeometricObject)
(circle instanceof Circle)
(object1 instanceof Circle)
```

(b) Are the following statements correct?

```
Circle circle = new Circle(5);
GeometricObject object = circle;
```

(c) Are the following statements correct?

```
GeometricObject object = new GeometricObject();
Circle circle = (Circle)object;
```

9.8 Suppose that `Fruit`, `Apple`, `Orange`, `Golden Delicious Apple`, and `Macintosh Apple` are declared, as shown in Figure 9.11. Assume that `fruit` is an instance of `GoldenDelicious` and `orange` is an instance of `Orange`. Answer the following questions:

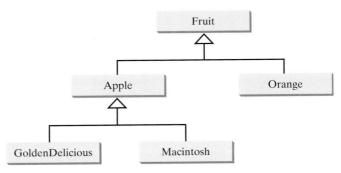

FIGURE 9.11 `GoldenDelicious` and `Macintosh` are subclasses of `Apple`, `Apple` and `Orange` are subclasses of `Fruit`.

(1) Is `fruit instanceof Orange`?
(2) Is `fruit instanceof Apple`?
(3) Is `fruit instanceof GoldenDelicious`?
(4) Is `fruit instanceof Macintosh`?
(5) Is `orange instanceof Orange`?
(6) Is `orange instanceof Fruit`?
(7) Is `orange instanceof Apple`?

(8) Suppose the method `makeApple` is defined in the `Apple` class. Can `fruit` invoke this method? Can `orange` invoke this method?

(9) Suppose the method `makeOrangeJuice` is defined in the `Orange` class. Can `orange` invoke this method? Can `fruit` invoke this method?

9.9 What is wrong in the following code?

```
1 public class Test {
2   public static void main(String[] args) {
3     Object fruit = new Fruit();
4     Object apple = (Apple)fruit;
5   }
6 }
7
8 class Apple extends Fruit {
9 }
10
11 class Fruit {
12 }
```

Section 9.9 The **ArrayList** Class

9.10 How do you create an `ArrayList`? How do you append an object to a list? How do you insert an object at the beginning of a list? How do you find the number of objects in a list? How do you remove a given object from a list? How do you remove the last object from the list? How do you check whether a given object is in a list? How do you retrieve an object at a specified index from a list?

9.11 Identify three errors in the following code:

```
ArrayList list = new ArrayList();
list.add("New York");
list.add("Austin");
list.add(new java.util.Date());
String city = list.get(0);
list.set(3, "Dallas");
System.out.println(list.get(3));
```

Section 9.11 The **protected** Data and Methods

9.12 What modifier should you use on a class so that a class in the same package can access it, but a class in a different package cannot access it?

9.13 What modifier should you use so that a class in a different package cannot access the class, but its subclasses in any package can access it?

9.14 In the following code, classes `A` and `B` are in the same package. If the question marks are replaced by blanks, can class `B` be compiled? If the question marks are replaced by `private`, can class `B` be compiled? If the question marks are replaced by `protected`, can class `B` be compiled?

```
package p1;

public class A {
  ?    int i;

  ?    void m() {
    ...
  }
}
```

```
package p1;

public class B extends A {
  public void m1(String[] args) {
    System.out.println(i);
    m();
  }
}
```

(a)   (b)

9.15 In the following code, classes **A** and **B** are in different packages. If the question marks are replaced by blanks, can class **B** be compiled? If the question marks are replaced by `private`, can class **B** be compiled? If the question marks are replaced by `protected`, can class **B** be compiled?

```
package p1;

public class A {
    ?    int i;

    ?    void m() {
        ...
    }
}
```
(a)

```
package p2;

public class B extends A {
    public void m1(String[] args) {
        System.out.println(i);
        m();
    }
}
```
(b)

Section 9.13 The Methods in the `Object` Class

9.16 When overriding the `equals` method, a common mistake is mistyping its signature in the subclass. For example, the `equals` method is incorrectly written as `equals(Circle circle)`, as shown in (a) in the following code, instead, it should be `equals(Object circle)`, as shown in (b). Show the output of running class **Test** with the **Circle** class in (a) and in (b).

```
public class Test {
  public static void main(String[] args) {
    Object circle1 = new Circle();
    Object circle2 = new Circle();
    System.out.println(circle1.equals(circle2));
  }
}
```

```
class Circle {
  double radius;

  public boolean equals(Circle circle) {
    return this.radius == circle.radius;
  }
}
```
(a)

```
class Circle {
  double radius;

  public boolean equals(Object circle) {
    return this.radius ==
        ((Circle)circle).radius;
  }
}
```
(b)

9.17 Where are the `equals`, `hashCode`, `finalize`, `clone`, and `getClass` methods defined? When is the `finalize` method invoked?

9.18 Since the `clone` method is defined in **Object**, every object can invoke this method. Is it true?

9.19 What is the return type of the `getClass` method? If two objects **o1** and **o2** have the same class type, is `o1.getClass()` same as `o2.getClass()`?

Section 9.14 Hiding Fields and Static Methods

9.20 Show the output of running class **Test**.

```
class A {                class B extend A {        public class Test {
  int i = 1;               int i = 2;                public static void main
  static int j = 3;        static int j = 4;             (String[] args) {
                                                       B b = new B();
  void m() {               void m() {                  System.out.println(b.i);
    i = 5;                   i = 6;                     System.out.println(b.j);
  }                         }
                                                       A a = new B();
  static void m1() {       static void m1() {          System.out.println(a.i);
    j = 7;                   j = 8;                     System.out.println(a.j);
  }                         }
}                         }                            a.m();
                                                       a.m1();
                                                       System.out.println(a.i);
                                                       System.out.println(a.j);
                                                     }
                                                   }
```

          (a)   (b)   (c)

9.21 For the HidingDemo class in Listing 9.10, what is the output if line 3 is replaced
      by B x = new B()? What error would occur if line 3 is replaced by A x = new A()?

Section 9.15 Initialization Blocks

9.22 Show the output of following program:

```
public class Test {                          public class Test {
  public static void main(String[] args) {     public static void main(String[] args) {
    A a = new A();                               A a = new A();
  }                                            }
}                                            }

class A {                                    class A extends B {
  int i = 1;                                   int i = 5;
  static int j = 2;                            static int j = 4;

  {                                            A() {
    System.out.println("i is " + i);            System.out.println("i is " + i);
  }                                             System.out.println("j is " + j);
                                               }
  static {
    System.out.println("j is " + j);           void m() {
  }                                             System.out.println("i is " + i);
}                                               System.out.println("j is " + j);
                                               }
                                             }

                                             class B {
                                               B() {
                                                 m();
                                               }

                                               void m() {
                                               }
                                             }
```

              (a)   (b)

9.23 For the InitializationDemo class in Listing 9.11, what is the output if line 3 is deleted?
      What is the output if line 3 is replaced by new N()? What is the output if line 3 is replaced by
      N object = new M()?

Comprehensive

9.24 Define the following terms: inheritance, superclass, subclass, the keywords `super` and `this`, casting objects, the modifiers `protected` and `final`.

9.25 Indicate true or false for the following statements:

- A protected datum or method can be accessed by any class in the same package.
- A protected datum or method can be accessed by any class in different packages.
- A protected datum or method can be accessed by its subclasses in any package.
- A final class can have instances.
- A final class can be extended.
- A final method can be overridden.
- You can always successfully cast an instance of a subclass to a superclass.
- You can always successfully cast an instance of a superclass to a subclass.
- The order in which modifiers appear before a method is important.

9.26 Describe the difference between method matching and method binding.

9.27 What are advantages of dynamic binding?

PROGRAMMING EXERCISES

Sections 9.2–9.4

9.1 (*The `Triangle` class*) Design a class named *`Triangle`* that extends `Geometric-Object`. The class contains:

- Three `double` data fields named `side1`, `side2`, and `side3` with default values `1.0` to denote three sides of the triangle.
- A no-arg constructor that creates a default triangle.
- A constructor that creates a rectangle with the specified `side1`, `side2`, and `side3`.
- The accessor methods for all three data fields.
- A method named `getArea()` that returns the area of this triangle.
- A method named `getPerimeter()` that returns the perimeter of this triangle.
- A method named `toString()` that returns a string description for the triangle.

For the formula to compute the area of a triangle, see Exercise 5.19. The `toString()` method is implemented as follows:

```
return "Triangle: side1 = " + side1 + " side2 = " + side2 +
   " side3 = " + side3;
```

Draw the UML diagram that involves the classes `Triangle` and `GeometricObject`. Implement the class. Write a test program that creates a `Triangle` object with sides 1, 1.5, 1, sets color `yellow` and filled `true`, and displays the area, perimeter, color, and whether filled or not.

Sections 9.5–9.9

9.2 (*The `Person`, `Student`, `Employee`, `Faculty`, and `Staff` classes*) Design a class named `Person` and its two subclasses named `Student` and `Employee`. Make `Faculty` and `Staff` subclasses of `Employee`. A person has a name, address, phone number, and email address. A student has a class status (freshman, sophomore, junior, or senior). Define the status as a constant. An employee has an office, salary, and date-hired. Define a class named `MyDate` that contains the fields `year`, `month`, and `day`. A faculty member has office hours and a rank. A staff member has a title. Override the `toString` method in each class to display the class name and the person's name.

Draw the UML diagram for the classes. Implement the classes. Write a test program that creates a `Person`, `Student`, `Employee`, `Faculty`, and `Staff`, and invokes their `toString()` methods.

9.3 (*Subclasses of Account*) In Exercise 7.3, the `Account` class was created to model a bank account. An account has the properties account number, balance, annual interest rate, and date created, and methods to deposit and withdraw. Create two subclasses for checking and saving accounts. A checking account has an overdraft limit, but a savings account cannot be overdrawn.

Draw the UML diagram for the classes. Implement the classes. Write a test program that creates objects of `Account`, `SavingsAccount`, and `CheckingAccount`, and invokes their `toString()` methods.

9.4 (*Implementing MyStack using inheritance*) In Listing 9.8, `MyStack` is implemented using composition. Create a new stack class that extends `MyArrayList`.

Draw the UML diagram for the classes. Implement `MyStack`.

9.5 (*The Course class*) Rewrite the `Course` class in Listing 7.11. Use an `ArrayList` to replace an array to store students.

9.6 (*Using ArrayList*) Write a program that creates an `ArrayList`, adds a `Loan` object, a `Date` object, a string, a `JFrame` object, and a `Circle` object to the list, and uses a loop to display all the elements in the list by invoking the object's `toString()` method.

CHAPTER 10

ABSTRACT CLASSES AND INTERFACES

Objectives

- To design and use abstract classes (§10.2).
- To process a calendar using the `Calendar` and `GregorianCalendar` classes (§10.3).
- To declare interfaces to model weak inheritance relationships (§10.4).
- To define a natural order using the `Comparable` interface (§10.4.1).
- To know the similarities and differences between an abstract class and an interface (§10.4.2).
- To declare custom interfaces (§10.4.3).
- (Optional) To make objects cloneable using the `Cloneable` interface (§10.4.4).
- To use wrapper classes (`Byte`, `Short`, `Integer`, `Long`, `Float`, `Double`, `Character`, and `Boolean`) to wrap primitive data values into objects (§10.5).
- (Optional) To use the `BigInteger` and `BigDecimal` classes for computing very large numbers with arbitrary precisions (§10.5.6).
- To create a generic sort method (§10.5).
- To simplify programming using JDK 1.5 automatic conversion between primitive types and wrapper class types (§10.6).
- (Optional GUI) To handle GUI events (§10.7).

10.1 Introduction

In the inheritance hierarchy, classes become more specific and concrete *with each new subclass*. If you move from a subclass back up to a superclass, the classes become more general and less specific. Class design should ensure that a superclass contains common features of its subclasses. Sometimes a superclass is so abstract that it cannot have any specific instances. Such a class is referred to as an *abstract class*.

abstract class

multiple inheritance
single inheritance

Sometimes it is necessary to derive a subclass from several classes. This capability is known as *multiple inheritance*. Java, however, does not allow multiple inheritance. A Java class may inherit directly from only one superclass. This restriction is known as *single inheritance*. If you use the **extends** keyword to define a subclass, it allows only one parent class. With interfaces, you can obtain the effect of multiple inheritance.

This chapter introduces abstract classes and interfaces, and discusses how to use wrapper classes for primitive data type values.

10.2 Abstract Classes

GeometricObject was declared as the superclass for Circle and Rectangle in the preceding chapter. GeometricObject models common features of geometric objects. Both Circle and Rectangle contain the getArea() and getPerimeter() methods for computing the area and perimeter of a circle and a rectangle. Since you can compute areas and perimeters for all geometric objects, it is better to declare the getArea() and getPerimeter() methods in the GeometricObject class. However, these methods cannot be implemented in the GeometricObject class because their implementation is dependent on the specific type of geometric object. Such methods are referred to as *abstract methods*. After you declare the methods in GeometricObject, GeometricObject becomes an abstract class. The new GeometricObject class is shown in Figure 10.1. In UML graphic notation, the names of abstract classes and their abstract methods are italicized, as shown in Figure 10.1. Listing 10.1 gives the source code for the new GeometricObject class.

abstract method

LISTING 10.1 GeometricObject.java

abstract class

```java
 1 public abstract class GeometricObject {
 2   private String color = "white";
 3   private boolean filled;
 4   private java.util.Date dateCreated;
 5
 6   /** Construct a default geometric object */
 7   protected GeometricObject() {
 8     dateCreated = new java.util.Date();
 9   }
10
11   /** Return color */
12   public String getColor() {
13     return color;
14   }
15
16   /** Set a new color */
17   public void setColor(String color) {
18     this.color = color;
19   }
20
21   /** Return filled. Since filled is boolean,
22       so, the get method name is isFilled */
```

```
23    public boolean isFilled() {
24       return filled;
25    }
26
27    /** Set a new filled */
28    public void setFilled(boolean filled) {
29       this.filled = filled;
30    }
31
32    /** Get dateCreated */
33    public java.util.Date getDateCreated() {
34       return dateCreated;
35    }
36
37    /** Return a string representation of this object */
38    public String toString() {
39       return "created on " + dateCreated + "\ncolor: " + color +
40         " and filled: " + filled;
41    }
42
43    /** Abstract method getArea */                               abstract method
44    public abstract double getArea();
45
46    /** Abstract method getPerimeter */                          abstract method
47    public abstract double getPerimeter();
48 }
```

The # sign indicates protected modifer

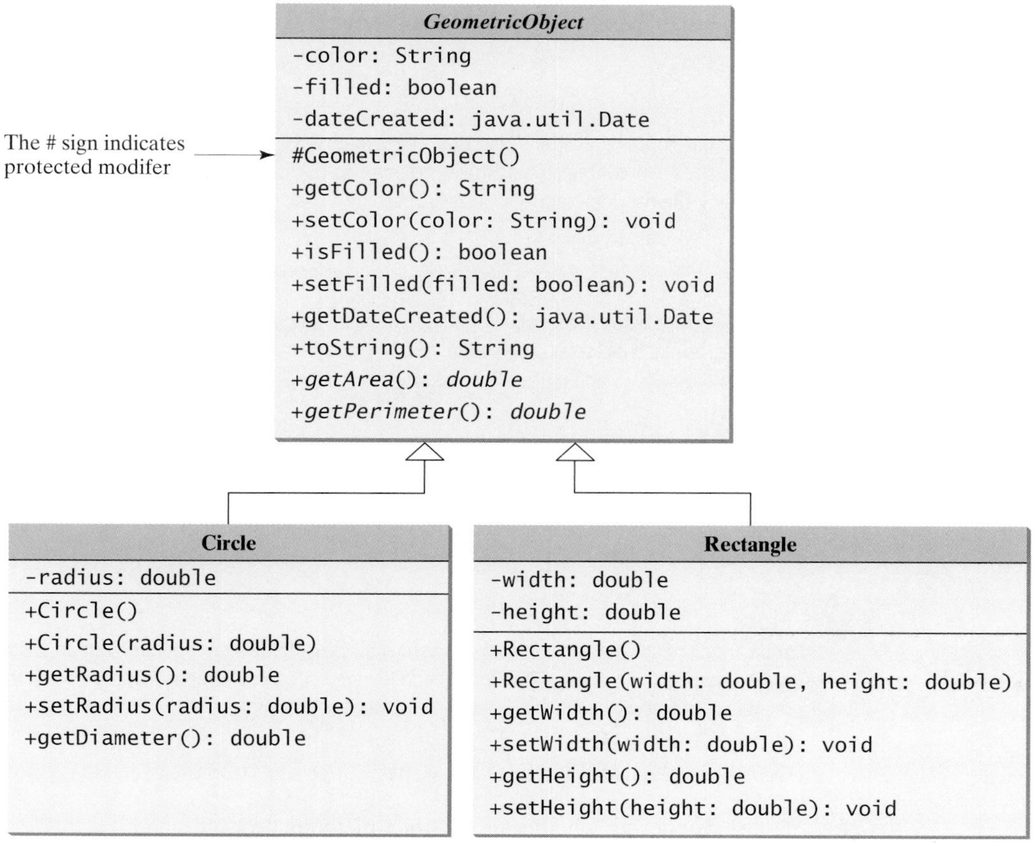

FIGURE 10.1 The new `GeometricObject` class contains abstract methods.

Abstract classes are like regular classes with data and methods, but you cannot create instances of abstract classes using the **new** operator. An abstract method is a method signature without implementation. Its implementation is provided by the subclasses. A class that contains abstract methods must be declared abstract.

The `GeometricObject` abstract class provides the common features (data and methods) for geometric objects. Because you don't know how to compute areas and perimeters of geometric objects, `getArea` and `getPerimeter` are defined as abstract methods. These methods are implemented in the subclasses. The implementation of `Circle` and `Rectangle` is the same as in Listings 9.2 and 9.3 except that they don't have the **package** statements. The new `GeometricObject.java`, `Circle.java`, and `Rectangle.java` are stored in `c:\book`. Note that the `GeometricObject`, `Circle`, and `Rectangle` classes in the preceding chapter are placed in a package named *chapter9* to avoid naming conflicts with the classes in this chapter.

abstract method in abstract class

Note

An abstract method cannot be contained in a nonabstract class. If a subclass of an abstract superclass does not implement all the abstract methods, the subclass must be declared abstract. In other words, in a nonabstract subclass extended from an abstract class, all the abstract methods must be implemented, even if they are not used in the subclass. Also note that abstract methods are non-static.

object cannot be created from abstract class

Note

An abstract class cannot be instantiated using the **new** operator, but you can still define its constructors, which are invoked in the constructors of its subclasses. For instance, the constructors of `GeometricObject` are invoked in the `Circle` class and the `Rectangle` class.

abstract class without abstract method

Note

A class that contains abstract methods must be abstract. However, it is possible to declare an abstract class that contains no abstract methods. In this case, you cannot create instances of the class using the **new** operator. This class is used as a base class for defining a new subclass.

superclass of abstract class may be concrete

Note

A subclass can be abstract even if its superclass is concrete. For example, the `Object` class is concrete, but its subclasses, such as `GeometricObject`, may be abstract.

concrete method overridden to be abstract

Note

A subclass can override a method from its superclass to declare it **abstract**. This is *very unusual*, but is useful when the implementation of the method in the superclass becomes invalid in the subclass. In this case, the subclass must be declared abstract.

abstract class as type

Note

You cannot create an instance from an abstract class using the **new** operator, but an abstract class can be used as a data type. Therefore, the following statement, which creates an array whose elements are of `GeometricObject` type, is correct.

```
GeometricObject[] objects = new GeometricObject[10];
```

You may be wondering whether the abstract methods `getArea` and `getPerimeter` should be removed from the `GeometricObject` class. The following example shows the benefits of retaining them in the `GeometricObject` class.

10.2.1 Example: Using the `GeometricObject` Class

This example presents a program that creates two geometric objects, a circle and a rectangle, invokes the **equalArea** method to check whether the two objects have equal areas, and invokes the **displayGeometricObject** method to display the objects.

Listing 10.2 gives the solution to the problem. A sample run of the program is shown in Figure 10.2.

LISTING 10.2 TestGeometricObject.java

```java
1 public class TestGeometricObject {
2   /** Main method */
3   public static void main(String[] args) {
4     // Declare and initialize two geometric objects
5     GeometricObject geoObject1 = new Circle(5);
6     GeometricObject geoObject2 = new Rectangle(5, 3);
7
8     System.out.println("The two objects have the same area? " +
9       equalArea(geoObject1, geoObject2));
10
11     // Display circle
12     displayGeometricObject(geoObject1);
13
14     // Display rectangle
15     displayGeometricObject(geoObject2);
16   }
17
18   /** A method for comparing the areas of two geometric objects */
19   public static boolean equalArea(GeometricObject object1,
20       GeometricObject object2) {
21     return object1.getArea() == object2.getArea();
22   }
23
24   /** A method for displaying a geometric object */
25   public static void displayGeometricObject(GeometricObject object) {
26     System.out.println();
27     System.out.println("The area is " + object.getArea());
28     System.out.println("The perimeter is " + object.getPerimeter());
29   }
30 }
```

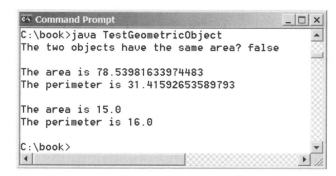

FIGURE 10.2 The program compares the areas of the objects and displays their properties.

The methods **getArea()** and **getPerimeter()** defined in the **GeometricObject** class are overridden in the **Circle** class and the **Rectangle** class. The statements (lines 5–6)

```java
GeometricObject geoObject1 = new Circle(5);
GeometricObject geoObject2 = new Rectangle(5, 3);
```

create a new circle and rectangle, and assign them to the variables `geoObject1` and `geoObject2`. These two variables are of the `GeometricObject` type.

When invoking `equalArea(geoObject1, geoObject2)` (line 9), the `getArea` method defined in the `Circle` class is used for `object1.getArea()`, since `geoObject1` is a circle, and the `getArea` method defined in the `Rectangle` class is used for `object2.getArea()`, since `geoObject2` is a rectangle.

Similarly, when invoking `displayGeometricObject(geoObject1)` (line 12), the methods `getArea` and `getPerimeter` defined in the `Circle` class are used, and when invoking `displayGeometricObject(geoObject2)` (line 15), the methods `getArea` and `getPerimeter` defined in the `Rectangle` class are used. The JVM dynamically determines which of these methods to invoke at runtime, depending on the type of object.

Note that if the `getArea` and `getPerimeter` methods were not defined in `GeometricObject`, you cannot define the `equalArea` and `displayObject` methods in this program. So, you now see the benefits of defining the abstract methods in `GeometricObject`.

10.3 The `Calendar` and `GregorianCalendar` Classes

An instance of `java.util.Date` represents a specific instant in time with millisecond precision. `java.util.Calendar` is an abstract base class for extracting detailed calendar information, such as year, month, date, hour, minute, and second. Subclasses of `Calendar` can implement specific calendar systems, such as the Gregorian calendar, the lunar calendar, and the Jewish calendar. Currently, `java.util.GregorianCalendar` for the Gregorian calendar is supported in Java, as shown in Figure 10.3.

java.util.Calendar

*java.util.Gregorian
Calendar*

You can use `new GregorianCalendar()` to construct a default `GregorianCalendar` with the current time and `new GregorianCalendar(year, month, date)` to construct a `GregorianCalendar` with the specified `year`, `month`, and `date`. The `month` parameter is 0-based, that is, 0 is for January.

constructing calendar

java.util.Calendar	
`#Calendar()`	Constructs a default calendar.
`+get(field: int): int`	Returns the value of the given calendar field.
`+set(field: int, value: int): void`	Sets the calendar field with the specified value.
`+set(year: int, month: int,` `  dayOfMonth: int): void`	Sets the calendar with the specified year, month, and date. The month parameter is 0-based, that is, 0 is for January.
`+getActualMaximum(field: int): int`	Returns the maximum value that the specified calendar field could have.
`+add(field: int, amount: int): void`	Adds or subtracts the specified amount of time to the given calendar field.
`+getTime(): java.util.Date`	Returns a Date object representing this calendar's time value (million-second offset from the Unix epoch).
`+setTime(date: java.util.Date): void`	Sets this calendar's time with the given Date object.

java.util.GregorianCalendar	
`+GregorianCalendar()`	Constructs a GregorianCalendar for the current time.
`+GregorianCalendar(year: int,` `  month: int, dayOfMonth: int)`	Constructs a GregorianCalendar for the specified year, month, and day of month.

`+GregorianCalendar(year: int,`
`  month: int, dayOfMonth: int,`
`  hour:int, minute: int, second: int)`
	Constructs a GregorianCalendar for the specified year, month, day of month, hour, minute, and second. The month parameter is 0-based, that is, 0 is for January.

FIGURE 10.3 The abstract `Calendar` class defines common features of various calendars.

The `get(int field)` method defined in the `Calendar` class is useful to extract the value for a given time field. The time fields are defined as constants, such as `YEAR`, `MONTH`, `DATE`, `HOUR` (for the twelve-hour clock), `HOUR_OF_DAY` (for the twenty-four-hour clock), `MINUTE`, `SECOND`, `DAY_OF_WEEK` (the day number within the current week, with `1` for Sunday), `DAY_OF_MONTH` (the day in the current month), `DAY_OF_YEAR` (the day number in the current year with `1` for the first day of the year), `WEEK_OF_MONTH` (the week number within the current month), and `WEEK_OF_YEAR` (the week number within the current year). For example, the following code

`get(field)`

```
// Construct a Gregorian calendar for the current date and time
java.util.Calendar calendar = new java.util.GregorianCalendar();
System.out.println("Year\tMonth\tDate\tHour\tHour24\tMinute\tSecond");
System.out.println(calendar.get(Calendar.YEAR) + "\t" +
  calendar.get(Calendar.MONTH) + "\t" + calendar.get(Calendar.DATE)
  + "\t" + calendar.get(Calendar.HOUR) + "\t" +
  calendar.get(Calendar.HOUR_OF_DAY) + "\t" +
  calendar.get(Calendar.MINUTE) + "\t" +
  calendar.get(Calendar.SECOND));
System.out.print("Day of week: " +
  calendar.get(Calendar.DAY_OF_WEEK) + "\t");
System.out.print("Day of month: " +
  calendar.get(Calendar.DAY_OF_MONTH) + "\t");
System.out.println("Day of year: " +
  calendar.get(Calendar.DAY_OF_YEAR));
System.out.print("Week of month: " +
  calendar.get(Calendar.WEEK_OF_MONTH) + "\t");
System.out.print("Week of year: " +
  calendar.get(Calendar.WEEK_OF_YEAR));
```

displays the information for the current date and time, as follows:

```
Year Month   Date   Hour   Hour24   Minute   Second
2003 2       9      8      20       17       39
Day of week: 1      Day of month: 9          Day of year: 68
Week of month: 3    Week of year: 11
```

The `set(int field, value)` method defined in the `Calendar` class can be used to set a field. For example, you can use `calendar.set(Calendar.DAY_OF_MONTH, 1)` to set the `calendar` to the first day of the month.

`set(field, value)`

The `add(field, value)` method adds or subtracts the specified amount to a given field. For example, to subtract five days from the current time of the calendar, you must call `add(Calendar.DAY_OF_MONTH, -5)`.

`add(field, amount)`

To obtain the number of days in a month, use `calendar.getActualMaximum (Calendar.DAY_OF_MONTH)`. For example, if the `calendar` were for March, this method would return `31`.

`getActualMaximum (field)`

You can set a time represented in a `Date` object for the `calendar` by invoking `calendar.setTime(date)` and retrieve the time by invoking `calendar.getTime()`.

`setTime(Date)`
`getTime()`

10.4 Interfaces

An *interface* is a classlike construct that contains only constants and abstract methods. In many ways, an interface is similar to an abstract class, but an abstract class can contain variables and concrete methods as well as constants and abstract methods.

interface

To distinguish an interface from a class, Java uses the following syntax to declare an interface:

```
modifier interface InterfaceName {
  /** Constant declarations */
  /** Method signatures */
}
```

An interface is treated like a special class in Java. Each interface is compiled into a separate bytecode file, just like a regular class. As with an abstract class, you cannot create an instance from an interface using the **new** operator, but in most cases you can use an interface more or less the same way you use an abstract class. For example, you can use an interface as a data type for a variable, as the result of casting, and so on.

Suppose you want to design a generic method to find the larger of two objects. The objects can be students, circles, or rectangles. Since compare methods are different for different types of objects, you need to define a generic compare method to determine the order of the two objects. Then you can tailor the method to compare students, circles, or rectangles. For example, you can use student ID as the key for comparing students, radius as the key for comparing circles, and area as the key for comparing rectangles. You can use an interface to define a generic **compareTo** method, as follows:

java.lang. Comparable

```
// Interface for comparing objects, defined in java.lang
package java.lang;

public interface Comparable {
  public int compareTo(Object o);
}
```

The **compareTo** method determines the order of this object with the specified object **o**, and returns a negative integer, zero, or a positive integer if this object is less than, equal to, or greater than the specified object **o**.

 Note

The **Comparable** interface has been available since JDK 1.2, and is included in the **java.lang** package.

Many classes in the Java library (e.g., **String** and **Date**) implement **Comparable** to define a natural order for the objects. If you examine the source code of these classes, you will see the keyword **implements** used in the classes, as shown below:

```
public class String extends Object
    implements Comparable {
  // class body omitted
}
```

```
public class Date extends Object
    implements Comparable {
  // class body omitted
}
```

Thus strings are comparable, and so are dates. Let **s** be a **String** object and **d** be a **Date** object. All the following expressions are all true:

```
s instanceof String
s instanceof Object
s instanceof Comparable
```

```
d instanceof java.util.Date
d instanceof Object
d instanceof Comparable
```

A generic **max** method for finding the larger of two objects can be declared, as shown in (a) or (b):

```
// Max.java: Find a maximum object
public class Max {
  /** Return the maximum of two objects */
  public static Comparable max
      (Comparable o1, Comparable o2) {
    if (o1.compareTo(o2) > 0)
      return o1;
    else
      return o2;
  }
}
```
(a)

```
// Max.java: Find a maximum object
public class Max {
  /** Return the maximum of two objects */
  public static Object max
      (Object o1, Object o2) {

    if (((Comparable)o1).compareTo(o2) > 0)
      return o1;
    else
      return o2;
  }
}
```
(b)

The `max` method in (a) *is simpler* than the one in (b). In the `Max` class in (b), `o1` is declared as `Object`, and `(Comparable)o1` tells the compiler to cast `o1` into `Comparable` so that the `compareTo` method can be invoked from `o1`. However, no casting is needed in the `Max` class in (a), since `o1` is declared as `Comparable`.

(a) is simpler

The `max` method in (a) *is more robust* than the one in (b). You must invoke the `max` method with two comparable objects. Suppose you invoke `max` with two noncomparable objects

(a) is more robust

```
Max.max(anyObject1, anyObject2);
```

The compiler will detect the error using the `max` method in (a), because `anyObject1` is not an instance of `Comparable`. Using the `max` method in (b), this line of code will compile fine, but will have a runtime `ClassCastException`, because `anyObject1` is not an instance of `Comparable` and cannot be cast into `Comparable`.

From now on, assume that the `max` method in (a) is in the text. Since strings are comparable and dates are comparable, you can use the `max` method to find the larger of two instances of `String` or `Date`. Here is an example:

```
String s1 = "abcdef";
String s2 = "abcdee";
String s3 = (String)Max.max(s1, s2);
```
```
Date d1 = new Date();
Date d2 = new Date();
Date d3 = (Date)Max.max(d1, d2);
```

The `return` value from the `max` method is of the `Comparable` type. So you need to cast it to `String` or `Date` explicitly.

10.4.1 Declaring Classes to Implement Comparable

You cannot use the `max` method to find the larger of two instances of `Rectangle`, because `Rectangle` does not implement `Comparable`. However, you can declare a new rectangle class that implements `Comparable`. The instances of this new class are comparable. Let this new class be named `ComparableRectangle`, as shown in Listing 10.3.

LISTING 10.3 ComparableRectangle.java

```
1 public class ComparableRectangle extends Rectangle
2     implements Comparable {
3   /** Construct a ComparableRectangle with specified properties */
4   public ComparableRectangle(double width, double height) {
5     super(width, height);
6   }
7
```

```
8    /** Implement the compareTo method defined in Comparable */
9    public int compareTo(Object o) {
10     if (getArea() > ((ComparableRectangle)o).getArea())
11       return 1;
12     else if (getArea() < ((ComparableRectangle)o).getArea())
13       return -1;
14     else
15       return 0;
16   }
17 }
```

ComparableRectangle extends Rectangle and implements Comparable, as shown in Figure 10.4. The keyword implements indicates that ComparableRectangle inherits all the constants from the Comparable interface and implements the methods in the interface. The compareTo method compares the areas of two rectangles. An instance of CompareRectangle is also an instance of Rectangle, GeometricObject, Object, and Comparable.

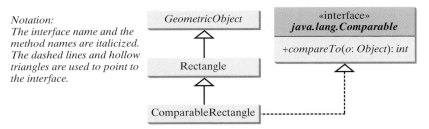

Notation:
The interface name and the method names are italicized. The dashed lines and hollow triangles are used to point to the interface.

FIGURE 10.4 ComparableRectangle extends Rectangle and implements Comparable.

You can now use the max method to find the larger of two objects of CompareRectangle. Here is an example:

```
ComparableRectangle rectangle1 = new ComparableRectangle(4, 5);
ComparableRectangle rectangle2 = new ComparableRectangle(3, 6);
System.out.println(Max.max(rectangle1, rectangle2));
```

An interface provides another form of generic programming. It would be difficult to use a generic max method to find the maximum of the objects without using an interface in this example, because multiple inheritance would be necessary to inherit Comparable and another class, such as Rectangle, at the same time.

The Object class contains the equals method, which is intended for the subclasses of the Object class to override in order to compare whether the contents of the objects are the same. Suppose that the Object class contains the compareTo method, as defined in the Comparable interface; the new max method can be used to compare a list of *any* objects. Whether a compareTo method should be included in the Object class is debatable. Since the compareTo method is not defined in the Object class, the Comparable interface is created in Java 2 to enable objects to be compared if they are instances of the Comparable interface. It is strongly recommended (though not required) that compareTo should be consistent with equals. That is, for two objects o1 and o2, o1.compareTo(o2) == 0 if and only if o1.equals(o2) is true.

10.4.2 Interfaces vs. Abstract Classes

An interface can be used the same way as an abstract class, but declaring an interface is different from declaring an abstract class. Table 10.1 summarizes the differences.

TABLE 10.1   Interfaces vs. Abstract Classes

	Variables	Constructors	Methods
Abstract class	No restrictions	Constructors are invoked by subclasses through constructor chaining. An abstract class cannot be instantiated using the new operator.	No restrictions
Interface	All variables must be `public static final`	No constructors. An interface cannot be instantiated using the new operator.	All methods must be public abstract instance methods

Note

Since all data fields are `public final static` and all methods are `public abstract` in an interface, Java allows these modifiers to be omitted. Therefore the following declarations are equivalent:

omitting modifiers

```
public interface T1 {
  public static final int K = 1;

  public abstract void p();
}
```

Equivalent

```
public interface T1 {
  int K = 1;

  void p();
}
```

Tip

A constant defined in an interface can be accessed using the syntax `Interface-Name.CONSTANT_NAME` (e.g., `T1.K`).

accessing constants

Java allows only single inheritance for class extension, but multiple extensions for interfaces. For example,

```
public class NewClass extends BaseClass
    implements Interface1, ..., InterfaceN {
  ...
}
```

An interface can inherit other interfaces using the **extends** keyword. Such an interface is called a *subinterface*. For example, `NewInterface` in the following code is a subinterface of `Interface1`, ..., and `InterfaceN`:

subinterface

```
public interface NewInterface extends Interface1, ..., InterfaceN {
  // constants and abstract methods
}
```

A class implementing `NewInterface` must implement the abstract methods defined in `NewInterface`, `Interface1`, ..., and `InterfaceN`. An interface can only extend other interfaces, not classes. A class can extend its superclass and implement multiple interfaces.

All classes share a single root, the `Object` class, but there is no single root for interfaces. Like a class, an interface also defines a type. A variable of an interface type can reference any instance of the class that implements the interface. If a class implements an interface, the interface is like a superclass for the class. You can use an interface as a data type and cast a variable of an interface type to its subclass, and vice versa. For example, suppose that `c` is an instance of `Class2` in Figure 10.5. `c` is also an instance of `Object`, `Class1`, `Interface1`, `Interface1_1`, `Interface1_2`, `Interface2_1`, and `Interface2_2`.

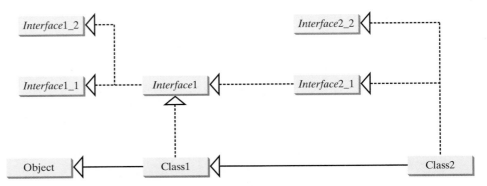

FIGURE 10.5 Abstract class *Class1* implements *Interface1*, *Interface1* extends *Interface1_1* and *Interface1_2*. *Class2* extends *Class1* and implements *Interface2_1* and *Interface2_2*.

Caution

conflict interfaces

On rare occasions, a class may implement two interfaces with conflict information (e.g., two identical constants with different values or two methods with the same signature but different return types). This type of error will be detected by the compiler.

Abstract classes and interfaces can both be used to model common features. How do you

is-a relationship

decide whether to use an interface or a class? In general, a *strong is-a relationship* that clearly describes a parent–child relationship should be modeled using classes. For example, a staff member is a person, so the relationship between them should be modeled using class inheri-

is-kind-of relationship

tance. A *weak is-a relationship*, also known as *an is-kind-of relationship*, indicates that an object possesses a certain property. A weak is-a relationship can be modeled using interfaces. For example, all strings are comparable, so the **String** class implements the **Comparable** interface. You can also use interfaces to circumvent the single-inheritance restriction if multiple inheritance is desired. In the case of multiple inheritance, you have to design one as a superclass and others as interfaces. See Chapter 11, "Object-Oriented Design," for more discussion.

Note

Class names are nouns. Interface names may be adjectives or nouns. For example, both **java.lang.Comparable** and **java.awt.event.ActionListener** are interfaces. **Comparable** is an adjective, and **ActionListener** is a noun. **ActionListener** will be introduced in Chapter 14, "Event-Driven Programming."

10.4.3 Creating Custom Interfaces

An example of implementing the **Comparable** interface is given in §10.4.1, "Declaring Classes to Implement Comparable". This section creates a custom interface. Suppose you want to describe whether an object is edible. You can declare the **Edible** interface:

```
public interface Edible {
  /** Describe how to eat */
  public String howToEat();
}
```

To denote that an object is edible, the class for the object must implement **Edible**. Let us create the following two sets of classes:

■ Create a class named **Animal** and its subclasses **Tiger**, **Chicken**, and **Elephant**. Since chicken is edible, implement the **Edible** interface for the **Chicken** class, as follows:

```
class Animal {
}
```

```
class Chicken extends Animal implements Edible, Comparable {
  int weight;

  public Chicken(int weight) {
    this.weight = weight;
  }

  public String howToEat() {
    return "Fry it";
  }

  public int compareTo(Object o) {
    return weight - ((Chicken)o).weight;
  }
}

class Tiger extends Animal {
}
```

A class may implement several interfaces. The Chicken class also implements the Comparable interface to compare two chickens according to their weight.

■ Create a class named Fruit and its subclasses Apple and Orange. Since all fruits are edible, implement the Edible interface for the Fruit class. The Fruit class is abstract, because you cannot implement the howToEat method without knowing exactly what the fruit is. In the Apple class and the Orange class, implement the howToEat method, as follows:

```
abstract class Fruit implements Edible {
}

class Apple extends Fruit {
  public String howToEat() {
    return "Make apple cider";
  }
}

class Orange extends Fruit {
  public String howToEat() {
    return "Make orange juice";
  }
}
```

To demonstrate how the Edible interface may be used, create the following program that creates an array with three objects. The showObject method invokes the howToEat() method if the object is edible.

```
public class TestEdible {
  public static void main(String[] args) {
    Object[] objects = {new Tiger(), new Chicken(), new Apple()};
    for (int i = 0; i < objects.length; i++)
      showObject(objects[i]);
  }

  public static void showObject(Object object) {
    if (object instanceof Edible)
      System.out.println(((Edible)object).howToEat());
  }
}
```

The program displays

```
Fry it
Make apple cider
```

10.4.4 (Optional) The Cloneable Interface

An interface contains constants and abstract methods, but the Cloneable interface is a special case. The Cloneable interface in the java.lang package is defined as follows:

java.lang.Cloneable

```java
package java.lang;

public interface Cloneable {
}
```

marker interface

This interface is empty. An interface with an empty body is referred to as a *marker interface*. A marker interface does not contain constants or methods. It is used to denote that a class possesses certain desirable properties. A class that implements the Cloneable interface is marked cloneable, and its objects can be cloned using the clone() method defined in the Object class.

Many classes in the Java library (e.g., Date, Calendar, and ArrayList) implement Cloneable. Thus, the instances of these classes can be cloned. For example, the following code

```java
Calendar calendar = new GregorianCalendar(2003, 2, 1);
Calendar calendarCopy = (Calendar)calendar.clone();
System.out.println("calendar == calendarCopy is " +
  (calendar == calendarCopy));
System.out.println("calendar.equals(calendarCopy) is " +
  calendar.equals(calendarCopy));
```

displays

```
calendar == calendarCopy is false
calendar.equals(calendarCopy) is true
```

how to implement
Cloneable

To declare a custom class that implements the Cloneable interface, the class must override the clone() method in the Object class. Listing 10.4 declares a class named House that implements Cloneable and Comparable.

LISTING 10.4 House.java

```java
 1  public class House implements Cloneable, Comparable {
 2    private int id;
 3    private double area;
 4    private java.util.Date whenBuilt;
 5
 6    public House(int id, double area) {
 7      this.id = id;
 8      this.area = area;
 9      whenBuilt = new java.util.Date();
10    }
11
12    public double getId() {
13      return id;
14    }
15
16    public double getArea() {
17      return area;
18    }
19
20    public java.util.Date getWhenBuilt() {
21      return whenBuilt;
22    }
23
```

```
24    /** Override the protected clone method defined in the Object
25       class, and strengthen its accessibility */
26    public Object clone() {
27      try {
28        return super.clone();
29      }
30      catch (CloneNotSupportedException ex) {
31        return null;
32      }
33    }
34
35    /** Implement the compareTo method defined in Comparable */
36    public int compareTo(Object o) {
37      if (area > ((House)o).area)
38        return 1;
39      else if (area < ((House)o).area)
40        return -1;
41      else
42        return 0;
43    }
44  }
```

This exception is thrown if House does not implement **Cloneable**

The House class overrides the clone method (lines 26–33) defined in the Object class. The clone method in the Object class is defined as follows:

```
protected native Object clone() throws CloneNotSupportedException;
```

The keyword native indicates that this method is not written in Java, but is implemented in the JVM for the native platform. The keyword protected restricts the method to be accessed in the same package or in a subclass. For this reason, the Cloneable class must override the method and change the visibility modifier to public so that the method can be used in any package. Since the clone method implemented for the native platform in the Object class performs the task of cloning objects, the clone method in the House class simply invokes super.clone(). The clone method defined in the Object class may throw CloneNotSupportedException. Thus, super.clone() must be placed in a try-catch block. Exceptions and the try-catch block are introduced in Chapter 17, "Exceptions and Assertions."

CloneNotSupported-Exception

The House class overrides the compareTo method (lines 36–43) defined in the Comparable interface. The method compares the areas of two houses.

You can now create an object of the House class and create an identical copy from it, as follows:

```
House house1 = new House(1, 1750.50);
House house2 = (House)house1.clone();
```

house1 and house2 are two different objects with identical contents. The clone method in the Object class copies each field from the original object to the target object. If the field is of a primitive type, its value is copied. For example, the value of area (double type) is copied from house1 to house2. If the field is of an object, the reference of the field is copied. For example, the field whenBuilt is of the Date class, so its reference is copied into house2, as shown in Figure 10.6. Therefore, house1.whenBuilt == house2.whenBuilt is true, although house1 == house2 is false. This is referred to as a *shallow copy* rather than a *deep copy*, meaning that if the field is of an object, the reference of the field is copied rather than its contents.

shallow copy

deep copy

If you want to perform a deep copy, you can override the clone method with custom cloning operations instead of invoking super.clone(). See Exercise 10.4.

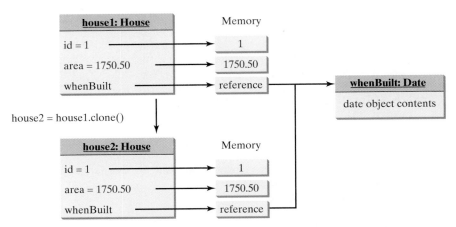

FIGURE 10.6 The `clone` method copies the values of primitive type fields and the references of object type fields.

Note

You learned how to use the `arraycopy` method to copy arrays in Chapter 6, "Arrays." This method provides shallow copies. It works fine for arrays of primitive data type elements, but not for arrays of object type elements. To support a deep copy, you have to deal with how to copy individual object elements in the array.

Caution

If the `House` class does not override the `clone()` method, the program will receive a syntax error because `clone()` is protected in `java.lang.Object`. If `House` does not implement `java.lang.Cloneable`, invoking `super.clone()` (line 28) in House.java would cause a `CloneNotSupportedException`. Thus, to enable cloning an object, the class for the object must override the `clone()` method and implement `Cloneable`.

10.5 Processing Primitive Data Type Values as Objects

Primitive data types are not used as objects in Java due to performance considerations. Because of the overhead of processing objects, the language's performance would be adversely affected if primitive data types were treated as objects. However, many Java methods require the use of objects as arguments. For example, the `add(object)` method in the `ArrayList` class adds an object to an `ArrayList`. Java offers a convenient way to incorporate, or wrap, a primitive data type into an object (e.g., wrapping `int` into the `Integer` class, and wrapping `double` into the `Double` class). The corresponding class is called a *wrapper class*. By using a wrapper object instead of a primitive data type variable, you can take advantage of generic programming.

wrapper class

Java provides `Boolean`, `Character`, `Double`, `Float`, `Byte`, `Short`, `Integer`, and `Long` wrapper classes for primitive data types. These classes are grouped in the `java.lang` package. Their inheritance hierarchy is shown in Figure 10.7.

Note

The wrapper class name for a primitive type is the same as the primitive data type name with the first letter capitalized. The exceptions are `Integer` and `Character`.

Each numeric wrapper class extends the abstract `Number` class, which contains the methods `doubleValue()`, `floatValue()`, `intValue()`, `longValue()`, `shortValue()`, and

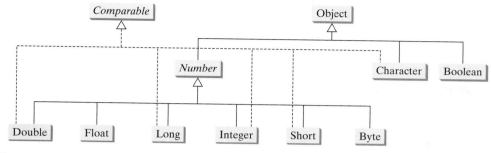

FIGURE 10.7 The Number class is an abstract superclass for Double, Float, Long, Integer, Short, and Byte.

byteValue(). These methods "convert" objects into primitive type values. The methods doubleValue(), floatValue(), intValue(), and longValue() are abstract. The methods byteValue() and shortValue() are not abstract; they simply return (byte)intValue() and (short)intValue(), respectively.

Each wrapper class overrides the toString, equals, and hashCode methods defined in the Object class. Since all the numeric wrapper classes and the Character class implement the Comparable interface, the compareTo method is implemented in these classes.

Wrapper classes are very similar. The Character class was introduced in Chapter 8, "Strings and Text I/O." The Boolean class is rarely used. The following sections use Integer and Double as examples to introduce the numeric wrapper classes. The key features of Integer and Double are shown in Figure 10.8.

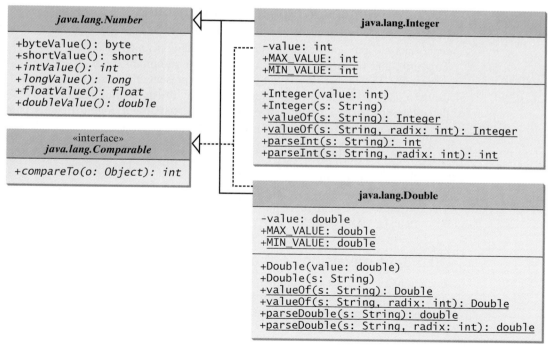

FIGURE 10.8 The wrapper classes provide constructors, constants, and conversion methods for manipulating various data types.

10.5.1   Numeric Wrapper Class Constructors

You can construct a wrapper object either from a primitive data type value or from a string representing the numeric value. The constructors for `Integer` and `Double` are:

```
public Integer(int value)
public Integer(String s)
public Double(double value)
public Double(String s)
```

For example, you can construct a wrapper object for `double` value `5.0` using either

```
Double doubleObject = new Double(5.0);
```

or

```
Double doubleObject = new Double("5.0");
```

You can construct a wrapper object for `int` value `5` using either

```
Integer integerObject = new Integer(5);
```

or

```
Integer integerObject = new Integer("5");
```

 Note

no no-arg constructor
immutable

(1) The wrapper classes do not have no-arg constructors. (2) The instances of all wrapper classes are *immutable*; this means that their internal values cannot be changed once the objects are created.

10.5.2   Numeric Wrapper Class Constants

Each numeric wrapper class has the constants `MAX_VALUE` and `MIN_VALUE`. `MAX_VALUE` represents the maximum value of the corresponding primitive data type. For `Byte`, `Short`, `Integer`, and `Long`, `MIN_VALUE` represents the minimum `byte`, `short`, `int`, and `long` values. For `Float` and `Double`, `MIN_VALUE` represents the minimum *positive* `float` and `double` values. The following statements display the maximum integer (2, 147, 483, 647), the minimum positive float (1.4E−45), and the maximum double floating-point number (1.79769313486231570e+308d):

```
System.out.println("The maximum integer is " + Integer.MAX_VALUE);
System.out.println("The minimum positive float is " +
  Float.MIN_VALUE);
System.out.println(
  "The maximum double precision floating-point number is " +
  Double.MAX_VALUE);
```

10.5.3   Conversion Methods

Each numeric wrapper class implements the abstract methods `doubleValue`, `floatValue`, `intValue`, `longValue`, and `shortValue`, which are defined in the `Number` class. These methods "convert" objects into primitive type values.

For example,

```
long l = doubleObject.longValue(); // Note it truncates
```

This converts `doubleObject`'s double value to a `long` variable `l`

```
int i = integerObject.intValue();
```

This assigns the `int` value of `integerObject` to `i`

```
double d = 5.9;
Double doubleObject = new Double(d);
String s = doubleObject.toString();
```

This converts `double d` to a string `s`.

10.5.4 The Static `valueOf` Methods

The numeric wrapper classes have a useful class method, `valueOf(String s)`. This method creates a new object initialized to the value represented by the specified string. For example,

```
Double doubleObject = Double.valueOf("12.4");
Integer integerObject = Integer.valueOf("12");
```

10.5.5 The Methods for Parsing Strings into Numbers

You have used the `parseInt` method in the `Integer` class to parse a numeric string into an `int` value and the `parseDouble` method in the `Double` class to parse a numeric string into a double value. Each numeric wrapper class has two overloaded parsing methods to parse a numeric string into an appropriate numeric value based on `10` (decimal) or any specified radix (e.g., `2` for binary, `8` for octal, and `16` for hexadecimal). These methods are shown below:

```
// These two methods are in the Byte class
public static byte parseByte(String s)
public static byte parseByte(String s, int radix)

// These two methods are in the Short class
public static short parseShort(String s)
public static short parseShort(String s, int radix)

// These two methods are in the Integer class
public static int parseInt(String s)
public static int parseInt(String s, int radix)

// These two methods are in the Long class
public static long parseLong(String s)
public static long parseLong(String s, int radix)

// These two methods are in the Float class
public static float parseFloat(String s)
public static float parseFloat(String s, int radix)

// These two methods are in the Double class
public static double parseDouble(String s)
public static double parseDouble(String s, int radix)
```

For example,

```
Integer.parseInt("11", 2) returns 3;
Integer.parseInt("12", 8) returns 10;
Integer.parseInt("13", 10) returns 13;
Integer.parseInt("1A", 16) returns 26;
```

`Integer.parseInt("12", 2)` would raise a runtime exception because `12` is not a binary number.

10.5.6 (Optional) `BigInteger` and `BigDecimal` Classes

If you need to compute with very large numbers and high precision, you can use the `BigInteger` and `BigDecimal` classes in the `java.math` package. They are wrapper classes for integer and decimal values. Both are *immutable*. Both extend the `Number` class and

immutable

implement the `Comparable` interface. The largest integer of the `long` type is 9223372036854775807. An instance of `BigInteger` can represent an integer of any size. You can use `new BigInteger(String)` and `new BigDecimal(String)` to create an instance of `BigInteger` and `BigDecimal` and use the `add`, `subtract`, `multiple`, and `divide` methods to perform numeric operations. For example, the following code creates two `BigInteger` objects and multiplies them:

```
BigInteger a = new BigInteger("9223372036854775807");
BigInteger b = new BigInteger("10000000");
BigInteger c = a.multiply(b);
System.out.println(c);
```

The output is 92233720368547758070000000.

There is no limit to the precision of a `BigDecimal` object. The `divide` method may throw an `ArithmeticException` if the result cannot be terminated. However, you can use the overloaded `divide(BigDecimal d, int scale, int roundingMode)` method to specify a scale and a rounding mode to avoid this exception. For example, the following code created two `BigDecimal` objects and performs division with scale 20 and rounding mode `BigDecimal.ROUND_UP`:

```
BigDecimal a = new BigDecimal(1.0);
BigDecimal b = new BigDecimal(3);
BigDecimal c = a.divide(b, 20, BigDecimal.ROUND_UP);
System.out.println(c);
```

The output is 0.33333333333333333334.

10.5.7 Example: Sorting an Array of Objects

This example presents a static generic method for sorting an array of comparable objects. The objects are instances of the `Comparable` interface, and they are compared using the `compareTo` method. The method can be used to sort an array of any objects as long as their classes implement the `Comparable` interface.

To test the method, the program sorts an array of integers, an array of double numbers, an array of characters, and an array of strings. The program is shown in Listing 10.5. Figure 10.9 shows a sample run of the code.

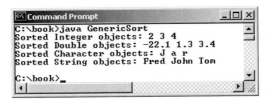

FIGURE 10.9 The program uses a generic sort method to sort an array of comparable objects.

LISTING 10.5 GenericSort.java

```
1 public class GenericSort {
2   public static void main(String[] args) {
3     // Create an Integer array
4     Integer[] intArray = {new Integer(2), new Integer(4),
5       new Integer(3)};
6
```

```
 7      // Create a Double array
 8      Double[] doubleArray = {new Double(3.4), new Double(1.3),
 9        new Double(-22.1)};
10
11      // Create a Character array
12      Character[] charArray = {new Character('a'),
13        new Character('J'), new Character('r')};
14
15      // Create a String array
16      String[] stringArray = {"Tom", "John", "Fred"};
17
18      // Sort the arrays
19      sort(intArray);                                              sort Integer objects
20      sort(doubleArray);                                           sort Double objects
21      sort(charArray);                                             sort Character objects
22      sort(stringArray);                                           sort String objects
23
24      // Display the sorted arrays
25      System.out.print("Sorted Integer objects: ");
26      printList(intArray);
27      System.out.print("Sorted Double objects: ");
28      printList(doubleArray);
29      System.out.print("Sorted Character objects: ");
30      printList(charArray);
31      System.out.print("Sorted String objects: ");
32      printList(stringArray);
33    }
34
35    /** Sort an array of comparable objects */
36    public static void sort(Object[] list) {                      generic sort method
37      Object currentMax;
38      int currentMaxIndex;
39
40      for (int i = list.length - 1; i >= 1; i--) {
41        // Find the maximum in the list[0..i]
42        currentMax = list[i];
43        currentMaxIndex = i;
44
45        for (int j = i - 1; j >= 0; j--) {
46          if (((Comparable)currentMax).compareTo(list[j]) < 0) {   compareTo
47            currentMax = list[j];
48            currentMaxIndex = j;
49          }
50        }
51
52        // Swap list[i] with list[currentMaxIndex] if necessary;
53        if (currentMaxIndex != i) {
54          list[currentMaxIndex] = list[i];
55          list[i] = currentMax;
56        }
57      }
58    }
59
60    /** Print an array of objects */
61    public static void printList(Object[] list) {
62      for (int i = 0; i < list.length; i++)
63        System.out.print(list[i] + " ");
64      System.out.println();
65    }
66  }
```

The algorithm for the **sort** method is the same as in §6.8.1, "Selection Sort." The sort method in §6.8.1 sorts an array of double values. The sort method in this example can sort an array of any object type, provided that the objects are also instances of the **Comparable** interface. This is another example of *generic programming*, a subject discussed in §9.7, "Polymorphism, Dynamic Binding, and Generic Programming." Generic programming enables a method to operate on arguments of generic types, making it reusable with multiple types.

Integer, **Double**, **Character**, and **String** implement **Comparable**, so the objects of these classes can be compared using the **compareTo** method. The sort method uses the **compareTo** method to determine the order of the objects in the array.

Tip

Java provides a static **sort** method for sorting an array of any object type in the **java.util.Arrays** class, provided that the elements in the array are comparable. Thus you can use the following code to sort arrays in this example:

```java
java.util.Arrays.sort(intArray);
java.util.Arrays.sort(doubleArray);
java.util.Arrays.sort(charArray);
java.util.Arrays.sort(stringArray);
```

Note

Arrays are objects. An array is an instance of the **Object** class. Furthermore, if **A** is a subtype of **B**, every instance of **A[]** is an instance of **B[]**. Therefore, the following statements are all true:

```java
new int[10] instanceof Object
new Integer[10] instanceof Object
new Integer[10] instanceof Comparable[]
new Integer[10] instanceof Number[]
new Number[10] instanceof Object[]
```

Caution

Although an **int** value can be assigned to a **double** type variable, **int[]** and **double[]** are two incompatible types. Therefore, you cannot assign an **int[]** array to a variable of **double[]** or **Object[]** type.

10.6 Automatic Conversion Between Primitive Types and Wrapper Class Types

JDK 1.5 allows primitive types and wrapper classes to be converted automatically. For example, the following statement in (a) can be simplified as in (b) due to autoboxing:

Integer intObject = new Integer(2);	Equivalent	Integer intObject = 2;
(a)	New JDK 1.5 autoboxing	(b)

boxing
unboxing

Converting a primitive value to a wrapper object is called *boxing*. The reverse conversion is called *unboxing*. The JDK 1.5 compiler will automatically box a primitive value that appears in a context requiring an object, and will unbox an object that appears in a context requiring a primitive value. Consider the following example:

```java
1 Integer[] intArray = {1, 2, 3};
2 System.out.println(intArray[0] + intArray[1] + intArray[2]);
```

In line 1, primitive values 1, 2, and 3 are automatically boxed into objects `new Integer(1)`, `new Integer(2)`, and `new Integer(3)`. In line 2, objects `intArray[0]`, `intArray[1]`, and `intArray[2]` are automatically converted into `int` values that are added together.

10.7 (Optional GUI) Handling GUI Events

When you run the program in Listing 9.12, it displays two buttons. If you click a button, there is no response. To respond, you need to write the code to process the clicking button action. The button is a *source object* where the action originates. You need to create an object capable of handling the action event on a button. This object is called a *listener*. Not all objects can be listeners for an action event. To be a listener, two requirements must be met:

    source object
    listener object

1. The object must be an instance of the `ActionListener` interface. The `Action-Listener` interface contains the `actionPerformed` method for processing the event.

    ActionListener interface

2. The `ActionListener` object `listener` must be registered with the source using the method `source.addActionListener(listener)`.

    addActionListener-
    (listener)

Listing 10.6 gives the code that processes the `ActionEvent` on the two buttons. When you click the OK button, the message "OK button clicked" is displayed. When you click the Cancel button, the message "Cancel button clicked" is displayed, as shown in Figure 10.10.

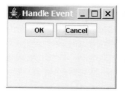 

FIGURE 10.10   The program responds to button-clicking action events.

LISTING 10.6 HandleEvent.java

```
1  import javax.swing.*;
2  import java.awt.*;
3  import java.awt.event.*;
4
5  public class HandleEvent extends JFrame {
6    public HandleEvent() {
7      // Set FlowLayout for the frame
8      FlowLayout layout = new FlowLayout();
9      setLayout(layout);
10
11     // Add two buttons to frame
12     JButton jbtOK = new JButton("OK");
13     JButton jbtCancel = new JButton("Cancel");
14     add(jbtOK);
15     add(jbtCancel);
16
17     // Register listeners
18     OKListenerClass listener1 = new OKListenerClass();
19     CancelListenerClass listener2 = new CancelListenerClass();
20     jbtOK.addActionListener(listener1);
21     jbtCancel.addActionListener(listener2);
22   }
23
```

    create listener

    register listener

```
24    public static void main(String[] args) {
25      JFrame frame = new HandleEvent();
26      frame.setTitle("Handle Event");
27      frame.setSize(200, 150);
28      frame.setLocation(200, 100);
29      frame.setDefaultCloseOperation(JFrame.EXIT_ON_CLOSE);
30      frame.setVisible(true);
31    }
32  }
33
34  class OKListenerClass implements ActionListener {
35    public void actionPerformed(ActionEvent e) {
36      System.out.println("OK button clicked");
37    }
38  }
39
40  class CancelListenerClass implements ActionListener {
41    public void actionPerformed(ActionEvent e) {
42      System.out.println("Cancel button clicked");
43    }
44  }
```

listener class
process event

listener class
process event

Two listener classes are declared in lines 34–44. Each listener class implements `ActionListener` to process `ActionEvent`. The object `listener1` is an instance of `OKListenerClass` (line 18), which is registered with the button `jbtOK` in line 20. When the OK button is clicked, the `actionPerformed(ActionEvent)` method (line 36) in `OKListenerClass` is invoked to process the event. The object `listener2` is an instance of `CancelListenerClass` (line 19), which is registered with the button `jbtCancel` in line 21. When the OK button is clicked, the `actionPerformed(ActionEvent)` method (line 42) in `CancelListenerClass` is invoked to process the event.

KEY TERMS

abstract class 342	multiple inheritance 342
abstract method 342	subinterface 351
deep copy 355	shallow copy 355
interface 347	single inheritance 342
marker interface 354	wrapper class 356

CHAPTER SUMMARY

■ Abstract classes are like regular classes with data and methods, but you cannot create instances of abstract classes using the `new` operator.

■ An abstract method cannot be contained in a nonabstract class. If a subclass of an abstract superclass does not implement all the inherited abstract methods of the superclass, the subclass must be declared abstract.

■ A class that contains abstract methods must be abstract. However, it is possible to declare an abstract class that contains no abstract methods.

■ A subclass can be abstract even if its superclass is concrete.

- An interface is a classlike construct that contains only constants and abstract methods. In many ways, an interface is similar to an abstract class, but an abstract class can contain constants and abstract methods as well as variables and concrete methods.

- An interface is treated like a special class in Java. Each interface is compiled into a separate bytecode file, just like a regular class.

- The `java.lang.Comparable` interface defines the `compareTo` method. Many classes in the Java library implement `Comparable`.

- The `java.lang.Cloneable` interface is a marker interface. An object of the class that implements the `Cloneable` interface is cloneable.

- A class can extend only one superclass but can implement one or more interfaces.

- An interface can extend one or more interfaces.

- Many Java methods require the use of objects as arguments. Java offers a convenient way to incorporate, or wrap, a primitive data type into an object (e.g., wrapping `int` into the `Integer` class, and wrapping double into the `Double` class). The corresponding class is called a *wrapper class*. By using a wrapper object instead of a primitive data type variable, you can take advantage of generic programming.

- The wrapper class for `byte` is `Byte`, for `short` is `Short`, for `int` is `Integer`, for `long` is `Long`, for `float` is `Float`, for `double` is `Double`, for `char` is `Character`, and for `boolean` is `Boolean`.

- The numeric wrapper classes extend the abstract `java.lang.Number` class and implement the `java.lang.Comparable` interface. The `Character` class also implements `java.lang.Comparable`.

REVIEW QUESTIONS

Section 10.2 Abstract Classes

10.1   Which of the following class definitions defines a legal abstract class?

```
class A {
  abstract void unfinished() {
  }
}
```
(a)

```
public class abstract A {
  abstract void unfinished();
}
```
(d)

```
class A {
  abstract void unfinished();
}
```
(b)

```
abstract class A {
  protected void unfinished();
}
```
(e)

```
abstract class A {
  abstract void unfinished();
}
```
(c)

```
abstract class A {
  abstract int unfinished();
}
```
(f)

10.2 The `getArea` and `getPerimeter` methods may be removed from the `GeometricObject` class. What are the benefits of defining `getArea` and `getPerimeter` as abstract methods in the `GeometricObject` class?

Section 10.4 Interfaces

10.3 Which of the following is a correct interface?

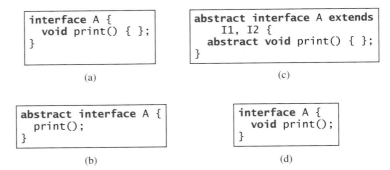

```
interface A {
  void print() { };
}
```
(a)

```
abstract interface A extends
    I1, I2 {
  abstract void print() { };
}
```
(c)

```
abstract interface A {
  print();
}
```
(b)

```
interface A {
  void print();
}
```
(d)

10.4 Two `max` methods are defined in §10.4. Explain why the `max` with the signature `max(Comparable, Comparable)` is better than the one with the signature `max(Object, Object)`.

Are these statements correct?

```
String s = Max.max("abc", "efg");
Date date = Max.max(new Date(), new Date());
```

10.5 You can define the `compareTo` method in a class without implementing the `Comparable` interface. What are the benefits of implementing the `Comparable` interface?

10.6 What would happen if the `House` class (defined in Listing 10.4) does not override the `clone()` method or if `House` does not implement `java.lang.Cloneable`?

10.7 Show the printout of the following code:

```
java.util.Date date = new java.util.Date();
java.util.Date date1 = (java.util.Date)(date.clone());
System.out.println(date == date1);
System.out.println(date.equals(date1));
```

10.8 Show the printout of the following code:

```
java.util.ArrayList list = new java.util.ArrayList();
list.add("New York"); list.add(new java.util.Date());
java.util.ArrayList list1 =
  (java.util.ArrayList)(list.clone());
System.out.println(list == list1);
System.out.println(list.get(0) == list1.get(0));
System.out.println(list.get(1) == list1.get(1));
```

10.9 What is wrong in the following code?

```
public class Test {
  public static void main(String[] args) {
    GeometricObject x = new Circle(3);
    GeometricObject y = x.clone();
    System.out.println(x == y);
  }
}
```

Section 10.5 Processing Primitive Data Type Values as Objects

10.10 Can you assign `new int[10]`, `new String[100]`, `new Object[50]`, or `new Calendar[20]` into a variable of `Object[]` type?

10.11 Describe primitive-type wrapper classes. Why do you need these wrapper classes?

10.12 Are the following statements correct?

```java
Integer i = new Integer("23");
Integer i = new Integer(23);
Integer i = Integer.valueOf("23");
Integer i = Integer.parseInt("23", 8);
Double d = new Double();
Double d = Double.valueOf("23.45");
int i = (Integer.valueOf("23")).intValue();
double d = (Double.valueOf("23.4")).doubleValue();
int i = (Double.valueOf("23.4")).intValue();
String s = (Double.valueOf("23.4")).toString();
```

10.13 How do you convert an integer into a string? How do you convert a numeric string into an integer? How do you convert a double number into a string? How do you convert a numeric string into a double value?

10.14 Why do the following two lines of code compile but cause a runtime error?

```java
Number numberRef = new Integer(0);
Double doubleRef = (Double)numberRef;
```

10.15 Why do the following two lines of code compile but cause a runtime error?

```java
Number[] numberArray = new Integer[2];
numberArray[0] = new Double(1.5);
```

10.16 What is wrong in the following code?

```java
public class Test {
  public static void main(String[] args) {
    Number x = new Integer(3);
    System.out.println(x.intValue());
    System.out.println(x.compareTo(new Integer(4)));
  }
}
```

10.17 What is wrong in the following code?

```java
public class Test {
  public static void main(String[] args) {
    Number x = new Integer(3);
    System.out.println(x.intValue());
    System.out.println((Integer)x.compareTo(new Integer(4)));
  }
}
```

10.18 What is the output of the following code?

```java
public class Test {
  public static void main(String[] args) {
    java.math.BigInteger x = new java.math.BigInteger("3");
    java.math.BigInteger y = new java.math.BigInteger("7");
    x.add(y);
    System.out.println(x);
  }
}
```

Section 10.6 Automatic Conversion Between Primitive Types and Wrapper Classes

10.19 Describe the boxing and unboxing features in JDK 1.5. Are the following statements correct in JDK 1.5?

```
Number x = 3;
Integer x = 3;
Double x = 3;
Double x = 3.0;
int x = new Integer(3);
int x = new Integer(3) + new Integer(4);
double y = 3.4;
y.intValue();

JOptionPane.showMessageDialog(null, 45.5);
```

Comprehensive

10.20 Define the following terms: abstract classes, interfaces. What are the similarities and differences between abstract classes and interfaces?

10.21 Indicate true or false for the following statements:

- An abstract class can have instances created using the constructor of the abstract class.
- An abstract class can be extended.
- An interface is compiled into a separate bytecode file.
- A subclass of a nonabstract superclass cannot be abstract.
- A subclass cannot override a concrete method in a superclass to declare it abstract.
- An abstract method must be non-static
- An interface can have static methods.
- An interface can extend one or more interfaces.
- An interface can extend an abstract class.
- An abstract class can extend an interface.

PROGRAMMING EXERCISES

Comprehensive

10.1* (*Enabling GeometricObject comparable*) Modify the GeometricObject class to implement the Comparable interface, and define a static max method in the GeometricObject class for finding the larger of two GeometricObject objects. Draw the UML diagram and implement the new GeometricObject class. Write a test program that uses the max method to find the larger of two circles and the larger of two rectangles.

10.2* (*The ComparableRectangle class*) Create a class named ComparableRectangle that extends Rectangle and implements Comparable. Draw the UML diagram and implement the compareTo method to compare the rectangles on the basis of area. Write a test class to find the larger of two instances of ComparableRectangle objects.

10.3* (*The Colorable interface*) Design an interface named Colorable with a void method named howToColor(). Every class of a colorable object must implement the Colorable interface. Design a class named Square that extends GeometricObject and implements Colorable. Implement howToColor to display a message on how to color the square.

Draw a UML diagram that involves `Colorable`, `Square`, and `Geometric-Object`. Write a test program that creates an array of five `Geometric-Objects`. For each object in the array, invoke its `howToColor` method if it is colorable.

10.4* (*Revising the House class*) Rewrite the `House` class in Listing 10.4 to perform a deep copy on the `whenBuilt` field.

10.5* (*Enabling Circle comparable*) Rewrite the `Circle` class in Listing 9.2 to extend `GeometricObject` and implement the `Comparable` interface. Override the `equals` and `hashCode` methods in the `Object` class. Two `Circle` objects are equal if their radii are the same. Draw the UML diagram that involves `Circle`, `GeometricObject`, and `Comparable`.

10.6* (*Enabling Rectangle comparable*) Rewrite the `Rectangle` class in Listing 9.3 to extend `GeometricObject` and implement the `Comparable` interface. Override the `equals` and `hashCode` methods in the `Object` class. Two `Rectangle` objects are equal if their areas are the same. Draw the UML diagram that involves `Rectangle`, `GeometricObject`, and `Comparable`.

10.7* (*The Octagon class*) Write a class named `Octagon` that extends `Geometric-Object` and implements the `Comparable` and `Cloneable` interfaces. Assume that all eight sides of the octagon are of equal size. The area can be computed using the following formula:

$$area = \left(2 + 4/\sqrt{2}\right) * side * side$$

Draw the UML diagram that involves `Octagon`, `GeometricObject`, `Comparable`, and `Cloneable`. Write a test program that creates an `Octagon` object with side value 5 and displays its area and perimeter. Create a new object using the `clone` method and compare the two objects using the `compareTo` method.

10.8* (*Summing the areas of geometric objects*) Write a method that sums the areas of all the geometric objects in an array. The method signature is:

public static double sumArea(GeometricObject[] a)

Write a test program that creates an array of three objects (a circle and a rectangle) and computes their total area using the `sumArea` method.

10.9* (*Finding the largest object*) Write a method that returns the largest object in an array of objects. The method signature is:

public static Object max(Object[] a)

All the objects are instances of the `Comparable` interface. The order of the objects in the array is determined using the `compareTo` method.

Write a test program that creates an array of ten strings, an array of ten integers, and an array of ten dates, and finds the largest string, integer, and date in the arrays.

10.10** (*Displaying calendars*) Rewrite the `PrintCalendar` class in Listing 5.8 to display a calendar for a specified month using the `Calendar` and `Gregorian-Calendar` classes. Your program receives the month and year from the command line. For example:

```
java Exercise10_10 6 2005
```

This displays the calendar shown in Figure 10.11.

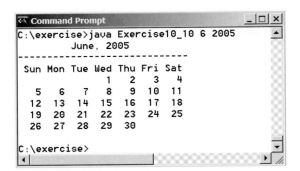

FIGURE 10.11 The program displays a calendar for June 2005.

You also can run the program without the year. In this case, the year is the current year. If you run the program without specifying a month and a year, the month is the current month.

OBJECT-ORIENTED DESIGN

Objectives

- To become familiar with the process of program development (§11.2).

- To learn the relationship types: association, aggregation, composition, dependency, strong inheritance, and weak inheritance (§11.3).

- To declare classes to represent the relationships among them (§11.3).

- To design systems by identifying the classes and discovering the relationships among these classes (§11.4).

- To implement the `Rational` class and process rational numbers using this class (§11.5).

- To design classes that follow the class-design guidelines (§11.6).

- To model dynamic behavior using sequence diagrams and statechart diagrams (§11.7 optional)

- To know the concept of framework-based programming using the Java API (§11.8).

11.1 Introduction

The preceding chapters introduced objects, classes, class inheritance, and interfaces. You learned the concepts of object-oriented programming. This chapter focuses on the development of software systems using the object-oriented approach, and introduces class modeling using the Unified Modeling Language (UML). You will learn class-design guidelines, and the techniques for designing reusable classes through the `Rational` class.

11.2 The Software Development Process

Developing a software project is an engineering process. Software products, no matter how large or how small, have the same developmental phases: requirements specification, analysis, design, implementation, testing, deployment, and maintenance, as shown in Figure 11.1.

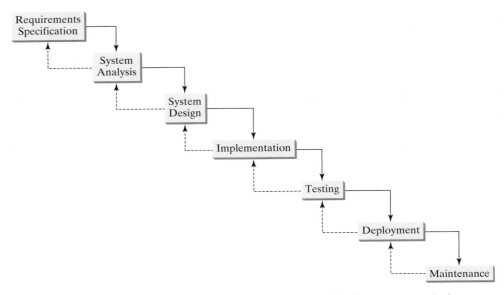

FIGURE 11.1 Developing a project involves requirements specification, system analysis, system design, implementation, testing, deployment, and maintenance.

requirements specification

Requirements specification is a formal process that seeks to understand the problem and document in detail what the software system needs to do. This phase involves close interaction between users and developers. Most of the examples in this book are simple, and their requirements are clearly stated. In the real world, however, problems are not well defined. You need to work closely with your customer and study a problem carefully to identify its requirements.

system analysis

System analysis seeks to analyze the business process in terms of data flow, and to identify the system's input and output. Part of the analysis entails modeling the system's behavior. The model is intended to capture the essential elements of the system and to define services to the system.

system design

System design is the process of designing the system's components. This phase involves the use of many levels of abstraction to decompose the problem into manageable components, identify classes and interfaces, and establish relationships among the classes and interfaces.

implementation

Implementation is translating the system design into programs. Separate programs are written for each component and put to work together. This phase requires the use of a programming language like Java. The implementation involves coding, testing, and debugging.

testing

Testing ensures that the code meets the requirements specification and weeds out bugs. An independent team of software engineers not involved in the design and implementation of the project usually conducts such testing.

Deployment makes the project available for use. For a Java applet, this means installing it on a Web server; for a Java application, installing it on the client's computer. A project usually consists of many classes. An effective approach for deployment is to package all the classes into a Java archive file, as will be introduced in §16.12, "Packaging and Deploying Java Projects."

deployment

Maintenance is concerned with changing and improving the product. A software product must continue to perform and improve in a changing environment. This requires periodic upgrades of the product to fix newly discovered bugs and incorporate changes.

maintenance

This chapter is mainly concerned with object-oriented design. While there are many object-oriented methodologies, UML has become the industry-standard notation for object-oriented modeling, and itself leads to a methodology. The process of designing classes calls for identifying the classes and discovering the relationships among them.

11.3 Discovering Class Relationships

The common relationships among classes are: *association*, *aggregation*, *composition*, *dependency*, and *inheritance*.

11.3.1 Association

Association is a general binary relationship that describes an activity between two classes. For example, a student taking a course is an association between the `Student` class and the `Course` class, and a faculty member teaching a course is an association between the `Faculty` class and the `Course` class. These associations can be represented in UML graphical notations, as shown in Figure 11.2.

association

An association is illustrated by a solid line between two classes with an optional label that describes the relationship. In Figure 11.2, the labels are *Take* and *Teach*. Each relationship may have an optional small black triangle that indicates the direction of the relationship. In Figure 11.2, the direction indicates that a student takes a course, as opposed to a course taking a student.

FIGURE 11.2 A student may take any number of courses, and a faculty member teaches at most three courses. A course may have from five to sixty students and is taught by only one faculty member.

Each class involved in the relationship may have a role name that describes the role it plays in the relationship. In Figure 11.2, *teacher* is the role name for `Faculty`.

Each class involved in an association may specify a *multiplicity*. A multiplicity could be a number or an interval that specifies how many objects of the class are involved in the relationship. The character $*$ means unlimited number of objects, and the interval $m..n$ means that the number of objects should be between m and n, inclusive. In Figure 11.2, each student may take any number of courses, and each course must have at least five students and at most sixty students. Each course is taught by only one faculty member, and a faculty member may teach from zero to three courses per semester.

Association may exist between objects of the same class. For example, a person may have a supervisor. This is illustrated in Figure 11.3.

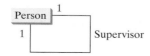

FIGURE 11.3 A person may have a supervisor.

In Java code, an association can be implemented using data fields and methods. The method in one class contains a parameter of the other class. For example, the relationships in Figure 11.2 may be implemented in the following classes:

```java
public class Student {
    private Course[]
        courseList;

    public void addCourse(
        Course s)
}
```

```java
public class Course {
    private Student[]
        classList;
    private Faculty faculty;

    public void addStudent(
        Student s)

    public void setFaculty(
        Faculty faculty)
}
```

```java
public class Faculty {
    private Course[]
        courseList;

    public void addCourse(
        Course c)
}
```

 Note

If you don't need to know the courses a student takes or a faculty member teaches, the data field `courseList` and the `addCourse` method in `Student` or `Faculty` can be omitted.

11.3.2 Aggregation and Composition

aggregation

aggregating object
aggregated object

Aggregation is a special form of association that represents an ownership relationship between two objects. Aggregation models *has-a* relationships. The owner object is called an *aggregating object*, and its class, an *aggregating class*. The subject object is called an *aggregated object*, and its class, an *aggregated class*. The association "a person has a supervisor" in Figure 11.3 is actually an aggregation.

composition

An object may be owned by several other aggregating objects. If an object is exclusively owned by an aggregating object, the relationship between the object and its aggregating object is referred to as *composition*. For example, "a student has a name" is a composition relationship between the `Student` class and the `Name` class, whereas "a student has an address" is an aggregation relationship between the `Student` class and the `Address` class, since an address may be shared by several students. In UML, a filled diamond is attached to an aggregating class (e.g., `Student`) to denote the composition relationship with an aggregated class (e.g., `Name`), and an empty diamond is attached to an aggregating class (e.g., `Student`) to denote the aggregation relationship with an aggregated class (e.g., `Address`), as shown in Figure 11.4.

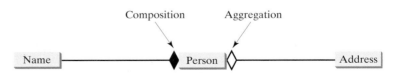

FIGURE 11.4 A student has a name and an address.

An aggregation relationship is usually represented as a data field in the aggregating class. For example, the relationship in Figure 11.4 can be represented as follows:

```
public class Name {
    ...
}
```
Aggregated class

```
public class Person {
    private Name name;
    private Address address;

    ...
}
```
Aggregating class

```
public class Address {
    ...
}
```
Aggregated class

In the relationship "a person has a supervisor," as shown in Figure 11.3, a supervisor can be represented as a data field in the **Person** class, as follows:

```
public class Person {
    private Person supervisor;
    ...
}
```

If a person has several supervisors, as shown in Figure 11.5, you may use an array or an **ArrayList** to store the supervisors.

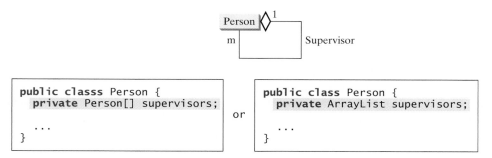

```
public classs Person {
    private Person[] supervisors;

    ...
}
```
or
```
public class Person {
    private ArrayList supervisors;

    ...
}
```

FIGURE 11.5   A person may have several supervisors.

Note

Since aggregation and composition relationships are translated into the same class template, for simplicity, both are called composition.

aggregation or composition

11.3.3   Dependency

A *dependency* describes a relationship between two classes where one (called **client**) uses the other (called *supplier*). In UML, draw a dashed line with an arrow from the client class to the supplier class. For example, the **ArrayList** class uses **Object** because you can add objects to an **ArrayList**. The relationship between **ArrayList** and **Object** can be described using dependency, as shown in Figure 11.6(a). The **Calendar** class uses **Date** because you can set a calendar with a specified **Date** object. The relationship between **Calendar** and **Date** can be described using dependency, as shown in Figure 11.6(b).

client

supplier

ArrayList - - - - - - ➤ Object   Calendar - - - - - - ➤ Date

(a)   (b)

FIGURE 11.6   (a) **ArrayList** uses **Object**. (b) **Calendar** uses **Date**.

In Java code, a dependency can be implemented using a method in the client class. The method contains a parameter of the supplier class type. For example, the `ArrayList` class has the `add(Object)` method that adds an object to the `ArrayList`. The `Calendar` class has the `setTime(Date)` method that sets a new time in the calendar.

```
public class ArrayList {
    public void add(Object o)


    ...
}
```

```
public abstract class Calendar {
    public void setTime(Date d)


    ...
}
```

dependency vs. association

Note

Both association and dependency describe one class as depending on another. Association is stronger than dependency. In association, the state of the object changes when its associated object changes. In dependency, the client object and the supplier object are loosely coupled. The association relationship is implemented using data fields and methods. There is a strong connection between the two classes. The dependency relationship is implemented using methods.

11.3.4 Inheritance

strong is-a
weak is-a

Inheritance models the *is-a* relationship between two classes. A *strong is-a* relationship describes a direct inheritance relationship between two classes. A *weak is-a* relationship describes that a class has certain properties. A strong is-a relationship can be represented using class inheritance. For example, the relationship "a faculty member is a person" (shown in Figure 11.7(a)) is a strong is-a relationship and can be represented using the class in Figure 11.7(b).

```
public class Faculty extends Person {
    ...
}
```

Person ◁——— Faculty

(a)   (b)

FIGURE 11.7 `Faculty` extends `Person`.

A weak is-a relationship can be represented using interfaces. For example, the weak is-a relationship "students are comparable based on their grades" (shown in Figure 11.8(a)) can be represented by implementing the `Comparable` interface, as shown in Figure 11.8(b).

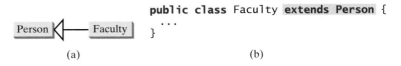

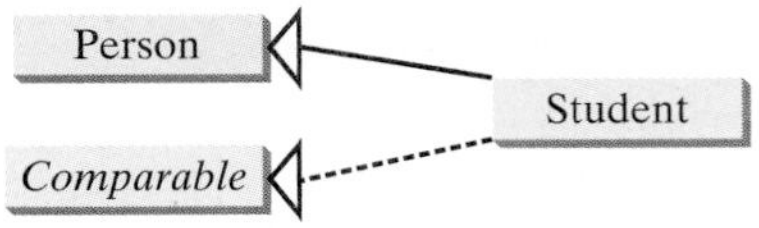

```
public class Student extends Person
       implements Comparable {
    ...

    /** Implement the compareTo method */
    public int compareTo(Object object) {
        ...
    }
}
```

Person ◁

Comparable ◁- - -

Student

(a)   (b)

FIGURE 11.8 `Student` extends `Person` and implements `Comparable`.

Note

Not all is-a relationships should be modeled using inheritance. For example, a square is a rectangle, but you should not declare a `Square` class to extend a `Rectangle` class, because there is nothing to extend (or supplement) from a rectangle to a square. For class `A` to extend class `B`, `A` should contain more detailed information than `B`.

nonextensible is-a

11.4 Case Study: Object-Oriented Design

The key to object-oriented programming is to model the application in terms of cooperative objects. Carefully designed classes are critical when a project is being developed. There are many levels of abstraction in system design. You have learned method abstraction and have applied it to the development of large programs. Methods are means to group statements. Classes extend abstraction to a higher level and provide a means of grouping methods. Classes do more than just group methods, however; they also contain data fields. Methods and data fields together describe the properties and behaviors of classes.

The power of classes is further extended by inheritance. Inheritance enables a class to extend the contract and the implementation of an existing class without knowing the details of the existing class. In the development of a Java program, class abstraction is applied to decompose the problem into a set of related classes, and method abstraction is applied to design individual classes.

This case study models borrowing loans to demonstrate how to identify classes, discover the relationships between classes, and apply class abstraction in object-oriented program development.

For simplicity, the example does not attempt to build a complete system for storing, processing, and manipulating loans for borrowers; instead it focuses on modeling borrowers and the loans for the borrowers. The following steps are usually involved in building an object-oriented system:

1. Identify classes for the system.

2. Establish relationships among classes.

3. Describe the attributes and methods in each class.

4. Implement the classes.

The first step is to *identify classes* for the system. There are many strategies for identifying classes in a system, one of which is to study how the system works and select a number of use cases, or scenarios. Since a borrower is a person who obtains a loan, and a person has a name and an address, you can identify the following classes: `Person`, `Name`, `Address`, `Borrower`, and `Loan`.

identify classes

Identifying objects is not easy for novice programmers. How do you find the right objects? There is no unique solution even for simple problems. Software development is more an art than a science. The quality of a program ultimately depends on the programmer's intuition, experience, and knowledge. This example identifies five classes: `Name`, `Address`, `Person`, `Borrower`, and `Loan`. There are several alternatives. One would combine `Name`, `Address`, `Person`, and `Borrower` into one class. This design is not clear because it puts too many entities into one class.

The second step is to *establish relationships* among the classes. The relationship is derived from the system analysis. The first two steps are intertwined. When you identify classes, you also think about the relationships among them. Establishing relationships among objects helps you understand the interactions among objects. An object-oriented system consists of a collection of interrelated cooperative objects. The relationships for the classes in this example are illustrated in Figure 11.9.

establish relationships

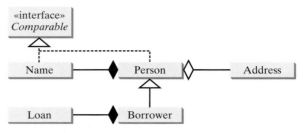

FIGURE 11.9 A borrower is a person who has a loan.

describe attributes

The third step is to describe the attributes and methods in each of the classes you have identified. The **Name** class has the properties **firstName**, **mi**, and **lastName**, their associated get and set methods, and the **getFullName** method for returning the full name. You can compare names in alphabetical order of their last name, first name, and mi. The **Address** class has the properties **street**, **city**, **state**, and **zip**, their associated **get** and **set** methods, and the **getAddress** method for returning the full address. The **Loan** class, presented in Listing 7.9, Loan.java, has the properties **annualInterestRate**, **numberOfYears**, and **loanAmount**, their associated property **get** and **set** methods, and **getMonthlyPayment** and **getTotalPayment** methods. The **Person** class has the properties **name** and **address**, their associated get and set methods, and the **toString** method for displaying complete information about the person. **Borrower** is a subclass of **Person**. Additionally, **Borrower** has the **loan** property and its associated **get** and **set** methods, and the **toString** method for displaying the person and the loan payments. You can compare persons according to their names. Figure 11.9 is expanded to Figure 11.10.

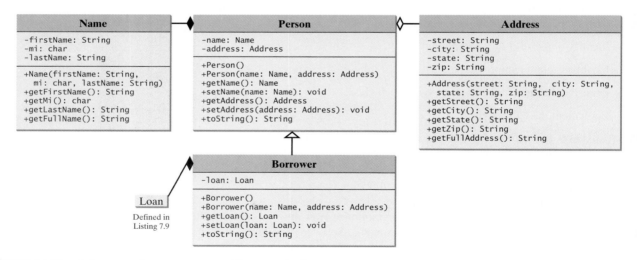

FIGURE 11.10 A borrower has a name, an address, and a loan.

coding

The fourth step is to write the code for the classes. The program is long, but most of the *coding* is for the **get** and **set** methods. Once an object is identified, its properties and methods can be defined by analyzing the requirements and scenarios of the system. It is a good practice to provide complete **get** and **set** methods. These may not be needed for your current project, but will be useful in other projects, because your classes are designed for reuse in future projects. Listings 11.1, 11.2, 11.3, and 11.4 give the **Name**, **Address**, **Person**, and **Borrower** classes.

Listing 11.1 `Name.java`

```java
1 public final class Name implements Comparable {
2   private String firstName;
3   private char mi;
4   private String lastName;
5
6   /** Construct a name with firstName, mi, and lastName */
7   public Name(String firstName, char mi, String lastName) {
8     this.firstName = firstName;
9     this.mi = mi;
10    this.lastName = lastName;
11  }
12
13  /** Return firstName */
14  public String getFirstName() {
15    return firstName;
16  }
17
18  /** Return middle name initial */
19  public char getMi() {
20    return mi;
21  }
22
23  /** Return lastName */
24  public String getLastname() {
25    return lastName;
26  }
27
28  /** Obtain full name */
29  public String getFullName() {
30    return firstName + ' ' + mi + ' ' + lastName;
31  }
32
33  /** Implement compareTo in the Comparable interface */
34  public int compareTo(Object o) {
35    if (!lastName.equals(((Name)o).lastName)) {
36      return lastName.compareTo(((Name)o).lastName);
37    }
38    else if (!firstName.equals(((Name)o).firstName)) {
39      return firstName.compareTo(((Name)o).firstName);
40    }
41    else {
42      return mi - ((Name)o).mi;
43    }
44  }
45 }
```

Listing 11.2 `Address.java`

```java
1 public final class Address {
2   private String street;
3   private String city;
4   private String state;
5   private String zip;
6
```

```java
7    /** Create an address with street, city, state, and zip */
8    public Address(String street, String city,
9      String state, String zip) {
10     this.street = street;
11     this.city = city;
12     this.state = state;
13     this.zip = zip;
14   }
15
16   /** Return street */
17   public String getStreet() {
18     return street;
19   }
20
21   /** Return city */
22   public String getCity() {
23     return city;
24   }
25
26   /** Return state */
27   public String getState() {
28     return state;
29   }
30
31   /** Return zip */
32   public String getZip() {
33     return zip;
34   }
35
36   /** Get full address */
37   public String getFullAddress() {
38     return street + '\n' + city + ", " + state + ' ' + zip + '\n';
39   }
40 }
```

LISTING 11.3 Person.java

```java
1  public class Person {
2    private Name name;
3    private Address address;
4
5    /** Construct a person with default properties */
6    public Person() {
7      this(new Name("Jill", 'S', "Barr"),
8        new Address("100 Main", "Savannah", "GA", "31411"));
9    }
10
11   /** Construct a person with specified name and address */
12   public Person(Name name, Address address) {
13     this.name = name;
14     this.address = address;
15   }
16
17   /** Return name */
18   public Name getName() {
19     return name;
20   }
21
```

```java
22   /** Set a new name */
23   public void setName(Name name) {
24     this.name = name;
25   }
26
27   /** Return address */
28   public Address getAddress() {
29     return address;
30   }
31
32   /** Set a new address */
33   public void setAddress(Address address) {
34     this.address = address;
35   }
36
37   /** Override the toString method */
38   public String toString() {
39     return '\n' + name.getFullName() + '\n' +
40       address.getFullAddress() + '\n';
41   }
42
43   /** Implement compareTo in the Comparable interface */
44   public int compareTo(Object o) {
45     return name.compareTo(((Person)o).name);
46   }
47 }
```

LISTING 11.4 Borrower.java

```java
1 public class Borrower extends Person {
2   private Loan loan;
3
4   /** Construct a borrower with default properties */
5   public Borrower() {
6     super();
7   }
8
9   /** Create a borrower with specified name and address */
10   public Borrower(Name name, Address address) {
11     super(name, address);
12   }
13
14   /** Return loan */
15   public Loan getLoan() {
16     return loan;
17   }
18
19   /** Set a new loan */
20   public void setLoan(Loan loan) {
21     this.loan = loan;
22   }
23
24   /** String representation for borrower */
25   public String toString() {
26     return super.toString() +
27       "Monthly payment is " + loan.getMonthlyPayment() + '\n' +
28       "Total payment is " + loan.getTotalPayment();
29   }
30 }
```

Listing 11.5 is a test program that uses the classes `Name`, `Address`, `Borrower`, and `Loan`. The output of the program is shown in Figure 11.11.

LISTING 11.5 `BorrowLoan.java`

```java
 1 import javax.swing.JOptionPane;
 2
 3 public class BorrowLoan {
 4   /** Main method */
 5   public static void main(String[] args) {
 6     // Create a name
 7     Name name = new Name("John", 'D', "Smith");
 8
 9     // Create an address
10     Address address = new Address("100 Main Street", "Savannah",
11       "GA", "31419");
12
13     // Create a loan
14     Loan loan = new Loan(5.5, 15, 250000);
15
16     // Create a borrower
17     Borrower borrower = new Borrower(name, address);
18
19     borrower.setLoan(loan);
20
21     // Display loan information
22     JOptionPane.showMessageDialog(null, borrower.toString());
23   }
24 }
```

FIGURE 11.11 The program creates name, address, and loan, stores the information in a `Borrower` object, and displays the information with the loan payment.

11.5 Case Study: The `Rational` Class

A rational number is a number with a numerator and a denominator in the form `a/b`, where `a` is the numerator and `b` is the denominator. For example, `1/3`, `3/4`, and `10/4` are rational numbers.

A rational number cannot have a denominator of `0`, but a numerator of `0` is fine. Every integer `a` is equivalent to a rational number `a/1`. Rational numbers are used in exact computations involving fractions; for example, `1/3 = 0.33333 ....` This number cannot be precisely represented in floating-point format using data type `double` or `float`. To obtain the exact result, it is necessary to use rational numbers.

Java provides data types for integers and floating-point numbers, but not for rational numbers. This section shows how to design a class to represent rational numbers.

Since rational numbers share many common features with integers and floating-point numbers, and Number is the base class for numeric wrapper classes, it is appropriate to define Rational as a subclass of Number. Since rational numbers are comparable, the Rational class should also implement the Comparable interface. Figure 11.12 illustrates the Rational class and its relationship to the Number class and the Comparable interface.

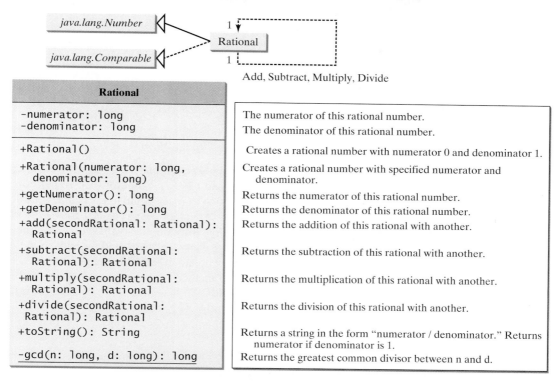

Rational	
-numerator: long	The numerator of this rational number.
-denominator: long	The denominator of this rational number.
+Rational()	Creates a rational number with numerator 0 and denominator 1.
+Rational(numerator: long, denominator: long)	Creates a rational number with specified numerator and denominator.
+getNumerator(): long	Returns the numerator of this rational number.
+getDenominator(): long	Returns the denominator of this rational number.
+add(secondRational: Rational): Rational	Returns the addition of this rational with another.
+subtract(secondRational: Rational): Rational	Returns the subtraction of this rational with another.
+multiply(secondRational: Rational): Rational	Returns the multiplication of this rational with another.
+divide(secondRational: Rational): Rational	Returns the division of this rational with another.
+toString(): String	Returns a string in the form "numerator / denominator." Returns numerator if denominator is 1.
-gcd(n: long, d: long): long	Returns the greatest common divisor between n and d.

FIGURE 11.12   The properties, constructors, and methods of the Rational class are illustrated in UML.

A rational number consists of a numerator and a denominator. There are many equivalent rational numbers; for example, $1/3 = 2/6 = 3/9 = 4/12$. For convenience, $1/3$ is used in this example to represent all rational numbers that are equivalent to $1/3$. The numerator and the denominator of $1/3$ have no common divisor except 1, so $1/3$ is said to be in lowest terms.

To reduce a rational number to its lowest terms, you need to find the greatest common divisor (GCD) of the absolute values of its numerator and denominator, and then divide both numerator and denominator by this value. You can use the method for computing the GCD of two integers n and d, as suggested in Listing 4.6, GreatestCommonDivisor.java. The numerator and denominator in a Rational object are reduced to their lowest terms.

As usual, let us first write a test program to create two Rational objects and test its methods. Listing 11.6 is a test program. Its output is shown in Figure 11.13.

```
C:\book>java TestRationalClass
2 + 2/3 = 8/3
2 - 2/3 = 4/3
2 * 2/3 = 4/3
2 / 2/3 = 3
2/3 is 0.6666666666666666

C:\book>
```

FIGURE 11.13   The program creates two Rational objects and displays their addition, subtraction, multiplication, and division.

LISTING 11.6 TestRationalClass.java

```
1  public class TestRationalClass {
2    /** Main method */
3    public static void main(String[] args) {
4      // Create and initialize two rational numbers r1 and r2.
5      Rational r1 = new Rational(4, 2);
6      Rational r2 = new Rational(2, 3);
7
8      // Display results
9      System.out.println(r1 + " + " + r2 + " = " + r1.add(r2));
10     System.out.println(r1 + " - " + r2 + " = " + r1.subtract(r2));
11     System.out.println(r1 + " * " + r2 + " = " + r1.multiply(r2));
12     System.out.println(r1 + " / " + r2 + " = " + r1.divide(r2));
13     System.out.println(r2 + " is " + r2.doubleValue());
14   }
15 }
```

The `main` method creates two rational numbers, `r1` and `r2` (lines 5–6), and displays the results of `r1 + r2`, `r1 - r2`, `r1 * r2`, and `r1 / r2` (lines 9–12). To perform `r1 + r2`, invoke `r1.add(r2)` to return a new `Rational` object. Similarly, `r1.subtract(r2)` is for `r1 - r2`, `r1.multiply(r2)` for `r1 * r2`, and `r1.divide(r2)` for `r1 / r2`.

The `doubleValue()` method displays the double value of `r2` (line 13). The `doubleValue()` method is defined in `java.lang.Number` and overridden in `Rational`.

Note that when a string is concatenated with an object using the plus sign (+), the object's string representation from the `toString()` method is used to concatenate with the string. So `r1 + " + " + r2 + " = " + r1.add(r2)` is equivalent to `r1.toString() + " + " + r2.toString() + " = " + r1.add(r2).toString()`.

The `Rational` class is implemented in Listing 11.7.

LISTING 11.7 Rational.java

```
1  public class Rational extends Number implements Comparable {
2    // Data fields for numerator and denominator
3    private long numerator = 0;
4    private long denominator = 1;
5
6    /** Construct a rational with default properties */
7    public Rational() {
8      this(0, 1);
9    }
10
11   /** Construct a rational with specified numerator and denominator */
12   public Rational(long numerator, long denominator) {
13     long gcd = gcd(numerator, denominator);
14     this.numerator = ((denominator > 0) ? 1 : -1) * numerator / gcd;
15     this.denominator = Math.abs(denominator) / gcd;
16   }
17
18   /** Find GCD of two numbers */
19   private static long gcd(long n, long d) {
20     long n1 = Math.abs(n);
21     long n2 = Math.abs(d);
22     int gcd = 1;
23
```

```
24      for (int k = 1; k <= n1 && k <= n2; k++) {
25        if (n1 % k == 0 && n2 % k == 0)
26          gcd = k;
27      }
28
29      return gcd;
30    }
31
32    /** Return numerator */
33    public long getNumerator() {
34      return numerator;
35    }
36
37    /** Return denominator */
38    public long getDenominator() {
39      return denominator;
40    }
41
42    /** Add a rational number to this rational */
43    public Rational add(Rational secondRational) {
44      long n = numerator * secondRational.getDenominator() +
45        denominator * secondRational.getNumerator();
46      long d = denominator * secondRational.getDenominator();
47      return new Rational(n, d);
48    }
49
50    /** Subtract a rational number from this rational */
51    public Rational subtract(Rational secondRational) {
52      long n = numerator * secondRational.getDenominator()
53        - denominator * secondRational.getNumerator();
54      long d = denominator * secondRational.getDenominator();
55      return new Rational(n, d);
56    }
57
58    /** Multiply a rational number to this rational */
59    public Rational multiply(Rational secondRational) {
60      long n = numerator * secondRational.getNumerator();
61      long d = denominator * secondRational.getDenominator();
62      return new Rational(n, d);
63    }
64
65    /** Divide a rational number from this rational */
66    public Rational divide(Rational secondRational) {
67      long n = numerator * secondRational.getDenominator();
68      long d = denominator * secondRational.numerator;
69      return new Rational(n, d);
70    }
71
72    /** Override the toString() method */
73    public String toString() {
74      if (denominator == 1)
75        return numerator + "";
76      else
77        return numerator + "/" + denominator;
78    }
79
80    /** Override the equals method in the Object class */
81    public boolean equals(Object parm1) {
```

$$\frac{a}{b} + \frac{c}{d} = \frac{ad + bc}{bd}$$

$$\frac{a}{b} - \frac{c}{d} = \frac{ad - bc}{bd}$$

$$\frac{a}{b} \times \frac{c}{d} = \frac{ac}{bd}$$

$$\frac{a}{b} \div \frac{c}{d} = \frac{ad}{bc}$$

```
82       if ((this.subtract((Rational)(parm1))).getNumerator() == 0)
83         return true;
84       else
85         return false;
86    }
87
88    /** Override the hashCode method in the Object class */
89    public int hashCode() {
90       return new Double(this.doubleValue()).hashCode();
91    }
92
93    /** Override the abstract intValue method in java.lang.Number */
94    public int intValue() {
95       return (int)doubleValue();
96    }
97
98    /** Override the abstract floatValue method in java.lang.Number */
99    public float floatValue() {
100      return (float)doubleValue();
101   }
102
103   /** Override the doubleValue method in java.lang.Number */
104   public double doubleValue() {
105      return numerator * 1.0 / denominator;
106   }
107
108   /** Override the abstract longValue method in java.lang.Number */
109   public long longValue() {
110      return (long)doubleValue();
111   }
112
113   /** Override the compareTo method in java.lang.Comparable */
114   public int compareTo(Object o) {
115      if ((this.subtract((Rational)o)).getNumerator() > 0)
116        return 1;
117      else if ((this.subtract((Rational)o)).getNumerator() < 0)
118        return -1;
119      else
120        return 0;
121   }
122 }
```

The rational number is encapsulated in a **Rational** object. Internally, a rational number is represented in its lowest terms (line 13), and the numerator determines its sign (line 14). The denominator is always positive (line 15).

The **gcd()** method (lines 19–30 in the **Rational** class) is private; it is not intended for use by clients. The **gcd()** method is only for internal use by the **Rational** class. The **gcd()** method is also static, since it is not dependent on any particular **Rational** object.

The **abs(x)** method (lines 20–21 in the **Rational** class) is defined in the **Math** class that returns the absolute value of **x**.

Two **Rational** objects can interact with each other to perform add, subtract, multiply, and divide operations. These methods return a new **Rational** object (lines 43–70).

The methods **toString**, **equals**, and **hashCode** in the **Object** class are overridden in the **Rational** class (lines 73–91). The **toString()** method returns a string representation of a **Rational** object in the form **numerator/denominator**, or simply **numerator** if **denominator** is 1. The **equals(Object other)** method returns **true** if this rational number is equal to the other rational number. By contract, if two objects are equal, their hash codes must be the same. For this reason, you should override **hashCode** whenever the **equals** method is overridden.

The abstract methods `intValue`, `longValue`, `floatValue`, and `doubleValue` in the `Number` class are implemented in the `Rational` class (lines 94–111). These methods return `int`, `long`, `float`, and `double` value for this rational number.

The `compareTo(Object other)` method in the `Comparable` interface is implemented in the `Rational` class (lines 114–121) to compare this rational number to the other rational number.

Tip

The get methods for the properties **numerator** and **denominator** are provided in the `Rational` class, but the set methods are not provided, so the contents of a `Rational` object cannot be changed once the object is created. The `Rational` class is *immutable*. A well-known example of an immutable class is the `String` class. The wrapper classes introduced in §10.5, "Processing Primitive Data Type Values as Objects," are also immutable.

immutable

Tip

The numerator and denominator are represented using two variables. It is possible to use an array of two integers to represent the numerator and denominator. See Exercise 11.2. The signatures of the public methods in the `Rational` class are not changed, although the internal representation of a rational number is changed. This is a good example to illustrate the idea that the data fields of a class should be kept private so as to encapsulate the implementation of the class from the use of the class.

encapsulation

11.6 Class Design Guidelines

You have learned how to design classes from the preceding two examples and from many other examples in the preceding chapters. Here are some guidelines.

11.6.1 Cohesion

A class should describe a single entity, and all the class operations should logically fit together to support a *coherent purpose*. You can use a class for students, for example, but you should not combine students and staff in the same class, because students and staff have different operations.

coherent purpose

A single entity with too many responsibilities can be broken into several classes to separate responsibilities. The classes `String`, `StringBuffer`, and `StringBuilder` all deal with strings, for example, but have different responsibilities. The `String` class deals with immutable strings, the `StringBuilder` class is for creating mutable strings, and the `StringBuffer` class is similar to `StringBuilder` except that `StringBuffer` contains synchronized methods for updating strings.

separating responsibilities

The `Date`, `Calendar`, and `GregorianCalendar` classes all deal with date and time, but have different responsibilities. The `Date` class represents a specific time. `Calendar` is an abstract class for extracting detailed calendar information from a specific time. `GregorianCalendar` implements a concrete calendar system.

11.6.2 Consistency

Follow standard Java programming style and naming conventions. Choose informative names for classes, data fields, and methods. A popular style is to place the data declaration before the constructor, and place constructors before methods.

naming conventions

Choose names consistently. It is not a good practice to choose different names for similar operations. For example, the `length()` method returns the size of a `String`, a `StringBuilder`, and a `StringBuffer`. But the `size()` method is used to return the size of a `Collection` and a `Map`. It is better to use the same name for consistency.

naming consistency

no-arg constructor

In general, you should consistently provide a public no-arg constructor for constructing a default instance. If a class does not support a no-arg constructor, document the reason. A public default no-arg constructor is assumed if no constructors are defined explicitly. A constructor invokes its superclass no-arg constructor by default if a constructor does not invoke an overloaded constructor or its superclass's constructor.

private constructor
protected constructor

If you want to prevent users from creating an object for a class, you may declare a private constructor in the class, as is the case for the `Math` class. The constructors in abstract classes should always be declared `protected`.

11.6.3 Encapsulation

encapsulating data fields

A class should use the `private` modifier to hide its data from direct access by clients. This makes the class easy to maintain.

Provide a `get` method only if you want the field to be readable, and provide a `set` method only if you want the field to be updateable. For example, the `Rational` class provides get methods for numerator and denominator, but no set methods, because `Rational` is an immutable class.

A class should also hide methods not intended for client use. The `gcd` method in the `Rational` class in the preceding section is private, for example, because it is only for internal use within the class.

private vs. protected

A class can present two contracts: one for the users of the class, and one for the extenders of the class. Make the fields `private` and the accessor and mutator methods `public` if they are intended for the users of the class. Make the fields or methods `protected` if they are intended for extenders of the class. The contract for extenders encompasses the contract for users. The extended class may increase the visibility of an instance method from `protected` to `public`, or may change its implementation, but you should never change the implementation in a way that violates the contract.

11.6.4 Clarity

Cohesion, consistency, and encapsulation are good guidelines for achieving design clarity. Additionally, a class should have a clear contract that is easy to explain and easy to understand.

easy to explain

Users can incorporate classes in many different combinations, orders, and environments. Therefore, you should design a class that imposes no restrictions on what or when the user can do with it, design the properties in a way that lets the user set them in any order and with any combination of values, and design methods that function independently of their order of occurrence. For example, the `Loan` class contains the properties `loanAmount`, `numberOfYears`, and `annualInterestRate`. The values of these properties can be set in any order.

independent methods

intuitive meaning

Methods should be defined intuitively without generating confusion. For example, the `substring(int beginIndex, int endIndex)` method in the `String` class is somehow confusing. The method returns a substring from `beginIndex` to `endIndex - 1`, rather than `endIndex`.

You should not declare a data field that can be derived from other data fields. For example, the following `Person` class has two data fields: `birthDate` and `age`. Since `age` can be derived from `birthDate`, age should not be declared as a data field.

independent properties

```java
public class Person {
  private java.util.Date birthDate;
  int age;

  ...
}
```

11.6.5 Completeness

Classes are designed for use by many different customers. In order to be useful in a wide range of applications, a class should provide a variety of ways for customization through properties and methods. For example, the String class contains more than fifty methods that are useful for a variety of applications. The Calendar class defines many time fields as constants, such as YEAR, MONTH, DATE, HOUR, HOUR_OF_DAY, MINUTE, SECOND, and DAY_OF_WEEK, and provides many methods for extracting date and time, and for setting a new date and time in the calendar.

11.6.6 Instance vs. Static

A variable or method that is dependent on a specific instance of the class should be an instance variable or method. A variable that is shared by all the instances of a class should be declared static. For example, the variable numberOfObjects in Circle2 in Listing 7.3, Circle2.java, is shared by all the objects of the Circle2 class, and therefore is declared static. A method that is not dependent on a specific instance should be declared as a static method. For instance, the getNumberOfObjects method in Circle2 and the gcd method in Rational are not tied to any specific instance, and therefore are declared as static methods.

Always reference static variables and methods from a class name (rather than a reference variable) to improve readability and avoid errors.

Do not pass a parameter from a constructor to initialize a static data field. It is better to use a set method to change the static data field. The following class in (a) is better replaced by (b).

```
public class SomeThing {
  int t1;
  static int t2;

  public SomeThing(int t1, int t2) {
    ...
  }
}
```

```
public class SomeThing {
  int t1;
  static int t2;

  public SomeThing(int t1) {
    ...
  }
  public static void setT2(int t2) {
    SomeThing.t2 = t2;
  }
}
```

(a)   (b)

Instance and static are integral parts of object-oriented programming. A data field or method is either instance or static. Do not mistakenly overlook static data fields or methods. It is a common design error to declare an instance method that should have been declared static. For example, the factorial(int n) method for computing the factorial of n should be declared static, because it is independent of any specific instance.

common design error

A constructor is always instance, because it is used to create a specific instance. A static variable or method can be invoked from an instance method, but an instance variable or method cannot be invoked from a static method.

11.6.7 Inheritance vs. Aggregation

The difference between inheritance and aggregation is the difference between an is-a relationship and a has-a relationship. For example, an apple is a fruit; thus, you would use inheritance to model the relationship between the classes Apple and Fruit. A person has a name; thus you would use aggregation to model the relationship between the classes Person and Name.

11.6.8 Interfaces vs. Abstract Classes

Both interfaces and abstract classes can be used to generalize common features. How do you decide whether to use an interface or a class? In general, a *strong is-a relationship* that clearly describes a parent–child relationship should be modeled using classes. For example, since an orange is a fruit, their relationship should be modeled using class inheritance. A *weak is-a relationship*, also known as an *is-kind-of relationship*, indicates that an object possesses a certain property. A weak is-a relationship can be modeled using interfaces. For example, all strings are comparable, so the `String` class implements the `Comparable` interface. A circle or a rectangle is a geometric object, so `Circle` can be designed as a subclass of `GeometricObject`. Circles are different and comparable based on their radii, so `Circle` can implement the `Comparable` interface.

Interfaces are more flexible than abstract classes, because a subclass can extend only one superclass but can implement any number of interfaces. However, interfaces cannot contain concrete methods. The virtues of interfaces and abstract classes can be combined by creating an interface with an abstract class that implements it. Then you can use the interface or the abstract class, whichever is convenient. For this reason, such classes are known as *convenience classes*. For example, in the Java Collections Framework, which is introduced in Chapter 22, "Java Collections Framework," the `AbstractCollection` class is a convenience class for the `Collection` interface, and the `AbstractSet` class is a convenience class for the `Set` interface.

11.7 (Optional) Modeling Dynamic Behavior Using Sequence Diagrams and Statecharts

The UML diagrams presented so far describe the properties and methods of a class or the static relationships among classes. This section introduces the sequence diagrams and statechart diagrams that model the dynamic behaviors of objects.

11.7.1 Sequence Diagrams

Sequence diagrams describe interactions among objects by depicting the time-ordering of method invocations. A sequence diagram consists of the following elements, as shown in Figure 11.14:

- **Class role** represents the roles the object plays. The objects at the top of the diagram represent class roles.

- **Lifeline** represents the existence of an object over a period of time. A vertical dotted line extending from the object is used to denote a lifeline.

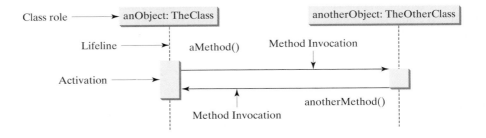

FIGURE 11.14 Sequence diagrams describe interactions between objects.

- **Activation** represents the time during which an object is performing an operation. Thin rectangles placed on lifelines are used to denote activations.

- **Method invocation** represents communication between objects. Horizontal arrows labeled with method calls are used to denote method invocations.

The interactions among the objects in the `BorrowLoan` class on page in Listing 11.5 are illustrated in Figure 11.15.

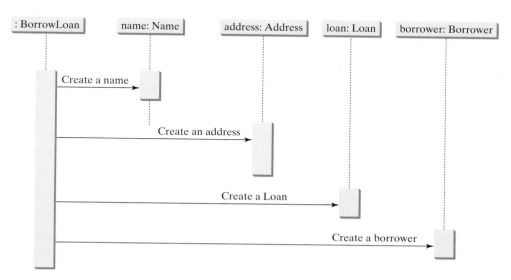

FIGURE 11.15 The `BorrowLoan` object invokes the methods in the `Name`, `Address`, `Loan`, and `Borrower` objects.

11.7.2 Statechart Diagrams

Statechart diagrams describe the flow of control of an object. A statechart diagram contains the following elements, as shown in Figure 11.16:

- **State** represents a situation during the life of an object in which it satisfies some condition, performs some action, or waits for some event to occur. All states have names. States are denoted by rectangles with rounded corners, except for the initial state, which is denoted by a small filled circle.

- **Transition** represents the relationship between two states, indicating that an object will perform some action to transfer from one state to the other. A solid arrow with appropriate method invocation denotes a transition.

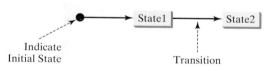

FIGURE 11.16 Statechart diagrams describe the flow of control of an object.

The life cycle of an object can be illustrated using a statechart diagram, as shown in Figure 11.17.

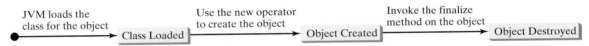

FIGURE 11.17 The life cycle of an object can be described using a statechart diagram.

11.8 Framework-Based Programming Using Java API

API

The Java API (*Application Program Interface*) consists of numerous classes and interfaces grouped into more than a dozen packages. You have used classes and interfaces in the `java.lang`, `javax.swing`, and `java.util` packages.

- `java.lang` contains core Java classes (e.g., `System`, `Math`, `Object`, `String`, `StringBuffer`, `Number`, `Character`, `Boolean`, `Byte`, `Short`, `Integer`, `Long`, `Float`, `Double`, `Comparable`, and `Cloneable`). This package is implicitly imported to every Java program.

- `javax.swing` contains the graphical user interface components for developing Swing GUI programs.

- `java.util` contains many utilities, such as `Arrays`, `ArrayList`, `Vector`, `Date`, `Calendar`, and `GregorianCalendar`.

These are just a few of the classes and interfaces you have learned. To create comprehensive projects, you have to use more classes and interfaces in the Java API. The classes and interfaces in the Java API establish a framework for programmers to develop applications using Java. For example, the classes and interfaces in the Java GUI API establish a framework for developing GUI programs. You have to use these classes and interfaces and follow their conventions and rules to create applications. This is referred to as *framework-based programming*.

framework-based programming

Once you understand the concept of Java and object-oriented programming, the most important lesson from now on is learning how to use the API to develop useful programs. The most effective way to achieve this is to imitate good examples. The book provides many carefully designed examples to demonstrate the concept of framework-based programming using the Java API. You will learn the Java GUI programming framework in Chapters 12–16, the Java exception-handling framework in Chapter 17, and the Java I/O framework in Chapter 18.

KEY TERMS

CHAPTER SUMMARY

- Developing a project involves *requirements specification, system analysis, system design, implementation, testing, deployment,* and *maintenance.* The process of designing classes calls for identifying the classes and discovering the relationships among them.

- The common relationships among classes are *association*, *aggregation*, *composition*, *dependency*, and *inheritance*.

- Some guidelines for class design are *cohesion*, *consistency*, *encapsulation*, *clarity*, and *completeness*.

- A property shared by all the instances of a class should be declared as a static property.

- Don't mistakenly overlook static data fields or methods. A method not tied to a specific instance should be declared static.

- The difference between inheritance and aggregation is the difference between an is-a relationship and a has-a relationship.

- Both interfaces and abstract classes can be used to generalize common features. How do you decide whether to use an interface or a class? In general, a *strong is-a relationship* that clearly describes a parent–child relationship should be modeled using classes.

- Interfaces are more flexible than abstract classes, because a subclass can extend only one superclass but can implement any number of interfaces. However, interfaces cannot contain concrete methods.

- Sequence diagrams describe interactions among objects by depicting the time-ordering of method invocations. Statechart diagrams describe the flow of control of an object.

REVIEW QUESTIONS

Section 11.3 Discovering Relationships Among Objects

11.1   What are the common types of relationships among classes? Describe the graphical notations for modeling the relationships among classes.

11.2   What relationship is appropriate for the following classes? Draw the relationships using UML diagrams.

- Company and Employee
- Course and Faculty
- Student and Person
- House and Window
- Account and Savings Account
- The JOptionPane class and the String class
- The Loan class and the Date class (§7.15)

Section 11.5 The Rational Class

11.3   Show the output of the following code:

```java
public class Test {
  public static void main(String[] args) {
    Rational r1 = new Rational(1, 3);
    Rational r2 = new Rational(2, 4);
    System.out.println(r1 + " + " + r2 + " = " + r1.add(r2));
    System.out.println(r2 + " + " + r1 + " = " + r2.add(r1));
    System.out.println(r1 + " - " + r2 + " = " + r1.subtract(r2));
    System.out.println(r2 + " - " + r1 + " = " + r2.subtract(r1));
```

```
System.out.println(r1 + " * " + r2 + " = " + r1.multiply(r2));
System.out.println(r2 + " * " + r1 + " = " + r2.multiply(r1));
System.out.println(r1 + " / " + r2 + " = " + r1.divide(r2));
System.out.println(r2 + " / " + r1 + " = " + r2.divide(r1));
System.out.println(r1 + " = " + r1.doubleValue());
System.out.println(r2 + " = " + r2.doubleValue());
    }
}
```

11.4 What is wrong in the following code?

```
Number r = new Rational();
System.out.println(r);
System.out.println(r.doubleValue());
System.out.println(r.add(new Rational()));
System.out.println((Rational)r.add(new Rational()));
System.out.println(((Rational)r).add(new Rational()));
```

11.5 What is wrong in the following code?

```
Number r = new Number();
System.out.println(r);
```

11.6 Is the following code correct?

```
Comparable r = new Rational();
System.out.println(r);
```

```
Comparable r = new Rational();
System.out.println(
    r.compareTo(new Rational()));
```

(a)   (b)

Section 11.6 Class Design Guidelines

11.7 What is cohesion? Give examples of cohesive class design.

11.8 What is consistency? Give examples of nonconsistent class design.

11.9 What is encapsulation? What are the benefits of data field encapsulation?

11.10 When is it appropriate to use the `protected` modifier?

11.11 Which of the following is poor design?

- A data field is derived from other data fields in the same class.
- A method must be invoked after/before invoking another method in the same class.
- A method is an instance method, but it does not reference any instance data fields or invoke instance methods.
- A parameter is passed from a constructor to initialize a static data field.

11.12 Which of the following is incorrect?

- A static method may reference instance data fields or invoke instance methods.
- An instance method may reference static data fields or invoke static methods.
- A constructor may be static.
- A constructor may be private.
- A constructor may invoke a static method.
- A constructor may invoke an overloaded constructor.
- A constructor invokes its superclass no-arg constructor by default if it does not invoke an overloaded constructor or its superclass's constructor.

- An abstract class contains constructors.
- The constructors in an abstract class are public.
- The constructors in an abstract class are private.
- You may declare a final abstract class.
- An interface may contain constructors.
- An interface may contain instance data fields.
- An interface may contain static methods.

PROGRAMMING EXERCISES

Section 11.5 The `Rational` Class

11.1 (*Using the `Rational` class*) Write a program that will compute the following summation series using the `Rational` class:

$$\frac{1}{2} + \frac{2}{3} + \frac{3}{4} + \cdots + \frac{98}{99} + \frac{99}{100}$$

11.2* (*Demonstrating the benefits of encapsulation*) Rewrite the `Rational` class in Section 11.5 using a new internal representation for numerator and denominator. Declare an array of two integers as follows:

```
private long[] r = new long[2];
```

Use `r[0]` to represent the numerator and `r[1]` to represent the denominator. The signatures of the methods in the `Rational` class are not changed, so a client application that uses the previous `Rational` class can continue to use this new `Rational` class without being recompiled.

11.3* (*Creating a rational number calculator*) Write a program similar to Listing 8.4, Calculator.java. Instead of using integers, use rationals, as shown in Figure 11.18. You will need to use the `split` method in the `String` class, introduced in §8.6.3, "Replacing and Splitting Strings," to retrieve the numerator string and denominator string, and convert strings into integers using the `Integer.parseInt` method.

```
Command Prompt                              _ □ ×
 19  20  21  22  23  24  25
 26  27  28  29  30

C:\exercise>java Exercise11_3 1/2 + 1/3
1/2 + 1/3 = 5/6

C:\exercise>java Exercise11_3 1/2 - 1/3
```

FIGURE 11.18 The program takes three arguments (operand1, operator, and operand2) from the command line and displays the expression and the result of the arithmetic operation.

Comprehensive

11.4** (*The `Person` and `Student` classes*) Design the `Student` class that extends `Person`. Implement the `compareTo` method in the `Person` class to compare persons in alphabetical order of their last name. Implement the `compareTo` method to compare students in alphabetical order of their major and last name. Draw a UML diagram that involves `Person`, `Student`, `Comparable`, and `Name`.

Write a test program with the following four methods:

```
/** Sort an array of comparable objects  */
public static void sort(Object[] list)
```

```
/** Print an array of objects */
public static void printList(Object[] object)
```

```
/** Return the max object in an array of comparable objects */
public static Object max(Object[] list)
```

main method: Test the **sort**, **printList**, and **max** methods using an array of four students, an array of four strings, an array of one hundred random rationals, and an array of one hundred random integers.

PART 3

GUI PROGRAMMING

Part 1, "Fundamentals of Programming," introduced basic programming concepts that are supported in all programming languages. Part 2, "Object-Oriented Programming," introduced object-oriented programming concepts, principles, and practices that are common in the object-oriented programming languages. Java is not simply a programming language. It is also a development and deployment platform with an extensive set of classes and interfaces in the API. You have to use the classes and interfaces in the API and follow their conventions and rules to develop your own projects. The design of the API for Java GUI programming is an excellent example of how the object-oriented principle is applied. In the chapters that follow, you will learn the framework of Java GUI API and use the GUI components to develop user-friendly interfaces for applications and applets.

Chapter 12
Getting Started with GUI Programming

Chapter 13
Graphics

Chapter 14
Event-Driven Programming

Chapter 15
Creating User Interfaces

Chapter 16
Applets and Multimedia

Prerequisites for Part 3

Part 3, "GUI Programming," may be intertwined with Part 2, "Object-Oriented Programming." You can cover GUI programming in Chapters 12 and 13, "Getting Started with GUI Programming" and "Graphics," after you have covered abstract classes in Chapter 10, "Abstract Classes and Interfaces."

GUI early

Interfaces in Chapter 10, "Abstract Classes and Interfaces," can be covered just before Chapter 14, "*Event-Driven Programming*."

event-driven programming

applets early

The concept and simple examples of using applets can be covered earlier after Chapter 12, "GUI Basics."

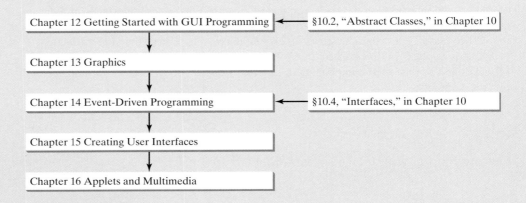

CHAPTER 12

GETTING STARTED WITH GUI PROGRAMMING

Objectives

- To get a glimpse of simple GUI components (§12.2).

- To describe the Java GUI API hierarchy (§12.3).

- To create user interfaces using frames, panels, and simple GUI components (§12.4).

- To understand the role of layout managers (§12.5).

- To use the FlowLayout, GridLayout, and BorderLayout managers to layout components in a container (§12.5).

- To specify colors and fonts using the Color and Font classes (§§12.6–12.7).

- To use JPanel as subcontainers (§12.8).

- To apply common features such as borders, tool tips, fonts, and colors on Swing components (§12.9).

- To use borders to visually group user-interface components (§12.9).

- To create image icons using the ImageIcon class (§12.10).

12.1 Introduction

Until now, you have only used dialog boxes and the command window for input and output. You used `JOptionPane.showInputDialog` to obtain input, and `JOptionPane.showMessageDialog` and `System.out.println` to display results. These approaches have limitations and are inconvenient. For example, to read ten numbers, you have to open ten input dialog boxes. Starting with this chapter, you will learn Java GUI programming. You will create custom graphical user interfaces (GUI, pronounced *goo-ee*) to obtain input and display output in the same user interface.

This chapter introduces the basics of Java GUI programming. Specifically, it discusses GUI components and their relationships, containers and layout managers, colors, fonts, borders, and tool tips.

12.2 GUI Components

You create graphical user interfaces using GUI objects such as buttons, labels, text fields, check boxes, radio buttons, and combo boxes. Each type of GUI object is defined in a class, such as `JButton`, `JLabel`, `JTextField`, `JCheckBox`, `JRadioButton`, and `JComboBox`. Each GUI component class provides several constructors that you can use to create GUI component objects. The following are examples to create buttons, labels, text fields, check boxes, radio buttons, and combo boxes:

```java
// Create a button with text OK
JButton jbtOK = new JButton("OK");

// Create a label with text "Enter your name: "
JLabel jlblName = new JLabel("Enter your name: ");

// Create a text field with text "Type Name Here"
JTextField jtfName = new JTextField("Type Name Here");

// Create a check box with text bold
JCheckBox jchkBold = new JCheckBox("Bold");

// Create a radio button with text red
JRadioButton jrbRed = new JRadioButton("Red");

// Create a combo box with choices red, green, and blue
JComboBox jcboColor = new JComboBox(new String[]{"Red",
  "Green", "Blue"});
```

Figure 12.1 shows these objects displayed in a frame. How to add components into a frame will be introduced in §12.4.2.

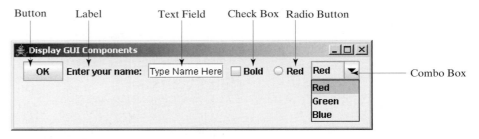

Figure 12.1   The GUI component objects can be displayed.

12.2.1 Swing vs. AWT

Why do the GUI component classes have the prefix *J*? Instead of `JButton`, why not name it simply `Button`? In fact, there is a class already named `Button` in the `java.awt` package.

When Java was introduced, the GUI classes were bundled in a library known as the Abstract Windows Toolkit (AWT). For every platform on which Java runs, the AWT components are automatically mapped to the platform-specific components through their respective agents, known as *peers*. AWT is fine for developing simple graphical user interfaces, but not for developing comprehensive GUI projects. Besides, AWT is prone to platform-specific bugs because its peer-based approach relies heavily on the underlying platform. With the release of Java 2, the AWT user-interface components were replaced by a more robust, versatile, and flexible library known as *Swing components*. Swing components are painted directly on canvases using Java code, except for components that are subclasses of `java.awt.Window` or `java.awt.Panel`, which must be drawn using native GUI on a specific platform. Swing components are less dependent on the target platform and use less of the native GUI resource. For this reason, Swing components that don't rely on native GUI are referred to as *lightweight components,* and AWT components are referred to as *heavyweight components.* lightweight
heavyweight

To distinguish new Swing component classes from their AWT counterparts, the names of Swing GUI component classes begin with a prefixed *J*. Although AWT components are still supported in Java 2, it is better to learn to how program using Swing components, because the AWT user-interface components will eventually fade away. This book uses Swing GUI components exclusively. why prefix J?

12.3 The Java GUI API

The design of the Java API for GUI programming is an excellent example of the use of classes, inheritance, and interfaces. The API contains the essential classes listed below. Their hierarchical relationships are shown in Figures 12.2 and 12.3.

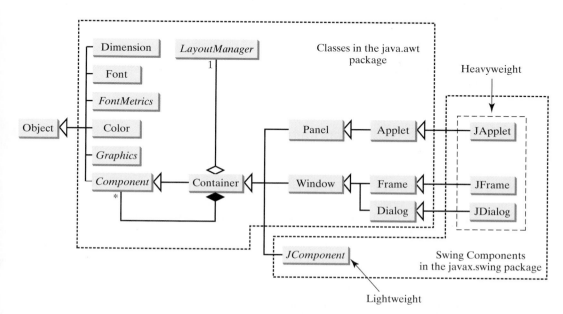

FIGURE 12.2 Java GUI programming utilizes the classes shown in this hierarchical diagram.

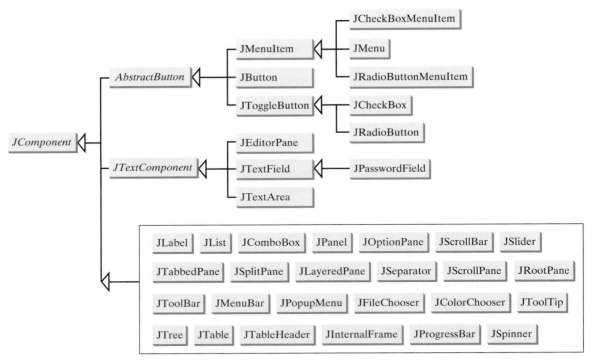

FIGURE 12.3 JComponent and its subclasses are the basic elements for building graphical user interfaces.

The GUI classes can be classified into three groups: *container classes*, *helper classes*, and *component classes*. The container classes, such as JFrame, JPanel, and JApplet, are used to contain other components. The helper classes, such as Graphics, Color, Font, FontMetrics, and Dimension, are used by components and containers to draw and place objects. The GUI component classes, such as JButton, JTextField, JTextArea, JComboBox, JList, JRadioButton, and JMenu, are subclasses of JComponent.

 Note

The JFrame, JApplet, JDialog, and JComponent classes and their subclasses are grouped in the javax.swing package. All the other classes in Figure 12.2 are grouped in the java.awt package.

12.3.1 Swing GUI Components

Component is a superclass of all the user-interface classes, and JComponent is a superclass of all the lightweight Swing components. Since JComponent is an abstract class, you cannot use new JComponent() to create an instance of JComponent. However, you can use the constructors of concrete subclasses of JComponent to create JComponent instances. It is important to become familiar with the class inheritance hierarchy. For example, the following statements all display true:

```
JButton jbtOK = new JButton("OK");
System.out.println(jbtOK instanceof JButton);
System.out.println(jbtOK instanceof AbstractButton);
System.out.println(jbtOK instanceof JComponent);
System.out.println(jbtOK instanceof Container);
System.out.println(jbtOK instanceof Component);
System.out.println(jbtOK instanceof Object);
```

12.3.2   Container Classes

Container classes are GUI components that are used as containers to contain other GUI components. `Window`, `Panel`, `Applet`, `Frame`, and `Dialog` are the container classes for AWT components. To work with Swing components, use `Component`, `Container`, `JFrame`, `JDialog`, `JApplet`, and `JPanel`.

- `Container` is used to group components. Frames, panels, and applets are examples of containers.

- `JFrame` is a window not contained inside another window. It is the container that holds other Swing user-interface components in Java GUI applications.

- `JDialog` is a popup window or message box generally used as a temporary window to receive additional information from the user or to provide notification that an event has occurred.

- `JApplet` is a subclass of `Applet`. You must extend `JApplet` to create a Swing-based Java applet.

- `JPanel` is an invisible container that holds user-interface components. Panels can be nested. You can place panels inside a container that includes a panel. `JPanel` can also be used as a canvas to draw graphics.

12.3.3   GUI Helper Classes

The helper classes, such as `Graphics`, `Color`, `Font`, `FontMetrics`, `Dimension`, and `LayoutManager`, are not subclasses of `Component`. They are used to describe the properties of GUI components, such as graphics context, colors, fonts, and dimension.

- `Graphics` is an abstract class that provides a graphical context for drawing strings, lines, and simple shapes.

- `Color` deals with the colors of GUI components. For example, you can specify background or foreground colors in components like `JFrame` and `JPanel`, or you can specify colors of lines, shapes, and strings in drawings.

- `Font` specifies fonts for the text and drawings on GUI components. For example, you can specify the font type (e.g., SansSerif), style (e.g., bold), and size (e.g., 24 points) for the text on a button.

- `FontMetrics` is an abstract class used to get the properties of the fonts.

- `Dimension` encapsulates the width and height of a component (in integer precision) in a single object.

- `LayoutManager` is an interface whose instances specify how components are arranged in a container.

Note
The helper classes are in the `java.awt` package. The Swing components do not replace all the classes in AWT, only the AWT GUI component classes (e.g., `Button`, `TextField`, `TextArea`). The AWT helper classes remain unchanged.

12.4   Frames

To create a user interface, you need to create either a frame or an applet to hold the user-interface components. Creating Java applets will be introduced in Chapter 16, "Applets and Multimedia." This section introduces frames.

12.4.1 Creating a Frame

To create a frame, use the `JFrame` class, as shown in Figure 12.4.

javax.swing.JFrame	
+JFrame()	Creates a default frame with no title.
+JFrame(title: String)	Creates a frame with the specified title.
+setSize(width: int, height: int): void	Specifies the size of the frame.
+setLocation(x: int, y: int): void	Specifies the upper-left-corner location of the frame.
+setVisible(visible: boolean): void	Sets true to display the frame.
+setDefaultCloseOperation(mode: int): void	Specifies the operation when the frame is closed.
+setLocationRelativeTo (c: Component): void	Sets the location of the frame relative to the specified component. If the component is null, the frame is centered on the screen.

FIGURE 12.4 Frame is a top-level container to hold GUI components.

The program in Listing 12.1 creates a frame.

LISTING 12.1 MyFrame.java

```
1 import javax.swing.*;
2
3 public class MyFrame {
4   public static void main(String[] args) {
5     JFrame frame = new JFrame("MyFrame"); // Create a frame
6     frame.setSize(400, 300); // Set the frame size
7     frame.setLocationRelativeTo(null); // New since JDK 1.4
8     frame.setDefaultCloseOperation(JFrame.EXIT_ON_CLOSE);
9     frame.setVisible(true); // Display the frame
10  }
11 }
```

import package (line 1)
create frame (line 5)
set size (line 6)
center frame (line 7)
close upon exit (line 8)
display the frame (line 9)

The frame is not displayed *until* the `frame.setVisible(true)` method is invoked. `frame.setSize(400, 300)` specifies that the frame is 400 pixels wide and 300 pixels high. If the `setSize` method is not used, the frame will be sized to display just the title bar. Since the `setSize` and `setVisible` methods are both defined in the `Component` class, they are inherited by the `JFrame` class. Later you will see that these methods are also useful in many other subclasses of `Component`.

When you run the `MyFrame` program, a window will be displayed on-screen (see Figure 12.5(a)).

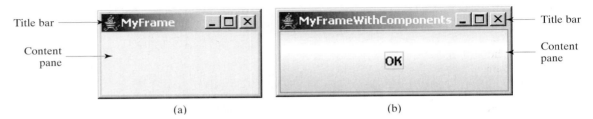

Title bar — MyFrame

Content pane

MyFrameWithComponents — Title bar

OK

Content pane

(a)   (b)

FIGURE 12.5 (a) The program creates and displays a frame with the title `MyFrame`. (b) An OK button is added to the frame.

Invoking `setLocationRelativeTo(null)` (line 7) centers the frame on the screen. Invoking `setDefaultCloseOperation(JFrame.EXIT ON CLOSE)` (line 8) tells the program to terminate when the frame is closed. If this statement is not used, the program does not terminate when the frame is closed. In that case, you have to stop the program by pressing Ctrl+C at the DOS prompt window in Windows or use the kill command to stop the process in Unix.

 Note

Recall that a pixel is the smallest unit of space for drawing on the screen. You can think of a pixel as a small rectangle and think of the screen as paved with pixels. The *resolution* specifies the number of pixels per square inch. The more pixels the screen has, the higher the screen's resolution. The higher the resolution, the more fine detail you can see.

pixel and resolution

12.4.2 Adding Components to a Frame

The frame shown in Figure 12.5(a) is empty. Using the **add** method, you can add components into the frame, as in Listing 12.2.

LISTING 12.2 MyFrameWithComponents.java

```
 1 import javax.swing.*;
 2
 3 public class MyFrameWithComponents {
 4   public static void main(String[] args) {
 5     JFrame frame = new JFrame("MyFrameWithComponents");
 6
 7     // Add a button into the frame
 8     JButton jbtOK = new JButton("OK");
 9     frame.add(jbtOK);
10
11     frame.setSize(400, 300);
12     frame.setDefaultCloseOperation(JFrame.EXIT_ON_CLOSE);
13     frame.setLocationRelativeTo(null); // Center the frame
14     frame.setVisible(true);
15   }
16 }
```

create a button
add to frame

set size
exit upon closing
  window
center the frame
set visible

Each **JFrame** contains a content pane. A content pane is an instance of **java.awt.Container**. The GUI components such as buttons are placed in the content pane in a frame. Prior to JDK 1.5, you have to use the **getContentPane** method in the **JFrame** class to return the content pane of the frame, and then invoke the content pane's **add** method to place a component into the content pane. This was cumbersome. JDK 1.5 allows you to place components to the content pane by invoking a frame's **add** method. This new feature is called *content pane delegation*. Strictly speaking, a component is added into the content pane of a frame. But for simplicity we say that a component is added to a frame.

content pane delegation

An object of **JButton** was created using **new JButton("OK")**, and this object was added to the content pane of the frame (line 9).

The **add(Component comp)** method defined in the **Container** class adds an instance of **Component** to the container. Since **JButton** is a subclass of **Component**, an instance of **JButton** is also an instance of **Component**. To remove a component from a container, use the **remove** method. The following statement removes the button from the container:

```
container.remove(jbtOK);
```

When you run the program **MyFrameWithComponents**, the window will be displayed as in Figure 12.5(b). The button is always centered in the frame and occupies the entire frame no matter how you resize it. This is because components are put in the frame by the content pane's layout manager, and the default layout manager for the content pane places the button in the center. In the next section, you will use several different layout managers to place components in other locations as desired.

12.5 Layout Managers

In many other window systems, the user-interface components are arranged by using hard-coded pixel measurements. For example, put a button at location (10, 10) in the window. Using hard-coded pixel measurements, the user interface might look fine on one system but be unusable on another. Java's layout managers provide a level of abstraction that automatically maps your user interface on all window systems.

Note

Java also supports hard-coded fixed layout, which will be covered in Chapter 28, "Containers, Layout Managers, and Borders." Since it is platform-dependent, it is rarely used in practice.

The Java GUI components are placed in containers, where they are arranged by the container's layout manager. In the preceding program, you did not specify where to place the OK button in the frame, but Java knows where to place it because the layout manager works behind the scenes to place components in the correct locations. A layout manager is created using a layout manager class. Every layout manager class implements the `LayoutManager` interface.

Layout managers are set in containers using the `setLayout(LayoutManager)` method. For example, you can use the following statements to create an instance of *X*Layout and set it in a container:

```
LayoutManager layoutManager = new XLayout();
container.setLayout(layoutManager);
```

This section introduces three basic layout managers: `FlowLayout`, `GridLayout`, and `BorderLayout`. More layout managers will be introduced in Chapter 28, "Containers, Layout Managers, and Borders."

12.5.1 FlowLayout

`FlowLayout` is the simplest layout manager. The components are arranged in the container from left to right in the order in which they were added. When one row is filled, a new row is started. You can specify the way the components are aligned by using one of three constants: `FlowLayout.RIGHT`, `FlowLayout.CENTER`, or `FlowLayout.LEFT`. You can also specify the gap between components in pixels. The constructors and methods in `FlowLayout` are shown in Figure 12.6.

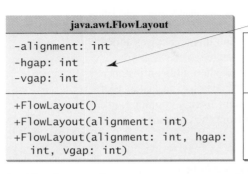

FIGURE 12.6 `FlowLayout` lays out components row by row.

Listing 12.3 gives a program that demonstrates flow layout. The program adds three labels and text fields into the frame with a `FlowLayout` manager. If you resize the frame, the components may be rearranged. In Figure 12.7(a), the first row has three components, but in Figure 12.7(b), the first row has four components, because the width has been increased.

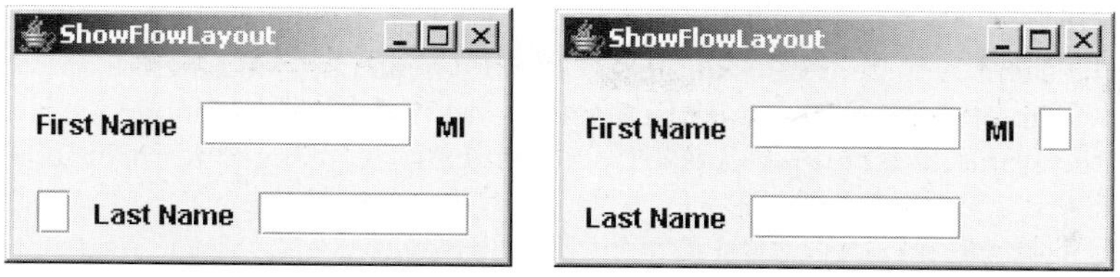

(a)   (b)

FIGURE 12.7   The components are added by the `FlowLayout` manager to fill in the rows in the container one after another.

LISTING 12.3   ShowFlowLayout.java

```java
1  import javax.swing.JLabel;
2  import javax.swing.JTextField;
3  import javax.swing.JFrame;
4  import java.awt.FlowLayout;
5
6  public class ShowFlowLayout extends JFrame {                          extends JFrame
7    public ShowFlowLayout() {
8      // Set FlowLayout, aligned left with horizontal gap 10
9      // and vertical gap 20 between components
10     setLayout (new FlowLayout(FlowLayout.LEFT, 10, 20));               set layout
11
12     // Add labels and text fields to the frame
13     add(new JLabel("First Name"));                                    add label
14     add(new JTextField(8));                                           add text field
15     add(new JLabel("MI"));
16     add(new JTextField(1));
17     add(new JLabel("Last Name"));
18     add(new JTextField(8));
19   }
20
21   /** Main method */
22   public static void main(String[] args) {
23     ShowFlowLayout frame = new ShowFlowLayout();                      create frame
24     frame.setTitle("ShowFlowLayout");
25     frame.setLocationRelativeTo(null); // Center the frame
26     frame.setDefaultCloseOperation(JFrame.EXIT_ON_CLOSE);
27     frame.setSize(200, 200);
28     frame.setVisible(true);                                           set visible
29   }
30 }
```

This example creates a program using a style different from the programs in the preceding section, where frames were created using the `JFrame` class. This example creates a class named `ShowFlowLayout` that extends the `JFrame` class (line 6). The `main` method in this program creates an instance of `ShowFlowLayout` (line 23). The constructor of `ShowFlowLayout` constructs and places the components in the frame. This is the preferred style of creating GUI applications for three reasons:

1. Creating a GUI application means creating a frame, so it is natural to define a frame to extend `JFrame`.

2. The frame may be further extended to add new components or functions.

3. The class can be easily reused. For example, you can create multiple frames by creating multiple instances of the class.

Using one style consistently makes programs easy to read. From now on, most of the GUI main classes will extend the `JFrame` class. The constructor of the main class constructs the user interface. The `main` method creates an instance of the main class and then displays the frame.

In this example, the `FlowLayout` manager is used to place components in a frame. If you resize the frame, the components are automatically rearranged to fit in it, as shown in Figure 12.7(b).

If you replace the `setLayout` statement (line 10) with `setLayout(new FlowLayout (FlowLayout.RIGHT, 0, 0))`, all the rows of buttons will be right-aligned with no gaps.

An anonymous `FlowLayout` object was created in the statement (line 10):

```
setLayout(new FlowLayout(FlowLayout.LEFT, 10, 20));
```

which is equivalent to:

```
FlowLayout layout = new FlowLayout(FlowLayout.LEFT, 10, 20);
setLayout(layout);
```

This code creates an explicit reference to the object `layout` of the `FlowLayout` class. The explicit reference is not necessary, because the object is not directly referenced in the `ShowFlowLayout` class.

The `setTitle` method (line 24) is defined in the `java.awt.Frame` class. Since `JFrame` is a subclass of `Frame`, you can use it to set a title for an object of `JFrame`.

Suppose you add the same button into the container ten times, will ten buttons appear in the container? No, only the last one will be displayed.

Caution
Do not forget to put the `new` operator before a layout manager class when setting a layout style; for example, `setLayout(new FlowLayout())`.

Note
The constructor `ShowFlowLayout()` does not explicitly invoke the constructor `JFrame()`, but the constructor `JFrame()` is invoked implicitly. See §9.3.2, "Constructor Chaining."

12.5.2 GridLayout   *(in a Matrix format decide the rows, columns)*

The `GridLayout` manager arranges components in a grid (matrix) formation with the number of rows and columns defined by the constructor. The components are placed in the grid from left to right, starting with the first row, then the second, and so on, in the order in which they are added. The constructors and methods in `GridLayout` are shown in Figure 12.8.

> The get and set methods for these data fields are provided in the class, but omitted in the UML diagram for brevity.

java.awt.GridLayout	
-rows: int	The number of rows in this layout manager (default: 1).
-columns: int	The number of columns in this layout manager (default: 1).
-hgap: int	The horizontal gap of this layout manager (default: 0).
-vgap: int	The vertical gap of this layout manager (default: 0).
+GridLayout()	Creates a default GridLayout manager.
+GridLayout(rows: int, columns: int)	Creates a GridLayout with a specified number of rows and columns.
+GridLayout(rows: int, columns: int, hgap: int, vgap: int)	Creates a GridLayout manager with a specified number of rows and columns, horizontal gap, and vertical gap.

FIGURE 12.8 `GridLayout` lays out components in equal-sized cells on a grid.

You can specify the number of rows and columns in the grid. The basic rules are as follows:

- The number of rows or the number of columns can be zero, but not both. If one is zero and the other is nonzero, the nonzero dimension is fixed, while the zero dimension is determined dynamically by the layout manager. For example, if you specify zero rows and three columns for a grid that has ten components, GridLayout creates three fixed columns of four rows, with the last row containing one component. If you specify three rows and zero columns for a grid that has ten components, GridLayout creates three fixed rows of four columns, with the last row containing two components.

- If both the number of rows and the number of columns are nonzero, the number of rows is the dominating parameter; that is, the number of rows is fixed, and the layout manager dynamically calculates the number of columns. For example, if you specify three rows and three columns for a grid that has ten components, GridLayout creates three fixed rows of four columns, with the last row containing two components.

Listing 12.4 gives a program that demonstrates grid layout. The program is similar to the one in Listing 12.3. It adds three labels and three text fields to the frame of GridLayout instead of FlowLayout, as shown in Figure 12.9.

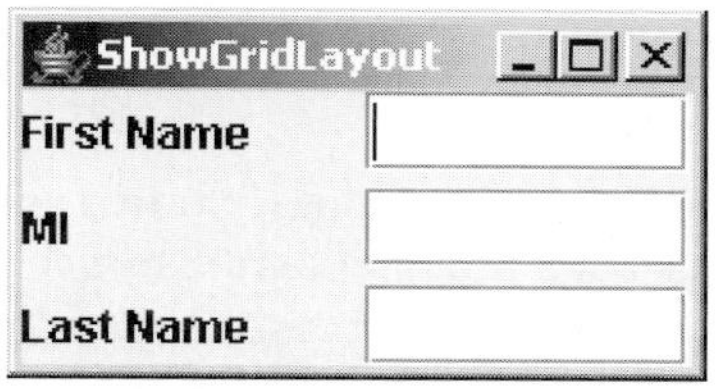

FIGURE 12.9 The GridLayout manager divides the container into grids, then the components are added to fill in the cells row by row.

LISTING 12.4 ShowGridLayout.java

```java
 1 import javax.swing.JLabel;
 2 import javax.swing.JTextField;
 3 import javax.swing.JFrame;
 4 import java.awt.GridLayout;
 5
 6 public class ShowGridLayout extends JFrame {
 7   public ShowGridLayout() {
 8     // Set GridLayout, 3 rows, 2 columns, and gaps 5 between
 9     // components horizontally and vertically
10     setLayout(new GridLayout(3, 2, 5, 5));               set layout
11
12     // Add labels and text fields to the frame
13     add(new JLabel("First Name"));                       add label
14     add(new JTextField(8));                              add text field
15     add(new JLabel("MI"));
16     add(new JTextField(1));
17     add(new JLabel("Last Name"));
18     add(new JTextField(8));
19   }
20
21   /** Main method */
22   public static void main(String[] args) {
23     ShowGridLayout frame = new ShowGridLayout();         create a frame
24     frame.setTitle("ShowGridLayout");
25     frame.setLocationRelativeTo(null); // Center the frame
26     frame.setDefaultCloseOperation(JFrame.EXIT_ON_CLOSE);
```

```
27     frame.setSize(200, 125);
28     frame.setVisible(true);
29   }
30 }
```

If you resize the frame, the layout of the buttons remains unchanged (i.e., the number of rows and columns does not change, and the gaps don't change either).

All components are given equal size in the container of `GridLayout`.

Replacing the `setLayout` statement (line 10) with `setLayout(new GridLayout(3, 10))` would still yield three rows and *two* columns. The columns parameter is ignored because the rows parameter is nonzero. The actual number of columns is calculated by the layout manager.

What would happen if the `setLayout` statement (line 10) is replaced with `setLayout (new GridLayout(4, 2))` or with `setLayout(new GridLayout(2, 2))`? Please try it yourself.

Note

In `FlowLayout` and `GridLayout`, the order in which the components are added to the container is important. It determines the location of the components in the container.

12.5.3 BorderLayout

The `BorderLayout` manager divides the window into five areas: East, South, West, North, and Center. Components are added to a `BorderLayout` by using **add(Component, index)**, where **index** is a constant `BorderLayout.EAST`, `BorderLayout.SOUTH`, `Border-Layout.WEST`, `BorderLayout.NORTH`, or `BorderLayout.CENTER`. The constructors and methods in `BorderLayout` are shown in Figure 12.10.

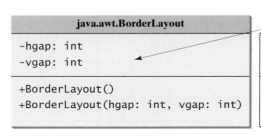

The get and set methods for these data fields are provided in the class, but omitted in the UML diagram for brevity.

java.awt.BorderLayout	
-hgap: int	The horizontal gap of this layout manager (default: 0).
-vgap: int	The vertical gap of this layout manager (default: 0).
+BorderLayout()	Creates a default BorderLayout manager.
+BorderLayout(hgap: int, vgap: int)	Creates a BorderLayout manager with a specified number of horizontal gap, and vertical gap.

FIGURE 12.10 `BorderLayout` lays out components in five areas.

The components are laid out according to their preferred sizes and where they are placed in the container. The North and South components can stretch horizontally; the East and West components can stretch vertically; the Center component can stretch both horizontally and vertically to fill any empty space.

Listing 12.5 gives a program that demonstrates border layout. The program adds five buttons labeled **East**, **South**, **West**, **North**, and **Center** into the frame with a `BorderLayout` manager, as shown in Figure 12.11.

LISTING 12.5 ShowBorderLayout.java

```
1 import javax.swing.JButton;
2 import javax.swing.JFrame;
3 import java.awt.BorderLayout;
4
```

```
 5 public class ShowBorderLayout extends JFrame {
 6   public ShowBorderLayout() {
 7     // Set BorderLayout with horizontal gap 5 and vertical gap 10
 8     setLayout(new BorderLayout(5, 10));                            set layout
 9
10     // Add buttons to the frame
11     add(new JButton("East"), BorderLayout.EAST);                   add buttons
12     add(new JButton("South"), BorderLayout.SOUTH);
13     add(new JButton("West"), BorderLayout.WEST);
14     add(new JButton("North"), BorderLayout.NORTH);
15     add(new JButton("Center"), BorderLayout.CENTER);
16   }
17
18   /** Main method */
19   public static void main(String[] args) {
20     ShowBorderLayout frame = new ShowBorderLayout();               create a frame
21     frame.setTitle("ShowBorderLayout");
22     frame.setLocationRelativeTo(null); // Center the frame
23     frame.setDefaultCloseOperation(JFrame.EXIT_ON_CLOSE);
24     frame.setSize(300, 200);
25     frame.setVisible(true);                                        set visible
26   }
27 }
```

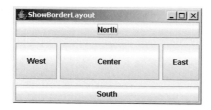

FIGURE 12.11 BorderLayout divides the container into five areas, each of which can hold a component.

The buttons are added to the frame (lines 11–15). Note that the **add** method for **BorderLayout** is different from the one for **FlowLayout** and **GridLayout**. With **BorderLayout** you specify where to put the components.

It is unnecessary to place components to occupy all the areas. If you remove the East button from the program and rerun it, you will see that the center stretches rightward to occupy the East area.

Note

For convenience, **BorderLayout** interprets the absence of an index specification as **BorderLayout.CENTER**. For example, **add(component)** is the same as **add(Component, BorderLayout.CENTER)**. If you add two components into a container of **BorderLayout**, as follows,

```
container.add(component1);
container.add(component2);
```

only the last component is displayed.

12.5.4   Properties of Layout Managers

Layout managers have properties that can be changed dynamically. **FlowLayout** has **alignment**, **hgap**, and **vgap** properties. You can use the **setAlignment**, **setHgap**, and setVgap methods to specify the alignment and the horizontal and vertical gaps. GridLayout has the rows, columns, hgap, and vgap properties. You can use the setRows, setColumns, setHgap, and setVgap methods to specify the number of rows, the number of columns, and the horizontal and vertical gaps. BorderLayout has the hgap and vgap properties. You can use the setHgap and setVgap methods to specify the horizontal and vertical gaps.

In the preceding sections, an anonymous layout manager is used because the properties of a layout manager do not change once it is created. If you have to change the properties of a layout manager dynamically, the layout manager must be explicitly referenced by a variable. You can then change the properties of the layout manager through the variable. For example, the following code creates a layout manager and sets its properties:

```
// Create a layout manager
FlowLayout flowLayout = new FlowLayout();

// Set layout properties
flowLayout.setAlignment(FlowLayout.RIGHT);
flowLayout.setHgap(10);
flowLayout.setVgap(20);
```

12.5.5 (Optional) The `validate` and `doLayout` Methods

validate()

A container can have only one layout manager at a time. You can change its layout manager by using the setLayout(aNewLayout) method and then use the validate() method to force the container to again layout the components in the container using the new layout manager.

doLayout()

If you use the same layout manager but change its properties, you need to use the doLayout() method to force the container to re-layout the components using the new properties of the layout manager.

12.6 The **Color** Class

You can set colors for GUI components by using the java.awt.Color class. Colors are made of red, green, and blue components, each of which is represented by an unsigned byte value that describes its intensity, ranging from 0 (darkest shade) to 255 (lightest shade). This is known as the *RGB model*.

You can create a color using the following constructor:

public Color(**int** r, **int** g, **int** b);

in which r, g, and b specify a color by its red, green, and blue components. For example,

Color color = **new** Color(128, 100, 100);

 Note
The arguments r, g, b are between 0 and 255. If a value beyond this range is passed to the argument, an IllegalArgumentException would throw.

IllegalArgument-
Exception

You can use the setBackground(Color c) and setForeground(Color c) methods defined in the java.awt.Component class to set a component's background and foreground colors. Here is an example of setting the background and foreground of a button:

```
JButton jbtOK = new JButton();
jbtOK.setBackground(color);
jbtOK.setForeground(new Color(100, 1, 1));
```

Alternatively, you can use one of the thirteen standard colors (black, blue, cyan, darkGray, gray, green, lightGray, magenta, orange, pink, red, white, yellow)

defined as constants in `java.awt.Color`. The following code, for instance, sets the foreground color of a button to red:

```
jbtOK.setForeground(Color.red);
```

Note

The standard color names are constants, but they are named as variables with lowercase for the first word and uppercase for the first letters of subsequent words. Thus the color names violate the Java naming convention. Since JDK 1.4, you can also use the new constants BLACK, BLUE, CYAN, DARK_GRAY, GRAY, GREEN, LIGHT_GRAY, MAGENTA, ORANGE, PINK, RED, WHITE, and YELLOW.

color constants

12.7 The **Font** Class

You can create a font using the `java.awt.Font` class and set fonts for the components using the `setFont` method in the `Component` class.

The constructor for `Font` is:

```
public Font(String name, int style, int size);
```

You can choose a font name from `SansSerif`, `Serif`, `Monospaced`, `Dialog`, or `DialogInput`, choose a style from `Font.PLAIN` (0), `Font.BOLD` (1), `Font.ITALIC` (2), and `Font.BOLD` + `Font.ITALIC` (3), and specify a font size of any positive integer. For example, the following statements create two fonts and set one font to a button:

```
Font font1 = new Font("SansSerif", Font.BOLD, 16);
Font font2 = new Font("Serif", Font.BOLD + Font.ITALIC, 12);

JButton jbtOK = new JButton("OK");
jbtOK.setFont(font1);
```

Tip (Optional)

If your system supports other fonts, such as "Times New Roman," you can use it to create a `Font` object. To find the fonts available on your system, you need to create an instance of `java.awt.GraphicsEnvironment` using its static method `getLocalGraphicsEnvironment()`. `GraphicsEnvironment` is an abstract class that describes the graphics environment on a particular system. You can use its `getAllFonts()` method to obtain all the available fonts on the system, and its `getAvailableFontFamilyNames()` method to obtain the names of all the available fonts. For example, the following statements print all the available font names in the system:

find available fonts

```
GraphicsEnvironment e =
  GraphicsEnvironment.getLocalGraphicsEnvironment();
String[] fontnames = e.getAvailableFontFamilyNames();

for (int i = 0; i < fontnames.length; i++)
  System.out.println(fontnames[i]);
```

12.8 Using Panels as Subcontainers

Suppose that you want to place ten buttons and a text field on a frame. The buttons are placed in grid formation, but the text field is placed on a separate row. It is difficult to achieve the desired look by placing all the components in a single container. With Java GUI programming, you can divide a window into panels. Panels act as subcontainers to group user-interface components. You add the buttons in one panel, and then add the panel into the frame. The Swing version of panel is `JPanel`. You can use `new JPanel()` to create a panel with a default `FlowLayout` manager or `new JPanel(LayoutManager)` to create a panel with the specified layout manager. Use the **add(Component)** method to add a component to the panel. For example, the following code creates a panel and adds a button to it:

```
JPanel p = new JPanel();
p.add(new JButton("OK"));
```

Panels can be placed inside a frame or inside another panel. The following statement places panel **p** into frame **f**:

```
f.add(p);
```

Listing 12.6 gives an example that demonstrates using panels as subcontainers. The program creates a user interface for a microwave oven, as shown in Figure 12.12.

FIGURE 12.12 The program uses panels to organize components.

LISTING 12.6 TestPanels.java

```
1  import java.awt.*;
2  import javax.swing.*;
3
4  public class TestPanels extends JFrame {
5    public TestPanels() {
6      // Create panel p1 for the buttons and set GridLayout
7      JPanel p1 = new JPanel();
8      p1.setLayout(new GridLayout(4, 3));
9
10     // Add buttons to the panel
11     for (int i = 1; i <= 9; i++) {
12       p1.add (new JButton("" + i));
13     }
14
15     p1.add(new JButton("" + 0));
16     p1.add(new JButton("Start"));
17     p1.add(new JButton("Stop"));
18
19     // Create panel p2 to hold a text field and p1
20     JPanel p2 = new JPanel(new BorderLayout());
21     p2.add (new JTextField("Time to be displayed here"),
22       BorderLayout.NORTH);
23     p2.add (p1, BorderLayout.CENTER);
24
25     // add contents into the frame
26     add(p2, BorderLayout.EAST);
27     add(new JButton("Food to be placed here"),
```

panel p1

panel p2

add p2 to frame

```
28        BorderLayout.CENTER);
29    }
30
31    /** Main method */
32    public static void main(String[] args) {
33      TestPanels frame = new TestPanels();
34      frame.setTitle("The Front View of a Microwave Oven");
35      frame.setLocationRelativeTo(null); // Center the frame
36      frame.setDefaultCloseOperation(JFrame.EXIT_ON_CLOSE);
37      frame.setSize(400, 250);
38      frame.setVisible(true);
39    }
40 }
```

The `setLayout` method is defined in `java.awt.Container`. Since `JPanel` is a subclass of `Container`, you can use `setLayout` to set a new layout manager in the panel (line 8). Lines 7–8 can be replaced by `JPanel p1 = new JPanel(new GridLayout(4, 3))`.

To achieve the desired layout, the program uses panel `p1` of `GridLayout` to group the number buttons, the Stop button, and the Start button, and panel `p2` of `BorderLayout` to hold a text field in the north and `p1` in the center. The button representing the food is placed in the center of the frame, and `p2` is placed in the east of the frame.

The statement (lines 21–22)

```
p2.add(new JTextField("Time to be displayed here"),
   BorderLayout.NORTH);
```

creates an instance of `JTextField` and adds it to `p2`. `JTextField` is a GUI component that can be used for user input as well as to display values.

Note

The `Container` class is the superclass for Swing GUI component classes, such as `JButton`. In theory, you could use the `setLayout` method to set the layout in a button and add components into a button, because all the public methods in the `Container` class are inherited into `JButton`, but for practical reasons you should not use buttons as containers.

12.9 Common Features of Swing GUI Components

You have used several GUI components (e.g., `JFrame`, `Container`, `JPanel`, `JButton`, `JLabel`, `JTextField`) in this chapter. Many more GUI components will be introduced in this book. It is important to understand the common features of Swing GUI components. The `Component` class is the root for all GUI components and containers. All Swing GUI components (except `JFrame`, `JApplet`, and `JDialog`) are subclasses of `JComponent`, as shown in Figures 12.2 and 12.3. Figure 12.13 lists some frequently used methods in `Component`, `Container`, and `JComponent` for manipulating properties like font, color, size, tool tip text, and border.

Component
Container
JComponent

A *tool tip* is a text displayed on a component when you move the mouse on the component. It is often used to describe the function of a component.

You can set a border on any object of the `JComponent` class. Swing has several types of borders. To create a titled border, use `new TitledBorder(String title)`. To create a line border, use `new LineBorder(Color color, int width)`, where `width` specifies the thickness of the line.

Listing 12.7 is an example to demonstrate Swing common features. The example creates a panel `p1` to hold three buttons (line 8) and a panel `p2` to hold two labels (line 25). The background of the button `jbtLeft` is set to `white` (line 12), and the foreground of the button `jbtCenter` is set to `green` (line 13). The tool tip of the button `jbtRight` is set in line 14.

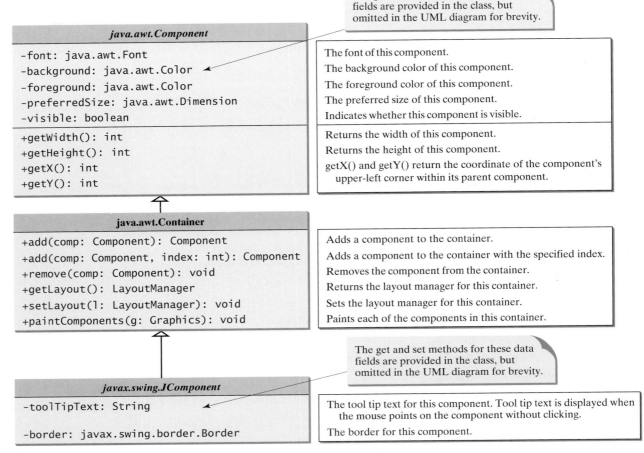

FIGURE 12.13 All the Swing GUI components inherit the public methods from Component, Container, and JComponent.

Titled borders are set on panels **p1** and **p2** (lines 18, 36), and line borders are set on the labels (lines 32–33).

LISTING 12.7 TestSwingCommonFeatures.java

```
1  import java.awt.*;
2  import javax.swing.*;
3  import javax.swing.border.*;
4
5  public class TestSwingCommonFeatures extends JFrame {
6    public TestSwingCommonFeatures() {
7      // Create a panel to group three buttons
8      JPanel p1 = new JPanel(new FlowLayout(FlowLayout.LEFT, 2, 2));
9      JButton jbtLeft = new JButton("Left");
10     JButton jbtCenter = new JButton("Center");
11     JButton jbtRight = new JButton("Right");
12     jbtLeft.setBackground(Color.WHITE);
13     jbtCenter.setForeground(Color.GREEN);
14     jbtRight.setToolTipText("This is the Right button");
15     p1.add(jbtLeft);
16     p1.add(jbtCenter);
17     p1.add(jbtRight);
18     p1.setBorder(new TitledBorder("Three Buttons"));
```

set background — 12
set foreground — 13
set tool tip text — 14
set titled border — 18

```
19
20      // Create a font and a line border
21      Font largeFont = new Font("TimesRoman", Font.BOLD, 20);        create a font
22      Border lineBorder = new LineBorder(Color.BLACK, 2);            create a border
23
24      // Create a panel to group two labels
25      JPanel p2 = new JPanel(new GridLayout(1, 2, 5, 5));
26      JLabel jlblRed = new JLabel("Red");
27      JLabel jlblOrange = new JLabel("Orange");
28      jlblRed.setForeground(Color.RED);                              set foreground
29      jlblOrange.setForeground(Color.ORANGE);
30      jlblRed.setFont(largeFont);                                    set font
31      jlblOrange.setFont(largeFont);
32      jlblRed.setBorder(lineBorder);                                 set line border
33      jlblOrange.setBorder(lineBorder);
34      p2.add(jlblRed);
35      p2.add(jlblOrange);
36      p2.setBorder(new TitledBorder("Two Labels"));                  set titled border
37
38      // Add two panels to the frame
39      setLayout(new GridLayout(2, 1, 5, 5));
40      add(p1);
41      add(p2);
42    }
43
44    public static void main(String[] args) {
45      // Create a frame and set its properties
46      JFrame frame = new TestSwingCommonFeatures();
47      frame.setTitle("TestSwingCommonFeatures");
48      frame.setSize(300, 150);
49      frame.setLocationRelativeTo(null); // Center the frame
50      frame.setDefaultCloseOperation(JFrame.EXIT_ON_CLOSE);
51      frame.setVisible(true);
52    }
53 }
```

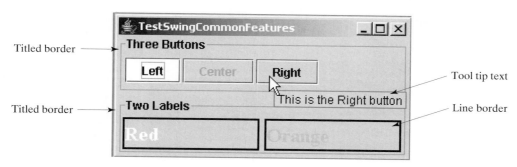

FIGURE 12.14   The font, color, border, and tool tip text are set in the message panel.

Note

The same property may have different default values in different components. For example, the `visible` property in `JFrame` is `false` by default, but it is `true` in every instance of `JComponent` (e.g., `JButton` and `JLabel`) by default. To display a `JFrame`, you have to invoke `setVisible(true)` to set the `visible` property `true`, but you don't have to set this property for a `JButton` or a `JLabel`, because it is already `true`. To make a `JButton` or a

property default values

JLabel invisible, you may invoke **setVisible(false)** on. Please run the program and see the effect after inserting the following two statements in line 37:

```
jbtLeft.setVisible(false);
jlblRed.setVisible(false);
```

12.10 Image Icons

Java uses the `javax.swing.ImageIcon` class to represent an icon. An icon is a fixed-size picture; typically it is small and used to decorate components. Images are normally stored in image files. You can use `new ImageIcon(filename)` to construct an image icon. For example, the following statement creates an icon from an image file `us.gif` in the `image` directory under the current class path:

create **ImageIcon**

```
ImageIcon icon = new ImageIcon("image/us.gif");
```

Note

"`image/us.gif`" is located in "`c:\book\image\us.gif`." The back slash (\) is the Windows file path notation. On Unix, the forward slash (/) should be used. In Java, the forward slash (/) is used to denote a relative file path under the Java classpath (e.g., `image/left.gif`, as in this example).

file path character

Note

Java currently supports three image formats: GIF (Graphics Interchange Format), JPEG (Joint Photographic Experts Group), and PNG (Portable Network Graphics). The image filenames for these types end with .gif, .jpg, and .png, respectively. If you have a bitmap file or image files in other formats, you can use image-processing utilities to convert them into GIF, JPEG, or PNG format for use in Java.

image file format

Note

File names are not case sensitive on Windows, but are case sensitive on Unix. To enable your programs to run on all platforms, name all the image files consistently, using lowercase.

naming files consistently

An image icon can be displayed in a label or a button using `new JLabel(imageIcon)` or `new JButton(imageIcon)`. Listing 12.8 demonstrates displaying icons in a label and a button. The example creates two labels and two buttons with icons, as shown in Figure 12.15.

FIGURE 12.15 The image icons are displayed in labels and buttons.

LISTING 12.8 TestImageIcon.java

```
1  import javax.swing.*;
2  import java.awt.*;
3
4  public class TestImageIcon extends JFrame {
5    private ImageIcon usIcon = new ImageIcon("image/us.gif");
6    private ImageIcon myIcon = new ImageIcon("image/my.jpg");
```

create image icons

```
7     private ImageIcon frIcon = new ImageIcon("image/fr.gif");
8     private ImageIcon ukIcon = new ImageIcon("image/uk.gif");
9
10    public TestImageIcon() {
11      setLayout(new GridLayout(1, 4, 5, 5));
12      add(new JLabel(usIcon));
13      add(new JLabel(myIcon));
14      add(new JButton(frIcon));
15      add(new JButton(ukIcon));
16    }
17
18    /** Main method */
19    public static void main(String[] args) {
20      TestImageIcon frame = new TestImageIcon();
21      frame.setTitle("TestImageIcon");
22      frame.setLocationRelativeTo(null); // Center the frame
23      frame.setDefaultCloseOperation(JFrame.EXIT_ON_CLOSE);
24      frame.setSize(200, 200);
25      frame.setVisible(true);
26    }
27 }
```

a label with image

a button with image

Note

GUI components cannot be shared by containers because a GUI component can appear in only one container at a time. Therefore, the relationship between a component and a container is the composition denoted by a solid diamond, as shown in Figure 12.2.

Note

Borders and icons can be shared. Thus you can create a border or icon and use it to set the **border** or **icon** property for any GUI component. For example, the following statements set a border **b** for two panels **p1** and **p2**:

sharing borders and icons

```
p1.setBorder(b);
p2.setBorder(b);
```

The following statements set an icon in two buttons **jbt1** and **jbt2**:

```
jbt1.setIcon(icon);
jbt2.setIcon(icon);
```

KEY TERMS

AWT 401	lightweight component 401
heavyweight component 401	Swing 401

CHAPTER SUMMARY

- Every container has a layout manager that is used to position and place components in the container in the desired locations. Three simple and useful layout managers are `FlowLayout`, `GridLayout`, and `BorderLayout`.

- You can use a `JPanel` as a subcontainer to group components to achieve a desired layout.

- Use the `add` method to place components to a `JFrame` or a `JPanel`. By default, the frame's layout is `BorderLayout`, and the `JPanel`'s layout is `FlowLayout`.

■ You can set colors for GUI components by using the `java.awt.Color` class. Colors are made of red, green, and blue components, each of which is represented by an unsigned byte value that describes its intensity, ranging from 0 (darkest shade) to 255 (lightest shade). This is known as the *RGB model*.

■ The syntax to create a `Color` object is `Color color = new Color(r, g, b)`, in which `r`, `g`, and `b` specify a color by its red, green, and blue components. Alternatively, you can use one of the thirteen standard colors (`black`, `blue`, `cyan`, `darkGray`, `gray`, `green`, `lightGray`, `magenta`, `orange`, `pink`, `red`, `white`, `yellow`) defined as constants in `java.awt.Color`.

■ Every Swing GUI component is a subclass of `javax.swing.JComponent`, and `JComponent` is a subclass of `java.awt.Component`. The properties `font`, `background`, `foreground`, `height`, `width`, and `preferredSize` in `Component` are inherited in these subclasses, as are `toolTipText` and `border` in `JComponent`.

■ You can use borders on any Swing components. You can create an image icon using the `ImageIcon` class and display it in a label and a button. Icons and borders can be shared.

REVIEW QUESTIONS

Sections 12.3–12.4

12.1 Which class is the root of the Java GUI component classes? Is a container class a subclass of `Component`? Which class is the root of the Swing GUI component classes?

12.2 Explain the difference between AWT GUI components, such as `java.awt.Button`, and Swing components, such as `javax.swing.JButton`.

12.3 How do you create a frame? How do you set the size for a frame? How do you get the size of a frame? How do you add components to a frame? What would happen if the statements `frame.setSize(400, 300)` and `frame.setVisible(true)` were swapped in the `MyFrameWithComponents` class in Section 12.4.2, "Adding Components to a Frame"?

12.4 Determine whether the following statements are true or false:

- You can add a button to a frame.
- You can add a frame to a panel.
- You can add a panel to a frame.
- You can add any number of components to a panel or a frame.
- You can derive a class from `JButton`, `JPanel`, `JFrame`, or `JApplet`.

12.5 The following program is supposed to display a button in a frame, but nothing is displayed. What is the problem?

```
1  public class Test extends javax.swing.JFrame {
2    public Test() {
3      add(new javax.swing.JButton("OK"));
4    }
5
6    public static void main(String[] args) {
7      javax.swing.JFrame frame = new javax.swing.JFrame();
8      frame.setSize(100, 200);
9      frame.setVisible(true);
10   }
11 }
```

12.6 Which of the following statements have syntax errors?

```
Component c1 = new Component();
JComponent c2 = new JComponent();
Component c3 = new JButton();
JComponent c4 = new JButton();
Container c5 = new JButton();
c5.add(c4);
Object c6 = new JButton();
c5.add(c6);
```

Section 12.5 Layout Managers

12.7 Why do you need to use layout managers? What is the default layout manager for a frame? How do you add a component to a frame?

12.8 Describe FlowLayout. How do you create a FlowLayout manager? How do you add a component to a FlowLayout container? Is there a limit to the number of components that can be added to a FlowLayout container?

12.9 Describe GridLayout. How do you create a GridLayout manager? How do you add a component to a GridLayout container? Is there a limit to the number of components that can be added to a GridLayout container?

12.10 Describe BorderLayout. How do you create a BorderLayout manager? How do you add a component to a BorderLayout container? Can you add multiple components in the same section?

Sections 12.6–12.7

12.11 How do you create a color? What is wrong about creating a Color using new Color(400, 200, 300)? Which of the following two colors are darker, new Color(10, 0, 0) or new Color(200, 0, 0)?

12.12 How do you create a font? How do you find all the available fonts on your system?

Section 12.8 Using Panels as Subcontainers

12.13 How do you create a panel with a specified layout manager?

12.14 What is the default layout manager for a JPanel? How do you add a component to a JPanel?

12.15 Can you use the setTitle method in a panel? What is the purpose of using a panel?

12.16 Since a GUI component class such as JButton is a subclass of Container, can you add components into a button?

Sections 12.9–12.10

12.17 How do you set background color, foreground color, font, and tool tip text on a Swing GUI component? Why is the tool tip text not displayed in the following code?

```
1 import javax.swing.*;
2
3 public class Test extends JFrame {
4   private JButton jbtOK = new JButton("OK");
5
6   public static void main(String[] args) {
7     // Create a frame and set its properties
8     JFrame frame = new Test();
9     frame.setTitle("Logic Error");
```

```
10       frame.setSize(200, 100);
11       frame.setDefaultCloseOperation(JFrame.EXIT_ON_CLOSE);
12       frame.setVisible(true);
13     }
14
15     public Test() {
16       jbtOK.setToolTipText("This is a button");
17       add(new JButton("OK"));
18     }
19 }
```

12.18 Show the output of the following code:

```
import javax.swing.*;

public class Test {
  public static void main(String[] args) {
    JButton jbtOK = new JButton("OK");
    System.out.println(jbtOK.isVisible());

    JFrame frame = new JFrame();
    System.out.println(frame.isVisible());
  }
}
```

12.19 How do you create an **ImageIcon** from the file image/us.gif in the class directory?

12.20 What happens if you add a button to a container several times, as shown below? Does it cause syntax errors? Does it cause runtime errors?

```
JButton jbt = new JButton();
JPanel panel = new JPanel();
panel.add(jbt);
panel.add(jbt);
panel.add(jbt);
```

12.21 Will the following code display three buttons? Will the buttons display the same icon?

```
1 import javax.swing.*;
2 import java.awt.*;
3
4 public class Test extends JFrame  {
5   public static void main(String[] args) {
6     // Create a frame and set its properties
7     JFrame frame = new Test();
8     frame.setTitle("ButtonIcons");
9     frame.setSize(200, 100);
10    frame.setDefaultCloseOperation(JFrame.EXIT_ON_CLOSE);
11    frame.setVisible(true);
12  }
13
14  public Test() {
15    ImageIcon usIcon = new ImageIcon("image/usIcon.gif");
16    JButton jbt1 = new JButton(usIcon);
17    JButton jbt2 = new JButton(usIcon);
18
19    JPanel p1 = new JPanel();
20    p1.add(jbt1);
```

```
21
22      JPanel p2 = new JPanel();
23      p2.add(jbt2);
24
25      JPanel p3 = new JPanel();
26      p2.add(jbt1);
27
28      add(p1, BorderLayout.NORTH);
29      add(p2, BorderLayout.SOUTH);
30      add(p3, BorderLayout.CENTER);
31    }
32 }
```

12.22 Can a border or an icon be shared by GUI components?

PROGRAMMING EXERCISES

Section 12.5 Layout Managers

12.1 (*Using the FlowLayout manager*) Write a program that meets the following requirements (see Figure 12.16):

- Create a frame and set its layout to FlowLayout.
- Create two panels and add them to the frame.
- Each panel contains three buttons. The panel uses FlowLayout.

FIGURE 12.16 Exercise 12.1 places three buttons in one panel and three buttons in another panel.

12.2 (*Using the BorderLayout manager*) Rewrite the preceding program to create the same user interface, but instead of using FlowLayout for the frame, use BorderLayout. Place one panel in the south of the frame and the other panel in the center.

12.3 (*Using the GridLayout manager*) Rewrite the preceding program to create the same user interface. Instead of using FlowLayout for the panels, use a GridLayout of two rows and three columns.

12.4 (*Using JPanel to group buttons*) Rewrite the preceding program to create the same user interface. Instead of creating buttons and panels separately, define a class that extends the JPanel class. Place three buttons in your panel class, and create two panels from the user-defined panel class.

12.5 (*Displaying labels*) Write a program that displays four lines of text in four labels, as shown in Figure 12.17(a). Add a line border on each label.

12.6 (*Displaying icons*) Write a program that displays four icons in four labels, as shown in Figure 12.17(b). Add a line border on each label. (Use any images of your choice or the ones in the book, which can be obtained along with the book's source code).

FIGURE 12.17 (a) Exercise 12.5 displays four labels. (b) Exercise 12.6 displays four icons.

12.7**(*Displaying a TicTacToe board*) Display a frame that contains nine labels. A label may display a cross image icon, a not image icon, or nothing, as shown in Figure 12.18(a). What to display is randomly decided. Use the `Math.random()` method to generate an integer 0, 1, or 2, which corresponds to displaying a cross image icon, a not image icon, or nothing. The cross and not images can be obtained from the `cross.gif` and `not.gif` files in the `image` directory on the Companion Website.

FIGURE 12.18 (a) A TicTacToe board is displayed with image icons in labels. (b) Six labels are placed in the frame.

12.8* (*Swing common features*) Display a frame that contains six labels. Set the background of the labels to white. Set the foreground of the labels to black, blue, cyan, green, magenta, and orange, respectively, as shown in Figure 12.18(b). Set the border of each label to a line border with the yellow color. Set the font of each label to TimesRoman, bold, and 20 pixels. Set the text and tool tip text of each label to the name of its foreground color.

GRAPHICS

Objectives

- To understand Java coordinate systems (§13.2).
- To draw things using the methods in the Graphics class (§13.3).
- To understand how and when a Graphics object is created (§13.3).
- To override the paintComponent method to draw things on a GUI component (§13.4).
- To use a panel as a canvas to draw things (§13.5).
- To draw strings, lines, rectangles, ovals, arcs, and polygons (§§13.6, 13.8–13.9).
- To obtain font properties using FontMetrics and know how to center a message (§13.10).
- (Optional) To display image in a GUI component (§13.13).
- To develop reusable GUI components FigurePanel, MessagePanel, StillClock, and ImageViewer (§§13.7, 13.11, 13.12 Optional, 13.14 Optional).

13.1 Introduction

The preceding chapter introduced GUI components and their relationships, containers and layout managers, colors, fonts, and image icons. This chapter introduces how to paint graphics on GUI components. You will learn how to draw strings, lines, rectangles, ovals, arcs, polygons, and images, and how to develop reusable GUI components.

13.2 Graphical Coordinate Systems

To paint, you need to know where to paint. Each component has its own coordinate system with the origin $(0, 0)$ at the upper-left corner of the component. The x coordinate increases to the right, and the y coordinate increases downward. Note that the Java coordinate system is different from the conventional coordinate system, as shown in Figure 13.1. The location of the upper-left corner of a component c1 (e.g., a button) inside its parent component c2 (e.g., a panel) can be located using c1.getX() and c1.getY(), as shown in Figure 13.2.

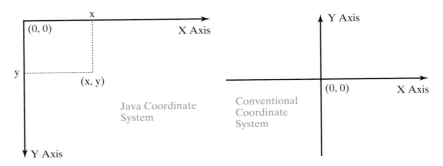

FIGURE 13.1 The Java coordinate system is measured in pixels, with $(0, 0)$ at its upper-left corner.

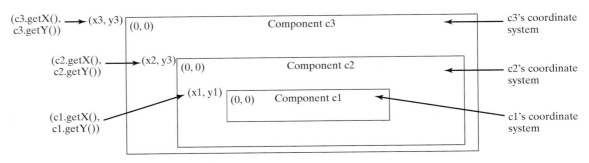

FIGURE 13.2 Each GUI component has its own coordinate system.

13.3 The Graphics Class

You can draw strings, lines, rectangles, ovals, arcs, polygons, and polylines, using the methods in the Graphics class, as shown in Figure 13.3.

The Graphics class is an abstract class that provides a device-independent graphics interface for displaying figures and images on the screen on different platforms. Whenever a component (e.g., a button, a label, a panel) is displayed, the JVM automatically creates a

java.awt.Graphics	
+setColor(color: Color): void	Sets a new color for subsequent drawings.
+setFont(font: Font): void	Sets a new font for subsequent drawings.
+drawString(s: String, x: int, y: int): void	Draws a string starting at point (x, y).
+drawLine(x1: int, y1: int, x2: int, y2: int): void	Draws a line from (x1, y1) to (x2, y2).
+drawRect(x:int, y: int, w: int, h: int): void	Draws a rectangle with specified upper-left-corner point at (x, y) and width w and height h.
+fillRect(x: int, y: int, w: int, h: int): void	Draws a filled rectangle with specified upper-left-corner point at (x, y) and width w and height h.
+drawRoundRect(x: int, y: int, w: int, h: int, aw: int, ah: int): void	Draws a round-cornered rectangle with specified arc width aw and arc height ah.
+fillRoundRect(x: int, y: int, w: int, h: int, aw: int, ah: int): void	Draws a filled round-cornered rectangle with specified arc width aw and arc height ah.
+draw3DRect(x: int, y: int, w: int, h: int, raised: boolean): void	Draws a 3-D rectangle raised above the surface or sunk into the surface.
+fill3DRect(x: int, y: int, w: int, h: int, raised: boolean): void	Draws a filled 3-D rectangle raised above the surface or sunk into the surface.
+drawOval(x: int, y: int, w: int, h: int): void	Draws an oval bounded by the rectangle specified by the parameters x, y, w, and h.
+fillOval(x: int, y: int, w: int, h: int): void	Draws a filled oval bounded by the rectangle specified by the parameters x, y, w, and h.
+drawArc(x: int, y: int, w: int, h: int, startAngle: int, arcAngle: int): void	Draws an arc conceived as part of an oval bounded by the rectangle specified by the parameters x, y, w, and h.
+fillArc(x: int, y: int, w: int, h: int, startAngle: int, arcAngle: int): void	Draws a filled arc conceived as part of an oval bounded by the rectangle specified by the parameters x, y, w, and h.
+drawPolygon(xPoints: int[], yPoints: int[], nPoints: int): void	Draws a closed polygon defined by arrays of x and y coordinates. Each pair of (x[i], y[i]) coordinates is a point.
+fillPolygon(xPoints: int[], yPoints: int[], nPoints: int): void	Draws a filled polygon defined by arrays of x and y coordinates. Each pair of (x[i], y[i]) coordinates is a point.
+drawPolygon(g: Polygon): void	Draws a closed polygon defined by a Polygon object.
+fillPolygon(g: Polygon): void	Draws a filled polygon defined by a Polygon object.
+drawPolyline(xPoints: int[], yPoints: int[], nPoints: int): void	Draws a polyline defined by arrays of x and y coordinates. Each pair of (x[i], y[i]) coordinates is a point.

FIGURE 13.3   The `Graphics` class contains the methods for drawing strings and shapes.

`Graphics` object for the component on the native platform. This object can be obtained using the `getGraphics()` method. For example, the `Graphics` object for a label `jlblBanner` can be obtained using

```
Graphics graphics = jlblBanner.getGraphics();
```

Think of a GUI component as a piece of paper and the `Graphics` object as a pencil or paintbrush. You can apply the methods in the `Graphics` class to draw things on a GUI component.

To fully understand the Graphics class, we first present an intuitive, but not practical example in Listing 13.1. The program creates a label in line 5. When the `main` method is executed, the constructor `TestGetGraphics` is executed (line 13) and the label is added to the frame (line 8). At this time, the `Graphics` object for the label has not been created because the label has not been displayed. Therefore, `jlblBanner.getGraphics()` returns `null` (line 9). After the frame is displayed in line 18, all the components in the frame are also displayed. The `Graphics` object for the label is obtained in line 21. A line is drawn from (0, 0) to (50, 50) on the label, as shown in Figure 13.4.

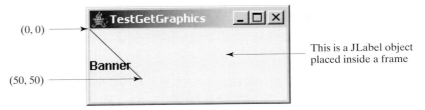

(0, 0)

(50, 50)

This is a JLabel object
placed inside a frame

FIGURE 13.4 A line is drawn on a label, and the label is placed inside the frame.

LISTING 13.1 TestGetGraphics.java

```
 1  import javax.swing.*;
 2  import java.awt.Graphics;
 3
 4  public class TestGetGraphics extends JFrame {
 5    private JLabel jlblBanner = new JLabel("Banner");
 6
 7    public TestGetGraphics() {
 8      add(jlblBanner);
 9      System.out.println(jlblBanner.getGraphics());
10    }
11
12    public static void main(String[] args) {
13      TestGetGraphics frame = new TestGetGraphics();
14      frame.setTitle("TestGetGraphics");
15      frame.setLocationRelativeTo(null); // Center the frame
16      frame.setDefaultCloseOperation(JFrame.EXIT_ON_CLOSE);
17      frame.setSize(200, 100);
18      frame.setVisible(true);
19      JOptionPane.showMessageDialog(null,
20        "Delay on purpose\nClick OK to dismiss the dialog");
21      Graphics graphics = frame.jlblBanner.getGraphics();
22      graphics.drawLine(0, 0, 50, 50);
23    }
24  }
```

create a label

add a label

create a frame

display frame
  for delay purpose

get graphics
draw line

When you run this program, the frame is displayed (line 18), then a message dialog box is displayed (line 19). What is the purpose of having a message dialog box in this program? The purpose is to delay the execution of lines 21 and 22. Without the delay, you might not see the line (line 22). The reason will be discussed in the next section.

When you create a label with a text such as new JLabel("Banner"), you see the text on the label when the label is displayed. The text is actually painted on the label using the drawString method in the Graphics class internally.

Every GUI component has a Graphics object that can be obtained using getGraphics() after the component is displayed. You may rewrite this example using a button, a text field, or a text area rather a label. Note that jlblBanner.getGraphics() returns null in line 9, because jlblBanner has not been displayed yet. It is displayed when the frame is set visible in line 18.

In line 9, jlblBanner.getGraphics() is used to return a Graphics object. In line 21, why do you have to use frame.jlblBanner.getGraphics() in the main method? This is because jlblBanner is an instance variable, and it cannot be referenced directly in a static method.

13.4 The **paintComponent** Method

The program in Listing 13.1 has two problems:

1. If you resize the frame, the line disappears.

2. It is awkward to program because you have to make sure that the component is displayed before obtaining its Graphics object using the getGraphics() method. For this reason, lines 21 and 22 are placed after the frame is displayed in line 18.

Because of these two problems, you should avoid programming using the getGraphics() method. To fix the first problem, you need to know its cause. When you resize the frame, the JVM automatically invokes the paintComponent method of a Swing component (e.g., a JLabel) to redisplay the graphics on the component. Since you did not draw a line in the paintComponent method, the line is gone when the frame is resized. To permanently display the line, you need to draw the line in the paintComponent method. The signature of the paintComponent method is as follows:

```
protected void paintComponent(Graphics g)
```

This method, defined in the JComponent class, is invoked whenever a component is first displayed or redisplayed. The Graphics object g is created automatically by the JVM for every visible GUI component. The JVM obtains the Graphics object and passes it to invoke paintComponent.

In order to draw things on a component (e.g., a JLabel) consistently, you need to declare a class that extends a Swing GUI component class and overrides its paintComponent method to specify what to draw. The program in Listing 13.1 can be rewritten as shown in Listing 13.2. The output is the same as shown in Figure 13.4. When you resize the frame, the JVM invokes the paintComponent method to repaint the line and the text.

LISTING 13.2 TestPaintComponent.java

```
 1 import javax.swing.*;
 2 import java.awt.Graphics;
 3
 4 public class TestPaintComponent extends JFrame {
 5   public TestPaintComponent() {
 6     add(new NewLabel("Banner"));                          create a label
 7   }
 8
 9   public static void main(String[] args) {
10     TestPaintComponent frame = new TestPaintComponent();
11     frame.setTitle("TestPaintComponent");
12     frame.setLocationRelativeTo(null); // Center the frame
13     frame.setDefaultCloseOperation(JFrame.EXIT_ON_CLOSE);
14     frame.setSize(200, 100);
15     frame.setVisible(true);
16   }
17 }
18
19 class NewLabel extends JLabel {
20   public NewLabel(String text) {                          new label class
21     super(text);
22   }
23
```

override
 paintComponent
draw things in the
 superclass **drawline**

```
24   protected void paintComponent(Graphics g) {
25     super.paintComponent(g);
26     g.drawLine(0, 0, 50, 50);
27   }
28 }
```

The **paintComponent** method is automatically invoked to paint graphics when the component is first displayed or whenever the component needs to be redisplayed. The text "banner" is drawn in the **paintComponent** method defined in the **JLabel** class. Invoking

super.paintComponent-
 (g)

super.paintComponent(g) (line 25) displays the text in the label, and invoking the **drawLine** method (line 26) draws a line.

protected
 paintComponent

The JVM invokes **paintComponent** to draw things on a component. The user should never invoke **paintComponent** directly. For this reason, the protected visibility is sufficient for **paintComponent**.

13.5 Drawing Graphics on Panels

Panels are invisible and are used as small containers that group components to achieve a desired layout. Another important use of **JPanel** is for drawing. You can draw things on any Swing GUI component, but normally you should use a **JPanel** as a canvas to draw things.

To draw in a **JPanel**, you create a new class that extends **JPanel** and overrides the **paintComponent** method to tell the panel how to draw things. Listing 13.3 is an example to demonstrate drawings on a panel. The example declares the **NewPanel** class, which extends **JPanel** and overrides the **paintComponent** method to draw a line (line 22) and a string (line 23), as shown in Figure 13.5.

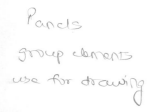

Panels
group elements
use for drawing

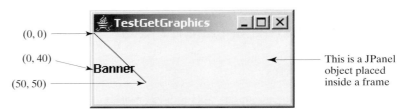

FIGURE 13.5   A line and a string are drawn on a panel.

LISTING 13.3   TestPanelDrawing.java

create a label

```
1 import javax.swing.*;
2 import java.awt.Graphics;
3
4 public class TestPanelDrawing extends JFrame {
5   public TestPanelDrawing() {
6     add(new NewPanel());
7   }
8
9   public static void main(String[] args) {
10     TestPanelDrawing frame = new TestPanelDrawing();
11     frame.setTitle("TestPanelDrawing");
12     frame.setLocationRelativeTo(null); // Center the frame
13     frame.setDefaultCloseOperation(JFrame.EXIT_ON_CLOSE);
14     frame.setSize(200, 100);
15     frame.setVisible(true);
16   }
17 }
18
```

```
19 class NewPanel extends JPanel {
20   protected void paintComponent(Graphics g) {
21     super.paintComponent(g);
22     g.drawLine(0, 0, 50, 50);
23     g.drawString("Banner", 0, 40);
24   }
25 }
```

new panel class

override
  paintComponent
draw things in the
  superclass
draw a line

All the drawing methods have parameters that specify the locations of the subjects to be drawn. All measurements in Java are made in pixels. The string "Banner" is drawn at location (0, 40).

Note

Invoking **super.paintComponent(g)** (line 21) is necessary to ensure that the viewing area is cleared before a new drawing is displayed.

super.paint-
  Component(g)

Tip

Some textbooks declare a canvas class by subclassing **JComponent**. The problem is that you have to write the code to paint the background color if you wish to set a background in the canvas. A simple **setBackground(Color color)** method will not set a background color in a **JComponent**.

extends **JComponent?**

13.6 Drawing Strings, Lines, Rectangles, and Ovals

The **drawString(String s, int x, int y)** method draws a string starting at the point (x, y), as shown in Figure 13.6(a).

drawString

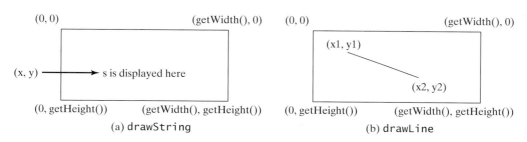

(a) drawString   (b) drawLine

FIGURE 13.6 (a) The **drawString(s, x, y)** method draws a string starting at (x, y). (b) The **drawLine(x1, y1, x2, y2)** method draws a line between two specified points.

The **drawLine(int x1, int y1, int x2, int y2)** method draws a straight line from point (x1, y1) to point (x2, y2), as shown in Figure 13.6(b).

drawLine

Java provides six methods for drawing rectangles in outline or filled with color. You can draw plain rectangles, round-cornered rectangles, or three-dimensional rectangles.

The **drawRect(int x, int y, int w, int h)** method draws a plain rectangle, and the **fillRect(int x, int y, int w, int h)** method draws a filled rectangle. The parameters x and y represent the upper-left corner of the rectangle, and w and h are its width and height (see Figure 13.7).

drawRect
fillRect

The **drawRoundRect(int x, int y, int w, int h, int aw, int ah)** method draws a round-cornered rectangle, and the **fillRoundRect(int x, int y, int w, int h, int aw, int ah)** method draws a filled round-cornered rectangle. Parameters x, y, w, and h are the same as in the **drawRect** method, parameter aw is the horizontal diameter

drawRoundRect

fillRoundRect

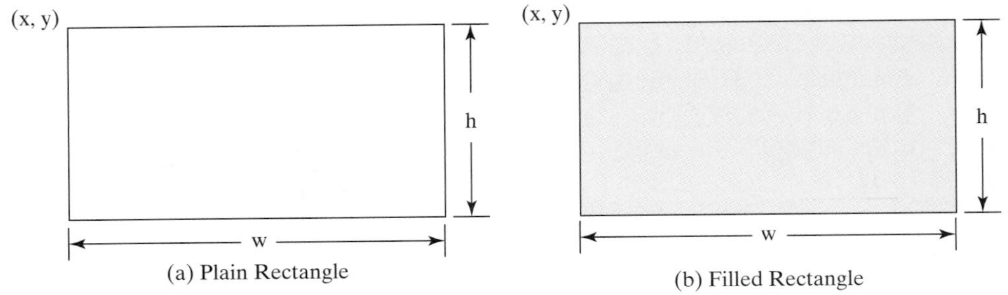

(x, y)

h

w

(a) Plain Rectangle

(x, y)

h

w

(b) Filled Rectangle

FIGURE 13.7 (a) The `drawRect(x, y, w, h)` method draws a rectangle. (b) The `fillRect(x, y, w, h)` method draws a filled rectangle.

of the arcs at the corner, and `ah` is the vertical diameter of the arcs at the corner (see Figure 13.8(a)). In other words, `aw` and `ah` are the width and the height of the oval that produces a quarter-circle at each corner.

draw3DRect

The `draw3DRect(int x, int y, int w, int h, boolean raised)` method draws a 3D rectangle and the `fill3DRect(int x, int y, int w, int h, boolean raised)` method draws a filled 3D rectangle. The parameters `x`, `y`, `w`, and `h` are the same as in the `drawRect` method. The last parameter, a Boolean value, indicates whether the rectangle is raised above the surface or sunk into the surface.

fill3DRect

drawOval
fillOval

Depending on whether you wish to draw an oval in outline or filled solid, you can use either the `drawOval(int x, int y, int w, int h)` method or the `fillOval(int x, int y, int w, int h)` method. An oval is drawn based on its bounding rectangle. Parameters `x` and `y` indicate the top-left corner of the bounding rectangle, and `w` and `h` indicate the width and height, respectively, of the bounding rectangle, as shown in Figure 13.8(b).

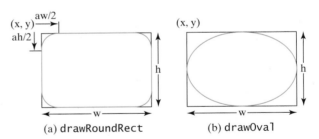

aw/2
(x, y)
ah/2

h

w

(a) drawRoundRect

(x, y)

h

w

(b) drawOval

FIGURE 13.8 (a) The `drawRoundRect(x, y, w, h, aw, ah)` method draws a round-cornered rectangle. (b) The `drawOval(x, y, w, h)` method draws an oval based on its bounding rectangle.

13.7 Case Study: The **FigurePanel** Class

This example develops a useful class for displaying various figures. The class enables the user to set the figure type and specify whether the figure is filled, and displays the figure on a panel. The UML diagram for the class is shown in Figure 13.9. The panel can display lines, rectangles, round-cornered rectangles, and ovals. Which figure to display is decided by the `type` property. If the `filled` property is `true`, the rectangle, round-cornered rectangle, and oval are filled in the panel.

The UML diagram serves as the contract for the `FigurePanel` class. The user can use the class without knowing how the class is implemented. Let us begin by writing a program in Listing 13.4 that uses the class to display six figure panels, as shown in Figure 13.10.

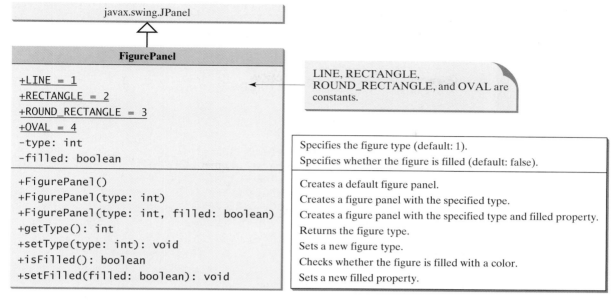

FIGURE 13.9   **FigurePanel** displays various types of figures on the panel.

LISTING 13.4   TestFigurePanel.java

```java
1  import java.awt.*;
2  import javax.swing.*;
3
4  public class TestFigurePanel extends JFrame {
5    public TestFigurePanel() {
6      setLayout(new GridLayout(2, 3, 5, 5));
7      add(new FigurePanel(FigurePanel.LINE));
8      add(new FigurePanel(FigurePanel.RECTANGLE));
9      add(new FigurePanel(FigurePanel.ROUND_RECTANGLE));
10     add(new FigurePanel(FigurePanel.OVAL));
11     add(new FigurePanel(FigurePanel.RECTANGLE, true));
12     add(new FigurePanel(FigurePanel.ROUND_RECTANGLE, true));
13   }
14
15   public static void main(String[] args) {
16     TestFigurePanel frame = new TestFigurePanel();
17     frame.setSize(400, 200);
18     frame.setTitle("TestFigurePanel");
19     frame.setLocationRelativeTo(null); // Center the frame
20     frame.setDefaultCloseOperation(JFrame.EXIT_ON_CLOSE);
21     frame.setVisible(true);
22   }
23 }
```

display lines
display a rectangle
round-cornered
    rectangle
display an oval
filled rectangle
filled round-
    cornered rectangle

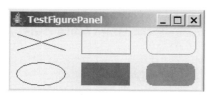

FIGURE 13.10   Six **FigurePanel** objects are created to display six figures.

The `FigurePanel` class is implemented in Listing 13.5. Four constants, `LINE`, `RECTANGLE`, `ROUND_RECTANGLE`, and `OVAL`, are declared in lines 6–9. Four types of figures are drawn according to the `type` property (line 37). The `setColor` method (lines 39, 44, 53, 62) sets a new color for the drawing.

LISTING 13.5 FigurePanel.java

```java
 1 import java.awt.*;
 2 import javax.swing.JPanel;
 3
 4 public class FigurePanel extends JPanel {
 5   // Define constants
 6   public static final int LINE = 1;
 7   public static final int RECTANGLE = 2;
 8   public static final int ROUND_RECTANGLE = 3;
 9   public static final int OVAL = 4;
10
11   private int type = 1;
12   private boolean filled;
13
14   /** Construct a default FigurePanel */
15   public FigurePanel() {
16   }
17
18   /** Construct a FigurePanel with the specified type */
19   public FigurePanel(int type) {
20     this.type = type;
21   }
22
23   /** Construct a FigurePanel with the specified type and filled */
24   public FigurePanel(int type, boolean filled) {
25     this.type = type;
26     this.filled = filled;
27   }
28
29   /** Draw a figure on the panel */
30   public void paintComponent(Graphics g) {
31     super.paintComponent(g);
32
33     // Get the appropriate size for the figure
34     int width = getSize().width;
35     int height = getSize().height;
36
37     switch (type) {
38     case LINE: // Display two cross lines
39       g.setColor(Color.BLACK);
40       g.drawLine(10, 10, width - 10, height - 10);
41       g.drawLine(width - 10, 10, 10, height - 10);
42       break;
43     case RECTANGLE: // Display a rectangle
44       g.setColor(Color.BLUE);
45       if (filled)
46         g.fillRect((int)(0.1 * width), (int)(0.1 * height),
47           (int)(0.8 * width), (int)(0.8 * height));
48       else
49         g.drawRect((int)(0.1 * width), (int)(0.1 * height),
50           (int)(0.8 * width), (int)(0.8 * height));
51       break;
```

constants

override
  paintComponent(g)

check type

draw lines

fill a rectangle

draw a rectangle

```
52        case ROUND_RECTANGLE: // Display a round-cornered rectangle
53          g.setColor(Color.RED);
54          if (filled)
55            g.fillRoundRect((int)(0.1 * width), (int)(0.1 * height),       fill round-cornered
56              (int)(0.8 * width), (int)(0.8 * height), 20, 20);              rect
57          else
58            g.drawRoundRect((int)(0.1 * width), (int)(0.1 * height),       draw round-cornered
59              (int)(0.8 * width), (int)(0.8 * height), 20, 20);              rect
60          break;
61        case OVAL: // Display an oval
62          g.setColor(Color.BLACK);
63          if (filled)
64            g.fillOval((int)(0.1 * width), (int)(0.1 * height),           fill an oval
65              (int)(0.8 * width), (int)(0.8 * height));
66          else
67            g.drawOval((int)(0.1 * width), (int)(0.1 * height),           draw an oval
68              (int)(0.8 * width), (int)(0.8 * height));
69      }
70    }
71
72    /** Set a new figure type */
73    public void setType(int type) {
74      this.type = type;
75      repaint();                                                          repaint panel
76    }
77
78    /** Return figure type */
79    public int getType() {
80      return type;
81    }
82
83    /** Set a new filled property */
84    public void setFilled(boolean filled) {
85      this.filled = filled;
86      repaint();                                                          repaint panel
87    }
88
89    /** Check if the figure is filled */
90    public boolean isFilled() {
91      return filled;
92    }
93
94    /** Specify preferred size */
95    public Dimension getPreferredSize() {                                 override
96      return new Dimension(80, 80);                                         getPreferredSize()
97    }
98  }
```

The `repaint` method (lines 75, 86) is defined in the `Component` class. Invoking `repaint` causes the `paintComponent` method to be called. The `repaint` method is invoked to refresh the viewing area. Typically, you call it if you have new things to display.

Caution

The `paintComponent` method should never be invoked directly. It is invoked either by the JVM whenever the viewing area changes or by the `repaint` method. You should override the `paintComponent` method to tell the system how to paint the viewing area, but never override the `repaint` method.

don't invoke
paintComponent

request repaint using
repaint()

Note

The `repaint` method lodges a request to update the viewing area and returns immediately. Its effect is asynchronous, and if several requests are outstanding, it is likely that only the last `paintComponent` will be done.

getPreferredSize()

The `getPreferredSize()` method (lines 95–97), defined in `Component`, is overridden in `FigurePanel` to specify the preferred size for the layout manager to consider when laying out a `FigurePanel` object. This property may or may not be considered by the layout manager, depending on its rules. For example, a component uses its preferred size in a container with a `FlowLayout` manager, but its preferred size may be ignored if it is placed in a container with a `GridLayout` manager. It is a good practice to override `getPreferredSize()` in a subclass of `JPanel` to specify a preferred size, because the default preferred size for a `JPanel` is 0 by 0.

13.8 Drawing Arcs

An arc is conceived as part of an oval bounded by a rectangle. The methods to draw or fill an arc are as follows:

```
drawArc(int x, int y, int w, int h, int startAngle, int arcAngle);
fillArc(int x, int y, int w, int h, int startAngle, int arcAngle);
```

Parameters x, y, w, and h are the same as in the `drawOval` method; parameter `startAngle` is the starting angle; `arcAngle` is the spanning angle (i.e., the angle covered by the arc). Angles are measured in degrees and follow the usual mathematical conventions (i.e., 0 degrees is in the easterly direction, and positive angles indicate counterclockwise rotation from the easterly direction); see Figure 13.11.

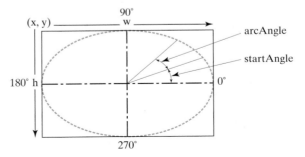

FIGURE 13.11 The `drawArc` method draws an arc based on an oval with specified angles.

Listing 13.6 is an example of how to draw arcs; the output is shown in Figure 13.12.

LISTING 13.6 DrawArcs.java

```
1 import javax.swing.JFrame;
2 import javax.swing.JPanel;
3 import java.awt.Graphics;
4
5 public class DrawArcs extends JFrame {
6   public DrawArcs() {
7     setTitle("DrawArcs");
```

```
 8       add(new ArcsPanel());
 9    }
10
11    /** Main method */
12    public static void main(String[] args) {
13      DrawArcs frame = new DrawArcs();
14      frame.setLocationRelativeTo(null); // Center the frame
15      frame.setDefaultCloseOperation(JFrame.EXIT_ON_CLOSE);
16      frame.setSize(250, 300);
17      frame.setVisible(true);
18    }
19 }
20
21 // The class for drawing arcs on a panel
22 class ArcsPanel extends JPanel {
23    // Draw four blazes of a fan
24    protected void paintComponent(Graphics g) {
25      super.paintComponent(g);
26
27      int xCenter = getWidth() / 2;
28      int yCenter = getHeight() / 2;
29      int radius = (int)(Math.min(getWidth(), getHeight()) * 0.4);
30
31      int x = xCenter - radius;
32      int y = yCenter - radius;
33
34      g.fillArc(x, y, 2 * radius, 2 * radius, 0, 30);
35      g.fillArc(x, y, 2 * radius, 2 * radius, 90, 30);
36      g.fillArc(x, y, 2 * radius, 2 * radius, 180, 30);
37      g.fillArc(x, y, 2 * radius, 2 * radius, 270, 30);
38    }
39 }
```

add a panel

override
    paintComponent

30° arc from 0°
30° arc from 90°
30° arc from 180°
30° arc from 270°

 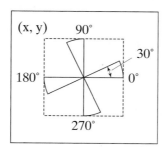

FIGURE 13.12   The program draws four filled arcs.

 Note

Angles may be negative. A negative starting angle sweeps clockwise from the easterly direction, as shown in Figure 13.13. A negative spanning angle sweeps clockwise from the starting angle. The following two statements draw the same arc:

negative degrees

```
g.fillArc(x, y, 2 * radius, 2 * radius, -30, -20);
g.fillArc(x, y, 2 * radius, 2 * radius, -50, 20);
```

The first statement uses negative starting angle −30 and negative spanning angle −20, as shown in Figure 13.13(a). The second statement uses negative starting angle −50 and positive spanning angle 20, as shown in Figure 13.13(b).

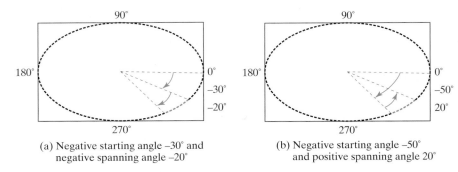

(a) Negative starting angle –30° and
negative spanning angle –20°

(b) Negative starting angle –50°
and positive spanning angle 20°

FIGURE 13.13 Angles may be negative.

13.9 The **Polygon** Class and Drawing Polygons and Polylines

The **Polygon** class encapsulates a description of a closed two-dimensional region within a coordinate space. This region is bounded by an arbitrary number of line segments, each of which is one side (or edge) of the polygon. Internally, a polygon comprises a list of (x, y) coordinate pairs in which each pair defines a vertex of the polygon, and two successive pairs are the endpoints of a line that is a side of the polygon. The first and final pairs of (x, y) points are joined by a line segment that closes the polygon.

The two constructors given below are used to create a **Polygon** object.

- **public** Polygon()
  Constructs an empty polygon.

- **public** Polygon(**int**[] xpoints, **int**[] ypoints, **int** npoints)
  Constructs and initializes a **Polygon** with specified points. Parameters **xpoints** and **ypoints** are arrays representing x-coordinates and y-coordinates, and **npoints** indicates the number of points.

To append a point to the polygon, use the **addPoint(int x, int y)** method. The **Polygon** class has the public data fields **xpoints**, **ypoints**, and **npoints**, which represent the array of x-coordinates and y-coordinates, and the total number of points.

Here is an example of creating a polygon and adding points into it:

```
Polygon polygon = new Polygon();
polygon.addPoint(40, 20);
polygon.addPoint(70, 40);
polygon.addPoint(60, 80);
polygon.addPoint(45, 45);
polygon.addPoint(20, 60);
```

To draw or fill a polygon, use one of the following methods:

```
drawPolygon(Polygon polygon);

fillPolygon(Polygon polygon);

drawPolygon(int[] xpoints, int[] ypoints, int npoints);

fillPolygon(int[] xpoints, int[] ypoints, int npoints);
```

For example:

```
int x[] = {40, 70, 60, 45, 20};
int y[] = {20, 40, 80, 45, 60};
g.drawPolygon(x, y, x.length);
```

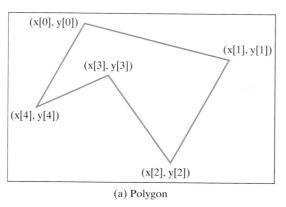

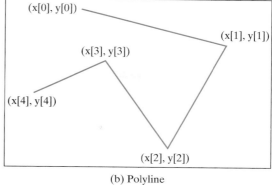

(a) Polygon

(b) Polyline

FIGURE 13.14   The **drawPolygon** method draws a polygon, and the **polyLine** method draws a polyline.

The drawing method opens the polygon by drawing lines between point (x[i], y[i]) and point (x[i+1], y[i+1]) for i = 0, ... , x.length-1; it closes the polygon by drawing a line between the first and last points (see Figure 13.14(a)).

To draw a polyline, use the **drawPolyline(int[] x, int[] y, int nPoints)** method, which draws a sequence of connected lines defined by arrays of x and y coordinates. For example, the following code draws the polyline, as shown in Figure 13.14(b):

```java
int x[] = {40, 70, 60, 45, 20};
int y[] = {20, 40, 80, 45, 60};
g.drawPolygon(x, y, x.length);
```

Listing 13.7 is an example of how to draw a hexagon, with the output shown in Figure 13.15.

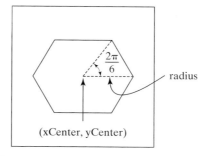

FIGURE 13.15   The program uses the **drawPolygon** method to draw a polygon.

LISTING 13.7 DrawPolygon.java

```java
1 import javax.swing.JFrame;
2 import javax.swing.JPanel;
3 import java.awt.Graphics;
4 import java.awt.Polygon;
5
6 public class DrawPolygon extends JFrame {
7   public DrawPolygon() {
8     setTitle("DrawPolygon");
9     add(new PolygonsPanel());                    add a panel
10  }
11
12  /** Main method */
13  public static void main(String[] args) {
14    DrawPolygon frame = new DrawPolygon();
```

```
15      frame.setLocationRelativeTo(null); // Center the frame
16      frame.setDefaultCloseOperation(JFrame.EXIT_ON_CLOSE);
17      frame.setSize(200, 250);
18      frame.setVisible(true);
19    }
20  }
21
22  // Draw a polygon in the panel
23  class PolygonsPanel extends JPanel {
24    protected void paintComponent(Graphics g) {
25      super.paintComponent(g);
26
27      int xCenter = getWidth() / 2;
28      int yCenter = getHeight() / 2;
29      int radius = (int)(Math.min(getWidth(), getHeight()) * 0.4);
30
31      // Create a Polygon object
32      Polygon polygon = new Polygon();
33
34      // Add points to the polygon
35      polygon.addPoint)(xCenter + radius, yCenter);
36      polygon.addPoint)((int)(xCenter + radius *
37        Math.cos(2 * Math.PI / 6)), (int)(yCenter - radius *
38        Math.sin(2 * Math.PI / 6)));
39      polygon.addPoint((int)(xCenter + radius *
40        Math.cos(2 * 2 * Math.PI / 6)), (int)(yCenter - radius *
41        Math.sin(2 * 2 * Math.PI / 6)));
42      polygon.addPoint((int)(xCenter + radius *
43        Math.cos(3 * 2 * Math.PI / 6)), (int)(yCenter - radius *
44        Math.sin(3 * 2 * Math.PI / 6)));
45      polygon.addPoint((int)(xCenter + radius *
46        Math.cos(4 * 2 * Math.PI / 6)), (int)(yCenter - radius *
47        Math.sin(4 * 2 * Math.PI / 6)));
48      polygon.addPoint((int)(xCenter + radius *
49        Math.cos(5 * 2 * Math.PI / 6)), (int)(yCenter - radius *
50        Math.sin(5 * 2 * Math.PI / 6)));
51
52      // Draw the polygon
53      g.drawPolygon(polygon);
54    }
55  }
```

override
paintComponent

add a point

draw polygon

13.10 Centering a Display Using the **FontMetrics** Class

You can display a string at any location in a panel. Can you display it centered? To do so, you need to use the FontMetrics class to measure the exact width and height of the string for a particular font. FontMetrics can measure the following attributes for a given font (see Figure 13.16):

- **Leading**, pronounced *ledding*, is the amount of space between lines of text.

- **Ascent** is the distance from the baseline to the ascent line. The top of most characters in the font will be under the ascent line, but some may extend above the ascent line.

- **Descent** is the distance from the baseline to the descent line. The bottom of most descending characters (e.g., *j*, *y*, and *g*) in the font will be above the descending line, but some may extend below the descending line.

- **Height** is the sum of leading, ascent, and descent.

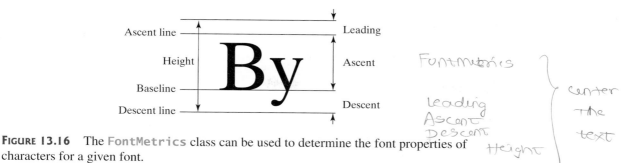

FIGURE 13.16   The FontMetrics class can be used to determine the font properties of characters for a given font.

FontMetrics is an abstract class. To get a FontMetrics object for a specific font, use the following getFontMetrics methods defined in the Graphics class:

- **public** FontMetrics getFontMetrics(Font font)
  Returns the font metrics of the specified font.

- **public** FontMetrics getFontMetrics()
  Returns the font metrics of the current font.

You can use the following instance methods in the FontMetrics class to obtain the attributes of a font and the width of a string when it is drawn using the font:

```
public int getAscent() // Return the ascent
public int getDescent() // Return the descent
public int getLeading() // Return the leading
public int getHeight() // Return the height
public int stringWidth(String str) // Return the width of the string
```

Listing 13.8 gives an example that displays a message in the center of the panel, as shown in Figure 13.17.

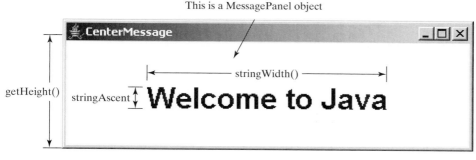

FIGURE 13.17   The program uses the FontMetrics class to measure the string width and height, and displays it at the center of the panel.

LISTING 13.8   TestCenterMessage.java

```
1  import javax.swing.*;
2  import java.awt.*;
3
4  public class TestCenterMessage extends JFrame {
5    public TestCenterMessage() {
6      CenterMessage messagePanel = new CenterMessage();
7      add(messagePanel);
8      messagePanel.setBackground(Color.WHITE);
```

create a message panel
add a message panel
set background

set font

```
 9       messagePanel.setFont(new Font("Californian FB", Font.BOLD, 30));
10     }
11
12   /** Main method */
13   public static void main(String[] args) {
14     TestCenterMessage frame = new TestCenterMessage();
15     frame.setLocationRelativeTo(null); // Center the frame
16     frame.setDefaultCloseOperation(JFrame.EXIT_ON_CLOSE);
17     frame.setSize(300, 150);
18     frame.setVisible(true);
19   }
20 }
21
22 class CenterMessage extends JPanel {
23   /** Paint the message */
24   protected void paintComponent(Graphics g) {
25     super.paintComponent(g);
26
27     // Get font metrics for the current font
28     FontMetrics fm = g.getFontMetrics();
29
30     // Find the center location to display
31     int stringWidth = fm.stringWidth("Welcome to Java");
32     int stringAscent = fm.getAscent();
33
34     // Get the position of the leftmost character in the baseline
35     int xCoordinate = getWidth() / 2 - stringWidth / 2;
36     int yCoordinate = getHeight() / 2 + stringAscent / 2;
37
38     g.drawString("Welcome to Java", xCoordinate, yCoordinate);
39   }
40 }
```

override **paintComponent** (line 24)

get **FontMetrics** (line 28)

The methods getWidth() and getHeight() (lines 35–36), defined in the Component class, return the component's width and height, respectively.

yCoordinate is the height of the baseline for the first character of the string to be displayed. When centered is true, yCoordinate should be getHeight() / 2 + h / 2, where h is the ascent of the string.

xCoordinate is the width of the baseline for the first character of the string to be displayed. When centered is true, xCoordinate should be getWidth() / 2 - stringWidth / 2.

13.11 Case Study: The **MessagePanel** Class

This case study develops a useful class that displays a message in a panel. The class enables the user to set the location of the message, center the message, and move the message with the specified interval. The contract of the class is shown in Figure 13.18.

Let us first write a test program in Listing 13.9 that uses the MessagePanel class to display four message panels, as shown in Figure 13.19.

LISTING 13.9 TestMessagePanel.java

```
1 import java.awt.*;
2 import javax.swing.*;
3
4 public class TestMessagePanel extends JFrame {
5   public TestMessagePanel() {
```

```
 6      MessagePanel messagePanel1 = new MessagePanel("Wecome to Java");          create message panel
 7      MessagePanel messagePanel2 = new MessagePanel("Java is fun");
 8      MessagePanel messagePanel3 = new MessagePanel("Java is cool");
 9      MessagePanel messagePanel4 = new MessagePanel("I love Java");
10      messagePanel1.setFont(new Font("SansSerif", Font.ITALIC, 20));            set font
11      messagePanel2.setFont(new Font("Courier", Font.BOLD, 20));
12      messagePanel3.setFont(new Font("Times", Font.ITALIC, 20));
13      messagePanel4.setFont(new Font("Californian FB", Font.PLAIN, 20));
14      messagePanel1.setBackground(Color.red);                                   set background
15      messagePanel2.setBackground(Color.cyan);
16      messagePanel3.setBackground(Color.green);
17      messagePanel4.setBackground(Color.white);
18      messagePanel1.setCentered(true);
19
20      setLayout(new GridLayout(2, 2));
21      add(messagePanel1);                                                       add message panel
22      add(messagePanel2);
23      add(messagePanel3);
24      add(messagePanel4);
25    }
26
27    public static void main(String[] args) {
28      TestMessagePanel frame = new TestMessagePanel();
29      frame.setSize(300, 200);
30      frame.setTitle("TestMessagePanel");
31      frame.setLocationRelativeTo(null); // Center the frame
32      frame.setDefaultCloseOperation(JFrame.EXIT_ON_CLOSE);
33      frame.setVisible(true);
34    }
35 }
```

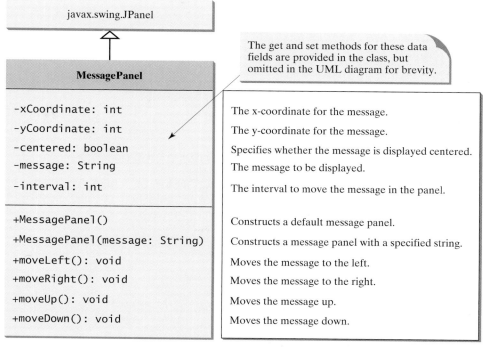

FIGURE 13.18   MessagePanel displays a message on the panel.

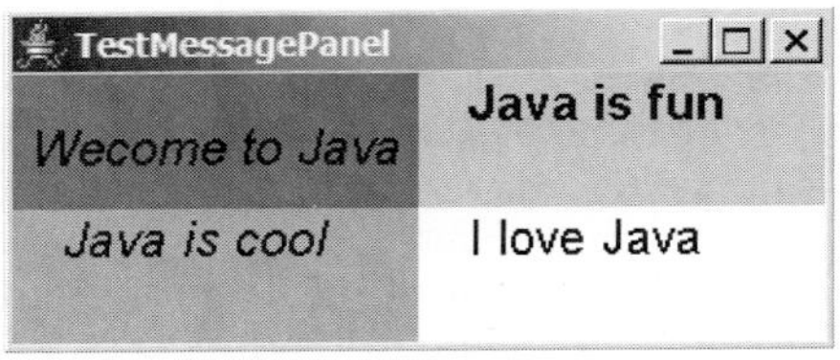

FIGURE 13.19 TestMessagePanel uses MessagePanel to display four message panels.

The MessagePanel class is implemented in Listing 13.10. The program seems long but is actually simple, because most of the methods are get and set methods, and each method is relatively short and easy to read.

LISTING 13.10 MessagePanel.java

```java
1  import java.awt.FontMetrics;
2  import java.awt.Dimension;
3  import java.awt.Graphics;
4  import javax.swing.JPanel;
5
6  public class MessagePanel extends JPanel {
7    /** The message to be displayed */
8    private String message = "Welcome to Java";
9
10   /** The x coordinate where the message is displayed */
11   private int xCoordinate = 20;
12
13   /** The y coordinate where the message is displayed */
14   private int yCoordinate = 20;
15
16   /** Indicate whether the message is displayed in the center */
17   private boolean centered;
18
19   /** The interval for moving the message horizontally and vertically */
20   private int interval = 10;
21
22   /** Construct with default properties */
23   public MessagePanel() {
24   }
25
26   /** Construct a message panel with a specified message */
27   public MessagePanel(String message) {
28     this.message = message;
29   }
30
31   /** Return message */
32   public String getMessage() {
33     return message;
34   }
35
36   /** Set a new message */
37   public void setMessage(String message) {
38     this.message = message;
39     repaint();
40   }
41
```

repaint panel

```
42    /** Return xCoordinator */
43    public int getXCoordinate() {
44      return xCoordinate;
45    }
46
47    /** Set a new xCoordinator */
48    public void setXCoordinate(int x) {
49      this.xCoordinate = x;
50      repaint();                                          repaint panel
51    }
52
53    /** Return yCoordinator */
54    public int getYCoordinate() {
55      return yCoordinate;
56    }
57
58    /** Set a new yCoordinator */
59    public void setYCoordinate(int y) {
60      this.yCoordinate = y;
61      repaint();                                          repaint panel
62    }
63
64    /** Return centered */
65    public boolean isCentered() {
66      return centered;
67    }
68
69    /** Set a new centered */
70    public void setCentered(boolean centered) {
71      this.centered = centered;
72      repaint();                                          repaint panel
73    }
74
75    /** Return interval */
76    public int getInterval() {
77      return interval;
78    }
79
80    /** Set a new interval */
81    public void setInterval(int interval) {
82      this.interval = interval;
83      repaint();                                          repaint panel
84    }
85
86    /** Paint the message */
87    protected void paintComponent(Graphics g) {           override
88      super.paintComponent(g);                              paintComponent
89
90      if (centered) {                                     check centered
91        // Get font metrics for the current font
92        FontMetrics fm = g.getFontMetrics();
93
94        // Find the center location to display
95        int stringWidth = fm.stringWidth(message);
96        int stringAscent = fm.getAscent();
97        // Get the position of the leftmost character in the baseline
98        xCoordinate = getWidth() / 2 - stringWidth / 2;
99        yCoordinate = getHeight() / 2 + stringAscent / 2;
100     }
101
```

```
102        g.drawString(message, xCoordinate, yCoordinate);
103      }
104
105      /** Move the message left */
106      public void moveLeft() {
107        xCoordinate -= interval;
108        repaint();
109      }
110
111      /** Move the message right */
112      public void moveRight() {
113        xCoordinate += interval;
114        repaint();
115      }
116
117      /** Move the message up */
118      public void moveUp() {
119        yCoordinate -= interval;
120        repaint();
121      }
122
123      /** Move the message down */
124      public void moveDown() {
125        yCoordinate += interval;
126        repaint();
127      }
128
129      /** Override get method for preferredSize */
130      public Dimension getPreferredSize() {
131        return new Dimension(200, 30);
132      }
133    }
```

override
getPreferredSize

The **paintComponent** method displays the message centered, if the **centered** property is **true** (line 90). **message** is initialized to **"Welcome to Java"** in line 8. If it is not initialized, a **NullPointerException** runtime error would occur when you create a **MessagePanel** using the no-arg constructor, because **message** would be **null** in line 102.

Caution

The **MessagePanel** class uses the properties **xCoordinate** and **yCoordinate** to specify the position of the message displayed on the panel. Do not use the property names **x** and **y**, because they are already defined in the **Component** class to return the position of the component in the parent's coordinate system using **getX()** and **getY()**.

Note

The **Component** class has the **setBackground**, **setForeground**, and **setFont** methods. These methods are for setting colors and fonts for the entire component. Suppose you want to draw several messages in a panel with different colors and fonts; you have to use the **setColor** and **setFont** methods in the **Graphics** class to set the color and font for the current drawing.

Note

design classes for reuse

One of the key features of Java programming is the reuse of classes. Throughout the book, reusable classes are developed and later reused. **MessagePanel** is an example of this, as are **Loan** in §7.15 and **FigurePanel** in §13.7. It can be reused whenever you need to display a message on a panel. To make your class reusable in a wide range of applications, you should provide a variety of ways to use it. **MessagePanel** provides many properties and methods that will be used in several examples in the book.

13.12 (Optional) Case Study: The StillClock Class

This case study develops a class that displays a clock on a panel. The contract of the class is shown in Figure 13.20.

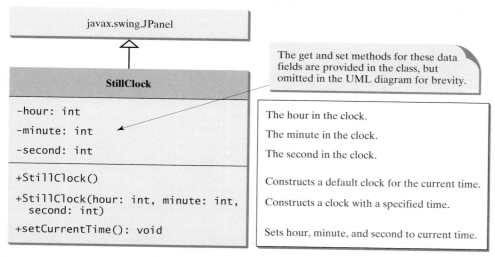

FIGURE 13.20   StillClock displays an analog clock.

Let us first write a test program in Listing 13.11 that uses the StillClock class to display an analog clock and uses the MessagePanel class to display the hour, minute, and second in a panel, as shown in Figure 13.21(a).

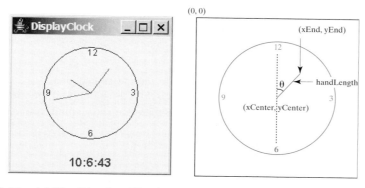

FIGURE 13.21   (a) The DisplayClock program displays a clock that shows the current time. (b) The end-point of a clock hand can be determined given the spanning angle, the hand length, and the center point.

LISTING 13.11   DisplayClock.java

```
1 import java.awt.*;
2 import javax.swing.*;
3
4 public class DisplayClock extends JFrame {
5   public DisplayClock() {
6     // Create an analog clock for the current time
7     StillClock clock = new StillClock();
8
```

create a clock

```
 9      // Display hour, minute, and seconds in the message panel
10      MessagePanel messagePanel = new MessagePanel(clock.getHour() +
11        ":"+ clock.getMinute() + ":"+ clock.getSecond());
12      messagePanel.setCentered(true);
13      messagePanel.setForeground(Color.blue);
14      messagePanel.setFont(new Font("Courier", Font.BOLD, 16));
15
16      // Add the clock and message panel to the frame
17      add(clock);
18      add(messagePanel, BorderLayout.SOUTH);
19    }
20
21    public static void main(String[] args) {
22      DisplayClock frame = new DisplayClock();
23      frame.setTitle("DisplayClock");
24      frame.setLocationRelativeTo(null); // Center the frame
25      frame.setDefaultCloseOperation(JFrame.EXIT_ON_CLOSE);
26      frame.setSize(300, 350);
27      frame.setVisible(true);
28    }
29 }
```

The rest of this section explains how to implement the StillClock class. Since you can use the class without knowing how it is implemented, you can skip the implementation if you wish.

To draw a clock, you need to draw a circle and three hands for second, minute, and hour. To draw a hand, you need to specify the two ends of the line. As shown in Figure 13.21(b), one end is the center of the clock at (xCenter, yCenter); the other end, at (xEnd, yEnd), is determined by the following formula:

```
xEnd = xCenter + handLength x sin(θ)
yEnd = yCenter - handLength x cos(θ)
```

Since there are sixty seconds in one minute, the angle for the second hand is

```
second x (2π/60)
```

The position of the minute hand is determined by the minute and second. The exact minute value combined with seconds is minute + second/60. For example, if the time is 3 minutes and 30 seconds, the total minutes are 3.5. Since there are sixty minutes in one hour, the angle for the minute hand is

```
(minute + second/60) x (2π/60)
```

Since one circle is divided into twelve hours, the angle for the hour hand is

```
(hour + minute/60 + second/(60 x 60))) x (2π/12)
```

For simplicity, you can omit the seconds in computing the angles of the minute hand and the hour hand, because they are very small and can be neglected. Therefore, the end-points for the second hand, minute hand, and hour hand can be computed as:

```
xSecond = xCenter + secondHandLength x sin(second x (2π/60))
ySecond = yCenter - secondHandLength x cos(second x (2π/60))
xMinute = xCenter + minuteHandLength x sin(minute x (2π/60))
yMinute = yCenter - minuteHandLength x cos(minute x (2π/60))
xHour = xCenter + hourHandLength x sin((hour + minute/60) x (2π/60)))
yHour = yCenter - hourHandLength x cos((hour + minute/60) x (2π/60)))
```

The StillClock class is implemented in Listing 13.12.

LISTING 13.12 StillClock.java

```
 1 import java.awt.*;
 2 import javax.swing.*;
 3 import java.util.*;
 4
 5 public class StillClock extends JPanel {
 6   private int hour;
 7   private int minute;
 8   private int second;
 9
10   /** Construct a default clock with the current time */
11   public StillClock() {
12     setCurrentTime();
13   }
14
15   /** Construct a clock with specified hour, minute, and second */
16   public StillClock(int hour, int minute, int second) {
17     this.hour = hour;
18     this.minute = minute;
19     this.second = second;
20   }
21
22   /** Return hour */
23   public int getHour() {
24     return hour;
25   }
26
27   /** Set a new hour */
28   public void setHour(int hour) {
29     this.hour = hour;
30     repaint();
31   }
32
33   /** Return minute */
34   public int getMinute() {
35     return minute;
36   }
37
38   /** Set a new minute */
39   public void setMinute(int minute) {
40     this.minute = minute;
41     repaint();
42   }
43
44   /** Return second */
45   public int getSecond() {
46     return second;
47   }
48
49   /** Set a new second */
50   public void setSecond(int second) {
51     this.second = second;
52     repaint();
53   }
54
55   /** Draw the clock */
56   protected void paintComponent(Graphics g) {
57     super.paintComponent(g);
58
```

repaint panel

repaint panel

repaint panel

override
paintComponent

```
59      // Initialize clock parameters
60      int clockRadius =
61        (int)(Math.min(getWidth(), getHeight()) * 0.8 * 0.5);
62      int xCenter = getWidth() / 2;
63      int yCenter = getHeight() / 2;
64
65      // Draw circle
66      g.setColor(Color.black);
67      g.drawOval(xCenter - clockRadius, yCenter - clockRadius,
68        2 * clockRadius, 2 * clockRadius);
69      g.drawString("12", xCenter - 5, yCenter - clockRadius + 12);
70      g.drawString("9", xCenter - clockRadius + 3, yCenter + 5);
71      g.drawString("3", xCenter + clockRadius - 10, yCenter + 3);
72      g.drawString("6", xCenter - 3, yCenter + clockRadius - 3);
73
74      // Draw second hand
75      int sLength = (int)(clockRadius * 0.8);
76      int xSecond = (int)(xCenter + sLength *
77        Math.sin(second * (2 * Math.PI / 60)));
78      int ySecond = (int)(yCenter - sLength *
79        Math.cos(second * (2 * Math.PI / 60)));
80      g.setColor(Color.red);
81      g.drawLine(xCenter, yCenter, xSecond, ySecond);
82
83      // Draw minute hand
84      int mLength = (int)(clockRadius * 0.65);
85      int xMinute = (int)(xCenter + mLength *
86        Math.sin(minute * (2 * Math.PI / 60)));
87      int yMinute = (int)(yCenter - mLength *
88        Math.cos(minute * (2 * Math.PI / 60)));
89      g.setColor(Color.blue);
90      g.drawLine(xCenter, yCenter, xMinute, yMinute);
91
92      // Draw hour hand
93      int hLength = (int)(clockRadius * 0.5);
94      int xHour = (int)(xCenter + hLength *
95        Math.sin((hour % 12 + minute / 60.0) * (2 * Math.PI / 12)));
96      int yHour = (int)(yCenter - hLength *
97        Math.cos((hour % 12 + minute / 60.0) * (2 * Math.PI / 12)));
98      g.setColor(Color.green);
99      g.drawLine(xCenter, yCenter, xHour, yHour);
100   }
101
102   public void setCurrentTime() {
103     // Construct a calendar for the current date and time
104     Calendar calendar = new GregorianCalendar();
105
106     // Set current hour, minute, and second
107     this.hour = calendar.get(Calendar.HOUR_OF_DAY);
108     this.minute = calendar.get(Calendar.MINUTE);
109     this.second = calendar.get(Calendar.SECOND);
110   }
111
112   public Dimension getPreferredSize() {
113     return new Dimension(200, 200);
114   }
115 }
```

get current time

override
getPreferredSize

The program enables the clock size to adjust as the frame resizes. Every time you resize the frame, the **paintComponent** method is automatically invoked to paint the new frame. The `paintComponent` method displays the clock in proportion to the panel width (`getWidth()`) and height (`getHeight()`) (lines 60–63 in `StillClock`).

> **Note**
> Like the `MessagePanel` class, the `StillClock` class is an example of a reusable class. `StillClock` will be used throughout the book. `StillClock` provides many properties and methods that enable it to be used in a wide range of applications.

design classes for reuse

13.13 (Optional) Displaying Images

You learned how to create image icons and display them in labels and buttons in §12.10, "Image Icons." For example, the following statements create an image icon and display it in a label:

```
ImageIcon icon = new ImageIcon("image/us.gif");
JLabel jlblImage = new JLabel(imageIcon);
```

An image icon displays a fixed-size image. To display an image in a flexible size, you need to use the `java.awt.Image` class. An image can be created from an image icon using the `getImage()` method as follows:

```
Image image = imageIcon.getImage();
```

Using a label as an area for displaying images is simple and convenient, but you don't have much control over how the image is displayed. A more flexible way to display images is to use the `drawImage` method of the `Graphics` class on a panel. Four versions of the `drawImage` method are shown in Figure 13.22.

java.awt.Graphics	
`+drawImage(image: Image, x: int, y: int, bgcolor: Color, observer: ImageObserver): void`	Draws the image in a specified location. The image's top-left corner is at (x, y) in the graphics context's coordinate space. Transparent pixels in the image are drawn in the specified color bgcolor. The observer is the object on which the image is displayed. The image is cut off if it is larger than the area it is being drawn on.
`+drawImage(image: Image, x: int, y: int, observer: ImageObserver): void`	Same as the preceding method except that it does not specify a background color.
`+drawImage(image: Image, x: int, y: int, width: int, height: int, observer: ImageObserver): void`	Draws a scaled version of the image that can fill all of the available space in the specified rectangle.
`+drawImage(image: Image, x: int, y: int, width: int, height: int, bgcolor: Color, observer: ImageObserver): void`	Same as the preceding method except that it provides a solid background color behind the image being drawn.

FIGURE 13.22 You can apply the `drawImage` method on a `Graphics` object to display an image in a GUI component.

`ImageObserver` is an asynchronous update interface that receives notifications of image information as the image is constructed. The `Component` class implements `ImageObserver`. Therefore, every GUI component is an instance of `ImageObserver`. To draw images using the `drawImage` method in a Swing component, such as `JPanel`, override the `paintComponent` method to tell the component how to display the image in the panel.

> **Note**
> You can also create an `ImageIcon` from an `Image` object using `new ImageIcon(image)`.

Listing 13.13 gives the code that displays an image from `image/us.gif`. The file `image/us.gif` (line 12) is under the **class** directory. The `Image` from the file is created in lines 11–14. The `drawImage` method displays the image to fill in the whole panel, as shown in Figure 13.23.

FIGURE 13.23 An image is displayed in a panel.

LISTING 13.13 DisplayImage.java

```
 1  import java.awt.*;
 2  import javax.swing.*;
 3
 4  public class DisplayImage extends JFrame {
 5    public DisplayImage() {
 6      add(new ImageCanvas());
 7    }
 8
 9    public static void main(String[] args) {
10      JFrame frame = new DisplayImage();
11      frame.setTitle("DisplayImage");
12      frame.setSize(300, 300);
13      frame.setLocationRelativeTo(null); // Center the frame
14      frame.setDefaultCloseOperation(JFrame.EXIT_ON_CLOSE);
15      frame.setVisible(true);
16    }
17  }
18
19  class ImageCanvas extends JPanel {
20    ImageIcon imageIcon = new ImageIcon("image/us.gif");
21    Image image = imageIcon.getImage();
22
23    /** Draw image on the panel */
24    public void paintComponent(Graphics g) {
25      super.paintComponent(g);
26
27      if (image != null)
28        g.drawImage(image, 0, 0, getWidth(), getHeight(), this);
29    }
30  }
```

add panel

create image icon
get image

override
  paintComponent

draw image

13.14 (Optional) Case Study: The **ImageViewer** Class

Displaying an image is a common task in Java programming. This case study develops a reusable component named **ImageViewer** that displays an image on a panel. The class contains the properties **image**, **stretched**, **xCoordinate**, and **yCoordinate**, with associated accessor and mutator methods, as shown in Figure 13.24.

You can use images in Swing components like `JLabel` and `JButton`, but these images are not stretchable. The image in an **ImageViewer** can be stretched.

Let us write a test program in Listing 13.14 that displays six images using the **ImageViewer** class. Figure 13.25 shows a sample run of the program.

stretchable image

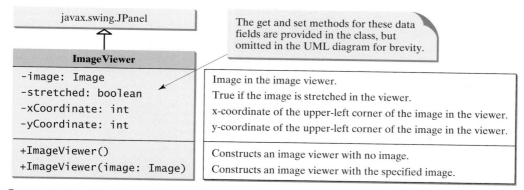

```
javax.swing.JPanel
```

The get and set methods for these data fields are provided in the class, but omitted in the UML diagram for brevity.

ImageViewer

```
-image: Image
-stretched: boolean
-xCoordinate: int
-yCoordinate: int
```

Image in the image viewer.
True if the image is stretched in the viewer.
x-coordinate of the upper-left corner of the image in the viewer.
y-coordinate of the upper-left corner of the image in the viewer.

```
+ImageViewer()
+ImageViewer(image: Image)
```

Constructs an image viewer with no image.
Constructs an image viewer with the specified image.

FIGURE 13.24   The `ImageViewer` class displays an image on a panel.

LISTING 13.14   SixFlags.java

```java
1  import javax.swing.*;
2  import java.awt.*;
3
4  public class SixFlags extends JFrame {
5    public SixFlags() {
6      Image image1 = new ImageIcon("image/us.gif").getImage();
7      Image image2 = new ImageIcon("image/ca.gif").getImage();
8      Image image3 = new ImageIcon("image/india.gif").getImage();
9      Image image4 = new ImageIcon("image/uk.gif").getImage();
10     Image image5 = new ImageIcon("image/china.gif").getImage();
11     Image image6 = new ImageIcon("image/norway.gif").getImage();
12
13     setLayout(new GridLayout(2, 0, 5, 5));
14     add(new ImageViewer(image1));
15     add(new ImageViewer(image2));
16     add(new ImageViewer(image3));
17     add(new ImageViewer(image4));
18     add(new ImageViewer(image5));
19     add(new ImageViewer(image6));
20   }
21
22   public static void main(String[] args) {
23     SixFlags frame = new SixFlags();
24     frame.setTitle("SixFlags");
25     frame.setLocationRelativeTo(null); // Center the frame
26     frame.setDefaultCloseOperation(JFrame.EXIT_ON_CLOSE);
27     frame.setSize(400, 320);
28     frame.setVisible(true);
29   }
30 }
```

create image

create image viewer

FIGURE 13.25   Six images are displayed in six `ImageViewer` components.

implementation

skip implementation?

The `ImageViewer` class is implemented in Listing 13.15. (*Note: You may skip the implementation.*) The accessor and mutator methods for the properties `image`, `stretched`, `xCoordinate`, and `yCoordinate` are easy to implement. The `paintComponent` method (lines 26–35) displays the image on the panel. Line 29 ensures that the image is not null before displaying it. Line 30 checks whether the image is stretched or not.

LISTING 13.15 ImageViewer.java

```java
1 import java.awt.*;
2 import javax.swing.*;
3
4 public class ImageViewer extends JPanel {
5   /** Hold value of property image. */
6   private java.awt.Image image;
7
8   /** Hold value of property stretched. */
9   private boolean stretched = true;
10
11   /** Hold value of property xCoordinate. */
12   private int xCoordinate;
13
14   /** Hold value of property yCoordinate. */
15   private int yCoordinate;
16
17   /** Construct an empty image viewer */
18   public ImageViewer() {
19   }
20
21   /** Construct an image viewer for a specified Image object */
22   public ImageViewer(Image image) {
23     this.image = image;
24   }
25
26   protected void paintComponent(Graphics g)  {
27     super.paintComponent(g);
28
29     if(image != null)
30       if (isStretched())
31         g.drawImage(image, xCoordinate, yCoordinate,
32           getSize().width, getSize().height, this);
33       else
34         g.drawImage(image, xCoordinate, yCoordinate, this);
35   }
36
37   /** Return value of property image */
38   public java.awt.Image getImage() {
39     return image;
40   }
41
42   /** Set a new value for property image */
43   public void setImage(java.awt.Image image) {
44     this.image = image;
45     repaint();
46   }
47
48   /** Return value of property stretched */
49   public boolean isStretched() {
50     return stretched;
51   }
52
```

properties

constructor

constructor

image null?

stretched

non-stretched

```
53    /** Set a new value for property stretched */
54    public void setStretched(boolean stretched) {
55      this.stretched = stretched;
56      repaint();
57    }
58
59    /** Return value of property xCoordinate */
60    public int getXCoordinate() {
61      return xCoordinate;
62    }
63
64    /** Set a new value for property xCoordinate */
65    public void setXCoordinate(int xCoordinate) {
66      this.xCoordinate = xCoordinate;
67      repaint();
68    }
69
70    /** Return value of property yCoordinate */
71    public int getYCoordinate() {
72      return yCoordinate;
73    }
74
75    /** Set a new value for property yCoordinate */
76    public void setYCoordinate(int yCoordinate) {
77      this.yCoordinate = yCoordinate;
78      repaint();
79    }
80 }
```

CHAPTER SUMMARY

■   Each component has its own coordinate system with the origin (0, 0) at the upper-left corner of the window. The *x*-coordinate increases to the right, and the *y*-coordinate increases downward.

■   The Graphics class is an abstract class for displaying figures and images on the screen on different platforms. The Graphics class is implemented on the native platform in the JVM. When you use the paintComponent(g) method to paint on a GUI component, this g is an instance of a concrete subclass of the abstract Graphics class for the specific platform. The Graphics class encapsulates the platform details and enables you to draw things uniformly without concern for the specific platform.

■   Invoking super.paintComponent(g) is necessary to ensure that the viewing area is cleared before a new drawing is displayed. The user can request the component to be redisplayed by invoking the repaint() method defined in the Component class. Invoking repaint() causes paintComponent to be invoked by the JVM. The user should never invoke paintComponent directly. For this reason, the protected visibility is sufficient for paintComponent.

■   Normally you use JPanel as a canvas. To draw on a JPanel, you create a new class that extends JPanel and overrides the paintComponent method to tell the panel how to draw things.

■   You can set fonts for the components or subjects you draw, and use font metrics to measure font size. Fonts and font metrics are encapsulated in the classes Font and

FontMetrics. FontMetrics can be used to compute the exact length and width of a string, which is helpful for measuring the size of a string in order to display it in the right position.

■   The Component class has the setBackground, setForeground, and setFont methods. These methods are used to set colors and fonts for the entire component. Suppose you want to draw several messages in a panel with different colors and fonts; you have to use the setColor and setFont methods in the Graphics class to set the color and font for the current drawing.

■   To display an image, first create an image icon. You can then use ImageIcon's getImage() method to get an Image object for the image and draw the image using the drawImage method in the java.awt.Graphics class.

REVIEW QUESTIONS

Sections 13.2–13.3

13.1   Suppose that you want to draw a new message below an existing message. Should the x, y coordinate increase or decrease?

13.2   Why does jlblBanner.getGraphics() in line 9 in Listing 13.1 return null? What is the reason for showing the message dialog box in line 19 in Listing 13.1? In line 9, jlblBanner.getGraphics() is used to return a Graphics object. In line 21, why do you have to use frame.jlblBanner.getGraphics() in the main method?

Sections 13.4–13.5

13.3   Describe the paintComponent method. Where is it defined? How is it invoked? Can it be directly invoked? Can the program cause this method to be invoked?

13.4   Why is the paintComponent method protected? What happens if you change it to public or private in a subclass? Why is super.paintComponent(g) invoked in line 25 in Listing 13.2 and in line 21 in Listing 13.3?

13.5   Can you draw things on any Swing GUI component? Why should you use a panel as a canvas for drawings rather than a label or a button?

Sections 13.6–13.9

13.6   Describe the methods for drawing strings, lines, rectangles, round-cornered rectangles, 3D rectangles, ovals, arcs, polygons, and polylines.

13.7   Describe the methods for filling rectangles, round-cornered rectangle, ovals, arcs, and polygons.

13.8   How do you get and set colors and fonts in a Graphics object?

13.9   Write a statement to draw the following shapes:

■   Draw a thick line from (10, 10) to (70, 30). You can draw several lines next to each other to create the effect of one thick line.

■   Draw/fill a rectangle of width 100 and height 50 with the upper-left corner at (10, 10).

■   Draw/fill a round-cornered rectangle with width 100, height 200, corner horizontal diameter 40, and corner vertical diameter 20.

■   Draw/fill a circle with radius 30.

- Draw/fill an oval with width 50 and height 100.
- Draw the upper half of a circle with radius 50.
- Draw/fill a polygon connecting the following points: (20, 40), (30, 50), (40, 90), (90, 10), (10, 30).
- Draw a 3-D cube like the one in Figure 13.26.

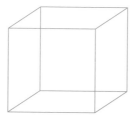

FIGURE 13.26   Use the drawLine method to draw a 3-D cube.

Sections 13.10–13.12

13.10 How do you find the leading, ascent, descent, and height of a font? How do you find the exact length of a string in a Graphics object?

13.11 If message is not initialized in line 8 in Listing 13.9, MessagePanel.java, what would happen when you create a MessagePanel using its no-arg constructor?

13.12 The following program is supposed to display a message on the panel, but nothing is displayed. There are problems in lines 2 and 14. Identify them.

```
 1 public class TestDrawMessage extends javax.swing.JFrame {
 2   public void TestDrawMessage() {
 3     add(new DrawMessage());
 4   }
 5
 6   public static void main(String[] args) {
 7     javax.swing.JFrame frame = new TestDrawMessage();
 8     frame.setSize(100, 200);
 9     frame.setVisible(true);
10   }
11 }
12
13 class DrawMessage extends javax.swing.JPanel {
14   protected void PaintComponent(java.awt.Graphics g) {
15     super.paintComponent(g);
16     g.drawString("Welcome to Java", 20, 20);
17   }
18 }
```

Sections 13.13–13.14

13.13 How do you create an Image object from the ImageIcon object?

13.14 How do you create an ImageIcon object from an Image object?

13.15 Describe the drawImage method in the Graphics class.

13.16 Explain the differences between displaying images in a JLabel and in a JPanel.

13.17 Which package contains ImageIcon, and which contains Image?

PROGRAMMING EXERCISES

Sections 13.2–13.9

13.1* (*Displaying a 3 × 3 grid*) Write a program that displays a 3 × 3 grid, as shown in Figure 13.27(a). Use red color for vertical lines and blue color for horizontal lines.

FIGURE 13.27 (a) Exercise 13.1 displays a grid. (b) Exercise 13.2 displays two objects of `OvalButton`. (c) Exercise 13.3 displays a checkerboard.

13.2** (*Creating a custom button class*) Develop a custom button class named `OvalButton` that extends `JButton` and displays the button text inside an oval. Figure 13.27(b) shows two buttons created using the `OvalButton` class.

13.3* (*Displaying a checkerboard*) Write a program that displays a checkerboard, as shown in Figure 13.27(c).

13.4* (*Displaying a multiplication table*) Write a program that displays a multiplication table in a panel using the drawing methods, as shown in Figure 13.28(a).

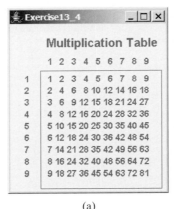 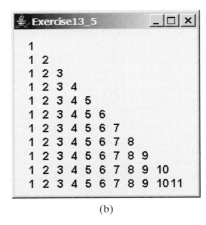

(a) (b)

FIGURE 13.28 (a) Exercise 13.4 displays a multiplication table. (b) Exercise 13.5 displays numbers in a triangle formation.

13.5** (*Displaying numbers in a triangular pattern*) Write a program that displays numbers in a triangular pattern, as shown in Figure 13.28(b). The number of lines in the display changes to fit the window as the window resizes.

13.6** (*Improving `FigurePanel`*) The `FigurePanel` class in Listing 13.5 can display lines, rectangles, round-cornered rectangles, and ovals. Add appropriate new code in the class to display arcs and polygons. Write a test program to display the shapes as shown in Figure 13.29(a), using the new `FigurePanel` class.

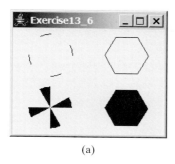
(a)
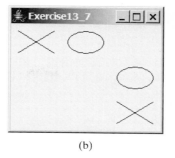
(b)
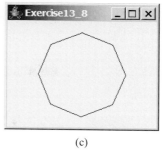
(c)

FIGURE 13.29 (a) Four panels of geometric figures are displayed in a frame of `GridLayout`. (b) `TicTacToe` cells display X, O, or nothing randomly. (c) Exercise 13.8 draws an octagon.

13.7** (*Displaying a TicTacToe board*) Create a custom panel that displays X, O, or nothing. What to display is randomly decided whenever a panel is repainted. Use the `Math.random()` method to generate an integer **0**, **1**, or **2**, which corresponds to displaying X, O, or nothing. Create a frame that contains nine custom panels, as shown in Figure 13.29(b).

13.8** (*Drawing an octagon*) Write a program that draws an octagon, as shown in Figure 13.29(c).

13.9* (*Creating four fans*) Write a program that places four fans in a frame of `GridLayout` with two rows and two columns, as shown in Figure 13.30(a).

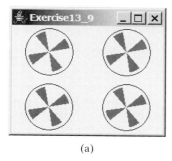
(a)
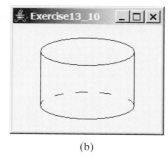
(b)
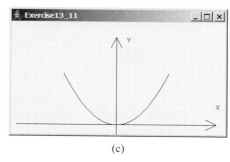
(c)

FIGURE 13.30 (a) Exercise 13.9 draws four fans. (b) Exercise 13.10 draws a cylinder. (c) Exercise 13.11 draws a diagram for function $f(x) = x^2$.

13.10* (*Creating a cylinder*) Write a program that draws a cylinder, as shown in Figure 13.30(b).

13.11** (*Plotting the square function*) Write a program that draws a diagram for the function $f(x) = x^2$ (see Figure 13.30(c)).

Hint
Add points to a polygon **p** using the following loop:

```
double scaleFactor = 0.1;
for (int x = -100; x <= 100; x++) {
  p.addPoint(x + 200, 200 - (int)(scaleFactor * x * x));
}
```

Connect the points using `g.drawPolyline(p.xpoints, p.ypoints, p.npoints)` for a `Graphics` object `g`. `p.xpoints` returns an array of x coordinates, `p.ypoints` returns an array of y coordinates, and `p.npoints` returns the number of points in `Polygon` object `p`.

13.12** *(Plotting the sine function)* Write a program that draws a diagram for the sine function, as shown in Figure 13.31(a).

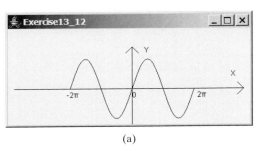

(a)

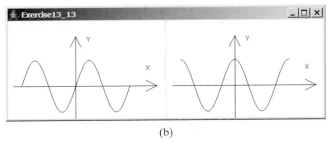

(b)

FIGURE 13.31   (a) Exercise 13.12 draws a diagram for function $f(x) = sin(x)$. (b) Exercise 13.13 draws the sine and cosine functions.

Hint

The Unicode for π is \u03c0. To display −2π use `g.drawString("-2\u03c0", x, y)`. For a trigonometric function like `sin(x)`, x is in radians. Use the following loop to add the points to a polygon `p`:

```
for (int x = -100; x <= 100; x++) {
  p.addPoint(x + 200,
    100 - (int)(50 * Math.sin((x / 100.0) * 2 * Math.PI)));
}
```

−2π is at (100, 100), the center of the axis is at (200, 100), and 2π is at (300, 100). Use the `drawPolyline` method in the `Graphics` class to connect the points.

13.13** *(Plotting functions using generic methods)* Write a generic class that draws the diagram for a function. The class is defined as follows:

```
public abstract class AbstractDrawFunction extends JPanel {
  /** Polygon to hold the points */
  private Polygon p = new Polygon();

  protected AbstractDrawFunction () {
    drawFunction();
  }

  /** Return the y coordinate */
  abstract double f(double x);

  /** Obtain points for x coordinates 100, 101, ..., 300 */
  public void drawFunction() {
    for (int x = -100; x <= 100; x++) {
      p.addPoint(x + 200, 200 - (int)f(x));
    }
  }

  /** Implement paintComponent to draw axes, labels, and
   *   connecting points
   */
```

```
     protected void paintComponent(Graphics g) {
       // To be completed by you
     }
   }
```

Test the class with the following functions:

```
   f(x) = x²;
   f(x) = sin(x);
   f(x) = cos(x);
   f(x) = tan(x);
   f(x) = cos(x) + 5sin(x);
   f(x) = cos(x) + 5sin(x);
   f(x) = log(x) + x²;
```

For each function, create a class that extends the **AbstractDrawFunction** class and implements the **f** method. Figure 13.31(b) displays the drawings for the sine function and the cosine function.

13.14** (*Displaying a bar chart*) Write a program that uses a bar chart to display the percentages of the overall grade represented by projects, quizzes, midterm exams, and the final exam, as shown in Figure 13.32(a). Suppose that projects take **20** percent and are displayed in red, quizzes take **10** percent and are displayed in blue, midterm exams take **30** percent and are displayed in green, and the final exam takes **40** percent and is displayed in orange.

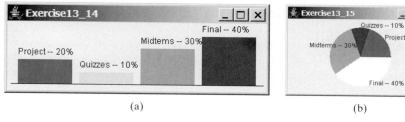

(a)   (b)

FIGURE 13.32   Exercise 13.14 and Exercise 13.15 use a bar chart and a pie chart to show the percentages of projects, quizzes, midterm exams, and final exam in the overall grade.

13.15** (*Displaying a pie chart*) Write a program that uses a pie chart to display the percentages of the overall grade represented by projects, quizzes, midterm exams, and the final exam, as shown in Figure 13.32(b). Suppose that projects take **20** percent and are displayed in red, quizzes take **10** percent and are displayed in blue, midterm exams take **30** percent and are displayed in green, and the final exam takes **40** percent and is displayed in orange.

13.16   (*Obtaining font information*) Write a program that displays the message "Java is fun" in a panel. Set the panel's font to TimesRoman, bold, and 20-pixel. Display the font's leading, ascent, descent, height, and the string width as a tool tip text for the panel, as shown in Figure 13.33(a).

(a)   (b)

FIGURE 13.33   (a) Exercise 13.16 displays font properties in a tool tip text. (b) Exercise 13.17 uses **MessagePanel** to display four strings.

13.17 (*Using the* `MessagePanel` *class*) Write a program that displays four messages, as shown in Figure 13.33(b).

13.18 (*Using the* `StillClock` *class*) Write a program that displays two clocks. The hour, minute, and second values are **4**, **20**, **45** for the first clock, and **22**, **46**, **15** for the second clock, as shown in Figure 13.34(a).

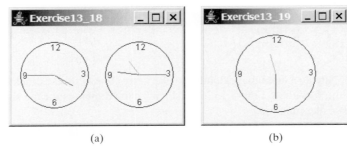

(a)   (b)   (c)

FIGURE 13.34 (a) Exercise 13.18 displays two clocks. (b) Exercise 13.19 displays a clock with random hour and minute values. (c) Exercise 13.20 displays a detailed clock.

13.19* (*Random time*) Modify the `StillClock` class with three new Boolean properties: `hourHandVisible`, `minuteHandVisible`, and `secondHandVisible`, and their associated accessor and mutator methods. You can use the set methods to make a hand visible or invisible. Write a test program that displays only the hour and minute hands. The hour and minute values are randomly generated. The hour is between **0** and **11**, and the minute is either **0** or **30**, as shown in Figure 13.34(b).

13.20** (*Drawing a detailed clock*) Modify the `StillClock` class in §13.12, "Case Study: The `StillClock` Class," to draw the clock with more details on the hours and minutes, as shown in Figure 13.34(c).

13.21** (*Displaying a TicTacToe board with images*) Rewrite Exercise 12.7 to display an image in a `JPanel` instead of displaying an image icon in a `JLabel`.

CHAPTER 14

EVENT-DRIVEN PROGRAMMING

Objectives

- To start learning about event-driven programming with a simple example (§14.1).
- To explain the concept of event-driven programming (§14.2).
- To understand events, event sources, and event classes (§14.2).
- To declare listener classes and write the code to handle events (§14.3).
- To register listener objects in the source object (§14.3).
- To declare inner classes and anonymous inner classes (§§14.3.1–14.3.2).
- To create listeners using inner classes and anonymous inner classes (§14.3.2).
- To understand how an event is handled (§14.3).
- To write programs to deal with `ActionEvent` (§14.3).
- To write programs to deal with `MouseEvent` (§14.4).
- To write programs to deal with `KeyEvent` (§14.5).
- (Optional) To use the `Timer` class to control animations (§14.6).

14.1 Introduction

event-driven programming

All the programs so far execute in a procedural order. This chapter introduces event-driven programming. In *event-driven programming*, code is executed when an event occurs (e.g., a button click or a mouse movement).

Before delving into event-driven programming, it is helpful to get a taste using a simple example. The example displays a button in the frame. A message is displayed on the console when a button is clicked, as shown in Figure 14.1.

FIGURE 14.1 A message is displayed when clicking the button.

The program is given in Listing 14.1. When a button is clicked, an event is fired from the button. The button is the source of the event. A listener object is created in line 11 and is registered with the button in line 12. When an action event occurs on the button, the button notifies the listener by invoking the listener's `actionPerformed` method (line 27).

LISTING 14.1 SimpleEventdemo.java

```java
1  import javax.swing.*;
2  import java.awt.event.*;
3  import java.awt.*;
4
5  public class SimpleEventDemo extends JFrame {
6    public SimpleEventDemo() {
7      JButton jbtOK = new JButton("OK");
8      setLayout(new FlowLayout());
9      add(jbtOK);
10
11     ActionListener listener = new OKListener();
12     jbtOK.addActionListener(listener);
13   }
14
15   /** Main method */
16   public static void main(String[] args) {
17     JFrame frame = new SimpleEventDemo();
18     frame.setTitle("SimpleEventDemo");
19     frame.setLocationRelativeTo(null); // Center the frame
20     frame.setDefaultCloseOperation(JFrame.EXIT_ON_CLOSE);
21     frame.setSize(220, 80);
22     frame.setVisible(true);
23   }
24 }
25
26 class OKListener implements ActionListener {
27   public void actionPerformed(ActionEvent e) {
28     System.out.println("It is OK");
29   }
30 }
```

create listener
register listener

listener class
handle event

Now that you have had a taste of event-driven programming, you probably have many questions, such as why a listener class is declared to implement the `ActionListener` interface. This chapter will give you all the answers.

14.2 Event and Event Source

When you run Java GUI programs, the program interacts with the user and the events drive its execution. An *event* can be defined as a signal to the program that something has happened. Events are triggered either by external user actions, such as mouse movements, button clicks, and keystrokes, or by internal program activities, such as a timer. The program can choose to respond to or ignore an event.

event

The component on which an event is *fired* or *generated* is called the *source object* or *source component*. For example, a button is the source object for a button-clicking action event. An event is an instance of an event class. The root class of the event classes is `java.util.EventObject`. The hierarchical relationships of some event classes are shown in Figure 14.2.

source object

fire event

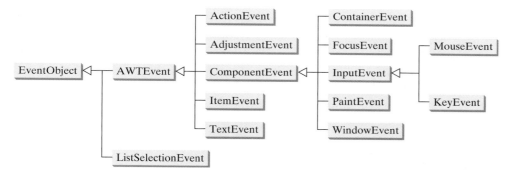

FIGURE 14.2 An event is an object of the `EventObject` class.

An event object contains whatever properties are pertinent to the event. You can identify the source object of an event using the `getSource()` instance method in the `EventObject` class. The subclasses of `EventObject` deal with special types of events, such as action events, window events, component events, mouse events, and key events. Table 14.1 lists external user actions, source objects, and event types fired.

getSource()

 Note
If a component can fire an event, any subclass of the component can fire the same type of event. For example, every GUI component can fire `MouseEvent`, `KeyEvent`, `FocusEvent`, and `ComponentEvent`, since `Component` is the superclass of all GUI components.

 Note
All the event classes in Figure 14.2 are included in the `java.awt.event` package except `ListSelectionEvent`, which is in the `javax.swing.event` package. AWT events were originally designed for AWT components, but many Swing components fire them.

14.3 Listeners, Registrations, and Handling Events

Java uses a delegation-based model for event handling: a source object fires an event, and an object interested in the event handles the event. The latter object is called a *listener*. Two things are needed for an object to be a listener for an event on a source object, as shown in Figure 14.3.

listener

TABLE 14.1 User Action, Source Object, and Event Type

User Action	Source Object	Event Type Fired
Click a button	`JButton`	`ActionEvent`
Press return on a text field	`JTextField`	`ActionEvent`
Select a new item	`JComboBox`	`ItemEvent, ActionEvent`
Select item(s)	`JList`	`ListSelectionEvent`
Click a check box	`JCheckBox`	`ItemEvent, ActionEvent`
Click a radio button	`JRadioButton`	`ItemEvent, ActionEvent`
Select a menu item	`JMenuItem`	`ActionEvent`
Move the scroll bar	`JScrollBar`	`AdjustmentEvent`
Window opened, closed, iconified, deiconified, or closing	`Window`	`WindowEvent`
Mouse pressed, released, clicked, entered, or exited	`Component`	`MouseEvent`
Mouse moved or dragged	`Component`	`MouseEvent`
Key released or pressed	`Component`	`KeyEvent`
Component added or removed from the container	`Container`	`ContainerEvent`
Component moved, resized, hidden, or shown	`Component`	`ComponentEvent`
Component gained or lost focus	`Component`	`FocusEvent`

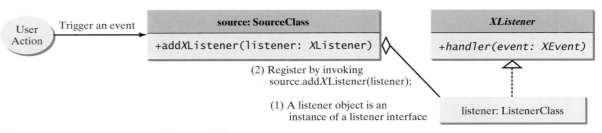

(a) A generic source component with a generic listener

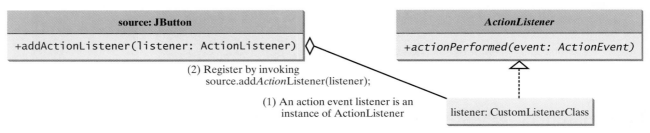

(b) A JButton source component with an ActionListener

FIGURE 14.3 A listener must be an instance of a listener interface and must be registered with a source component.

1. The listener object must be an instance of the corresponding event-listener interface to ensure that the listener has the correct method for processing the event. Java provides a *listener interface* for every type of GUI event. The listener interface is usually named *X*Listener for *X*Event, with the exception of MouseMotionListener. For example, the corresponding listener interface for ActionEvent is ActionListener; each listener for ActionEvent should implement the ActionListener interface. Table 14.2 lists event types, the corresponding listener interfaces, and the methods defined in the listener interfaces. The listener interface contains the method(s), known as the *handler(s)*, invoked by the source object to process the event.

listener interface
*X*Event/*X*Listener
ActionEvent/Action-
   Listener

handler

TABLE 14.2   Events, Event Listeners, and Listener Methods

Event Class (Handlers)	Listener Interface	Listener Methods
ActionEvent	ActionListener	actionPerformed(ActionEvent)
ItemEvent	ItemListener	itemStateChanged(ItemEvent)
MouseEvent	MouseListener	mousePressed(MouseEvent)
		mouseReleased(MouseEvent)
		mouseEntered(MouseEvent)
		mouseExited(MouseEvent)
		mouseClicked(MouseEvent)
	MouseMotionListener	mouseDragged(MouseEvent)
		mouseMoved(MouseEvent)
KeyEvent	KeyListener	keyPressed(KeyEvent)
		keyReleased(KeyEvent)
		keyTyped(KeyEvent)
WindowEvent	WindowListener	windowClosing(WindowEvent)
		windowOpened(WindowEvent)
		windowIconified(WindowEvent)
		windowDeiconified(WindowEvent)
		windowClosed(WindowEvent)
		windowActivated(WindowEvent)
		windowDeactivated(WindowEvent)
ContainerEvent	ContainerListener	componentAdded(ContainerEvent)
		componentRemoved(ContainerEvent)
ComponentEvent	ComponentListener	componentMoved(ComponentEvent)
		componentHidden(ComponentEvent)
		componentResized(ComponentEvent)
		componentShown(ComponentEvent)
FocusEvent	FocusListener	focusGained(FocusEvent)
		focusLost(FocusEvent)
AdjustmentEvent	AdjustmentListener	adjustmentValueChanged (AdjustmentEvent)

register listener

2. The listener object must be registered by the source object. Registration methods are dependent on the event type. For **ActionEvent**, the method is **addActionListener**. In general, the method is named **add*X*Listener** for *X*Event. A source object may fire several types of events. For each event, the source object maintains a list of listeners and notifies all the registered listeners by invoking the *handler* on the listener object to respond to the event, as shown in Figure 14.4. (Figure 14.4 shows the internal implementation of a source class. It addresses the question how a handler is invoked.)

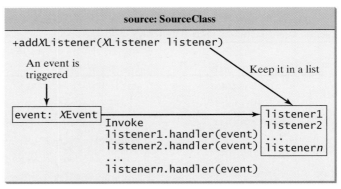

(a) Internal function of a generic source object

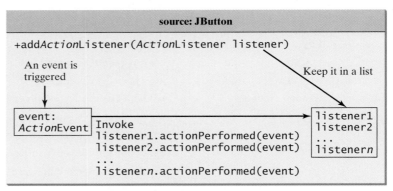

(b) Internal function of a JButton object

FIGURE 14.4 The source object notifies the listeners of the event by invoking the handler of the listener object.

Now you have the answers to all your questions about the simple example in Listing 14.1. Since a **JButton** object fires **ActionEvent**, a listener object for **ActionEvent** must be an instance of **ActionListener**, so the listener class implements **ActionListener** in line 26. The source object invokes **addActionListener(listener)** to register a listner, as follows:

create source object
create listener object

```java
JButton jbt = new JButton("OK"); // Line 7 in Listing 14.1
ActionListener listener = new OKListener(); // Line 11 in Listing 14.1
jbt.addActionListener(listener ); // Line 12 in Listing 14.1
```

register listener

When you click the button, the **JButton** object fires an **ActionEvent** and passes it to invoke the listener's **actionPerformed** method to handle the event.

The event object contains information pertinent to the event, which can be obtained using the methods, as shown in Figure 14.5. For example, you can use **e.getSource()** to obtain

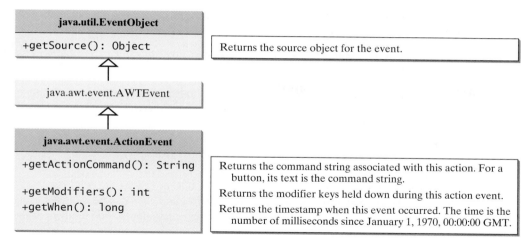

FIGURE 14.5   You can obtain useful information from an event object.

the source object in order to determine whether it is a button, a check box, or a radio button. For an action event, you can use `e.getWhen()` to obtain the time when the event occurs.

14.3.1   Inner Class Listeners

A listener class is designed specifically to create a listener object for a GUI component (e.g., a button). The listener class will not be shared by other applications and therefore is appropriately defined inside the frame class as an inner class.

An *inner class*, or *nested class,* is a class defined within the scope of another class. The   inner class
code in Figure 14.6(a) declares two separate classes, `Test` and `A`. The code in Figure 14.6(b) declares `A` as an inner class in `Test`.

```java
public class Test {
    ...
}
public class A {
    ...
}
```

(a)

```java
public class Test {
    ...
    // Inner class
    public class A {
        ...
    }
}
```

(b)

```java
// OuterClass.java: inner class demo
public class OuterClass {
    private int data;

    /** A method in the outer class */
    public void m() {
        // Do something
    }

    // An inner class
    class InnerClass {
        /** A method in the inner class */
        public void mi() {
            // Directly reference data and method
            // defined in its outer class
            data++;
            m();
        }
    }
}
```

(c)

FIGURE 14.6   Inner classes combine dependent classes into the primary class.

The class `InnerClass` defined inside `OuterClass` in Figure 14.6(c) is another example of an inner class. An inner class may be used just like a regular class. Normally, you declare a class an inner class if it is only used by its outer class. An inner class has the following features:

- An inner class is compiled into a class named *OuterClassName$InnerClassName*.class. For example, the inner class **A** in **Test** is compiled into *Test$A*.class in Figure 14.6(b).

- An inner class can reference the data and methods defined in the outer class in which it nests, so you do not need to pass the reference of an object of the outer class to the constructor of the inner class. For this reason, inner classes can make programs simple and concise.

- An inner class can be declared with a visibility modifier subject to the same visibility rules applied to a member of the class.

- An inner class can be declared **static**. A **static** inner class can be accessed using the outer class name. A **static** inner class cannot access non-static members of the outer class.

- Objects of an inner class are often created in the outer class. But you can also create an object of an inner class from another class. If the inner class is non-static, you must first create an instance of the outer class, then use the following syntax to create an object for the inner class:

  ```
  OuterClass.InnerClass innerObject = outerObject.new InnerClass();
  ```

- If the inner class is static, use the following syntax to create an object for it:

  ```
  OuterClass.InnerClass innerObject = new OuterClass.InnerClass();
  ```

Tip

A simple use of inner classes is to combine dependent classes into a primary class. This reduces the number of source files. It also makes class files easy to organize, since all the class files are named with the primary class as the prefix. For example, rather than creating two source files, Test.java and A.java, in Figure 14.6(a), you can combine class **A** into class **Test** and create just one source file, Test.java, in Figure 14.6(b). The resulting class files are Test.class and Test$A.class.

Listing 14.1 can now be modified using an inner class.

LISTING 14.2 SimpleEventDemoInnerClass.java

```
1  import javax.swing.*;
2  import java.awt.event.*;
3  import java.awt.*;
4
5  public class SimpleEventDemoInnerClass extends JFrame {
6    public SimpleEventDemoInnerClass() {
7      JButton jbtOK = new JButton("OK");
8      setLayout(new FlowLayout());
9      add(jbtOK);
10
11     ActionListener listener = new OKListener();
12     jbtOK.addActionListener(listener);
13   }
14
15   /** Main method */
16   public static void main(String[] args) {
17     JFrame frame = new SimpleEventDemoInnerClass();
18     frame.setTitle("SimpleEventDemoInnerClass");
```

create listener

register listener

```
19    frame.setLocationRelativeTo(null); // Center the frame
20    frame.setDefaultCloseOperation(JFrame.EXIT_ON_CLOSE);
21    frame.setSize(220, 80);
22    frame.setVisible(true);
23  }
24
25  private class OKListener implements ActionListener {
26    public void actionPerformed(ActionEvent e) {
27      System.out.println("It is OK");
28    }
29  }
30 }
```

Inner class

listener class
handle event

Listing 14.2 is the same as Listing 14.1 except that the `OKListener` class is now an inner class. As an inner class, it can conveniently reference data and methods in the frame class. Since the listener class will not be used by applications outside the frame class, it is declared `private`.

The interaction between the source and the listener is shown in Figure 14.7.

1. `jbtOK` registers `listener` by invoking `addActionListener(listener)`.

2. `jbtOK` invokes `listener`'s `actionPerformed` method to process an `ActionEvent`.

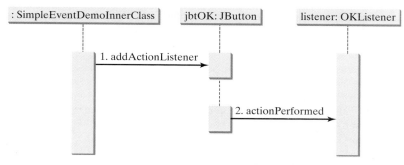

FIGURE 14.7   The source invokes `actionPerformed` in the listener (`OKListener`) to handle an `ActionEvent`.

14.3.2   Anonymous Inner Class Listeners

Inner class listeners can be shortened using anonymous inner classes. An *anonymous inner class* is an inner class without a name. It combines declaring an inner class and creating an instance of the class in one step. An anonymous inner class is declared as follows:

anonymous inner class

```
new SuperClassName/InterfaceName() {
  // Implement or override methods in superclass or interface
  // Other methods if necessary
}
```

Since an anonymous inner class is a special kind of inner class, it is treated like an inner class in many ways. In addition, it has the following features:

- An anonymous inner class must always extend a superclass or implement an interface, but it cannot have an explicit `extends` or `implements` clause.

- An anonymous inner class must implement all the abstract methods in the superclass or in the interface.

- An anonymous inner class always uses the no-arg constructor from its superclass to create an instance. If an anonymous inner class implements an interface, the constructor is `Object()`.

- An anonymous inner class is compiled into a class named OuterClassName$n.class. For example, if the outer class Test has two anonymous inner classes, they are compiled into Test$1.class and Test$2.class.

Listing 14.3 is an example of rewriting the preceding example using anonymous inner classes.

LISTING 14.3 `SimpleEventDemoAnonymousInnerClass.java`

```
 1  import javax.swing.*;
 2  import java.awt.event.*;
 3  import java.awt.*;
 4
 5  public class SimpleEventDemoAnonymousInnerClass extends JFrame {
 6    public SimpleEventDemoAnonymousInnerClass() {
 7      JButton jbtOK = new JButton("OK");
 8      setLayout(new FlowLayout());
 9      add(jbtOK);
10
11      // Create and register anonymous inner class listener
12      jbtOK.addActionListener(new ActionListener() {
13        public void actionPerformed(ActionEvent e) {
14          System.out.println("It is OK");
15        }
16      });
17    }
18
19    /** Main method */
20    public static void main(String[] args) {
21      JFrame frame = new SimpleEventDemoAnonymousInnerClass();
22      frame.setTitle("SimpleEventDemoAnonymousInnerClass");
23      frame.setLocationRelativeTo(null); // Center the frame
24      frame.setDefaultCloseOperation(JFrame.EXIT_ON_CLOSE);
25      frame.setSize(220, 80);
26      frame.setVisible(true);
27    }
28  }
```

anonymous listener
handle event

The anonymous listener (lines 12–16) in this example works the same way as the inner class listener in the preceding example. The program is condensed using an anonymous inner class.

Anonymous inner classes are compiled into `OuterClassName$#.class`, where # starts at 1 and is incremented for each anonymous class encountered by the compiler. In this example, the anonymous inner class is compiled into `SimpleEventDemoAnonymous InnerClass$1.class`.

Pedagogical Note

anonymous adapter
advantages

Anonymous adapters make programs simple and concise, and enable handlers to access data and methods in the outer class. From here on, this book will use anonymous inner class event adapters to implement listeners.

14.3.3   Example: Handling Simple Action Events

This example writes a program that displays two buttons, OK and Cancel, in a frame. A message is displayed on the console to indicate which button and when it is clicked, as shown in Figure 14.8. The program is given in Listing 14.4.

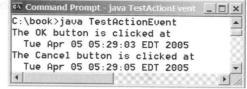

FIGURE 14.8 The program responds to the button action events.

LISTING 14.4 TestActionEvent.java

```java
 1 import javax.swing.*;
 2 import java.awt.*;
 3 import java.awt.event.*;
 4
 5 public class TestActionEvent extends JFrame {
 6   private JButton jbtOK = new JButton("OK");                          create buttons
 7   private JButton jbtCancel = new JButton("Cancel");
 8
 9   public TestActionEvent() {
10     setLayout(new FlowLayout());                                     set FlowLayout
11
12     add(jbtOK);                                                      add components
13     add(jbtCancel);
14
15     jbtOK.addActionListener(new ActionListener() {                   create a listener
16       public void actionPerformed(ActionEvent e) {
17         System.out.println("The " + e.getActionCommand() + " button "
18           + "is clicked at\n  " + new java.util.Date(e.getWhen()));
19       }
20     });
21
22     jbtCancel.addActionListener(new ActionListener() {               create a listener
23       public void actionPerformed(ActionEvent e) {
24         System.out.println("The " + e.getActionCommand() + " button "
25           + "is clicked at\n  " + new java.util.Date(e.getWhen()));
26       }
27     });
28   }
29
30   /** Main method */
31   public static void main(String[] args) {
32     TestActionEvent frame = new TestActionEvent();
33     frame.setTitle("TestActionEvent");
34     frame.setDefaultCloseOperation(JFrame.EXIT_ON_CLOSE);
35     frame.setSize(220, 80);
36     frame.setVisible(true);
37   }
38 }
```

The button objects **jbtOK** and **jbtCancel** are the source of **ActionEvent**. Anonymous inner class listeners are used to create listeners for **jbtOK** and **jbtCancel** in lines 15 and 22.

Clicking a button causes the **actionPerformed** method in the listener to be invoked. The **e.getActionCommand()** method returns the action command from the button (line 17). By default, a button's action command is the text of the button.

The **e.getWhen()** method returns the time of the action in milliseconds since January 1, 1970, 00:00:00 GMT. The **Date** class converts the time to year, month, date, hours, minutes, and seconds (line 18).

14.3.4 Example: Handling Window Events

This example writes a program that demonstrates handling window events. Any subclass of the `Window` class can fire the following window events: window opened, closing, closed, activated, deactivated, iconified, and deiconified. The program in Listing 14.5 creates a frame, listens to the window events, and displays a message to indicate the occurring event. Figure 14.9 shows a sample run of the program.

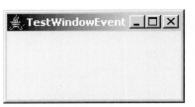 

FIGURE 14.9 The window events are displayed on the console when you run the program from a DOS prompt.

LISTING 14.5 TestWindowEvent.java

```
1 import java.awt.event.*;
2 import javax.swing.JFrame;
3
4 public class TestWindowEvent extends JFrame {
5   public static void main(String[] args) {
6     TestWindowEvent frame = new TestWindowEvent();
7     frame.setLocationRelativeTo(null); // Center the frame
8     frame.setDefaultCloseOperation(JFrame.EXIT_ON_CLOSE);
9     frame.setTitle("TestWindowEvent");
10    frame.setSize(220, 80);
11    frame.setVisible(true);
12  }
13
14  public TestWindowEvent() {
15    addWindowListener(new WindowListener() {
16      /**
17       * Handler for window deiconified event
18       * Invoked when a window is changed from a minimized
19       * to a normal state.
20       */
21      public void windowDeiconified(WindowEvent event) {
22        System.out.println("Window deiconified");
23      }
24
25      /**
26       * Handler for window iconified event
27       * Invoked when a window is changed from a normal to a
28       * minimized state. For many platforms, a minimized window
29       * is displayed as the icon specified in the window's
30       * iconImage property.
31       */
32      public void windowIconified(WindowEvent event) {
33        System.out.println("Window iconified");
34      }
35
36      /**
37       * Handler for window activated event
38       * Invoked when the window is set to be the user's
39       * active window, which means the window (or one of its
```

anonymous listener (line 15)

override handler (line 21)

override handler (line 32)

```
40              * subcomponents) will receive keyboard events.
41              */
42             public void windowActivated(WindowEvent event) {          override handler
43               System.out.println("Window activated");
44             }
45
46             /**
47              * Handler for window deactivated event
48              * Invoked when a window is no longer the user's active
49              * window, which means that keyboard events will no longer
50              * be delivered to the window or its subcomponents.
51              */
52             public void windowDeactivated(WindowEvent event) {         override handler
53               System.out.println("Window deactivated");
54             }
55
56             /**
57              * Handler for window opened event
58              * Invoked the first time a window is made visible.
59              */
60             public void windowOpened(WindowEvent event) {
61               System.out.println("Window opened");
62             }
63
64             /**
65              * Handler for window closing event
66              * Invoked when the user attempts to close the window
67              * from the window's system menu.  If the program does not
68              * explicitly hide or dispose the window while processing
69              * this event, the window close operation will be cancelled.
70              */
71             public void windowClosing(WindowEvent event) {             override handler
72               System.out.println("Window closing");
73             }
74
75             /**
76              * Handler for window closed event
77              * Invoked when a window has been closed as the result
78              * of calling dispose on the window.
79              */
80             public void windowClosed(WindowEvent event) {              override handler
81               System.out.println("Window closed");
82             }
83           });
84     }
85 }
```

The `WindowEvent` can be fired by the `Window` class or by any subclass of `Window`. Since `JFrame` is a subclass of `Window`, it can fire `WindowEvent`.

`TestWindowEvent` extends `JFrame` and implements `WindowListener`. The `Window-Listener` interface defines several abstract methods (`windowActivated`, `windowClosed`, `windowClosing`, `windowDeactivated`, `windowDeiconified`, `windowIconified`, `windowOpened`) for handling window events when the window is activated, closed, closing, deactivated, deiconified, iconified, or opened.

When a window event, such as activation, occurs, the `windowActivated` method is triggered. Implement the `windowActivated` method with a concrete response if you want the event to be processed.

14.3.5 Listener Interface Adapters

Because the methods in the `WindowListener` interface are abstract, you must implement all of them even if your program does not care about some of the events. For convenience, Java provides support classes, called *convenience adapters*, which provide default implementations for all the methods in the listener interface. The default implementation is simply an empty body. Java provides convenience listener adapters for every AWT listener interface with multiple handlers. A convenience listener adapter is named *X*Adapter for *X*Listener. For example, `WindowAdapter` is a convenience listener adapter for `WindowListener`. Table 14.3 lists the convenience adapters.

convenience adapter

TABLE 14.3 Convenience Adapters

Adapter	Interface
WindowAdapter	WindowListener
MouseAdapter	MouseListener
MouseMotionAdapter	MouseMotionListener
KeyAdapter	KeyListener
ContainerAdapter	ContainerListener
ComponentAdapter	ComponentListener
FocusAdapter	FocusListener

Using `WindowAdapter`, the preceding example can be simplified as shown in Listing 14.6 if you are only interested in the window activated event. The `WindowAdapter` class is used to create an anonymous listener instead of `WindowListener` (line 15). The `windowActivated` handler is implemented in line 16.

LISTING 14.6 TestWindowEvent.java

```
1  import java.awt.event.*;
2  import javax.swing.JFrame;
3
4  public class AdapterDemo extends JFrame {
5    public static void main(String[] args) {
6      AdapterDemo frame = new AdapterDemo();
7      frame.setLocationRelativeTo(null); // Center the frame
8      frame.setDefaultCloseOperation(JFrame.EXIT_ON_CLOSE);
9      frame.setTitle("AdapterDemo");
10     frame.setSize(220, 80);
11     frame.setVisible(true);
12   }
13
14   public AdapterDemo() {
15     addWindowListener(new WindowAdapter() {
16       public void windowActivated(WindowEvent event) {
17         System.out.println("Window activated");
18       }
19     });
20   }
21 }
```

register listener
override handler

14.4 Mouse Events

A mouse event is fired whenever a mouse is pressed, released, clicked, moved, or dragged on a component. The mouse event object captures the event, such as the number of clicks associated with it or the location (x and y coordinates) of the mouse, as shown in Figure 14.10.

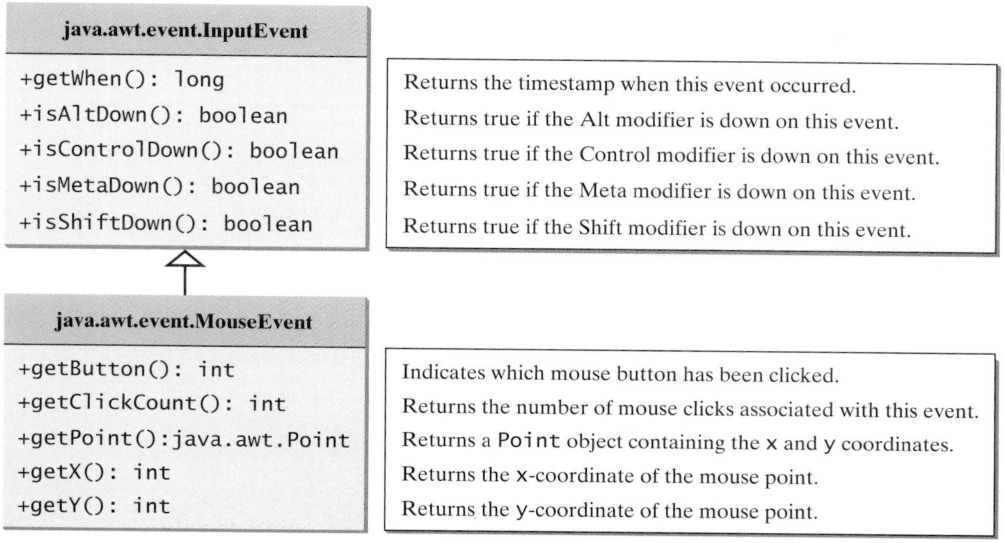

java.awt.event.InputEvent	
+getWhen(): long	Returns the timestamp when this event occurred.
+isAltDown(): boolean	Returns true if the Alt modifier is down on this event.
+isControlDown(): boolean	Returns true if the Control modifier is down on this event.
+isMetaDown(): boolean	Returns true if the Meta modifier is down on this event.
+isShiftDown(): boolean	Returns true if the Shift modifier is down on this event.

java.awt.event.MouseEvent	
+getButton(): int	Indicates which mouse button has been clicked.
+getClickCount(): int	Returns the number of mouse clicks associated with this event.
+getPoint():java.awt.Point	Returns a Point object containing the x and y coordinates.
+getX(): int	Returns the x-coordinate of the mouse point.
+getY(): int	Returns the y-coordinate of the mouse point.

FIGURE 14.10 The MouseEvent class encapsulates information for mouse events.

Since the MouseEvent class inherits InputEvent, you can use the methods defined in the InputEvent class on a MouseEvent object.

The java.awt.Point class represents a point on a component. The class contains two public variables, x and y, for coordinates. To create a Point, use the following constructor:

Point class

```
Point(int x, int y)
```

This constructs a Point object with the specified x and y coordinates. Normally, the data fields in a class should be private. This class has two public data fields, which is not a good practice.

Java provides two listener interfaces, MouseListener and MouseMotionListener, to handle mouse events, as shown in Figure 14.11. Implement the MouseListener interface to listen for such actions as pressing, releasing, entering, exiting, or clicking the mouse, and implement the MouseMotionListener interface to listen for such actions as dragging or moving the mouse.

14.4.1   Example: Moving a Message on a Panel Using a Mouse

This example writes a program that displays a message in a panel, as shown in Listing 14.7. You can use the mouse to move the message. The message moves as the mouse drags and is always displayed at the mouse point. A sample run of the program is shown in Figure 14.12.

static — does not reference any instance members

java.awt.event.MouseListener	
+mousePressed(e: MouseEvent): void	Invoked after the mouse button has been pressed on the source component.
+mouseReleased(e: MouseEvent): void	Invoked after the mouse button has been released on the source component.
+mouseClicked(e: MouseEvent): void	Invoked after the mouse button has been clicked (pressed and released) on the source component.
+mouseEntered(e: MouseEvent): void	Invoked after the mouse enters the source component.
+mouseExited(e: MouseEvent): void	Invoked after the mouse exits the source component.

java.awt.event.MouseMotionListener	
+mouseDragged(e: MouseEvent): void	Invoked after a mouse button is moved with a button pressed.
+mouseMoved(e: MouseEvent): void	Invoked after a mouse button is moved without a button pressed.

FIGURE 14.11 The `MouseListener` interface handles mouse pressed, released, clicked, entered, and exited events. The `MouseMotionListener` interface handles mouse dragged and moved events.

FIGURE 14.12 You can move the message by dragging the mouse.

LISTING 14.7 MoveMessageDemo.java

```
 1 import java.awt.*;
 2 import java.awt.event.*;
 3 import javax.swing.*;
 4
 5 public class MoveMessageDemo extends JFrame {
 6   public MoveMessageDemo() {
 7     // Create a MovableMessagePanel instance for moving a message
 8     MovableMessagePanel p = new MovableMessagePanel("Welcome to Java");
 9
10     // Place the message panel in the frame
11     getContentPane().setLayout(new BorderLayout());
12     getContentPane().add(p);
13   }
14
15   /** Main method */
16   public static void main(String[] args) {
17     MoveMessageDemo frame = new MoveMessageDemo();
18     frame.setTitle("MoveMessageDemo");
19     frame.setLocationRelativeTo(null); // Center the frame
20     frame.setDefaultCloseOperation(JFrame.EXIT_ON_CLOSE);
21     frame.setSize(200, 100);
22     frame.setVisible(true);
23   }
24
```

create a panel

```
25    // Inner class: MovableMessagePanel draws a message
26    static class MovableMessagePanel extends JPanel {          inner class
27      private String message = "Welcome to Java";
28      private int x = 20;
29      private int y = 20;
30
31      /** Construct a panel to draw string s */
32      public MovableMessagePanel(String s) {
33        message = s;                                            set a new message
34        addMouseMotionListener(new MouseMotionAdapter() {       anonymous listener
35          /** Handle mouse dragged event */
36          public void mouseDragged(MouseEvent e) {              override handler
37            // Get the new location and repaint the screen
38            x = e.getX();                                       new location
39            y = e.getY();
40            repaint();                                          repaint
41          }
42        });
43      }
44
45      /** Paint the component */
46      protected void paintComponent(Graphics g) {
47        super.paintComponent(g);
48        g.drawString(message, x, y);
49      }
50    }
51  }
```

The `MovableMessagePanel` class extends `JPanel` to draw a message (line 26). Additionally, it handles redisplaying the message when the mouse is dragged. This class is declared as an inner class inside the main class because it is only used in this class. Furthermore, the inner class is declared static because it does not reference any instance members of the main class.

The `MouseMotionListener` interface contains two handlers, `mouseMoved` and `mouseDragged`, for handling mouse-motion events. When you move the mouse with the button pressed, the `mouseDragged` method is invoked to repaint the viewing area and display the message at the mouse point. When you move the mouse without pressing the button, the `mouseMoved` method is invoked.

Because the listener is only interested in the mouse dragged event, the anonymous inner class listener extends `MouseMotionAdapter` to override the `mouseDragged` method. If the inner class implements the `MouseMotionListener` interface, you would have to implement all of the handlers even if your listener does not care about some of the events.

The `mouseDragged` method is invoked when you move the mouse with a button pressed. This method obtains the mouse location using `getX` and `getY` methods (lines 38–39) in the `MouseEvent` class. This becomes the new location for the message. Invoking the `repaint()` method (line 40) causes `paintComponent` to be invoked (line 46), which displays the message in a new location.

14.5 Key Events

Key events enable the use of the keys to control and perform actions or get input from the keyboard. A key event is fired whenever a key is pressed, released, or typed on a component. The `KeyEvent` object describes the nature of the event (namely, that a key has been pressed, released, or typed) and the value of the key, as shown in Figure 14.13. Java provides the `KeyListener` to handle key events, as shown in Figure 14.14.

The `keyPressed` handler is invoked when a key is pressed, the `keyReleased` handler is invoked when a key is released, and the `keyTyped` handler is invoked when a Unicode

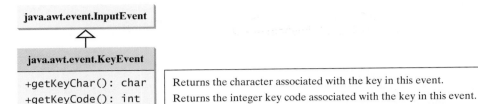

FIGURE 14.13 The KeyEvent class encapsulates information about key events.

java.awt.event.KeyListener	
+*keyPressed(e: KeyEvent): void*	Invoked after a key is pressed on the source component.
+*keyReleased(e: KeyEvent): void*	Invoked after a key is released on the source component.
+*keyTyped(e: KeyEvent): void*	Invoked after a key is pressed and then released on the source component.

FIGURE 14.14 The KeyListener interface handles key pressed, released, and typed events.

character is entered. If a key does not have a Unicode (e.g., function keys, modifier keys, action keys, and control keys), the keyTyped handler will be not be invoked.

Every key event has an associated key character or key code that is returned by the getKeyChar() or getKeyCode() method in KeyEvent. The key codes are constants defined in Table 14.4. For a key of the Unicode character, the key code is the same as the Unicode value. For the key pressed and key released events, getKeyCode() returns the value as defined in the table. For the key typed event, getKeyCode() returns VK_UNDEFINED.

TABLE 14.4 Key Constants

Constant	Description	Constant	Description
VK_HOME	The Home key	VK_SHIFT	The Shift key
VK_END	The End key	VK_BACK_SPACE	The Backspace key
VK_PGUP	The Page Up key	VK_CAPS_LOCK	The Caps Lock key
VK_PGDN	The Page Down key	VK_NUM_LOCK	The Num Lock key
VK_UP	The up-arrow key	VK_ENTER	The Enter key
VK_DOWN	The down-arrow key	VK_UNDEFINED	The keyCode unknown
VK_LEFT	The left-arrow key	VK_F1 to VK_F12	The function keys from F1 to F12
VK_RIGHT	The right-arrow key		
VK_ESCAPE	The Esc key	VK_0 to VK_9	The number keys from 0 to 9
VK_TAB	The Tab key	VK_A to VK_Z	The letter keys from A to Z
VK_CONTROL	The Control key		

The program in Listing 14.8 displays a user-input character. The user can move the character up, down, left, and right, using the arrow keys VK_UP, VK_DOWN, VK_LEFT, and VK_RIGHT. Figure 14.15 contains a sample run of the program.

LISTING 14.8 KeyEventDemo.java

```java
1 import java.awt.*;
2 import java.awt.event.*;
3 import javax.swing.*;
```

```
 4
 5 public class KeyEventDemo extends JFrame {
 6   private KeyboardPanel keyboardPanel = new KeyboardPanel();              create a panel
 7
 8   /** Initialize UI */
 9   public KeyEventDemo() {
10     // Add the keyboard panel to accept and display user input
11     add(keyboardPanel);
12
13     // Set focus
14     keyboardPanel.setFocusable(true);                                      focusable
15   }
16
17   /** Main method */
18   public static void main(String[] args) {
19     KeyEventDemo frame = new KeyEventDemo();
20     frame.setTitle("KeyEventDemo");
21     frame.setLocationRelativeTo(null); // Center the frame
22     frame.setDefaultCloseOperation(JFrame.EXIT_ON_CLOSE);
23     frame.setSize(300, 300);
24     frame.setVisible(true);
25   }
26
27   // Inner class: KeyboardPanel for receiving key input
28   static class KeyboardPanel extends JPanel {                             inner class
29     private int x = 100;
30     private int y = 100;
31     private char keyChar = 'A'; // Default key
32
33     public KeyboardPanel() {
34       addKeyListener(new KeyAdapter() {                                   register listener
35         public void keyPressed(KeyEvent e) {                             override handler
36           switch (e.getKeyCode()) {
37             case KeyEvent.VK_DOWN: y += 10; break;
38             case KeyEvent.VK_UP: y -= 10; break;
39             case KeyEvent.VK_LEFT: x -= 10; break;
40             case KeyEvent.VK_RIGHT: x += 10; break;
41             default: keyChar = e.getKeyChar();                           get the key pressed
42           }
43
44           repaint();                                                     repaint
45         }
46       });
47     }
48
49     /** Draw the character */
50     protected void paintComponent(Graphics g) {
51       super.paintComponent(g);
52
53       g.setFont(new Font("TimesRoman", Font.PLAIN, 24));
54       g.drawString(String.valueOf(keyChar), x, y);                       redraw character
55     }
56   }
57 }
```

The **KeyboardPanel** class extends **JPanel** to display a character (line 28). This class is declared as an inner class inside the main class because it is only used in this class. Furthermore, the inner class is declared static because it does not reference any instance members of the main class.

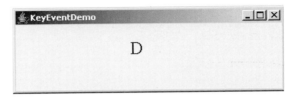

FIGURE 14.15   The program responds to key events by displaying a character and moving it up, down, left, or right.

Because the program gets input from the keyboard, it listens for `KeyEvent` and extends `KeyAdapter` to handle key input (line 34).

When a key is pressed, the `keyPressed` handler is invoked. The program uses `e.getKeyCode()` to obtain the key code and `e.getKeyChar()` to get the character for the key. When a non-arrow key is pressed, the key is displayed (line 41). When an arrow key is pressed, the character moves in the direction indicated by the arrow key (lines 37–40).

focusable

Only a focused component can receive `KeyEvent`. To make a component *focusable*, set its `isFocusable` property to `true` (line 14).

efficient?

Every time the component is repainted, a new font is created for the `Graphics` object in line 53. This is not efficient. It is better to create the font one time as a data field.

14.6 (Optional) Animation Using the **Timer** Class

Not all source objects are GUI components. The `javax.swing.Timer` class is a source component that fires an `ActionEvent` at a predefined rate. Figure 14.16 lists some of the methods in the class.

javax.swing.Timer	
+Timer(delay: int, listener: ActionListener)	Creates a Timer object with a specified delay in milliseconds and an ActionListener.
+addActionListener(listener: ActionListener): void	Adds an ActionListener to the timer.
+start(): void	Starts this timer.
+stop(): void	Stops this timer.
+setDelay(delay: int): void	Sets a new delay value for this timer.

FIGURE 14.16   A `Timer` object fires an `ActionEvent` at a fixed rate.

A `Timer` object serves as the source of an `ActionEvent`. The listeners must be instances of `ActionListener` and registered with a `Timer` object. You create a `Timer` object using its sole constructor with a delay and a listener, where `delay` specifies the number of milliseconds between two action events. You can add additional listeners using the `addActionListener` method, and adjust the `delay` using the `setDelay` method . To start the timer, invoke the `start()` method. To stop the timer, invoke the `stop()` method.

The `Timer` class can be used to control animations. For example, you can use it to display a moving message, as shown in Figure 14.17, with the code in Listing 14.9.

FIGURE 14.17   A message moves in the panel.

LISTING 14.9 AnimationDemo.java

```java
 1 import java.awt.*;
 2 import java.awt.event.*;
 3 import javax.swing.*;
 4
 5 public class AnimationDemo extends JFrame {
 6   public AnimationDemo() {
 7     // Create a MovingMessagePanel for displaying a moving message
 8     add(new MovingMessagePanel("message moving?"));              create panel
 9   }
10
11   /** Main method */
12   public static void main(String[] args) {
13     AnimationDemo frame = new AnimationDemo();
14     frame.setTitle("AnimationDemo");
15     frame.setLocationRelativeTo(null); // Center the frame
16     frame.setDefaultCloseOperation(JFrame.EXIT_ON_CLOSE);
17     frame.setSize(280, 100);
18     frame.setVisible(true);
19   }
20
21   //Inner class: Displaying a moving message
22   static class MovingMessagePanel extends JPanel {
23     private String message = "Welcome to Java";
24     private int xCoordinate = 0;
25     private int yCoordinate = 20;
26
27     public MovingMessagePanel(String message) {
28       this.message = message;                                   set message
29
30       // Create a timer
31       Timer timer = new Timer(1000, new TimerListener());       create timer
32       timer.start();                                            start timer
33     }
34
35     /** Paint message */
36     public void paintComponent(Graphics g) {
37       super.paintComponent(g);
38
39       if (xCoordinate > getWidth()) {
40         xCoordinate = -20;                                      reset x-coordinate
41       }
42       xCoordinate += 5;
43       g.drawString(message, xCoordinate, yCoordinate);          move message
44     }
45
46     class TimerListener implements ActionListener {             listener class
47       /** Handle ActionEvent */                                 event handler
48       public void actionPerformed(ActionEvent e) {
49         repaint();                                              repaint
50       }
51     }
52   }
53 }
```

The MovingMessagePanel class extends JPanel to display a message (line 22). This class
is declared as an inner class inside the main class because it is only used in this class.

Furthermore, the inner class is declared static because it does not reference any instance members of the main class.

An inner class listener is declared in line 46 to listener for `ActionEvent`. Line 31 creates a `Timer` for the listener. The timer is started in line 32. The timer fires an `ActionEvent` every second, and the listener responds in line 49 to repaint the panel. When a panel is painted, its x coordinate is increased (line 42), so the message is displayed to the right. When the x coordinate exceeds the bound of the panel, it is reset to −20 (line 40), so the message continues moving from left to right.

In §13.12, "Case Study: The `StillClock` Class," you drew a `StillClock` to show the current time. The clock does not tick after it is displayed. What can you do to make the clock display a new current time every second? The key to making the clock tick is to repaint it every second with a new current time. You can use a timer to control the repainting of the clock with the code in Listing 14.10.

LISTING 14.10 ClockAnimation.java

```java
 1  import java.awt.event.*;
 2  import javax.swing.*;
 3
 4  public class ClockAnimation extends StillClock {
 5    public ClockAnimation() {
 6      // Create a timer with delay 1000 ms
 7      Timer timer = new Timer(1000, new TimerListener());
 8      timer.start();
 9    }
10
11    private class TimerListener implements ActionListener {
12      /** Handle the action event */
13      public void actionPerformed(ActionEvent e) {
14        // Set new time and repaint the clock to display current time
15        setCurrentTime();
16        repaint();
17      }
18    }
19
20    /** Main method */
21    public static void main(String[] args) {
22      JFrame frame = new JFrame("ClockAnimation");
23      ClockAnimation clock = new ClockAnimation();
24      frame.add(clock);
25      frame.setLocationRelativeTo(null); // Center the frame
26      frame.setDefaultCloseOperation(JFrame.EXIT_ON_CLOSE);
27      frame.setSize(200, 200);
28      frame.setVisible(true);
29    }
30  }
```

create timer
start timer

listener class

implement handler

set new time
repaint

The program displays a running clock, as shown in Figure 14.18. `ClockAnimation` extends `StillClock` and repaints the clock every 1 second triggered by a timer. Line 7 creates a `Timer` for a `ClockAnimation`. The timer is started in line 8 when a `ClockAnimation` is constructed. The timer fires an `ActionEvent` every second, and the listener responds in line 15 to set a new time and repaint the clock. The `setCurrentTime()` method defined in `StillClock` sets the current time in the clock.

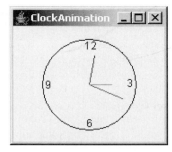  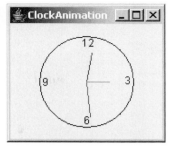

FIGURE 14.18   A live clock is displayed in the panel.

KEY TERMS

anonymous inner class   471
convenience listener adapter   476
event   465
event delegation   465
event handler   467
event listener   464

event listener interface   467
event object   465
event registration   467
event source (source object)   465
event-driven programming   464
inner class?   469

CHAPTER SUMMARY

- The root class of the event classes is `java.util.EventObject`. The subclasses of `EventObject` deal with special types of events, such as action events, window events, component events, mouse events, and key events. You can identify the source object of an event using the `getSource()` instance method in the `EventObject` class. If a component can fire an event, any subclass of the component can fire the same type of event.

- The listener object's class must implement the corresponding event-listener interface. Java provides a listener interface for every event class. The listener interface is usually named *X*`Listener` for *X*`Event`, with the exception of `MouseMotionListener`. For example, the corresponding listener interface for `ActionEvent` is `ActionListener`; each listener for `ActionEvent` should implement the `ActionListener` interface. The listener interface contains the method(s), known as the *handler(s)*, which process the events.

- The listener object must be registered by the source object. Registration methods are dependent on the event type. For `ActionEvent`, the method is `addActionListener`. In general, the method is named `add`*X*`Listener` for *X*`Event`.

- An *inner class*, or *nested class,* is a class defined within the scope of another class. An inner class can reference the data and methods defined in the outer class in which it nests, so you do not need to pass the reference of the outer class to the constructor of the inner class.

- Convenience adapters are support classes that provide default implementations for all the methods in the listener interface. Java provides convenience listener adapters for every AWT listener interface with multiple handlers. A convenience listener adapter is named *X*Adapter for *X*Listener.

■ A source object may fire several types of events. For each event, the source object maintains a list of listeners and notifies all the registered listeners by invoking the *handler* on the listener object to process the event.

■ A mouse event is fired whenever a mouse is clicked, released, moved, or dragged on a component. The mouse-event object captures the event, such as the number of clicks associated with it or the location (x- and y-coordinates) of the mouse point.

■ Java provides two listener interfaces, `MouseListener` and `MouseMotionListener`, to handle mouse events, implement the `MouseListener` interface to listen for such actions as mouse pressed, released, clicked, entered, or exited, and implement the `MouseMotionListener` interface to listen for such actions as mouse dragged or moved.

■ A `KeyEvent` object describes the nature of the event (namely, that a key has been pressed, released, or typed) and the value of the key.

■ The `keyPressed` handler is invoked when a key is pressed, the `keyReleased` handler is invoked when a key is released, and the `keyTyped` handler is invoked when a Unicode character is entered. If a key does not have a Unicode (e.g., function keys, modifier keys, action keys, and control keys), the `keyTyped` handler will be not be invoked.

■ You can use the `Timer` class to control Java animations. A timer fires an `ActionEvent` at a fixed rate. The listener updates the painting to simulate an animation.

REVIEW QUESTIONS

Sections 14.2–14.3

14.1 Can a button fire a `WindowEvent`? Can a button fire a `MouseEvent`? Can a button fire an `ActionEvent`?

14.2 Why must a listener be an instance of an appropriate listener interface? Explain how to register a listener object and how to implement a listener interface.

14.3 Can a source have multiple listeners? Can a listener listen on multiple sources? Can a source be a listener for itself?

14.4 How do you override a method defined in the listener interface? Do you need to override all the methods defined in the listener interface?

14.5 Can an inner class be used in a class other than the class in which it nests?

14.6 Can the modifiers `public`, `private`, and `static` be used on inner classes?

14.7 If class A is an inner class in class B, what is the `.class` file for A? If class B contains two anonymous inner classes, what are the `.class` file names for these two classes?

14.8 What is wrong in the following code?

```
import java.swing.*;
import java.awt.*;

public class Test extends JFrame {
  public Test() {
    JButton jbtOK = new JButton("OK");
    add(jbtOK);
  }

  private class Listener
      implements ActionListener {
    public void actionPerform
        (ActionEvent e) {
      System.out.println
        (jbtOK.getActionCommand());
    }
  }

  /** Main method omitted */
}
```
(a)

```
import java.awt.event.*;
import javax.swing.*;

public class Test extends JFrame {
  public Test() {
    JButton jbtOK = new JButton("OK");
    add(jbtOK);
    jbtOK.addActionListener(
      new ActionListener() {
        public void actionPerformed
          (ActionEvent e) {
          System.out.println
            (jbtOK.getActionCommand());
        }
    } // Something missing here
  }

  /** Main method omitted */
}
```
(b)

Sections 14.4–14.5

14.9 What method do you use to get the source of an event? What method do you use to get the timestamp for an action event, a mouse event or a key event? What method do you use to get the mouse point position for a mouse event? What method do you use to get the key character for a key event?

14.10 What is the listener interface for mouse pressed, released, clicked, entered, and exited? What is the listener interface for mouse moved and dragged?

14.11 Does every key in the keyboard have a Unicode? Is a key code in the KeyEvent class equivalent to a Unicode?

14.12 Is the keyPressed handler invoked after a key is pressed? Is the keyReleased handler invoked after a key is released? Is the keyTyped handler invoked after *any* key is typed?

Section 14.6 (Optional) Animation Using the Timer Class

14.13 How do you create a timer? How do you start a timer? How do you stop a timer?

14.14 Does the Timer class have a no-arg constructor? Can you add multiple listeners to a timer?

PROGRAMMING EXERCISES

Sections 14.2–14.3

14.1 (*Finding which button has been clicked on the console*) Add the code to Exercise 12.1 that will display a message on the console indicating which button has been clicked.

14.2 (*Using ComponentEvent*) Any GUI component can fire a ComponentEvent. The ComponentListener defines the componentMoved, componentResized, componentShown, and componentHidden methods for processing component events. Write a test program to demonstrate ComponentEvent.

14.3* (*Finding which button has been clicked on a panel*) Write a program that creates a user interface with two buttons named OK and Cancel and a message panel for displaying a message. When you click the OK button, a message "The OK button has been clicked" is displayed. When you click the Cancel button, a message "The Cancel button has been clicked" is displayed, as shown in Figure 14.19(a).

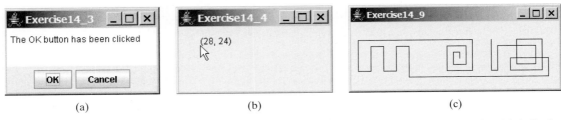

(a)   (b)   (c)

FIGURE 14.19 (a) Exercise 14.3 displays which button is clicked on a message panel. (b) Exercise 14.4 displays the mouse position. (c) Exercise 14.9 uses the arrow keys to draw the lines.

Section 14.4 Mouse Events

14.4* (*Displaying the mouse position*) Write two programs, one displays the mouse position when the mouse is clicked (see Figure 14.19(b)), and the other displays the mouse position when the mouse is pressed and the display disappears when the mouse is released.

14.5* (*Setting background color using a mouse*) Write a program that displays the background color of a panel as black when the mouse is pressed and as white when the mouse is released.

14.6** (*Alternating two messages*) Write a program to rotate two messages "Java is fun" and "Java is powerful" displayed on a panel with a mouse click.

Section 14.5 Key Events

14.7** (*Entering and displaying a string*) Write a program that receives a string from the keyboard and displays it on a panel. The Enter key signals the end of a string. Whenever a new string is entered, it is displayed on the panel.

14.8* (*Displaying a character*) Write a program to get a character input from the keyboard and display the character where the mouse points.

14.9* (*Drawing lines using the arrow keys*) Write a program that draws line segments using the arrow keys. The line starts from the center of the frame and draws toward east, north, west, or south when the right-arrow key, up-arrow key, left-arrow key, or down-arrow key is clicked, as shown in Figure 14.19(c).

Section 14.6 (Optional) Animation Using the Timer Class

14.10* (*Displaying a flashing label*) Write a program that displays a flashing label.

Hint
To make the label flash, you need to repaint the panel alternately with the label and without the label (blank screen) at a fixed rate. Use a boolean variable to control the alternation.

14.11* (*Controlling a moving label*) Modify Listing 14.9, AnimationDemo.java, to control a moving label using the mouse. The label freezes when the mouse is pressed, and moves again when the button is released.

14.12** (*Displaying a running fan*) Listing 13.6, DrawArcs.java, displays a motionless fan. Write a program that displays a running fan.

14.13** (*Slides show*) Twenty-five slides are stored as image files (slide0.jpg, slide1.jpg, ..., slide24.jpg) in the image directory downloadable along with the source code in the book. The size of each image is 800 × 600 pixels. Write a Java application that automatically displays the slides repeatedly. Each slide is shown for a second. The slides are displayed in order. When the last slide finishes, the first slide is redisplayed, and so on. (Hint: place a label in the frame and set a slide as an image icon in the label.)

14.14** (*Raising flag*) Write a Java program that animates raising a flag, as shown in Figure 14.20. (See §13.13, "Displaying Images," on how to display images.)

FIGURE 14.20 A flag is rising upward.

14.15** (*Racing car*) Write a Java program that simulates car racing, as shown in Figure 14.21(a). The car moves from left to right. When it hits the right end, it restarts from the left and continues the same process. You can use a timer to control the animation. Redraw the car with new base coordinates (x, y), as shown in Figure 14.21(b).

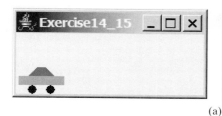  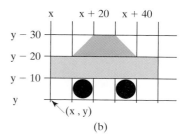

(a)

(b)

FIGURE 14.21 (a) Exercise 14.15 displays a moving car. (b) You can redraw a car with a new base point.

CREATING USER INTERFACES

Objectives

- To create graphical user interfaces with various user-interface components: JButton, JCheckBox, JRadioButton, JLabel, JTextField, JTextArea, JComboBox, JList, JScrollBar, and JSlider (§§15.2–15.11).

- To create listeners for various types of events (§§15.2–15.11).

- To display multiple windows in an application (§15.12).

15.1 Introduction

A graphical user interface (*GUI*) makes a system user-friendly and easy to use. Creating a GUI requires creativity and knowledge of how GUI components work. Since the GUI components in Java are very flexible and versatile, you can create a wide assortment of useful user interfaces.

Many Java IDEs provide tools for visually designing and developing GUI interfaces. This enables you to rapidly assemble the elements of a user interface (UI) for a Java application or applet with minimum coding. Tools, however, cannot do everything. You have to modify the programs they produce. Consequently, before you begin to use the visual tools, it is imperative that you understand the basic concepts of Java GUI programming.

Previous chapters briefly introduced several GUI components. This chapter introduces the frequently used GUI components in detail (see Figure 15.1).

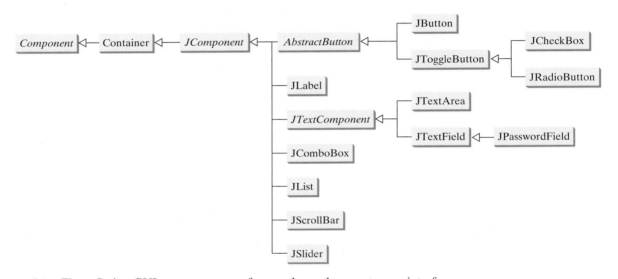

FIGURE 15.1 These Swing GUI components are frequently used to create user interfaces.

Note

Throughout this book, the prefixes `jbt`, `jchk`, `jrb`, `jlbl`, `jtf`, `jpf`, `jta`, `jcbo`, `jlst`, `jscb`, and `jsld` are used to name reference variables for `JButton`, `JCheckBox`, `JRadioButton`, `JLabel`, `JTextField`, `JPasswordField`, `JTextArea`, `JComboBox`, `JList`, `JScrollBar`, and `JSlider`.

15.2 Buttons

A *button* is a component that triggers an action event when clicked. Swing provides regular buttons, toggle buttons, check box buttons, and radio buttons. The common features of these buttons are represented in `javax.swing.AbstractButton`, as shown in Figure 15.2.

This section introduces the regular buttons defined in the `JButton` class. `JButton` inherits `AbstractButton` and provides several constructors to create buttons, as shown in Figure 15.3.

15.2.1 Icons, Pressed Icons, and Rollover Icons

A regular button has a default icon, pressed icon, and rollover icon. Normally, you use the default icon. The other icons are for special effects. A pressed icon is displayed when a button is pressed, and a rollover icon is displayed when the mouse is over the button but not

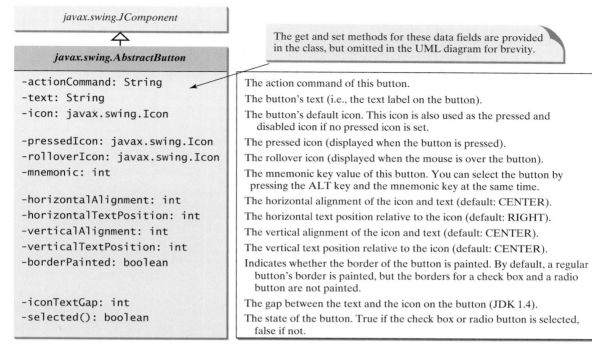

FIGURE 15.2   `AbstractButton` defines common features of different types of buttons.

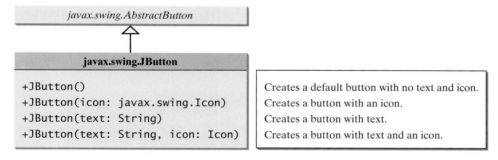

FIGURE 15.3   `JButton` defines a regular push button.

pressed. For example, Listing 15.1 displays the American flag as a regular icon, the Canadian flag as a pressed icon, and the British flag as a rollover icon, as shown in Figure 15.4.

LISTING 15.1   TestButtonIcons.java

```java
1 import javax.swing.*;
2
3 public class TestButtonIcons extends JFrame  {
4   public static void main(String[] args) {
5     // Create a frame and set its properties
6     JFrame frame = new TestButtonIcons();
7     frame.setTitle("ButtonIcons");
8     frame.setSize(200, 100);
9     frame.setLocationRelativeTo(null); // Center the frame
10    frame.setDefaultCloseOperation(JFrame.EXIT_ON_CLOSE);
11    frame.setVisible(true);
12  }
13
```

```
14    public TestButtonIcons() {
15      ImageIcon usIcon = new ImageIcon("image/usIcon.gif");
16      ImageIcon caIcon = new ImageIcon("image/caIcon.gif");
17      ImageIcon ukIcon = new ImageIcon("image/ukIcon.gif");
18
19      JButton jbt = new JButton("Click it", usIcon);
20      jbt.setPressedIcon(caIcon);
21      jbt.setRolloverIcon(ukIcon);
22
23      add(jbt);
24    }
25  }
```

create icons

regular icon
pressed icon
rollover icon

add a button

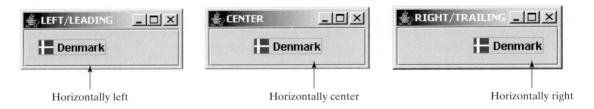

(a) Default icon   (b) Pressed icon   (c) Rollover icon

FIGURE 15.4 A button can have several types of icons.

15.2.2 Alignments

horizontal alignment

Horizontal alignment specifies how the icon and text are placed horizontally on a button. You can set the horizontal alignment using `setHorizontalAlignment(int)` with one of the five constants `LEADING`, `LEFT`, `CENTER`, `RIGHT`, `TRAILING`, as shown in Figure 15.5. At present, `LEADING` and `LEFT` are the same, and `TRAILING` and `RIGHT` are the same. Future implementation may distinquish them. The default horizontal alignment is `Swing-Constants.TRAILING`.

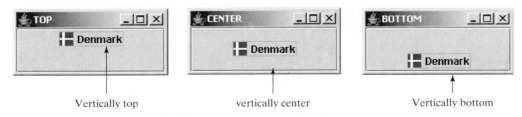

Horizontally left   Horizontally center   Horizontally right

FIGURE 15.5 You can specify how the icon and text are placed on a button horizontally.

vertical alignment

Vertical alignment specifies how the icon and text are placed vertically on a button. You can set the vertical alignment using `setVerticalAlignment(int)` with one of the three constants `TOP`, `CENTER`, `BOTTOM`, as shown in Figure 15.6. The default vertical alignment is `SwingConstants.CENTER`.

Vertically top   vertically center   Vertically bottom

FIGURE 15.6 You can specify how the icon and text are placed on a button vertically.

15.2.3 Text Positions

Horizontal text position specifies the horizontal position of the text relative to the icon. You can set the horizontal text position using `setHorizontalTextPosition(int)` with one of the five constants `LEADING`, `LEFT`, `CENTER`, `RIGHT`, `TRAILING`, as shown in Figure 15.7. At present, `LEADING` and `LEFT` are the same, and `TRAILING` and `RIGHT` are the same. Future implementation may distinquish them. The default horizontal text position is `SwingConstants.RIGHT`.

horizontal text position

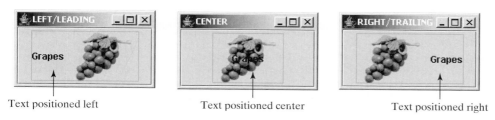

Text positioned left   Text positioned center   Text positioned right

FIGURE 15.7 You can specify the horizontal position of the text relative to the icon.

Vertical text position specifies the vertical position of the text relative to the icon. You can set the vertical text position using `setVerticalTextPosition(int)` with one of the three constants `TOP`, `CENTER`, `BOTTOM`, as shown in Figure 15.8. The default vertical text position is `SwingConstants.CENTER`.

vertical text position

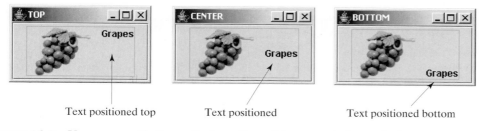

Text positioned top   Text positioned   Text positioned bottom

FIGURE 15.8 You can specify the vertical position of the text relative to the icon.

Note

The constants `LEFT`, `CENTER`, `RIGHT`, `LEADING`, `TRAILING`, `TOP`, and `BOTTOM` used in `AbstractButton` are also used in many other Swing components. These constants are centrally defined in the `javax.swing.SwingConstants` interface. Since all Swing GUI components implement `SwingConstants`, you can reference the constants through `SwingConstants` or a GUI component. For example, `SwingConstants.CENTER` is the same as `JButton.CENTER`.

SwingConstants

`JButton` can generate many types of events, but often you need to respond to an `ActionEvent`. When a button is pressed, it generates an `ActionEvent`.

15.2.4 Example: Using Buttons

This example presents a program, shown in Listing 15.2, that displays a message on a panel and uses two buttons, <= and =>, to move the message on the panel to the left or right. The layout of the UI and the output of the program are shown in Figure 15.9.

Here are the major steps in the program:

1. Create the user interface.
   Create a `MessagePanel` object to display the message. The `MessagePanel` class was created in §13.11, "Case Study: The `MessagePanel` Class." Place it in the center of the frame. Create two buttons, <= and =>, on a panel. Place the panel in the south of the frame.

FIGURE 15.9 Clicking the <= and => buttons causes the message on the panel to move to the left and right, respectively.

2. Process the event.
   Create and register listeners for processing the action event to move the message left or right according to whether the left or right button was clicked.

LISTING 15.2 ButtonDemo.java

```java
 1  import java.awt.*;
 2  import java.awt.event.ActionListener;
 3  import java.awt.event.ActionEvent;
 4  import javax.swing.*;
 5
 6  public class ButtonDemo extends JFrame {
 7    // Create a panel for displaying message
 8    protected MessagePanel messagePanel
 9      = new MessagePanel("Welcome to Java");
10
11    // Declare two buttons to move the message left and right
12    private JButton jbtLeft = new JButton("<=");
13    private JButton jbtRight = new JButton("=>");
14
15    public static void main(String[] args) {
16      ButtonDemo frame = new ButtonDemo();
17      frame.setTitle("ButtonDemo");
18      frame.setLocationRelativeTo(null); // Center the frame
19      frame.setDefaultCloseOperation(JFrame.EXIT_ON_CLOSE);
20      frame.setSize(250, 100);
21      frame.setVisible(true);
22    }
23
24    public ButtonDemo() {
25      // Set the background color of messagePanel
26      messagePanel.setBackground(Color.white);
27
28      // Create Panel jpButtons to hold two Buttons "<=" and "right =>"
29      JPanel jpButtons = new JPanel();
30      jpButtons.setLayout(new FlowLayout());
31      jpButtons.add(jbtLeft);
32      jpButtons.add(jbtRight);
33
34      // Set keyboard mnemonics
35      jbtLeft.setMnemonic('L');
36      jbtRight.setMnemonic('R');
37
38      // Set icons and remove text
39      // jbtLeft.setIcon(new ImageIcon("image/left.gif"));
40      // jbtRight.setIcon(new ImageIcon("image/right.gif"));
```

create frame

create UI

mnemonic

```
41        // jbtLeft.setText(null);
42        // jbtRight.setText(null);
43
44        // Set tool tip text on the buttons
45        jbtLeft.setToolTipText("Move message to left");          tool tip
46        jbtRight.setToolTipText("Move message to right");
47
48        // Place panels in the frame
49        setLayout(new BorderLayout());
50        add(messagePanel, BorderLayout.CENTER);
51        add(jpButtons, BorderLayout.SOUTH);
52
53        // Register listeners with the buttons
54        jbtLeft.addActionListener(new ActionListener() {          register listener
55          public void actionPerformed(ActionEvent e) {
56            messagePanel.moveLeft();
57          }
58        });
59        jbtRight.addActionListener(new ActionListener() {         register listener
60          public void actionPerformed(ActionEvent e) {
61            messagePanel.moveRight();
62          }
63        });
64      }
65 }
```

`messagePanel` (line 8) is deliberately declared `protected` so that it can be referenced by a subclass in future examples.

You can set an icon image on the button by using the `setIcon` method. If you uncomment the following code in lines 39–42:

```
// jbtLeft.setIcon(new ImageIcon("image/left.gif"));
// jbtRight.setIcon(new ImageIcon("image/right.gif"));
// jbtLeft.setText(null);
// jbtRight.setText(null);
```

the texts are replaced by the icons, as shown in Figure 15.10(a). `"image/left.gif"` is located in `"c:\book\image\left.gif"`. Note that the back slash is the Windows file path notation. In Java, the forward slash should be used.

(a)   (b)   (c)

FIGURE 15.10 You can set an icon on a `JButton` and access a button using mnemonic keys.

You can set text and an icon on a button at the same time, if you wish, as shown in Figure 15.10(b). By default, the text and icon are centered horizontally and vertically.

The button can also be accessed by using the keyboard mnemonics. Pressing ALT+L is equivalent to clicking the <= button, since you set the mnemonic property to `'L'` in the left button (line 35). If you change the left button text to "Left" and the right button to "Right," the L and R in the captions of these buttons will be underlined, as shown in Figure 15.10(b).

Each button has a tool-tip text (lines 45–46), which appears when the mouse is set on the button without clicking, as shown in Figure 15.10(c).

locating **MessagePanel**

Note

Since `MessagePanel` is not in the Java API, you should place MessagePanel.java in the same directory with ButtonDemo.java.

15.3 Check Boxes

toggle button

A *toggle button* is a two-state button like a light switch. `JToggleButton` inherits `Abstract-Button` and implements a toggle button. Often `JToggleButton`'s subclasses `JCheckBox` and `JRadioButton` are used to enable the user to toggle a choice on or off. This section introduces `JCheckBox`. `JRadioButton` will be introduced in the next section.

`JCheckBox` inherits all the properties from `AbstractButton`, such as `text`, `icon`, `mnemonic`, `verticalAlignment`, `horizontalAlignment`, `horizontalTextPosition`, `verticalTextPosition`, and `selected`, and provides several constructors to create check boxes, as shown in Figure 15.11.

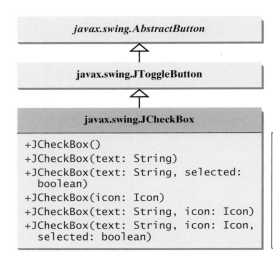

FIGURE 15.11 `JCheckBox` defines a check box button.

Here is an example of a check box with text Student, red foreground, white background, mnemonic key 'S', and initially selected.

```java
JCheckBox jchk = new JCheckBox("Student", true);
jchk.setForeground(Color.red);
jchk.setBackground(Color.white);
jchk.setMnemonic('S');
```

When a check box is clicked (checked or unchecked), it fires an `ItemEvent` and then an `ActionEvent`. To see if a check box is selected, use the `isSelected()` method.

Listing 15.3 gives a program that adds three check boxes named *Centered*, *Bold*, and *Italic* into the preceding example to let the user specify whether the message is centered, bold, or italic, as shown in Figure 15.12.

There are at least two approaches to writing this program. The first is to revise the preceding `ButtonDemo` class to insert the code for adding the check boxes and processing their events. The second is to create a subclass that extends `ButtonDemo`. Please implement the first approach as an exercise. Listing 15.3 gives the code to implement the second approach.

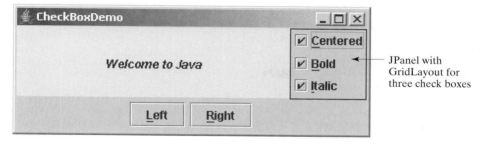

FIGURE 15.12 Three check boxes are added to specify how the message is displayed.

LISTING 15.3 CheckBoxDemo.java

```java
1  import java.awt.*;
2  import java.awt.event.*;
3  import javax.swing.*;
4
5  public class CheckBoxDemo extends ButtonDemo {
6    // Create three check boxes to control the display of message
7    private JCheckBox jchkCentered = new JCheckBox("Centered");
8    private JCheckBox jchkBold = new JCheckBox("Bold");
9    private JCheckBox jchkItalic = new JCheckBox("Italic");
10
11   public static void main(String[] args) {
12     CheckBoxDemo frame = new CheckBoxDemo();
13     frame.setTitle("CheckBoxDemo");
14     frame.setLocationRelativeTo(null); // Center the frame
15     frame.setDefaultCloseOperation(JFrame.EXIT_ON_CLOSE);
16     frame.setSize(500, 200);
17     frame.setVisible(true);
18   }
19
20   public CheckBoxDemo() {
21     // Set mnemonic keys
22     jchkCentered.setMnemonic('C');
23     jchkBold.setMnemonic('B');
24     jchkItalic.setMnemonic('I');
25
26     // Create a new panel to hold check boxes
27     JPanel jpCheckBoxes = new JPanel();
28     jpCheckBoxes.setLayout(new GridLayout(3, 1));
29     jpCheckBoxes.add(jchkCentered);
30     jpCheckBoxes.add(jchkBold);
31     jpCheckBoxes.add(jchkItalic);
32     add(jpCheckBoxes, BorderLayout.EAST);
33
34     // Register listeners with the check boxes
35     jchkCentered.addActionListener(new ActionListener() {
36       public void actionPerformed(ActionEvent e) {
37         messagePanel.setCentered(jchkCentered.isSelected());
38       }
39     });
40     jchkBold.addActionListener(new ActionListener() {
41       public void actionPerformed(ActionEvent e) {
42         setNewFont();
43       }
44     });
```

create frame

create UI

register listener

register listener

ButtonDemo

CheckBoxDemo

register listener

```
45    jchkItalic.addActionListener(new ActionListener() {
46      public void actionPerformed(ActionEvent e) {
47        setNewFont();
48      }
49    });
50  }
51
```

set a new font

```
52  private void setNewFont() {
53    // Determine a font style
54    int fontStyle = Font.PLAIN;
55    fontStyle += (jchkBold.isSelected() ? Font.BOLD : Font.PLAIN);
56    fontStyle += (jchkItalic.isSelected() ? Font.ITALIC : Font.PLAIN);
57
58    // Set font for the message
59    Font font = messagePanel.getFont();
60    messagePanel.setFont(
61      new Font(font.getName(), fontStyle, font.getSize()));
62  }
63 }
```

CheckBoxDemo extends ButtonDemo and adds three check boxes to control how the message is displayed. When a CheckBoxDemo is constructed (line 12), its superclass's no-arg constructor is invoked, so you don't have to rewrite the code that is already in the constructor of ButtonDemo.

When a check box is checked or unchecked, the listener's actionPerformed method is invoked to process the event. When the "Centered" check box is checked or unchecked, the centered property of the MessagePanel class is set to true or false.

The current font name and size used in MessagePanel are obtained from messagePanel.getFont() using the getName() and getSize() methods. The font styles (Font.BOLD and Font.ITALIC) are specified in the check boxes. If no font style is selected, the font style is Font.PLAIN. Font styles are combined by adding together the selected integers representing the fonts.

The keyboard mnemonics 'C', 'B', and 'I' are set on the check boxes "Centered," "Bold," and "Italic," respectively (lines 22–24). You can use a mouse gesture or a shortcut key to select a check box.

The setFont method (line 60) defined in the Component class is inherited in the MessagePanel class. This method automatically invokes the repaint method. Invoking setFont in messagePanel automatically repaints the message.

A check box fires an ActionEvent and an ItemEvent when it is clicked. You could process either the ActionEvent or the ItemEvent to redisplay the message. The example processes the ActionEvent. If you wish to process the ItemEvent, you could create a listener for ItemEvent and register it with a check box, as shown below:

```
public class CheckBoxDemoUsingItemEvent extends ButtonDemo {
  ... // Same as in CheckBoxDemo.java, so omitted

  public CheckBoxDemoUsingItemEvent() {
    ... // Same as in CheckBoxDemo.java, so omitted

    // To listen for ItemEvent
    jchkCentered.addItemListener(newItemListener() {
      /** Handle ItemEvent */
      public void itemStateChanged(ItemEvent e) {
        messagePanel.setCentered(jchkCentered.isSelected());
      }
    });
  }
}
```

15.4 Radio Buttons

Radio buttons, also known as *option buttons*, enable you to choose a single item from a group of choices. In appearance radio buttons resemble check boxes, but check boxes display a square that is either checked or blank, whereas radio buttons display a circle that is either filled (if selected) or blank (if not selected).

JRadioButton inherits AbstractButton and provides several constructors to create radio buttons, as shown in Figure 15.13. These constructors are similar to the constructors for JCheckBox.

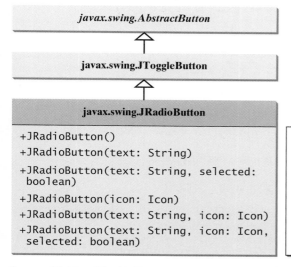

javax.swing.JRadioButton	
+JRadioButton()	Creates a default radio button with no text and icon.
+JRadioButton(text: String)	Creates a radio button with text.
+JRadioButton(text: String, selected: boolean)	Creates a radio button with text and specifies whether the radio button is initially selected.
+JRadioButton(icon: Icon)	Creates a radio button with an icon.
+JRadioButton(text: String, icon: Icon)	Creates a radio button with text and an icon.
+JRadioButton(text: String, icon: Icon, selected: boolean)	Creates a radio button with text and an icon, and specifies whether the radio button is initially selected.

FIGURE 15.13   JRadioButton defines a radio button.

Here is an example of a radio button with text Student, red foreground, white background, mnemonic key 'S', and initially selected.

```java
JRadioButton jrb = new JRadioButton("Student", true);
jrb.setForeground(Color.red);
jrb.setBackground(Color.white);
jrb.setMnemonic('S');
```

To group radio buttons, you need to create an instance of java.swing.ButtonGroup and use the add method to add them to it, as follows:

```java
ButtonGroup group = new ButtonGroup();
group.add(jrb1);
group.add(jrb2);
```

This code creates a radio button group for radio buttons jrb1 and jrb2 so that jrb1 and jrb2 are selected mutually exclusively. Without grouping, jrb1 and jrb2 would be independent.

Note

ButtonGroup is not a subclass of java.awt.Component, so a ButtonGroup object cannot be added to a container.

When a radio button is clicked (selected or deselected), it fires an ItemEvent and then an ActionEvent. To see if a radio button is selected, use the isSelected() method.

Listing 15.4 gives a program that adds three radio buttons named *Red*, *Green*, and *Blue* into the preceding example to let the user choose the color of the message, as shown in Figure 15.14.

GUI helper class

Again there are at least two approaches to writing this program. The first is to revise the preceding CheckBoxDemo class to insert the code for adding the radio buttons and processing

JPanel with
GridLayout
for three
radio buttons

FIGURE 15.14 Three radio buttons are added to specify the color of the message.

their events. The second is to create a subclass that extends CheckBoxDemo. Listing 15.4 gives
the code to implement the second approach.

LISTING 15.4 RadioButtonDemo.java

```
1  import java.awt.*;
2  import java.awt.event.*;
3  import javax.swing.*;
4
5  public class RadioButtonDemo extends CheckBoxDemo {
6    // Declare radio buttons
7    private JRadioButton jrbRed, jrbGreen, jrbBlue;
8
9    public static void main(String[] args) {
10     RadioButtonDemo frame = new RadioButtonDemo();
11     frame.setLocationRelativeTo(null); // Center the frame
12     frame.setDefaultCloseOperation(JFrame.EXIT_ON_CLOSE);
13     frame.setTitle("RadioButtonDemo");
14     frame.setSize(500, 200);
15     frame.setVisible(true);
16   }
17
18   public RadioButtonDemo() {
19     // Create a new panel to hold check boxes
20     JPanel jpRadioButtons = new JPanel();
21     jpRadioButtons.setLayout(new GridLayout(3, 1));
22     jpRadioButtons.add(jrbRed = new JRadioButton("Red"));
23     jpRadioButtons.add(jrbGreen = new JRadioButton("Green"));
24     jpRadioButtons.add(jrbBlue = new JRadioButton("Blue"));
25     add(jpRadioButtons, BorderLayout.WEST);
26
27     // Create a radio button group to group three buttons
28     ButtonGroup group = new ButtonGroup();
29     group.add(jrbRed);
30     group.add(jrbGreen);
31     group.add(jrbBlue);
32
33     // Set keyboard mnemonics
34     jrbRed.setMnemonic('E');
35     jrbGreen.setMnemonic('G');
36     jrbBlue.setMnemonic('U');
37
38     // Register listeners for check boxes
39     jrbRed.addActionListener(new ActionListener() {
40       public void actionPerformed(ActionEvent e) {
41         messagePanel.setForeground(Color.red);
42       }
43     });
```

create frame

create UI

group buttons

register listener

```
44      jrbGreen.addActionListener(new ActionListener() {          register listener
45        public void actionPerformed(ActionEvent e) {
46          messagePanel.setForeground(Color.green);
47        }
48      });
49      jrbBlue.addActionListener(new ActionListener() {           register listener
50        public void actionPerformed(ActionEvent e) {
51          messagePanel.setForeground(Color.blue);
52        }
53      });
54
55      // Set initial message color to blue
56      jrbBlue.setSelected(true);
57      messagePanel.setForeground(Color.blue);
58    }
59  }
```

RadioButtonDemo extends **CheckBoxDemo** and adds three radio buttons to specify the message color. When a radio button is clicked, the radio button's action event listener sets the corresponding foreground color in **messagePanel**.

The keyboard mnemonics 'R' and 'B' are already set for the Right button and Bold check box. To avoid conflict, the keyboard mnemonics 'E', 'G', and 'U' are set on the radio buttons "Red", "Green", and "Blue", respectively (lines 34–36).

The program creates a **ButtonGroup group** and puts three **JRadioButton** instances (**jrbRed**, **jrbGreen**, and **jrbBlue**) in the group (lines 28–31).

A radio button fires an **ActionEvent** and an **ItemEvent** when it is selected or deselected. You could process either the **ActionEvent** or the **ItemEvent** to choose a color. The example processes the **ActionEvent**. Please rewrite the code using the **ItemEvent** as an exercise.

15.5 Labels

A *label* is a display area for a short text, an image, or both. It is often used to label other components (usually text fields). Figure 15.15 lists the constructors and methods in **JLabel**.

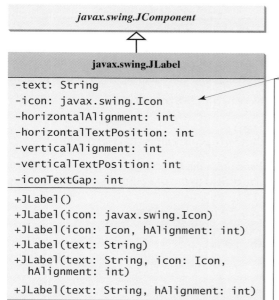

> The get and set methods for these data fields are provided in the class, but omitted in the UML diagram for brevity.

javax.swing.JLabel	
-text: String	The label's text.
-icon: javax.swing.Icon	The label's image icon.
-horizontalAlignment: int	The horizontal alignment of the text and icon on the label.
-horizontalTextPosition: int	The horizontal text position relative to the icon on the label.
-verticalAlignment: int	The vertical alignment of the text and icon on the label.
-verticalTextPosition: int	The vertical text position relative to the icon on the label.
-iconTextGap: int	The gap between the text and the icon on the label (JDK 1.4).
+JLabel()	Creates a default label with no text and icon.
+JLabel(icon: javax.swing.Icon)	Creates a label with an icon.
+JLabel(icon: Icon, hAlignment: int)	Creates a label with an icon and the specified horizontal alignment.
+JLabel(text: String)	Creates a label with text.
+JLabel(text: String, icon: Icon, hAlignment: int)	Creates a label with text, an icon, and the specified horizontal alignment.
+JLabel(text: String, hAlignment: int)	Creates a label with text and the specified horizontal alignment.

FIGURE 15.15 **JLabel** displays text or an icon, or both.

JLabel inherits all the properties from **JComponent** and has many properties similar to the ones in **JButton**, such as **text**, **icon**, **horizontalAlignment**, **verticalAlignment**, **horizontalTextPosition**, **verticalTextPosition**, and **iconTextGap**. For example, the following code displays a label with text and an icon:

```
// Create an image icon from an image file
ImageIcon icon = new ImageIcon("image/grapes.gif");

// Create a label with text, an icon,
// with centered horizontal alignment
JLabel jlbl = new JLabel("Grapes", icon, SwingConstants.CENTER);

// Set label's text alignment and gap between text and icon
jlbl.setHorizontalTextPosition(SwingConstants.CENTER);
jlbl.setVerticalTextPosition(SwingConstants.BOTTOM);
jlbl.setIconTextGap(5);
```

15.6 Text Fields

A *text field* can be used to enter or display a string. **JTextField** is a subclass of **JText-Component**. Figure 15.16 lists the constructors and methods in **JTextField**.

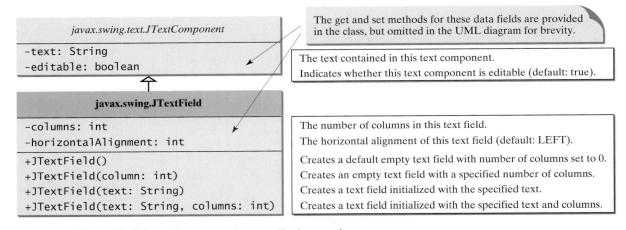

FIGURE 15.16 **JTextField** enables you to enter or display a string.

JTextField inherits **JTextComponent**, which inherits **JComponent**. Here is an example of creating a non-editable text field with red foreground color and right horizontal alignment:

```
JTextField jtfMessage = new JTextField("T-Strom");
jtfMessage.setEditable(false);
jtfMessage.setForeground(Color.red);
jtfMessage.setHorizontalAlignment(SwingConstants.RIGHT);
```

When you move the cursor in the text field and press the Enter key, it fires an **ActionEvent**.

Listing 15.5 gives a program that adds a text field to the preceding example to let the user set a new message, as shown in Figure 15.17.

Listing 15.5 creates a subclass that extends **RadioButtonDemo**.

LISTING 15.5 TextFieldDemo.java

```
1 import java.awt.*;
2 import java.awt.event.*;
3 import javax.swing.*;
4
```

```
5  public class TextFieldDemo extends RadioButtonDemo {
6    private JTextField jtfMessage = new JTextField(10);
7
8    /** Main method */
9    public static void main(String[] args) {
10     TextFieldDemo frame = new TextFieldDemo();
11     frame.pack();
12     frame.setTitle("TextFieldDemo");
13     frame.setLocationRelativeTo(null); // Center the frame
14     frame.setDefaultCloseOperation(JFrame.EXIT_ON_CLOSE);
15     frame.setVisible(true);
16   }
17
18   public TextFieldDemo() {
19     // Create a new panel to hold label and text field
20     JPanel jpTextField = new JPanel();
21     jpTextField.setLayout(new BorderLayout(5, 0));
22     jpTextField.add(
23       new JLabel("Enter a new message"), BorderLayout.WEST);
24     jpTextField.add(jtfMessage, BorderLayout.CENTER);
25     add(jpTextField, BorderLayout.NORTH);
26
27     jtfMessage.setHorizontalAlignment(JTextField.RIGHT);
28
29     // Register listener
30     jtfMessage.addActionListener(new ActionListener() {
31       /** Handle ActionEvent */
32       public void actionPerformed(ActionEvent e) {
33         messagePanel.setMessage(jtfMessage.getText());
34         jtfMessage.requestFocusInWindow();
35       }
36     });
37   }
38 }
```

create frame
pack frame

create UI

listener

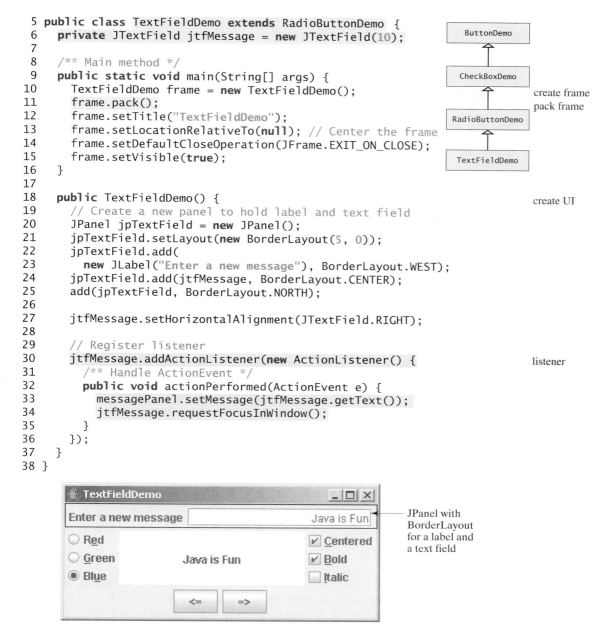

FIGURE 15.17   A label and a text field are added to set a new message.

TextFieldDemo extends RadioButtonDemo and adds a label and a text field to let the user enter a new message. After you set a new message in the text field and press the Enter key, a new message is displayed. Pressing the Enter key on the text field triggers an action event. The listener sets a new message in messagePanel (line 33).

Instead of using the setSize method to set the size for the frame, the program uses the pack() method (line 11), which automatically sizes up the frame according to the size of the components placed in it.

pack()

The requestFocusInWindow() method (line 34) defined in the Component class requests the component to receive input focus. Thus, jtfMessage.request-FocusInWindow() (line 34) requests the input focus on jtfMessage. You will see the cursor on jtfMessage after the actionPerformed method is invoked.

requestFocus-
 InWindow()

JPasswordField

Note

If a text field is used for entering a password, use `JPasswordField` to replace `JTextField`. `JPasswordField` extends `JTextField` and hides the input text with echo characters (e.g., `******`). By default, the echo character is `*`. You can specify a new echo character using the `setEchoChar(char)` method.

15.7 Text Areas

If you want to let the user enter multiple lines of text, you have to create several instances of `JTextField`. A better alternative is to use `JTextArea`, which enables the user to enter multiple lines of text. Figure 15.18 lists the constructors and methods in `JTextArea`.

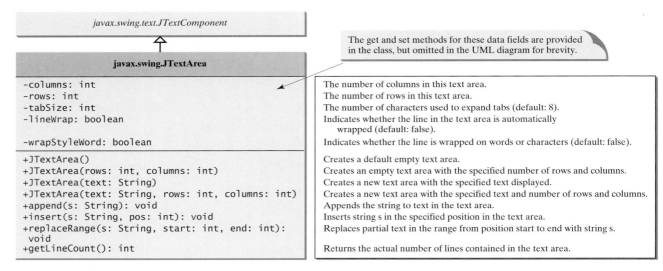

FIGURE 15.18 `JTextArea` enables you to enter or display multiple lines of characters.

Like `JTextField`, `JTextArea` inherits `JTextComponent`, which contains the methods `getText`, `setText`, `isEditable`, and `setEditable`. Here is an example of creating a text area with five rows and twenty columns, line-wrapped on words, red foreground color, and Courier font, bold, 20 pixels.

```
JTextArea jtaNote = new JTextArea("This is a text area", 5, 20);
jtaNote.setLineWrap(true);
jtaNote.setWrapStyleWord(true);
jtaNote.setForeground(Color.red);
jtaNote.setFont(new Font("Courier", Font.BOLD, 20));
```

wrap line
wrap word

`JTextArea` does not handle scrolling, but you can create a `JScrollPane` object to hold an instance of `JTextArea` and let `JScrollPane` handle scrolling for `JTextArea`, as follows:

```
// Create a scroll pane to hold text area
JScrollPane scrollPane = new JScrollPane(jta = new JTextArea());
add(scrollPane, BorderLayout.CENTER);
```

Listing 15.6 gives a program that displays an image and a text in a label, and a text in a text area, as shown in Figure 15.19.

Here are the major steps in the program:

1. Create a class named `DescriptionPanel` that extends `JPanel`. This class contains a text area inside a scroll pane, a label for displaying an image icon, and a title. This class is used in the present example and will be reused in later examples.

A label showing an image and a text →

DescriptionPanel with Border Layout →

Text inside a scroll pane →

FIGURE 15.19 The program displays an image in a label, a title in a label, and a text in the text area.

2. Create a class named TextAreaDemo that extends JFrame. Create an instance of DescriptionPanel and add it to the center of the frame. The relationship between DescriptionPanel and TextAreaDemo is shown in Figure 15.20.

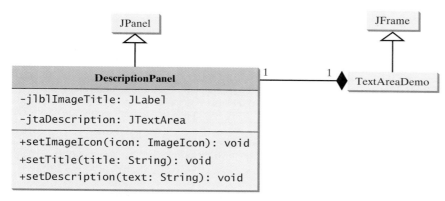

FIGURE 15.20 TextAreaDemo uses DescriptionPanel to display an image, title, and text description of a national flag.

LISTING 15.6 TextAreaDemo.java

```
1  import java.awt.*;
2  import javax.swing.*;
3
4  public class TextAreaDemo extends JFrame {
5    // Declare and create a description panel
6    private DescriptionPanel descriptionPanel = new DescriptionPanel();
7
8    public static void main(String[] args) {
9      TextAreaDemo frame = new TextAreaDemo();                    create frame
10     frame.pack();
11     frame.setLocationRelativeTo(null); // Center the frame
12     frame.setDefaultCloseOperation(JFrame.EXIT_ON_CLOSE);
13     frame.setTitle("TextAreaDemo");
14     frame.setVisible(true);
15   }
16
17   public TextAreaDemo() {
18     // Set title, text and image in the description panel        create UI
19     descriptionPanel.setTitle("Canada");
20     String description = "The Maple Leaf flag \n\n" +
21       "The Canadian National Flag was adopted by the Canadian " +
22       "Parliament on October 22, 1964 and was proclaimed into law " +
23       "by Her Majesty Queen Elizabeth II (the Queen of Canada) on " +
```

```
24              "February 15, 1965. The Canadian Flag (colloquially known " +
25              "as The Maple Leaf Flag) is a red flag of the proportions " +
26              "two by length and one by width, containing in its center a " +
27              "white square, with a single red stylized eleven-point " +
28              "mapleleaf centered in the white square.";
29          descriptionPanel.setDescription(description);
30          descriptionPanel.setImageIcon(new ImageIcon("image/ca.gif"));
31
32          // Add the description panel to the frame
33          setLayout(new BorderLayout());
34          add(descriptionPanel, BorderLayout.CENTER);
35      }
36  }
37
38  // Define a panel for displaying image and text
39  class DescriptionPanel extends JPanel {
40      /** Label for displaying an image icon and a text */
41      private JLabel jlblImageTitle = new JLabel();
42
43      /** Text area for displaying text */
44      private JTextArea jtaDescription = new JTextArea();
45
46      public DescriptionPanel() {
47          // Center the icon and text and place the text under the icon
48          jlblImageTitle.setHorizontalAlignment(JLabel.CENTER);
49          jlblImageTitle.setHorizontalTextPosition(JLabel.CENTER);
50          jlblImageTitle.setVerticalTextPosition(JLabel.BOTTOM);
51
52          // Set the font in the label and the text field
53          jlblImageTitle.setFont(new Font("SansSerif", Font.BOLD, 16));
54          jtaDescription.setFont(new Font("Serif", Font.PLAIN, 14));
55
56          // Set lineWrap and wrapStyleWord true for the text area
57          jtaDescription.setLineWrap(true);
58          jtaDescription.setWrapStyleWord(true);
59          jtaDescription.setEditable(false);
60
61          // Create a scroll pane to hold the text area
62          JScrollPane scrollPane = new JScrollPane(jtaDescription);
63
64          // Set BorderLayout for the panel, add label and scrollpane
65          setLayout(new BorderLayout(5, 5));
66          add(scrollPane, BorderLayout.CENTER);
67          add(jlblImageTitle, BorderLayout.WEST);
68      }
69
70      /** Set the title */
71      public void setTitle(String title) {
72          jlblImageTitle.setText(title);
73      }
74
75      /** Set the image icon */
76      public void setImageIcon(ImageIcon icon) {
77          jlblImageTitle.setIcon(icon);
78      }
79
80      /** Set the text description */
81      public void setDescription(String text) {
82          jtaDescription.setText(text);
83      }
84  }
```

label

text area

wrap line
wrap word
read only

scroll pane

TextAreaDemo simply creates an instance of DescriptionPanel (line 6), and sets the title (line 19), image (line 30), and text in the description panel (line 29). DescriptionPanel is a subclass of JPanel. DescriptionPanel contains a label for displaying an image icon and a text title, and a text area for displaying a description of the image.

It is not necessary to create a separate class for DescriptionPanel in this example. Nevertheless, this class was created for reuse in the next example, where you will use it to display a description panel for various images.

The text area is inside a JScrollPane (line 62), which provides scrolling functions for the text area. Scroll bars automatically appear if there is more text than the physical size of the text area, and disappear if the text is deleted and the remaining text does not exceed the text area size.

The lineWrap property is set to true (line 57) so that the line is automatically wrapped when the text cannot fit in one line. The wrapStyleWord property is set to true (line 58) so that the line is wrapped on words rather than characters. The text area is set non-editable (line 59), so you cannot edit the description in the text area.

15.8 Combo Boxes

A *combo box*, also known as a *choice list* or *drop-down list*, contains a list of items from which the user can choose. It is useful in limiting a user's range of choices and avoids the cumbersome validation of data input. Figure 15.21 lists several frequently used constructors and methods in JComboBox.

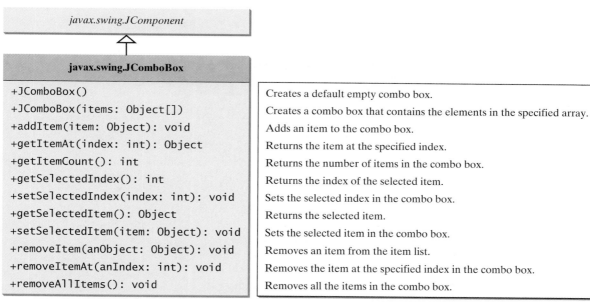

FIGURE 15.21 JComboBox enables you to select an item from a set of items.

The following statements create a combo box with four items, red foreground, white background, and the second item selected:

```
JComboBox jcb = new JComboBox(new Object[]
  {"Item 1", "Item 2", "Item 3", "Item 4"});
jcb.setForeground(Color.red);
jcb.setBackground(Color.white);
jcb.setSelectedItem("Item 2");
```

JComboBox can generate ActionEvent and ItemEvent, among many other events. Whenever an item is selected, an ActionEvent is fired. Whenever a new item is selected,

JComboBox generates ItemEvent twice, once for deselecting the previously selected item, and the other for selecting the currently selected item. Note that no ItemEvent is fired if the current item is reselected. To respond to an ItemEvent, you need to implement the itemStateChanged(ItemEvent e) handler for processing a choice. To get data from a JComboBox menu, you can use getSelectedItem() to return the currently selected item, or e.getItem() method to get the item from the itemStateChanged(ItemEvent e) handler.

Listing 15.7 gives a program that lets users view an image and a description of a country's flag by selecting the country from a combo box, as shown in Figure 15.22.

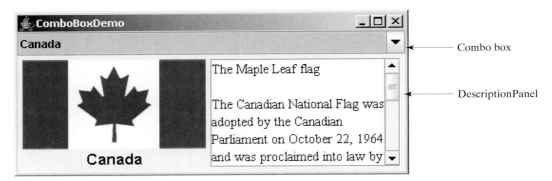

FIGURE 15.22 A country's info, including a flag image and a description of the flag, is displayed when the country is selected in the combo box.

Here are the major steps in the program:

1. Create the user interface.
   Create a combo box with country names as its selection values. Create a DescriptionPanel object. The DescriptionPanel class was introduced in the preceding example. Place the combo box in the north of the frame and the description panel in the center of the frame.

2. Process the event.
   Create a listener to implement the itemStateChanged handler to set the flag title, image, and text in the description panel for the selected country name.

LISTING 15.7 ComboBoxDemo.java

```java
1 import java.awt.*;
2 import java.awt.event.*;
3 import javax.swing.*;
4
5 public class ComboBoxDemo extends JFrame {
6   // Declare an array of Strings for flag titles
7   private String[] flagTitles = {"Canada", "China", "Denmark",
8     "France", "Germany", "India", "Norway", "United Kingdom",
9     "United States of America"};
10
11   // Declare an ImageIcon array for the national flags of 9 countries
12   private ImageIcon[] flagImage = {
13     new ImageIcon("image/ca.gif"),
14     new ImageIcon("image/china.gif"),
15     new ImageIcon("image/denmark.gif"),
16     new ImageIcon("image/fr.gif"),
17     new ImageIcon("image/germany.gif"),
18     new ImageIcon("image/india.gif"),
```

country

image icon

```
19       new ImageIcon("image/norway.gif"),
20       new ImageIcon("image/uk.gif"),
21       new ImageIcon("image/us.gif")
22     };
23
24     // Declare an array of strings for flag descriptions
25     private String[] flagDescription = new String[9];                    description
26
27     // Declare and create a description panel
28     private DescriptionPanel descriptionPanel = new DescriptionPanel();
29
30     // Create a combo box for selecting countries
31     private JComboBox jcbo = new JComboBox(flagTitles);                   combo box
32
33     public static void main(String[] args) {
34       ComboBoxDemo frame = new ComboBoxDemo();
35       frame.pack();
36       frame.setTitle("ComboBoxDemo");
37       frame.setLocationRelativeTo(null); // Center the frame
38       frame.setDefaultCloseOperation(JFrame.EXIT_ON_CLOSE);
39       frame.setVisible(true);
40     }
41
42     public ComboBoxDemo() {                                               create UI
43       // Set text description
44       flagDescription[0] = "The Maple Leaf flag \n\n" +
45         "The Canadian National Flag was adopted by the Canadian " +
46         "Parliament on October 22, 1964 and was proclaimed into law " +
47         "by Her Majesty Queen Elizabeth II (the Queen of Canada) on " +
48         "February 15, 1965. The Canadian Flag (colloquially known " +
49         "as The Maple Leaf Flag) is a red flag of the proportions " +
50         "two by length and one by width, containing in its center a " +
51         "white square, with a single red stylized eleven-point " +
52         "mapleleaf centered in the white square.";
53       flagDescription[1] = "Description for China ... ";
54       flagDescription[2] = "Description for Denmark ... ";
55       flagDescription[3] = "Description for France ... ";
56       flagDescription[4] = "Description for Germany ... ";
57       flagDescription[5] = "Description for India ... ";
58       flagDescription[6] = "Description for Norway ... ";
59       flagDescription[7] = "Description for UK ... ";
60       flagDescription[8] = "Description for US ... ";
61
62       // Set the first country (Canada) for display
63       setDisplay(0);
64
65       // Add combo box and description panel to the list
66       add(jcbo, BorderLayout.NORTH);
67       add(descriptionPanel, BorderLayout.CENTER);
68
69       // Register listener
70       jcbo.addItemListener(new ItemListener() {                          listener
71         /** Handle item selection */
72         public void itemStateChanged(ItemEvent e) {
73           setDisplay(jcbo.getSelectedIndex());
74         }
75       });
76     }
77
```

```
78    /** Set display information on the description panel */
79    public void setDisplay(int index) {
80      descriptionPanel.setTitle(flagTitles[index]);
81      descriptionPanel.setImageIcon(flagImage[index]);
82      descriptionPanel.setDescription(flagDescription[index]);
83    }
84  }
```

The listener listens to `ItemEvent` from the combo box and implements `ItemListener` (lines 70–75). Instead of using `ItemEvent`, you may rewrite the program to use `ActionEvent` for handling combo box item selection.

The program stores the flag information in three arrays: `flagTitles`, `flagImage`, and `flagDescription` (lines 7–25). The array `flagTitles` contains the names of nine countries, the array `flagImage` contains images of the nine countries' flags, and the array `flagDescription` contains descriptions of the flags.

The program creates an instance of `DescriptionPanel` (line 28), which was presented in Listing 15.6, TextAreaDemo.java. The program creates a combo box with initial values from `flagTitles` (line 31). When the user selects an item in the combo box, the `ItemStateChanged` handler is executed, finds the selected index, and sets its corresponding flag title, flag image, and flag description on the panel.

15.9 Lists

A *list* is a component that basically performs the same function as a combo box but enables the user to choose a single value or multiple values. The Swing `JList` is very versatile. Figure 15.23 lists several frequently used constructors and methods in `JList`.

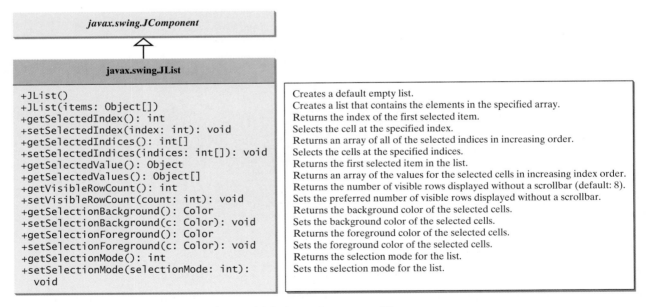

FIGURE 15.23 `JList` enables you to select multiple items from a set of items.

`selectionMode` is one of the three values (`SINGLE_SELECTION`, `SINGLE_INTERVAL_SELECTION`, `MULTIPLE_INTERVAL_SELECTION`) defined in `javax.swing.SelectionModel` that indicate whether a single item, single-interval item, or multiple-interval item can be selected. Single selection allows only one item to be selected. Single-interval selection allows multiple selections, but the selected items must be contiguous. Multiple-interval selection allows selections of multiple contiguous items without restrictions, as shown in Figure 15.24. The default value is MULTIPLE_INTERVAL_SELECTION.

(a) Single selection   (b) Single-interval selection   (c) Multiple-interval selection

FIGURE 15.24 JList has three selection modes: single selection, single-interval selection, and multiple-interval selection.

The following statements create a list with six items, red foreground, white background, pink selection foreground, black selection background, and visible row count 4:

```
JList jlst = new JList(new Object[]
   {"Item 1", "Item 2", "Item 3", "Item 4", "Item 5", "Item 6"});
jlst.setForeground(Color.red);
jlst.setBackground(Color.white);
jlst.setSelectionForeground(Color.pink);
jlst.setSelectionBackground(Color.black);
jlst.setVisibleRowCount(4);
```

Lists do not scroll automatically. To make a list scrollable, create a scroll pane and add the list to it. Text areas are made scrollable in the same way.

JList generates javax.swing.event.ListSelectionEvent to notify the listeners of the selections. The listener must implement the valueChanged handler in the javax.swing.event.ListSelectionListener interface to process the event.

Listing 15.8 gives a program that lets users select countries in a list and display the flags of the selected countries in the labels. Figure 15.25 shows a sample run of the program.

JList inside a scroll pane →   ← JPanel with GridLayout

← An image is displayed on a JLabel

FIGURE 15.25 When the countries in the list are selected, corresponding images of their flags are displayed in the labels.

Here are the major steps in the program:

1. Create the user interface.
   Create a list with nine country names as selection values, and place the list inside a scroll pane. Place the scroll pane in the west of the frame. Create nine labels to be used to display the countries' flag images. Place the labels in the panel, and place the panel in the center of the frame.

2. Process the event.

Create a listener to implement the **valueChanged** method in the **ListSelection-Listener** interface to set the selected countries' flag images in the labels.

LISTING 15.8 `ListDemo.java`

```
1  import java.awt.*;
2  import javax.swing.*;
3  import javax.swing.event.*;
4
5  public class ListDemo extends JFrame {
6    final int NUMBER_OF_FLAGS = 9;
7
8    // Declare an array of Strings for flag titles
9    private String[] flagTitles = {"Canada", "China", "Denmark",
10     "France", "Germany", "India", "Norway", "United Kingdom",
11     "United States of America"};
12
13   // The list for selecting countries
14   private JList jlst = new JList(flagTitles);
15
16   // Declare an ImageIcon array for the national flags of 9 countries
17   private ImageIcon[] imageIcons = {
18     new ImageIcon("image/ca.gif"),
19     new ImageIcon("image/china.gif"),
20     new ImageIcon("image/denmark.gif"),
21     new ImageIcon("image/fr.gif"),
22     new ImageIcon("image/germany.gif"),
23     new ImageIcon("image/india.gif"),
24     new ImageIcon("image/norway.gif"),
25     new ImageIcon("image/uk.gif"),
26     new ImageIcon("image/us.gif")
27   };
28
29   // Arrays of labels for displaying images
30   private JLabel[] jlblImageViewer = new JLabel[NUMBER_OF_FLAGS];
31
32   public static void main(String[] args) {
33     ListDemo frame = new ListDemo();
34     frame.setSize(650, 500);
35     frame.setTitle("ListDemo");
36     frame.setLocationRelativeTo(null); // Center the frame
37     frame.setDefaultCloseOperation(JFrame.EXIT_ON_CLOSE);
38     frame.setVisible(true);
39   }
40
41   public ListDemo() {
42     // Create a panel to hold nine labels
43     JPanel p = new JPanel(new GridLayout(3, 3, 5, 5));
44
45     for (int i = 0; i < NUMBER_OF_FLAGS; i++) {
46       p.add(jlblImageViewer[i] = new JLabel());
47       jlblImageViewer[i].setHorizontalAlignment
48         (SwingConstants.CENTER);
49     }
50
51     // Add p and the list to the frame
52     add(p, BorderLayout.CENTER);
53     add(new JScrollPane(jlst), BorderLayout.WEST);
54
```

create frame

create UI

```
55      // Register listeners
56      jlst.addListSelectionListener(new ListSelectionListener() {
57        /** Handle list selection */
58        public void valueChanged(ListSelectionEvent e) {
59          // Get selected indices
60          int[] indices = jlst.getSelectedIndices();
61
62          int i;                                              handler
63          // Set icons in the labels
64          for (i = 0; i < indices.length; i++) {
65            jlblImageViewer[i].setIcon(imageIcons[indices[i]]);
66          }
67
68          // Remove icons from the rest of the labels
69          for (; i < NUMBER_OF_FLAGS; i++) {
70            jlblImageViewer[i].setIcon(null);
71          }
72        }
73      });
74    }
75 }
```

The anonymous inner class listener listens to `ListSelectionEvent` for handling the selection of country names in the list (lines 56–73). `ListSelectionEvent` and `ListSelection Listener` are defined in the `javax.swing.event` package, so this package is imported in the program (line 3).

The program creates an array of nine labels for displaying flag images for nine countries. The program loads the images of the nine countries into an image array (lines 17–27) and creates a list of the nine countries in the same order as in the image array (lines 9–11). Thus the index 0 of the image array corresponds to the first country in the list.

The list is placed in a scroll pane (line 53) so that it can be scrolled when the number of items in the list extends beyond the viewing area.

By default, the selection mode of the list is multiple-interval, which allows the user to select multiple items from different blocks in the list. When the user selects countries in the list, the `valueChanged` handler (lines 58–72) is executed, which gets the indices of the selected item and sets their corresponding image icons in the label to display the flags.

15.10 Scroll Bars

`JScrollBar` is a component that enables the user to select from a range of values, as shown in Figure 15.26.

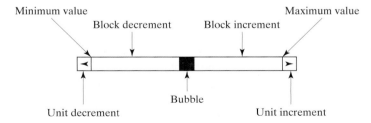

FIGURE 15.26 A scroll bar represents a range of values graphically.

Normally, the user changes the value of the scroll bar by making a gesture with the mouse. For example, the user can drag the scroll bar's bubble up and down, or click in the scroll bar's unit-increment or block-increment areas. Keyboard gestures can also be mapped to the scroll bar. By convention, the Page Up and Page Down keys are equivalent to clicking in the scroll bar's block-increment and block-decrement areas.

 Note
The width of the scroll bar's track corresponds to `maximum + visibleAmount`. When a scroll bar is set to its maximum value, the left side of the bubble is at `maximum`, and the right side is at `maximum + visibleAmount`.

`JScrollBar` has the following properties, as shown in Figure 15.27.

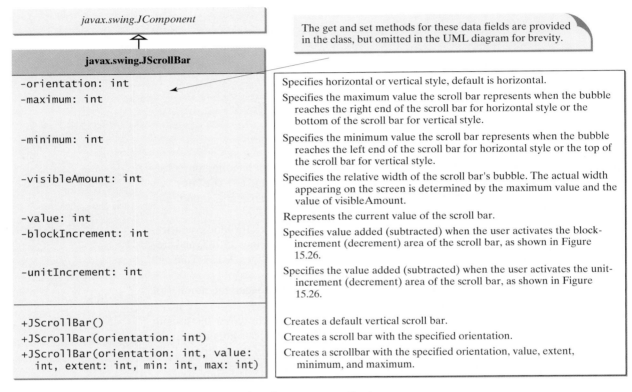

FIGURE 15.27 `JScrollBar` enables you to select from a range of values.

Normally, a program changes a scroll bar's value by calling the `setValue` method. The `setValue` method simultaneously and synchronously sets the minimum, maximum, visible amount, and value properties of a scroll bar, so that they are mutually consistent.

When the user changes the value of the scroll bar, the scroll bar generates an instance of `AdjustmentEvent`, which is passed to every registered listener. An object that wishes to be notified of changes to the scroll bar's value must implement the `adjustmentValueChanged` method in the `AdjustmentListener` interface defined in the package `java.awt.event`.

Listing 15.9 gives a program that uses horizontal and vertical scroll bars to control a message displayed on a panel. The horizontal scroll bar is used to move the message to the left or the right, and the vertical scroll bar to move it up and down. A sample run of the program is shown in Figure 15.28.

Here are the major steps in the program:

1. Create the user interface.
   Create a `MessagePanel` object and place it in the center of the frame. Create a vertical scroll bar and place it in the east of the frame. Create a horizontal scroll bar and place it in the south of the frame.

Figure 15.28 The scroll bars move the message on a panel horizontally and vertically.

2. Process the event.

Create a listener to implement the **adjustmentValueChanged** handler to move the message according to the bar movement in the scroll bars.

Listing 15.9 ScrollBarDemo.java

```java
1  import java.awt.*;
2  import java.awt.event.*;
3  import javax.swing.*;
4
5  public class ScrollBarDemo extends JFrame {
6    // Create horizontal and vertical scroll bars
7    private JScrollBar jscbHort =
8      new JScrollBar(JScrollBar.HORIZONTAL);                  horizontal scroll bar
9    private JScrollBar jscbVert =
10     new JScrollBar(JScrollBar.VERTICAL);                    vertical scroll bar
11
12   // Create a MessagePanel
13   private MessagePanel messagePanel =
14     new MessagePanel("Welcome to Java");
15
16   public static void main(String[] args) {
17     ScrollBarDemo frame = new ScrollBarDemo();               create frame
18     frame.setTitle("ScrollBarDemo");
19     frame.setLocationRelativeTo(null); // Center the frame
20     frame.setDefaultCloseOperation(JFrame.EXIT_ON_CLOSE);
21     frame.pack();
22     frame.setVisible(true);
23   }
24
25   public ScrollBarDemo() {                                   create UI
26     // Add scroll bars and message panel to the frame
27     setLayout(new BorderLayout());
28     add(messagePanel, BorderLayout.CENTER);
29     add(jscbVert, BorderLayout.EAST);                       add scroll bar vertical
30     add(jscbHort, BorderLayout.SOUTH);
31
32     // Register listener for the scroll bars
33     jscbHort.addAdjustmentListener(new AdjustmentListener() {  adjustment listener
34       public void adjustmentValueChanged(AdjustmentEvent e) {
35         // getValue() and getMaximumValue() return int, but for better
36         // precision, use double
37         double value = jscbHort.getValue();
38         double maximumValue = jscbHort.getMaximum();
39         double newX = (value * messagePanel.getWidth()
40           / maximumValue);
41         messagePanel.setXCoordinate((int) newX);
42       }
43     });
```

adjustment listener

```
44    jscbVert.addAdjustmentListener(new AdjustmentListener() {
45      public void adjustmentValueChanged(AdjustmentEvent e) {
46        // getValue() and getMaximumValue() return int, but for better
47        // precision, use double
48        double value = jscbVert.getValue();
49        double maximumValue = jscbVert.getMaximum();
50        double newY = (value * messagePanel.getHeight()
51          / maximumValue);
52        messagePanel.setYCoordinate((int)newY);
53      }
54    });
55  }
56 }
```

The program creates two scroll bars (`jscbVert` and `jscbHort`) (lines 7–10) and an instance of `MessagePanel` (`messagePanel`) (lines 13–14). `messagePanel` is placed in the center of the frame; `jscbVert` and `jscbHort` are placed in the east and south sections of the frame (lines 29–30), respectively.

You can specify the orientation of the scroll bar in the constructor or use the `set-Orientation` method. By default, the property value is `100` for `maximum`, `0` for `minimum`, `10` for `blockIncrement`, and `10` for `visibleAmount`.

When the user drags the bubble, or clicks the increment or decrement unit, the value of the scroll bar changes. An instance of `AdjustmentEvent` is generated and passed to the listener by invoking the `adjustmentValueChanged` handler. The listener for the vertical scroll bar moves the message up and down (lines 34–42), and the listener for the horizontal bar moves the message to right and left (lines 43–53).

The maximum value of the vertical scroll bar corresponds to the height of the panel, and the maximum value of the horizontal scroll bar corresponds to the width of the panel. The ratio between the current and maximum values of the horizontal scroll bar is the same as the ratio between the x value and the width of the message panel. Similarly, the ratio between the current and maximum values of the vertical scroll bar is the same as the ratio between the y value and the height of the message panel. The x-coordinate and y-coordinate are set in response to the scroll bar adjustments (lines 39, 50).

15.11 Sliders

`JSlider` is similar to `JScrollBar`, but `JSlider` has more properties and can appear in many forms. Figure 15.29 shows two sliders.

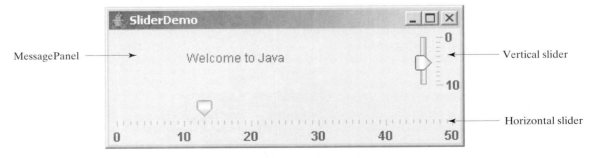

FIGURE 15.29 The sliders move the message on a panel horizontally and vertically.

`JSlider` lets the user graphically select a value by sliding a knob within a bounded interval. The slider can show both major tick marks and minor tick marks between them. The number of pixels between the tick marks is controlled by the `majorTickSpacing` and `minorTickSpacing` properties. Sliders can be displayed horizontally or vertically, with or without ticks, and with or without labels. The frequently used constructors and properties in JSlider are shown in Figure 15.30.

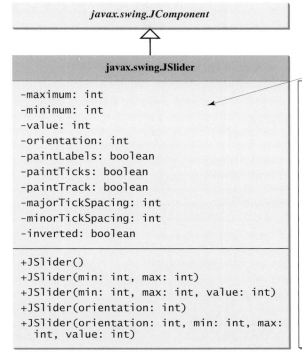

The get and set methods for these data fields are provided in the class, but omitted in the UML diagram for brevity.

javax.swing.JComponent

javax.swing.JSlider

-maximum: int	The maximum value represented by the slider (default: 100).
-minimum: int	The minimum value represented by the slider (default: 0).
-value: int	The current value represented by the slider.
-orientation: int	The orientation of the slider (default: JSlider. HORIZONTAL).
-paintLabels: boolean	True if the labels are painted at tick marks (default: false).
-paintTicks: boolean	True if the ticks are painted on the slider (default: false).
-paintTrack: boolean	True if the track is painted on the slider (default: true).
-majorTickSpacing: int	The number of units between major ticks (default: 0)
-minorTickSpacing: int	The number of units between minor ticks (default: 0)
-inverted: boolean	True to reverse the value range, and false to put the value range in the normal order (default: false).
+JSlider()	Creates a default horizontal slider.
+JSlider(min: int, max: int)	Creates a horizontal slider using the specified min and max.
+JSlider(min: int, max: int, value: int)	Creates a horizontal slider using the specified min, max, and value.
+JSlider(orientation: int)	Creates a slider with the specified orientation.
+JSlider(orientation: int, min: int, max: int, value: int)	Creates a slider with the specified orientation, min, max, and value.

FIGURE 15.30   JSlider enables you to select from a range of values.

Note
The values of a vertical scroll bar increase from top to bottom, but the values of a vertical slider decrease from top to bottom.

Note
All the properties listed in Figure 15.30 have the associated get and set methods, which are omitted for brevity. By convention, the get method for a Boolean property is named *is<PropertyName>()*. In the JSlider class, the get methods for **paintLabels**, **paintTicks()**, **paintTrack()**, and **inverted** are **getPaintLabels()**, **getPaintTicks()**, **getPaintTrack()**, and **getInverted()**, which violate the naming convention.

When the user changes the value of the slider, the slider generates an instance of javax.swing.event.ChangeEvent, which is passed to any registered listeners. Any object that wishes to be notified of changes to the slider's value must implement **stateChanged** method in the **ChangeListener** interface defined in the package javax.swing.event.

Listing 15.10 writes a program that uses the sliders to control a message displayed on a panel, as shown in Figure 15.29. Here are the major steps in the program:

1. Create the user interface.
   Create a MessagePanel object and place it in the center of the frame. Create a vertical slider and place it in the east of the frame. Create a horizontal slider and place it in the south of the frame.

2. Process the event.
   Create a listener to implement the **stateChanged** handler in the **ChangeListener** interface to move the message according to the knot movement in the slider.

LISTING 15.10 SliderBarDemo.java

```java
1  import java.awt.*;
2  import javax.swing.*;
3  import javax.swing.event.*;
4
5  public class SliderDemo extends JFrame {
6    // Create horizontal and vertical sliders
7    private JSlider jsldHort = new JSlider(JSlider.HORIZONTAL);
8    private JSlider jsldVert = new JSlider(JSlider.VERTICAL);
9
10   // Create a MessagePanel
11   private MessagePanel messagePanel =
12     new MessagePanel("Welcome to Java");
13
14   public static void main(String[] args) {
15     SliderDemo frame = new SliderDemo();
16     frame.setTitle("SliderDemo");
17     frame.setLocationRelativeTo(null); // Center the frame
18     frame.setDefaultCloseOperation(JFrame.EXIT_ON_CLOSE);
19     frame.pack();
20     frame.setVisible(true);
21   }
22
23   public SliderDemo() {
24     // Add sliders and message panel to the frame
25     setLayout(new BorderLayout(5, 5));
26     add(messagePanel, BorderLayout.CENTER);
27     add(jsldVert, BorderLayout.EAST);
28     add(jsldHort, BorderLayout.SOUTH);
29
30     // Set properties for sliders
31     jsldHort.setMaximum(50);
32     jsldHort.setPaintLabels(true);
33     jsldHort.setPaintTicks(true);
34     jsldHort.setMajorTickSpacing(10);
35     jsldHort.setMinorTickSpacing(1);
36     jsldHort.setPaintTrack(false);
37     jsldVert.setInverted(true);
38     jsldVert.setMaximum(10);
39     jsldVert.setPaintLabels(true);
40     jsldVert.setPaintTicks(true);
41     jsldVert.setMajorTickSpacing(10);
42     jsldVert.setMinorTickSpacing(1);
43
44     // Register listener for the sliders
45     jsldHort.addChangeListener(new ChangeListener() {
46       /** Handle scroll bar adjustment actions */
47       public void stateChanged(ChangeEvent e) {
48         // getValue() and getMaximumValue() return int, but for better
49         // precision, use double
50         double value = jsldHort.getValue();
51         double maximumValue = jsldHort.getMaximum();
52         double newX = (value * messagePanel.getWidth()
53           / maximumValue);
54         messagePanel.setXCoordinate((int)newX);
55       }
56     });
57     jsldVert.addChangeListener(new ChangeListener() {
```

Margin notes:
- horizontal slider (line 7)
- vertical slider (line 8)
- create frame (line 15)
- create UI (line 23)
- slider properties (line 31)
- listener (line 45)
- listener (line 57)

```
58        /** Handle scroll bar adjustment actions */
59        public void stateChanged(ChangeEvent e) {
60          // getValue() and getMaximumValue() return int, but for better
61          // precision, use double
62          double value = jsldVert.getValue();
63          double maximumValue = jsldVert.getMaximum();
64          double newY = (value * messagePanel.getHeight()
65            / maximumValue);
66          messagePanel.setYCoordinate((int)newY);
67        }
68      });
69    }
70 }
```

JSlider is similar to JScrollBar, but JSlider has more features. As shown in this example, you can specify maximum, labels, major ticks, and minor ticks on a JSlider (lines 31–35). You can also choose to hide the track (line 36). Since the values of a vertical slider decrease from top to bottom, the setInverted method reverses the order (line 37).

JSlider fires ChangeEvent when the slider is changed. The listener needs to implement the stateChanged handler in ChangeListener (lines 45–69). Note that JScrollBar fires AdjustmentEvent when the scroll bar is adjusted.

15.12 Creating Multiple Windows

Occasionally, you may want to create multiple windows in an application. The application opens a new window to perform the specified task. The new windows are called *subwindows*, and the main frame is called the *main window*.

To create a subwindow from an application, you need to create a subclass of JFrame that defines the task and tells the new window what to do. You can then create an instance of this subclass in the application and launch the new window by setting the frame instance to be visible.

Listing 15.11 gives a program that creates a main window with a text area in the scroll pane and a button named "Show Histogram." When the user clicks the button, a new window appears that displays a histogram to show the occurrences of the letters in the text area. Figure 15.31 contains a sample run of the program.

 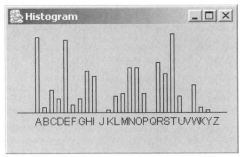

FIGURE 15.31 The histogram is displayed in a separate frame.

Here are the major steps in the program:

1. Create a main class for the frame named MultipleWindowsDemo in Listing 15.11. Add a text area inside a scroll pane, and place the scroll pane in the center of the frame. Create a button "Show Histogram" and place it in the south of the frame.

2. Create a subclass of JPanel named Histogram in Listing 15.12. The class contains a data field named count of the int[] type, which counts the occurrences of twenty-six letters. The values in count are displayed in the histogram.

3. Implement the actionPerformed handler in MultipleWindowsDemo, as follows:

   a. Create an instance of Histogram. Count the letters in the text area and pass the count to the Histogram object.

   b. Create a new frame and place the Histogram object in the center of frame. Display the frame.

LISTING 15.11 MultipleWindowsDemo.java

```java
1  import java.awt.*;
2  import java.awt.event.*;
3  import javax.swing.*;
4
5  public class MultipleWindowsDemo extends JFrame {
6    private JTextArea jta;
7    private JButton jbtShowHistogram = new JButton("Show Histogram");
8    private Histogram histogram = new Histogram();
9
10   // Create a new frame to hold the histogram panel
11   private JFrame histogramFrame = new JFrame();
12
13   public MultipleWindowsDemo() {
14     // Store text area in a scroll pane
15     JScrollPane scrollPane = new JScrollPane(jta = new JTextArea());
16     scrollPane.setPreferredSize(new Dimension(300, 200));
17     jta.setWrapStyleWord(true);
18     jta.setLineWrap(true);
19
20     // Place scroll pane and button in the frame
21     add(scrollPane, BorderLayout.CENTER);
22     add(jbtShowHistogram, BorderLayout.SOUTH);
23
24     // Register listener
25     jbtShowHistogram.addActionListener(new ActionListener() {
26       /** Handle the button action */
27       public void actionPerformed(ActionEvent e) {
28         // Count the letters in the text area
29         int[] count = countLetters();
30
31         // Set the letter count to histogram for display
32         histogram.showHistogram(count);
33
34         // Show the frame
35         histogramFrame.setVisible(true);
36       }
37     });
38
39     // Create a new frame to hold the histogram panel
40     histogramFrame.add(histogram);
41     histogramFrame.pack();
42     histogramFrame.setTitle("Histogram");
43   }
44
```

Margin notes:
create subframe (line 8)
create subframe (line 11)
create UI (line 13)
display subframe (line 35)

```
45    /** Count the letters in the text area */
46    private int[] countLetters() {
47      // Count for 26 letters
48      int[] count = new int[26];
49
50      // Get contents from the text area
51      String text = jta.getText();
52
53      // Count occurrence of each letter (case insensitive)
54      for (int i = 0; i < text.length(); i++) {
55        char character = text.charAt(i);
56
57        if ((character >= 'A') && (character <= 'Z')) {
58          count[(int)character - 65]++; // The ASCII for 'A' is 65
59        }
60        else if ((character >= 'a') && (character <= 'z')) {
61          count[(int)character - 97]++; // The ASCII for 'a' is 97
62        }
63      }
64
65      return count; // Return the count array
66    }
67
68    public static void main(String[] args) {
69      MultipleWindowsDemo frame = new MultipleWindowsDemo();        create main frame
70      frame.setLocationRelativeTo(null); // Center the frame
71      frame.setDefaultCloseOperation(JFrame.EXIT_ON_CLOSE);
72      frame.setTitle("MultipleWindowsDemo");
73      frame.pack();
74      frame.setVisible(true);
75    }
76  }
```

LISTING 15.12 Histogram.java

```
1  import javax.swing.*;
2  import java.awt.*;
3
4  public class Histogram extends JPanel {
5    // Count the occurrence of 26 letters
6    private int[] count;
7
8    /** Set the count and display histogram */
9    public void showHistogram(int[] count) {
10     this.count = count;
11     repaint();
12   }
13
14   /** Paint the histogram */
15   protected void paintComponent(Graphics g) {
16     if (count == null) return; // No display if count is null        paint histogram
17
18     super.paintComponent(g);
19
20     // Find the panel size and bar width and interval dynamically
21     int width = getWidth();
22     int height = getHeight();
```

```
23      int interval = (width - 40) / count.length;
24      int individualWidth = (int)(((width - 40) / 24) * 0.60);
25
26      // Find the maximum count. The maximum count has the highest bar
27      int maxCount = 0;
28      for (int i = 0; i < count.length; i++) {
29        if (maxCount < count[i])
30          maxCount = count[i];
31      }
32
33      // x is the start position for the first bar in the histogram
34      int x = 30;
35
36      // Draw a horizontal base line
37      g.drawLine(10, height - 45, width - 10, height - 45);
38      for (int i = 0; i < count.length; i++) {
39        // Find the bar height
40        int barHeight =
41          (int)((((double)count[i] / (double)maxCount) * (height - 55));
42
43        // Display a bar (i.e., rectangle)
44        g.drawRect(x, height - 45 - barHeight, individualWidth,
45          barHeight);
46
47        // Display a letter under the base line
48        g.drawString((char)(65 + i) + " ", x, height - 30);
49
50        // Move x for displaying the next character
51        x += interval;
52      }
53    }
54
```

preferredSize
```
55    /** Override getPreferredSize */
56    public Dimension getPreferredSize() {
57      return new Dimension(300, 300);
58    }
59 }
```

The program contains two classes: `MultipleWindowsDemo` and `Histogram`. Their relationship is shown in Figure 15.32.

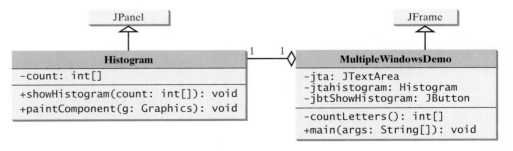

FIGURE 15.32 `MultipleWindowsDemo` uses `Histogram` to display a histogram of the occurrences of the letters in a text area in the frame.

`MultipleWindowsDemo` is a frame that holds a text area in a scroll pane and a button. `Histogram` is a subclass of `JPanel` that displays a histogram for the occurrences of letters in the text area.

When the user clicks the "Show Histogram" button, the handler counts the occurrences of letters in the text area. Letters are counted regardless of their case. Nonletter characters are not counted. The count is stored in an `int` array of twenty-six elements. The first element stores the count for letter '*a*' or '*A*,' and the last element in the array stores the count for letter '*z*' or '*Z*.' The count array is passed to the histogram for display.

The `MultipleWindowsDemo` class contains a `main` method. The `main` method creates an instance of `MultipleWindowsDemo` and displays the frame. The `MultipleWindowsDemo` class also contains an instance of `JFrame`, named `histogramFrame`, which holds an instance of `Histogram`. When the user clicks the "Show Histogram" button, `histogramFrame` is set visible to display the histogram.

The height and width of the bars in the histogram are determined dynamically according to the window size of the histogram.

You cannot add an instance of `JFrame` to a container. For example, adding `histogramFrame` to the main frame would cause a runtime exception. However, you can create a frame instance and set it visible to launch a new window.

CHAPTER SUMMARY

- You learned how to create graphical user interfaces using Swing GUI components `JButton`, `JCheckBox`, `JRadioButton`, `JLabel`, `JTextField`, `JTextArea`, `JComboBox`, `JList`, `JScrollBar`, and `JSlider`. You also learned how to handle events on these components.

- You can display a text and icon on buttons (`JButton`, `JCheckBox`, `JRadioButton`) and labels.

REVIEW QUESTIONS

Sections 15.2–15.4

15.1   How do you create a button labeled "OK"? How do you change text on a button? How do you set an icon, pressed icon, and rollover icon in a button?

15.2   Given a `JButton` object `jbtOK`, write statements to set the button's foreground to red, background to yellow, mnemonic to 'K', tool tip text to "Click OK to proceed", horizontal alignment to RIGHT, vertical alignment to BOTTOM, horizontal text position to LEFT, vertical text position to TOP, and icon text gap to 5.

15.3   How do you create a check box? How do you create a check box with the box checked initially? How do you determine whether a check box is selected?

15.4   What is wrong if the statement `super.actionPerformed(e)` in `CheckBoxDemo` is omitted?

15.5   How do you create a radio button? How do you create a radio button with the button selected initially? How do you group the radio buttons together? How do you determine whether a radio button is selected?

Sections 15.5–15.9

15.6   How do you create a label named "Address"? How do you change the name on a label? How do you set an icon in a label?

15.7   Given a `JLabel` object `jlblMap`, write statements to set label's foreground to red, background to yellow, mnemonic to 'K', tool tip text to "Click OK to proceed", horizontal alignment to RIGHT, vertical alignment to BOTTOM, horizontal text position to LEFT, vertical text position to TOP, and icon text gap to 5.

15.8   How do you create a text field with ten columns and the default text "Welcome to Java"? How do you write the code to check whether a text field is empty?

15.9   How do you create a text area with ten rows and twenty columns? How do you insert three lines into the text area? How do you create a scrollable text area?

15.10   How do you create a combo box, add three items to it, and retrieve a selected item?

15.11   How do you create a list with an array of strings?

Sections 15.10–15.12

15.12   How do you create a horizontal scroll bar? What event can a scroll bar generate?

15.13   How do you create a vertical slider? What event can a slider generate?

15.14   Explain how to create and show multiple frames in an application.

PROGRAMMING EXERCISES

Sections 15.2–15.5

15.1*   (*Revising Listing 15.2, ButtonDemo.java*) Rewrite Listing 15.2 to add a group of radio buttons to select background colors. The available colors are red, yellow, white, gray, and green (see Figure 15.33).

FIGURE 15.33   The <= and => buttons move the message on the panel, and you can also set the background color for the message.

15.2*   (*Selecting geometric figures*) Write a program that draws various figures, as shown in Figure 15.34. The user selects a figure from a radio button and specifies whether it is filled in a check box. (Hint: Use the **FigurePanel** class introduced in §13.7 to display a figure.)

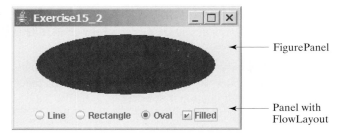

FIGURE 15.34   The program displays lines, rectangles, and ovals when you select a shape type.

15.3** (*Traffic lights*) Write a program that simulates a traffic light. The program lets the user select one of three lights: red, yellow, or green. When a radio button is selected, the light is turned on, and only one light can be on at a time (see Figure 15.35). No light is on when the program starts.

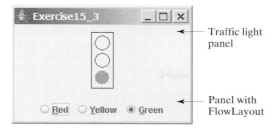

FIGURE 15.35 The radio buttons are grouped to let you select only one color in the group to control a traffic light.

Sections 15.6–15.10

15.4* (*Creating a simple calculator*) Write a program to perform add, subtract, multiply, and divide operations (see Figure 15.36).

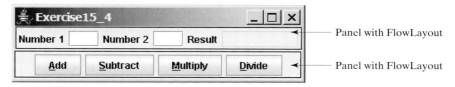

FIGURE 15.36 The program does addition, subtraction, multiplication, and division on double numbers.

15.5* (*Creating a miles/kilometers converter*) Write a program that converts miles and kilometers, as shown in Figure 15.37. If you enter a value in the Mile text field and press the Enter key, the corresponding kilometer is displayed in the Kilometer text field. Likewise, if you enter a value in the Kilometer text field and press the Enter key, the corresponding mile is displayed in the Mile text field.

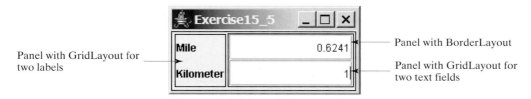

FIGURE 15.37 The program converts miles to kilometers, and vice versa.

15.6* (*Creating an investment value calculator*) Write a program that calculates the future value of an investment at a given interest rate for a specified number of years. The formula for the calculation is as follows:

$$\text{futureValue} = \text{investmentAmount} * (1 + \text{monthlyInterestRate})^{\text{years}*12}$$

Use text fields for interest rate, investment amount, and years. Display the future amount in a text field when the user clicks the Calculate button, as shown in Figure 15.38.

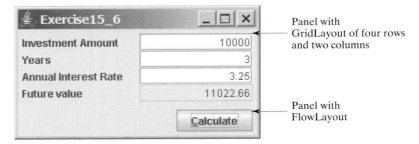

Panel with GridLayout of four rows and two columns

Panel with FlowLayout

FIGURE 15.38 The user enters the investment amount, years, and interest rate to compute future value.

15.7* (*Setting clock time*) Write a program that displays a clock time and sets the clock time with the input from three text fields, as shown in Figure 15.39. Use the StillClock in §13.12, "Case Study: The StillClock Class."

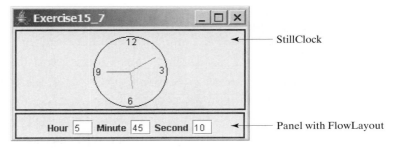

StillClock

Panel with FlowLayout

FIGURE 15.39 The program displays the time specified in the text fields.

15.8** (*Selecting a font*) Write a program that can dynamically change the font of a message to be displayed on a panel. The message can be displayed in bold and italic at the same time, or can be displayed in the center of the panel. You can select the font name or font size from combo boxes, as shown in Figure 15.40. The available font names can be obtained using getAvailableFontFamilyNames() in GraphicsEnvironment (§12.7, "The Font Class"). The combo box for font size is initialized with numbers from 1 to 100.

Panel with BorderLayout

Panel with BorderLayout

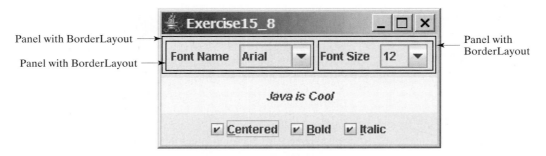

Panel with BorderLayout

FIGURE 15.40 You can dynamically set the font for the message.

15.9** (*Demonstrating JLabel properties*) Write a program to let the user dynamically set the properties horizontalAlignment, verticalAlignment, horizontalTextAlignment, and verticalTextAlignment, as shown in Figure 15.41.

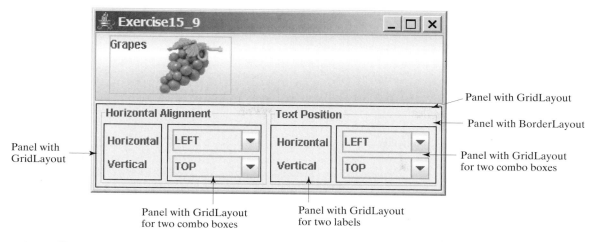

FIGURE 15.41 You can set the alignment and text-position properties of a button dynamically.

15.10* (*Adding new features into Listing 15.2, ButtonDemo.java, incrementally*) Improve Listing 15.2 incrementally, as follows (see Figure 15.42):

1. Add a text field labeled "Enter a new message" in the same panel with the buttons. Upon typing a new message in the text field and pressing the Enter key, the new message is displayed in the message panel.

2. Add a combo box labeled "Select an interval" in the same panel with the buttons. The combo box enables the user to select a new interval for moving the message. The selection values range from 5 to 100 with interval 5. The user can also type a new interval in the combo box.

3. Add three radio buttons that enable the user to select the foreground color for the message as Red, Green, and Blue. The radio buttons are grouped in a panel, and the panel is placed in the north of the frame's content pane.

4. Add three check boxes that enable the user to center the message and display it in italic or bold. Place the check boxes in the same panel with the radio buttons.

5. Add a border titled "Message Panel" on the message panel, add a border titled "South Panel" on the panel for buttons, and add a border titled "North Panel" on the panel for radio buttons and check boxes.

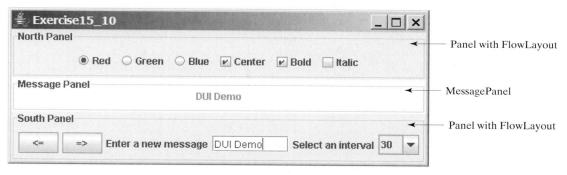

FIGURE 15.42 The program uses buttons, labels, text fields, combo boxes, radio buttons, check boxes, and borders.

15.11* (*Demonstrating `JTextField` properties*) Write a program that sets the horizontal-alignment and column-size properties of a text field dynamically, as shown in Figure 15.43.

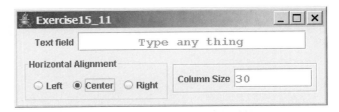

FIGURE 15.43 You can set the horizontal-alignment and column-size properties of a text field dynamically.

15.12* (*Demonstrating JTextArea properties*) Write a program that demonstrates the wrapping styles of the text area. The program uses a check box to indicate whether the text area is wrapped. In the case where the text area is wrapped, you need to specify whether it is wrapped by characters or by words, as shown in Figure 15.44.

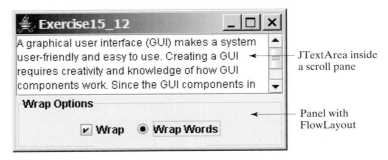

FIGURE 15.44 You can set the options to wrap a text area by characters or by words dynamically.

15.13* (*Comparing loans with various interest rates*) Rewrite Exercise 4.21 to create a user interface, as shown in Figure 15.45. Your program should let the user enter the loan amount and loan period in number of years from a text field, and should display the monthly and total payments for each interest rate starting from 5 percent to 8 percent, with increments of one-eighth, in a text area.

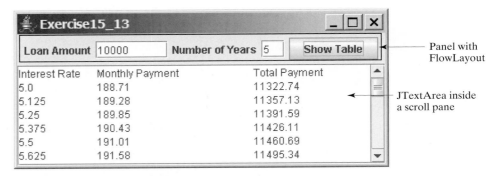

FIGURE 15.45 The program displays a table for monthly payments and total payments on a given loan based on various interest rates.

15.14* (*Using JComboBox and JList*) Write a program that demonstrates selecting items in a list. The program uses a combo box to specify a selection mode, as shown in Figure 15.46. When you select items, they are displayed in a label below the list.

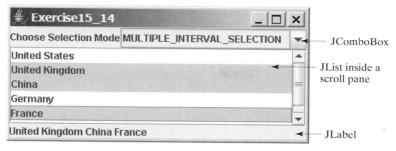

FIGURE 15.46 You can choose single selection, single-interval selection, or multiple-interval selection in a list.

Sections 15.11–15.13

15.15**(*Using* `JScrollBar`) Write a program that uses scroll bars to select the foreground color for a label, as shown in Figure 15.47. Three horizontal scroll bars are used for selecting the red, green, and blue components of the color. Use a title border on the panel that holds the scroll bars.

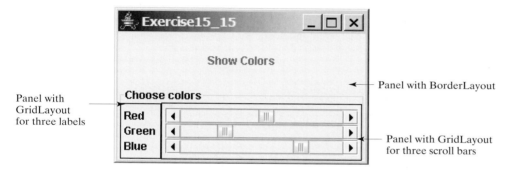

FIGURE 15.47 The foreground color changes in the label as you adjust the scroll bars.

15.16**(*Using* `JSlider`) Revise the preceding exercise using sliders.

15.17***(*Displaying a calendar*) Write a program that displays the calendar for the current month, as shown in Figure 15.48. Use labels, and set texts on the labels to display the calendar. Use the `GregorianCalendar` class in §10.3, "The

Exercise15_17						
			6/2005			
Sunday	Monday	Tuesday	Wednesday	Thursday	Friday	Saturday
			1	2	3	4
5	6	7	8	9	10	11
12	13	14	15	16	17	18
19	20	21	22	23	24	25
26	27	28	29	30		

JPanel with GridLayout

Each cell is a JLabel

FIGURE 15.48 The program displays the calendar for the current month.

Calendar and GregorianCalendar classes," to obtain the information about month, year, first day of the month, and number of days in the month.

15.18* (*Revising Listing 15.11, MultipleWindowsDemo.java*) Instead of displaying the occurrences of the letters using the Histogram component in Listing 15.11, use a bar chart, so that the display is as shown in Figure 15.49.

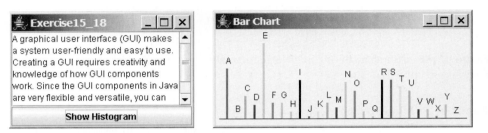

FIGURE 15.49 The number of occurrences of each letter is displayed in a bar chart.

Three exercises involving text I/O using Scanner

15.19** (*Text Viewer*) Write a program that displays a text file in a text area, as shown in Figure 15.50. The user enters a filename in a text field and clicks the View button; the file is then displayed in a text area.

FIGURE 15.50 The program displays a histogram that shows the occurrences of each letter in the file.

15.20** (*Displaying country flag and flag description*) Listing 15.7, ComboBoxDemo.java, gives a program that lets users view a country's flag image and description by selecting the country from a combo box. The description is a string coded in the program. Rewrite the program to read the text description from a file. Suppose that the descriptions are stored in the file description0.txt, ..., and description8.txt under the text directory for the nine countries Canada, China, Denmark, France, Germany, India, Norway, the United Kingdom, and the United States, in this order.

15.21** (*Creating a histogram for occurrences of letters*) In Listing 15.11, MultipleWindowsDemo.java, you developed a program that displays a histogram to show the occurrences of each letter in a text area. Reuse the Histogram class created in Listing 15.12 to write a program that will display a histogram on a panel. The histogram should show the occurrences of each letter in a text file, as shown in Figure 15.51. Assume that the letters are not case-sensitive.

- Place a panel that will display the histogram in the center of the frame.
- Place a label and a text field in a panel, and put the panel in the south side of the frame. The text file will be entered from this text field.
- Pressing the Enter key on the text field causes the program to count the occurrences of each letter and display the count in a histogram.

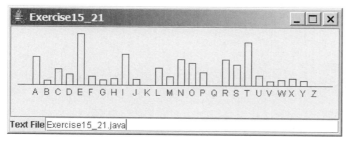

FIGURE 15.51 The program displays a histogram that shows the occurrences of each letter in the file.

15.22** (*Slideshow*) Exercise 14.13 developed a slideshow using images. Rewrite Exercise 14.13 to develop a slideshow using text files. Suppose ten text files named slide0.txt, slide1.txt, ..., and slide9.txt are stored in the text directory downloadable along with the source code in the book. Each slide displays the text from one file. Each slide is shown for a second. The slides are displayed in order. When the last slide finishes, the first slide is redisplayed, and so on. Use a text area to display the slide.

CHAPTER 16

APPLETS AND MULTIMEDIA

Objectives

- To explain how the Web browser controls and executes applets (§16.2).
- To describe the `init`, `start`, `stop`, and `destroy` methods in the `Applet` class (§§16.2.1–16.2.4).
- To develop Swing applets using the `JApplet` class (§16.3).
- To know how to embed applets in Web pages (§16.4).
- To run applets from the appletviewer and from Web browsers (§§16.4.1–16.4.2).
- To write a Java program that can run as both an application and an applet (§16.5).
- To pass string values to applets from HTML (§16.6).
- (Optional) To locate resource (images and audio) using the `URL` class (§16.9).
- (Optional) To play audio (§16.10).
- (Optional) To package and deploy Java projects using Java archive files (§16.12).

16.1 Introduction

Java's early success has been attributed to applets. Running from a Java-enabled Web browser, applets bring dynamic interaction and live animation to an otherwise static HTML page. It is safe to say that Java would be nowhere today without applets. They made Java instantly appealing, attractive, and popular during its infancy. Java is now used not only for applets, but also for standalone applications and as a programming language for developing server-side applications and for mobile devices.

In this book so far, you have only used Java applications. Everything you have learned about writing applications, however, also applies to writing applets. Applications and applets share many common programming features, although they differ slightly in some respects. For example, every application must have a `main` method, which is invoked by the Java interpreter. Java applets, on the other hand, do not need a `main` method. They run in the Web browser environment. Because applets are invoked from a Web page, Java provides special features that enable applets to run from a Web browser.

In this chapter, you will learn how to write Java applets, discover the relationship between applets and the Web browser, and explore the similarities and differences between applications and applets. You will also learn how to create multimedia applets with images and audio.

16.2 The **Applet** Class

The `Applet` class provides the essential framework that enables applets to be run from a Web browser. While every Java application has a `main` method that is executed, when the application starts, applets do not have a `main` method. Instead they depend on the browser to call the methods in the `Applet` class. Every applet is a subclass of `java.applet.Applet`, as outlined below:

subclass of **Applet**

no-arg constructor required

```
public class MyApplet extends java.applet.Applet {
  ...
  /** The no-arg constructor is called by the browser when the Web
   *  page containing this applet is initially loaded, or reloaded
   */
  public MyApplet() {
    ...
  }

  /** Called by the browser after the applet is loaded
   */
  public void init() {
    ...
  }

  /** Called by the browser after the init() method, or
   *  every time the Web page is visited
   */
  public void start() {
    ...
  }

  /** Called by the browser when the page containing this
   *  applet becomes inactive
   */
  public void stop() {
    ...
  }

  /** Called by the browser when the Web browser exits */
  public void destroy() {
    ...
  }

  /** Other methods if necessary... */
}
```

When the applet is loaded, the Web browser creates an instance of the applet by invoking the applet's *no-arg constructor*. So the applet must have a no-arg constructor declared either explicitly or implicitly. The browser uses the `init`, `start`, `stop`, and `destroy` methods to control the applet. By default, these methods do nothing. To perform specific functions, they need to be modified in the user's applet so that the browser can call your code properly. Figure 16.1(a) shows how the browser calls these methods, and Figure 16.1(b) illustrates the flow of control of an applet using a statechart diagram.

no-arg constructor

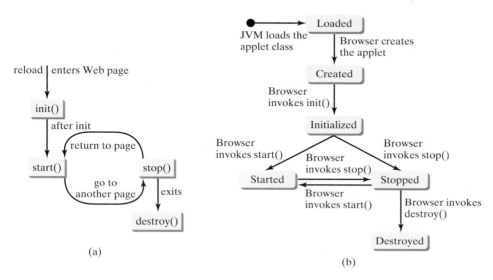

(a)

(b)

FIGURE 16.1   The Web browser uses the `init`, `start`, `stop`, and `destroy` methods to control the applet.

16.2.1   The `init` Method

The `init` method is invoked after the applet is created. A subclass of **Applet** should override this method if the subclass has an initialization to perform. The functions usually implemented in this method include setting up user-interface components, loading resources such as images and audio, and getting string parameter values from the `<applet>` tag in the HTML page.

init()

16.2.2   The `start` Method

The `start` method is invoked after the `init` method. It is also called when the user returns to the Web page containing the applet after surfing other pages.

start()

A subclass of **Applet** overrides this method if it has any operation that needs to be performed whenever the Web page containing the applet is visited. An applet with animation, for example, might start the timer to resume animation.

16.2.3   The `stop` Method

The `stop` method is the opposite of the `start` method. The `start` method is called when the user moves back to the page that contains the applet. The `stop` method is invoked when the user leaves the page.

stop()

A subclass of **Applet** overrides this method if it has any operation that needs to be performed each time the Web page containing the applet is no longer visible. An applet with animation, for example, might stop the timer to pause animation.

16.2.4 The destroy Method

destroy()

The destroy method is invoked when the browser exits normally to inform the applet that it is no longer needed and should release any resources it has allocated. The stop method is always called before the destroy method.

A subclass of Applet overrides this method if it has any operation that needs to be performed before it is destroyed. Usually, you won't need to override this method unless you wish to release specific resources that the applet created.

16.3 The JApplet Class

The Applet class is an AWT class and is not designed to work with Swing components. To use Swing components in Java applets, it is necessary to create a Java applet that extends javax.swing.JApplet, which is a subclass of java.applet.Applet. JApplet inherits all the methods from the Applet class. In addition, it provides support for laying out Swing components.

To add a component to an applet, you add it to the content pane of an applet, which is similar to adding a component to the content pane of a frame. By default, the content pane of JApplet uses BorderLayout. Here is an example of a simple applet that uses JLabel to display a message.

```java
// WelcomeApplet.java: Applet for displaying a message
import javax.swing.*;

public class WelcomeApplet extends JApplet {
  /** Initialize the applet */
  public void init() {
    add(new JLabel("Welcome to Java", JLabel.CENTER));
  }
}
```

add a label in applet

Note

content pane delegation

The *content pane delegation* feature in JDK 1.5 allows you to invoke the **add** method from an applet to place components to the content pane of an applet. Strictly speaking, a component is added into the content pane of an applet. But for simplicity we say that a component is added to an applet.

You cannot run this applet standalone, because it does not have a main method. To run this applet, you have to create an HTML file with the applet tag that references the applet. When you write Java GUI applications, you must create a frame to hold graphical components, set the frame size, and make the frame visible. Applets are run from the Web browser. The Web browser automatically places the applet inside it and makes it visible. The following section shows how to create HTML files for applets.

Note

alternative coding

You may rewrite the WelcomeApplet by moving the code in the init method to the no-arg constructor, as follows:

```java
// WelcomeApplet.java: Applet for displaying a message
import javax.swing.*;

public class WelcomeApplet extends JApplet {
  /** Construct the applet */
  public WelcomeApplet() {
    add(new JLabel("Welcome to Java", JLabel.CENTER));
  }
}
```

16.4 The HTML File and the **\<applet\>** Tag

HTML is a markup language that presents static documents on the Web. It uses tags to instruct the Web browser how to render a Web page and contains a tag called \<applet\> that incorporates applets into a Web page.

The following HTML file named WelcomeApplet.html invokes the WelcomeApplet.class:

```html
<html>
  <head>
    <title>Welcome Java Applet</title>
  </head>
  <body>
    <applet
      code = "WelcomeApplet.class"
      width = 350
      height = 200>
    </applet>
  </body>
</html>
```

applet class

A *tag* is an instruction to the Web browser. The browser interprets the tag and decides how to display or otherwise treat the subsequent contents of the HTML document. Tags are enclosed inside brackets. The first word in a tag, called the *tag name*, describes tag functions. Tags can have additional attributes, sometimes with values after an equals sign, which further define the tag's action. For example, in the preceding HTML file, \<applet\> is the tag name, and `code`, `width`, and `height` are the attributes. The `width` and `height` attributes specify the rectangular viewing area of the applet.

Most tags have a *start tag* and a corresponding *end tag*. The tag has a specific effect on the region between the start tag and the end tag. For example, \<applet...\>...\</applet\> tells the browser to display an applet. An end tag is always the start tag's name preceded by a slash.

An HTML document begins with the \<html\> tag, which declares that the document is written in HTML. Each document has two parts, a *head* and a *body*, defined by \<head\> and \<body\> tags, respectively. The head part contains the document title, using the \<title\> tag and other information the browser can use when rendering the document, and the body part contains the actual contents of the document. The header is optional. For more information, refer to Supplement VI.A, "HTML and XHTML Tutorial."

HTML tag

The complete syntax of the \<applet\> tag is as follows:

\<applet\> tag

```html
<applet
  [codebase = applet_url]
  code = classfilename.class
  width = applet_viewing_width_in_pixels
  height = applet_viewing_height_in_pixels
  [archive = archivefile]
  [vspace = vertical_margin]
  [hspace = horizontal_margin]
  [align = applet_alignment]
  [alt = alternative_text]
>
<param name = param_name1 value = param_value1>
<param name = param_name2 value = param_value2>
...
<param name = param_name3 value = param_value3>
</applet>
```

\<param\> tag

The `code`, `width`, and `height` attributes are required; all the others are optional. The \<param\> tag is introduced in §16.6, "Passing Strings to Applets." The other attributes are explained below.

codebase attribute

- **codebase** specifies a base where your classes are loaded. If this attribute is not used, the Web browser loads the applet from the directory in which the HTML page is located. If your applet is located in a different directory from the HTML page, you must specify the `applet_url` for the browser to load the applet. This attribute enables you to load the class from anywhere on the Internet. The classes used by the applet are dynamically loaded when needed.

archive attribute

- **archive** instructs the browser to load an archive file that contains all the class files needed to run the applet. Archiving allows the Web browser to load all the classes from a single compressed file at one time, thus reducing loading time and improving performance. To create archives, see §16.12, "Packaging and Deploying Java Projects."

- **vspace** and **hspace** specify the size, in pixels, of the blank margin to pad around the applet vertically and horizontally.

- **align** specifies how the applet will be aligned in the browser. One of nine values is used: `left`, `right`, `top`, `texttop`, `middle`, `absmiddle`, `baseline`, `bottom`, or `absbottom`.

- **alt** specifies the text to be displayed in case the browser cannot run Java.

16.4.1 Viewing Applets Using the Applet Viewer Utility

appletviewer

You can test the applet using the applet viewer utility, which can be invoked from the DOS prompt using the *appletviewer* command from `c:\book`, as shown in Figure 16.2. Its output is shown in Figure 16.3.

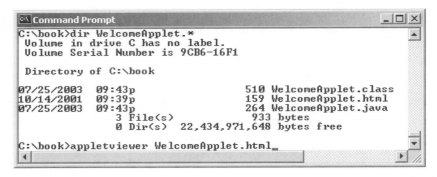

FIGURE 16.2 The appletviewer command runs a Java applet in the applet viewer utility.

FIGURE 16.3 The WelcomeApplet program is running from the applet viewer.

16.4.2 Viewing Applets from a Web Browser

Applets are eventually displayed in a Web browser. Using the applet viewer, you do not need to start a Web browser. The applet viewer functions as a browser. It is convenient for testing applets during development. However, you should also test the applets from a Web browser before deploying them on a Web site. To display an applet from a Web browser, open the applet's HTML file (e.g., WelcomeApplet.html). Its output is shown in Figure 16.4.

FIGURE 16.4 The WelcomeApplet program is displayed in Internet Explorer.

To make your applet accessible on the Web, you need to store the WelcomeApplet.class and WelcomeApplet.html on a Web server. You can view the applet from an appropriate URL. For example, I have uploaded these two files on Web server www.cs.armstrong.edu/. As shown in Figure 16.5, you can access the applet from www.cs.armstrong.edu/liang/intro6e/book/WelcomeApplet.html.

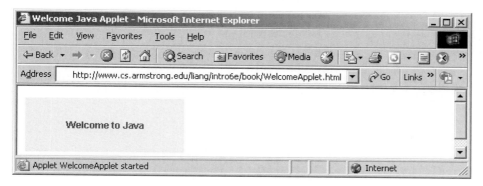

FIGURE 16.5 The `WelcomeApplet` program is downloaded from the Web server.

16.4.3 Example: The Loan Applet

This example writes an applet that computes loan payments. The applet enables the user to enter the interest rate, the number of years, and the loan amount. Clicking the Compute Payment button displays the monthly payment and the total payment, as shown in Figure 16.6. The applet is given in Listing 16.1.

FIGURE 16.6 The applet computes the monthly payment and the total payment when provided with the interest rate, number of years, and loan amount.

LISTING 16.1 LoanApplet.java

```java
 1  import java.awt.*;
 2  import java.awt.event.*;
 3  import javax.swing.*;
 4  import javax.swing.border.TitledBorder;
 5
 6  public class LoanApplet extends JApplet {
 7    // Declare and create text fields for interest rate
 8    // year, loan amount, monthly payment, and total payment
 9    private JTextField jtfAnnualInterestRate = new JTextField();
10    private JTextField jtfNumberOfYears = new JTextField();
11    private JTextField jtfLoanAmount = new JTextField();
12    private JTextField jtfMonthlyPayment = new JTextField();
13    private JTextField jtfTotalPayment = new JTextField();
14
15    // Declare and create a Compute Payment button
16    private JButton jbtComputeLoan = new JButton("Compute Payment");
17
18    /** Initialize user interface */
19    public void init() {
20      // Set properties on the text fields
21      jtfMonthlyPayment.setEditable(false);
22      jtfTotalPayment.setEditable(false);
23
24      // Right align text fields
25      jtfAnnualInterestRate.setHorizontalAlignment(JTextField.RIGHT);
26      jtfNumberOfYears.setHorizontalAlignment(JTextField.RIGHT);
27      jtfLoanAmount.setHorizontalAlignment(JTextField.RIGHT);
28      jtfMonthlyPayment.setHorizontalAlignment(JTextField.RIGHT);
29      jtfTotalPayment.setHorizontalAlignment(JTextField.RIGHT);
30
31      // Panel p1 to hold labels and text fields
32      JPanel p1 = new JPanel(new GridLayout(5, 2));
33      p1.add(new JLabel("Annual Interest Rate"));
34      p1.add(jtfAnnualInterestRate);
35      p1.add(new JLabel("Number of Years"));
36      p1.add(jtfNumberOfYears);
37      p1.add(new JLabel("Loan Amount"));
38      p1.add(jtfLoanAmount);
39      p1.add(new JLabel("Monthly Payment"));
40      p1.add(jtfMonthlyPayment);
41      p1.add(new JLabel("Total Payment"));
42      p1.add(jtfTotalPayment);
43      p1.setBorder(new
44        TitledBorder("Enter interest rate, year and loan amount"));
45
46      // Panel p2 to hold the button
47      JPanel p2 = new JPanel(new FlowLayout(FlowLayout.RIGHT));
48      p2.add(jbtComputeLoan);
49
50      // Add the components to the applet
51      add(p1, BorderLayout.CENTER);
52      add(p2, BorderLayout.SOUTH);
53
54      // Register listener
55      jbtComputeLoan.addActionListener(new ButtonListener());
56    }
57
```

create text fields (lines 9–13)

create a button (line 16)

create UI (line 19)

titled border (lines 43–44)

add to applet (lines 51–52)

```
58    /** Handle the Compute Payment button */
59    private class ButtonListener implements ActionListener {          listener class
60      public void actionPerformed(ActionEvent e) {
61        // Get values from text fields
62        double interest =
63          Double.parseDouble(jtfAnnualInterestRate.getText());
64        int year =
65          Integer.parseInt(jtfNumberOfYears.getText());
66        double loanAmount =
67          Double.parseDouble(jtfLoanAmount.getText());
68
69        // Create a loan object
70        Loan loan = new Loan(interest, year, loanAmount);                create Loan object
71
72        // Display monthly payment and total payment
73        jtfMonthlyPayment.setText(String.format("%.2f",
74          loan.getMonthlyPayment()));
75        jtfTotalPayment.setText(String.format("%.2f",
76          loan.getTotalPayment()));
77      }
78    }
79 }
```

You need to use the `public` modifier for the `LoanApplet`; otherwise, the Web browser   public applet
cannot load it (line 6).

The `init` method initializes the user interface (lines 19–56). The program overrides this
method to create user-interface components (labels, text fields, and a button), and places them
in the applet.

The only event handled is the Compute Payment button. When this button is clicked, the
`actionPerformed` method gets the interest rate, number of years, and loan amount from the
text fields. It then creates a `Loan` object (line 70) to obtain the monthly payment and the total
payment. Finally, it displays the monthly and total payments in their respective text fields.
The `Loan` class is responsible for computing the payments. This class was introduced in
§7.15, "Case Study: The `Loan` Class."

To run the applet, embed it in the HTML file, as shown in Listing 16.2.

LISTING 16.2 LoanApplet.html

```
<!-- HTML code, this code is separated from the preceding Java code -->
<html>
  <head>
    <title>Loan Applet</title>
  </head>
  <body>
    This is a loan calculator. Enter your input for interest, year,
    and loan amount. Click the "Compute Payment" button, you will
    get the payment information. <p>
    <applet
      code = "LoanApplet.class"
      width = 300
      height = 150
      alt = "You must have a Java 2-enabled browser to view the applet">
    </applet>
  </body>
</html>
```

Applet demos

Tip
Many interesting applets are included in the JDK demo. To run them, change the directory to

`c:\Program Files\Java\jdk1.5.0\demo\applets`

Use the **dir** command to list the contents in the directory, as shown in Figure 16.7(a). Change to a subdirectory (e.g., using the command **cd Animator**). There are one or several .html files in that directory for executing applets (e.g., **example1.html**). In the command window, type the following to run the applet, as shown in Figure 16.7(b):

`appletviewer example1.html`

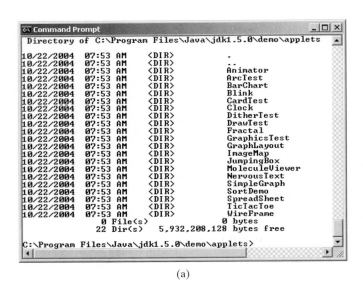
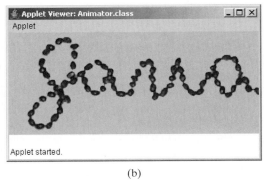

(a) (b)

FIGURE 16.7 You can find applet examples in the JDK demo directory.

16.5 Enabling Applets to Run as Applications

The `JFrame` class and the `JApplet` class have a lot in common despite some differences. Since they both are subclasses of the `Container` class, all their user-interface components, layout managers, and event-handling features are the same. Applications, however, are invoked from the static `main` method by the Java interpreter JVM, and applets are run by the Web browser. The Web browser creates an instance of the applet using the applet's no-arg constructor and controls and executes the applet through the `init`, `start`, `stop`, and `destroy` methods.

For security reasons, the restrictions listed below are imposed on applets to prevent destructive programs from damaging the system on which the browser is running.

- Applets are not allowed to read from, or write to, the file system of the computer. Otherwise, they could damage the files and spread viruses.

- Applets are not allowed to run programs on the browser's computer. Otherwise, they might call destructive local programs and damage the local system on the user's computer.

- Applets are not allowed to establish connections between the user's computer and any other computer, except for the server where the applets are stored. This restriction prevents the applet from connecting the user's computer to another computer without the user's knowledge.

Note

A new security protocol was introduced in Java 2 to allow *trusted applets* to circumvent the security restrictions. See http://www.developer.com/java/ent/article.php/3303561 for detailed instructions on how to create trusted applets.

trusted applet

In general, an applet can be converted to an application without loss of functionality. An application can be converted to an applet as long as it does not violate the security restrictions imposed on applets. You can implement a `main` method in an applet to enable the applet to run as an application. This feature has both theoretical and practical implications. Theoretically, it blurs the difference between applets and applications. You can write a class that is both an applet and an application. From the standpoint of practicality, it is convenient to be able to run a program in two ways.

It is not difficult to write such programs on your own. Suppose you have an applet named `MyApplet`. To enable it to run as an application, all you need to do is add a `main` method in the applet with the implementation, as follows:

```java
 1 public static void main(String[] args) {
 2   // Create a frame
 3   JFrame frame = new JFrame("Applet is in the frame");
 4
 5   // Create an instance of the applet
 6   MyApplet applet = new MyApplet();
 7
 8   // Add the applet to the frame
 9   frame.add(applet, BorderLayout.CENTER);
10
11   // Invoke init and start
12   applet.init();
13   applet.start();
14
15   // Display the frame
16   frame.setLocationRelativeTo(null); // Center the frame
17   frame.setDefaultCloseOperation(JFrame.EXIT_ON_CLOSE);
18   frame.setSize(300, 300);
19   frame.setVisible(true);
20 }
```

create frame

create applet

add applet

init()
start()

show frame

The `main` method creates a frame to hold an applet (line 13). When the applet is run from a Web browser, the Web browser invokes the `init` and `start` methods of the applet. When the applet is run standalone, you have to manually invoke the `init` and `start` methods in order to perform the operations in these methods (lines 12–13).

You can revise the `LoanApplet` class in Listing 16.1 to enable `LoanApplet` to run standalone by adding a `main` method in Listing 16.3.

LISTING 16.3 New `LoanApplet.java` with a **main** Method

```java
 1 import java.awt.*;
 2 import java.awt.event.*;
 3 import javax.swing.*;
 4 import javax.swing.border.TitledBorder;
 5
 6 public class LoanApplet extends JApplet {
 7   // Same code in Listing 16.1 from line 7 to line 78
 8   ...
 9
10   public static void main(String[] args) {
11     // Create a frame
12     JFrame frame = new JFrame("Applet is in the frame");
```

code omitted

new **main** method

```
13
14      // Create an instance of the applet
15      LoanApplet applet = new LoanApplet();
16
17      // Add the applet to the frame
18      frame.add(applet, BorderLayout.CENTER);
19
20      // Invoke applet's init method
21      applet.init();
22
23      // Display the frame
24      frame.setLocationRelativeTo(null); // Center the frame
25      frame.setDefaultCloseOperation(JFrame.EXIT_ON_CLOSE);
26      frame.setSize(300, 300);
27      frame.setVisible(true);
28    }
29 }
```

16.6 Passing Strings to Applets

In §8.5, "Command-Line Arguments," you learned how to pass strings to Java applications from a command line. Strings are passed to the `main` method as an array of strings. When the application starts, the `main` method can use these strings. There is no `main` method in an applet, however, and applets are not run from the command line by the Java interpreter.

How, then, can applets accept arguments? In this section, you will learn how to pass strings to Java applets. To be passed to an applet, a parameter must be declared in the HTML file, and must be read by the applet when it is initialized. Parameters are declared using the `<param>` tag. The `<param>` tag must be embedded in the `<applet>` tag and has no end tag. The syntax for the `<param>` tag is given below:

```
<param name = parametername value = stringvalue />
```

This tag specifies a parameter and its corresponding string value.

Note
There is no comma separating the parameter name from the parameter value in the HTML code. The HTML parameter names are not case sensitive.

Suppose you want to write an applet to display a message. The message is passed as a parameter. In addition, you want the message to be displayed at a specific location with x-coordinate and y-coordinate, which are passed as two parameters. The parameters and their values are listed in Table 16.1.

TABLE 16.1 Parameter Names and Values for the `DisplayMessage` Applet

Parameter Name	Parameter Value
MESSAGE	"Welcome to Java"
X	20
Y	30

The HTML source file is given in Listing 16.4.

LISTING 16.4 DisplayMessage.html

```html
<html>
  <head>
    <title>Passing Strings to Java Applets</title>
  </head>
  <body>
    <p>This applet gets a message from the HTML
       page and displays it.</p>
    <applet
      code = "DisplayMessage.class"
      width = 200
      height = 50
      alt = "You must have a Java 2-enabled browser to view the applet"
    >
      <param name = MESSAGE value = "Welcome to Java" />
      <param name = X value = 20 />
      <param name = Y value = 30 />
    </applet>
  </body>
</html>
```

To read the parameter from the applet, use the following method defined in the **Applet** class:

```java
public String getParameter(String parametername);
```

This returns the value of the specified parameter.

The applet is given in Listing 16.5. A sample run of the applet is shown in Figure 16.8.

FIGURE 16.8   The applet displays the message Welcome to Java passed from the HTML page.

LISTING 16.5 DisplayMessage.java

```java
1 import javax.swing.*;
2
3 public class DisplayMessage extends JApplet {
4   /** Initialize the applet */
5   public void init() {
6     // Get parameter values from the HTML file
7     String message = getParameter("MESSAGE");                     getParameter
8     int x = Integer.parseInt(getParameter("X"));
9     int y = Integer.parseInt(getParameter("Y"));
10
11    // Create a message panel
12    MessagePanel messagePanel = new MessagePanel(message);
13    messagePanel.setXCoordinate(x);
14    messagePanel.setYCoordinate(y);
15
```

add to applet

```
16       // Add the message panel to the applet
17       add(messagePanel);
18    }
19 }
```

The program gets the parameter values from the HTML in the `init` method. The values are strings obtained using the `getParameter` method (lines 7–9). Because `x` and `y` are `int`, the program uses `Integer.parseInt(string)` to parse a digital string into an `int` value.

If you change `Welcome to Java` in the HTML file to `Welcome to HTML`, and reload the HTML file in the Web browser, you should see `Welcome to HTML` displayed. Similarly, the `x` and `y` values can be changed to display the message in a desired location.

 Caution

The `Applet`'s `getParameter` method can be invoked only after an instance of the applet is created. Therefore, this method cannot be invoked in the constructor of the applet class. You should invoke it from the `init` method.

You can add a `main` method to enable this applet to run standalone. The applet takes the parameters from the HTML file when it runs as an applet and takes the parameters from the command line when it runs standalone. The program, as shown in Listing 16.6, is identical to `DisplayMessage` except for the addition of a new `main` method and of a variable named `isStandalone` to indicate whether it is running as an applet or as an application.

LISTING 16.6   `DisplayMessageApp.java`

isStandalone

applet params

```
 1 import javax.swing.*;
 2 import java.awt.Font;
 3 import java.awt.BorderLayout;
 4
 5 public class DisplayMessageApp extends JApplet {
 6   private String message = "A default message"; // Message to display
 7   private int x = 20; // Default x coordinate
 8   private int y = 20; // Default y coordinate
 9
10   /** Determine if it is application */
11   private boolean isStandalone = false;
12
13   /** Initialize the applet */
14   public void init() {
15     if (!isStandalone) {
16       // Get parameter values from the HTML file
17       message = getParameter("MESSAGE");
18       x = Integer.parseInt(getParameter("X"));
19       y = Integer.parseInt(getParameter("Y"));
20     }
21
22     // Create a message panel
23     MessagePanel messagePanel = new MessagePanel(message);
24     messagePanel.setFont(new Font("SansSerif", Font.BOLD, 20));
25     messagePanel.setXCoordinate(x);
26     messagePanel.setYCoordinate(y);
27
28     // Add the message panel to the applet
29     add(messagePanel);
30   }
31
32   /** Main method to display a message
33      @param args [0] x coordinate
```

```
34        @param args [1] y coordinate
35        @param args [2] message
36      */
37    public static void main(String[] args) {
38      // Create a frame
39      JFrame frame = new JFrame("DisplayMessageApp");
40
41      // Create an instance of the applet
42      DisplayMessageApp applet = new DisplayMessageApp();
43
44      // It runs as an application
45      applet.isStandalone = true;
46
47      // Get parameters from the command line
48      applet.getCommandLineParameters(args);
49
50      // Add the applet instance to the frame
51      frame.add(applet, BorderLayout.CENTER);
52
53      // Invoke applet's init method
54      applet.init();
55      applet.start();
56
57      // Display the frame
58      frame.setSize(300, 300);
59      frame.setLocationRelativeTo(null); // Center the frame
60      frame.setDefaultCloseOperation(JFrame.EXIT_ON_CLOSE);
61      frame.setVisible(true);
62    }
63
64    /** Get command line parameters */
65    private void getCommandLineParameters(String[] args) {
66      // Check usage and get x, y and message
67      if (args.length != 3) {
68        System.out.println(
69          "Usage: java DisplayMessageApp x y message");
70        System.exit(0);
71      }
72      else {
73        x = Integer.parseInt(args[0]);
74        y = Integer.parseInt(args[1]);
75        message = args[2];
76      }
77    }
78 }
```

standalone

command params

When you run the program as an applet, the **main** method is ignored. When you run it as an application, the **main** method is invoked. A sample run of the program as an application and as an applet is shown in Figure 16.9.

FIGURE 16.9   The `DisplayMessageApp` class can run as an application and as an applet.

The `main` method creates a `JFrame` object `frame` and creates a `JApplet` object `applet`, then places the applet `applet` into the frame `frame` and invokes its `init` method. The application runs just like an applet.

The `main` method sets `isStandalone true` (line 45) so that it does not attempt to retrieve HTML parameters when the `init` method is invoked.

The `setVisible(true)` method (line 61) is invoked *after* the components are added to the applet, and the applet is added to the frame to ensure that the components will be visible. Otherwise, the components are not shown when the frame starts.

omitting **main** method

Important Pedagogical Note

From now on, all the GUI examples will be created as applets with a `main` method. Thus you will be able to run the program either as an applet or as an application. For brevity, the `main` method is not listed in the text.

 ## 16.7 (Optional) Case Study: TicTacToe

You have learned about objects, classes, arrays, class inheritance, GUI, event-driven programming, and applets from the many examples in this chapter and the preceding chapters. Now it is time to put what you have learned to work in developing comprehensive projects. In this section, you will develop a Java applet with which to play the popular game of TicTacToe.

In a game of TicTacToe, two players take turns marking an available cell in a 3 × 3 grid with their respective tokens (either X or O). When one player has placed three tokens in a horizontal, vertical, or diagonal row on the grid, the game is over and that player has won. A draw (no winner) occurs when all the cells on the grid have been filled with tokens and neither player has achieved a win. Figure 16.10 shows two representative sample runs of the example.

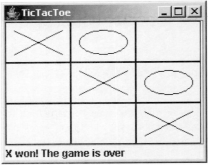

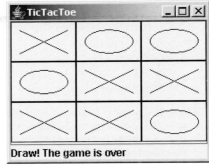

(a) The x player won the game

(b) Draw—no game winners

FIGURE 16.10 Two players play a TicTacToe game.

All the examples you have seen so far show simple behaviors that are easy to model with classes. The behavior of the TicTacToe game is somewhat more complex. To create classes that model the behavior, you need to study and understand the game.

Assume that all the cells are initially empty, and that the first player takes the X token, and the second player takes the O token. To mark a cell, the player points the mouse to the cell and clicks it. If the cell is empty, the token (X or O) is displayed. If the cell is already filled, the player's action is ignored.

From the preceding description, it is obvious that a cell is a GUI object that handles the mouse-click event and displays tokens. Such an object could be either a button or a panel. Drawing on panels is more flexible than on buttons, because the token (X or O) can be drawn on a panel in any size, but on a button it can only be displayed as a text label. Therefore, a panel should be used to model a cell. How do you know the state of the cell (empty, X, or O)? You use a property named `token` of `char` type in the `Cell` class. The `Cell` class is responsible for drawing the token when an empty cell is clicked. So you need to write the code for listening to the `MouseEvent` and for painting the shapes for tokens X and O. The `Cell` class can be defined as shown in Figure 16.11.

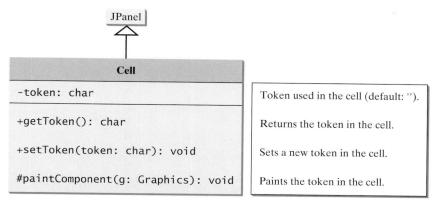

| JPanel |

Cell	
-token: char	Token used in the cell (default: '').
+getToken(): char	Returns the token in the cell.
+setToken(token: char): void	Sets a new token in the cell.
#paintComponent(g: Graphics): void	Paints the token in the cell.

FIGURE 16.11 The `Cell` class paints the token on a cell.

The TicTacToe board consists of nine cells, declared using `new Cell[3][3]`. To determine which player's turn it is, you can introduce a variable named `whoseTurn` of `char` type. `whoseTurn` is initially X, then changes to O, and subsequently changes between X and O whenever a new cell is occupied. When the game is over, set `whoseTurn` to ' '.

How do you know whether the game is over, whether there is a winner, and who the winner, if any, is? You can create a method named `isWon(char token)` to check whether a specified token has won and a method named `isFull()` to check whether all the cells are occupied.

Clearly, two classes emerge from the foregoing analysis. One is the `Cell` class, which handles operations for a single cell; and the other is the `TicTacToe` class, which plays the whole game and deals with all the cells. The relationship between these two classes is shown in Figure 16.12.

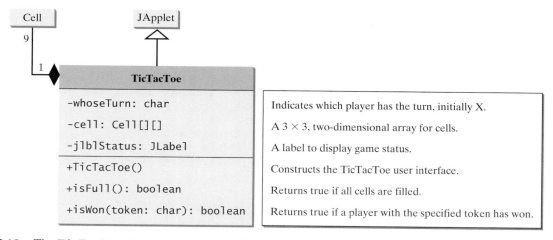

Cell		JApplet

9

1

TicTacToe	
-whoseTurn: char	Indicates which player has the turn, initially X.
-cell: Cell[][]	A 3 × 3, two-dimensional array for cells.
-jlblStatus: JLabel	A label to display game status.
+TicTacToe()	Constructs the TicTacToe user interface.
+isFull(): boolean	Returns true if all cells are filled.
+isWon(token: char): boolean	Returns true if a player with the specified token has won.

FIGURE 16.12 The `TicTacToe` class contains nine cells.

Since the `Cell` class is only to support the `TicTacToe` class, it can be defined as an inner class in `TicTacToe`. The complete program is given in Listing 16.7.

LISTING 16.7 `TicTacToe.java`

```
 1 import java.awt.*;
 2 import java.awt.event.*;
 3 import javax.swing.*;
 4 import javax.swing.border.LineBorder;
 5
 6 public class TicTacToe extends JApplet {
 7   // Indicate which player has a turn, initially it is the X player
 8   private char whoseTurn = 'X';
 9
10   // Create and initialize cells
11   private Cell[][] cells =  new Cell[3][3];
12
13   // Create and initialize a status label
14   private JLabel jlblStatus = new JLabel("X's turn to play");
15
16   /** Initialize UI */
17   public TicTacToe() {
18     // Panel p to hold cells
19     JPanel p = new JPanel(new GridLayout(3, 3, 0, 0));
20     for (int i = 0; i < 3; i++)
21       for (int j = 0; j < 3; j++)
22         p.add(cells[i][j] = new Cell());
23
24     // Set line borders on the cells panel and the status label
25     p.setBorder(new LineBorder(Color.red, 1));
26     jlblStatus.setBorder(new LineBorder(Color.yellow, 1));
27
28     // Place the panel and the label to the applet
29     add(p, BorderLayout.CENTER);
30     add(jlblStatus, BorderLayout.SOUTH);
31   }
32
33   /** Determine if the cells are all occupied */
34   public boolean isFull() {
35     for (int i = 0; i < 3; i++)
36       for (int j = 0; j < 3; j++)
37         if (cells[i][j].getToken() == ' ')
38           return false;
39
40     return true;
41   }
42
43   /** Determine if the player with the specified token wins */
44   public boolean isWon(char token) {
45     for (int i = 0; i < 3; i++)
46       if ((cells[i][0].getToken() == token)
47           && (cells[i][1].getToken() == token)
48           && (cells[i][2].getToken() == token)) {
49         return true;
50       }
51
52     for (int j = 0; j < 3; j++)
53       if ((cells[0][j].getToken() ==  token)
54           && (cells[1][j].getToken() == token)
55           && (cells[2][j].getToken() == token)) {
56         return true;
57       }
58
```

main class **TicTacToe**

check **isFull**

check rows

check columns

```
59      if ((cells[0][0].getToken() == token)                                    check major diagonal
60          && (cells[1][1].getToken() == token)
61          && (cells[2][2].getToken() == token)) {
62        return true;
63      }
64
65      if ((cells[0][2].getToken() == token)                                    check subdiagonal
66          && (cells[1][1].getToken() == token)
67          && (cells[2][0].getToken() == token)) {
68        return true;
69      }
70
71      return false;
72    }
73
74    // An inner class for a cell
75    public class Cell extends JPanel {                                         inner class Cell
76      // Token used for this cell
77      private char token = ' ';
78
79      public Cell() {
80        setBorder(new LineBorder(Color.black, 1)); // Set cell's border
81        addMouseListener(new MouseListener()); // Register listener            register listener
82      }
83
84      /** Return token */
85      public char getToken() {
86        return token;
87      }
88
89      /** Set a new token */
90      public void setToken(char c) {
91        token = c;
92        repaint();
93      }
94
95      /** Paint the cell */
96      protected void paintComponent(Graphics g) {                              paint cell
97        super.paintComponent(g);
98
99        if (token == 'X') {
100         g.drawLine(10, 10, getWidth() - 10, getHeight() - 10);
101         g.drawLine(getWidth() - 10, 10, 10, getHeight() - 10);
102       }
103       else if (token == 'O') {
104         g.drawOval(10, 10, getWidth() - 20, getHeight() - 20);
105       }
106     }
107
108     private class MouseListener extends MouseAdapter {                        listener class
109       /** Handle mouse click on a cell */
110       public void mouseClicked(MouseEvent e) {
111         // If cell is empty and game is not over
112         if (token == ' ' && whoseTurn != ' ') {
113           setToken(whoseTurn); // Set token in the cell
114
115           // Check game status
116           if (isWon(whoseTurn)) {
117             jlblStatus.setText(whoseTurn + " won! The game is over");
118             whoseTurn = ' '; // Game is over
```

```
119                    }
120                    else if (isFull()) {
121                       jlblStatus.setText("Draw! The game is over");
122                       whoseTurn = ' '; // Game is over
123                    }
124                    else {
125                       whoseTurn = (whoseTurn == 'X') ? 'O': 'X';
126                       jlblStatus.setText(whoseTurn + "'s turn");
127                    }
128                 }
129              }
130           }
131     }
132 }
```

main method omitted

The `TicTacToe` class initializes the user interface with nine cells placed in a panel of `GridLayout` (lines 19–22). A label named `jlblStatus` is used to show the status of the game (line 14). The variable `whoseTurn` (line 8) is used to track the next type of token to be placed in a cell. The methods `isFull` (lines 34–41) and `isWon` (lines 44–72) are for checking the status of the game.

Since `Cell` is an inner class in `TicTacToe`, the variable (`whoseTurn`) and methods (`isFull` and `isWon`) defined in `TicTacToe` can be referenced from the `Cell` class. The inner class makes programs simple and concise. If `Cell` were not declared as an inner class of `TicTacToe`, you would have to pass an object of `TicTacToe` to `Cell` in order for the variables and methods in `TicTacToe` to be used in `Cell`. You will rewrite the program without using an inner class in Exercise 16.6.

The listener for `MouseEvent` is registered for the cell (line 81). If an empty cell is clicked and the game is not over, a token is set in the cell (line 113). If the game is over, `whoseTurn` is set to ' ' (lines 118, 122). Otherwise, `whoseTurn` is alternated to a new turn (line 125).

Tip

incremental development and testing

Use an incremental approach in developing and testing a Java project of this kind. The foregoing program can be divided into five steps.

1. Lay out the user interface and display a fixed token X on a cell.

2. Enable the cell to display a fixed token X upon a mouse click.

3. Coordinate between the two players so as to display tokens X and O alternately.

4. Check whether a player wins, or whether all the cells are occupied without a winner.

5. Implement displaying a message on the label upon each move by a player.

 ## 16.8 (Optional) Case Study: Bouncing Ball

This section presents an applet that displays a ball bouncing in a panel. Use two buttons to suspend and resume the movement, and use a scroll bar to control the bouncing speed, as shown in Figure 16.13.

FIGURE 16.13 The ball's movement is controlled by the Suspend and Resume buttons and the scroll bar.

Here are the major steps to complete this example.

1. Create a subclass of **JPanel** named **Ball** to display a ball bouncing, as shown in Listing 16.8.

2. Create a subclass of **JPanel** named **BallControl** to contain the ball with a scroll bar and two control buttons *Suspend* and *Resume*, as shown in Listing 16.9.

3. Create an applet named **BounceBallApp** to contain an instance of **BallControl** and enable the applet to run standalone, as shown in Listing 16.10.

The relationship among these classes is shown in Figure 16.14.

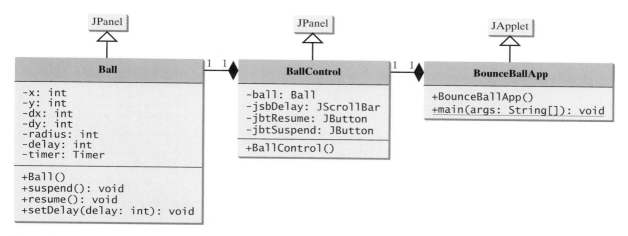

FIGURE 16.14 **BounceBallApp** contains **BallControl**, and **BallControl** contains **Ball**.

LISTING 16.8 Ball.java

```
1  import javax.swing.Timer;
2  import java.awt.*;
3  import javax.swing.*;
4  import java.awt.event.*;
5
6  public class Ball extends JPanel {
7    private int delay = 10;                                        timer delay
8
9    // Create a timer with delay 1000 ms
10   protected Timer timer = new Timer(delay, new TimerListener());  create timer
11
12   private int x = 0; private int y = 0; // Current ball position
13   private int radius = 5; // Ball radius
14   private int dx = 2; // Increment on ball's x-coordinate
15   private int dy = 2; // Increment on ball's y-coordinate
16
17   public Ball() {
18     timer.start();                                               start timer
19   }
20
21   private class TimerListener implements ActionListener {        timer listener
22     /** Handle the action event */
23     public void actionPerformed(ActionEvent e) {
24       repaint();                                                 repaint ball
25     }
26   }
```

paint ball

```
27
28  protected void paintComponent(Graphics g) {
29    super.paintComponent(g);
30
31    g.setColor(Color.red);
32
33    // Check boundaries
34    if (x < radius) dx = Math.abs(dx);
35    if (x > getWidth() - radius) dx = -Math.abs(dx);
36    if (y < radius) dy = Math.abs(dy);
37    if (y > getHeight() - radius) dy = -Math.abs(dy);
38
39    // Adjust ball position
40    x += dx;
41    y += dy;
42    g.fillOval(x - radius, y - radius, radius * 2, radius * 2);
43  }
44
45  public void suspend() {
46    timer.stop(); // Suspend timer
47  }
48
49  public void resume() {
50    timer.start(); // Resume timer
51  }
52
53  public void setDelay(int delay) {
54    this.delay = delay;
55    timer.setDelay(delay);
56  }
57 }
```

Using **Timer** to control animation was introduced in §14.6, "Animation Using the **Timer** Class." **Ball** extends **JPanel** to display a moving ball. The timer listener implements **ActionListener** to listen for **ActionEvent** (line 21). Line 10 creates a **Timer** for a **Ball**. The timer is started in line 18 when a **Ball** is constructed. The timer fires an **ActionEvent** at a fixed rate. The listener responds in line 24 to repaint the ball to animate ball movement. The center of the ball is at (**x**, **y**), which changes to (**x** + **dx**, **y** + **dy**) on the next display. The **suspend** and **resume** methods (lines 45–51) can be used to stop and start the timer. The **setDelay(int)** method (lines 53–56) sets a new delay.

LISTING 16.9 BallControl.java

```
1 import javax.swing.*;
2 import java.awt.event.*;
3 import java.awt.*;
4
5 public class BallControl extends JPanel {
6   private Ball ball = new Ball();
7   private JButton jbtSuspend = new JButton("Suspend");
8   private JButton jbtResume = new JButton("Resume");
9   private JScrollBar jsbDelay = new JScrollBar();
10
11  public BallControl() {
12    // Group buttons in a panel
13    JPanel panel = new JPanel();
14    panel.add(jbtSuspend);
15    panel.add(jbtResume);
```

button

scroll bar

create UI

```
16
17      // Add ball and buttons to the panel
18      ball.setBorder(new javax.swing.border.LineBorder(Color.red));
19      jsbDelay.setOrientation(JScrollBar.HORIZONTAL);
20      ball.setDelay(jsbDelay.getMaximum());
21      setLayout(new BorderLayout());
22      add(jsbDelay, BorderLayout.NORTH);
23      add(ball, BorderLayout.CENTER);
24      add(panel, BorderLayout.SOUTH);
25
26      // Register listeners
27      jbtSuspend.addActionListener(new ActionListener() {          register listener
28        public void actionPerformed(ActionEvent e) {
29          ball.suspend();                                          suspend
30        }
31      });
32      jbtResume.addActionListener(new ActionListener() {           register listener
33        public void actionPerformed(ActionEvent e) {
34          ball.resume();                                           resume
35        }
36      });
37      jsbDelay.addAdjustmentListener(new AdjustmentListener() {     register listener
38        public void adjustmentValueChanged(AdjustmentEvent e) {
39          ball.setDelay(jsbDelay.getMaximum() - e.getValue());     new delay
40        }
41      });
42    }
43 }
```

The **BallControl** class extends **JPanel** to display the ball with a scroll bar and two control buttons. When the *Suspend* button is clicked, the ball's **suspend()** method is invoked to suspend the ball movement (line 29). When the *Resume* button is clicked, the ball's **resume()** method is invoked to resume the ball movement (line 34). The bouncing speed can be changed using the scroll bar.

LISTING 16.10 BounceBallApp.java

```
1 import java.awt.*;
2 import java.awt.event.*;
3 import java.applet.*;
4 import javax.swing.*;
5
6 public class BounceBallApp extends JApplet {
7   public BounceBallApp() {
8     add(new BallControl());                                        add BallControl
9   }
10 }                                                                 main method omitted
```

The **BounceBallApp** class simply places an instance of **BallControl** in the applet. The **main** method is provided in the applet (not displayed in the listing for brevity) so that you can also run it standalone.

16.9 (Optional) Locating Resource Using the **URL** Class

You have used the **ImageIcon** class to create an icon from an image file and used the **setIcon** method or the constructor to place the icon in a GUI component, such as a button or a label. For example, the following statements create an **ImageIcon** and set it on a **JLabel** object **jlbl**:

```
ImageIcon imageIcon = new ImageIcon("c:\\book\\image\\us.gif");
jlbl.setIcon(imageIcon);
```

This approach presents a problem. The file location is fixed, because it uses the absolute file path on Windows. As a result, the program cannot run on other platforms and cannot run as an applet. Assume that **image/us.gif** is under the class directory. You can circumvent this problem by using a relative path, as follows:

```
ImageIcon imageIcon = new ImageIcon("image/us.gif");
```

This works fine with Java applications on all platforms, but does not work with Java applets because applets cannot load local files. To make it to work with both applications and applets, you need to locate the file using the **URL** class.

why **URL** class?

The **java.net.URL** class can be used to identify files (image, audio, text, etc.) on the Internet. In general, a URL (Uniform Resource Locator) is a pointer to a "resource" on the World Wide Web on a local machine or a remote host. A resource can be something as simple as a file or a directory.

An URL for a file can also be accessed by class code in a way that is independent of the location of the file as long as the file is located in the class directory. Recall that the class directory is where the class (i.e., the .class file) is stored. For example, all the classes in this book are stored in c:\book. So the class directory is **c:\book**.

As discussed in §9.13.5, "The **getClass** Method," when a class is loaded, the JVM creates a meta-object for the class, which can be obtained using

```
java.lang.Class metaObject = this.getClass();
```

The **Class** class provides access to useful information about the class, such as the data fields, constructors, and methods. It also contains the **getResource(filename)** method, which can be used to obtain the URL of a given file name in the class directory.

To obtain the URL of a file in the class directory, use

```
URL url = metaObject.getResource(filename);
```

For example, if the class directory is **c:\book**, the following statements create a URL for c:\book\image\us.gif:

```
Class metaObject = this.getClass();
URL url = metaObject.getResource("image/us.gif");
```

You can now create an **ImageIcon** using

```
ImageIcon imageIcon = new ImageIcon(url);
```

Listing 16.11 gives the code that displays an image from **image/us.gif** in the class directory. The file **image/us.gif** is under the class directory, and its URL is obtained using the **getResource** method (line 5). A label with an image icon is created in line 6. The image icon is obtained from the URL.

LISTING 16.11 DisplayImageWithURL.java

```
1  import javax.swing.*;
2
3  public class DisplayImageWithURL extends JApplet {
4    public DisplayImageWithURL() {
5      java.net.URL url = this.getClass().getResource("image/us.gif");
6      add(new JLabel(new ImageIcon(url)));
7    }
8  }
```

get image URL
create a label

main method omitted

If you replace the code in lines 5–6 with the following code,

```
add(new JLabel(new ImageIcon("image/us.gif")));
```

you can still run the program standalone, but not from a browser.

16.10 (Optional) Playing Audio

There are several formats for audio files. Prior to Java 2, sound files in the AU format used on the UNIX operating system were the only ones Java was able to play. With Java 2, you can play sound files in the WAV, AIFF, MIDI, AU, and RMF formats, with better sound quality.

To play an audio file in an applet, first create an *audio clip object* for the audio file. The audio clip is created once and can be played repeatedly without reloading the file. To create an audio clip, use the static method `newAudioClip()` in the `java.applet.Applet` class:

```
AudioClip audioClip = Applet.newAudioClip(url);
```

Audio was originally used with Java applets. For this reason, the `AudioClip` interface is in the `java.applet` package.

The following statements, for example, create an `AudioClip` for the `beep.au` audio file in the class directory:

```
Class metaObject = this.getClass();
URL url = metaObject.getResource("beep.au");
AudioClip audioClip = Applet.newAudioClip(url);
```

To manipulate a sound for an audio clip, use the `play()`, `loop()`, and `stop()` methods in `java.applet.AudioClip`, as shown in Figure 16.15.

«interface» *java.applet.AudioClip*	
+*play()*	Starts playing this audio clip. Each time this method is called, the clip is restarted from the beginning.
+*loop()*	Plays the clip repeatedly.
+*stop()*	Stops playing the clip.

FIGURE 16.15 The `AudioClip` interface provides the methods for playing sound.

Listing 16.12 gives the code that displays the Danish flag and plays the Danish national anthem repeatedly. The image file **image/denmark.gif** and audio file **audio/denmark.mid** are stored under the class directory. Line 12 obtains the audio file URL. Line 13 creates an audio clip for the file. Line 14 repeatedly plays the audio.

LISTING 16.12 DisplayImagePlayAudio.java

```
1 import javax.swing.*;
2 import java.net.URL;
3 import java.applet.*;
4
5 public class DisplayImagePlayAudio extends JApplet {
6   private AudioClip audioClip;
7
8   public DisplayImagePlayAudio() {
9     URL urlForImage = getClass().getResource("image/denmark.gif");     get image URL
10    add(new JLabel(new ImageIcon(urlForImage)));                        create a label
```

get audio URL
create an audio clip
play audio repeatedly

```
11
12    URL urlForAudio = getClass().getResource("audio/denmark.mid");
13    audioClip = Applet.newAudioClip(urlForAudio);
14    audioClip.loop();
15   }
16
17   public void start() {
18     if (audioClip != null) audioClip.loop();
19   }
20
21   public void stop() {
22     if (audioClip != null) audioClip.stop();
23   }
24 }
```

start audio

stop audio

main method omitted

The **stop** method (lines 21–23) stops the audio when the applet is not displayed, and the **start** method (lines 17–19) restarts the audio when the applet is redisplayed. Please try to run this applet from a browser and observe the effect without the **stop** and **start** methods.

16.11 (Optional) Case Study: Multimedia Animations

This case study presents a multimedia animation with images and audio. The images are for seven national flags, named **flag0.gif**, **flag1.gif**, ..., **flag6.gif** for Denmark, Germany, China, India, Norway, the UK, and the US. They are stored under the **image** directory in the class path. The audio consists of national anthems for these seven nations, named **anthem0.mid**, **anthem1.mid**, ..., and **anthem6.mid**. They are stored under the **audio** directory in the class path.

The program presents the nations, starting from the first one. For each nation, it displays its flag and plays its anthem. When the audio finishes, the next nation is presented, and so on. When the last nation is presented, the program starts to present all the nations again. You may suspend animation by clicking the Suspend button and resume it by clicking the Resume button, as shown in Figure 16.16. You can also directly select a nation from a combo box.

FIGURE 16.16 The applet displays a sequence of images and plays audio.

The program is given in Listing 16.13. A timer is created to control the animation (line 15). The timer delay for each presentation is the play time for the anthem. You can find the play time for an audio file using RealPlayer or Windows Media on Windows. The delay times are stored in an array named **delays** (lines 13–14). The delay time for the first audio file (the Danish anthem) is 48 seconds.

LISTING 16.13 ImageAudioAnimation.java

```java
1  import java.awt.*;
2  import java.awt.event.*;
3  import javax.swing.*;
4  import java.applet.*;
5
6  public class ImageAudioAnimation extends JApplet {
7    private final static int NUMBER_OF_NATIONS = 7;
8    private int current = 0;
9    private ImageIcon[] icons = new ImageIcon[NUMBER_OF_NATIONS];          image icons
10   private AudioClip[] audioClips = new AudioClip[NUMBER_OF_NATIONS];     audio clips
11   private AudioClip currentAudioClip;                                    current audio clip
12
13   private int[] delays =                                                 audio play time
14     {48000, 54000, 59000, 54000, 59000, 31000, 68000};
15   private Timer timer = new Timer(delays[0], new TimerListener());       timer
16
17   private JLabel jlblImageLabel = new JLabel();                          GUI components
18   private JButton jbtResume = new JButton("Resume");
19   private JButton jbtSuspend = new JButton("Suspend");
20   private JComboBox jcboNations = new JComboBox(new Object[]
21     {"Denmark", "Germany", "China", "India", "Norway", "UK", "US"});
22
23   public ImageAudioAnimation() {
24     // Load image icons and audio clips
25     for (int i = 0; i < NUMBER_OF_NATIONS; i++) {
26       icons[i] = new ImageIcon(getClass().getResource(                  create icons
27         "image/flag" + i + ".gif"));
28       audioClips[i] = Applet.newAudioClip(                              create audio clips
29         getClass().getResource("audio/anthem" + i + ".mid"));
30     }
31
32     JPanel panel = new JPanel();                                        create UI
33     panel.add(jbtResume);
34     panel.add(jbtSuspend);
35     panel.add(new JLabel("Select"));
36     panel.add(jcboNations);
37     this.getContentPane().add(jlblImageLabel, BorderLayout.CENTER);
38     this.getContentPane().add(panel, BorderLayout.SOUTH);
39
40     jbtResume.addActionListener(new ActionListener() {                  register listener
41       public void actionPerformed(ActionEvent e) {
42         start();                                                        start animation
43       }
44     });
45     jbtSuspend.addActionListener(new ActionListener() {                 register listener
46       public void actionPerformed(ActionEvent e) {
47         stop();                                                         stop animation
48       }
49     });
50     jcboNations.addActionListener(new ActionListener() {                register listener
51       public void actionPerformed(ActionEvent e) {
52         stop();
53         current = jcboNations.getSelectedIndex();                       select a nation
54         presentNation(current);                                         present a nation
55         timer.start();
56       }
57     });
58
```

```
59       timer.start();
60       jlblImageLabel.setIcon(icons[0]);
61       jlblImageLabel.setHorizontalAlignment(JLabel.CENTER);
62       currentAudioClip = audioClips[0];
63       currentAudioClip.play();
64     }
65
66     private class TimerListener implements ActionListener {
67       public void actionPerformed(ActionEvent e) {
68         current = (current + 1) % NUMBER_OF_NATIONS;
69         presentNation(current);
70       }
71     }
72
73     private void presentNation(int index) {
74       jlblImageLabel.setIcon(icons[index]);
75       jcboNations.setSelectedIndex(index);
76       currentAudioClip = audioClips[index];
77       currentAudioClip.play();
78       timer.setDelay(delays[index]);
79     }
80
81     public void start() {
82       timer.start();
83       currentAudioClip.play();
84     }
85
86     public void stop() {
87       timer.stop();
88       currentAudioClip.stop();
89     }
90 }
```

set a new delay (line 78)

stop audio clip (line 88)

main method omitted (line 90)

A label is created in line 17 to display a flag image. An array of flag images for seven nations is created in lines 26–27. An array of audio clips is created in lines 28–29. Each audio clip is created for an audio file through the URL of the current class. The audio files are stored in the same directory with the applet class file.

The combo box for country names is created in lines 20–21. When a new country name in the combo box is selected, the current presentation is stopped and a new selected nation is presented (line 52–55).

The `presentNation(index)` method (lines 73–79) presents a nation with the specified index. It sets a new image in the label (line 74), synchronizes with the combo box by setting the selected index (line 75), plays the new audio, and sets a new delay time (line 78).

The applet's `start` and `stop` methods are overridden to resume and suspend the animation (lines 81–89).

16.12 (Optional) Packaging and Deploying Java Projects

Your project may consist of many classes and supporting files, such as image files and audio files. To make your programs run on the end-user side, you need to provide end-users with all these files. For convenience, Java supports an archive file that can be used to group all the project files in a compressed file.

Archiving makes it possible for Java applications, applets, and their requisite components (.class files, images, and sounds) to be transported in a single file. This single file can be deployed on an end-user's machine as an application. It also can be downloaded to a browser in a single HTTP transaction, rather than opening a new connection for each piece. This greatly simplifies application deployment and improves the speed with which an applet can be loaded onto a web page and begin functioning.

You can use the JDK **jar** command to create an archive file. The following command creates an archive file named TicTacToe.jar for classes TicTacToe.class and TicTacToe$Cell.class (inner class).

```
jar -cf TicTacToe.jar TicTacToe.class TicTacToe$Cell.class
```

The **-c** option is for creating a new archive file, and the **-f** option specifies the archive file's name.

 Note

The Java archive file format (JAR) is based on the popular ZIP file format. You can view the contents of a .jar file using WinZip, a popular compression utility for Windows, as shown in Figure 16.17.

viewing .jar contents

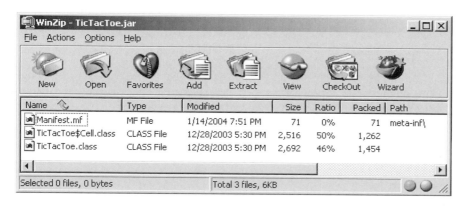

FIGURE 16.17 You can view the files contained in the archive file using the WinZip utility.

16.12.1 The Manifest File

As shown in Figure 16.17, a manifest file was created with the path name `meta-inf\`. The manifest is a special file that contains information about the files packaged in a JAR file. For instance, the manifest file in Figure 16.17 contains the following information:

```
Manifest-Version: 1.0

Name: TicTacToe.class
Java-Bean: True

Name: TicTacToe$Cell.class
Java-Bean: True
```

You can modify the information contained in the manifest file to enable the JAR file to be used for a variety of purposes. For example, you can add information to specify a `main` class to run an application using the .jar file.

16.12.2 Running Archived Projects

You can package all the class files and dependent resource files in an archive file for distribution to the end-user. If the project is a Java application, the user should have a Java-running environment already installed. If it is not installed, the user can download the Java Runtime Environment (JRE) from java.sun.com and install it.

 Note

The Java Runtime Environment is the minimum standard Java platform for running Java programs. It contains the Java interpreter, Java core classes, and supporting files. The JRE does not contain any development tools (such as Applet Viewer or javac) or classes that pertain only to a development environment. The JRE is a subset of JDK.

JRE

To run `TicTacToe` as an application, take the following steps:

1. Update the manifest file to insert an entry for the main class. You need to create a text file containing the following two lines:

```
Main-Class: TicTacToe

Sealed: true
```

The first line specifies the main class. The second line is necessary to ensure that the first line can be inserted into an existing manifest file in a jar. Assume that these two lines are contained in the file temp.mf.

2. Execute the `jar` command to insert the main class line into the manifest file in TicTac-Toe.jar, as follows:

```
jar -uvmf temp.mf TicTacToe.jar
```

The **-u** option is for updating an existing jar file, the **-v** option is for displaying command output, the **-m** option is for appending the contents in temp.mf to the manifest file in the archive, and the **-f** option specifies the archive file's name.

3. Run the .jar file using the java command from the directory that contains TicTacToe.jar, as follows:

```
java -jar TicTacToe.jar
```

 Note
You can write an installation procedure that creates the necessary directories and subdirectories on the end-user's computer. The installation can also create an icon that the end-user can double-click to start the program. For information on creating Windows desktop icons, please see Supplement I.E, "Creating Shortcuts for Java Applications on Windows."

To run `TicTacToe` as an applet, modify the `<applet>` tag in the HTML file to include an archive attribute. The archive attribute specifies the archive file in which the applet is contained. For example, the HTML file for running `TicTacToe` can be modified as shown below:

```
<applet
   code     = "TicTacToe.class"
   archive  = "TicTacToe.jar"
   width    = 400
   height   = 300
   hspace   = 0
   vspace   = 0
   align    = middle
>
</applet>
```

KEY TERMS

applet   536
HTML   539
.html or .htm   539

tag   539
JAR   563

CHAPTER SUMMARY

■   The Web browser controls and executes applets through the `init`, `start`, `stop`, and `destroy` methods in the `Applet` class. Applets always extend the `Applet` class and implement these methods, if applicable, so that they can be run by a Web browser.

- `JApplet` is a subclass of `Applet`. It should be used for developing Java applets with Swing components.

- The applet bytecode must be specified, using the `<applet>` tag in an HTML file to tell the Web browser where to find the applet. The applet can accept string parameters from HTML using the `<param>` tag.

- When an applet is loaded, the Web browser creates an instance of the applet by invoking its no-arg constructor. The `init` method is invoked after the applet is created. The `start` method is invoked after the `init` method. It is also called whenever the applet becomes active again after the page containing the applet is revisited. The `stop` method is invoked when the applet becomes inactive.

- The `destroy` method is invoked when the browser exits normally to inform the applet that it is no longer needed and should release any resources it has allocated. The `stop` method is always called before the `destroy` method.

- The procedures for writing applications and writing applets are very similar. An applet can easily be converted into an application, and vice versa. Moreover, an applet can be written with the additional capability of running as an application.

- You can pass arguments to an applet using the `param` attribute in the applet's tag in HTML. To retrieve the value of the parameter, invoke the `getParameter(paramName)` method.

- The `Applet`'s `getParameter` method can be invoked only after an instance of the applet is created. Therefore, this method cannot be invoked in the constructor of the applet class. You should invoke this method from the `init` method.

- You learned how to incorporate images and audio in Java applications and applets. To load audio and images for Java applications and applets, you have to create a URL for the audio and image. You can create a `URL` from a file under the class directory or from an Internet source.

- To play an audio, create an audio clip from the `URL` for the audio source. You can use the `AudioClip`'s `play()` method to play it once, the `loop()` method to play it repeatedly, and the `stop()` method to stop it.

REVIEW QUESTIONS

Sections 16.2–16.4

16.1 Is every applet an instance of `java.applet.Applet`? Is every applet an instance of `javax.swing.JApplet`?

16.2 Describe the `init()`, `start()`, `stop()`, and `destroy()` methods in the `Applet` class.

16.3 How do you add components to a `JApplet`? What is the default layout manager of the content pane of `JApplet`?

16.4 Why does the applet in (a) display nothing? Why does the applet in (b) have a runtime `NullPointerException` on line 12?

```java
import javax.swing.*;

public class WelcomeApplet extends JApplet {
  public void WelcomeApplet() {
    JLabel jlblMessage =
      new JLabel("It is Java");
  }
}
```

(a)

```java
import javax.swing.*;

public class WelcomeApplet extends JApplet {
  private JLabel jlblMessage;

  public WelcomeApplet() {
    JLabel jlblMessage =
      new JLabel("It is Java");
  }

  public void init() {
    getContentPane().add(jlblMessage);
  }
}
```

(b)

Sections 16.5–16.6

16.5 Describe the `<applet>` HTML tag. How do you pass parameters to an applet?

16.6 Where is the `getParameter` method defined?

16.7 What is wrong if the `DisplayMessage` applet is revised as follows?

```java
public class DisplayMessage extends JApplet {
  /** Initialize the applet */
  public DisplayMessage() {
    // Get parameter values from the HTML file
    String message = getParameter("MESSAGE");
    int x =
      Integer.parseInt(getParameter("X"));
    int y =
      Integer.parseInt(getParameter("Y"));

    // Create a message panel
    MessagePanel messagePanel =
      new MessagePanel(message);
    messagePanel.setXCoordinate(x);
    messagePanel.setYCoordinate(y);

    // Add the message panel to the applet
    getContentPane().add(messagePanel);
  }
}
```

(a) Revision 1

```java
public class DisplayMessage extends JApplet {
  private String message;
  private int x;
  private int y;

  /** Initialize the applet */
  public void init() {
    // Get parameter values from the HTML file
    message = getParameter("MESSAGE");
    x = Integer.parseInt(getParameter("X"));
    y = Integer.parseInt(getParameter("Y"));
  }

  public DisplayMessage() {
    // Create a message panel
    MessagePanel messagePanel =
      new MessagePanel(message);
    messagePanel.setXCoordinate(x);
    messagePanel.setYCoordinate(y);

    // Add the message panel to the applet
    getContentPane().add(messagePanel);
  }
}
```

(b) Revision 2

16.8 What are the differences between applications and applets? How do you run an application, and how do you run an applet? Is the compilation process different for applications and applets? List some security restrictions on applets.

16.9 Can you place a frame in an applet?

16.10 Can you place an applet in a frame?

16.11 Delete `super.paintComponent(g)` on line 97 in TicTacToe.java in Listing 16.7 and run the program to see what happens.

Sections 16.9 Locating Resource Using the URL Class

16.12 How do you create a `URL` object for the file http://www.cs.armstrong.edu/liang/intro6e/book/audio/us.mid on the Internet? How do you create a `URL` object for the file http://www.cs.armstrong.edu/liang/audio/us.mid in the class directory?

16.13 How do you create an `ImageIcon` from the file image/us.gif in the class directory? How do you create an `ImageIcon` from www.cs.armstrong.edu/liang/intro6e/book/image/us.gif?

Section 16.10 Playing Audio

16.14 What types of audio files are used in Java?

16.15 How do you create an audio clip from a file anthem/us.mid in the class directory? How do you create an audio clip from http://www.cs.armstrong.edu/liang/intro6e/book/audio/us.mid?

16.16 How do you play, repeatedly play, and stop an audio clip?

PROGRAMMING EXERCISES

Sections 16.2–16.4

16.1 (*Converting applications to applets*) Convert Listing 15.2, ButtonDemo.java, into an applet.

Sections 16.5–16.6

16.2* (*Passing strings to applets*) Rewrite Listing 16.5, DisplayMessage.java, to display a message with a standard color, font, and size. The `message`, `x`, `y`, `color`, `fontname`, and `fontsize` are parameters in the `<applet>` tag, as shown below:

```
<applet
  code = "Exercise16_2.class"
  width = 200
  height = 50
  alt = "You must have a Java-enabled browser to view the applet"
>
  <param name = MESSAGE value = "Welcome to Java" />
  <param name = X value = 40 />
  <param name = Y value = 50 />
  <param name = COLOR value = "red" />
  <param name = FONTNAME value = "Monospaced" />
  <param name = FONTSIZE value = 20 />
</applet>
```

16.3 (*Enabling applets to run standalone*) Rewrite the `LoanApplet` in Listing 16.1, LoanApplet.Java, to enable it to run as an application as well as an applet.

16.4* (*Creating multiple windows from an applet*) Write an applet that contains two buttons called *Investment Calculator* and *Loan Calculator*. When you click Investment Calculator, a frame appears in a new window for calculating future investment values. When you click *Loan Calculator*, a frame appears in a separate new window for computing loan payments (see Figure 16.18).

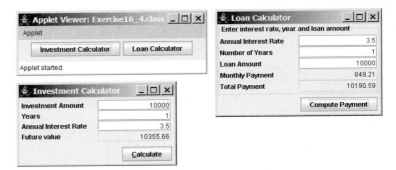

FIGURE 16.18 You can show frames in the applets.

16.5**(*A clock learning tool*) Develop a clock applet to show a first-grade student how to read a clock. Modify Exercise 13.20 to display a detailed clock with an hour hand and minute hand in an applet, as shown in Figure 16.19(a). The hour and minute values are randomly generated. The hour is between 0 and 11, and the minute is 0, 15, 30, or 45. A new random time is displayed upon a mouse click on the clock. Enable the applet to run standalone.

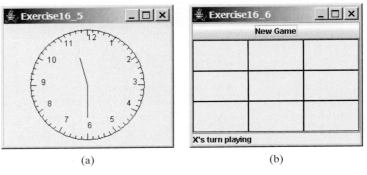

(a)   (b)

FIGURE 16.19 (a) Upon a mouse click on the clock, the clock time is randomly displayed. (b) The New Game button starts a new game.

16.6**(*TicTacToe*) Rewrite the program in Listing 16.7, TicTacToe.java, with the following modifications:

- Declare **Cell** as a separate class rather than an inner class.
- Add a button named *New Game*, as shown in Figure 16.19(b). The New Game button starts a new game.

16.7** (*Tax calculator*) Create an applet to compute tax, as shown in Figure 16.20. The applet lets the user select the tax status and enter the taxable income to compute

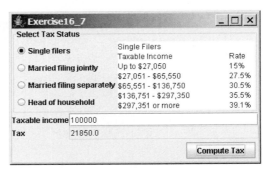

FIGURE 16.20 The tax calculator computes the tax for the specified taxable income and tax status.

the tax based on the 2001 federal tax rates, as shown in Exercise 7.14. Enable it to run standalone.

16.8* *(Creating a calculator)* Use various panels of `FlowLayout`, `GridLayout`, and `BorderLayout` to lay out the following calculator and to implement addition (+), subtraction (−), division (/), square root (sqrt), and modulus (%) functions (see Figure 16.21(a)). Enable it to run standalone.

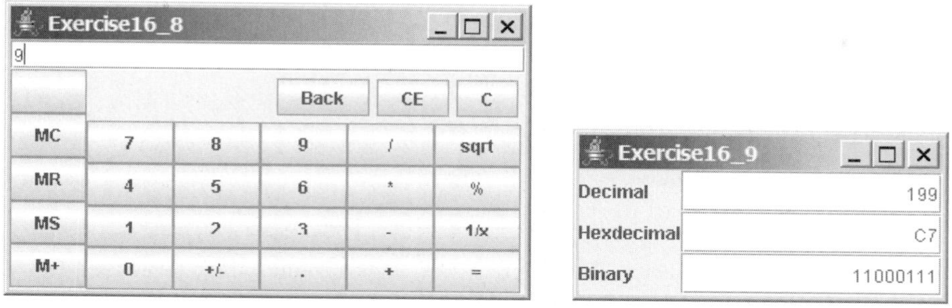

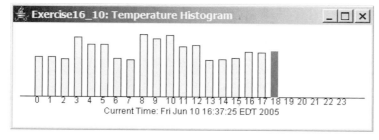

(a)   (b)

FIGURE 16.21 (a) Exercise 16.8 is a Java implementation of a popular calculator. (b) Exercise 16.9 converts between decimal, hex, and binary numbers.

16.9* *(Converting numbers)* Write an applet that converts between decimal, hex, and binary numbers, as shown in Figure 16.21(b). When you enter a decimal value on the decimal value text field and press the Enter key, its corresponding hex and binary numbers are displayed in the other two text fields. Likewise, you can enter values in the other fields and convert them accordingly. Enable it to run standalone.

16.10* *(Repainting a partial area)* When you repaint the entire viewing area of a panel, sometimes only a tiny portion of the viewing area is changed. You can improve the performance by only repainting the affected area, but do not invoke `super.paintComponent(g)` when repainting the panel, because this will cause the entire viewing area to be cleared. Use this approach to write an applet to display the temperatures of each hour during the last twenty-four hours in a histogram. Suppose that the temperatures between 50 and 90 degrees Fahrenheit are obtained randomly and are updated every hour. The temperature of the current hour needs to be redisplayed, while the others remain unchanged. Use a unique color to highlight the temperature for the current hour (see Figure 16.22).

FIGURE 16.22 The histogram displays the average temperature of every hour in the last twenty-four hours.

16.11* *(Showing a running fan)* Write a Java applet that simulates a running fan, as shown in Figure 16.23. The buttons Start, Stop, and Reverse control the fan.

The scrollbar controls the fan's speed. Create a class named **Fan**, a subclass of **JPanel**, to display the fan. This class also contains the methods to suspend and resume the fan, set its speed, and reverse its direction. Create a class named **FanControl** that contains a fan, and three buttons and a scroll bar to control the fan. Create a Java applet that contains an instance of **FanControl**. Enable the applet to run standalone.

FIGURE 16.23 The program simulates a running fan.

16.12**(*Controlling a group of fans*) Write a Java applet that displays three fans in a group, with control buttons to start and stop all of them, as shown in Figure 16.24. Use the **FanControl** to control and display a single fan. Enable the applet to run standalone.

FIGURE 16.24 The program runs and controls a group of fans.

16.13***(*Creating an elevator simulator*) Write an applet that simulates an elevator going up and down (see Figure 16.25). The buttons on the left indicate the floor where the passenger is now located. The passenger must click a button on the left to request that the elevator come to his or her floor. On entering the elevator, the passenger clicks a button on the right to request that it go to the specified floor. Enable the applet to run standalone.

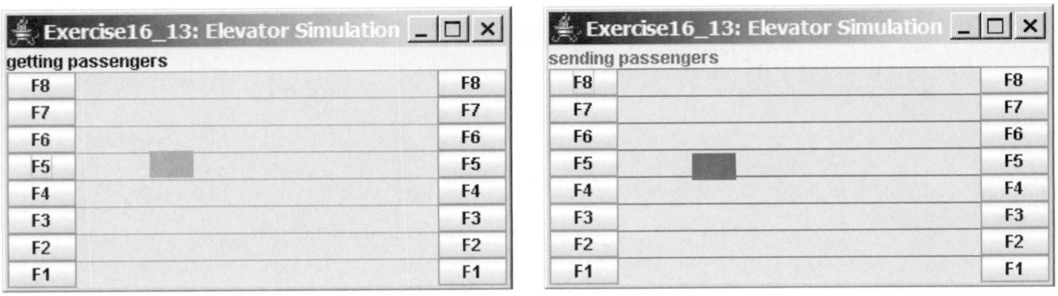

FIGURE 16.25 The program simulates elevator operations.

16.14* (*Controlling a group of clocks*) Write a Java applet that displays three clocks in a group, with control buttons to start and stop all of them, as shown in Figure 16.26. Use the `ClockControl` to control and display a single clock. Enable the applet to run standalone.

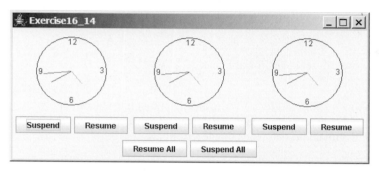

FIGURE 16.26   Three clocks run independently with individual control and group control.

Section 16.9 Displaying Images

16.15* (*Enlarging and shrinking an image*) Write an applet that will display a sequence of images from a single image file in different sizes. Initially, the viewing area for this image has a width of 300 and a height of 300. Your program should continuously shrink the viewing area by 1 in width and 1 in height until it reaches a width of 50 and a height of 50. At that point, the viewing area should continuously enlarge by 1 in width and 1 in height until it reaches a width of 300 and a height of 300. The viewing area should shrink and enlarge (alternately) to create animation for the single image. Enable the applet to run standalone.

16.16*** (*Simulating a stock ticker*) Write a Java applet that displays a stock index ticker (see Figure 16.27). The stock index information is passed from the `<param>` tag in the HTML file. Each index has four parameters: Index Name (e.g., S&P 500), Current Time (e.g., 15:54), the index from the previous day (e.g., 919.01), and Change (e.g., 4.54). Enable the applet to run standalone.

FIGURE 16.27   The program displays a stock index ticker.

Use at least five indexes, such as Dow Jones, S&P 500, NASDAQ, NIKKEI, and Gold & Silver Index. Display positive changes in green, and negative changes in red. The indexes move from right to left in the applet's viewing area. The applet freezes the ticker when the mouse button is pressed; it moves again when the mouse button is released.

16.17** (*Racing cars*) Write an applet that simulates four cars racing, as shown in Figure 16.28. You can set the speed for each car with 1 the highest.

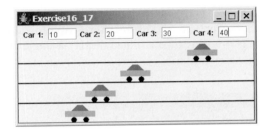

FIGURE 16.28 You can set speed for each car.

16.18**(*Showing national flags*) Write an applet that introduces national flags, one after the other, by presenting each one's image, name, and description (see Figure 16.29) along with audio that reads the description.

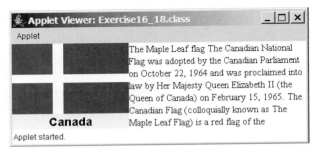

FIGURE 16.29 This applet shows each country's flag, name, and description, one after another, and reads the description that is currently shown.

Suppose your applet displays the flags of eight countries. Assume that the photo image files, named flag0.gif, flag1.gif, and so on, up to flag7.gif, are stored in a subdirectory named image in the applet's directory. The length of each audio is less than 10 seconds. Assume that the name and description of each country's flag are passed from the HTML using the parameter **name0**, **name1**, ..., **name7**, and **description0**, **description1**, ..., and **description7**. Pass the number of countries as an HTML parameter using **numberOfCountries**. Here is an example:

```
<param name="numberOfCountries" value=8>
<param name="name0" value="Canada">
<param name="description0" value=
"The Maple Leaf flag
The Canadian National Flag was adopted by the Canadian
Parliament on October 22, 1964 and was proclaimed into law
by Her Majesty Queen Elizabeth II (the Queen of Canada) on
February 15, 1965. The Canadian Flag (colloquially known
as The Maple Leaf Flag) is a red flag of the proportions
two by length and one by width, containing in its center a
white square, with a single red stylized eleven-point
mapleleaf centered in the white square.">
```

Hint

Use the **DescriptionPanel** class to display the image, name, and the text. The **DescriptionPanel** class was introduced in Listing 15.6, TextAreaDemo.java.

16.19*** (*Bouncing balls*) The example in §16.8 simulates a bouncing ball. Extend the example to allow multiple balls, as shown in Figure 16.30. You may use the +*1* or −*1* button to increase or decrease the number of the balls, and use the *Suspend* and *Resume* buttons to freeze the balls or resume bouncing.

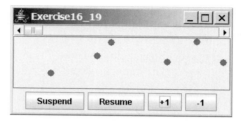

FIGURE 16.30   The applet allows you to add or remove bouncing balls.

Section 16.12 Playing Audio

16.20* (*Playing, looping, and stopping a sound clip*) Write an applet that meets the following requirements:

- Get an audio file. The file is in the class directory.
- Place three buttons labeled Play, Loop, and Stop, as shown in Figure 16.31.
- If you click the Play button, the audio file is played once. If you click the Loop button, the audio file keeps playing repeatedly. If you click the Stop button, the playing stops.
- The applet can run as an application.

FIGURE 16.31   Click Play to play an audio clip once, click Loop to play an audio repeatedly, and click Stop to terminate playing.

16.21** (*Creating an alarm clock*) Write an applet that will display a digital clock with a large display panel that shows hour, minute, and second. This clock should allow the user to set an alarm. Figure 16.32(a) shows an example of such a clock. To turn on the alarm, check the Alarm check box. To specify the alarm time, click the "Set alarm" button to display a new frame, as shown in Figure 16.32(b). You can set the alarm time in the frame. Enable the applet to run standalone.

   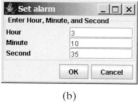

(a)   (b)

FIGURE 16.32   The program displays current hour, minute, and second, and enables you to set an alarm.

16.22**(*Creating an image animator with audio*) Create animation using the applet (see Figure 16.33) to meet the following requirements:

■ Allow the user to specify the animation speed. The user can enter the speed in a text field.

■ Get the number of frames and the image filename prefix from the user. For example, if the user enters **n** for the number of frames and **L** for the image prefix, then the files are **L1**, **L2**, and so on, to **Ln**. Assume that the images are stored in the **image** directory, a subdirectory of the applet's directory.

■ Allow the user to specify an audio filename. The audio file is stored in the same directory as the applet. The sound is played while the animation runs.

■ Enable the applet to run standalone.

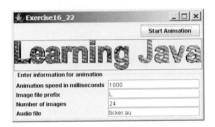

FIGURE 16.33 This applet lets the user select image files, audio file, and animation speed.

16.23**(*Raising flag and playing anthem*) Create an applet that displays a flag rising up, as shown in Figure 14.20. As the national flag rises, play the national anthem. (You may use a flag image and anthem audio file from Listing 16.13.)

PART 4

EXCEPTION HANDLING, I/O, AND RECURSION

This part introduces the use of exception handling and assertions to make your programs robust and correct, the use of input and output to manage and process a large quantity of binary data, and the use of recursion to write methods for solving inherently recursive problems.

Prerequisites for Part 4

flexible ordering

All the chapters after Chapter 17 are designed to minimize dependencies so that they can be reordered flexibly.

Chapter 17, "Exceptions and Assertions," can be covered after Chapter 9, "Inheritance and Polymorphism." Chapter 18, "Binary I/O," is usually covered after Chapter 17.

Chapter 19

The concept of recursion and how to write simple recursive programs in §§19.1–19.3 can be covered after Chapter 6, "Arrays."

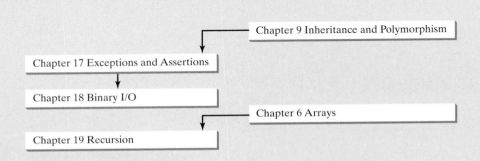

EXCEPTIONS AND ASSERTIONS

Objectives

- To understand exceptions and exception handling (§§17.2–17.3).
- To distinguish exception types: `Error` (fatal) vs. `Exception` (non-fatal), and checked vs. unchecked (§17.3).
- To declare exceptions in a method header (§17.4.1).
- To throw exceptions in a method (§17.4.2).
- To write a `try-catch` block to handle exceptions (§17.4.3).
- To explain how an exception is propagated (§17.4.3).
- To use the `finally` clause in a `try-catch` block (§17.5).
- To know when to use exceptions (§17.6).
- To rethrow exceptions in a `try-catch` block (§17.7).
- To create chained exceptions (§17.8).
- (Optional) To declare custom exception classes (§17.9).
- (Optional) To apply assertions to help ensure program correctness (§17.10).

17.1 Introduction

Three categories of errors (syntax errors, runtime errors, and logic errors) were introduced in §2.15, "Programming Errors." *Syntax errors* arise because the rules of the language have not been followed. They are detected by the compiler. *Runtime errors* occur while the program is running if the environment detects an operation that is impossible to carry out. *Logic errors* occur when a program doesn't perform the way it was intended to. In general, syntax errors are easy to find and easy to correct because the compiler indicates where they came from and why they occurred. You can use the debugging techniques introduced in §2.16, "Debugging," to find logic errors. This chapter introduces using exception handling to deal with runtime errors and using assertions to help ensure program correctness.

17.2 Exception-Handling Overview

An exception is a runtime error. A program that does not provide code for *catching* and *handling* exceptions will terminate abnormally, and may cause serious problems. For example, if your program attempts to transfer money from a savings account to a checking account, but because of a runtime error is terminated *after* the money is drawn from the savings account and *before* the money is deposited in the checking account, the customer will lose money.

Exceptions occur for various reasons. The user may enter an invalid input, for example, or the program may attempt to open a file that doesn't exist, or the network connection may hang up, or the program may attempt to access an out-of-bounds array element.

You have already been briefly introduced to exceptions in earlier chapters. In Chapter 6, "Arrays," you learned that an `ArrayIndexOutOfBoundsException` occurs if you access an element past the end of an array. In Chapter 7, "Objects and Classes," you learned that a `NullPointerException` occurs when you invoke a method on a reference variable with `null` value. In Chapter 8, "Strings and Text I/O," you learned that a `StringIndexOutOfBoundsException` occurs when you access a character in a string using an out-of-bound index. You also learned that text I/O operations may throw exceptions.

When an exception occurs, the normal execution flow of the program will be interrupted. Java provides programmers with the capability to handle runtime exceptions. With this capability, referred to as *exception handling*, you can develop robust programs for mission-critical computing.

exception handling

Here is an example. The program in Listing 17.1 terminates abnormally if you enter a floating-point value instead of an integer, as shown in Figure 17.1.

LISTING 17.1 ExceptionDemo.java

```
1  import java.util.Scanner;
2
3  public class ExceptionDemo {
4    public static void main(String[] args) {
5      Scanner scanner = new Scanner(System.in);
6      System.out.print("Enter an integer: ");
7      int number = scanner.nextInt();
8
9      // Display the result
10     System.out.println(
11       "The number entered is " + number);
12    }
13  }
```

If an exception occurs on this line, the rest of the lines in the method are skipped and the program is terminated.

Terminated.

Stack trace →

```
Command Prompt                                          _ □ X
C:\book>java ExceptionDemo
Enter an integer: 3.5
Exception in thread "main" java.util.InputMismatchException
        at java.util.Scanner.throwFor(Scanner.java:819)
        at java.util.Scanner.next(Scanner.java:1431)
        at java.util.Scanner.nextInt(Scanner.java:2040)
        at java.util.Scanner.nextInt(Scanner.java:2000)
        at ExceptionDemo.main(ExceptionDemo.java:7)

C:\book>
```

FIGURE 17.1   An exception occurs when you enter an invalid input.

Note that several lines of information are displayed in Figure 17.1 in response to this invalid input. This information, known as the *stack trace*, includes the name of the exception (`java.util.InputMismatchException`) followed by the method call stack at the time the exception occurred. The stack trace helps in debugging a program. Starting from the last line of the stack trace, you see that the exception was detected in line 7 of the `main` method. Each line of the stack trace contains the class name and method (`ExceptionDemo.main`) along with the file name and line number (`ExceptionDemo.java: 7`). Moving up the stack trace, you see that the exception occurred in line 2000 in the `nextInt` method of the `Scanner` class, the exception occurred in line 2040 in the overloaded `nextInt` method of the `Scanner` class, the exception occurred in line 1431 in the `next` method of the `Scanner` class, the exception occurred in line 819 in the `throwFor` method of the `Scanner` class. The last method in the call chain actually threw an `InputMismatchException`.

Java allows the program to catch and process exceptions. You can revise Listing 17.1 to handle the `InputMismatchException` using a new construct called the **try-catch** *block*, as shown in Listing 17.2.

stack trace

try-catch block

LISTING 17.2   HandleExceptionDemo.java

```
 1   import java.util.*;
 2
 3   public class HandleExceptionDemo {
 4     public static void main(String[] args) {
 5       Scanner scanner = new Scanner(System.in);
 6       boolean continueInput = true;
 7
 8       do {
 9         try{
10           System.out.print("Enter an integer: ");
11           int number = scanner.nextInt();
12
13           // Display the result
14           System.out.println(
15             "The number entered is " + number);
16
17           continueInput = false;
18         }
19         catch (InputMismatchException ex) {
20           System.out.println("Try again. (" +
21             "Incorrect input: an integer is required)");
22           scanner.nextLine(); // discard input
23         }
24       } while (continueInput);
25     }
```

If an exception occurs on this line, the rest of lines in the try block are skipped and the control is transferred to the catch block.

A `try` block begins with the keyword `try` followed by a block of statements in curly braces (`{}`). A `try` block contains the statements that might throw exceptions. A `catch` block begins with the keyword `catch` followed by an exception parameter in parentheses and a block of statements for handling the exception in curly braces. When a statement in a `try` block throws an exception, the rest of the statements in the `try` block are skipped and control is transferred to the `catch` block.

Suppose you enter `3.5` when executing line 11, as shown in Figure 17.2. An `InputMismatchException` occurs and the control is transferred to the `catch` block. The statements in the `catch` block are now executed. The statement `scanner.nextLine()` in line 22 discards the current input line so that the user can enter a new line of input. The variable `continueInput` controls the loop. Its initial value is `true` (line 6), and it is changed to `false` (line 17) when a valid input is received.

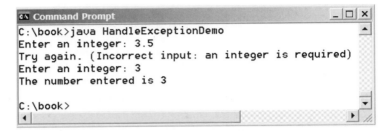

FIGURE 17.2 An exception is caught and handled in the program.

17.3 Exceptions and Exception Types

A Java exception is an instance of a class derived from `Throwable`. The `Throwable` class is contained in the `java.lang` package, and subclasses of `Throwable` are contained in various packages. Errors related to GUI components are included in the `java.awt` package; numeric exceptions are included in the `java.lang` package because they are related to the `java.lang.Number` class. You can create your own exception classes by extending `Throwable` or a subclass of `Throwable`. Figure 17.3 shows some of Java's predefined exception classes.

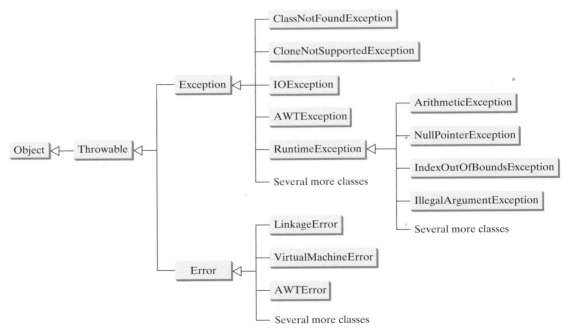

FIGURE 17.3 Exceptions thrown are instances of the classes shown in this diagram, or of subclasses of one of these classes.

Note

The class names `Error`, `Exception`, and `RuntimeException` are somewhat confusing. All three of these classes are exceptions, and all of the errors discussed here occur at runtime.

The exception classes can be classified into three major types: system errors, exceptions, and runtime exceptions.

■ *System errors* are thrown by the JVM and represented in the `Error` class. The `Error` class describes internal system errors. Such errors rarely occur. If one does, there is little you can do beyond notifying the user and trying to terminate the program gracefully. Examples of subclasses of `Error` are listed in Table 17.1.

system error

TABLE 17.1   Examples of Subclasses of `Error`

Class	Possible Reason for Exception
`LinkageError`	A class has some dependency on another class, but the latter class has changed incompatibly after the compilation of the former class.
`VirtualMachineError`	The JVM is broken or has run out of the resources necessary for it to continue operating.
`AWTError`	A fatal error in the GUI runtime system.
`AssertionError`	An assertion has failed. Assertions will be introduced in §17.8, "Assertions."

■ *Exceptions* are represented in the `Exception` class, which describes errors caused by your program and by external circumstances. These errors can be caught and handled by your program. Examples of subclasses of `Exception` are listed in Table 17.2.

exception

TABLE 17.2   Examples of Subclasses of `Exception`

Class	Possible Reason for Exception
`ClassNotFoundException`	Attempt to use a class that does not exist. This exception would occur, for example, if you tried to run a nonexistent class using the **java** command, or if your program was composed of, say, three class files, only two of which could be found.
`CloneNotSupported Exception`	Attempt to clone an object whose defining class does not implement the `Cloneable` interface. Cloning objects were introduced in Chapter 10, "Abstract Classes and Interfaces."
`IOException`	Related to input/output operations, such as invalid input, reading past the end of a file, and opening a nonexistent file. Examples of subclasses of `IOException` are `InterruptedIOException`, `EOFException` (EOF is short for End Of File), and `FileNotFound Exception`.
`AWTException`	Exceptions in GUI components.

■ *Runtime exceptions* are represented in the `RuntimeException` class, which describes programming errors, such as bad casting, accessing an out-of-bounds array, and numeric errors. Runtime exceptions are generally thrown by the JVM. Examples of subclasses are listed in Table 17.3.

runtime exception

TABLE 17.3 Examples of Subclasses of `RuntimeException`

Class	Possible Reason for Exception
ArithmeticException	Dividing an integer by zero. Note that floating-point arithmetic does not throw exceptions. See Appendix E, "Special Floating-Point Values."
NullPointerException	Attempt to access an object through a `null` reference variable.
IndexOutOfBoundsException	Index to an array is out of range.
IllegalArgumentException	A method is passed an argument that is illegal or inappropriate.

unchecked exception
checked exception

`RuntimeException`, `Error`, and their subclasses are known as *unchecked exceptions*. All other exceptions are known as *checked exceptions*, meaning that the compiler forces the programmer to check and deal with them.

In most cases, unchecked exceptions reflect programming logic errors that are not recoverable. For example, a `NullPointerException` is thrown if you access an object through a reference variable before an object is assigned to it; an `IndexOutOfBoundsException` is thrown if you access an element in an array outside the bounds of the array. These are logic errors that should be corrected in the program. Unchecked exceptions can occur anywhere in a program. To avoid cumbersome overuse of `try-catch` blocks, Java does not mandate that you write code to catch or declare unchecked exceptions.

Caution

integer overflow

At present, Java does not throw *integer overflow* exceptions. The following statement adds 1 to the maximum integer.

```
int number = Integer.MAX_VALUE + 1;
System.out.println(number);
```

It displays −2147483648, which is logically incorrect. The cause of this problem is overflow, that is, the result exceeds the maximum for an `int` value.

A future version of Java may fix this problem by throwing an overflow exception.

Tip

BigInteger

For processing large integral values, use the `BigInteger` class, introduced in §10.5.6, "`BigInteger` and `BigDecimal` Classes."

17.4 Understanding Exception Handling

Java's exception-handling model is based on three operations: *declaring an exception*, *throwing an exception*, and *catching an exception*, as shown in Figure 17.4.

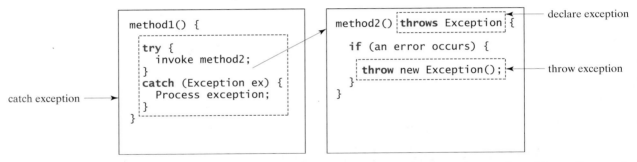

FIGURE 17.4 Exception handling in Java consists of declaring exceptions, throwing exceptions, and catching and processing exceptions.

17.4.1 Declaring Exceptions

In Java, the statement currently being executed belongs to a method. The Java interpreter invokes the **main** method for a Java application, and the Web browser invokes the applet's no-arg constructor and then the **init** method for a Java applet. Every method must state the types of checked exceptions it might throw. This is known as *declaring exceptions*. Because system errors and runtime errors can happen to any code, Java does not require that you declare **Error** and **RuntimeException** (unchecked exceptions) explicitly in the method. However, all other exceptions thrown by the method must be explicitly declared in the method declaration so that the caller of the method is informed of the exception.

declare exception

To declare an exception in a method, use the **throws** keyword in the method declaration, as in this example:

```
public void myMethod() throws IOException
```

The **throws** keyword indicates that **myMethod** might throw an **IOException**. If the method might throw multiple exceptions, add a list of the exceptions, separated by commas, after **throws**:

```
public void myMethod()
    throws Exception1, Exception2, ..., ExceptionN
```

Note

If a method does not declare exceptions in the superclass, you cannot override it to declare exceptions in the subclass.

17.4.2 Throwing Exceptions

A program that detects an error can create an instance of an appropriate exception type and throw it. This is known as *throwing an exception*. Here is an example: Suppose the program detected that an argument passed to the method violates the method contract (e.g., the argument must be non-negative, but a negative argument is passed); the program can create an instance of **IllegalArgumentException** and throw it, as follows:

throw exception

```
IllegalArgumentException ex =
    new IllegalArgumentException("Wrong Argument");
throw ex;
```

Or if you prefer, you can use the following:

```
throw new IllegalArgumentException("Wrong Argument");
```

Note

IllegalArgumentException is an exception class in the Java API. In general, each exception class in the Java API has at least two constructors: a no-arg constructor, and a constructor with a **String** argument that describes the exception. This argument is called the *exception message*, which can be obtained using **getMessage()**.

exception message

Tip

The keyword to declare an exception is **throws**, and the keyword to throw an exception is **throw**.

throws and **throw**

17.4.3 Catching Exceptions

You now know how to declare an exception and how to throw an exception. When an exception is thrown, it can be caught and handled in a **try-catch** block, as follows:

catch exception

```
try {
  statements;   // Statements that may throw exceptions
}
```

```
      catch (Exception1 exVar1) {
        handler for exception1;
      }
      catch (Exception2 exVar2) {
        handler for exception2;
      }
      ...
      catch (ExceptionN exVar3) {
        handler for exceptionN;
      }
```

If no exceptions arise during the execution of the **try** block, the **catch** blocks are skipped.

If one of the statements inside the **try** block throws an exception, Java skips the remaining statements in the **try** block and starts the process of finding the code to handle the exception. The code that handles the exception is called the *exception handler*; it is found by propagating the exception backward through a chain of method calls, starting from the current method. Each **catch** block is examined in turn, from first to last, to see whether the type of the exception object is an instance of the exception class in the **catch** block. If so, the exception object is assigned to the variable declared and the code in the **catch** block is executed. If no handler is found, Java exits this method, passes the exception to the method that invoked the method, and continues the same process to find a handler. If no handler is found in the chain of methods being invoked, the program terminates and prints an error message on the console. The process of finding a handler is called *catching an exception*.

exception handler

Suppose the **main** method invokes **method1**, **method1** invokes **method2**, **method2** invokes **method3**, and an exception occurs in **method3**, as shown in Figure 17.5. Consider the following scenario:

- If **method3** cannot handle the exception, **method3** is aborted and the control is returned to **method2**. If the exception type is **Exception3**, it is caught by the **catch** block for handling exception **ex3** in **method2**. **statement5** is skipped, and **statement6** is executed.

- If the exception type is **Exception2**, **method2** is aborted, the control is returned to **method1**, and the exception is caught by the **catch** block for handling exception **ex2** in **method1**. **statement3** is skipped, and **statement4** is executed.

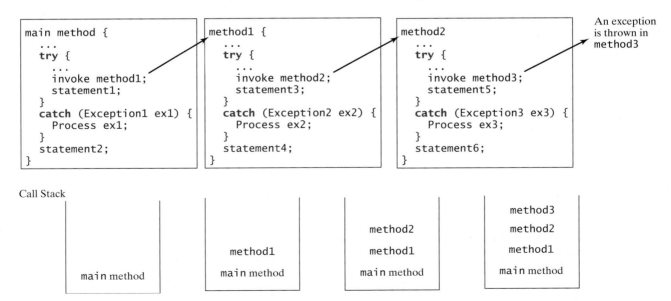

FIGURE 17.5 If an exception is not caught in the current method, it is passed to its caller. The process is repeated until the exception is caught or passed to the **main** method.

- If the exception type is `Exception1`, `method1` is aborted, the control is returned to the `main` method, and the exception is caught by the `catch` block for handling exception `ex1` in the `main` method. `statement1` is skipped, and `statement2` is executed.

- If the exception type is not `Exception1`, `Exception2`, or `Exception3`, the exception is not caught and the program terminates. `statement1` and `statement2` are not executed.

Note

Various exception classes can be derived from a common superclass. If a `catch` block catches exception objects of a superclass, it can catch all the exception objects of the subclasses of that superclass.

catch block

Note

The order in which exceptions are specified in `catch` blocks is important. A compilation error will result if a `catch` block for a superclass type appears before a `catch` block for a subclass type. For example, the ordering in (a) is erroneous, because `RuntimeException` is a subclass of `Exception`. The correct ordering should be as shown in (b).

order of exception handlers

```
try {
    ...
}
catch (Exception ex) {
    ...
}
catch (RuntimeException ex) {
    ...
}
```
(a) Wrong order

```
try {
    ...
}
catch (RuntimeException ex) {
    ...
}
catch (Exception ex) {
    ...
}
```
(b) Correct order

Note

Java forces you to deal with checked exceptions. If a method declares a checked exception (i.e., an exception other than `Error` or `RuntimeException`), you must invoke it in a `try-catch` block or declare to throw the exception in the calling method. For example, suppose that method `p1` invokes method `p2`, and `p2` may throw a checked exception (e.g., `IOException`), you have to write the code as shown in (a) or (b).

catch or declare checked exceptions

```
void p1() {
    try {
        p2();
    }
    catch (IOException ex) {
        ...
    }
}
```
(a) catch exception

```
void p1() throws IOException {

    p2();

}
```
(b) throw exception

17.4.4 Getting Information from Exceptions

An exception object contains valuable information about the exception. You may use the following instance methods in the `java.lang.Throwable` class to get information regarding the exception, as shown in Figure 17.6. The `printStackTrace()` method prints stack trace information on the console. The `getStackTrace()` method provides programmatic access to the stack trace information printed by `printStackTrace()`.

methods in **Throwable**

java.lang.Throwable	
+getMessage(): String	Returns the message of this object.
+toString(): String	Returns the concatenation of three strings: (1) the full name of the exception class; (2) ":" (a colon and a space); (3) the getMessage() method.
+printStackTrace(): void	Prints the Throwable object and its call stack trace information on the console.
+getStackTrace(): StackTraceElement[]	Returns an array of stack trace elements representing the stack trace pertaining to this throwable.

FIGURE 17.6 `Throwable` is the root class for all exception objects.

Listing 17.3 gives an example that uses the methods in `Throwable` to display exception information. Line 4 invokes the sum method to return the sum of all the elements in the array. There is an error in line 23 that causes the `ArrayIndexOutOfBoundsException`, a subclass of `IndexOutOfBoundsException`. This exception is caught in the `try-catch` block. Lines 7, 8, 9 display the stack trace, exception message, and exception object and message using the `printStackTrace()`, `getMessage()`, and `toString()` methods, as shown in Figure 17.7. Line 12 obtains stack trace elements into an array. Each element represents a method call. You can obtain the method (line 14), class name (line 15), and exception line number (line 16) for each element.

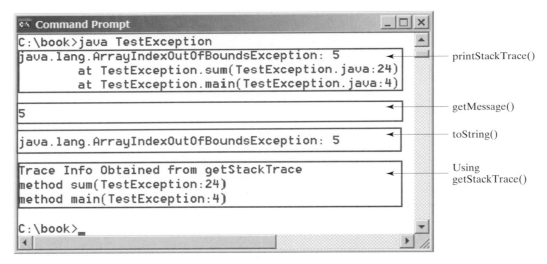

FIGURE 17.7 You can use the `printStackTrace()`, `getMessage()`, `toString()`, and `getStackTrace()` methods to obtain information from exception objects.

LISTING 17.3 TestException.java

```
1 public class TestException {
2   public static void main(String[] args) {
3     try {
4       System.out.println(sum(new int[] {1, 2, 3, 4, 5}));
5     }
6     catch (Exception ex) {
7       ex.printStackTrace();
8       System.out.println("\n" + ex.getMessage());
9       System.out.println("\n" + ex.toString());
10
11      System.out.println("\nTrace Info Obtained from getStackTrace");
12      StackTraceElement[] traceElements = ex.getStackTrace();
```

invoke sum

printStackTrace()
getMessage()
toString()

```
13          for (int i = 0; i < traceElements.length; i++) {
14            System.out.print("method " + traceElements[i].getMethodName());
15            System.out.print("(" + traceElements[i].getClassName() + ":");    error
16            System.out.println(traceElements[i].getLineNumber() + ")");
17          }
18        }
19      }
20
21      private static int sum(int[] list) {
22        int result = 0;
23        for (int i = 0; i <= list.length; i++)
24          result += list[i];
25        return result;
26      }
27    }
```

17.4.5 Example: Declaring, Throwing, and Catching Exceptions

This example demonstrates declaring, throwing, and catching exceptions by modifying the
setRadius method in the Circle2 class in Listing 7.3. The new setRadius method throws
an exception if the radius is negative.

Rename the circle class given in Listing 17.4 as CircleWithException, which is the
same as Circle2 except that the setRadius(double newRadius) method throws an
IllegalArgumentException if the argument newRadius is negative.

LISTING 17.4 CircleWithException.java

```
1 public class CircleWithException {
2   /** The radius of the circle */
3   private double radius;
4
5   /** The number of the objects created */
6   private static int numberOfObjects = 0;
7
8   /** Construct a circle with radius 1 */
9   public CircleWithException() {
10    this(1.0);
11  }
12
13  /** Construct a circle with a specified radius */
14  public CircleWithException(double newRadius) {
15    setRadius(newRadius);
16    numberOfObjects++;
17  }
18
19  /** Return radius */
20  public double getRadius() {
21    return radius;
22  }
23
24  /** Set a new radius */
25  public void setRadius(double newRadius)
26      throws IllegalArgumentException {                          declare exception
27    if (newRadius >= 0)
28      radius = newRadius;
29    else
30      throw new IllegalArgumentException(                        throw exception
```

```
31              "Radius cannot be negative");
32    }
33
34    /** Return numberOfObjects */
35    public static int getNumberOfObjects() {
36      return numberOfObjects;
37    }
38
39    /** Return the area of this circle */
40    public double findArea() {
41      return radius * radius * 3.14159;
42    }
43 }
```

A test program that uses the new `Circle` class is given in Listing 17.5. Figure 17.8 shows a sample run of the test program.

FIGURE 17.8 The exception is thrown when the radius is negative.

LISTING 17.5 TestCircleWithException.java

```
1 public class TestCircleWithException {
2    /** Main method */
3    public static void main(String[] args) {
4      try {
5        CircleWithException c1 = new CircleWithException(5);
6        CircleWithException c2 = new CircleWithException(-5);
7        CircleWithException c3 = new CircleWithException(0);
8      }
9      catch (IllegalArgumentException ex) {
10       System.out.println(ex);
11     }
12
13     System.out.println("Number of objects created: " +
14       CircleWithException.getNumberOfObjects());
15   }
16 }
```

try

catch

The original `Circle2` class remains intact except that the class name is changed to `CircleWithException`, a new constructor `CircleWithException(newRadius)` is added, and the `setRadius` method now declares an exception and throws it if the radius is negative.

The `setRadius` method declares to throw `IllegalArgumentException` in the method declaration (lines 25–26 in CircleWithException.java). The `CircleWithException` class would still compile if the `throws IllegalArgumentException` clause were removed from the method declaration, since it is a subclass of `RuntimeException` and every method can throw `RuntimeException` (unchecked exception) regardless of whether it is declared in the method header.

The test program creates three `CircleWithException` objects, `c1`, `c2`, and `c3`, to test how to handle exceptions. Invoking `new CircleWithException(-5)` (line 6 in Listing 17.5) causes the setRadius method to be invoked, which throws an IllegalArgumentException, because the radius is negative. In the catch block, the type of the object ex is IllegalArgumentException, which matches the exception object thrown by the setRadius method. So this exception is caught by the catch block.

The exception handler prints a short message, ex.toString() (line 10), about the exception, using System.out.println(ex).

Note that the execution continues in the event of the exception. If the handlers had not caught the exception, the program would have abruptly terminated.

The test program would still compile if the try statement were not used, because the method throws an instance of IllegalArgumentException, a subclass of RuntimeException (unchecked exception). If a method throws an exception other than RuntimeException and Error, the method must be invoked within a try-catch block.

Note

As you will learn in Chapter 24, "Multithreading" Java supports multithreading. One program can have many threads. Methods are executed on threads. If an exception occurs on a thread, the thread is terminated if the exception is not caught. If a program has only one thread, an uncaught exception will cause the program to terminate. If a program has *multiple threads*, an uncaught exception will terminate only the thread where the exception occurred. However, since certain threads may rely on the terminated thread, terminating a thread may affect the rest of the program.

multiple threads

17.5 The **finally** Clause

Occasionally, you may want some code to be executed regardless of whether an exception occurs or is caught. Java has a finally clause that can be used to accomplish this objective. The syntax for the finally clause might look like this:

```
try {
  statements;
}
catch (TheException ex) {
  handling ex;
}
finally {
  finalStatements;
}
```

The code in the finally block is executed under all circumstances, regardless of whether an exception occurs in the try block or is caught. Consider three possible cases:

- If no exception arises in the try block, finalStatements is executed, and the next statement after the try statement is executed.

- If one of the statements causes an exception in the try block that is caught in a catch block, the other statements in the try block are skipped, the catch block is executed, and the finally clause is executed. If the catch block does not rethrow an exception, the next statement after the try statement is executed. If it does, the exception is passed to the caller of this method.

- If one of the statements causes an exception that is not caught in any catch block, the other statements in the try block are skipped, the finally clause is executed, and the exception is passed to the caller of this method.

- The finally block executes even if there is a return statement prior to reaching the finally block.

omitting **catch** block

Note

The **catch** block may be omitted when the **finally** clause is used.

A common use of the **finally** clause is in I/O programming. To ensure that a file is closed under all circumstances, you may place a file closing statement in the **finally** block, as shown in Listing 17.6.

LISTING 17.6   FinallyDemo.java

```
 1 public class FinallyDemo {
 2   public static void main(String[] args) {
 3     java.io.PrintWriter output = null;
 4
 5     try {
 6       // Create a file
 7       output = new java.io.Printwriter("text.txt");
 8
 9       // Write formatted output to the file
10       output.println("Welcome to Java");
11     }
12     catch (java.io.IOException ex) {
13       ex.printStackTrace();
14     }
15     finally {
16       // Close the file
17       if (output != null) output.close();
18     }
19   }
20 }
```

try

catch

finally

The statements in lines 7 and 10 may throw an **IOException**, so they are placed inside a **try** block. The statement **output.close()** closes the **PrintWriter** object output in the **finally** block. This statement is executed regardless of whether an exception occurs in the **try** block or is caught.

17.6 When to Use Exceptions

The **try** block contains the code that are executed in normal circumstances. The **catch** block contains the code that are executed in exceptional circumstances. Exception handling separates error-handling code from normal programming tasks, thus making programs easier to read and to modify. Be aware, however, that exception handling usually requires more time and resources because it requires instantiating a new exception object, rolling back the call stack, and propagating the exception through the chain of methods invoked to search for the handler.

An exception occurs in a method. If you want the exception to be processed by its caller, you should create an exception object and throw it. If you can handle the exception in the method where it occurs, there is no need to throw or use exceptions.

In general, common exceptions that may occur in multiple classes in a project are candidates for exception classes. Simple errors that may occur in individual methods are best handled locally without throwing exceptions.

When should you use a **try-catch** block in the code? Use it when you have to deal with unexpected error conditions. Do not use a **try-catch** block to deal with simple, expected situations. For example, the following code

```
try {
  System.out.println(refVar.toString());
}
```

```
  catch (NullPointerException ex) {
    System.out.println("refVar is null");
  }
```

is better replaced by

```
  if (refVar != null)
    System.out.println(refVar.toString());
  else
    System.out.println("refVar is null");
```

Which situations are exceptional and which are expected is sometimes difficult to decide. The point is not to abuse exception handling as a way to deal with a simple logic test.

17.7 Rethrowing Exceptions

Java allows an exception handler to rethrow the exception if the handler cannot process the exception or the handler simply wants to let its caller be notified of the exception. The syntax may look like this:

```
  try {
    statements;
  }
  catch (TheException ex) {
    perform operations before exits;
    throw ex;
  }
```

The statement **throw ex** rethrows the exception so that other handlers get a chance to process the exception **ex**.

17.8 (Optional) Chained Exceptions

In the preceding section, the **catch** block rethrows the original exception. Sometimes, you may need to throw a new exception (with additional information) along with the original exception. This is called *chained exceptions*. Listing 17.7 gives an example that demonstrates how to create and throw chained exceptions.

LISTING 17.7 ChainedExceptionDemo.java

```
 1 public class ChainedExceptionDemo {
 2   public static void main(String[] args) {
 3     try {
 4       method1();
 5     }
 6     catch (Exception ex) {
 7       ex.printStackTrace();                              stack trace
 8     }
 9   }
10
11   public static void method1() throws Exception {
12     try {
13         method2();
14     }
15     catch (Exception ex) {
16       throw new Exception("New info from method1", ex);  chained exception
17     }
18   }
19
20   public static void method2() throws Exception {
```

throw exception

```
21      throw new Exception("New info from method2");
22  }
23 }
```

The `main` method invokes `method1` (line 4), `method1` invokes `method2` (line 13), and `method2` throws an exception (line 21). This exception is caught in the `catch` block in `method1` and is wrapped in a new exception in line 16. The new exception is thrown and caught in the `catch` block in the `main` method in line 6. Figure 17.9 shows the output from the `printStackTrace()` method in line 7. The new exception thrown from `method1` is displayed first, followed by the original exception thrown from `method2`.

```
Command Prompt
C:\book>java ChainedExceptionDemo
java.lang.Exception: New info from method1
        at ChainedExceptionDemo.method1(ChainedExceptionDemo.java:16)
        at ChainedExceptionDemo.main(ChainedExceptionDemo.java:4)
Caused by: java.lang.Exception: New info from method2
        at ChainedExceptionDemo.method2(ChainedExceptionDemo.java:21)
        at ChainedExceptionDemo.method1(ChainedExceptionDemo.java:13)
        ... 1 more

C:\book>
```

FIGURE 17.9   The stack trace displayed the chained exceptions.

 ## 17.9 (Optional) Creating Custom Exception Classes

Java provides quite a few exception classes. Use them whenever possible instead of creating your own exception classes. However, if you run into a problem that cannot be adequately described by the predefined exception classes, you can create your own exception class, derived from `Exception` or from a subclass of `Exception`, such as `IOException`.

In Listing 17.4, CircleWithException.java, the `setRadius` method throws an exception if the radius is negative. Suppose you wish to pass the radius to the handler. In that case, you may create a custom exception class, as shown in Listing 17.8.

LISTING 17.8   InvalidRadiusException.java

```java
1 public class InvalidRadiusException extends Exception {
2   private double radius;
3
4   /** Construct an exception */
5   public InvalidRadiusException(double radius) {
6     super("Invalid radius " + radius);
7     this.radius = radius;
8   }
9
10  /** Return the radius */
11  public double getRadius() {
12    return radius;
13  }
14 }
```

This custom exception class extends `java.lang.Exception` (line 1). The `Exception` class extends `java.lang.Throwable`. All the methods (e.g., `getMessage()`, `toString()`, and `printStackTrace()`) in `Exception` are inherited from `Throwable`. The `Exception` class contains four constructors. Among them, the following two constructors are often used:

Exception constructors

■ **public** Exception() Constructs an exception with no message.

■ **public** Exception(String message) Constructs an exception with the specified message.

Line 6 invokes the superclass's constructor with a message. This message will be set in the exception object and can be obtained by invoking `getMessage()` on the object.

Tip
Most exception classes in the Java API contain two constructors: a no-arg constructor and a constructor with a message parameter.

To create an `InvalidRadiusException`, you have to pass a radius. So the `setRadius` method in Listing 17.4 can be modified as follows:

```
/** Set a new radius */
public void setRadius(double newRadius)
    throws InvalidRadiusException {
  if (newRadius >= 0)
    radius = newRadius;
  else
    throw new InvalidRadiusException(newRadius);
}
```

The following code creates a circle object and sets its radius to -5:

```
try {
  CircleWithException1 c = new CircleWithException1(4);
  c.setRadius(-5);
}
catch (InvalidRadiusException ex) {
  System.out.println("The invalid radius is " + ex.getRadius());
}
```

Invoking `setRadius(-5)` throws an `InvalidRadiusException`, which is caught by the handler. The handler displays the radius in the exception object `ex`.

Tip
Can you declare a custom exception class by extending `RuntimeException`? Yes, but it is not good, because it makes your custom exception unchecked. It is better to make a custom exception checked so that the complier can force these exceptions to be caught in your program.

checked custom exception

17.10 (Optional) Assertions

An *assertion* is a Java statement that enables you to assert an assumption about your program. An assertion contains a Boolean expression that should be true during program execution. Assertions can be used to ensure program correctness and avoid logic errors.

assertion

17.10.1   Declaring Assertions

An *assertion* is declared using the new Java keyword `assert` in JDK 1.4, as follows:

    assert *assertion*;

or

    assert *assertion* : *detailMessage*;

where *assertion* is a Boolean expression and *detailMessage* is a primitive-type or an `Object` value.

When an assertion statement is executed, Java evaluates the `assertion`. If it is `false`, an `AssertionError` will be thrown. The `AssertionError` class has a no-arg constructor and seven overloaded single-parameter constructors of type `int`, `long`, `float`, `double`, `boolean`, `char`, and `Object`. For the first `assert` statement with no detailed message, the no-arg constructor of `AssertionError` is used. For the second `assert` statement with a detailed message, an appropriate `AssertionError` constructor is used to match the data type of the message. `AssertionError` is a subclass of `Error`, so when an assertion becomes false, the program displays a message on the console and exits.

Here is an example of using assertions:

```
 1 public class AssertionDemo {
 2   public static void main(String[] args) {
 3     int i; int sum = 0;
 4     for (i = 0; i < 10; i++) {
 5       sum += i;
 6     }
 7     assert i == 10;
 8     assert sum > 10 && sum < 5 * 10 : "sum is " + sum;
 9   }
10 }
```

The statement `assert i == 10` asserts that `i` is `10` when the statement is executed. If `i` is not `10`, an `AssertionError` is thrown. The statement `assert sum > 10 && sum < 5 * 10 : "sum is " + sum` asserts that `sum > 10` and `sum < 5 * 10`. If `false`, an `AssertionError` with the message `"sum is " + sum` is thrown.

Suppose you typed `i < 100` instead of `i < 10` by mistake in line 4, the following `AssertionError` would be thrown:

```
Exception in thread "main" java.lang.AssertionError
        at AssertionDemo.main(AssertionDemo.java:7)
```

Suppose you typed `sum += 1` instead of `sum += i` by mistake in line 5, the following `AssertionError` would be thrown:

```
Exception in thread "main" java.lang.AssertionError: sum is 10
        at AssertionDemo.main(AssertionDemo.java:8)
```

17.10.2   Running Programs with Assertions

By default, assertions are disabled at runtime. To enable them, use the switch –enableassertions, or –ea for short, as follows:

java –ea AssertionDemo

Assertions can be selectively enabled or disabled at the class level or the package level. The disable switch is –disableassertions, or –da for short. For example, the following command enables assertions in package `package1` and disables assertions in class `Class1`:

java –ea:package1 –da:Class1 AssertionDemo

17.10.3   Using Exception Handling or Assertions

Assertion should not be used to replace exception handling. Exception handling deals with unusual circumstances during program execution. Assertions are intended to ensure the correctness of the program. Exception handling addresses robustness, whereas assertion addresses correctness. Like exception handling, assertions are not used for normal tests, but for internal consistency and validity checks. Assertions are checked at runtime and can be turned on or off at startup time.

Do not use assertions for argument checking in public methods. Valid arguments that may be passed to a public method are considered to be part of the method's contract. The contract must always be obeyed whether assertions are enabled or disabled. For example, the following code in (a) should be rewritten using exception handling, as shown in (b):

```
public void setRadius(double newRadius) {
  assert newRadius >= 0;
  radius = newRadius;
}
```
(a)

```
public void setRadius(double newRadius) {
  if (newRadius >= 0)
    radius = newRadius;
  else
    throw new IllegalArgumentException(
      "Radius cannot be negative");
}
```
(b)

Use assertions to reaffirm assumptions. This will increase your confidence in the program's correctness. A common use of assertions is to replace assumptions with assertions in the code. For example, the following code in (a) can be replaced by (b):

```
if (even) {
  ...
}
else { // even is false
  ...
}
```
(a)

```
if (even) {
  ...
}
else {
  assert !even;
  ...
}
```
(b)

Similarly, the following code in (a) can also be replaced by (b):

```
if (numberOfDollars > 1) {
  ...
}
else if (numberOfDollars == 1) {
  ...
}
```
(a)

```
if (numberOfDollars > 1) {
  ...
}
else if (numberOfDollars == 1) {
  ...
}
else
    assert false : numberOfDollars;
```
(b)

Another good use of assertions is to place them in a `switch` statement without a default case. For example,

```
switch (month) {
  case 1: ... ; break;
  case 2: ... ; break;
  ...
  case 12: ... ; break;
  default: assert false : "Invalid month: " + month
}
```

KEY TERMS

CHAPTER SUMMARY

■ When an exception occurs, Java creates an object that contains the information for the exception. You can use the information to handle the exception.

■ A Java exception is an instance of a class derived from `java.lang.Throwable`. Java provides a number of predefined exception classes, such as `Error`, `Exception`, `RuntimeException`, `ClassNotFoundException`, `NullPointerException`, and `ArithmeticException`. You can also define your own exception class by extending `Exception`.

■ Exceptions occur during the execution of a method. `RuntimeException` and `Error` are unchecked exceptions; all other exceptions are checked exceptions.

■ When declaring a method, you have to declare a checked exception if the method might throw that checked exception, thus telling the compiler what can go wrong.

■ The keyword for declaring an exception is `throws`, and the keyword for throwing an exception is `throw`.

■ To invoke the method that declares checked exceptions, you must enclose the method call in a `try` statement. When an exception occurs during the execution of the method, the `catch` block catches and handles the exception.

■ If an exception is not caught in the current method, it is passed to its caller. The process is repeated until the exception is caught or passed to the `main` method.

■ If an exception of a subclass of `Exception` occurs in a GUI component, Java prints the error message on the console, but the program goes back to its user-interface-processing loop to run continuously. The exception is ignored.

■ Various exception classes can be derived from a common superclass. If a `catch` block catches the exception objects of a superclass, it can also catch all the exception objects of the subclasses of that superclass.

■ The order in which exceptions are specified in a `catch` block is important. A compilation error will result if you do not specify an exception object of a class before an exception object of the superclass of that class.

■ When an exception occurs in a method, the method exits immediately if it does not catch the exception. If the method is required to perform some task before exiting, you can catch the exception in the method and then rethrow it to the real handler.

■ The code in the `finally` block is executed under all circumstances, regardless of whether an exception occurs in the `try` block or is caught.

■ Exception handling separates error-handling code from normal programming tasks, thus making programs easier to read and to modify.

■ Exception handling should not be used to replace simple tests. You should test simple exceptions whenever possible, and reserve exception handling for dealing with situations that cannot be handled with `if` statements.

■ Exceptions address robustness, whereas assertions address correctness. Exceptions and assertions are not meant to substitute for simple tests. Avoid using exception handling if a simple `if` statement is sufficient. Never use assertions to check normal conditions.

REVIEW QUESTIONS

Sections 17.2–17.3

17.1 Describe the Java `Throwable` class, its subclasses, and the types of exceptions. What `RunTimeException` will the following programs throw, if any?

```java
public class Test {
  public static void main(String[] args) {
    System.out.println(1 / 0);
  }
}
```

(a)

```java
public class Test {
  public static void main(String[] args) {
    int[] list = new int[5];
    System.out.println(list[5]);
  }
}
```

(b)

```java
public class Test {
  public static void main(String[] args) {
    String s = "abc";
    System.out.println(s.charAt(3));
  }
}
```

(c)

```java
public class Test {
  public static void main(String[] args) {
    Object o = new Object();
    String d = (String)o;
  }
}
```

(d)

```java
public class Test {
  public static void main(String[] args) {
    Object o = null;
    System.out.println(o.toString());
  }
}
```

(e)

```java
public class Test {
  public static void main(String[] args) {
    System.out.println(1.0 / 0);
  }
}
```

(f)

17.2 Show the output of the following code:

```java
public class Test {
  public static void main(String[] args) {
    for (int i = 0; i < 2; i++) {
      System.out.print(i + " ");
      try {
        System.out.println(1 / 0);
      }
      catch (Exception ex) {
      }
    }
  }
}
```

(a)

```java
public class Test {
  public static void main(String[] args) {
    try {
      for (int i = 0; i < 2; i++) {
        System.out.print(i + " ");
        System.out.println(1 / 0);
      }
    }
    catch (Exception ex) {
    }
  }
}
```

(b)

17.3 Point out the problem in the following code. Does the code throw any exceptions?

```java
long value = Long.MAX_VALUE + 1;
System.out.println(value);
```

17.4 What is the purpose of declaring exceptions? How do you declare an exception, and where? Can you declare multiple exceptions in a method declaration?

17.5 What is a checked exception, and what is an unchecked exception?

17.6 How do you throw an exception? Can you throw multiple exceptions in one **throw** statement?

17.7 What is the keyword **throw** used for? What is the keyword **throws** used for?

17.8 What does the JVM do when an exception occurs? How do you catch an exception?

17.9 What is the printout of the following code?

```java
public class Test {
  public static void main(String[] args) {
    try {
      int value = 30;
      if (value < 40)
        throw new Exception("value is too small");
    }
    catch (Exception ex) {
      System.out.println(ex.getMessage());
    }
    System.out.println("Continue after the catch block");
  }
}
```

What would be the printout if the line

```java
int value = 30;
```

is changed to

```java
int value = 50;
```

17.10 Suppose that **statement2** causes an exception in the following **try-catch** block:

```java
try {
  statement1;
  statement2;
  statement3;
}
catch (Exception1 ex1) {
}
catch (Exception2 ex2) {
}
statement4;
```

Answer the following questions:

- Will **statement3** be executed?
- If the exception is not caught, will **statement4** be executed?
- If the exception is caught in the **catch** block, will **statement4** be executed?
- If the exception is passed to the caller, will **statement4** be executed?

17.11 What is displayed when the following program is run?

```java
public class Test {
  public static void main(String[] args) {
    try {
      int [] list = new int [10];
      System.out.println("list[10] is " + list[10]);
    }
```

```
      catch (ArithmeticException ex) {
        System.out.println("ArithmeticException");
      }
      catch (RuntimeException ex) {
        System.out.println("RuntimeException");
      }
      catch (Exception ex) {
        System.out.println("Exception");
      }
    }
  }
```

17.12 What is displayed when the following program is run?

```
public class Test {
  public static void main(String[] args) {
    try {
      method();
      System.out.println("After the method call");
    }
    catch (ArithmeticException ex) {
      System.out.println("ArithmeticException");
    }
    catch (RuntimeException ex) {
      System.out.println("RuntimeException");
    }
    catch (Exception e) {
      System.out.println("Exception");
    }
  }

  static void method() throws Exception {
    System.out.println(1 / 0);
  }
}
```

17.13 What is displayed when the following program is run?

```
public class Test {
  public static void main(String[] args) {
    try {
      method();
      System.out.println("After the method call");
    }
    catch (RuntimeException ex) {
      System.out.println("RuntimeException in main");
    }
    catch (Exception ex) {
      System.out.println("Exception in main");
    }
  }

  static void method() throws Exception {
    try {
      String s = "abc";
      System.out.println(s.charAt(3));
    }
    catch (RuntimeException ex) {
      System.out.println("RuntimeException in method()");
    }
```

```
      catch (Exception ex) {
        System.out.println("Exception in method()");
      }
    }
  }
}
```

17.14 If an exception is not caught in a non-GUI application, what will happen? If an exception is not caught in a GUI application, what will happen?

17.15 What does the method `printStackTrace` do?

17.16 Does the presence of a `try-catch` block impose overhead when no exception occurs?

17.17 Correct a compilation error in the following code:

```java
public void m(int value) {
  if (value < 40)
    throw new Exception("value is too small");
}
```

Sections 17.4–17.7

17.18 Suppose that `statement2` causes an exception in the following statement:

```java
try {
  statement1;
  statement2;
  statement3;
}
catch (Exception1 ex1) {
}
catch (Exception2 ex2) {
}
catch (Exception3 ex3) {
  throw ex3;
}
finally {
  statement4;
};
statement5;
```

Answer the following questions:

- Will `statement5` be executed if the exception is not caught?
- If the exception is of type `Exception3`, will `statement4` be executed, and will `statement5` be executed?

17.19 Suppose the `setRadius` method throws the `RadiusException` declared in §17.7. What is displayed when the following program is run?

```java
public class Test {
  public static void main(String[] args) {
    try {
      method();
      System.out.println("After the method call");
    }
    catch (RuntimeException ex) {
      System.out.println("RuntimeException in main");
    }
    catch (Exception ex) {
      System.out.println("Exception in main");
    }
  }
```

```
      static void method() throws Exception {
        try {
          Circle c1 = new Circle(1);
          c1.setRadius(-1);
          System.out.println(c1.getRadius());
        }
        catch (RuntimeException ex) {
          System.out.println("RuntimeException in method()");
        }
        catch (Exception ex) {
          System.out.println("Exception in method()");
          throw ex;
        }
      }
    }
```

Section 17.10 Assertions

17.20 What is assertion for? How do you declare assertions? How do you compile code with assertions? How do you run programs with assertions?

17.21 What happens when you run the following code?

```
public class Test {
  public static void main(String[] args) {
    int i; int sum = 0;
    for (i = 0; i < 11; i++) {
      sum += i;
    }
    assert i == 10: "i is " + i;
  }
}
```

Comprehensive

17.22 A student wrote a method that checks whether a string is a numeric string, as follows:

```
public static boolean isNumeric(String token) {
  try {
    Double.parseDouble(token);
    return true;
  }
  catch (java.lang.NumberFormatException ex) {
    return false;
  }
}
```

Is it correct? Rewrite it without using exceptions.

PROGRAMMING EXERCISES

Sections 17.2–17.4

17.1* (*NumberFormatException*) Listing 8.4, Calculator.java, is a simple command-line calculator. Note that the program terminates if any operand is non-numeric. Write a program with an exception handler that deals with non-numeric operands; then write another program without using an exception handler to achieve the same objective. Your program should display a message that informs the user of the wrong operand type before exiting (see Figure 17.10).

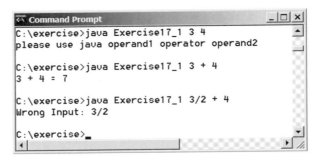

FIGURE 17.10   The program performs arithmetic operations and detects input errors.

17.2* (*ArithmeticException* and *NumberFormatException*) Write a program
that creates a user interface to perform integer divisions, as shown in Figure 17.11.
The user enters two numbers in the text fields, Number 1 and Number 2. The division of Number 1 and Number 2 is displayed in the Result field when the Divide
button is clicked. If Number 1 or Number 2 were not an integer, the program
would throw a NumberFormatException. If Number 2 were zero, the program
would throw an ArithmeticException. Display the exception in a message
dialog box, as shown in Figure 17.11.

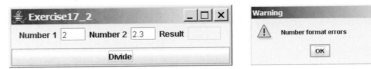

FIGURE 17.11   The program displays an error message in the dialog box if the number is
not well formatted.

17.3* (*ArrayIndexOutBoundsException*) Write a program that meets the following
requirements:

- Create an array with one hundred randomly chosen integers.
- Create a text field to enter an array index and another text field to display the
  array element at the specified index (see Figure 17.12).
- Create a Show Element button to cause the array element to be displayed. If
  the specified index is out of bounds, display the message **Out of Bound**.

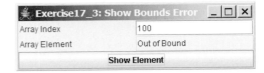

FIGURE 17.12   The program displays the array element at the specified index or displays
the message *Out of Bound* if the index is out of bounds.

17.4* (*IllegalArgumentException*) Modify the Loan class in §7.15, "Case Study:
The Loan Class," to throw IllegalArgumentException if the loan amount,
interest rate, or number of years is less than or equal to zero.

17.5* (*IllegalTriangleException*) Exercise 9.1 defined the Triangle class
with three sides. In a triangle, the sum of any two sides is greater than the other
side. The Triangle class must adhere to this rule. Create the IllegalTriangleException class, and modify the constructor of the Triangle class to

throw an `IllegalTriangleException` object if a triangle is created with sides that violate the rule, as follows:

```
/** Construct a triangle with the specified sides */
public Triangle(double side1, double side2, double side3)
  throws IllegalTriangleException {
  // Implement it
}
```

17.6* (*NumberFormatException*) Exercise 8.7 specifies the `parseHex(String hexString)` method, which converts a hex string into a decimal number. Implement the `parseHex` method to throw a `NumberFormatException` if the string is not a hex string.

17.7* (*NumberFormatException*) Exercise 8.8 specifies the `parseBinary(String binaryString)` method, which converts a binary string into a decimal number. Implement the `parseBinary` method to throw a `NumberFormatException` if the string is not a binary string.

17.8* (*HexFormatException*) Exercise 17.6 implements the `parseHex` method to throw a `NumberFormatException` if the string is not a hex string. Define a custom exception called `HexFormatException`. Implement the `parseHex` method to throw a `HexFormatException` if the string is not a hex string.

17.9* (*BinaryFormatException*) Exercise 17.7 implements the `parseBinary` method to throw a `BinaryFormatException` if the string is not a binary string. Define a custom exception called `BinaryFormatException`. Implement the `parseBinary` method to throw a `BinaryFormatException` if the string is not a binary string.

BINARY I/O

Objectives

- To understand how I/O is processed in Java (§18.2).

- To distinguish between text I/O and binary I/O (§18.3).

- To read and write bytes using `FileInputStream` and `FileOutputStream` (§18.4.1).

- To read and write primitive values and strings using `DataInputStream`/`DataOutputStream` (§18.4.3).

- To store and restore objects using `ObjectOutputStream` and `ObjectInputStream`, and to understand how objects are serialized and what kind of objects can be serialized (§18.6).

- To use the `Serializable` interface to enable objects to be serializable (§18.6.1).

- To know how to serialize arrays (§18.6.2).

- (Optional) To use `RandomAccessFile` for both read and write (§18.7).

18.1 Introduction

text file
binary file

Data stored in a *text file* is represented in human-readable form. Data stored in a *binary file* is represented in binary form. You cannot read binary files. They are designed to be read by programs. For example, Java source programs are stored in text files and can be read by a text editor, but Java classes are stored in binary files and are read by the JVM. The advantage of binary files is that they are more efficient to process than text files.

Although it is not technically precise and correct, you can envision a text file as consisting of a sequence of characters and a binary file as consisting of a sequence of bits. For example, the decimal integer **199** is stored as the sequence of three characters, **'1'**, **'9'**, **'9'**, in a text file, and the same integer is stored as a **byte**-type value **C7** in a binary file, because decimal **199** equals hex **C7** ($199 = 12 \times 16^1 + 7$).

Java offers many classes for performing file input and output. These classes can be categorized as *text I/O classes* and *binary I/O classes.* You learned how to read/write strings and numeric values from/to a text file using **Scanner** and **PrintWriter** in §8.8, "Text I/O." This section introduces the classes for performing binary I/O.

text I/O
binary I/O

18.2 How is I/O Handled in Java?

Recall that a **File** object encapsulates the properties of a file or a path, but does not contain the methods for reading/writing data from/to a file. In order to perform I/O, you need to create objects using appropriate Java I/O classes. The objects contain the methods for reading/writing data from/to a file. For example, to write text to a file named **temp.txt**, you may create an object using the **PrintWriter** class, as follows:

```
PrintWriter output = new PrintWriter("temp.txt");
```

You can now invoke **PrintWriter** from the object to write a string into the file. For example, the following statement writes **"Java 101"** to the file:

```
output.print("Java 101");
```

The next statement closes the file.

```
output.close();
```

There are many I/O classes for various purposes. In general, these can be classified as input classes and output classes. An input class contains the methods to read data, and an output class contains the methods to write data. **PrintWriter** is an example of an output class, and **Scanner** is an example of an input class. The following code shows an example of creating an input object for the file **temp.txt** and reading data from the file:

```
Scanner input = new Scanner(new File("temp.txt"));
System.out.println(input.nextLine());
```

If **temp.txt** contains **"Java 101"**, **input.nextLine()** returns string **"Java 101"**.

Figure 18.1 illustrates Java I/O programming. An input object reads a stream of data from a file, and an output object writes a stream of data to a file. An input object is also called an *input stream*, and an output object is also called an *output stream*.

input stream
output stream

18.3 Text I/O vs. Binary I/O

Computers do not differentiate binary files and text files. All files are stored in binary format, and thus all files are essentially binary files. Text I/O is built upon binary I/O to provide a level of abstraction for character encoding and decoding, as shown in Figure 18.2(a). Encoding and decoding are automatically performed for text I/O. The JVM converts a

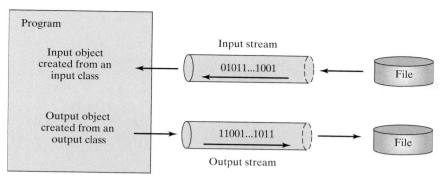

FIGURE 18.1   The program receives data through an input object and sends data through an output object.

Unicode to a file-specific encoding when writing a character and converts a file-specific encoding to a Unicode when reading a character. For example, suppose you write string **"199"** using text I/O to a file. Each character is written to the file. Since the Unicode for character '1' is **0x0031**, the Unicode **0x0031** is converted to a code that depends on the encoding scheme for the file. (Note that the prefix **0x** denotes a hex number.) In the United States, the default encoding for text files on Windows is ASCII. The ASCII code for character '1' is **49** (**0x31** in hex) and for character '9' is **57** (**0x39** in hex). So to write the characters "**199**", three bytes, **0x31**, **0x39**, and **0x39**, are sent to the output, as shown in Figure 18.2(a).

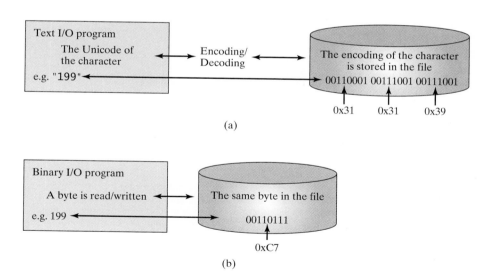

FIGURE 18.2   Text I/O requires encoding and decoding, whereas binary I/O does not.

Note

JDK 1.5 supports *supplementary Unicode*. For simplicity, however, this book considers only the original Unicode from **0** to **FFFF**.

supplementary Unicode

Binary I/O does not require conversions. If you write a numeric value to a file using binary I/O, the exact value in the memory is copied into the file. For example, a byte-type value **199** is represented as **0xC7** ($199 = 12 \times 16^1 + 7$) in the memory and appears exactly as **0xC7** in the file, as shown in Figure 18.2(b). When you read a byte using binary I/O, one byte value is read from the input.

In general, you should use text input to read a file created by a text editor or a text output program, and use binary input to read a file created by a Java binary output program.

Binary I/O is more efficient than text I/O, because binary I/O does not require encoding and decoding. Binary files are independent of the encoding scheme on the host machine and thus are portable. Java programs on any machine can read a binary file created by a Java program. This is why Java class files are binary files. Java class files can run on a JVM on any machine.

 Note

For consistency, this book uses the extension `.txt` to name text files and `.dat` to name binary files.

.txt and .dat

18.4 Binary I/O Classes

The design of the Java I/O classes is a good example of applying inheritance, where common operations are generalized in superclasses, and subclasses provide specialized operations. Figure 18.3 lists some of the classes for performing binary I/O. **InputStream** is the root for binary input classes, and **OutputStream** is the root for binary output classes. Figures 18.4 and 18.5 list all the methods in **InputStream** and **OutputStream**.

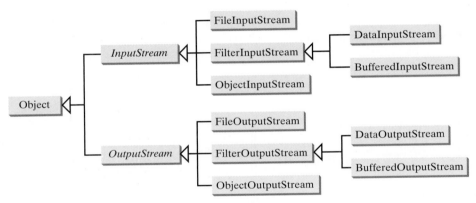

FIGURE 18.3 InputStream, OutputStream, and their subclasses are for binary I/O.

java.io.InputStream	
+read(): int	Reads the next byte of data from the input stream. The value byte is returned as an int value in the range 0 to 255. If no byte is available because the end of the stream has been reached, the value –1 is returned.
+read(b: byte[]): int	Reads up to b.length bytes into array b from the input stream and returns the actual number of bytes read. Returns –1 at the end of the stream.
+read(b: byte[], off: int, len: int): int	Reads bytes from the input stream and stores them in b[off], b[off+1], ..., b[off+len–1]. The actual number of bytes read is returned. Returns –1 at the end of the stream.
+available(): int	Returns the number of bytes that can be read from the input stream.
+close(): void	Closes this input stream and releases any system resources associated with it.
+skip(n: long): long	Skips over and discards n bytes of data from this input stream. The actual number of bytes skipped is returned.
+markSupported(): boolean	Tests whether this input stream supports the mark and reset methods.
+mark(readlimit: int): void	Marks the current position in this input stream.
+reset(): void	Repositions this stream to the position at the time the mark method was last called on this stream.

FIGURE 18.4 The abstract InputStream class defines the methods for the input stream of bytes.

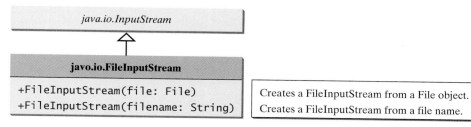

FIGURE 18.5 The abstract `OutputStream` class defines the methods for the output stream of bytes.

Note

All the methods in the binary I/O classes are declared to throw `java.io.IOException` or a subclass of `java.io.IOException`.

throws **IOException**

18.4.1 FileInputStream/FileOutputStream

`FileInputStream/FileOutputStream` is for reading/writing bytes from/to files. All the methods in these classes are inherited from `InputStream` and `OutputStream`. `FileInputStream/FileOutputStream` does not introduce new methods. To construct a `FileInputStream`, use the following constructors, as shown in Figure 18.6:

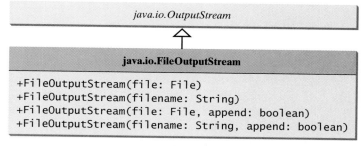

FIGURE 18.6 `FileInputStream` inputs stream of bytes from a file.

A `java.io.FileNotFoundException` will occur if you attempt to create a `FileInputStream` with a nonexistent file.

**FileNotFound-
Exception**

To construct a `FileOutputStream`, use the following constructors, as shown in Figure 18.7.

java.io.OutputStream	
java.io.FileOutputStream	
+FileOutputStream(file: File)	Creates a FileOutputStream from a File object.
+FileOutputStream(filename: String)	Creates a FileOutputStream from a file name.
+FileOutputStream(file: File, append: boolean)	If append is true, data is appended to the existing file.
+FileOutputStream(filename: String, append: boolean)	If append is true, data is appended to the existing file.

FIGURE 18.7 `FileOutputStream` outputs stream of bytes to a file.

If the file does not exist, a new file will be created. If the file already exists, the first two constructors will delete the current content of the file. To retain the current content and append new data into the file, use the last two constructors by passing **true** to the **append** parameter.

IOException

Almost all the methods in the I/O classes throw `java.io.IOException`. Therefore you have to declare `java.io.IOException` to throw in the method or place the code in a **try-catch** block, as shown below:

Declaring exception in the method

```
public static void main(String[] args)
    throws IOException {
    // Perform I/O operations
}
```

Using **try-catch** block

```
public static void main(String[] args) {
    try {
        // Perform I/O operations
    }
    catch (IOException ex) {
        ex.printStackTrace();
    }
}
```

Listing 18.1 uses binary I/O to write ten byte values from 1 to 10 to a file named **temp.dat** and reads them back from the file.

LISTING 18.1 TestFileStream.java

import

output stream

output

input stream

input

```
 1  import java.io.*;
 2
 3  public class TestFileStream {
 4    public static void main(String[] args) throws IOException {
 5      // Create an output stream to the file
 6      FileOutputStream output = new FileOutputStream("temp.dat");
 7
 8      // Output values to the file
 9      for (int i = 1; i <= 10; i++)
10        output.write(i);
11
12      // Close the output stream
13      output.close();
14
15      // Create an input stream for the file
16      FileInputStream input = new FileInputStream("temp.dat");
17
18      // Read values from the file
19      int value;
20      while ((value = input.read()) != -1)
21        System.out.print(value + " ");
22
23      // Close the output stream
24      input.close();
25    }
26  }
```

A `FileOutputStream` is created for file temp.dat in line 6. The **for** loop writes ten byte values into the file (lines 9–10). Invoking `write(i)` is the same as invoking `write((byte)i)`. Line 13 closes the output stream. Line 16 creates a `FileInputStream` for file temp.dat. Values are read from the file and displayed on the console in lines 19–21. The expression `((value = input.read()) != -1)` (line 20) reads a byte from `input.read()`, assigns it to `value`, and checks whether it is -1. The input value of -1 signifies the *end of a file*.

end of a file

The file `temp.dat` created in this example is a binary file. It can be read from a Java program but not from a text editor, as shown in Figure 18.8.

Tip

close stream

When a stream is no longer needed, always close it using the `close()` method. Not closing streams may cause data corruption in the output file, or other programming errors.

Binary data ——→

FIGURE 18.8 A binary file cannot be displayed in text mode.

 Note

Text I/O is built upon binary I/O. `PrinterWriter` and `Scanner` are implemented using binary I/O classes. An instance of `FileInputStream` can be used as an argument to construct a `Scanner`, and an instance of `FileOutputStream` can be used as an argument to construct a `PrintWriter`. You can create a `PrintWriter` to append text into a file using

```
new PrintWriter(new FileOutputStream("temp.txt", true));
```

If temp.txt does not exist, it is created. If temp.txt already exists, new data is appended to the file.

appending to text file

18.4.2 FilterInputStream/FilterOutputStream

Filter streams are streams that filter bytes for some purpose. The basic byte input stream provides a read method that can only be used for reading bytes. If you want to read integers, doubles, or strings, you need a filter class to wrap the byte input stream. Using a filter class enables you to read integers, doubles, and strings instead of bytes and characters. `FilterInputStream` and `FilterOutputStream` are the base classes for filtering data. When you need to process primitive numeric types, use `DataInputStream` and `DataOutputStream` to filter bytes.

18.4.3 DataInputStream/DataOutputStream

`DataInputStream` reads bytes from the stream and converts them into appropriate primitive type values or strings. `DataOutputStream` converts primitive type values or strings into bytes and outputs the bytes to the stream.

`DataInputStream` extends `FilterInputStream` and implements the `DataInput` interface, as shown in Figure 18.9. `DataOutputStream` extends `FilterOutputStream` and implements the `DataOutput` interface, as shown in Figure 18.10.

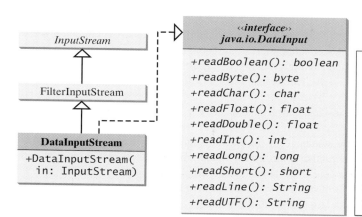

FIGURE 18.9 `DataInputStream` filters input stream of bytes into primitive data type values and strings.

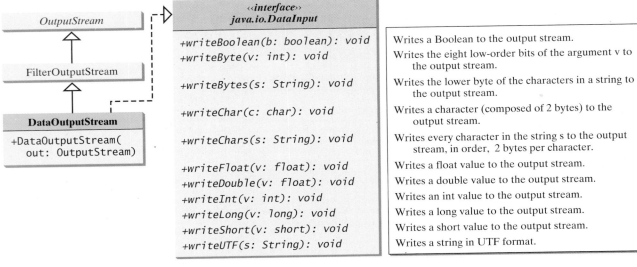

FIGURE 18.10 `DataOutputStream` enables you to write primitive data type values and strings into an output stream.

`DataInputStream` implements the methods defined in the `DataInput` interface to read primitive data type values and strings. `DataOutputStream` implements the methods defined in the `DataOutput` interface to write primitive data type values and strings. Primitive values are copied from memory to the output without any conversions. Characters in a string may be written in several ways, as discussed in the next section.

Characters and Strings in Binary I/O

A Unicode consists of two bytes. The `writeChar(char c)` method writes the Unicode of character `c` to the output. The `writeChars(String s)` method writes the Unicode for each character in the string `s` to the output. The `writeBytes(String s)` method writes the lower byte of the Unicode for each character in the string `s` to the output. The high byte of the Unicode is discarded. The `writeBytes` method is suitable for strings that consist of ASCII characters, since an ASCII code is stored only in the lower byte of a Unicode. If a string consists of non-ASCII characters, you have to use the `writeChars` method to write the string.

The `writeUTF(String s)` method writes two bytes of length information to the output stream, followed by the modified UTF-8 representation of every character in the string s. UTF-8 is a coding scheme that allows systems to operate with both ASCII and Unicode. Most operating systems use ASCII. Java uses Unicode. The ASCII character set is a subset of the Unicode character set. Since most applications need only the ASCII character set, it is a waste to represent an 8-bit ASCII character as a 16-bit Unicode character. The modified UTF-8 scheme stores a character using one, two, or three bytes. ASCII values less than `0x7F` are coded in one byte. Unicode values less than `0x7FF` are coded in two bytes. Other Unicode values are coded in three bytes.

UTF-8 scheme

The initial bits of a UTF-8 character indicate whether a character is stored in one byte, two bytes, or three bytes. If the first bit is 0, it is a one-byte character. If the first bits are `110`, it is the first byte of a two-byte sequence. If the first bits are `1110`, it is the first byte of a three-byte sequence. The information that indicates the number of characters in a string is stored in the first two bytes preceding the UTF-8 characters. For example, `writeUTF("ABCDEF")` actually writes eight bytes to the file because the first two bytes store the number of characters in the string.

The `writeUTF(String s)` method converts a string into a series of bytes in the UTF-8 format and writes them into a binary stream. The `readUTF()` method reads a string that has been written using the `writeUTF` method.

The UTF-8 format has the advantage of saving a byte for each ASCII character, because a Unicode character takes up two bytes and an ASCII character in UTF-8 takes up only one byte. If most of characters in a long string are regular ASCII characters, using UTF-8 is more efficient.

Using `DataInputStream`/`DataOutputStream`

Data streams are used as wrappers on existing input, and output streams to filter data in the original stream. They are created using the following constructors (see Figure 18.9 and Figure 18.10):

```
public DataInputStream(InputStream instream)
public DataOutputStream(OutputStream outstream)
```

The statements given below create data streams. The first statement creates an input stream for file `in.dat`; the second statement creates an output stream for file `out.dat`:

```
DataInputStream infile =
  new DataInputStream (new FileInputStream("in.dat"));
DataOutputStream outfile =
  new DataOutputStream (new FileOutputStream("out.dat"));
```

Listing 18.2 writes student names and scores to a file named `temp.dat` and reads the data back from the file.

LISTING 18.2 TestDataStream.java

```
 1 import java.io.*;
 2
 3 public class TestDataStream {
 4   public static void main(String[] args) throws IOException {
 5     // Create an output stream for file temp.dat
 6     DataOutputStream output =                                      output stream
 7       new DataOutputStream(new FileOutputStream("temp.dat"));
 8
 9     // Write student test scores to the file
10     output.writeUTF("John");                                       output
11     output.writeDouble(85.5);
12     output.writeUTF("Jim");
13     output.writeDouble(185.5);
14     output.writeUTF("George");
15     output.writeDouble(105.25);
16
17     // Close output stream
18     output.close();                                                close stream
19
20     // Create an input stream for file temp.dat
21     DataInputStream input =                                        input stream
22       new DataInputStream(new FileInputStream("temp.dat"));
23
24     // Read student test scores from the file
25     System.out.println(input.readUTF() + " " + input.readDouble());  input
26     System.out.println(input.readUTF() + " " + input.readDouble());
27     System.out.println(input.readUTF() + " " + input.readDouble());
28   }
29 }
```

A `DataOutputStream` is created for file `temp.dat` in lines 6–7. Student names and scores are written to the file in lines 10–15. Line 18 closes the output stream. A `DataInputStream` is created for the same file in lines 21–22. Student names and scores are read back from the file and displayed on the console in lines 25–27.

`DataInputStream` and `DataOutputStream` read and write Java primitive type values and strings in a machine-independent fashion, thereby enabling you to write a data file on one machine and read it on another machine that has a different operating system or file structure. An application uses a data output stream to write data that can later be read by a program using a data input stream.

Caution

You have to read data in the same order and format in which they are stored. For example, since names are written in UTF-8 using **writeUTF**, you must read names using **readUTF**.

Tip

If you keep reading data at the end of a **DataInputStream**, an **EOFException** will occur. How, then, do you check the end of a file? Use **input.available()** to check it. **input.available() == 0** indicates the end of a file.

18.4.4 BufferedInputStream/BufferedOutputStream

BufferedInputStream/BufferedOutputStream can be used to speed up input and output by reducing the number of reads and writes. BufferedInputStream/BufferedOutputStream does not contain new methods. All the methods in BufferedInputStream/BufferedOutputStream are inherited from the InputStream/OutputStream classes. BufferedInputStream/BufferedOutputStream adds a buffer in the stream for storing bytes for efficient processing.

You may wrap a BufferedInputStream/BufferedOutputStream on any InputStream/OutputStream using the following constructors, as shown in Figure 18.11 and Figure 18.12:

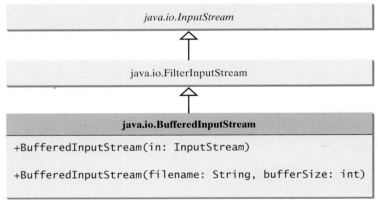

FIGURE 18.11 BufferedInputStream buffers input stream.

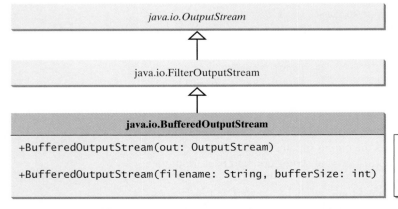

FIGURE 18.12 BufferedOutputStream buffers output stream.

If no buffer size is specified, the default size is 512 bytes. A buffered input stream reads as many data as possible into its buffer in a single read call. By contrast, a buffered output stream calls the write method only when its buffer fills up or when the `flush()` method is called.

You can improve the performance of the `TestDataStream` program in the preceding example by adding buffers in the stream in lines 6–7 and 21–22, as follows:

```
DataOutputStream output = new DataOutputStream(
  new BufferedOutputStream (new FileOutputStream("temp.dat")));

DataInputStream input = new DataInputStream(
  new BufferedInputStream (new FileInputStream("temp.dat")));
```

18.5 Case Study: Copying File

This case study develops a program that copies files. The user needs to provide a source file and a target file as command-line arguments using the following command:

java Copy source target

The program copies a source file to a target file and displays the number of bytes in the file. If the source does not exist, tell the user that the file has not been found. If the target file already exists, tell the user that the file exists. A sample run of the program is shown in Figure 18.13.

File exists
Delete file
Copy
Source not exist

FIGURE 18.13   The program copies a file.

To copy the contents from a source to a target file, it is appropriate to use a binary input stream to read bytes from the source file and a binary output stream to send bytes to the target file, regardless of the contents of the file. The source file and the target file are specified from the command line. Create an `InputFileStream` for the source file and an `OutputFileStream` for the target file. Use the `read()` method to read a byte from the input stream, and then use the `write(b)` method to write the byte to the output stream. Use `BufferedInputStream` and `BufferedOutputStream` to improve the performance. Listing 18.3 gives the solution to the problem.

LISTING 18.3 Copy.java

```
 1 import java.io.*;
 2
 3 public class Copy {
 4   /** Main method
 5      @param args[0] for source file
 6      @param args[1] for target file
 7   */
 8   public static void main(String[] args) throws IOException {
 9     // Check command line parameter usage
10     if (args.length != 2) {
```

check usage

```
11          System.out.println(
12            "Usage: java CopyFile sourceFile targetfile");
13          System.exit(0);
14        }
15
16        // Check if source file exists
17        File sourceFile = new File(args[0]);
18        if (!sourceFile.exists()) {
19          System.out.println("Source file " + args[0] + " not exist");
20          System.exit(0);
21        }
22
23        // Check if target file exists
24        File targetFile = new File(args[1]);
25        if (targetFile.exists()) {
26          System.out.println("Target file " + args[1] + " already exists");
27          System.exit(0);
28        }
29
30        // Create an input stream
31        BufferedInputStream input =
32          new BufferedInputStream(new FileInputStream(sourceFile));
33
34        // Create an output stream
35        BufferedOutputStream output =
36          new BufferedOutputStream(new FileOutputStream(targetFile));
37
38        // Display the file size
39        System.out.println("The file " + args[0] + " has " +
40          input.available()  + " bytes");
41
42        // Continuously read a byte from input and write it to output
43        int r;
44        while ((r = input.read() ) != -1)
45          output.write((byte)r);
46
47        // Close streams
48        input.close();
49        output.close();
50
51        System.out.println("Copy done!");
52      }
53    }
```

Margin notes:
- source file (line 17)
- target file (line 24)
- input stream (line 31)
- output stream (line 35)
- read (line 44)
- write (line 45)
- close stream (line 48)

- The program first checks whether the user has passed two required arguments from the command line in lines 10–14.

- The program uses the **File** class to check whether the source file and target file exist. If the source file does not exist (lines 18–21) or if the target file already exists, exit the program.

- An input stream is created using **BufferedInputStream** wrapped on **FileInputStream** in lines 31–32, and an output stream is created using **BufferedOutputStream** wrapped on **FileOutputStream** in lines 35–36.

- The **available()** method (line 40) defined in the **InputStream** class returns the number of bytes remaining in the input stream.

- The expression **((r = input.read()) != -1)** (line 44) reads a byte from **input.read()**, assigns it to **r**, and checks whether it is **-1**. The input value of **-1** signifies the end of a file. The program continuously reads bytes from the input stream and sends them to the output stream until all of the bytes have been read.

18.6 Object I/O

`DataInputStream`/`DataOutputStream` enables you to perform I/O for primitive type values and strings. `ObjectInputStream`/`ObjectOutputStream` enables you to perform I/O for objects in addition to primitive type values and strings. Since `ObjectInputStream`/`ObjectOutputStream` contains all the functions of `DataInputStream`/`DataOutputStream`, you can replace `DataInputStream`/`DataOutputStream` completely with `ObjectInputStream`/`ObjectOutputStream`.

`ObjectInputStream` extends `InputStream` and implements `ObjectInput` and `ObjectStreamConstants`, as shown in Figure 18.14. `ObjectInput` is a subinterface of `DataInput`. `DataInput` is shown in Figure 18.9. `ObjectStreamConstants` contains the constants to support `ObjectInputStream`/`ObjectOutputStream`.

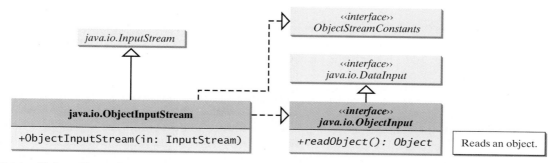

FIGURE 18.14 `ObjectInputStream` can read objects, primitive type values, and strings.

`ObjectOutputStream` extends `OutputStream` and implements `ObjectOutput` and `ObjectStreamConstants`, as shown in Figure 18.15. `ObjectOutput` is a subinterface of `DataOutput`. `DataOutput` is shown in Figure 18.10.

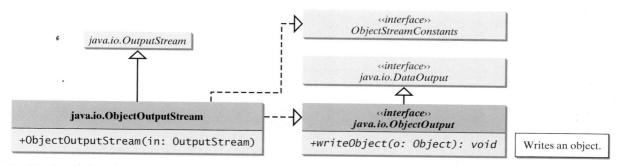

FIGURE 18.15 `ObjectOutputStream` can write objects, primitive type values, and strings.

You may wrap an `ObjectInputStream`/`ObjectOutputStream` on any `InputStream`/`OutputStream` using the following constructors:

```
// Create an ObjectInputStream
public ObjectInputStream(InputStream in)

// Create an ObjectOutputStream
public ObjectOutputStream(OutputStream out)
```

Listing 18.4 writes student names, scores, and current date to a file named `object.dat`.

LISTING 18.4 TestObjectOutputStream.java

```
1 import java.io.*;
2
3 public class TestObjectOutputStream {
```

output stream

output

```
 4   public static void main(String[] args) throws IOException {
 5     // Create an output stream for file object.dat
 6     ObjectOutputStream output =
 7       new ObjectOutputStream(new FileOutputStream("object.dat"));
 8
 9     // Write a string, double value, and object to the file
10     output.writeUTF("John");
11     output.writeDouble(85.5);
12     output.writeObject(new java.util.Date());
13
14     // Close output stream
15     output.close();
16   }
17 }
```

An `ObjectOutputStream` is created to write data into file `object.dat` in lines 6–7. A string, a double value, and an object are written to the file in lines 10–12. To improve performance, you may add a buffer in the stream using the following statement to replace lines 6–7:

```
ObjectOutputStream output = new ObjectOutputStream(
  new BufferedOutputStream(new FileOutputStream("object.dat")));
```

Multiple objects or primitives can be written to the stream. The objects must be read back from the corresponding `ObjectInputStream` with the same types and in the same order as they were written. Java's safe casting should be used to get the desired type. Listing 18.5 reads data back from `object.dat`.

LISTING 18.5 TestObjectInputStream.java

input stream

input

```
 1 import java.io.*;
 2
 3 public class TestObjectInputStream {
 4   public static void main(String[] args)
 5       throws ClassNotFoundException, IOException {
 6     // Create an input stream for file object.dat
 7     ObjectInputStream input =
 8       new ObjectInputStream(new FileInputStream("object.dat"));
 9
10     // Write a string, double value, and object to the file
11     String name = input.readUTF();
12     double score = input.readDouble();
13     java.util.Date date = (java.util.Date)(input.readObject());
14     System.out.println(name + " " + score + " " + date);
15
16     // Close output stream
17     input.close();
18   }
19 }
```

ClassNotFoundException

The `readObject()` method may throw `java.lang.ClassNotFoundException`. The reason is that when the JVM restores an object, it first loads the class for the object if the class has not been loaded. Since `ClassNotFoundException` is a checked exception, the `main` method declares to throw it in line 5. An `ObjectInputStream` is created to read input from `object.dat` in lines 7–8. You have to read the data from the file in the same order and format as they were written to the file. A string, a double value, and an object are read in lines 11–13. Since `readObject()` returns an `Object`, it is cast into `Date` and assigned to a `Date` variable in line 13.

18.6.1 The `Serializable` Interface

Not every object can be written to an output stream. Objects that can be written to an object stream are said to be *serializable*. A serializable object is an instance of the `java.io.Serializable` interface, so the class of a serializable object must implement `Serializable`.

serializable

The `Serializable` interface is a marker interface. Since it has no methods, you don't need to add additional code in your class that implements `Serializable`. Implementing this interface enables the Java serialization mechanism to automate the process of storing objects and arrays.

To appreciate this automation feature and understand how an object is stored, consider what you need to do in order to store an object without using this feature. Suppose you want to store a `JButton` object. To do this you need to store all the current values of the properties (e.g., color, font, text, alignment) in the object. Since `JButton` is a subclass of `AbstractButton`, the property values of `AbstractButton` have to be stored as well as the properties of all the superclasses of `AbstractButton`. If a property is of an object type (e.g., `background` of the `Color` type), storing it requires storing all the property values inside this object. As you can see, this is a very tedious process. Fortunately, you don't have to go through it manually. Java provides a built-in mechanism to automate the process of writing objects. This process is referred to as *object serialization*, which is implemented in `ObjectOutputStream`. In contrast, the process of reading objects is referred to as *object deserialization*, which is implemented in `ObjectInputStream`.

serialization
deserialization

Many classes in the Java API implement `Serializable`. The utility classes, such as `java.util.Date`, and all the Swing GUI component classes implement `Serializable`. Attempting to store an object that does not support the `Serializable` interface would cause a `NotSerializableException`.

NotSerializable-
Exception

When a serializable object is stored, the class of the object is encoded; this includes the class name and the signature of the class, the values of the object's instance variables, and the closure of any other objects referenced from the initial object. The values of the object's static variables are not stored.

Note

If an object is an instance of `Serializable` but contains nonserializable instance data fields, can it be serialized? The answer is no. To enable the object to be serialized, mark these data fields with the `transient` keyword to tell the JVM to ignore them when writing the object to an object stream. Consider the following class:

non-serializable fields

transient

```java
public class Foo implements java.io.Serializable {
  private int v1;
  private static double v2;
  private transient A v3 = new A();
}

class A { } // A is not serializable
```

When an object of the `Foo` class is serialized, only variable `v1` is serialized. Variable `v2` is not serialized because it is a static variable, and variable `v3` is not serialized because it is marked `transient`. If `v3` were not marked `transient`, a `java.io.NotSerializable Exception` would occur.

Note

If an object is written to an object stream more than once, will it be stored in multiple copies? The answer is no. When an object is written for the first time, a serial number is created for it. The JVM writes the complete content of the object along with the serial number into the object stream. After the first time, only the serial number is stored if the same object is written again.

duplicate objects

When the objects are read back, their references are the same, since only one object is actually created in the memory.

18.6.2 Serializing Arrays

An array is serializable if all its elements are serializable. An entire array can be saved using **writeObject** into a file and later can be restored using **readObject**. Listing 18.6 stores an array of five **int** values, an array of three strings, and an array of two **JButton** objects, and reads them back to display on the console.

LISTING 18.6 TestObjectStreamForArray.java

```
1 import java.io.*;
2 import javax.swing.*;
3
4 public class TestObjectStreamForArray {
5   public static void main(String[] args)
6       throws ClassNotFoundException, IOException {
7     int[] numbers = {1, 2, 3, 4, 5};
8     String[] strings = {"John", "Jim", "Jake"};
9     JButton[] buttons = {new JButton("OK"), new JButton("Cancel")};
10
11     // Create an output stream for file array.dat
12     ObjectOutputStream output =
13       new ObjectOutputStream (new FileOutputStream("array.dat", true));
14
15     // Write arrays to the object output stream
16     output.writeObject(numbers);
17     output.writeObject(strings);
18     output.writeObject(buttons);
19
20     // Close the stream
21     output.close();
22
23     // Create an input stream for file array.dat
24     ObjectInputStream input =
25       new ObjectInputStream(new FileInputStream("array.dat"));
26
27     int[] newNumbers = (int[])(input.readObject());
28     String[] newStrings = (String[])(input.readObject());
29     JButton[] newButtons = (JButton[])(input.readObject());
30
31     // Display arrays
32     for (int i = 0; i < newNumbers.length; i++)
33       System.out.print(newNumbers[i] + " ");
34     System.out.println();
35
36     for (int i = 0; i < newStrings.length; i++)
37       System.out.print(newStrings[i] + " ");
38     System.out.println();
39
40     for (int i = 0; i < newButtons.length; i++)
41       System.out.print(newButtons[i].getText() + " ");
42   }
43 }
```

output stream (line 12)

store array (line 16)

input stream (line 24)

restore array (line 27)

Lines 16–18 write three arrays into file **array.dat**. Lines 27–29 read three arrays back in the same order they were written. Since **readObject()** returns **Object**, casting is used to cast the objects into **int[]**, **String[]**, and **JButton[]**.

18.7 (Optional) Random Access Files

All of the streams you have used so far are known as *read-only* or *write-only* streams. The external files of these streams are *sequential* files that cannot be updated without creating a new file. It is often necessary to modify files or to insert new records into files. Java provides the `RandomAccessFile` class to allow a file to be read from and written to at random locations.

read-only
write-only
sequential

The `RandomAccessFile` class implements the `DataInput` and `DataOutput` interfaces, as shown in Figure 18.16. The `DataInput` interface shown in Figure 18.9 defines the methods (e.g., `readInt`, `readDouble`, `readChar`, `readBoolean`, `readUTF`) for reading primitive type values and strings, and the `DataOutput` interface shown in Figure 18.10 defines the methods (e.g., `writeInt`, `writeDouble`, `writeChar`, `writeBoolean`, `writeUTF`) for writing primitive type values and strings.

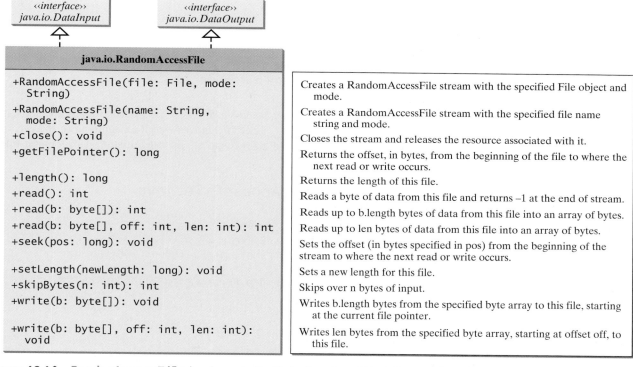

FIGURE 18.16 `RandomAccessFile` implements the `DataInput` and `DataOutput` interfaces with additional methods to support random access.

When creating a `RandomAccessFile`, you can specify one of two modes (`"r"` or `"rw"`). Mode `"r"` means that the stream is read-only, and mode `"rw"` indicates that the stream allows both read and write. For example, the following statement creates a new stream, `raf`, that allows the program to read from and write to the file `test.dat`:

```
RandomAccessFile raf = new RandomAccessFile("test.dat", "rw");
```

If `test.dat` already exists, `raf` is created to access it; if `test.dat` does not exist, a new file named `test.dat` is created, and `raf` is created to access the new file. The method `raf.length()` returns the number of bytes in `test.dat` at any given time. If you append new data into the file, `raf.length()` increases.

Tip

Open the file with the `"r"` mode if the file is not intended to be modified. This prevents unintentional modification of the file.

file pointer

A random access file consists of a sequence of bytes. There is a special marker called *file pointer* that is positioned at one of these bytes. A read or write operation takes place at the location of the file pointer. When a file is opened, the file pointer is set at the beginning of the file. When you read or write data to the file, the file pointer moves forward to the next data item. For example, if you read an **int** value using **readInt()**, the JVM reads 4 bytes from the file pointer and now the file pointer is 4 bytes ahead of the previous location, as shown in Figure 18.17.

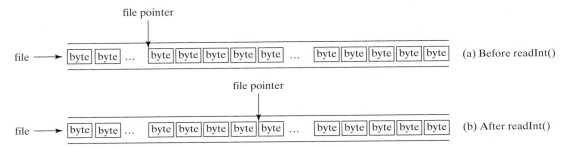

FIGURE 18.17 After reading an **int** value, the file pointer is moved 4 bytes ahead.

For a RandomAccessFile raf, you can use **raf.seek(position)** method to move the file pointer to a specified position. **raf.seek(0)** moves it to the beginning of the file, and **raf.seek(raf.length())** moves it to the end of the file. Listing 18.7 demonstrates RandomAccessFile.

LISTING 18.7 TestRandomAccessFile.java

```
1  import java.io.*;
2
3  public class TestRandomAccessFile {
4    public static void main(String[] args) throws IOException {
5      // Create a random access file
6      RandomAccessFile inout = new RandomAccessFile("inout.dat", "rw");
7
8      // Clear the file to destroy the old contents if exists
9      inout.setLength(0);
10
11     // Write new integers to the file
12     for (int i = 0; i < 200; i++)
13       inout.writeInt(i);
14
15     // Display the current length of the file
16     System.out.println("Current file length is " + inout.length());
17
18     // Retrieve the first number
19     inout.seek(0); // Move the file pointer to the beginning
20     System.out.println("The first number is " + inout.readInt());
21
22     // Retrieve the second number
23     inout.seek(1 * 4); // Move the file pointer to the second number
24     System.out.println("The second number is " + inout.readInt());
25
26     // Retrieve the tenth number
27     inout.seek(9 * 4); // Move the file pointer to the tenth number
28     System.out.println("The tenth number is " + inout.readInt());
29
30     // Modify the eleventh number
31     inout.writeInt(555);
```

RandomAccessFile (line 6)

empty file (line 9)

write (line 13)

move pointer (line 19)
read (line 20)

```
32
33     // Append a new number
34     inout.seek(inout.length()); // Move the file pointer to the end
35     inout.writeInt(999);
36
37     // Display the new length
38     System.out.println("The new length is " + inout.length());
39
40     // Retrieve the new eleventh number
41     inout.seek(10 * 4); // Move the file pointer to the eleventh number
42     System.out.println("The eleventh number is " + inout.readInt());
43
44     inout.close();                                                      close file
45   }
46 }
```

- A `RandomAccessFile` is created for the file named `inout.dat` with mode "rw" to allow both read and write operations in line 6.

- `inout.setLength(0)` sets the length to `0` in line 9. This, in effect, destroys the old contents of the file.

- The `for` loop writes two hundred `int` values from `0` to `199` into the file in lines 12–13. Since each `int` value takes 4 bytes, the total length of the file returned from `inout.length()` is now 800 (line 16), as shown in Figure 18.18.

- Invoking `inout.seek(0)` in line 19 sets the file pointer to the beginning of the file. `inout.readInt()` reads the first value in line 20 and moves the file pointer to the next number. The second number is read in line 24.

- `inout.seek(9 * 4)` (line 27) moves the file pointer to the tenth number. `inout.readInt()` reads the tenth number and moves the file pointer to the eleventh number in line 28. `inout.write(555)` writes a new eleventh number at the current position (line 31). The previous eleventh number is destroyed.

- `inout.seek(inout.length())` moves the file pointer to the end of the file (line 34). `inout.writeInt(999)` writes 999 to the file. Now the length of the file is increased by 4, so `inout.length()` returns 804 (line 38).

- `inout.seek(10 * 4)` moves the file pointer to the eleventh number in line 41. The new eleventh number, 555, is displayed in line 42.

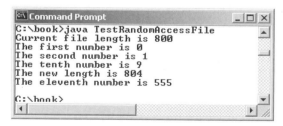

FIGURE 18.18   `TestRandomAccessFile` manipulates a `RandomAccessFile`.

18.8 (Optional) Case Study: Address Book

Now let us use `RandomAccessFile` to create a useful project for storing and viewing an address book. The user interface of the program is shown in Figure 18.19. The *Add* button stores a new address at the end of the file. The *First, Next, Previous,* and *Last* buttons retrieve the first, next, previous, and last addresses from the file, respectively.

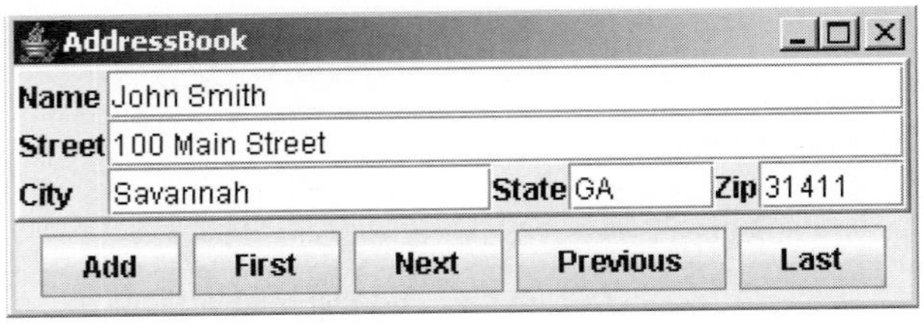

FIGURE 18.19 AddressBook stores and retrieves addresses from a file.

Random access files are often used to process files of records. For convenience, fixed-length records are used in random access files so that a record can be located easily, as shown in Figure 18.20. A record consists of a fixed number of fields. A field can be a string or a primitive data type. A string in a *fixed-length record* has a maximum size. If a string is smaller than the maximum size, the rest of the string is padded with blanks.

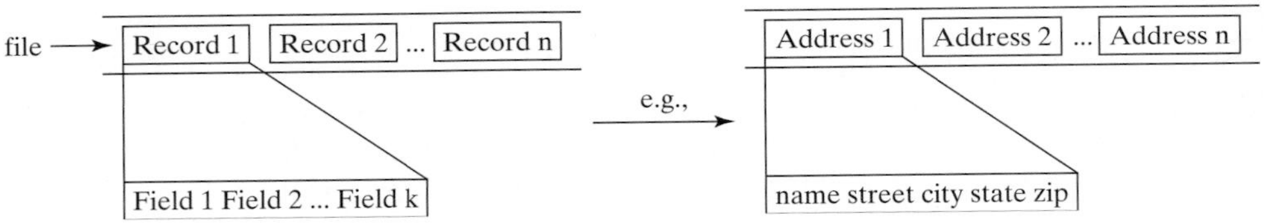

fixed-length record

FIGURE 18.20 Random access files are often used to process files of fixed-length records.

Let `address.dat` be the file to store addresses. A `RandomAccessFile` for both read and write can be created using

```
RandomAccessFile raf = new RandomAccessFile("address.dat", "rw");
```

Let each address consist of a name (32 characters), street (32 characters), city (20 characters), state (2 characters), and zip (5 characters). If the actual size of a field (e.g., name) is less than the fixed maximum size, fill it with blank characters. If the actual size of a field is greater than the fixed maximum size, truncate the string. Thus the total size of an address is $32 + 32 + 20 + 2 + 5 = 91$ characters. Since each character occupies two bytes, one address takes $2*91 = 182$ bytes. After an address record is read, the file pointer is 182 bytes ahead of the previous file pointer.

For convenience, Listing 18.8 contains two methods for reading and writing a fixed-length string.

LISTING 18.8 FixedLengthStringIO.java

```
 1  import java.io.*;
 2
 3  public class FixedLengthStringIO {
 4    /** Read fixed number of characters from a DataInput stream */
 5    public static String readFixedLengthString(int size,
 6        DataInput in) throws IOException {
 7      // Declare an array of characters
 8      char[] chars = new char[size];
 9
10      // Read fixed number of characters to the array
11      for (int i = 0; i < size; i++)
12        chars[i] = in.readChar();
13
```

read characters

```
14      return new String(chars);
15    }
16
17    /** Write fixed number of characters to a DataOutput stream */
18    public static void writeFixedLengthString(String s, int size,
19        DataOutput out) throws IOException {
20      char[] chars = new char[size];
21
22      // Fill in string with characters
23      s.getChars(0, Math.min(s.length(), size), chars, 0);          fill string
24
25      // Fill in blank characters in the rest of the array
26      for (int i = Math.min(s.length(), size); i < chars.length; i++)
27        chars[i] = ' ';                                              fill blank
28
29      // Create and write a new string padded with blank characters
30      out.writeChars(new String(chars));                            write string
31    }
32 }
```

The `writeFixedLengthString(String s, int size, DataOutput out)` method writes a string in a fixed size to a `DataOutput` stream. If the string is longer than the specified size, it is truncated (line 23); if it is shorter than the specified size, blanks are padded into it (lines 26–27). In any case, a new fixed-length string is written to a specified output stream. Since `RandomAccessFile` implements `DataOutput`, this method can be used to write a string to a `RandomAccessFile`. For example, invoking `writeFixedLengthString("John", 2, raf)` actually writes `"Jo"` to the `RandomAccessFile raf`, since the size is `2`. Invoking `writeFixedLengthString("John", 6, raf)` actually writes `"John "` to the `Random AccessFile raf`, since the size is `6`.

The `readFixedLengthString(int size, InputOutput in)` method reads a fixed number of characters from an `InputStream` and returns as a string. Since `RandomAccessFile` implements `InputOutput`, this method can be used to read a string from a `writeFixedLengthString(String s, int size, DataOutput out)`.

The rest of the work can be summarized in the following steps:

1. Create the user interface.

2. Add a record to the file.

3. Read a record from the file.

4. Write the code to implement the button actions.

The program is shown in Listing 18.9.

LISTING 18.9   AddressBook.java

```
1 import java.io.*;
2 import java.awt.*;
3 import java.awt.event.*;
4 import javax.swing.*;
5 import javax.swing.border.*;
6
7 public class AddressBook extends JFrame {
8   // Specify the size of five string fields in the record
9   final static int NAME_SIZE = 32;                          constant
10   final static int STREET_SIZE = 32;
11   final static int CITY_SIZE = 20;
12   final static int STATE_SIZE = 2;
13   final static int ZIP_SIZE = 5;
```

```
14  final static int RECORD_SIZE =
15    (NAME_SIZE + STREET_SIZE + CITY_SIZE + STATE_SIZE + ZIP_SIZE);
16
17  // Access address.dat using RandomAccessFile
18  private RandomAccessFile raf;
19
20  // Text fields
21  private JTextField jtfName = new JTextField(NAME_SIZE);
22  private JTextField jtfStreet = new JTextField(STREET_SIZE);
23  private JTextField jtfCity = new JTextField(CITY_SIZE);
24  private JTextField jtfState = new JTextField(STATE_SIZE);
25  private JTextField jtfZip = new JTextField(ZIP_SIZE);
26
27  // Buttons
28  private JButton jbtAdd = new JButton("Add");
29  private JButton jbtFirst = new JButton("First");
30  private JButton jbtNext = new JButton("Next");
31  private JButton jbtPrevious = new JButton("Previous");
32  private JButton jbtLast = new JButton("Last");
33
34  public AddressBook() {
35    // Open or create a random access file
36    try {
37      raf = new RandomAccessFile("address.dat", "rw");
38    }
39    catch(IOException ex) {
40      System.out.print("Error: " + ex);
41      System.exit(0);
42    }
43
44    // Panel p1 for holding labels Name, Street, and City
45    JPanel p1 = new JPanel();
46    p1.setLayout(new GridLayout(3, 1));
47    p1.add(new JLabel("Name"));
48    p1.add(new JLabel("Street"));
49    p1.add(new JLabel("City"));
50
51    // Panel jpState for holding state
52    JPanel jpState = new JPanel();
53    jpState.setLayout(new BorderLayout());
54    jpState.add(new JLabel("State"), BorderLayout.WEST);
55    jpState.add(jtfState, BorderLayout.CENTER);
56
57    // Panel jpZip for holding zip
58    JPanel jpZip = new JPanel();
59    jpZip.setLayout(new BorderLayout());
60    jpZip.add(new JLabel("Zip"), BorderLayout.WEST);
61    jpZip.add(jtfZip, BorderLayout.CENTER);
62
63    // Panel p2 for holding jpState and jpZip
64    JPanel p2 = new JPanel();
65    p2.setLayout(new BorderLayout());
66    p2.add(jpState, BorderLayout.WEST);
67    p2.add(jpZip, BorderLayout.CENTER);
68
69    // Panel p3 for holding jtfCity and p2
70    JPanel p3 = new JPanel();
71    p3.setLayout(new BorderLayout());
72    p3.add(jtfCity, BorderLayout.CENTER);
73    p3.add(p2, BorderLayout.EAST);
74
```

raf

GUI component

open file

create UI

```
75      // Panel p4 for holding jtfName, jtfStreet, and p3
76      JPanel p4 = new JPanel();
77      p4.setLayout(new GridLayout(3, 1));
78      p4.add(jtfName);
79      p4.add(jtfStreet);
80      p4.add(p3);
81
82      // Place p1 and p4 into jpAddress
83      JPanel jpAddress = new JPanel(new BorderLayout());
84      jpAddress.add(p1, BorderLayout.WEST);
85      jpAddress.add(p4, BorderLayout.CENTER);
86
87      // Set the panel with line border
88      jpAddress.setBorder(new BevelBorder(BevelBorder.RAISED));
89
90      // Add buttons to a panel
91      JPanel jpButton = new JPanel();
92      jpButton.add(jbtAdd);
93      jpButton.add(jbtFirst);
94      jpButton.add(jbtNext);
95      jpButton.add(jbtPrevious);
96      jpButton.add(jbtLast);
97
98      // Add jpAddress and jpButton to the frame
99      add(jpAddress, BorderLayout.CENTER);
100     add(jpButton, BorderLayout.SOUTH);
101
102     jbtAdd.addActionListener(new ActionListener() {              register listener
103       public void actionPerformed(ActionEvent e) {
104         writeAddress();                                         add address
105       }
106     });
107     jbtFirst.addActionListener(new ActionListener() {           register listener
108       public void actionPerformed(ActionEvent e) {
109         try {
110           if (raf.length() > 0) readAddress(0);                 first record
111         }
112         catch (IOException ex) {
113           ex.printStackTrace();
114         }
115       }
116     });
117     jbtNext.addActionListener(new ActionListener() {            register listener
118       public void actionPerformed(ActionEvent e) {
119         try {
120           long currentPosition = raf.getFilePointer();
121           if (currentPosition < raf.length())
122             readAddress(currentPosition);                       next address
123         }
124         catch (IOException ex) {
125           ex.printStackTrace();
126         }
127       }
128     });
129     jbtPrevious.addActionListener(new ActionListener() {
130       public void actionPerformed(ActionEvent e) {
131         try {
132           long currentPosition = raf.getFilePointer();
133           if (currentPosition - 2 * RECORD_SIZE > 0)
134             // Why 2 * 2 * RECORD_SIZE? See the follow-up remarks
135             readAddress(currentPosition - 2 * 2 * RECORD_SIZE);
```

```
136          else
137            readAddress(0);
138        }
139        catch (IOException ex) {
140          ex.printStackTrace();
141        }
142      }
143    });
```

register listener

```
144    jbtLast.addActionListener(new ActionListener() {
145      public void actionPerformed(ActionEvent e) {
146        try {
147          long lastPosition = raf.length();
148          if (lastPosition > 0)
149            // Why 2 * RECORD_SIZE? See the follow-up remarks
150            readAddress(lastPosition - 2 * RECORD_SIZE);
151        }
152        catch (IOException ex) {
153          ex.printStackTrace();
154        }
155      }
156    });
157
158    // Display the first record if exists
159    try {
160      if (raf.length() > 0) readAddress(0);
161    }
162    catch (IOException ex) {
163      ex.printStackTrace();
164    }
165  }
166
167  /** Write a record at the end of the file */
168  public void writeAddress() {
169    try {
170      raf.seek(raf.length());
171      FixedLengthStringIO.writeFixedLengthString(
172        jtfName.getText(), NAME_SIZE, raf);
173      FixedLengthStringIO.writeFixedLengthString(
174        jtfStreet.getText(), STREET_SIZE, raf);
175      FixedLengthStringIO.writeFixedLengthString(
176        jtfCity.getText(), CITY_SIZE, raf);
177      FixedLengthStringIO.writeFixedLengthString(
178        jtfState.getText(), STATE_SIZE, raf);
179      FixedLengthStringIO.writeFixedLengthString(
180        jtfZip.getText(), ZIP_SIZE, raf);
181    }
182    catch (IOException ex) {
183      ex.printStackTrace();
184    }
185  }
186
187  /** Read a record at the specified position */
188  public void readAddress(long position) throws IOException {
189    raf.seek(position);
190    string name = FixedLengthStringIO.readFixedLengthString(
191      NAME_SIZE, raf);
192    String street = FixedLengthStringIO.readFixedLengthString(
193      STREET_SIZE, raf);
```

last address

first address

```
194        String city = FixedLengthStringIO.readFixedLengthString(
195          CITY_SIZE, raf);
196        String state = FixedLengthStringIO.readFixedLengthString(
197          STATE_SIZE, raf);
198        String zip = FixedLengthStringIO.readFixedLengthString(
199          ZIP_SIZE, raf);
200
201        jtfName.setText(name);
202        jtfStreet.setText(street);
203        jtfCity.setText(city);
204        jtfState.setText(state);
205        jtfZip.setText(zip);
206      }
207
208      public static void main(String[] args) {
209        AddressBook frame = new AddressBook();
210        frame.pack();
211        frame.setTitle("AddressBook");
212        frame.setDefaultCloseOperation(JFrame.EXIT_ON_CLOSE);
213        frame.setVisible(true);
214      }
215    }
```

■ A random access file, `address.dat`, is created to store address information if the file does not yet exist (line 37). If it already exists, the file is opened. A random file object, `raf`, is used for both write and read operations. The size of each field in the record is fixed and therefore defined as a constant in lines 9–15.

■ The user interface is created in lines 44–100. The listeners are registered in lines 102–156. When the program starts, it displays the first record, if it exists, in lines 159–164.

■ The `writeAddress()` method sets the file pointer to the end of the file (line 170) and writes a new record to the file (lines 171–180).

■ The `readAddress()` method sets the file pointer at the specified position (line 189) and reads a record from the file (lines 190–199). The record is displayed in lines 201–205.

■ To add a record, you need to collect the address information from the user interface and write the address into the file (line 104).

■ The code to process button events is implemented in lines 102–156. For the *First* button, read the record from position `0` (line 110). For the *Next* button, read the record from the current file pointer (line 122). When a record is read, the file pointer is moved `2 * RECORD_SIZE` number of bytes ahead of the previous file pointer. For the *Previous* button, you need to display the record prior to the one being displayed now. So you have to move the file pointer two records before the current file pointer (line 135). For the *Last* button, read the record from the position at `raf.length() - 2 * RECORD_SIZE`.

KEY TERMS

binary I/O 606	sequential access file 621
deserialization 619	serialization 619
file pointer 622	stream 606
random access file 621	text I/O 606

CHAPTER SUMMARY

■ I/O can be classified into text I/O and binary I/O. Text I/O interprets data in sequences of characters. Binary I/O interprets data as raw binary values. How text is stored in a file is dependent on the encoding scheme for the file. Java automatically performs encoding and decoding for text I/O.

■ The `InputStream` and `OutputStream` classes are the roots of all binary I/O classes. `FileInputStream`/`FileOutputStream` associates a file for binary input/output. `BufferedInputStream`/`BufferedOutputStream` can be used to wrap on any binary I/O stream to improve performance. `DataInputStream`/`DataOutputStream` can be used to read/write primitive values and strings.

■ `ObjectInputStream`/`ObjectOutputStream` can be used to read/write objects in addition to primitive values and strings. To enable object serialization, the object's defining class must implement the `java.io.Serializable` marker interface.

■ The `RandomAccessFile` class enables you to read and write data to a file. You can open a file with the `"r"` mode to indicate that it is read-only, or with the `"rw"` mode to indicate that it is updateable. Since the `RandomAccessFile` class implements `DataInput` and `DataOutput` interfaces, many methods in `RandomAccessFile` are the same as those in `DataInputStream` and `DataOutputStream`.

REVIEW QUESTIONS

Sections 18.1–18.2

18.1 What is a text file, and what is a binary file? Can you view a text file or a binary file using a text editor?

18.2 How do you read or write data in Java? What is a stream?

Section 18.3 Text I/O vs. Binary I/O

18.3 What are the differences between text I/O and binary I/O?

18.4 How is a Java character represented in the memory, and how is a character represented in a text file?

18.5 If you write string `"ABC"` to an ASCII text file, what values are stored in the file?

18.6 If you write string `"100"` to an ASCII text file, what values are stored in the file? If you write a numeric byte-type value `100` using binary I/O, what values are stored in the file?

18.7 What is the encoding scheme for representing a character in a Java program? By default, what is the encoding scheme for a text file on Windows?

Section 18.4 Binary I/O Classes

18.8 Why do you have to declare to throw `IOException` in the method or use a `try-catch` block to handle `IOException` for Java IO programs?

18.9 Why should you always close streams?

18.10 `InputStream` reads bytes. Why does the `read()` method return an `int` instead of a byte? Find the abstract methods in `InputSteam` and `OutputStream`.

18.11 Does `FileInputStream`/`FileOutputStream` introduce any new methods? How do you create a `FileInputStream`/`FileOutputStream`?

18.12 What will happen if you attempt to create an input stream on a nonexistent file? What will happen if you attempt to create an output stream on an existing file? Can you append data to an existing file?

18.13 How do you append data to an existing text file using `java.io.PrintWriter`?

18.14 Suppose `input` is a `DataInputStream`, `input.available()` returns 100. After invoking `read()`, what is `input.available()`? After invoking `readInt()`, what is `input.available()`? After invoking `readChar()`, what is `input.available()`? After invoking `readDouble()`, what is `input.available()`?

18.15 What is written to a file using `writeByte(91)` on a `FileOutputStream`?

18.16 How do you check the end of a file in a binary input stream (`FileInputStream`, `DataInputStream`)?

18.17 What is wrong in the following code?

```java
import java.io.*;

public class Test {
  public static void main(String[] args) {
    try {
      FileInputStream fis = new FileInputStream("test.dat");
    }
    catch (IOException ex) {
      ex.printStackTrace();
    }
    catch (FileNotFoundException ex) {
      ex.printStackTrace();
    }
  }
}
```

18.18 Suppose you run the program on Windows using the default ASCII encoding. After the program is finished, how many bytes are in the file `t.txt`? Show the contents of each byte.

```java
public class Test {
  public static void main(String[] args) throws
      java.io.IOException {
    java.io.PrintWriter output = new
    java.io.PrintWriter("t.txt");
    output.printf("%s", "1234");
    output.printf("%s", "5678");
    output.close();
  }
}
```

18.19 After the program is finished, how many bytes are in the file `t.dat`? Show the contents of each byte.

```java
import java.io.*;

public class Test {
  public static void main(String[] args) throws IOException {
    DataOutputStream output = new DataOutputStream(
      new FileOutputStream("t.dat"));
    output.writeInt(1234);
    output.writeInt(5678);
    output.close();
  }
}
```

18.20 For each of the following statements on a `DataOutputStream out`, how many bytes are sent to the output?

```
output.writeChar('A');
output.writeChars("BC");
output.writeUTF("DEF");
```

18.21 What are the advantages of using buffered streams? Are the following statements correct?

```
BufferedInputStream input1 =
  new BufferedInputStream(new FileInputStream("t.dat"));

DataInputStream input2 = new DataInputStream(
  new BufferedInputStream(new FileInputStream("t.dat")));

ObjectInputStream input3 = new ObjectInputStream(
  new BufferedInputStream(new FileInputStream("t.dat")));
```

Section 18.6 Object I/O

18.22 What types of objects can be stored using the `ObjectOutputStream`? What is the method for writing an object? What is the method for reading an object? What is the return type of the method that reads an object from `ObjectInputStream`?

18.23 If you serialize two objects of the same type, will they take same space?

18.24 Is it true that any instance of `java.io.Serializable` can be successfully serialized? Are the static variables in an object serialized? How do you mark an instance variable not to be serialized?

18.25 Can you write an array to an `ObjectOutputStream`?

18.26 Is it true that `DataInputStream`/`DataOutputStream` can always be replaced by `ObjectInputStream`/`ObjectOutputStream`?

18.27 What will happen when you attempt to run the following code?

```java
import java.io.*;

public class Test {
  public static void main(String[] args) throws IOException {
    ObjectOutputStream output =
      new ObjectOutputStream(new
        FileOutputStream("object.dat"));

    output.writeObject(new A());
  }
}

class A implements Serializable {
  B b = new B();
}

class B {
}
```

Section 18.7 (Optional) Random Access Files

18.28 Can `RandomAccessFile` streams read and write a data file created by `DataOutputStream`? Can `RandomAccessFile` streams read and write objects?

18.29 Create a `RandomAccessFile` stream for the file `address.dat` to allow the updating of student information in the file. Create a `DataOutputStream` for the file `address.dat`. Explain the differences between these two statements.

18.30 What happens if the file `test.dat` does not exist when you attempt to compile and run the following code?

```
import java.io.*;

public class Test {
  public static void main(String[] args) {
    try {
      RandomAccessFile raf =
        new RandomAccessFile("test.dat", "r");
      int i = raf.readInt();
    }
    catch (IOException ex) {
      System.out.println("IO exception");
    }
  }
}
```

PROGRAMMING EXERCISES

Section 18.3 Text I/O vs. Binary I/O

18.1* (*Creating a text file*) Write a program to create a file named `Exercise18_1.txt` if it does not exist. Append new data to it if the file already exists. Write one hundred integers created randomly into the file using text I/O. Integers are separated by a space.

Section 18.4 Binary I/O Classes

18.2* (*Creating a binary data file*) Write a program to create a file named `Exercise18_2.dat` if it does not exist. Append new data to it if the file already exists. Write one hundred integers created randomly into the file using binary I/O.

18.3* (*Summing all the integers in a binary data file*) Suppose a binary data file named `Exercise18_3.dat` has been created using `writeInt(int)` in `DataOutputStream`. The file contains an unspecified number of integers. Write a program to find the total of integers.

18.4* (*Converting a text file into UTF*) Write a program that reads lines of characters from a text and writes each line as a UTF-8 string into a binary file. Display the sizes of the text file and the binary file. Use the following command to run the program:

```
java Exercise18_4 Welcome.java Welcome.utf
```

Section 18.6 Object I/O

18.5* (*Storing objects and arrays into a file*) Write a program that stores an array of five `int` values 1, 2, 3, 4 and 5, a `Date` object for current time, and a double value 5.5 into the file named `Exercise18_5.dat.`

18.6* (*Storing Loan objects*) The `Loan` class, introduced in §7.15, "Case Study: The Loan Class," does not implement `Serializable`. Rewrite the `Loan` class to implement `Serializable`. Write a program that creates five `Loan` objects and stores them in a file named `Exercise18_6.dat.`

18.7* (*Restoring objects from a file*) Suppose a file named `Exercise18_7.dat` has been created using the `ObjectOutputStream`. Write a program that reads the `Loan` objects from the file and computes the total loan amount. Suppose you don't know how many `Loan` objects are in the file. Use `EOFException` to end the loop.

Section 18.7 (Optional) Random Access Files

18.8* (*Updating count*) Suppose you want to track how many times a program has been executed. You may store an `int` to count the file. Increase the count by 1 each time this program is executed. Let the program be `Exercise18_8`, and store the count in `Exercise18_8.dat`.

18.9** (*Updating address*) Modify `AddressBook` in Listing 18.9, AddressBook.java, to add an *Update* button, as shown in Figure 18.21, to enable the user to modify an address that is being displayed.

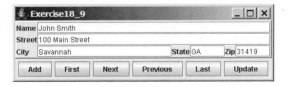

FIGURE 18.21 You can update the address record that is currently displayed.

RECURSION

Objectives

- To know what a recursive method is and the benefits of using recursive methods (§19.1).
- To determine the base cases in a recursive method (§§19.2–19.5).
- To understand how recursive method calls are handled in a call stack (§§19.2–19.3).
- To solve problems using recursion (§§19.2–19.7).
- To use an overloaded helper method to derive a recursive method (§19.5).
- To solve the Towers of Hanoi problem using recursion (§19.6).
- To draw fractals using recursion (§19.7).
- To understand the relationship and difference between recursion and iteration (§19.8).

19.1 Introduction

recursive method

A *recursive method* is a method that invokes itself directly or indirectly. Recursion is a useful programming technique. In some cases, using recursion enables you to develop a natural, straightforward, simple solution to a problem that would otherwise be difficult to solve. This chapter introduces the concepts and techniques of recursive programming and uses examples demonstrating how to "think recursively."

19.2 Example: Factorials

Many mathematical functions are defined using recursion. The factorial of a number n can be recursively defined as follows:

```
0! = 1;
n! = n x (n - 1)!; n > 0
```

How do you find $n!$ for a given n? It is easy to find $1!$ because you know that $0!$ and $1!$ is $1 \times 0!$. Assuming that you know $(n-1)!$, $n!$ can be obtained immediately using $n \times (n - 1)!$. Thus, the problem of computing $n!$ is reduced to computing $(n - 1)!$. When computing $(n - 1)!$, you can apply the same idea recursively until n is reduced to 0.

Let `factorial(n)` be the method for computing $n!$. If you call the method with $n = 0$, it immediately returns the result. The method knows how to solve the simplest case, which is referred to as the *base case* or the *stopping condition*. If you call the method with $n > 0$, it reduces the problem into a subproblem for computing the factorial of $n - 1$. The subproblem is essentially the same as the original problem, but is simpler or smaller than the original. Because the subproblem has the same property as the original, you can call the method with a different argument, which is referred to as a *recursive call*.

base case or stopping
condition

recursive call

The recursive algorithm for computing `factorial(n)` can be simply described as follows:

```
if (n == 0)
    return 1;
else
    return n * factorial(n - 1);
```

A recursive call can result in many more recursive calls because the method is dividing a subproblem into new subproblems. For a recursive method to terminate, the problem must eventually be reduced to a stopping case. When it reaches a stopping case, the method returns a result to its caller. The caller then performs a computation and returns the result to its own caller. This process continues until the result is passed back to the original caller. The original problem can now be solved by multiplying n with the result of `factorial(n - 1)`.

Listing 19.1 gives a complete program that prompts the user to enter a non-negative integer and displays the factorial for the number.

LISTING 19.1 ComputeFactorial.java

```
1 import javax.swing.JOptionPane;
2
3 public class ComputeFactorial {
4    /** Main method */
5    public static void main(String[] args) {
6        // Prompt the user to enter an integer
7        String intString = JOptionPane.showInputDialog(
8            "Please enter a non-negative integer:");
9
```

```
10      // Convert string into integer
11      int n = Integer.parseInt(intString);
12
13      // Display factorial
14      JOptionPane.showMessageDialog(null,
15        "Factorial of " + n + " is " + factorial(n));
16    }
17
18    /** Return the factorial for a specified number */
19    public static long factorial(int n) {
20      if (n == 0) // Base case                                    base case
21        return 1;
22      else
23        return n * factorial(n - 1); // Recursive call            recursion
24    }
25  }
```

The `factorial` method (lines 19–24) is essentially a direct translation of the recursive mathematical definition for the factorial into Java code. The call to `factorial` is recursive because it calls itself. The parameter passed to `factorial` is decremented until it reaches the base case of 0.

Figure 19.1 illustrates the execution of the recursive calls, starting with n = 4. The use of stack space for recursive calls is shown in Figure 19.2.

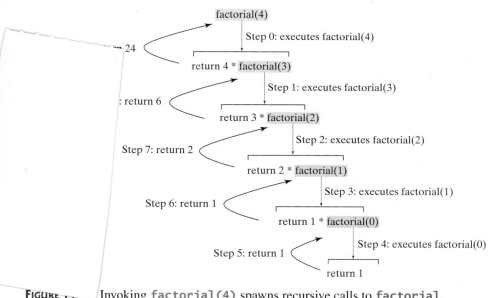

FIGURE 19.1 Invoking `factorial(4)` spawns recursive calls to `factorial`.

 Caution

Infinite recursion can occur if recursion does not reduce the problem in a manner that allows it to   infinite recursion
eventually converge into the base case. For example, if you mistakenly write the `factorial`
method as follows:

```
public static long factorial(int n) {
  return n * factorial(n - 1);
}
```

The method runs infinitely and causes a `StackOverflowError`.

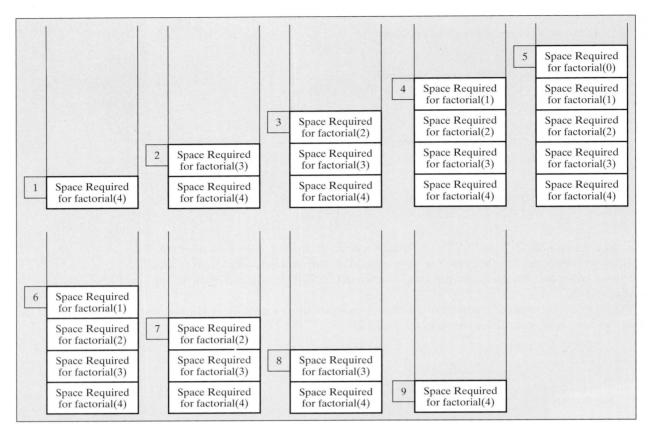

FIGURE 19.2 When `factorial(4)` is being executed, the `factorial` method is called recursively, causing memory space to dynamically change.

 Pedagogical Note

It is simpler and more efficient to implement the `factorial` method using a loop. However, the recursive `factorial` method is a good example to demonstrate the concept of recursion.

19.3 Example: Fibonacci Numbers

The `factorial` method in the preceding section could easily be rewritten without using recursion. In some cases, however, using recursion enables you to give a natural, straightforward, simple solution to a program that would otherwise be difficult to solve. Consider the well-known Fibonacci series problem, as follows:

The series: 0   1   1   2   3   5   8   13   21   34   55   89   . . .
indices: 0   1   2   3   4   5   6   7   8   9   10   11

The Fibonacci series begins with 0 and 1, and each subsequent number is the sum of the preceding two numbers in the series. The series can be recursively defined as follows:

```
fib(0) = 0;
fib(1) = 1;
fib(index) = fib(index - 2) + fib(index - 1); index >= 2
```

The Fibonacci series was named for Leonardo Fibonacci, a medieval mathematician, who originated it to model the growth of the rabbit population. It can be applied in numeric optimization and in various other areas.

How do you find `fib(index)` for a given `index`? It is easy to find `fib(2)` because you know `fib(0)` and `fib(1)`. Assuming that you know `fib(index - 2)` and `fib(index - 1)`, `fib(index)` can be obtained immediately. Thus, the problem of computing `fib(index)` is reduced to computing `fib(index - 2)` and `fib(index - 1)`. When computing `fib(index - 2)` and `fib(index - 1)`, you apply the idea recursively until `index` is reduced to 0 or 1.

The base case is `index = 0` or `index = 1`. If you call the method with `index = 0` or `index = 1`, it immediately returns the result. If you call the method with `index >= 2`, it divides the problem into two subproblems for computing `fib(index - 1)` and `fib(index - 2)` using recursive calls. The recursive algorithm for computing `fib(index)` can be simply described as follows:

```
if (index == 0)
   return 0;
else if (index == 1)
   return 1;
else
   return fib(index - 1) + fib(index - 2);
```

Listing 19.2 gives a complete program that prompts the user to enter an index and computes the Fibonacci number for the index.

LISTING 19.2   ComputeFibonacci.java

```
 1 import javax.swing.JOptionPane;
 2
 3 public class ComputeFibonacci {
 4   /** Main method */
 5   public static void main(String args[]) {
 6     // Read the index
 7     String intString = JOptionPane.showInputDialog(
 8       "Enter an index for the Fibonacci number:");
 9
10     // Convert string into integer
11     int index = Integer.parseInt(intString);
12
13     // Find and display the Fibonacci number
14     JOptionPane.showMessageDialog(null,
15       "Fibonacci number at index " + index + " is " + fib(index));
16   }
17
18   /** The method for finding the Fibonacci number */
19   public static long fib(long index) {
20     if (index == 0) // Base case                                    base case
21       return 0;
22     else if (index == 1) // Base case
23       return 1;
24     else  // Reduction and recursive calls
25       return fib(index - 1) + fib(index - 2);                       recursion
26   }
27 }
```

The program does not show the considerable amount of work done behind the scenes by the computer. Figure 19.3, however, shows successive recursive calls for evaluating `fib(4)`. The original method, `fib(4)`, makes two recursive calls, `fib(3)` and `fib(2)`, and then returns `fib(3)` + `fib(2)`. But in what order are these methods called? In Java, operands are evaluated from left to right. The labels in Figure 19.3 show the order in which methods are called.

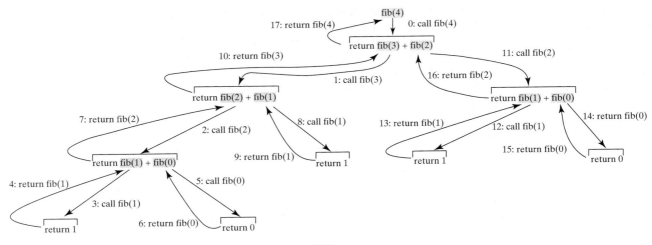

FIGURE 19.3 Invoking `fib(4)` spawns recursive calls to `fib`.

As shown in Figure 19.3, there are many duplicated recursive calls. For instance, `fib(2)` is called twice, `fib(1)` is called three times, and `fib(0)` is called twice. In general, computing `fib(index)` requires twice as many recursive calls as are needed for computing `fib(index - 1)`. As you try larger index values, the number of calls substantially increases.

Besides the large number of recursive calls, the computer requires more time and space to run recursive methods.

 Pedagogical Note

The recursive implementation of the `fib` method is very simple and straightforward, but not efficient. See Exercise 19.2 for an efficient solution using loops. The recursive `fib` method is a good example to demonstrate how to write recursive methods, though it is not practical.

19.4 Problem Solving Using Recursion

The preceding sections presented two classic recursion examples. All recursive methods have the following characteristics:

recursion characteristics

if-else

- The method is implemented using an `if-else` or a `switch` statement that leads to different cases.

base cases

- One or more *base cases* (the simplest case) are used to stop recursion.

reduction

- Every recursive call reduces the original problem, bringing it increasingly closer to a base case until it becomes that case.

In general, to solve a problem using recursion, you break it into subproblems. If a subproblem resembles the original problem, you can apply the same approach to solve the subproblem recursively. This subproblem is almost the same as the original problem in nature but with a smaller size.

Let us consider the simple problem of printing a message for n times. You can break the problem into two subproblems: one is to print the message one time and the other is to print the message n - 1 times. The second problem is the same as the original problem with a smaller size. The base case for the problem is n == 0. You can solve this problem using recursion as follows:

```
public static void nPrintln(String message, int times) {
  if (times >= 1) {
    System.out.println(message);
    nPrintln(message, times - 1);
  } // The base case is n == 0
}
```

recursive call

Note that the `fib` method in the preceding example returns a value to its caller, but the `nPrintln` method is `void` and does not return a value to its caller.

Many of the problems presented in the early chapters can be solved using recursion if you *think recursively*. Consider the palindrome problem in Listing 7.1. Recall that a string is a palindrome if it reads the same from the left and from the right. For example, mom and dad are palindromes, but uncle and aunt are not. The problem to check whether a string is a palindrome can be divided into two subproblems:

think recursively

- Check whether the first character and the last character of the string are equal.

- Ignore the two end characters and check whether the rest of the substring is a palindrome.

The second subproblem is the same as the original problem but with a smaller size. There are two base cases: (1) the two end characters are not same; (2) the string size is 0 or 1. In case 1, the string is not a palindrome; and in case 2, the string is a palindrome. The recursive method for this problem can be implemented in Listing 19.3.

LISTING 19.3 Recursive Palindrome Method

```
1 public static boolean isPalindrome(String s) {
2   if (s.length() <= 1) // Base case
3     return true;
4   else if (s.charAt(0) != s.charAt(s.length() - 1)) // Base case
5     return false;
6   else
7     return isPalindrome(s.substring(1, s.length() - 1));
8 }
```

recursive call

The `substring` method in line 7 creates a new string that is the same as the original string except without the first and last characters in the original string. Checking whether a string is a palindrome is equivalent to checking whether the substring is a palindrome if the two end characters in the original string are the same.

19.5 Recursive Helper Methods

The preceding recursive `isPalindrome` method is not efficient, because it creates a new string for every recursive call. To avoid creating new strings, you can use the low and high indices to indicate the range of the substring. These two indices must be passed to the recursive method. Since the original method is `isPalindrome(String s)`, you have to create a new method `isPalindrome(String s, int low, int high)` to accept additional information on the string, as shown in Listing 19.4.

LISTING 19.4 Palindrome Using a Helper Method

```
1 public static boolean isPalindrome(String s) {
2   return isPalindrome(s, 0, s.length() - 1);
3 }
4
5 public static boolean isPalindrome(String s, int low, int high) {
6   if (high <= low) // Base case
7     return true;
8   else if (s.charAt(low) != s.charAt(high)) // Base case
9     return false;
10  else
11    return isPalindrome(s, low + 1, high - 1);
12 }
```

recursive call

Two overloaded `isPalindrome` methods are declared. The first method, `isPalindrome` `(String s)`, checks whether a string is a palindrome, and the second method, `isPalindrome`

(String s, int low, int high), checks whether a substring s(low..high) is a palindrome. The first method passes the string s with low = 0 and high = s.length() – 1 to the second method. The second method can be invoked recursively to check a palindrome in an ever-shrinking substring. It is a common design technique in recursive programming to declare a second method that receives additional parameters. Such a method is known as a *recursive helper method*.

recursive helper method

Helper methods are very useful to design recursive solutions for problems involving strings and arrays. The following sections present two more examples.

19.5.1 Selection Sort

Selection sort was introduced in §6.8.1, "Selection Sort." Recall that selection sort finds the largest number in the list and places it last. It then finds the largest number remaining and places it next to last, and so on until the list contains only a single number. The problem can be divided into two subproblems:

- Find the largest number in the list and swap it with the last number.

- Ignore the last number and sort the remaining smaller list recursively.

The base case is that the list contains only one number. Listing 19.5 gives the recursive sort method.

LISTING 19.5 Recursive Sort Method

```
 1 public static void sort(double[] list) {
 2   sort(list, list.length - 1);
 3 }
 4
 5 public static void sort(double[] list, int high) {
 6   if (high > 1) {
 7     // Find the largest number and its index
 8     int indexOfMax = 0;
 9     double max = list[0];
10     for (int i = 1; i <= high; i++) {
11       if (list[i] > max) {
12         max = list[i];
13         indexOfMax = i;
14       }
15     }
16
17     // Swap the largest with the last number in the list
18     list[indexOfMax] = list[high];
19     list[high] = max;
20
21     // Sort the remaining list
22     sort(list, high - 1);
23   }
24 }
```

base case

recursive call

Two overloaded sort methods are declared. The first method, sort(double[] list), sorts an array in list[0..list.length - 1], and the second method, sort(double[] list, int high), sorts an array in list[0..high]. The second method can be invoked recursively to sort an ever-shrinking subarray.

19.5.2 Binary Search

Binary search was introduced in §6.7.2, "The Binary Search Approach." For binary search to work, the elements in the array must already be ordered. The binary search first compares the key with the element in the middle of the array. Consider the following three cases:

- Case 1: If the key is less than the middle element, recursively search the key in the first half of the array.

- Case 2: If the key is equal to the middle element, the search ends with a match.

- Case 3: If the key is greater than the middle element, recursively search the key in the second half of the array.

Case 1 and Case 3 reduce the search in a smaller list. Case 2 is a base case when there is a match. Another base case is that the search is exhausted without a match. Listing 19.6 gives a clear, simple solution for the binary search problem using recursion.

LISTING 19.6 Recursive Binary Search Method

```
1 public static int recursiveBinarySearch(int[] list, int key) {
2    int low = 0;
3    int high = list.length - 1;
4    return recursiveBinarySearch(list, key, low, high);
5 }
6
7 public static int recursiveBinarySearch(int[] list, int key,
8        int low, int high) {                                            base case
9    if (low > high) // The list has been exhausted without a match
10       return -low - 1; // Return -insertion point - 1
11
12   int mid = (low + high) / 2;
13   if (key < list[mid])
14       return recursiveBinarySearch(list, key, low, mid - 1);         recursive call
                                                                         base case
15   else if (key == list[mid])
16       return mid;
17   else
18       return recursiveBinarySearch(list, key, mid + 1, high);        recursive call
19 }
```

The first method finds a key in the whole list. The second method finds a key in the list with index from `low` to `high`.

The first `binarySearch` method passes the initial array with `low = 0` and `high = list.length - 1` to the second `binarySearch` method. The second method is invoked recursively to find the key in an ever-shrinking subarray.

19.6 Tower of Hanoi

The Tower of Hanoi problem is another classic recursion example. The problem can be solved easily using recursion, but is difficult to solve without using recursion.

The problem involves moving a specified number of disks of distinct sizes from one tower to another while observing the following rules:

- There are n disks labeled 1, 2, 3, ..., n, and three towers labeled A, B, and C.

- No disk can be on top of a smaller disk at any time.

- All the disks are initially placed on tower A.

- Only one disk can be moved at a time, and it must be the top disk on the tower.

The objective of the problem is to move all the disks from A to B with the assistance of C. For example, if you have three disks, as shown in Figure 19.4, the following steps will move all of the disks from A to B:

1. Move disk 1 from A to B.

2. Move disk 2 from A to C.

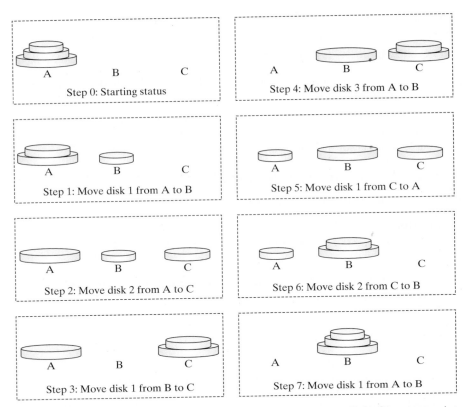

FIGURE 19.4 The goal of the Towers of Hanoi problem is to move disks from tower A to tower B without breaking the rules.

3. Move disk 1 from B to C.

4. Move disk 3 from A to B.

5. Move disk 1 from C to A.

6. Move disk 2 from C to B.

7. Move disk 1 from A to B.

 Note

The Towers of Hanoi is a classic computer science problem. There are many Websites devoted to this problem. The Website `www.cut-the-knot.com/recurrence/hanoi.html` is worth seeing.

In the case of three disks, you can find the solution manually. However, the problem is quite complex for a larger number of disks—even for four. Fortunately, the problem has an inherently recursive nature, which leads to a straightforward recursive solution.

The base case for the problem is `n = 1`. If `n == 1`, you could simply move the disk from A to B. When `n > 1`, you could split the original problem into three subproblems and solve them sequentially.

1. Move the first `n - 1` disks from A to C with the assistance of tower B.

2. Move disk `n` from A to B.

3. Move `n - 1` disks from C to B with the assistance of tower A.

The following method moves *n* disks from the `fromTower` to the `toTower` with the assistance of the `auxTower`:

```
void moveDisks(int n, char fromTower, char toTower, char auxTower)
```

The algorithm for the method can be described as follows:

```
if (n == 1) // Stopping condition
  Move disk 1 from the fromTower to the toTower;
else {
  moveDisks(n - 1, fromTower, auxTower, toTower);
  Move disk n from the fromTower to the toTower;
  moveDisks(n - 1, auxTower, toTower, fromTower);
}
```

Listing 19.7 gives a program that prompts the user to enter the number of disks and invokes the recursive method `moveDisks` to display the solution for moving the disks. A sample run of the following program appears in Figure 19.5.

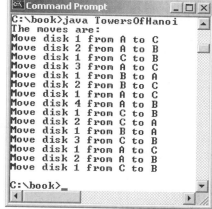

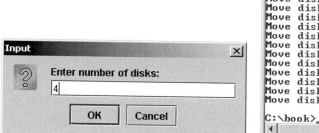

FIGURE 19.5   The program prompts the user to enter the number of disks and then displays the steps that must be followed to solve the Towers of Hanoi problem.

LISTING 19.7   TowersOfHanoi.java

```
 1  import javax.swing.JOptionPane;
 2
 3  public class TowersOfHanoi {
 4    /** Main method */
 5    public static void main(String[] args) {
 6      // Read number of disks, n
 7      String intString = JOptionPane.showInputDialog(
 8        "Enter number of disks:");
 9
10      // Convert string into integer
11      int n = Integer.parseInt(intString);
12
13      // Find the solution recursively
14      System.out.println("The moves are:");
15      moveDisks(n, 'A', 'B', 'C');
16    }
17
18    /** The method for finding the solution to move n disks
19        from fromTower to toTower with auxTower */
```

```
20   public static void moveDisks(int n, char fromTower,
21       char toTower, char auxTower) {
22     if (n == 1) // Stopping condition
23       System.out.println("Move disk " + n + " from " +
24         fromTower + " to " + toTower);
25     else {
26       moveDisks(n - 1, fromTower, auxTower, toTower);
27       System.out.println("Move disk " + n + " from " +
28         fromTower + " to " + toTower);
29       moveDisks(n - 1, auxTower, toTower, fromTower);
30     }
31   }
32 }
```

recursion

recursion

This problem is inherently recursive. Using recursion makes it possible to find a natural, simple solution. It would be difficult to solve the problem without using recursion.

Consider tracing the program for n = 3. The successive recursive calls are shown in Figure 19.6. As you can see, writing the program is easier than tracing the recursive calls. The system uses stacks to trace the calls behind the scenes. To some extent, recursion provides a level of abstraction that hides iterations and other details from the user.

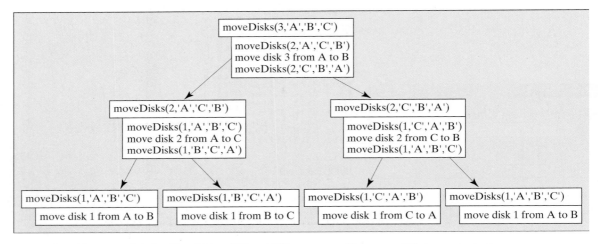

FIGURE 19.6 Invoking moveDisks(3, 'A', 'B', 'C') spawns calls to moveDisks recursively.

19.7 Fractals

A fractal is a geometrical figure, but unlike triangles, circles, and rectangles, fractals can be divided into parts that are each a reduced-size copy of the whole. There are many interesting examples of fractals. This section introduces a simple fractal, called the *Sierpinski triangle*, named after a famous Polish mathematician.

A Sierpinski triangle is created as follows:

1. It begins with an equilateral triangle, which is considered to be a Sierpinski fractal of order (or level) 0, as shown in Figure 19.7(a).

2. Connect the midpoints of the sides of the triangle of order 0 to create a Sierpinski triangle of order 1, as shown in Figure 19.7(b).

3. Leave the center triangle intact. Connect the midpoints of the sides of the three other triangles to create a Sierpinski of order 2, as shown in Figure 19.7(c).

4. You can repeat the same process recursively to create a Sierpinski triangle of order 3, 4, ..., and so on, as shown in Figure 19.7(d).

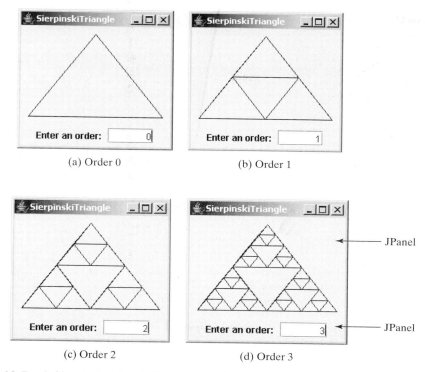

(a) Order 0   (b) Order 1

(c) Order 2   (d) Order 3

FIGURE 19.7   A Sierpinski triangle is a pattern of triangles.

The problem is inherently recursive. How do you develop a recursive solution for this problem? Consider the base case when the order is 0. It is easy to draw a Sierpinski triangle of order 0. How do you draw a Sierpinski triangle of order 1? The problem can be reduced by drawing three Sierpinski triangles of order 0. How do you draw a Sierpinski triangle of order 2? The problem can be reduced to drawing three Sierpinski triangles of order 1. So the problem of drawing a Sierpinski triangle of order n can be reduced to drawing three Sierpinski triangles of order $n - 1$.

Listing 19.8 gives a Java applet that displays a Sierpinski triangle of any order, as shown in Figure 19.7. You can enter an order in a text field to display a Sierpinski triangle of the specified order.

LISTING 19.8   SierpinskiTriangle.java

```
1 import javax.swing.*;
2 import java.awt.*;
3 import java.awt.event.*;
4
5 public class SierpinskiTriangle extends JApplet {
6   private JTextField jtfOrder = new JTextField(5); // To hold order
7   private SierpinskiTrianglePanel trianglePanel =
8     new SierpinskiTrianglePanel(); // To display the pattern
9
10  public SierpinskiTriangle() {
11    // Panel to hold label, text field, and a button
12    JPanel panel = new JPanel();
13    panel.add(new JLabel("Enter an order: "));
14    panel.add(jtfOrder);
15    jtfOrder.setHorizontalAlignment(SwingConstants.RIGHT);
16
17    // Add a Sierpinski Triangle panel to the applet
18    getContentPane().add(trianglePanel);
```

<table>
<tr><td>listener</td></tr>
<tr><td>set a new order</td></tr>
</table>

```
19      getContentPane().add(panel, BorderLayout.SOUTH);
20
21      // Register a listener
22      jtfOrder.addActionListener(new ActionListener() {
23        public void actionPerformed(ActionEvent e) {
24          trianglePanel.setOrder(Integer.parseInt(jtfOrder.getText()));
25        }
26      });
27    }
28
29    static class SierpinskiTrianglePanel extends JPanel {
30      private int order = 0;
31
32      /** Set a new order */
33      public void setOrder(int order) {
34        this.order = order;
35        repaint();
36      }
37
38      public void paintComponent(Graphics g) {
39        super.paintComponent(g);
40
41        // Select three points in proportion to the panel size
42        Point p1 = new Point(getWidth() / 2, 10);
43        Point p2 = new Point(10, getHeight() - 10);
44        Point p3 = new Point(getWidth() - 10, getHeight() - 10);
45
46        displayTriangles(g, order, p1, p2, p3);
47      }
48
49      private static void displayTriangles(Graphics g, int order,
50          Point p1, Point p2, Point p3) {
51        if (order >= 0) {
52          // Draw a triangle to connect three points
53          g.drawLine(p1.x, p1.y, p2.x, p2.y);
54          g.drawLine(p1.x, p1.y, p3.x, p3.y);
55          g.drawLine(p2.x, p2.y, p3.x, p3.y);
56
57          // Get three midpints in the triangle
58          Point midBetweenP1P2 = midpoint(p1, p2);
59          Point midBetweenP2P3 = midpoint(p2, p3);
60          Point midBetweenP3P1 = midpoint(p3, p1);
61
62          // Recursively display three triangles
63          displayTriangles(g, order - 1,
64            p1, midBetweenP1P2, midBetweenP3P1);
65          displayTriangles(g, order - 1,
66            midBetweenP1P2, p2, midBetweenP2P3);
67          displayTriangles(g, order - 1,
68            midBetweenP3P1, midBetweenP2P3, p3);
69        }
70      }
71
72      private static Point midpoint(Point p1, Point p2) {
73        return new Point((p1.x + p2.x) / 2, (p1.y + p2.y) / 2);
74      }
75    }
76  }
```

Margin notes:
- three initial points (line 42)
- draw a triangle (line 53)
- top subtriangle (line 62)
- left subtriangle (line 64)
- right subtriangle (line 66)
- **main** method omitted (line 75)

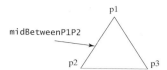

The initial triangle has three points set in proportion to the panel size (lines 42–44). The `displayTriangles(g, order, p1, p2, p3)` method performs the following tasks if `order >= 0`:

1. Display a triangle to connect three points `p1`, `p2`, and `p3` in lines 53–55.

2. Obtain a midpoint between `p1` and `p2` (line 58), a midpoint between `p2` and `p3` (line 59), and a midpoint between `p3` and `p1` (line 60).

3. Recursively invoke `displayTriangles` with a reduced order to display three smaller triangles (lines 63–68).

A Sierpinski triangle is displayed in a `SierpinskiTrianglePanel`. The `order` property in the inner class `SierpinskiTrianglePanel` specifies the order for the Sierpinski triangle. The `Point` class, introduced in §14.4, "Mouse Events," represents a point on a component. The `midpoint(Point p1, Point p2)` method returns the midpoint between `p1` and `p2` (lines 72–74).

19.8 Recursion versus Iteration

Recursion is an alternative form of program control. It is essentially repetition without a loop control. When you use loops, you specify a loop body. The repetition of the loop body is controlled by the loop-control structure. In recursion, the method itself is called repeatedly. A selection statement must be used to control whether to call the method recursively or not.

Recursion bears substantial overhead. Each time the program calls a method, the system must assign space for all of the method's local variables and parameters. This can consume considerable memory and requires extra time to manage the additional space.

Any problem that can be solved recursively can be solved nonrecursively with iterations. Recursion has many negative aspects: it uses up too much time and too much memory. Why, then, should you use it? In some cases, using recursion enables you to specify a clear, simple solution that would otherwise be difficult to obtain.

The decision whether to use recursion or iteration should be based on the nature of the problem you are trying to solve and your understanding of the problem. The rule of thumb is to use whichever of the two approaches can best develop an intuitive solution that naturally mirrors the problem. If an iterative solution is obvious, use it. It will generally be more efficient than the recursive option.

Note

Your recursive program could run out of memory, causing a `StackOverflowError`.

StackOverflowError

Tip

If you are concerned about your program's performance, avoid using recursion, because it takes more time and consumes more memory than iteration.

performance concern

KEY TERMS

base case   636
infinite recursion   637
recursive helper method   641

recursive method   636
stopping condition   636

CHAPTER SUMMARY

- A recursive method is a method that invokes itself directly or indirectly. For a recursive method to terminate, there must be one or more base cases.

- Recursion is an alternative form of program control. It is essentially repetition without a loop control. It can be used to specify simple, clear solutions for inherently recursive problems that would otherwise be difficult to solve.

- Sometimes the original method needs to be modified to receive additional parameters in order to be invoked recursively. A recursive helper method can be declared for this purpose.

- Recursion bears substantial overhead. Each time the program calls a method, the system must assign space for all of the method's local variables and parameters. This can consume considerable memory and requires extra time to manage the additional space.

REVIEW QUESTIONS

Sections 19.1–19.3

19.1 What is a recursive method? Describe the characteristics of recursive methods. What is an infinite recursion?

19.2 Write a recursive mathematical definition for computing 2^n for a positive integer n.

19.3 Write a recursive mathematical definition for computing x^n for a positive integer n and a real number x.

19.4 Write a recursive mathematical definition for computing $1 + 2 + 3 + \cdots + n$ for a positive integer n.

19.5 How many times is the `factorial` method in Listing 19.1 invoked for `factorial(6)`?

19.6 How many times is the `fib` method in Listing 19.2 invoked for `fib(6)`?

19.7 Show the output of the following program:

```
public class Test {
  public static void main(String[] args) {
    System.out.println(
      "Sum is " + xMethod(5));
  }

  public static int xMethod(int n) {
    if (n == 1)
      return 1;
    else
      return n + xMethod(n - 1);
  }
}
```

```
public class Test {
  public static void main(String[] args) {
    xMethod(1234567);
  }

  public static void xMethod(int n) {
    if (n > 0) {
      System.out.print(n % 10);
      xMethod(n / 10);
    }
  }
}
```

19.8   Show the output of the following two programs:

```java
public class Test {
  public static void main(String[] args) {
    xMethod(5);
  }

  public static void xMethod(int n) {
    if (n > 0) {
      System.out.print(n + " ");
      xMethod(n - 1);
    }
  }
}
```

```java
public class Test {
  public static void main(String[] args) {
    xMethod(5);
  }

  public static void xMethod(int n) {
    if (n > 0) {
      xMethod(n - 1);
      System.out.print(n + " ");
    }
  }
}
```

19.9   What is wrong in the following method?

```java
public class Test {
  public static void main(String[] args) {
    xMethod(1234567);
  }

  public static void xMethod(double n) {
    if (n != 0) {
      System.out.print(n);
      xMethod(n / 10);
    }
  }
}
```

```java
public class Test {
  public static void main(String[] args) {
    Test test = new Test();
    System.out.println(test.toString());
  }

  public Test() {
    Test test = new Test();
  }
}
```

Sections 19.4–19.6

19.10   Show the call stack for `isPalindrome("abcba")` using the methods declared in Listing 19.3 and Listing 19.4, respectively.

19.11   Show the call stack for `selectionSort(new double[]{2, 3, 5, 1})` using the method declared in Listing 19.5.

19.12   What is a recursive helper method?

Section 19.6 Towers of Hanoi

19.13   How many times is the `moveDisks` method in Listing 19.7 invoked for `moveDisks(5, 'A', 'B', 'C')`?

Section 19.8 Recursion versus Iteration

19.14   Which of the following statements are true?

- Any recursive method can be converted into a non-recursive method.
- Recursive methods take more time and memory to execute than non-recursive methods.
- Recursive methods are *always* simpler than non-recursive methods.
- There is always a condition statement in a recursive method to check whether a base case is reached.

19.15   What is the cause for the stack overflow exception?

PROGRAMMING EXERCISES

Sections 19.2–19.3

19.1 (*Computing factorials*) Rewrite the `factorial` method in Listing 19.1 using iterations.

19.2* (*Fibonacci numbers*) Rewrite the `fib` method in Listing 19.2 using iterations.

Hint

To compute `fib(n)` without recursion, you need to obtain `fib(n - 2)` and `fib(n - 1)` first. Let `f0` and `f1` denote the two previous Fibonacci numbers. The current Fibonacci number would then be `f0 + f1`. The algorithm can be described as follows:

```
f0 = 0; // For fib(0)
f1 = 1; // For fib(1)

for (int i = 1; i <= n; i++) {
  currentFib = f0 + f1;
  f0 = f1;
  f1 = currentFib;
}

// After the loop, currentFib is fib(n)
```

19.3* (*Computing greatest common divisor using recursion*) The `gcd(m, n)` can also be defined recursively as follows:

- If `m % n` is 0, gcd `(m, n)` is `n`.
- Otherwise, `gcd(m, n)` is `gcd(n, m % n)`.

Write a recursive method to find the GCD. Write a test program that computes `gcd(24, 16)` and `gcd(255, 25)`.

19.4 (*Summing series*) Write a recursive method to compute the following series:

$$m(i) = 1 + \frac{1}{2} + \frac{1}{3} + \cdots + \frac{1}{i}$$

19.5 (*Summing series*) Write a recursive method to compute the following series:

$$m(i) = \frac{1}{3} + \frac{2}{5} + \frac{3}{7} + \frac{4}{9} + \frac{5}{11} + \frac{6}{13} + \cdots + \frac{i}{2i + 1}$$

19.6** (*Summing the series*) Write a recursive method to compute the following series:

$$m(i) = \frac{1}{2} + \frac{2}{3} + \cdots + \frac{i}{i + 1}$$

19.7* (*Fibonacci series*) Modify Listing 19.2, ComputeFibonacci.java, so that the program finds the number of times the `fib` method is called.

Hint

Use a static variable and increment it every time the method is called.

Section 19.4 Problem Solving Using Recursion

19.8** (*Printing the digits in an integer reversely*) Write a recursive method that displays an `int` value reversely on the console using the following header:

public static void reverseDisplay(**int** value)

For example, `reverseDisplay(12345)` displays `54321`.

19.9** (*Printing the characters in a string reversely*) Write a recursive method that displays a string reversely on the console using the following header:

```
public static void reverseDisplay(String value)
```

For example, `reverseDisplay("abcd")` displays dcba.

19.10* (*Occurrences of a specified character in a string*) Write a recursive method that finds the number of occurrences of a specified letter in a string using the following method header:

```
public static int count(String str, char a)
```

For example, `count("Welcome", 'e')` returns 2.

19.11** (*Summing the digits in an integer using recursion*) Write a recursive method that computes the sum of the digits in an integer. Use the following method header:

```
public static int sumDigits(long n)
```

For example, `sumDigits(234)` returns 2 + 3 + 4 = 9.

Section 19.5 Recursion Helper Methods

19.12** (*Printing the characters in a string reversely*) Rewrite Exercise 19.9 using a helper method to pass the substring high index to the method. The helper method header is:

```
public static void reverseDisplay(String value, int high)
```

19.13** (*Finding the largest number in an array*) Write a recursive method that returns the largest integer in an array.

19.14* (*Finding the number of uppercase letters in a string*) Write a recursive method to return the number of uppercase letters in a string.

19.15* (*Occurrences of a specified character in a string*) Rewrite Exercise 19.10 using a helper method to pass the substring high index to the method. The helper method header is:

```
public static int count(String str, char a, int high)
```

19.16* (*Finding the number of uppercase letters in an array*) Write a recursive method to return the number of uppercase letters in an array of characters. You need to declare the following two methods. The second one is a recursive helper method.

```
public static int count(char[] chars)
public static int count(char[] chars, int high)
```

19.17* (*Occurrences of a specified character in an array*) Write a recursive method that finds the number of occurrences of a specified character in an array. You need to declare the following two methods. The second one is a recursive helper method.

```
public static int count(char[] chars, char ch)
public static int count(char[] chars, char ch, int high)
```

Sections 19.6 Tower of Hanoi

19.18* (*Towers of Hanoi*) Modify Listing 19.7, TowersOfHanoi.java, so that the program finds the number of moves needed to move *n* disks from tower A to tower B. (Hint: Use a static variable and increment it every time the method is called.)

19.19* (*Sierpinski triangle*) Revise Listing 19.8 to develop an applet that lets the user use the Increase and Decrease buttons to increase or decrease the current order by 1, as shown in Figure 19.8(a). The initial order is 0. If the current order is 0, the Decrease button is ignored.

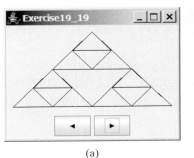 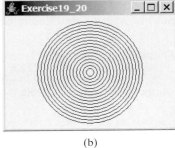

(a)   (b)

FIGURE 19.8 (a) Exercise 19.19 uses the Increase and Decrease buttons to increase or decrease the current order by 1. (b) Exercise 19.10 draws ovals using a recursive method.

19.20*(*Displaying circles*) Write a Java applet that displays ovals, as shown in Figure 19.8(b). The ovals are centered in the panel. The gap between two adjacent ovals is 10 pixels, and the gap between the panel and the largest oval is also 10.

Comprehensive

19.21***(*String permutation*) Write a recursive method to print all the permutations of a string. For example, for a string abc, the printout is

```
abc
acb
bac
bca
cab
cba
```

Hint

Declare the following two methods. The second is a helper method.

public static void displayPermutation(String s)
public static void displayPermutation(String s1, String s2)

The first method simply invokes **displayPermutation("", s)**. The second method uses a loop to move a character from **s2** to **s1** and recursively invoke it with a new **s1** and **s2**. The base case is that **s2** is empty and prints **s1** to the console.

19.22***(*Creating a maze*) Write an applet that will find a path in a maze, as shown in Figure 19.9(a). The applet should also run as an application. The maze is represented by an 8 × 8 board. The path must meet the following conditions:

- The path is between the upper-left corner cell and the lower-right corner cell in the maze.

■ The applet enables the user to insert or remove a mark on a cell. A path consists of adjacent unmarked cells. Two cells are said to be adjacent if they are horizontal or vertical neighbors, but not if they are diagonal neighbors.

■ The path does not contain cells that form a square. The path in Figure 19.9(b), for example, does not meet this condition. (The condition makes a path easy to identify on the board.)

(a) Correct path

(b) Illegal path

FIGURE 19.9   The program finds a path from the upper-left corner to the bottom-right corner.

19.23*(*Koch snowflake fractal*) The text presented the Sierpinski triangle fractal. In this exercise, you will write an applet to display another fractal, called the *Koch snowflake*, named after a famous Swedish mathematician. A Koch snowflake is created as follows:

1. It begins with an equilateral triangle, which is considered to be the Koch fractal of order (or level) 0, as shown in Figure 19.10(a).
2. Divide each line in the shape into three equal line segments and draw an outward equilateral triangle with the middle line segment as the base to create a Koch fractal of order 1, as shown in Figure 19.10(b).
3. Repeat step 2 to create a Koch fractal of order 2, 3, ..., and so on, as shown in Figure 19.10(c).

(a)

(b)

(c)

(d)

FIGURE 19.10   A Koch snowflake is a fractal starting with a triangle.

DATA STRUCTURES

The design and implementation of efficient data structures is an important subject in computer science. Data structures such as lists, stacks, queues, sets, maps, heaps, and binary trees have many applications in compiler construction, computer operating systems, and file management. Java provides the data structures for lists, stacks, sets, and maps in the collections framework. This part of the book introduces the main subjects in a typical data structures course. You will learn the concepts and implementation of several popular data structures in Chapter 20, "Lists, Stacks, Queues, Trees, and Heaps," JDK 1.5 generics in Chapter 21, "Generics," the Java collection framework in Chapter 22, "Java Collections Framework," and finally, algorithm efficiency and sorting algorithms in Chapter 23 "Algorithm Efficiency and Sorting."

Chapter 20
Lists, Stacks, Queues, Trees, and Heaps

Chapter 21
Generics

Chapter 22
Java Collections Framework

Chapter 23
Algorithm Efficiency and Sorting

Prerequisites for Part 5

All the chapters after Chapter 16, "Applets and Multimedia," are designed with minimal dependencies so that they can be reordered flexibly.

flexible ordering

Chapter 20

Chapter 20, "Lists, Stacks, Queues, Trees, and Heaps," can be covered after Chapter 10, "Abstract Classes and Interfaces."

Chapter 21

Chapter 21, "Generics," can be intertwined with Chapter 11, "Object-Oriented Design."

Chapter 22

Chapter 22, "Java Collections Framework," can be covered after Chapter 11, "Object-Oriented Design," and Chapter 21, "Generics."

Chapter 23

Chapter 23, "Algorithm Efficiency and Sorting," can be covered after Chapter 19, "Recursion."

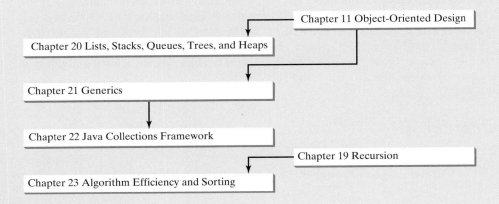

LISTS, STACKS, QUEUES, TREES, AND HEAPS

Objectives

- To describe what a data structure is (§20.1).

- To explain the limitations of arrays (§20.1).

- To design and implement a dynamic list using an array (§20.2.1).

- To design and implement a dynamic list using a linked structure (§20.2.2).

- To design and implement a stack using an array list (§20.3).

- To design and implement a queue using a linked list (§20.3).

- (Optional) To design and implement a binary search tree (§20.4).

- (Optional) To design and implement a heap (§20.5).

- (Optional) To design and implement a priority queue (§20.6).

20.1 Introduction

A data structure is a collection of data organized in some fashion. A data structure not only stores data, but also supports the operations for accessing and manipulating data in the structure. For example, an array is a data structure that holds a collection of data in sequential order. You can find the size of the array, and store, retrieve, and modify data in the array. Arrays are simple and easy to use, but they have two limitations: (1) once an array is created, its size cannot be altered; (2) an array does not provide adequate support for insertion and deletion operations. This chapter introduces dynamic data structures that grow and shrink at runtime. `ArrayList`, introduced in §9.9, are examples of dynamic data structures. You have used this class. You will learn how to design and implement it in this chapter.

Five classic dynamic data structures are introduced in this chapter: lists, stacks, queues, binary trees, and heaps. A *list* is a collection of data stored sequentially. It supports insertion and deletion anywhere in the list. A *stack* can be perceived as a special type of list where insertions and deletions take place only at one end, referred to as the *top* of the stack. A *queue* represents a waiting list, where insertions take place at the back (also referred to as the tail) of the queue, and deletions take place from the front (also referred to as the head) of the queue. A *binary tree* is a data structure that supports searching, sorting, inserting, and deleting data efficiently. A *heap* is a data structure that can be used to develop efficient sorting and priority queue algorithms.

In object-oriented thinking, a data structure is an object that stores other objects, referred to as data or elements. Some people refer to data structures as *container objects* or *collection objects*. To define a data structure is essentially to declare a class. The class for a data structure should use data fields to store data and provide methods to support such operations as insertion and deletion. To create a data structure is therefore to create an instance from the class. You can then apply the methods on the instance to manipulate the data structure, such as inserting an element into the data structure or deleting an element from the data structure.

The focus of this chapter is to introduce the design and implementation of the interfaces and classes for data structures: lists, stacks, queues, binary trees, heaps, and priority queues. These are classic data structures typically covered in a data structures course. Lists, stacks, queues, and heaps are supported in the Java API. Chapter 22, "Java Collections Framework," introduces how to use these data structures in the Java API. Some useful applications of data structures are provided in Supplement Part 3 on the Companion Website. Since knowledge of implementing data structures is not required for learning the Java collections framework, this chapter is designed independently of Chapter 22 and therefore can be skipped.

20.2 Lists

A list is a popular data structure for storing data in sequential order. For example, a list of students, a list of available rooms, a list of cities, and a list of books can all be stored using lists. The operations listed below are typical of most lists:

- Retrieve an element from a list.

- Insert a new element to a list.

- Delete an element from a list.

- Find how many elements are in a list.

- Find whether an element is in a list.

- Find whether a list is empty.

There are two ways to implement a list. One is to use an *array* to store the elements. Arrays are dynamically created. If the capacity of the array is exceeded, create a new, larger array and copy all the elements from the current array to the new array. The other approach is to

use a *linked structure*. A linked structure consists of nodes. Each node is dynamically created to hold an element. All the nodes are linked together to form a list. Thus you can declare
two classes for lists. For convenience, let's name these two classes `MyArrayList` and
`MyLinkedList`. These two classes have common operations but different data fields. The
common operations can be generalized in an interface or an abstract class. As discussed in
§11.6.8, "Interfaces vs. Abstract Classes," a good strategy is to combine the virtues of interfaces and abstract classes by providing both an interface and an abstract class in the design so
that the user can use either of them, whichever is convenient. Such an abstract class is known
as a *convenience class*.

convenience class

Let us name the interface `MyList` and the convenience class `MyAbstractList`. Figure 20.1
shows the relationship of `MyList`, `MyAbstractList`, `MyArrayList`, and `MyLinkedList`.
The methods in `MyList` and the methods implemented in `MyAbstractList` are shown in
Figure 20.2. Listing 20.1 gives the source code for `MyList`.

FIGURE 20.1 `MyList` defines a common interface for `MyAbstractList`, `MyArrayList`,
and `MyLinkedList`.

LISTING 20.1 MyList.java

```java
1  public interface MyList {
2    /** Add a new element o at the end of this list */
3    public void add(Object o);
4
5    /** Add a new element o at the specified index in this list */
6    public void add(int index, Object o);
7
8    /** Clear the list */
9    public void clear();
10
11   /** Return true if this list contains the element o */
12   public boolean contains(Object o);
13
14   /** Return the element from this list at the specified index */
15   public Object get(int index);
16
17   /** Return the index of the first matching element in this list.
18    *  Return -1 if no match. */
19   public int indexOf(Object o);
20
21   /** Return true if this list contains no elements */
22   public boolean isEmpty();
23
24   /** Return the index of the last matching element in this list
25    *  Return -1 if no match. */
26   public int lastIndexOf(Object o);
27
28   /** Remove the first occurrence of the element o from this list.
29    *  Shift any subsequent elements to the left.
30    *  Return true if the element is removed. */
31   public boolean remove(Object o);
32
```

```
33   /** Remove the element at the specified position in this list
34    *  Shift any subsequent elements to the left.
35    *  Return the element that was removed from the list. */
36   public Object remove(int index);
37
38   /** Replace the element at the specified position in this list
39    *  with the specified element and return the new set. */
40   public Object set(int index, Object o);
41
42   /** Return the number of elements in this list */
43   public int size();
44 }
```

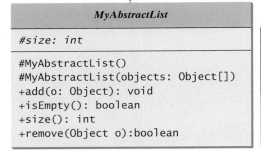

«interface» *MyList*	
+add(o: Object): void	Appends a new element o at the end of this list.
+add(index: int, o: Object): void	Adds a new element o at the specified index in this list.
+clear(): void	Removes all the elements from this list.
+contains(o: Object): boolean	Returns true if this list contains the element o.
+get(index: int): Object	Returns the element from this list at the specified index.
+indexOf(o: Object): int	Returns the index of the first matching element in this list.
+isEmpty(): boolean	Returns true if this list contains no elements.
+lastIndexOf(o: Object): int	Returns the index of the last matching element in this list.
+remove(o: Object): boolean	Removes the element o from this list.
+size(): int	Returns the number of elements in this list.
+remove(index: int): Object	Removes the element at the specified index and returns the removed element.
+set(index: int, o: Object): Object	Sets the element at the specified index and returns the element you are replacing.

MyAbstractList	
#size: int	The size of the list.
#MyAbstractList()	Creates a default list.
#MyAbstractList(objects: Object[])	Creates a list from an array of objects.
+add(o: Object): void	Implements the add method.
+isEmpty(): boolean	Implements the isEmpty method.
+size(): int	Implements the size method.
+remove(Object o):boolean	Implements the remove method.

FIGURE 20.2 `MyList` supports many methods for manipulating a list. `MyAbstractList` provides a partial implementation of the `MyList` interface.

`MyAbstractList` declares variable `size` to indicate the number of elements in the list. The methods `isEmpty` and `size` can be implemented in the class in Listing 20.2.

LISTING 20.2 MyAbstractList.java

size

no-arg constructor

```
1 public abstract class MyAbstractList implements MyList {
2    protected int size = 0; // The size of the list
3
4    /** Create a default list */
5    protected MyAbstractList() {
6    }
7
```

```
 8    /** Create a list from an array of objects */
 9    protected MyAbstractList(Object[] objects) {                    constructor
10      for (int i = 0; i < objects.length; i++)
11        this.add(objects[i]);
12    }
13
14    /** Add a new element o at the end of this list */
15    public void add(Object o) {
16      add(size, o);
17    }
18
19    /** Return true if this list contains no elements */
20    public boolean isEmpty() {
21      return size == 0;
22    }
23
24    /** Return the number of elements in this list */
25    public int size() {
26      return size;
27    }
28
29    /** Remove the first occurrence of the element o from this list.
30     *  Shift any subsequent elements to the left.
31     *  Return true if the element is removed. */
32    public boolean remove(Object o) {
33      if (indexOf(o) >= 0) {
34        remove(indexOf(o));
35        return true;
36      }
37      else
38        return false;
39    }
40 }
```

The following sections give the implementation for **MyArrayList** and **MyLinkedList**, respectively.

20.2.1   Array Lists

Array is a fixed-size data structure. Once an array is created, its size cannot be changed. Nevertheless, you can still use arrays to implement dynamic data structures. The trick is to create a larger new array to replace the current array if the current array cannot hold new elements in the list. This section shows how to use arrays to implement **MyArrayList**.

Initially, an array, say **data** of **Object[]** type, is created with a default size. When inserting a new element into the array, first make sure that there is enough room in the array. If not, create a new array twice as large as the current one. Copy the elements from the current array to the new array. The new array now becomes the current array. Before inserting a new element at a specified index, shift all the elements after the index to the right and increase the list size by 1, as shown in Figure 20.3.

Note

The data array is of type **Object[]**. Each cell in the array actually stores the reference of an object.

To remove an element at a specified index, shift all the elements after the index to the left by one position and decrease the list size by 1, as shown in Figure 20.4.

MyArrayList uses an array to implement **MyAbstractList**, as shown in Figure 20.5. Its implementation is given in Listing 20.3.

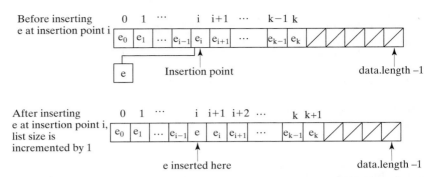

FIGURE 20.3 Inserting a new element to the array requires that all the elements after the insertion point be shifted one position to the right so that the new element can be inserted at the insertion point.

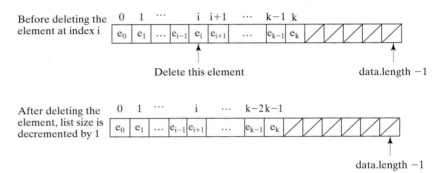

FIGURE 20.4 Deleting an element from the array requires that all the elements after the deletion point be shifted one position to the left.

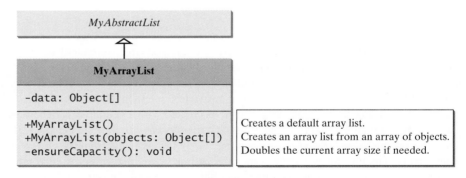

FIGURE 20.5 `MyArrayList` implements a list using an array.

LISTING 20.3 MyArrayList.java

initial capacity
array

```java
1  public class MyArrayList extends MyAbstractList {
2    public static final int INITIAL_CAPACITY = 16;
3    private Object[] data = new Object[INITIAL_CAPACITY];
4
```

```
 5    /** Create a default list */
 6    public MyArrayList() {
 7    }
 8
 9    /** Create a list from an array of objects */
10    public MyArrayList(Object[] objects) {
11      data = objects;
12      size = objects.length;
13    }
14
15    /** Add a new element o at the specified index in this list */
16    public void add(int index, Object o) {
17      ensureCapacity();
18
19      // Move the elements to the right after the specified index
20      for (int i = size - 1; i >= index; i--)
21        data[i + 1] = data[i];
22
23      // Insert new element to data[index]
24      data[index] = o;
25
26      // Increase size by 1
27      size++;
28    }
29
30    /** Create a new larger array, double the current size */
31    private void ensureCapacity() {
32      if (size >= data.length) {
33        Object[] newData = new Object[data.length * 2];          double capacity
34        System.arraycopy(data, 0, newData, 0, data.length);
35        data = newData;
36      }
37    }
38
39    /** Clear the list */
40    public void clear() {
41      data = new Object[INITIAL_CAPACITY];
42    }
43
44    /** Return true if this list contains the element o */
45    public boolean contains(Object o) {
46      for (int i = 0; i < size; i++)
47        if (o.equals(data[i])) return true;
48
49      return false;
50    }
51
52    /** Return the element from this list at the specified index */
53    public Object get(int index) {
54      return data[index];
55    }
56
57    /** Return the index of the first matching element in this list.
58     *  Return -1 if no match. */
59    public int indexOf(Object o) {
60      for (int i = 0; i < size; i++)
61        if (o.equals(data[i])) return i;
62
```

```
63        return -1;
64    }
65
66    /** Return the index of the last matching element in this list
67     *  Return -1 if no match. */
68    public int lastIndexOf(Object o) {
69      for (int i = size - 1; i >= 0; i--)
70        if (o.equals(data[i])) return i;
71
72      return -1;
73    }
74
75    /** Remove the element at the specified position in this list
76     *  Shift any subsequent elements to the left.
77     *  Return the element that was removed from the list. */
78    public Object remove(int index) {
79      Object o = data[index];
80
81      // Shift data to the left
82      for (int j = index; j < size - 1; j++)
83        data[j] = data[j + 1];
84
85      // Decrement size
86      size--;
87
88      return o;
89    }
90
91    /** Replace the element at the specified position in this list
92     *  with the specified element. */
93    public Object set(int index, Object o) {
94      Object old = data[index];
95      data[index] = o;
96      return old;
97    }
98
99    /** Override toString() to return elements in the list */
100   public String toString() {
101     StringBuffer result = new StringBuffer("[");
102
103     for (int i = 0; i < size; i++) {
104       result.append(data[i]);
105       if (i < size - 1) result.append(", ");
106     }
107
108     return result.toString() + "]";
109   }
110 }
```

The constant `INITIAL_CAPACITY` (line 2) is used to create an initial array `data` of type `Object` (line 3).

The `add(int index, Object o)` method (lines 16–28) adds element `o` at the specified `index` in the array. This method first invokes `ensureCapacity()` (line 17), which ensures that there is a space in the array for the new element. It then shifts all the elements after the index one position to the right before inserting the element (lines 20–21). After the element is added, `size` is incremented by 1 (line 27). Note that variable `size` is defined as `protected` in `MyAbstractList`, so it can be accessed in `MyArrayList`.

The `ensureCapacity()` method (lines 31–37) checks whether the array is full. If so, create a new array that doubles the current array size, copy the current array to the new array using the `System.arraycopy` method, and set the new array as the current array.

The `clear()` method (lines 40–42) creates a brand-new array with initial capacity.

The `contains(Object o)` method (lines 45–50) checks whether element o is contained in the array by comparing o with each element in the array using the `equals` method.

The `get(int index)` method (lines 53–55) simply returns `data[index]`. The implementation of this method is simple and efficient.

The `indexOf(Object o)` method (lines 59–64) compares element o with the elements in the array starting from the first one. If a match is found, the index of the element is returned; otherwise, it returns −1.

The `lastIndexOf(Object o)` method (lines 68–73) compares element o with the elements in the array starting from the last one. If a match is found, the index of the element is returned; otherwise, it returns −1.

The `remove(int index)` method (lines 78–89) shifts all the elements before the index one position to the left and decrements `size` by 1.

The `set(int index, Object o)` method (lines 93–97) simply assigns o to `data[index]` to replace the element at the specified index with element o.

The `toString()` method (lines 100–107) overrides the `toString` method in the `Object` class to return a string representing all the elements in the list.

Listing 20.4 gives an example that creates a list using `MyArrayList`. It uses the `add` method to add strings to the list and the `remove` method to remove strings from the list. A sample run of the program is shown in Figure 20.6.

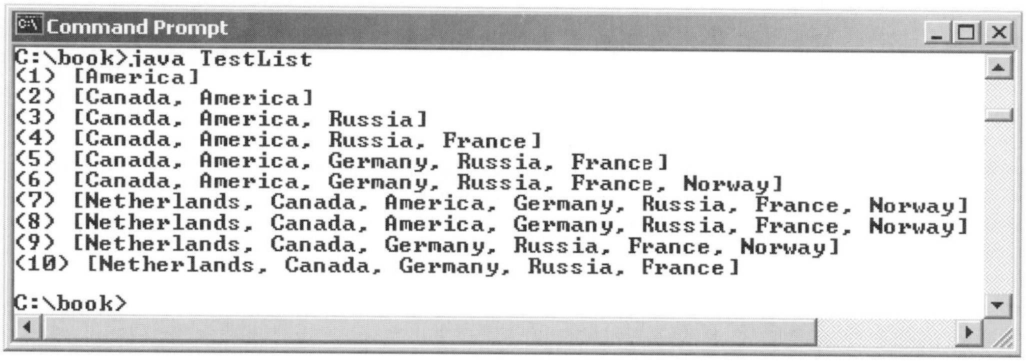

FIGURE 20.6 The program uses a list to store and process strings.

LISTING 20.4 TestList.java

```java
1 public class TestList {
2   public static void main(String[] args) {
3     // Create a list
4     MyList list = new MyArrayList();
5
6     // Add elements to the list
7     list.add("America"); // Add it to the list
8     System.out.println("(1) " + list);
9
10    list.add(0, "Canada"); // Add it to the beginning of the list
11    System.out.println("(2) " + list);
12
13    list.add("Russia"); // Add it to the end of the list
14    System.out.println("(3) " + list);
15
16    list.add("France"); // Add it to the end of the list
17    System.out.println("(4) " + list);
18
```

```
19      list.add(2, "Germany"); // Add it to the list at index 2
20      System.out.println("(5) " + list);
21
22      list.add(5, "Norway"); // Add it to the list at index 5
23      System.out.println("(6) " + list);
24
25      list.add(0, "Netherlands"); // Same as list.addFirst("Daniel")
26      System.out.println("(7) " + list);
27
28      // Remove elements from the list
29      list.remove("Australia"); // Same as list.remove(0) in this case
30      System.out.println("(8) " + list);
31
32      list.remove(2); // Remove the element at index 2
33      System.out.println("(9) " + list);
34
35      list.remove(list.size() - 1); // Remove the last element
36      System.out.println("(10) " + list);
37    }
38 }
```

MyArrayList is implemented using arrays. Although an array is a fixed-size data structure, **MyArrayList** is a dynamic data structure. The user can create an instance of **MyArrayList** to store any number of elements. The internal array in **MyArrayList** is encapsulated. The user manipulates the list through the public methods in **MyArrayList**.

The list can hold any objects. A primitive data type value cannot be directly stored in a list. However, you can create an object for a primitive data type value using the corresponding wrapper class. For example, to store number **10**, use one of the following methods:

```
list.add(new Integer(10));
list.add(10); // JDK 1.5 autoboxing
```

20.2.2 Linked Lists

Since **MyArrayList** is implemented using an array, the methods **get(int index)** and **set(int index, Object o)** for accessing and modifying an element through an index and the **add(Object o)** for adding an element at the end of the list are efficient. However, the methods **add(int index, Object o)** and **remove(int index)** are inefficient because they require shifting a potentially large number of elements. You can use a linked structure to implement a list to improve efficiency for adding and removing an element anywhere in a list.

A linked list consists of nodes, as shown in Figure 20.7. Each node contains an element, and each node is linked to its next neighbor. Thus a node can be defined as a class, as follows:

```
class Node {
  Object element;
  Node next;

  public Node(Object o) {
    element = o;
  }
}
```

FIGURE 20.7 A linked list consists of any number of nodes chained together.

The variable `first` refers to the first node in the list, and the variable `last` refers to the last node in the list. If the list is empty, both are `null`. For example, you can create three nodes to store three circle objects (radius 1, 2, and 3) in a list:

```
Node first, last;

// Create a node to store the first circle object
first = new Node(new Circle(1));
last = first;

// Create a node to store the second circle object
last.next = new Node(new Circle(2));
last = last.next;

// Create a node to store the third circle object
last.next = new Node(new Circle(3));
last = last.next;
```

The process of creating a new linked list and adding three nodes is shown in Figure 20.8.

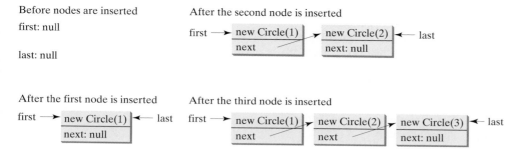

FIGURE 20.8   Three nodes are added to a new linked list.

`MyLinkedList` uses a linked structure to implement a dynamic list. It extends `MyAbstractList`. In addition, it provides the methods `addFirst`, `addLast`, `removeFirst`, `removeLast`, `getFirst`, and `getLast`, as shown in Figure 20.9. Its implementation is given in Listing 20.5.

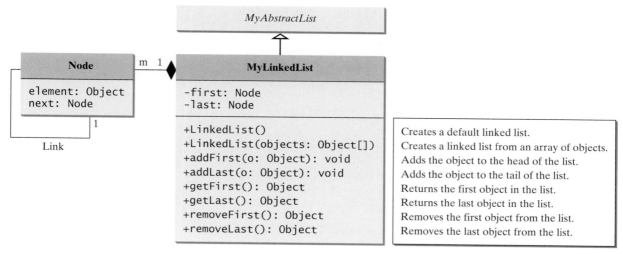

FIGURE 20.9   `MyLinkedList` implements a list using a linked list of nodes.

LISTING 20.5 MyLinkedList.java

```java
public class MyLinkedList extends MyAbstractList {
  private Node first, last;

  /** Create a default list */
  public MyLinkedList() {
  }

  /** Create a list from an array of objects */
  public MyLinkedList(Object[] objects) {
    super(objects);
  }

  /** Return the first element in the list */
  public Object getFirst() {
    if (size == 0) return null;
    else return first.element;
  }

  /** Return the last element in the list */
  public Object getLast() {
    if (size == 0) return null;
    else return last.element;
  }

  /** Add an element to the beginning of the list */
  public void addFirst(Object o) {
    Node newNode = new Node(o);
    newNode.next = first;
    first = newNode;
    size++;

    if (last == null)
      last = first;
  }

  /** Add an element to the end of the list */
  public void addLast(Object o) {
    if (last == null) {
      first = last = new Node(o);
    }
    else {
      last.next = new Node(o);
      last = last.next;
    }

    size++;
  }

  /** Adds a new element o at the specified index in this list
   * The index of the first element is 0 */
  public void add(int index, Object o) {
    if (index == 0) addFirst(o);
    else if (index >= size) addLast(o);
    else {
      Node current = first;
```

addFirst
create node

addLast

add

```
56      for (int i = 1; i < index; i++)
57        current = current.next;
58      Node temp = current.next;
59      current.next = new Node(o);
60      (current.next).next = temp;
61      size++;
62    }
63  }
64
65  /** Remove the first node and
66   *  return the object that is contained in the removed node. */
67  public Object removeFirst() {                                    removeFirst
68    if (size == 0) return null;
69    else {
70      Node temp = first;
71      first = first.next;
72      size--;
73      if (first == null) last = null;
74      return temp.element;
75    }
76  }
77
78  /** Remove the last node and
79   * return the object that is contained in the removed node. */
80  public Object removeLast() {                                     removeLast
81    // Implementation left as an exercise
82    return null;
83  }
84
85  /** Removes the element at the specified position in this list.
86   *  Returns the element that was removed from the list. */
87  public Object remove(int index) {
88    if ((index < 0) || (index >= size)) return null;
89    else if (index == 0) return removeFirst();
90    else if (index == size - 1) return removeLast();
91    else {
92      Node previous = first;
93
94      for (int i = 1; i < index; i++) {
95        previous = previous.next;
96      }
97
98      Node current = previous.next;
99      previous.next = current.next;
100     size--;                                                     addFirst
101     return current.element;
102   }
103 }
104
105 /** Override toString() to return elements in the list */
106 public String toString() {
107   StringBuffer result = new StringBuffer("[");
108
109   Node current = first;
110   for (int i = 0; i < size; i++) {
111     result.append(current.element);
112     current = current.next;
```

```
113        if (current != null)
114          result.append(","); // Separate two elements with a comma
115        else
116          result.append("]"); // Insert the closing ] in the string
117      }
118
119      return result.toString();
120    }
121
121    /** Clear the list */
121    public void clear() {
122      first = last = null;
123    }
124
125    /** Return true if this list contains the element o */
126    public boolean contains(Object o) {
127      // Implementation left as an exercise
128      return true;
129    }
130
131    /** Return the element from this list at the specified index */
132    public Object get(int index) {
133      // Implementation left as an exercise
134      return null;
135    }
136
137    /** Returns the index of the first matching element in this list.
138     *   Returns -1 if no match. */
139    public int indexOf(Object o) {
140      // Implementation left as an exercise
141      return 0;
142    }
143
144    /** Returns the index of the last matching element in this list
145     *   Returns -1 if no match. */
146    public int lastIndexOf(Object o) {
147      // Implementation left as an exercise
148      return 0;
149    }
150
151    /** Replace the element at the specified position in this list
152     *   with the specified element. */
153    public Object set(int index, Object o) {
154      // Implementation left as an exercise
155      return null;
156    }
157
158    private static class Node {
159      Object element;
160      Node next;
161
162      public Node(Object o) {
163        element = o;
164      }
165    }
166 }
```

The variables **first** and **last** (line 2) refer to the first and last nodes in the list, respectively. The **getFirst()** and **getLast()** methods (lines 14–23) return the first and last elements in the list, respectively.

Since variable `size` is defined as `protected` in `MyAbstractList`, it can be accessed in `MyLinkedList`. When a new element is added to the list, `size` is incremented by 1, and when an element is removed from the list, `size` is decremented by 1. The `add-First(Object o)` method (line 26–34) creates a new node to store the element and insert the node to the beginning of the list. After the insertion, `first` should refer to this new element node (line 29), as shown in Figure 20.10.

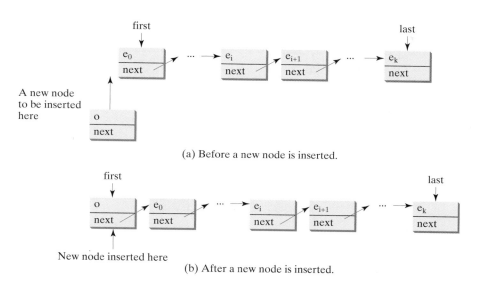

(a) Before a new node is inserted.

(b) After a new node is inserted.

FIGURE 20.10 A new element `o` is added to the beginning of the list.

The `addLast(Object o)` method (lines 37–47) creates a node to hold element `o` and inserts the node at the end of the list. After the insertion, `last` should refer to this new element node (line 43), as shown in Figure 20.11.

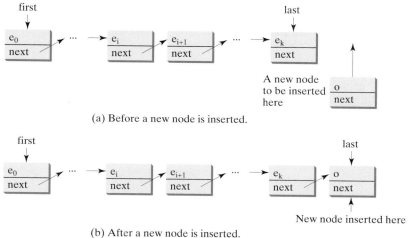

(a) Before a new node is inserted.

(b) After a new node is inserted.

FIGURE 20.11 A new element `o` is added at the end of the list.

The `add(int index, Object o)` method (lines 51–63) adds an element `o` to the list at the specified index. Consider three cases: (1) if `index` is 0, invoke `addFirst(o)` to insert the element at the beginning of the list; (2) if `index` is greater than or equal to `size`, invoke `addLast(o)` to insert the element at the end of the list; (3) create a new node to store the new element and locate where to insert it. As shown in Figure 20.12, the new node is to be inserted between the nodes `current` and `temp`. The method assigns the new node to `current.next` and assigns `temp` to the new node's `next`.

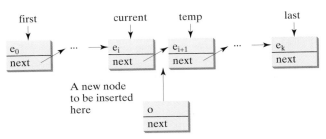

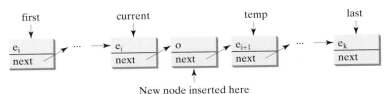

(a) Before a new node is inserted.

(b) After a new node is inserted.

FIGURE 20.12 A new element is inserted in the middle of the list.

The `removeFirst()` method (lines 67–76) removes the first node from the list by pointing `first` to the second node, as shown in Figure 20.13.

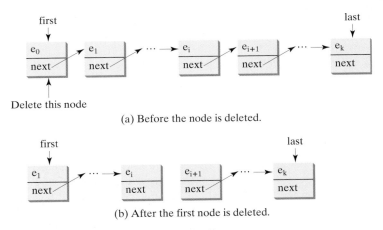

(a) Before the node is deleted.

(b) After the first node is deleted.

FIGURE 20.13 The first node is deleted from the list.

The `remove(int index)` method (lines 87–103) finds the node at the specified index and then removes it. Consider four cases: (1) if `index` is beyond the range of the list (i.e., `index < 0 || index >= size`), return `null`; (2) if `index` is 0, invoke `removeFirst()` to remove the first node; (3) if `index` is `size - 1`, invoke `removeLast()` to remove the last node; (4) locate the node at the specified `index`, let `current` denote this node and `previous` denote the node before this node, as shown in Figure 20.14, and assign `current.next` to `previous.next` to eliminate the current node.

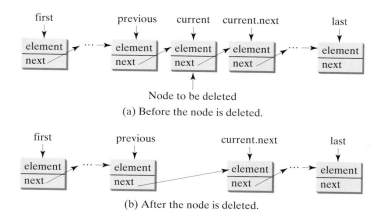

(a) Before the node is deleted.

(b) After the node is deleted.

FIGURE 20.14   A node is deleted from the list.

The implementation of methods `removeLast()`, `clear()`, `contains(Object o)`, `get(int index)`, `indexOf(Object o)`, `lastIndexOf(Object o)`, and `set(int index, Object o)` is omitted and left as an exercise.

To test `MyLinkedList`, simply replace `MyArrayList` in line 7 by `MyLinkedList` in `TestList` in Listing 20.4. The output should be the same as shown in Figure 20.6.

20.3 Stacks and Queues

A stack can be viewed as a special type of list whose elements are accessed, inserted, and deleted only from the end (top) of the stack. A queue represents a waiting list. A queue can be viewed as a special type of list whose elements are inserted into the end (tail) of the queue, and are accessed and deleted from the beginning (head) of the queue.

Since the insertion and deletion operations on a stack are made only at the end of the stack, it is more efficient to implement a stack with an array list than with a linked list. Since deletions are made at the beginning of the list, it is more efficient to implement a queue using a linked list than an array list. This section implements a stack class using an array list and a queue using a linked list.

There are two ways to design the stack and queue classes:

- Using *inheritance*: You can declare a stack class by extending the array list class, and a queue class by extending the linked list class.   inheritance

- Using *composition*: You can declare an array list as a data field in the stack class, and a linked list as a data field in the queue class.   composition

Both designs are fine, but using composition is better because it enables you to declare a completely new stack class and queue class without inheriting the unnecessary and inappropriate methods from the array list and linked list. The implementation of the stack class using the composition approach was given in Listing 9.8, MyStack.java. Listing 20.6 implements the queue class using the composition approach. Figure 20.15 shows the UML of the class.

LISTING 20.6   MyQueue.java

```
1 public class MyQueue {
2   private MyLinkedList list = new MyLinkedList();    linked list
3
4   public void enqueue(Object o) {
5     list.addLast(o);
6   }
7
```

```
 8    public Object dequeue() {
 9      return list.removeFirst();
10    }
11
12    public int getSize() {
13      return list.size();
14    }
15
16    public String toString() {
17      return "Queue: " + list.toString();
18    }
19 }
```

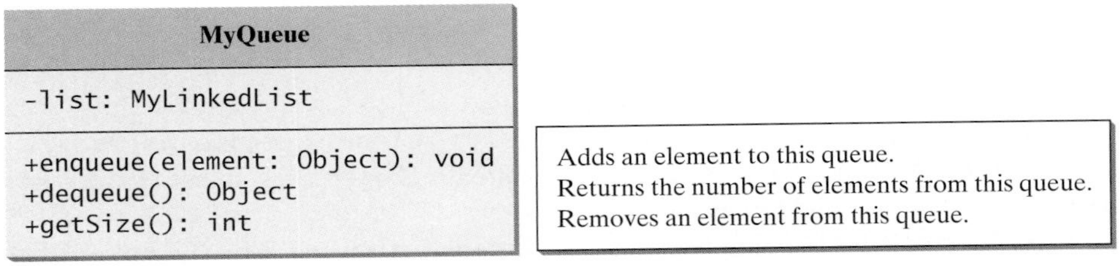

MyQueue
-list: MyLinkedList
+enqueue(element: Object): void +dequeue(): Object +getSize(): int

Adds an element to this queue.
Returns the number of elements from this queue.
Removes an element from this queue.

FIGURE 20.15 MyQueue uses a linked list to provide a first-in/first-out data structure.

A linked list is created to store the elements in a queue (line 2). The `enqueue(Object o)` method (lines 4–6) adds element `o` into the tail of the queue. The `dequeue()` method (lines 8–10) removes an element from the head of the queue and returns the removed element. The `getSize()` method (lines 12–14) returns the number of elements in the queue.

Listing 20.7 gives an example that creates a stack using `MyStack` and a queue using `MyQueue`. It uses the `push (enqueue)` method to add strings to the stack (queue) and the `pop (dequeue)` method to remove strings from the stack (queue). A sample run of the program is shown in Figure 20.16.

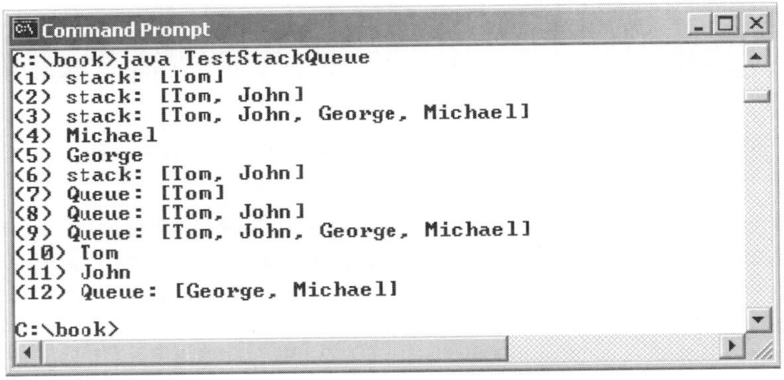

```
Command Prompt                                        _ |□| x|
C:\book>java TestStackQueue
(1) stack: [Tom]
(2) stack: [Tom, John]
(3) stack: [Tom, John, George, Michael]
(4) Michael
(5) George
(6) stack: [Tom, John]
(7) Queue: [Tom]
(8) Queue: [Tom, John]
(9) Queue: [Tom, John, George, Michael]
(10) Tom
(11) John
(12) Queue: [George, Michael]

C:\book>
```

FIGURE 20.16 The program uses a stack and a queue to store and process strings.

LISTING 20.7 TestStackQueue.java

```
1 public class TestStackQueue {
2   public static void main(String[] args) {
3     // Create a stack
4     MyStack stack = new MyStack();
5
```

```
 6        // Add elements to the stack
 7        stack.push("Tom"); // Push it to the stack
 8        System.out.println("(1) " + stack);
 9
10        stack.push("John"); // Push it to the stack
11        System.out.println("(2) " + stack);
12
13        stack.push("George"); // Push it to the stack
14        stack.push("Michael"); // Push it to the stack
15        System.out.println("(3) " + stack);
16
17        // Remove elements from the stack
18        System.out.println("(4) " + stack.pop());
19        System.out.println("(5) " + stack.pop());
20        System.out.println("(6) " + stack);
21
22        // Create a queue
23        MyQueue queue = new MyQueue();
24
25        // Add elements to the queue
26        queue.enqueue("Tom"); // Add it to the queue
27        System.out.println("(7) " + queue);
28
29        queue.enqueue("John"); // Add it to the queue
30        System.out.println("(8) " + queue);
31
32        queue.enqueue("George"); // Add it to the queue
33        queue.enqueue("Michael"); // Add it to the queue
34        System.out.println("(9) " + queue);
35
36        // Remove elements from the queue
37        System.out.println("(10) " + queue.dequeue());
38        System.out.println("(11) " + queue.dequeue());
39        System.out.println("(12) " + queue);
40    }
41 }
```

For a stack, the **push(o)** method adds an element to the top of the stack, and the **pop()** method removes the top element from the stack and returns the removed element.

For a queue, the **enqueue(o)** method adds an element to the tail of the queue, and the **dequeue()** method removes the element from the head of the queue.

20.4 Binary Trees

A list, stack, or queue is a linear structure that consists of a sequence of elements. A binary tree is a hierarchical structure. It is either empty or consists of an element called the *root* and two distinct binary trees called the *left subtree* and *right subtree*. Examples of binary trees are shown in Figure 20.17.

root
left subtree
right subtree

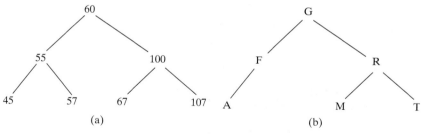

(a)   (b)

FIGURE 20.17   Each node in a binary tree has zero, one, or two branches.

leaf
binary search tree

The root of a left (right) subtree of a node is called a *left (right) child* of the node. A node without children is called a *leaf*. A special type of binary tree called a *binary search tree* is often useful. A binary search tree (with no duplicate elements) has the property that for every node in the tree, the value of any node in its left subtree is less than the value of the node, and the value of any node in its right subtree is greater than the value of the node. The binary trees in Figure 20.17 are all binary search trees. This section is concerned with binary search trees.

20.4.1 Representing Binary Trees

A binary tree can be represented using a set of linked nodes. Each node contains a value and two links named *left* and *right* that reference the left child and right child, respectively, as shown in Figure 20.18.

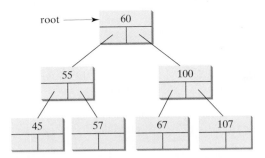

FIGURE 20.18 A binary tree can be represented using a set of linked nodes.

A node can be defined as a class, as follows:

```
class TreeNode {
   Object element;
   TreeNode left;
   TreeNode right;

   public TreeNode(Object o) {
      element = o;
   }
}
```

The variable **root** refers to the root node of the tree. If the tree is empty, **root** is **null**. The following code creates the first three nodes of the tree in Figure 20.18:

```
// Create the root node
TreeNode root = new TreeNode(new Integer(60));

// Create the left child node
root.left = new TreeNode(new Integer(55));

// Create the right child node
root.right = new TreeNode(new Integer(100));
```

20.4.2 Inserting an Element into a Binary Search Tree

If a binary tree is empty, create a root node with the new element. Otherwise, locate the parent node for the new element node. If the new element is less than the parent element, the node for the new element becomes the left child of the parent. If the new element is greater than the parent element, the node for the new element becomes the right child of the parent. Here is the algorithm:

```
if (root == null)
  root = new TreeNode(element);
else {
  // Locate the parent node
  current = root;
  while (current != null)
    if (element value < the value in current.element) {
      parent = current;
      current = current.left;
    }
    else if (element value > the value in current.element) {
      parent = current;
      current = current.right;
    }
    else
      return false; // Duplicate node not inserted

  // Create the new node and attach it to the parent node
  if (element < parent.element)
    parent.left = new TreeNode(element);
  else
    parent.right = new TreeNode(element);

  return true; // Element inserted
}
```

For example, to insert 101 into the tree in Figure 20.18, the parent is the node for 107. The new node for 101 becomes the left child of the parent. To insert 59 into the tree, the parent is the node for 57. The new node for 59 becomes the right child of the parent. Both of these insertions are shown in Figure 20.19.

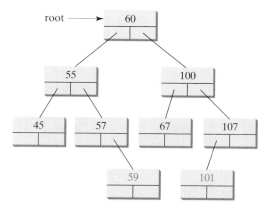

FIGURE 20.19 Two new elements are inserted into the tree.

20.4.3 Tree Traversal

Tree traversal is the process of visiting each node in the tree exactly once. There are several ways to traverse a tree. This section presents *inorder, preorder, postorder, depth-first, and breadth-first* traversals.

With *inorder* traversal, the left subtree of the current node is visited first, then the current node, and finally the right subtree of the current node. The inorder traversal displays all the nodes in a binary search tree in increasing order.

inorder

With *postorder* traversal, the left subtree of the current node is visited first, then the right subtree of the current node, and finally the current node itself.

postorder

preorder
depth-first

With *preorder* traversal, the current node is visited first, then the left subtree of the current node, and finally the right subtree of the current node. *Depth-first* traversal is the same as preorder traversal.

breadth-first

With *breadth-first* traversal, the nodes are visited level by level. First the root is visited, then all the children of the root from left to right, then the grandchildren of the root from left to right, and so on.

For example, in the tree in Figure 20.19, the inorder is 45 55 57 59 60 67 100 101 107. The postorder is 45 59 57 55 67 101 107 100 60. The preorder is 60 55 45 57 59 100 67 101 101. The breadth-first traversal is 60 55 100 45 57 67 107 59 101.

20.4.4 The Binary Tree Class

Let us define a binary tree class named **BinaryTree** with insert, inorder traversal, postorder traversal, and preorder traversal, as shown in Figure 20.20. Its implementation is given in Listing 20.8.

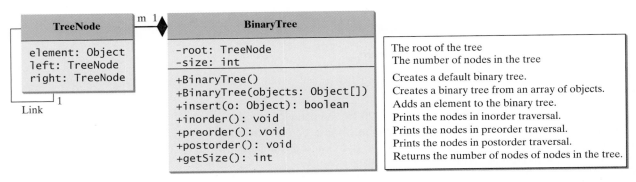

FIGURE 20.20 **BinaryTree** implements a binary tree with operations **insert**, **inorder**, **preorder**, and **postorder**.

LISTING 20.8 BinaryTree.java

```
1  public class BinaryTree {
2    private TreeNode root;
3    private int size = 0;
4
5    /** Create a default binary tree */
6    public BinaryTree() {
7    }
8
9    /** Create a binary tree from an array of objects */
10   public BinaryTree(Object[] objects) {
11     for (int i = 0; i < objects.length; i++)
12       insert(objects[i]);
13   }
14
15   /** Insert element o into the binary tree
16    * Return true if the element is inserted successfully */
17   public boolean insert(Object o) {
18     if (root == null)
19       root = new TreeNode(o); // Create a new root
20     else {
21       // Locate the parent node
22       TreeNode parent = null;
```

no-arg constructor

constructor

insert

```
23        TreeNode current = root;
24        while (current != null)
25          if (((Comparable)o).compareTo(current.element) < 0) {
26            parent = current;
27            current = current.left;
28          }
29          else if (((Comparable)o).compareTo(current.element) > 0) {
30            parent = current;
31            current = current.right;
32          }
33          else
34            return false; // Duplicate node not inserted
35
36        // Create the new node and attach it to the parent node
37        if (((Comparable)o).compareTo(parent.element) < 0)
38          parent.left = new TreeNode(o);
39        else
40          parent.right = new TreeNode(o);
41      }
42
43      size++;
44      return true; // Element inserted
45    }
46
47    /** Inorder traversal */
48    public void inorder() {
49      inorder(root);
50    }
51
52    /** Inorder traversal from a subtree */
53    private void inorder(TreeNode root) {
54      if (root == null) return;
55      inorder(root.left);
56      System.out.print(root.element + " ");
57      inorder(root.right);
58    }
59
60    /** Postorder traversal */
61    public void postorder() {
62      postorder(root);
63    }
64
65    /** Postorder traversal from a subtree */
66    private void postorder(TreeNode root) {
67      if (root == null) return;
68      postorder(root.left);
69      postorder(root.right);
70      System.out.print(root.element + " ");
71    }
72
73    /** Preorder traversal */
74    public void preorder() {
75      preorder(root);
76    }
77
78    /** Preorder traversal from a subtree */
79    private void preorder(TreeNode root) {
80      if (root == null) return;
81      System.out.print(root.element + " ");
82      preorder(root.left);
```

compare objects

increase size

inorder

recursive helper
method

postorder

recursive helper
method

preorder

recursive helper
method

```
83        preorder(root.right);
84      }
85
86      /** Inner class tree node */
87      private static class TreeNode {
88        Object element;
89        TreeNode left;
90        TreeNode right;
91
92        public TreeNode(Object o) {
93          element = o;
94        }
95      }
96
97      /** Get the number of nodes in the tree */
98      public int getSize() {
99        return size;
100     }
101   }
```

tree node

The `insert(Object o)` method (lines 17–45) creates a node for element `o` and inserts it into the tree. If the tree is empty, the node becomes the root. Otherwise, the method finds an appropriate parent for the node to maintain the order of the tree. If the element is already in the tree, the method returns `false`; otherwise it returns `true`.

The `inorder()` method (lines 48–50) invokes `inorder(root)` to traverse the entire tree. The method `inorder(TreeNode root)` traverses the tree with the specified root. This is a recursive method. It recursively traverses the left subtree, then the root, and finally the right subtree. The traversal ends when the tree is empty.

The `postorder()` method (lines 61–63) and the `preorder()` method (lines 74–76) are implemented similarly using recursion.

Listing 20.9 gives an example that creates a binary tree using `BinaryTree`. Add strings into the binary tree and traverse the tree in inorder, postorder, and preorder. A sample run of the program is shown in Figure 20.21.

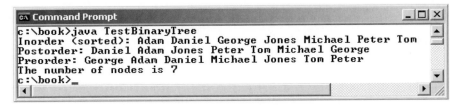

FIGURE 20.21 The program creates a tree, inserts elements into it, and displays them in inorder, postorder, and preorder.

LISTING 20.9 TestBinaryTree.java

```
1 public class TestBinaryTree {
2   public static void main(String[] args) {
3     BinaryTree tree = new BinaryTree();
4     tree.insert("George");
5     tree.insert("Michael");
6     tree.insert("Tom");
7     tree.insert("Adam");
8     tree.insert("Jones");
9     tree.insert("Peter");
10    tree.insert("Daniel");
11    System.out.print("Inorder (sorted): ");
```

create tree
insert

inorder

```
12      tree.inorder();
13      System.out.print("\nPostorder: ");                              postorder
14      tree.postorder();
15      System.out.print("\nPreorder: ");                               preorder
16      tree.preorder();
17      System.out.print("\nThe number of nodes is " + tree.getSize());  getSize
18    }
19  }
```

After all the elements are inserted, the tree should appear as shown in Figure 20.22.

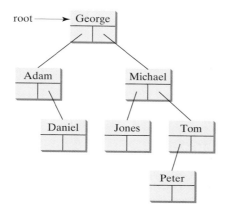

FIGURE 20.22 The binary search tree is pictured here after line 10 is executed.

If the elements are inserted in a different order (e.g., Daniel, Adam, Jones, Peter, Tom, Michael, George), the tree will look different. However, the inorder is the same as long as the set of elements is the same. The inorder displays a sorted list.

20.5 Heaps

Heaps are a useful data structure for designing efficient sorting algorithms and priority queues. A *heap* is a binary tree with the following properties:

heap

- It is a complete binary tree.

- Each node is greater than or equal to any of its children.

A binary tree is *complete* if every level of the tree is full, except that the last level may not be full and all the leaves on the last level are placed left-most. For example, in Figure 20.23, the binary trees in (a) and (b) are complete, but the binary trees in (c) and (d) are not complete. Further, the binary tree in (a) is a heap, but the binary tree in (b) is not a heap, because the root (39) is less than its right child (42).

complete binary tree

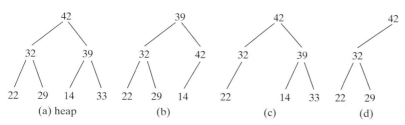

FIGURE 20.23 A heap is a special complete binary tree.

20.5.1 Representing a Heap

A heap is a binary tree, so it can be represented using a binary tree data structure. However, a more efficient representation for a heap is using an array or an array list if the heap size is known in advance. The heap in Figure 20.24(a) can be represented using an array in Figure 20.24(b). The root is at position 0, and its two children are at positions 1 and 2. For a node at position i, its left child is at position $2i + 1$, its right child is at position $2i + 2$, and its parent is $(i − 1)/2$. For example, the node for element 39 is at position 4, so its left child (element 14) is at 9 ($2 \times 4 + 1$), its right child (element 33) is at 10 ($2 \times 4 + 2$), and its parent (element 42) is at 1 (($4 − 1$)/2).

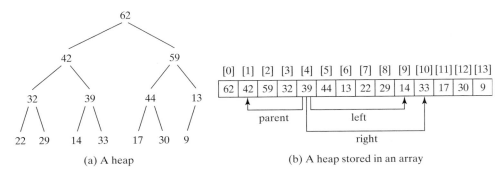

(a) A heap   (b) A heap stored in an array

FIGURE 20.24   A binary heap can be implemented using an array.

If the heap size is not known in advance, it is better to use an array list to store a heap.

20.5.2   Removing the Root

Often you need to remove the root from a heap. After the root is removed, the tree must be rebuilt to maintain the heap property. The algorithm for building the tree can be described as follows:

```
Move the last node to replace the root;
Let the root be the current node;
while (the current node has children and the current node is
        smaller than one of its children) {
  Swap the current node with the larger of its children;
  Now the current node is one level down;
}
```

Figure 20.25 shows the process of rebuilding a heap after the root 62 is removed from Figure 20.24(a). Move the last node 9 to the root, as shown in Figure 20.25(a). Swap 9 with 59 as shown in Figure 20.25(b). Swap 9 with 44 as shown in Figure 20.25(c). Swap 9 with 30 as shown in Figure 20.25(d).

20.5.3   Adding a New Node

To add a new node to the heap, first add it to the end of the heap and then rebuild the tree as follows:

```
Let the last node be the current node;
while (the current node is greater than its parent) {
  Swap the current node with its parent;
  Now the current node is one level up;
}
```

Figure 20.26 shows the process of rebuilding a heap after adding a new node 88 to the heap in Figure 20.25(d). Place the new node 88 at the end of the tree, as shown in Figure 20.26(a).

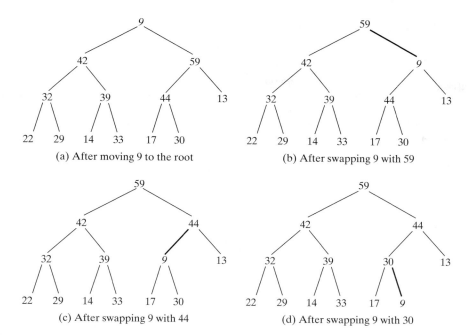

FIGURE 20.25 Rebuild the heap after the root is removed.

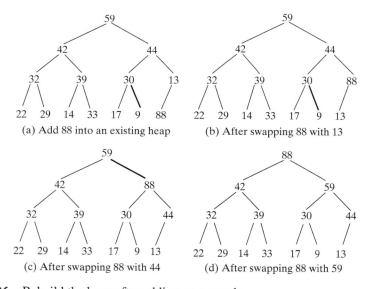

FIGURE 20.26 Rebuild the heap after adding a new node.

Swap 88 with 13, as shown in Figure 20.26(b). Swap 88 with 44, as shown in Figure 20.26(c). Swap 88 with 59, as shown in Figure 20.26(d).

20.5.4 The Heap Class

Now you are ready to design and implement the Heap class. The class diagram is shown in Figure 20.27. Its implementation is given in Listing 20.10.

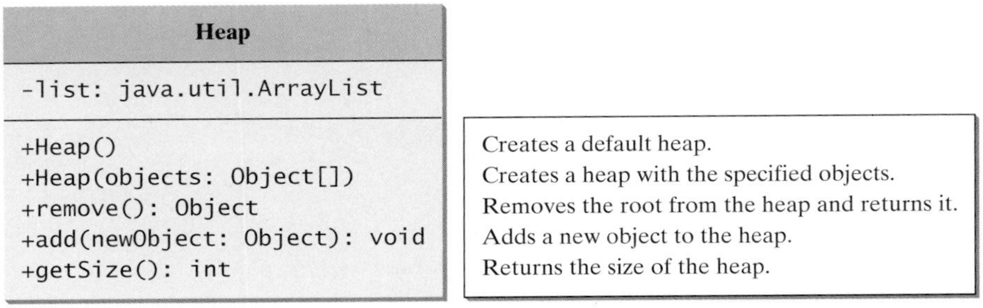

Heap
-list: java.util.ArrayList
+Heap() +Heap(objects: Object[]) +remove(): Object +add(newObject: Object): void +getSize(): int

Creates a default heap.
Creates a heap with the specified objects.
Removes the root from the heap and returns it.
Adds a new object to the heap.
Returns the size of the heap.

FIGURE 20.27 Heap provides operations for manipulating a heap.

LISTING 20.10 Heap.java

```
 1  public class Heap {
 2    private java.util.ArrayList list = new java.util.ArrayList();
 3
 4    /** Create a default heap */
 5    public Heap() {
 6    }
 7
 8    /** Create a heap from an array of objects */
 9    public Heap(Object[] objects) {
10      for (int i = 0; i < objects.length; i++)
11        add(objects[i]);
12    }
13
14    /** Add a new object into the heap */
15    public void add(Object newObject) {
16      list.add(newObject); // Append to the heap
17      int currentIndex = list.size() - 1; // The index of the last node
18
19      while (currentIndex > 0) {
20        int parentIndex = (currentIndex - 1) / 2;
21        // Swap if the current object is greater than its parent
22        if (((Comparable)(list.get(currentIndex))).compareTo(
23            list.get(parentIndex)) > 0) {
24          Object temp = list.get(currentIndex);
25          list.set(currentIndex, list.get(parentIndex));
26          list.set(parentIndex, temp);
27        }
28        else
29          break; // the tree is a heap now
30
31        currentIndex = parentIndex;
32      }
33    }
34
35    /** Remove the root from the heap */
36    public Object remove() {
37      if (list.size() == 0) return null;
38
39      Object removedObject = list.get(0);
40      list.set(0, list.get(list.size() - 1));
41      list.remove(list.size() - 1);
42
43      int currentIndex = 0;
44      while (currentIndex < list.size()) {
```

internal heap representation (line 2)

no-arg constructor (line 5)

constructor (line 9)

add a new object (line 15)
append the object (line 17)

swap with parent (line 24)

heap now (line 29)

remove the root (line 36)
empty heap (line 37)

root (line 39)
new root (line 40)
remove the last (line 41)

adjust the tree (line 44)

```
45        int leftChildIndex = 2 * currentIndex + 1;
46        int rightChildIndex = 2 * currentIndex + 2;
47
48        // Find the maximum between two children
49        if (leftChildIndex >= list.size()) break; // The tree is a heap
50        int maxIndex = leftChildIndex;
51        if (rightChildIndex < list.size()) {
52          if (((Comparable)(list.get(maxIndex))).compareTo(           compare two children
53              list.get(rightChildIndex)) < 0) {
54            maxIndex = rightChildIndex;
55          }
56        }
57
58        // Swap if the current node is less than the maximum
59        if (((Comparable)(list.get(currentIndex))).compareTo(
60            list.get(maxIndex)) < 0) {
61          Object temp = list.get(maxIndex);
62          list.set(maxIndex, list.get(currentIndex));            swap with the
63          list.set(currentIndex, temp);                          larger child
64          currentIndex = maxIndex;
65        }
66        else
67          break; // The tree is a heap
68      }
69
70      return removedObject;
71    }
72
73    /** Get the number of nodes in the tree */
74    public int getSize() {
75      return list.size();
76    }
77 }
```

A heap is represented using an array list internally (line 2). You may change it to other data structures, but the **Heap** class contract will remain unchanged. See Exercise 20.9.

The **add(Object newObject)** method (lines 15–33) appends the object to the tree and then swaps it with its parent if it is greater than its parent. This process continues until the new object becomes the root or is not greater than its parent.

The **remove()** method (lines 36–71) removes and returns the root. To maintain the heap property, the method moves the last object to the root position and swaps it with its larger child if it is less than the larger child. This process continues until the last object becomes a leaf or is not less than its children.

Listing 20.11 gives an example of using a heap to sort numbers. Line 3 creates a heap from an array of integers. The loop in lines 5–7 displays all the elements in the heap in decreasing order.

LISTING 20.11   TestHeap.java

```
1 public class TestHeap {
2   public static void main(String[] args) {
3     Heap heap = new Heap(new Integer[]{8, 9, 2, 3, 4, 1, 5, 6, 7});    create a heap
4
5     while (heap.getSize() > 0)                                       heap not empty?
6       System.out.print(heap.remove() + " ");                        remove the root
7   }
8 }
```

The printout from Listing 20.11 is

9 8 7 6 5 4 3 2 1

20.6 Priority Queues

A regular queue is a first-in/first-out data structure. Elements are appended to the end of the queue and are removed from the beginning of the queue. In a priority queue, elements are assigned with priorities. When accessing elements, the element with the highest priority is removed first. A priority queue has a largest-in/first-out behavior. For example, the emergency room in a hospital assigns priority numbers to patients; the patient with the highest priority is treated first.

A priority queue can be implemented using a heap, where the root is the object with the highest priority in the queue. The class diagram for the priority queue is shown in Figure 20.28. Its implementation is given in Listing 20.12.

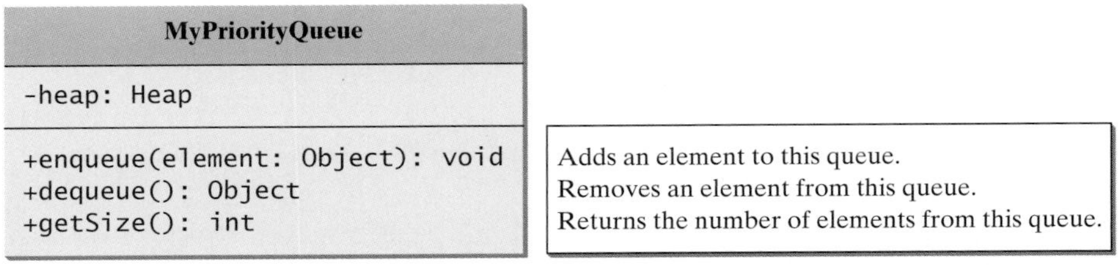

MyPriorityQueue
-heap: Heap
+enqueue(element: Object): void +dequeue(): Object +getSize(): int

> Adds an element to this queue.
> Removes an element from this queue.
> Returns the number of elements from this queue.

FIGURE 20.28 `MyPriorityQueue` uses a heap to provide a largest-in/first-out data structure.

LISTING 20.12 MyPriorityQueue.java

heap for priority
queue

add to queue

remove from queue

queue size

```java
 1 public class MyPriorityQueue {
 2   private Heap heap = new Heap();
 3
 4   public void enqueue(Object newObject) {
 5     heap.add(newObject);
 6   }
 7
 8   public Object dequeue() {
 9     return heap.remove();
10   }
11
12   public int getSize() {
13     return heap.getSize();
14   }
15 }
```

Listing 20.13 gives an example of using a priority queue for patients. The `Patient` class is declared in lines 18–34. Four patients are created with associated priority values in lines 3–6. Line 8 creates a priority queue. The patients are enqueued in lines 9–12. Line 15 dequeues a patient from the queue.

LISTING 20.13 TestPriorityQueue.java

create a patient

```java
 1 public class TestPriorityQueue {
 2   public static void main(String[] args) {
 3     Patient patient1 = new Patient("John", 2);
 4     Patient patient2 = new Patient("Jim", 1);
 5     Patient patient3 = new Patient("Tim", 5);
 6     Patient patient4 = new Patient("Cindy", 7);
 7
```

```
 8        MyPriorityQueue priorityQueue = new MyPriorityQueue();          create a priority
 9        priorityQueue.enqueue(patient1);                                   queue
10        priorityQueue.enqueue(patient2);
11        priorityQueue.enqueue(patient3);                               add to queue
12        priorityQueue.enqueue(patient4);
13
14        while (priorityQueue.getSize() > 0)
15          System.out.print(priorityQueue.dequeue() + " ");             remove from queue
16      }
17
18      static class Patient implements Comparable {                     inner class Patient
19        private String name;
20        private int priority;
21
22        public Patient(String name, int priority) {
23          this.name = name;
24          this.priority = priority;
25        }
26
27        public String toString() {
28          return name + "(priority:" + priority + ")";
29        }
30
31        public int compareTo(Object o) {                               compareTo
32          return this.priority - ((Patient)o).priority;
33        }
34      }
35 }
```

The printout from Listing 20.13 is

```
Cindy(priority:7) Tim(priority:5) John(priority:2) Jim(priority:1)
```

KEY TERMS

CHAPTER SUMMARY

■ You have learned the concept of object-oriented data structures and how to create lists, stacks, queues, binary trees, heaps, and priority queues using the object-oriented approach.

■ To define a data structure is essentially to declare a class. The class for a data structure should use data fields to store data and provide methods to support such operations as insertion and deletion.

■ To create a data structure is to create an instance from the class. You can then apply the methods on the instance to manipulate the data structure, such as inserting an element to the data structure or deleting an element from the data structure.

REVIEW QUESTIONS

Sections 20.1–20.2

20.1 What is a data structure? What is an object-oriented data structure?

20.2 What are the limitations of the array data type?

20.3 `MyArrayList` is implemented using an array, and an array is a fixed-size data structure. Why is `MyArrayList` considered a dynamic data structure?

20.4 What are the benefits of defining both the `MyList` interface and the `MyAbstractList` class? What is a convenience class?

20.5 What is wrong in the following code?

```
MyArrayList list = new MyArrayList();
list.add(100);
```

20.6 What is wrong if lines 11–12 in Listing 20.3, MyArrayList.java

```
data = objects;
size = objects.length;
```

are replaced by

```
super(objects);
```

20.7 If the number of elements in the program is fixed, what data structure should you use? If the number of elements in the program changes, what data structure should you use?

20.8 If you have to add or delete the elements anywhere in a list, should you use `ArrayList` or `LinkedList`?

Section 20.3 Stacks and Queues

20.9 You can use inheritance or composition to design the data structures for stacks and queues. Discuss the pros and cons of these two approaches.

20.10 Which lines of the following code are wrong?

```
MyList list = new MyArrayList();
list.add("Tom");
list = new MyLinkedList();
list.add("Tom");
list = new MyStack();
list.add("Tom");
```

Section 20.4 Binary Trees

20.11 If a set of the same elements is inserted into a binary tree in two different orders, will the two corresponding binary trees look the same? Will the inorder traversal be the same? Will the postorder traversal be the same? Will the preorder traversal be the same?

Section 20.5 Heaps

20.12 What is a complete binary tree? What is a heap? Describe how to remove the root from a heap and how to add a new object to a heap.

20.13 What is the return value from invoking the `remove` method if the heap is empty?

Section 20.6 Priority Queues

20.14 What is a priority queue?

PROGRAMMING EXERCISES

Section 20.2 Lists

20.1 (*Adding set operations in* `MyAbstractList`) Add and implement the following methods in `MyAbstractList`:

```
/** Add the elements in otherList to this list.
  * Returns true if this list changed after the call */
public boolean addAll(MyList otherList)

/** Remove all the elements in otherList from this list
  * Returns true if this list changed after the call */
public boolean removeAll(MyList otherList)

/** Retain the elements if they are also in otherList
  * Returns true if this list changed after the call */
public boolean retainAll(MyList otherList)
```

Write a test program that creates two `MyArrayLists`, `list1` and `list2`, with the initial values {"Tom", "George", "Peter", "Jean", "Jane"} and {"Tom", "George", "Michael", "Michelle", "Daniel"}, then invokes `list1.addAll(list2)`, `list1.removeAll(list2)`, and `list1.retainAll(list2)`, and displays the resulting new `list1`.

20.2* (*Completing the implementation of* `MyLinkedList`) The implementations of methods `removeLast()`, `clear()`, `contains(Object o)`, `get(int index)`, `indexOf(Object o)`, `lastIndexOf(Object o)`, and `set(int index, Object o)` are omitted in the text. Implement these methods.

20.3* (*Creating a two-way linked list*) The `MyLinkedList` class used in Listing 20.5 is a one-way directional linked list that enables one-way traversal of the list. Modify the `Node` class to add the new field name `previous` to refer to the previous node in the list, as follows:

```
public class TreeNode {
  Object element;
  TreeNode next;
  TreeNode previous;

  public TreeNode(Object o) {
    element = o;
  }
}
```

Simplify the implementation of the `add(Object element, int index)` and `remove(int index)` methods to take advantage of the bi-directional linked list.

Section 20.3 Stacks and Queues

20.4 (*Using the* `Stack` *class*) Write a program that displays the first fifty prime numbers in descending order. Use a stack to store prime numbers.

20.5 (*Implementing* `MyQueue` *using inheritance*) In §20.3, "Stacks and Queues," `MyQueue` is implemented using composition. Create a new queue class that extends `MyLinkedList`.

Section 20.4 Binary Trees

20.6* (*Adding new methods in BinaryTree*) Add the following new methods in BinaryTree:

```
/** Search element o in this binary tree */
public boolean search(Object o)
```

```
/** Display the nodes in breadth-first traversal */
public void breadthFirstTraversal()
```

```
/** Return the depth of this binary tree. Depth is the
 * number of the nodes in the longest path of the tree */
public int depth()
```

20.7** (*Implementing inorder traversal using a stack*) Implement the inorder method in BinaryTree using a stack instead of recursion.

Section 20.5 Heaps

20.8** (*Sorting using a heap*) Implement the following sort method using a heap:

```
public static void sort(Object[] list)
```

20.9***(*Implementing heap using a binary tree*) The Heap class in the text is implemented using an array list. Implement it using a binary tree.

GENERICS

Objectives

- To use generic classes and interfaces (§21.2).

- To declare generic classes and interfaces (§21.3).

- To understand why generic types can improve reliability and readability (§21.3).

- To declare and use generic methods and bounded generic types (§21.4).

- To use raw types for backward compatibility (§21.5).

- To know wildcard types and understand why they are necessary (§21.6).

- To understand that all instances of a generic class share the same runtime class file (§21.7).

- To convert legacy code using JDK 1.5 generics (§21.8).

- (Optional) To design and implement a generic matrix class (§21.9).

21.1 Introduction

Generics is the capability to parameterize types. You can declare a generic type in a class, interface, or method and specify a concrete type when using the class, interface, or method.

This chapter introduces how to declare and use generic classes, interfaces, and methods, and demonstrates how generics can be used to improve software reliability and readability. This chapter can be intertwined with Chapter 10, "Abstract Classes and Interfaces."

21.2 Motivations

JDK 1.5 allows you to declare generic classes, interfaces, and methods. Several interfaces and classes in the Java API are modified using generics. For example, the `java.lang.Comparable` interface was declared as shown in Figure 21.1(a) prior to JDK 1.5, but is modified as shown in Figure 21.1(b) in JDK 1.5.

```
package java.lang;

public interface Comparable {
  public int compareTo(Object o)
}
```
(a) Prior to JDK 1.5

```
package java.lang;

public interface Comparable<T> {
  public int compareTo(T o)
}
```
(b) JDK 1.5

FIGURE 21.1 The `java.lang.Comparable` interface is redefined in JDK 1.5 with a generic type.

formal generic type
actual concrete type
generic instantiation

Here, `<T>` represents a *formal generic type*, which can be substituted with an *actual concrete type* later. Substituting a generic type is called a *generic instantiation*. By convention, a single capital letter such as `E` or `T` is used to denote a formal generic type.

The statement in Figure 21.2(a) declares that `c` is a reference variable whose type was `Comparable` prior to JDK 1.5 and invokes the `compareTo` method to compare a `Date` object with a string. The code compiles fine, but has a runtime error because a string cannot be compared with a date.

```
Comparable c = new Date();
System.out.println(c.compareTo("red"));
```
(a) Prior to JDK 1.5

```
Comparable<Date> c = new Date();
System.out.println(c.compareTo("red"));
```
(b) JDK 1.5

FIGURE 21.2 The new generic type detects possible errors at compile time.

The statement in Figure 21.2(b) declares that `c` is a reference variable whose type is `Comparable<Date>` in JDK 1.5 and invokes the `compareTo` method to compare a `Date` object with a string. The code has a compile error, because the argument passed to the `compareTo` method must be of the `Date` type. Since the errors can be detected at compile time rather than at runtime, the generic type makes the program more *reliable*.

> **Note**
>
>
> Generic types must be reference types. You cannot substitute a generic type with a primitive type such as `int`, `double`, or `char`.

`ArrayList` was introduced in §9.9, "The `ArrayList` Class." This class is a generic class in JDK 1.5. Figure 21.3 shows the class diagrams for `ArrayList` prior to JDK 1.5 and in JDK 1.5, respectively.

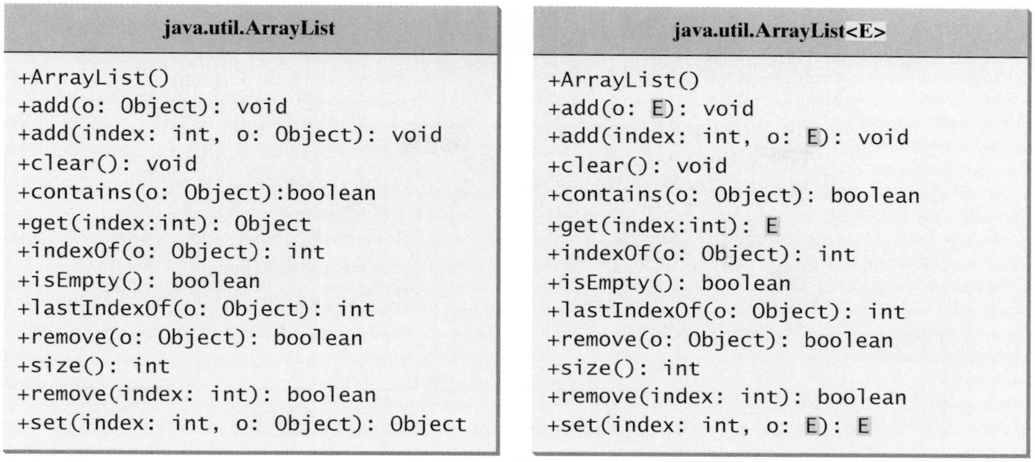

java.util.ArrayList
+ArrayList()
+add(o: Object): void
+add(index: int, o: Object): void
+clear(): void
+contains(o: Object):boolean
+get(index:int): Object
+indexOf(o: Object): int
+isEmpty(): boolean
+lastIndexOf(o: Object): int
+remove(o: Object): boolean
+size(): int
+remove(index: int): boolean
+set(index: int, o: Object): Object

java.util.ArrayList<E>
+ArrayList()
+add(o: E): void
+add(index: int, o: E): void
+clear(): void
+contains(o: Object): boolean
+get(index:int): E
+indexOf(o: Object): int
+isEmpty(): boolean
+lastIndexOf(o: Object): int
+remove(o: Object): boolean
+size(): int
+remove(index: int): boolean
+set(index: int, o: E): E

(a) ArrayList before JDK 1.5   (b) ArrayList in JDK 1.5

FIGURE 21.3 `ArrayList` is a generic class in JDK 1.5.

For example, the following statement creates a list for strings:

```
ArrayList<String> list = new ArrayList<String>();
```

You can now add only strings into the list. For example,

```
list.add("Red");
```

If you attempt to add a non-string, a compile time error will occur. For example, the following statement is now illegal because `list` can only contain strings:

```
list.add(new Integer(1));
```

Casting is not needed to retrieve a value from a list with a specified element type because the compiler already knows the element type. For example, the following statements create a list that contains only double values, add elements to the list, and retrieve elements from the list:

no casting needed

```
1 ArrayList<Double> list = new ArrayList<Double>();
2 list.add(5.5); // 5.5 is automatically converted to new Double(5.5)
3 list.add(3.0); // 3.0 is automatically converted to new Double(3.0)
4 Double doubleObject = list.get(0); // No casting is needed
5 double d = list.get(1); // Automatically converted to double
```

In lines 2 and 3, `5.5` and `3.0` are automatically converted into `Double` objects and added to `list`. In line 4, the first element in `list` is assigned to a `Double` variable. No casting is necessary because list is declared for `Double` objects. In line 5, the second element in `list` is assigned to a `double` variable. The object in `list.get(1)` is automatically converted into a primitive type value.

21.3 Declaring Generic Classes and Interfaces

Let us revise the stack class in §9.10, "A Custom Stack Class," to generalize the element type with a generic type. The new stack class, named `GenericStack`, is shown in Figure 21.4 and is implemented in Listing 21.1.

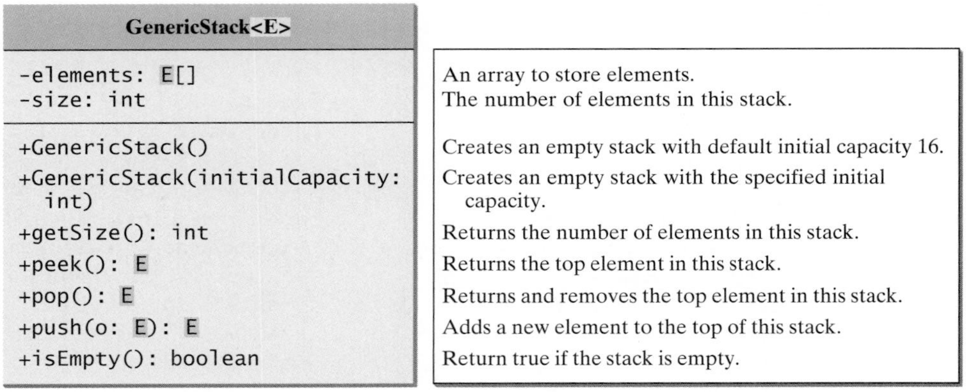

GenericStack<E>	
-elements: E[] -size: int	An array to store elements. The number of elements in this stack.
+GenericStack()	Creates an empty stack with default initial capacity 16.

+GenericStack(initialCapacity:
  int)
	Creates an empty stack with the specified initial
	  capacity.

+getSize(): int	Returns the number of elements in this stack.
+peek(): E	Returns the top element in this stack.
+pop(): E	Returns and removes the top element in this stack.
+push(o: E): E	Adds a new element to the top of this stack.
+isEmpty(): boolean	Return true if the stack is empty.

FIGURE 21.4 The MyStack class encapsulates the stack storage and provides the operations for manipulating the stack.

LISTING 21.1 GenericStack.java

```
1  public class GenericStack<E> {                              generic type E declared
2    public final static int INITIAL_SIZE = 16;
3    private E[] elements;                                      generic type E[]
4    private int size;
5
6    /** Construct a stack with the default initial capacity */
7    public GenericStack() {
8      this(INITIAL_SIZE);
9    }
10
11   /** Construct a stack with the specified initial capacity */
12   public GenericStack(int initialCapacity) {
13     elements = (E[])new Object[initialCapacity];             cast to E[]
14   }
15
16   /** Push a new element into the top of the stack */
17   public E push(E value) {                                   generic type E
18     if (size >= elements.length) {
19       E[] temp = (E[])new Object[elements.length * 2];       cast to E[]
20       System.arraycopy(elements, 0, temp, 0, elements.length);
21       elements = temp;
22     }
23
24     return elements[size++] = value;
25   }
26
27   /** Return and remove the top element from the stack */
28   public E pop() {                                           generic type E
29     return elements[--size];
30   }
31
32   /** Return the top element from the stack */
33   public E peek() {                                          generic type E
34     return elements[size - 1];
35   }
36
37   /** Test whether the stack is empty */
38   public boolean isEmpty() {
```

```
39        return size == 0;
40    }
41
42    /** Return the number of elements in the stack */
43    public int getSize() {
44        return size;
45    }
46 }
```

Here is an example that creates a stack to hold strings and adds three strings to the stack:

```
GenericStack<String> stack1 = new GenericStack<String>();
stack1.push("London");
stack1.push("Paris");
stack1.push("Berlin");
```

Here is another example that creates a stack to hold integers and adds three integers to the stack:

```
GenericStack<Integer> stack2 = new GenericStack<Integer>();
stack2.push(1); // auto boxing 1 to new Integer(1)
stack2.push(2);
stack2.push(3);
```

Note

Instead of using a generic type in Listing 21.1, you could simply make the type element `Object`, which can accommodate any object type. However, using generic types can improve software reliability and readability because certain errors can be detected at compile time rather than at runtime. For example, since `stack1` is declared `GenericStack<String>`, only strings can be added to the stack. It would be a compilation error if you attempted to add an integer to `stack1`.

benefits of using generic types

You cannot create an instance using a generic type parameter. For example, the expression `new E()` or `new E[10]` would be wrong. To circumvent this limitation, an array of the `Object` type is created in line 12, and cast into `E[]`. You need to compile the program with the option *–Xlint:unchecked*,

generic type limitation

compile with **–Xlint**

```
javac –Xlint:unchecked GenericStack.java
```

The compiler, however, issues a warning about this casting:

```
GenericStack.java:12: warning: [unchecked] unchecked cast
found    : java.lang.Object[]
required: E[]
elements = (E[])new Object[capacity];
```

The reason for this warning is that the compiler cannot ensure that casting will always succeed. For example, if `E` is `String` and `new Object[]` is an array of `Integer` objects, `(String[])(new Object[])` would cause a `ClassCastException`. Note that `ClassCast-Exception` will never occur in this case, because every object pushed to the stack must be an instance of the generic type `E`.

Caution

To create a stack of strings, you use `new GenericStack<String>()`. This could mislead you into thinking that the constructor of `GenericStack` should be declared as

generic class constructor

```
public GenericStack<E>()
```

This is wrong. It should be declared

```
public GenericStack()
```

Caution

primitive type?

You cannot substitute a generic type with a *primitive type* such as `int`, `double`, `char`, etc., because a generic type must be a reference type. However, you can use wrapper classes such as `Integer`, `Double`, `Character`, etc, instead.

Caution

generic exception class?

A generic class cannot be a subclass of `java.lang.Throwable`, so the following class declaration would be illegal:

```
public class MyException<T> extends Exception {

}
```

Note

multiple generic parameters

Occasionally, a generic class may have more than one parameter. In this case, place the parameters together inside the brackets, separated by commas, such as `<E1, E2, E3>`.

21.4 Generic Methods

generic method

You can declare generic interfaces (e.g., the `Comparable` interface in Figure 21.1(b)) and classes (e.g., the `GenericStack` class in Listing 21.1). You can also use generic types to declare generic methods. For example, Listing 21.2 declares a *generic method* `print` (lines 10–14) to print an array of objects. Line 6 passes an array of integer objects to invoke the generic `print` method. Line 7 invokes `print` with an array of strings.

LISTING 21.2   GenericMethodDemo.java

```
 1 public class GenericMethodDemo {
 2   public static void main(String[] args ) {
 3     Integer[] integers = {1, 2, 3, 4, 5};
 4     String[] strings = {"London", "Paris", "New York", "Austin"};
 5
 6     GenericMethodDemo.<Integer>print(integers);
 7     GenericMethodDemo.<Integer>print(strings);
 8   }
 9
```
generic method
```
10     public static <E> void print(E [] list) {
11       for (int i = 0; i < list.length; i++)
12         System.out.print(list[i] + " ");
13       System.out.println();
14     }
15 }
```

invoke generic method

To invoke a generic method, prefix the method name with the actual type in angle brackets. For example,

```
GenericMethodDemo.<Integer>print(integers);
GenericMethodDemo.<String>print(strings);
```

bounded generic type

A generic type can be bounded. For example, Listing 21.3 revises the `equalArea` method in Listing 10.2, TestGeometricObject.java to test whether two geometric objects have the same area. The *bounded generic type* `<E extends GeometricObject>` (line 9) specifies that `E` is a generic subtype of `GeometricObject`. You must invoke `equalArea` by passing two instances of `GeometricObject`.

LISTING 21.3   BoundedTypeDemo.java

```
 1 public class BoundedTypeDemo {
 2   public static void main(String[] args) {
 3     Rectangle rectangle = new Rectangle(2, 2);
 4     Circle9 circle = new Circle9(2);
 5
 6     System.out.println("Same area? " +
 7       BoundTypeDemo.<GeometricObject>equalArea(rectangle, circles);
 8   }
 9
10   public static <E extends GeometricObject> boolean equalArea(
11       E object1, E object2) {
12     return object1.findArea() == object2.findArea();
13   }
14 }
```

bounded type

Note

An unbounded generic type <E> is the same as <E extends Object>.

Note

To declare a generic type for a class, place the generic type after the class name, such as GenericStack<E>. To declare a generic type for a method, place the generic type before the method return type, such as <E> void max(E o1, E o2).

generic class parameter vs. generic method parameter

21.5 Raw Type and Backward Compatibility

You may use a generic class without specifying a concrete type like this:

```
GenericStack stack = new GenericStack(); // raw type
```

This is roughly equivalent to

```
GenericStack<Object> stack = new GenericStack<Object>();
```

A class such as **GenericStack** used without a type parameter is called a *raw type*. The use of raw type is allowed in JDK 1.5 for *backward compatibility* with the earlier versions of JDK. For example, generic type is used in **java.lang.Comparable** in JDK 1.5, but a lot of code still uses the raw type **Comparable**, as shown in Listing 21.4 (also see the **Max** class in §10.4, "Interfaces"):

raw type

backward compatibility

LISTING 21.4   Max.java

```
 1 // Max.java: Find a maximum object
 2 public class Max {
 3   /** Return the maximum between two objects */
 4   public static Comparable max(Comparable o1, Comparable o2) {
 5     if (o1.compareTo(o2) > 0)
 6       return o1;
 7     else
 8       return o2;
 9   }
10 }
```

raw type

Comparable o1 and **Comparable o2** are raw type declarations. *Raw type is unsafe.* For example, you may invoke the **max** method using

```
Max.max("Welcome", 23); // 23 is autoboxed into new Integer(23)
```

This would cause a runtime error because you cannot compare a string with an integer object. The new JDK 1.5 compiler displays a warning on line 5 when compiled with the option *–Xlint:unchecked*, as shown in Figure 21.5.

```
Command Prompt                                                    _ |□| x|
C:\book>javac -Xlint:unchecked Max.java
Max.java:5: warning: [unchecked] unchecked call to compareTo(T) as a member of t
he raw type java.lang.Comparable
    if (o1.compareTo(o2) > 0)
           ^
1 warning

C:\book>_
```

FIGURE 21.5 The unchecked warnings are displayed using the compiler option *–Xlint:unchecked*.

A better way to write the **max** method is to use a generic type, as shown in Listing 21.5.

LISTING 21.5 Max1.java

```
1  // Max1.java: Find a maximum object
2  public class Max1 {
3    /** Return the maximum between two objects */
4    public static <E extends Comparable<E>> E  max(E o1 , E o2 ) {
5      if (o1.compareTo(o2) > 0)
6        return o1;
7      else
8        return o2;
9    }
10 }
```

bounded type

If you invoke the **max** method using

```
Max1.max("Welcome", 23); // 23 is autoboxed into new Integer(23)
```

a compilation error will be displayed because two arguments of the **max** method in **Max1** must have the same type (e.g., two strings or two integer objects). Furthermore, the type **E** must be a subtype of **Comparable<E>**.

As another example in the following code, you may declare a raw type **stack** in line 1, assign **new GenericStack<String>** to it in line 2, and push a string and an integer object to the stack in lines 3 and 4.

```
1 GenericStack stack;
2 stack = new GenericStack<String>();
3 stack.push("Welcome to Java");
4 stack.push(new Integer(2));
```

Line 4 is unsafe because the stack is intended to store strings, but an **Integer** object is added into the stack. Line 3 should be OK, but the compiler will show warnings on both line 3 and line 4, because it cannot follow the semantic meaning of the program. All the compiler knows is that stack is a raw type and it is unsafe to perform certain operations. Therefore, warnings are displayed to alert potential programs.

Tip
Since raw types are unsafe, this book will not use them from here on.

21.6 Wildcards

What are wildcards? Listing 21.6 gives an example to demonstrate the needs they address. The example declares a generic `max` method for finding the maximum in a stack of numbers (lines 12–22). The `main` method creates a stack of integer objects, adds three integers to the stack, and invokes the `max` method to find the maximum number in the stack.

LISTING 21.6 WildCardDemo1.java

```
 1 public class WildCardDemo1 {
 2   public static void main(String[] args) {
 3     GenericStack<Integer> intStack = new GenericStack<Integer>();
 4     intStack.push(1); // 1 is autoboxed into new Integer(1)
 5     intStack.push(2);
 6     intStack.push(-2);
 7
 8     System.out.print("The max number is " + max(intStack));
 9   }
10
11   // Find the maximum in a stack of numbers
12   public static double max(GenericStack<Number> stack) {
13     double max = stack.pop().doubleValue(); // initialize max
14
15     while (!stack.isEmpty()) {
16       double value = stack.pop().doubleValue();
17       if (value > max)
18         max = value;
19     }
20
21     return max;
22   }
23 }
```

GenericStack
<Integer> type

GenericStack
<Number> type

The program in Listing 21.6 has a compilation error in line 8 because `intStack` is not an instance of `GenericStack<Number>`. So you cannot invoke `max(intStack)`.

The fact is that `Integer` is a subtype of `Number`, but `GenericStack<Integer>` is not a subtype of `GenericStack<Number>`. To circumvent this problem, JDK 1.5 introduces wildcards. A wildcard represents a type in the form of `?`, `? extends T`, or `? super T`, where `T` is a type.

The first form, `?`, called an *unbounded wildcard*, is the same as `? extends Object`. The second form, `? extends T`, called a *bounded wildcard*, represents `T` or an unknown subtype of `T`. The third form, `? super T`, called a *lower bound wildcard*, denotes `T` or an unknown supertype of `T`.

unbounded wildcard
bounded wildcard
lower bound wildcard

You can fix the error by replacing line 11 in Listing 21.6 as follows:

```
public static double max(GenericStack<? extends Number> stack) {
```

`<? extends Number>` is a wildcard type that represents `Number` or a subtype of `Number`. So it is legal to invoke `max(new GenericStack<Integer>())` or `max(new GenericStack<Double>())`.

Listing 21.7 shows an example of using the `?` wildcard in the `print` method that prints objects in a stack and empties the stack. `<?>` is a wildcard that represents any object type. It is equivalent to `<? Extends Object>`. What happens if you replace `GenericStack<?>` by `GenericStack<Object>`? It would be wrong to invoke `print(intStack)`, because instack is not an instance of GenericStack<Object>. Please note that GenericStack<Integer> is not a subtype of GenericStack<Object>, although Integer is a subtype of Object.

LISTING 21.7 WildCardDemo2.java

```
 1 public class WildCardDemo2 {
 2   public static void main(String[] args) {
 3     GenericStack<Integer> intStack = new GenericStack<Integer>();
 4     intStack.push(1); // 1 is autoboxed into new Integer(1)
 5     intStack.push(2);
 6     intStack.push(-2);
 7
 8     print(intStack);
 9   }
10
11   /** Print objects and empties the stack */
12   public static void print(GenericStack<?> stack) {
13     while (!stack.isEmpty()) {
14       System.out.print(stack.pop() + " ");
15     }
16   }
17 }
```

GenericStack
<Integer> type

wild card type

When is the wildcard <? super T> needed? Consider the example in Listing 21.8. The example creates a stack of strings in stack1 (line 3) and a stack of objects in stack2 (line 4) and invokes add(stack1, stack2) (line 9) to add the strings in stack1 into stack2. GenericStack<? super T> is used to declare stack2 in line 12. If <? super T> is replaced by <T>, a compilation error would occur on add(stack1, stack2) in line 9, because stack1's type is GenericStack<String> and stack2's type is GenericStack <Object>. <? super T> represents type T or a supertype of T. GenericStack<Object> is a subtype of GenericStack<? super String>.

LISTING 21.8 WildCardDemo3.java

```
 1 public class WildCardDemo3 {
 2   public static void main(String[] args) {
 3     GenericStack<String> stack1 = new GenericStack<String>();
 4     GenericStack<Object> stack2 = new GenericStack<Object>();
 5     stack2.push("Java");
 6     stack2.push(2);
 7     stack1.push("Sun");
 8     add(stack1, stack2);
 9     WildCardDemo2.print(stack2);
10   }
11
12   public static <T> void add(GenericStack<T> stack1,
13       GenericStack<? super T> stack2) {
14     while (!stack1.isEmpty())
15       stack2.push(stack1.pop());
16   }
17 }
```

GenericStack
<Integer> type

GenericStack
<?> type

The relationship among generic types and wildcard types is summarized in Figure 21.6. In this figure, A and B represent classes or interfaces, and E is a generic type parameter.

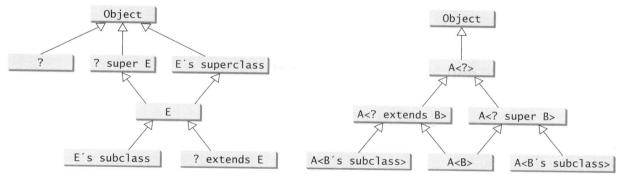

FIGURE 21.6   The relationship between generic types and wildcard types.

21.7 Important Facts

It is important to note that a generic class is shared by all its instances regardless of its actual concrete type. Suppose `stack1` and `stack2` are created as follows:

```
GenericStack<String> stack1 = new GenericStack<String>();
GenericStack<Integer> stack2 = new GenericStack<Integer>();
```

Although `GenericStack<String>` and `GenericStack<Integer>` are two types, there is only one `GenericStack` class loaded into the JVM. `stack1` and `stack2` are both instances of `GenericStack`. So the following statements display `true`:

```
System.out.println(stack1 instanceof GenericStack);
System.out.println(stack1 instanceof GenericStack<?>);
System.out.println(stack2 instanceof GenericStack);
System.out.println(stack2 instanceof GenericStack<?>);
```

But the expression `stack1 instanceof GenericStack<String>` is wrong. Since `GenericStack<String>` is not stored as a separate class in the JVM, it makes no sense to use it in casting or `instanceof` expression. The following expressions are illegal:

```
stack1 instanceof GenericStack<String>
(GenericStack<String>)stack1
```

Since all instances of a generic class have the same runtime class, the static variables and methods of a generic class are shared by all its instances. Therefore, it is illegal to refer to a generic type parameter for a class in a static method or initializer. For example, the following code is illegal:

```
public class Test<E> {
  public static void m(E o1) { // illegal
  }

  static {
    E o2; // illegal
  }
}
```

21.8 Avoiding Unsafe Raw Types

Raw types are unsafe in JDK 1.5. If you try to use them, you will get a compilation warning "unchecked operation." To fix it, instantiate generic types. For example, Listing 9.7, TestArrayList.java, uses an array list to store strings. The compiler reports unchecked operation warnings on the **add** method. These warnings can be avoided if you revise the program, as shown in Listing 21.9. A list to store strings is created in line 6, and strings are added to the list in lines 9–14. A list to store circles is created in line 39, and circles are added to the list in lines 42–43.

LISTING 21.9 `TestArrayListNew.java`

```
 1 import java.util.*;
 2
 3 public class TestArrayListNew {
 4   public static void main(String[] args) {
 5     // Create a list to store cities
 6     ArrayList<String> cityList = new ArrayList<String>();
 7
 8     // Add some cities in the list
 9     cityList.add("London");
10     cityList.add("New York");
11     cityList.add("Paris");
12     cityList.add("Toronto");
13     cityList.add("Hong Kong");
14     cityList.add("Singapore");
15
16     System.out.println("List size? " + cityList.size());
17     System.out.println("Is Toronto in the list? " +
18       cityList.contains("Toronto"));
19     System.out.println("The location of New York in the list? "
20       + cityList.indexOf("New York"));
21     System.out.println("Is the list empty? " +
22       cityList.isEmpty()); // Print false
23
24     // Insert a new city at index 2
25     cityList.add(2, "Beijing");
26
27     // Remove a city from the list
28     cityList.remove("Toronto");
29
30     // Remove a city at index 1
31     cityList.remove(1);
32
33     // Display London Beijing Paris Hong Kong Singapore
34     for (int i = 0; i < cityList.size(); i++)
35       System.out.print(cityList.get(i) + " ");
36     System.out.println();
37
38     // Create a list to store two circles
39     ArrayList<Circle> list = new ArrayList<Circle>();
40
41     // Add a circle and a cylinder
42     list.add(new Circle(2));
43     list.add(new Circle(3));
44
45     // Display the area of the first circle in the list
46     System.out.println("The area of the circle? " +
47       ((Circle)list.get(0)).findArea());
48   }
49 }
```

instantiate generic type

add string

instantiate generic type

add circle

The **sort** method in Listing 10.5, GenericSort.java, has "unchecked operation" warning. It can be fixed as shown in Listing 21.10. The generic type **E** is a subtype of **Comparable<E>**. When invoking the **sort** method, you must pass an array of comparable objects.

LISTING 21.10   GenericSortNew.java

```
 1 public class GenericSortNew {
 2    /** Sort an array of comparable objects */
 3    public static <E extends Comparable<E>> void sort(E[] list) {
 4       E currentMax;
 5       int currentMaxIndex;
 6
 7       for (int i = list.length - 1; i >= 1; i--) {
 8          // Find the maximum in the list[0..i]
 9          currentMax = list[i];
10          currentMaxIndex = i;
11
12          for (int j = i - 1; j >= 0; j--) {
13             if (currentMax.compareTo(list[j]) < 0) {
14                currentMax = list[j];
15                currentMaxIndex = j;
16             }
17          }
18
19          // Swap list[i] with list[currentMaxIndex] if necessary;
20          if (currentMaxIndex != i) {
21             list[currentMaxIndex] = list[i];
22             list[i] = currentMax;
23          }
24       }
25    }
26
27    public static void main(String[] args) {
28       // Create a String array
29       String[] stringArray = {"Tom", "John", "Fred"};
30
31       sort(stringArray);
32
33       for (int i = 0; i < stringArray.length; i++)
34          System.out.print(stringArray[i] + " ");
35    }
36 }
```

generic sort method
generic type E

invoke sort

21.9 (Optional) Case Study: Generic Matrix Class

This supplement presents a case study on designing classes for matrix operations using generic types. The addition and multiplication operations for all matrices are similar except that their element types differ. Therefore, you can design a superclass that describes the common operations shared by matrices of all types regardless of their element types, and you can create subclasses tailored to specific types of matrices. This case study gives implementations for two types: `int` and `Rational`. For the `int` type, the wrapper class `Integer` should be used to wrap an `int` value into an object, so that the object is passed in the methods for operations.

The class diagram is shown in Figure 21.7. The methods `addMatrix` and `multiplyMatrix` add and multiply two matrices of a generic type `E[][]`. The static method `printResult` displays the matrices, the operations, and their result. The methods `add`, `multiply`, and `zero` are abstract methods because their implementations are dependent on the specific type of the array elements. For example, the `zero()` method returns 0 for the `Integer` type and 0/1 for the `Rational` type. These methods will be implemented in the subclasses in which the matrix element type is specified.

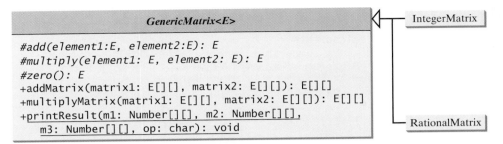

FIGURE 21.7   The `GenericMatrix` class is an abstract superclass for `IntegerMatrix` and `RationalMatrix`.

`IntegerMatrix` and `RationalMatrix` are concrete subclasses of `GenericMatrix`. These two classes implement the `add`, `multiply`, and `zero` methods defined in the `GenericMatrix` class.

Listing 21.11 implements the `GenericMatrix` class. `<E extends Number>` in line 1 specifies that the generic type is a subtype of `Number`. Three abstract methods—`add`, `multiply`, and `zero`—are defined in lines 3, 6, and 9. These methods are abstract because they cannot be implemented without knowing the exact type of the elements. The `addMaxtrix` (lines 12–30) and `multiplyMatrix` (lines 33–56) methods implement the methods for adding and multiplying two matrices. All these methods must be non-static because they use generic type `E`. The `printResult` method (lines 59–83) is static because it is not tied to specific instances.

The matrix element type is generic. This enables you to use an object of any class as long as you can implement the abstract `add`, `multiply`, and `zero` methods in subclasses.

The `addMatrix` and `multiplyMatrix` methods (lines 12–57) are concrete methods. They are ready to use as long as the `add`, `multiply`, and `zero` methods are implemented in the subclasses.

The `addMatrix` and `multiplyMatrix` methods check the bounds of the matrices before performing operations. If the two matrices have incompatible bounds, the program throws an exception (lines 16, 36).

LISTING 21.11   GenericMatrix.java

bounded generic type

abstract method

abstract method

abstract method

add two matrices

```java
 1 public abstract class GenericMatrix <E extends Number> {
 2   /** Abstract method for adding two elements of the matrices */
 3   protected abstract E add(E o1, E o2);
 4
 5   /** Abstract method for multiplying two elements of the matrices */
 6   protected abstract E multiply(E o1, E o2);
 7
 8   /** Abstract method for defining zero for the matrix element */
 9   protected abstract E zero();
10
11   /** Add two matrices */
12   public E[][] addMatrix(E[][] matrix1, E[][] matrix2) {
13     // Check bounds of the two matrices
14     if ((matrix1.length != matrix2.length) ||
15         (matrix1[0].length != matrix2.length)) {
16       throw new RuntimeException(
17         "The matrices do not have the same size");
18     }
19
```

```
20      E[][] result =
21        (E[][])new Number[matrix1.length][matrix1[0].length];
22
23      // Perform addition
24      for (int i = 0; i < result.length; i++)
25        for (int j = 0; j < result[i].length; j++) {
26          result[i][j] = add(matrix1[i][j], matrix2[i][j]);
27        }
28
29      return result;
30    }
31
32    /** Multiply two matrices */
33    public E[][] multiplyMatrix(E[][] matrix1, E[][] matrix2) {
34      // Check bounds
35      if (matrix1[0].length != matrix2.length) {
36        throw new RuntimeException(
37          "The matrices do not have compatible size");
38      }
39
40      // Create result matrix
41      E[][] result =
42        (E[][])new Number[matrix1.length][matrix2[0].length];
43
44      // Perform multiplication of two matrices
45      for (int i = 0; i < result.length; i++) {
46        for (int j = 0; j < result[0].length; j++) {
47          result[i][j] = zero();
48
49          for (int k = 0; k < matrix1[0].length; k++) {
50            result[i][j] = add(result[i][j],
51              multiply(matrix1[i][k], matrix2[k][j]));
52          }
53        }
54      }
55
56      return result;
57    }
58
59    /** Print matrices, the operator, and their operation result */
60    public static void printResult(
61        Number[][] m1, Number[][] m2, Number[][] m3, char op) {
62      for (int i = 0; i < m1.length; i++) {
63        for (int j = 0; j < m1[0].length; j++)
64          System.out.print(" " + m1[i][j]);
65
66        if (i == m1.length / 2)
67          System.out.print( "   " + op + "   " );
68        else
69          System.out.print( "       " );
70
71        for (int j = 0; j < m2.length; j++)
72          System.out.print(" " + m2[i][j]);
73
74        if (i == m1.length / 2)
75          System.out.print( "   =   " );
76        else
77          System.out.print( "       " );
78
```

multiply two matrices

display result

```
79        for (int j = 0; j < m3.length; j++)
80          System.out.print(m3[i][j] + " ");
81
82        System.out.println();
83      }
84    }
85 }
```

Listing 21.12 implements the `IntegerMatrix` class. The class extends `Generic-Matrix<Integer>` in line 1. After the generic instantiation, the `add` method in `GenericMatrix<Integer>` is now `Integer add(Integer o1, Integer o2)`. The `add`, `multiply`, and `zero` methods are implemented for `Integer` objects. These methods are still protected, because they are only invoked by the `addMatrix` and `multiplyMatrix` methods.

LISTING 21.12 IntegerMatrix.java

extends generic type

implement add

implement multiply

implement zero

```java
1 public class IntegerMatrix extends GenericMatrix<Integer> {
2   /** Implement the add method for adding two matrix elements */
3   protected Integer add(Integer o1, Integer o2) {
4     return new Integer(o1.intValue() + o2.intValue());
5   }
6
7   /** Implement the multiply method for multiplying two
8       matrix elements */
9   protected Integer multiply(Integer o1, Integer o2) {
10     return new Integer(o1.intValue() * o2.intValue());
11   }
12
13   /** Implement the zero method to specify zero for Integer */
14   protected Integer zero() {
15     return new Integer(0);
16   }
17 }
```

Listing 21.13 implements the `RationalMatrix` class. The `Rational` class was introduced in §11.5, "Case Study: The `Rational` Class." `Rational` is a subtype of `Number`. The `RationalMatrix` class extends `GenericMatrix<Rational>` in line 1. After the generic instantiation, the `add` method in `GenericMatrix<Rational>` is now `Rational add(Rational o1, Rational o2)`. The `add`, `multiply`, and `zero` methods are implemented for `Rational` objects. These methods are still protected, because they are only invoked by the `addMatrix` and `multiplyMatrix` methods.

LISTING 21.13 RationalMatrix.java

extends generic type

implement add

implement multiply

```java
1 public class RationalMatrix extends GenericMatrix<Rational> {
2   /** Implement the add method for adding two rational elements */
3   protected Rational add(Rational r1, Rational r2) {
4     return r1.add(r2);
5   }
6
7   /** Implement the multiply method for multiplying
8       two rational elements */
9   protected Rational multiply(Rational r1, Rational r2) {
10     return r1.multiply(r2);
11   }
12
```

```
13    /** Implement the zero method to specify zero for Rational */
14    protected Rational zero() {                                          implement zero
15      return new Rational(0,1);
16    }
17 }
```

Listing 21.14 gives a program that creates two `Integer` matrices (lines 4–5) and an `IntegerMatrix` object (line 8), and adds and multiplies two matrices in lines 12 and 16. The output is shown in Figure 21.8.

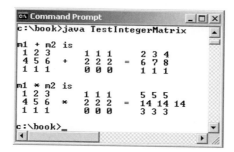

FIGURE 21.8 The program creates two `Integer` matrices and performs addition and multiplication on them.

LISTING 21.14 TestIntegerMatrix.java

```
1 public class TestIntegerMatrix {
2   public static void main(String[] args) {
3     // Create Integer arrays m1, m2
4     Integer[][] m1 = new Integer[][]{{1, 2, 3}, {4, 5, 6}, {1, 1, 1}};    create matrices
5     Integer[][] m2 = new Integer[][]{{1, 1, 1}, {2, 2, 2}, {0, 0, 0}};
6
7     // Create an instance of IntegerMatrix
8     IntegerMatrix integerMatrix = new IntegerMatrix();                    create IntegerMatrix
9
10    System.out.println("\nm1 + m2 is ");
11    integerMatrix.printResult(
12      m1, m2, integerMatrix.addMatrix(m1, m2), '+');                      add two matrices
13
14    System.out.println("\nm1 * m2 is ");
15    integerMatrix.printResult(
16      m1, m2, integerMatrix.multiplyMatrix(m1, m2), '*');                multiply two matrices
17  }
18 }
```

Listing 21.15 gives a program that creates two `Rational` matrices (lines 4–10) and a `RationalMatrix` object (line 13), and adds and multiplies two matrices in lines 17 and 21. The output is shown in Figure 21.9.

LISTING 21.15 TestRationalMatrix.java

```
1 public class TestRationalMatrix {
2   public static void main(String[] args) {
3     // Create two Rational arrays m1 and m2
4     Rational[][] m1 = new Rational[3][3];                                 create matrices
5     Rational[][] m2 = new Rational[3][3];
6     for (int i = 0; i < m1.length; i++)
```

create **RationalMatrix**

add two matrices

multiply two matrices

```
7       for (int j = 0; j < m1[0].length; j++) {
8         m1[i][j] = new Rational(i + 1, j + 5);
9         m2[i][j] = new Rational(i + 1, j + 6);
10      }
11
12      // Create an instance of RationalMatrix
13      RationalMatrix rationalMatrix = new RationalMatrix();
14
15      System.out.println("\nm1 + m2 is ");
16      rationalMatrix.printResult(
17        m1, m2, rationalMatrix.addMatrix(m1, m2), '+');
18
19      System.out.println("\nm1 * m2 is ");
20      rationalMatrix.printResult(
21        m1, m2, rationalMatrix.multiplyMatrix(m1, m2), '*');
22    }
23 }
```

```
Command Prompt                                                    _ □ ×
c:\book>java TestRationalMatrix

m1 + m2 is
  1/5 1/6 1/7        1/6 1/7 1/8        11/30 13/42 15/56
  2/5 1/3 2/7    +   1/3 2/7 1/4    =   11/15 13/21 15/28
  3/5 1/2 3/7        1/2 3/7 3/8        11/10 13/14 45/56

m1 * m2 is
  1/5 1/6 1/7        1/6 1/7 1/8        101/630 101/735 101/840
  2/5 1/3 2/7    *   1/3 2/7 1/4    =   101/315 202/735 101/420
  3/5 1/2 3/7        1/2 3/7 3/8        101/210 101/245 101/280

c:\book>
```

FIGURE 21.9   The program creates two matrices of rational numbers and performs addition and multiplication on them.

KEY TERMS

actual concrete type 694	raw type 699
bounded generic type 698	<?> type 701
formal generic type 694	<? extends E> type 701
generic instantiation 694	<? super E> type 701

REVIEW QUESTIONS

Sections 21.2–21.4

21.1   Are there any compilation errors in (a) and (b)?

```
ArrayList dates = new ArrayList();
dates.add(new Date());
dates.add(new String());
```

(a)

```
ArrayList<Date> dates = new ArrayList<Date>();
dates.add(new Date());
dates.add(new String());
```

(b)

21.2   What is wrong in (a)? Is the code in (b) correct?

```
ArrayList dates = new ArrayList();
dates.add(new Date());
Date date = dates.get(0);
```

(a)

```
ArrayList<Date> dates = new ArrayList<Date>();
dates.add(new Date());
Date date = dates.get(0);
```

(b)

21.3   What are the benefits of using generic types?

21.4   Can you create an instance using a generic type, for example, `new E()` or new `E[20]`?

21.5   Since you create an instance of `ArrayList` of strings using `new ArrayList<String>()`, should the constructor in the `ArrayList` class be declared as

```
public ArrayList<E>()
```

21.6   Can a generic class have multiple generic parameters?

21.7   How do you declare a generic type in a class? How do you declare a generic type in a method?

21.8   What is a bounded generic type?

Sections 21.5–21.7

21.9   What is a raw type? Is `GenericStack` the same as `GenericStack<Object>`?

21.10   What are an unbounded wildcard, a bounded wildcard, and a lower bounded wildcard?

21.11   If your program uses `ArrayList<String>` and `ArrayList<Date>`, does the JVM load both of them?

21.12   Can a method that uses a generic class parameter be static? Why?

PROGRAMMING EXERCISES

21.1   Revise `MyList`, `MyAbstractList`, `MyArrayList`, and `MyLinkedList` in Chapter 20, using a generic parameter for objects.

21.2   Revise `MyQueue` in Listing 20.6, using a generic parameter for objects.

21.3   Revise `BinaryTree` in Listing 20.8, using a generic parameter for objects.

21.4   Revise `Heap` in Listing 20.10, using a generic parameter for objects.

21.5   Revise `PriorityQueue` in Listing 20.12, using a generic parameter for objects.

JAVA COLLECTIONS FRAMEWORK

Objectives

- To describe the Java Collections Framework hierarchy (§22.1).

- To use the common methods defined in the `Collection` interface for operating sets and lists (§22.2).

- To use the `Iterator` interface to traverse a collection (§22.3).

- To use the JDK 1.5 `foreach` loop to replace an iterator for traversing a collection (§22.3).

- To discover the `Set` interface, and know how and when to use `HashSet`, `LinkedHashSet`, or `TreeSet` to store elements (§22.3).

- To compare elements using the `Comparator` interface (§22.4).

- To explore the `List` interface, and know how and when to use `ArrayList` or `LinkedList` to store elements (§22.5).

- To know how to use the static methods in the `Collections` class for lists and collections (§22.6).

- To distinguish `Vector` and `ArrayList`, and know how to use `Vector` and `Stack` (§22.7).

- To explore the relationships among `Collection`, `Queue`, `LinkedList`, and `PriorityQueue` and to create priority queues using the `PriorityQueue` class (§22.8).

- (Optional) To understand the differences between `Collection` and `Map`, and know how and when to use `HashMap`, `LinkedHashMap`, and `TreeMap` to store values associated with keys (§22.9).

- To obtain singleton sets, lists, and maps, and unmodifiable sets, lists, and maps using the static methods in the `Collections` class (§22.10).

22.1 Introduction

Java Collection Framework

Chapter 20 introduced several data structures such as linked lists, stacks, queues, heaps, and priority queues. These popular data structures are widely used in many applications. Java provides an API known as the *Collections Framework* for these and many other useful data structures. So you can use them without having to reinvent the wheel.

The focus of this chapter is on how to use the classes and interfaces in the collections framework. Since knowledge of implementing data structures is not required for learning the Java Collections Framework, this chapter need not be used in conjunction with Chapter 20.

collection
set
list
map

A *collection* is a container object that stores a group of objects, often referred to as *elements*. The Java Collections Framework supports three major types of collections: *set, list,* and *map.* They are defined in the interfaces **Set**, **List**, and **Map**. An instance of **Set** stores a group of nonduplicate elements. An instance of **List** stores an ordered collection of elements. An instance of **Map** stores a group of objects, each of which is associated with a key. The relationships of the major interfaces and classes in the Java Collections Framework are shown in Figures 22.1 and 22.2. These interfaces and classes provide a unified API for efficiently storing and processing a collection of objects. You will learn how to use these interfaces and classes in this chapter.

Note

All the interfaces and classes defined in the Java Collections Framework are grouped in the **java.util** package.

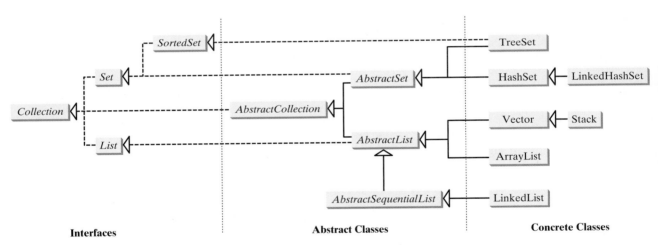

FIGURE 22.1 **Set** and **List** are subinterfaces of **Collection**.

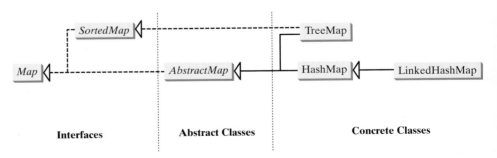

FIGURE 22.2 An instance of **Map** stores a group of objects and their associated keys.

Note

The design of the Java Collections Framework is a good example of using interfaces, abstract classes, and concrete classes. The interfaces define the framework. The abstract classes provide partial implementation for convenience. The concrete classes implement the interfaces with concrete data structures.

Note

All the concrete classes in the Java Collections Framework implement the `Cloneable` and `Serializable` interfaces. Thus their instances can be cloned and serialized.

`Cloneable`
`Serializable`

22.2 The **Collection** Interface and the **AbstractCollection** Class

The `Collection` interface is the root interface for manipulating a collection of objects. Its public methods are listed in Figure 22.3. The `AbstractCollection` class is a convenience class that provides partial implementation for the `Collection` interface. It implements all the methods in `Collection` except the `size` and `iterator` methods. These are implemented in appropriate subclasses.

«interface» *java.util.Collection<E>*	
+add(o: E): boolean	Adds a new element o to this collection.
+addAll(c: Collection<? extends E>): boolean	Adds all the elements in the collection c to this collection.
+clear(): void	Removes all the elements from this collection.
+contains(o: Object): boolean	Returns true if this collection contains the element o.
+containsAll(c: Collection<?>): boolean	Returns true if this collection contains all the elements in c.
+equals(o: Object): boolean	Returns true if this collection is equal to another collection o.
+hashCode(): int	Returns the hash code for this collection.
+isEmpty(): boolean	Returns true if this collection contains no elements.
+iterator(): Iterator	Returns an iterator for the elements in this collection.
+remove(o: Object): boolean	Removes the element o from this collection.
+removeAll(c: Collection<?>): boolean	Removes all the elements in c from this collection.
+retainAll(c: Collection<?>): boolean	Retains the elements that are both in c and in this collection.
+size(): int	Returns the number of elements in this collection.
+toArray(): Object[]	Returns an array of Object for the elements in this collection.

«interface» *java.util.Iterator<E>*	
+hasNext(): boolean	Returns true if this iterator has more elements to traverse.
+next(): E	Returns the next element from this iterator.
+remove(): void	Removes the last element obtained using the next method.

FIGURE 22.3   The `Collection` interface contains the methods for manipulating the elements in a collection, and each collection object contains an iterator for traversing elements in the collection.

The `Collection` interface provides the *basic operations* for adding and removing elements in a collection. The **add** method adds an element to the collection. The **addAll** method

basic operations

adds all the elements in the specified collection to this collection. The `remove` method removes an element from the collection. The `removeAll` method removes the elements from this collection that are present in the specified collection. The `retainAll` method retains the elements in this collection that are also present in the specified collection. All these methods return `boolean`. The return value is `true` if the collection is changed as a result of the method execution. The `clear()` method simply removes all the elements from the collection.

Note

The methods `addAll`, `removeAll`, and `retainAll` are similar to the set union, difference, and intersection operations.

set operations

query operations

The `Collection` interface provides various *query operations*. The `size` method returns the number of elements in the collection. The `contains` method checks whether the collection contains the specified element. The `containsAll` method checks whether the collection contains all the elements in the specified collection. The `isEmpty` method returns true if the collection is empty.

The `Collection` interface provides the `toArray()` method that returns an array representation for the collection.

iterator

A collection may be a set or a list. The `Iterator` interface provides a uniform way for traversing elements in various types of collections. The `iterator` method in the `Collection` interface returns an instance of the `Iterator` interface, as shown in Figure 22.3, which provides sequential access to the elements in the collection using the `next()` method. You can also use the `hasNext()` method to check whether there are more elements in the iterator, and the `remove()` method to remove the last element returned by the iterator.

Note

unsupported operations

Some of the methods in the `Collection` interface cannot be implemented in the concrete subclass. In this case, the method would throw `java.lang.UnsupportedOperation-Exception`, a subclass of `RuntimeException`. This is a good design that you can use in your project. If a method has no meaning in the subclass, you can implement it as follows:

```
public void someMethod() {
  throw new UnsupportedOperationException("Method not supported");
}
```

22.3 Sets

The `Set` interface extends the `Collection` interface. It does not introduce new methods or constants, but it stipulates that an instance of `Set` contains *no duplicate* elements. The concrete classes that implement `Set` must ensure that no duplicate elements can be added to the set. That is, no two elements `e1` and `e2` can be in the set such that `e1.equals(e2)` is `true`.

no duplicates

The `AbstractSet` class is a convenience class that extends `AbstractCollection` and implements `Set`. The `AbstractSet` class provides concrete implementations for the `equals` method and the `hashCode` method. The hash code of a set is the sum of the hash codes of all the elements in the set. Since the `size` method and `iterator` method are not implemented in the `AbstractSet` class, `AbstractSet` is an abstract class.

Three concrete classes of `Set` are `HashSet`, `LinkedHashSet`, and `TreeSet`, as shown in Figure 22.4.

22.3.1 HashSet

The `HashSet` class is a concrete class that implements `Set`. You can create an empty hash set using its no-arg constructor or create a hash set from an existing collection. A `HashSet` can be used to store duplicate-free elements. For efficiency, objects added to a hash set need

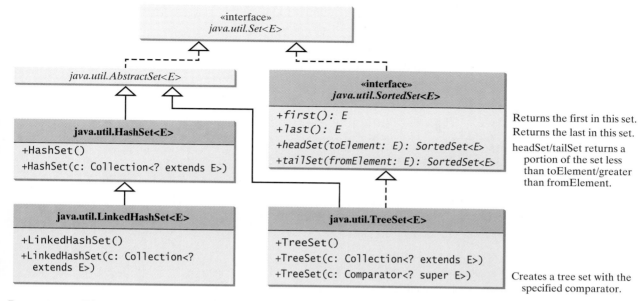

FIGURE 22.4   The Java Collections Framework provides three concrete set classes.

to implement the hashCode method in a manner that properly disperses the hash code. Most of the classes in the Java API implement the hashCode method. For example, the hashCode in the Integer class returns its int value. The hashCode in the Character class returns the Unicode of the character. The hashCode in the String class returns $s_0*31^{n-1} + s_1*31^{n-2} + \cdots + s_{n-1}$, where s_i is s.charAt(i).

Recall that the hash codes of two objects must be the same if the two objects are equal. Two unequal objects may have the same hash code, but you should implement the hashCode method to avoid too many such cases. Additionally, it is required that invoking the hashCode method multiple times returns the same integer during one execution of the program.

hashCode()

Listing 22.1 gives a program that finds all the words used in a text. The program creates a hash set to store the words extracted from the text, and uses an iterator to traverse the elements in the set. The output of the program is shown in Figure 22.5.

```
Command Prompt                                    _ □ ×
C:\book>java TestHashSet
[Paris, Beijing, London, San Francisco, New York]
Paris Beijing London San Francisco New York
C:\book>
```

FIGURE 22.5   The program adds string elements to a hash set, displays the elements using the toString method, and traverses the elements using an iterator.

LISTING 22.1   TestHashSet.java

```java
1  import java.util.*;
2
3  public class TestHashSet {
4    public static void main(String[] args) {
5      // Create a hash set
6      Set<String> set = new HashSet<String>();
7
```

create set

add element

get iterator

traverse iterator

```
 8    // Add strings to the set
 9    set.add("London");
10    set.add("Paris");
11    set.add("New York");
12    set.add("San Francisco");
13    set.add("Beijing");
14    set.add("New York");
15
16    System.out.println(set);
17
18    // Obtain an iterator for the hash set
19    Iterator iterator = set.iterator();
20
21    // Display the elements in the hash set
22    while (iterator.hasNext()) {
23      System.out.print(iterator.next() + " ");
24    }
25  }
26 }
```

The strings are added to the set (lines 9–14). **"New York"** is added to the set more than once, but only one is stored, because a set does not allow duplicates.

As shown in Figure 22.5, the strings are not stored in the order in which they are inserted into the set. There is no particular order for the elements in a hash set. To impose an order on them, you need to use the **LinkedHashSet** class, which is introduced in the next section.

JDK 1.5 **foreach** loop

Tip
You can simplify the code in lines 18–24 using a *JDK 1.5* **foreach** *loop* without using an iterator, as follows:

```
for (Object element: set)
  System.out.print(element.toString() + " ");
```

This loop reads as "for each element in the set, do the following." The **foreach** loop can be used for arrays (see §6.2.7) as well as any instance of **Collection**.

Caution
Since **set** is declared as **Set<String>** in line 6, all elements added to **set** must be strings. A compilation error would occur if a non-string object is added to **set**.

22.3.2 LinkedHashSet

LinkedHashSet was added in JDK 1.4. It extends **HashSet** with a linked list implementation that supports an ordering of the elements in the set. The elements in a **HashSet** are not ordered, but the elements in a **LinkedHashSet** can be retrieved in the order in which they were inserted into the set. A **LinkedHashSet** can be created by using its no-arg constructor.

Listing 22.2 rewrites the preceding example using **LinkedHashSet**. Simply replace **HashSet** by **LinkedHashSet**. The output of the program is shown in Figure 22.6.

LISTING 22.2 TestLinkedHashSet.java

```
1 import java.util.*;
2
3 public class TestLinkedHashSet {
4   public static void main(String[] args) {
```

```
5      // Create a hash set
6      Set<String> set = new LinkedHashSet<String>();
7
8      // Add strings to the set
9      set.add("London");
10     set.add("Paris");
11     set.add("New York");
12     set.add("San Francisco");
13     set.add("Beijing");
14     set.add("New York");
15
16     System.out.println(set);
17
18     // Display the elements in the hash set
19     for (Object element: set)
20        System.out.print(element.toString() + " ");
21   }
22 }
```

create linked hash set

add element

display elements

```
Command Prompt                                    _ □ ×
C:\book>java TestLinkedHashSet
[London, Paris, New York, San Francisco, Beijing]
London Paris New York San Francisco Beijing
C:\book>_
```

FIGURE 22.6   The program adds string elements to a linked hash set, displays the elements using the `toString` method, and traverses the elements using an iterator.

A `LinkedHashSet` is created in line 6. As shown in Figure 22.6, the strings are stored in the order in which they are inserted. Since `LinkedHashSet` is a set, it does not store duplicate elements.

The `LinkedHashSet` maintains the order in which the elements are inserted. To impose a different order (e.g., increasing or decreasing order), you can use the `TreeSet` class introduced in the next section.

 Tip
If you don't need to maintain the order in which the elements are inserted, use `HashSet`, which is more efficient than `LinkedHashSet`.

22.3.3   TreeSet

`SortedSet` is a subinterface of `Set`, which guarantees that the elements in the set are sorted. Additionally, it provides the methods `first()` and `last()` for returning the first and last elements in the set, and `headSet(toElement)` and `tailSet(fromElement)` for returning a portion of the set whose elements are less than `toElement` and greater than `fromElement`.

`TreeSet` is a concrete class that implements the `SortedSet` interface. To create a `TreeSet`, use its no-arg constructor or use `new TreeSet(Collection)`. You can add objects into a tree set as long as they can be compared with each other. There are two ways to compare objects.

■ Use the `Comparable` interface. Since the objects added to the set are instances of `Comparable`, they can be compared using the `compareTo` method. The `Comparable`

Comparable

interface was introduced in §10.4, "Interfaces." Several classes in the Java API, such as `String`, `Date`, `Calendar`, and all the wrapper classes for the primitive types, implement the `Comparable` interface. This approach is referred to as *natural order*.

■ If the class for the elements does not implement the `Comparable` interfaces, or if you don't want to use the `compareTo` method in the class that implements the `Comparable` interface, specify a comparator for the elements in the set. This approach is referred to as *order by comparator*. It will be introduced in §22.4, "The `Comparator` Interface."

Comparator

Listing 22.3 gives an example of ordering elements using the `Comparable` interface. The preceding example in Listing 22.2 displays all the words used in a text. The words are displayed in their insertion order. This example rewrites the preceding example to display the words in alphabetical order using the `TreeSet` class. Figure 22.7 shows a sample run of the program.

LISTING 22.3 TestTreeSet.java

```
 1 import java.util.*;
 2
 3 public class TestTreeSet {
 4   public static void main(String[] args) {
 5     // Create a hash set
 6     Set<String> set = new HashSet<String>();
 7
 8     // Add strings to the set
 9     set.add("London");
10     set.add("Paris");
11     set.add("New York");
12     set.add("San Francisco");
13     set.add("Beijing");
14     set.add("New York");
15
16     TreeSet<String> treeSet = new TreeSet<String>(set);
17     System.out.println(treeSet);
18
19     // Display the elements in the hash set
20     for (Object element: set)
21       System.out.print(element.toString() + " ");
22   }
23 }
```

create hash set

create tree set

display elements

```
Command Prompt
C:\book>java TestTreeSet
[Beijing, London, New York, Paris, San Francisco]
Paris Beijing London San Francisco New York
C:\book>_
```

FIGURE 22.7 The program demonstrates the differences between hash sets and tree sets.

The example creates a hash set filled with strings, and then creates a tree set for the same strings. The strings are sorted in the tree set using the `compareTo` method in the `Comparable` interface.

The elements in the set are sorted once you create a `TreeSet` object from a `HashSet` object using `new TreeSet(hashSet)` (line 17). You may rewrite the program to create an instance of `TreeSet` using its no-arg constructor, and add the strings into the `TreeSet` object. Then, every time a string is added to the `TreeSet` object, the elements in it will be reordered. The approach used in the example is generally more efficient because it requires only a one-time sorting.

Note

All the classes in Figure 22.1 have at least two constructors. One is the no-arg constructor that constructs an empty collection. The other constructs instances from a collection. Thus the `TreeSet` class has the constructor `TreeSet(Collection c)` for constructing a `TreeSet` from a collection `c`. In this example, `new TreeSet(hashSet)` creates an instance of `TreeSet` from the collection `hashSet`.

Tip

If you don't need to maintain a sorted set when updating a set, you can use a hash set, because it takes less time to insert and remove elements in a hash set. When you need a set to be sorted, you can convert it into a tree set.

22.4 The **Comparator** Interface

Sometimes you want to insert elements of different types into a tree set. The elements may not be instances of `java.lang.Comparable`. You can define a comparator to compare these elements. To do so, create a class that implements the `java.util.Comparator` interface. The `Comparator` interface has two methods, `compare` and `equals`.

- **public int** compare(Object element1, Object element2)
  Returns a negative value if `element1` is less than `element2`, a positive value if `element1` is greater than `element2`, and zero if they are equal

- **public boolean** equals(Object element).
  Returns `true` if the specified object is also a comparator and imposes the same ordering as this comparator.

Note

The `equals` method is also defined in the `Object` class. Therefore, you will not get a compilation error even if you don't implement the `equals` method in your custom comparator class. However, in some cases implementing this method may improve performance by allowing programs to determine quickly whether two distinct comparators impose the same order.

Listing 22.4 declares a `Comparator` for geometric objects. The `GeometricObject` class was introduced in §10.2, "Abstract Classes." Line 4 implements `Comparator<GeometricObject>`. Line 5 overrides the `compare` method to compare two geometric objects. The comparator class also implements `Serializable`. It is generally a good idea for comparators to implement `Serializable`, as they may be used as ordering methods in serializable data structures such as `TreeSet`. In order for the data structure to serialize successfully, the comparator (if provided) must implement `Serializable`.

LISTING 22.4 GeometricComparator.java

```
1 import java.util.Comparator;
2
3 public class GeometricObjectComparator
4   implements Comparator<GeometricObject> , java.io.Serializable {          implements Comparator
5   public int compare(GeometricObject o1, GeometricObject o2) {             implements compare
6     double area1 = o1.getArea();
7     double area2 = o2.getArea();
8
9     if (area1 < area2)
10      return -1;
```

```
11        else if (area1 == area2)
12          return 0;
13        else
14          return 1;
15    }
16 }
```

If you create a TreeSet using its no-arg constructor, the compareTo method is used to compare the elements in the set, assuming that the class of the elements implements the Comparable interface. To use a comparator, you have to use the constructor TreeSet(Comparator comparator) to create a sorted set that uses the compare method in the comparator to order the elements in the set.

Listing 22.5 gives a program that demonstrates how to sort elements in a tree set using the Comparator interface. The example creates a tree set of geometric objects in lines 6–7. The geometric objects are sorted using the compare method in the Comparator interface. The output of the program is shown in Figure 22.8.

LISTING 22.5 TestTreeSetWithComparator.java

```
1 import java.util.*;
2
3 public class TestTreeSetWithComparator {
4   public static void main(String[] args) {
5     // Create a tree set for geometric objects using a comparator
6     Set<GeometricObject> set =
7       new TreeSet<GeometricObject>(new GeometricObjectComparator());
8     set.add(new Rectangle(4, 5));
9     set.add(new Circle(40));
10    set.add(new Circle(40));
11    set.add(new Rectangle(4, 1));
12
13    // Display geometric objects in the tree set
14    System.out.println("A sorted set of geometric objects");
15    for (GeometricObject element: set)
16      System.out.println("area = " + element.getArea());
17  }
18 }
```

tree set

display elements

```
Command Prompt                              _ □ ×

C:\book>java TestTreeSetWithComparator
A sorted set of geometric objects
area = 4.0
area = 20.0
area = 5026.548245743669

C:\book>
```

FIGURE 22.8 The program demonstrates the use of the Comparator interface.

The Circle and Rectangle classes were defined in §10.2, "Abstract Classes." They are all subclasses of GeometricObject.

Two circles of the same radius are added to the set in the tree set (lines 9–10), but only one is stored, because the two circles are equal and the set does not allow duplicates.

Note

Comparable is used to compare two objects of the same type, but Comparator can be used to compare two objects of different types.

Comparable vs. Comparator

22.5 Lists

A set stores nonduplicate elements. To allow duplicate elements to be stored in a collection, you need to use a list. A list can not only store duplicate elements, but also allows the user to specify where they are stored. The user can access elements by an index. The `List` interface extends `Collection` to define an ordered collection with duplicates allowed. The `List` interface adds position-oriented operations, as well as a new list iterator that enables the user to traverse the list bi-directionally. The new methods in the `List` interface are shown in Figure 22.9.

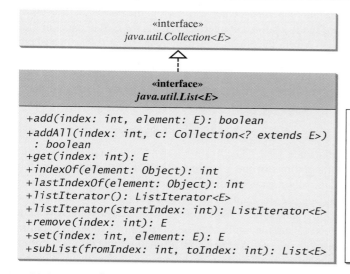

FIGURE 22.9   The `List` interface stores elements in sequence, permitting duplicates.

The `add(index, element)` method is used to insert an element at a specified index, and the `addAll(index, collection)` method to insert a collection at a specified index. The `remove(index)` method is used to remove an element at the specified index from the list. A new element can be set at the specified index using the `set(index, element)` method.

The `indexOf(element)` method is used to obtain the index of the first occurrence of the specified element in the list, and the `lastIndexOf(element)` method to obtain the index of the last occurrence of the specified element in the list. A sublist can be obtained by using the `subList(fromIndex, toIndex)` method.

The `listIterator()` or `listIterator(startIndex)` method returns an instance of `ListIterator`. The `ListIterator` interface extends the `Iterator` interface to add bi-directional traversal of the list. The methods in `ListIterator` are listed in Figure 22.10.

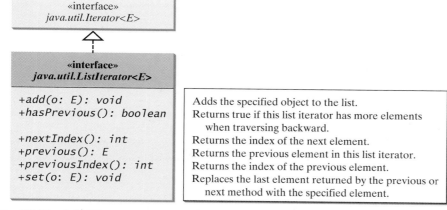

FIGURE 22.10   `ListIterator` enables traversal of a list bi-directionally.

The `add(element)` method inserts the specified element into the list. The element is inserted immediately before the next element that would be returned by the `next()` method defined in the `Iterator` interface, if any, and after the element that would be returned by the `previous()` method, if any. If the list contains no elements, the new element becomes the sole element in the list. The `set(element)` method can be used to replace the last element returned by the `next` method or the `previous` method with the specified element.

The `hasNext()` method defined in the `Iterator` interface is used to check whether the iterator has more elements when traversed in the forward direction, and the `hasPrevious()` method to check whether the iterator has more elements when traversed in the backward direction.

The `next()` method defined in the `Iterator` interface returns the next element in the iterator, and the `previous()` method returns the previous element in the iterator. The `nextIndex()` method returns the index of the next element in the iterator, and the `previousIndex()` returns the index of the previous element in the iterator.

The `AbstractList` class provides a partial implementation for the `List` interface. The `AbstractSequentialList` class extends `AbstractList` to provide support for linked lists.

22.5.1 The `ArrayList` and `LinkedList` Classes

The `ArrayList` class (introduced in §9.9, "The `Array List` Class") and the `LinkedList` class are two concrete implementations of the `List` interface. `ArrayList` stores elements in an array. The array is dynamically created. If the capacity of the array is exceeded, create a larger new array and copy all the elements from the current array to the new array. `LinkedList` stores elements in a linked list. Which of the two classes you use depends on your specific needs. If you need to support random access through an index without inserting or removing elements except at the end, `ArrayList` offers the most efficient collection. If, however, your application requires the insertion or deletion of elements anywhere in the list, you should choose `LinkedList`. A list can grow or shrink dynamically. An array is fixed once it is created. If your application does not require the insertion or deletion of elements, an array is the most efficient data structure.

`ArrayList` is a resizable-array implementation of the `List` interface. In addition to implementing the `List` interface, this class provides methods for manipulating the size of the array that is used internally to store the list, as shown in Figure 22.11. Each `ArrayList` instance has a capacity. The capacity is the size of the array used to store the elements in the list. It is always at least as large as the list size. As elements are added to an `ArrayList`, its capacity grows automatically. An `ArrayList` does not automatically shrink. You can use the `trimToSize()`

`trimToSize()`

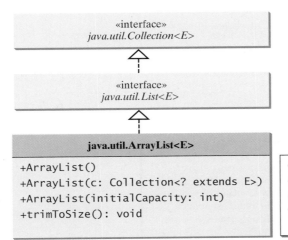

FIGURE 22.11 `ArrayList` implements `List` using an array.

method to reduce the array capacity to the size of the list. An `ArrayList` can be constructed using its no-arg constructor, `ArrayList(Collection)`, or `ArrayList(intialCapacity)`.

`LinkedList` is a linked list implementation of the `List` interface. In addition to implementing the `List` interface, this class provides the methods for retrieving, inserting, and removing elements from both ends of the list, as shown in Figure 22.12. A `LinkedList` can be constructed using its no-arg constructor or `LinkedList(Collection)`.

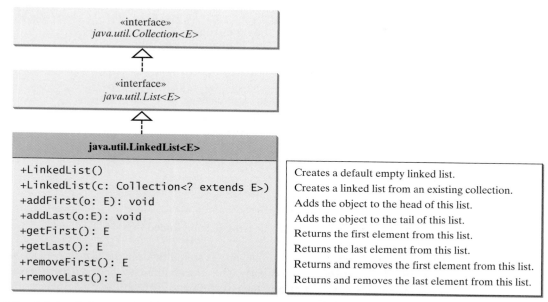

FIGURE 22.12 `LinkedList` provides methods for adding and inserting elements at both ends of the list.

Listing 22.6 gives a program that creates an array list filled with numbers and inserts new elements into specified locations in the list. The example also creates a linked list from the array list, and inserts and removes elements from the list. Finally, the example traverses the list forward and backward. The output of the program is shown in Figure 22.13.

LISTING 22.6 TestArrayAndLinkedList.java

```java
1  import java.util.*;
2
3  public class TestArrayAndLinkedList {
4    public static void main(String[] args) {
5      List<Integer> arrayList = new ArrayList<Integer>();          array list
6      arrayList.add(1); // 1 is autoboxed to new Integer(1)
7      arrayList.add(2);
8      arrayList.add(3);
9      arrayList.add(1);
10     arrayList.add(4);
11     arrayList.add(0, 10);
12     arrayList.add(3, 30);
13
14     System.out.println("A list of integers in the array list:");
15     System.out.println(arrayList);
16
17     LinkedList<Object> linkedList = new LinkedList<Object>(arrayList);   linked list
18     linkedList.add(1, "red");
19     linkedList.removeLast();
20     linkedList.addFirst("green");
21
```

<table>
<tr><td>list iterator</td><td>

```
22    System.out.println("Display the linked list forward:");
23    ListIterator listIterator = linkedList.listIterator();
24    while (listIterator.hasNext()) {
25      System.out.print(listIterator.next() + " ");
26    }
27    System.out.println();
28
29    System.out.println("Display the linked list backward:");
30    listIterator = linkedList.listIterator(linkedList.size());
31    while (listIterator.hasPrevious()) {
32      System.out.print(listIterator.previous() + " ");
33    }
34  }
35 }
```
</td></tr>
</table>

list iterator (line 23)

list iterator (line 30)

```
C:\book>java TestArrayAndLinkedList
A list of integers in the array list:
[10, 1, 2, 30, 3, 1, 4]
Display the linked list forward:
green 10 red 1 2 30 3 1
Display the linked list backward:
1 3 30 2 1 red 10 green
C:\book>_
```

FIGURE 22.13   The program uses an array list and linked lists.

A list can hold identical elements. Integer 1 is stored twice in the list (lines 6, 9). **ArrayList** and **LinkedList** are operated similarly. The critical difference between them pertains to internal implementation, which affects their performance. **ArrayList** is efficient for retrieving elements, and for inserting and removing elements from the end of the list. **LinkedList** is efficient for inserting and removing elements anywhere in the list.

Tip

`Arrays.asList(T...a)` method

Java provides the static **asList** method for creating a list from a variable-length argument list of a generic type. Thus you can use the following code to create a list of strings:

```
List<String> list = Arrays.asList("red", "green", "blue");
```

22.6 Static Methods for Lists and Collections

You can use **TreeSet** to store sorted elements in a set. But there is no sorted list. However, the Java Collections Framework provides static methods in the **Collections** class that can be used to sort a list. The **Collections** class also contains the **binarySearch**, **reverse**, **shuffle**, **copy**, and **fill** methods on lists, and **max**, **min**, **disjoint**, and **frequency** methods on collections, as shown in Figure 22.14.

You can sort the comparable elements in a list in its natural order through the **compareTo** method in the **Comparable** interface. You may also specify a comparator to sort elements. For example, the following code sorts strings in a list:

sort list

```
List<String> list = Arrays.asList("red", "green", "blue");
Collections.sort(list);
System.out.println(list);
```

The output is [blue, green, red].

ascending order

descending order

The preceding code sorts a list in *ascending order*. To sort it in *descending order*, you may simply use the **Collections.reverseOrder()** method to return a **Comparator** object

java.util.Collections	
+sort(list: List): void	Sorts the specified list.
+sort(list: List, c: Comparator): void	Sorts the specified list with the comparator.
+binarySearch(list: List, key: Object): int	Searches the key in the sorted list using binary search.
+binarySearch(list: List, key: Object, c: Comparator): int	Searches the key in the sorted list using binary search with the comparator.
+reverse(list: List): void	Reverses the specified list.
+reverseOrder(): Comparator	Returns a comparator with the reverse ordering.
+shuffle(list: List): void	Shuffles the specified list randomly.
+shuffle(list: List): void	Shuffles the specified list with a random object.
+copy(des: List, src: List): void	Copies from the source list to the destination list.
+nCopies(n: int, o: Object): List	Returns a list consisting of n copies of the object.
+fill(list: List, o: Object): void	Fills the list with the object.
+max(c: Collection): Object	Returns the max object in the collection.
+max(c: Collection, c: Comparator): Object	Returns the max object using the comparator.
+min(c: Collection): Object	Returns the min object in the collection.
+min(c: Collection, c: Comparator): Object	Returns the min object using the comparator.
+disjoint(c1: Collection, c2: Collection): boolean	Returns true if c1 and c2 have no elements in common.
+frequency(c: Collection, o: Object): int	Returns the number of occurrences of the specified element in the collection.

Labels: List, Collection (row group labels at left)

FIGURE 22.14 The `Collections` class contains static methods for manipulating lists and collections.

that orders the elements in reverse order. For example, the following code sorts a list of strings in descending order:

```
List<String> list = Arrays.asList("green", "red", "yellow", "blue");
Collections.sort(list, Collections.reverseOrder());
System.out.println(list);
```

The output is `[yellow, red, green, blue]`.

You can use the `binarySearch` method to search for a key in a list. The list must be presorted in increasing order. If the key is not in the list, the method returns –(insertion point + 1). Recall that the insertion point is where the item would fall in the list if it were present. For example, the following code searches the keys in a list of integers and a list of strings:

binarySearch

```
List<Integer> list1 = Arrays.asList(2, 4, 7, 10, 11, 45, 50, 59, 60, 66);
System.out.println("(1) Index: " + Collections.binarySearch(list1, 7));
System.out.println("(2) Index: " + Collections.binarySearch(list1, 9));

List<String> list2 = Arrays.asList("blue", "green", "red");
System.out.println("(3) Index: " + Collections.binarySearch(list2, "red"));
System.out.println("(4) Index: " + Collections.binarySearch(list2, "cyan"));
```

The output of the preceding code is

(1) Index: 2

(2) Index: –4

(3) Index: 2

(4) Index: –2

reverse

You can use the `reverse` method to reverse the elements in a list. For example, the following code displays [blue, green, red, yellow]:

```
List<String> list = Arrays.asList("yellow", "red", "green", "blue");
Collections.reverse(list);
System.out.println(list);
```

shuffle

You can use the `shuffle(List)` method to randomly reorder the elements in a list. For example, the following code shuffles the elements in `list`:

```
List<String> list = Arrays.asList("yellow", "red", "green", "blue");
Collections.shuffle(list);
System.out.println(list);
```

You can also use the `shuffle(List, Random)` method to randomly reorder the elements in a list with a specified `Random` object. Using a specified `Random` object is useful to generate a list with identical sequences of elements for the same original list. For example, the following code shuffles the elements in `list`:

```
List<String> list1 = Arrays.asList("yellow", "red", "green", "blue");
List<String> list2 = Arrays.asList("yellow", "red", "green", "blue");
Collections.shuffle(list1, new Random(20));
Collections.shuffle(list2, new Random(20));
System.out.println(list1);
System.out.println(list2);
```

You will see that `list1` and `list2` have the same sequence of elements before and after the shuffling.

copy

You can use the `copy(det, src)` method to copy all the elements from a source list to a destination list on the same index. The destination must be as long as the source list. If it is longer, the remaining elements in the source list are not affected. For example, the following code copies `list2` to `list1`:

```
List<String> list1 = Arrays.asList("yellow", "red", "green", "blue");
List<String> list2 = Arrays.asList("white", "black");
Collections.copy(list1, list2);
System.out.println(list1);
```

The output for `list1` is [white, black, green, blue]. The `copy` method performs a shallow copy. Only the references of the elements from the source list are copied.

nCopies

You can use the `nCopies(int n, Object o)` method to create an immutable list that consists of n copies of the specified object. For example, the following code creates a list with five `Calendar` objects:

```
List<GregorianCalendar> list1 = Collections.nCopies
    (5, new GregorianCalendar(2005, 0, 1));
```

The list created from the `nCopies` method is immutable, so you cannot add, remove, or update elements in the list. All the elements have the same references.

fill

You can use the `fill(List list, Object o)` method to replace all the elements in the list with the specified element. For example, the following code displays [black, black, black]:

```
List<String> list = Arrays.asList("red", "green", "blue");
Collections.fill(list, "black");
System.out.println(list);
```

You can use the `max` and `min` methods for finding the maximum and minimum elements in a collection. The elements must be comparable using the `Comparable` interface or the `Comparator` interface. For example, the following code displays the largest and smallest strings in a collection:

`max` and `min` methods

```
Collection<String> collection = Arrays.asList("red", "green", "blue");
System.out.println(Collections.max(collection));
System.out.println(Collections.min(collection));
```

The `disjoint(collection1, collection2)` method returns `true` if the two collections have no elements in common. For example, in the following code, `disjoint(collection1, collection2)` returns `false`, but `disjoint(collection1, collection3)` returns `true`:

`disjoint` method

```
Collection<String> collection1 = Arrays.asList("red", "cyan");
Collection<String> collection2 = Arrays.asList("red", "blue");
Collection<String> collection3 = Arrays.asList("pink", "tan");
System.out.println(Collections.disjoint(collection1, collection2));
System.out.println(Collections.disjoint(collection1, collection3));
```

The `frequency(collection, element)` method finds the number of occurrences of the element in the collection. For example, `frequency(collection, "red")` returns `2` in the following code:

`frequency` method

```
Collection<String> collection = Arrays.asList("red", "cyan", "red");
System.out.println(Collections.frequency(collection, "red"));
```

22.7 The **Vector** and **Stack** Classes

The Java Collections Framework was introduced with Java 2. Several data structures were supported prior to Java 2. Among them were the `Vector` and `Stack` classes. These classes were redesigned to fit into the Java Collections Framework, but all their old-style methods are retained for compatibility.

`Vector` is the same as `ArrayList`, except that it contains synchronized methods for accessing and modifying the vector. Synchronized methods can prevent data corruption when a vector is accessed and modified by two or more threads concurrently. For the many applications that do not require synchronization, using `ArrayList` is more efficient than using `Vector`.

The `Vector` class implements the `List` interface. It also has the methods contained in the original `Vector` class defined prior to Java 2, as shown in Figure 22.15.

Most of the additional methods in the `Vector` class listed in the UML diagram in Figure 22.15 are similar to the methods in the `List` interface. These methods were introduced before the Java Collections Framework. For example, `addElement(Object element)` is the same as the `add(Object element)` method, except that `addElement` method is synchronized. Use the `ArrayList` class if you don't need synchronization. It works much faster than `Vector`.

Note

The `elements()` method returns an `Enumeration`. The `Enumeration` interface was introduced prior to Java 2 and was superseded by the `Iterator` interface.

Note

`Vector` is widely used in Java programming because it was the Java resizable array implementation before Java 2. Many of the Swing data models use vectors.

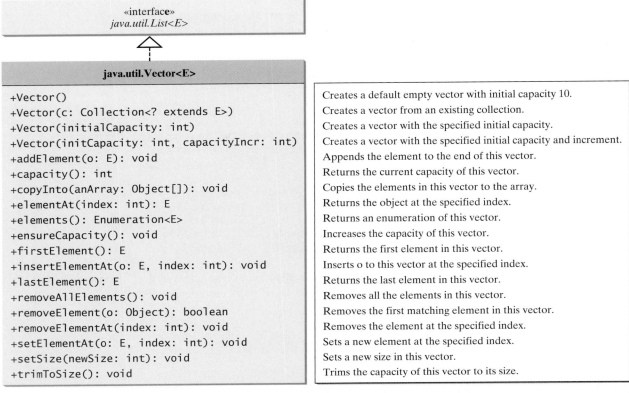

«interface»
java.util.List<E>

java.util.Vector<E>

+Vector()	Creates a default empty vector with initial capacity 10.
+Vector(c: Collection<? extends E>)	Creates a vector from an existing collection.
+Vector(initialCapacity: int)	Creates a vector with the specified initial capacity.
+Vector(initCapacity: int, capacityIncr: int)	Creates a vector with the specified initial capacity and increment.
+addElement(o: E): void	Appends the element to the end of this vector.
+capacity(): int	Returns the current capacity of this vector.
+copyInto(anArray: Object[]): void	Copies the elements in this vector to the array.
+elementAt(index: int): E	Returns the object at the specified index.
+elements(): Enumeration<E>	Returns an enumeration of this vector.
+ensureCapacity(): void	Increases the capacity of this vector.
+firstElement(): E	Returns the first element in this vector.
+insertElementAt(o: E, index: int): void	Inserts o to this vector at the specified index.
+lastElement(): E	Returns the last element in this vector.
+removeAllElements(): void	Removes all the elements in this vector.
+removeElement(o: Object): boolean	Removes the first matching element in this vector.
+removeElementAt(index: int): void	Removes the element at the specified index.
+setElementAt(o: E, index: int): void	Sets a new element at the specified index.
+setSize(newSize: int): void	Sets a new size in this vector.
+trimToSize(): void	Trims the capacity of this vector to its size.

FIGURE 22.15 The `Vector` class in Java 2 implements `List` and also retains all the methods in the original `Vector` class.

In the Java Collections Framework, `Stack` is implemented as an extension of `Vector`, as illustrated in Figure 22.16.

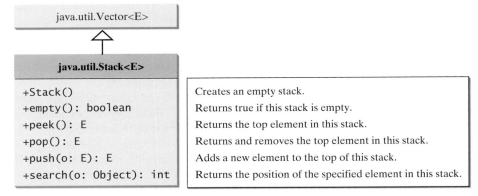

java.util.Vector<E>

java.util.Stack<E>

+Stack()	Creates an empty stack.
+empty(): boolean	Returns true if this stack is empty.
+peek(): E	Returns the top element in this stack.
+pop(): E	Returns and removes the top element in this stack.
+push(o: E): E	Adds a new element to the top of this stack.
+search(o: Object): int	Returns the position of the specified element in this stack.

FIGURE 22.16 The `Stack` class extends `Vector` to provide a last-in/first-out data structure.

The `Stack` class was introduced prior to Java 2. The methods shown in Figure 22.16 were used before Java 2. The `empty()` method is the same as `isEmpty()`. The `peek()` method looks at the element at the top of the stack without removing it. The `pop()` method removes the top element from the stack and returns it. The `push(Object element)` method adds the specified element to the stack. The `search(Object element)` method checks whether the specified element is in the stack.

22.8 Queues and Priority Queues

A queue is a first-in/first-out data structure. Elements are appended to the end of the queue and are removed from the beginning of the queue. In a priority queue, elements are assigned priorities. When accessing elements, the element with the highest priority is removed first. The design and implementation of queues and priority queues were introduced in §20.3, "Stacks and Queues"and §20.6 "Priority Queues". This section introduces queues and priority queues in the Java API.

JDK 1.5 introduced the `Queue` interface that extends `java.util.Collection` with additional insertion, extraction, and inspection operations, as shown in Figure 22.17.

Queue interface

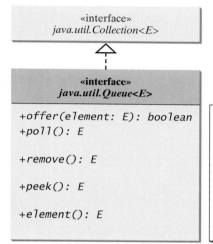

+offer(element: E): boolean	Inserts an element to the queue.
+poll(): E	Returns and removes the head of this queue, or returns null if this queue is empty.
+remove(): E	Returns and removes the head of this queue and throws an exception if this queue is empty.
+peek(): E	Returns, but does not remove, the head of this queue, returning null if this queue is empty.
+element(): E	Returns, but does not remove, the head of this queue, throwing an exception if this queue is empty.

FIGURE 22.17 The `Queue` interface extends `Collection` to provide additional insertion, extraction, and inspection operations.

The `offer` method is used to add an element to the queue. This method is similar to the `add` method in the `Collection` interface, but the `offer` method is preferred for queues. The `poll` and `remove` methods are similar except that `poll()` returns `null` if the queue is empty, whereas `remove()` throws an exception. The `peek` and `element` methods are similar except that `peek()` returns `null` if the queue is empty, whereas `element()` throws an exception.

queue operations

In JDK 1.5, the `LinkedList` class implements the `Queue` interfaces, so you can use `LinkedList` to create a queue. Listing 22.7 shows an example of using a queue to store strings. Line 3 creates a queue using `LinkedList`. Four strings are added to the queue in lines 4–7. The `size()` method defined in the `Collection` interface returns the number of elements in the queue (line 9). The `remove()` method retrieves and removes the element at the head of the queue (line 10). Figure 22.18 shows the output of the program.

LinkedList queue

LISTING 22.7 TestQueue.java

```
1 public class TestQueue {
2   public static void main(String[] args) {
3     java.util.Queue<String> queue = new java.util.LinkedList<String>();
4     queue.offer("Oklahoma");
5     queue.offer("Indiana");
6     queue.offer("Georgia");
7     queue.offer("Texas");
8
```

creates a queue

inserts an element

queue size
remove element

```
 9    while (queue.size() > 0)
10      System.out.print(queue.remove() + " ");
11  }
12 }
```

```
Command Prompt                    _ □ X
C:\book>java TestQueue
Oklahoma Indiana Georgia Texas
C:\book>_
```

FIGURE 22.18 The program adds string elements to a queue and removes the elements from the queue.

PriorityQueue class

The `PriorityQueue` class in JDK 1.5 implements a priority queue, as shown in Figure 22.19. By default, the priority queue orders its elements according to their natural ordering using `Comparable`. The element with the least value is assigned the highest priority, and thus is removed from the queue first. If there are several elements with the same highest priority, the tie is broken arbitrarily. You can also specify an ordering using `Comparator` using the constructor `PriorityQueue(initialCapacity, comparator)`.

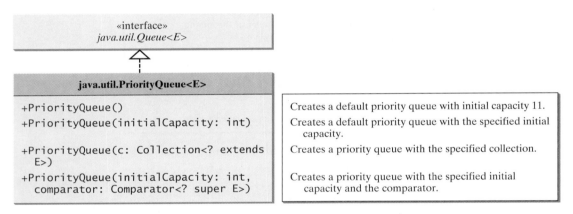

FIGURE 22.19 The `PriorityQueue` class implements a priority queue.

Listing 22.8 shows an example of using a priority queue to store strings. Line 5 creates a priority queue for strings using its no-arg constructor. This priority queue orders the strings using their natural order, so the strings are removed from the queue in increasing order. Line 16 creates a priority queue using the comparator obtained from `Collections.reverseOrder()`, which orders the elements in reverse order, so the strings are removed from the queue in decreasing order. Figure 22.20 shows the output of the program.

LISTING 22.8 PriorityQueueDemo.java

a default queue
inserts an element

```
 1 import java.util.*;
 2
 3 public class PriorityQueueDemo {
 4   public static void main(String[] args) {
 5     PriorityQueue<String> queue1 = new PriorityQueue<String>();
 6     queue1.offer("Oklahoma");
 7     queue1.offer("Indiana");
 8     queue1.offer("Georgia");
 9     queue1.offer("Texas");
10
```

```
11        System.out.println("Priority queue using Comparable:");
12        while (queue1.size() > 0) {
13          System.out.print(queue1.remove() + " ");
14        }
15
16        PriorityQueue<String> queue2 = new PriorityQueue<String>(
17          4, Collections.reverseOrder());
18        queue2.offer("Oklahoma");
19        queue2.offer("Indiana");
20        queue2.offer("Georgia");
21        queue2.offer("Texas");
22
23        System.out.println("\nPriority queue using Comparator:");
24        while (queue2.size() > 0) {
25          System.out.print(queue2.remove() + " ");
26        }
27    }
28 }
```

a queue with comparator

```
Command Prompt                          _ □ ×
C:\book>java PriorityQueueDemo
Priority queue using Comparable:
Georgia Indiana Oklahoma Texas
Priority queue using Comparator:
Texas Oklahoma Indiana Georgia
C:\book>
```

FIGURE 22.20   The program creates priority queues using `Comparable` and `Comparator`.

22.9 (Optional) Maps

The `Collection` interface represents a collection of elements stored in a set or a list. The `Map` interface maps keys to the elements. The keys are like indexes. In `List`, the indexes are integers. In `Map`, the keys can be any objects. A map cannot contain duplicate keys. Each key maps to one value. The `Map` interface provides the methods for querying, updating, and obtaining a collection of values and a set of keys, as shown in Figure 22.21.

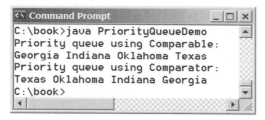

java.util.Map<K, V>	
`+clear(): void`	Removes all mappings from this map.
`+containsKey(key: Object): boolean`	Returns true if this map contains a mapping for the specified key.
`+containsValue(value: Object): boolean`	Returns true if this map maps one or more keys to the specified value.
`+entrySet(): Set`	Returns a set consisting of the entries in this map.
`+get(key: Object): V`	Returns the value for the specified key in this map.
`+isEmpty(): boolean`	Returns true if this map contains no mappings.
`+keySet(): Set<K>`	Returns a set consisting of the keys in this map.
`+put(key: K, value: V): V`	Puts a mapping in this map.
`+putAll(m: Map): void`	Adds all the mappings from m to this map.
`+remove(key: Object): V`	Removes the mapping for the specified key.
`+size(): int`	Returns the number of mappings in this map.
`+values(): Collection<V>`	Returns a collection consisting of the values in this map.

FIGURE 22.21   The `Map` interface maps keys to values.

The update methods include `clear`, `put`, `putAll`, and `remove`. The `clear()` method removes all mappings from the map. The `put(Object key, Object value)` method associates the specified value with the specified key in the map. If the map formerly contained a mapping for this key, the old value associated with the key is returned. The `putAll(Map m)` method adds the specified map to this map. The `remove(Object key)` method removes the map elements for the specified key from the map.

The query methods include `containsKey`, `containsValue`, `isEmpty`, and `size`. The `containsKey(Object key)` method checks whether the map contains a mapping for the specified key. The `containsValue(Object value)` method checks whether the map contains a mapping for this value. The `isEmpty()` method checks whether the map contains any mappings. The `size()` method returns the number of mappings in the map.

You can obtain a set of the keys in the map using the `keySet()` method, and a collection of the values in the map using the `values()` method. The `entrySet()` method returns a collection of objects that implement the `Map.Entry` interface, where `Entry` is an inner interface for the `Map` interface. Each object in the collection is a specific key-value pair in the underlying map.

The `AbstractMap` class is a convenience class that implements all the methods in the `Map` interface except the `entrySet()` method. The `SortedMap` interface extends the `Map` interface to maintain the mapping in ascending order of keys with additional methods `firstKey()` and `lastKey()` for returning the lowest and highest key, `headMap(toKey)` for returning the portion of the map whose keys are less than `toKey`, and `tailMap(fromKey)` for returning the portion of the map whose keys are greater than or equal to `fromKey`.

The `HashMap`, `LinkedHashMap`, and `TreeMap` classes are three concrete implementations of the `Map` interface, as shown in Figure 22.22.

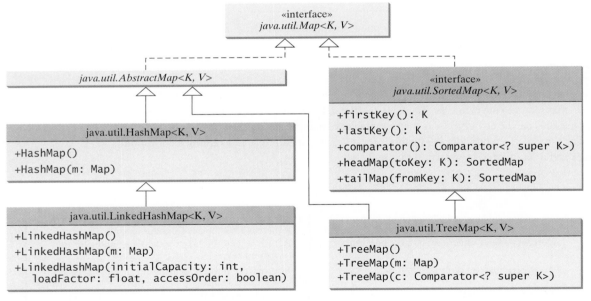

FIGURE 22.22   The Java Collections Framework provides three concrete map classes.

The `HashMap` class is efficient for locating a value, inserting a mapping, and deleting a mapping.

`LinkedHashMap` was introduced in JDK 1.4. It extends `HashMap` with a linked list implementation that supports an ordering of the entries in the map. The entries in a `HashMap` are not ordered, but the entries in a `LinkedHashMap` can be retrieved either in the order in which they were inserted into the map (known as the *insertion order*) or in the order in which they were last accessed, from least recently accessed to most recently accessed (*access order*).

The no-arg constructor constructs a LinkedHashMap with the insertion order. To construct a LinkedHashMap with the access order, use the LinkedHashMap(initialCapacity, loadFactor, true).

The TreeMap class, implementing SortedMap, is efficient for traversing the keys in a sorted order. The keys can be sorted using the Comparable interface or the Comparator interface. If you create a TreeMap using its no-arg constructor, the compareTo method in the Comparable interface is used to compare the elements in the set, assuming that the class of the elements implements the Comparable interface. To use a comparator, you have to use the TreeMap(Comparator comparator) constructor to create a sorted map that uses the compare method in the comparator to order the elements in the map based on the keys.

Note

Prior to JDK 1.2, Map was supported in java.util.Hashtable. Hashtable was redesigned to fit into the Java Collections Framework with all its methods retained for compatibility. Hashtable implements the Map interface and is used in the same way as HashMap except that Hashtable is synchronized.

Listing 22.9 gives an example that creates a hash map, a linked hash map, and a tree map that map students to ages. The program first creates a hash map with the student's name as its key and the age as its value. The program then creates a tree map from the hash map and displays the mappings in ascending order of the keys. Finally, the program creates a linked hash map, adds the same entries to the map, and displays the entries. The output of the program is shown in Figure 22.23.

LISTING 22.9 TestMap.java

```java
 1 import java.util.*;
 2
 3 public class TestMap {
 4   public static void main(String[] args) {
 5     // Create a HashMap
 6     Map<String, Integer> hashMap = new HashMap<String, Integer>();   create map
 7     hashMap.put("Smith", 30);                                        add entry
 8     hashMap.put("Anderson", 31);
 9     hashMap.put("Lewis", 29);
10     hashMap.put("Cook", 29);
11
12     System.out.println("Display entries in HashMap");
13     System.out.println(hashMap);
14
15     // Create a TreeMap from the previous HashMap
16     Map<String, Integer> treeMap =
17       new TreeMap<String, Integer>(hashMap);                         tree map
18     System.out.println("\nDisplay entries in ascending order of key");
19     System.out.println(treeMap);
20
21     // Create a LinkedHashMap                                        linked hash map
22     Map<String, Integer> linkedHashMap =
23       new LinkedHashMap<String, Integer>(16, 0.75f, true);
24     linkedHashMap.put("Smith", 30);
25     linkedHashMap.put("Anderson", 31);
26     linkedHashMap.put("Lewis", 29);
27     linkedHashMap.put("Cook", 29);
28
29     // Display the age for Lewis
30     System.out.println("The age for " + "Lewis is " +
31       linkedHashMap.get("Lewis").intValue());
```

```
32
33        System.out.println("\nDisplay entries in LinkedHashMap");
34        System.out.println(linkedHashMap);
35    }
36 }
```

```
Command Prompt                                    _ □ ×
C:\book>java TestMap
Display entries in HashMap
{Cook=29, Smith=30, Lewis=29, Anderson=31}

Display entries in ascending order of key
{Anderson=31, Cook=29, Lewis=29, Smith=30}
The age for Lewis is 29

Display entries in LinkedHashMap
{Smith=30, Anderson=31, Cook=29, Lewis=29}

C:\book>
```

FIGURE 22.23 The program demonstrates the use of `HashMap`, `LinkedHashMap`, and `TreeMap`.

As shown in Figure 22.23, the entries in the `HashMap` are in random order. The entries in the `TreeMap` are in increasing order of the keys. The entries in the `LinkedHashMap` are in the order of their access, from least recently accessed to most recently.

All the concrete classes that implement the `Map` interface have at least two constructors. One is the no-arg constructor that constructs an empty map, and the other constructs a map from an instance of `Map`. Thus `new TreeMap<String, Integer>(hashMap)` (line 16) constructs a tree map from a hash map.

You can create an insertion-ordered or access-ordered linked hash map. An access-ordered linked hash map is created in line 22. The most recently accessed entry is placed at the end of the map. The entry with the key Lewis is last accessed in line 30, so it is displayed last in line 33.

Tip
If you don't need to maintain an order in a map when updating it, use a `HashMap`, because less time is needed to insert and remove mappings in a `HashMap`. When you need to maintain the insertion order or access order in the map, use a `LinkedHashMap`. When you need the map to be sorted on keys, convert it to a tree map.

22.9.1 Case Study: Occurrences of Words

This case study writes a program that counts the occurrences of words in a text and displays the words and their occurrences in ascending order of word frequency. The program uses a hash map to store a pair consisting of a word and its count. For each word, check whether it is already a key in the map. If not, add the key and value 1 to the map. Otherwise, increase the value for the word (key) by 1 in the map. To sort the map, convert it to a tree map.

Listing 22.10 gives the solution to the problem. The output of the program is shown in Figure 22.24.

LISTING 22.10 `CountOccurrenceOfWords.java`

```java
1 import java.util.*;
2
3 public class CountOccurrenceOfWords {
4   public static void main(String[] args) {
5     // Text in a string
6     String text = "Have a good day. Have a good class. " +
7       "Have a good visit. Have fun!";
8
```

```
 9      // Create a hash map to hold words as key and count as value
10      Map<String, Integer> hashMap = new HashMap<String, Integer>();          hash map
11
12      String[] words = text.split("[ .!?]");                                   split string
13      for (int i = 0; i < words.length; i++) {
14        if (words[i].length() > 1) {
15          if (hashMap.get(words[i]) != null) {
16            int value = hashMap.get(words[i]).intValue();
17            value++;
18            hashMap.put(words[i], value);                                      add entry
19          }
20          else
21            hashMap.put(words[i], 1);                                          add entry
22        }
23      }
24
25      // Create a tree map from the hash map
26      Map<String, Integer> treeMap =
27        new TreeMap<String, Integer>(hashMap);                                 tree map
28
29      // Display mappings
30      System.out.println("Display words and their count in " +
31        "ascending order of the words");
32      System.out.print(treeMap);
33    }
34 }
```

```
Command Prompt                                                    _ □ ×
C:\book>java CountOccurrenceOfWords
Display words and their count in ascending order of the words
{Have=4, a=3, class=1, day=1, fun=1, good=3, visit=1}
C:\book>_
```

Figure 22.24   The program finds the occurrences of each word in a text.

The pairs of words and their occurrence counts are stored in the map. The words serve as the keys. Since all elements in the map must be stored as objects, the count is wrapped in an `Integer` object.

The program extracts a word from a text using the `split` method in the `String` class and checks whether it is already stored as a key in the map (Line 15). If not, a new pair consisting of the word and its initial count (1) is stored to the map (line 21). Otherwise, the count for the word is incremented by 1 (lines 16–18).

The program first stores the pairs in a hash map, then creates a tree map from the hash map (line 26). It then displays all the entries in the set. Each entry consists of a word and its count connected by the = sign in ascending order of word frequency. To display them in ascending order of the occurrence counts, see Exercise 22.7.

22.10 Singleton and Unmodifiable Collections and Maps

The `Collections` class contains the static methods for lists and collections. It also contains the methods for creating singleton sets, lists, and maps, and for creating unmodifiable sets, lists, and maps, as shown in Figure 22.25.

The `Collections` class defines three constants: one for an empty set, one for an empty list, and one for an empty map (`EMPTY_SET`, `EMPTY_LIST`, and `EMPTY_MAP`). The class also provides the `singleton(Object o)` method for creating an immutable set containing only

java.util.Collections	
+singleton(o: Object): Set	Returns a singleton set containing the specified object.
+singletonList(o: Object): List	Returns a singleton list containing the specified object.
+singletonMap(key: Object, value: Object): Map	Returns a singleton map with the key and value pair.
+unmodifiedCollection(c: Collection): Collection	Returns an unmodified collection.
+unmodifiableList(list: List): List	Returns an unmodified list.
+unmodifiableMap(m: Map): Map	Returns an unmodified map.
+unmodifiableSet(s: Set): Set	Returns an unmodified set.
+unmodifiableSortedMap(s: SortedMap): SortedMap	Returns an unmodified sorted map.
+unmodifiableSortedSet(s: SortedSet): SortedSet	Returns an unmodified sorted set.

FIGURE 22.25 The `Collections` class contains the static methods for creating singleton and unmodifiable sets, lists, and maps.

a single item, the `singletonList(Object o)` method for creating an immutable list containing only a single item, and the `singletonMap(Object key, Object value)` method for creating an immutable map containing only a single mapping.

The `Collections` class also provides six static methods for creating read-only collections: `unmodifiableCollection(Collection c)`, `unmodifiableList(List list)`, `unmodifiableMap(Map m)`, `unmodifiableSet(Set set)`, `unmodifiableSortedMap-(SortedMap m)`, and `unmodifiableSortedSet(SortedSet s)`. The read-only collections prevent the data in the collections from being modified, and, as well, offer better performance for read-only operations.

KEY TERMS

collection   714
comparator   720
hash map   734
hash set   716
linked hash map   734
linked hash set   716
linked list   724

list   723
map   733
priority queue   732
queue   731
set   716
tree map   735
tree set   717

CHAPTER SUMMARY

■ The Java Collections Framework supports three types of collections: *sets*, *lists*, and *maps*. They are defined in the interfaces `Set`, `List`, and `Map`. A *set* stores a group of nonduplicate elements. A *list* stores an ordered collection of elements. A *map* stores a group of objects, each of which is associated with a key.

■ A set stores nonduplicate elements. To allow duplicate elements to be stored in a collection, you need to use a list. A list can not only store duplicate elements, it also allows the user to specify where they are stored. The user can access elements by an index.

■ Three types of sets are supported: `HashSet`, `LinkedHashSet`, and `TreeSet`. `HashSet` stores elements in an unpredictable order. `LinkedHashSet` stores elements in the order they were inserted. `TreeSet` stores elements sorted. All the methods in `HashSet`, `LinkedHashSet`, and `TreeSet` are inherited from the `Collection` interface.

■ Two types of lists are supported: `ArrayList` and `LinkedList`. `ArrayList` is a resizable-array implementation of the `List` interface. All the methods in `ArrayList` are defined in `List`. `LinkedList` is a linked list implementation of the `List` interface. In addition to implementing the `List` interface, this class provides the methods for retrieving, inserting, and removing elements from both ends of the list.

■ The `Vector` class implements the `List` interface. In Java 2, `Vector` is the same as `ArrayList`, except that it contains synchronized methods for accessing and modifying the vector. The `Stack` class extends the `Vector` class and provides several methods for manipulating the stack.

■ The `Collection` interface represents a collection of elements stored in a set or a list. The `Map` interface maps keys to the elements. The keys are like indexes. In `List`, the indexes are integers. In `Map`, the keys can be any objects. A map cannot contain duplicate keys. Each key can map to at most one value. The `Map` interface provides the methods for querying, updating, and obtaining a collection of values and a set of keys.

■ The `Queue` interface represents a queue. The `PriorityQueue` class implements `Queue` for a priority queue.

■ Three types of maps are supported: `HashMap`, `LinkedHashMap`, and `TreeMap`. `HashMap` is efficient for locating a value, inserting a mapping, and deleting a mapping. `LinkedHashMap` supports ordering of the entries in the map. The entries in a `HashMap` are not ordered, but the entries in a `LinkedHashMap` can be retrieved either in the order in which they were inserted into the map (known as the *insertion order*) or in the order in which they were last accessed, from least recently accessed to most recently (*access order*). `TreeMap` is efficient for traversing the keys in a sorted order. The keys can be sorted using the `Comparable` interface or the `Comparator` interface.

REVIEW QUESTIONS

Sections 22.1–22.2

22.1 Describe the Java Collections Framework. List the interfaces, convenience abstract classes, and concrete classes.

22.2 Can a collection object be cloned and serialized?

22.3 The `hashCode` method and the `equals` method are defined in the `Object` class. Why are they redefined in the `Collection` interface?

22.4 Find the default implementation for the `equals` method and the `hashCode` method in the `Object` class from the source code of Object.java.

Section 22.3 Sets

22.5 How do you create an instance of `Set`? How do you insert a new element in a set? How do you remove an element from a set? How do you find the size of a set?

22.6 What are the differences between `HashSet`, `LinkedHashSet`, and `TreeSet`?

22.7 How do you traverse the elements in a set? Can you traverse the elements in a set in an arbitrary order?

22.8 How do you sort the elements in a set using the `compareTo` method in the `Comparable` interface? How do you sort the elements in a set using the

`Comparator` interface? What would happen if you added an element that cannot be compared with the existing elements in a tree set?

22.9 Suppose that `set1` is a set that contains the strings "**red**", "**yellow**", "**green**", and that `set2` is another set that contains the strings "**red**", "**yellow**", "**blue**". Answer the following questions:

- What are `set1` and `set2` after executing `set1.addAll(set2)`?
- What are `set1` and `set2` after executing `set1.add(set2)`?
- What are `set1` and `set2` after executing `set1.removeAll(set2)`?
- What are `set1` and `set2` after executing `set1.remove(set2)`?
- What are `set1` and `set2` after executing `set1.retainAll(set2)`?
- What is `set1` after executing `set1.clear()`?

Section 22.4 The **Comparator** Interface

22.10 What are the differences between the `Comparable` interface and the `Comparator` interface? Which package is `Comparable` in, and which package is `Comparator` in?

22.11 The `Comparator` interface contains the `equals` method. Why is the method not implemented in the `GeometricObjectComparator` class in this section?

Section 22.5 Lists

22.12 How do you add and remove elements from a list? How do you traverse a list in both directions?

22.13 Suppose that `list1` is a list that contains the strings "**red**", "**yellow**", "**green**", and that `list2` is another list that contains the strings "**red**", "**yellow**", "**blue**". Answer the following questions:

- What are `list1` and `list2` after executing `list1.addAll(list2)`?
- What are `list1` and `list2` after executing `list1.add(list2)`?
- What are `list1` and `list2` after executing `list1.removeAll(list2)`?
- What are `list1` and `list2` after executing `list1.remove(list2)`?
- What are `list1` and `list2` after executing `list1.retainAll(list2)`?
- What is `list1` after executing `list1.clear()`?

22.14 What are the differences between `ArrayList` and `LinkedList`? Are all the methods in `ArrayList` also in `LinkedList`? What methods are in `LinkedList` but not in `ArrayList`?

22.15 How do you create a set or a list from an array of objects?

Section 22.6 Static Methods for Lists and Collections

22.16 Are all the methods in the `Collections` class static?

22.17 Which of the following static methods in the `Collections` class are for lists, and which are for collections?

```
sort, binarySearch, reverse, shuffle, max, min, disjoint,
  frequency
```

22.18 Show the printout of the following code:

```java
import java.util.*;

public class Test {
  public static void main(String[] args) {
    List<String> list = Arrays.asList("yellow", "red", "green",
      "blue");
    Collections.reverse(list);
    System.out.println(list);
```

```
        List<String> list1 = Arrays.asList("yellow", "red", "green",
            "blue");
        List<String> list2 = Arrays.asList("white", "black");
        Collections.copy(list1, list2);
        System.out.println(list1);

        Collection<String> collection1 = Arrays.asList("red", "cyan");
        Collection<String> collection2 = Arrays.asList("red", "blue");
        Collection<String> collection3 = Arrays.asList("pink", "tan");
        System.out.println(Collections.disjoint(collection1,
            collection2));
        System.out.println(Collections.disjoint(collection1,
            collection3));

        Collection<String> collection = Arrays.asList("red", "cyan",
            "red");
        System.out.println(Collections.frequency(collection, "red"));
    }
}
```

22.19 Which method can you use to sort the elements in an `ArrayList` or a `LinkedList`? Which method can you use to sort an array of strings?

22.20 Which method can you use to perform binary search for elements in an `ArrayList` or a `LinkedList`? Which method can you use to perform binary search for an array of strings?

22.21 Write a statement to find the largest element in an array of comparable objects?

Section 22.7 Vectors and Stacks

22.22 How do you create an instance of `Vector`? How do you add or insert a new element into a vector? How do you remove an element from a vector? How do you find the size of a vector?

22.23 How do you create an instance of `Stack`? How do you add a new element into a stack? How do you remove an element from a stack? How do you find the size of a stack?

22.24 Does Listing 22.1, TestHashSet.java, compile and run if line 7 (`Set set = new HashSet()`) is replaced by one of the following statements?

```
Collection set = new LinkedHashSet();
Collection set = new TreeSet();
Collection set = new ArrayList();
Collection set = new LinkedList();
Collection set = new Vector();
Collection set = new Stack();
```

Section 22.8 Queues and Priority Queues

22.25 Is `java.util.Queue` a subinterface of `java.util.Collection`, `java.util.Set`, or `java.util.List`? Does `LinkedList` implement `Queue`?

22.26 How do you create a priority queue for integers? By default, how are elements ordered in a priority queue? Is the element with the least value assigned the highest priority in a priority queue?

22.27 How do you create a priority queue that reverses the natural order of the elements?

Section 22.9 Maps

22.28 How do you create an instance of Map? How do you add a pair consisting of an element and a key into a map? How do you remove an entry from a map? How do you find the size of a map? How do you traverse entries in a map?

22.29 Describe and compare HashMap, LinkedHashMap, and TreeMap.

22.30 Show the printout of the following code:

```java
public class Test {
  public static void main(String[] args) {
    Map map = new LinkedHashMap();
    map.put("123", "John Smith");
    map.put("111", "George Smith");
    map.put("123", "Steve Yao");
    map.put("222", "Steve Yao");
    System.out.println("(1) " + map);
    System.out.println("(2) " + new TreeMap(map));
  }
}
```

PROGRAMMING EXERCISES

Section 22.3 Sets

22.1 (*Performing set operations on hash sets*) Create two hash sets {"George", "Jim", "John", "Blake", "Kevin", "Michael"} and {"George", "Katie", "Kevin", "Michelle", "Ryan"}, and find their union, difference, and intersection. (You may clone the sets to preserve the original sets from being changed by these set methods.)

22.2 (*Displaying nonduplicate words in ascending order*) Write a program that reads words from a text file and displays all the nonduplicate words in ascending order. The text file is passed as a command-line argument.

22.3** (*Counting the keywords in Java source code*) Write a program that reads a Java source code file and reports the number of keywords in the file. Pass the Java file name from the command line.

 Hint
Create a set to store all the Java keywords.

Section 22.4 Lists

22.4 (*Performing set operations on array lists*) Create two array lists {"George", "Jim", "John", "Blake", "Kevin", "Michael"} and {"George", "Katie", "Kevin", "Michelle", "Ryan"}, and find their union, difference, and intersection. (You may clone the lists to preserve the original lists from being changed by these methods.)

22.5* (*Displaying words in ascending alphabetical order*) Write a program that reads words from a text file and displays all the words (duplicates allowed) in ascending alphabetical order. The text file is passed as a command-line argument.

Section 22.6 Static Methods for Lists and Collections

22.6* (*Storing numbers in a linked list*) Write a program that lets the user enter numbers from a graphical user interface and display them in a text area, as shown in Figure 22.26. Use a linked list to store the numbers. Do not store duplicate numbers. Add the buttons *Sort*, *Shuffle*, and *Reverse* to sort, shuffle, and reverse the list.

FIGURE 22.26 The program stores numbers in a list.

Section 22.9 Maps

22.7* (*Counting the occurrences of numbers entered*) Write a program that reads an unspecified number of integers and finds the one that has the most occurrences. Your input ends when the input is **0**. For example, if you entered **2 3 40 3 5 4 –3 3 3 2 0**, the number **3** occurred most often. Please enter one number at a time. If not one but several numbers have the most occurrences, all of them should be reported. For example, since **9** and **3** appear twice in the list **9 30 3 9 3 2 4**, both should be reported.

22.8** (*Revising Listing 22.10, CountOccurrenceOfWords.java*) Rewrite Listing 22.10 to display the words in ascending order of occurrence counts.

Hint

Create a class named `WordOccurrence` that implements the `Comparable` interface. The class contains two fields, `word` and `count`. The `compareTo` method compares the counts. For each pair in the hash set in Listing 22.10, create an instance of `WordOccurrence` and store it in an array list. Sort the array list using the `Collections.sort` method. What would be wrong if you stored the instances of `WordOccurrence` in a tree set?

22.9** (*Counting the occurrences of words in a text file*) Rewrite Listing 22.10 to read the text from a text file. The text file is passed as a command-line argument.

22.10***(*Syntax highlighting*) Write a program that converts a Java file into an HTML file. In the HTML file, the keywords, comments, and literals are displayed in bold navy, green, and blue, respectively. Use the command line to pass a Java file and an HTML file. For example, the following command

java Exercise22_10 ComputeArea.java ComputeArea.HTML

converts Test.java into Test.HTML. Figure 22.27(a) shows a Java file. The corresponding HTML file is shown in Figure 22.27(b).

```
public class ComputeArea {
  /** Main method */
  public static void main(String[] args) {
    double radius; // Declare radius
    double area; // Declare area

    // Assign a radius
    radius = 20; // New value in radius

    // Compute area
    area = radius * radius * 3.14159; // New value in area

    // Display results
    System.out.println("The area for the circle of radius " +
      radius + " is " + area);
  }
}
```

FIGURE 22.27 The Java code in plain text in (a) is displayed in HTML with syntax-highlighted in (b).

ALGORITHM EFFICIENCY AND SORTING

Objectives

- To estimate algorithm efficiency using the Big O notation (§23.2).

- To understand growth rates and why constants and smaller terms can be ignored in the estimation (§23.2).

- To know the examples of algorithms with constant time, logarithmic time, linear time, log-linear time, quadratic time, and exponential time (§23.2).

- To analyze linear search, binary search, selection sort, and insertion sort (§23.2).

- To design, implement, and analyze bubble sort (§23.3).

- To design, implement, and analyze merge sort (§23.4).

- To design, implement, and analyze quick sort (§23.5).

- To design, implement, and analyze heap sort (§23.6).

- To sort large data in a file (§23.7).

23.1 Introduction

Sorting is a classic subject in computer science. There are three reasons for studying sorting algorithms. First, sorting algorithms illustrate many creative approaches to problem solving and these approaches can be applied to solve other problems. Second, sorting algorithms are good for practicing fundamental programming techniques using selection statements, loops, methods, and arrays. Third, sorting algorithms are excellent examples to demonstrate algorithm performance.

The data to be sorted might be integers, doubles, characters, or objects. §6.8, "Sorting Arrays," presented selection sort and insertion sort for numeric values. The selection sort algorithm was extended to sort an array of objects in §10.5.7, "Example: Sorting an Array of Objects." The Java API contains several overloaded sort methods for sorting primitive type values and objects in the `java.util.Arrays` and `java.util.Collections` class. For simplicity, this section assumes:

1. data to be sorted are integers,

2. data are sorted in ascending order, and

3. data are stored in an array.

The programs can be easily modified to sort other types of data, to sort in descending order, or to sort data in an `ArrayList` or a `LinkedList`.

There are many algorithms on sorting. In order to analyze and compare the complexities of these algorithms, this chapter first introduces the Big O notation for estimating algorithm efficiency. The whole chapter is optional. No chapter in the book is dependent on this chapter.

23.2 Estimating Algorithm Efficiency

Suppose two algorithms perform the same task such as search (linear search vs. binary search) and sorting (selection sort vs. insertion sort). Which one is better? One possible approach to answer this question is to implement these algorithms in Java and run the programs to get *execution time*. But there are two problems for this approach:

1. First, there are many tasks running concurrently on a computer. The execution time of a particular program is dependent on the system load.

2. Second, the execution time is dependent on specific input. Consider linear search and binary search for example. If an element to be searched happens to be the first in the list, linear search will find the element quicker than binary search.

It is very difficult to compare algorithms by measuring their execution time. To overcome these problems, a theoretical approach was developed to analyze algorithms independent of computers and specific input. This approach approximates the effect of a change on the size of the input. In this way, you can see how fast an algorithm's execution time increases as the input size increases, so you can compare two algorithms by examining their *growth rates*.

23.2.1 Big O Notation

Consider linear search. The linear search algorithm compares the key with the elements in the array sequentially until the key is found or the array is exhausted. If the key is not in the array, it requires n comparisons for an array of size n. If the key is in the array, it requires $n/2$ comparisons on average. The algorithm's execution time is proportional to the size of the array. If you double the size of the array, you will expect the number of comparisons to double. The algorithm grows at a linear rate. The growth rate has an order of magnitude of n. Computer scientists use the *Big O notation* to abbreviate for "order of magnitude." Using this notation, the complexity of the linear search algorithm is $O(n)$, pronounced as "*order of n.*"

For the same input size, an algorithm's execution time may vary, depending on the input. An input that results in the shortest execution time is called the *best-case* input and an input that results in the longest execution time is called the *worst-case* input. Best-case and worst-case are not representative, but worst-case analysis is very useful. You can show that the algorithm will never be slower than the worst-case. An *average-case* analysis attempts to determine the average amount of time among all possible input of the same size. Average-case analysis is ideal, but difficult to perform, because it is hard to determine the relative probabilities and distributions of various input instances for many problems. Worst-case analysis is easier to obtain and is thus common. So, the analysis is generally conducted for the worst-case. worst-case

average-case

The linear search algorithm requires n comparisons in the worst-case and $n/2$ comparisons in the average-case. Using the Big O notation, both cases require $O(n)$ time. The multiplicative constant $(1/2)$ can be omitted. Algorithm analysis is focused on growth rate. The multiplicative constants have no impact on growth rates. The growth rate for $n/2$ or $100n$ is the same as n, i.e., $O(n) = O(n/2) = O(100n)$. ignoring multiplicative constants

Consider the algorithm for finding the maximum number in an array of n elements. If n is 2, it takes one comparison to find the maximum number. If n is 3, it takes two comparisons to find the maximum number. In general, it takes $n - 1$ times of comparisons to find the maximum number in a list of n elements. Algorithm analysis is for *large input size*. If the input size is small, there is no significance to estimate an algorithm's efficiency. As n grows larger, the n part in the expression $n - 1$ dominates the complexity. The Big O notation allows you to ignore the non-dominating part (e.g., -1 in the expression $n - 1$) and highlight the important part (e.g., n in the expression $n - 1$). So, the complexity of this algorithm is $O(n)$. large input size

ignoring non-dominating terms

The Big O notation estimates the execution time of an algorithm in relation to the input size. If the time is not related to the input size, the algorithm is said to take *constant time* with the notation $O(1)$. For example, a method that retrieves an element at a given index in an array takes constant time, because it does not grow as the size of the array increases. constant time

23.2.2 Analyzing Binary Search

The binary search algorithm presented in Listing 6.7, BinarySearch.java, searches a key in a sorted array. Each iteration in the algorithm contains a fixed number of operations, denoted by c. Let $T(n)$ denote the time complexity for a binary search on a list of n elements. Without loss of generality, assume n is a power of 2 and $k = \log n$. Since binary search eliminates half of the input after two comparisons,

$$T(n) = T\left(\frac{n}{2}\right) + c = T\left(\frac{n}{2^2}\right) + c + c = \cdots = T\left(\frac{n}{2^k}\right) + ck$$

$$= T(1) + c \log n = 1 + c \log n$$

Ignoring constants and smaller terms, the complexity of the binary search algorithm is $O(\log n)$. An algorithm with the $O(\log n)$ time complexity is called a *logarithmic algorithm*. The base of the log is 2, but the base does not affect a logarithmic growth rate, so it can be omitted. The logarithmic algorithm grows slowly as the problem size increases. If you square the input size, the time for the algorithm is doubled. logarithmic time

23.2.3 Analyzing Selection Sort

The selection sort algorithm presented in Listing 6.8, SelectionSort.java, finds the largest number in the list and places it last. It then finds the largest number remaining and places it next to last, and so on until the list contains only a single number. The number of comparisons is $n - 1$ for the first iteration, $n - 2$ for the second iteration, and so on. Let $T(n)$ denote the complexity for selection sort and c denote the total number of other operations such as assignments and additional comparisons in each iteration. So,

$$T(n) = (n - 1) + c + (n - 2) + c \ldots + 2 + c + 1 + c = \frac{n^2}{2} - \frac{n}{2} + cn$$

Ignoring constants and smaller terms, the complexity of the selection sort algorithm is $O(n^2)$.

quadratic time

An algorithm with the $O(n^2)$ time complexity is called a *quadratic algorithm*. The quadratic algorithm grows quickly as the problem size increases. If you double the input size, the time for the algorithm is quadrupled. Algorithms with two nested loops are often quadratic.

23.2.4 Analyzing Insertion Sort

The insertion sort algorithm presented in Listing 6.9, InsertionSort.java, sorts a list of values by repeatedly inserting a new element into a sorted partial array until the whole array is sorted. At the kth iteration, to insert an element to a array of size k, it may take k comparisons to find the insertion position, and k moves to insert the element. So, the total number of operations is $2k$. Let $T(n)$ denote the complexity for insertion sort and c denote the total number of other operations such as assignments and additional comparisons in each iteration. So,

$$T(n) = 2 + c + 2 \times 2 + c \ldots + 2 \times (n - 1) + c = n^2 - n + c(n - 1)$$

Ignoring constants and smaller terms, the complexity of the insertion sort algorithm is $O(n^2)$.

23.2.5 Analyzing Towers of Hanoi

The Towers of Hanoi problem presented in Listing 19.7, TowersOfHanoi.java, moves n disks from tower A to tower B with the assistance of tower C recursively as follows:

1. Move the first n – 1 disks from A to C with the assistance of tower B.

2. Move disk n from A to B.

3. Move n – 1 disks from C to B with the assistance of tower A.

Let $T(n)$ denote the complexity for the algorithm that moves n disks and c denote the constant time to move one disk, i.e., $T(1)$ is c. So,

$$T(n) = T(n - 1) + c + T(n - 1) = 2T(n - 1) + c$$
$$= 2(2(T(n - 2) + c) + c) = 2^n T(1) + c2^{n-1} + \ldots + c2 + c$$
$$= c2^n + c2^{n-1} + \ldots + c2 + c = c(2^{n+1} - 1) = O(2^n)$$

exponential time

An algorithm with the $O(c^n)$ time complexity is called an *exponential algorithm*. As the input size increases, the time for the exponential algorithm grows exponentially. The exponential algorithms are not practical for large input size.

23.2.6 Comparing Common Growth Functions

The preceding sections analyzed the complexity of several algorithms. Table 23.1 lists some common growth functions. These functions are ordered as follows:

$$O(1) < O(\log n) < O(n) < O(n \log n) < O(n^2) < O(n^3) < O(2^n)$$

TABLE 23.1 Common Growth Functions

Big-O Function	Name
$O(1)$	Constant time
$O(\log n)$	Logarithmic time
$O(n)$	Linear time
$O(n \log n)$	log-linear time
$O(n^2)$	Quadratic time
$O(n^3)$	Cubic time
$O(2^n)$	Exponential time

Table 23.2 shows how growth rates change as the input size doubles from $n = 25$ to $n = 50$.

TABLE 23.2 Change of Growth Rates

Function	$n = 25$	$n = 50$	$f(50)/f(25)$
$O(1)$	1	1	1
$O(\log n)$	4.64	5.64	1.21
$O(n)$	25	50	2
$O(n \log n)$	116	282	2.431
$O(n^2)$	625	2500	4
$O(n^3)$	15625	125000	8
$O(2^n)$	3.36×10^7	1.27×10^{15}	3.35×10^7

23.3 Bubble Sort

The bubble sort algorithm makes several passes through the array. On each pass, successive neighboring pairs are compared. If a pair is in decreasing order, its values are swapped; otherwise, the values remain unchanged. The technique is called a *bubble sort* or *sinking sort* because the smaller values gradually "bubble" their way to the top and the larger values sink to the bottom. After first pass, the last element becomes the largest in the array. After the second pass, the second last element becomes the second largest in the array. Continue the process until all elements are sorted.

Figure 23.1(a) shows the first pass of a bubble sort of an array of six elements (2 9 5 4 8 1). Compare the elements in the first pair (2 and 9), and no swap is needed because they are already in order. Compare the elements in the second pair (9 and 5), and swap 9 with 5 because 9 is greater than 5. Compare the elements in the third pair (9 and 4), and swap 9 with 4. Compare the elements in the fourth pair (9 and 8), and swap 9 with 8. Compare the elements in the fifth pair (9 and 1), swap 9 with 1. The pairs being compared are highlighted and the numbers that are already sorted are italicized.

bubble sort illustration

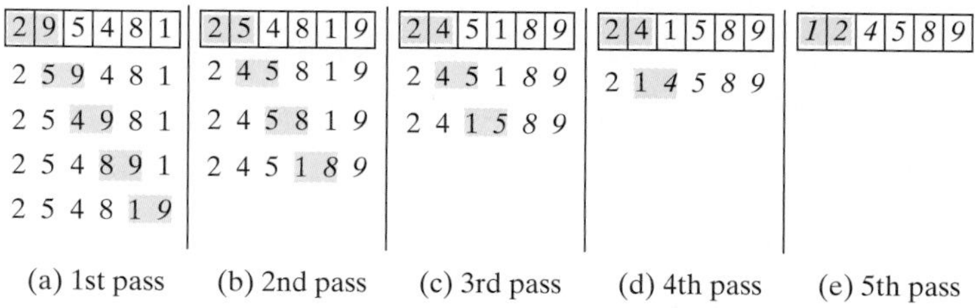

(a) 1st pass   (b) 2nd pass   (c) 3rd pass   (d) 4th pass   (e) 5th pass

FIGURE 23.1   Each pass compares and orders the pairs of elements sequentially.

The first pass places the largest number (9) as the last in the array. In the second pass, as shown in Figure 23.1(b), you compare and order pairs of elements sequentially. There is no need to consider the last pair, because the last element in the array is already the largest. In the third pass, as shown in Figure 23.1(c), you compare and order pairs of elements sequentially except the last two elements, because they are already ordered. So in the *k*th pass, you don't need to consider the last $k - 1$ elements, because they are already ordered.

The *algorithm* for bubble sort is described in Listing 23.1.

algorithm

LISTING 23.1   Bubble Sort Algorithm

```
1 for (int k = 1; k < list.length; k++) {
2    // Perform the kth pass
3    for (int i = 0; i < list.length - k; i++) {
4      if (list[i] > list[i + 1])
5        swap list[i] with list[i + 1];
6    }
7 }
```

Note that if no swap takes place in a pass, there is no need to perform the next pass, because all the elements are already sorted. You may improve the preceding algorithm by utilizing this property as in Listing 23.2.

LISTING 23.2 Improved Bubble Sort Algorithm

```
1 boolean needNextPass = true;
2 for (int k = 1; k < list.length && needNextPass; k++) {
3    // Array may be sorted and next pass not needed
4    needNextPass = false;
5    // Perform the kth pass
6    for (int i = 0; i < list.length - k; i++) {
7      if (list[i] > list[i + 1]) {
8        swap list[i] with list[i + 1];
9        needNextPass = true; // Next pass still needed
10     }
11   }
12 }
```

The algorithm can be implemented as shown in Listing 23.3.

LISTING 23.3 BubbleSort.java

```
1 public class BubbleSort {
2    /** The method for sorting the numbers */
3    public static void bubbleSort(int[] list) {
4      boolean needNextPass = true;
5
6      for (int k = 1; k < list.length; k++) {
7        // Array may be sorted and next pass not needed
8        needNextPass = false;
9        for (int i = 0; i < list.length - k; i++) {
10         if (list[i] > list[i + 1]) {
11           // swap list[i] with list[i + 1]
12           int temp = list[i];
13           list[i] = list[i + 1];
14           list[i + 1] = temp;
15
16           needNextPass = true; // Next pass still needed
17         }
18       }
19     }
20   }
21 }
```

23.3.1 Bubble Sort Time

In the best-case, the bubble sort algorithm needs just the first pass to find out that the array is already sorted. No next pass is needed. Since the number of comparisons is $n - 1$ in the first pass, the best-case time for bubble sort is $O(n)$.

In the worst case, the bubble sort algorithm requires $n - 1$ passes. The first pass takes $n - 1$ comparisons; the second pass takes $n - 2$ comparisons; and so on; the last pass takes 1 comparison. So, the total number of comparisons is:

$$(n - 1) + (n - 2) + \cdots + 2 + 1 = \frac{n^2}{2} - \frac{n}{2}$$

Therefore, the worst-case time for bubble sort is $O(n^2)$.

23.4 Merge Sort

The merge sort algorithm can be described recursively as follows: The algorithm divides the array into two halves and applies merge sort on each half recursively. After the two halves are sorted, merge them. The algorithm is described in Listing 23.4.

LISTING 23.4 Merge Sort Algorithm

```
1 public static void mergeSort(int[] list) {
2   if (list.length > 1) {
3     mergeSort(list[0 ... list.length / 2]);
4     mergeSort(list[list.length / 2 + 1 ... list.length]);
5     merge list[0 ... list.length / 2] with
6       list[list.length / 2 + 1 ... list.length];
7   }
8 }
```

base condition
sort first half
sort second half
merge two halves

Figure 23.2 illustrates a merge sort of an array of eight elements (2 9 5 4 8 1 6 7). The original array is split into (2 9 5 4) and (8 1 6 7). Apply merge sort on this two subarrays recursively to split (1 9 5 4) into (1 9) and (5 4) and (8 1 6 7) into (8 1) and (6 7). This process continues until the subarray contains only one element. For example, array (2 9) is split into subarrays (2) and (9). Since array (2) contains a single element, it cannot be further split. Now merge (2) with (9) into a new sorted array (2 9), merge (5) with (4) into a new sorted array (4 5). Merge (2 9) with (4 5) into a new sorted array (2 4 5 9), and finally merge (2 4 5 9) with (1 6 7 8) into a new sorted array (1 2 4 5 6 7 8 9).

merge sort illustration

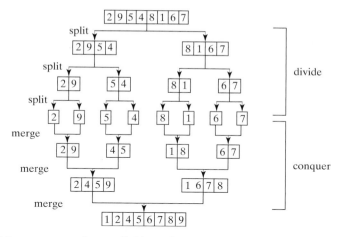

FIGURE 23.2 Merge sort employs a divide-and-conquer approach to sort the array.

The recursive call continues dividing the array into subarrays until each subarray contains only one element. The algorithm then merges these small subarrays into larger sorted subarrays until one sorted array results. The method for merging two sorted arrays is given in Listing 23.5.

LISTING 23.5 Method for Merging Two Arrays

```
1 private static int[] merge(int[] list1, int[] list2) {
2   int[] temp = new int[list1.length + list2.length];
3
4   int current1 = 0; // Index in list1
5   int current2 = 0; // Index in list2
6   int current3 = 0; // Index in temp
7
```

create a new array

sort second half
merge two halves

move to temp

```
8   while (current1 < list1.length && current2 < list2.length) {
9     if (list1[current1] < list2[current2])
10      temp[current3++] = list1[current1++];
11    else
12      temp[current3++] = list2[current2++];
13  }
14
15  while (current1 < list1.length)
16    temp[current3++] = list1[current1++];
17
18  while (current2 < list2.length)
19    temp[current3++] = list2[current2++];
20
21  return temp;
22 }
```

This method merges arrays `list1` and `list2` into a temporary array `temp`. So, `temp.length` is `list1.length + list2.length` (line 2). `current1` and `current2` point to the current element to be considered in `list1` and `list2` (lines 4–5). The method repeatedly compares the current elements from `list1` and `list2` and moves the smaller one to `temp`. `current1` is increased by 1 (line 10) if the smaller one is in `list1` and `current2` is increased by 1 (line 12) if the smaller one is in `list2`. Finally, all the elements in one of the lists are moved to `temp`. If there are still unmoved elements in `list1`, copy them to `temp` (lines 15–16). If there are still unmoved elements in `list2`, copy them to `temp` (lines 18–19). The method returns `temp` as the new sorted array in line 21.

Figure 23.3 illustrates how to merge two arrays `list1` (2 4 5 9) and `list2` (1 6 7 8). Initially the current elements to be considered in the arrays are 2 and 1. Compare them and move the smaller element 1 to `temp`, as shown in Figure 23.3(a). `current2` and `current3` are increased by 1. Continue to compare the current elements in the two arrays and move the smaller one to `temp` until one of the arrays is completely moved. As shown in Figure 23.3(b), all the elements in `list2` are moved to `temp` and `current1` points to element 9 in `list1`. Copy 9 to `temp`, as shown in Figure 23.3(c).

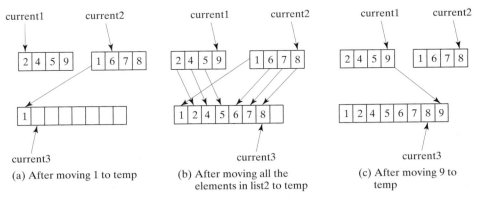

(a) After moving 1 to temp

(b) After moving all the elements in list2 to temp

(c) After moving 9 to temp

FIGURE 23.3 Two sorted arrays are merged into one sorted array.

The merge sort algorithm is implemented in Listing 23.6.

LISTING 23.6 MergeSort.java

```
1 public class MergeSort {
2   /** The method for sorting the numbers */
3   public static void mergeSort(int[] list) {
```

```
4      if (list.length > 1) {                                          base case
5        // Merge sort the first half
6        int[] firstHalf = new int[list.length / 2];
7        System.arraycopy(list, 0, firstHalf, 0, list.length / 2);
8        mergeSort(firstHalf);                                        sort first half
9
10       // Merge sort the second half
11       int secondHalfLength = list.length - list.length / 2;
12       int[] secondHalf = new int[secondHalfLength];
13       System.arraycopy(list, list.length / 2,
14         secondHalf, 0, secondHalfLength);
15       mergeSort(secondHalf);                                       sort second half
16
17       // Merge firstHalf with secondHalf
18       int[] temp = merge(firstHalf, secondHalf);                  merge two halves
19       System.arraycopy(temp, 0, list, 0, temp.length);            copy to original array
20     }
21   }
22
23   private static int[] merge(int[] list1, int[] list2) {
24     // Same as in Listing 23.5, so omitted
25   }
26 }
```

The algorithm creates a new array `firstHalf`, which is a copy of the first half of `list` (line 7). The algorithm invokes `mergeSort` recursively on `firstHalf` (line 8). The length of the `firstHalf` is `list.length / 2` and the length of the `secondHalf` is `list.length - list.length / 2`. The new array `secondHalf` was created to contain the second part of the original array `list`. The algorithm invokes `mergeSort` recursively on `secondHalf` (line 15). After `firstHalf` and `secondHalf` are sorted, they are merged to become a new sorted array in `temp` (line 18). Finally, `temp` is assigned to the original array `list` (line 19). So, array `list` is now sorted.

23.4.1 Merge Sort Time

Let $T(n)$ denote the time required for sorting an array of n elements using merge sort. Without loss of generality, assume n is a power of 2. The merge sort algorithm splits the array into two subarrays, sorts the subarrays using the same algorithm recursively, and then merges the subarrays. So,

time analysis

$$T(n) = T\left(\frac{n}{2}\right) + T\left(\frac{n}{2}\right) + mergetime$$

The first $T\left(\frac{n}{2}\right)$ is the time for sorting the first half of the array and the second $T\left(\frac{n}{2}\right)$ is the time for sorting the second half. To merge two subarrays, it takes at most $n - 1$ comparisons to compare the elements from the two subarrays and n moves to move elements to the temporary array. So, the total time is $2n - 1$. Therefore,

$$T(n) = 2T\left(\frac{n}{2}\right) + 2n - 1 = 2\left(2T\left(\frac{n}{4}\right) + 2\frac{n}{2} - 1\right) + 2n - 1$$

$$= 2^2 T\left(\frac{n}{2^2}\right) + 2n - 2 + 2n - 1$$

$$= 2^k T\left(\frac{n}{2^k}\right) + 2n - 2^{k-1} + \cdots + 2n - 2 + 2n - 1$$

$$= 2^{\log n}\, T\left(\frac{n}{2^{\log n}}\right) + 2n - 2^{\log n-1} + \cdots + 2n - 2 + 2n - 1$$

$$= n + 2n \log n - 2^{\log n} + 1 = 2n \log n + 1 = O(n \log n)$$

O(n log n) merge sort

The complexity of merge sort is $O(n \log n)$. This algorithm is better than selection sort, insertion sort, and bubble sort. The `sort` method in the `java.util.Arrays` class is implemented using a variation of the merge sort algorithm.

23.5 Quick Sort

Quick sort, developed by C. A. R. Hoare (1962), works as follows: The algorithm selects an element, called the *pivot*, in the array. Divide the array into two parts such that all the elements in the first part are less than or equal to the pivot and all the elements in the second part are greater than the pivot. Recursively apply the quick sort algorithm to the first part and then the second part. The algorithm is described in Listing 23.7.

LISTING 23.7 Quick Sort Algorithm

base condition
select the pivot
partition the list

sort first part
sort second part

```
 1 public static void quickSort(int[] list) {
 2   if (list.length > 1) {
 3     select a pivot;
 4     partition list into list1 and list2 such that
 5       all elements in list1 <= pivot and all elements
 6       in list2 > pivot;
 7     quickSort(list1);
 8     quickSort(list2);
 9   }
10 }
```

how to partition

Each partition places the pivot in the right place. The selection of the pivot affects the performance of the algorithm. Ideally, you should choose the pivot that divides the two parts evenly. For simplicity, assume the first element in the array is chosen as the pivot. Exercise 23.4 proposes an alternative strategy for selecting the pivot.

quick sort illustration

Figure 23.4 illustrates how to sort an array (5 2 9 3 8 4 0 1 6 7) using quick sort. Choose the first element 5 as the pivot. The array is partitioned into two parts, as shown in Figure 23.4(b). The highlighted pivot is placed in the right place in the array. Apply quick sort on two partial arrays (4 2 1 3 0) and then (8 9 6 7). The pivot 4 partitions (4 2 1 3 0) into just one partial array (0 2 1 3), as shown in Figure 23.4(c). Apply quick sort on (0 2 1 3). The pivot 0 partitions it to just one partial array (2 1 3), as shown in Figure 23.4(d). Apply quick sort on (2 1 3). The pivot 2 partitions it to (1) and (3), as shown in Figure 23.4(e). Apply quick sort on (1). Since the array contains just one element, no further partition is needed.

Now turn attention to partition. To partition an array or a partial array, search for the first element from left forward in the array that is greater than the pivot, then search for the first element from right backward in the array that is less than or equal to the pivot. Swap these two elements. Repeat the same search and swap operations until all the elements are searched. Listing 23.8 gives a method that partitions a partial array `list[first..last]`. The first element in the partial array is chosen as the pivot (line 3). Initially `low` points to the second element in the partial array and `high` points to the last element in the partial array. The method returns the new index for the pivot that divides the partial array into two parts.

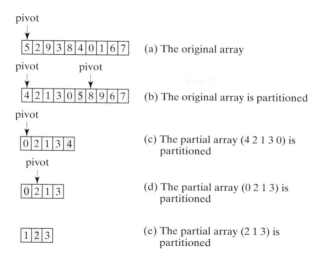

FIGURE 23.4 The quick sort algorithm is recursively applied to partial arrays.

LISTING 23.8 Partition Method

```java
 1  /** Partition the array list[first..last] */
 2  private static int partition(int[] list, int first, int last) {
 3    int pivot = list[first]; // Choose the first element as the pivot
 4    int low = first + 1; // Index for forward search
 5    int high = last; // Index for backward search
 6
 7    while (high > low) {
 8      // Search forward from left
 9      while (low <= high && list[low] <= pivot)
10        low++;                                                    forward
11
12      // Search backward from right
13      while (low <= high && list[high] > pivot)
14        high--;                                                   backward
15
16      // Swap two elements in the list
17      if (high > low) {
18        int temp = list[high];                                    swap
19        list[high] = list[low];
20        list[low] = temp;
21      }
22    }
23
24    while (high > first && list[high] >= pivot)                   place pivot
25      high--;
26
27    // Swap pivot with list[high]
28    if (pivot > list[high]) {
29      list[first] = list[high];
30      list[high] = pivot;
31      return high;                                                pivot's new index
32    }
33    else {
34      return first;                                               pivot's new index
35    }
36  }
```

partition illustration

Figure 23.5 illustrates how to partition an array (5 2 9 3 8 4 0 1 6 7). Choose the first element 5 as the pivot. Initially `low` is the index that points to element 2 and `high` points to element 7, as shown in Figure 23.5(a). Advance index `low` forward to search for the first element (9) that is greater than the pivot and move index `high` backward to search for the first element (1) that is less than or equal to the pivot, as shown in Figure 23.5(b). Swap 9 with 1, as shown in Figure 23.5(c). Continue the search and move `low` to point to element 8 and `high` to point to element 0, as shown in Figure 23.5(d). Swap element 8 with 0, as shown in Figure 23.5(e). Continue to move `low` until it passes `high`, as shown in Figure 23.5(f). Now all the elements are examined. Swap the pivot with element 4 at index `high`. The final partition is shown in Figure 23.5(g). The index of the pivot is returned when the method is finished.

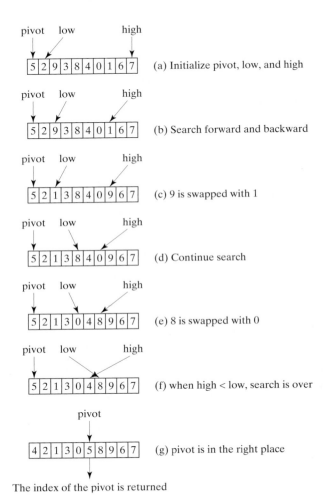

FIGURE 23.5 The partition method returns the index of the pivot after it is put in the right place.

The quick sort algorithm is implemented in Listing 23.9. There are two overloaded `quickSort` methods in the class. The first method (line 2) is used to sort an array. The second is a helper method (line 6) that sorts a partial array with a specified range.

LISTING 23.9 QuickSort.java

sort method

```
1 public class QuickSort {
2     public static void quickSort(int[] list) {
```

```
3          quickSort(list, 0, list.length - 1);
4      }
5
6      private static void quickSort(int[] list, int first, int last) {        helper method
7          if (last > first) {
8              int pivotIndex = partition(list, first, last);
9              quickSort(list, first, pivotIndex - 1);
10             quickSort(list, pivotIndex + 1, last);                          recursive call
11         }
12     }
13
14     /** Partition the array list[first..last] */
15     private static int partition(int[] list, int first, int last) {
16         // Same as in Listing 23.8, so omitted
17     }
18 }
```

23.5.1 Quick Sort Time

To partition an array of n elements, it takes n comparisons and n moves in the worst case. So, the time required for partition is $O(n)$.

$O(n)$ partition time

In the worst case, each time the pivot divides the array into one big subarray with the other empty. The size of the big subarray is one less than the one before divided. The algorithm requires $(n - 1) + (n - 2) + \cdots + 2 + 1 = O(n^2)$ time.

$O(n^2)$ worst-case time

In the best case, each time the pivot divides the array into two parts of about the same size. Let $T(n)$ denote the time required for sorting an array of n elements using quick sort. So,

$O(n \log n)$ best-case time

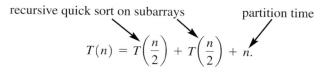

recursive quick sort on subarrays   partition time

$$T(n) = T\left(\frac{n}{2}\right) + T\left(\frac{n}{2}\right) + n.$$

Similar to the merge sort analysis, $T(n) = O(n \log n)$.

On the average, each time the pivot will not divide the array into two parts of the same size nor one empty part. Statistically, the sizes of the two parts are very close. So the average time is $O(n \log n)$. The exact average-case analysis is beyond the scope of this book.

$O(n \log n)$ average-case time

Both merge sort and quick sort employ the divide-and-conquer approach. For merge sort, the bulk of work is to merge two sublists, which takes place *after* the sublists are sorted. For quick sort, the bulk of work is to partition the list into two sublists, which takes place *before* the sublists are sorted. Merge sort is more efficient than quick sort in the worst case, but the two are equally efficient in the average case. Merge sort requires a temporary array for merging two subarrays. Quick sort does not need additional array space. So, quick sort is more space efficient than merge sort.

quick sort vs. merge sort

23.6 Heap Sort

Heap sort uses a binary heap to sort an array. The binary heap, introduced in §20.5, "Heaps," can be visualized as a complete binary tree. Each node in the tree is greater than or equal to its descendants, as shown in Figure 23.6(a). Recall that a binary heap can be implemented using an array, as shown in Figure 23.6(b). The root is at position 0, and its two children are at positions 1 and 2. For a node at position i, its left child is at position $2i + 1$ and its right child is at position $2i + 2$, and its parent is $(i - 1)/2$. For example, the node for element 39 is at position 4, so its left child (element 14) is at 9 ($2 \times 4 + 1$), its right child (element 33) is at 10 ($2 \times 4 + 2$), and its parent (element 42) is at 1 ($(4 - 1)/2$).

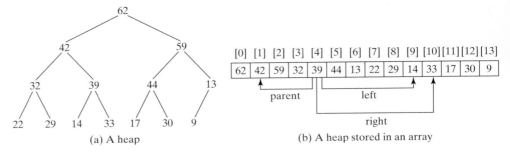

(a) A heap   (b) A heap stored in an array

FIGURE 23.6   A binary heap can be implemented using an array.

23.6.1 Sorting an Array from a Heap

Once you have such a heap, it is easy to obtain a sorted array as follows: Swap the root (i.e., the first element in the array) with the last leaf in the binary heap (i.e, the last element in the array). Remove the last element from the heap and rebuild heap. Repeat the swap and rebuild operations until the heap is empty. Figure 23.7(a) shows the tree after swapping the root with the last leaf. After this swap, the tree is no longer a heap. To rebuild a heap, use the following algorithm:

LISTING 23.10 Algorithm for Rebuilding a Heap

```
Let the root be the current node;
while (the current node has children and the current node is
        smaller than one of its children) {
  Swap the current node with the larger of its children;
  Now the current node is one level down;
}
```

Figure 23.7 shows the process of rebuilding a heap by swapping 9 with 59 in (b), swapping 9 with 44 in (c), and swapping 9 with 30 in (d).

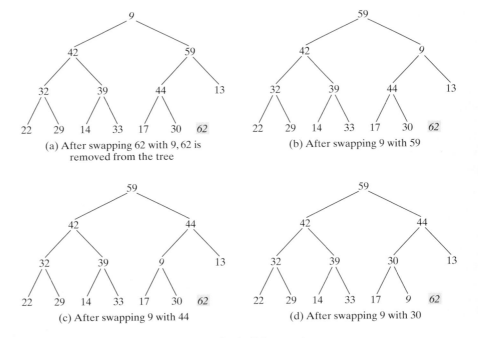

FIGURE 23.7   Heap sort performs swap and rebuild operations.

The algorithm is implemented in Listing 23.11.

LISTING 23.11 Method for Rebuilding a Heap

```
1  private static void rebuildHeap(int[] list, int last) {
2    int currentIndex = 0;
3    boolean isHeap = false;
4
5    while (!isHeap) {
6      int leftChildIndex = 2 * currentIndex + 1;
7      int rightChildIndex = 2 * currentIndex + 2;
8      int maxIndex = currentIndex;
9
10     if (leftChildIndex <= last &&
11       list[maxIndex] < list[leftChildIndex]) {
12       maxIndex = leftChildIndex;
13     }
14
15     if (rightChildIndex <= last &&
16       list[maxIndex] < list[rightChildIndex]) {
17       maxIndex = rightChildIndex;
18     }
19
20     if (maxIndex != currentIndex) {
21       // Swap list[currentIndex] with list[maxIndex]
22       int temp = list[currentIndex];
23       list[currentIndex] = list[maxIndex];
24       list[maxIndex] = temp;
25       currentIndex = maxIndex;
26     }
27     else {
28       isHeap = true;
29     }
30   }
31 }
```

starts with `list[0]`

continue examining the current node
left child index
right child index
initialize `maxIndex`

update `maxIndex` *with left child*

update `maxIndex` *with right child*

The method rebuilds a heap in array `list[0..last]`. Before invoking the method, all the nodes in the tree represented in array `list[0..last]` satisfy the heap property except `list[0]`. The method starts from `list[0]`, compares it with its children, and stores the index of the largest value in `maxIndex`. Line 20 checks whether `maxIndex` is `currentIndex`. If so, the current node is greater than its children. In this case, the tree is a heap now (line 27). If not, swap the current node with the larger of its two children at position `maxIndex` and continue to move the current node down to the next level.

23.6.2 Creating an Initial Heap

You know how to produce a sorted array from a heap. Now the question is how to create a heap from an arbitrary array `list` initially. You may create a heap by adding a node to the tree one at a time. The heap initially contains `list[0]` as the root. Add `list[1]` to the heap. Swap `list[0]` with `list[1]` if `list[0]` < `list[1]`. Suppose that `list[0..k-1]` is already a heap. To add `list[k]` into the heap, consider `list[k]` as the last node in the existing heap. Compare it with its parent and swap them if `list[k]` is greater than its parent. Continue the compare and swap operations until `list[k]` is put in the right place in the heap. Figure 23.8 illustrates the process of adding element 88 to an existing heap (59 42 44 32 39 30 13 22 29 14 33 17).

Listing 23.12 presents a method for making `list[0..k]` a heap, assume that `list[0..k-1]` is already a heap.

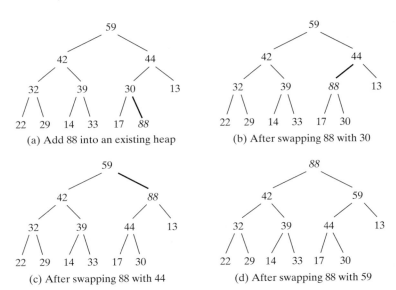

(a) Add 88 into an existing heap
(b) After swapping 88 with 30

(c) After swapping 88 with 44
(d) After swapping 88 with 59

FIGURE 23.8 A new element is added to the heap.

LISTING 23.12 Method for Making a Heap

```
 1  /** Assume list[0..k-1] is a heap, add list[k] to the heap */
 2  private static void makeHeap(int[] list, int k) {
 3     int currentIndex = k;
 4
 5     while (currentIndex > 0 &&
 6        list[currentIndex] > list[(currentIndex - 1) / 2]) {
 7        // Swap list[currentIndex] with list[(currentIndex - 1) / 2]
 8        int temp = list[currentIndex];
 9        list[currentIndex] = list[(currentIndex - 1) / 2];
10        list[(currentIndex - 1) / 2] = temp;
11
12        currentIndex = (currentIndex - 1) / 2;
13     }
14  }
```

*starts with **currentIndex*** (line 3)

check if swap needed (lines 5–6)

swap (lines 8–10)

currentIndex *moved up* (line 12)

The method constructs a heap in array `list[0..k]`. Before invoking the method, all the nodes in the tree represented in array `list[0..k-1]` already form a heap. The method starts from `list[k]`, compares it with its parent, and swaps it with its parent if `list[k]` is greater than its parent (lines 8–10). Continue to move the new element up to the root or it is less than its parent in the `while` loop.

23.6.3 Heap Sort Implementation

The complete heap sort algorithm can be implemented in Listing 23.13. The algorithm first creates a heap by adding one element from an array at a time (lines 4–6), and then sorts the array by repeatedly removing the root from the heap (line 9–15).

LISTING 23.13 HeapSort.java

```
1  public class HeapSort {
2     public static void heapSort(int list[]) {
3        // Create a heap from the list
```

```
4        for (int i = 1; i < list.length; i++) {
5          makeHeap(list, i);
6        }
7
8        // Produce a sorted array from the heap
9        for (int last = list.length - 1; last > 0; ) {
10         // Swap list[0] with list[last]
11         int temp = list[last];
12         list[last] = list[0];
13         list[0] = temp;
14         rebuildHeap(list, --last);
15       }
16     }
17
18     /** Assume list[0..k-1] is a heap, add list[k] to the heap */
19     private static void makeHeap(int[] list, int k) {
20       // Same as in Listing 23.12, so omitted
21     }
22
23     private static void rebuildHeap(int[] list, int last) {
24       // Same as in Listing 23.11, so omitted
25     }
26   }
```

create a heap

sort from a heap

23.6.4 Heap Sort Analysis

Let h denote the height for a heap of n elements. Since a heap is a complete binary tree, the first level has 1 node, the second level has 2 nodes, the kth level has 2^{k-1} nodes, the $h - 1$th level has 2^{h-2} nodes, and the hth level has at least one node and at most 2^{h-1} nodes. Therefore,

height of a heap

$$1 + 2 + \cdots + 2^{h-2} < n \le 1 + 2 + \cdots + 2^{h-2} + 2^{h-1}$$

i.e.,

$$2^{h-1} - 1 < n \le 2^h - 1$$

So, $\log(n + 1) \le h < \log(n + 1) + 1$. Hence, the height of the heap is $O(\log n)$.

Since the makeHeap method traces a path from a leaf to a root, it takes at most h steps to add a new element to the heap. Since the makeHeap method is invoked n times, the total time for constructing an initial heap is $O(n \log n)$. Since the rebuildHeap method traces a path from a root to a leaf, it takes at most h steps to rebuild a heap after removing the root from the heap. Since the rebuildHeap method is invoked n times, the total time for producing a sorted array from a heap is $O(n \log n)$.

$O(n \log n)$ worst-case time

Both merge sort and heap sort requires $O(n \log n)$ time. Merge sort requires a temporary array for merging two subarrays. Heap sort does not need additional array space. So, heap sort is more space efficient than merge sort.

heap sort vs. merge sort

23.7 External Sort

All the sort algorithms discussed in the preceding sections assume that all data to be sorted is available at one time in internal memory such as an array. To sort data stored in an external file, you may first bring data to the memory, then sort it internally. However, if the file is too large, all data in the file cannot be brought to memory at one time. This section discusses how to sort data in a large external file.

For simplicity, assume that two million **int** values are stored in a binary file named large-data.dat. This file was created using the following program:

LISTING 23.14 CreateLargeFile.java

```
1 import java.io.*;
2
3 public class CreateLargeFile {
4   public static void main(String[] args) throws Exception {
5     DataOutputStream output = new DataOutputStream(
6     new BufferedOutputStream
7     (new FileOutputStream("largedata.dat")));
8
9     for (int i = 0; i < 2000000; i++)
10      output.writeInt((int)(Math.random() × 1000000));
11
12    output.close();
13  }
14 }
```

a binary output stream

output an **int** value

close the file

A variation of merge sort can be used to sort this file in two phases:

PHASE I: Repeatedly bring data from the file to an array, sort the array using an internal sorting algorithm, and output the data from the array to a temporary file. This process is shown in Figure 23.9. Ideally, you want to create a large array, but the maximum size of the array is dependent on how much memory is allocated to the JVM by the operating system. Assume that the maximum array size is of 100000 **int** values. In the temporary file, every 100000 **int** values are sorted. They are denoted as $S_1, S_2, \ldots$, and S_k, where S_k may contain less than 100000 values.

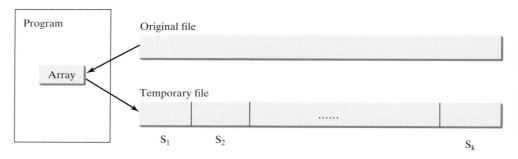

FIGURE 23.9 The original file is sorted by pieces.

PHASE II: Merge a pair of sorted segments (e.g., S_1 with S_2, S_3 with $S_4, \ldots$, and so on) into a larger sorted segment and save the new segment into a new temporary file. Continue the same process until one sorted segment results. Figure 23.10 shows how to merge eight segments.

Note
It is not necessary to merge two successive segments. For example, you may merge S_1 with S_5, S_2 with S_6, S_3 with S_7, and S_4 with S_8, in the first merge step.

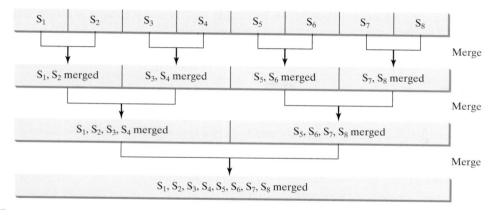

FIGURE 23.10 Sorted segments are merged iteratively.

23.7.1 Implementing Phase I

Assume `MAX_ARRAY_SIZE` is declared as a constant 100000. Listing 23.15 gives the method that sorts every 100000 in largedata.dat and stores the sorted segments into a new file named f1.dat. The method returns the number of segments.

LISTING 23.15 Creating Initial Sorted Segments

```
1  /** Sort original file into sorted segments */
2  private static int initializeSegments (int segmentSize,
3      String originalFile, String f1) throws Exception {
4    int[] list = new int[segmentSize];
5    DataInputStream input = new DataInputStream(
6      new BufferedInputStream(new FileInputStream(originalFile)));
7    DataOutputStream output = new DataOutputStream(
8      new BufferedOutputStream(new FileOutputStream(f1)));
9
10   int numberOfSegments = 0;
11   while (input.available() > 0) {
12     numberOfSegments++;
13     int i = 0;
14     for ( ; input.available() > 0 && i < segmentSize; i++) {
15       list[i] = input.readInt();
16     }
17
18     // Sort an array list[0..i-1]
19     java.util.Arrays.sort(list, 0, i);
20
21     // Write the array to f1.dat
22     for (int j = 0; j < i; j++) {
23       output.writeInt(list[j]);
24     }
25   }
26
27   input.close();
28   output.close();
29   return numberOfSegments;
30 }
```

The method declares an array with the max size in line 5, declares a data input stream for the original file in line 6, and declares a data output stream for a temporary file in line 8. Buffered streams are used to improve performance. Assume `BFFER_SIZE` is a constant 50000.

Lines 15–17 read a segment of data from the file into the array. Line 20 sorts the array. Lines 23–25 write the data in the array to the temporary file.

The number of the segments is returned in line 37. Note that every segment has `MAX_ARRAY_SIZE` number of elements except the last segment that may have a smaller number of elements.

23.7.2 Implementing Phase II

Each merge step merges two sorted segments to form a new segment. The new segment doubles the number elements. So the number of segments is reduced by half after each merge step. A segment is too large to be brought to an array in memory. To implement a merge step, copy half the number of segments from file f1.dat to a temporary file f2.dat. Then merge the first remaining segment in f1.dat with the first segment in f2.dat into a temporary file named f3.dat, as shown in Figure 23.11.

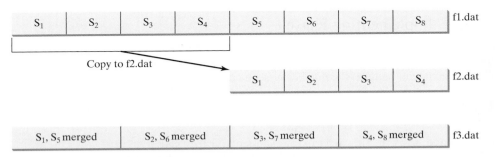

FIGURE 23.11 Sorted segments are merged iteratively.

 Note

f1.dat may have more than one segment than f2.dat. If so, move the last segment into f3.dat after the merge.

Listing 23.16 gives a method that copies the first half of the segments in f1.dat to f2.dat. Listing 23.17 gives a method that merges a pair of segments in f1.dat and f2.dat. Listing 23.18 gives a method that merges two segments.

LISTING 23.16 Copying First Half Segments

input stream **f1**
output stream **f2**

segments copied

```
1 private static void copyHalfToF2(int numberOfSegments,
2     int segmentSize, DataInputStream f1, DataOutputStream f2)
3     throws Exception {
4   for (int i = 0; i < (numberOfSegments / 2) * segmentSize; i++) {
5     f2.writeInt(f1.readInt());
6   }
7 }
```

LISTING 23.17 Merging All Segments

input streams **f1** and **f2**
output stream **f3**

merge two segments

```
1 private static void mergeSegments(int numberOfSegments,
2     int segmentSize, DataInputStream f1, DataInputStream f2,
3     DataOutputStream f3) throws Exception {
4   for (int i = 0; i < numberOfSegments; i++) {
5     mergeTwoSegments(segmentSize, f1, f2, f3);
6   }
7
```

```
 8    // f1 may have one extra segment, copy it to f3
 9    while (f1.available() > 0) {                              extra segment in f1
10      f3.writeInt(f1.readInt());
11    }
12  }
```

LISTING 23.18 Merging Two Segments

```
 1  private static void mergeTwoSegments(int segmentSize,
 2      DataInputStream f1, DataInputStream f2,                  input streams f1 and f2
 3      DataOutputStream f3) throws Exception {                  output stream f3
 4    int intFromF1 = f1.readInt();                              read from f1
 5    int intFromF2 = f2.readInt();                              read from f2
 6    int f1Count = 1;
 7    int f2Count = 1;
 8
 9    while (true) {
10      if (intFromF1 < intFromF2) {
11        f3.writeInt(intFromF1);                                write to f3
12        if (f1.available() == 0 || f1Count++ >= segmentSize) {
13          f3.writeInt(intFromF2);
14          break;                                               segment in f1 finished
15        }
16        else {
17          intFromF1 = f1.readInt();
18        }
19      }
20      else {
21        f3.writeInt(intFromF2);                                write to f3
22        if (f2.available() == 0 || f2Count++ >= segmentSize) {
23          f3.writeInt(intFromF1);
24          break;                                               segment in f2 finished
25        }
26        else {
27          intFromF2 = f2.readInt();
28        }
29      }
30    }
31
32    while (f1.available() > 0 && f1Count++ < segmentSize) {    remaining f1 segment
33      f3.writeInt(f1.readInt());
34    }
35
36    while (f2.available() > 0 && f2Count++ < segmentSize) {    remaining f2 segment
37      f3.writeInt(f2.readInt());
38    }
39  }
```

23.7.3 Combining Two Phases

Listing 23.19 gives the complete program for sorting int values in largedata.dat and storing the sorted data in sortedlargedata.dat.

LISTING 23.19 SortLargeFile.java

```
 1  import java.io.*;
 2
```

```
 3  public class SortLargeFile {
 4    public static final int MAX_ARRAY_SIZE = 100000;
 5    public static final int BFFER_SIZE = 100000;
 6
 7    public static void main(String[] args) throws Exception {
 8      // Implement Phase 1: Create initial segments
 9      int numberOfSegments =
10        initializeSegments(MAX_ARRAY_SIZE, "largedata.dat", "f1.dat");
11
12      // Implement Phase 2: Merge segments recursively
13      merge(numberOfSegments, MAX_ARRAY_SIZE,
14        "f1.dat", "f2.dat", "f3.dat");
15    }
16
17    /** Sort original file into sorted segments */
18    private static int initializeSegments (int segmentSize,
19        String originalFile, String f1) throws Exception {
20      // Same as Listing 23.14, so omitted
21    }
22
23    private static void merge(int numberOfSegments, int segmentSize,
24        String f1, String f2, String f3) throws Exception {
25      if (numberOfSegments > 1) {
26        mergeOneStep(numberOfSegments, segmentSize, f1, f2, f3);
27        merge((numberOfSegments + 1) / 2, segmentSize * 2, f3, f1, f2);
28      }
29      else { // rename f1 as the final sorted file
30        File sortedFile = new File("sortedlargedata.dat");
31        if (sortedFile.exists()) sortedFile.delete();
32        new File(f1).renameTo(sortedFile);
33      }
34    }
35
36    private static void mergeOneStep(int numberOfSegments,
37        int segmentSize, String f1, String f2, String f3) throws
38        Exception {
39      DataInputStream f1Input = new DataInputStream(
40        new BufferedInputStream(new FileInputStream(f1), BFFER_SIZE));
41      DataOutputStream f2Output = new DataOutputStream(
42        new BufferedOutputStream(new FileOutputStream(f2), BFFER_SIZE));
43
44      // Copy half number of segments from f1.dat to f2.dat
45      copyHalfToF2(numberOfSegments, segmentSize, f1Input, f2Output);
46      f2Output.close();
47
48      // Merge remaining segments in f1 with segments in f2 into f3
49      DataInputStream f2Input = new DataInputStream(
50        new BufferedInputStream(new FileInputStream(f2), BFFER_SIZE));
51      DataOutputStream f3Output = new DataOutputStream(
52        new BufferedOutputStream(new FileOutputStream(f3), BFFER_SIZE));
53
54      mergeSegments(numberOfSegments / 2,
55        segmentSize, f1Input, f2Input, f3Output);
56
57      f1Input.close();
58      f2Input.close();
59      f3Output.close();
60    }
61
```

Margin annotations:

- max array size (line 4)
- I/O stream buffer size (line 5)
- create segments (line 10)
- merge recursively (line 13)
- merge one step (line 26)
- merge recursively (line 27)
- final sorted file (line 29)
- input stream **f1Input** (line 39)
- output stream **f2Output** (line 41)
- copy half segments to **f2** (line 45)
- close **f2Output** (line 46)
- input stream **f2Input** (line 49)
- output stream **f3Output** (line 51)
- merge two segments (line 54)
- close streams (line 57)

```
62    /** Copy first half number of segments from f1.dat to f2.dat */
63    private static void copyHalfToF2(int numberOfSegments,
64        int segmentSize, DataInputStream f1, DataOutputStream f2)
65        throws Exception {
66      // Same as Listing 23.15, so omitted
67    }
68
69    /** Merge all segments */
70    private static void mergeSegments(int numberOfSegments,
71        int segmentSize, DataInputStream f1, DataInputStream f2,
72        DataOutputStream f3) throws Exception {
73      // Same as Listing 23.16, so omitted
74    }
75
76    /** Merge two segments */
77    private static void mergeTwoSegments(int segmentSize,
78        DataInputStream f1, DataInputStream f2,
79        DataOutputStream f3) throws Exception {
80      // Same as Listing 23.17, so omitted
81    }
82  }
```

Line 10 creates initial segments from the original array and stores the sorted segments in a new file f1.dat. Line 13 produces a sorted file in sortedlargedata.dat. The **merge** method

```
merge(int numberOfSegments,
      int segmentSize, String f1, String f2, String f3)
```

merges the segments in **f1** into **f3** using **f2** to assist the merge. The **merge** method is invoked recursively with many merge steps. Each merge step reduces the **numberOfSegments** by half and doubles the sorted segment size. After completing one merge step, the next merge step merges the new segments in **f3** to **f2** using **f1** to assist the merge. So the statement to invoke the new merge method is

```
merge((numberOfSegments + 1) / 2, segmentSize * 2, f3, f1, f2);
```

The **numberOfSegments** for the next merge step is **(numberOfSegments + 1) / 2**. For example, if **numberOfSegments** is 5, **numberOfSegments** is 3 for the next merge step, because every two segments are merged but there is one left unmerged.

The recursive **merge** method ends when **numberOfSegments** is 1. In this case, **f1** contains sorted data. Rename it to sortedlargedata.dat in line 32.

KEY TERMS

average-case analysis   747
best-case analysis   746
big O notation   746
bubble sort   749
constant time   747
exponential time   748
growth rate   746

heap sort   757
logarithmic time   747
quadratic time   748
merge sort   751
quick sort   754
worst-case analysis   747

CHAPTER SUMMARY

■ The Big *O* notation is a theoretical approach for analyzing the performance of the algorithm. It estimates how fast an algorithm's execution time increases as the input size increases. So you can compare two algorithms by examining their *growth rates*.

■ An input that results in the shortest execution time is called the *best-case* input and an input that results in the longest execution time is called the *worst-case* input. Best-case and worst-case are not representative, but worst-case analysis is very useful. You can show that the algorithm will never be slower than the worst-case.

■ An average-case analysis attempts to determine the average amount of time among all possible input of the same size. Average-case analysis is ideal, but difficult to perform, because it is hard to determine the relative probabilities and distributions of various input instances for many problems.

■ If the time is not related to the input size, the algorithm is said to take *constant time* with the notation $O(1)$.

■ Linear search takes $O(n)$ time. An algorithm with the $O(n)$ time complexity is called a *linear algorithm*. Binary search takes $O(\log n)$ time. An algorithm with the $O(\log n)$ time complexity is called a *logarithmic algorithm*.

■ The worst time complexity for selection sort, insertion sort, bubble sort, and quick sort is $O(n^2)$. An algorithm with the $O(n^2)$ time complexity is called a *quadratic algorithm*.

■ The average-time and worst-time complexity for merge sort and heap sort is $O(n \log n)$. The average time for quick sort is also $O(n \log n)$. An algorithm with the $O(n \log n)$ time complexity is called a log-linear time.

■ A variation of merge sort can be applied to sort large data from external files.

REVIEW QUESTIONS

Sections 23.2 Estimating Algorithm Efficiency

23.1 Put the following growth functions in order:

$$\frac{5n^3}{4032}, \quad 44 \log n, \quad 10n\log n, \quad 500, \quad 2n^2, \quad \frac{2^n}{45}, \quad 3n$$

23.2 Use the Big O notation to estimate the time complexity of the following methods:

```java
public static void mA(int n) {
  for (int i = 0; i < n; i++) {
    System.out.print(Math.random());
  }
}
```

```java
public static void mB(int n) {
  for (int i = 0; i < n; i++) {
    for (int j = 0; j < i; j++)
      System.out.print(Math.random());
  }
}
```

```java
public static void mC(int[] m) {
  for (int i = 0; i < m.length; i++) {
    System.out.print(m[i]);
  }

  for (int i = m.length - 1; i >= 0; )
  {
    System.out.print(m[i]);
    i--;
  }
}
```

```java
public static void mD(int[] m) {
  for (int i = 0; i < m.length; i++) {
    for (int j = 0; j < i; j++)
      System.out.print(m[i] * m[j]);
  }
}
```

23.3   Estimate the time complexity for adding two $n \times m$ matrices, and for multiplying a $n \times m$ matrix with a $m \times k$ matrix.

Sections 23.3–23.7

23.4   Use Figure 23.1 as an example to show how to apply bubble sort on {45, 11, 50, 59, 60, 2, 4, 7, 10}.

23.5   Use Figure 23.2 as an example to show how to apply merge sort on {45, 11, 50, 59, 60, 2, 4, 7, 10}.

23.6   Use Figure 23.4 as an example to show how to apply quick sort on {45, 11, 50, 59, 60, 2, 4, 7, 10}.

23.7   Show the steps of creating a heap using {45, 11, 50, 59, 60, 2, 4, 7, 10}.

23.8   Given the following heap, show the steps of removing all nodes from the heap.

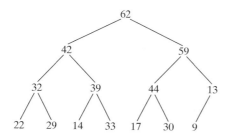

23.9   There are 10 numbers {2, 3, 4, 0, 5, 6, 7, 9, 8, 1} stored in the external file large-data.dat. Trace the SortLargeFile program by hand with `MAX_ARRAY_SIZE` 2.

PROGRAMMING EXERCISES

23.1   (*Generic bubble sort*) Write the following two generic methods using bubble sort. The first method sorts the elements using the `Comparable` interface and the second uses the `Comparator` interface.

```
public static <E extends Comparable<E>> void bubbleSort(E[] list)
public static <E> void bubbleSort(E[] list, Comparator comparator)
```

23.2   (*Generic merge sort*) Write the following two generic methods using merge sort. The first method sorts the elements using the `Comparable` interface and the second uses the `Comparator` interface.

```
public static <E extends Comparable<E>> void mergeSort(E[] list)
public static <E> void mergeSort(E[] list, Comparator comparator)
```

23.3   (*Generic quick sort*) Write the following two generic methods using quick sort. The first method sorts the elements using the `Comparable` interface and the second uses the `Comparator` interface.

```
public static <E extends Comparable<E>> void quickSort(E[] list)
public static <E> void quickSort(E[] list, Comparator comparator)
```

23.4   (*Improving quick sort*) The quick sort algorithm presented in the book selects the first element in the list as the pivot. Revise it by selecting the medium among the first, middle, and last elements in the list.

23.5 (*Generic heap sort*) Write the following two generic methods using heap sort. The first method sorts the elements using the `Comparable` interface and the second uses the `Comparator` interface.

```
public static <E extends Comparable<E>> void heapSort(E[] list)
public static <E> void heapSort(E[] list, Comparator comparator)
```

23.6 (*Checking order*) Write the following overloaded methods that check whether an array is ordered in ascending order, or descending order. By default, the method checks ascending order. To check descending order, pass `false` to the ascending argument in the method.

```
public static boolean ordered(int[] list)
public static boolean ordered(byte[] list, boolean ascending)
public static boolean ordered(double[] list)
public static boolean ordered(double[] list, boolean descending)
public static <E extends Comparable<E>> boolean ordered(E[] list)
public static <E extends Comparable<E>> boolean ordered(E[] list,
  boolean ascending)
public static <E> Boolean ordered(E[] list, Comparator comparator,
  boolean ascending)
```

CONCURRENCY, NETWORKING, AND INTERNATIONALIZATION

This part of the book is devoted to three unique and useful features of Java. Chapter 24 treats the use of multithreading to make programs more responsive and interactive. Chapter 25 introduces how to write programs that talk with each other from different hosts over the Internet. Chapter 26 covers the use of internationalization support to develop projects for international audiences.

Chapter 24
Multithreading

Chapter 25
Networking

Chapter 26
Internationalization

Prerequisites for Part 6

Chapter 24, "Multithreading," or Chapter 26, "Internationalization," can be covered after Chapter 16, "Applets and Multimedia." Chapter 25, "Networking," is dependent on Chapter 24, "Multithreading," and Chapter 18, "Binary I/O."

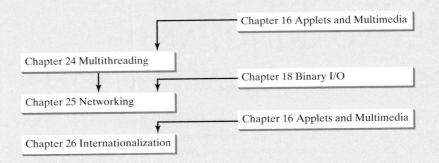

MULTITHREADING

Objectives

- To understand the concept of multithreading and apply it to develop concurrent programs (§24.2).

- To develop task classes by implementing the `Runnable` interface (§24.3).

- To create threads to run tasks using the `Thread` class (§24.3).

- To control threads using the methods in the `Thread` class (§24.4).

- To control animations using threads (§§24.5, 24.7).

- To run code in the event dispatcher thread (§24.6).

- To execute tasks in a thread pool (§24.8).

- To use synchronized methods or blocks to synchronize threads to avoid race conditions (§24.9).

- To synchronize threads using locks (§24.10).

- To facilitate thread communications using conditions on locks (§§24.11–24.12).

- (Optional) To use blocking queues to synchronize access to an array queue, linked queue, and priority queue (§24.13).

- (Optional) To restrict the number of accesses to a shared resource using semaphores (§24.14).

- (Optional) To use the resource-ordering technique to avoid deadlocks (§24.15).

- To understand the life cycle of a thread (§24.16).

- To create synchronized collections using the static methods in the `Collections` class (§24.17).

- (Optional) To display the completion status of a task using `JProgressBar` (§24.18).

24.1 Introduction

multithreading

One of the powerful features of Java is its built-in support for multithreading. *Multithreading* is the capability of running multiple tasks concurrently within a program. In many programming languages, you have to invoke system-dependent procedures and functions to implement multi-threading. This chapter introduces the concepts of threads and how to develop multithreading programs in Java.

24.2 Thread Concepts

thread
task

A *thread* is the flow of execution, from beginning to end, of a task in a program. A *task* is a program unit that is executed independently of other parts of the program. A thread provides the mechanism for running a task. With Java, you can launch multiple threads from a program concurrently. These threads can be executed simultaneously in multiprocessor systems, as shown in Figure 24.1(a).

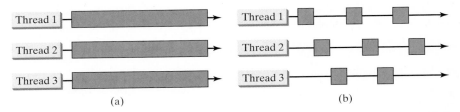

FIGURE 24.1 (a) Here multiple threads are running on multiple CPUs. (b) Here multiple threads share a single CPU.

In single-processor systems, as shown in Figure 24.1(b), the multiple threads share CPU time, and the operating system is responsible for scheduling and allocating resources to them. This arrangement is practical because most of the time the CPU is idle. It does nothing, for example, while waiting for the user to enter data.

Multithreading can make your program more responsive and interactive, as well as enhance performance. For example, a good word processor lets you print or save a file while you are typing. In some cases, multithreaded programs run faster than single-threaded programs even on single-processor systems. Java provides exceptionally good support for creating and running threads and for locking resources to prevent conflicts.

Java task

runnable object
thread

When your program executes as an application, the Java interpreter starts a thread for the **main** method. When your program executes as an applet, the Web browser starts a thread to run the applet. You can create additional threads to run concurrent tasks in the program. In Java, each task is an instance of the **Runnable** interface, also called a *runnable object*. A *thread* is essentially an object that facilitates the execution of a task.

24.3 Creating Tasks and Threads

Thread class
Runnable interface
run() method

Tasks are objects. To create tasks, you have to first declare a class for tasks. A task class must implement the **Runnable** interface. The **Runnable** interface is rather simple. All it contains is the **run** method. You need to implement this method to tell the system how your thread is going to run. A template for developing a task class is shown in Figure 24.2(a).

Once you have declared a **TaskClass**, you can create a task using its constructor. For example,

creating a task

```
TaskClass task = new TaskClass(...);
```

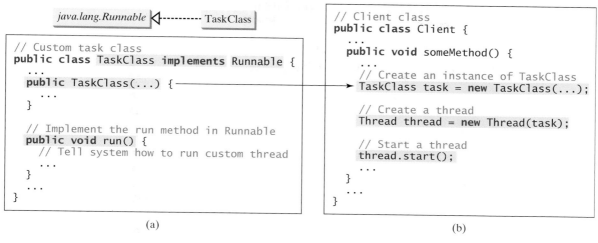

FIGURE 24.2 Define a task class by implementing the **Runnable** interface.

A task must be executed in a thread. The **Thread** class contains the constructors for creating threads and many useful methods for controlling threads. To create a thread for a task, use

```
Thread thread = new Thread(task);
```
creating a thread

You can then invoke the **start()** method to tell the JVM that the thread is ready to run, as follows:

```
thread.start();
```
starting a thread

The JVM will execute the task by invoking the task's **run()** method. Figure 24.2(b) outlines the major steps for creating a task, a thread, and start the thread.

Listing 24.1 gives a program that creates three tasks and three threads to run them:

- The first task prints the letter **a** one hundred times.

- The second task prints the letter **b** one hundred times.

- The third task prints the integers **1** through **100**.

If you run this program on a multiple-CPU system, all three threads will execute simultaneously. If you run the program on a single-CPU system, the three threads will share the CPU and take turns printing letters and numbers on the console. This is known as *time-sharing*. *time-sharing* Figure 24.3 shows a sample run of the program.

```
Command Prompt                                            _ □ ×
C:\book>java TaskThreadDemo
aaaaaaaaaaaaaaaaab 1b 2b 3b 4b 5b 6b 7b 8 9 10 11 12 13 14 15 16 17 18 19 20 21 2
2 23 24 25 26bababababababababababa 27 28 29 30 31 32 33 34 35 36 37 38 39 40 41 42
43 44 45 46 47 48 49 50 51 52 53 54 55 56 57 58 59 60 61ababababababababababbbbbbbb
bbbbbbbbbbbbba 62a 63a 64a 65a 66a 67a 68a 69a 70 71 72 73 74 75 76 77 78 79 80 8
1 82 83 84 85 86 87 88abababababababababbbbbbbbbbbbbbbbbbbbba 89a 90a 91a 92a 93a
94a 95a 96a 97 98 99 100aaaaaaaaaaaaaaaaaaaabbbbbbbbbbbbbbbbbbbbbbbbbbbbaaaaaaaaaa
aaaaaaaaaaaa
C:\book>
```

FIGURE 24.3 Tasks **printA**, **printB**, and **print100** are executed simultaneously to display the letter **a** one hundred times, the letter **b** one hundred times, and the numbers from 1 to 100.

LISTING 24.1 TaskThreadDemo.java

create tasks

create threads

start threads

task class

run

task class

run

```java
 1  public class TaskThreadDemo {
 2    public static void main(String[] args) {
 3      // Create tasks
 4      Runnable printA = new PrintChar('a', 100);
 5      Runnable printB = new PrintChar('b', 100);
 6      Runnable print100 = new PrintNum(100);
 7
 8      // Create threads
 9      Thread thread1 = new Thread(printA);
10      Thread thread2 = new Thread(printB);
11      Thread thread3 = new Thread(print100);
12
13      // Start threads
14      thread1.start();
15      thread2.start();
16      thread3.start();
17    }
18  }
19
20  // The task for printing a specified character in specified times
21  class PrintChar implements Runnable {
22    private char charToPrint; // The character to print
23    private int times; // The times to repeat
24
25    /** Construct a task with specified character and number of
26     *  times to print the character
27     */
28    public PrintChar(char c, int t) {
29      charToPrint = c;
30      times = t;
31    }
32
33    /** Override the run() method to tell the system
34     *  what the task to perform
35     */
36    public void run() {
37      for (int i = 0; i < times; i++) {
38        System.out.print(charToPrint);
39      }
40    }
41  }
42
43  // The task class for printing number from 1 to n for a given n
44  class PrintNum implements Runnable {
45    private int lastNum;
46
47    /** Construct a task for printing 1, 2, ... i */
48    public PrintNum(int n) {
49      lastNum = n;
50    }
51
52    /** Tell the thread how to run */
53    public void run() {
54      for (int i = 1; i <= lastNum; i++) {
55        System.out.print(" " + i);
56      }
57    }
58  }
```

The program creates three tasks (lines 4–6). To run them concurrently, three threads are created (lines 9–11). The `start()` method (lines 14–16) is invoked to start a thread that causes the `run()` method in the task to be executed. When the `run()` method completes, the thread terminates.

Because the first two tasks, `printA` and `printB`, have similar functionality, they can be defined in one task class `PrintChar` (lines 21–41). The `PrintChar` class implements `Runnable` and overrides the `run()` method (lines 36–40) with the print-character action. This class provides a framework for printing any single character a given number of times. The runnable objects `printA` and `printB` are instances of the `PrintChar` class.

The `PrintNum` class (lines 44–58) implements `Runnable` and overrides the `run()` method (lines 53–57) with the print-number action. This class provides a framework for printing numbers from *1* to *n*, for any integer *n*. The runnable object `print100` is an instance of the class `printNum` class.

Important Note

The `run()` method in a task specifies how to perform the task. This method is automatically invoked by the JVM. You should not invoke it. Invoking `run()` directly merely executes this method in the same thread and no new thread is started.

run() method

24.4 The **Thread** Class

The `Thread` class contains the constructors for creating threads for tasks, and the methods for controlling threads, as shown in Figure 24.4.

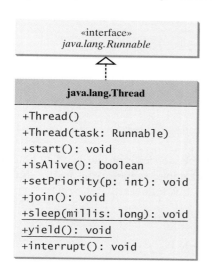

«interface»
java.lang.Runnable

java.lang.Thread

`+Thread()`	Creates a default thread.
`+Thread(task: Runnable)`	Creates a thread for a specified task.
`+start(): void`	Starts the thread that causes the run() method to be invoked by the JVM.
`+isAlive(): boolean`	Tests whether the thread is currently running.
`+setPriority(p: int): void`	Sets priority p (ranging from 1 to 10) for this thread.
`+join(): void`	Waits for this thread to finish.
`+sleep(millis: long): void`	Puts the runnable object to sleep for a specified time in milliseconds.
`+yield(): void`	Causes this thread to temporarily pause and allow other threads to execute.
`+interrupt(): void`	Interrupts this thread.

FIGURE 24.4 The `Thread` class contains the methods for controlling threads.

Note

Since the `Thread` class implements `Runnable`, you could declare a class that extends `Thread` and implements the `run` method, as shown in Figure 24.5(a), and then create an object from the class and invoke its `start` method in a client program to start the thread, as shown in Figure 24.5(b).

This approach is, however, not recommended, because it mixes the task and the mechanism of running the task. Separating the task from the thread is a preferred design.

separating task from thread

Note

The `Thread` class also contains the `stop()`, `suspend()`, and `resume()` methods. As of Java 2, these methods are *deprecated* (or *outdated*) because they are known to be inherently unsafe. Instead of using the `stop()` method, you should assign `null` to a `Thread` variable to indicate that it is stopped.

deprecated method

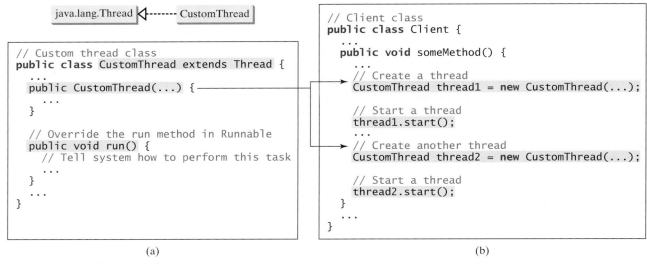

FIGURE 24.5 Define a thread class by extending the `Thread` class.

`yield()`

You can use the `yield()` method to temporarily release time for other threads. For example, suppose you modify the code in the `run()` method (lines 53–57 in `PrintNum` in TaskThreadDemo.java) in Listing 24.1 as follows:

```java
public void run() {
  for (int i = 1; i <= lastNum; i++) {
    System.out.print(" " + i);
    Thread.yield();
  }
}
```

Every time a number is printed, the `print100` thread is yielded. So each number is followed by some characters.

`sleep(long)`

The `sleep(long mills)` method puts the thread to sleep for the specified time in milliseconds to allow other threads to execute. For example, suppose you modify the code in lines 53–57 in TaskThreadDemo.java in Listing 24.1 as follows:

```java
public void run() {
  try {
    for (int i = 1; i <= lastNum; i++) {
      System.out.print(" " + i);
      if (i >= 50) Thread.sleep(1);
    }
  }
  catch (InterruptedException ex) {
  }
}
```

`InterruptedException`

Every time a number (>= 50) is printed, the `print100` thread is put to sleep for 1 millisecond. The `sleep` method may throw an `InterruptedException`, which is a checked exception. Such an exception may occur when a sleeping thread's `interrupt()` method is called. The `interrupt()` method is very rarely invoked on a thread, so an `InterruptedException` is unlikely to occur. But since Java forces you to catch checked exceptions, you have to put it in a `try-catch` block. If a `sleep` method is invoked in a loop, you should wrap the loop in a `try-catch` block, as shown in (a) below. If the loop is outside the `try-catch` block, as shown in (b), the thread may continue to execute even though it is being interrupted.

```java
public void run() {
  try {
    while (...) {
      ...
      Thread.sleep(1000);
    }
  }
  catch (InterruptedException ex) {
    ex.printStackTrace();
  }
}
```
(a) Correct

```java
public void run() {
  while (...) {
    try {
      ...
      Thread.sleep(sleepTime);
    }
    catch (InterruptedException ex) {
      ex.printStackTrace();
    }
  }
}
```
(b) Incorrect

You can use the `join()` method to force one thread to wait for another thread to finish. For example, suppose you modify the code in lines 53–57 in TaskThreadDemo.java in Listing 24.1 as follows:

`join()`

```java
public void run() {
  Thread thread4 = new Thread(
    new PrintChar('c', 40));
    thread4.start();
  try {
    for (int i = 1; i <= lastNum; i++) {
      System.out.print (" " + i);
      If (i == 50) thread4.join();
    }
  }
  catch (InterruptException ex) {
  }
}
```

Thread print100   Thread thread4

thread4.join()

Wait for thread4 to finish

thread4 finished

A new `thread4` is created. It prints character `c` forty times. The numbers from `50` to `100` are printed after thread `thread4` is finished.

Java assigns every thread a priority. By default, a thread inherits the priority of the thread that spawned it. You can increase or decrease the priority of any thread by using the `setPriority` method, and you can get the thread's priority by using the `getPriority` method. Priorities are numbers ranging from `1` to `10`. The `Thread` class has the `int` constants `MIN_PRIORITY`, `NORM_PRIORITY`, and `MAX_PRIORITY`, representing `1`, `5`, and `10`, respectively. The priority of the main thread is `Thread.NORM_PRIORITY`.

`setPriority(int)`

The JVM always picks the currently runnable thread with the highest priority. If several runnable threads have equally high priorities, the CPU is allocated to all of them in round-robin fashion. A lower-priority thread can run only when no higher-priority threads are running. For example, suppose you insert the following code in line 16 in TaskThreadDemo.java in Listing 24.1:

```java
print100.setPriority(Thread.MAX_PRIORITY);
```

The `print100` thread will be finished first.

Tip
The priority numbers may be changed in a future version of Java. To minimize the impact of any changes, use the constants in the **Thread** class to specify thread priorities.

Tip
A thread may never get a chance to run if there is always a higher-priority thread running or a same-priority thread that never yields. This situation is known as *contention* or *starvation*. To avoid contention, the thread with high priority must periodically invoke the sleep or yield method to give a thread with a lower or the same priority a chance to run.

contention or starvation

24.5 Example: Flashing Text

The use of a `Timer` object to control animations was introduced in §14.6, "Animation Using the `Timer` Class." You can also use a thread to control animation. Listing 24.2 gives an example that displays a flashing text on a label, as shown in Figure 24.6.

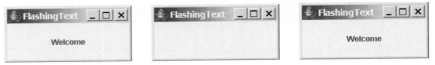

FIGURE 24.6 The text Welcome blinks.

LISTING 24.2 FlashingText.java

```java
 1  import javax.swing.*;
 2
 3  public class FlashingText extends JApplet implements Runnable {
 4    private JLabel jlblText = new JLabel("Welcome", JLabel.CENTER);
 5
 6    public FlashingText() {
 7      add(jlblText);
 8      new Thread(this).start();
 9    }
10
11    /** Set the text on/off every 200 milliseconds */
12    public void run() {
13      try {
14        while (true) {
15          if (jlblText.getText() == null)
16            jlblText.setText("Welcome");
17          else
18            jlblText.setText(null);
19
20          Thread.sleep(200);
21        }
22      }
23      catch (InterruptedException ex) {
24      }
25    }
26  }
```

implements Runnable
create a label

add a label
start a thread

how to run

sleep

main method omitted

thread vs. timer

`FlashingText` implements `Runnable` (line 3), so it is a task class. Line 8 wraps the task in a thread and starts the thread. The `run` method dictates how to run the thread. It sets a text in the label if the label does not have a text (line 15), and sets its text `null` (line 17) if the label has a text. The text is set and unset to simulate a flashing effect.

You can use a timer or a thread to control animation. Which one is better? A timer is a source component that fires an `ActionEvent` at a "fixed rate." When an action event occurs, the timer invokes the listener's `actionPerformed` method to handle the event. The timer and event-handling run on the same event dispatcher thread. If it takes a long time to handle the event, the actual delay time between two events will be longer than the requested delay time. In this case, you should run event-handling on a separate thread. The next section will give an example to illustrate the problem and fix it by running the event-handling on a separate thread. In general, threads are more reliable and responsive than timers. If you need a precise delay time or a quick response, it is better to use a thread. Otherwise, using a timer is simpler and more efficient than using a thread. Timers consume fewer system resources than threads because timers run on the GUI event dispatcher thread so you don't need to spawn new threads for timers.

24.6 GUI Event Dispatcher Thread

GUI event handling and painting code executes in a single thread called the *event dispatcher thread*. This ensures that each event handler finishes executing before the next one executes and the painting isn't interrupted by events.

In certain situations, you need to run the code in the event dispatcher thread to avoid possible deadlock. You can use the static methods, `invokeLater` and `invokeAndWait`, in the `javax.swing.SwingUtilities` class to run the code in the event dispatcher thread. You must put this code in the `run` method of a `Runnable` object and specify the `Runnable` object as the argument to `invokeLater` and `invokeAndWait`. The `invokeLater` method returns immediately, without waiting for the event dispatcher thread to execute the code. The `invokeAndWait` method is just like `invokeLater`, except that `invokeAndWait` doesn't return until the event-dispatching thread has executed the specified code.

So far, you have launched your GUI application from the `main` method by creating a frame and making it visible. This works fine for most applications. In certain situations, however, it could cause problems. To avoid possible thread deadlock, you should launch GUI creation from the event dispatcher thread, as follows:

```java
public static void main(String[] args) {
  SwingUtilities.invokeLater(new Runnable() {
    public void run() {
      // Place the code for creating a frame and setting it properties
    }
  });
}
```

For example, Listing 24.3 gives a simple program that launches the frame from the event dispatcher thread.

LISTING 24.3 EventDispatcherThreadDemo.java

```java
1 import javax.swing.*;
2
3 public class EventDispatcherThreadDemo extends JApplet {
4   public EventDispatcherThreadDemo() {
5     add(new JLabel("Hi, it runs from an event dispatcher thread"));
6   }
7
8   /** Main method */
9   public static void main(String[] args) {
10    SwingUtilities.invokeLater(new Runnable() {
11      public void run() {
12        JFrame frame = new JFrame("EventDispatcherThreadDemo");
13        frame.add(new EventDispatcherThreadDemo());
14        frame.setLocationRelativeTo(null); // Center the frame
15        frame.setDefaultCloseOperation(JFrame.EXIT_ON_CLOSE);
16        frame.setSize(200, 200);
17        frame.setVisible(true);
18      }
19    });
20  }
21 }
```

24.7 (Optional) Case Study: Clock with Audio

The example creates an applet that displays a running clock and announces the time at one-minute intervals. For example, if the current time is 6:30:00, the applet announces, "six o'clock thirty minutes A.M." If the current time is 20:20:00, the applet announces, "eight o'clock twenty minutes P.M." Also add a label to display the digital time, as shown in Figure 24.7.

FIGURE 24.7 The applet displays a clock and announces the time every minute.

To announce the time, the applet plays three *audio clips*. The first clip announces the hour, the second announces the minute, and the third announces AM or PM. All of the *audio files* are stored in the directory `audio`, a subdirectory of the applet's class directory. The twelve audio files that are used to announce the hours are stored in the files **hour0.au**, **hour1.au**, and so on, to **hour11.au**. The sixty audio files that are used to announce the minutes are stored in the files **minute0.au**, **minute1.au**, and so on, to **minute59.au**. The two audio files that are used to announce AM or PM are stored in the file **am.au** and **pm.au**.

You need to play three audio clips on a separate thread to avoid animation delays. To illustrate the problem, let us first write a program without playing the audio on a separate thread.

In §13.12, the `StillClock` class was developed to draw a still clock to show the current time. Create an applet named `ClockWithAudio` (Listing 24.4) that contains an instance of `StillClock` to display an analog clock, and an instance of `JLabel` to display the digit time. Override the `init` method to load the audio files. Use a `Timer` object to set and display the current time continuously at a fixed rate. When the second is zero, announce the current time.

LISTING 24.4 ClockWithAudio.java

```java
1  import java.applet.*;
2  import javax.swing.*;
3  import java.awt.event.*;
4  import java.awt.*;
5
6  public class ClockWithAudio extends JApplet {
7    protected AudioClip[] hourAudio = new AudioClip[12];
8    protected AudioClip[] minuteAudio = new AudioClip[60];
9
10   // Create audio clips for pronouncing am and pm
11   protected AudioClip amAudio =
12     Applet.newAudioClip(this.getClass().getResource("audio/am.au"));
13   protected AudioClip pmAudio =
14     Applet.newAudioClip(this.getClass().getResource("audio/pm.au"));
15
16   // Create a clock
17   private StillClock clock = new StillClock();
18
19   // Create a timer
20   private Timer timer = new Timer(1000, new TimerListener());
21
```

audio clips
audio files

audio clips

am clip

pm clip

still clock

timer

```
22    // Create a label to display time
23    private JLabel jlblDigitTime = new JLabel("", JLabel.CENTER);              label
24
25    /** Initialize the applet */
26    public void init() {
27      // Create audio clips for pronouncing hours
28      for (int i = 0; i < 12; i++)
29        hourAudio[i] = Applet.newAudioClip(                                    create audio clips
30          this.getClass().getResource("audio/hour" + i + ".au"));
31
32      // Create audio clips for pronouncing minutes
33      for (int i = 0; i < 60; i++)
34        minuteAudio[i] = Applet.newAudioClip(
35          this.getClass().getResource("audio/minute" + i + ".au"));
36
37      // Add clock and time label to the content pane of the applet
38      add(clock, BorderLayout.CENTER);
39      add(jlblDigitTime, BorderLayout.SOUTH);
40    }
41
42    /** Override the applet's start method */
43    public void start() {
44      timer.start(); // Resume clock                                           start timer
45    }
46
47    /** Override the applet's stop method */
48    public void stop() {
49      timer.stop(); // Suspend clock                                           stop timer
50    }
51
52    private class TimerListener implements ActionListener {                    timer listener
53      public void actionPerformed(ActionEvent e) {
54        clock.setCurrentTime();                                               set new time
55        clock.repaint();
56        jlblDigitTime.setText(clock.getHour() + ":" + clock.getMinute()
57          + ":" + clock.getSecond());
58        if (clock.getSecond() == 0)
59          announceTime(clock.getHour(), clock.getMinute());                   announce time
60      }
61    }
62
63    /** Announce the current time at every minute */
64    public void announceTime(int hour, int minute) {
65      // Announce hour
66      hourAudio[hour % 12].play();                                            announce hour
67
68      try {
69        // Time delay to allow hourAudio play to finish
70        Thread.sleep(1500);
71
72        // Announce minute
73        minuteAudio[minute].play();                                          announce minute
74
75        // Time delay to allow minuteAudio play to finish
76        Thread.sleep(1500);
77      }
78      catch(InterruptedException ex) {
79      }
80
81      // Announce am or pm
82      if (hour < 12)                                                         announce am
```

```
83        amAudio.play();
84      else
85        pmAudio.play();
86    }
87 }
```

The `hourAudio` is an array of twelve audio clips that are used to announce the twelve hours of the day (line 7); the `minuteAudio` is an audio clip that is used to announce the minutes in an hour (line 8). The `amAudio` announces A.M. (line 11); the `pmAudio` announces P.M. (line 13).

The `init()` method creates hour audio clips (lines 29–30) and minute audio clips (lines 34–35), and places a clock and a label in the applet (lines 38–39).

An `ActionEvent` is fired by the timer every second. In the listener's `actionPerformed` method (lines 53–60), the clock is repainted with the new current time, and the digital time is displayed in the label.

In the `announceTime` method (lines 64–86), the `sleep()` method (lines 70, 76) is purposely invoked to ensure that one clip finishes before the next clip starts, so that the clips do not interfere with each other.

The applet's `start()` and `stop()` methods (lines 43–50) are overridden to ensure that the timer starts or stops when the applet is restarted or stopped.

When you run the preceding program, you will notice that the second hand does not display at the first, second, and third seconds of the minute. This is because `sleep(1500)` is invoked twice in the `announceTime()` method, which takes three seconds to announce the time at the beginning of each minute. Thus, the next action event is delayed for three seconds during the first three seconds of each minute. As a result of this delay, the time is not updated and the clock was not repainted for these three seconds. To fix this problem, you should announce the time on a separate thread. This can be accomplished by modifying the `announceTime` method. Listing 24.5 gives the new program.

abnormal problem

LISTING 24.5 ClockWithAudioOnSeparateThread.java

omitted

omitted

create a thread

task class

run thread

```
1  // same import statements as in Listing 24.4, so omitted
2
3  public class ClockWithAudioOnSeparateThread extends JApplet {
4    // same as in lines 7-61, so omitted
5
6    /** Announce the current time at every minute */
7    public void announceTime(int h, int m) {
8      new Thread(new AnnounceTimeOnSeparateThread(h, m)).start();
9    }
10
11   /** Inner class for announcing time */
12   class AnnounceTimeOnSeparateThread implements Runnable {
13     private int hour, minute;
14
15     /** Get Audio clips */
16     public AnnounceTimeOnSeparateThread(int hour, int minute) {
17       this.hour = hour;
18       this.minute = minute;
19     }
20
21     public void run() {
22       // Announce hour
23       hourAudio[hour % 12].play();
24
25       try {
26         // Time delay to allow hourAudio play to finish
27         Thread.sleep(1500);
28
```

```
29        // Announce minute
30        minuteAudio[minute].play();
31
32        // Time delay to allow minuteAudio play to finish
33        Thread.sleep(1500);
34      }
35      catch (InterruptedException ex) {
36      }
37
38      // Announce am or pm
39      if (hour < 12)
40        amAudio.play();
41      else
42        pmAudio.play();
43    }
44  }
45 }
```

main omitted

The new class `ClockWithAudioOnSeparateThread` is the same as `ClockWithAudio` except that the `announceTime` method is new. The new `announceTime` method creates a thread (line 8) for the task of announcing time. The task class is declared an inner class (lines 12–44). The `run` method (line 21) announces the time on a separate thread.

When running this program, you will discover that the audio does not interfere with the clock animation because an instance of `AnnounceTimeOnSeparateThread` starts on a separate thread to announce the current time. This thread is independent of the thread on which the `actionPerformed` method runs.

24.8 Thread Pools

In §24.3, "Creating Tasks and Threads," you learned how to declare a task class by implementing `java.lang.Runnable`, and how to create a thread to run a task like this:

```
Runnable task = new TaskClass(task);
new Thread(task).start();
```

This approach is convenient for a single task execution, but it is not efficient for a large number of tasks, because you have to create a thread for each task. Starting a new thread for each task could limit throughput and cause poor performance. A thread pool is ideal to manage the number of tasks executing concurrently. JDK 1.5 uses the `Executor` interface for executing tasks in a thread pool and the `ExecutorService` interface for managing and controlling tasks. `ExecutorService` is a subinterface of `Executor`, as shown in Figure 24.8.

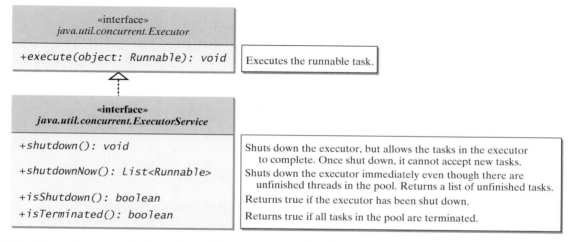

Figure 24.8 `Executor` executes threads, and `ExecutorService` manages threads.

To create an `Executor` object, use the static methods in the `Executors` class, as shown in Figure 24.9. The `newFixedThreadPool(int)` method creates a fixed number of threads in a pool. If a thread completes executing a task, it can be reused to execute another task. If a thread terminates due to a failure prior to shutdown, a new thread will be created to replace it if all the threads in the pool are not idle and there are tasks waiting for execution. The `newCachedThreadPool()` method creates a new thread if all the threads in the pool are not idle and there are tasks waiting for execution. A thread in a cached pool will be terminated if it has not been used for 60 seconds. A cached pool is efficient for many short tasks.

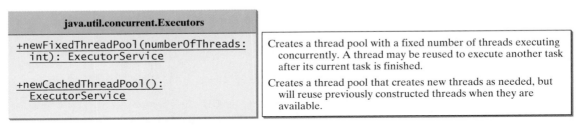

FIGURE 24.9 The `Executors` class provides static methods for creating `Executor` objects.

Listing 24.6 shows how to rewrite Listing 24.1, TaskThreadDemo.java, using a thread pool.

LISTING 24.6 `ExecutorDemo.java`

```
1 import java.util.concurrent.*;
2
3 public class ExecutorDemo {
4   public static void main(String[] args) {
5     // Create a fixed thread pool with maximum three threads
6     ExecutorService executor = Executors.newFixedThreadPool(3);
7
8     // Submit runnable tasks to the executor
9     executor.execute(new PrintChar('a', 100));
10    executor.execute(new PrintChar('b', 100));
11    executor.execute(new PrintNum(100));
12
13    // Shutdown the executor
14    executor.shutdown();
15  }
16 }
```

create executor

submit task

shut down executor

Line 6 creates a thread pool executor with three threads maximum. Classes **PrintChar** and **PrintNum** were declared in TaskThreadDemo.java in Listing 24.1. Line 9 creates a task new **PrintChar('a', 100)** and adds it to the pool. Another two runnable tasks are created and added to the same pool in lines 10–11. The executor creates three threads to execute three tasks concurrently. What will happen if you replace line 6 by

```
ExecutorService executor = Executors.newFixedThreadPool(1);
```

The three runnable tasks will be executed sequentially, because there is only one thread in the pool.

What will happen if you replace line 6 by

```
ExecutorService executor = Executors.newCachedThreadPool();
```

New threads will be created for each waiting task, so all the tasks will be executed concurrently.

The `shutdown()` method in line 14 tells the executor to shut down. No new tasks can be accepted, but the existing task will continue to finish.

Tip

If you need to create a thread for one task, use the **Thread** class. If you need to create threads for multiple tasks, it is better to use a thread pool.

24.9 Thread Synchronization

A shared resource may be corrupted if it is accessed simultaneously by multiple threads. The following example demonstrates the problem.

Suppose that you create and launch one hundred threads, each of which adds a penny to an account. Create a class named **Account** to model the account, a class named **AddAPennyTask** to add a penny to the account, and a main class that creates and launches threads. The relationships of these classes are shown in Figure 24.10. The program is given in Listing 24.7.

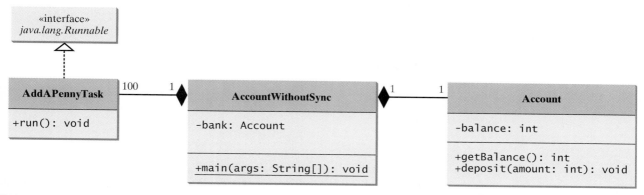

FIGURE 24.10 **AccountWithoutSync** contains an instance of **Account** and one hundred threads of **AddAPennyTask**.

LISTING 24.7 `AccountWithoutSync.java`

```java
1 import java.util.concurrent.*;
2
3 public class AccountWithoutSync {
4   private static Account account = new Account();
5
6   public static void main(String[] args) {
7     ExecutorService executor = Executors.newCachedThreadPool();       // create executor
8
9     // Create and launch 100 threads
10    for (int i = 0; i < 100; i++) {
11      executor.execute(new AddAPennyTask());                          // submit task
12    }
13
14    executor.shutdown();                                             // shut down executor
15
16    // Wait until all tasks are finished
17    while (!executor.isTerminated()) {                               // wait for all tasks
18    }                                                                //   to terminate
19
20    System.out.println("What is balance ? " + account.getBalance());
21  }
22
```

```
23    // A thread for adding a penny to the account
24    private static class AddAPennyTask implements Runnable {
25      public void run() {
26        account.deposit(1);
27      }
28    }
29
30    // An inner class for account
31    private static class Account {
32      private int balance = 0;
33
34      public int getBalance() {
35        return balance;
36      }
37
38      public void deposit(int amount) {
39        int newBalance = balance + amount;
40
41        // This delay is deliberately added to magnify the
42        // data-corruption problem and make it easy to see.
43        try {
44          Thread.sleep(5);
45        }
46        catch (InterruptedException ex) {
47        }
48
49        balance = newBalance;
50      }
51    }
52  }
```

The classes **AddAPennyTask** and **Account** in lines 23–51 are inner classes. Line 4 creates an **Account** with initial balance **0**. Line 11 creates a task to add a penny to the account and submit the task to the executor. Line 11 is repeated one hundred times in lines 10–12. The program repeatedly checks whether all tasks are completed in lines 17–18. The account balance is displayed in line 20 after all tasks are completed.

The program creates one hundred threads executed in a thread pool **executor** (lines 10–12). The **isTerminated()** method (line 17) is used to test whether the thread is terminated.

The balance of the account is initially **0** (line 32). When all the threads are finished, the balance should be **100**, but the output is unpredictable. As can be seen in Figure 24.11, the answers are wrong in the sample run. This demonstrates the data-corruption problem that occurs when all the threads have access to the same data source simultaneously.

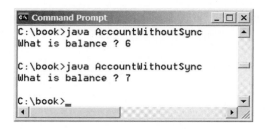

FIGURE 24.11 The **AccountWithoutSync** program causes data inconsistency.

Lines 39–49 could be replaced by one statement:

```
balance = balance + amount;
```

However, it is highly unlikely, although plausible, that the problem can be replicated using this single statement. The statements in lines 39–49 are deliberately designed to magnify the data-corruption problem and make it easy to see. If you run the program several times but still do not see the problem, increase the sleep time in line 26. This will increase the chances for showing the problem of data inconsistency.

What, then, caused the error in this program? Here is a possible scenario, as shown in Figure 24.12.

Step	balance	Task 1	Task 2
1	0	newBalance = balance + 1;	
2	0		newBalance = balance + 1;
3	1	balance = newBalance;	
4	1		balance = newBalance;

FIGURE 24.12 Task 1 and Task 2 both add 1 to the same balance.

In Step 1, Task 1 gets the balances from the account. In Step 2, Task 2 gets the same balances from the account. In Step 3, Task 1 writes a new balance to the account. In Step 4, Task 2 writes a new balance to the account.

The effect of this scenario is that Task 1 does nothing, because in Step 4 Task 2 overrides Task 1's result. Obviously, the problem is that Task 1 and Task 2 are accessing a common resource in a way that causes conflict. This is a common problem, known as a *race condition*, in multithreaded programs. A class is said to be *thread-safe* if an object of the class does not cause a race condition in the presence of multiple threads. As demonstrated in the preceding example, the `Account` class is not thread-safe.

race condition

thread-safe

24.9.1 The `synchronized` Keyword

To avoid race conditions, it is necessary to prevent more than one thread from simultaneously entering a certain part of the program, known as the *critical region*. The critical region in Listing 24.7 is the entire `deposit` method. You can use the keyword `synchronized` to synchronize the method so that only one thread can access the method at a time. There are several ways to correct the problem in Listing 24.7. One approach is to make `Account` thread-safe by adding the keyword `synchronized` in the `deposit` method in line 38, as follows:

critical region

```
public synchronized void deposit(double amount)
```

A synchronized method acquires a lock before it executes. In the case of an instance method, the lock is on the object for which the method was invoked. In the case of a static method, the lock is on the class. If one thread invokes a synchronized instance method (respectively, static method) on an object, the lock of that object (respectively, class) is acquired first, then the method is executed, and finally the lock is released. Another thread invoking the same method of that object (respectively, class) is blocked until the lock is released.

With the `deposit` method synchronized, the preceding scenario cannot happen. If Task 1 starts to enter the method, and Task 2 is already in the method, Task 2 is blocked until Task 1 finishes the method, as shown in Figure 24.13.

Suppose you are not allowed to modify `Account`. You could add a new, synchronized method that invokes `deposit(1)` and invoke this new method from the `run()` method.

24.9.2 Synchronizing Statements

Invoking a synchronized instance method of an object acquires a lock on the object, and invoking a synchronized static method of a class acquires a lock on the class. A synchronized statement can be used to acquire a lock on any object, not just *this* object, when executing a

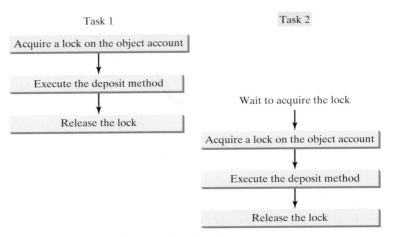

FIGURE 24.13 Task 1 and Task 2 are synchronized.

block of the code in a method. This block is referred to as a *synchronized block*. The general form of a synchronized statement is as follows:

```
synchronized (expr) {
  statements;
}
```

The expression **expr** must evaluate to an object reference. If the object is already locked by another thread, the thread is blocked until the lock is released. When a lock is obtained on the object, the statements in the synchronized block are executed, and then the lock is released.

Synchronized statements enable you to synchronize part of the code in a method instead of the entire method. This increases concurrency. Synchronized statements enable you to acquire a lock on any object so that you can synchronize the access to an object instead of to a method. You can make Listing 24.7 thread-safe by placing the statement in line 26 inside a synchronized block:

```
synchronized (account) {
  account.deposit(1);
}
```

 Note

Any synchronized instance method can be converted into a synchronized statement. For example, the following synchronized instance method in (a) is equivalent to (b):

```
public synchronized void xMethod() {
  // method body
}
```

```
public void xMethod() {
  synchronized (this) {
    // method body
  }
}
```

(a)   (b)

24.10 (Optional) Synchronization Using Locks

In Listing 24.7, one hundred tasks deposit a penny to the same account concurrently, which causes conflict. To avoid it, you can simply use the **synchronized** keyword in the **deposit** method, as follows:

```
public synchronized void deposit(double amount)
```

A synchronized instance method implicitly acquires a lock on the instance before it executes the method.

JDK 1.5 enables you to use locks explicitly. The new locking features are flexible and give you more control for coordinating threads. A lock is an instance of the Lock interface, which declares the methods for acquiring and releasing locks, as shown in Figure 24.14. A lock may also use the newCondition() method to create any number of Condition objects, which can be used for thread communications.

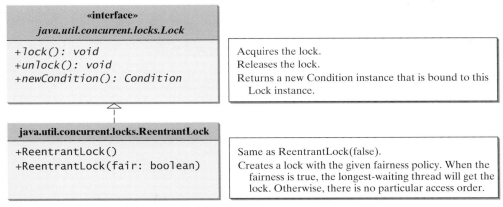

FIGURE 24.14   The ReentrantLock class implements the Lock interface to represent a lock.

ReentrantLock is a concrete implementation of Lock for creating mutually exclusive locks. You can create a lock with the specified *fairness policy*. True fairness policies guarantee that the longest-wait thread will obtain the lock first. False fairness policies grant a lock to a waiting thread without any access order. Programs using fair locks accessed by many threads may have poorer overall performance than those using the default setting, but have smaller variances in times to obtain locks and guarantee lack of starvation.

fairness policy

Listing 24.8 revises AccountWithoutSync.java in Listing 24.7 to synchronize the account modification using explicit locks.

LISTING 24.8   AccountWithSyncUsingLock.java

```
1 import java.util.concurrent.*;
2 import java.util.concurrent.locks.* ;
3
4 public class AccountWithSyncUsingLock {
5   private static Account account = new Account();
6
7   public static void main(String[] args) {
8     ExecutorService executor = Executors.newCachedThreadPool();
9
10    // Create and launch 100 threads
11    for (int i = 0; i < 100; i++) {
12      executor.execute(new AddAPennyTask());
13    }
14
15    executor.shutdown();
16
17    // Wait until all tasks are finished
18    while (!executor.isTerminated()) {
19    }
```

package for locks

```
20
21      System.out.println("What is balance ? " + account.getBalance());
22    }
23
24    // A thread for adding a penny to the account
25    public static class AddAPennyTask implements Runnable {
26      public void run() {
27        account.deposit(1);
28      }
29    }
30
31    // An inner class for account
32    public static class Account {
33      private static Lock lock = new ReentrantLock(); // Create a lock
34      private int balance = 0;
35
36      public int getBalance() {
37        return balance;
38      }
39
40      public void deposit(int amount) {
41        lock.lock(); // Acquire the lock
42
43        try {
44          int newBalance = balance + amount;
45
46          // This delay is deliberately added to magnify the
47          // data-corruption problem and make it easy to see.
48          Thread.sleep(5);
49
50          balance = newBalance;
51        }
52        catch (InterruptedException ex) {
53        }
54        finally {
55          lock.unlock(); // Release the lock
56        }
57      }
58    }
59  }
```

create a lock — line 33

acquire the lock — line 41

release the lock — line 55

Line 33 creates a lock, line 41 acquires the lock, and line 55 releases the lock.

 Tip

It is a good practice to always immediately follow a call to `lock()` with a `try-catch` block and release the lock in the `finally` clause, as shown in lines 41–56, to ensure that the lock is always released.

The example in Listing 24.7 using the synchronized method is simpler than the example in Listing 24.8 using a lock. In general, using **synchronized** methods or statements is simpler than using explicit locks for mutual exclusion. However, using explicit locks is more intuitive and flexible to synchronize threads with conditions, as you will see in the next section.

24.11 (Optional) Cooperation Among Threads

Thread synchronization suffices to avoid race conditions by ensuring the mutual exclusion of multiple threads in the critical region, but sometimes you also need a way for threads to cooperate. Conditions can be used to facilitate communications among threads. A thread can specify what to do under a certain condition. Conditions are objects created by invoking the `newCondition()` method on a `Lock` object. Once a condition is created, you can use its `await()`, `signal()`, and `signalAll()` methods for thread communications, as shown in Figure 24.15. The `await()` method causes the current thread to wait until the condition is signaled. The `signal()` method wakes up one waiting thread, and the `signalAll()` method wakes all waiting threads.

«interface»	
java.util.concurrent.Condition	
+await(): void	Causes the current thread to wait until the condition is signaled.
+signal(): void	Wakes up one waiting thread.
+signalAll(): Condition	Wakes up all waiting threads.

FIGURE 24.15   The `Condition` interface defines the methods for performing synchronization.

Let us use an example to demonstrate thread communications. Suppose that you create and launch two tasks, one that deposits to an account, and one that withdraws from the same account. The withdraw task has to wait if the amount to be withdrawn is more than the current balance in the account. Whenever new funds are deposited to the account, the deposit task notifies the withdraw thread to resume. If the amount is still not enough for a withdrawal, the withdraw thread has to continue to wait for a new deposit.

thread cooperation example

To synchronize the operations, use a lock with a condition: `newDeposit` (i.e., a new deposit added to the account). If the balance is less than the amount to be withdrawn, the withdraw task will wait for the `newDeposit` condition. When the deposit task adds money to the account, the task signals the waiting withdraw task to try again. The interaction between the two tasks is shown in Figure 24.16.

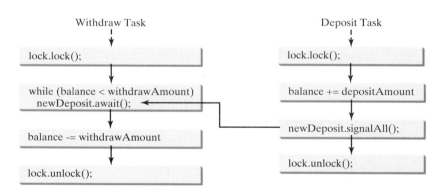

FIGURE 24.16   The condition `newDeposit` is used for communications between the two threads.

You create a condition from a `Lock` object. To use a condition, you have to first obtain a lock. The `await()` method causes the thread to wait and automatically releases the lock on the condition. Once the condition is right, the thread reacquires the lock and continues executing.

Assume that the initial balance is `0` and the amounts to deposit and withdraw are randomly generated. Listing 24.9 gives the program. A sample run of the program is shown in Figure 24.17.

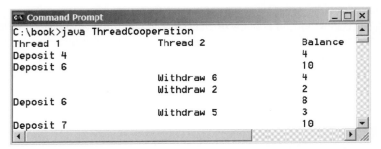

FIGURE 24.17 Withdraw task waits if there are not sufficient funds to withdraw.

LISTING 24.9 ThreadCooperation.java

```
1  import java.util.concurrent.*;
2  import java.util.concurrent.locks.*;
3
4  public class ThreadCooperation {
5    private static Account account = new Account();
6
7    public static void main(String[] args) {
8      // Create a thread pool with two threads
9      ExecutorService executor = Executors.newFixedThreadPool(2);
10     executor.execute(new DepositTask());
11     executor.execute(new WithdrawTask());
12     executor.shutdown();
13
14     System.out.println("Thread 1\t\tThread 2\t\tBalance");
15   }
16
17   // A task for adding an amount to the account
18   public static class DepositTask implements Runnable {
19     public void run() {
20       try { // Purposely delay it to let the withdraw method proceed
21         while (true) {
22           account.deposit((int)(Math.random() * 10) + 1);
23           Thread.sleep(1000);
24         }
25       }
26       catch (InterruptedException ex) {
27         ex.printStackTrace();
28       }
29     }
30   }
31
32   // A task for subtracting an amount from the account
33   public static class WithdrawTask implements Runnable {
34     public void run() {
35       while (true) {
36         account.withdraw((int)(Math.random() * 10) + 1);
37       }
38     }
39   }
40
41   // An inner class for account
42   private static class Account {
43     // Create a new lock
44     private static Lock lock = new ReentrantLock();
45
```

create two threads

create a lock

```
46        // Create a condition
47        private static Condition newDeposit = lock.newCondition();          create a condition
48
49        private int balance = 0;
50
51        public int getBalance() {
52          return balance;
53        }
54
55        public void withdraw(int amount) {
56          lock.lock(); // Acquire the lock                                   acquire the lock
57          try {
58            while (balance < amount)
59              newDeposit.await();                                           wait on the condition
60
61            balance -= amount;
62            System.out.println("\t\t\tWithdraw " + amount +
63              "\t\t" + getBalance());
64          }
65          catch (InterruptedException ex) {
66            ex.printStackTrace();
67          }
68          finally {
69            lock.unlock(); // Release the lock                              release the lock
70          }
71        }
72
73        public void deposit(int amount) {
74          lock.lock(); // Acquire the lock                                   acquire the lock
75          try {
76            balance += amount;
77            System.out.println("Deposit " + amount +
78              "\t\t\t\t\t" + getBalance());
79
80            // Signal thread waiting on the condition
81            newDeposit.signalAll();                                         signal threads
82          }
83          finally {
84            lock.unlock(); // Release the lock                              release the lock
85          }
86        }
87      }
88    }
```

The example creates a new inner class named **Account** to model the account with two methods, **deposit(int)** and **withdraw(int)**, a class named **DepositTask** to add an amount to the balance, a class named **WithdrawTask** to withdraw an amount from the balance, and a main class that creates and launches two threads.

The program creates and submits the deposit task (line 10) and the withdraw task (line 11). The deposit task is purposely put to sleep (line 23) to let the withdraw task run. When there are not enough funds to withdraw, the withdraw task waits (line 59) for notification of the balance change from the deposit task (line 81).

A lock is created in line 44. A condition named **newDeposit** on the lock is created in line 47. A condition is bound to a lock. Before waiting or signaling the condition, a thread must first acquire the lock for the condition. The withdraw task acquires the lock in line 56, waits for the **newDeposit** condition (line 59) when there is not a sufficient amount to withdraw, and releases the lock in line 69. The deposit task acquires the lock in line 74, and signals all waiting threads (line 81) for the **newDeposit** condition after a new deposit is made.

What will happen if you replace the `while` loop in lines 58–59 with the following `if` statement?

```
if (balance < amount)
  newDeposit.await();
```

The deposit task will notify the withdraw task whenever the balance changes. (`balance < amount`) may still be true when the withdraw task is awakened. Using the loop statement, the withdraw task will have a chance to recheck the condition. But using the if statement will not recheck the condition.

Caution

ever-waiting threads

Once a thread invokes `await()` on a condition, the thread is put to wait for a signal to resume. If you forget to call `signal()` or `signalAll()` on the condition, the thread will wait forever.

Caution

`IllegalMonitor-StateException`

A condition is created from a `Lock` object. To invoke any method (e.g., `await()`, `signal()`, and `signalAll()`), you must first own the lock. If you invoke these methods without acquiring the lock, an `IllegalMonitorStateException` will be thrown.

24.11.1   (Optional) Java's Built-In Monitor

Locks and conditions are new in Java 5. Prior to Java 5, thread communications were programmed using the object's built-in monitors. Locks and conditions are more powerful and flexible than the built-in monitor, and in consequence, this section can be completely ignored. However, if you are working with legacy Java code, you may encounter Java's built-in monitor.

A *monitor* is an object with mutual exclusion and synchronization capabilities. Only one thread can execute a method at a time in the monitor. A thread enters the monitor by acquiring a lock on the monitor and exits by releasing the lock. *Any object can be a monitor*. An object becomes a monitor once a thread locks it. Locking is implemented using the `synchronized` keyword on a method or a block. A thread must acquire a lock before executing a synchronized method or block. A thread can wait in a monitor if the condition is not right for it to continue executing in the monitor. You can invoke the `wait()` method on the monitor object to release the lock so that some other thread can get in the monitor and perhaps change the state of the monitor. When the condition is right, the other thread can invoke the `notify()` or `notifyAll()` method to signal one or all waiting threads to regain the lock and resume execution. The template for invoking these methods is shown in Figure 24.18.

Task 1

```
synchronized (anObject) {
  try {
    // Wait for the condition to become true
    while (!condition)
      anObject.wait();          resume

    // Do something when condition is true
  }
  catch (InterruptedException ex) {
    ex.printStackTrace();
  }
}
```

Task 2

```
synchronized (anObject) {
  // When condition becomes true
  anObject.notify(); or anObject.notifyAll();
  ...
}
```

FIGURE 24.18   The `wait()`, `notify()`, and `notifyAll()` methods coordinate thread communication.

The `wait()`, `notify()`, and `notifyAll()` methods must be called in a synchronized method or a synchronized block on the receiving object of these methods. Otherwise, an `IllegalMonitorStateException` will occur.

When `wait()` is invoked, it pauses the thread and simultaneously releases the lock on the object. When the thread is restarted after being notified, the lock is automatically reacquired.

The `wait()`, `notify()`, and `notifyAll()` methods on an object are analogous to the `await()`, `signal()`, and `signalAll()` methods on a condition.

24.12 (Optional) Case Study: Producer/Consumer

Consider the classic Consumer/Producer example. Suppose you use a buffer to store integers. The buffer size is limited. The buffer provides the method `write(int)` to add an `int` value to the buffer and the method `read()` to read and delete an `int` value from the buffer. To synchronize the operations, use a lock with two conditions: `notEmpty` (i.e., buffer is not empty) and `notFull` (i.e., buffer is not full). When a task adds an `int` to the buffer, if the buffer is full, the task will wait for the `notFull` condition. When a task deletes an `int` from the buffer, if the buffer is empty, the task will wait for the `notEmpty` condition. The interaction between the two tasks is shown in Figure 24.19.

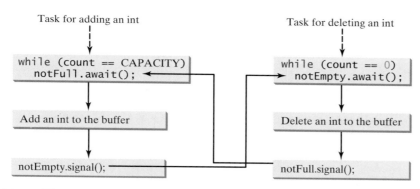

FIGURE 24.19   The conditions `notFull` and `notEmpty` are used to coordinate task interactions.

Listing 24.10 presents the complete program. The program contains the `Buffer` class (lines 48–95) and two tasks for repeatedly producing and consuming numbers to and from the buffer (lines 16–45). The `write(int)` method (line 60) adds an integer to the buffer. The `read()` method (line 77) deletes and returns an integer from the buffer.

For simplicity, the buffer is implemented using a linked list (lines 50–51). Recall that linked list implements the queue interface in JDK 1.5. The conditions `notEmpty` and `notFull` on the lock are created in lines 57–58. The conditions are bound to a lock. A lock must be acquired before a condition can be applied. If you use the `wait()` and `notify()` methods to rewrite this example, you have to designate two objects as monitors.

LISTING 24.10   ConsumerProducer.java

```
1 import java.util.concurrent.*;
2 import java.util.concurrent.locks.*;
3
4 public class ConsumerProducer {
5   private static Buffer buffer = new Buffer();          create a buffer
6
7   public static void main(String[] args) {
8     // Create a thread pool with two threads
```

```
                          9    ExecutorService executor = Executors.newFixedThreadPool(2);
create two threads        10   executor.execute(new ProducerTask());
                          11   executor.execute(new ConsumerTask());
                          12   executor.shutdown();
                          13 }
                          14
                          15 // A task for adding an int to the buffer
producer task             16 private static class ProducerTask implements Runnable {
                          17   public void run() {
                          18     try {
                          19       int i = 1;
                          20       while (true) {
                          21         System.out.println("Producer writes " + i);
                          22         Buffer.write(i++); // Add a value to the buffer
                          23         // Put the thread into sleep
                          24         Thread.sleep((int)(Math.random() * 10000));
                          25       }
                          26     } catch (InterruptedException ex) {
                          27       ex.printStackTrace();
                          28     }
                          29   }
                          30 }
                          31
                          32 // A task for reading and deleting an int from the buffer
consumer task             33 private static class ConsumerTask implements Runnable {
                          34   public void run() {
                          35     try {
                          36       while (true) {
                          37         System.out.println("\t\t\tConsumer reads " + buffer.read());
                          38         // Put the thread into sleep
                          39         Thread.sleep((int)(Math.random() * 10000));
                          40       }
                          41     } catch (InterruptedException ex) {
                          42       ex.printStackTrace();
                          43     }
                          44   }
                          45 }
                          46
                          47 // An inner class for buffer
                          48 private static class Buffer {
                          49   private static final int CAPACITY = 1; // buffer size
                          50   private java.util.LinkedList<Integer> queue =
                          51     new java.util.LinkedList<Integer>();
                          52
                          53   // Create a new lock
create a lock             54   private static Lock lock = new ReentrantLock();
                          55
                          56   // Create two conditions
create a condition        57   private static Condition notEmpty = lock.newCondition();
                          58   private static Condition notFull = lock.newCondition();
                          59
                          60   public void write(int value) {
acquire the lock          61     lock.lock(); // Acquire the lock
                          62     try {
                          63       while (queue.size() == CAPACITY) {
                          64         System.out.println("Wait for notFull condition");
wait on notFull           65         notFull.await();
                          66       }
                          67
```

```
68            queue.offer(value);
69            notEmpty.signal(); // Signal notEmpty condition
70          } catch (InterruptedException ex) {
71            ex.printStackTrace();
72          } finally {
73            lock.unlock(); // Release the lock
74          }
75        }
76
77        public int read() {
78          int value = 0;
79          lock.lock(); // Acquire the lock
80          try {
81            while (queue.isEmpty()) {
82              System.out.println("\t\t\tWait for notEmpty condition");
83              notEmpty.await();
84            }
85
86            value = queue.remove();
87            notFull.signal(); // Signal notFull condition
88          } catch (InterruptedException ex) {
89            ex.printStackTrace();
90          } finally {
91            lock.unlock(); // Release the lock
92            return value;
93          }
94        }
95      }
96    }
```

signal **notEmpty**

release the lock

acquire the lock

wait on **notEmpty**

signal **notFull**

release the lock

A sample run of the program is shown in Figure 24.20.

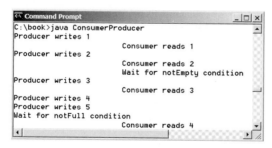

FIGURE 24.20   Locks and conditions are used for communications between the Producer and Consumer threads.

24.13 (Optional) Blocking Queues

The discussion in §22.8 introduced queues and priority queues. A *blocking queue* causes a thread to block when you try to add an element to a full queue or to remove an element from an empty queue. The **BlockingQueue** interface extends **java.util.Queue** and provides the synchronized **put** and **take** methods for adding an element to the head of the queue and for removing an element from the tail of the queue, as shown in Figure 24.21.

blocking queue

Three concrete blocking queues, **ArrayBlockingQueue**, **LinkedBlockingQueue**, and **PriorityBlockingQueue**, are supported in JDK 1.5, as shown in Figure 24.22. All are in the **java.util.concurrent** package. **ArrayBlockingQueue** implements a blocking queue using an array. You have to specify a capacity or an optional fairness to construct an **ArrayBlockingQueue**. **LinkedBlockingQueue** implements a blocking queue using a

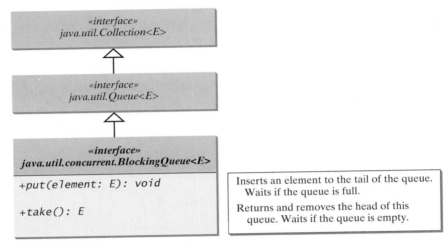

FIGURE 24.21 BlockingQueue is a subinterface of Queue.

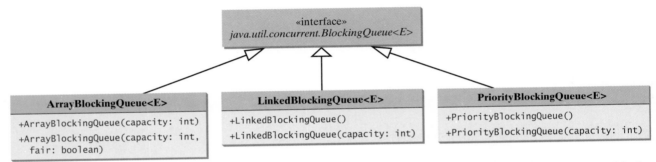

FIGURE 24.22 ArrayBlockingQueue, LinkedBlockingQueue, and PriorityBlockingQueue are concrete blocking queues.

linked list. You may create an unbounded or bounded LinkedBlockingQueue. PriorityBlockingQueue is a priority queue. You may create an unbounded or bounded priority queue.

Note

You may create an unbounded LinkedBlockingQueue or PriorityBlockingQueue. For an *unbounded queue*, the **put** method will never block.

unbounded queue

Listing 24.11 gives an example of using an ArrayBlockingQueue to simplify the Consumer/Producer example in Listing 24.10. Line 5 creates an ArrayBlockingQueue to store integers. The Producer thread puts an integer into the queue (line 22), and the Consumer thread takes an integer from the queue (line 37).

LISTING 24.11 ConsumerProducerUsingBlockingQueue.java

```
1 import java.util.concurrent.*;
2
3 public class ConsumerProducerUsingBlockingQueue {
4   private static ArrayBlockingQueue<Integer> buffer =
5     new ArrayBlockingQueue<Integer>(2);
6
7   public static void main(String[] args) {
8     // Create a thread pool with two threads
```

create a buffer

```
9     ExecutorService executor = Executors.newFixedThreadPool(2);        create two threads
10    executor.execute(new ProducerTask());
11    executor.execute(new ConsumerTask());
12    executor.shutdown();
13  }
14
15  // A task for adding an int to the buffer
16  private static class ProducerTask implements Runnable {               producer task
17    public void run() {
18      try {
19        int i = 1;
20        while (true) {
21          System.out.println("Producer writes " + i);
22          buffer.put(i++); // Add any value to the buffer, say, 1       put
23          // Put the thread into sleep
24          Thread.sleep((int)(Math.random() * 10000));
25        }
26      } catch (InterruptedException ex) {
27        ex.printStackTrace();
28      }
29    }
30  }
31
32  // A task for reading and deleting an int from the buffer
33  private static class ConsumerTask implements Runnable {               consumer task
34    public void run() {
35      try {
36        while (true) {
37          System.out.println("\t\t\tConsumer reads " + buffer.take()); take
38          // Put the thread into sleep
39          Thread.sleep((int)(Math.random() * 10000));
40        }
41      } catch (InterruptedException ex) {
42        ex.printStackTrace();
43      }
44    }
45  }
46 }
```

In Listing 24.10, you used locks and conditions to synchronize the Producer and Consumer threads. In this program, there is no need to hand-code it, because synchronization is already implemented in `ArrayBlockingQueue`.

24.14 (Optional) Semaphores

Semaphores can be used to restrict the number of threads that access a shared resource. Before accessing the resource, a thread must acquire a permit from the semaphore. After finishing with the resource, the thread must return the permit back to the semaphore, as shown in Figure 24.23.

To create a semaphore, you have to specify the number of permits with an optional fairness policy, as shown in Figure 24.24. A task acquires a permit by invoking the semaphore's `acquire()` method and releases the permit by invoking the semaphore's `release()` method. Once a permit is acquired, the total number of available permits in a semaphore is reduced by 1. Once a permit is released, the total number of available permits in a semaphore is increased by 1.

A semaphore with just one permit can be used to simulate a mutually exclusive lock. Listing 24.12 revises the `Account` inner class in Listing 24.10 using a semaphore to ensure that only one thread can access the `deposit` method at a time.

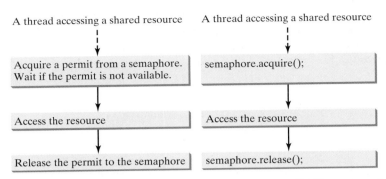

FIGURE 24.23 A limited number of threads can access a shared resource controlled by a semaphore.

java.util.concurrent.Semaphore	
+Semaphore(numberOfPermits: int)	Creates a semaphore with the specified number of permits. The fairness policy is false.
+Semaphore(numberOfPermits: int, fair: boolean)	Creates a semaphore with the specified number of permits and the fairness policy.
+acquire(): void	Acquires a permit from this semaphore. If no permit is available, the thread is blocked until one is available.
+release(): void	Releases a permit back to the semaphore.

FIGURE 24.24 The Semaphore class contains the methods for accessing a semaphore.

LISTING 24.12 New Account Inner Class

```
1  // An inner class for account
2  private static class Account {
3    // Create a semaphore
4    private static Semaphore semaphore = new Semaphore(1);
5    private int balance = 0;
6
7    public int getBalance() {
8      return balance;
9    }
10
11   public void deposit(int amount) {
12     try {
13       semaphore.acquire(); // Acquire a permit
14       int newBalance = balance + amount;
15
16       // This delay is deliberately added to magnify the
17       // data-corruption problem and make it easy to see.
18       Thread.sleep(5);
19
20       balance = newBalance;
21     }
22     catch (InterruptedException ex) {
23     }
24     finally {
25       semaphore.release(); // Release a permit
26     }
27   }
28 }
```

create a semaphore *(line 4)*

acquire a permit *(line 13)*

release a permit *(line 25)*

A semaphore with one permit is created in line 4. A thread first acquires a permit when executing the `deposit` method in line 13. After the balance is updated, the thread releases the permit in line 25. It is a good practice to always place the `release()` method in the `finally` clause to ensure that the permit is finally released even in the case of exceptions.

24.15 Avoiding Deadlocks

Sometimes two or more threads need to acquire the locks on several shared objects. This could cause a *deadlock*, in which each thread has the lock on one of the objects and is waiting for the lock on the other object. Consider the scenario with two threads and two objects, as shown in Figure 24.25. Thread 1 has acquired a lock on `object1`, and Thread 2 has acquired a lock on `object2`. Now Thread 1 is waiting for the lock on `object2`, and Thread 2 for the lock on `object1`. Each thread waits for the other to release the lock it needs, and until that happens neither can continue to run.

deadlock

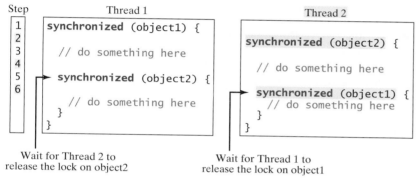

FIGURE 24.25   Thread 1 and Thread 2 are deadlocked.

Deadlock is easily avoided by using a simple technique known as *resource ordering*. With this technique, you assign an order on all the objects whose locks must be acquired and ensure that each thread acquires the locks in that order. For the example in Figure 24.25, suppose that the objects are ordered as `object1` and `object2`. Using the resource ordering technique, Thread 2 must acquire a lock on `object1` first, then on `object2`. Once Thread 1 acquires a lock on `object1`, Thread 2 has to wait for a lock on `object1`. So Thread 1 will be able to acquire a lock on `object2` and no deadlock will occur.

resource ordering

24.16 Thread States

Tasks are executed in threads. Threads can be in one of five states: New, Ready, Running, Blocked, or Finished (see Figure 24.26).

When a thread is newly created, it enters the ***New*** *state*. After a thread is started by calling its `start()` method, it enters the ***Ready*** *state*. A ready thread is runnable but may not be running yet. The operating system has to allocate CPU time to it.

When a ready thread begins executing, it enters the ***Running*** *state*. A running thread may enter the ***Ready*** state if its given CPU time expires or its `yield()` method is called.

A thread can enter the ***Blocked*** *state* (i.e., become inactive) for several reasons. It may have invoked the `join()`, `sleep()`, `wait()`, or `lock()` method, or some other thread may have invoked these methods. It may be waiting for an I/O operation to finish. A blocked thread may be reactivated when the action inactivating it is reversed. For example, if a thread has been put to sleep and the sleep time has expired, the thread is reactivated and enters the **Ready** state.

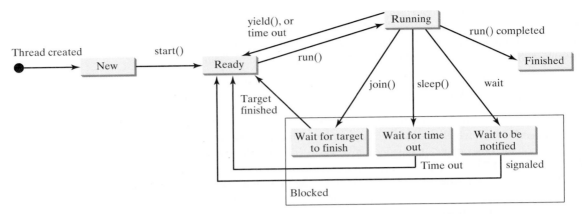

FIGURE 24.26 A thread can be in one of five states: New, Ready, Running, Blocked, or Finished.

Finally, a thread is *finished* if it completes the execution of its `run()` method.

The `isAlive()` method is used to find out the state of a thread. It returns `true` if a thread is in the **Ready**, **Blocked**, or **Running** state; it returns `false` if a thread is new and has not started or if it is finished.

The `interrupt()` method interrupts a thread in the following way: If a thread is currently in the **Ready** or **Running** state, its interrupted flag is set; if a thread is currently blocked, it is awakened and enters the **Ready** state, and a `java.lang.InterruptedException` is thrown.

24.17 Synchronized Collections

The classes in the Java Collections Framework are not thread-safe, that is, their contents may be corrupted if they are accessed and updated concurrently by multiple threads. You can protect the data in a collection by locking the collection or by using synchronized collections.

synchronized collection

The `Collections` class provides six static methods for wrapping a collection into a synchronized version, as shown in Figure 24.27. The collections created using these methods are called *synchronization wrappers*.

synchronization wrapper

java.util.Collections	
+synchronizedCollection(c: Collection): Collection	Returns a synchronized collection.
+synchronizedList(list: List): List	Returns a synchronized list from the specified list.
+synchronizedMap(m: Map): Map	Returns a synchronized map from the specified map.
+synchronizedSet(s: Set): Set	Returns a synchronized set from the specified set.
+synchronizedSortedMap(s: SortedMap): SortedMap	Returns a synchronized sorted map from the specified sorted map.
+synchronizedSortedSet(s: SortedSet): SortedSet	Returns a synchronized sorted set.

FIGURE 24.27 You can obtain synchronized collections using the methods in the `Collections` class.

Invoking `synchronizedCollection(Collection c)` returns a new `Collection` object, in which all the methods that access and update the original collection `c` are synchronized. These methods are implemented using the `synchronized` keyword . For example, the `add` method is implemented like this:

```java
public boolean add(E o) {
    synchronized (this) { return c.add(o); }
}
```

Synchronized collections can be safely accessed and modified by multiple threads concurrently.

Note

The methods in `java.util.Vector`, `java.util.Stack`, and `java.util.Hashtable` are already synchronized. These are old classes introduced in JDK 1.0. In JDK 1.5, you should use `java.util.ArrayList` to replace `Vector`, `java.util.LinkedList` to replace `Stack`, and `java.util.Map` to replace `java.util.Hashtable`. If synchronization is needed, use a synchronization wrapper.

The synchronization wrapper classes are thread-safe, but the iterator is *fail-fast*. This means that if you are using an iterator to traverse a collection while the underlying collection is being modified by another thread, then the iterator will immediately fail by throwing `java.util.ConcurrentModificationException`, which is a subclass of `RuntimeException`. To avoid this error, you need to create a synchronized collection object and acquire a lock on the object when traversing it. For example, suppose you want to traverse a set, you have to write the code like this:

fail-fast

```
Set hashSet = Collections.synchronizedSet(new HashSet());
synchronized (hashSet) { // Must synchronize it
  Iterator iterator = hashSet.iterator();

  while (iterator.hasNext()) {
    System.out.println(iterator.next());
  }
}
```

Failure to do so may result in nondeterministic behavior, such as `Concurrent-ModificationException`.

24.18 (Optional) **JProgressBar**

`JProgressBar` is a component that displays a value graphically within a bounded interval. A progress bar is typically used to show the percentage of completion of a lengthy operation; it comprises a rectangular bar that is "filled in" from left to right horizontally or from bottom to top vertically as the operation is performed. It provides the user with feedback on the progress of the operation. For example, when a file is being read, it alerts the user to the progress of the operation, thereby keeping the user attentive.

`JProgressBar` is often implemented using a thread to monitor the completion status of other threads. The progress bar can be displayed horizontally or vertically, as determined by its `orientation` property. The `minimum`, `value`, and `maximum` properties determine the minimum, current, and maximum lengths on the progress bar, as shown in Figure 24.28. Figure 24.29 lists frequently used features of `JProgressBar`.

$$percentComplete = \frac{value}{maximum}$$

FIGURE 24.28 `JProgressBar` displays the progress of a task.

To demonstrate `JProgressBar`, let us write a GUI application that copies files. A progress bar is used to show the progress of the copying operation, as shown in Figure 24.30.

Place a `JProgressBar` in the north of the frame. Place a button in a panel, and place the panel in the south of the frame. Place the two text fields in two panels, set the titles on the borders of the panels, and place the panels in another panel of the `GridLayout` with two rows. Place the panel in the center of the frame.

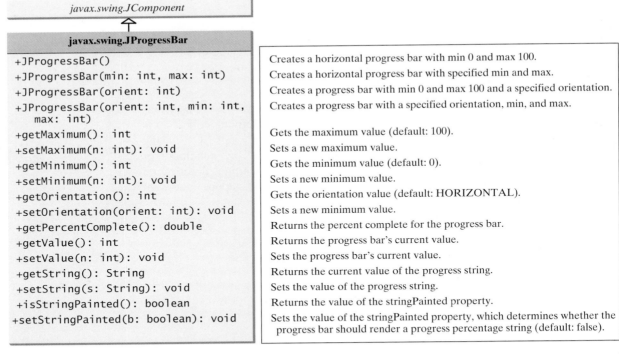

FIGURE 24.29 `JProgressBar` is a Swing component with many properties that enable you to customize a progress bar.

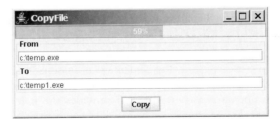

FIGURE 24.30 The user enters the files in the text fields and clicks the Copy button to start copying files.

While copying the data from a source file to a destination file on one thread, the progress bar is updated on another thread. You need to create a thread that copies a file and another thread that updates the progress bar. Every time some bytes of the file are copied, the current value in the progress bar is updated to show the progress.

Create a main class named `CopyFile` that lays out the user interface. Declare an inner class named `CopyFileTask` that implements `Runnable` to copy files. When the Copy button is pressed, a thread for copying a file is created and started in line 41. The progress bar is updated in line 87 as a file is being copied. The complete program is given in Listing 24.13.

LISTING 24.13 CopyFile.java

```
1 import java.awt.*;
2 import java.awt.event.*;
3 import javax.swing.*;
4 import javax.swing.border.*;
5 import java.io.*;
6
7 public class CopyFile extends JFrame {
8    private JProgressBar jpb = new JProgressBar();
```

progress bar

```
9    private JButton jbtCopy = new JButton("Copy");
10   private JTextField jtfFrom = new JTextField();
11   private JTextField jtfTo = new JTextField();
12
13   public CopyFile() {
14     JPanel jPanel2 = new JPanel();
15     jPanel2.setLayout(new BorderLayout());
16     jPanel2.setBorder(new TitledBorder("From"));
17     jPanel2.add(jtfFrom, BorderLayout.CENTER);
18
19     JPanel jPanel3 = new JPanel();
20     jPanel3.setLayout(new BorderLayout());
21     jPanel3.setBorder(new TitledBorder("To"));
22     jPanel3.add(jtfTo, BorderLayout.CENTER);
23
24     JPanel jPanel1 = new JPanel();
25     jPanel1.setLayout(new GridLayout(2, 1));
26     jPanel1.add(jPanel2);
27     jPanel1.add(jPanel3);
28
29     JPanel jPanel4 = new JPanel();
30     jPanel4.add(jbtCopy);
31
32     this.add(jpb, BorderLayout.NORTH);
33     this.add(jPanel1, BorderLayout.CENTER);
34     this.add(jPanel4, BorderLayout.SOUTH);
35
36     jpb.setStringPainted(true); // Paint the percent in a string
37
38     jbtCopy.addActionListener(new ActionListener() {
39       public void actionPerformed(ActionEvent e) {
40         // Create a thread for copying files
41         new Thread(new CopyFileTask()).start();
42       }
43     });
44   }
45
46   public static void main(String[] args) {
47     CopyFile frame = new CopyFile();
48     frame.setDefaultCloseOperation(JFrame.EXIT_ON_CLOSE);
49     frame.setTitle("CopyFile");
50     frame.setSize(400, 180);
51     frame.setVisible(true);
52   }
53
54   // Copy file and update progress bar in a separate thread
55   class CopyFileTask implements Runnable {
56     private int currentValue;
57
58     public void run() {
59       BufferedInputStream in = null;
60       BufferedOutputStream out = null;
61       try {
62         // Create file input stream
63         File inFile = new File(jtfFrom.getText().trim());
64         in = new BufferedInputStream(new FileInputStream(inFile));
65
66         // Create file output stream
67         File outFile = new File(jtfTo.getText());
68         out = new BufferedOutputStream(new FileOutputStream(outFile));
```

create UI

thread class

```
69
70          // Get total bytes in the file
71          long totalBytes = in.available();
72
73          // Start progress meter bar
74          jpb.setValue(0);
75          jpb.setMaximum(100);
76
77          int r;
78          long bytesRead = 0;
79          // You may increase buffer size to improve IO speed
80          byte[] b = new byte[10];
81          while ((r = in.read(b, 0, b.length)) != -1) {
82            out.write(b, 0, r);
83            bytesRead += r;
84            currentValue = (int)(bytesRead * 100 / totalBytes);
85
86            // Update the progress bar
87            jpb.setValue(currentValue);
88          }
89        }
90        catch (FileNotFoundException ex) {
91          ex.printStackTrace();
92        }
93        catch (IOException ex) {
94          ex.printStackTrace();
95        }
96        finally {
97          try {
98            if (in != null) in.close();
99            if (out != null) out.close();
100          }
101          catch (Exception ex) {}
102        }
103      }
104    }
105 }
```

progress bar value

The class **CopyFileTask** is a task class. The program creates a task for copying a file on a separate thread. What would happen if copying a file is not run on a separate thread? The progress bar will not be updated until the copy ends. This is because the operation for repainting the progress bar runs on the thread with the **actionPerformed** method. As long as the copy operation continues, the progress bar never gets a chance to be repainted. Running the copy operation on a separate thread will enable the progress bar to be repainted simultaneously with the copy operation.

KEY TERMS

condition   793
deadlock   803
event dispatcher thread   781
fail-fast   805
fairness policy   791
lock   790
monitor   796

multithreading   774
race condition   789
synchronization wrapper   804
synchronized   789
thread   774
thread-safe   789

CHAPTER SUMMARY

■ Each task is an instance of the `Runnable` interface. A *thread* is an object that facilitates the execution of a task. You can declare a task class by implementing the `Runnable` interface and create a thread by wrapping a task using a `Thread` constructor.

■ After a thread object is created, use the `start()` method to start a thread, and the `sleep(long)` method to put a thread to sleep so that other threads get a chance to run.

■ A thread object never directly invokes the `run` method. The JVM invokes the `run` method when it is time to execute the thread. Your class must override the `run` method to tell the system what the thread will do when it runs.

■ To prevent threads from corrupting a shared resource, use synchronized methods or blocks. A synchronized method acquires a lock before it executes. In the case of an instance method, the lock is on the object for which the method was invoked. In the case of a static (class) method, the lock is on the class.

■ A synchronized statement can be used to acquire a lock on any object, not just *this* object, when executing a block of the code in a method. This block is referred to as a *synchronized block*.

■ You can use explicit locks and conditions to facilitate the communications among threads, as well as using the built-in monitor for objects.

■ *Deadlock* occurs when two or more threads acquire locks on multiple objects and each has a lock on one object and is waiting for the lock on the other object. The *resource ordering technique* can be used to avoid deadlock.

■ You can use a `JProgressBar` to track the progress of a thread.

REVIEW QUESTIONS

Sections 24.1–24.4

24.1 Why do you need multithreading? How can multiple threads run simultaneously in a single-processor system?

24.2 How do you declare a task class? How do you create a thread for a task?

24.3 What would happen if you replace the `start()` method by the `run()` method in lines 14–16 in Listing 24.1?

```
print100.start();          print100.run();
printA.start();            printA.run();
printB.start();            printB.run();
```
Replaced by

24.4 What is wrong in the following two programs? Correct the errors.

```
public class Test implements Runnable {
  public static void main(String[] args) {
    new Test();
  }

  public Test() {
    Test task = new Test();
    new Thread(task).start();
  }

  public void run(){
    System.out.println("test");
  }
}
```

(a)

```
public class Test implements Runnable {
  public static void main(String[] args) {
    newTest();
  }

  public Test() {
    Thread t = new Thread(this);
    t.start();
    t.start();
  }

  public void run() {
    System.out.println("test");
  }
}
```

(b)

24.5 Which of the following methods are instance methods in `java.lang.Thread`? Which method may throw an `InterruptedException`? Which of them are deprecated in Java 2?

run, start, stop, suspend, resume, sleep, interrupt, yield, join

24.6 If a loop contains a method that throws an `InterruptedException`, why should the loop be placed inside a `try-catch` block?

24.7 How do you set a priority for a thread? What is the default priority?

Sections 24.5–24.7

24.8 When should you use a timer or a thread to control animation? What are the advantages and disadvantages of using a thread and a timer?

24.9 What is the event dispatcher thread? How do you let a task run from the event dispatcher thread?

Section 24.8 Thread Pools

24.10 What are the benefits of using a thread pool?

24.11 How do you create a thread pool with three fixed threads? How do you submit a task to the thread pool? How do you know that all the tasks are finished?

Sections 24.9–24.12

24.12 Give some examples of possible resource corruption when running multiple threads. How do you synchronize conflicting threads?

24.13 Suppose you place the statement in line 26 of Listing 24.7, AccountWithoutSync.java, inside a synchronized block to avoid race conditions, as follows:

```
synchronized (this) {
  account.deposit(1);
}
```

Does it work?

24.14 How do you create a lock object? How do you acquire a lock and release a lock?

24.15 How do you create a condition on a lock? What are the `await()`, `signal()`, and `signalAll()` methods for?

24.16 What would happen if the `while` loop in lines 58–59 of Listing 24.9, ThreadCooperation.java, is changed to an `if` statement?

```
while (balance < amount)      Replaced by      if (balance < amount)
    wait();                                        wait();
```

24.17 Why does the following class have a syntax error?

```java
 1 import javax.swing.*;
 2
 3 public class Test extends JApplet implements Runnable {
 4   public void init() throws InterruptedException {
 5     Thread thread = new Thread(this);
 6     thread.sleep(1000);
 7   }
 8
 9   public synchronized void run() {
10   }
11 }
```

24.18 What is the possible cause for `IllegalMonitorStateException`?

24.19 Can `wait()`, `notify()`, and `notifyAll()` be invoked from any object? What is the purpose of these methods?

24.20 What is wrong in the following code?

```java
synchronized (object1) {
  try {
    while (!condition) object2.wait();
  }
  catch (InterruptedException ex) {
  }
}
```

Section 24.13 Blocking Queues

24.21 What blocking queues are supported in JDK 1.5?

24.22 What method do you use to add an element to an `ArrayBlockingQueue`? What happens if the queue is full?

24.23 What method do you use to retrieve an element from an `ArrayBlockingQueue`? What happens if the queue is empty?

Section 24.14 Semaphores

24.24 What are the similarities and differences between a lock and a semaphore?

24.25 How do you create a semaphore that allows three concurrent threads? How do you acquire a semaphore? How do you release a semaphore?

Section 24.15 Avoiding Deadlocks

24.26 What is deadlock? How can you avoid deadlock?

Section 24.17 Synchronized Collections

24.27 What is a synchronized collection? Is `ArrayList` synchronized? How do you make it synchronized?

24.28 Explain why an iterator is fail-fast.

Section 24.18 JProgressBar

24.29 For a JProgressBar, what is the property that displays the percentage of work completed? How do you set its orientation?

PROGRAMMING EXERCISES

Sections 24.1–24.5

24.1* *(Revising Listing 24.1)* Rewrite Listing 24.1 to display the output in a text area, as shown in Figure 24.31.

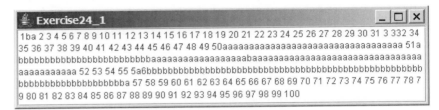

FIGURE 24.31 The output from three threads is displayed in a text area.

24.2 *(Racing cars)* Rewrite Exercise 16.17 using a thread to control car racing. Compare the program with Exercise 16.17 by setting the delay time to 10 in both programs. Which one runs animation faster?

24.3 *(Raising flags)* Rewrite Exercise 16.23 using a thread to animate flag rising. Compare the program with Exercise 16.23 by setting the delay time to 10 in both programs. Which one runs animation faster?

Sections 24.8–24.12

24.4 *(Synchronizing threads)* Write a program that launches one thousand threads. Each thread adds 1 to a variable sum that initially is zero. You need to pass sum by reference to each thread. In order to pass it by reference, define an Integer wrapper object to hold sum. Run the program with and without synchronization to see its effect.

24.5 *(Running fans)* Rewrite Exercise 16.11 using a thread to control fan animation.

24.6 *(Bouncing balls)* Rewrite Exercise 16.19 using a thread to animate ball movements.

24.7 *(Controlling a group of clocks)* Rewrite Exercise 16.14 using a thread to control clock animation.

24.8 *(Account synchronization)* Rewrite Listing 24.9, ThreadCoorperation.java, using object's wait() and notifyAll() methods.

24.9 *(Demonstrating ConcurrentModificationException)* The iterator is *fail-fast*. Write a program to demonstrate it by creating two threads that concurrently access and modify a set. The first thread creates a hash set filled with numbers, and adds a new number to the set every second. The second thread obtains an iterator for the set and traverses the set back and forth through the iterator every second. You will receive a ConcurrentModificationException because the underlying set is being modified in the first thread while the set in the second thread is being traversed.

24.10* (*Using synchronized sets*) Using synchronization, correct the problem in the preceding exercise so that the second thread does not throw `Concurrent-ModificationException`.

Section 24.15 Avoiding Deadlocks

24.11* (*Demonstrating deadlock*) Write a program that demonstrates deadlock.

Section 24.18 `JProgressBar`

24.12* (*Using JProgressBar*) Create a program that displays an instance of `JProgressBar` and sets its `value` property randomly every 500 milliseconds infinitely.

NETWORKING

Objectives

- To comprehend socket-based communication in Java (§25.2).
- To understand client/server computing (§25.2).
- To implement Java networking programs using stream sockets (§25.2).
- To obtain Internet addresses using the `InetAddress` class (§25.3).
- To develop servers for multiple clients (§25.4).
- To develop applets that communicate with the server (§25.5).
- To send and receive objects on a network (§25.6).
- To create applications or applets to retrieve files from a network (§25.7).
- To render HTML files using the `JEditorPane` class (§25.8).
- (Optional) To implement Java networking programs using datagram sockets (§25.10).

25.1 Introduction

To browse the Web or send email, your computer must be connected to the Internet. The Internet is the global network of millions of computers. Your computer may connect to the Internet through an Internet Service Provider (ISP) using dialup, DSL, or cable modem, or through a local area network (LAN).

IP address

When a computer needs to communicate with another computer, it needs to know the address of the other computer. This is called an *Internet Protocol* (IP) address that uniquely identifies the computer on the Internet. An *IP address* consists of four dotted decimal numbers between 0 and 255, such as 130.254.204.36. Since it is not easy to remember so many numbers, they are often mapped to meaningful names called *domain names*, such as drake.armstrong.edu. There are special servers on the Internet that translate host names into IP addresses. These servers are called *Domain Name Servers* (DNS). When a computer contacts drake.armstrong.edu, it first asks the DNS to translate this domain name into a numeric IP address and then sends the request using the IP address.

domain name

domain name server

TCP

The Internet Protocol is a low-level protocol for delivering data from one computer to another across the Internet in packets. Two higher-level protocols used in conjunction with the IP are the *Transmission Control Protocol* (*TCP*) and the *User Datagram Protocol* (UDP). TCP enables two hosts to establish a connection and exchange streams of data. TCP guarantees delivery of data and also guarantees that packets will be delivered in the same order in which they were sent. UDP is a standard, low-overhead, connectionless, host-to-host protocol that is used over the IP. UDP allows an application program on one computer to send a datagram to an application program on another computer.

stream socket
datagram socket

Java supports stream sockets and datagram sockets. *Stream sockets* use TCP (Transmission Control Protocol) for data transmission, whereas *datagram sockets* use UDP (User Datagram Protocol). Since TCP can detect lost transmissions and resubmit them, transmissions are lossless and reliable. UDP, in contrast, cannot guarantee lossless transmission. Because of this, stream sockets are used in most areas of Java programming, and that is why the most of discussion in this chapter is based on stream sockets. Datagram socket programming is introduced in the last section of the chapter.

25.2 Client/Server Computing

socket-based

Networking is tightly integrated in Java. *Socket-based communication* is provided that enables programs to communicate through designated sockets. *Sockets* are the endpoints of logical connections between two hosts and can be used to send and receive data. Java treats socket communications much as it treats I/O operations; thus programs can read from or write to sockets as easily as they can read from or write to files.

Network programming usually involves a server and one or more clients. The client sends requests to the server, and the server responds to the requests. The client begins by attempting to establish a connection to the server. The server can accept or deny the connection. Once a connection is established, the client and the server communicate through sockets.

The server must be running when a client starts. The server waits for a connection request from a client. The statements needed to create a server and a client are shown in Figure 25.1.

25.2.1 Server Sockets

To establish a server, you need to create a *server socket* and attach it to a port, which is where the server listens for connections. The port identifies the TCP service on the socket. Port numbers range from 0 to 65536, but port numbers 0 to 1024 are reserved for privileged services. For instance, the email server runs on port 25, and the Web server usually runs on port 80.

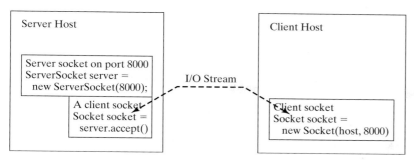

FIGURE 25.1 The server creates a server socket and, once a connection to a client is established, connects to the client with a client socket.

You can choose any port number that is not currently used by any other process. The following statement creates a server socket `serverSocket`:

```
ServerSocket serverSocket = new ServerSocket(port);
```

server socket

Note

Attempting to create a server socket on a port already in use would cause the `java.net.BindException`.

BindException

25.2.2 Client Sockets

After a server socket is created, the server can use the following statement to listen for connections:

```
Socket socket = serverSocket.accept();
```

This statement waits until a client connects to the server socket. The client issues the following statement to request a connection to a server:

connect to client

```
Socket socket = new Socket(serverName, port);
```

This statement opens a socket so that the client program can communicate with the server. *serverName* is the server's Internet host name or IP address. The following statement creates a socket at port `8000` on the client machine to connect to the host `130.254.204.36`:

client socket

```
Socket socket = new Socket("130.254.204.36", 8000)
```

Alternatively, you can use the domain name to create a socket, as follows:

use IP address

```
Socket socket = new Socket("drake.armstrong.edu", 8000);
```

When you create a socket with a host name, the JVM asks the DNS to translate the host name into the IP address.

use domain name

Note

A program can use the host name `localhost` or the IP address `127.0.0.1` to refer to the machine on which a client is running.

localhost

Note

The `Socket` constructor throws a `java.net.UnknownHostException` if the host cannot be found.

UnknownHostException

25.2.3 Data Transmission through Sockets

After the server accepts the connection, communication between server and client is conducted the same as for I/O streams. The statements needed to create the streams and to exchange data between them are shown in Figure 25.2.

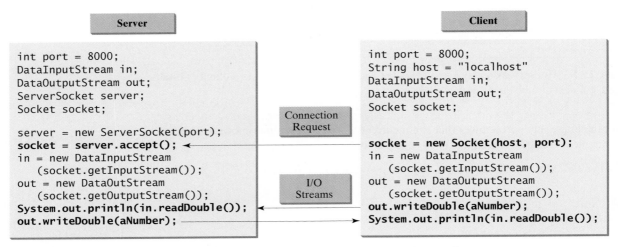

FIGURE 25.2 The server and client exchange data through I/O streams on top of the socket.

To get an input stream and an output stream, use the `getInputStream()` and `getOutputStream()` methods on a socket object. For example, the following statements create an `InputStream` stream called `input` and an `OutputStream` stream called `output` from a socket:

```
InputStream input = socket.getInputStream();
OutputStream output = socket.getOutputStream();
```

The `InputStream` and `OutputStream` streams are used to read or write bytes. You can use `DataInputStream`, `DataOutputStream`, `BufferedReader`, and `PrintWriter` to wrap on the `InputStream` and `OutputStream` to read or write data, such as `int`, `double`, or `String`. The following statements, for instance, create a `DataInputStream` stream, `input`, and a `DataOutput` stream, `output`, to read and write primitive data values:

```
DataInputStream input = new DataInputStream
   (socket.getInputStream());
DataOutputStream output = new DataOutputStream
   (socket.getOutputStream());
```

The server can use `input.readDouble()` to receive a double value from the client, and `output.writeDouble(d)` to send double value `d` to the client.

 Tip

Recall that binary I/O is more efficient than text I/O because text I/O requires encoding and decoding. Therefore it is better to use binary I/O for transmitting data between a server and a client to improve performance.

25.2.4 A Client/Server Example

This example presents a client program and a server program. The client sends data to a server. The server receives the data, uses it to produce a result, and then sends the result back to the client. The client displays the result on the console. In this example, the data sent from the client comprises the radius of a circle, and the result produced by the server is the area of the circle (see Figure 25.3).

FIGURE 25.3   The client sends the radius to the server; the server computes the area and sends it to the client.

The client sends the radius through a `DataOutputStream` on the output stream socket, and the server receives the radius through the `DataInputStream` on the input stream socket, as shown in Figure 25.4(a). The server computes the area and sends it to the client through a `DataOutputStream` on the output stream socket, and the client receives the area through a `DataInputStream` on the input stream socket, as shown in Figure 25.4(b). The server and client programs are given in Listings 25.1 and 25.2. Figure 25.5 contains a sample run of the server and the client.

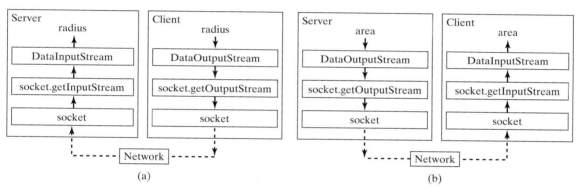

FIGURE 25.4   (a) The client sends the radius to the server. (b) The server sends the area to the client.

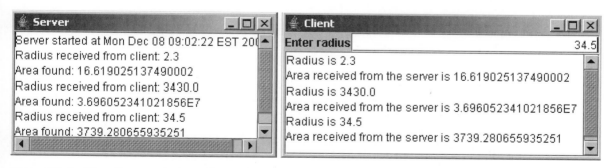

FIGURE 25.5   The client sends the radius to the server. The server receives it, computes the area, and sends the area to the client.

LISTING 25.1   Server.java

```
1 import java.io.*;
2 import java.net.*;
3 import java.util.*;
4 import java.awt.*;
5 import javax.swing.*;
6
```

```
 7 public class Server extends JFrame {
 8   // Text area for displaying contents
 9   private JTextArea jta = new JTextArea();
10
11   public static void main(String[] args) {
12     new Server();
13   }
14
15   public Server() {
16     // Place text area on the frame
17     setLayout(new BorderLayout());
18     add(new JScrollPane(jta), BorderLayout.CENTER);
19
20     setTitle("Server");
21     setSize(500, 300);
22     setDefaultCloseOperation(JFrame.EXIT_ON_CLOSE);
23     setVisible(true); // It is necessary to show the frame here!
24
25     try {
26       // Create a server socket
27       ServerSocket serverSocket = new ServerSocket(8000);
28       jta.append("Server started at " + new Date() + '\n');
29
30       // Listen for a connection request
31       Socket socket = serverSocket.accept();
32
33       // Create data input and output streams
34       DataInputStream inputFromClient = new DataInputStream(
35         socket.getInputStream());
36       DataOutputStream outputToClient = new DataOutputStream(
37         socket.getOutputStream());
38
39       while (true) {
40         // Receive radius from the client
41         double radius = inputFromClient.readDouble();
42
43         // Compute area
44         double area = radius * radius * Math.PI;
45
46         // Send area back to the client
47         outputToClient.writeDouble(area);
48
49         jta.append("Radius received from client: " + radius + '\n');
50         jta.append("Area found: " + area + '\n');
51       }
52     }
53     catch(IOException ex) {
54       System.err.println(ex);
55     }
56   }
57 }
```

The following marginal notes appear alongside the code:

- launch server (line 12)
- server socket (line 27)
- connect client (line 31)
- input from client (line 34)
- output to client (line 36)
- read radius (line 41)
- write area (line 47)

LISTING 25.2 Client.java

```
1 import java.io.*;
2 import java.net.*;
3 import java.awt.*;
4 import java.awt.event.*;
5 import javax.swing.*;
6
```

```java
 7 public class Client extends JFrame {
 8   // Text field for receiving radius
 9   private JTextField jtf = new JTextField();
10
11   // Text area to display contents
12   private JTextArea jta = new JTextArea();
13
14   // IO streams
15   private DataOutputStream toServer;
16   private DataInputStream fromServer;
17
18   public static void main(String[] args) {
19     new Client();                                          launch client
20   }
21
22   public Client() {
23     // Panel p to hold the label and text field
24     JPanel p = new JPanel();
25     p.setLayout(new BorderLayout());
26     p.add(new JLabel("Enter radius"), BorderLayout.WEST);
27     p.add(jtf, BorderLayout.CENTER);
28     jtf.setHorizontalAlignment(JTextField.RIGHT);
29
30     setLayout(new BorderLayout());
31     add(p, BorderLayout.NORTH);
32     add(new JScrollPane(jta), BorderLayout.CENTER);
33
34     jtf.addActionListener(new ButtonListener()); // Register listener    register listener
35
36     setTitle("Client");
37     setSize(500, 300);
38     setDefaultCloseOperation(JFrame.EXIT_ON_CLOSE);
39     setVisible(true); // It is necessary to show the frame here!
40
41     try {
42       // Create a socket to connect to the server
43       Socket socket = new Socket("localhost", 8000);          request connection
44       // Socket socket = new Socket("130.254.204.36", 8000);
45       // Socket socket = new Socket("drake.Armstrong.edu", 8000);
46
47       // Create an input stream to receive data from the server
48       fromServer = new DataInputStream(                        input from server
49         socket.getInputStream());
50
51       // Create an output stream to send data to the server
52       toServer =                                               output to server
53         new DataOutputStream(socket.getOutputStream());
54     }
55     catch (IOException ex) {
56       jta.append(ex.toString() + '\n');
57     }
58   }
59
60   private class ButtonListener implements ActionListener {
61     public void actionPerformed(ActionEvent e) {
62       try {
63         // Get the radius from the text field
64         double radius = Double.parseDouble(jtf.getText().trim());
65
66         // Send the radius to the server
```

write radius

read radius

```
67            toServer.writeDouble(radius);
68            toServer.flush();
69
70            // Get area from the server
71            double area = fromServer.readDouble();
72
73            // Display to the text area
74            jta.append("Radius is " + radius + "\n");
75            jta.append("Area received from the server is "
76              + area + '\n');
77        }
78        catch (IOException ex) {
79          System.err.println(ex);
80        }
81      }
82    }
83  }
```

You start the server program first, then start the client program. In the client program, enter a radius in the text field and press Enter to send the radius to the server. The server computes the area and sends it back to the client. This process is repeated until one of the two programs terminates.

The networking classes are in the package `java.net`. This should be imported when writing Java network programs.

The `Server` class creates a `ServerSocket serverSocket` and attaches it to port 8000, using this statement (line 27 in Server.java):

```
ServerSocket serverSocket = new ServerSocket(8000);
```

The server then starts to listen for connection requests, using the following statement (line 31 in Server.java):

```
Socket socket = serverSocket.accept();
```

The server waits until a client requests a connection. After it is connected, the server reads the radius from the client through an input stream, computes the area, and sends the result to the client through an output stream.

The `Client` class uses the following statement to create a socket that will request a connection to the server on the same machine (localhost) at port 8000 (line 43 in Client.java):

```
Socket socket = new Socket("localhost", 8000);
```

If you run the server and the client on different machines, replace `localhost` with the server machine's host name or IP address. In this example, the server and the client are running on the same machine.

If the server is not running, the client program terminates with a `java.net.ConnectException`. After it is connected, the client gets input and output streams—wrapped by data input and output streams—in order to receive and send data to the server.

If you receive a `java.net.BindException` when you start the server, the server port is currently in use. You need to terminate the process that is using the server port and then restart the server.

What happens if the `setVisible(true)` statement in line 23 in Server.java is moved after the `try-catch` block in line 56 in Server.java? The frame would not be displayed, because the `while` loop in the `try-catch` block will not finish until the program terminates.

25.3 The `InetAddress` Class

Occasionally, you would like to know who is connecting to the server. You can use the `InetAddress` class to find the client's host name and IP address. The `InetAddress` class models an IP address. You can use the statement shown below to create an instance of `InetAddress` for the client on a socket:

```
InetAddress inetAddress = socket.getInetAddress();
```

Next, you can display the client's host name and IP address, as follows:

```
System.out.println("Client's host name is " +
  inetAddress.getHostName());
System.out.println("Client's IP Address is " +
  inetAddress.getHostAddress());
```

You can also create an instance of `InetAddress` from a host name or IP address using the static `getByName` method. For example, the following statement creates an `InetAddress` for the host `liang.armstrong.edu`:

```
InetAddress address = InetAddress.getByName("liang.armstrong.edu");
```

Listing 25.3 gives a program that identifies the host name and IP address of the arguments you pass in from the command line. Line 7 creates an `InetAddress` using the `getByName` method. Lines 8–9 use the `getHostName` and `getHostAddress` methods to get the host name and IP address. Figure 25.6 shows a sample run of the program.

LISTING 25.3   IdentifyHostNameIP.java

```
 1  import java.net.*;
 2
 3  public class IdentifyHostNameIP {
 4    public static void main(String[] args) {
 5      for (int i = 0; i < args.length; i++) {
 6        try {
 7          InetAddress address = InetAddress.getByName(args[i]);      get an InetAddress
 8          System.out.println("Host name: " + address.getHostName());  get host name
 9          System.out.println("IP address: " + address.getHostAddress() );  get host IP
10        }
11        catch (UnknownHostException ex) {
12          System.err.println("Unknown host or IP address " + args[i]);
13        }
14      }
15    }
16  }
```

```
Command Prompt                                      _ □ x
C:\book>java IdentifyHostNameIP www.whitehouse.gov 130.254.204.34
Host name: www.whitehouse.gov
IP address: 199.77.203.17
Host name: panda.Armstrong.EDU
IP address: 130.254.204.34

C:\book>_
```

FIGURE 25.6   The program identifies host names and IP addresses.

25.4 Serving Multiple Clients

Multiple clients are quite often connected to a single server at the same time. Typically, a server runs constantly on a server computer, and clients from all over the Internet may want to connect to it. You can use threads to handle the server's multiple clients simultaneously. Simply create a thread for each connection. Here is how the server handles a connection:

```
while (true) {
   Socket socket = serverSocket.accept();
   Thread thread = new ThreadClass(socket);
   thread.start();
}
```

The server socket can have many connections. Each iteration of the `while` loop creates a new connection. Whenever a connection is established, a new thread is created to handle communication between the server and the new client; and this allows multiple connections to run at the same time.

Listing 25.4 creates a server class that serves multiple clients simultaneously. For each connection, the server starts a new thread. This thread continuously receives input (the radius of a circle) from clients and sends the results (the area of the circle) back to them (see Figure 25.7). The client program is the same as in Listing 25.2. A sample run of the server with two clients is shown in Figure 25.8.

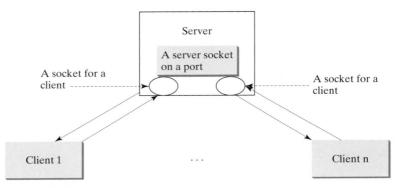

FIGURE 25.7 Multithreading enables a server to handle multiple independent clients.

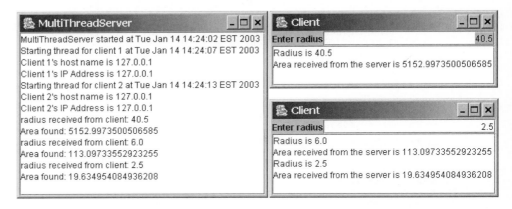

FIGURE 25.8 The server spawns a thread in order to serve a client.

LISTING 25.4 MultiThreadServer.java

```
1 import java.io.*;
2 import java.net.*;
3 import java.util.*;
4 import java.awt.*;
5 import javax.swing.*;
6
7 public class MultiThreadServer extends JFrame {
```

```
 8      // Text area for displaying contents
 9      private JTextArea jta = new JTextArea();
10
11      public static void main(String[] args) {
12        new MultiThreadServer();
13      }
14
15      public MultiThreadServer() {
16        // Place text area on the frame
17        setLayout(new BorderLayout());
18        add(new JScrollPane(jta), BorderLayout.CENTER);
19
20        setTitle("MultiThreadServer");
21        setSize(500, 300);
22        setDefaultCloseOperation(JFrame.EXIT_ON_CLOSE);
23        setVisible(true); // It is necessary to show the frame here!
24
25        try {
26          // Create a server socket
27          ServerSocket serverSocket = new ServerSocket(8000);          server socket
28          jta.append("MultiThreadServer started at " + new Date() + '\n');
29
30          // Number a client
31          int clientNo = 1;
32
33          while (true) {
34            // Listen for a new connection request
35            Socket socket = serverSocket.accept();                     connect client
36
37            // Display the client number
38            jta.append("Starting thread for client " + clientNo +
39              " at " + new Date() + '\n');
40
41            // Find the client's host name, and IP address
42            InetAddress inetAddress = socket.getInetAddress();          network information
43            jta.append("Client " + clientNo + "'s host name is "
44              + inetAddress.getHostName() + "\n");
45            jta.append("Client " + clientNo + "'s IP Address is "
46              + inetAddress.getHostAddress() + "\n");
47
48            // Create a new task for the connection
49            HandleAClient task = new HandleAClient(socket);             create thread
50
51            // Start the new thread
52            task.start();                                              start thread
53
54            // Increment clientNo
55            clientNo++;
56          }
57        }
58        catch(IOException ex) {
59          System.err.println(ex);
60        }
61      }
62
63      // Inner class
64      // Define the thread class for handling new connection
65      class HandleAClient implements Runnable {                        thread class
66        private Socket socket; // A connected socket
67
```

I/O

```
68      /** Construct a thread */
69      public HandleAClient(Socket socket) {
70        this.socket = socket;
71      }
72
73      /** Run a thread */
74      public void run() {
75        try {
76          // Create data input and output streams
77          DataInputStream inputFromClient = new DataInputStream(
78            socket.getInputStream());
79          DataOutputStream outputToClient = new DataOutputStream(
80            socket.getOutputStream());
81
82          // Continuously serve the client
83          while (true) {
84            // Receive radius from the client
85            double radius = inputFromClient.readDouble();
86
87            // Compute area
88            double area = radius * radius * Math.PI;
89
90            // Send area back to the client
91            outputToClient.writeDouble(area);
92
93            jta.append("radius received from client: " +
94              radius + '\n');
95            jta.append("Area found: " + area + '\n');
96          }
97        }
98        catch(IOException e) {
99          System.err.println(e);
100        }
101      }
102    }
103  }
```

The server creates a server socket at port 8000 (line 27) and waits for a connection (line 35). When a connection with a client is established, the server creates a new thread to handle the communication (line 49). It then waits for another connection in an infinite `while` loop (lines 33–56).

The threads, which run independently of one another, communicate with designated clients. Each thread creates data input and output streams that receive and send data to a client.

This server accepts an unlimited number of clients. To limit the number of concurrent connections, you can use a thread pool with a fixed size and add tasks to the pool.

25.5 Applet Clients

Because of security constraints, applets can only connect to the host from which they were loaded. Therefore, the HTML file must be located on the machine on which the server is running. You can obtain the server's host name by invoking `getCodeBase().getHost()` on an applet, you can write the applet without the host name fixed. Below is an example of how to use an applet to connect to a server.

The applet shows the number of visits made to a Web page. The count should be stored in a file on the server side. Every time the page is visited or reloaded, the applet sends a request to the server, and the server increases the count and sends it to the applet. The applet then displays the new count in a message, such as **You are visitor number 11**, as shown in Figure 25.9. The server and client programs are given in Listings 25.5 and 25.6.

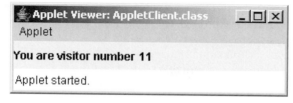

FIGURE 25.9   The applet displays the access count on a Web page.

LISTING 25.5   CountServer.java

```
1 import java.io.*;
2 import java.net.*;
3
4 public class CountServer {
5   private RandomAccessFile raf;
6   private int count; // Count the access to the server
7
8   public static void main(String[] args) {
9     new CountServer();                                          launch server
10   }
11
12   public CountServer() {
13     try {
14       // Create a server socket
15       ServerSocket serverSocket = new ServerSocket(8000);      server socket
16       System.out.println("Server started ");
17
18       // Create or open the count file
19       raf = new RandomAccessFile("count.dat", "rw");           random access file
20
21       // Get the count
22       if (raf.length() == 0)
23         count = 0;                                             new file
24       else
25         count = raf.readInt();                                 get count
26
27       while (true) {
28         // Listen for a new connection request
29         Socket socket = serverSocket.accept();                 connect client
30
31         // Create a DataOutputStream for the socket
32         DataOutputStream outputToClient =                      send to client
33           new DataOutputStream(socket.getOutputStream());
34
35         // Increase count and send the count to the client
36         count++;                                               update count
37         outputToClient.writeInt(count);
38
39         // Write new count back to the file
40         raf.seek(0);
41         raf.writeInt(count);
42       }
43     }
44     catch(IOException ex) {
45       ex.printStackTrace();
46     }
47   }
48 }
```

The server creates a ServerSocket in line 15 and creates or opens a file using RandomAccessFile in line 19. It reads the count from the file in lines 22–25. The server then waits for a connection request from a client (line 29). After a connection with a client is established, the server creates an output stream to the client (lines 32–33), increases the count (line 36), sends the count to the client (line 37), and writes the new count back to the file. This process continues in an infinite while loop to handle all clients.

LISTING 25.6 AppletClient.java

```java
 1 import java.io.*;
 2 import java.net.*;
 3 import java.awt.BorderLayout;
 4 import javax.swing.*;
 5
 6 public class AppletClient extends JApplet {
 7   // Label for displaying the visit count
 8   private JLabel jlblCount = new JLabel();
 9
10   // Indicate if it runs as application
11   private boolean isStandAlone = false;
12
13   // Host name or ip
14   private String host = "localhost";
15
16   /** Initialize the applet */
17   public void init() {
18     add(jlblCount);
19
20     try {
21       // Create a socket to connect to the server
22       Socket socket;
23       if (isStandAlone)
24         socket = new Socket(host, 8000);
25       else
26         socket = new Socket(getCodeBase().getHost(), 8000);
27
28       // Create an input stream to receive data from the server
29       DataInputStream inputFromServer =
30         new DataInputStream(socket.getInputStream());
31
32       // Receive the count from the server and display it on label
33       int count = inputFromServer.readInt();
34       jlblCount.setText("You are visitor number " + count);
35
36       // Close the stream
37       inputFromServer.close();
38     }
39     catch (IOException ex) {
40       ex.printStackTrace();
41     }
42   }
43 }
44   /** Run the applet as an application */
45   public static void main(String[] args) {
46     // Create a frame
47     JFrame frame = new JFrame("Applet client");
48
49     // Create an instance of the applet
50     AppletClient applet = new AppletClient();
51     applet.isStandAlone = true;
```

for standalone

for applet

receive count

```
52
53    // Get host
54    if (args.length == 1) applet.host = args[0];
55
56    // Add the applet instance to the frame
57    frame.getContentPane().add(applet, BorderLayout.CENTER);
58
59    // Invoke init() and start()
60    applet.init();
61    applet.start();
62
63    // Display the frame
64    frame.pack();
65    frame.setVisible(true);
66    }
67 }
```

The client is an applet. When it runs as an applet, it uses **getCodeBase().getHost()** (line 26) to return the IP address for the server. When it runs as an application, it passes the URL from the command line (line 54). If the URL is not passed from the command line, by default "localhost" is used for the URL (line 14).

The client creates a socket to connect to the server (lines 23–26), creates an input stream from the socket (lines 29–30), receives the count from the server (line 33), and displays it in the text field (line 34).

25.6 Sending and Receiving Objects

In the preceding examples, you learned how to send and receive data of primitive types. You can also send and receive objects using **ObjectOutputStream** and **ObjectInputStream** on socket streams. To enable passing, the objects must be serializable. The following example demonstrates how to send and receive objects.

The example consists of three classes: Student.java (Listing 25.7), StudentClient.java (Listing 25.8), and StudentServer.java (Listing 25.9). The client program collects student information from a client and sends it to a server, as shown in Figure 25.10.

The **Student** class contains the student information: name, street, state, and zip. The **Student** class implements the **Serializable** interface. Therefore, it can be sent and received using the object output and input streams.

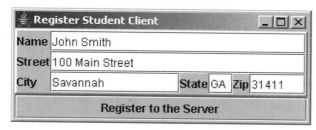

FIGURE 25.10 The client sends the student information in an object to the server.

LISTING 25.7 Student.java

```
1 public class Student implements java.io.Serializable {
2   private String name;
3   private String street;
4   private String city;
5   private String state;
6   private String zip;
7
```

serialized

```
 8    public Student(String name, String street, String city,
 9        String state, String zip) {
10      this.name = name;
11      this.street = street;
12      this.city = city;
13      this.state = state;
14      this.zip = zip;
15    }
16
17    public String getName() {
18      return name;
19    }
20
21    public String getStreet() {
22      return street;
23    }
24
25    public String getCity() {
26      return city;
27    }
28
29    public String getState() {
30      return state;
31    }
32
33    public String getZip() {
34      return zip;
35    }
36 }
```

The client sends a `Student` object through an `ObjectOutputStream` on the output stream socket, and the server receives the `Student` object through the `ObjectInputStream` on the input stream socket, as shown in Figure 25.11. The client uses the `writeObject` method in the `ObjectOutputStream` class to send a student to the server, and the server receives the student using the `readObject` method in the `ObjectInputStream` class. The server and client programs are given in Listings 25.8 and 25.9.

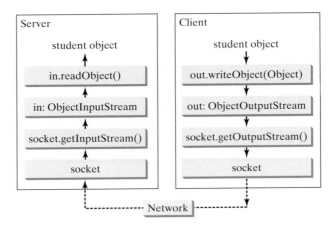

FIGURE 25.11 The client sends a `Student` object to the server.

LISTING 25.8 StudentClient.java

```
1 import java.io.*;
2 import java.net.*;
3 import java.awt.*;
```

```
 4 import java.awt.event.*;
 5 import javax.swing.*;
 6 import javax.swing.border.*;
 7
 8 public class StudentClient extends JApplet {
 9   private JTextField jtfName = new JTextField(32);
10   private JTextField jtfStreet = new JTextField(32);
11   private JTextField jtfCity = new JTextField(20);
12   private JTextField jtfState = new JTextField(2);
13   private JTextField jtfZip = new JTextField(5);
14
15   // Button for sending a student to the server
16   private JButton jbtRegister = new JButton("Register to the Server");
17
18   // Indicate if it runs as application
19   private boolean isStandAlone = false;
20
21   // Host name or ip
22   String host = "localhost";
23
24   public void init() {
25     // Panel p1 for holding labels Name, Street, and City
26     JPanel p1 = new JPanel();                                            create UI
27     p1.setLayout(new GridLayout(3, 1));
28     p1.add(new JLabel("Name"));
29     p1.add(new JLabel("Street"));
30     p1.add(new JLabel("City"));
31
32     // Panel jpState for holding state
33     JPanel jpState = new JPanel();
34     jpState.setLayout(new BorderLayout());
35     jpState.add(new JLabel("State"), BorderLayout.WEST);
36     jpState.add(jtfState, BorderLayout.CENTER);
37
38     // Panel jpZip for holding zip
39     JPanel jpZip = new JPanel();
40     jpZip.setLayout(new BorderLayout());
41     jpZip.add(new JLabel("Zip"), BorderLayout.WEST);
42     jpZip.add(jtfZip, BorderLayout.CENTER);
43
44     // Panel p2 for holding jpState and jpZip
45     JPanel p2 = new JPanel();
46     p2.setLayout(new BorderLayout());
47     p2.add(jpState, BorderLayout.WEST);
48     p2.add(jpZip, BorderLayout.CENTER);
49
50     // Panel p3 for holding jtfCity and p2
51     JPanel p3 = new JPanel();
52     p3.setLayout(new BorderLayout());
53     p3.add(jtfCity, BorderLayout.CENTER);
54     p3.add(p2, BorderLayout.EAST);
55
56     // Panel p4 for holding jtfName, jtfStreet, and p3
57     JPanel p4 = new JPanel();
58     p4.setLayout(new GridLayout(3, 1));
59     p4.add(jtfName);
60     p4.add(jtfStreet);
61     p4.add(p3);
62
63     // Place p1 and p4 into StudentPanel
64     JPanel studentPanel = new JPanel(new BorderLayout());
```

register listener

get server name

server socket

output stream

send to server

```
65      studentPanel.setBorder(new BevelBorder(BevelBorder.RAISED));
66      studentPanel.add(p1, BorderLayout.WEST);
67      studentPanel.add(p4, BorderLayout.CENTER);
68
69      // Add the student panel and button to the applet
70      add(studentPanel, BorderLayout.CENTER);
71      add(jbtRegister, BorderLayout.SOUTH);
72
73      // Register listener
74      jbtRegister.addActionListener(new ButtonListener());
75
76      // Find the IP address of the Web server
77      if (!isStandAlone)
78        host = getCodeBase().getHost();
79    }
80
81    /** Handle button action */
82    private class ButtonListener implements ActionListener {
83      public void actionPerformed(ActionEvent e) {
84        try {
85          // Establish connection with the server
86          Socket socket = new Socket(host, 8000);
87
88          // Create an output stream to the server
89          ObjectOutputStream toServer =
90            new ObjectOutputStream(socket.getOutputStream());
91
92          // Get text field
93          String name = jtfName.getText().trim();
94          String street = jtfStreet.getText().trim();
95          String city = jtfCity.getText().trim();
96          String state = jtfState.getText().trim();
97          String zip = jtfZip.getText().trim();
98
99          // Create a Student object and send to the server
100         Student s = new Student(name, street, city, state, zip);
101         toServer.writeObject(s);
102       }
103       catch (IOException ex) {
104         System.err.println(ex);
105       }
106     }
107   }
108
109   /** Run the applet as an application */
110   public static void main(String[] args) {
111     // Create a frame
112     JFrame frame = new JFrame("Register Student Client");
113
114     // Create an instance of the applet
115     StudentClient applet = new StudentClient();
116     applet.isStandAlone = true;
117
118     // Get host
119     if (args.length == 1) applet.host = args[0];
120
121     // Add the applet instance to the frame
122     frame.add(applet, BorderLayout.CENTER);
123
```

```
124       // Invoke init() and start()
125       applet.init();
126       applet.start();
127
128       // Display the frame
129       frame.pack();
130       frame.setVisible(true);
131   }
132 }
```

LISTING 25.9 StudentServer.java

```
1 import java.io.*;
2 import java.net.*;
3
4 public class StudentServer {
5   private ObjectOutputStream outputToFile;
6   private ObjectInputStream inputFromClient;
7
8   public static void main(String[] args) {
9     new StudentServer();
10   }
11
12   public StudentServer() {
13     try {
14       // Create a server socket
15       ServerSocket serverSocket = new ServerSocket(8000);        server socket
16       System.out.println("Server started ");
17
18       // Create an object ouput stream
19       outputToFile = new ObjectOutputStream(                     output to file
20         new FileOutputStream("student.dat", true));
21
22       while (true) {
23         // Listen for a new connection request
24         Socket socket = serverSocket.accept();                   connect to client
25
26         // Create an input stream from the socket
27         inputFromClient =                                        input stream
28           new ObjectInputStream(socket.getInputStream());
29
30         // Read from input
31         Object object = inputFromClient.readObject();             get from client
32
33         // Write to the file
34         outputToFile.writeObject(object);                        write to file
35         System.out.println("A new student object is stored");
36       }
37     }
38     catch(ClassNotFoundException ex) {
39       ex.printStackTrace();
40     }
41     catch(IOException ex) {
42       ex.printStackTrace();
43     }
44     finally {
45       try {
46         inputFromClient.close();
```

```
47              outputToFile.close();
48          }
49        catch (Exception ex) {
50            ex.printStackTrace();
51        }
52      }
53    }
54 }
```

On the client side, when the user clicks the "Register to the Server" button, the client creates a socket to connect to the host (line 86), creates an `ObjectOutputStream` on the output stream of the socket (lines 89–90), and invokes the `writeObject` method to send the `Student` object to the server through the object output stream (line 101).

On the server side, when a client connects to the server, the server creates a thread to process the client registration (line 24). The thread creates an `ObjectInputStream` on the input stream of the socket (lines 27–28), invokes the `readObject` method to receive the `Student` object through the object input stream (line 31), and writes the object to a file (line 34).

This program can run either as an applet or as an application. To run it as an application, the host name is passed as a command-line argument.

25.7 Retrieving Files from Web Servers

You developed client/server applications in the preceding sections. Java allows you to develop clients that retrieve files on a remote host through a Web server. In this case, you don't have to create a custom server program. The Web server can be used to send the files, as shown in Figure 25.12.

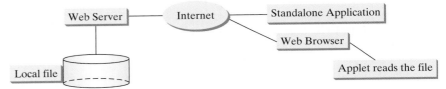

FIGURE 25.12 The applet client or the application client retrieves files from a Web server.

To retrieve a file, first create a `URL` object for the file. The `java.net.URL` class was introduced in §16.9, "Locating Resource Using the `URL` Class." You can create a URL object using the following constructor:

public URL(String spec) **throws** MalformedURLException

For example, the statement given below creates a `URL` object for http://www.cs.armstrong.edu/liang/index.html:

```
try {
   URL url = new URL("http://www.cs.armstrong.edu/liang/index.html");
}
catch (MalformedURLException ex) {
}
```

A `MalformedURLException` is thrown if the URL string has a syntax error. For example, the URL string "http:/www.cs.armstrong.edu/liang/index.html" would cause a `Malformed-URLException` runtime error because two slashes (`//`) are required after the colon (`:`).

You can then use the `openStream()` method defined in the `URL` class to open an input stream to the file's URL.

```
InputStream inputStream = url.openStream();
```

Now you can read the data from the input stream. Listing 25.10 gives an example that demonstrates how to retrieve a file from a Web server. The program can run as an application or an applet. The user interface includes a text field in which to enter the URL of the filename, a text area in which to show the file, and a button that can be used to submit an action. A label is added at the bottom of the applet to indicate the status, such as *File loaded successfully* or *Network connection problem*. A sample run of the program is shown in Figure 25.13.

FIGURE 25.13 The program displays the contents of a specified file on the Web server.

LISTING 25.10 ViewRemoteFile.java

```java
1 import java.awt.*;
2 import java.awt.event.*;
3 import java.io.*;
4 import java.net.*;
5 import javax.swing.*;
6
7 public class ViewRemoteFile extends JApplet {
8   // Button to view the file
9   private JButton jbtView = new JButton("View");
10
11   // Text field to receive file name
12   private JTextField jtfURL = new JTextField(12);
13
14   // Text area to store file
15   private JTextArea jtaFile = new JTextArea();
16
17   // Label to display status
18   private JLabel jlblStatus = new JLabel();
19
20   /** Initialize the applet */
21   public void init() {
22     // Create a panel to hold a label, a text field, and a button
23     JPanel p1 = new JPanel();
24     p1.setLayout(new BorderLayout());                         create UI
25     p1.add(new JLabel("Filename"), BorderLayout.WEST);
26     p1.add(jtfURL, BorderLayout.CENTER);
27     p1.add(jbtView, BorderLayout.EAST);
28
29     // Place text area and panel p to the applet
30     setLayout(new BorderLayout());
31     add(new JScrollPane(jtaFile), BorderLayout.CENTER);
32     add(p1, BorderLayout.NORTH);
33     add(jlblStatus, BorderLayout.SOUTH);
34
```

```
35      // Register listener to handle the "View" button
36      jbtView.addActionListener(new ActionListener() {
37        public void actionPerformed(ActionEvent e) {
38          showFile();
39        }
40      });
41    }
42
43    private void showFile() {
44      // Declare buffered stream for reading text for the URL
45      BufferedReader infile = null;
46      URL url = null;
47
48      try {
49        // Obtain URL from the text field
50        url = new URL(jtfURL.getText().trim());
51
52        // Create a buffered stream
53        InputStream is = url.openStream();
54        infile = new BufferedReader(new InputStreamReader(is));
55
56        // Get file name from the text field
57        String inLine;
58
59        // Read a line and append the line to the text area
60        while ((inLine = infile.readLine()) != null) {
61          jtaFile.append(inLine + '\n');
62        }
63
64        jlblStatus.setText("File loaded successfully");
65      }
66      catch (FileNotFoundException e) {
67        jlblStatus.setText("URL " + url + " not found.");
68      }
69      catch (IOException e) {
70        jlblStatus.setText(e.getMessage());
71      }
72      finally {
73        try {
74          if (infile != null) infile.close();
75        }
76        catch (IOException ex) {}
77      }
78    }
79 }
```

register listener · line 36

get URL · line 50

input stream · line 53

main method omitted · line 79

Line 54 `new URL(jtfURL.getText().trim())` creates a `URL` for the filename entered from the text field. Line 57 `url.openStream()` creates an `InputStream` from the URL. After the input stream is established, reading data from the remote file is just like reading data locally. A `BufferedReader` object is created from the input stream (line 58). The text from the file is displayed in the text area (line 65).

25.8 JEditorPane

Swing provides a GUI component named `javax.swing.JEditorPane` that can display plain text, HTML, and RTF files automatically. Using it you don't have to write code to explicitly read data from the files. `JEditorPane` is a subclass of `JTextComponent`. Thus it inherits all the behavior and properties of `JTextComponent`.

To display the content of a file, use the `setPage(URL)` method, as follows:

```
public void setPage(URL url) throws IOException
```

JEditorPane generates `javax.swing.event.HyperlinkEvent` when a hyperlink in the editor pane is clicked. Through this event, you can get the URL of the hyperlink and display it using the `setPage(url)` method.

Listing 25.11 gives an example that creates a simple Web browser to render HTML files. The program lets the user enter an HTML file in a text field and press the Enter key to display it in an editor pane, as shown in Figure 25.14.

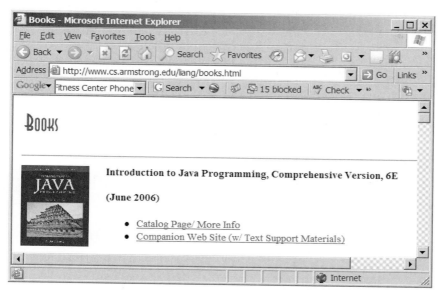

FIGURE 25.14   You can specify a URL in the text field and display the HTML file in an editor pane.

LISTING 25.11   WebBrowser.java

```java
1  import java.awt.*;
2  import java.awt.event.*;
3  import javax.swing.*;
4  import java.net.URL;
5  import javax.swing.event.*;
6  import java.io.*;
7
8  public class WebBrowser extends JApplet {
9    // JEditor pane to view HTML files
10   private JEditorPane jep = new JEditorPane();
11
12   // Label for URL
13   private JLabel jlblURL = new JLabel("URL");
14
15   // Text field for entering URL
16   private JTextField jtfURL = new JTextField();
17
18   /** Initialize the applet */
19   public void init() {
20     // Create a panel jpURL to hold the label and text field
21     JPanel jpURL = new JPanel();
22     jpURL.setLayout(new BorderLayout());
23     jpURL.add(jlblURL, BorderLayout.WEST);
24     jpURL.add(jtfURL, BorderLayout.CENTER);
25
26     // Create a scroll pane to hold JEditorPane
27     JScrollPane jspViewer = new JScrollPane();
```

create UI

```
28      jspViewer.getViewport().add(jep, null);
29
30      // Place jpURL and jspViewer in the applet
31      add(jspViewer, BorderLayout.CENTER);
32      add(jpURL, BorderLayout.NORTH);
33
34      // Set jep noneditable
35      jep.setEditable(false);
36
37      // Register listener
38      jep.addHyperlinkListener(new HyperlinkListener() {
39        public void hyperlinkUpdate(HyperlinkEvent e) {
40          try {
41            jep.setPage(e.getURL());
42          }
43          catch (IOException ex) {
44            System.out.println(ex);
45          }
46        }
47      });
48      jtfURL.addActionListener(new ActionListener() {
49        public void actionPerformed(ActionEvent e) {
50          try {
51            // Get the URL from text field
52            URL url = new URL(jtfURL.getText().trim());
53
54            // Display the HTML file
55            jep.setPage(url);
56          }
57          catch (IOException ex) {
58            System.out.println(ex);
59          }
60        }
61      });
62    }
63  }
```

register listener (line 38)

register listener (line 48)

get URL (line 52)

display HTML (line 55)

main method omitted (line 63)

In this example, a simple Web browser is created using the **JEditorPane** class (line 10). **JEditorPane** is capable of displaying files in HTML format. To enable scrolling, the editor pane is placed inside a scroll pane (lines 27–28).

The user enters the URL of the HTML file in the text field and presses the Enter key to fire an action event to display the URL in the editor pane. To display the URL in the editor pane, simply set the URL in the **page** property of the editor pane (line 55).

The editor pane does not have all the functions of a commercial Web browser, but it is convenient for displaying HTML files, including embedded images.

There are two shortcomings in this program: (1) it cannot view a local HTML file, and (2) to view a remote HTML file, you have to enter a URL beginning with http://. In Exercise 25.9, you will modify the program so that it can also view an HTML file from the local host and accept URLs beginning with either http:// or www.

25.9 (Optional) Case Studies: Distributed TicTacToe Games

In §16.7, "Case Study: TicTacToe," you developed an applet for the TicTacToe game that enables two players to play on the same machine. In this section, you will learn how to develop a distributed TicTacToe game using multithreads and networking with socket streams. A distributed TicTacToe game enables users to play on different machines from anywhere on the Internet.

You need to develop a server for multiple clients. The server creates a server socket, and accepts connections from every two players to form a session. Each session is a thread that communicates with the two players and determines the status of the game. The server can establish any number of sessions, as shown in Figure 25.15.

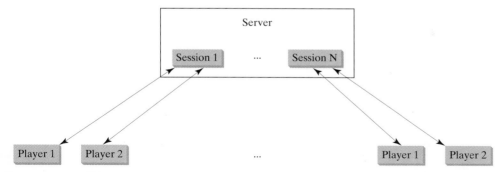

FIGURE 25.15   The server can create many sessions, each of which facilitates a TicTacToe game for two players.

For each session, the first client connecting to the server is identified as Player 1 with token 'X', and the second client connecting to the server is identified as Player 2 with token 'O'. The server notifies the players of their respective tokens. Once two clients are connected to it, the server starts a thread to facilitate the game between the two players by performing the steps repeatedly, as shown in Figure 25.16.

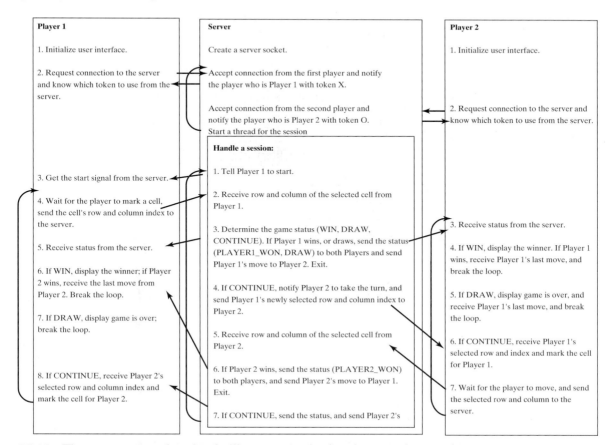

FIGURE 25.16   The server starts a thread to facilitate communications between the two players.

The server does not have to be a graphical component, but creating it as a frame in which game information can be viewed is user-friendly. You can create a scroll pane to hold a text area in the frame and display game information in the text area. The server creates a thread to handle a game session when two players are connected to the server.

The client is responsible for interacting with the players. It creates a user interface with nine cells, and displays the game title and status to the players in the labels. The client class is very similar to the TicTacToe class presented in §16.7, "Case Study: TicTacToe." However, the client in this example does not determine the game status (win or draw), it simply passes the moves to the server and receives the game status from the server.

Based on the foregoing analysis, you can create the following classes:

- `TicTacToeServer` serves all the clients in Listing 25.13.

- `HandleASession` facilitates the game for two players in Listing 25.13. It is in the same file with TicTacToeServer.java.

- `TicTacToeClient` models a player in Listing 25.14.

- `Cell` models a cell in the game in Listing 25.14. It is an inner class in `TicTacToe-Client`.

- `TicTacToeConstants` is an interface that defines the constants shared by all the classes in the example in Listing 25.12.

The relationships of these classes are shown in Figure 25.17.

LISTING 25.12 TicTacToeConstants.java

```java
1 public interface TicTacToeConstants {
2   public static int PLAYER1 = 1; // Indicate player 1
3   public static int PLAYER2 = 2; // Indicate player 2
4   public static int PLAYER1_WON = 1; // Indicate player 1 won
5   public static int PLAYER2_WON = 2; // Indicate player 2 won
6   public static int DRAW = 3; // Indicate a draw
7   public static int CONTINUE = 4; // Indicate to continue
8 }
```

LISTING 25.13 TicTacToeServer.java

```java
1 import java.io.*;
2 import java.net.*;
3 import javax.swing.*;
4 import java.awt.*;
5 import java.util.Date;
6
7 public class TicTacToeServer extends JFrame
8     implements TicTacToeConstants {
9   public static void main(String[] args) {
10     TicTacToeServer frame = new TicTacToeServer();
11   }
12
13   public TicTacToeServer() {
14     JTextArea jtaLog = new JTextArea();
15
16     // Create a scroll pane to hold text area
17     JScrollPane scrollPane = new JScrollPane(jtaLog);
18
19     // Add the scroll pane to the frame
20     add(scrollPane, BorderLayout.CENTER);
21
```

run server

create UI

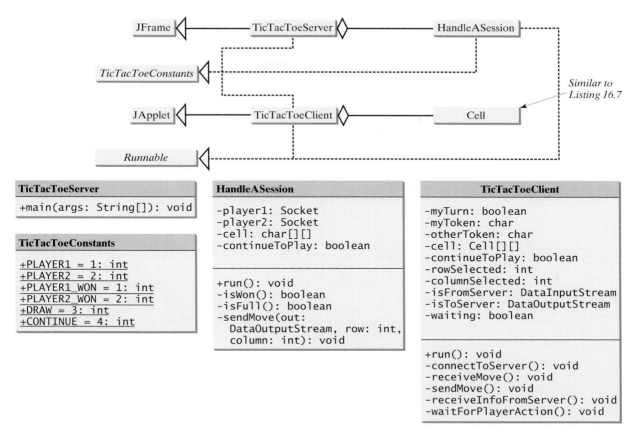

FIGURE 25.17 `TicTacToeServer` creates an instance of `HandleASession` for each session of two players. `TicTacToeClient` creates nine cells in the UI.

```
22    setDefaultCloseOperation(JFrame.EXIT_ON_CLOSE);
23    setSize(300, 300);
24    setTitle("TicTacToeServer");
25    setVisible(true);
26
27    try {
28      // Create a server socket
29      ServerSocket serverSocket = new ServerSocket(8000);          server socket
30      jtaLog.append(new Date() +
31        ": Server started at socket 8000\n");
32
33      // Number a session
34      int sessionNo = 1;
35
36      // Ready to create a session for every two players
37      while (true) {
38        jtaLog.append(new Date() +
39          ": Wait for players to join session " + sessionNo + '\n');
40
41        // Connect to player 1
42        Socket player1 = serverSocket.accept();                    connect to client
43
44        jtaLog.append(new Date() + ": Player 1 joined session " +
45          sessionNo + '\n');
```

```
46        jtaLog.append("Player 1's IP address" +
47          player1.getInetAddress().getHostAddress() + '\n');
48
49        // Notify that the player is Player 1
```
to **player1**
```
50        new DataOutputStream(
51          player1.getOutputStream()).writeInt(PLAYER1);
52
53        // Connect to player 2
54        Socket player2 = serverSocket.accept();
55
56        jtaLog.append(new Date() +
57          ": Player 2 joined session " + sessionNo + '\n');
58        jtaLog.append("Player 2's IP address" +
59          player2.getInetAddress().getHostAddress() + '\n');
60
61        // Notify that the player is Player 2
```
to **player2**
```
62        new DataOutputStream(
63          player2.getOutputStream()).writeInt(PLAYER2);
64
65        // Display this session and increment session number
66        jtaLog.append(new Date() + ": Start a thread for session " +
67          sessionNo++ + '\n');
68
```
a session for two players
```
69        // Create a new thread for this session of two players
70        HandleASession task = new HandleASession(player1, player2);
71
72        // Start the new thread
73        new Thread(task).start();
74      }
75    }
76    catch(IOException ex) {
78      System.err.println(ex);
79    }
80  }
81 }
82
83 // Define the thread class for handling a new session for two players
84 class HandleASession implements Runnable, TicTacToeConstants {
85   private Socket player1;
86   private Socket player2;
87
88   // Create and initialize cells
89   private char[][] cell =  new char[3][3];
90
91   private DataInputStream fromPlayer1;
92   private DataOutputStream toPlayer1;
93   private DataInputStream fromPlayer2;
94   private DataOutputStream toPlayer2;
95
96   // Continue to play
97   private boolean continueToPlay = true;
98
99   /** Construct a thread */
100  public HandleASession(Socket player1, Socket player2) {
101    this.player1 = player1;
102    this.player2 = player2;
103
104    // Initialize cells
105    for (int i = 0; i < 3; i++)
106      for (int j = 0; j < 3; j++)
107        cell[i][j] = ' ';
```

```
108    }
109
110    /** Implement the run() method for the thread */
111    public void run() {
112      try {
113        // Create data input and output streams
114        DataInputStream fromPlayer1 = new DataInputStream(
115          player1.getInputStream());
116        DataOutputStream toPlayer1 = new DataOutputStream(
117          player1.getOutputStream());
118        DataInputStream fromPlayer2 = new DataInputStream(
119          player2.getInputStream());
120        DataOutputStream toPlayer2 = new DataOutputStream(
121          player2.getOutputStream());
122
123        // Write anything to notify player 1 to start
124        // This is just to let player 1 know to start
125        toPlayer1.writeInt(1);
126
127        // Continuously serve the players and determine and report
128        // the game status to the players
129        while (true) {
130          // Receive a move from player 1
131          int row = fromPlayer1.readInt();
132          int column = fromPlayer1.readInt();
133          cell[row][column] = 'X';
134
135          // Check if Player 1 wins
136          if (isWon('X')) {
137            toPlayer1.writeInt(PLAYER1_WON);
138            toPlayer2.writeInt(PLAYER1_WON);
139            sendMove(toPlayer2, row, column);
140            break; // Break the loop
141          }
142          else if (isFull()) { // Check if all cells are filled
143            toPlayer1.writeInt(DRAW);
144            toPlayer2.writeInt(DRAW);
145            sendMove(toPlayer2, row, column);
146            break;
147          }
148          else {
149            // Notify player 2 to take the turn
150            toPlayer2.writeInt(CONTINUE);
151
152            // Send player 1's selected row and column to player 2
153            sendMove(toPlayer2, row, column);
154          }
155
156          // Receive a move from Player 2
157          row = fromPlayer2.readInt();
158          column = fromPlayer2.readInt();
159          cell[row][column] = 'O';
160
161          // Check if Player 2 wins
162          if (isWon('O')) {
163            toPlayer1.writeInt(PLAYER2_WON);
164            toPlayer2.writeInt(PLAYER2_WON);
165            sendMove(toPlayer1, row, column);
166            break;
167          }
168          else {
```

```
169              // Notify player 1 to take the turn
170              toPlayer1.writeInt(CONTINUE);
171
172              // Send player 2's selected row and column to player 1
173              sendMove(toPlayer1, row, column);
174          }
175        }
176      }
177      catch(IOException ex) {
178        System.err.println(ex);
179      }
180    }
181
182    /** Send the move to other player */
183    private void sendMove(DataOutputStream out, int row, int column)
184        throws IOException {
185      out.writeInt(row); // Send row index
186      out.writeInt(column); // Send column index
187    }
188
189    /** Determine if the cells are all occupied */
190    private boolean isFull() {
191      for (int i = 0; i < 3; i++)
192        for (int j = 0; j < 3; j++)
193          if (cell[i][j] == ' ')
194            return false; // At least one cell is not filled
195
196      // All cells are filled
197      return true;
198    }
199
200    /** Determine if the player with the specified token wins */
201    private boolean isWon(char token) {
202      // Check all rows
203      for (int i = 0; i < 3; i++)
204        if ((cell[i][0] == token)
205            && (cell[i][1] == token)
206            && (cell[i][2] == token)) {
207          return true;
208        }
209
210      /** Check all columns */
211      for (int j = 0; j < 3; j++)
212        if ((cell[0][j] == token)
213            && (cell[1][j] == token)
214            && (cell[2][j] == token)) {
215          return true;
216        }
217
218      /** Check major diagonal */
219      if ((cell[0][0] == token)
220          && (cell[1][1] == token)
221          && (cell[2][2] == token)) {
222        return true;
223      }
224
225      /** Check subdiagonal */
226      if ((cell[0][2] == token)
227          && (cell[1][1] == token)
228          && (cell[2][0] == token)) {
```

```
229          return true;
230      }
231
232      /** All checked, but no winner */
233      return false;
234    }
235  }
```

LISTING 25.14 TicTacToeClient.java

```java
1 import java.awt.*;
2 import java.awt.event.*;
3 import javax.swing.*;
4 import javax.swing.border.LineBorder;
5 import java.io.*;
6 import java.net.*;
7
8 public class TicTacToeClient extends JApplet
9     implements Runnable, TicTacToeConstants {
10   // Indicate whether the player has the turn
11   private boolean myTurn = false;
12
13   // Indicate the token for the player
14   private char myToken = ' ';
15
16   // Indicate the token for the other player
17   private char otherToken = ' ';
18
19   // Create and initialize cells
20   private Cell[][] cell =  new Cell[3][3];
21
22   // Create and initialize a title label
23   private JLabel jlblTitle = new JLabel();
24
25   // Create and initialize a status label
26   private JLabel jlblStatus = new JLabel();
27
28   // Indicate selected row and column by the current move
29   private int rowSelected;
30   private int columnSelected;
31
32   // Input and output streams from/to server
33   private DataInputStream fromServer;
34   private DataOutputStream toServer;
35
36   // Continue to play?
37   private boolean continueToPlay = true;
38
39   // Wait for the player to mark a cell
40   private boolean waiting = true;
41
42   // Indicate if it runs as application
43   private boolean isStandAlone = false;
44
45   // Host name or ip
46   private String host = "localhost";
47
48   /** Initialize UI */
49   public void init() {                              create UI
50     // Panel p to hold cells
51     JPanel p = new JPanel();
```

```
52      p.setLayout(new GridLayout(3, 3, 0, 0));
53      for (int i = 0; i < 3; i++)
54        for (int j = 0; j < 3; j++)
55          p.add(cell[i][j] = new Cell(i, j));
56
57      // Set properties for labels and borders for labels and panel
58      p.setBorder(new LineBorder(Color.black, 1));
59      jlblTitle.setHorizontalAlignment(JLabel.CENTER);
60      jlblTitle.setFont(new Font("SansSerif", Font.BOLD, 16));
61      jlblTitle.setBorder(new LineBorder(Color.black, 1));
62      jlblStatus.setBorder(new LineBorder(Color.black, 1));
63
64      // Place the panel and the labels to the applet
65      add(jlblTitle, BorderLayout.NORTH);
66      add(p, BorderLayout.CENTER);
67      add(jlblStatus, BorderLayout.SOUTH);
68
69      // Connect to the server
70      connectToServer();
71    }
72
73    private void connectToServer() {
74      try {
75        // Create a socket to connect to the server
76        Socket socket;
77        if (isStandAlone)
78          socket = new Socket(host, 8000);
79        else
80          socket = new Socket(getCodeBase().getHost(), 8000);
81
82        // Create an input stream to receive data from the server
83        fromServer = new DataInputStream(socket.getInputStream());
84
85        // Create an output stream to send data to the server
86        toServer = new DataOutputStream(socket.getOutputStream());
87      }
88      catch (Exception ex) {
89        System.err.println(ex);
90      }
91
92      // Control the game on a separate thread
93      Thread thread = new Thread(this);
94      thread.start();
95    }
96
97    public void run() {
98      try {
99        // Get notification from the server
100        int player = fromServer.readInt();
101
102        // Am I player 1 or 2?
103        if (player == PLAYER1) {
104          myToken = 'X';
105          otherToken = 'O';
106          jlblTitle.setText("Player 1 with token 'X'");
107          jlblStatus.setText("Waiting for player 2 to join");
108
109          // Receive startup notification from the server
110          fromServer.readInt(); // Whatever read is ignored
111
112          // The other player has joined
```

connect to server

standalone

applet

input from server

output to server

```
113              jlblStatus.setText("Player 2 has joined. I start first");
114
115              // It is my turn
116              myTurn = true;
117            }
118            else if (player == PLAYER2) {
119              myToken = 'O';
120              otherToken = 'X';
121              jlblTitle.setText("Player 2 with token 'O'");
122              jlblStatus.setText("Waiting for player 1 to move");
123            }
124
125            // Continue to play
126            while (continueToPlay) {
127              if (player == PLAYER1) {
128                waitForPlayerAction(); // Wait for player 1 to move
129                sendMove(); // Send the move to the server
130                receiveInfoFromServer(); // Receive info from the server
131              }
132              else if (player == PLAYER2) {
133                receiveInfoFromServer(); // Receive info from the server
134                waitForPlayerAction(); // Wait for player 2 to move
135                sendMove(); // Send player 2's move to the server
136              }
137            }
138          }
139          catch (Exception ex) {
140          }
141      }
142
143      /** Wait for the player to mark a cell */
144      Private void waitForPlayerAction() throws InterruptedException {
145        while (waiting) {
146          Thread.sleep(100);
147        }
148
149        waiting = true;
150      }
151
152      /** Send this player's move to the server */
153      private void sendMove() throws IOException {
154        toServer.writeInt(rowSelected); // Send the selected row
155        toServer.writeInt(columnSelected); // Send the selected column
156      }
157
158      /** Receive info from the server */
159      private void receiveInfoFromServer() throws IOException {
160        // Receive game status
161        int status = fromServer.readInt();
162
163        if (status == PLAYER1_WON) {
164          // Player 1 won, stop playing
165          continueToPlay = false;
166          if (myToken == 'X') {
167            jlblStatus.setText("I won! (X)");
168          }
169          else if (myToken == 'O') {
170            jlblStatus.setText("Player 1 (X) has won!");
171            receiveMove();
172          }
173        }
```

```
174      else if (status == PLAYER2_WON) {
175        // Player 2 won, stop playing
176        continueToPlay = false;
177        if (myToken == '0') {
178          jlblStatus.setText("I won! (0)");
179        }
180        else if (myToken == 'X') {
181          jlblStatus.setText("Player 2 (0) has won!");
182            receiveMove();
183        }
184      }
185      else if (status == DRAW) {
186        // No winner, game is over
187        continueToPlay = false;
188        jlblStatus.setText("Game is over, no winner!");
189
190        if (myToken == '0') {
191          receiveMove();
192        }
193      }
194      else {
195        receiveMove();
196        jlblStatus.setText("My turn");
197        myTurn = true; // It is my turn
198      }
199    }
200
201    private void receiveMove() throws IOException {
202      // Get the other player's move
203      int row = fromServer.readInt();
204      int column = fromServer.readInt();
205      cell[row][column].setToken(otherToken);
206    }
207
208    // An inner class for a cell
209    public class Cell extends JPanel {
210      // Indicate the row and column of this cell in the board
211      private int row;
212      private int column;
213
214      // Token used for this cell
215      private char token = ' ';
216
217      public Cell(int row, int column) {
218        this.row = row;
219        this.column = column;
220        setBorder(new LineBorder(Color.black, 1)); // Set cell's border
221        addMouseListener(new ClickListener());  // Register listener
222      }
223
224      /** Return token */
225      public char getToken() {
226        return token;
227      }
228
229      /** Set a new token */
230      public void setToken(char c) {
231        token = c;
232        repaint();
233      }
234
```

model a cell

register listener

```
235      /** Paint the cell */
236      protected void paintComponent(Graphics g) {
237        super.paintComponent(g);
238
239        if (token == 'X') {
240          g.drawLine(10, 10, getWidth() - 10, getHeight() - 10);
241          g.drawLine(getWidth() - 10, 10, 10, getHeight() - 10);
242        }
243        else if (token == 'O') {
244          g.drawOval(10, 10, getWidth() - 20, getHeight() - 20);
245        }
246      }
247
248      /** Handle mouse click on a cell */
249      private class ClickListener extends MouseAdapter {
250        public void mouseClicked(MouseEvent e) {
251          // If cell is not occupied and the player has the turn
252          if ((token == ' ') && myTurn) {
253            setToken(myToken); // Set the player's token in the cell
254            myTurn = false;
255            rowSelected = row;
256            columnSelected = column;
257            jlblStatus.setText("Waiting for the other player to move");
258            waiting = false; // Just completed a successful move
259          }
260        }
261      }
262   }
263 }
```

draw X *(line 240)*

draw O *(line 244)*

mouse listener *(line 249)*

main method omitted *(line 263)*

The server can serve any number of sessions. Each session takes care of two players. The client can be a Java applet or a Java application. To run a client as a Java applet from a Web browser, the server must run from a Web server. Figures 25.18 and 25.19 show sample runs of the server and the clients.

FIGURE 25.18   TicTacToeServer accepts connection requests and creates sessions to serve pairs of players.

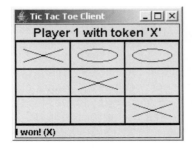 

FIGURE 25.19   TicTacToeClient can run as an applet or an application.

The `TicTacToeConstants` interface defines the constants shared by all the classes in the project. Each class that uses the constants needs to implement the interface. Centrally defining constants in an interface is a common practice in Java. For example, all the constants shared by Swing classes are defined in `java.swing.SwingConstants`.

Once a session is established, the server receives moves from the players in alternation. Upon receiving a move from a player, the server determines the status of the game. If the game is not finished, the server sends the status (`CONTINUE`) and the player's move to the other player. If the game is won or drawn, the server sends the status (`PLAYER1_WON`, `PLAYER2_WON`, or `DRAW`) to both players.

The implementation of Java network programs at the socket level is tightly synchronized. An operation to send data from one machine requires an operation to receive data from the other machine. As shown in this example, the server and the client are tightly synchronized to send or receive data.

25.10 (Optional) Datagram Socket

Clients and servers that communicate via a stream socket have a dedicated point-to-point channel between them. To communicate, they establish a connection, transmit the data, and then close the connection. The stream sockets use TCP (Transmission Control Protocol) for data transmission. Since TCP can detect lost transmissions and resubmit them, transmissions are lossless and reliable. All data sent via a stream socket is received in the same order in which it was sent.

datagram

In contrast, clients and servers that communicate via a datagram socket do not have a dedicated point-to-point channel. Data is transmitted using packets. Datagram sockets use UDP (User Datagram Protocol), which cannot guarantee that the packets are not lost, or not received in duplicate, or received in the order in which they were sent. A *datagram* is an independent, self-contained message sent over the network whose arrival, arrival time, and content are not guaranteed.

packet

In an analogy, a stream socket communication between a client and a server is like a telephone connection with a dedicated link. A datagram communication is like sending a letter through the post office. Your letter is contained in an envelope (*packet*). If the letter is too large, it may be sent in several envelopes (packets). There is no guarantee that your letter will arrive or that the envelopes will arrive in the order they were sent. One difference is that the letter will not arrive in duplicate, whereas a datagram packet may arrive in duplicate.

Most applications require reliable transmission between clients and servers. In such cases, it is best to use stream socket network communication. Some applications that you write to communicate over the network will not require the reliable, point-to-point channel provided by TCP. In such cases, datagram communication is more efficient.

25.10.1 The `DatagramPacket` and `DatagramSocket` Classes

The `java.net` package contains two classes to help you write Java programs that use datagrams to send and receive packets over the network: `DatagramPacket` and `DatagramSocket`. An application can send and receive `DatagramPackets` through a `DatagramSocket`.

The DatagramPacket Class

The `DatagramPacket` class represents a datagram packet. Datagram packets are used to implement a connectionless packet-delivery service. Each message is routed from one machine to another based solely on information contained within the packet.

To create a `DatagramPacket` for delivery from a client, use the `DatagramPacket(byte[] buf, int length, InetAddress host, int port)` constructor. To create all other `DatagramPackets`, use the `DatagramPacket(byte[] buf, int length)` constructor, as shown in Figure 25.20. Once a datagram packet is created, you can use the `getData` and `setData` methods to obtain and set data in the packet.

java.net.DatagramPacket	
length: int	Specifies the length of the buffer with get and set methods.
address: InetAddress	Specifies the address of the machine where the packet is sent or received with get and set methods.
port: int	Specifies the port of the machine where the packet is sent or received with get and set methods.
+DatagramPacket(buf: byte[], length: int, host: InetAddress, port: int)	Constructs a datagram packet in a byte array buf of the specified length with the host and the port for which the packet is sent. This constructor is often used to construct a packet for delivery from a client.
+DatagramPacket(buf: byte[], length: int)	Constructs a datagram packet in a byte array buf of the specified length.
+getData(): byte[]	Returns the data from the packet.
+setData(buf: byte[]): void	Sets the data in the packet.

FIGURE 25.20 The DatagramPacket class contains the data and information about data.

DatagramSocket

The DatagramSocket class represents a socket for sending and receiving datagram packets. A datagram socket is the sending or receiving point for a packet-delivery service. Each packet sent or received on a datagram socket is individually addressed and routed. Multiple packets sent from one machine to another may be routed differently, and may arrive in any order.

To create a server DatagramSocket, use the constructor DatagramSocket(int port), which binds the socket with the specified port on the local host machine.

To create a client DatagramSocket, use the constructor DatagramSocket(), which binds the socket with any available port on the local host machine.

To send data, you need to create a packet, fill in the contents, specify the Internet address and port number for the receiver, and invoke the send(packet) method on a DatagramSocket.

To receive data, you have to create an empty packet and invoke the receive(packet) method on a DatagramSocket.

construct datagram socket

send packet

receive packet

25.10.2 Datagram Programming

Datagram programming is different from stream socket programming in the sense that there is no concept of a ServerSocket for datagrams. Both client and server use DatagramSocket to send and receive packets, as shown in Figure 25.21.

Normally, you designate one application as the server and create a DatagramSocket with the specified port using the constructor DatagramSocket(port). A client can create a DatagramSocket without specifying a port number. The port number will be dynamically chosen at runtime. When a client sends a packet to the server, the client's IP address and port number are contained in the packet. The server can retrieve it from the packet and use it to send the packet back to the client.

To demonstrate, let us rewrite the client and server programs in Listings 25.1 and 25.2 using datagrams rather than socket streams. The client sends the radius to a server. The server receives this information, uses it to find the area, and then sends the area to the client.

Listing 25.15 gives the server, and Listing 25.16 gives the client. A sample run of the program is shown in Figure 25.22.

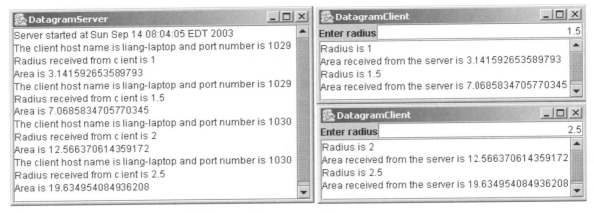

DatagramServer
```
DatagramSocket socket;
socket = new DatagramSocket(8000);

byte[] buf= new byte[256];

DatagramPacket receivePacket = new
  DatagramPacket(buf, bef.length)

socket.receive(receivePacket);

get data from buf or receivePacket.getData();

DatagramPacket sendPacket = new
  DatagramPacket(buf, bef.length)

set client's InetAddree and port into sendPacket;

fill in the contents in buf;
socket.send(sendPacket);
```

DatagramClient
```
DatagramSocket socket;
socket = new DatagramSocket();

byte[] buf= new byte[256];

InetAddress address = new
  InetAddress(serverName);

DatagramPacket sendPacket = new
  DatagramPacket(buf, bef.length, address, 8000)

fill in the contentsin buf;
socket.send(sendPacket);

DatagramPacket receivePacket = new
  DatagramPacket(buf, bef.length)

socket.receive(receivePacket);

get data from buf or receivePacket.getData();
```

FIGURE 25.21 The programs send and receive packets via datagram sockets.

FIGURE 25.22 The server receives a radius from a client, computes the area, and sends the area to the client. The server can serve multiple clients.

LISTING 25.15 DatagramServer.java

```java
1 import java.io.*;
2 import java.net.*;
3 import java.util.*;
4 import java.awt.*;
5 import javax.swing.*;
6
7 public class DatagramServer extends JFrame {
8   // Text area for displaying contents
9   private JTextArea jta = new JTextArea();
10
11  // The byte array for sending and receiving datagram packets
12  private byte[] buf = new byte[256];
13
```

```
14    public static void main(String[] args) {
15      new DatagramServer();
16    }
17
18    public Server() {
19      // Place text area on the frame
20      setLayout(new BorderLayout());                                        create UI
21      add(new JScrollPane(jta), BorderLayout.CENTER);
22
23      setTitle("DatagramServer");
24      setSize(500, 300);
25      setDefaultCloseOperation(JFrame.EXIT_ON_CLOSE);
26      setVisible(true); // It is necessary to show the frame here!
27
28      try {
29        // Create a server socket
30        DatagramSocket socket = new DatagramSocket(8000);                   datagram socket
31        jta.append("Server started at " + new Date() + '\n');
32
33        // Create a packet for receiving data
34        DatagramPacket receivePacket =                                      incoming packet
35          new DatagramPacket(buf, buf.length);
36
37        // Create a packet for sending data
38        DatagramPacket sendPacket =                                         outgoing packet
39          new DatagramPacket(buf, buf.length);
40
41        while (true) {
42          // Initialize buffer for each iteration
43          Arrays.fill(buf, (byte)0);
44
45          // Receive radius from the client in a packet
46          socket.receive(receivePacket);                                    receive packet
47          jta.append("The client host name is " +
48            receivePacket.getAddress().getHostName() +
49            " and port number is " + receivePacket.getPort() + '\n');
50          jta.append("Radius received from client is " +
51            new String(buf).trim() +  '\n');
52
53          // Compute area
54          double radius = Double.parseDouble(new String(buf).trim());
55          double area = radius * radius * Math.PI;
56          jta.append("Area is " + area + '\n');
57
58          // Send area to the client in a packet
59          sendPacket.setAddress(receivePacket.getAddress());
60          sendPacket.setPort(receivePacket.getPort());                      packet address
61          sendPacket.setData(new Double(area).toString().getBytes());
62          socket.send(sendPacket);
63        }                                                                   send packet
64      }
65      catch(IOException ex) {
66        ex.printStackTrace();
67      }
68    }
69  }
```

LISTING 25.16 DatagramClient.java

```java
1  import java.io.*;
2  import java.net.*;
3  import java.util.*;
4  import java.awt.*;
5  import java.awt.event.*;
6  import javax.swing.*;
7
8  public class DatagramClient extends JFrame {
9    // Text field for receiving radius
10   private JTextField jtf = new JTextField();
11
12   // Text area to display contents
13   private JTextArea jta = new JTextArea();
14
15   // Datagram socket
16   private DatagramSocket socket;
17
18   // The byte array for sending and receiving datagram packets
19   private byte[] buf = new byte[256];
20
21   // Server InetAddress
22   private InetAddress address;
23
24   // The packet sent to the server
25   private DatagramPacket sendPacket;
26
27   // The packet received from the server
28   private DatagramPacket receivePacket;
29
30   public static void main(String[] args) {
31     new DatagramClient();
32   }
33
34   public DatagramClient() {
35     // Panel p to hold the label and text field
36     JPanel p = new JPanel();
37     p.setLayout(new BorderLayout());
38     p.add(new JLabel("Enter radius"), BorderLayout.WEST);
39     p.add(jtf, BorderLayout.CENTER);
40     jtf.setHorizontalAlignment(JTextField.RIGHT);
41
42     setLayout(new BorderLayout());
43     add(p, BorderLayout.NORTH);
44     add(new JScrollPane(jta), BorderLayout.CENTER);
45
46     jtf.addActionListener(new ButtonListener()); // Register listener
47
48     setTitle("DatagramClient");
49     setSize(500, 300);
50     setDefaultCloseOperation(JFrame.EXIT_ON_CLOSE);
51     setVisible(true); // It is necessary to show the frame here!
52
53     try {
54       // get a datagram socket
55       socket = new DatagramSocket();
56       address = InetAddress.getByName("localhost");
57       sendPacket =
58         new DatagramPacket(buf, buf.length, address, 8000);
```

create UI

datagram socket

outgoing packet

```
59        receivePacket = new DatagramPacket(buf, buf.length);                    incoming packet
60      }
61    catch (IOException ex) {
62        ex.printStackTrace();
63      }
64    }
65
66    private class ButtonListener implements ActionListener {
67      public void actionPerformed(ActionEvent e) {
68        try {
69          // Initialize buffer for each iteration
70          Arrays.fill(buf, (byte)0);
71
72          // Send radius to the server in a packet
73          sendPacket.setData(jtf.getText().trim().getBytes());
74          socket.send(sendPacket);                                               send packet
75
76          // Receive area from the server in a packet
77          socket.receive(receivePacket);                                         receive packet
78
79          // Display to the text area
80          jta.append("Radius is " + jtf.getText().trim() + "\n");
81          jta.append("Area received from the server is "
82            +  Double.parseDouble(new String(buf).trim()) + '\n');
83        }
84      catch (IOException ex) {
85          ex.printStackTrace();
86        }
87      }
88    }
89 }
```

Since datagrams are connectionless, a DatagramPacket can be sent to multiple clients, and multiple clients can receive a packet from the same server. As shown in this example, you can launch multiple clients. Each client sends the radius to the server, and the server sends the area back to the client.

The server creates a DatagramSocket on port 8000 (line 30 in DatagramServer.java). No DatagramSocket can be created again on the same port. The client creates a DatagramSocket on an available port (line 55 in DatagramClient.java). The port number is dynamically assigned to the socket. You can launch multiple clients simultaneously, and each client's datagram socket will be different.

The client creates a DatagramPacket named sendPacket for delivery to the server (lines 57–58 in DatagramClient.java). The DatagramPacket contains the server address and port number. The client creates another DatagramPacket named receivePacket (line 59), which is used for receiving packets from the server. This packet does not need to contain any address or port number.

A user enters a radius in the text field in the client. When the user presses the Enter key on the text field, the radius value in the text field is put into the packet and sent to the server (lines 73–74 in DatagramClient.java). The server receives the packet (line 46 in DatagramServer.java), extracts the data from the byte array buf, and computes the area (lines 54–55 in DatagramServer.java). The server then builds a packet that contains the area value in the buffer, the client's address, and the port number, and sends the packet to the client (lines 59–62). The client receives the packet (line 77 in DatagramClient.java) and displays the result in the text area.

The data in the packet is stored in a byte array. To send a numerical value, you need to convert it into a string and then store it in the array as bytes, using the getBytes() method in the String class (line 62 in DatagramServer.java and line 74 in DatagramClient.java). To convert the array into a number, first convert it into a string, and then convert it into a number using the static `parseDouble` method in the `Double` class (line 54 in DatagramServer.java and line 82 in DatagramClient.java).

Note

The port numbers for the stream socket and the datagram socket are not related. You can use the same port number for a stream socket and a datagram socket simultaneously.

CHAPTER SUMMARY

- Java supports stream sockets and datagram sockets. *Stream sockets* use TCP (Transmission Control Protocol) for data transmission, whereas *datagram sockets* use UDP (User Datagram Protocol). Since TCP can detect lost transmissions and resubmit them, transmissions are lossless and reliable. UDP, in contrast, cannot guarantee lossless transmission.

- To create a server, you must first obtain a server socket, using `new ServerSocket-(port)`. After a server socket is created, the server can start to listen for connections, using the `accept()` method on the server socket. The client requests a connection to a server by using `new socket(serverName, port)` to create a client socket.

- Stream socket communication is very much like input/output stream communication after the connection between a server and a client is established. You can obtain an input stream using the `getInputStream()` method and an output stream using the `getOutputStream()` method on the socket.

- A server must often work with multiple clients at the same time. You can use threads to handle the server's multiple clients simultaneously by creating a thread for each connection.

- Applets are good for deploying multiple clients. They can be run anywhere with a single copy of the program. However, because of security restrictions, an applet client can only connect to the server where the applet is loaded.

- Java programs can retrieve data from a file on a remote host through a Web server. To do so, first create a URL object using `new URL(urlString)`, then use `openStream()` to get an `InputStream` to read the data from the file.

- Swing provides a GUI component named `javax.swing.JEditorPane` that can be used to display text, HTML, and RTF files automatically without writing the code to read data from the file explicitly.

- Clients and servers that communicate via a datagram socket do not have a dedicated point-to-point channel. Data is transmitted using packets. Datagram sockets use UDP (User Datagram Protocol), which cannot guarantee that the packets are not lost, or not received in duplicate, or received in the order in which they were sent. A *datagram* is an independent, self-contained message sent over the network whose arrival, arrival time, and content are not guaranteed.

REVIEW QUESTIONS

Section 25.2 Client/Server Computing

25.1 How do you create a server socket? What port numbers can be used? What happens if a requested port number is already in use? Can a port connect to multiple clients?

25.2   What are the differences between a server socket and a client socket?

25.3   How does a client program initiate a connection?

25.4   How does a server accept a connection?

25.5   How is data transferred between a client and a server?

Sections 25.3–25.4

25.6   How do you find the IP address of a client that connects to a server?

25.7   How do you make a server serve multiple clients?

Sections 25.5–25.6

25.8   Can an applet connect to a server that is different from the machine where the applet is located?

25.9   How do you find the host name of an applet?

25.10 How do you send and receive an object?

Sections 25.7–25.8

25.11 Can an application retrieve a file from a remote host? Can an application update a file on a remote host?

25.12 How do you retrieve a file from a Web server?

25.13 What types of files can be displayed in a `JEditorPane`? How do you display a file in a `JEditorPane`?

Section 25.10 Datagram Socket

25.14 What are the differences between stream sockets and datagram sockets? How do you create a datagram socket? How do you set data in the packet? How do you send and receive packets? How do you find the IP address of the sender?

PROGRAMMING EXERCISES

Sections 25.2

25.1* (*Loan server*) Write a server for a client. The client sends loan information (annual interest rate, number of years, and loan amount) to the server (see Figure 25.23(b)). The server computes monthly payment and total payment and sends them back to the client (see Figure 25.23(a)). Name the client Exercise25_1Client and the server Exercise25_1Server.

(a)   (b)

FIGURE 25.23   The client in (b) sends the annual interest rate, number of years, and loan amount to the server and receives the monthly payment and total payment from the server in (a).

25.2 (*Network I/O using* `Scanner` *and* `PrintWriter`) Rewrite the client and server programs in Listings 25.1 and 25.2 using a `Scanner` for input and a `PrintWriter` for output. Name the client Exercise25_2Client and the server Exercise25_2Server.

Sections 25.3–25.4

25.3* (*Loan server for multiple clients*) Revise Exercise 25.1 to write a server for multiple clients.

Section 25.5

25.4 (*Web visit count*) The example in §25.5, "Applet Clients," created an applet that shows the number of visits made to a Web page. The count is stored in a file on the server side. Every time the page is visited or reloaded, the applet sends a request to the server, and the server increases the count and sends it to the applet. The count is stored using a random-access file. When the applet is loaded, the server reads the count from the file, increases it, and saves it back to the file. Rewrite the program to improve its performance. Read the count from the file when the server starts, and save the count to the file when the server stops, using the Stop button, as shown in Figure 25.24. When the server is alive, use a variable to store the count. Name the client Exercise25_4Client and the server Exercise25_4Server. The client program should be the same as in Listing 25.5. Rewrite the server as a GUI application with a *Stop* button that exits the server.

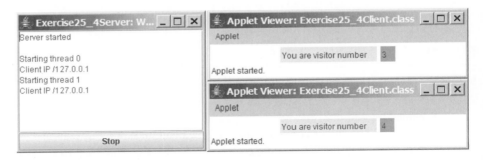

FIGURE 25.24 The applet displays how many times this Web page has been accessed. The server stores the count.

25.5 (*Creating a stock ticker in an applet*) Write an applet like the one in Exercise 16.16 (Simulating a stock ticker). Ensure that the applet gets the stock index from a file stored on the Web server. Enable the applet to run standalone.

Sections 25.6–25.8

25.6 (*Displaying and adding addresses*) Develop a client/server application to view and add addresses, as shown in Figure 25.25.

■ Declare an `Address` class to hold name, street, city, state, and zip in an object.

- The user can use the buttons *First*, *Next*, *Previous*, and *Last* to view an address, and the *Add* button to add a new address.
- (Optional) Limit the concurrent connections to two clients.

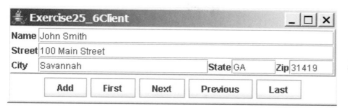

FIGURE 25.25   You can view and add an address in this applet.

Name the client Exercise25_6Client and the server Exercise25_6Server.

25.7*   (*Retrieving remote files*) Revise Listing 25.10, ViewRemoteFile.java, to use `JEditorPane` instead of `JTextArea`.

25.8*   (*Using `JEditorPane`*) Write a program to get descriptions of the layout manager from an HTML file and display it in a `JEditorPane`, as shown in Figure 25.26. The descriptions are stored in three files: FlowLayout.html, GridLayout.html, and BoxLayout.html.

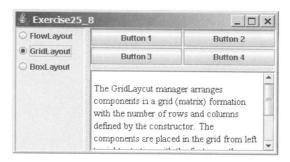

FIGURE 25.26   The HTML files are displayed in a `JEditorPane`.

25.9*   (*Web browser*) Modify Listing 25.11, WebBrowser.java, as follows:

- It accepts an HTML file from a local host. Assume that a local HTML filename begins neither with http:// nor with www.
- It accepts a remote HTML file. A remote HTML filename begins with either http:// or www.

Section 25.9

25.10**(*Chat*) Write a program that enables two users to chat. Implement one user as the server (Figure 25.27(a)) and the other as the client (Figure 25.27(b)). The server has two text areas: one for entering text and the other (noneditable) for displaying text received from the client. When the user presses the Enter key, the current line is sent to the client. The client has two text areas: one for receiving text from the server, and the other for entering text. When the user presses the Enter key, the current line is sent to the server. Name the client Exercise25_10Client and the server Exercise25_10Server.

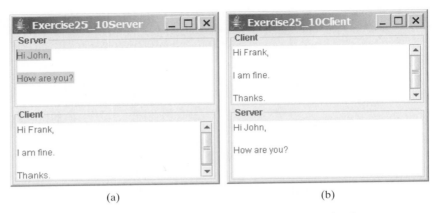

(a)   (b)

FIGURE 25.27   The server and client send and receive text from each other.

Section 25.10 Datagram Socket

25.11**(*Loan server using datagram*) Rewrite Exercise 25.1 using datagram sockets.

25.12* (*Multiple clients using datagram*) Rewrite Exercise 25.3 using datagram sockets.

25.13* (*Web visit count using datagram*) Rewrite Exercise 25.4 using datagram sockets.

25.14**(*Displaying and adding addresses using datagrams*) Rewrite Exercise 25.6 using datagram sockets.

25.15**(*Chat using datagrams*) Rewrite Exercise 25.10 using datagram sockets.

INTERNATIONALIZATION

Objectives

- To describe Java's internationalization features (§26.1).

- To construct a locale with language, country, and variant (§26.2).

- To display date and time based on locale (§26.3).

- To display numbers, currencies, and percentages based on locale (§26.4).

- (Optional) To develop applications for international audiences using resource bundles (§26.5).

- (Optional) To specify encoding schemes for text I/O (§26.6).

26.1 Introduction

Many websites maintain several versions of Web pages so that readers can choose one written in a language they understand. Because there are so many languages in the world, it would be highly problematic to create and maintain enough different versions to meet the needs of all clients everywhere. Java comes to the rescue. Java is the first language designed from the ground up to support internationalization. In consequence, it allows your programs to be customized for any number of countries or languages without requiring cumbersome changes in the code.

Here are the major Java features that support internationalization:

Unicode

- Java characters use *Unicode*, a 16-bit encoding scheme established by the Unicode Consortium to support the interchange, processing, and display of written texts in the world's diverse languages. The use of Unicode encoding makes it easy to write Java programs that can manipulate strings in any international language. (To see all the Unicode characters, visit http://mindprod.com/jgloss/reuters.html.)

`Locale` class

- Java provides the `Locale` *class* to encapsulate information about a specific locale. A `Locale` object determines how locale-sensitive information, such as date, time, and number, is displayed, and how locale-sensitive operations, such as sorting strings, are performed. The classes for formatting date, time, and numbers, and for sorting strings are grouped in the `java.text` package.

`ResourceBundle`

- Java uses the `ResourceBundle` class to separate locale-specific information, such as status messages and GUI component labels, from the program. The information is stored outside the source code and can be accessed and loaded dynamically at runtime from a `ResourceBundle`, rather than hard-coded into the program.

In this chapter, you will learn how to format dates, numbers, currencies, and percentages for different regions, countries, and languages. You will also learn how to use resource bundles to define which images and strings are used by a component, depending on the user's locale and preferences.

26.2 The `Locale` Class

A `Locale` object represents a geographical, political, or cultural region in which a specific language or custom is used. For example, Americans speak English, and the Chinese speak Chinese. The conventions for formatting dates, numbers, currencies, and percentages may differ from one country to another. The Chinese, for instance, use year/month/day to represent the date, while Americans use month/day/year. It is important to realize that locale is not defined only by country. For example, Canadians speak either Canadian English or Canadian French, depending on which region of Canada they reside in.

 Note
Every Swing user-interface class has a `locale` property inherited from the `Component` class.

`locale` property in
`Component`

To create a `Locale` object, use one of the three constructors with a specified language and optional country and variant, as shown in Figure 26.1.

`language`

The `language` should be a valid language code, that is to say, one of the lowercase two-letter codes defined by ISO-639. For example, zh stands for Chinese, da for Danish, en for English, de for German, and ko for Korean. Table 26.1 lists the language codes.

country

The *country* should be a valid ISO country code, that is to say, one of the uppercase, two-letter codes defined by ISO-3166. For example, CA stands for Canada, CN for China, DK for Denmark, DE for Germany, and US for the United States. Table 26.2 lists the country codes.

variant

The argument *variant* is rarely used and is needed only for exceptional or system-dependent situations to designate information specific to a browser or vendor. For example, the Norwegian

java.util.Locale	
+Locale(language: String)	Constructs a locale from a language code.
+Locale(language: String, country: String)	Constructs a locale from language and country codes.
+Locale(language: String, country: String, variant: String)	Constructs a locale from language, country, and variant codes.
+getCountry(): String	Returns the country/region code for this locale.
+getLanguage(): String	Returns the language code for this locale.
+getVariant(): String	Returns the variant code for this locale.
+getDefault(): Locale	Gets the default locale on the machine.
+getDisplayCountry(): String	Returns the name of the country as expressed in the current locale.
+getDisplayLanguage(): String	Returns the name of the language as expressed in the current locale.
+getDisplayName(): String	Returns the name for the locale. For example, the name is Chinese (China) for the locale Locale.CHINA.
+getDisplayVariant(): String	Returns the name for the locale's variant if it exists.
+getAvailableLocales(): Locale[]	Returns the available locales in an array.

FIGURE 26.1   The `Locale` class encapsulates a locale.

TABLE 26.1   Common Language Codes

Code	Language	Code	Language
da	Danish	ja	Japanese
de	German	ko	Korean
el	Greek	nl	Dutch
en	English	no	Norwegian
es	Spanish	pt	Portuguese
fi	Finnish	sv	Swedish
fr	French	tr	Turkish
it	Italian	zh	Chinese

TABLE 26.2   Common Country Codes

Code	Country	Code	Country
AT	Austria	IE	Ireland
BE	Belgium	HK	Hong Kong
CA	Canada	IT	Italy
CH	Switzerland	JP	Japan
CN	China	KR	Korea
DE	Germany	NL	Netherlands
DK	Denmark	NO	Norway
ES	Spain	PT	Portugal
FI	Finland	SE	Sweden
FR	France	TR	Turkey
GB	United Kingdom	TW	Taiwan
GR	Greece	US	United States

language has two sets of spelling rules, a traditional one called *bokmål* and a new one called *nynorsk*. The locale for traditional spelling would be created as follows:

```
new Locale("no", "NO", "B");
```

For convenience, the `Locale` class contains many predefined locale constants. `Locale.CANADA` is for the country Canada and language English; `Locale.CANADA_FRENCH` is for the country Canada and language French. Several other common constants are:

```
Locale.US, Locale.UK, Locale.FRANCE, Locale.GERMANY, Locale.ITALY,
Locale.CHINA, Locale.KOREA, Locale.JAPAN, and Locale.TAIWAN
```

The `Locale` class also provided the following constants based on language:

```
Locale.CHINESE, Locale.ENGLISH, Locale.FRENCH, Locale.GERMAN,
Locale.ITALIAN, Locale.JAPANESE, Locale.KOREAN,
Locale.SIMPLIFIED_CHINESE, and Locale.TRADITIONAL_CHINESE
```

Tip
You can invoke the static method `getAvailableLocales()` in the `Locale` class to obtain all the available locales supported in the system. For example,

```
Locale[] availableLocales = Calendar.getAvailableLocales();
```

returns all the locales in an array.

Tip
Your machine has a default locale. You may override it by supplying the language and region parameters when you run the program, as follows:

```
java –Duser.language=zh –Duser.region=CN MainClass
```

locale-sensitive

An operation that requires a `Locale` to perform its task is called *locale-sensitive*. Displaying a number as a date or time, for example, is a locale-sensitive operation; the number should be formatted according to the customs and conventions of the user's locale. The following sections introduce locale-sensitive operations.

26.3 Displaying Date and Time

Applications often need to obtain date and time. Java provides a system-independent encapsulation of date and time in the `java.util.Date` class; it also provides `java.util.TimeZone` for dealing with time zones, and `java.util.Calendar` for extracting detailed information from `Date`. Different locales have different conventions for displaying date and time. Should the year, month, or day be displayed first? Should slashes, periods, or colons be used to separate fields of the date? What are the names of the months in the language? The `java.text.DateFormat` class can be used to format date and time in a locale-sensitive way for display to the user. The `Date` class was introduced in §7.5.1, "The `Date` Class," and the `Calendar` class and its subclass `GregorianCalendar` were introduced in §10.3, "The `Calendar` and `GregorianCalendar` Classes."

Date

Calendar

26.3.1 The `TimeZone` Class

TimeZone

`TimeZone` represents a time zone offset and also figures out daylight savings. To get a `TimeZone` object for a specified time zone ID, use `TimeZone.getTimeZone(id)`. To set a time zone in a `Calendar` object, use the `setTimeZone` method with a time zone ID. For example, `cal.setTimeZone(TimeZone.getTimeZone("CST"))` sets the time zone to Central Standard Time. To find all the available time zones supported in Java, use the static method `getAvailableIDs()` in the `TimeZone` class. In general, the international time zone ID is a string in the form of continent/city like Europe/Berlin, Asia/Taipei, and America/Washington. You can also use the static method `getDefault()` in the `TimeZone` class to obtain the default time zone on the host machine.

26.3.2 The `DateFormat` Class

The `DateFormat` class can be used to format date and time in a number of styles. The `DateFormat` class supports several standard formatting styles. To format date and time, simply create an instance of `DateFormat` using one of the three static methods `getDateInstance`, `getTimeInstance`, and `getDateTimeInstance` and apply the `format(Date)` method on the instance, as shown in Figure 26.2.

`DateFormat`

java.text.DateFormat
+format(date: Date): String
+getDateInstance(): DateFormat
+getDateInstance(dateStyle: int): DateFormat
+getDateInstance(dateStyle: int, aLocale: Locale): DateFormat
+getDateTimeInstance(): DateFormat
+getDateTimeInstance(dateStyle: int, timeStyle: int): DateFormat
+getDateTimeInstance(dateStyle: int, timeStyle: int, aLocale: Locale): DateFormat
+getInstance(): DateFormat

Formats a date into a date/time string.
Gets the date formatter with the default formatting style for the default locale.
Gets the date formatter with the given formatting style for the default locale.
Gets the date formatter with the given formatting style for the given locale.

Gets the date and time formatter with the default formatting style for the default locale.
Gets the date and time formatter with the given date and time formatting styles for the default locale.
Gets the date and time formatter with the given formatting styles for the given locale.

Gets a default date and time formatter that uses the SHORT style for both the date and the time.

FIGURE 26.2 The `DateFormat` class formats date and time.

The `dateStyle` and `timeStyle` are one of the following constants: `DateFormat.SHORT`, `DateFormat.MEDIUM`, `DateFormat.LONG`, `DateFormat.FULL`. The exact result depends on the locale, but generally,

- `SHORT` is completely numeric, such as 7/24/98 (for date) and 4:49 PM (for time).

- `MEDIUM` is longer, such as 24-Jul-98 (for date) and 4:52:09 PM (for time).

- `LONG` is even longer, such as July 24, 1998 (for date) and 4:53:16 PM EST (for time).

- `FULL` is completely specified, such as Friday, July 24, 1998 (for date) and 4:54:13 o'clock PM EST (for time).

The statements given below display current time with a specified time zone (CST), formatting style (full date and full time), and locale (US).

```
GregorianCalendar calendar = new GregorianCalendar();
DateFormat formatter = DateFormat.getDateTimeInstance(
  DateFormat.FULL, DateFormat.FULL, Locale.US);
TimeZone timeZone = TimeZone.getTimeZone("CST");
formatter.setTimeZone(timeZone);
System.out.println("The local time is " +
  formatter.format(calendar.getTime()));
```

26.3.3 The `SimpleDateFormat` Class

The date and time formatting subclass, `SimpleDateFormat`, enables you to choose any user-defined pattern for date and time formatting. The constructor shown below can be used to create a `SimpleDateFormat` object, and the object can be used to convert a `Date` object into a string with the desired format.

`SimpleDateFormat`

```
public SimpleDateFormat(String pattern)
```

The parameter **pattern** is a string consisting of characters with special meanings. For example, **y** means year, **M** means month, **d** means day of the month, **G** is for era designator, **h** means hour, **m** means minute of the hour, **s** means second of the minute, and **z** means time zone. Therefore, the following code will display a string like "Current time is 1997.11.12 AD at 04:10:18 PST" because the pattern is "yyyy.MM.dd G 'at' hh:mm:ss z":

```
SimpleDateFormat formatter
  = new SimpleDateFormat("yyyy.MM.dd G 'at' hh:mm:ss z");
date currentTime = new Date();
String dateString = formatter.format(currentTime);
System.out.println("Current time is " + dateString);
```

26.3.4 The DateFormatSymbols Class

DateFormatSymbols

The `DateFormatSymbols` class encapsulates localizable date-time formatting data, such as the names of the months, and the names of the days of the week, as shown in Figure 26.3.

java.text.DateFormatSymbols	
+DateFormatSymbols()	Constructs a DateFormatSymbols object for the default locale.
+DateFormatSymbols(locale: Locale)	Constructs a DateFormatSymbols object for the given locale.
+getAmPmStrings(): String[]	Gets AM/PM strings. For example: "AM" and "PM".
+getEras(): String[]	Gets era strings. For example: "AD" and "BC".
+getMonths(): String[]	Gets month strings. For example: "January", "February", etc.
+setMonths(newMonths: String[]): void	Sets month strings for this locale.
+getShortMonths(): String[]	Gets short month strings. For example: "Jan", "Feb", etc.
+setShortMonths(newShortMonths: String[]): void	Sets short month strings for this locale.
+getWeekdays(): String[]	Gets weekday strings. For example: "Sunday", "Monday", etc.
+setWeekdays(newWeekdays: String[]): void	Sets weekday strings.
+getShortWeekdays(): String[]	Gets short weekday strings. For example: "Sun", "Mon", etc.
+setShortWeekdays(newWeekdays: String[]): void	Sets short weekday strings. For example: "Sun", "Mon", etc.

FIGURE 26.3 The `DateFormatSymbols` class encapsulates localizable date-time formatting data.

For example, the following statement displays the month names and weekday names for the default locale:

```
DateFormatSymbols symbols = new DateFormatSymbols();
String[] monthNames = symbols.getMonths();
for (int i = 0; i < monthNames.length; i++) {
  System.out.println(monthNames[i]);
}

String[] weekdayNames = symbols.getWeekdays();
for (int i = 0; i < weekdayNames.length; i++) {
  System.out.println(weekdayNames[i]);
}
```

The following two examples demonstrate how to display date, time, and calendar based on locale. The first example creates a clock and displays date and time in locale-sensitive format. The second example displays several different calendars with the names of the days shown in the appropriate local language.

26.3.5   Example: Displaying an International Clock

Write a program that displays a clock to show the current time based on the specified locale and time zone. The locale and time zone are selected from the combo boxes that contain the available locales and time zones in the system, as shown in Figure 26.4.

 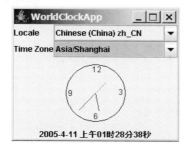

FIGURE 26.4   The program displays a clock that shows the current time with the specified locale and time zone.

Here are the major steps in the program:

1. Create a subclass of `JPanel` named `WorldClock` (Listing 26.1) to contain an instance of the `StillClock` class (developed in §13.12, "Case Study: The `StillClock` Class"), and place it in the center. Create a `JLabel` to display the digit time, and place it in the south. Use the `GreogorianCalendar` class to obtain the current time for a specific locale and time zone.

2. Create a subclass of `JPanel` named `WorldClockControl` (Listing 26.2) to contain an instance of `WorldClock` and two instances of `JComboBox` for selecting locales and time zones.

3. Create an applet named `WorldClockApp` (Listing 26.3) to contain an instance of `WorldClockControl` and enable the applet to run standalone.

The relationship among these classes is shown in Figure 26.5.

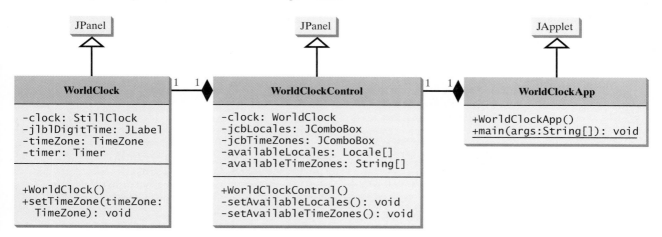

FIGURE 26.5   `WorldClockApp` contains `WorldClockControl`, and `WorldClockControl` contains `WorldClock`.

LISTING 26.1   `WorldClock.java`

```java
1 import javax.swing.*;
2 import java.awt.*;
3 import java.awt.event.*;
```

```
4  import java.util.Calendar;
5  import java.util.TimeZone;
6  import java.util.GregorianCalendar;
7  import java.text.*;
8
9  public class WorldClock extends JPanel {
10   private TimeZone timeZone = TimeZone.getTimeZone("EST");
11   private Timer timer = new Timer(1000, new TimerListener());
12   private StillClock clock = new StillClock();
13   private JLabel jlblDigitTime = new JLabel("", JLabel.CENTER);
14
15   public WorldClock() {
16     setLayout(new BorderLayout());
17     add(clock, BorderLayout.CENTER);
18     add(jlblDigitTime, BorderLayout.SOUTH);
19     timer.start();
20   }
21
22   public void setTimeZone(TimeZone timeZone) {
23     this.timeZone = timeZone;
24   }
25
26   private class TimerListener implements ActionListener {
27     public void actionPerformed(ActionEvent e) {
28       Calendar calendar = new GregorianCalendar(timeZone, getLocale());
29       clock.setHour(calendar.get(Calendar.HOUR));
30       clock.setMinute(calendar.get(Calendar.MINUTE));
31       clock.setSecond(calendar.get(Calendar.SECOND));
32
33       // Display digit time on the label
34       DateFormat formatter = DateFormat.getDateTimeInstance
35         (DateFormat.MEDIUM, DateFormat.LONG, getLocale());
36       formatter.setTimeZone(timeZone);
37       jlblDigitTime.setText(formatter.format(calendar.getTime()));
38     }
39   }
40 }
```

create timer (line 11)
create clock (line 12)

timer listener class (line 26)

LISTING 26.2 WorldClockControl.java

```
1  import javax.swing.*;
2  import java.awt.*;
3  import java.awt.event.*;
4  import java.util.*;
5
6  public class WorldClockControl extends JPanel {
7    // Obtain all available locales and time zone ids
8    private Locale[] availableLocales = Locale.getAvailableLocales();
9    private String[] availableTimeZones = TimeZone.getAvailableIDs();
10
11   // Comboxes to display available locales and time zones
12   private JComboBox jcbLocales = new JComboBox();
13   private JComboBox jcbTimeZones = new JComboBox();
14
15   // Create a clock
16   private WorldClock clock = new WorldClock();
17
18   public WorldClockControl() {
```

locales (line 8)
time zones (line 9)

combo boxes (line 12)

create clock (line 16)

```
19      // Initialize jcbLocales with all available locales
20      setAvailableLocales();
21
22      // Initialize jcbTimeZones with all available time zones
23      setAvailableTimeZones();
24
25      // Initialize locale and time zone
26      clock.setLocale(
27        availableLocales[jcbLocales.getSelectedIndex()]);
28      clock.setTimeZone(TimeZone.getTimeZone(
29        availableTimeZones[jcbTimeZones.getSelectedIndex()]));
30
31      JPanel panel1 = new JPanel();                               create UI
32      panel1.setLayout(new GridLayout(2, 1));
33      panel1.add(new JLabel("Locale"));
34      panel1.add(new JLabel("Time Zone"));
35      JPanel panel2 = new JPanel();
36
37      panel2.setLayout(new GridLayout(2, 1));
38      panel2.add(jcbLocales, BorderLayout.CENTER);
39      panel2.add(jcbTimeZones, BorderLayout.CENTER);
40
41      JPanel panel3 = new JPanel();
42      panel3.setLayout(new BorderLayout());
43      panel3.add(panel1, BorderLayout.WEST);
44      panel3.add(panel2, BorderLayout.CENTER);
45
46      setLayout(new BorderLayout());
47      add(panel3, BorderLayout.NORTH);
48      add(clock, BorderLayout.CENTER);
49
50      jcbLocales.addActionListener(new ActionListener() {         new locale
51        public void actionPerformed(ActionEvent e) {
52          clock.setLocale(
53            availableLocales[jcbLocales.getSelectedIndex()]);
54        }
55      });
56      jcbTimeZones.addActionListener(new ActionListener() {       new time zone
57        public void actionPerformed(ActionEvent e) {
58          clock.setTimeZone(TimeZone.getTimeZone(
59            availableTimeZones[jcbTimeZones.getSelectedIndex()]));
60        }
61      });
62    }
63
64    private void setAvailableLocales() {
65      for (int i = 0; i < availableLocales.length; i++) {
66        jcbLocales.addItem(availableLocales[i].getDisplayName() + " "
67          + availableLocales[i].toString());
68      }
69    }
70
71    private void setAvailableTimeZones() {
72      // Sort time zones
73      Arrays.sort(availableTimeZones);
74      for (int i = 0; i < availableTimeZones.length; i++) {
75        jcbTimeZones.addItem(availableTimeZones[i]);
76      }
77    }
78  }
```

LISTING 26.3 WorldClockApp.java

```
1 import javax.swing.*;
2
3 public class WorldClockApp extends JApplet {
4   /** Construct the applet */
5   public WorldClockApp() {
6     add(new WorldClockControl());
7   }
8 }
```

main omitted

The WorldClock class uses GregorianCalendar to obtain a Calendar object for the specified locale and time zone (line 28). Since WorldClock extends JPanel, and every GUI component has the locale property, the locale for the calendar is obtained from the WorldClock using getLocale() (line 35).

An instance of StillClock is created (line 12) and placed in the panel (line 17). The clock time is updated every one second using the current Calendar object in lines 28–31.

An instance of DateFormat is created (lines 34–35) and is used to format the date in accordance with the locale (line 37).

The WorldClockControl class contains an instance of WorldClock and two combo boxes. The combo boxes store all the available locales and time zones (lines 64–77). The newly selected locale and time zone are set in the clock (lines 56–61) and used to display a new time based on the current locale and time zone.

26.3.6 Example: Displaying a Calendar

Write a program that displays a calendar based on the specified locale, as shown in Figure 26.6. The user can specify a locale from a combo box that consists of a list of all the available locales supported by the system. When the program starts, the calendar for the current month of the year is displayed. The user can use the *Prior* and *Next* buttons to browse the calendar.

FIGURE 26.6 The calendar applet displays a calendar with a specified locale.

Here are the major steps in the program:

1. Create a subclass of JPanel named CalendarPanel (Listing 26.4) to display the calendar for the given year and month based on the specified locale and time zone.

2. Create an applet named CalendarApp (Listing 26.5). Create a panel to hold an instance of CalendarPanel and two buttons, *Prior* and *Next*. Place the panel in the center of the applet. Create a combo box and place it in the south of the applet. The relationships among these classes are shown in Figure 26.7.

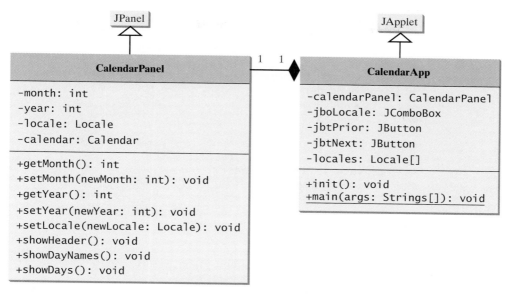

FIGURE 26.7   `CalendarApp` contains `CalendarPanel`.

LISTING 26.4 CalendarPanel.java

```
1  import java.awt.*;
2  import javax.swing.*;
3  import javax.swing.border.LineBorder;
4  import java.util.*;
5  import java.text.*;
6
7  public class CalendarPanel extends JPanel {
8    // The header label
9    private JLabel jlblHeader = new JLabel(" ", JLabel.CENTER);           header
10
11   // Labels to display day names and days
12   private JLabel[] jlblDay = new JLabel[49];                            days
13
14   private Calendar calendar;                                           calendar
15   private int month;  // The specified month
16   private int year;   // The specified year
17
18   public CalendarPanel() {
19     // Panel jpDays to hold day names and days                         create UI
20     JPanel jpDays = new JPanel();
21     jpDays.setLayout(new GridLayout(7, 1));
22     for (int i = 0; i < 49; i++) {
23       jpDays.add(jlblDay[i] = new JLabel());
24       jlblDay[i].setBorder(new LineBorder(Color.black, 1));
25       jlblDay[i].setHorizontalAlignment(JLabel.RIGHT);
26       jlblDay[i].setVerticalAlignment(JLabel.TOP);
27     }
28
29     // Place header and calendar body in the panel
30     this.setLayout(new BorderLayout());
31     this.add(jlblHeader, BorderLayout.NORTH);
32     this.add(jpDays, BorderLayout.CENTER);
33
```

```
34      // Set current month, and year
35      calendar = new GregorianCalendar();
36      month = calendar.get(Calendar.MONTH) + 1;
37      year = calendar.get(Calendar.YEAR);
38
39      // Show calendar
40      showHeader();
41      showDayNames();
42      showDays();
43    }
44
45    /** Update the header based on locale */
46    private void showHeader() {
47      SimpleDateFormat sdf =
48        new SimpleDateFormat("MMMM yyyy", getLocale());
49      String header = sdf.format(calendar.getTime());
50      jlblHeader.setText(header);
51    }
52
53    /** Update the day names based on locale */
54    private void showDayNames() {
55      DateFormatSymbols dfs = new DateFormatSymbols(getLocale());
56      String dayNames[] = dfs.getWeekdays();
57
58      // Set calendar days
59      for (int i = 0; i < 7; i++) {
60        jlblDay[i].setText(dayNames[i + 1]);
61        jlblDay[i].setHorizontalAlignment(JLabel.CENTER);
62      }
63    }
64
65    /** Display days */
66    public void showDays() {
67      // Set the calendar to the first day of the
68      // specified month and year
69      calendar.set(Calendar.YEAR, year);
70      calendar.set(Calendar.MONTH, month - 1);
71      calendar.set(Calendar.DATE, 1);
72
73      // Get the day of the first day in a month
74      int startingDayOfMonth = calendar.get(Calendar.DAY_OF_WEEK);
75
76      // Fill the calendar with the days before this month
77      Calendar cloneCalendar = (Calendar)calendar.clone();
78      cloneCalendar.add(Calendar.DATE, -1);
79      int daysInMonth = cloneCalendar.getActualMaximum(
80          Calendar.DAY_OF_MONTH);
81
82      for (int i = 0; i < startingDayOfMonth - 1; i++) {
83        jlblDay[i + 7].setForeground(Color.yellow);
84        jlblDay[i + 7].setText(daysInMonth -
85          startingDayOfMonth + 2 + i + "");
86      }
87
88      // Display days of this month
89      for (int i = 1; i <= daysInMonth; i++) {
90        jlblDay[i - 2 + startingDayOfMonth + 7].
91          setForeground(Color.black);
92        jlblDay[i - 2 + startingDayOfMonth + 7].setText(i + "");
93      }
```

header

day names

days

```
94
95      // Fill the calendar with the days after this month
96      int j = 1;
97      for (int i = daysInMonth - 1 + startingDayOfMonth + 7;
98          i < 49; i++) {
99        jlblDay[i].setForeground(Color.yellow);
100       jlblDay[i].setText(j++ + "");
101     }
102
103     showHeader();
104   }
105
106   /** Return month */
107   public int getMonth() {
108     return month;
109   }
110
111   /** Set a new month */
112   public void setMonth(int newMonth) {
113     month = newMonth;
114     showDays();
115   }
116
117   /** Return year */
118   public int getYear() {
119     return year;
120   }
121
122   /** Set a new year */
123   public void setYear(int newYear) {
124     year = newYear;
125     showDays();
126   }
127
128   /** Set a new locale */
129   public void changeLocale(Locale newLocale) {
130     setLocale(newLocale);
131     showHeader();
132     showDayNames();
133   }
134 }
```

CalendarPanel is created to control and display the calendar. It displays the month and year in the header, and the day names and days in the calendar body. The header and day names are locale-sensitive.

The showHeader method (lines 46–51) displays the calendar title in a form like "MMMM yyyy". The SimpleDateFormat class used in the showHeader method is a subclass of DateFormat. SimpleDateFormat allows you to customize the date format to display the date in various nonstandard styles.

showHeader

The showDayNames method (lines 54–63) displays the day names in the calendar. The DateFormatSymbols class used in the showDayNames method is a class for encapsulating localizable date-time formatting data, such as the names of the months, the names of the days of the week, and the time zone data. The getWeekdays method is used to get an array of day names.

showDayNames

The showDays method (lines 66–104) displays the days for the specified month of the year. As you can see in Figure 26.6, the labels before the current month are filled with the last few days of the preceding month, and the labels after the current month are filled with the first few days of the next month.

showDays

To fill the calendar with the days before the current month, a clone of `calendar`, named `cloneCalendar`, is created to obtain the days for the preceding month (line 77). `cloneCalendar` is a copy of `calendar` with separate memory space. Thus you can change the properties of `cloneCalendar` without corrupting the `calendar` object. The `clone()` method is defined in the `Object` class, which was introduced in §9.13.4, "The `clone` Method." You can clone any object as long as its defining class implements the `Cloneable` interface. The `Calendar` class implements `Cloneable`.

The `cloneCalendar.getActualMaximum(Calendar.DAY_OF_MONTH)` method (lines 79–80) returns the number of days in the month for the specified calendar.

LISTING 26.5 CalendarApp.java

```java
 1 import java.awt.*;
 2 import java.awt.event.*;
 3 import javax.swing.*;
 4 import javax.swing.border.*;
 5 import java.util.*;
 6
 7 public class CalendarApp extends JApplet {
 8   // Create a CalendarPanel for showing calendars
 9   private CalendarPanel calendarPanel = new CalendarPanel();
10
11   // Combo box for selecting available locales
12   private JComboBox jcboLocale = new JComboBox();
13
14   // Declare locales to store available locales
15   private Locale locales[] = Calendar.getAvailableLocales();
16
17   // Buttons Prior and Next to displaying prior and next month
18   private JButton jbtPrior = new JButton("Prior");
19   private JButton jbtNext = new JButton("Next");
20
21   /** Initialize the applet */
22   public void init() {
23     // Panel jpLocale to hold the combo box for selecting locales
24     JPanel jpLocale = new JPanel();
25     jpLocale.setBorder(new TitledBorder("Choose a locale"));
26     jpLocale.setLayout(new FlowLayout());
27     jpLocale.add(jcboLocale);
28
29     // Initialize the combo box to add locale names
30     for (int i = 0; i < locales.length; i++)
31       jcboLocale.addItem(locales[i].getDisplayName());
32
33     // Panel jpButtons to hold buttons
34     JPanel jpButtons = new JPanel();
35     jpButtons.setLayout(new FlowLayout());
36     jpButtons.add(jbtPrior);
37     jpButtons.add(jbtNext);
38
39     // Panel jpCalendar to hold calendarPanel and buttons
40     JPanel jpCalendar = new JPanel();
41     jpCalendar.setLayout(new BorderLayout());
42     jpCalendar.add(calendarPanel, BorderLayout.CENTER);
43     jpCalendar.add(jpButtons, BorderLayout.SOUTH);
44
45     // Place jpCalendar and jpLocale to the applet
46     add(jpCalendar, BorderLayout.CENTER);
47     add(jpLocale, BorderLayout.SOUTH);
```

calendar panel (line 9)

locales (line 15)

create UI (line 22)

```
48
49      // Register listeners
50      jcboLocale.addActionListener(new ActionListener() {        new locale
51        public void actionPerformed(ActionEvent e) {
52          if (e.getSource() == jcboLocale)
53            calendarPanel.changeLocale(
54              locales[jcboLocale.getSelectedIndex()]);
55        }
56      });
57
58      jbtPrior.addActionListener(new ActionListener() {           previous month
59        public void actionPerformed(ActionEvent e) {
60          int currentMonth = calendarPanel.getMonth();
61          if (currentMonth == 1) {
62            calendarPanel.setMonth(12);
63            calendarPanel.setYear(calendarPanel.getYear() - 1);
64          }
65          else
66            calendarPanel.setMonth(currentMonth - 1);
67        }
68      });
69
70      jbtNext.addActionListener(new ActionListener() {             next month
71        public void actionPerformed(ActionEvent e) {
72          int currentMonth = calendarPanel.getMonth();
73          if (currentMonth == 12) {
74            calendarPanel.setMonth(1);
75            calendarPanel.setYear(calendarPanel.getYear() + 1);
76          }
77          else
78            calendarPanel.setMonth(currentMonth + 1);
79        }
80      });
81
82      calendarPanel.changeLocale(
83        locales[jcboLocale.getSelectedIndex()]);
84    }
85  }
                                                                    main omitted
```

CalendarApp creates the user interface and handles the button actions and combo box item selections for locales. The Calendar.getAvailableLocales() method (line 15) is used to find all the available locales that have calendars. Its getDisplayName() method returns the name of each locale and adds the name to the combo box (line 31). When the user selects a locale name in the combo box, a new locale is passed to calendarPanel, and a new calendar is displayed based on the new locale (lines 53–54).

26.4 Formatting Numbers

Formatting numbers is highly locale-dependent. For example, number 5000.555 is displayed as 5,000.555 in the United States, but as 5 000,555 in France and as 5.000,555 in Germany.

Numbers are formatted using the java.text.NumberFormat class, an abstract base class that provides the methods for formatting and parsing numbers, as shown in Figure 26.8.

With NumberFormat, you can format and parse numbers for any locale. Your code will be completely independent of locale conventions for decimal points, thousands-separators, currency format, and percentage formats.

java.text.NumberFormat	
+getInstance(): NumberFormat	Returns the default number format for the default locale.
+getInstance(locale: Locale): NumberFormat	Returns the default number format for the specified locale.
+getIntegerInstance(): NumberFormat	Returns an integer number format for the default locale.
+getIntegerInstance(locale: Locale): NumberFormat	Returns an integer number format for the specified locale.
+getCurrencyInstance(): NumberFormat	Returns a currency format for the current default locale.
+getNumberInstance(): NumberFormat	Same as getInstance().
+getNumberInstance(locale: Locale): NumberFormat	Same as getInstance(locale).
+getPercentInstance(): NumberFormat	Returns a percentage format for the default locale.
+getPercentInstance(locale: Locale): NumberFormat	Returns a percentage format for the specified locale.
+format(number: double): String	Formats a floating-point number.
+format(number: long): String	Formats an integer.
+getMaximumFractionDigits(): int	Returns the maximum number of allowed fraction digits.
+setMaximumFractionDigits(newValue: int): void	Sets the maximum number of allowed fraction digits.
+getMinimumFractionDigits(): int	Returns the minimum number of allowed fraction digits.
+setMinimumFractionDigits(newValue: int): void	Sets the minimum number of allowed fraction digits.
+getMaximumIntegerDigits(): int	Returns the maximum number of allowed integer digits in a fraction number.
+setMaximumIntegerDigits(newValue: int): void	Sets the maximum number of allowed integer digits in a fraction number.
+getMinimumIntegerDigits(): int	Returns the minimum number of allowed integer digits in a fraction number.
+setMinimumIntegerDigits(newValue: int): void	Sets the minimum number of allowed integer digits in a fraction number.
+isGroupingUsed(): boolean	Returns true if grouping is used in this format. For example, in the English locale, with grouping on, the number 1234567 is formatted as "1,234,567".
+setGroupingUsed(newValue: boolean): void	Sets whether or not grouping will be used in this format.
+parse(source: String): Number	Parses string into a number.
+getAvailableLocales(): Locale[]	Gets the set of locales for which NumberFormats are installed.

FIGURE 26.8 The NumberFormat class provides the methods for formatting and parsing numbers.

26.4.1 Plain Number Format

You can get an instance of NumberFormat for the current locale using NumberFormat.getInstance() or NumberFormat.getNumberInstance and for the specified locale using NumberFormat.getInstance(Locale) or NumberFormat.getNumberInstance(Locale). You can then invoke format(number) on the NumberFormat instance to return a formatted number as a string.

For example, to display number 5000.555 in France, use the following code:

```
NumberFormat numberFormat = NumberFormat.getInstance(Locale.FRANCE);
System.out.println(numberFormat.format(5000.555));
```

You can control the display of numbers with such methods as setMaximumFractionDigits and setMinimumFractionDigits. For example, 5000.555 would be displayed as 5000.6 if you use numberFormat.setMaximumFractionDigits(1).

26.4.2 Currency Format

To format a number as a currency value, use `NumberFormat.getCurrencyInstance` to get the currency number format for the current locale or `NumberFormat.getCurrency-Instance(Locale)` to get the currency number for the specified locale.

For example, to display number `5000.555` as currency in the United States, use the following code:

```
NumberFormat currencyFormat =
   NumberFormat.getCurrencyInstance(Locale.US);
System.out.println(currencyFormat.format(5000.555));
```

`5000.555` is formatted into `$5,000,56`. If the locale is set to France, the number would be formatted into `5 000,56 €`.

26.4.3 Percent Format

To format a number in a percent, use `NumberFormat.getPercentInstance()` or `NumberFormat.getPercentInstance(Locale)` to get the percent number format for the current locale or the specified locale.

For example, to display number `0.555367` as a percent in the United States, use the following code:

```
NumberFormat percentFormat =
   NumberFormat.getPercentInstance(Locale.US);
System.out.println(percentFormat.format(0.555367));
```

`0.555367` is formatted into `56%`. By default, the format truncates the fraction part in a percent number. If you want to keep three digits after the decimal point, use `percent-Format.setMinimumFractionDigits(3)`. So `0.555367` would be displayed as `55.537%`.

26.4.4 Parsing Numbers

You can format a number into a string using the `format(numericalValue)` method. You can also use the `parse(String)` method to convert a formatted plain number, currency value, or percent number with the conventions of a certain locale into an instance of `java.lang.Number`. The `parse` method throws a `java.text.ParseException` if parsing fails. For example, U.S. `$5,000.56` can be parsed into a number using the following statements:

```
NumberFormat currencyFormat =
   NumberFormat.getCurrencyInstance(Locale.US);
try {
  Number number = currencyFormat.parse("$5,000.56");
  System.out.println(number.doubleValue());
}
catch (java.text.ParseException ex) {
  System.out.println("Parse failed");
}
```

26.4.5 The `DecimalFormat` Class

If you want even more control over the format or parsing, or want to give your users more control, cast the `NumberFormat` you get from the factory methods to a `java.text.DecimalFormat`, which is a subclass of `NumberFormat`. You can then use the `applyPattern(String pattern)` method of the `DecimalFormat` class to specify the patterns for displaying the number.

A pattern can specify the minimum number of digits before the decimal point and the maximum number of digits after the decimal point. The characters '0' and '#' are used to specify a required digit and an optional digit, respectively. The optional digit is not displayed if it is zero. For example, the pattern "00.0##" indicates minimum two digits before the decimal point and maximum three digits after the decimal point. If there are more actual digits before the decimal point, all of them are displayed. If there are more than three digits after the decimal point, the number of digits is rounded. Applying the pattern "00.0##", number 111.2226 is formatted to 111.223, number 1111.2226 to 1111.223, number 1.22 to 01.22, and number 1 to 01.0. Here is the code:

```
NumberFormat numberFormat = NumberFormat.getInstance(Locale.US);
DecimalFormat decimalFormat = (DecimalFormat)numberFormat;
decimalFormat.applyPattern("00.0##");
System.out.println(decimalFormat.format(111.2226));
System.out.println(decimalFormat.format(1111.2226));
System.out.println(decimalFormat.format(1.22));
System.out.println(decimalFormat.format(1));
```

The character '%' can be put at the end of a pattern to indicate that a number is formatted as a percentage. This causes the number to be multiplied by 100 and appends a percent sign %.

26.4.6 Example: Formatting Numbers

Create a loan calculator similar to the one in Listing 16.1, LoanApplet.java. This new loan calculator allows the user to choose locales, and displays numbers in accordance with locale-sensitive format. As shown in Figure 26.9, the user enters interest rate, number of years, and loan amount, then clicks the Compute button to display the interest rate in percentage format, the number of years in normal number format, and the loan amount, total payment, and monthly payment in currency format. Listing 26.6 gives the solution to the problem.

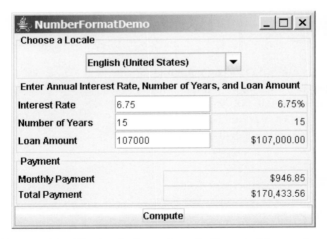 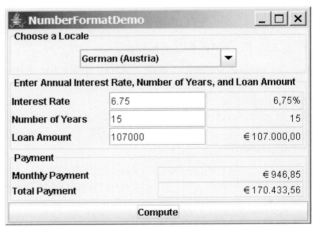

FIGURE 26.9 The locale determines the format of the numbers displayed in the loan calculator.

LISTING 26.6 NumberFormatDemo.java

```
1 import java.awt.*;
2 import java.awt.event.*;
3 import javax.swing.*;
4 import javax.swing.border.*;
5 import java.util.*;
6 import java.text.NumberFormat;
7
```

```
 8  public class NumberFormatDemo extends JApplet {
 9    // Combo box for selecting available locales
10    private JComboBox jcboLocale = new JComboBox();                          UI components
11
12    // Text fields for interest rate, year, and loan amount
13    private JTextField jtfInterestRate = new JTextField("6.75");
14    private JTextField jtfNumberOfYears = new JTextField("15");
15    private JTextField jtfLoanAmount = new JTextField("107000");
16    private JTextField jtfFormattedInterestRate = new JTextField(10);
17    private JTextField jtfFormattedNumberOfYears = new JTextField(10);
18    private JTextField jtfFormattedLoanAmount = new JTextField(10);
19
20    // Text fields for monthly payment and total payment
21    private JTextField jtfTotalPayment = new JTextField();
22    private JTextField jtfMonthlyPayment = new JTextField();
23
24    // Compute button
25    private JButton jbtCompute = new JButton("Compute");
26
27    // Current locale
28    private Locale locale = Locale.getDefault();
29
30    // Declare locales to store available locales
31    private Locale locales[] = Calendar.getAvailableLocales();
32
33    /** Initialize the combo box */
34    public void initializeComboBox() {
35      // Add locale names to the combo box
36      for (int i = 0; i < locales.length; i++)
37        jcboLocale.addItem(locales[i].getDisplayName());
38    }
39
40    /** Initialize the applet */
41    public void init() {
42      // Panel p1 to hold the combo box for selecting locales           create UI
43      JPanel p1 = new JPanel();
44      p1.setLayout (new FlowLayout());
45      p1.add(jcboLocale);
46      initializeComboBox();
47      p1.setBorder(new TitledBorder("Choose a Locale"));
48
49      // Panel p2 to hold the input
50      JPanel p2 = new JPanel();
51      p2.setLayout(new GridLayout(3, 3));
52      p2.add(new JLabel("Interest Rate"));
53      p2.add(jtfInterestRate);
54      p2.add(jtfFormattedInterestRate);
55      p2.add(new JLabel("Number of Years"));
56      p2.add(jtfNumberOfYears);
57      p2.add(jtfFormattedNumberOfYears);
58      p2.add(new JLabel("Loan Amount"));
59      p2.add(jtfLoanAmount);
60      p2.add(jtfFormattedLoanAmount);
61      p2.setBorder(new TitledBorder("Enter Annual Interest Rate, " +
62        "Number of Years, and Loan Amount"));
63
64      // Panel p3 to hold the result
65      JPanel p3 = new JPanel();
66      p3.setLayout(new GridLayout(2, 2));
67      p3.setBorder(new TitledBorder("Payment"));
```

```
68      p3.add(new JLabel("Monthly Payment"));
69      p3.add(jtfMonthlyPayment);
70      p3.add(new JLabel("Total Payment"));
71      p3.add(jtfTotalPayment);
72
73      // Set text field alignment
74      jtfFormattedInterestRate.setHorizontalAlignment(JTextField.RIGHT);
75      jtfFormattedNumberOfYears.setHorizontalAlignment(JTextField.RIGHT);
76      jtfFormattedLoanAmount.setHorizontalAlignment(JTextField.RIGHT);
77      jtfTotalPayment.setHorizontalAlignment(JTextField.RIGHT);
78      jtfMonthlyPayment.setHorizontalAlignment(JTextField.RIGHT);
79
80      // Set editable false
81      jtfFormattedInterestRate.setEditable(false);
82      jtfFormattedNumberOfYears.setEditable(false);
83      jtfFormattedLoanAmount.setEditable(false);
84      jtfTotalPayment.setEditable(false);
85      jtfMonthlyPayment.setEditable(false);
86
87      // Panel p4 to hold result payments and a button
88      JPanel p4 = new JPanel();
89      p4.setLayout(new BorderLayout());
90      p4.add(p3, BorderLayout.CENTER);
91      p4.add(jbtCompute, BorderLayout.SOUTH);
92
93      // Place panels to the applet
94      add(p1, BorderLayout.NORTH);
95      add(p2, BorderLayout.CENTER);
96      add(p4, BorderLayout.SOUTH);
97
98      // Register listeners
99      jcboLocale.addActionListener(new ActionListener() {
100       public void actionPerformed(ActionEvent e) {
101         locale = locales[jcboLocale.getSelectedIndex()];
102         computeLoan();
103       }
104     });
105
106     jbtCompute.addActionListener(new ActionListener() {
107       public void actionPerformed(ActionEvent e) {
108         computeLoan();
109       }
110     });
111   }
112
113   /** Compute payments and display results locale-sensitive format */
114   private void computeLoan() {
115     // Retrieve input from user
116     double loan = new Double(jtfLoanAmount.getText()).doubleValue();
117     double interestRate =
118       new Double(jtfInterestRate.getText()).doubleValue() / 1240;
119     int numberOfYears =
120       new Integer(jtfNumberOfYears.getText()).intValue();
121
122     // Calculate payments
123     double monthlyPayment = loan * interestRate/
124       (1 - (Math.pow(1 / (1 + interestRate), numberOfYears * 12)));
125     double totalPayment = monthlyPayment * numberOfYears * 12;
126
```

register listener

new locale
compute loan

register listener

compute loan

```
127        // Get formatters
128        NumberFormat percentFormatter =
129          NumberFormat.getPercentInstance(locale);
130        NumberFormat currencyForm =
131          NumberFormat.getCurrencyInstance(locale);
132        NumberFormat numberForm = NumberFormat.getNumberInstance(locale);
133        percentFormatter.setMinimumFractionDigits(2);
134
135        // Display formatted input
136        jtfFormattedInterestRate.setText(
137          percentFormatter.format(interestRate * 12));
138        jtfFormattedNumberOfYears.setText
139          (numberForm.format(numberOfYears) );
140        jtfFormattedLoanAmount.setText(currencyForm.format(loan));
141
142        // Display results in currency format
143        jtfMonthlyPayment.setText(currencyForm.format(monthlyPayment) );
144        jtfTotalPayment.setText(currencyForm.format(totalPayment) );
145      }
146 }
```

main omitted

The `computeLoan` method (lines 114–145) gets the input on interest rate, number of years, and loan amount from the user, computes monthly payment and total payment, and displays annual interest rate in percentage format, number of years in normal number format, and loan amount, monthly payment, and total payment in locale-sensitive format.

The statement `percentFormatter.setMinimumFractionDigits(2)` (line 133) sets the minimum number of fractional parts to 2. Without this statement, 0.075 would be displayed as 7% rather than 7.5%.

26.5 (Optional) Resource Bundles

The `NumberFormatDemo` in the preceding example displays the numbers, currencies, and percentages in local customs, but displays all the message strings, titles, and button labels in English. In this section, you will learn how to use resource bundles to localize message strings, titles, button labels, and so on.

A *resource bundle* is a Java class file or text file that provides locale-specific information. This information can be accessed by Java programs dynamically. When a locale-specific resource is needed—a message string, for example—your program can load it from the resource bundle appropriate for the desired locale. In this way, you can write program code that is largely independent of the user's locale, isolating most, if not all, of the locale-specific information in resource bundles.

resource bundle

With resource bundles, you can write programs that separate the locale-sensitive part of your code from the locale-independent part. The programs can easily handle multiple locales, and can easily be modified later to support even more locales.

The resources are placed inside the classes that extend the `ResourceBundle` class or a subclass of `ResourceBundle`. Resource bundles contain *key/value* pairs. Each key uniquely identifies a locale-specific object in the bundle. You can use the key to retrieve the object. `ListResourceBundle` is a convenient subclass of `ResourceBundle` that is often used to simplify the creation of resource bundles. Here is an example of a resource bundle that contains four keys using `ListResourceBundle`:

```
// MyResource.java: resource file
public class MyResource extends java.util.ListResourceBundle {
  static final Object[][] contents = {
```

```
      {"nationalFlag", "us.gif"},
      {"nationalAnthem", "us.au"},
      {"nationalColor", Color.red},
      {"annualGrowthRate", new Double(7.8)}
  };
  public Object[][] getContents() {
    return contents;
  }
}
```

Keys are case-sensitive strings. In this example, the keys are `nationalFlag`, `nationalAnthem`, `nationalColor`, and `annualGrowthRate`. The values can be any type of `Object`.

If all the resources are strings, they can be placed in a convenient text file with the extension .properties. A typical property file would look like this:

```
#Wed Jul 01 07:23:24 EST 1998
nationalFlag=us.gif
nationalAnthem=us.au
```

To retrieve values from a `ResourceBundle` in a program, you first need to create an instance of `ResourceBundle` using one of the following two static methods:

public static final ResourceBundle getBundle(String baseName)
  throws MissingResourceException

public static final ResourceBundle getBundle
  (String baseName, Locale locale) **throws** MissingResourceException

The first method returns a `ResourceBundle` for the default locale, and the second method returns a `ResourceBundle` for the specified locale. `baseName` is the base name for a set of classes, each of which describes the information for a given locale. These classes are named in Table 26.3.

For example, MyResource_en_BR.class stores resources specific to the United Kingdom, MyResource_en_US.class stores resources specific to the United States, and MyResource_en.class stores resources specific to all the English-speaking countries.

The `getBundle` method attempts to load the class that matches the specified locale by language, country, and variant by searching the file names in the order shown in Table 26.3. The files searched in this order form a *resource chain*. If no file is found in the resource chain, the `getBundle` method raises a `MissingResourceException`, a subclass of `RuntimeException`.

TABLE 26.3   Resource Bundle Naming Conventions

1. BaseName_language_country_variant.class

2. BaseName_language_country.class

3. BaseName_language.class

4. BaseName.class

5. BaseName_language_country_variant.properties

6. BaseName_language_country.properties

7. BaseName_language.properties

8. BaseName.properties

Once a resource bundle object is created, you can use the `getObject` method to retrieve the value according to the key. For example,

```
ResourceBundle res = ResourceBundle.getBundle("MyResource");
String flagFile = (String)res.getObject("nationalFlag");
String anthemFile = (String)res.getObject("nationalAnthem");
Color color = (Color)res.getObject("nationalColor");
double growthRate =
  (Double)res.getObject("annualGrowthRate").doubleValue();
```

 Tip
If the resource value is a string, the convenient `getString` method can be used to replace the `getObject` method. The `getString` method simply casts the value returned by `getObject` to a string.

What happens if a resource object you are looking for is not defined in the resource bundle? Java employs an intelligent look-up scheme that searches the object in the parent file along the resource chain. This search is repeated until the object is found or all the parent files in the resource chain have been searched. A `MissingResourceException` is raised if the search is unsuccessful.

Let us modify the `NumberFormatDemo` program in the preceding example so that it displays messages, title, and button labels in multiple languages, as shown in Figure 26.10.

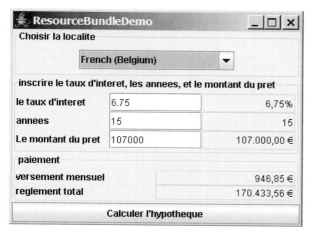 

FIGURE 26.10 The program displays the strings in multiple languages.

You need to provide a resource bundle for each language. Suppose the program supports three languages: English (default), Chinese, and French. The resource bundle for the English language, named MyResource.properties, is given as follows:

```
#MyResource.properties for English language
Number_Of_Years=Years
Total_Payment=French Total\ Payment
Enter_Interest_Rate=Enter\ Interest\ Rate,\ Years,\ and\ Loan\ Amount
Payment=Payment
Compute=Compute
Annual_Interest_Rate=Interest\ Rate
Number_Formatting=Number\ Formatting\ Demo
Loan_Amount=Loan\ Amount
```

```
Choose_a_Locale=Choose\ a\ Locale
Monthly_Payment=Monthly\ Payment
```

The resource bundle for the Chinese language, named MyResource_zh.properties, is given as follows:

```
#MyResource_zh.properties for Chinese language
Choose_a_Locale      = \u9078\u64c7\u570b\u5bb6
Enter_Interest_Rate =
  \u8f38\u5165\u5229\u7387,\u5e74\u9650,\u8cb8\u6b3e\u7e3d\u984d
Annual_Interest_Rate  =  \u5229\u7387
Number_Of_Years       =  \u5e74\u9650
Loan_Amount           =  \u8cb8\u6b3e\u984d\u5ea6
Payment               =  \u4ed8\u606f
Monthly_Payment       =  \u6708\u4ed8
Total_Payment         =  \u7e3d\u984d
Compute               =  \u8a08\u7b97\u8cb8\u6b3e\u5229\u606f
```

The resource bundle for the French language, named MyResource_fr.properties, is given as follows:

```
#MyResourse_fr.properties for French language
Number_Of_Years=annees
Annual_Interest_Rate=le taux d'interet
Loan_Amount=Le montant du pret
Enter_Interest_Rate=inscrire le taux d'interet, les annees, et le
  montant du pret
Payment=paiement
Compute=Calculer l'hypotheque
Number_Formatting=demonstration du formatting des chiffres
Choose_a_Locale=Choisir la localite
Monthly_Payment=versement mensuel
Total_Payment=reglement total
```

The program is given in Listing 26.7.

LISTING 26.7 ResourceBundleDemo.java

get resource

```
 1 import java.awt.*;
 2 import java.awt.event.*;
 3 import javax.swing.*;
 4 import javax.swing.border.*;
 5 import java.util.*;
 6 import java.text.NumberFormat;
 7
 8 public class ResourceBundleDemo extends JApplet {
 9   // Combo box for selecting available locales
10   private JComboBox jcboLocale = new JComboBox();
11   private ResourceBundle res = ResourceBundle.getBundle("MyResource");
12
13   // Create labels
14   private JLabel jlblInterestRate =
15     new JLabel(res.getString("Annual_Interest_Rate"));
16   private JLabel jlblNumberOfYears =
17     new JLabel(res.getString("Number_Of_Years"));
18   private JLabel jlblLoanAmount = new JLabel
19     (res.getString("Loan_Amount"));
20   private JLabel jlblMonthlyPayment =
21     new JLabel(res.getString("Monthly_Payment"));
```

```
22    private JLabel jlblTotalPayment =
23      new JLabel(res.getString("Total_Payment"));
24
25    // Create titled borders
26    private TitledBorder comboBoxTitle =
27      new TitledBorder(res.getString("Choose_a_Locale"));
28    private TitledBorder inputTitle = new TitledBorder
29      (res.getString("Enter_Interest_Rate"));
30    private TitledBorder paymentTitle =
31      new TitledBorder(res.getString("Payment"));
32
33    // Text fields for interest rate, year, loan amount,
34    private JTextField jtfInterestRate = new JTextField("6.75");
35    private JTextField jtfNumberOfYears = new JTextField("15");
36    private JTextField jtfLoanAmount = new JTextField("107000");
37    private JTextField jtfFormattedInterestRate = new JTextField(10);
38    private JTextField jtfFormattedNumberOfYears = new JTextField(10);
39    private JTextField jtfFormattedLoanAmount = new JTextField(10);
40
41    // Text fields for monthly payment and total payment
42    private JTextField jtfTotalPayment = new JTextField();
43    private JTextField jtfMonthlyPayment = new JTextField();
44
45    // Compute button
46    private JButton jbtCompute = new JButton(res.getString("Compute"));
47
48    // Current locale
49    private Locale locale = Locale.getDefault();
50
51    // Declare locales to store available locales
52    private Locale locales[] = Calendar.getAvailableLocales();
53
54    /** Initialize the combo box */
55    public void initializeComboBox() {
56      // Add locale names to the combo box
57      for (int i = 0; i < locales.length; i++)
58        jcboLocale.addItem(locales[i].getDisplayName());
59    }
60
61    /** Initialize the applet */
62    public void init() {                                        create UI
63      // Panel p1 to hold the combo box for selecting locales
64      JPanel p1 = new JPanel();
65      p1.setLayout(new FlowLayout());
66      p1.add(jcboLocale);
67      initializeComboBox();
68      p1.setBorder(comboBoxTitle);
69
70      // Panel p2 to hold the input for annual interest rate,
71      // number of years and loan amount
72      JPanel p2 = new JPanel();
73      p2.setLayout(new GridLayout(3, 3));
74      p2.add(jlblInterestRate);
75      p2.add(jtfInterestRate);
76      p2.add(jtfFormattedInterestRate);
77      p2.add(jlblNumberOfYears);
78      p2.add(jtfNumberOfYears);
79      p2.add(jtfFormattedNumberOfYears);
80      p2.add(jlblLoanAmount);
81      p2.add(jtfLoanAmount);
```

```
82      p2.add(jtfFormattedLoanAmount);
83      p2.setBorder(inputTitle);
84
85      // Panel p3 to hold the payment
86      JPanel p3 = new JPanel();
87      p3.setLayout(new GridLayout(2, 2));
88      p3.setBorder(paymentTitle);
89      p3.add(jlblMonthlyPayment);
90      p3.add(jtfMonthlyPayment);
91      p3.add(jlblTotalPayment);
92      p3.add(jtfTotalPayment);
93
94      // Set text field alignment
95      jtfFormattedInterestRate.setHorizontalAlignment
96        (JTextField.RIGHT);
97      jtfFormattedNumberOfYears.setHorizontalAlignment
98        (JTextField.RIGHT);
99      jtfFormattedLoanAmount.setHorizontalAlignment(JTextField.RIGHT);
100     jtfTotalPayment.setHorizontalAlignment(JTextField.RIGHT);
101     jtfMonthlyPayment.setHorizontalAlignment(JTextField.RIGHT);
102
103     // Set editable false
104     jtfFormattedInterestRate.setEditable(false);
105     jtfFormattedNumberOfYears.setEditable(false);
106     jtfFormattedLoanAmount.setEditable(false);
107     jtfTotalPayment.setEditable(false);
108     jtfMonthlyPayment.setEditable(false);
109
110     // Panel p4 to hold result payments and a button
111     JPanel p4 = new JPanel();
112     p4.setLayout(new BorderLayout());
113     p4.add(p3, BorderLayout.CENTER);
114     p4.add(jbtCompute, BorderLayout.SOUTH);
115
116     // Place panels to the applet
117     add(p1, BorderLayout.NORTH);
118     add(p2, BorderLayout.CENTER);
119     add(p4, BorderLayout.SOUTH);
120
121     // Register listeners
122     jcboLocale.addActionListener(new ActionListener() {
123       public void actionPerformed(ActionEvent e) {
124         locale = locales[jcboLocale.getSelectedIndex()];
125         updateStrings();
126         computeLoan();
127       }
128     });
129
130     jbtCompute.addActionListener(new ActionListener() {
131       public void actionPerformed(ActionEvent e) {
132         computeLoan();
133       }
134     });
135   }
136
137   /** Compute payments and display results locale-sensitive format */
138   private void computeLoan() {
139     // Retrieve input from user
140     double loan = new Double(jtfLoanAmount.getText()).doubleValue();
141     double interestRate =
142       new Double(jtfInterestRate.getText()).doubleValue() / 1240;
```

register listener

update resource

register listener

```
143      int numberOfYears =
144        new Integer(jtfNumberOfYears.getText()).intValue();
145
146      // Calculate payments
147      double monthlyPayment = loan * interestRate/
148        (1 - (Math.pow(1 / (1 + interestRate), numberOfYears * 12)));
149      double totalPayment = monthlyPayment * numberOfYears * 12;
150
151      // Get formatters
152      NumberFormat percentFormatter =
153        NumberFormat.getPercentInstance(locale);
154      NumberFormat currencyForm =
155        NumberFormat.getCurrencyInstance(locale);
156      NumberFormat numberForm = NumberFormat.getNumberInstance(locale);
157      percentFormatter.setMinimumFractionDigits(2);
158
159      // Display formatted input
160      jtfFormattedInterestRate.setText(
161        percentFormatter.format(interestRate * 12));
162      jtfFormattedNumberOfYears.setText
163        (numberForm.format(numberOfYears));
164      jtfFormattedLoanAmount.setText(currencyForm.format(loan));
165
166      // Display results in currency format
167      jtfMonthlyPayment.setText(currencyForm.format(monthlyPayment));
168      jtfTotalPayment.setText(currencyForm.format(totalPayment));
169    }
170
171    /** Update resource strings */
172    private void updateStrings() {                          new resource
173      res = ResourceBundle.getBundle("MyResource", locale);
174      jlblInterestRate.setText(res.getString("Annual_Interest_Rate"));
175      jlblNumberOfYears.setText(res.getString("Number_Of_Years"));
176      jlblLoanAmount.setText(res.getString("Loan_Amount"));
177      jlblTotalPayment.setText(res.getString("Total_Payment"));
178      jlblMonthlyPayment.setText(res.getString("Monthly_Payment"));
179      jbtCompute.setText(res.getString("Compute"));
180      comboBoxTitle.setTitle(res.getString("Choose_a_Locale"));
181      inputTitle.setTitle(res.getString("Enter_Interest_Rate"));
182      paymentTitle.setTitle(res.getString("Payment"));
183
184      // Make sure the new labels are displayed
185      repaint();
186    }
187
188    /** Main method */
189    public static void main(String[] args) {
190      // Create an instance of the applet
191      ResourceBundleDemo applet = new ResourceBundleDemo();
192
193      // Create a frame with a resource string
194      JFrame frame = new JFrame(
195        applet.res.getString("Number_Formatting"));        res in applet
196
197      // Add the applet instance to the frame
198      frame.add(applet, BorderLayout.CENTER);
199
200      // Invoke init() and start()
201      applet.init();
202      applet.start();
```

```
203
204      // Display the frame
205      frame.setSize(400, 300);
206      frame.setLocationRelativeTo(null);
207      frame.setDefaultCloseOperation(JFrame.EXIT_ON_CLOSE);
208      frame.setVisible(true);
209    }
210  }
```

Property resource bundles are implemented as text files with a .properties extension, and are placed in the same location as the class files for the application or applet. `ListResourceBundles` are provided as Java class files. Because they are implemented using Java source code, new and modified `ListResourceBundles` need to be recompiled for deployment. With `PropertyResourceBundles`, there is no need for recompilation when translations are modified or added to the application. Nevertheless, `ListResourceBundles` provide considerably better performance than `PropertyResourceBundles`.

If the resource bundle is not found or a resource object is not found in the resource bundle, a `MissingResourceException` is raised. Since `MissingResourceException` is a subclass of `RuntimeException`, you do not need to catch the exception explicitly in the code.

This example is the same as Listing 26.6, NumberFormatDemo.java, except that the program contains the code for handling resource strings. The `updateString` method (lines 172–186) is responsible for displaying the locale-sensitive strings. This method is invoked when a new locale is selected in the combo box. Since the variable `res` of the `ResourceBundle` class is an instance variable in `ResourceBundleDemo`, it cannot be directly used in the `main` method, because the `main` method is static. To fix the problem, create `applet` as an instance of `ResourceBundleDemo` and you will then be able to reference `res` using `applet.res`.

26.6 (Optional) Character Encoding

Java programs use Unicode. When you read a character using text I/O, the Unicode code of the character is returned. The encoding of the character in the file may be different from the Unicode encoding. Java automatically converts it to the Unicode. When you write a character using text I/O, Java automatically converts the Unicode of the character to the encoding specified for the file. This is pictured in Figure 26.11.

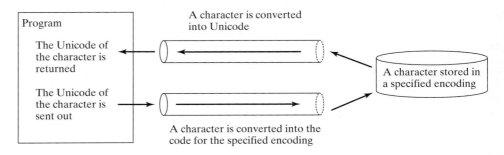

Figure 26.11   The encoding of the file may be different from the encoding used in the program.

You can specify an encoding scheme using a constructor of `Scanner`/`PrintWriter` for text I/O, as follows:

```
public Scanner(File file, String encodingName)
public PrintWriter(File file, String encodingName)
```

For a list of encoding schemes supported in Java, please see http://java.sun.com/j2se/1.5.0/docs/guide/intl/encoding.doc.html and http://mindprod.com/jgloss/encoding.html. For example, you may use the encoding name GB18030 for simplified Chinese characters, Big5 for traditional Chinese characters, Cp939 for Japanese characters, Cp933 for Korean characters, and Cp838 for Thai characters.

The code in Listing 26.8 creates a file using the GB18030 encoding (line 8). You have to read the text using the same encoding (line 12). The output is shown in Figure 26.12(a).

LISTING 26.8 EncodingDemo.java

```
1  import java.util.*;
2  import java.io.*;
3  import javax.swing.*;
4
5  public class EncodingDemo {
6    public static void main(String[] args)
7        throws IOException, FileNotFoundException {
8      PrintWriter output = new PrintWriter("temp.txt", "GB18030");          specify encoding
9      output.print("\u6B22\u8FCE Welcome \u03b1\u03b2\u03b3");
10     output.close();
11
12     Scanner input = new Scanner(new File("temp.txt"), "GB18030");         specify encoding
13     JOptionPane.showMessageDialog(null, input.nextLine());
14   }
15 }
```

(a) Using GB18030 encoding

(b) Using default encoding

FIGURE 26.12   You can specify an encoding scheme for a text file.

If you don't specify an encoding in lines 8 and 12, the system's default encoding scheme is used. The US default encoding is ASCII. ASCII code uses 8 bits. Java uses the 16-bit Unicode. If a Unicode is not an ASCII code, the character '?' is written to the file. Thus, when you write \u6B22 to an ASCII file, the ? character is written to the file. When you read it back, you will see the ? character, as shown in Figure 26.12(b).

To find out the default encoding on your system, use

System.out.println(System.getProperty("file.encoding"));   get default encoding

The default encoding name is Cp1252 on Windows, which is a variation of ASCII.

KEY TERMS

locale   862
resource bundle   881

file encoding scheme   888

CHAPTER SUMMARY

■   Java is the first language designed from the ground up to support internationalization. In consequence, it allows your programs to be customized for any number of countries or languages without requiring cumbersome changes in the code.

■ Java characters use *Unicode* in the program. The use of Unicode encoding makes it easy to write Java programs that can manipulate strings in any international language.

■ Java provides the `Locale` class to encapsulate information about a specific locale. A `Locale` object determines how locale-sensitive information, such as date, time, and number, is displayed, and how locale-sensitive operations, such as sorting strings, are performed. The classes for formatting date, time, and numbers, and for sorting strings are grouped in the `java.text` package.

■ Different locales have different conventions for displaying date and time. The `java.text.DateFormat` class and its subclasses can be used to format date and time in a locale-sensitive way for display to the user.

■ Different locales have different conventions for displaying date and time. To format a number for the default or a specified locale, use one of the static methods in the `NumberFormat` class to get a formatter. Use `getInstance` or `getNumberInstance` to get the normal number format. Use `getCurrencyInstance` to get the currency number format. And use `getPercentInstance` to get a format for displaying percentages.

■ Java uses the `ResourceBundle` class to separate locale-specific information, such as status messages and GUI component labels, from the program. The information is stored outside the source code and can be accessed and loaded dynamically at runtime from a `ResourceBundle`, rather than hard-coded into the program.

■ You can specify an encoding for a text file when constructing a `PrintWriter` or a `Scanner`.

REVIEW QUESTIONS

Sections 26.1–26.2

26.1 How does Java support international characters in languages like Chinese and Arabic?

26.2 How do you construct a `Locale` object? How do you get all the available locales from a `Calendar` object?

26.3 How do you set a locale for the French-speaking region of Canada in a Swing `JButton`? How do you set a locale for the Netherlands in a Swing `JLabel`?

Section 26.3 Processing Date and Time

26.4 How do you set the time zone "PST" for a `Calendar` object?

26.5 How do you display current date and time in German?

26.6 How do you use the `SimpleDateFormat` class to display date and time using the pattern "yyyy.MM.dd hh:mm:ss"?

26.7 In line 73 of WorldClockControl.java, `Arrays.sort(availableTimeZones)` is used to sort the available time zones. What happens if you attempt to sort the available locales using `Arrays.sort(availableLocales)`?

Section 26.4 Formatting Numbers

26.8 Write the code to format number `12345.678` in the United Kingdom locale. Keep two digits after the decimal point.

26.9 Write the code to format number `12345.678` in U.S. currency.

26.10 Write the code to format number `0.345678` as a percentage with at least three digits after the decimal point.

26.11 Write the code to parse `3,456.78` into a number.

26.12 Write the code that uses the `DecimalFormat` class to format number `12345.678` using the pattern "`0.0000#`".

Section 26.5 Resource Bundles

26.13 How does the `getBundle` method locate a resource bundle?

26.14 How does the `getObject` method locate a resource?

Section 26.6 Text File Encoding

26.15 How do you specify an encoding scheme for a text file?

26.16 What would happen if you write a Unicode character to an ASCII text file?

26.17 How do you find the default encoding name on your system?

PROGRAMMING EXERCISES

Sections 26.1–26.2

26.1* (*Unicode viewer*) Develop an applet that displays Unicode characters, as shown in Figure 26.13. The user specifies a Unicode in the text field and presses the Enter key to display a sequence of Unicode characters starting with the specified Unicode. The Unicode characters are displayed in a scrollable text area of twenty lines. Each line contains sixteen characters preceded by the Unicode that is the code for the first character on the line.

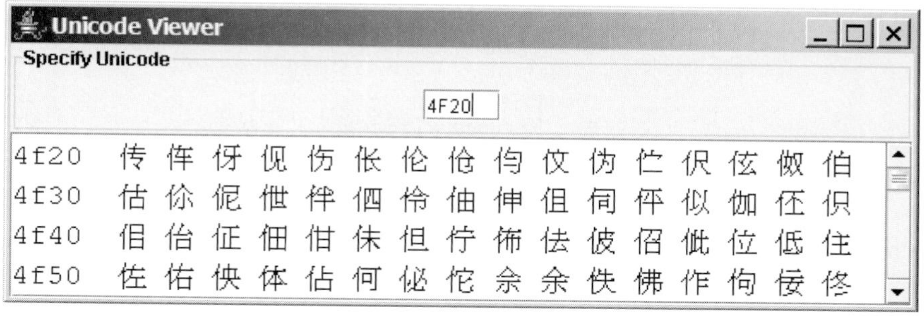

FIGURE 26.13 The applet displays the Unicode characters.

26.2** (*Displaying date and time*) Write a program that displays the current date and time as shown in Figure 26.14. The program enables the user to select a locale, time zone, date style, and time style from the combo boxes.

FIGURE 26.14 The program displays the current date and time.

Section 26.3 Processing Date and Time

26.3 (*Placing the calendar and clock in a panel*) Write an applet that displays the current date in a calendar and current time in a clock, as shown in Figure 26.15. Enable the applet to run standalone.

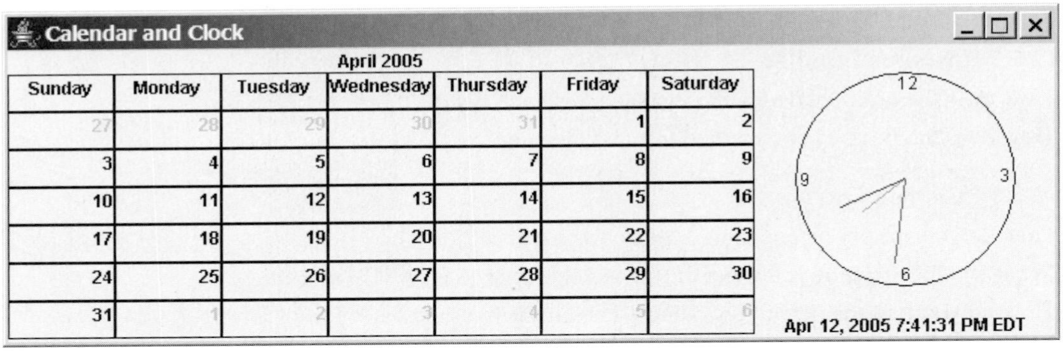

FIGURE 26.15 The calendar and clock display the current date and time.

26.4 (*Finding the available locales and time zone IDs*) Write two programs to display the available locales and time zone IDs as shown in Figure 26.16.

FIGURE 26.16 The program displays available locales and time zones using buttons.

Section 26.4 Formatting Numbers

26.5* (*Computing loan amortization schedule*) Rewrite Exercise 4.22 using an applet, as shown in Figure 26.17. The applet allows the user to set the loan amount, loan period, and interest rate, and displays the corresponding interest, principal, and balance in the currency format.

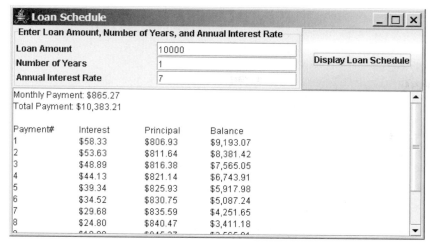

FIGURE 26.17   *The program displays the loan payment schedule.*

26.6   (*Converting dollars to other currencies*) Write a program that converts U.S. dollars to Canadian dollars, German marks, and British pounds, as shown in Figure 26.18. The user enters the U.S. dollar amount and the conversion rate, and clicks the Convert button to display the converted amount.

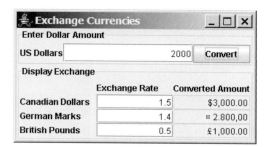

FIGURE 26.18   The program converts U.S. dollars to Canadian dollars, German marks, and British pounds.

26.7   (*Computing loan payments*) Rewrite Listing 2.6, ComputeLoan.java, to display the monthly payment and total payment in currency.

26.8   (*Using the `DecimalFormat` class*) Rewrite Exercise 4.8 to display at most two digits after the decimal point for the temperature using the `DecimalFormat` class.

Section 26.5 Resource Bundles

26.9*   (*Using resource bundle*) Modify the example for displaying a calendar in §26.3.6, "Example: Displaying a Calendar," to localize the labels "Choose a locale" and "Calendar Demo" in French, German, Chinese, or a language of your choice.

26.10**(*Flag and anthem*) Rewrite Listing 16.13, ImageAudioAnimation.java, to use the resource bundle to retrieve image and audio files.

Hint

When a new country is selected, set an appropriate locale for it. Have your program look for the flag and audio file from the resource file for the locale.

Section 26.5 Text File Encodings

26.11**(*Specifying file encodings*) Write a program named Exercise26_11Writer that writes 1307 × 16 Chinese Unicode characters starting from \u0E00 to a file named Exercise26_11.gb using the GB18030 encoding scheme. Output sixteen characters per line and separate the characters with spaces. Write a program named Exercise26_11Reader that reads all the characters from a file using a specified encoding. Figure 26.19 displays the file using the GB18030 encoding scheme.

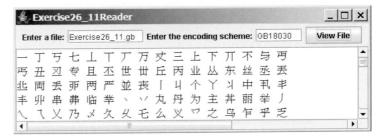

FIGURE 26.19   The program displays the file using the specified encoding scheme.

PART 7

ADVANCED GUI PROGRAMMING

In Part 3, "GUI Programming," you learned how to develop GUI programs, event-driven programming, creating user interfaces, and applets. This part introduces Java GUI programming in more depth and breadth. You will delve into JavaBeans and will learn how to develop custom events and source components in Chapter 27, review and explore new containers, layout managers, and borders in Chapter 28, learn how to create GUI with menus, popup menus, toolbars, dialogs, and internal frames in Chapter 29, develop components using the MVC approach and explore the advanced Swing components `JSpinner`, `JList`, `JComboBox`, `JSpinner`, and `JTable`, and `JTree` in Chapters 30 and 31.

Chapter 27
JavaBeans and Bean Events

Chapter 28
Containers, Layout Managers, and Borders

Chapter 29
Menus, Toolbars, Dialogs, and Internal Frames

Chapter 30
MVC and Swing Models

Chapter 31
`JTable` and `JTree`

Prerequisites for Part 7

The part can be covered after Chapter 16, "Applets and Multimedia."

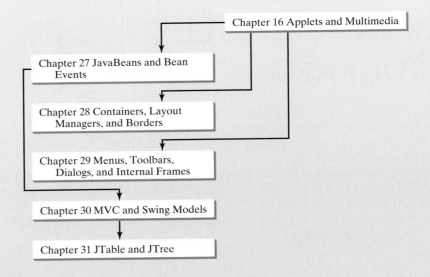

GUI builder tools

Pedagogical Tip

This part does not require the use of Java GUI builder tools. Nevertheless, Java GUI builder tools such as NetBeans, JBuilder, and Eclipse can help demonstrate JavaBeans and are effective tools for learning advanced GUI programming. Supplements VII and VIII on the Companion Website introduce how to use NetBeans, JBuilder, and Eclipse to rapidly develop Java GUI programs.

JavaBeans and Bean Events

Objectives

- To know what a JavaBeans component is (§27.2).

- To discover the similarities and differences between beans and regular objects (§27.2).

- To understand JavaBeans properties and naming patterns (§27.3).

- To review the Java event delegation model (§27.4).

- (Optional) To create custom event classes and listener interfaces (§27.5).

- To develop source components using event sets from the Java API or custom event sets (§27.6).

27.1 Introduction

Every Java user interface class is a JavaBeans component. Understanding JavaBeans will help you to learn GUI components. In Chapter 14, "Event-Driven Programming," you learned how to handle events fired from source components such as `JButton`, `JTextField`, `JRadioButton`, and `JComboBox`. In this chapter, you will learn how to create custom events and develop your own source components that can fire events. By developing your own events and source components, you will gain a better understanding of the Java event model and GUI components.

27.2 JavaBeans

JavaBeans_

JavaBeans is a software component architecture that extends the power of the Java language by enabling well-formed objects to be manipulated visually at design time in a pure Java builder tool, such as NetBeans, JBuilder, or Eclipse. Such well-formed objects are referred to as *JavaBeans* or simply *beans*. The classes that define the beans, referred to as *JavaBeans components* or *bean components*, or simply *components*, conform to the JavaBeans component model with the following requirements:

- A bean must be a public class.

- A bean must have a public no-arg constructor, though it can have other constructors if needed. For example, a bean named `MyBean` must either have a constructor with the signature

  public MyBean();

  or have no constructor if its superclass has a no-arg constructor.

Serializable_

- A bean must implement the `java.io.Serializable` interface to ensure a persistent state.

accessor_
mutator_

- A bean usually has properties with correctly constructed public *accessor* (get) methods and *mutator* (set) methods that enable the properties to be seen and updated visually by a builder tool.

event registration_

- A bean may have events with correctly constructed public registration and deregistration methods that enable it to add and remove listeners. If the bean plays a role as the source of events, it must provide registration methods for registering listeners. For example, you can register a listener for `ActionEvent` using the `addActionListener` method of a `JButton` bean.

The first three requirements must be observed, and therefore are referred to as *minimum JavaBeans component requirements*. The last two requirements are dependent on implementations. It is possible to write a bean without get/set methods and event registration/deregistration methods.

A JavaBeans component is a special kind of Java class. The relationship between JavaBeans components and Java classes is illustrated in Figure 27.1.

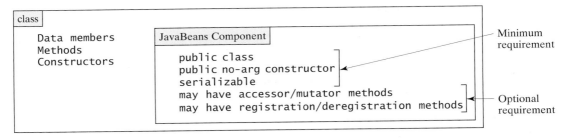

FIGURE 27.1 A JavaBeans component is a serializable public class with a public no-arg constructor.

Every GUI class is a JavaBeans component, because

1. it is a public class,

2. it has a public no-arg constructor, and

3. it is an extension of `java.awt.Component`, which implements `java.io.-Serializable`.

27.3 Bean Properties

Properties are discrete, named attributes of a Java bean that can affect its appearance or behavior. They are often data fields of a bean. For example, the `JButton` component has a property named `text` that represents the text to be displayed on the button. Private data fields are often used to hide specific implementations from the user and prevent the user from accidentally corrupting the properties. Accessor and mutator methods are provided instead to let the user read and write the properties.

27.3.1 Property-Naming Patterns

The bean property-naming pattern is a convention of the JavaBeans component model that simplifies the bean developer's task of presenting properties. A property can be a primitive data type or an object type. The property type dictates the signature of the accessor and mutator methods.

In general, the accessor method is named `get<PropertyName>()`, which takes no parameters and returns a primitive type value or an object of a type identical to the property type. For example,

```java
public String getMessage() { }
public int getXCoordinate() { }
public int getYCoordinate() { }
```

For a property of `boolean` type, the *accessor method* should be named `is<PropertyName>()`, which returns a `boolean` value. For example,

```java
public boolean isCentered() { }
```

The mutator method should be named `set<PropertyName>(dataType p)`, which takes a single parameter identical to the property type and returns `void`. For example,

```java
public void setMessage(String s) { }
public void setXCoordinate(int x) { }
public void setYCoordinate(int y) { }
public void setCentered(boolean centered) { }
```

accessor method

boolean accessor method

mutator method

 Note
You may have multiple get and set methods, but there must be one get or set method with a signature conforming to the naming patterns.

27.3.2 Properties and Data Fields

Properties describe the state of the bean. Naturally, data fields are used to store properties. However, a bean property is not necessarily a data field. For example, in the `MessagePanel` class in §13.11, "Case Study: The `MessagePanel` Class," you may create a new property named `messageLength` that represents the number of characters in `message`. The get method for the property may be defined as follows:

```java
public int getMessageLength() {
  return message.length();
}
```

read-only property
write-only property

> **Note**
> A property may be *read-only* with a get method but no set method, or *write-only* with a set method but no get method.

27.4 Java Event Model Review

A bean may communicate with other beans. The Java event delegation model provides the foundation for beans to send, receive, and handle events. Let us review the Java event model that was introduced in Chapter 14, "Event-Driven Programming." The Java event model consists of the following three types of elements, as shown in Figure 14.3:

- The event object
- The source object
- The event listener object

event

source object

listener

An *event* is a signal to the program that something has happened. It can be triggered by external user actions, such as mouse movements, mouse button clicks, and keystrokes, or by the operating system, such as a timer. An *event object* contains the information that describes the event. A *source object* is where the event originates. When an event occurs on a source object, an event object is created. An object interested in the event receives the event. Such an object is called a *listener*. Not all objects can receive events. To become a listener, an object must be registered as a listener by the source object. The source object maintains a list of listeners and notifies all the registered listeners by invoking the event-handling method implemented on the listener object. The handlers are defined in the class known as the *event listener interface*. Each class of an event object has a corresponding event listener interface. The Java event model is referred to as a *delegation-based model* because the source object delegates the event to the listeners for processing.

27.4.1 Event Classes and Event Listener Interfaces

An event object is created using an event class, such as `ActionEvent`, `MouseEvent`, and `ItemEvent`, as shown in Figure 14.2. All the event classes extend `java.util.EventObject`. The event class contains whatever data values and methods are pertinent to the particular event type. For example, the `KeyEvent` class describes the data values related to a key event and contains the methods, such as `getKeyChar()`, for retrieving the key associated with the event.

handler

Every event class is associated with an event listener interface that defines one or more methods referred to as *handlers*. An event listener interface is a subinterface of `java.util.EventListener`. The handlers are implemented by the listener components. The source component invokes the listeners' handlers when an event is detected.

event set

Since an event class and its listener interface are coexistent, they are often referred to as an *event set* or *event pair*. The event listener interface must be named *X*Listener for the *X*Event. For example, the listener interface for `ActionEvent` is `ActionListener`. The parameter list of a handler always consists of an argument of the event class type. Table 14.2 lists some commonly used events and their listener interfaces. Figure 27.2 shows the pair of `ActionEvent` and `ActionListener`.

27.4.2 Source Components

The component on which an event is generated is referred to as an *event source*. Every Java GUI component is an *event source* for one or more events. For example, `JButton` is an event source for `ActionEvent`. A `JButton` object fires a `java.awt.event.ActionEvent` when it is clicked. `JComboBox` is an event source for `ActionEvent` and `ItemEvent`. A `JComboBox`

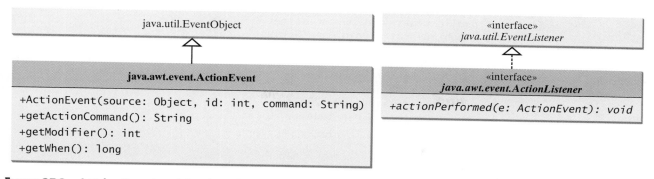

FIGURE 27.2   `ActionEvent` and `ActionListener` are examples of an event pair.

object fires a `java.awt.event.ActionEvent` and a `java.awt.event.ItemEvent` when a new item is selected in the combo box.

The source component contains the code that detects an external or internal action that triggers the event. Upon detecting the action, the source should fire an event to the listeners by invoking the event handler defined by the listeners. The source component must also contain methods for registering and deregistering listeners, as shown in Figure 27.3.

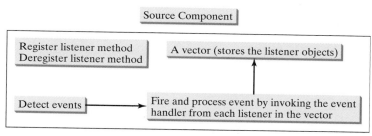

FIGURE 27.3   The source component detects events and processes them by invoking the event listeners' handlers.

27.4.3   Listener Components

A listener component for an event must implement the event listener interface. The object of the listener component cannot receive event notifications from a source component unless the object is registered as a listener of the source.

A listener component may implement any number of listener interfaces to listen to several types of events. A source component may register many listeners. A source component may register itself as a listener.

Listing 27.1 gives an example that creates a source object (line 8) and a listener object (line 14), and registers the listener with the source object (line 17). Figure 27.4 highlights the relationship between the source and the listener. The listener is registered with the source by invoking the `addActionListener` method. Once the button is clicked, an `ActionEvent` is generated by the source. The source object then notifies the listener by invoking the listener's `actionPerformed` method.

LISTING 27.1   `TestSourceListener.java`

```
1 import javax.swing.*;
2 import java.awt.event.*;
3
```

```
 4 public class TestSourceListener {
 5   public static void main(String[] args) {
 6     JFrame frame = new JFrame("TestSourceListener");
 7     // Create a source object
 8     JButton jbt = new JButton("OK");
 9     frame.add(jbt);
10     frame.setSize(200, 200);
11     frame.setVisible(true);
12
13     // Create listeners
14     MyListener listener = new MyListener();
15
16     // Register listeners
17     jbt.addActionListener(listener);
18   }
19 }
20
21 /** MyListener class */
22 class MyListener implements ActionListener{
23   public void actionPerformed(ActionEvent e) {
24     System.out.println("I will process it!");
25   }
26 }
```

source object — line 8

listener object — line 14

registration — line 17

listener class — line 22

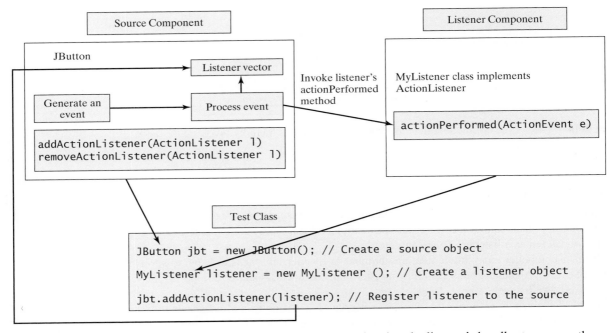

FIGURE 27.4 The listener is registered with the source, and the source invokes the listener's handler to process the event.

27.5 Creating Custom Source Components

You have used source components such as **JButton**. This section demonstrates how to create a custom source component.

registration method

A source component must have the appropriate registration and deregistration methods for adding and removing listeners. Events can be unicasted (only one listener object is notified of the event) or multicasted (each object in a list of listeners is notified of the event). The naming pattern for adding a unicast listener is

```
public void add<Event>Listener(<Event>Listener l)
  throws TooManyListenersException;
```
unicast

The naming pattern for adding a multicast listener is the same, except that it does not throw the TooManyListenersException.

```
public void add<Event>Listener(<Event>Listener l)
```
multicast

The naming pattern for removing a listener (either unicast or multicast) is:

deregistration method

```
public void remove<Event>Listener(<Event>Listener l)
```

A source component contains the code that creates an event object and passes it to the listening components by calling a method in the listener's event listener interface. You may use a standard Java event class like ActionEvent to create event objects or may define your own event classes if necessary.

The Course class in §7.16, "Case Study: The Course Class," models the courses. Suppose a Course object fires an ActionEvent when the number of students for the course exceeds a certain enrollment cap. The new class named CourseWithActionEvent is shown in Figure 27.5.

CourseWithActionEvent	
-name: String	The name of the course.
-students: ArrayList\<String>	The students who take the course.
-enrollmentCap: int	The maximum enrollment (default: 10).
+Course()	Creates a default course.
+Course(name: String)	Creates a course with the specified name.
+getName(): String	Returns the course name.
+addStudent(student: String): void	Adds a new student to the course list.
+getStudents(): String[]	Returns the students for the course as an array.
+getNumberOfStudents(): int	Returns the number of students for the course.
+getEnrollmentCap(): int	Returns the enrollment cap.
+setEnrollmentCap(enrollmentCap: int): void	Sets a new enrollment cap.
+addActionListener(e: ActionEvent): void	Adds a new ActionEvent listener.
+removeActionListener(e: ActionEvent): void	Deletes an ActionEvent listener.
-processEvent(e: ActionEvent): void	Processes an ActionEvent.

FIGURE 27.5   The new CourseWithActionEvent class can fire an ActionEvent.

The source component is responsible for registering listeners, creating events, and notifying listeners by invoking the methods defined in the listeners' interfaces. The CourseWithActionEvent component is capable of registering multiple listeners, generating ActionEvent objects when the enrollment exceeds the cap, and notifying the listeners by invoking the listeners' actionPerformed method. Listing 27.2 implements the new class.

LISTING 27.2 CourseWithActionEvent.java

```
1 import java.util.*;
2 import java.awt.event.*;
3
```

```
 4  public class CourseWithActionEvent {
 5    private String name = "default name";
 6    private ArrayList<String> students = new ArrayList<String>();
 7    private int enrollmentCap = 10;
 8
 9    private ArrayList<ActionListener> actionListenerList;
10
11    public CourseWithActionEvent() {
12    }
13
14    public CourseWithActionEvent(String name) {
15      this.name = name;
16    }
17
18    public void addStudent(String student) {
19      students.add(student);
20
21      if (students.size() > enrollmentCap) {
22        // Fire ActionEvent
23        processEvent(new ActionEvent(this,
24          ActionEvent.ACTION_PERFORMED, null));
25      }
26    }
27
28    public String[] getStudents() {
29      return (String[])students.toArray();
30    }
31
32    public int getNumberOfStudents() {
33      return students.size();
34    }
35
36    public int getEnrollmentCap() {
37      return enrollmentCap;
38    }
39
40    public void setEnrollmentCap(int enrollmentCap) {
41      this.enrollmentCap = enrollmentCap;
42    }
43
44    /** Register an action event listener */
45    public synchronized void addActionListener
46        (ActionListener listener) {
47      if (actionListenerList == null) {
48        actionListenerList = new ArrayList<ActionListener>(2);
49      }
50
51      if (!actionListenerList.contains(listener)) {
52        actionListenerList.add(listener);
53      }
54    }
55
56    /** Remove an action event listener */
57    public synchronized void removeActionListener
58        (ActionListener listener) {
59      if (actionListenerList !=
60          null && actionListenerList.contains(listener)) {
61        actionListenerList.remove(listener);
62      }
63    }
64
```

store students
enrollmentCap

store listeners

no-arg constructor

constructor

create event

register listener

remove listener

```
65   /** Fire ActionEvent */
66   private void processEvent(ActionEvent e) {                    process event
67     ArrayList list;
68
69     synchronized (this) {
70       if (actionListenerList == null) return;
71       list = (ArrayList)actionListenerList.clone();
72     }
73
74     for (int i = 0; i < list.size(); i++) {
75       ActionListener listener = (ActionListener)list.get(i);
76       listener.actionPerformed(e);
77     }
78   }
79 }
```

Since the source component is designed for multiple listeners, a `java.util.ArrayList` instance `actionListenerList` is used to hold all the listeners for the source component (line 9). The data type of the elements in the array list is `ActionListener`. To add a listener, `listener`, to `actionListenerList`, use

```
actionListenerList.add(listener); (line 52)
```

To remove a listener, `listener`, from `actionListenerList`, use

```
actionListenerList.remove(listener); (line 61)
```

The `if` statement (lines 47–49) ensures that the `addActionListener` method does not add the listener twice if it is already in the list. The `removeActionListener` method removes a listener if it is in list. `actionListenerList` is an instance of `ArrayList`, which functions as a flexible array that can grow or shrink dynamically. Initially, `actionListenerList` is new `ArrayList(2)` (line 48), which implies that the capacity of the list is 2, but the capacity can be changed dynamically. If more than two listeners are added to `actionListenerList`, the list size will be automatically increased.

 Note

Instead of using `ArrayList`, you can also use `javax.swing.event.EventListenerList` to store listeners. Using `EventListenerList` is preferred, since it provides the support for   storing listeners
synchronization and is efficient in the case of no listeners.

The `addActionListener` and `removeActionListener` methods are synchronized to prevent data corruption on `actionListenerList` when attempting to register multiple listeners concurrently (lines 45, 57).

The `addStudent` method adds a new student to the course and checks whether the number of students is more than the enrollment cap. If so, it creates an `ActionEvent` and invokes the `processEvent` method to process the event (lines 23–24).

The UML diagram for `ActionEvent` is shown in Figure 27.2. To create an `ActionEvent`, use the constructor

```
ActionEvent(Object source, int id, String command)
```

where `source` specifies the source component, `id` identifies the event, and `command` specifies a command associated with the event. Use `ActionEvent.ACTION_PERFORMED` for the `id`. If you don't want to associate a command with the event, use `null`.

The `processEvent` method (lines 66–78) is invoked when an `ActionEvent` is generated. This notifies the listeners in `actionListenerList` by calling each listener's `actionPerformed` method to process the event. It is possible that a new listener may be added or an existing listener may be removed when `processEvent` is running. To avoid corruption on `actionListenerList`, a clone `list` of `actionListenerList` is created for use to notify listeners. To avoid corruption when creating the clone, invoke it in a synchronized block, as in lines 69–72:

```
synchronized (this) {
  if (actionListenerList == null) return;
  list = (ArrayList)actionListenerList.clone();
}
```

Listing 27.3 gives a test program that creates a course using the new class (line 5), sets the enrollment cap to 2 (line 8), registers a listener (line 10), and adds three students to the course (lines 11–13). When line 13 is executed, the `addStudent` method adds student Tim to the course and fires an `ActionEvent` because the course exceeds the enrollment cap. The course object invokes the listener's `actionPerformed` method to process the event and displays a message `Enrollment cap exceeded`.

LISTING 27.3 `TestCourseWithActionEvent.java`

```
 1 import java.awt.event.*;
 2
 3 public class TestCourseWithActionEvent {
 4   CourseWithActionEvent course =
 5     new CourseWithActionEvent("Java Programming");
 6
 7   public TestCourseWithActionEvent() {
 8     course.setEnrollmentCap(2);
 9     ActionListener listener = new Listener();
10     course.addActionListener(listener);
11     course.addStudent("John");
12     course.addStudent("Jim");
13     course.addStudent("Tim");
14   }
15
16   public static void main(String[] args) {
17     new TestCourseWithActionEvent();
18   }
19
20   private class Listener implements ActionListener {
21     public void actionPerformed(ActionEvent e) {
22       System.out.println("Enrollment cap exceeded");
23     }
24   }
25 }
```

create course

set **enrollmentCap**
create listener
register listener
add students

The flow of event processing from the source to the listener is shown in Figure 27.6.

27.6 (Optional) Creating Custom Event Sets

The Java API provides many event sets. You used the event set `ActionEvent`/ `ActionListener` in the preceding section. A course object fires an `ActionEvent` when the enrollment cap is exceeded. It is convenient to use the existing event sets in the Java API, but they are not always adequate. Sometimes you need to declare custom event classes in order to obtain information not available in the existing API event classes. For example, suppose you want to know the enrollment cap and the number of students in the course; an `ActionEvent` object does not provide such information. You have to declare your own event class and event listener interface.

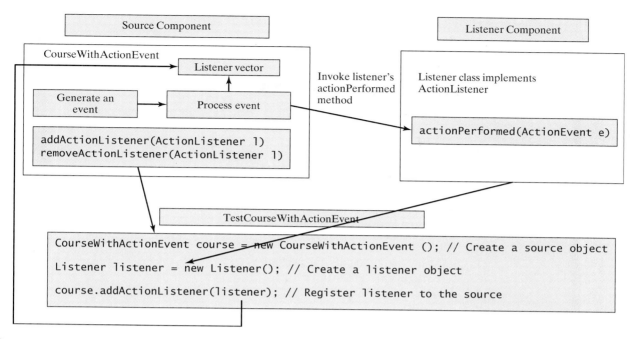

FIGURE 27.6   The listener is registered with the source `course`, and the source invokes the listener's handler `actionPerformed` to process the event.

A custom event class must extend `java.util.EventObject` or a subclass of `java.util.EventObject`. Additionally, it may provide constructors to create events, data members, and methods to describe events.

A custom event listener interface must extend `java.util.EventListener` or a subinterface of `java.util.EventListener`, and define the signature of the handlers for the event. By convention, the listener interface should be named <Event>Listener for the corresponding event class named <Event>. For example, `ActionListener` is the listener interface for `ActionEvent`.

Let us declare `EnrollmentEvent` as the event class for describing the enrollment event and its corresponding listener interface `EnrollmentListener` for defining a handler, as shown in Figure 27.7.

The source code for the enrollment event set is given in Listings 27.4 and 27.5.

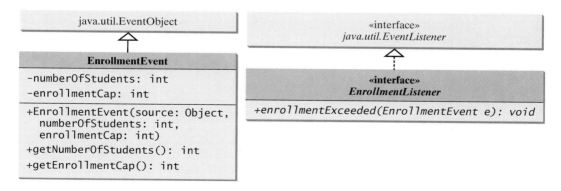

FIGURE 27.7   `EnrollmentEvent` and `EnrollmentListener` comprise an event set for enrollment event.

LISTING 27.4 EnrollmentEvent.java

extends **EventObject**

```
 1  public class EnrollmentEvent extends java.util.EventObject {
 2    private int numberOfStudents;
 3    private int enrollmentCap;
 4
 5    /** Construct an EnrollmentEvent */
 6    public EnrollmentEvent(Object source, int numberOfStudents,
 7        int enrollmentCap) {
 8      super(source);
 9      this.numberOfStudents = numberOfStudents;
10      this.enrollmentCap = enrollmentCap;
11    }
12
13    public long getNumberOfStudents() {
14      return numberOfStudents;
15    }
16
17    public long getEnrollmentCap() {
18      return enrollmentCap;
19    }
20  }
```

constructor

invoke superclass constructor

LISTING 27.5 EnrollmentListener.java

extends **EventListener**

handler

```
 1  public interface EnrollmentListener extends java.util.EventListener {
 2    /** Handle an EnrollmentEvent, to be implemented by a listener */
 3    public void enrollmentExceeded(EnrollmentEvent e);
 4  }
```

An event class is an extension of `EventObject`. To construct an event, the constructor of `EventObject` must be invoked by passing a source object as the argument. In the constructor for `EnrollmentEvent`, `super(source)` (line 8) invokes the superclass's constructor with the source object as the argument. `EnrollmentEvent` contains the information pertaining to the event, such as the number of students and the enrollment cap.

`EnrollmentListener` simply extends `EventListener` and defines the `enrollmentExceeded` method for handling enrollment events.

 Note

specifying a source for an event

An event class does not have a no-arg constructor, because you must always specify a source for the event when creating an event.

Let us revise `CourseWithActionEvent` in Listing 27.2 to use `EnrollmentEvent`/`EnrollmentListener` instead of `ActionEvent`/`ActionListener`. The new class named `CouseWithEnrollmentEvent` in Listing 27.6 is very similar to `CourseWithActionEvent` in Listing 27.2.

LISTING 27.6 CourseWithEnrollmentEvent.java

store students

enrollmentCap

store listeners

```
 1  import java.util.*;
 2
 3  public class CourseWithEnrollmentEvent {
 4    private String name = "default name";
 5    private ArrayList<String> students = new ArrayList<String>();
 6    private int enrollmentCap = 10;
 7
 8    private ArrayList<EnrollmentListener> enrollmentListenerList;
 9
```

```
10    public CourseWithEnrollmentEvent() {                              no-arg constructor
11    }
12
13    public CourseWithEnrollmentEvent(String name) {                   constructor
14      this.name = name;
15    }
16
17    public void addStudent(String student) {
18      students.add(student);
19
20      if (students.size() > enrollmentCap) {
21        // Fire EnrollmentEvent
22        processEvent(new EnrollmentEvent(this,                        create event
23          getNumberOfStudents(), getEnrollmentCap()));
24      }
25    }
26
27    public String[] getStudents() {
28      return (String[])students.toArray();
29    }
30
31    public int getNumberOfStudents() {
32      return students.size();
33    }
34
35    public int getEnrollmentCap() {
36      return enrollmentCap;
37    }
38
39    public void setEnrollmentCap(int enrollmentCap) {
40      this.enrollmentCap = enrollmentCap;
41    }
42
43    /** Register an action event listener */
44    public synchronized void addEnrollmentListener                    register listener
45        (EnrollmentListener listener) {
46      if (enrollmentListenerList == null) {
47        enrollmentListenerList = new ArrayList<EnrollmentListener>(2);
48      }
49
50      if (!enrollmentListenerList.contains(listener)) {
51        enrollmentListenerList.add(listener);
52      }
53    }
54
55    /** Remove an action event listener */
56    public synchronized void removeEnrollmentListener                 remove listener
57        (EnrollmentListener listener) {
58      if (enrollmentListenerList !=
59          null && enrollmentListenerList.contains(listener)) {
60        enrollmentListenerList.remove(listener);
61      }
62    }
63
64    /** Fire EnrollmentEvent */
65    private void processEvent(EnrollmentEvent e) {                    process event
66      ArrayList list;
67
```

```
68      synchronized (this) {
69        if (enrollmentListenerList == null) return;
70        list = (ArrayList)enrollmentListenerList.clone();
71      }
72
73      for (int i = 0; i < list.size(); i++) {
74        EnrollmentListener listener = (EnrollmentListener)list.get(i);
75        listener.enrollmentExceeded(e);
76      }
77    }
78 }
```

Line 8 creates a `java.util.ArrayList` instance `enrollmentListenerList` for holding all the listeners for the source component. The data type of the elements in the array list is `EnrollmentListener`. The registration and deregistration methods for `EnrollmentListener` are declared in lines 44, 56.

The `addStudent` method adds a new student to the course and checks whether the number of students is more than the enrollment cap. If so, it creates an `EnrollmentEvent` and invokes the `processEvent` method to process the event (lines 22–23). To create an `EnrollmentEvent`, use the constructor

```
EnrollmentEvent(Object source, int numberOfStudents, int enrollmentCap)
```

where `source` specifies the source component.

The `processEvent` method (lines 65–77) is invoked when an `EnrollmentEvent` is generated. This notifies the listeners in `enrollmentListenerList` by calling each listener's `enrollmentExceeded` method to process the event.

Let us revise the test program in Listing 27.3 to use `EnrollmentEvent/EnrollmentListener` instead of `ActionEvent/ActionListener`. The new program, given in Listing 27.7, creates a course using `CourseWithEnrollmentEvent` (line 3), sets the enrollment cap to 2 (line 6), creates an enrollment listener (line 7), registers it (line 8), and adds three students to the course (lines 9–11). When line 11 is executed, the `addStudent` method adds student Tim to the course and fires an `EnrollmentEvent` because the course exceeds the enrollment cap. The course object invokes the listener's `enrollmentExceeded` method to process the event and displays the number of students in the course and the enrollment cap.

LISTING 27.7 TestCourseWithEnrollmentEvent.java

create course

set **enrollmentCap**
create listener
register listener
add students

```
1  public class TestCourseWithEnrollmentEvent {
2    CourseWithEnrollmentEvent course =
3      new CourseWithEnrollmentEvent("Java Programming");
4
5    public TestCourseWithEnrollmentEvent() {
6      course.setEnrollmentCap(2);
7      EnrollmentListener listener = new NewListener();
8      course.addEnrollmentListener(listener);
9      course.addStudent("John");
10     course.addStudent("Jim");
11     course.addStudent("Tim");
12   }
13
14   public static void main(String[] args) {
15     new TestCourseWithEnrollmentEvent();
16   }
17
```

```
18    private class NewListener implements EnrollmentListener {
19      public void enrollmentExceeded(EnrollmentEvent e) {
20        System.out.println(e.getNumberOfStudents() + " enrolled" +
21          " and the enrollment cap is " + e.getEnrollmentCap());
22      }
23    }
24  }
```

The flow of event processing from the source to the listener is shown in Figure 27.8.

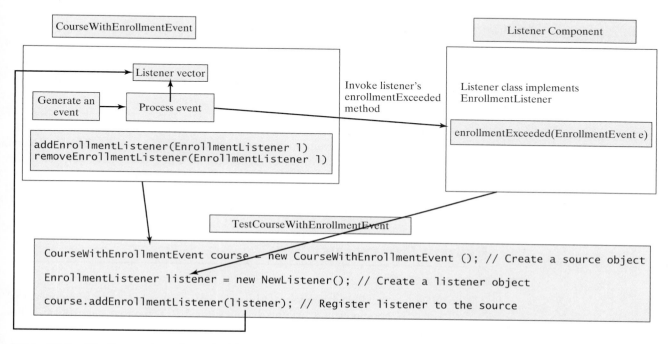

FIGURE 27.8 The listener is registered with the source `course`, and the source invokes the listener's handler `enrollmentExceeded` to process the event.

Tip

Using the `ActionEvent`/`ActionListener` event set is sufficient in most cases. Normally, the information about the event can be obtained from the source. For example, the number of students in the course and the enrollment can all be obtained from a course object. The source can be obtained by invoking `e.getSource()` for any event `e`.

ActionEvent

Note

The `EnrollmentEvent` component is created from scratch. If you build a new component that extends a component capable of generating events, the new component inherits the ability to generate the same type of events. For example, since `JButton` is a subclass of `java.awt.Component` that can fire `MouseEvent`, `JButton` can also detect and generate mouse events. You don't need to write the code to generate these events and register listeners for them, since the code is already given in the superclass. However, you still need to write the code to make your component capable of firing events not supported in the superclass.

inheriting features

KEY TERMS

event set	900	JavaBeans events	900
JavaBeans component	898	JavaBeans properties	899

CHAPTER SUMMARY

■ JavaBeans is a software component architecture that extends the power of the Java language for building reusable software components. JavaBeans properties describe the state of the bean. Naturally, data fields are used to store properties. However, a bean property is not necessarily a data field.

■ A source component must have the appropriate registration and deregistration methods for adding and removing listeners. Events can be unicasted (only one listener object is notified of the event) or multicasted (each object in a list of listeners is notified of the event).

■ An event object is created using an event class, such as `ActionEvent`, `MouseEvent`, and `ItemEvent`. All event classes extend `java.util.EventObject`. Every event class is associated with an event listener interface that defines one or more methods referred to as *handlers*. An event listener interface is a subinterface of `java.util.EventListener`. Since an event class and its listener interface are coexistent, they are often referred to as an *event set* or *event pair*.

REVIEW QUESTIONS

Sections 27.1–27.4

27.1 What is a JavaBeans component? Is every GUI class a JavaBeans component? Is every GUI component a JavaBeans component? Is it true that a JavaBeans component must be a GUI component?

27.2 Describe the naming conventions for accessor and mutator methods in a JavaBeans component.

27.3 Describe the naming conventions for JavaBeans registration and deregistration methods.

27.4 What is an event pair? How do you declare an event class? How do you declare an event listener interface?

PROGRAMMING EXERCISES

Sections 27.1–27.6

27.1* (*Enabling MessagePanel to fire ActionEvent*) The `MessagePanel` class in §13.11, "Case Study: The `MessagePanel` Class," is a subclass of `JPanel`; it can fire a `MouseEvent`, `KeyEvent`, and `ComponentEvent`, but not an `ActionEvent`. Modify the `MessagePanel` class so that it can fire an `ActionEvent` when an instance of the `MessagePanel` class is clicked. Name the new class `MessagePanelWithActionEvent`. Test it with a Java applet that displays the current time in a message panel whenever the message panel is clicked, as shown in Figure 27.9.

Thu Jun 23 00:24:16 EDT 2005

FIGURE 27.9   The current time is displayed whenever you click on the message panel.

27.2*   *(Creating custom event sets and source components)* Develop a project that meets the following requirements:

- Create a source component named `MemoryWatch` for monitoring memory. The component generates a `MemoryEvent` when the free memory space exceeds a specified `highLimit` or is below a specified `lowLimit`. The `highLimit` and `lowLimit` are customizable properties in `MemoryWatch`.
- Create an event set named `MemoryEvent` and `MemoryListener`. The `MemoryEvent` simply extends `java.util.EventObject` and contains two methods, `freeMemory` and `totalMemory`, which return the free memory and total memory of the system. The `MemoryListener` interface contains two handlers, `sufficientMemory` and `insufficientMemory`. The `sufficientMemory` method is invoked when the free memory space exceeds the specified high limit, and `insufficientMemory` is invoked when the free memory space is less than the specified low limit. The free memory and total memory in the system can be obtained using

```
Runtime runtime = Runtime.getRuntime();
runtime.freeMemory();
runtime.totalMemory();
```

- Develop a listener component that displays free memory, total memory, and whether the memory is sufficient or insufficient when a `MemoryEvent` occurs. Make the listener an applet with a `main` method to run standalone.

27.3**   *(The `Hurricane` source component)* Create a class named `Hurricane` with properties `name` and `category` and its accessor methods. The `Hurricane` component generates an `ActionEvent` whenever its `category` property is changed. Write a listener that displays the hurricane category. If the category is 2 or greater, a message "Hurricane Warning!!!" is displayed, as shown in Figure 27.10.

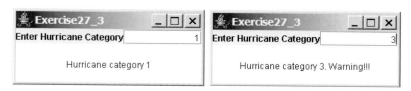

FIGURE 27.10   Whenever the hurricane category is changed, an appropriate message is displayed in the message panel.

27.4**   *(The `Clock` source component)* Create a JavaBeans component for displaying an analog clock. This bean allows the user to customize a clock through the properties, as shown in Figure 27.11. Write a test program that displays four clocks, as shown in Figure 27.12.

27.5*   *(Creating `ClockWithAlarm` from `Clock`)* Create an alarm clock, named `ClockWithAlarm`, which extends the `Clock` component built in the preceding exercise, as shown in Figure 27.13. This component contains two new properties, `alarmDate` and `alarmTime`. `alarmDate` is a string consisting of year, month, and day, separated by commas. For example, 1998,5,13 represents the year 1998,

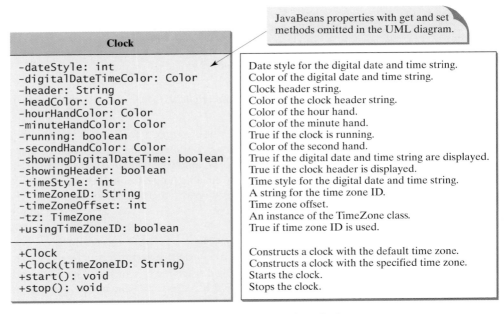

JavaBeans properties with get and set methods omitted in the UML diagram.

Clock
-dateStyle: int
-digitalDateTimeColor: Color
-header: String
-headColor: Color
-hourHandColor: Color
-minuteHandColor: Color
-running: boolean
-secondHandColor: Color
-showingDigitalDateTime: boolean
-showingHeader: boolean
-timeStyle: int
-timeZoneID: String
-timeZoneOffset: int
-tz: TimeZone
+usingTimeZoneID: boolean
+Clock
+Clock(timeZoneID: String)
+start(): void
+stop(): void

Date style for the digital date and time string.
Color of the digital date and time string.
Clock header string.
Color of the clock header string.
Color of the hour hand.
Color of the minute hand.
True if the clock is running.
Color of the second hand.
True if the digital date and time string are displayed.
True if the clock header is displayed.
Time style for the digital date and time string.
A string for the time zone ID.
Time zone offset.
An instance of the TimeZone class.
True if time zone ID is used.

Constructs a clock with the default time zone.
Constructs a clock with the specified time zone.
Starts the clock.
Stops the clock.

FIGURE 27.11 The `Clock` component displays an analog clock.

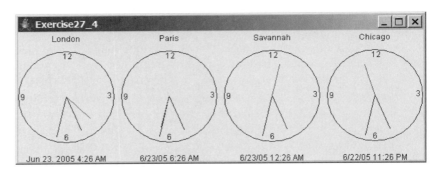

FIGURE 27.12 The program displays four clocks using the `Clock` component.

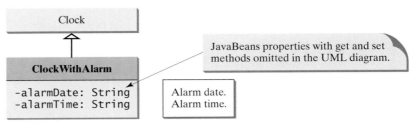

Clock

JavaBeans properties with get and set methods omitted in the UML diagram.

ClockWithAlarm
-alarmDate: String
-alarmTime: String

Alarm date.
Alarm time.

FIGURE 27.13 The `ClockWithAlarm` component extends `Clock` with alarm functions.

month 5, and day 13. `alarmTime` is a string consisting of hour, minute, and second, separated by commas. For example, 10,45,2 represents 10 hours, 45 minutes, and 2 seconds. When the clock time matches the alarm time, `ClockWithAlarm` fires an `ActionEvent`. Write a test program that displays the alert message "You have an appointment now" on a dialog box at a specified time (e.g., date: 2004,1,1 and time: 10,30,0).

27.6*(*The Tick source component*) Create a custom source component that is capable of generating tick events at variant time intervals, as shown in Figure 27.14. The `Tick` component is similar to `javax.swing.Timer`. The `Timer` class generates a timer at fixed time intervals. This `Tick` component can generate tick events at variant time intervals as well as at fixed time intervals.

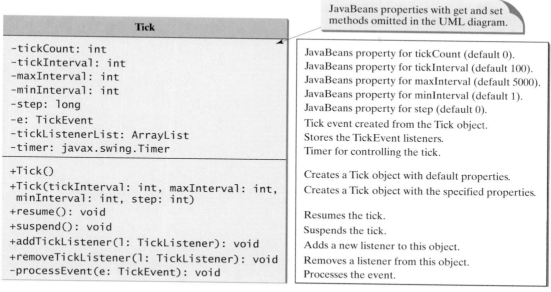

FIGURE 27.14   `Tick` is a component that generates `TickEvent`.

The component contains the properties `tickCount`, `tickInterval`, `maxInterval`, `minInterval`, and `step`. The component adjusts the `tickInterval` by adding `step` to it after a tick event occurs. If `step` is 0, `tickInterval` is unchanged. If `step > 0`, `tickInterval` is increased. If `step < 0`, `tickInterval` is decreased. If `tickInterval > maxInterval` or `tickInterval < minInterval`, the component will no longer generate tick events.

The `Tick` component is capable of registering multiple listeners, generating `TickEvent` objects at variant time intervals, and notifying the listeners by invoking the listeners' `handleTick` method. The UML diagram for `TickEvent` and `TickListener` is shown in Figure 27.15.

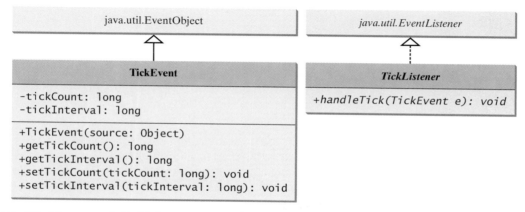

FIGURE 27.15   `TickEvent` and `TickListener` comprise an event set for a tick event.

Create an applet named `DisplayMovingMessage`, and create a panel named `MovingMessage` to display the message. Place an instance of the panel in the applet. To enable the message to move rightward, redraw the message with a new incremental *x*-coordinate. Use a `Tick` object to generate a tick event and invoke the **repaint** method to redraw the message when a tick event occurs. To move the message at a decreasing pace, use a positive step (e.g., 10) when constructing a `Tick` object.

CHAPTER 28

CONTAINERS, LAYOUT MANAGERS, AND BORDERS

Objectives

- To know the internal structures of the Swing container (§28.2).

- To understand how a layout manager works in Java (§28.3).

- To know how to use CardLayout, GridBagLayout, BoxLayout, LayeredLayout, and SpringLayout (§28.3).

- To create custom layout managers (§28.4).

- To use JScrollPane to create scroll panes (§28.5).

- To use JTabbedPane to create tabbed panes (§28.6).

- To use JSplitPane to create split panes (§28.7).

- To use various borders for Swing components (§28.8).

- (Optional) To use Swing pluggable look-and-feel (§28.9).

28.1 Introduction

container

layout manager

Chapter 12, "GUI Basics," introduced the concept of containers and the role of layout managers. You learned how to add components into a *container* and how to use `FlowLayout`, `BorderLayout`, and `GridLayout` to arrange components in a container. A *container* is an object that holds and groups components. A *layout manager* is a special object used to place components in a container. Containers and layout managers play a crucial role in creating user interfaces. This chapter presents a conceptual overview of containers, reviews the layout managers in Java, and introduces several new containers and layout managers. You will also learn how to create custom layout managers and use various borders.

28.2 Swing Container Structures

User interface components like `JButton` cannot be displayed without being placed in a container. A container is a component that is capable of containing other components. You do not display a user interface component; you place it in a container, and the container displays the components it contains.

The base class for all containers is `java.awt.Container`, which is a subclass of `java.awt.Component`. The `Container` class has the following essential functions:

- It adds and removes components using various **add** and **remove** methods.

- It maintains a `layout` property for specifying a layout manager that is used to lay out components in the container. Every container has a default layout manager.

- It provides registration methods for the `java.awt.event.ContainerEvent`.

In AWT programming, the `java.awt.Frame` class is used as a top-level container for Java applications, the `java.awt.Applet` class is used for all Java applets, and `java.awt.Dialog` is used for dialog windows. These classes do not work properly with Swing lightweight components. Special versions of `Frame`, `Applet`, and `Dialog` named `JFrame`, `JApplet`, and `JDialog` have been developed to accommodate Swing components. `JFrame` is a subclass of `Frame`, `JApplet` is a subclass of `Applet`, and `JDialog` is a subclass of `Dialog`. `JFrame` and `JApplet` inherit all the functions of their heavyweight counterparts, but they have a more complex internal structure with several layered panes, as shown in Figure 28.1.

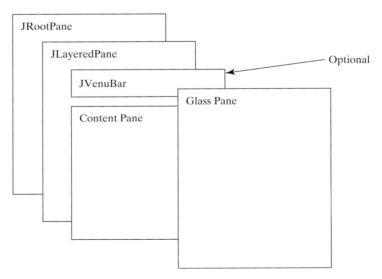

FIGURE 28.1 Swing top-level containers use layers of panes to group lightweight components and make them work properly.

`javax.swing.JRootPane` is a lightweight container used behind the scenes by Swing's top-level containers, such as `JFrame`, `JApplet`, and `JDialog`. `javax.swing.JLayeredPane` is a container that manages the optional menu bar and the content pane. The content pane is an instance of `Container`. By default, it is a `JPanel` with `BorderLayout`. This is the container where the user interface components are added. To obtain the content pane in a `JFrame` or in a `JApplet`, use the `getContentPane()` method. If you wish to set an instance of `Container` to be a new content pane, use the `setContentPane` method. The glass pane floats on top of everything. `javax.swing.JGlassPane` is a hidden pane by default. If you make the glass pane visible, then it's like a sheet of glass over all the other parts of the root pane. It's completely transparent unless you implement the glass pane's `paint` method so that it does something, and it intercepts input events for the root pane. In general, `JRootPane`, `JLayeredPane`, and `JGlassPane` are not used directly.

Now let us review the three most frequently used Swing containers: `JFrame`, `JApplet`, and `JPanel`.

28.2.1   JFrame

`JFrame`, a Swing version of `Frame`, is a top-level container for Java graphics applications. Like `Frame`, `JFrame` is displayed as a standalone window with a title bar and a border. The following properties are often useful in `JFrame`:

- `contentPane` is the content pane of the frame.

- `iconImage` is the image that represents the frame. This image replaces the default Java image on the frame's title bar and is also displayed when the frame is minimized. This property type is `Image`. You can get an image using the `ImageIcon` class, as follows:

  ```
  Image image = (new ImageIcon(filename)).getImage();
  ```

- `jMenuBar` is the optional menu bar for the frame.

- `resizable` is a `boolean` value indicating whether the frame is resizable. The default value is `true`.

- `title` specifies the title of the frame.

28.2.2   JApplet

`JApplet` is a Swing version of `Applet`. Since it is a subclass of `Applet`, it has all the functions required by the Web browser. Here are the four essential methods defined in `Applet`:

```
// Called by the browser when the Web page containing
// this applet is initially loaded
public void init()

// Called by the browser after the init() method and
// every time the Web page is visited.
public void start()

// Called by the browser when the page containing this
// applet becomes inactive.
public void stop()

// Called by the browser when the Web browser exits.
public void destroy()
```

Additionally, `JApplet` has the `contentPane` and `jMenuBar` properties, among others. As with `JFrame`, you do not place components directly into `JApplet`; instead you place them into the content pane of the applet. The `Applet` class cannot have a menu bar, but the `JApplet` class allows you to set a menu bar using the `setJMenuBar` method.

 Note

When an applet is loaded, the Web browser creates an instance of the applet by invoking the applet's no-arg constructor. So the constructor is invoked before the init method.

28.2.3   JPanel

Panels act as subcontainers for grouping user interface components. `javax.swing.JPanel` is different from `JFrame` and `JApplet`. First, `JPanel` is not a top-level container; it must be placed inside another container, and it can be placed inside another `JPanel`. Second, since `JPanel` is a subclass of `JComponent`, it is a lightweight component, but `JFrame` and `JApplet` are heavyweight components.

`JPanel` is a Swing version of `Panel`, but it is not a subclass of `Panel`. Nevertheless, you can use `JPanel` the same way you use `Panel`. As a subclass of `JComponent`, `JPanel` can take advantage of `JComponent`, such as double buffering and borders. You should draw figures on `JPanel` rather than `JFrame` or `JApplet`, because `JPanel` supports double buffering, which is the technique for eliminating flickers.

28.3 Layout Managers

Every container has a layout manager that is responsible for arranging its components. The container's `setLayout` method can be used to set a layout manager. Certain types of containers have default layout managers. For instance, the content pane of `JFrame` or `JApplet` uses `BorderLayout`, and `JPanel` uses `FlowLayout`.

The layout manager places the components in accordance with its own rules and property settings, and with the constraints associated with each component. Every layout manager has its own specific set of rules. For example, the `FlowLayout` manager places components in rows from left to right and starts a new row when the previous row is filled. The `BorderLayout` manager places components in the north, south, east, west, or center of the container. The `GridLayout` manager places components in a grid of cells in rows and columns from left to right in order.

Some layout managers have properties that can affect the sizing and location of the components in the container. For example, `BorderLayout` has properties called `hgap` (horizontal gap) and `vgap` (vertical gap) that determine the distance between components horizontally and vertically. `FlowLayout` has properties that can be used to specify the alignment (left, center, right) of the components and properties for specifying the horizontal or vertical gap between the components. `GridLayout` has properties that can be used to specify the horizontal or vertical gap between columns and rows and properties for specifying the number of rows and columns. These properties can be retrieved and set using their accessor and mutator methods.

The size of a component in a container is determined by many factors, such as:

- The type of layout manager used by the container.

- The layout constraints associated with each component.

- The size of the container.

- Certain properties common to all components (such as `preferredSize`, `minimumSize`, `maximumSize`, `alignmentX`, and `alignmentY`).

The `preferredSize` property indicates the ideal size at which the component looks best. Depending on the rules of the particular layout manager, this property may or may not be considered. For example, the preferred size of a component is used in a container with a `FlowLayout` manager, but ignored if it is placed in a container with a `GridLayout` manager.

The `minimumSize` property specifies the minimum size at which the component is useful. For most GUI components, `minimumSize` is the same as `preferredSize`. Layout managers generally respect `minimumSize` more than `preferredSize`.

The `maximumSize` property specifies the maximum size needed by a component, so that the layout manager won't wastefully give space to a component that does not need it. For instance, `BorderLayout` limits the center component's size to its maximum size, and gives the space to edge components.

The `alignmentX` (`alignmentY`) property specifies how the component would like to be aligned relative to other components along the *x*-axis (*y*-axis). This value should be a number between 0 and 1, where 0 represents alignment along the origin, 1 is aligned the farthest away from the origin, 0.5 is centered, and so on. These two properties are used in the `BoxLayout` and `OverlayLayout`.

Java provides a variety of layout managers. You have learned how to use `BorderLayout`, `FlowLayout`, and `GridLayout`. The following sections introduce `CardLayout`, `GridBagLayout`, `Null` layout, `BoxLayout`, `OverlayLayout`, and `SpringLayout`.

Tip

If you set a new layout manager in a container, invoke the container's `validate()` method to force the container to again lay out the components. If you change the properties of a layout manager in a `JFrame` or `JApplet`, invoke the `doLayout()` method to force the container to again layout the components using the new layout properties. If you change the properties of a layout manager in a `JPanel`, invoke either `doLayout()` or `revalidate()` method to force it to again layout the components using the new layout properties, but it is better to use `revalidate()`. Note that `validate()` is a public method defined in `java.awt.Container`, `revalidate()` is a public method defined in `javax.swing.JComponent`, and `doLayout()` is a public method defined in `java.awt.Container`.

`validate()`

`doLayout()`

`revalidate()`

28.3.1   CardLayout

`CardLayout` places components in the container as cards. Only one card is visible at a time, and the container acts as a stack of cards. The ordering of cards is determined by the container's own internal ordering of its component objects. You can specify the size of the horizontal and vertical gaps surrounding a stack of components in a `CardLayout` manager, as shown in Figure 28.2.

`CardLayout` defines a set of methods that allow an application to flip through the cards sequentially or to show a specified card directly, as shown in Figure 28.3.

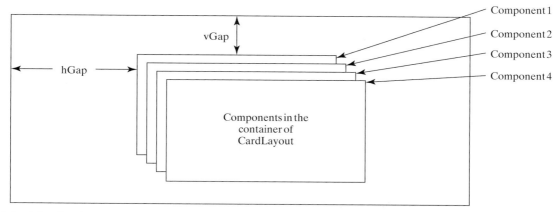

FIGURE 28.2   The `CardLayout` places components in the container as a stack of cards.

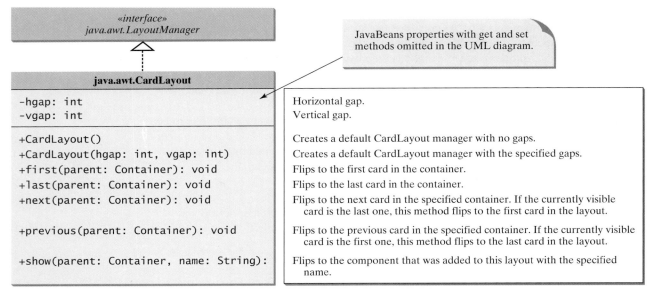

FIGURE 28.3 `CardLayout` contains the methods to flip the card.

To add a component into a container, use the **add(Component c, String name)** method defined in the **Container** class interface. The **String** parameter, **name**, gives an explicit identity to the component in the container.

Listing 28.1 gives a program that creates two panels in a frame. The first panel uses **CardLayout** to hold six labels for displaying images. The second panel uses **FlowLayout** to group four buttons named First, Next, Previous, and Last, and a combo box labeled **Image**, as shown in Figure 28.4.

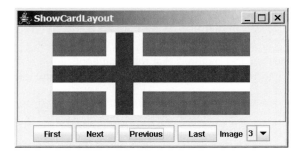

FIGURE 28.4 The program shows images in a panel of `CardLayout`.

These buttons control which image will be shown in the **CardLayout** panel. When the user clicks the button named First, for example, the first image in the **CardLayout** panel appears. The combo box enables the user to directly select an image.

LISTING 28.1 ShowCardLayout.java

```
1 import java.awt.*;
2 import java.awt.event.*;
3 import javax.swing.*;
4
```

```
5  public class ShowCardLayout extends JApplet {
6    private CardLayout cardLayout = new CardLayout(20, 10);            card layout
7    private JPanel cardPanel = new JPanel(cardLayout) ;
8    private JButton jbtFirst, jbtNext, jbtPrevious, jbtLast;
9    private JComboBox jcboImage;
10   private final int NUM_OF_FLAGS = 6;
11
12   public ShowCardLayout() {
13     cardPanel.setBorder(                                            create UI
14       new javax.swing.border.LineBorder(Color.red));
15
16     // Add 9 labels for displaying images into cardPanel
17     for (int i = 1; i <= NUM_OF_FLAGS; i++) {
18       JLabel label =
19         new JLabel(new ImageIcon("image/flag" + i + ".gif"));
20       cardPanel.add(label, String.valueOf(i));
21     }
22
23     // Panel p to hold buttons and a combo box
24     JPanel p = new JPanel();
25     p.add(jbtFirst = new JButton("First"));
26     p.add(jbtNext = new JButton("Next"));
27     p.add(jbtPrevious= new JButton("Previous"));
28     p.add(jbtLast = new JButton("Last"));
29     p.add(new JLabel("Image"));
30     p.add(jcboImage = new JComboBox());
31
32     // Initialize combo box items
33     for (int i = 1; i <= NUM_OF_FLAGS; i++)
34       jcboImage.addItem(String.valueOf(i));
35
36     // Place panels in the frame
37     add(cardPanel, BorderLayout.CENTER);
38     add(p, BorderLayout.SOUTH);
39
40     // Register listeners with the source objects
41     jbtFirst.addActionListener(new ActionListener() {               register listener
42       public void actionPerformed(ActionEvent e) {
43         // Show the first component in cardPanel
44         cardLayout.first(cardPanel);                                first component
45       }
46     });
47     jbtNext.addActionListener(new ActionListener() {                register listener
48       public void actionPerformed(ActionEvent e) {
49         // Show the first component in cardPanel
50         cardLayout.next(cardPanel);                                 next component
51       }
52     });
53     jbtPrevious.addActionListener(new ActionListener() {            register listener
54       public void actionPerformed(ActionEvent e) {
55         // Show the first component in cardPanel
56         cardLayout.previous(cardPanel);                             previous component
57       }
58     });
59     jbtLast.addActionListener(new ActionListener() {                register listener
60       public void actionPerformed(ActionEvent e) {
61         // Show the first component in cardPanel
62         cardLayout.last(cardPanel);                                 last component
63       }
64     });
```

register listener

```
65    jcboImage.addItemListener(new ItemListener() {
66      public void itemStateChanged(ItemEvent e) {
67        // Show the component at specified index
```

selected component

```
68        cardLayout.show(cardPanel, (String)e.getItem());
69      }
70    });
71  }
```

main omitted

```
72 }
```

An instance of `CardLayout` is created in line 6, and a panel of `CardLayout` is created in line 7. You have already used such statements as `setLayout(new FlowLayout())` to create an anonymous layout object and set the layout for a container, instead of declaring and creating a separate instance of the layout manager, as in this program. The `cardLayout` object, however, is useful later in the program to show components in `cardPanel`. You have to use `cardLayout.first(cardPanel)` (line 44), for example, to view the first component in `cardPanel`.

The statement in lines 17–21 adds the image label with the identity `String.valueOf(i)`. Later, when the user selects an image with number `i`, the identity `String.valueOf(i)` is used in the `show` method (line 68) to view the image with the specified identity.

 ## 28.3.2 (Optional) The `GridBagLayout` Manager

The `GridBagLayout` manager is the most flexible and the most complex. It is similar to the `GridLayout` manager in the sense that both layout managers arrange components in a grid. The components of `GridBagLayout` can vary in size, however, and can be added in any order. For example, with `GridBagLayout` you can create the layout shown in Figure 28.5.

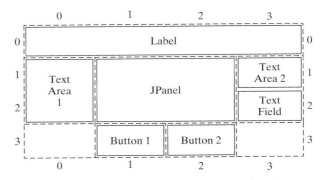

FIGURE 28.5 A `GridBagLayout` manager divides the container into cells. A component can occupy several cells.

The constructor `GridBagLayout()` is used to create a new `GridBagLayout`. In `GridLayout`, the grid size (the number of rows and columns) may be specified in the constructor. It is not specified in `GridBagLayout`. The actual size is dynamically determined by the constraints associated with the components added to the container of `GridBagLayout`.

Each `GridBagLayout` uses a dynamic rectangular grid of cells, with each component occupying one or more cells called its *display area*. Each component managed by a `GridBagLayout` is associated with a `GridBagConstraints` instance that specifies how the component is laid out within its display area. How a `GridBagLayout` places a set of components depends on the `GridBagConstraints` and minimum size of each component, as well as the preferred size of the component's container.

To use `GridBagLayout` effectively, you must customize the `GridBagConstraints` of one or more of its components. You customize a `GridBagConstraints` object by setting one or more of its public instance variables. These variables specify the component's location, size, growth factor, anchor, inset, filling, and padding.

Location

The variables `gridx` and `gridy` specify the cell at the upper left of the component's display area, where the upper-leftmost cell has the address `gridx=0`, `gridy=0`. Note that `gridx` specifies the column in which the component will be placed, and `gridy` specifies the row in which it will be placed. In Figure 28.5, Button 1 has a `gridx` value of `1` and a `gridy` value of `3`, and Label has a `gridx` value of 0 and a `gridy` value of 0.

You can assign `GridBagConstraints.RELATIVE` to `gridx` to specify that the component be placed immediately after the component that was just added to the container. You can assign `GridBagConstraints.RELATIVE` to `gridy` to specify that the component be placed immediately below the component that was just added to the container.

Size

The variables `gridwidth` and `gridheight` specify the number of cells in a row (for `gridheight`) or column (for `gridwidth`) in the component's display area. The default value is `1`. In Figure 28.5, the `JPanel` in the center occupies two columns and two rows, so its `gridwidth` is `2`, and its `gridheight` is `2`. Text Area 2 occupies one row and one column; therefore its `gridwidth` is `1`, and its `gridheight` is `1`.

You can assign `GridBagConstraints.RELATIVE.REMAINDER` to `gridwidth` (`gridheight`) to specify that the component is to be the last one in its row (column).

Growth Weight

The variables `weightx` and `weighty` specify the extra horizontal and vertical space to allocate for the component when the resulting layout is smaller horizontally than the area it needs to fill.

The `GridBagLayout` manager calculates the weight of a column to be the maximum `weightx` (`weighty`) of all the components in a column (row). The extra space is distributed to each column (row) in proportion to its weight.

Unless you specify a weight for at least one component in a row (`weightx`) and a column (`weighty`), all the components clump together in the center of their container. This is because, when the weight is zero (the default), the `GridBagLayout` puts any extra space between its grid of cells and the edges of the container. You will see the effect of these parameters in Listing 28.2.

Anchor

The variable `anchor` specifies where in the area the component is placed when it does not fill the entire area. Valid values are:

```
GridBagConstraints.CENTER (the default)
GridBagConstraints.NORTH
GridBagConstraints.NORTHEAST
GridBagConstraints.EAST
GridBagConstraints.SOUTHEAST
GridBagConstraints.SOUTH
GridBagConstraints.SOUTHWEST
GridBagConstraints.WEST
GridBagConstraints.NORTHWEST
```

Filling

The variable `fill` specifies how the component should be resized if its viewing area is larger than its current size. Valid values are `GridBagConstraints.NONE` (the default), `GridBagConstraints.HORIZONTAL` (makes the component wide enough to fill its display area horizontally, but doesn't change its height), `GridBagConstraints.VERTICAL` (makes the component tall enough to fill its display area vertically, but doesn't change its width), and `GridBagConstraints.BOTH` (makes the component totally fill its display area).

Insets

The variable **insets** specifies the external padding of the component, the minimum amount of space between the component and the edges of its display area. The default value is **new Insets(0, 0, 0, 0)**.

Padding

The variables **ipadx** and **ipady** specify the internal padding of the component: how much space to add to its minimum width and height. The width of the component is at least its minimum width plus (**ipadx** * 2) pixels, and the height of the component is at least its minimum height plus (**ipady** * 2) pixels. The default value of these variables is **0**. The **insets** variable specifies the external padding, while the **ipadx** and **ipady** variables specify the internal padding, as shown in Figure 28.6.

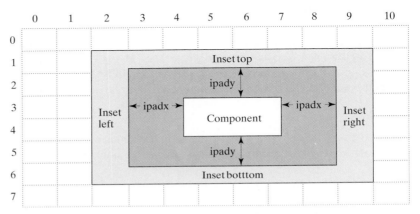

FIGURE 28.6 You can specify the external insets and internal padding for a component in the container of the **GridBagLayout** manager.

Constructing a **GridBagConstraints** Object

There are two constructors for creating a **GridBagConstraints** object:

- **public** GridBagConstraints()

  Constructs a **GridBagConstraints** object with all of its fields set to their default values.

- **public** GridBagConstraints(**int** gridx, **int** gridy, **int** gridwidth, **int** gridheight, **double** weightx, **double** weighty, **int** anchor, **int** fill, Insets insets, **int** ipadx, **int** ipady)

  Constructs a **GridBagConstraints** object with the specified field values.

Adding a Component to the Container of GridBagLayout

To add a component to the container of **GridBagLayout**, use the following method in the container:

  public void add(Component comp, Object gbConstraints)

Adds a component to the container with the specified **GridBagConstraints**.

Example: Using **GridBagLayout**

Listing 28.2 gives a program that uses the **GridBagLayout** manager to create a layout for Figure 28.5. The output of the program is shown in Figure 28.7.

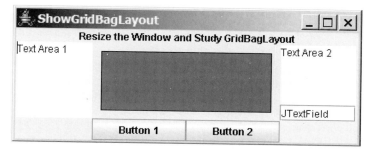

FIGURE 28.7 The components are placed in the frame of `GridBagLayout`.

LISTING 28.2 ShowGridBagLayout.java

```
1  import java.awt.*;
2  import javax.swing.*;
3
4  public class ShowGridBagLayout extends JApplet {
5    private JLabel jlbl = new JLabel(
6      "Resize the Window and Study GridBagLayout", JLabel.CENTER);
7    private JTextArea jta1 = new JTextArea("Text Area 1", 5, 15 );
8    private JTextArea jta2 = new JTextArea("Text Area 2", 5, 15 );
9    private JTextField jtf = new JTextField("JTextField");
10   private JPanel jp = new JPanel();
11   private JButton jbt1 = new JButton("Button 1");
12   private JButton jbt2 = new JButton("Button 2");
13
14   public ShowGridBagLayout() {
15     // Set GridBagLayout in the container
16     setLayout(new GridBagLayout());
17
18     // Create an GridBagConstraints object
19     GridBagConstraints gbConstraints = new GridBagConstraints();
20
21     gbConstraints.fill = GridBagConstraints.BOTH;
22     gbConstraints.anchor = GridBagConstraints.CENTER;
23
24     Container container = getContentPane();
25
26     // Place JLabel to occupy row 0 (the first row)
27     addComp(jlbl, container, gbConstraints, 0, 0, 1, 4, 0, 0);
28
29     // Place text area 1 in row 1 and 2, and column 0
30     addComp(jta1, container, gbConstraints, 1, 0, 2, 1, 5, 1);
31
32     // Place text area 2 in row 1 and column 3
33     addComp(jta2, container, gbConstraints, 1, 3, 1, 1, 5, 1);
34
35     // Place text field in row 2 and column 3
36     addComp(jtf, container, gbConstraints, 2, 3, 1, 1, 5, 0);
37
38     // Place JButton 1 in row 3 and column 1
39     addComp(jbt1, container, gbConstraints, 3, 1, 1, 1, 5, 0);
40
41     // Place JButton 2 in row 3 and column 2
42     addComp(jbt2, container, gbConstraints, 3, 2, 1, 1, 5, 0);
43
44     // Place Panel in row 1 and 2, and column 1 and 2
45     jp.setBackground(Color.red);
46     jp.setBorder(new javax.swing.border.LineBorder(Color.black));
```

UI components

create UI

```
47    gbConstraints.insets = new Insets(10, 10, 10, 10);
48    addComp(jp, container, gbConstraints, 1, 1, 2, 2, 10, 1);
49  }
50
51  /** Add a component to the container of GridBagLayout */
52  private void addComp(Component c, Container container,
53                       GridBagConstraints gbConstraints,
54                       int row, int column,
55                       int numberOfRows, int numberOfColumns,
56                       double weightx, double weighty) {
57    // Set parameters
58    gbConstraints.gridx     = column;
59    gbConstraints.gridy     = row;
60    gbConstraints.gridwidth  = numberOfColumns;
61    gbConstraints.gridheight = numberOfRows;
62    gbConstraints.weightx    = weightx;
63    gbConstraints.weighty    = weighty;
64
65    // Add component to the container with the specified layout
66    container.add(c, gbConstraints);
67  }
68 }
```

The program defines the **addComp** method (lines 52–67) to add a component to the container of **GridBagLayout** with the specified constraints. The **GridBagConstraints** object **gbConstraints** created in line 19 is used to specify the layout constraints for each component. Before adding a component to the container, set the constraints in **gbConstraints** and then use **container.add(c, gbConstraints)** (line 66) to add the component to the container.

What would happen if you change the **weightx** parameter for **jbt2** to **10** in line 41? Now **jbt2**'s **weightx** is larger than **jbt1**'s. When you enlarge the window, **jbt2** will get larger horizontally than **jbt1**.

The **weightx** and **weighty** for all the other components are **0**. Whether the size of these components grows or shrinks depends on the **fill** parameter. The program defines **fill = BOTH** for all the components added to the container (line 27).

Consider this scenario: Suppose that you enlarge the window. The display area for text area **jta1** will increase. Because **fill** is **BOTH** for **jta1**, **jta1** fills in its new display area. If you set **fill** to **NONE** for **jta1**, **jta1** will not expand or shrink when you resize the window.

The **insets** parameter is (**0**, **0**, **0**, **0**) by default. For the panel **jp**, **insets** is set to (**10, 10, 10, 10**) (line 47).

28.3.3 Using No Layout Manager

If you have used a Windows-based RAD tool like Visual Basic, you know that it is easier to create user interfaces with Visual Basic than with Java. This is mainly because the components are placed in absolute positions and sizes in Visual Basic, whereas they are placed in containers using a variety of layout managers in Java. Absolute positions and sizes are fine if the application is developed and deployed on the same platform, but what looks fine on a development system may not look right on a deployment system. To solve this problem, Java provides a set of layout managers that place components in containers in a way that is independent of fonts, screen resolutions, and platform differences.

For convenience, Java also supports an absolute layout that enables you to place components at fixed locations. In this case, the component must be placed using the component's instance method **setBounds()** (defined in **java.awt.Component**), as follows:

```
public void setBounds(int x, int y, int width, int height);
```

This sets the location and size for the component, as in the next example:

```
JButton jbt = new JButton("Help");
jbt.setBounds(10, 10, 40, 20);
```

The upper-left corner of the Help button is placed at (10, 10); the button width is 40, and the height is 20.

You perform the following steps in order not to use a layout manager:

1. Use this statement to specify no layout manager:

```
setLayout(null);
```

set **null** layout

2. Add the component to the container:

```
add(jbt);
```

3. Specify the location where the component is to be placed, using the **setBounds** method:

```
JButton jbt = new JButton("Help");
jbt.setBounds(10, 10, 40, 20);
```

setBounds

Listing 28.3 gives a program that places the same components in the same layout as in the preceding example but without using a layout manager. Figure 28.8 contains the sample output.

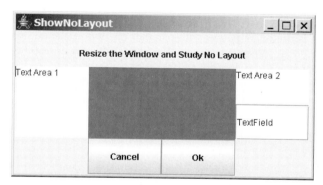

FIGURE 28.8   The components are placed in the frame without using a layout manager.

LISTING 28.3   ShowNoLayout.java

```
1 import java.awt.*;
2 import javax.swing.*;
3
4 public class ShowNoLayout extends JApplet {
5   private JLabel jlbl =
6     new JLabel("Resize the Window and Study No Layout",
7       JLabel.CENTER);
8   private JTextArea jta1 = new JTextArea("Text Area 1", 5, 10 );
9   private JTextArea jta2 = new JTextArea("Text Area 2", 5, 10 );
10  private JTextField jtf = new JTextField("TextField");
11  private JPanel jp = new JPanel();
12  private JButton jbt1 = new JButton("Cancel" );
13  private JButton jbt2 = new JButton("Ok" );
14  private GridBagLayout gbLayout;
15  private GridBagConstraints gbConstraints;
16
17  public ShowNoLayout() {
18    // Set background color for the panel
19    jp.setBackground(Color.red);
```

UI components

create UI

```
20
21      // Specify no layout manager
22      setLayout(null);
23
24      // Add components to frame
25      add(jlbl);
26      add(jp);
27      add(jta1);
28      add(jta2);
29      add(jtf);
30      add(jbt1);
31      add(jbt2);
32
33      // Put components in the right place
34      jlbl.setBounds(0, 10, 400, 40);
35      jta1.setBounds(0, 50, 100, 100);
36      jp.setBounds(100, 50, 200, 100);
37      jta2.setBounds(300, 50, 100, 50);
38      jtf.setBounds(300, 100, 100, 50);
39      jbt1.setBounds(100, 150, 100, 50);
40      jbt2.setBounds(200, 150, 100, 50);
41    }
42 }
```

main omitted

If you run this program on Windows with 640 × 480 resolution, the layout size is just right. When the program is run on Windows with a higher resolution, the components appear very small and clump together. When it is run on Windows with a lower resolution, they cannot be shown in their entirety.

If you resize the window, you will see that the location and size of the components are not changed, as shown in Figure 28.9.

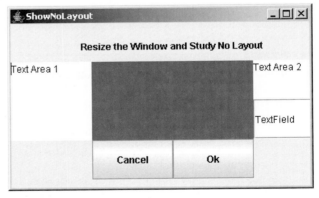

FIGURE 28.9 With no layout manager, the size and positions of the components are fixed.

 Tip
Do not use the no-layout-manager option to develop platform-independent applications.

28.3.4 BoxLayout

`javax.swing.BoxLayout` is a Swing layout manager that arranges components in a row or a column. To create a `BoxLayout`, use the following constructor:

```
public BoxlayLayout(Container target, int axis)
```

This constructor is different from other layout constructors. It creates a layout manager that is dedicated to the given target container. The `axis` parameter is `BoxLayout.X_AXIS` or `BoxLayout.Y_AXIS`, which specifies whether the components are laid out horizontally or vertically. For example, the following code creates a horizontal `BoxLayout` for panel `p1`:

```
JPanel p1 = new JPanel();
BoxLayout boxLayout = new BoxLayout(p1, BoxLayout.X_AXIS);
p1.setLayout(boxLayout);
```

You still need to invoke the `setLayout` method on `p1` to set the layout manager.

You can use `BoxLayout` in any container, but it is simpler to use the `Box` class, which is a container of `BoxLayout`. To create a `Box` container, use one of the following two static methods:

```
Box box1 = Box.createHorizontalBox();
Box box2 = Box.createVerticalBox();
```

The former creates a box that contains components horizontally, and the latter creates a box that contains components vertically.

You can add components to a box in the same way that you add them to the containers of `FlowLayout` or `GridLayout` using the `add` method, as follows:

```
box1.add(new JButton("A Button"));
```

You can remove components from a box in the same way that you drop components to a container. The components are laid left to right in a horizontal box, and top to bottom in a vertical box.

`BoxLayout` is similar to `GridLayout` but has many unique features.

First, `BoxLayout` respects a component's preferred size, maximum size, and minimum size. If the total preferred size of all the components in the box is less than the box size, then the components are expanded up to their maximum size. If the total preferred size of all the components in the box is greater than the box size, then the components are shrunk down to their minimum size. If the components do not fit at their minimum width, some of them will not be shown. In the `GridLayout`, the container is divided into cells of equal size, and the components are fit in regardless of their preferred maximum or minimum size.

Second, unlike other layout managers, `BoxLayout` considers the component's `alignmentX` or `alignmentY` property. The `alignmentX` property is used to place the component in a vertical box layout, and the `alignmentY` property is used to place it in a horizontal box layout.

Third, `BoxLayout` does not have gaps between the components, but you can use fillers to separate components. A filler is an invisible component. There are three kinds of fillers: struts, rigid areas, and glues.

A *strut* simply adds some space between components. The static method `createHorizontalStrut(int)` in the `Box` class is used to create a horizontal strut, and the static method `createVerticalStrut(int)` to create a vertical strut. For example, the code shown below adds a vertical strut of 8 pixels between two buttons in a vertical box:

strut

```
box2.add(new JButton("Button 1"));
box2.add(Box.createVerticalStrut(8));
box2.add(new JButton("Button 2"));
```

A *rigid area* is a two-dimensional space that can be created using the static method `createRigidArea(dimension)` in the `Box` class. For example, the next code adds a rigid area 10 pixels wide and 20 pixels high into a box.

rigid area

```
box2.add(Box.createRigidArea(new Dimension(10, 20)));
```

glue

A *glue* separates components as much as possible. For example, by adding a glue between two components in a horizontal box, you place one component at the left end and the other at the right end. A glue can be created using the `Box.createGlue()` method.

Listing 28.4 shows an example that creates a horizontal box and a vertical box. The horizontal box holds two buttons with print and save icons. The vertical box holds four buttons for selecting flags. When a button in the vertical box is clicked, a corresponding flag icon is displayed in the label centered in the applet, as shown in Figure 28.10.

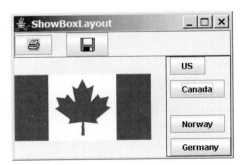

FIGURE 28.10 The components are placed in the containers of `BoxLayout`.

LISTING 28.4 ShowBoxLayout.java

UI components
BoxLayout container
BoxLayout container

create icons

buttons

create UI

add to box

```
1  import java.awt.*;
2  import java.awt.event.*;
3  import javax.swing.*;
4
5  public class ShowBoxLayout extends JApplet {
6    // Create two box containers
7    private Box box1 = Box.createHorizontalBox();
8    private Box box2 = Box.createVerticalBox();
9
10   // Create a label to display flags
11   private JLabel jlblFlag = new JLabel();
12
13   // Create image icons for flags
14   private ImageIcon imageIconUS =
15     new ImageIcon(getClass().getResource("/image/us.gif"));
16   private ImageIcon imageIconCanada =
17     new ImageIcon(getClass().getResource("/image/ca.gif"));
18   private ImageIcon imageIconNorway =
19     new ImageIcon(getClass().getResource("/image/norway.gif"));
20   private ImageIcon imageIconGermany =
21     new ImageIcon(getClass().getResource("/image/germany.gif"));
22   private ImageIcon imageIconPrint =
23     new ImageIcon(getClass().getResource("/image/print.gif"));
24   private ImageIcon imageIconSave =
25     new ImageIcon(getClass().getResource("/image/save.gif"));
26
27   // Create buttons to select images
28   private JButton jbtUS = new JButton("US");
29   private JButton jbtCanada = new JButton("Canada");
30   private JButton jbtNorway = new JButton("Norway");
31   private JButton jbtGermany = new JButton("Germany");
32
33   public ShowBoxLayout() {
34     box1.add(new JButton(imageIconPrint));
35     box1.add(Box.createHorizontalStrut(20));
36     box1.add(new JButton(imageIconSave));
```

```
37
38    box2.add(jbtUS);
39    box2.add(Box.createVerticalStrut(8));
40    box2.add(jbtCanada);
41    box2.add(Box.createGlue());
42    box2.add(jbtNorway);
43    box2.add(Box.createRigidArea(new Dimension(10, 8)));;
44    box2.add(jbtGermany);
45
46    box1.setBorder(new javax.swing.border.LineBorder(Color.red));
47    box2.setBorder(new javax.swing.border.LineBorder(Color.black));
48
49    add(box1, BorderLayout.NORTH);
50    add(box2, BorderLayout.EAST);
51    add(jlblFlag, BorderLayout.CENTER);
52
53    // Register listeners
54    jbtUS.addActionListener(new ActionListener() {
55      public void actionPerformed(ActionEvent e) {
56        jlblFlag.setIcon(imageIconUS);
57      }
58    });
59    jbtCanada.addActionListener(new ActionListener() {
60      public void actionPerformed(ActionEvent e) {
61        jlblFlag.setIcon(imageIconCanada);
62      }
63    });
64    jbtNorway.addActionListener(new ActionListener() {
65      public void actionPerformed(ActionEvent e) {
66        jlblFlag.setIcon(imageIconNorway);
67      }
68    });
69    jbtGermany.addActionListener(new ActionListener() {
70      public void actionPerformed(ActionEvent e) {
71        jlblFlag.setIcon(imageIconGermany);
72      }
73    });
74  }
75 }
```

main omitted

Two containers of the Box class are created in lines 7–8 using the convenient static methods createHorizontalBox() and createVerticalBox(). You could also create it using the constructor Box(int axis). The box containers always use the BoxLayout manager. You cannot reset the layout manager for the box containers.

The image icons are created from image files (lines 14–25) through resource bundles, which was introduced in §16.9, "Locating Resource Using the URL Class."

Two buttons with print and save icons are added into the horizontal box (lines 34–36). A horizontal strut with size 20 is added between these two buttons (line 35).

Four buttons with texts US, Canada, Norway, and Germany are added into the vertical box (lines 38–44). A horizontal strut with size 8 is added to separate the US button and the Canada button (line 39). A rigid area is inserted between the Norway button and the Germany button (line 43). A glue is inserted to separate the Canada button and the Norway button as far as possible in the vertical box (line 41).

The strut, rigid area, and glue are instances of Component, so they can be added to the box container. In theory, you can add them to a container other than the box container. But they may be ignored and have no effect in other containers.

28.3.5 (Optional) OverlayLayout

`OverlayLayout` is a Swing layout manager that arranges components on top of each other. To create an `OverlayLayout`, use the following constructor:

> **public** OverlayLayout(Container target)

The constructor creates a layout manager that is dedicated to the given target container. For example, the following code creates an `OverlayLayout` for panel `p1`:

```
JPanel p1 = new JPanel();
OverlayLayout overlayLayout = new OverlayLayout(p1);
p1.setLayout(overlayLayout);
```

You still need to invoke the `setLayout` method on `p1` to set the layout manager.

A component is on top of another component if it is added to the container before the other one. Suppose components `p1`, `p2`, and `p3` are added to a container of the `OverlayLayout` in this order, then `p1` is on top of `p2`, and `p2` is on top of `p3`.

Listing 28.5 gives an example that overlays two buttons in a panel of `OverlayLayout`, as shown in Figure 28.11. The first button is on top of the second button. The program enables the user to set the `alignmentX` and `alignmentY` properties of the two buttons dynamically. You can also set the `opaque` (blocked) property of the first button. When the `opaque` property is set to `true`, the first button blocks the scene of the second button, as shown in Figure 28.11(a). When the `opaque` property is set to `false`, the first button becomes transparent to allow the second button to be seen through the first button, as shown in Figure 28.11(b).

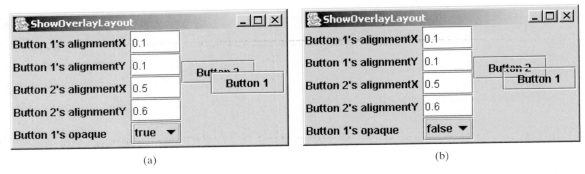

FIGURE 28.11 The components are overlaid in the container of `OverlayLayout`.

LISTING 28.5 ShowOverLayLayout.java

```
1 import java.awt.*;
2 import java.awt.event.*;
3 import javax.swing.*;
4
5 public class ShowOverlayLayout extends JApplet {
6   private JButton jbt1 = new JButton("Button 1");
7   private JButton jbt2 = new JButton("Button 2");
8
9   private JTextField jtfButton1AlignmentX = new JTextField(4);
10   private JTextField jtfButton1AlignmentY = new JTextField(4);
11   private JTextField jtfButton2AlignmentX = new JTextField(4);
12   private JTextField jtfButton2AlignmentY = new JTextField(4);
13   private JComboBox jcboButton1Opaque = new JComboBox(
14     new Object[]{new Boolean(true), new Boolean(false)});
```

```
15
16   // Panel p1 to hold two buttons
17   private JPanel p1 = new JPanel();
18
19   public ShowOverlayLayout() {
20     // Add two buttons to p1 of OverlayLayout
21     p1.setLayout(new OverlayLayout(p1));
22     p1.add(jbt1);
23     p1.add(jbt2);
24
25     JPanel p2 = new JPanel();
26     p2.setLayout(new GridLayout(5, 1));
27     p2.add(new JLabel("Button 1's alignmentX"));
28     p2.add(new JLabel("Button 1's alignmentY"));
29     p2.add(new JLabel("Button 2's alignmentX"));
30     p2.add(new JLabel("Button 2's alignmentY"));
31     p2.add(new JLabel("Button 1's opaque"));
32
33     JPanel p3 = new JPanel();
34     p3.setLayout(new GridLayout(5, 1));
35     p3.add(jtfButton1AlignmentX);
36     p3.add(jtfButton1AlignmentY);
37     p3.add(jtfButton2AlignmentX);
38     p3.add(jtfButton2AlignmentY);
39     p3.add(jcboButton1Opaque);
40
41     JPanel p4 = new JPanel();
42     p4.setLayout(new BorderLayout(4, 4));
43     p4.add(p2, BorderLayout.WEST);
44     p4.add(p3, BorderLayout.CENTER);
45
46     add(p1, BorderLayout.CENTER);
47     add(p4, BorderLayout.WEST);
48
49     jtfButton1AlignmentX.addActionListener(new ActionListener() {
50       public void actionPerformed(ActionEvent e) {
51         jbt1.setAlignmentX(
52           Float.parseFloat(jtfButton1AlignmentX.getText()));
53         p1.revalidate(); // Cause the components to be rearranged
54         p1.repaint(); // Cause the viewing area to be repainted
55       }
56     });
57     jtfButton1AlignmentY.addActionListener(new ActionListener() {
58       public void actionPerformed(ActionEvent e) {
59         jbt1.setAlignmentY(
60           Float.parseFloat(jtfButton1AlignmentY.getText()));
61         p1.revalidate(); // Cause the components to be rearranged
62         p1.repaint(); // Cause the viewing area to be repainted
63       }
64     });
65     jtfButton2AlignmentX.addActionListener(new ActionListener() {
66       public void actionPerformed(ActionEvent e) {
67         jbt2.setAlignmentX(
68           Float.parseFloat(jtfButton2AlignmentX.getText()));
69         p1.revalidate(); // Cause the components to be rearranged
70         p1.repaint(); // Cause the viewing area to be repainted
71       }
72     });
73     jtfButton2AlignmentY.addActionListener(new ActionListener() {
74       public void actionPerformed(ActionEvent e) {
```

overlay layout

```
75           jbt2.setAlignmentY(
76             Float.parseFloat(jtfButton2AlignmentY.getText()));
77           p1.revalidate(); // Cause the components to be rearranged
78           p1.repaint(); // Cause the viewing area to be repainted
79         }
80       });
81       jcboButton1Opaque.addActionListener(new ActionListener() {
82         public void actionPerformed(ActionEvent e) {
83           jbt1.setOpaque(((Boolean)(jcboButton1Opaque.
84             getSelectedItem())).booleanValue());
85           p1.revalidate(); // Cause the components to be rearranged
86           p1.repaint(); // Cause the viewing area to be repainted
87         }
88       });
89     }
90 }
```

main omitted

A panel `p1` of `OverlayLayout` is created (line 21) to hold two buttons (lines 22–23). Since Button 1 is added before Button 2, Button 1 is on top of Button 2.

The `alignmentX` and `alignmentY` properties specify how the two buttons are aligned relative to each other along the *x*-axis and *y*-axis (lines 51, 59). These two properties are used in `BoxLayout` and `OverlayLayout`, but are ignored by other layout managers. Note that the alignment is a `float` type number between `0` and `1`.

The `opaque` property is defined in `JComponent` for all Swing lightweight components. By default, it is `true` for `JButton`, which means that the button is nontransparent. So if Button 1's `opaque` is `true`, you cannot see any other components behind JButton 1. To enable the components behind Button 1 to be seen, set Button 1's `opaque` property to `false` (lines 83–86).

28.3.6   (Optional) SpringLayout

`SpringLayout` is a new Swing layout manager introduced in JDK 1.4. The idea of `SpringLayout` is to put a flexible spring around a component. The spring may compress or expand to place the components in desired locations.

To create a `SpringLayout`, use its no-arg constructor:

public SpringLayout()

A spring is an instance of the `Spring` class that can be created using one of the following two static methods:

■ **public static** Spring constant(**int** pref)

Returns a spring whose minimum, preferred, and maximum values each have the value `pref`.

■ **public static** Spring constant(**int** min, **int** pref, **int** max)

Returns a spring with the specified minimum, preferred, and maximum values.

Each spring has a preferred value, minimum value, maximum value, and actual value. The `getPreferredValue()`, `getMinimumValue()`, `getMaximumValue()`, and `getValue()` methods retrieve these values. The `setValue(int value)` method can be used to set an actual value.

The `Spring` class defines the static `sum(Spring s1, Spring s2)` to produce a combined new spring, the static `minus(Spring s)` to produce a new spring running in the opposite direction, and the static `max(Spring s1, Spring s2)` to produce a new spring with larger values from `s1` and `s2`.

To add a spring or a fixed space to separate components in the container, use one of the following two methods in the SpringLayout class:

■ **public void** putConstraint(String e1, Component c1, Spring s, String e2, Component c2)

Places a spring between edge e1 of component c1 and edge e2 of component c2, anchored on c2. Each edge must have one of the following values: SpringLayout.NORTH, SpringLayout.SOUTH, SpringLayout.EAST, SpringLayout.WEST.

■ **public void** putConstraint(String e1, Component c1, **int** pad, String e2, Component c2)

Places a fixed pad between edge e1 of component c1 and edge e2 of component c2, anchored on c2.

In the preceding methods, e2 and c2 are referred to as the *anchor edge* and *anchor component*, and e1 and c1 as the *dependent edge* and *dependent component*.

Listing 28.6 gives an example that places a button in the center of the container, as shown in Figure 28.12.

FIGURE 28.12 The button is centered in the container of SpringLayout.

LISTING 28.6 ShowSpringLayout.java

```
1 import java.awt.*;
2 import javax.swing.*;
3
4 public class ShowSpringLayout extends JApplet {
5   public ShowSpringLayout() {
6     SpringLayout springLayout = new SpringLayout();          spring layout
7     JPanel p1 = new JPanel(springLayout);
8     JButton jbt1 = new JButton("Button 1");
9     p1.add(jbt1);
10
11    Spring spring = Spring.constant(0, 1000, 2000);          spring
12    springLayout.putConstraint(SpringLayout.WEST, jbt1, spring,   spring constraints
13                      SpringLayout.WEST, p1);
14    springLayout.putConstraint(SpringLayout.EAST, p1, spring,
15                      SpringLayout.EAST, jbt1);
16    springLayout.putConstraint(SpringLayout.NORTH, jbt1, spring,
17                      SpringLayout.NORTH, p1);
18    springLayout.putConstraint(SpringLayout.SOUTH, p1, spring,
19                      SpringLayout.SOUTH, jbt1);
20
21    add(p1, BorderLayout.CENTER);
22  }
23 }
```

main omitted

A SpringLayout named springLayout is created in line 6 and is set in JPanel p1 (line 7). An instance of Spring is created using the static constant method with minimum value 0, preferred value 1000, and maximum value 2000 (line 11).

Like icons and borders, an instance of `Spring` can be shared. The **putConstraint** method in `SpringLayout` puts a spring between two components. In lines 12–13, the spring is padded between the west of the button and the west of the panel `p1`, anchored at `p1`. In lines 14–15, the same spring is padded between the east of the panel and the east of the button, anchored at the button. The selection of the anchor components is important. For example, if lines 12–13 were replaced by the following code,

```
springLayout.putConstraint(SpringLayout.WEST, p1, spring,
                           SpringLayout.WEST, jbt1);
```

the button would be pushed all the way to the east, as shown in Figure 28.13(a). If lines 12–13 were replaced by the following code,

```
springLayout.putConstraint(SpringLayout.NORTH, p1, spring,
                           SpringLayout.NORTH, jbt1);
```

the button would be pushed all the way to the top, as shown in Figure 28.13(b).
If lines 14–15 were replaced by the following code,

```
springLayout.putConstraint(SpringLayout.EAST, p1,
    Spring.sum(spring, spring), SpringLayout.EAST, jbt1);
```

the spring on the right of the button is twice strong as the left spring of the button, as shown in Figure 28.13(c).

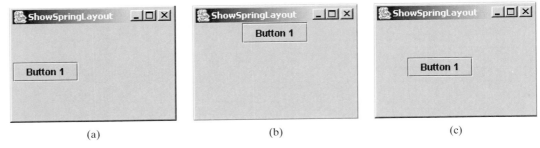

(a)   (b)   (c)

FIGURE 28.13 The selection of the anchor component can affect the layout.

28.4 Creating Custom Layout Managers

In addition to the layout managers provided in Java, you can create your own layout managers. To do so, you need to understand how a layout manager lays out components. A container's `setLayout` method specifies a layout manager for the container. The layout manager is responsible for laying out the components and displaying them in a desired location with an appropriate size. Every layout manager must directly or indirectly implement the `LayoutManager` interface. For instance, `FlowLayout` directly implements `LayoutManager`, and `BorderLayout` implements `LayoutManager2`, a subclass of `LayoutManager`. The `LayoutManager` interface provides the following methods for laying out components in a container:

- **public void** addLayoutComponent(String name, Component comp)

  Adds the specified component with the specified name to the container.

- **public void** layoutContainer(Container parent)

  Lays out the components in the specified container. In this method, you should provide concrete instructions that specify where the components are to be placed.

- **public** Dimension minimumLayoutSize(Container parent)

  Calculates the minimum size dimensions for the specified panel, given the components in the specified parent container.

- **public** Dimension preferredLayoutSize(Container parent)

  Calculates the preferred size dimensions for the specified panel, given the components in the specified parent container.

- **public void** removeLayoutComponent(Component comp)

  Removes the specified component from the layout.

These methods in LayoutManager are invoked by the methods in the java.awt.Container class through the layout manager in the container. Container contains a property named layout (an instance of LayoutManager) and the methods for adding and removing components from the container. There are five overloading add methods defined in Container for adding components with various options. The remove method removes a component from the container. The add method invokes addImpl, which then invokes the addLayoutComponent method defined in the LayoutManager interface. The layoutContainer method in the LayoutManager interface is indirectly invoked by validate through several calls. The remove method invokes removeLayoutComponent in LayoutManager. The validate method is invoked to refresh the container after the components it contains have been added to or modified. The relationship of Container and LayoutManager is shown in Figure 28.14.

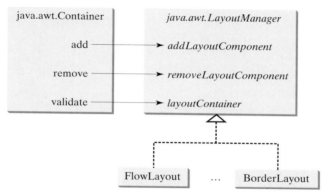

FIGURE 28.14   The add, remove, and validate methods in Container invoke the methods defined in the LayoutManager interface.

Let us declare a custom layout manager named DiagonalLayout that places the components in a diagonal. To test DiagonalLayout, the example creates an applet with radio buttons named "FlowLayout," "GridLayout," and "DiagonalLayout," as shown in Figure 28.15. You can dynamically select one of these three layouts in the panel.

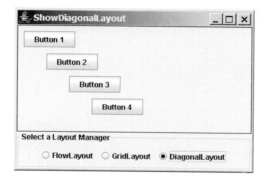

FIGURE 28.15   The DiagonalLayout manager places the components in a diagonal in the container.

The **DiagonalLayout** class is similar to **FlowLayout**. **DiagonalLayout** arranges components along a diagonal using each component's natural **preferredSize**. It contains three constraints, **gap**, **lastFill**, and **majorDiagonal**, as shown in Figure 28.16. The source code for **DiagonalLayout** is given in Listing 28.7.

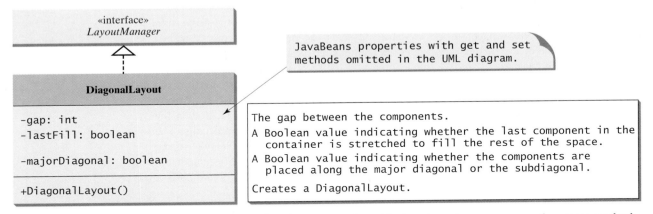

FIGURE 28.16 The **DiagonalLayout** manager has three properties with the supporting accessor and mutator methods.

LISTING 28.7 DiagonalLayout.java

properties

```
1 import java.awt.*;
2
3 public class DiagonalLayout implements LayoutManager,
4     java.io.Serializable {
5   /** Vertical gap between the components */
6   private int gap = 10;
7
8   /** True if components are placed along the major diagonal */
9   private boolean majorDiagonal = true;
10
11  /* True if the last component is stretched to fill the space */
12  private boolean lastFill = false;
13
14  /** Constructor */
15  public DiagonalLayout() {
16  }
17
18  public void addLayoutComponent(String name, Component comp) {
19    // TODO: implement this java.awt.LayoutManager method
20  }
21
22  public void removeLayoutComponent(Component comp) {
23    // TODO: implement this java.awt.LayoutManager method
24  }
25
26  public Dimension preferredLayoutSize(Container parent) {
27    // TODO: implement this java.awt.LayoutManager method
28    return minimumLayoutSize(parent);
29  }
30
31  public Dimension minimumLayoutSize(Container parent) {
32    // TODO: implement this java.awt.LayoutManager method;
```

```
33        return new Dimension(0, 0);
34      }
35
36      public void layoutContainer(Container parent) {                    layout container
37        // TODO: implement this java.awt.LayoutManager method;
38        int numberOfComponents = parent.getComponentCount();
39
40        Insets insets = parent.getInsets();
41        int w = parent.getSize().width - insets.left - insets.right;
42        int h = parent.getSize().height - insets.bottom - insets.top;
43
44        if (majorDiagonal) {
45          int x = 10, y = 10;
46
47          for (int j = 0; j < numberOfComponents; j++) {
48            Component c = parent.getComponent(j);
49            Dimension d = c.getPreferredSize();
50
51            if (c.isVisible())
52              if (lastFill && (j == numberOfComponents - 1))
53                c.setBounds(x, y, w - x, h - y);
54              else
55                c.setBounds(x, y, d.width, d.height);
56            x += d.height + gap;
57            y += d.height + gap;
58          }
59        }
60        else { // It is subdiagonal
61          int x = w - 10, y = 10;
62
63          for (int j = 0; j < numberOfComponents; j++) {
64            Component c = parent.getComponent(j);
65            Dimension d = c.getPreferredSize();
66
67            if (c.isVisible())
68              if (lastFill & (j == numberOfComponents - 1))
69                c.setBounds(0, y, x, h - y);
70              else
71                c.setBounds(x, d.width, y, d.height);
72
73            x -= (d.height + gap);
74            y += d.height + gap;
75          }
76        }
77      }
78
79      public int getGap() {
80        return gap;
81      }
82
83      public void setGap(int gap) {
84        this.gap = gap;
85      }
86
87      public void setMajorDiagonal(boolean newMajorDiagonal) {
88        majorDiagonal = newMajorDiagonal;
89      }
90
91      public boolean isMajorDiagonal() {
92        return majorDiagonal;
```

```
93    }
94
95    public void setLastFill(boolean newLastFill) {
96      lastFill = newLastFill;
97    }
98
99    public boolean isLastFill() {
100     return lastFill;
101   }
102 }
```

The `DiagonalLayout` class implements the `LayoutManger` and `Serializable` interfaces (lines 3–4). The reason to implement `Serializable` is to make it a JavaBeans component.

The `Insets` class describes the size of the borders of a container. It contains the variables `left`, `right`, `bottom`, and `top`, which correspond to the measurements for the *left border*, *right border*, *top border*, and *bottom border* (lines 40–42).

The `Dimension` class used in `DiagonalLayout` encapsulates the width and height of a component in a single object. The class is associated with certain properties of components. Several methods defined by the `Component` class and the `LayoutManager` interface return a `Dimension` object.

Listing 28.8 gives a test program that uses `DiagonalLayout`.

LISTING 28.8   ShowDiagonalLayout.java

```
1  import javax.swing.*;
2  import javax.swing.border.*;
3  import java.awt.*;
4  import java.awt.event.*;
5
6  public class ShowDiagonalLayout extends JApplet {
7    private FlowLayout flowLayout = new FlowLayout();
8    private GridLayout gridLayout = new GridLayout(2, 2);
9    private DiagonalLayout diagonalLayout = new DiagonalLayout();
10
11   private JButton jbt1 = new JButton("Button 1");
12   private JButton jbt2 = new JButton("Button 2");
13   private JButton jbt3 = new JButton("Button 3");
14   private JButton jbt4 = new JButton("Button 4");
15
16   private JRadioButton jrbFlowLayout =
17     new JRadioButton("FlowLayout");
18   private JRadioButton jrbGridLayout =
19     new JRadioButton("GridLayout");
20   private JRadioButton jrbDiagonalLayout =
21     new JRadioButton("DiagonalLayout", true);
22
23   private JPanel jPanel2 = new JPanel();
24
25   public ShowDiagonalLayout() {
26     // Set default layout in jPanel2
27     jPanel2.setLayout(diagonalLayout);
28     jPanel2.add(jbt1);
29     jPanel2.add(jbt2);
30     jPanel2.add(jbt3);
31     jPanel2.add(jbt4);
32     jPanel2.setBorder(new LineBorder(Color.black));
```

diagonal layout (margin note at line 9)

create UI (margin note at line 27)

```
33
34      JPanel jPanel1 = new JPanel();
35      jPanel1.setBorder(new TitledBorder("Select a Layout Manager"));
36      jPanel1.add(jrbFlowLayout);
37      jPanel1.add(jrbGridLayout);
38      jPanel1.add(jrbDiagonalLayout);
39
40      ButtonGroup buttonGroup1 = new ButtonGroup();
41      buttonGroup1.add(jrbFlowLayout);
42      buttonGroup1.add(jrbGridLayout);
43      buttonGroup1.add(jrbDiagonalLayout);
44
45      add(jPanel1, BorderLayout.SOUTH);
46      add(jPanel2, BorderLayout.CENTER);
47
48      jrbFlowLayout.addActionListener(new ActionListener() {          register listener
49        public void actionPerformed(ActionEvent e) {
50          jPanel2.setLayout(flowLayout);
51          jPanel2.validate();
52        }
53      });
54      jrbGridLayout.addActionListener(new ActionListener() {          register listener
55        public void actionPerformed(ActionEvent e) {
56          jPanel2.setLayout(gridLayout);
57          jPanel2.validate();
58        }
59      });
60      jrbDiagonalLayout.addActionListener(new ActionListener() {      register listener
61        public void actionPerformed(ActionEvent e) {
62          jPanel2.setLayout(diagonalLayout);
63          jPanel2.validate();
64        }
65      });
66    }
67 }                                                                    main omitted
```

The `TestDiagonalLayout` class enables you to dynamically set the layout in `jPanel2`. When you select a new layout, the layout manager is set in `jPanel2`, and the `validate()` method is invoked (lines 51, 57, 63), which in turn invokes the `layoutContainer` method in the `LayoutManager` interface to display the components in the container.

28.5 **JScrollPane**

Often you need to use a scrollbar to scroll the contents of an object that does not fit completely into the viewing area. `JScrollBar` and `JSlider` can be used for this purpose, but you have to *manually* write the code to implement scrolling with them. `JScrollPane` is a component that supports *automatic* scrolling without coding. It was used to scroll the text area in Listing 15.6, TextAreaDemo.java, and to scroll a list in Listing 15.8, ListDemo.java. In fact, it can be used to scroll any subclass of `JComponent`.

A `JScrollPane` can be viewed as a specialized container with a view port for displaying the contained component. In addition to horizontal and vertical scrollbars, a `JScrollPane` can have a column header, a row header, and corners, as shown in Figure 28.17.

The *view port* is an instance of `JViewport` through which a scrollable component is dis-   view port
played. When you add a component to a scroll pane, you are actually placing it in the scroll pane's view port. Figure 28.18 shows the frequently used properties, constructors, and methods in `JScrollPane`.

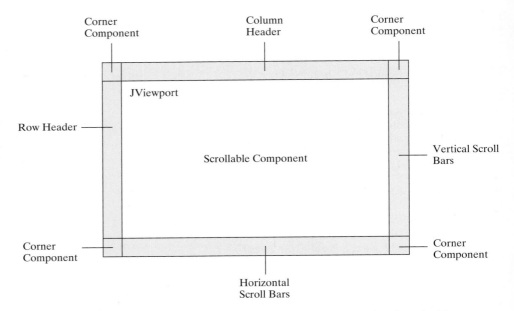

FIGURE 28.17 A JScrollPane has a view port, optional horizontal and vertical bars, optional column and row headers, and optional corners.

The constructor always creates a view port regardless of whether the viewing component is specified. Normally, you have the component and you want to place it in a scroll pane. A convenient way to create a scroll pane for a component is to use the JScrollPane(component) constructor.

The vsbPolicy parameter can be one of the following three values:

```
JScrollPane.VERTICAL_SCROLLBAR_AS_NEEDED
JScrollPane.VERTICAL_SCROLLBAR_NEVER
JScrollPane.VERTICAL_SCROLLBAR_ALWAYS
```

The hsbPolicy parameter can be one of the following three values:

```
JScrollPane.HORIZONTAL_SCROLLBAR_AS_NEEDED
JScrollPane.HORIZONTAL_SCROLLBAR_NEVER
JScrollPane.HORIZONTAL_SCROLLBAR_ALWAYS
```

To set a corner component, you can use the setCorner(String key, Component corner) method. The legal values for the key are:

```
JScrollPane.LOWER_LEFT_CORNER
JScrollPane.LOWER_RIGHT_CORNER
JScrollPane.UPPER_LEFT_CORNER
JScrollPane.UPPER_RIGHT_CORNER
```

Listing 28.9 shows an example that displays a map in a label and places the label in a scroll pane so that a large map can be scrolled. The program lets you choose a map from a combo box and display it in the scroll pane, as shown in Figure 28.19.

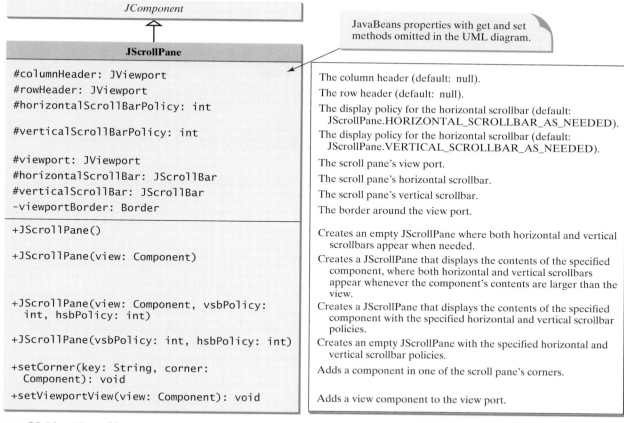

JComponent

JavaBeans properties with get and set methods omitted in the UML diagram.

JScrollPane

#columnHeader: JViewport
#rowHeader: JViewport
#horizontalScrollBarPolicy: int

#verticalScrollBarPolicy: int

#viewport: JViewport
#horizontalScrollBar: JScrollBar
#verticalScrollBar: JScrollBar
-viewportBorder: Border

+JScrollPane()

+JScrollPane(view: Component)

+JScrollPane(view: Component, vsbPolicy: int, hsbPolicy: int)

+JScrollPane(vsbPolicy: int, hsbPolicy: int)

+setCorner(key: String, corner: Component): void
+setViewportView(view: Component): void

The column header (default: null).
The row header (default: null).
The display policy for the horizontal scrollbar (default: JScrollPane.HORIZONTAL_SCROLLBAR_AS_NEEDED).
The display policy for the horizontal scrollbar (default: JScrollPane.VERTICAL_SCROLLBAR_AS_NEEDED).
The scroll pane's view port.
The scroll pane's horizontal scrollbar.
The scroll pane's vertical scrollbar.
The border around the view port.

Creates an empty JScrollPane where both horizontal and vertical scrollbars appear when needed.
Creates a JScrollPane that displays the contents of the specified component, where both horizontal and vertical scrollbars appear whenever the component's contents are larger than the view.
Creates a JScrollPane that displays the contents of the specified component with the specified horizontal and vertical scrollbar policies.
Creates an empty JScrollPane with the specified horizontal and vertical scrollbar policies.
Adds a component in one of the scroll pane's corners.
Adds a view component to the view port.

FIGURE 28.18 `JScrollPane` provides methods for displaying and manipulating the components in a scroll pane.

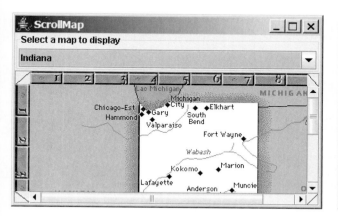
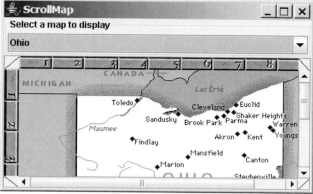

FIGURE 28.19 The scroll pane can be used to scroll contents automatically.

LISTING 28.9 ScrollMap.java

```java
1 import java.awt.*;
2 import java.awt.event.*;
3 import javax.swing.*;
```

```
 4  import javax.swing.border.*;
 5
 6  public class ScrollMap extends JApplet {
 7    // Create images in labels
 8    private JLabel lblIndianaMap = new JLabel(
 9      new ImageIcon(getClass().getResource("image/indianaMap.gif")));
10    private JLabel lblOhioMap = new JLabel(
11      new ImageIcon(getClass().getResource("image/ohioMap.gif")));
12
13    // Create a scroll pane to scroll map in the labels
14    private JScrollPane jspMap = new JScrollPane(lblIndianaMap);
15
16    public ScrollMap() {
17      // Create a combo box for selecting maps
18      JComboBox jcboMap = new JComboBox(new String[]{"Indiana",
19        "Ohio"});
20
21      // Panel p to hold combo box
22      JPanel p = new JPanel();
23      p.setLayout(new BorderLayout());
24      p.add(jcboMap);
25      p.setBorder(new TitledBorder("Select a map to display"));
26
27      // Set row header, column header and corner header
28      jspMap.setColumnHeaderView(new JLabel(new ImageIcon(getClass().
29        getResource("image/horizontalRuler.gif"))));
30      jspMap.setRowHeaderView(new JLabel(new ImageIcon(getClass().
31        getResource("image/verticalRuler.gif"))));
32      jspMap.setCorner(JScrollPane.UPPER_LEFT_CORNER,
33        new CornerPanel(JScrollPane.UPPER_LEFT_CORNER));
34      jspMap.setCorner(ScrollPaneConstants.UPPER_RIGHT_CORNER,
35        new CornerPanel(JScrollPane.UPPER_RIGHT_CORNER));
36      jspMap.setCorner(JScrollPane.LOWER_RIGHT_CORNER,
37        new CornerPanel(JScrollPane.LOWER_RIGHT_CORNER));
38      jspMap.setCorner(JScrollPane.LOWER_LEFT_CORNER,
39        new CornerPanel(JScrollPane.LOWER_LEFT_CORNER));
40
41      // Add the scroll pane and combo box panel to the frame
42      add(jspMap, BorderLayout.CENTER);
43      add(p, BorderLayout.NORTH);
44
45      // Register listener
46      jcboMap.addItemListener(new ItemListener() {
47        /** Show the selected map */
48        public void itemStateChanged(ItemEvent e) {
49          String selectedItem = (String)e.getItem();
50          if (selectedItem.equals("Indiana")) {
51            // Set a new view in the view port
52            jspMap.setViewportView(lblIndianaMap);
53          }
54          else if (selectedItem.equals("Ohio")) {
55            // Set a new view in the view port
56            jspMap.setViewportView(lblOhioMap);
57          }
58
59          // Revalidate the scroll pane
60          jspMap.revalidate();
61        }
62      });
63    }
```

labels

create UI

scroll pane

register listener

```
64 }
65
66 // A panel displaying a line used for scroll pane corner
67 class CornerPanel extendsJPanel {
68   // Line location
69   private String location;
70
71   public CornerPanel(String location) {
72     this.location = location;
73   }
74
75   /** Draw a line depending on the location */
76   protected void paintComponent(Graphics g) {
77     super.paintComponents(g);
78
79     if (location == "UPPER_LEFT_CORNER")
80       g.drawLine(0, getHeight(), getWidth(), 0);
81     else if (location == "UPPER_RIGHT_CORNER")
82       g.drawLine(0, 0, getWidth(), getHeight());
83     else if (location == "LOWER_RIGHT_CORNER")
84       g.drawLine(0, getHeight(), getWidth(), 0);
85     else if (location == "LOWER_LEFT_CORNER")
86       g.drawLine(0, 0, getWidth(), getHeight());
87   }
88 }
```

main omitted

The program creates a scroll pane to view image maps. The images are created from image files and displayed in labels (lines 8–11). To view an image, the label that contains the image is placed in the scroll pane's view port (line 14).

The scroll pane has a main view, a header view, a column view, and four corner views. Each view is a subclass of Component. Since ImageIcon is not a subclass of Component, it cannot be directly used as a view in the scroll pane. Instead the program places an ImageIcon to a label and uses the label as a view.

The CornerPanel (lines 67–88) is a subclass of JPanel that is used to display a line. How the line is drawn depends on the location of the corner. The location is a string passed in as a parameter in the CornerPanel's constructor.

Whenever a new map is selected, the label for displaying the map image is set to the scroll pane's view port. The revalidate() method (line 60) must be invoked to cause the new image to be displayed. The revalidate() method causes a container to lay out its sub-components again after the components it contains have been added to or modified.

28.6 JTabbedPane

JTabbedPane is a useful Swing container that provides a set of mutually exclusive tabs for accessing multiple components, as shown in Figure 28.20.

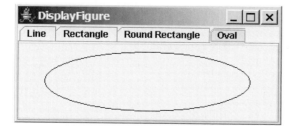

FIGURE 28.20   JTabbedPane displays components through the tabs.

Usually you place the panels inside a `JTabbedPane` and associate a tab with each panel. `JTabbedPane` is easy to use, because the selection of the panel is handled automatically by clicking the corresponding tab. You can switch between a group of panels by clicking on a tab with a given title and/or icon. Figure 28.21 shows the frequently used properties, constructors, and methods in `JTabbedPane`.

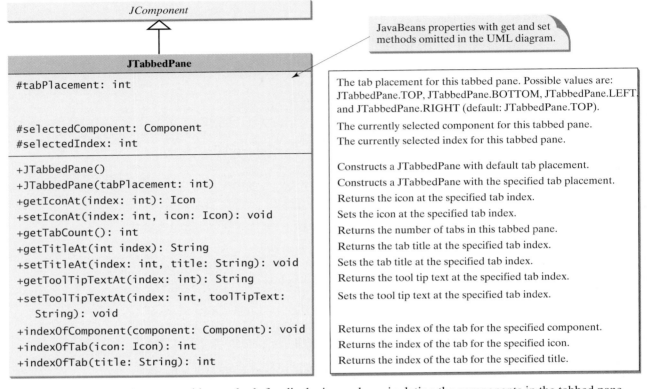

FIGURE 28.21 `JTabbedPane` provides methods for displaying and manipulating the components in the tabbed pane.

Listing 28.10 gives an example that uses a tabbed pane with four tabs to display four types of figures: line, rectangle, rounded rectangle, and oval. You can select a figure to display by clicking the corresponding tab, as shown in Figure 28.20. The `FigurePanel` class for displaying a figure was presented in §13.7, "Case Study: The `FigurePanel` Class." You can use the `type` property to specify a figure type.

LISTING 28.10 DisplayFigure.java

```
1  import java.awt.*;
2  import javax.swing.*;
3
4  public class DisplayFigure extends JApplet {
5    private JTabbedPane jtpFigures = new JTabbedPane();
6    private FigurePanel squarePanel = new FigurePanel();
7    private FigurePanel rectanglePanel = new FigurePanel();
8    private FigurePanel circlePanel = new FigurePanel();
9    private FigurePanel ovalPanel = new FigurePanel();
10
11   public DisplayFigure() {
12     squarePanel.setType(FigurePanel.LINE);
13     rectanglePanel.setType(FigurePanel.RECTANGLE);
14     circlePanel.setType(FigurePanel.ROUND_RECTANGLE);
15     ovalPanel.setType(FigurePanel.OVAL);
```

tabbed pane

set type

```
16
17      add(jtpFigures, BorderLayout.CENTER);                    add tabs
18      jtpFigures.add(squarePanel, "Line");
19      jtpFigures.add(rectanglePanel, "Rectangle");
20      jtpFigures.add(circlePanel, "Round Rectangle");
21      jtpFigures.add(ovalPanel, "Oval");
22                                                               set tool tips
23      jtpFigures.setToolTipTextAt(0, "Line");
24      jtpFigures.setToolTipTextAt(1, "Rectangle");
25      jtpFigures.setToolTipTextAt(2, "Round Rectangle");
26      jtpFigures.setToolTipTextAt(3, "Oval");
27    }                                                          main omitted
28 }
```

The program creates a tabbed pane to hold four panels, each of which displays a figure. A panel is associated with a tab. The tabs are titled Line, Rectangle, Rounded Rectangle, and Oval.

By default, the tabs are placed at the top of the tabbed pane. You can select a different placement using the `tabPlacement` property.

28.7 **JSplitPane**

JSplitPane is a convenient Swing container that contains two components with a separate bar known as a *divider*, as shown in Figure 28.22.

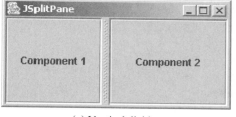
(a) Vertical divider

(b) Horizontal divider

FIGURE 28.22   JSplitPane divides a container into two parts.

The bar can divide the container horizontally or vertically, and can be dragged to change the amount of space occupied by each component. Figure 28.23 shows the frequently used properties, constructors, and methods in JSplitPane.

Listing 28.11 gives an example that uses radio buttons to let the user select a FlowLayout, GridLayout, or BoxLayout manager dynamically for a panel. The panel contains four buttons, as shown in Figure 28.24. The description of the currently selected layout manager is displayed in a text area. The radio buttons, buttons, and text area are placed in two split panes.

LISTING 28.11   ShowLayout.java

```
1 import java.awt.*;
2 import java.awt.event.*;
3 import java.net.*;
4 import javax.swing.*;
5
6 public class ShowLayout extends JApplet {
7   // Get the url for HTML files
8   private String flowLayoutDesc = "FlowLayout arranges components " +      descriptions
9     "according to their preferredSize in " +
10    "a left-to-right flow, much like lines of text in a paragraph.";
11  private String gridLayoutDesc = "GridLayout arranges ...";
```

```
12   private String boxLayoutDesc = "BoxLayout arranges ...";
13
14   private JRadioButton jrbFlowLayout =
15     new JRadioButton("FlowLayout");
16   private JRadioButton jrbGridLayout =
17     new JRadioButton("GridLayout", true);
18   private JRadioButton jrbBoxLayout =
19     new JRadioButton("BoxLayout");
20
21   private JPanel jpComponents = new JPanel();
22   private JTextArea jtfDescription = new JTextArea();
23
24   // Create layout managers
25   private FlowLayout flowLayout = new FlowLayout();
26   private GridLayout gridLayout = new GridLayout(2, 2, 3, 3);
27   private BoxLayout boxLayout =
28     new BoxLayout(jpComponents, BoxLayout.X_AXIS);
29
30   public ShowLayout() {
31     // Create a box to hold radio buttons
32     Box jpChooseLayout = Box.createVerticalBox();
33     jpChooseLayout.add(jrbFlowLayout);
34     jpChooseLayout.add(jrbGridLayout);
35     jpChooseLayout.add(jrbBoxLayout);
36
37     // Group radio buttons
38     ButtonGroup btg = new ButtonGroup();
39     btg.add(jrbFlowLayout);
40     btg.add(jrbGridLayout);
41     btg.add(jrbBoxLayout);
42
43     // Wrap lines and words
44     jtfDescription.setLineWrap(true);
45     jtfDescription.setWrapStyleWord(true);
46
47     // Add fours buttons to jpComponents
48     jpComponents.add(new JButton("Button 1"));
49     jpComponents.add(new JButton("Button 2"));
50     jpComponents.add(new JButton("Button 3"));
51     jpComponents.add(new JButton("Button 4"));
52
53     // Create two split panes to hold jpChooseLayout, jpComponents,
54     // and jtfDescription
55     JSplitPane jSplitPane2 = new JSplitPane(
56       JSplitPane.VERTICAL_SPLIT, jpComponents,
57       new JScrollPane(jtfDescription));
58     JSplitPane jSplitPane1 = new JSplitPane(
59       JSplitPane.HORIZONTAL_SPLIT, jpChooseLayout, jSplitPane2);
60
61     // Set FlowLayout as default
62     jpComponents.setLayout(flowLayout);
63     jpComponents.validate();
64     jtfDescription.setText(flowLayoutDesc);
65
66     add(jSplitPane1 , BorderLayout.CENTER);
67
68     // Register listeners
69     jrbFlowLayout.addActionListener(new ActionListener() {
70       public void actionPerformed(ActionEvent e) {
71         jpComponents.setLayout(flowLayout);
```

radio buttons

layout managers

split pane

split pane

```
72        jtfDescription.setText(flowLayoutDesc);
73        jpComponents.revalidate();
74      }
75    });
76    jrbGridLayout.addActionListener(new ActionListener() {        register listener
77      public void actionPerformed(ActionEvent e) {
78        jpComponents.setLayout(gridLayout);
79        jtfDescription.setText(gridLayoutDesc);
80        jpComponents.revalidate();                                 validate
81      }
82    });
83    jrbBoxLayout.addActionListener(new ActionListener() {         register listener
84      public void actionPerformed(ActionEvent e) {
85        jpComponents.setLayout(boxLayout);
86        jtfDescription.setText(boxLayoutDesc);
87        jpComponents.revalidate();                                 validate
88      }
89    });
90  }
91 }                                                                 main omitted
```

JComponent

JavaBeans properties with get and set methods omitted in the UML diagram.

JSplitPane	
#continuousLayout: boolean	A Boolean value indicating whether or not the views are continuously redisplayed while resizing.
#dividerSize: int	Size of the divider.
#lastDividerLocation: int	Previous location of the divider.
#leftComponent: Component	The left or top component.
#oneTouchExpandable: boolean	A Boolean property with the default value false. If the property is true, the divider has an expanding and contracting look, so that it can expand and contract with one touch.
#orientation: int	Specifies whether the container is divided horizontally or vertically. The possible values are JSplitPane.HORIZONTAL_SPLIT and JSplitPane.VERTICAL_SPLIT. The default value is JSplitPane.HORIZONTAL_SPLIT, which divides the container into a left part and a right part.
#rightComponent: Component	The right or bottom component.
+JSplitPane()	Creates a JSplitPane configured to arrange the child components side-by-side horizontally with no continuous layout.
+JSplitPane(newOrientation: int)	Creates a JSplitPane configured with the specified orientation and no continuous layout.
+JSplitPane(newOrientation: int, newContinuousLayout: boolean)	Creates a JSplitPane with the specified orientation and continuous layout.
+JSplitPane(newOrientation: int, newContinuousLayout: boolean, newLeftComponent: Component, newRightComponent: Component)	Creates a JSplitPane with the specified orientation and continuous layout, and the left (top) and right (bottom) components.
+JSplitPane(newOrientation: int, newLeftComponent: Component, newRightComponent: Component)	Creates a JSplitPane with the specified orientation, and the left (top) and right (bottom) components. No continuous layout.

FIGURE 28.23 JSplitPane provides methods to specify the properties of a split pane and for manipulating the components in a split pane.

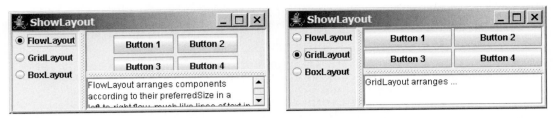

FIGURE 28.24 The split pane lets you adjust the component size in the split panes.

Split panes can be embedded. Adding a split pane to an existing split results in three split panes. The program creates two split panes (lines 55–59) to hold a panel for radio buttons, a panel for buttons, and a scroll pane.

The radio buttons are used to select layout managers. A selected layout manager is used in the panel for laying out the buttons (lines 69–89). The scroll pane contains a `JTextField` for displaying the text that describes the selected layout manager (line 57).

28.8 Swing Borders

Swing provides a variety of borders that you can use to decorate components. You learned how to create titled borders and line borders in §12.9, "Common Features of Swing GUI Components." This section introduces borders in more detail.

A Swing border is defined in the `Border` interface. Every instance of `JComponent` can set a border through the `border` property defined in `JComponent`. If a border is present, it replaces the inset. The `AbstractBorder` class implements an empty border with no size. This provides a convenient base class from which other border classes can easily be derived. There are eight concrete border classes, `BevelBorder`, `SoftBevelBorder`, `CompoundBorder`, `EmptyBorder`, `EtchedBorder`, `LineBorder`, `MatteBorder`, and `TitledBorder`, as shown in Figure 28.25.

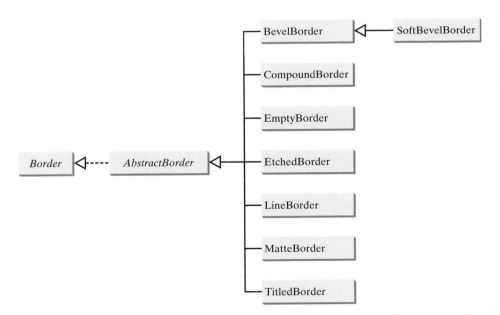

FIGURE 28.25 Every instance of `JComponent` can have a border derived from the `Border` interface.

- **BevelBorder** is a 3D-look border that can be lowered or raised. BevelBorder has the following constructors, which create a BevelBorder with the specified bevelType (BevelBorder.LOWERED or BevelBorder.RAISED) and colors:

```
BevelBorder(int bevelType)
BevelBorder(int bevelType, Color highlight, Color shadow)
BevelBorder(int bevelType, Color highlightOuterColor,
            Color highlightInnerColor, Color shadowOuterColor,
            Color shadowInnerColor)
```

- **SoftBevelBorder** is a raised or lowered bevel with softened corners. SoftBevelBorder has the following constructors:

```
SoftBevelBorder(int bevelType)
SoftBevelBorder(int bevelType, Color highlight, Color shadow)
SoftBevelBorder(int bevelType, Color highlightOuterColor,
                Color highlightInnerColor, Color
                shadowOuterColor, Color shadowInnerColor)
```

- **EmptyBorder** is a border with border space but no drawings. EmptyBorder has the following constructors:

```
EmptyBorder(Insets borderInsets)
EmptyBorder(int top, int left, int bottom, int right)
```

- **EtchedBorder** is an etched border that can be etched-in or etched-out. EtchedBorder has the property etchType with the value LOWERED or RAISED. EtchedBorder has the following constructors:

```
EtchedBorder() // default constructor with a lowered border
EtchedBorder(Color highlight, Color shadow)
EtchedBorder(int etchType)
EtchedBorder(int etchType, Color highlight, Color shadow)
```

- **LineBorder** draws a line of arbitrary thickness and a single color around the border. LineBorder has the following constructors:

```
LineBorder(Color color) // Thickness 1
LineBorder(Color color, int thickness)
LineBorder(Color color, int thickness, boolean roundedCorners)
```

- **MatteBorder** is a matte-like border padded with the icon images. MatteBorder has the following constructors:

```
MatteBorder(Icon tileIcon)
MatteBorder(Insets borderInsets, Color matteColor)
MatteBorder(Insets borderInsets, Icon tileIcon)
MatteBorder(int top, int left, int bottom, int right,
  Color matteColor)
MatteBorder(int top, int left, int bottom, int right, Icon
  tileIcon)
```

- **CompoundBorder** is used to compose two Border objects into a single border by nesting an inside Border object within the insets of an outside Border object using the following constructor:

```
CompoundBorder(Border outsideBorder, Border insideBorder)
```

■ **TitledBorder** is a border with a string title in a specified position. Titled border can be composed with other borders. **TitledBorder** has the following constructors:

```
TitledBorder(String title)
TitledBorder(Border border) // Empty title on another border
TitledBorder(Border border, String title)
TitledBorder(Border border, String title,
             int titleJustification, int titlePosition)
TitledBorder(Border border, String title,
             int titleJustification, int titlePosition,
             Font titleFont)
TitledBorder(Border border, String title, int
             titleJustification, int titlePosition,
             Font titleFont, Color titleColor)
```

For convenience, Java also provides the `javax.swing.BorderFactory` class, which contains the static methods for creating borders shown in Figure 28.26.

javax.swing.BorderFactory
+createBevelBorder(type: int): Border
+createBevelBorder(type: int, highlight: Color, shadow: Color): Border
+createBevelBorder(type: int, highlightOuter: Color, highlightInner: Color, shadowOuter: Color, shadowInner: Color): Border
+createCompoundBorder(): CompoundBorder
+createCompoundBorder(outsideBorder: Border, insideBorder: Border): CompoundBorder
+createEmptyBorder(): Border
+createEmptyBorder(top: int, left: int, bottom: int, right: int): Border
+createEtchedBorder(): Border
+createEtchedBorder(highlight: Color, shadow: Color): Border
+createEtchedBorder(type: int): Border
+createEtchedBorder(type: int, highlight: Color, shadow: Color): Border
+createLineBorder(color: Color): Border
+createLineBorder(color: Color, thickness: int): Border
+createLoweredBevelBorder(): Border
+createMatteBorder(top: int, left: int, bottom: int, right: int, color: Color): MatteBorder
+createMatteBorder(top: int, left: int, bottom: int, right: int, tileIcon: Icon): MatteBorder
+createRaisedBevelBorder(): Border
+createTitledBorder(border: Border): TitledBorder
+createTitledBorder(border: Border, title: String): TitledBorder
+createTitledBorder(border: Border, title: String, titleJustification: int, titlePosition: int): TitledBorder
+createTitledBorder(border: Border, title: String, titleJustification: int, titlePosition: int, titleFont: Font): TitledBorder
+createTitledBorder(border: Border, title: String, titleJustification: int, titlePosition: int, titleFont: Font, titleColor: Color): TitledBorder
+createTitledBorder(title: String): TitledBorder

FIGURE 28.26 BorderFactory contains the static methods for creating various types of borders.

For example, to create an etched border, use the following statement:

```
Border border = BorderFactory.createEtchedBorder();
```

 Note

All the border classes and interfaces are grouped in the package `javax.swing.border` except `javax.swing.BorderFactory`.

Note

Borders and icons can be shared. Thus you can create a border or icon and use it to set the **border** or **icon** property for any GUI component. For example, the following statements set a border **b** for two panels **p1** and **p2**:

```
p1.setBorder(b);
p2.setBorder(b);
```

Listing 28.12 gives an example that creates and displays various types of borders. You can select a border with a title or without a title. For a border without a title, you can choose a border style from Lowered Bevel, Raised Bevel, Etched, Line, Matte, or Empty. For a border with a title, you can specify the title position and justification. You can also embed another border into a titled border. Figure 28.27 displays a sample run of the program.

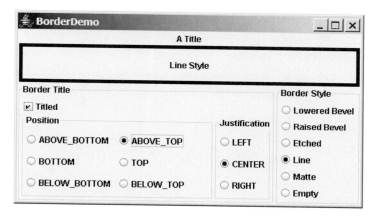

FIGURE 28.27   The program demonstrates various types of borders.

Here are the major steps in the program:

1. Create the user interface.

   a. Create a `JLabel` object and place it in the center of the frame.

   b. Create a panel named `jpPosition` to group the radio buttons for selecting the border title position. Set the border of this panel in the titled border with the title "Position".

   c. Create a panel named `jpJustification` to group the radio buttons for selecting the border title justification. Set the border of this panel in the titled border with the title "Justification".

   d. Create a panel named `jpTitleOptions` to hold the `jpPosition` panel and the `jpJustification` panel.

   e. Create a panel named `jpTitle` to hold a check box named "Titled" and the `jpTitleOptions` panel.

   f. Create a panel named `jpBorderStyle` to group the radio buttons for selecting border styles.

   g. Create a panel named `jpAllChoices` to hold the panels `jpTitle` and `jpBorderStyle`. Place `jpAllChoices` in the south of the frame.

2. Process the event.

Create and register listeners to implement the `actionPerformed` handler to set the border for the label according to the events from the check box, and from all the radio buttons.

LISTING 28.12   BorderDemo.java

```
1  import java.awt.*;
2  import java.awt.event.ActionListener;
3  import java.awt.event.ActionEvent;
4  import javax.swing.*;
5  import javax.swing.border.*;
6
7  public class BorderDemo extends JApplet {
8    // Declare a label for displaying message
9    private JLabel jLabel1 = new JLabel("Display the border type",
10     JLabel.CENTER);
11
12   // A check box for selecting a border with or without a title
13   private JCheckBox jchkTitled;
14
15   // Radio buttons for border styles
16   private JRadioButton jrbLoweredBevel, jrbRaisedBevel,
17     jrbEtched, jrbLine, jrbMatte, jrbEmpty;
18
19   // Radio buttons for titled border options
20   private JRadioButton jrbAboveBottom, jrbBottom,
21     jrbBelowBottom, jrbAboveTop, jrbTop, jrbBelowTop,
22     jrbLeft, jrbCenter, jrbRight;
23
24   // TitledBorder for the label
25   private TitledBorder jLabel1Border;
26
27   /** Constructor */
28   public BorderDemo() {
29     // Create a JLabel instance and set colors
30     jLabel1.setBackground(Color.yellow);
31     jLabel1.setBorder(jLabel1Border);
32
33     // Place title position radio buttons
34     JPanel jpPosition = new JPanel();
35     jpPosition.setLayout(new GridLayout(3, 2));
36     jpPosition.add(
37       jrbAboveBottom = new JRadioButton("ABOVE_BOTTOM"));
38     jpPosition.add(jrbAboveTop = new JRadioButton("ABOVE_TOP"));
39     jpPosition.add(jrbBottom = new JRadioButton("BOTTOM"));
40     jpPosition.add(jrbTop = new JRadioButton("TOP"));
41     jpPosition.add(
42       jrbBelowBottom = new JRadioButton("BELOW_BOTTOM"));
43     jpPosition.add(jrbBelowTop = new JRadioButton("BELOW_TOP"));
44     jpPosition.setBorder(new TitledBorder("Position"));
45
46     // Place title justification radio buttons
47     JPanel jpJustification = new JPanel();
48     jpJustification.setLayout(new GridLayout(3,1));
49     jpJustification.add(jrbLeft = new JRadioButton("LEFT"));
50     jpJustification.add(jrbCenter = new JRadioButton("CENTER"));
51     jpJustification.add(jrbRight = new JRadioButton("RIGHT"));
52     jpJustification.setBorder(new TitledBorder("Justification"));
53
54     // Create panel jpTitleOptions to hold jpPosition and
55     // jpJustification
56     JPanel jpTitleOptions = new JPanel();
57     jpTitleOptions.setLayout(new BorderLayout());
```

create UI

```
58      jpTitleOptions.add(jpPosition, BorderLayout.CENTER);
59      jpTitleOptions.add(jpJustification, BorderLayout.EAST);
60
61      // Create Panel jpTitle to hold a check box and title position
62      // radio buttons, and title justification radio buttons
63      JPanel jpTitle = new JPanel();
64      jpTitle.setBorder(new TitledBorder("Border Title"));
65      jpTitle.setLayout(new BorderLayout());
66      jpTitle.add(jchkTitled = new JCheckBox("Titled"),
67        BorderLayout.NORTH);
68      jpTitle.add(jpTitleOptions, BorderLayout.CENTER);
69
70      // Group radio buttons for title position
71      ButtonGroup btgTitlePosition = new ButtonGroup();
72      btgTitlePosition.add(jrbAboveBottom);
73      btgTitlePosition.add(jrbBottom);
74      btgTitlePosition.add(jrbBelowBottom);
75      btgTitlePosition.add(jrbAboveTop);
76      btgTitlePosition.add(jrbTop);
77      btgTitlePosition.add(jrbBelowTop);
78
79      // Group radio buttons for title justification
80      ButtonGroup btgTitleJustification = new ButtonGroup();
81      btgTitleJustification.add(jrbLeft);
82      btgTitleJustification.add(jrbCenter);
83      btgTitleJustification.add(jrbRight);
84
85      // Create Panel jpBorderStyle to hold border style radio buttons
86      JPanel jpBorderStyle = new JPanel();
87      jpBorderStyle.setBorder(new TitledBorder("Border Style"));
88      jpBorderStyle.setLayout(new GridLayout(6, 1));
89      jpBorderStyle.add(jrbLoweredBevel =
90        new JRadioButton("Lowered Bevel"));
91      jpBorderStyle.add(jrbRaisedBevel =
92        new JRadioButton("Raised Bevel"));
93      jpBorderStyle.add(jrbEtched = new JRadioButton("Etched"));
94      jpBorderStyle.add(jrbLine = new JRadioButton("Line"));
95      jpBorderStyle.add(jrbMatte = new JRadioButton("Matte"));
96      jpBorderStyle.add(jrbEmpty = new JRadioButton("Empty"));
97
98      // Group radio buttons for border styles
99      ButtonGroup btgBorderStyle = new ButtonGroup();
100     btgBorderStyle.add(jrbLoweredBevel);
101     btgBorderStyle.add(jrbRaisedBevel);
102     btgBorderStyle.add(jrbEtched);
103     btgBorderStyle.add(jrbLine);
104     btgBorderStyle.add(jrbMatte);
105     btgBorderStyle.add(jrbEmpty);
106
107     // Create Panel jpAllChoices to place jpTitle and jpBorderStyle
108     JPanel jpAllChoices = new JPanel();
109     jpAllChoices.setLayout(new BorderLayout());
110     jpAllChoices.add(jpTitle, BorderLayout.CENTER);
111     jpAllChoices.add(jpBorderStyle, BorderLayout.EAST);
112
113     // Place panels in the frame
114     setLayout(new BorderLayout());
115     add(jLabel1, BorderLayout.CENTER);
116     add(jpAllChoices, BorderLayout.SOUTH);
117
```

```
118      // Register listeners
119      ActionListener listener = new EventListener();
120      jchkTitled.addActionListener(listener);
121      jrbAboveBottom.addActionListener(listener);
122      jrbBottom.addActionListener(listener);
123      jrbBelowBottom.addActionListener(listener);
124      jrbAboveTop.addActionListener(listener);
125      jrbTop.addActionListener(listener);
126      jrbBelowTop.addActionListener(listener);
127      jrbLeft.addActionListener(listener);
128      jrbCenter.addActionListener(listener);
129      jrbRight.addActionListener(listener);
130      jrbLoweredBevel.addActionListener(listener);
131      jrbRaisedBevel.addActionListener(listener);
132      jrbLine.addActionListener(listener);
133      jrbEtched.addActionListener(listener);
134      jrbMatte.addActionListener(listener);
135      jrbEmpty.addActionListener(listener);
136    }
137
138    private class EventListener implements ActionListener {
139      /** Handle ActionEvents on check box and radio buttons */
140      public void actionPerformed(ActionEvent e) {
141        // Get border style
142        Border border = new EmptyBorder(2, 2, 2, 2);
143
144        if (jrbLoweredBevel.isSelected()) {
145          border = new BevelBorder(BevelBorder.LOWERED);
146          jLabel1.setText("Lowered Bevel Style");
147        }
148        else if (jrbRaisedBevel.isSelected()) {
149          border = new BevelBorder(BevelBorder.RAISED);
150          jLabel1.setText("Raised Bevel Style");
151        }
152        else if (jrbEtched.isSelected()) {
153          border = new EtchedBorder();
154          jLabel1.setText("Etched Style");
155        }
156        else if (jrbLine.isSelected()) {
157          border = new LineBorder(Color.black, 5);
158          jLabel1.setText("Line Style");
159        }
160        else if (jrbMatte.isSelected()) {
161          border = new MatteBorder(15, 15, 15, 15,
162            new imageIcon(getClass().getResource("image/caIcon.gif")));
163          jLabel1.setText("Matte Style");
164        }
165        else if (jrbEmpty.isSelected()) {
166          border = new EmptyBorder(2, 2, 2, 2);
167          jLabel1.setText("Empty Style");
168        }
169
170        if (jchkTitled.isSelected()) {
171          // Get the title position and justification
172          int titlePosition = TitledBorder.DEFAULT_POSITION;
173          int titleJustification = TitledBorder.DEFAULT_JUSTIFICATION;
174
175          if (jrbAboveBottom.isSelected())
176            titlePosition = TitledBorder.ABOVE_BOTTOM;
177          else if (jrbBottom.isSelected())
```

empty border

bevel border

bevel border

etched border

line border

mette border

empty border

```
178              titlePosition = TitledBorder.BOTTOM;
179            else if (jrbBelowBottom.isSelected())
180              titlePosition = TitledBorder.BELOW_BOTTOM;
181            else if (jrbAboveTop.isSelected())
182              titlePosition = TitledBorder.ABOVE_TOP;
183            else if (jrbTop.isSelected())
184              titlePosition = TitledBorder.TOP;
185            else if (jrbBelowTop.isSelected())
186              titlePosition = TitledBorder.BELOW_TOP;
187
188            if (jrbLeft.isSelected())
189              titleJustification = TitledBorder.LEFT;
190            else if (jrbCenter.isSelected())
191              titleJustification = TitledBorder.CENTER;
192            else if (jrbRight.isSelected())
193              titleJustification = TitledBorder.RIGHT;
194
195            jLabel1Border = new TitledBorder("A Title");        border on border
196            jLabel1Border.setBorder(border);
197            jLabel1Border.setTitlePosition(titlePosition);
198            jLabel1Border.setTitleJustification(titleJustification);
199            jLabel1.setBorder(jLabel1Border);
200          }
201          else {
202            jLabel1.setBorder(border);
203          }
204        }
205      }
206 }
```

main omitted

This example uses many panels to group UI components to achieve the desired look. Figure 28.27 illustrates the relationship of the panels. The Border Title panel groups all the options for setting title properties. The position options are grouped in the Position panel. The justification options are grouped in the Justification panel. The Border Style panel groups the radio buttons for choosing Lowered Bevel, Raised Bevel, Etched, Line, Matte, and Empty borders.

The label displays the selected border with or without a title, depending on the selection of the title check box. The label also displays a text indicating which type of border is being used, depending on the selection of the radio button in the Border Style panel.

The `TitledBorder` can be mixed with other borders. To do so, simply create an instance of `TitledBorder`, and use the `setBorder` method to embed a new border in `TitledBorder`.

The `MatteBorder` can be used to display icons on the border, as shown in Figure 28.28.

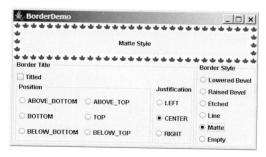

FIGURE 28.28   `MatteBorder` can display icons on the border.

28.9 (Optional) Pluggable Look-and-Feel

Lightweight components consume fewer resources and can be transparent, but they lack the AWT's platform-specific look-and-feel advantage. To address this problem, a new pluggable look-and-feel feature was introduced in Java.

The pluggable look-and-feel feature lets you design a single set of GUI components that automatically has the look-and-feel of any OS platform. The implementation of this feature is independent of the underlying native GUI, yet it can imitate the native behavior of the native GUI.

Currently, Java supports the following three look-and-feel styles:

- Metal

- Motif

- Windows

To see an example that demonstrates these three styles, change the directory to `c:\book`, and type the following command at the DOS prompt: **java –jar SimpleExample.jar**.

Figure 28.29 shows a sample run of the program.

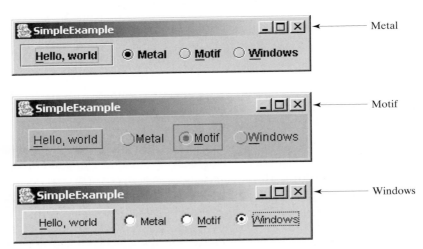

FIGURE 28.29   SimpleExample demonstrates three look-and-feel styles.

The Metal style, also known as the *Java style*, gives you a consistent look regardless of operating system. The Windows style is currently only available on Windows due to Windows copyright restrictions. The Motif style is used on Unix operating systems.

The `javax.swing.UIManager` class manages the look-and-feel of the user interface. You can use one of the following three methods to set the look-and-feel for Metal, Motif, or Windows:

```
UIManager.setLookAndFeel
  (UIManager.getCrossPlatformLookAndFeelClassName());
UIManager.setLookAndFeel
  (new com.sun.java.swing.plaf.motif.MotifLookAndFeel());
UIManager.setLookAndFeel
  (new com.sun.java.swing.plaf.windows.WindowsLookAndFeel());
```

The `setLookAndFeel` method throws `UnsupportedLookAndFeelException`, so you have to put the method inside a `try-catch` block for it to compile. To ensure that the setting takes effect, the `setLookAndFeel` method should be executed before any of the components are instantiated. Thus, you can put the code in a static block, as shown below:

```
static {
  try {
    // Set a look-and-feel, e.g.,
    // UIManager.setLookAndFeel
    //    (UIManager.getCrossPlatformLookAndFeelClassName());
  }
  catch (UnsupportedLookAndFeelException ex) {}
}
```

Static initialization blocks are executed when the class is loaded. For more information on static initialization blocks, please refer to §9.15, "Initialization Blocks."

CHAPTER SUMMARY

- `javax.swing.JRootPane` is a lightweight container used behind the scenes by Swing's top-level containers, such as `JFrame`, `JApplet`, and `JDialog`. `javax.swing.JLayeredPane` is a container that manages the optional menu bar and the content pane. The content pane is an instance of `Container`. By default, it is a `JPanel` with `BorderLayout`. This is the container where the user interface components are added. To obtain the content pane in a `JFrame` or in a `JApplet`, use the `getContentPane()` method. You can set any instance of `Container` to be a new content pane using the `setContentPane` method.

- Every container has a layout manager that is responsible for arranging its components. The container's `setLayout` method can be used to set a layout manager. Certain types of containers have default layout managers.

- Java provides `FlowLayout`, `GridLayout`, `BorderLayout`, `CardLayout`, `GridBagLayout`, `BoxLayout`, `OverlayLayout`, and `SpringLayout`. The layout manager places the components in accordance with its own rules and property settings, and with the constraints associated with each component. Every layout manager has its own specific set of rules. Some layout managers have properties that can affect the sizing and location of the components in the container.

- Java also supports absolute layout, which enables you to place components at fixed locations. In this case, the component must be placed using the component's instance method `setBounds` (defined in `java.awt.Component`). Absolute positions and sizes are fine if the application is developed and deployed on the same platform, but what looks fine on a development system may not look right on a deployment system on a different platform. To solve this problem, Java provides a set of layout managers that place components in containers in a way that is independent of fonts, screen resolutions, and operating systems.

- In addition to the layout managers provided in Java, you can create custom layout managers by implementing the `LayoutManager` interface.

- Java provides specialized containers `Box`, `JScrollPane`, `JTabbedPane`, and `JSplitPane` with fixed layout managers.

- A Swing border is defined in the `Border` interface. Every instance of `JComponent` can set a border through the `border` property defined in `JComponent`. If a border is present, it replaces the inset. There are eight concrete border classes: `BevelBorder`, `SoftBevelBorder`, `CompoundBorder`, `EmptyBorder`, `EtchedBorder`, `LineBorder`, `MatteBorder`, and `TitledBorder`. You can use the constructors of these classes or the static methods in `javax.swing.BorderFactory` to create borders.

REVIEW QUESTIONS

Section 28.2 Swing Container Structures

28.1 Since JButton is a subclass of Container, can you add a button inside a button?

28.2 How do you set an image icon in a JFrame's title bar? Can you set an image icon in a JApplet's title bar?

28.3 Which of the following are the properties in JFrame, JApplet, and JPanel?

```
contentPane, iconImage, jMenuBar, resizable, title
```

Section 28.3 Layout Managers

28.4 How does the layout in Java differ from the ones in Visual Basic and Delphi?

28.5 Discuss the factors that determine the size of the components in a container.

28.6 Discuss the properties preferredSize, minimumSize, and maximumSize.

28.7 Discuss the properties alignmentX and alignmentY.

28.8 What is a CardLayout manager? How do you create a CardLayout manager?

28.9 What is a GridBagLayout manager? How do you create a GridBagLayout manager?

28.10 Can you use absolute positioning in Java? How do you use absolute positioning? Why should you avoid using absolute positioning?

28.11 What is BoxLayout? How do you use BoxLayout? How do you use fillers to separate the components?

28.12 What is OverlayLayout? How do you use OverlayLayout?

28.13 What is SpringLayout? How do you use SpringLayout?

Sections 28.4–28.7

28.14 How do you create a custom layout manager?

28.15 What is JScrollPane? How do you use JScrollPane?

28.16 What is JTabbedPane? How do you use JTabbedPane?

28.17 What is JSplitPane? How do you use JSplitPane?

28.18 Can you specify a layout manager in Box, JScrollPane, JTabbedPane, and JSplitPane?

Section 28.8 Swing Borders

28.19 How do you create a titled border, a line border, a bevel border, and an etched border?

28.20 Can you set a border for every Swing GUI component? Can a border object be shared by different GUI components?

28.21 What package contains Border, BevelBorder, CompoundBorder, EmptyBorder, EtchedBorder, LineBorder, MatteBorder, TitledBorder, and BorderFactory?

PROGRAMMING EXERCISES

Section 28.3 Layout Managers

28.1* (*Demonstrating FlowLayout properties*) Create a program that enables the user to set the properties of a FlowLayout manager dynamically, as shown in Figure 28.30. The FlowLayout manager is used to place fifteen components in a panel. You can set the alignment, hgap, and vgap properties of the FlowLayout dynamically.

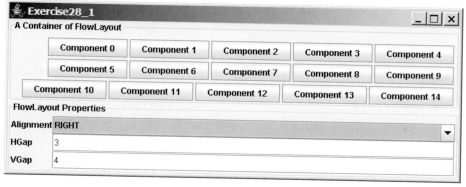

FIGURE 28.30 The program enables you to set the properties of a `FlowLayout` manager dynamically.

28.2* (*Demonstrating `GridLayout` properties*) Create a program that enables the user to set the properties of a `GridLayout` manager dynamically, as shown in Figure 28.31. The `GridLayout` manager is used to place fifteen components in a panel. You can set the `rows`, `columns`, `hgap`, and `vgap` properties of the `GridLayout` dynamically.

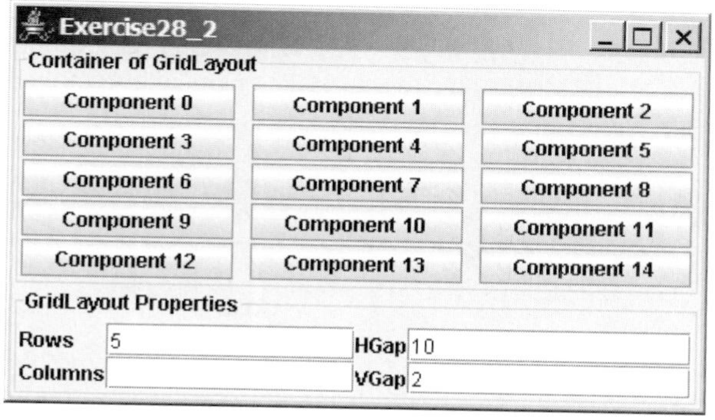

FIGURE 28.31 The program enables you to set the properties of a `GridLayout` manager dynamically.

28.3* (*Demonstrating `BorderLayout` properties*) Create a program that enables the user to set the properties of a `BorderLayout` manager dynamically, as shown in Figure 28.32. The `BorderLayout` manager is used to place five components in a panel. You can set the `hgap` and `vgap` properties of the `BorderLayout` dynamically.

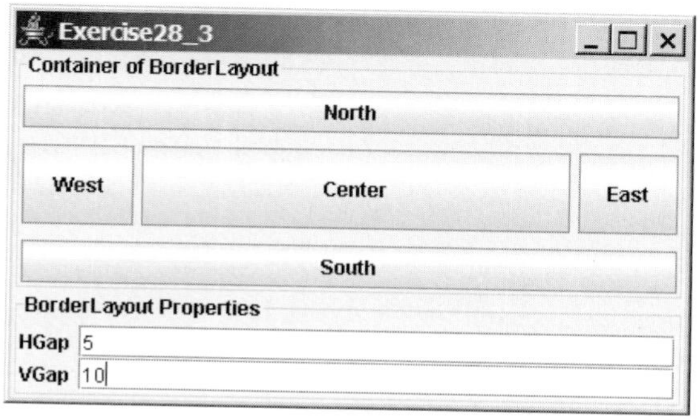

FIGURE 28.32 The program enables you to set the properties of a `BorderLayout` manager dynamically.

28.4* (*Using* `CardLayout`) Write an applet that does arithmetic on integers and rationals. The program uses two panels in a `CardLayout` manager, one for integer arithmetic and the other for rational arithmetic.

The program provides a combo box with two items Integer and Rational. When the user chooses the Integer item, the integer panel is activated. When the user chooses the rational item, the rational panel is activated (see Figure 28.33).

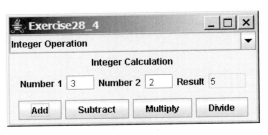 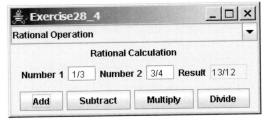

FIGURE 28.33 `CardLayout` is used to select panels that perform integer operations and rational number operations.

28.5* (*Using* `GridBagLayout`) Use `GridBagLayout` to lay out a calculator, as shown in Figure 16.21(a).

Sections 28.4–28.8

28.6* (*Using tabbed panes*) Modify Listing 28.10, DisplayFigure.java, to add a panel of radio buttons for specifying the tab placement of the tabbed pane, as shown in Figure 28.34.

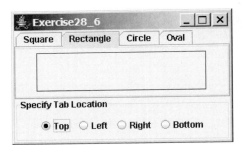 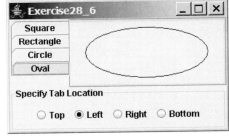

FIGURE 28.34 The radio buttons let you choose the tab placement of the tabbed pane.

28.7* (*Using tabbed pane*) Rewrite Exercise 28.4 using tabbed panes instead of `CardLayout` (see Figure 28.35).

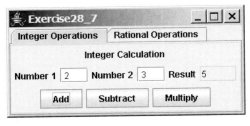 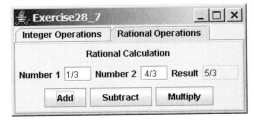

FIGURE 28.35 A tabbed pane is used to select panels that perform integer operations and rational number operations.

28.8* (*Using* `JSplitPane`) Create a program that displays four figures in split panes, as shown in Figure 28.36. Use the `FigurePanel` class defined in §13.7, "Case Study: The `FigurePanel` Class."

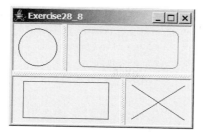

FIGURE 28.36   Four figures are displayed in split panes.

28.9*   (*Demonstrating* **JSplitPane** *properties*) Create a program that enables the user to set the properties of a split pane dynamically, as shown in Figure 28.37.

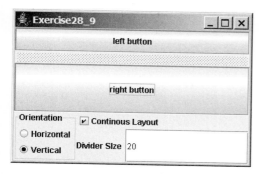 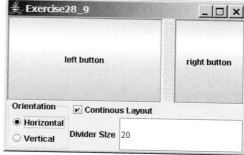

FIGURE 28.37   The program enables you to set the properties of a split pane dynamically.

MENUS, TOOLBARS, DIALOGS, AND INTERNAL FRAMES

Objectives

- To create menus using components `JMenuBar`, `JMenu`, `JMenuItem`, `JCheckBoxMenuItem`, and `JRadioButtonMenuItem` (§29.2).

- To create popup menus using components `JPopupMenu`, `JMenuItem`, `JCheckBoxMenuItem`, and `JRadioButtonMenuItem` (§29.3).

- To use `JToolBar` to create tool bars (§29.4).

- To use `Action` objects to generalize the code for processing actions (§29.5).

- To create standard dialogs using the `JOptionPane` class (§29.6).

- To extend the `JDialog` class to create custom dialogs (§29.7).

- To select colors using `JColorChooser` (§29.8).

- To use `JFileChooser` to display Open and Save File dialogs (§29.9).

- (Optional) To create internal frames using `JInternalFrame` (§29.10).

29.1 Introduction

Java provides a comprehensive solution for building graphical user interfaces. This chapter introduces menus, popup menus, tool bars, dialogs, and internal frames. You will also learn how to use `Action` objects to generalize the code for processing actions.

29.2 Menus

menu

Menus make selection easier and are widely used in window applications. Java provides five classes that implement menus: `JMenuBar`, `JMenu`, `JMenuItem`, `JCheckBoxMenuItem`, and `JRadioButtonMenuItem`.

menu item

`JMenuBar` is a top-level menu component used to hold menus. A menu consists of *menu items* that the user can select (or toggle on or off). A menu item can be an instance of `JMenuItem`, `JCheckBoxMenuItem`, or `JRadioButtonMenuItem`. Menu items can be associated with icons, keyboard mnemonics, and keyboard accelerators. Menu items can be separated using separators.

29.2.1 Creating Menus

The sequence of implementing menus in Java is as follows:

1. Create a menu bar and associate it with a frame or an applet by using the `setJMenuBar` method. For example, the following code creates a frame and a menu bar, and sets the menu bar in the frame:

```
JFrame frame = new JFrame();
frame.setSize(300, 200);
frame.setVisible(true);
JMenuBar jmb = new JMenuBar();
frame.setJMenuBar(jmb); // Attach a menu bar to a frame
```

2. Create menus and associate them with the menu bar. You can use the following constructor to create a menu:

```
public JMenu(String label)
```

Here is an example of creating menus:

```
JMenu fileMenu = new JMenu("File");
JMenu helpMenu = new JMenu("Help");
```

This creates two menus labeled `File` and `Help`, as shown in Figure 29.1(a). The menus will not be seen until they are added to an instance of `JMenuBar`, as follows:

```
jmb.add(fileMenu);
jmb.add(helpMenu);
```

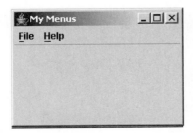
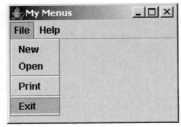

FIGURE 29.1 (a) The menu bar appears below the title bar on the frame. (b) Clicking a menu on the menu bar reveals the items under the menu. (c) Clicking a menu item reveals the submenu items under the menu item.

3. Create menu items and add them to the menus.

```
fileMenu.add(new JMenuItem("New"));
fileMenu.add(new JMenuItem("Open"));
fileMenu.addSeparator();
fileMenu.add(new JMenuItem("Print"));
fileMenu.addSeparator();
fileMenu.add(new JMenuItem("Exit"));
```

This code adds the menu items New, Open, a separator bar, Print, another separator bar, and Exit, in this order, to the File menu, as shown in Figure 29.1(b). The `addSeparator()` method adds a separator bar in the menu.

3.1. Creating submenu items. You can also embed menus inside menus so that the embedded menus become submenus. Here is an example:

```
JMenu softwareHelpSubMenu = new JMenu("Software");
JMenu hardwareHelpSubMenu = new JMenu("Hardware");
helpMenu.add(softwareHelpSubMenu);
helpMenu.add(hardwareHelpSubMenu);
softwareHelpSubMenu.add(new JMenuItem("Unix"));
softwareHelpSubMenu.add(new JMenuItem("NT"));
softwareHelpSubMenu.add(new JMenuItem("Win95"));
```

This code adds two submenus, `softwareHelpSubMenu` and `hardwareHelp-SubMenu`, in `helpMenu`. The menu items `Unix`, `NT`, and `Win95` are added to `softwareHelpSubMenu` (see Figure 29.1(c)).

3.2. Creating check box menu items. You can also add a `JCheckBoxMenuItem` to a `JMenu`. `JCheckBoxMenuItem` is a subclass of `JMenuItem` that adds a Boolean state to the `JMenuItem`, and displays a check when its state is true. You can click a menu item to turn it on or off. For example, the following statement adds the check box menu item `Check it` (see Figure 29.2(a)):

```
helpMenu.add(new JCheckBoxMenuItem("Check it"));
```

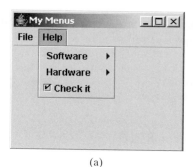
(a)

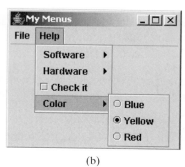
(b)

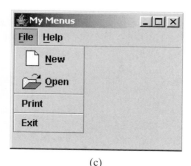
(c)

FIGURE 29.2 (a) A check box menu item lets you check or uncheck a menu item just like a check box. (b) You can use `JRadioButtonMenuItem` to choose among mutually exclusive menu choices. (c) You can set image icons, keyboard mnemonics, and keyboard accelerators in menus.

3.3. Creating radio button menu items. You can also add radio buttons to a menu, using the `JRadioButtonMenuItem` class. This is often useful when you have a group of mutually exclusive choices in the menu. For example, the following statements add a submenu named Color and a set of radio buttons for choosing a color (see Figure 29.2(b)):

```
JMenu colorHelpSubMenu = new JMenu("Color");
helpMenu.add(colorHelpSubMenu);
```

```
JRadioButtonMenuItem jrbmiBlue, jrbmiYellow, jrbmiRed;
colorHelpSubMenu.add(jrbmiBlue =
  new JRadioButtonMenuItem("Blue"));
colorHelpSubMenu.add(jrbmiYellow =
  new JRadioButtonMenuItem("Yellow"));
colorHelpSubMenu.add(jrbmiRed =
  new JRadioButtonMenuItem("Red"));

ButtonGroup btg = new ButtonGroup();
btg.add(jrbmiBlue);
btg.add(jrbmiYellow);
btg.add(jrbmiRed);
```

4. The menu items generate `ActionEvent`. Your listener class must implement the `ActionListener` and the `actionPerformed` handler to respond to the menu selection.

29.2.2 Image Icons, Keyboard Mnemonics, and Keyboard Accelerators

The menu components `JMenu`, `JMenuItem`, `JCheckBoxMenuItem`, and `JRadioButtonMenuItem` have the `icon` and `mnemonic` properties. For example, using the following code, you can set icons for the New and Open menu items, and set keyboard mnemonics for File, Help, New, and Open:

```
JMenuItem jmiNew, jmiOpen;
fileMenu.add(jmiNew = new JMenuItem("New"));
fileMenu.add(jmiOpen = new JMenuItem("Open"));
jmiNew.setIcon(new ImageIcon("image/new.gif"));
jmiOpen.setIcon(new ImageIcon("image/open.gif"));
helpMenu.setMnemonic('H');
fileMenu.setMnemonic('F');
jmiNew.setMnemonic('N');
jmiOpen.setMnemonic('O');
```

The new icons and mnemonics are shown in Figure 29.2(c). You can also use `JMenuItem` constructors like the ones that follow to construct and set an icon or mnemonic in one statement:

```
public JMenuItem(String label, Icon icon);
public JMenuItem(String label, int mnemonic);
```

By default, the text is at the right of the icon. Use `setHorizontalTextPosition(SwingConstants.LEFT)` to set the text to the left of the icon.

To select a menu, press the ALT key and the mnemonic key. For example, press ALT+F to select the File menu, and then press ALT+O to select the Open menu item. Keyboard mnemonics are useful, but only let you select menu items from the currently open menu. Key accelerators, however, let you select a menu item directly by pressing the CTRL and *accelerator* keys. For example, by using the following code, you can attach the key CTRL+O to the Open menu item:

accelerator

```
jmiOpen.setAccelerator(KeyStroke.getKeyStroke
  (KeyEvent.VK_O, ActionEvent.CTRL_MASK));
```

The `setAccelerator` method takes a `KeyStroke` object. The static method `getKeyStroke` in the `KeyStroke` class creates an instance of the keystroke. `VK_O` is a constant representing the O key, and `CTRL_MASK` is a constant indicating that the CTRL key is associated with the keystroke.

Note
As shown in Figure 15.3, **AbstractButton** is the superclass for **JButton** and **JMenuItem**, and **JMenuItem** is a superclass for **JCheckBoxMenuItem**, **JMenu**, and **JRadioButtonMenuItem**. The menu components are very similar to buttons.

29.2.3 Example: Using Menus

This section gives an example that creates a user interface to perform arithmetic. The interface contains labels and text fields for Number 1, Number 2, and Result. The Result text field displays the result of the arithmetic operation between Number 1 and Number 2. Figure 29.3 contains a sample run of the program.

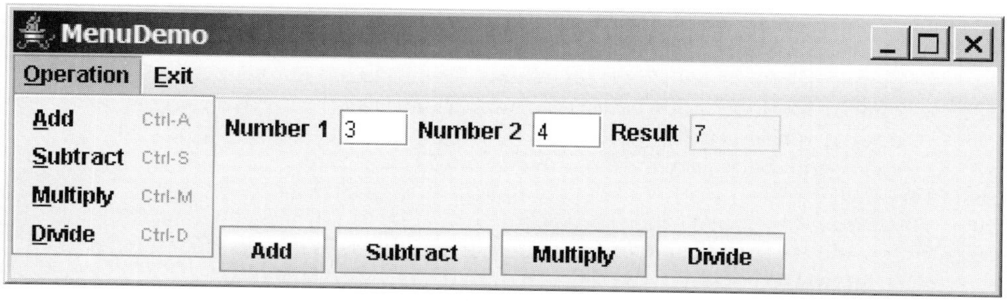

FIGURE 29.3 Arithmetic operations can be performed by clicking buttons or by choosing menu items from the Operation menu.

Here are the major steps in the program (Listing 29.1):

1. Create a menu bar and set it in the applet. Create the menus Operation and Exit, and add them to the menu bar. Add the menu items Add, Subtract, Multiply, and Divide under the Operation menu, and add the menu item Close under the Exit menu.

2. Create a panel to hold labels and text fields, and place the panel in the center of the applet.

3. Create a panel to hold the four buttons labeled Add, Subtract, Multiply, and Divide. Place the panel in the south of the applet.

4. Implement the **actionPerformed** handler to process the events from the menu items and the buttons.

LISTING 29.1 MenuDemo.java

```java
1  import java.awt.*;
2  import java.awt.event.*;
3  import javax.swing.*;
4
5  public class MenuDemo extends JApplet {
6    // Text fields for Number 1, Number 2, and Result
7    private JTextField jtfNum1, jtfNum2, jtfResult;
8
9    // Buttons "Add", "Subtract", "Multiply" and "Divide"
10   private JButton jbtAdd, jbtSub, jbtMul, jbtDiv;
11
12   // Menu items "Add", "Subtract", "Multiply", "Divide" and "Close"
13   private JMenuItem jmiAdd, jmiSub, jmiMul, jmiDiv, jmiClose;
14
15   public MenuDemo() {
16     // Create menu bar
17     JMenuBar jmb = new JMenuBar();
```

menu bar

set menu bar

exit menus

add menu items

accelerator

buttons

register listener

```java
18
19      // Set menu bar to the applet
20      setJMenuBar(jmb);
21
22      // Add menu "Operation" to menu bar
23      JMenu operationMenu = new JMenu("Operation");
24      operationMenu.setMnemonic('O');
25      jmb.add(operationMenu);
26
27      // Add menu "Exit" to menu bar
28      JMenu exitMenu = new JMenu("Exit");
29      exitMenu.setMnemonic('E');
30      jmb.add(exitMenu);
31
32      // Add menu items with mnemonics to menu "Operation"
33      operationMenu.add(jmiAdd= new JMenuItem("Add", 'A'));
34      operationMenu.add(jmiSub = new JMenuItem("Subtract", 'S'));
35      operationMenu.add(jmiMul = new JMenuItem("Multiply", 'M'));
36      operationMenu.add(jmiDiv = new JMenuItem("Divide", 'D'));
37      exitMenu.add(jmiClose = new JMenuItem("Close", 'C'));
38
39      // Set keyboard accelerators
40      jmiAdd.setAccelerator(
41        KeyStroke.getKeyStroke(KeyEvent.VK_A, ActionEvent.CTRL_MASK));
42      jmiSub.setAccelerator(
43        KeyStroke.getKeyStroke(KeyEvent.VK_S, ActionEvent.CTRL_MASK));
44      jmiMul.setAccelerator(
45        KeyStroke.getKeyStroke(KeyEvent.VK_M, ActionEvent.CTRL_MASK));
46      jmiDiv.setAccelerator(
47        KeyStroke.getKeyStroke(KeyEvent.VK_D, ActionEvent.CTRL_MASK));
48
49      // Panel p1 to hold text fields and labels
50      JPanel p1 = new JPanel(new FlowLayout());
51      p1.add(new JLabel("Number 1"));
52      p1.add(jtfNum1 = new JTextField(3));
53      p1.add(new JLabel("Number 2"));
54      p1.add(jtfNum2 = new JTextField(3));
55      p1.add(new JLabel("Result"));
56      p1.add(jtfResult = new JTextField(4));
57      jtfResult.setEditable(false);
58
59      // Panel p2 to hold buttons
60      JPanel p2 = new JPanel(new FlowLayout());
61      p2.add(jbtAdd = new JButton("Add"));
62      p2.add(jbtSub = new JButton("Subtract"));
63      p2.add(jbtMul = new JButton("Multiply"));
64      p2.add(jbtDiv = new JButton("Divide"));
65
66      // Add panels to the frame
67      setLayout(new BorderLayout());
68      add(p1, BorderLayout.CENTER);
69      add(p2, BorderLayout.SOUTH);
70
71      // Register listeners
72      jbtAdd.addActionListener(new ActionListener() {
73        public void actionPerformed(ActionEvent e) {
74          calculate('+');
75        }
76      });
```

```
77      jbtSub.addActionListener(new ActionListener() {
78        public void actionPerformed(ActionEvent e) {
79          calculate('-');
80        }
81      });
82      jbtMul.addActionListener(new ActionListener() {
83        public void actionPerformed(ActionEvent e) {
84          calculate('*');
85        }
86      });
87      jbtDiv.addActionListener(new ActionListener() {
88        public void actionPerformed(ActionEvent e) {
89          calculate('/');
90        }
91      });
92      jmiAdd.addActionListener(new ActionListener() {
93        public void actionPerformed(ActionEvent e) {
94          calculate('+');
95        }
96      });
97      jmiSub.addActionListener(new ActionListener() {
98        public void actionPerformed(ActionEvent e) {
99          calculate('-');
100       }
101     });
102     jmiMul.addActionListener(new ActionListener() {
103       public void actionPerformed(ActionEvent e) {
104         calculate('*');
105       }
106     });
107     jmiDiv.addActionListener(new ActionListener() {
108       public void actionPerformed(ActionEvent e) {
109         calculate('/');
110       }
111     });
112     jmiClose.addActionListener(new ActionListener() {
113       public void actionPerformed(ActionEvent e) {
114         System.exit(0);
115       }
116     });
117   }
118
119   /** Calculate and show the result in jtfResult */
120   private void calculate(char operator) {
121     // Obtain Number 1 and Number 2
122     int num1 = (Integer.parseInt(jtfNum1.getText().trim()));
123     int num2 = (Integer.parseInt(jtfNum2.getText().trim()));
124     int result = 0;
125
126     // Perform selected operation
127     switch (operator) {
128       case '+': result = num1 + num2;
129                 break;
130       case '-': result = num1 - num2;
131                 break;
132       case '*': result = num1 * num2;
133                 break;
134       case '/': result = num1 / num2;
135     }
```

register listener

register listener

register listener

register listener

register listener

register listener

register listener

register listener

calculator

```
136
137      // Set result in jtfResult
138      jtfResult.setText(String.valueOf(result));
139  }
140 }
```

main omitted

The program creates a menu bar, jmb, which holds two menus: operationMenu and exitMenu (lines 17–30). The operationMenu contains four menu items for doing arithmetic: Add, Subtract, Multiply, and Divide. The exitMenu contains the menu item Close for exiting the program. The menu items in the Operation menu are created with keyboard mnemonics and accelerators.

The user enters two numbers in the number fields. When an operation is chosen from the menu, its result, involving two numbers, is displayed in the Result field. The user can also click the buttons to perform the same operation.

The private method calculate(char operator) (lines 120–139) retrieves operands from the text fields in Number 1 and Number 2, applies the binary operator on the operands, and sets the result in the Result text field.

 Note

The menu bar is usually attached to the window using the setJMenuBar method. However, like any other component, it can be placed in a container. For instance, you can place a menu bar in the south of the container with BorderLayout.

29.3 Popup Menus

popup menu

A *popup menu*, also known as *a context menu*, is like a regular menu, but does not have a menu bar and can float anywhere on the screen. Creating a popup menu is similar to creating a regular menu. First, you create an instance of JPopupMenu, then you can add JMenuItem, JCheckBoxMenuItem, JRadioButtonMenuItem, and separators to the popup menu. For example, the following code creates a JPopupMenu and adds JMenuItems into it:

```
JPopupMenu jPopupMenu = new JPopupMenu();
jPopupMenu.add(new JMenuItem("New"));
jPopupMenu.add(new JMenuItem("Open"));
```

A regular menu is always attached to a menu bar using the setJMenuBar method, but a popup menu is associated with a parent component and is displayed using the show method in the JPopupMenu class. You specify the parent component and the location of the popup menu, using the coordinate system of the parent like this:

```
jPopupMenu.show(component, x, y);
```

popup trigger

The popup menu usually contains the commands for an object. Customarily, you display a popup menu by pointing to the object and clicking a certain mouse button, the so-called *popup trigger*. Popup triggers are system-dependent. In Windows, the popup menu is displayed when the right-mouse button is released. In Motif, the popup menu is displayed when the third mouse button is pressed and held down.

Listing 29.2 gives an example that creates a text area in a scroll pane. When the mouse points to the text area, it triggers the popup menu display, as shown in Figure 29.4.

Here are the major steps in the program (Listing 29.2):

1. Create a popup menu using JPopupMenu. Create menu items for New, Open, Print, and Exit using JMenuItem. For the menu items with both labels and icons, it is convenient to use the JMenuItem(label, icon) constructor.

2. Add the menu items into the popup menu.

3. Create a scroll pane and add a text area into it. Place the scroll pane in the center of the applet.

4. Implement the `actionPerformed` handler to process the events from the menu items.

5. Implement the `mousePressed` and `mouseReleased` methods to process the events for handling popup triggers.

FIGURE 29.4   A popup menu is displayed when the popup trigger is issued on the text area.

LISTING 29.2   PopupMenuDemo.java

```
1 import javax.swing.*;
2 import java.awt.*;
3 import java.awt.event.*;
4
5 public class PopupMenuDemo extends JApplet {
6   private JPopupMenu jPopupMenu1 = new JPopupMenu();                              popup menu
7   private JMenuItem jmiNew = new JMenuItem("New",
8     new ImageIcon(getClass().getResource("image/new.gif")));
9   private JMenuItem jmiOpen = new JMenuItem("Open",
10    new ImageIcon(getClass().getResource("image/open.gif")));
11  private JMenuItem jmiPrint = new JMenuItem("Print",
12    new ImageIcon(getClass().getResource("image/print.gif")));
13  private JMenuItem jmiExit = new JMenuItem("Exit");
14  private JTextArea jTextArea1 = new JTextArea();
15
16  public PopupMenuDemo() {
17    jPopupMenu1.add(jmiNew);                                                      add menu items
18    jPopupMenu1.add(jmiOpen);
19    jPopupMenu1.addSeparator();
20    jPopupMenu1.add(jmiPrint);
21    jPopupMenu1.addSeparator();
22    jPopupMenu1.add(jmiExit);
23    jPopupMenu1.add(jmiExit);
24
25    add(new JScrollPane(jTextArea1), BorderLayout.CENTER);
26
27    jmiNew.addActionListener(new ActionListener() {                              register listener
28      public void actionPerformed(ActionEvent e) {
29        System.out.println("Process New");
30      }
31    });
32    jmiOpen.addActionListener(new ActionListener() {                             register listener
33      public void actionPerformed(ActionEvent e) {
34        System.out.println("Process Open");
35      }
36    });
37    jmiPrint.addActionListener(new ActionListener() {                            register listener
38      public void actionPerformed(ActionEvent e) {
39        System.out.println("Process Print");
40      }
```

register listener

```
41      });
42      jmiExit.addActionListener(new ActionListener() {
43        public void actionPerformed(ActionEvent e) {
44          System.exit(0);
45        }
46      });
```

register listener

```
47      jTextArea1.addMouseListener(new MouseAdapter() {
48        public void mousePressed(MouseEvent e) { // For Motif
```

show popup menu

```
49          showPopup(e);
50        }
51
52        public void mouseReleased(MouseEvent e) { // For Windows
```

show popup menu

```
53          showPopup(e);
54        }
55      });
56    }
57
58    /** Display popup menu when triggered */
59    private void showPopup(java.awt.event.MouseEvent evt) {
60      if (evt.isPopupTrigger())
61        jPopupMenu1.show(evt.getComponent(), evt.getX(), evt.getY());
62    }
```

main omitted

```
63 }
```

The process of creating popup menus is similar to the process for creating regular menus. To create a popup menu, create a **JPopupMenu** as the basis (line 6), and add **JMenuItem**s to the popup menu (lines 17–23).

To show a popup menu, use the **show** method by specifying the parent component and the location for the popup menu (line 47). The **show** method is invoked when the popup menu is triggered by a particular mouse click on the text area. Popup triggers are system-dependent. The listener implements the **mouseReleased** handler for displaying the popup menu in Windows (lines 52–54) and the **mousePressed** handler for displaying the popup menu in Motif (lines 48–50).

 Tip

JDK 1.5 provides a new **setComponentPopupMenu(JPopupMenu)** method in the **JComponent** class, which can be used to add a popup menu on a component. This method automatically handles mouse listener registration and popup display. Using this method, you may delete the **showPopup** method in lines 59–62 and replace the code in lines 47–55 with the following statement:

simplifying popup menu

```
jTextArea1.setComponentPopupMenu(jPopupMenu1);
```

Due to a bug, **this** method does not work with **JPanel**.

29.4 JToolBar

toolbar

In user interfaces, a *toolbar* is often used to hold commands that also appear in the menus. Frequently used commands are placed in a toolbar for quick access. Clicking a command in the toolbar is faster than choosing it from the menu.

Swing provides the **JToolBar** class as the container to hold tool bar components. **JToolBar** uses **BoxLayout** to manage components by default. You can set a different layout manager if desired. The components usually appear as icons. Since icons are not components, they cannot be placed into a tool bar directly. Instead you place buttons into the tool bar and set the icons on the buttons. An instance of **JToolBar** is like a regular container. Often it is placed in the north, west, or east of a container of **BorderLayout**.

The following properties in the `JToolBar` class are often useful:

- `orientation` specifies whether the items in the tool bar appear horizontally or vertically. The possible values are `JToolBar.HORIZONTAL` and `JToolBar.VERTICAL`. The default value is `JToolBar.HORIZONTAL`.

- `floatable` is a `boolean` value that specifies whether the tool bar can be floated. By default, a tool bar is floatable.

Listing 29.3 gives an example that creates a `JToolBar` to hold three buttons with the icons representing the commands New, Open, and Print, as shown in Figure 29.5.

FIGURE 29.5   The tool bar contains the icons representing the commands New, Open, and Print.

Listing 29.3 shows the program.

LISTING 29.3   `ToolBarDemo.java`

```java
 1 import javax.swing.*;
 2 import java.awt.*;
 3
 4 public class ToolBarDemo extends JApplet {
 5   private JButton jbtNew = new JButton(
 6     new ImageIcon(getClass().getResource("image/new.gif")));      buttons
 7   private JButton jbtOpen = new JButton(
 8     new ImageIcon(getClass().getResource("image/open.gif")));
 9   private JButton jbPrint = new JButton(
10     new ImageIcon(getClass().getResource("image/print.gif")));
11
12   public ToolBarDemo() {
13     JToolBar jToolBar1 = new JToolBar("My Tool Bar");           tool bar
14     jToolBar1.setFloatable(true);
15     jToolBar1.add(jbtNew);
16     jToolBar1.add(jbtOpen);
17     jToolBar1.add(jbPrint);
18
19     jbtNew.setToolTipText("New");
20     jbtOpen.setToolTipText("Open");
21     jbPrint.setToolTipText("Print");
22
23     jbtNew.setBorderPainted(false);
24     jbtOpen.setBorderPainted(false);
25     jbPrint.setBorderPainted(false);
26
27     add(jToolBar1, BorderLayout.NORTH);                         add tool bar
28   }
29 }
                                                                  main omitted
```

A `JToolBar` is created in line 13. The tool bar is a container with `BoxLayout` by default. Using the `orientation` property, you can specify whether components in the tool bar are organized horizontally or vertically. By default, it is horizontal.

By default, the tool bar is floatable, and a floatable controller is displayed in front of its components. You can drag the floatable controller to move the tool bar to different locations of the window or can show the tool bar in a separate window, as shown in Figure 29.6.

FIGURE 29.6   The toolbar buttons are floatable.

You can also set a title for the floatable tool bar, as shown in Figure 29.7(a). To do so, create a tool bar using the `JToolBar(String title)` constructor. If you set `floatable` false, the floatable controller is not displayed, as shown in Figure 29.7(b). If you set a border (e.g., a line border), as shown in Figure 29.7(c), the line border is displayed and the floatable controller is not displayed.

FIGURE 29.7   The toolbar buttons can be customized in many forms.

Tip

For the floatable feature to work properly, do the following: (1) place a tool bar to one side of the container of `BorderLayout` and add no components to the other sides; (2) don't set border on a tool bar. Setting a border would make it non-floatable.

29.5 Processing Actions Using the `Action` Interface

Often menus and tool bars contain some common actions. For example, you can save a file by choosing *File*, *Save*, or by clicking the save button in the tool bar. Swing provides the `Action` interface, which can be used to create action objects for processing actions. Using `Action` objects, common action processing can be centralized and separated from the other application code.

The `Action` interface is a subinterface of `ActionListener`, as shown in Figure 29.8. Additionally, it defines several methods for checking whether the action is enabled, for enabling and disabling the action, and for retrieving and setting the associated action value using a key. The key can be any string, but four keys have predefined meanings:

Key	Description
`Action.NAME`	A name for the action
`Action.SMALL_ICON`	A small icon for the action
`Action.SHORT_DESCRIPTION`	A tool tip for the action
`Action.LONG_DESCRIPTION`	A description for online help

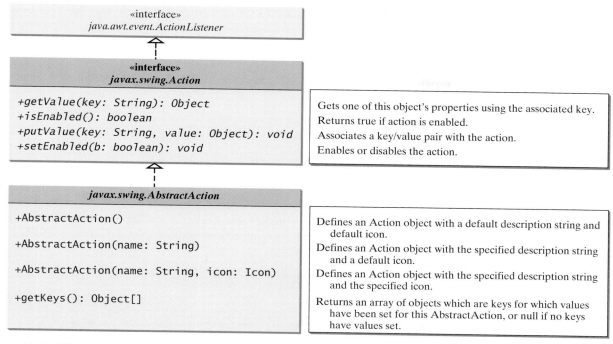

FIGURE 29.8   The **Action** interface provides a useful extension to the **ActionListener** interface in cases where the same functionality may be accessed by several controls. The **AbstractAction** class provides a default implementation for **Action**.

AbstractAction is a default implementation of the **Action** interface, as shown in Figure 29.8. It implements all the methods in the **Action** interface except the **actionPerformed** method. Additionally, it defines the **getKeys()** method.

Since **AbstractAction** is an abstract class, you cannot create an instance using its constructor. However, you can create a concrete subclass of **AbstractAction** and implement the **actionPerformed** method. This subclass can be conveniently defined as an anonymous inner class. For example, the following code creates an **Action** object for terminating a program:

```
Action exitAction = new AbstractAction("Exit") {
  public void actionPerformed(ActionEvent e) {
    System.exit(0);
  }
};
```

Certain containers, such as **JMenu** and **JToolBar**, know how to add an **Action** object. When an **Action** object is added to such a container, the container automatically creates an appropriate component for the **Action** object and registers a listener with the **Action** object. Here is an example of adding an **Action** object to a menu and a tool bar:

```
jMenu.add(exitAction);
jToolBar.add(exitAction);
```

Several Swing components, such as **JButton**, **JRadioButton**, and **JCheckBox**, contain constructors to create instances from **Action** objects. For example, you can create a **JButton** from an **Action** object, as follows:

```
JButton jbt = new JButton(exitAction);
```

`Action` objects can also be associated with mnemonic and accelerator keys. To associate actions with a mnemonic key (e.g., ALT+E), use the following statement:

```
exitAction.putValue(Action.MNEMONIC_KEY, new Integer(KeyEvent.VK_E));
```

To associate actions with an accelerator key (e.g., CTRL+E), use the following statement:

```
KeyStroke exitKey =
  KeyStroke.getKeyStroke(KeyEvent.VK_E, KeyEvent.CTRL_MASK);
exitAction.putValue(Action.ACCELERATOR_KEY, exitKey);
```

Listing 29.4 gives an example that creates three menu items, Left, Center, and Right, three tool bar buttons, Left, Center, and Right, and three regular buttons, Left, Center, and Right, in a panel, as shown in Figure 29.9. The panel that holds the buttons uses the `FlowLayout`. The actions of the left, center, and right buttons set the alignment of the `FlowLayout` to left, right, and center, respectively. The actions of the menu items, the tool bar buttons, and the buttons in the panel can be processed through common action handlers using the `Action` interface.

FIGURE 29.9 Left, Center, and Right appear in the menu, in the toolbar, and in regular buttons.

LISTING 29.4 `ActionInterfaceDemo.java`

```
1  import java.awt.*;
2  import java.awt.event.*;
3  import javax.swing.*;
4
5  public class ActionInterfaceDemo extends JApplet {
6    private JPanel buttonPanel = new JPanel();
7    private FlowLayout flowLayout = new FlowLayout();
8
9    public ActionInterfaceDemo() {
10     // Create image icons
11     ImageIcon leftImageIcon = new ImageIcon(getClass().getResource(
12       "image/leftAlignment.png"));
13     ImageIcon centerImageIcon = new ImageIcon(getClass().getResource(
14       "image/centerAlignment.png"));
15     ImageIcon rightImageIcon = new ImageIcon(getClass().getResource(
16       "image/rightAlignment.png"));
17
18     // Create actions
19     Action leftAction = new MyAction("Left", leftImageIcon,
20       "Left alignment for the buttons in the panel",
21       new Integer(KeyEvent.VK_L),
22       KeyStroke.getKeyStroke(KeyEvent.VK_L, ActionEvent.CTRL_MASK));
23     Action centerAction = new MyAction("Center", centerImageIcon,
24       "Center alignment for the buttons in the panel",
25       new Integer(KeyEvent.VK_C),
26       KeyStroke.getKeyStroke(KeyEvent.VK_C, ActionEvent.CTRL_MASK));
```

image icon

create action

```
27    Action rightAction = new MyAction("Right", rightImageIcon,
28      "Right alignment for the buttons in the panel",
29      new Integer(KeyEvent.VK_R),
30      KeyStroke.getKeyStroke(KeyEvent.VK_R, ActionEvent.CTRL_MASK));
31
32    // Create menus
33    JMenuBar jMenuBar1 = new JMenuBar();                              menu
34    JMenu jmenuAlignment = new JMenu("Alignment");
35    setJMenuBar(jMenuBar1);
36    jMenuBar1.add(jmenuAlignment);
37
38    // Add actions to the menu
39    jmenuAlignment.add(leftAction);
40    jmenuAlignment.add(centerAction);
41    jmenuAlignment.add(rightAction);
42
43    // Add actions to the toolbar
44    JToolBar jToolBar1 = new JToolBar(JToolBar.VERTICAL);             toolbar
45    jToolBar1.setBorder(BorderFactory.createLineBorder(Color.red));
46    jToolBar1.add(leftAction);
47    jToolBar1.add(centerAction);
48    jToolBar1.add(rightAction);
49
50    // Add buttons to the button panel
51    buttonPanel.setLayout(flowLayout);
52    JButton jbtLeft = new JButton(leftAction);                       button
53    JButton jbtCenter = new JButton(centerAction);
54    JButton jbtRight = new JButton(rightAction);
55    buttonPanel.add(jbtLeft);
56    buttonPanel.add(jbtCenter);
57    buttonPanel.add(jbtRight);
58
59    // Add tool bar to the east and panel to the center
60    add(jToolBar1, BorderLayout.EAST);
61    add(buttonPanel, BorderLayout.CENTER);
62  }
63
64  private class MyAction extends AbstractAction {                     custom action
65    String name;
66
67    MyAction(String name, Icon icon) {                                constructor
68      super(name, icon);
69      this.name = name;
70    }
71
72    MyAction(String name, Icon icon, String desc, Integer mnemonic,   constructor
73      KeyStroke accelerator) {
74      super(name, icon);
75      putValue(Action.SHORT_DESCRIPTION, desc);
76      putValue(Action.MNEMONIC_KEY, mnemonic);
77      putValue(Action.ACCELERATOR_KEY, accelerator);
78      this.name = name;
79    }
80
81    public void actionPerformed(ActionEvent e) {                      handler
82      if (name.equals("Left"))
83        flowLayout.setAlignment(FlowLayout.LEFT);
84      else if (name.equals("Center"))
85        flowLayout.setAlignment(FlowLayout.CENTER);
86      else if (name.equals("Right"))
87        flowLayout.setAlignment(FlowLayout.RIGHT);
```

```
88
89        buttonPanel.revalidate();
90      }
91    }
92 }
```

The inner class **MyAction** extends **AbstractAction** with a constructor to construct an action with a name and an icon (lines 67–70) and another constructor to construct an action with a name, icon, description, mnemonic, and accelerator (lines 72–79). The constructors invoke the **putValue** method to associate the name, icon, description, mnemonic, and accelerator. It implements the **actionPerformed** method to set a new alignment in the panel of the **FlowLayout** (lines 81–90). The **revalidate()** method validates the new alignment (line 89) .

Three actions, **leftAction**, **centerAction**, and **rightAction**, were created from the **MyAction** class (lines 19–30). Each action has a name, icon, decription, mnemonic, and accelerator. The actions are for the menu items and the buttons in the tool bar and in the panel. The menu and toolbar know how to add these objects automatically (lines 39–41, 46–48). Three regular buttons are created with the properties taken from the actions (lines 51–54).

29.6 JOptionPane Dialogs

You have used **JOptionPane** to create input and output dialog boxes. This section provides a comprehensive introduction to **JOptionPane** and other dialog boxes. A *dialog box* is normally used as a temporary window to receive additional information from the user or to provide notification that some event has occurred. Java provides the **JOptionPane** class, which can be used to create standard dialogs. You can also build custom dialogs by extending the **JDialog** class.

The **JOptionPane** class can be used to create four kinds of standard dialogs:

- **Message dialog** shows a message and waits for the user to click OK.

- **Confirmation dialog** shows a question and asks for confirmation, such as OK or Cancel.

- **Input dialog** shows a question and gets the user's input from a text field, combo box, or list.

- **Option dialog** shows a question and gets the user's answer from a set of options.

These dialogs are created using the static methods **show*Xxx*Dialog** and generally appear as shown in Figure 29.10(a).

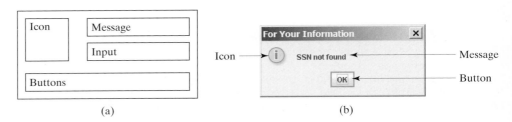

(a)   (b)

FIGURE 29.10   (a) A **JOptionPane** dialog can display an icon, a message, an input, and option buttons. (b) The message dialog displays a message and waits for the user to click OK.

For example, you can use the following method to create a message dialog box, as shown in Figure 29.10(b):

```
JOptionPane.showMessageDialog(null, "SSN not found",
  "For Your Information", JOptionPane.INFORMATION_MESSAGE);
```

29.6.1   Message Dialogs

A *message dialog* box displays a message that alerts the user and waits for the user to click the OK button to close the dialog. The methods for creating message dialogs are:

```
public static void showMessageDialog(Component parentComponent,
                                     Object message)
public static void showMessageDialog(Component parentComponent,
                                     Object message,
                                     String title,
                                     int messageType)
public static void showMessageDialog(Component parentComponent,
                                     Object message,
                                     String title,
                                     int messageType,
                                     Icon icon)
```

The **parentComponent** can be any component or **null**. The **message** is an object, but often a string is used. These two parameters must always be specified. The **title** is a string displayed in the title bar of the dialog with the default value "Message".

The **messageType** is one of the following constants:

```
JOptionPane.ERROR_MESSAGE
JOptionPane.INFORMATION_MESSAGE
JOptionPane.PLAIN_MESSAGE
JOptionPane.WARNING_MESSAGE
JOptionPane.QUESTION_MESSAGE
```

By default, **messageType** is **JOptionPane.INFORMATION_MESSAGE**. Each type has an associated icon except the **PLAIN_MESSAGE** type, as shown in Figure 29.11. You can also supply your own icon in the **icon** parameter.

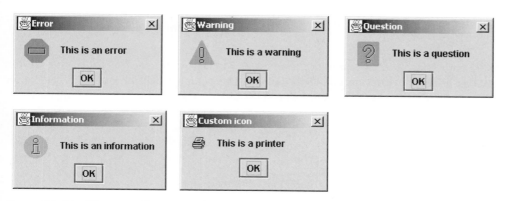

FIGURE 29.11   There are five types of message dialog boxes.

The **message** parameter is an object. If it is a GUI component, the component is displayed. If it is a non-GUI component, the string representation of the object is displayed. For example, the following statement displays a clock in a message dialog, as shown in Figure 29.12:

```
JOptionPane.showMessageDialog(null, new StillClock(),
   "Current Time", JOptionPane.PLAIN_MESSAGE);
```

29.6.2   Confirmation Dialogs

A message dialog box displays a message and waits for the user to click the OK button to dismiss the dialog. The message dialog does not return any value. A *confirmation dialog* asks a question and requires the user to respond with an appropriate button. The confirmation dialog returns a value that corresponds to a selected button.

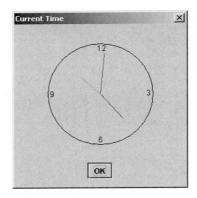

FIGURE 29.12 A clock is displayed in a message dialog.

The methods for creating confirmation dialogs are:

```
public static int showConfirmDialog(Component parentComponent,
                                    Object message)
public static int showConfirmDialog(Component parentComponent,
                                    Object message,
                                    String title,
                                    int optionType)
public static int showConfirmDialog(Component parentComponent,
                                    Object message,
                                    String title,
                                    int optionType,
                                    int messageType)
public static int showConfirmDialog(Component parentComponent,
                                    Object message,
                                    String title,
                                    int optionType,
                                    int messageType,
                                    Icon icon)
```

The parameters `parentComponent`, `message`, `title`, `icon`, and `messageType` are the same as in the `showMessageDialog` method. The default value for `title` is "Select an Option" and for `messageType` is `QUESTION_MESSAGE`. The `optionType` determines which buttons are displayed in the dialog. The possible values are:

```
JOptionPane.YES_NO_OPTION
JOptionPane.YES_NO_CANCEL_OPTION
JOptionPane.OK_CANCEL_OPTION
```

Figure 29.13 shows the confirmation dialogs with these options.

 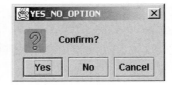 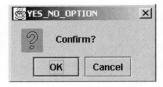

FIGURE 29.13 The confirmation dialog displays a question and three types of option buttons, and requires responses from the user.

The `showConfirmDialog` method returns one of the following `int` values corresponding to the selected option:

```
JOptionPane.YES_OPTION
JOptionPane.NO_OPTION
```

```
JOptionPane.CANCEL_OPTION
JOptionPane.OK_OPTION
JOptionPane.CLOSED_OPTION
```

These options correspond to the button that was activated, except for the CLOSED_OPTION, which implies that the dialog box is closed without buttons activated.

29.6.3 Input Dialogs

An *input dialog* box is used to receive input from the user. The input can be entered from a text field or selected from a combo box or a list. Selectable values can be specified in an array, and one of them can be designated as the initial selected value. If no selectable value is specified when an input dialog is created, a text field is used for entering input. If fewer than twenty selection values are specified, a combo box is displayed in the input dialog. If twenty or more selection values are specified, a list is used in the input dialog.

The methods for creating input dialogs are shown below:

```
public static String showInputDialog(Object message)
public static String showInputDialog(Component parentComponent,
                                     Object message)
public static String showInputDialog(Component parentComponent,
                                     Object message,
                                     String title,
                                     int messageType)
public static Object showInputDialog(Component parentComponent,
                                     Object message,
                                     int messageType,
                                     Icon icon,
                                     Object[] selectionValues,
                                     Object initialSelectionValue)
```

The first three methods listed above use a text field for input, as shown in Figure 29.14(a). The last method listed above specifies an array of **Object** type as selection values in addition to an object specified as an initial selection. The first three methods return a **String** that is entered from the text field in the input dialog. The last method returns an **Object** selected from a combo box or a list. The input dialog displays a combo box if there are fewer than twenty selection values, as shown in Figure 29.14(b); it displays a list if there are twenty or more selection values, as shown in Figure 29.14(c).

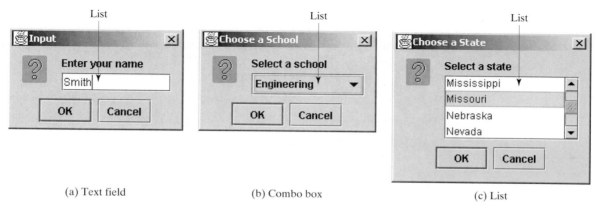

(a) Text field   (b) Combo box   (c) List

FIGURE 29.14   (a) When creating an input dialog without specifying selection values, the input dialog displays a text field for data entry. (b) When creating an input dialog with selection values, the input dialog displays a combo box if there are fewer than twenty selection values. (c) When creating an input dialog with selection values, the input dialog displays a list if there are twenty or more selection values.

Note
The `showInputDialog` method does not have the `optionType` parameter. The buttons for input dialog are not configurable. The OK and Cancel buttons are always used.

29.6.4 Option Dialogs

An *option dialog* allows you to create custom buttons. You can create an option dialog using the following method:

```
public static int showOptionDialog(Component parentComponent,
                                    Object message,
                                    String title,
                                    int optionType,
                                    int messageType,
                                    Icon icon,
                                    Object[] options,
                                    Object initialValue)
```

The buttons are specified using the `options` parameter. The `initialValue` parameter allows you to specify a button to receive initial focus. The `showOptionDialog` method returns an `int` value indicating the button that was activated. For example, here is the code that creates an option dialog, as shown in Figure 29.15:

```
int value =
  JOptionPane.showOptionDialog(null, "Select a button",
    "Option Dialog", JOptionPane.DEFAULT_OPTION,
    JOptionPane.PLAIN_MESSAGE, null,
    new Object[]{"Button 0", "Button 1", "Button 2"}, "Button 1");
```

FIGURE 29.15 The option dialog displays the custom buttons.

29.6.5 Example: Creating `JOptionPane` Dialogs

This section gives an example that demonstrates the use of `JOptionPane` dialogs. The program prompts the user to select the annual interest rate from a list in an input dialog, the number of years from a combo box in an input dialog, and the loan amount from an input dialog, and it displays the loan payment schedule in a text area inside a `JScrollPane` in a message dialog, as shown in Figure 29.16.

Here are the major steps in the program (Listing 29.5):

1. Display an input dialog box to let the user select an annual interest rate from a list.

2. Display an input dialog box to let the user select the number of years from a combo box.

3. Display an input dialog box to let the user enter the loan amount.

4. Compute the monthly payment, total payment, and loan payment schedule, and display the result in a text area in a message dialog box.

LISTING 29.5 JOptionPaneDemo.java

```
1 import javax.swing.*;
2
3 public class JOptionPaneDemo {
4   public static void main(String args[]) {
```

```
5     // Create an array for annual interest rates
6     Object[] rateList = new Object[25];
7     int i = 0;
8     for (double rate = 5; rate <= 8; rate += 1.0 / 8)
9       rateList[i++] = new Double(rate);
10
11    // Prompt the user to select an annual interest rate
12    Object annualInterestRateObject = JOptionPane.showInputDialog(
13      null, "Select annual interest rate:", "JOptionPaneDemo",
14      JOptionPane.QUESTION_MESSAGE, null, rateList, null);
15    double annualInterestRate =
16      ((Double)annualInterestRateObject).doubleValue();
17
18    // Create an array for number of years
19    Object[] yearList = {new Integer(7), new Integer(15),
20      new Integer(30)};
21
22    // Prompt the user to enter number of years
23    Object numberOfYearsObject = JOptionPane.showInputDialog(null,
24      "Select number of years:", "JOptionPaneDemo",
25      JOptionPane.QUESTION_MESSAGE, null, yearList, null);
26    int numberOfYears = ((Integer)numberOfYearsObject).intValue();
27
28    // Prompt the user to enter loan amount
29    String loanAmountString = JOptionPane.showInputDialog(null,
30      "Enter loan amount,\nfor example, 150000 for $150000",
31      "JOptionPaneDemo", JOptionPane.QUESTION_MESSAGE);
32    double loanAmount = Double.parseDouble(loanAmountString);
33
34    // Obtain monthly payment and total payment
35    Loan loan = new Loan(
36      annualInterestRate, numberOfYears, loanAmount);
37    double monthlyPayment = loan.getMonthlyPayment();
38    double totalPayment = loan.getTotalPayment();
39
40    // Prepare output string
41    String output = "Interest Rate: " + annualInterestRate + "%" +
42      " Number of Years: " + numberOfYears + " Loan Amount: $"
43      + loanAmount;
44    output += "\nMonthly Payment: " + "$" +
45      (int)(monthlyPayment * 100) / 100.0;
46    output += "\nTotal Payment: $" +
47      (int)(monthlyPayment * 12 * numberOfYears * 100) / 100.0 + "\n";
48
49    // Obtain monthly interest rate
50    double monthlyInterestRate = annualInterestRate / 1200;
51
52    double balance = loanAmount;
53    double interest;
54    double principal;
55
56    // Display the header
57    output += "\nPayment#\tInterest\tPrincipal\tBalance\n";
58
59    for (i = 1; i <= numberOfYears * 12; i++) {
60      interest = (int)(monthlyInterestRate * balance * 100) / 100.0;
61      principal = (int)((monthlyPayment - interest) * 100) / 100.0;
62      balance = (int)((balance - principal) * 100) / 100.0;
63      output += i + "\t" + interest + "\t" + principal + "\t" +
64        balance + "\n";
65    }
```

input dialog

input dialog

input dialog

```
66
67      // Display monthly payment and total payment
68      JScrollPane jsp = new JScrollPane(new JTextArea(output));
69      jsp.setPreferredSize(new java.awt.Dimension(400, 200));
70      JOptionPane.showMessageDialog(null, jsp,
71        "JOptionPaneDemo", JOptionPane.INFORMATION_MESSAGE, null);
72    }
73  }
```

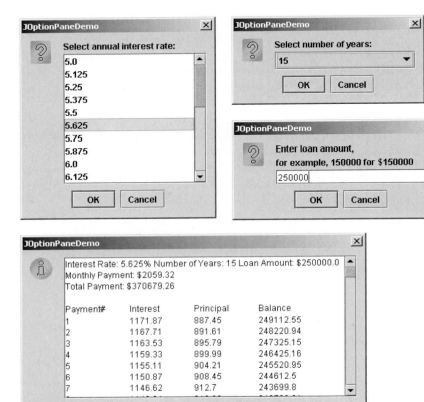

FIGURE 29.16 The input dialogs can contain a list or a combo box for selecting input, and the message dialogs can contain GUI objects like `JScrollPane`.

The `JOptionPane` dialog boxes are *modal*, which means that no other window can be accessed until a dialog box is dismissed.

You have used the input dialog box to enter input from a text field. This example shows that input dialog boxes can also contain a list (lines 12–14) or a combo box (lines 23–25) to list input options. The elements of the list are objects. The return value from these input dialog boxes is of the `Object` type. To obtain a `double` value or an `int` value, you have to cast the return object into `Double` or `Integer`, then use the `doubleValue` or `intValue` method to get the `double` or `int` value (lines 15–16 and 26).

You have already used the message dialog box to display a string. This example shows that the message dialog box can also contain GUI objects. The output string is contained in a text area, the text area is inside a scroll pane, and the scroll pane is placed in the message dialog box (lines 68–71).

29.7 Creating Custom Dialogs

Standard `JOptionPane` dialogs are sufficient in most cases. Occasionally, you need to create custom dialogs. In Swing, the `JDialog` class can be extended to create custom dialogs.

As with `JFrame`, components are added to the **contentPane** of `JDialog`. Creating a custom dialog usually involves laying out user interface components in the dialog, adding buttons for dismissing the dialog, and installing listeners that respond to button actions.

The standard dialog is *modal*, which means that no other window can be accessed before the dialog is dismissed. However, the custom dialogs derived from `JDialog` are not modal by default. To make a dialog modal, set its **modal** property to **true**. To display an instance of `JDialog`, set its **visible** property to **true**.

Let us create a custom dialog box for choosing colors, as shown in Figure 29.17(a). Use this dialog to choose the color for the foreground of the button, as shown in Figure 29.17(b). When the user clicks the *Change Button Text Color* button, the Choose Color dialog box is displayed.

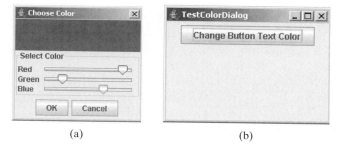

(a)   (b)

FIGURE 29.17   The custom dialog allows you to choose a color for the label's foreground.

Create a custom dialog component named `ColorDialog` by extending `JDialog`. Use three sliders to specify red, green, and blue components of a color. The program is given in Listing 29.6.

LISTING 29.6 `ColorDialog.java`

```
1  import java.awt.*;
2  import java.awt.event.*;
3  import javax.swing.*;
4  import javax.swing.event.*;
5
6  public class ColorDialog extends JDialog {
7    // Declare color component values and selected color
8    private int redValue, greenValue, blueValue;              color value
9    private Color color = null;
10
11   // Create sliders
12   private JSlider jslRed = new JSlider(0, 128);             sliders
13   private JSlider jslGreen = new JSlider(0, 128);
14   private JSlider jslBlue = new JSlider(0, 128);
15
16   // Create two buttons
17   private JButton jbtOK = new JButton("OK");               buttons
18   private JButton jbtCancel = new JButton("Cancel");
19
20   // Create a panel to display the selected color
21   private JPanel jpSelectedColor = new JPanel();
22
```

constructor

```
23  public ColorDialog() {
24    this(null, true);
25  }
26
27  public ColorDialog(java.awt.Frame parent, boolean modal) {
28    super(parent, modal);
29    setTitle("Choose Color");
30
31    // Group two buttons OK and Cancel
32    JPanel jpButtons = new JPanel();
33    jpButtons.add(jbtOK);
34    jpButtons.add(jbtCancel);
35
36    // Group labels
37    JPanel jpLabels = new JPanel();
38    jpLabels.setLayout(new GridLayout(3, 0));
39    jpLabels.add(new JLabel("Red"));
40    jpLabels.add(new JLabel("Green"));
41    jpLabels.add(new JLabel("Blue"));
42
43    // Group sliders for selecting red, green, and blue colors
44    JPanel jpSliders = new JPanel();
45    jpSliders.setLayout(new GridLayout(3, 0));
46    jpSliders.add(jslRed);
47    jpSliders.add(jslGreen);
48    jpSliders.add(jslBlue);
49
50    // Group jpLabels and jpSliders
51    JPanel jpSelectColor = new JPanel();
52    jpSelectColor.setLayout(new BorderLayout());
53    jpSelectColor.setBorder(
54      BorderFactory.createTitledBorder("Select Color"));
55    jpSelectColor.add(jpLabels, BorderLayout.WEST);
56    jpSelectColor.add(jpSliders, BorderLayout.CENTER);
57
58    // Group jpSelectColor and jpSelectedColor
59    JPanel jpColor = new JPanel();
60    jpColor.setLayout(new BorderLayout());
61    jpColor.add(jpSelectColor, BorderLayout.SOUTH);
62    jpColor.add(jpSelectedColor, BorderLayout.CENTER);
63
64    // Place jpButtons and jpColor into the dialog box
65    add(jpButtons, BorderLayout.SOUTH);
66    add(jpColor, BorderLayout.CENTER);
67    pack();
68
69    jbtOK.addActionListener(new ActionListener() {
70      public void actionPerformed(ActionEvent e) {
71        setVisible(false);
72      }
73    });
74
75    jbtCancel.addActionListener(new ActionListener() {
76      public void actionPerformed(ActionEvent e) {
77        color = null;
78        setVisible(false);
79      }
80    });
81
```

The left margin annotations read: "constructor" (line 23), "constructor" (line 27), "create UI" (line 29), "listeners" (line 69).

```
82        jslRed.addChangeListener(new ChangeListener() {
83          public void stateChanged(ChangeEvent e) {
84            redValue = jslRed.getValue();
85            color = new Color(redValue, greenValue, blueValue);
86            jpSelectedColor.setBackground(color);
87          }
88        });
89
90        jslGreen.addChangeListener(new ChangeListener() {
91          public void stateChanged(ChangeEvent e) {
92            greenValue = jslGreen.getValue();
93            color = new Color(redValue, greenValue, blueValue);
94            jpSelectedColor.setBackground(color);
95          }
96        });
97
98        jslBlue.addChangeListener(new ChangeListener() {
99          public void stateChanged(ChangeEvent e) {
100            blueValue = jslBlue.getValue();
101            color = new Color(redValue, greenValue, blueValue);
102            jpSelectedColor.setBackground(color);
103          }
104        });
105      }
106
107      public Dimension getPreferredSize() {
108        return new java.awt.Dimension(200, 200);
109      }
110
111      /** Return color */
112      public Color getColor() {
113        return color;
114      }
115 }
```

Create a test class to use the color dialog to select the color for the foreground color of the button in Listing 29.7.

LISTING 29.7 TestColorDialog.java

```
1  import javax.swing.*;
2  import java.awt.*;
3  import java.awt.event.*;
4
5  public class TestColorDialog extends JApplet {
6    private ColorDialog colorDialog1 = new ColorDialog();
7    private JButton jbtChangeColor = new JButton("Choose color");
8
9    public TestColorDialog() {
10     setLayout(new java.awt.FlowLayout());
11     jbtChangeColor.setText("Change Button Text Color");
12     jbtChangeColor.addActionListener(new ActionListener() {     listener
13       public void actionPerformed(ActionEvent e) {
14         colorDialog1.setVisible(true);
15
16         if (colorDialog1.getColor() != null)
17           jbtChangeColor.setForeground(colorDialog1.getColor());
18       }
19     });
```

```
20      add(jbtChangeColor);
21   }
22 }
```

The custom dialog box allows the user to use the sliders to select colors. The selected color is stored in the **color** variable. When the user clicks the *Cancel* button, color becomes **null**, which implies that no selection has been made.

The dialog box is displayed when the user clicks the "Change Button Text Color" button and is closed when the OK button or the Cancel button is clicked.

Tip

Not setting the dialog modal when needed is a common mistake. In this example, the dialog is set modal in line 24 in ColorDialog.java (Listing 29.6). If the dialog is not modal, all the statements in the "Change Button Text Color" button handler are executed before the color is selected from the dialog box.

29.8 JColorChooser

You created a color dialog in the preceding example as a subclass of **JDialog**, which is a subclass of **java.awt.Dialog** (a top-level heavy-weight component). Therefore, it cannot be added to a container as a component. Color dialogs are commonly used in GUI programming. Swing provides a convenient and versatile color dialog named **javax.-swing.JColorChooser**. **JColorChooser** is a lightweight component inherited from **JComponent**. It can be added to any container. For example, the following code places a **JColorChooser** in an applet, as shown in Figure 29.18:

create **JColorChooser**

```
public class JColorChooserDemo extends javax.swing.JApplet {
  public JColorChooserDemo() {
    this.add(new javax.swing.JColorChooser());
  }
}
```

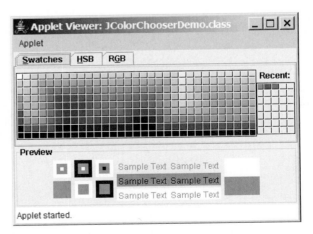

FIGURE 29.18   An instance of **JColorChooser** is displayed in an applet.

Often an instance of **JColorChooser** is displayed in a dialog box using **JColorChooser**'s static **showDialog** method:

```
public static Color showDialog(Component parentComponent,
                               String title,
                               Color initialColor)
```

For example, the following code creates a JColorChooser in an applet, as shown in Figure 29.18:

```java
import javax.swing.*;
import java.awt.Color;

public class JColorChooserDemo extends javax.swing.JApplet {
    public void init() {
        Color color = JColorChooser.showDialog(this, "Choose a color",
            Color.YELLOW);
    }
}
```

create JColorChooser

The showDialog method creates an instance of JDialog with three buttons, OK, Cancel, and Reset, to hold a JColorChooser object, as shown in Figure 29.19. The method displays a modal dialog. If the user clicks the *OK* button, the method dismisses the dialog and returns the selected color. If the user clicks the *Cancel* button or closes the dialog, the method dismisses the dialog and returns null.

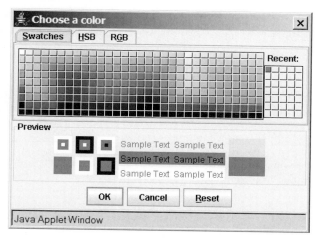

FIGURE 29.19 An instance of JColorChooser is displayed in a dialog box with the OK, Cancel, and Reset buttons.

JColorChooser consists of a tabbed pane and a color preview panel. The tabbed pane has three tabs for choosing colors using Swatches, HSB, and RGB, as shown in Figure 29.20. The preview panel shows the effect of the selected color.

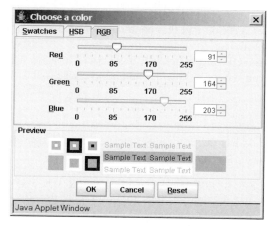

FIGURE 29.20 The JColorChooser class contains a tabbed pane with three tabs for selecting colors using Swatches, HSB, and RGB.

Note

JColorChooser is very flexible. It allows you to replace the tabbed pane or the color preview panel with custom components. The default tabbed pane and the color preview panel are sufficient. You rarely need to use custom components.

29.9 JFileChooser

The javax.swing.JFileChooser class displays a dialog box from which the user can navigate through the file system and select files for loading or saving, as shown in Figure 29.21.

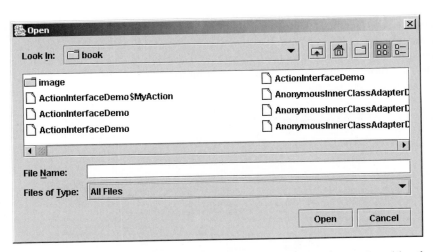

FIGURE 29.21 The Swing JFileChooser shows files and directories, and enables the user to navigate through the file system visually.

Like JColorChooser, JFileChooser is a lightweight component inherited from JComponent. It can be added to any container if desired, but often you create an instance of JFileChooser and display it standalone.

JFileChooser is a subclass of JComponent. There are several ways to construct a file dialog box. The simplest is to use JFileChooser's no-arg constructor.

The file dialog box can appear in two types: open and save. The *open type* is for opening a file, and the *save type* is for storing a file. To create an open file dialog, use the following method:

```
public int showOpenDialog(Component parent)
```

This method creates a dialog box that contains an instance of JFileChooser for opening a file. The method returns an int value, either APPROVE_OPTION or CANCEL_OPTION, which indicates whether the OK button or the Cancel button was clicked.

Similarly, you can use the following method to create a dialog for saving files:

```
public int showSaveDialog(Component parent)
```

The file dialog box created with showOpenDialog or showSaveDialog is modal. The JFileChooser class has the properties inherited from JComponent. It also has the following useful properties:

- dialogType specifies the type of this dialog. Use OPEN_DIALOG when you want to bring up a file chooser that the user can use to open a file. Likewise, use SAVE_DIALOG to let the user choose a file for saving.

- dialogTitle is the string that is displayed in the title bar of the dialog box.

- `currentDirectory` is the current directory of the file. The type of this property is `java.io.File`. If you want the current directory to be used, use `setCurrent-Directory(new File("."))`.

- `selectedFile` is the file you have selected. You can use `getSelectedFile()` to return the selected file from the dialog box. The type of this property is `java.io.File`. If you have a default file name that you expect to use, use `setSelectedFile(new File(filename))`.

- `selectedFiles` is a list of the files selected if the file chooser is set to allow multi-selection. The type of this property is `File[]`.

- `multiSelectionEnabled` is a `boolean` value indicating whether multiple files can be selected. By default, it is `false`.

Let us create an example of a simple text editor that uses Swing menus, tool bar, file chooser, and color chooser, as shown in Figure 29.22, which allows the user to open and save text files, clear text, and change the color and font of the text. Listing 29.8 shows the program.

  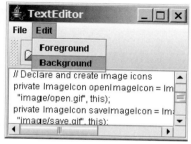

FIGURE 29.22 The editor enables you to open and save text files from the File menu or from the tool bar, and to change the color and font of the text from the Edit menu.

LISTING 29.8 TextEditor.java

```java
1 import java.io.*;
2 import java.awt.*;
3 import java.awt.event.*;
4 import javax.swing.*;
5
6 public class TextEditor extends JApplet {
7   // Declare and create image icons
8   private ImageIcon openImageIcon =
9     new ImageIcon(getClass().getResource("image/open.gif"));
10  private ImageIcon saveImageIcon =
11    new ImageIcon(getClass().getResource("image/save.gif"));
12
13  // Create menu items
14  private JMenuItem jmiOpen = new JMenuItem("Open", openImageIcon);
15  private JMenuItem jmiSave = new JMenuItem("Save", saveImageIcon);
16  private JMenuItem jmiClear = new JMenuItem("Clear");
17  private JMenuItem jmiExit = new JMenuItem("Exit");
18  private JMenuItem jmiForeground = new JMenuItem("Foreground");
19  private JMenuItem jmiBackground = new JMenuItem("Background");
20
21  // Create buttons to be placed in a tool bar
22  private JButton jbtOpen = new JButton(openImageIcon);
23  private JButton jbtSave = new JButton(saveImageIcon);
24  private JLabel jlblStatus = new JLabel();
```

create UI

```java
25
26   // Create a JFileChooser with the current directory
27   private JFileChooser jFileChooser1
28     = new JFileChooser(new File("."));
29
30   // Create a text area
31   private JTextArea jta = new JTextArea();
32
33   public TextEditor() {
34     // Add menu items to the menu
35     JMenu jMenu1 = new JMenu("File");
36     jMenu1.add(jmiOpen);
37     jMenu1.add(jmiSave);
38     jMenu1.add(jmiClear);
39     jMenu1.addSeparator();
40     jMenu1.add(jmiExit);
41
42     // Add menu items to the menu
43     JMenu jMenu2 = new JMenu("Edit");
44     jMenu2.add(jmiForeground);
45     jMenu2.add(jmiBackground);
46
47     // Add menus to the menu bar
48     JMenuBar jMenuBar1 = new JMenuBar();
49     jMenuBar1.add(jMenu1);
50     jMenuBar1.add(jMenu2);
51
52     // Set the menu bar
53     setJMenuBar(jMenuBar1);
54
55     // Create tool bar
56     JToolBar jToolBar1 = new JToolBar();
57     jToolBar1.add(jbtOpen);
58     jToolBar1.add(jbtSave);
59
60     jmiOpen.addActionListener(new ActionListener() {
61       public void actionPerformed(ActionEvent e) {
62         open();
63       }
64     });
65
66     jmiSave.addActionListener(new ActionListener() {
67       public void actionPerformed(ActionEvent evt) {
68         save();
69       }
70     });
71
72     jmiClear.addActionListener(new ActionListener() {
73       public void actionPerformed(ActionEvent evt) {
74         jta.setText(null);
75       }
76     });
77
78     jmiExit.addActionListener(new ActionListener() {
79       public void actionPerformed(ActionEvent evt) {
80         System.exit(0);
81       }
82     });
83
```

```
84    jmiForeground.addActionListener(new ActionListener() {
85      public void actionPerformed(ActionEvent evt) {
86        Color selectedColor =
87          JColorChooser.showDialog(null, "Choose Foreground Color",
88            jta.getForeground());
89
90        if (selectedColor != null)
91          jta.setForeground(selectedColor);
92      }
93    });
94
95    jmiBackground.addActionListener(new ActionListener() {
96      public void actionPerformed(ActionEvent evt) {
97        Color selectedColor =
98          JColorChooser.showDialog(null, "Choose Background Color",
99            jta.getForeground());
100
101       if (selectedColor != null)
102         jta.setBackground(selectedColor);
103     }
104   });
105
106   jbtOpen.addActionListener(new ActionListener() {
107     public void actionPerformed(ActionEvent evt) {
108       open();
109     }
110   });
111
112   jbtSave.addActionListener(new ActionListener() {
113     public void actionPerformed(ActionEvent evt) {
114       save();
115     }
116   });
117
118   add(jToolBar1, BorderLayout.NORTH);
119   add(jlblStatus, BorderLayout.SOUTH);
120   add(new JScrollPane(jta), BorderLayout.CENTER);
121 }
122
123 /** Open file */
124 private void open() {
125   if (jFileChooser1.showOpenDialog(this) ==
126     JFileChooser.APPROVE_OPTION )
127     open(jFileChooser1.getSelectedFile());
128 }
129
130 /** Open file with the specified File instance */
131 private void open(File file) {
132   try {
133     // Read from the specified file and store it in jta
134     BufferedInputStream in = new BufferedInputStream(
135       new FileInputStream(file));
136     byte[] b = new byte[in.available()];
137     in.read(b, 0, b.length);
138     jta.append(new String(b, 0, b.length));
139     in.close();
140
141     // Display the status of the Open file operation in jlblStatus
142     jlblStatus.setText(file.getName() + " Opened");
143   }
```

color chooser

color chooser

file chooser

```
144        catch (IOException ex) {
145          jlblStatus.setText("Error opening " + file.getName());
146        }
147      }
148
149      /** Save file */
150      private void save() {
151        if (jFileChooser1.showSaveDialog(this) ==
152          JFileChooser.APPROVE_OPTION) {
153          save(jFileChooser1.getSelectedFile());
154        }
155      }
156
157      /** Save file with specified File instance */
158      private void save(File file) {
159        try {
160          // Write the text in jta to the specified file
161          BufferedOutputStream out = new BufferedOutputStream(
162            new FileOutputStream(file));
163          byte[] b = (jta.getText()).getBytes();
164          out.write(b, 0, b.length);
165          out.close();
166
167          // Display the status of the save file operation in jlblStatus
168          jlblStatus.setText(file.getName()  + " Saved ");
169        }
170        catch (IOException ex) {
171          jlblStatus.setText("Error saving " + file.getName());
172        }
173      }
174    }
```

main omitted

The program creates the File and Edit menus (lines 34–45). The File menu contains the menu commands Open for loading a file, Save for saving a file, Clear for clearing the text editor, and Exit for terminating the program. The Edit menu contains the menu commands Foreground Color and Background Color for setting foreground color and background color in the text. The Open and Save menu commands can also be accessed from the tool bar, which is created in lines 56–58. The status of executing Open and Save is displayed in the status label, which is created in line 24.

jFileChooser1, an instance of JfileChooser, is created for displaying the file dialog box to open and save files (lines 27–28). new File(".") is used to set the current directory to the directory where the class is stored.

The open method is invoked when the user clicks the Open menu command or the Open tool bar button (lines 62, 108). The showOpenDialog method (line 125) displays an Open dialog box, as shown in Figure 29.21. Upon receiving the selected file, the method open(file) (line 127) is invoked to load the file to the text area using a BufferedInputStream wrapped on a FileInputStream.

The save method is invoked when the user clicks the Save menu command or the Save tool bar button (lines 68, 114). The showSaveDialog method (line 151) displays a Save dialog box. Upon receiving the selected file, the method save(file) (line 153) is invoked to save the contents from the text area to the file using a BufferedOutputStream wrapped on a FileOutputStream.

The color dialog is displayed using the static method showDialog (lines 87, 98) of JColorChooser. Thus you don't need to create an instance of JFileChooser. The showDialog method returns the selected color if the OK button is clicked after a color is selected.

29.10 (Optional) Creating Internal Frames

You can create multiple windows, as discussed in §15.12, "Creating Multiple Windows." Java also allows you to use the `JInternalFrame` class to create windows within a window. This user interface is commonly known as a *multiple document interface* or *MDI*. It was once quite popular and was used in the earlier versions of many popular Windows software programs. Now, however, MDI is rarely used. That is why this section is marked optional.

MDI

The `JInternalFrame` class is almost the same as the external `JFrame` class. The components are added to the internal frame in the same way as they are added to the external frame. An internal frame can have menus, title, Close icon, Minimize icon, and Maximize icon just like an external frame. The following are the major differences:

- `JInternalFrame` extends `JComponent`, and `JFrame` extends the AWT `Frame` class. Therefore, `JInternalFrame` is a Swing lightweight component, and `JFrame` is a Swing heavyweight component.

- Both `JInternalFrame` and `JFrame` are used to hold other components. `JFrame` is a top-level window component, and `JInternalFrame` must be contained inside a `JDesktopPane` of a `JFrame` or a `JApplet`.

Here are the steps to create an internal frame inside another window:

1. Use a `JFrame` or a `JApplet` as the outer window.

2. Create a `JDesktopPane` and add it to the content pane of a `JFrame` or `JApplet`. Usually, the `JDesktopPane` is added to the center of the content pane.

3. Create a `JInternalFrame` and add it to the `JDesktopPane` using the **add** method.

4. Use the `setVisible(true)` method to display the internal frame.

Listing 29.9 gives an example that creates internal frames to display flags in an applet. You can select flags from the Flags menu. Clicking a menu item causes a flag to be displayed in an internal frame, as shown in Figure 29.23.

FIGURE 29.23 The flag image is displayed in an internal frame.

LISTING 29.9 ShowInternalFrame.java

```
 1 import java.awt.*;
 2 import java.awt.event.*;
 3 import javax.swing.*;
 4
 5 public class ShowInternalFrame extends JApplet {
 6   // Create image icons
 7   private ImageIcon USIcon =
 8     new ImageIcon(getClass().getResource("image/usIcon.gif"));
 9   private ImageIcon CanadaIcon =
10     new ImageIcon(getClass().getResource("image/caIcon.gif"));
11
```

desktop pane

internal frame

add frame

set frame icon

add label

main omitted

```
12    private JMenuBar jMenuBar1 = new JMenuBar();
13    private JMenuItem jmiUS = new JMenuItem("US");
14    private JMenuItem jmiCanada = new JMenuItem("Canada");
15    private JLabel jlblImage = new JLabel(USIcon, JLabel.CENTER);
16
17    // Create JDesktopPane to hold the internal frame
18    private JDesktopPane desktop = new JDesktopPane();
19    private JInternalFrame internalFrame =
20      new JInternalFrame("US", true, true, true, true);
21
22    public ShowInternalFrame() {
23      desktop.add(internalFrame);
24
25      this.setSize(new Dimension(400, 300));
26      this.getContentPane().add(desktop, BorderLayout.CENTER);
27
28      jlblImage.setIcon(USIcon);
29      internalFrame.setFrameIcon(USIcon);
30
31      internalFrame.add(jlblImage);
32      internalFrame.setLocation(20, 20);
33      internalFrame.setSize(100, 100);
34      internalFrame.setVisible(true);
35
36      JMenu jMenu1 = new JMenu("Flags");
37      jMenuBar1.add(jMenu1);
38      jMenu1.add(jmiUS);
39      jMenu1.add(jmiCanada);
40
41      this.setJMenuBar(jMenuBar1);
42
43      jmiUS.addActionListener(new ActionListener() {
44        public void actionPerformed(ActionEvent e) {
45          jlblImage.setIcon(USIcon);
46          internalFrame.setFrameIcon(USIcon);
47          internalFrame.setTitle("US");
48        }
49      });
50
51      jmiCanada.addActionListener(new ActionListener() {
52        public void actionPerformed(ActionEvent e) {
53          jlblImage.setIcon(CanadaIcon);
54          internalFrame.setFrameIcon(CanadaIcon);
55          internalFrame.setTitle("Canada");
56        }
57      });
58    }
59 }
```

An image icon is displayed on a label (line 15). The label is placed inside an internal frame (line 31). As shown in Figure 29.23, an internal frame looks like an external frame. Internal frames can be used much the same way as external frames, except that internal frames are always placed inside a `JDesktopPane`. `JDesktopPane` is a subclass of `JLayeredPane`. Since `JDesktopPane` is also a subclass of `JComponent`, it can be placed into the content pane of a `JFrame` or a `JApplet`.

The properties of `JInternalFrame` and `JFrame` are very similar. You can set a title, internal frame icon, size, and visible for an internal frame. You may modify this example to add menus to the internal frame too.

CHAPTER SUMMARY

- Menus make selection easier and are widely used in window applications. Java provides five classes that implement menus: `JMenuBar`, `JMenu`, `JMenuItem`, `JCheckBoxMenuItem`, and `JRadioButtonMenuItem`. These classes are subclasses of `AbstractButton`. They are very similar to buttons.

- `JMenuBar` is a top-level menu component used to hold menus. A menu consists of *menu items* that the user can select (or toggle on or off). A menu item can be an instance of `JMenuItem`, `JCheckBoxMenuItem`, or `JRadioButtonMenuItem`. Menu items can be associated with icons, keyboard mnemonics, and keyboard accelerators. Menu items can be separated using separators.

- A popup menu, also known as *a context menu*, is like a regular menu, but does not have a menu bar and can float anywhere on the screen. Creating a popup menu is similar to creating a regular menu. First, you create an instance of `JPopupMenu`, then you can add `JMenuItem`, `JCheckBoxMenuItem`, `JRadioButtonMenuItem`, and separators to the popup menu.

- A popup menu usually contains the commands for an object. Customarily, you display a popup menu by pointing to the object and clicking a certain mouse button, the so-called *popup trigger*. Popup triggers are system-dependent. In Windows, the popup menu is displayed when the right mouse button is released. In Motif, the popup menu is displayed when the third mouse button is pressed and held down.

- Swing provides the `JToolBar` class as the container to hold tool bar components. `JToolBar` uses `BoxLayout` to manage components. The components usually appear as icons. Since icons are not components, they cannot be placed into a tool bar directly. Instead you place buttons into the tool bar and set the icons on the buttons. An instance of `JToolBar` is like a regular container. Often it is placed in the north, west, or east of a container of `BorderLayout`.

- Swing provides the `Action` interface, which can be used to create action objects for processing actions. Using `Action` objects, common action processing for menu items and tool bar buttons can be centralized and separated from the other application code.

- The `JOptionPane` class contains the static methods for creating message dialogs, confirmation dialogs, input dialogs, and option dialogs. You can also create custom dialogs by extending the `JDialog` class.

- Swing provides a convenient and versatile color dialog named `javax.swing.JColorChooser`. Like `JOptionPane`, `JColorChooser` is a lightweight component inherited from `JComponent`. It can be added to any container.

- Swing provides the `javax.swing.JFileChooser` class that displays a dialog box from which the user can navigate through the file system and select files for loading or saving.

- You can create internal frames using the `JInternalFrame` class. This user interface is commonly known as a *multiple document interface* or *MDI*. The `JInternalFrame` class is almost the same as the external `JFrame` class. The components are added to the internal frame in the same way as they are added to the external frame. An internal frame can have menus, a title, a Close icon, a Minimize icon, and a Maximize icon just like an external frame.

REVIEW QUESTIONS

Section 29.2 Menus

29.1 How do you create a menu bar?

29.2 How do you create a submenu? How do you create a check box menu item? How do you create a radio button menu item?

29.3 How do you add a separator in a menu?

29.4 How do you set an icon and a text in a menu item? How do you associate keyboard mnemonics and accelerators in a menu item?

Section 29.3 Popup Menus

29.5 How do you create a popup menu? How do you show a popup menu?

29.6 Describe a popup trigger.

Section 29.4 `JToolBar`

29.7 What is the layout manager used in `JToolBar`? Can you change the layout manager?

29.8 How do you add buttons into a `JToolBar`? How do you add a `JToolBar` into a frame or an applet?

Section 29.5 Processing Actions Using the `Action` Interface

29.9 What is the `Action` interface for?

29.10 How do you add an `Action` object to a `JToolBar`, `JMenu`, `JButton`, `JRadioButton`, and `JCheckBox`?

Section 29.6 `JOptionPane` Dialogs

29.11 Describe the standard dialog boxes created using the `JOptionPane` class.

29.12 How do you create a message dialog? What are the message types? What is the button in the message dialog?

29.13 How do you create a confirmation dialog? What are the button option types?

29.14 How do you create an input dialog with a text field for entering input? How do you create a combo box dialog for selecting values as input? How do you create a list dialog for selecting values as input?

Sections 29.7–29.10

29.15 How do you show an instance of `JDialog`? Is a standard dialog box created using the static methods in `JOptionPane` modal? Is an instance of `JDialog` modal?

29.16 How do you display an instance of `JColorChooser`? Is an instance of `JColorChooser` modal? How do you obtain the selected color?

29.17 How do you display an instance of `JFileChooser`? Is an instance of `JFileChooser` modal? How do you obtain the selected file? What is the return type for `getSelectedFile()` and `getSelectedDirectory()`? How do you set the current directory as the default directory for a `JFileChooser` dialog?

29.18 How do you create an internal frame?

PROGRAMMING EXERCISES

Sections 29.2–29.3

29.1* (*Creating an investment value calculator*) Write a program that calculates the future value of an investment at a given interest rate for a specified number of years. The formula for the calculation is as follows:

$$futureValue = investmentAmount \times (1 + monthlyInterestRate)^{years \times 12}$$

Use text fields for interest rate, investment amount, and years. Display the future amount in a text field when the user clicks the Calculate button or chooses Calculate from the Operation menu (see Figure 29.24). Show a message dialog box when the user clicks the About menu item from the Help menu.

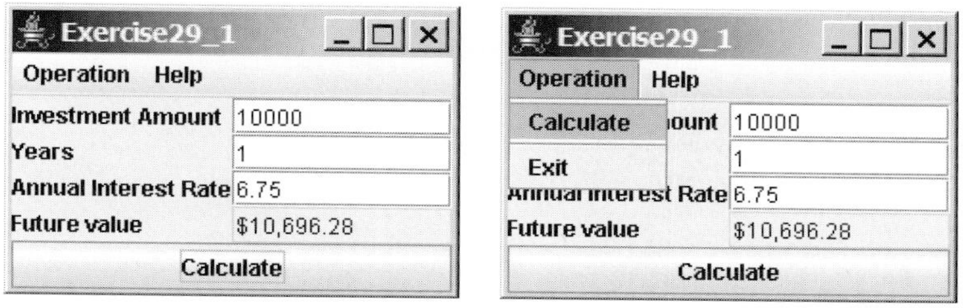

FIGURE 29.24   The user enters the investment amount, years, and interest rate to compute future value.

29.2* (*Using popup menus*) Modify Listing 29.1, MenuDemo.java, to create a popup menu that contains the menus Operations and Exit, as shown in Figure 29.25. The popup is displayed when you click the right-mouse button on the panel that contains the labels and the text fields.

FIGURE 29.25   The popup menu contains the commands to perform arithmetic operations.

Sections 29.4–29.5

29.3**(*A paint utility*) Write a program that emulates a paint utility. Your program should enable the user to choose options and draw shapes or get characters from the keyboard based on the selected options (see Figure 29.26). The options are displayed in a tool bar. To draw a line, the user first clicks the line icon in the tool bar and then uses the mouse to draw a line in the same way you would draw using Microsoft Paint.

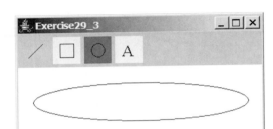

FIGURE 29.26 This exercise produces a prototype drawing utility that enables you to draw lines, rectangles, ovals, and characters.

29.4* (*Using actions*) Write a program that contains the menu items and tool bar buttons that can be used to select flags to be displayed in an `ImageViewer`, as shown in Figure 29.27. Use the `Action` interface to centralize the processing for the actions.

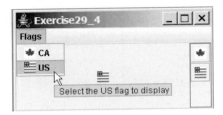

FIGURE 29.27 The menu items and tool buttons are used to display selected images in the `ImageViewer`.

Sections 29.6–29.10

29.5* (*Demonstrating JOptionPane*) Write a program that creates option panes of all types, as shown in Figure 29.28. Each menu item invokes a static `showXxxDialog` method to display a dialog box.

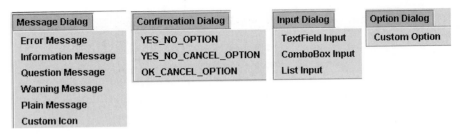

FIGURE 29.28 You can display a dialog box by clicking a menu item.

29.6* (*Creating custom dialog*) Write a program that creates a custom dialog box to gather user information, as shown in Figure 29.29.

FIGURE 29.29   The custom dialog box prompts the user to enter username and password.

29.7* (*Using* `JFileChooser`) Write a program that enables the user to select a file from a file open dialog box. A file open dialog box is displayed when the Browse button is clicked, as shown in Figure 29.30. The file is displayed in the text area, and the filename is displayed in the text field when the OK button is clicked in the file open dialog box. You can also enter the filename in the text field and press the Enter key to display the file in the text area.

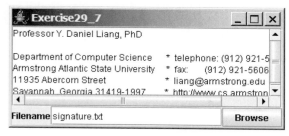

FIGURE 29.30   The program enables the user to view a file by selecting it from a file open dialog box.

29.8* (*Selecting an audio file*) Write a program that selects an audio file using the file dialog box, and use three buttons, Play, Loop, and Stop, to control the audio, as shown in Figure 29.31. If you click the Play button, the audio file is played once. If you click the Loop button, the audio file keeps playing repeatedly. If you click the Stop button, the playing stops. The selected audio files are stored in the folder named **audio** under the exercise directory.

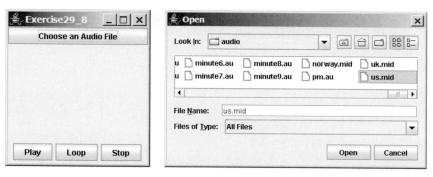

FIGURE 29.31   The program allows you to choose an audio file from a dialog box and use the buttons to play, repeatedly play, or stop the audio.

29.9**(*Playing TicTacToe with a computer*) The game in §16.7, "Case Study: TicTac-Toe," facilitates two players. Write a new game that enables a player to play against the computer. Add a File menu with two items, New Game and Exit, as shown in Figure 29.32. When you click New Game, it displays a dialog box. From this dialog box, you can decide whether to let the computer go first.

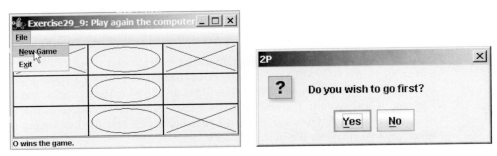

FIGURE 29.32 The new TicTacToe game enables you to play against the computer.

MVC and Swing Models

Objectives

- To use the model-view-controller approach to separate data and logic from the presentation of data (§30.2).

- To implement the model-view-controller components using the JavaBeans event model (§30.2).

- To understand the Swing model-view-controller architecture (§30.4).

- To use `JSpinner` to scroll the next and previous values (§30.5).

- To create custom spinner models and editors (§30.6).

- To use `JList` to select single or multiple items in a list (§30.7).

- To add and remove items using `ListModel` and `Default-ListModel` (§30.8).

- To render list cells using a default or custom cell renderer (§30.9).

- To create custom combo box models and renderers (§30.10).

30.1 Introduction

The Swing user interface components are implemented using variations of the MVC architecture. You have used simple Swing components without concern for their supporting models, but in order to use advanced Swing components, you have to use their models to store, access, and modify data. This chapter introduces the MVC architecture and Swing models. Specifically, you will learn how to use the models in `JSpinner`, `JList`, and `JComboBox`. The next chapter will introduce `JTable` and `JTree`.

30.2 MVC

model
view

controller

The model-view-controller (MVC) approach is a way of developing components by separating data storage and handling from the visual representation of the data. The component for storing and handling data, known as a *model*, contains the actual contents of the component. The component for presenting the data, known as a *view*, handles all essential component behaviors. It is the view that comes to mind when you think of the component. It does all the displaying of the components. The *controller* is a component that is usually responsible for obtaining data, as shown in Figure 30.1.

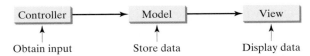

FIGURE 30.1 The controller obtains data and stores it in a model. The view displays the data stored in the model.

MVC benefits

Separating a component into a model and a view has two major benefits:

- It makes multiple views possible so that data can be shared through the same model. For example, a model storing student names can simultaneously be displayed in a combo box and a list box.

- It simplifies the task of writing complex applications and makes the components scalable and easy to maintain. Changes can be made to the view without affecting the model, and vice versa.

A model contains data, whereas a view makes the data visible. Once a view is associated with a model, it is synchronized with the model. This ensures that all of the model's views display the same data consistently. To achieve consistency and synchronization with its dependent views, the model should notify the views when there is a change in any of its properties that are used in the view. In response to a change notification, the view is responsible for redisplaying the viewing area affected by the property change.

Prior to JDK 1.1, you would create a model by extending the `java.util.Observable` class, and would create a view by implementing the `java.util.Observer` interface. `Observable` and `Observer` were introduced in JDK 1.0, and their use is not consistent with the JDK 1.1 event model. With the arrival of the new Java event delegation model, using `Observable` and `Observer` became obsolete. The JDK event delegation model provides a superior architecture for supporting MVC component development. The model can be implemented as a source with appropriate event and event listener registration methods. The view can be implemented as a listener. Thus, if data is changed in the model, the view will be notified. To enable the selection of the model from the view, simply add the model as a property in the view with a set method.

Let us use an example to demonstrate the development of components using the MVC approach. The example creates a model named `CircleModel`, a view named `CircleView`, and a controller named `CircleControl`. `CircleModel` stores the properties (`radius`, filled, and color) that describe a circle. filled is a boolean value that indicates whether a circle is filled. CircleView draws a circle according to the properties of the circle. CircleControl enables the user to enter circle properties from a graphical user interface. Create an applet with two buttons named *Show Controller* and *Show View,* as shown in Figure 30.2(a). When you click the Show Controller button, the controller is displayed in a frame, as shown in Figure 30.2(b). When you click the Show View button, the view is displayed in a separate frame, as shown in Figure 30.2(c).

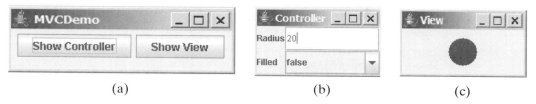

(a)   (b)   (c)

FIGURE 30.2 The controller obtains circle properties and stores them in a circle model. The view displays the circle specified by the circle model.

The circle model contains the properties **radius**, **filled**, and **color**, as well as the registration/deregistration methods for the action event, as shown in Figure 30.3.

date model

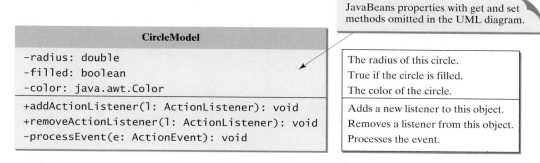

FIGURE 30.3 The circle model stores the data and notifies the listeners if the data changes.

When a property value is changed, the listeners are notified. The complete source code for CircleModel is given in Listing 30.1.

LISTING 30.1 CircleModel.java

```
1 import java.awt.event.*;
2 import java.util.*;
3
4 public class CircleModel {
5   /** Property radius. */
6   private double radius = 20;
7
8   /** Property filled. */
9   private boolean filled;
10
11  /** Property color. */
12  private java.awt.Color color;
13
14  /** Utility field used by event firing mechanism. */
15  private ArrayList<ActionListener> actionListenerList;
16
```

properties

```
17    public double getRadius() {
18      return radius;
19    }
20
21    public void setRadius(double radius) {
22      this.radius = radius;
23
24      // Notify the listener for the change on radius
25      processEvent(
26        new ActionEvent(this, ActionEvent.ACTION_PERFORMED, "radius"));
27    }
28
29    public boolean isFilled() {
30      return filled;
31    }
32
33    public void setFilled(boolean filled) {
34      this.filled = filled;
35
36      // Notify the listener for the change on filled
37      processEvent(
38        new ActionEvent(this, ActionEvent.ACTION_PERFORMED, "filled"));
39    }
40
41    public java.awt.Color getColor() {
42      return color;
43    }
44
45    public void setColor(java.awt.Color color) {
46      this.color = color;
47
48      // Notify the listener for the change on color
49      processEvent(
50        new ActionEvent(this, ActionEvent.ACTION_PERFORMED, "color"));
51    }
52
53    /** Register an action event listener */
54    public synchronized void addActionListener(ActionListener l) {
55      if (actionListenerList == null)
56        actionListenerList = new ArrayList<ActionListener>();
57
58      actionListenerList.add(l);
59    }
60
61    /** Remove an action event listener */
62    public synchronized void removeActionListener(ActionListener l) {
63      if (actionListenerList != null && actionListenerList.contains(l))
64        actionListenerList.remove(l);
65    }
66
67    /** Fire TickEvent */
68    private void processEvent(ActionEvent e) {
69      ArrayList list;
70
71      synchronized (this) {
72        if (actionListenerList == null) return;
73        list = (ArrayList)actionListenerList.clone();
74      }
75
```

fire event (line 25)
fire event (line 37)
fire event (line 49)
standard code (line 54)
standard code (line 62)
standard code (line 68)

```
76        for (int i = 0; i < list.size(); i++) {
77          ActionListener listener = (ActionListener)list.get(i);
78          listener.actionPerformed(e);
79        }
80      }
81 }
```

Note

The registration/deregistration/processEvent methods (lines 54–80) are the same as in Listing 27.2, CourseWithActionEvent.java. If you use a GUI builder tool such as NetBeans, JBuilder, or Eclipse, the code can be generated automatically.

The *view* implements `ActionListener` to listen for notifications from the model. It contains the model as its property. When a model is set in the view, the view is registered with the model. The view extends `JPanel` and overrides the `paintComponent` method to draw the circle according to the property values specified in the mode. The UML diagram for `CircleView` is shown in Figure 30.4, and its source code is given in Listing 30.2.

view

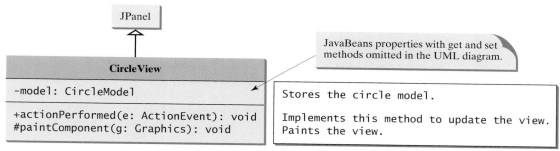

FIGURE 30.4 The view displays the circle according to the model.

LISTING 30.2 CircleView.java

```
1 import java.awt.*;
2 import java.awt.event.*;
3
4 public class CircleView extends javax.swing.JPanel
5     implements ActionListener {
6   private CircleModel model;                                model
7
8   public void actionPerformed(ActionEvent actionEvent) {
9     repaint();
10  }
11
12  /** Set a model */
13  public void setModel(CircleModel newModel) {             set model
14    model = newModel;
15
16    if (model != null)
16      // Register the view as listener for the model
18      model.addActionListener(this);
19
20    repaint();
21  }
22
23  public CircleModel getModel() {
```

```
24      return model;
25    }
26
27    public void paintComponent(Graphics g) {
28      super.paintComponent(g);
29
30      if (model == null) return;
31
32      g.setColor(model.getColor());
33
34      int xCenter = getWidth() / 2;
35      int yCenter = getHeight() / 2;
36      int radius = (int)model.getRadius();
37
38      if (model.isFilled()) {
39        g.fillOval(xCenter - radius, yCenter - radius,
40          2 * radius, 2 * radius);
41      }
42      else {
43        g.drawOval(xCenter - radius, yCenter - radius,
44          2 * radius, 2 * radius);
45      }
46    }
47 }
```

The controller presents a GUI interface that enables the user to enter circle properties `radius`, `filled`, and `color`. It contains the model as its property. You can use the `setModel` method to associate a circle model with the controller. It uses a text field to obtain a new radius and a combo box to obtain a Boolean value to specify whether the circle is filled. The source code for `CircleController` is given in Listing 30.3.

LISTING 30.3 CircleController.java

```
1 import java.awt.event.*;
2 import java.awt.*;
3 import javax.swing.*;
4
5 public class CircleController extends JPanel {
6   private CircleModel model;
7   private JTextField jtfRadius = new JTextField();
8   private JComboBox jcboFilled = new JComboBox(new Boolean[]{
9     new Boolean(false), new Boolean(true)});
10
11   /** Creates new form CircleController */
12   public CircleController() {
13     // Panel to group labels
14     JPanel panel1 = new JPanel();
15     panel1.setLayout(new GridLayout(2, 1));
16     panel1.add(new JLabel("Radius"));
17     panel1.add(new JLabel("Filled"));
18
19     // Panel to group text field, combo box, and another panel
20     JPanel panel2 = new JPanel();
21     panel2.setLayout(new GridLayout(2, 1));
22     panel2.add(jtfRadius);
23     panel2.add(jcboFilled);
24
25     setLayout(new BorderLayout());
26     add(panel1, BorderLayout.WEST);
27     add(panel2, BorderLayout.CENTER);
```

paint view

model

create UI

```
28
29       // Register listeners
30       jtfRadius.addActionListener(new ActionListener() {
31         public void actionPerformed(ActionEvent e) {
32           if (model == null) return; // No model associated yet. Do nothing
33           model.setRadius(new Double(jtfRadius.getText()).doubleValue());
34         }
35       });
36       jcboFilled.addActionListener(new ActionListener() {
37         public void actionPerformed(ActionEvent e) {
38           if (model == null) return; // No model associated yet. Do nothing
39           model.setFilled(
40             ((Boolean)jcboFilled.getSelectedItem()).booleanValue());
41         }
42       });
43     }
44
45     public void setModel(CircleModel newModel) {                    set model
46       model = newModel;
47     }
48
49     public CircleModel getModel() {
50       return model;
51     }
52 }
```

Finally, let us create an applet named MVCDemo with two buttons, **Show Controller** and **Show View**. The Show Controller button displays a controller in a frame, and the Show View button displays a view in a separate frame. The program is shown in Listing 30.4.

LISTING 30.4 MVCDemo.java

```
1  import java.awt.*;
2  import java.awt.event.*;
3  import javax.swing.*;
4
5  public class MVCDemo extends JApplet {
6    private JButton jbtController = new JButton("Show Controller");
7    private JButton jbtView = new JButton("Show View");
8    private CircleModel model = new CircleModel();                 create model
9
10   public MVCDemo() {                                             create UI
11     setLayout(new FlowLayout());
12     add(jbtController);
13     add(jbtView);
14
15     jbtController.addActionListener(new ActionListener() {
16       public void actionPerformed(ActionEvent e) {
17         JFrame frame = new JFrame("Controller");
18         CircleController controller = new CircleController();
19         controller.setModel(model);                             set model
20         frame.add(controller);
21         frame.setSize(200, 200);
22         frame.setLocation(200, 200);
23         frame.setVisible(true);
24       }
25     });
26
27     jbtView.addActionListener(new ActionListener() {
28       public void actionPerformed(ActionEvent e) {
```

set model

```
29          JFrame frame = new JFrame("View");
30          CircleView view = new CircleView();
31          view.setModel(model);
32          frame.add(view);
33          frame.setSize(500, 200);
34          frame.setLocation(200, 200);
35          frame.setVisible(true);
36        }
37     });
38   }
39 }
```

The model stores and handles data, and the views are responsible for presenting data. The fundamental issue in the model-view approach is to ensure consistency between the views and the model. Any change in the model should be notified to the dependent views, and all the views should display the same data consistently. The data in the model is changed through the controller.

The methods `setRadius` and `setFilled`, and `setColor` (lines 21, 33, 45) in `CircleModel` invoke the `processEvent` method to notify the listeners of any change in the properties. The `setModel` method in `CircleView` sets a new model and registers the view with the model by invoking the model's `addActionListener` method (line 18). When the data in the model is changed, the view's `actionPerformed` method is invoked to repaint the circle (line 9).

The controller `CircleController` presents a GUI. You can enter the radius from the radius text field. You can specify whether the circle is filled from the combo box that contains two `Boolean` objects, `new Boolean(false)` and `new Boolean(true)` (lines 8–9). Several controllers or views can share a model. Every time you click the Show Controller button, a new controller is created (line 18). Every time you click the Show View button, a new view is created (line 30). All the controllers and views share the same model.

30.3 MVC Variations

A variation of the model-view-controller architecture combines the controller with the view. In this case, a view not only presents the data, but is also used as an interface to interact with the user and accept user input, as shown in Figure 30.5.

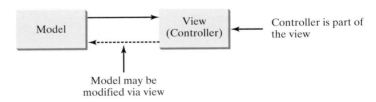

FIGURE 30.5 The view can interact with the user as well as display data.

For example, you can modify the view in the preceding example to enable the user to change the circle's radius using the mouse. When the left mouse button is clicked, the radius is increased by 5 pixels. When the right mouse button is clicked, the radius is decreased by 5 pixels. The new view, named `ViewController`, can be implemented by extending `CircleView`, as follows:

```
public class ViewController extends CircleView {
  public ViewController() {
    // Register mouse listener
    addMouseListener(new java.awt.event.MouseAdapter() {
      public void mousePressed(java.awt.event.MouseEvent e) {
        CircleModel model = getModel(); // Get model
```

```
        if (model == null) return;

        if (e.isMetaDown())
          model.setRadius(model.getRadius() - 5); // Right button
        else
          model.setRadius(model.getRadius() + 5); // Left button
      }
    });
  }
}
```

Another variation of the model-view-controller architecture adds some of the data from the model to the view so that frequently used data can be accessed directly from the view. Swing components are designed using the MVC architecture. Each Swing GUI component is a view that uses a model to store data. A Swing GUI component contains some data in the model so that it can be accessed directly from the component.

30.4 Swing Model-View-Controller Architecture

Every Swing user interface component (except some containers and dialog boxes, such as `JPanel`, `JSplitPane`, `JFileChooser`, and `JColorChooser`) has a property named `model` that refers to its data model. The data model is defined in an interface whose name ends with `Model`. For example, the model for button component is `ButtonModel`. Most model interfaces have a default implementation class that is commonly named `DefaultX`, where *X* is its model interface name. For example, the default implementation class for `ButtonModel` is `DefaultButtonModel`. The relationship of a Swing component, its model interface, and its default model implementation class is illustrated in Figure 30.6.

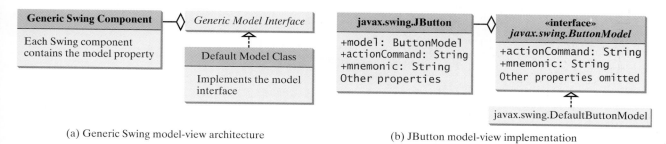

(a) Generic Swing model-view architecture   (b) JButton model-view implementation

FIGURE 30.6 Swing components are implemented using the MVC architecture.

For convenience, most Swing components contain some properties of their models, and these properties can be accessed and modified directly from the component without knowing the existence of the model. For example, the properties `actionCommand` and `mnemonic` are defined in both `ButtonModel` and `JButton`. Actually, these properties are in the `AbstractButton` class. Since `JButton` is a subclass of `AbstractButton`, it inherits all the properties from `AbstractButton`.

When you create a Swing component without specifying a model, a default data model is assigned to the `model` property. For example, the following code sets the `actionCommand` and `mnemonic` properties of a button through its model:

```
public class TestSwingModel1 {
  public static void main(String[] args) {
    javax.swing.JButton jbt = new javax.swing.JButton();
```

get model

```
                     // Obtain the default model from the component
                     javax.swing.ButtonModel model = jbt.getModel();
```

get model properties

```
                     // Set properties in the model
                     model.setActionCommand("OK");
                     model.setMnemonic('O');

                     // Display the property values from the component
                     System.out.println("actionCommand is " + jbt.getActionCommand());
                     System.out.println("mnemonic is " + (char)(jbt.getMnemonic()));
                   }
                 }
```

The output is

```
    actionCommand is OK
    mnemonic is O
```

You can also create a new model and assign it to a Swing component. For example, the following code creates an instance of **ButtonModel** and assigns it to an instance of **JButton**:

```
    public class TestSwingModel2 {
      public static void main(String[] args) {
        javax.swing.JButton jbt = new javax.swing.JButton();

        // Create a new button model
        javax.swing.ButtonModel model =
          new javax.swing.DefaultButtonModel();
```

create model

set model properties

```
        // Set properties in the model
        model.setActionCommand("OK");
        model.setMnemonic('O');
```

set a new model

```
        // Assign the model to the button
        jbt.setModel(model);

        // Display the property values from the component
        System.out.println("actionCommand is " + jbt.getActionCommand());
        System.out.println("mnemonic is " + jbt.getMnemonic());
      }
    }
```

It is unnecessary to use the models for simple Swing components, such as **JButton**, **JToggleButton**, **JCheckBox**, **JRadioButton**, **JTextField**, and **JTextArea**, because the frequently used properties in their models are also in these components. You can access and modify these properties directly through the components. For advanced components, such as **JSpinner**, **JList**, **JComboBox**, **JTable**, and **JTree**, you have to work with their models to store, access, and modify data.

30.5 JSpinner

A spinner is a text field with a pair of tiny arrow buttons on its right side that enable the user to select numbers, dates, or values from an ordered sequence, as shown in Figure 30.7. The keyboard up/down arrow keys also cycle through the elements. The user may also be allowed to type a (legal) value directly into the spinner. A spinner is similar to a combo box, but a spinner is sometimes preferred because it doesn't require a drop-down list that can obscure important data.

Spinner   Spinner

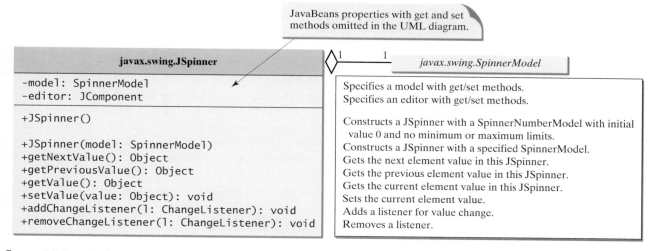

FIGURE 30.7 Two JSpinner components enable the user to select a month and a year for the calendar.

Figure 30.8 shows the constructors and commonly used methods in JSpinner. A JSpinner's sequence value is defined by the SpinnerModel interface, which manages a potentially unbounded sequence of elements. The model doesn't support indexed random access to sequence elements. Only three sequence elements are accessible at a time, current, next, and previous, using the methods getValue(), getNextValue(), and getPreviousValue(), respectively. The current sequence element can be modified using the setValue method. When the current value in a spinner is changed, the model invokes the stateChanged-(javax.swing.event.ChangeEvent e) method of the registered listeners. The listeners must implement javax.swing.event.ChangeListener. All these methods in SpinnerModel are also defined in JSpinner for convenience, so you can access the data in the model from JSpinner directly.

JavaBeans properties with get and set methods omitted in the UML diagram.

javax.swing.JSpinner		*javax.swing.SpinnerModel*
-model: SpinnerModel -editor: JComponent		Specifies a model with get/set methods. Specifies an editor with get/set methods.
+JSpinner() +JSpinner(model: SpinnerModel) +getNextValue(): Object +getPreviousValue(): Object +getValue(): Object +setValue(value: Object): void +addChangeListener(l: ChangeListener): void +removeChangeListener(l: ChangeListener): void		Constructs a JSpinner with a SpinnerNumberModel with initial value 0 and no minimum or maximum limits. Constructs a JSpinner with a specified SpinnerModel. Gets the next element value in this JSpinner. Gets the previous element value in this JSpinner. Gets the current element value in this JSpinner. Sets the current element value. Adds a listener for value change. Removes a listener.

FIGURE 30.8 JSpinner uses a spinner model to store data.

Note

If you create a JSpinner object without specifying a model, the spinner displays a sequence of integers.

Listing 30.5 gives an example that creates a JSpinner object for a sequence of numbers and displays the previous, current, and next numbers from the spinner on a label, as shown in Figure 30.9.

FIGURE 30.9 The previous, current, and next values in the spinner are displayed on the label.

LISTING 30.5 SimpleSpinner.java

```
1  import javax.swing.*;
2  import javax.swing.event.*;
3  import java.awt.BorderLayout;
4
5  public class SimpleSpinner extends JApplet {
6    // Create a JSpinner
7    private JSpinner spinner = new JSpinner();
8
9    // Create a JLabel
10   private JLabel label = new JLabel(" ", JLabel.CENTER);
11
12   public SimpleSpinner() {
13     // Add spinner and label to the UI
14     add(spinner, BorderLayout.NORTH);
15     add(label, BorderLayout.CENTER);
16
17     // Register and create a listener
18     spinner.addChangeListener(new ChangeListener() {
19       public void stateChanged(javax.swing.event.ChangeEvent e) {
20         label.setText("Previous value: " + spinner.getPreviousValue()
21           + " Current value: " + spinner.getValue()
22           + " Next value: " + spinner.getNextValue());
23       }
24     });
25   }
26 }
```

margin notes: spinner · spinner listener · **main** omitted

A JSpinner object is created using its no-arg constructor (line 7). By default, a spinner displays a sequence of integers.

An anonymous inner class event adapter is created to process the value change event on the spinner (lines 18–24). The previous, current, and next values in a spinner can be obtained using the JSpinner's instance methods getPreviousValue(), getValue(), and getNextValue().

To display a sequence of values other than integers, you have to use spinner models.

30.6 Spinner Models and Editors

SpinnerModel is an interface for all spinner models. AbstractSpinnerModel is a convenient abstract class that implements SpinnerModel and provides the implementation for its registration/deregistration methods. SpinnerListModel, SpinnerNumberModel, and SpinnerDateModel are concrete implementations of SpinnerModel. The relationship among them is illustrated in Figure 30.10. Besides these models, you can create a custom spinner model that extends AbstractSpinnerModel or directly implements SpinnerModel.

30.6.1 SpinnerListModel

SpinnerListModel (see Figure 30.11) is a simple implementation of SpinnerModel whose values are stored in a java.util.List.

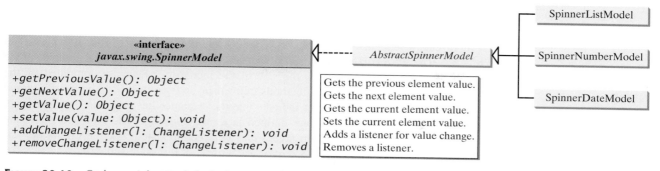

FIGURE 30.10 `SpinnerListModel`, `SpinnerNumberModel`, and `SpinnerDateModel` are concrete implementations of `SpinnerModel`.

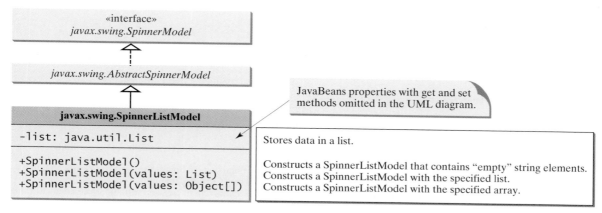

FIGURE 30.11 `SpinnerListModel` uses a `java.util.List` to store a sequence of data in the model.

You can create a `SpinnerListModel` using an array or a list. For example, the following code creates a model that consists of the values Freshman, Sophomore, Junior, Senior, and Graduate in an array:

```
// Create an array
String[] grades = {"Freshman", "Sophomore", "Junior",
  "Senior", "Graduate"};

// Create a model from an array
model = new SpinnerListModel(grades);
```

Alternatively, the following code creates a model using a list:

```
// Create an array
String[] grades = {"Freshman", "Sophomore", "Junior",
  "Senior", "Graduate"};

// Create an array list from the array
list = new ArrayList(Arrays.asList(grades));

// Create a model from list
model = new SpinnerListModel(list);
```

The alternative code seems unnecessary. However, it is useful if you need to add or remove elements from the model. The size of an array is fixed once an array is created. The list is a flexible data structure that enables you to add or remove elements dynamically.

30.6.2 SpinnerNumberModel

SpinnerNumberModel (see Figure 30.12) is a concrete implementation of SpinnerModel that represents a sequence of numbers. It contains the properties maximum, minimum, and stepSize. The maximum and minimum properties specify the upper and lower bounds of the sequence. The stepSize specifies the size of the increase or decrease computed by the nextValue and previousValue methods defined in SpinnerModel. The minimum and maximum properties can be null to indicate that the sequence has no lower or upper limit. All of the properties in this class are defined in terms of two generic types, Number and Comparable, so that all Java numeric types may be accommodated. Internally, only the values with type Double, Float, Long, Integer, Short, or Byte are supported.

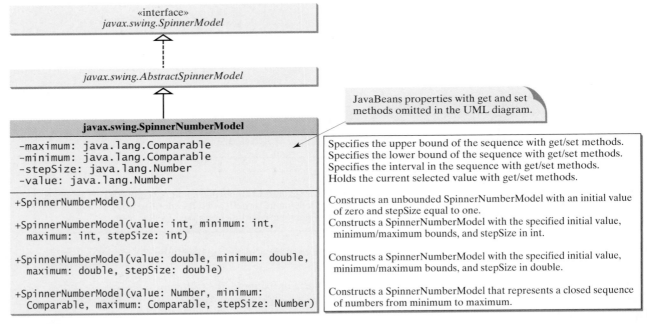

FIGURE 30.12 SpinnerNumberModel represents a sequence of numbers.

You can create a SpinnerNumberModel with integers or double. For example, the following code creates a model that represents a sequence of numbers from 0 to 3000 with initial value 2004 and interval 1:

```
// Create a spinner number model
SpinnerNumberModel model = new SpinnerNumberModel(2004, 0, 3000, 1);
```

The following code creates a model that represents a sequence of numbers from 0 to 120 with initial value 50 and interval 0.1:

```
// Create a spinner number model
SpinnerNumberModel model = new SpinnerNumberModel(50, 0, 120, 0.1);
```

30.6.3 SpinnerDateModel

SpinnerDateModel (see Figure 30.13) is a concrete implementation of SpinnerModel that represents a sequence of dates. The upper and lower bounds of the sequence are defined by properties called start and end, and the size of the increase or decrease computed by the nextValue and previousValue methods is defined by a property called calendarField.

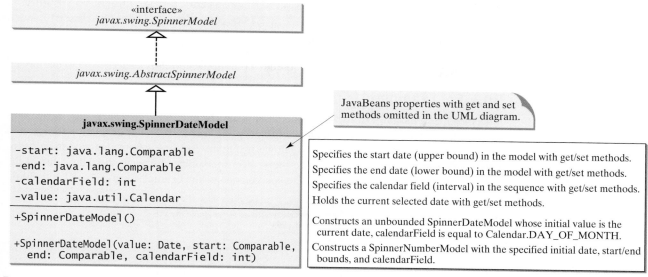

FIGURE 30.13 `SpinnerDateModel` represents a sequence of dates.

The `start` and `end` properties can be `null` to indicate that the sequence has no lower or upper limit. The value of the `calendarField` property must be one of the `java.util.Calendar` constants that specify a field within a Calendar. The `getNextValue` and `getPreviousValue` methods change the date forward or backward by this amount. For example, if `calendarField` is `Calendar.DAY_OF_WEEK`, then `nextValue` produces a date that is twenty-four hours after the current value, and `previousValue` produces a date that is twenty-four hours earlier.

For example, the following code creates a spinner model that represents a sequence of dates, starting from the current date without a lower or upper limit and with calendar field on month.

```
SpinnerDateModel model = new SpinnerDateModel(
  new Date(), null, null, Calendar.MONTH);
```

30.6.4 Spinner Editors

A `JSpinner` has a single child component, called the *editor*, which is responsible for displaying the current element or value of the model. Four editors are defined as static inner classes inside `JSpinner`.

- `JSpinner.DefaultEditor` is a simple base class for all other specialized editors to display a read-only view of the model's current value with a `JFormatted-TextField`. `JFormattedTextField` extends `JTextField` adding support for formatting arbitrary values, as well as retrieving a particular object once the user has edited the text.

- `JSpinner.NumberEditor` is a specialized editor for a `JSpinner` whose model is a `SpinnerNumberModel`. The value of the editor is displayed with a `JFormatted-TextField` whose format is defined by a `NumberFormatter` instance.

- `JSpinner.DateEditor` is a specialized editor for a `JSpinner` whose model is a `SpinnerDateModel`. The value of the editor is displayed with a `JFormatted-TextField` whose format is defined by a `DateFormatter` instance.

- `JSpinner.ListEditor` is a specialized editor for a `JSpinner` whose model is a `SpinnerListModel`. The value of the editor is displayed with a `JFormatted-TextField`.

The **JSpinner**'s constructor creates a **NumberEditor** for **SpinnerNumberModel**, a **DateEditor** for **SpinnerDateModel**, a **ListEditor** for **SpinnerListModel**, and a **DefaultEditor** for all other models. The editor can also be changed using the **setEditor** method. The **JSpinner**'s editor stays in sync with the model by listening for **ChangeEvent**s. The **commitEdit()** method should be used to commit the currently edited value to the model.

30.6.5 Example: Using Spinner Models and Editors

This example uses a **JSpinner** component to display the date and three other **JSpinner** components to display the day in a sequence of numbers, the month in a sequence of strings, and the year in a sequence of numbers, as shown in Figure 30.14. All four components are synchronized. For example, if you change the year in the spinner for year, the date value in the date spinner is updated accordingly. The source code of the example is given in Listing 30.6.

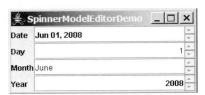

FIGURE 30.14 The four spinner components are synchronized to display the date in one field and the day, month, and year in three separate fields.

LISTING 30.6 SpinnerModelEditorDemo.java

```java
1  import javax.swing.*;
2  import javax.swing.event.*;
3  import java.util.*;
4  import java.text.*;
5  import java.awt.*;
6
7  public class SpinnerModelEditorDemo extends JApplet {
8    // Create four spinners for date, day, month, and year
9    private JSpinner spinnerDate =
10     new JSpinner(new SpinnerDateModel());
11   private JSpinner spinnerDay =
12     new JSpinner(new SpinnerNumberModel(1, 1, 31, 1));
13   private String[] monthNames = new DateFormatSymbols().getMonths();
14   private JSpinner spinnerMonth = new JSpinner
15     (new SpinnerListModel(Arrays.asList(monthNames).subList(0, 12)));
16   private JSpinner spinnerYear =
17     new JSpinner(new SpinnerNumberModel(2004, 1, 3000, 1));
18
19   public SpinnerModelEditorDemo() {
20     // Group labels
21     JPanel panel1 = new JPanel();
22     panel1.setLayout(new GridLayout(4, 1));
23     panel1.add(new JLabel("Date"));
24     panel1.add(new JLabel("Day"));
25     panel1.add(new JLabel("Month"));
26     panel1.add(new JLabel("Year"));
27
28     // Group spinners
29     JPanel panel2 = new JPanel();
30     panel2.setLayout(new GridLayout(4, 1));
31     panel2.add(spinnerDate);
32     panel2.add(spinnerDay);
33     panel2.add(spinnerMonth);
```

spinners (margin note at lines 9)

create UI (margin note at line 20)

```
34      panel2.add(spinnerYear);
35
36      // Add spinner and label to the UI
37      add(panel1, BorderLayout.WEST);
38      add(panel2, BorderLayout.CENTER);
39
40      // Set editor for date
41      JSpinner.DateEditor dateEditor =
42        new JSpinner.DateEditor(spinnerDate, "MMM dd, yyyy");
43      spinnerDate.setEditor(dateEditor);
44
45      // Set editor for year
46      JSpinner.NumberEditor yearEditor =
47        new JSpinner.NumberEditor(spinnerYear, "####");
48      spinnerYear.setEditor(yearEditor);
49
50      // Update date to synchronize with the day, month, and year
51      updateDate();
52
53      // Register and create a listener for spinnerDay
54      spinnerDay.addChangeListener(new ChangeListener() {
55        public void stateChanged(javax.swing.event.ChangeEvent e) {
56          updateDate();
57        }
58      });
59
60      // Register and create a listener for spinnerMonth
61      spinnerDay.addChangeListener(new ChangeListener() {
62        public void stateChanged(javax.swing.event.ChangeEvent e) {
63          updateDate();
64        }
65      });
66
67      // Register and create a listener for spinnerYear
68      spinnerMonth.addChangeListener(new ChangeListener() {
69        public void stateChanged(javax.swing.event.ChangeEvent e) {
70          updateDate();
71        }
72      });
73    }
74
75    // Update date spinner to synchronize with the other three spinners
76    private void updateDate() {
77      // Get current month and year in int
78      int month = ((SpinnerListModel)spinnerMonth.getModel()).
79         getList().indexOf(spinnerMonth.getValue());
80      int year = ((Integer)spinnerYear.getValue()).intValue();
81
82      // Set a new maximum number of days for the new month and year
83      SpinnerNumberModel numberModel =
84        (SpinnerNumberModel)spinnerDay.getModel();
85      numberModel.setMaximum(new Integer(maxDaysInMonth(year, month)));
86
87      // Set a new current day if it exceeds the maximum
88      if (((Integer)(numberModel.getValue())).intValue() >
89         maxDaysInMonth(year, month))
90       numberModel.setValue(new Integer(maxDaysInMonth(year, month)));
91
92      // Get the current day
93      int day = ((Integer)spinnerDay.getValue()).intValue();
```

spinner listener

spinner listener

spinner listener

```
94
95      // Set a new date in the date spinner
96      spinnerDate.setValue(
97        new GregorianCalendar(year, month, day).getTime());
98    }
99
100   /** Return the maximum number of days in a month. For example,
101      Feb 2004 has 29 days. */
102   private int maxDaysInMonth(int year, int month) {
103     Calendar calendar = new GregorianCalendar(year, month, 1);
104     return calendar.getActualMaximum(Calendar.DAY_OF_MONTH);
105   }
106 }
```

main omitted

A `JSpinner` object for dates, `spinnerDate`, is created with a default `SpinnerDateModel` (lines 9–10). The format of the date displayed in the spinner is MMM dd, yyyy (e.g., Feb 01, 2006). This format is created using the `JSpinner`'s inner class constructor `DateEditor` (lines 41–42) and is set as `spinnerDate`'s editor (line 43).

A `JSpinner` object for days, `spinnerDay`, is created with a `SpinnerNumberModel` with a sequence of integers between `1` and `31` in which the initial value is `1` and the interval is `1` (lines 11–12). The maximum number is reset in the `updateDate()` method based on the current month and year (lines 88–90). For example, February 2004 has twenty-nine days, so the maximum in `spinnerDay` is set to 29 for February 2004.

A `JSpinner` object for months, `spinnerMonth`, is created with a `SpinnerListModel` with a list of month names (lines 14–15). Month names are locale-specific and can be obtained using the `new DateFormatSymbols().getMonths()` (line 13). Some calendars can have thirteen months. `Arrays.asList(monthNames)` creates a list from an array of strings, and `subList(0, 12)` returns the first twelve elements in the list.

A `JSpinner` object for years, `spinnerYear`, is created with a `SpinnerNumberModel` with a sequence of integers between `1` and `3000` in which the initial value is 2004 and the interval is `1` (lines 16–17). By default, locale-specific number separators are used. For example, 2004 would be displayed as 2,004 in the spinner. To display the number without separators, the number pattern #### is specified to construct a new `NumberEditor` for `spinnerYear` (lines 46–47). The editor is set as `spinnerYear`'s editor (line 48).

The `updateDate()` method synchronizes the date spinner with the day, month, and year spinners. Whenever a new value is selected in the day, month, or year spinner, a new date is set in the date spinner. The `maxDaysInMonth` method (lines 102–105) returns the maximum number of days in a month. For example, February 2004 has twenty nine days.

A `JSpinner` object can fire `javax.swing.event.ChangeEvent` to notify the listeners of the state change in the spinner. The anonymous event adapters are created to process spinner state changes for the day, month, and year spinners (lines 53–72). Whenever a new value is selected in one of these three spinners, the date spinner value is updated accordingly. In Exercise 30.3, you will improve the example to synchronize the day, month, and year spinners with the date spinner. Then, when a new value is selected in the date spinner, the values in the day, month, and year spinners will be updated accordingly.

This example uses `SpinnerNumberModel`, `SpinnerDateModel`, and `SpinnerList-Model`. They are predefined concrete spinner models in the API. You can also create custom spinner models (see Exercise 30.4).

30.7 JList

The basic features of `JList` were introduced in §15.9, "Lists," without using list models. You learned how to create a list and how to respond to list selections. However, you cannot add or remove elements from a list without using list models. This section introduces list models and gives a detailed discussion on how to use `JList`.

JList has two supporting models: a list model and a list-selection model. The *list model* is for storing and processing data. The *list-selection model* is for selecting items. By default, items are rendered as strings or icons. You can also create a custom renderer implementing the **ListCellRenderer** interface. The relationship of these interfaces and classes is shown in Figure 30.15.

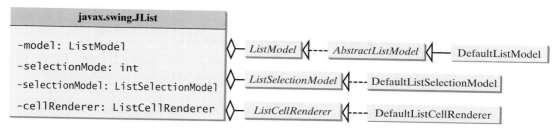

FIGURE 30.15 **JList** contains several supporting interfaces and classes.

30.7.1 **JList** Constructors, Properties, and Methods

Figure 30.16 shows the properties and constructors of **JList**. You can create a list from a list model, an array of objects, or a vector.

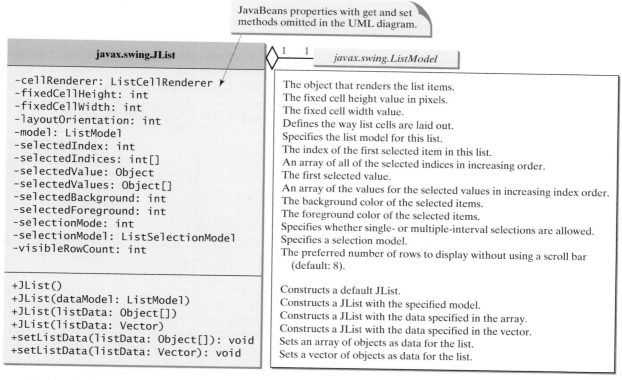

FIGURE 30.16 **JList** displays elements in a list.

30.7.2 List Layout Orientations

The **layoutOrientation** property, introduced in JDK 1.4, specifies the layout of the items using one of the following three values:

- **JList.VERTICAL** specifies that the cells should be laid out vertically in one column. This is the default value.

- **JList.HORIZONTAL_WRAP** specifies that the cells should be laid out horizontally, wrapping to a new row as necessary. The number of rows to use is determined by the **visibleRowCount** property if its value is greater than **0**; otherwise the number of rows is determined by the width of the **JList**.

- **JList.VERTICAL_WRAP** specifies that the cells should be laid out vertically, wrapping to a new column as necessary. The number of rows to use is determined by the **visibleRowCount** property if its value is greater than **0**; otherwise the number of rows is determined by the height of the **JList**.

For example, suppose there are five elements (item1, item2, item3, item4, and item5) in the list and the **visibleRowCount** is **2**. Figure 30.17 shows the layout in these three cases.

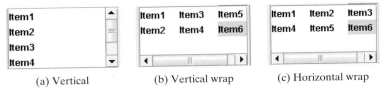

(a) Vertical   (b) Vertical wrap   (c) Horizontal wrap

FIGURE 30.17 Layout orientation specifies how elements are laid out in a list.

30.7.3 List-Selection Modes and List-Selection Models

The **selectionMode** property is one of the three values (**SINGLE_SELECTION**, **SINGLE_INTERVAL_SELECTION**, **MULTIPLE_INTERVAL_SELECTION**) that indicate whether a single item, single-interval item, or multiple-interval item can be selected, as shown in Figure 30.18. Single selection allows only one item to be selected. Single-interval selection allows multiple selections, but the selected items must be contiguous. These items can be selected all together by holding down the SHIFT key. Multiple-interval selection allows selections of multiple contiguous items without restrictions. These items can be selected by holding down the CTRL key. The default value is **MULTIPLE_INTERVAL_SELECTION**.

(a) Single-Selection   (b) Single-Interval Selection   (c) Multiple-Interval Selection

FIGURE 30.18 A list has three selection modes.

The **selectionModel** property specifies an object that tracks list selection. **JList** has two models: a list model and a list-selection model. *List models* handle data management, and *list-selection models* deal with data selection. A list-selection model must implement the **ListSelectionModel** interface, which defines constants for three selection modes (**SINGLE_SELECTION**, **SINGLE_INTERVAL_SELECTION**, and **MULTIPLE_INTERVAL_SELECTION**), and registration methods for **ListSectionListener**. It also defines the methods for adding and removing selection intervals, and the access methods for the properties, such as **selectionMode**, **anchorSelectionIndex**, **leadSelectionIndex**, and **valueIsAdjusting**.

By default, an instance of **JList** uses **DefaultListSelectionModel**, which is a concrete implementation of **ListSelectionModel**. Usually, you do not need to provide a custom list-selection model, because the **DefaultListSelectionModel** class is sufficient in most cases. List-selection models are rarely used explicitly, because you can set the selection mode directly in **JList**.

30.7.4 Example: List Properties Demo

This example creates a list of a fixed number of items displayed as strings. The example enables you to dynamically set `visibleRowCount` from a spinner, `layoutOrientation` from a combo box, and `selectionMode` from a combo box, as shown in Figure 30.19. When you select one or more items, their values are displayed in a status label below the list. The source code of the example is given in Listing 30.7.

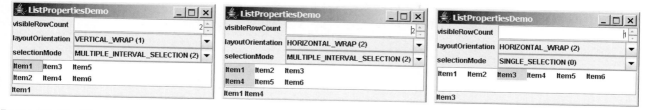

FIGURE 30.19 You can dynamically set the properties for `visibleRowCount`, `layoutOrientation`, and `selectionMode` in a list.

LISTING 30.7 ListPropertiesDemo.java

```java
 1 import java.awt.*;
 2 import java.awt.event.*;
 3 import javax.swing.*;
 4 import javax.swing.event.*;
 5
 6 public class ListPropertiesDemo extends JApplet {
 7   private JList jlst = new JList(new String[] {"Item1",          // list
 8     "Item2", "Item3", "Item4", "Item5", "Item6"});
 9   private JSpinner jspinnerVisibleRowCount =                      // spinner
10     new JSpinner(new SpinnerNumberModel(8, -1, 20, 1));
11   private JComboBox jcboLayoutOrientation =                       // combo box
12     new JComboBox(new String[]{"VERTICAL (0)",
13       "VERTICAL_WRAP (1)", "HORIZONTAL_WRAP (2)"});
14   private JComboBox jcboSelectionMode =                           // combo box
15     new JComboBox(new String[]{"SINGLE_SELECTION (0)",
16       "SINGLE_INTERVAL_SELECTION (1)",
17       "MULTIPLE_INTERVAL_SELECTION (2)"});
18   private JLabel jlblStatus = new JLabel();
19
20   /** Construct the applet */
21   public ListPropertiesDemo() {
22     // Place labels in a panel
23     JPanel panel1 = new JPanel();                                 // create UI
24     panel1.setLayout(new GridLayout(3, 1));
25     panel1.add(new JLabel("visibleRowCount"));
26     panel1.add(new JLabel("layoutOrientation"));
27     panel1.add(new JLabel("selectionMode"));
28
29     // Place text fields in a panel
30     JPanel panel2 = new JPanel();
31     panel2.setLayout(new GridLayout(3, 1));
32     panel2.add(jspinnerVisibleRowCount);
33     panel2.add(jcboLayoutOrientation);
34     panel2.add(jcboSelectionMode);
35
36     // Place panel1 and panel2
37     JPanel panel3 = new JPanel();
38     panel3.setLayout(new BorderLayout(5, 5));
```

```
39        panel3.add(panel1, BorderLayout.WEST);
40        panel3.add(panel2, BorderLayout.CENTER);
41
42        // Place elements in the applet
43        add(panel3, BorderLayout.NORTH);
44        add(new JScrollPane(jlst), BorderLayout.CENTER);
45        add(jlblStatus, BorderLayout.SOUTH);
46
47        // Set initial property values
48        jlst.setFixedCellWidth(50);
49        jlst.setFixedCellHeight(20);
50        jlst.setSelectionMode(ListSelectionModel.SINGLE_SELECTION);
51
52        // Register listeners
53        jspinnerVisibleRowCount.addChangeListener(new ChangeListener() {
54          public void stateChanged(ChangeEvent e) {
55            jlst.setVisibleRowCount(
56              ((Integer)jspinnerVisibleRowCount.getValue()).intValue());
57          }
58        });
59
60        jcboLayoutOrientation.addActionListener(new ActionListener() {
61          public void actionPerformed(ActionEvent e) {
62            jlst.setLayoutOrientation(
63              jcboLayoutOrientation.getSelectedIndex());
64          }
65        });
66
67        jcboSelectionMode.addActionListener(new ActionListener() {
68          public void actionPerformed(ActionEvent e) {
69            jlst.setSelectionMode(
70              jcboSelectionMode.getSelectedIndex());
71          }
72        });
73
74        jlst.addListSelectionListener(new ListSelectionListener() {
75          public void valueChanged(ListSelectionEvent e) {
76            Object[] values = jlst.getSelectedValues();
77            String display = " ";
78
79            for (int i = 0; i < values.length; i++) {
80              display += (String)values[i] + " ";
81            }
82
83            jlblStatus.setText(display);
84          }
85        });
86      }
87 }
```

Labels in the left margin:
- spinner listener (line 53)
- combo box listener (line 60)
- combo box listener (line 67)
- list listener (line 74)
- **main** omitted (line 87)

A `JList` is created with six string values (lines 7–8). A `JSpinner` is created using a `SpinnerNumberModel` with initial value 8, minimum value –1, maximum value 20, and step 1 (lines 9–10). A `JComboBox` is created with string values `VERTICAL` (0), `VERTICAL_WRAP` (1), and `HORIZONTAL_WRAP` (2) for choosing layout orientation (lines 11–13). A `JComboBox` is created with string values `SINGLE_SELECTION` (0), `INTERVAL_SELECTION` (1), and `MULTIPLE_INTERVAL_SELECTION` (2) for choosing a selection mode (lines 14–17). A `JLabel` is created to display the selected elements in the list (lines 18).

A `JList` does not support scrolling. To create a scrollable list, create a `JScrollPane` and add an instance of `JList` to it (line 44).

The fixed list cell width and height are specified in lines 48–49. The default selection mode is multiple-interval selection. Line 50 sets the selection mode to single selection.

When a new visible row count is selected from the spinner, the `setVisibleRowCount` method is used to set the count (lines 53–58). When a new layout orientation is selected from the `jcboLayoutOrientation` combo box, the `setLayoutOrientation` method is used to set the layout orientation (lines 60–65). Note that the constant values for `VERTICAL`, `VERTICAL_WRAP`, and `HORIZONTAL_WRAP` are `0`, `1`, and `2`, which correspond to the index values of these items in the combo box. When a new selection mode is selected from the `jcboSelectionMode` combo box, the `setSelectionMode` method is used to set the selection mode (lines 67–72). Note that the constant values for `SINGLE_SELECTION`, `SINGLE_INTERVAL_SELECTION`, and `MULTIPLE_INTERVAL_SELECTION` are `0`, `1`, and `2`, which correspond to the index values of these items in the combo box.

`JList` generates `javax.swing.event.ListSelectionEvent` to notify the listeners of the selections. The listener must implement the `valueChanged` handler to process the event. When the user selects an item in the list, the `valueChanged` handler is executed, which gets the selected items and displays all the items in the label (lines 74–85).

30.8 List Models

The preceding example constructs a list with a fixed set of strings. If you want to add new items to the list or delete existing items, you have to use a list model. This section introduces list models.

The `JList` class delegates the responsibilities of storing and maintaining data to its data model. The `JList` class itself does not have methods for adding or removing items from the list. These methods are supported in `ListModel`, as shown in Figure 30.20.

All list models implement the `ListModel` interface, which defines the registration methods for `ListDataEvent`. The instances of `ListDataListener` are notified when the items in the list are modified. `ListModel` also defines the methods `getSize` and `getElementAt`. The `getSize` method returns the length of the list, and the `getElementAt` method returns the element at the specified index.

`AbstractListModel` implements the `ListModel` and `Serializable` interfaces. `AbstractListModel` implements the registration methods in `ListModel`, but does not implement the `getSize` and `getElementAt` methods.

`DefaultListModel` extends `AbstractListModel` and implements the two methods `getSize` and `getElementAt`, which are not implemented by `AbstractListModel`.

The methods in `DefaultListModel` are similar to those in the `java.util.Vector` class. You use the `add` method to insert an element to the list, the `remove` method to remove an element from the list, the `clear` method to clear the list, the `getSize` method to return the number of elements in the list, and the `getElementAt` method to retrieve an element. In fact, the `DefaultListModel` stores data in an instance of `Vector`, which is essentially a resizable array. Swing components were developed before the Java Collections Framework. In future implementations, `Vector` may be replaced by `java.util.ArrayList`.

Note

In most cases, if you create a Swing GUI object without specifying a model, an instance of the default model class is created. But this is not true for `JList`. By default, the `model` property in `JList` is not an instance of `DefaultListModel`. To use a list model, you should explicitly create one using `DefaultListModel`.

default list model

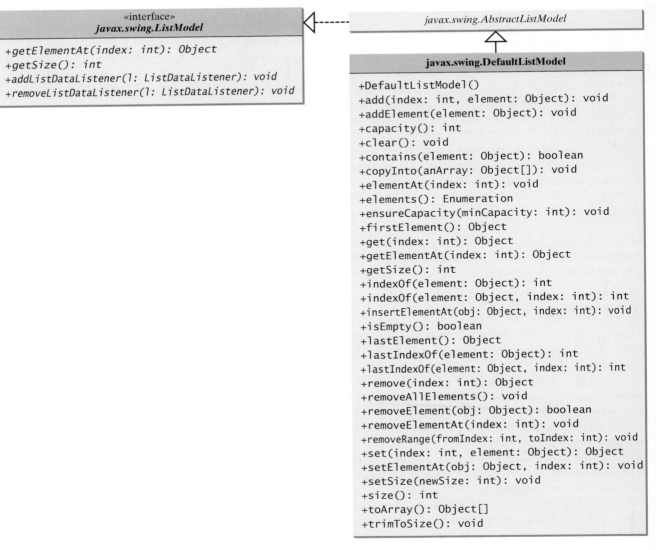

FIGURE 30.20 `ListModel` stores and manages data in a list.

Listing 30.8 gives an example that creates a list using a list model and allows the user to add and delete items in the list, as shown in Figure 30.21. When the user clicks the *Add new item* button, an input dialog box is displayed to receive a new item.

FIGURE 30.21 You can add elements and remove elements in a list using list models.

LISTING 30.8 `ListModelDemo.java`

```java
 1 import java.awt.*;
 2 import java.awt.event.*;
 3 import javax.swing.*;
 4
 5 public class ListModelDemo extends JApplet {
 6   private DefaultListModel listModel = new DefaultListModel();
 7   private JList jlst = new JList(listModel);
 8   private JButton jbtAdd = new JButton("Add new item");
 9   private JButton jbtRemove = new JButton("Remove selected item");
10
11   /** Construct the applet */
12   public ListModelDemo() {
13     // Add items to the list model
14     listModel.addElement("Item1");
15     listModel.addElement("Item2");
16     listModel.addElement("Item3");
17     listModel.addElement("Item4");
18     listModel.addElement("Item5");
19     listModel.addElement("Item6");
20
21     JPanel panel = new JPanel();
22     panel.add(jbtAdd);
23     panel.add(jbtRemove);
24
25     add(panel, BorderLayout.NORTH);
26     add(new JScrollPane(jlst), BorderLayout.CENTER);
27
28     // Register listeners
29     jbtAdd.addActionListener(new ActionListener() {
30       public void actionPerformed(ActionEvent e) {
31         String newItem =
32           JOptionPane.showInputDialog("Enter a new item");
33
34         if (newItem != null)
35           if (jlst.getSelectedIndex() == -1)
36             listModel.addElement(newItem);
37           else
38             listModel.add(jlst.getSelectedIndex(), newItem);
39       }
40     });
41
42     jbtRemove.addActionListener(new ActionListener() {
43       public void actionPerformed(ActionEvent e) {
44         listModel.remove(jlst.getSelectedIndex());
45       }
46     });
47   }
48 }
```

list model
list

add items

button listener

button listener

main omitted

The program creates `listModel` (line 6), which is an instance of `DefaultListModel`, and uses it to manipulate data in the list. The model enables you to add and remove items in the list.

A list is created from the list model (line 7). The initial elements are added into the model using the `addElement` method (lines 14–19).

To add an element, the user clicks the *Add new item* button to display an input dialog box. Type a new item in the dialog box. The new item is inserted before the currently selected element in the list (line 38). If no element is selected, the new element is appended to the list (line 36).

To remove an element, the user has to select the element and then click the *Remove select-ed item* button. Note that only the first selected item is removed. You can modify the program to remove all the selected items (see Exercise 30.6).

What would happen if you click the *Remove selected item* button but no items are currently selected? This would cause an error. To fix it, see Exercise 30.6.

30.9 List Cell Renderer

The preceding example displays items as strings in a list. JList is very flexible and versa-tile, and it can be used to display images and GUI components in addition to simple text. This section introduces list cell renderers for displaying graphics.

In addition to delegating data storage and processing to list models, JList delegates the ren-dering of list cells to list cell renderers. All list cell renderers implement the ListCellRenderer interface, which defines a single method, getListCellRendererComponent, as follows:

```
public Component getListCellRendererComponent
    (JList list, Object value, int index, boolean isSelected,
    boolean cellHasFocus)
```

This method is passed with a list, the value associated with the cell, the index of the value, and information regarding whether the value is selected and whether the cell has the focus. The component returned from the method is painted on the cell in the list. By default, JList uses DefaultListCellRenderer to render its cells. The DefaultListCellRenderer class implements ListCellRenderer, extends JLabel, and can display either a string or an icon, but not both in the same cell.

For example, you can use JList's default cell renderer to display strings, as shown in Figure 30.22(a), using the following code:

```
JList list = new JList(new String[]{"Denmark", "Germany",
    "China", "India", "Norway", "UK", "US"});
```

You can use JList's default cell renderer to display icons, as shown in Figure 30.22(b), using the following code:

```
ImageIcon denmarkIcon = new ImageIcon(getClass().getResource(
    "image/denmarkIcon.gif"));
...
JList list = new JList(new ImageIcon[]{denmarkIcon, germanyIcon,
    chinaIcon, indiaIcon, norwayIcon, ukIcon, usIcon});
```

How do you display a string along with an icon in one cell, as shown in Figure 30.22(c)? You need to create a custom renderer by implementing ListCellRenderer, as shown in Figure 30.23.

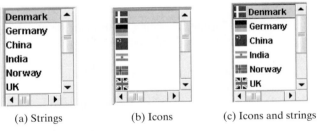

(a) Strings   (b) Icons   (c) Icons and strings

FIGURE 30.22   The cell renderer displays list items in a list.

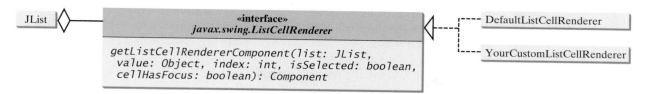

FIGURE 30.23 ListCellRenderer defines how cells are rendered in a list.

Suppose a list is created as follows:

```
JList list = new JList(new Object[][][]{{denmarkIcon, "Denmark"},
  {germanyIcon, "Germany"}, {chinaIcon, "China"},
  {indiaIcon, "India"}, {norwayIcon, "Norway"}, {ukIcon, "UK"},
  {usIcon, "US"}});
```

Each item in the list is an array that consists of an icon and a string. You can create a custom cell renderer that retrieves an icon and a string from the list data model and displays them in a label. The custom cell renderer class is given in Listing 30.9.

LISTING 30.9 MyListCellRenderer.java

```
 1  import java.awt.*;
 2  import javax.swing.*;
 3  import javax.swing.border.*;
 4
 5  public class MyListCellRenderer implements ListCellRenderer {
 6    private JLabel jlblCell = new JLabel(" ", JLabel.LEFT);          cell component
 7    private Border lineBorder =
 8      BorderFactory.createLineBorder(Color.black, 1);
 9    private Border emptyBorder =
10      BorderFactory.createEmptyBorder(2, 2, 2, 2);
11
12    /** Implement this method in ListCellRenderer */
13    public Component getListCellRendererComponent
14      (JList list, Object value, int index, boolean isSelected,
15      boolean cellHasFocus) {
16      Object[] pair = (Object[])value; // Cast value into an array
17      jlblCell.setOpaque(true);
18      jlblCell.setIcon((ImageIcon)pair[0]);                          set icon
19      jlblCell.setText(pair[1].toString());                         set text
20
21      if (isSelected) {
22        jlblCell.setForeground(list.getSelectionForeground());     cell selected
23        jlblCell.setBackground(list.getSelectionBackground());
24      }
25      else {
26        jlblCell.setForeground(list.getForeground());
27        jlblCell.setBackground(list.getBackground());
28      }
29
30      jlblCell.setBorder(cellHasFocus ? lineBorder : emptyBorder);
31
32      return jlblCell;                                              return rendering cell
33    }
34  }
```

The MyListCellRenderer class implements the getListCellRendererComponent method in the ListCellRenderer interface. This method is passed with the parameters list, value, index, isSelected, and isFocused (lines 13–15). The value represents the current item value. In this case, it is an array consisting of two elements. The first element is an image icon (line 18). The second element is a string (line 19). Both image icon and string are displayed on a label. The `getListCellRendererComponent` method returns the label (line 32), which is painted on the cell in the list.

If the cell is selected, the background and foreground of the cell are set to the list's selection background and foreground (lines 22–23). If the cell is focused, the cell's border is set to the line border (line 30); otherwise, it is set to the empty border (line 39). The empty border serves as a divider between the cells.

Note

any GUI renderer

The example in Listing 30.9 uses a `JLabel` as a renderer. You may use any GUI component as a renderer, returned from the `getListCellRendererComponent` method.

Let us develop an example that creates a list of countries and displays the flag image and name for each country as one item in the list, as shown in Figure 30.24. When a country is selected in the list, its flag is displayed in a label next to the list.

small icon ——

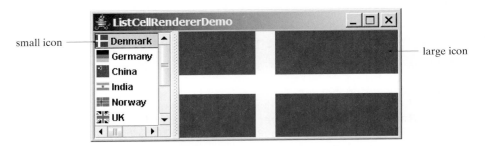

large icon

FIGURE 30.24 The image and the text are displayed in the list cell.

Two types of icons are used in this program. The small icons are created from files `flagIcon0.gif`, ..., `flagIcon6.gif` (lines 31–32). The small icons are rendered inside the list. The large icons are created from files `flag0.gif`, ..., `flag6.gif` (lines 35–36) and are displayed on a label on the right side of the split pane. Listing 30.10 gives the program.

LISTING 30.10 `ListCellRendererDemo.java`

```
 1  import javax.swing.*;
 2  import javax.swing.event.*;
 3  import java.awt.*;
 4
 5  public class ListCellRendererDemo extends JApplet {
 6    private final static int NUMBER_OF_NATIONS = 7;
 7    private String[] nations = new String[]
 8      {"Denmark", "Germany", "China", "India", "Norway", "UK", "US"};
 9    private ImageIcon[] icons = new ImageIcon[NUMBER_OF_NATIONS];
10    private ImageIcon[] bigIcons = new ImageIcon[NUMBER_OF_NATIONS];
11
12    // Create a list model
13    private DefaultListModel listModel = new DefaultListModel();
14
15    // Create a list using the list model
16    private JList jlstNations = new JList(listModel);
17
18    // Create a list cell renderer
19    private ListCellRenderer renderer = new MyListCellRenderer();
20
21    // Create a split pane
22    private JSplitPane jSplitPane1 = new JSplitPane();
23
```

nation strings

small icons
big icons

list model

list

list cell renderer

split pane

```
24    // Create a label for displaying image
25    private JLabel jlblImage = new JLabel("", JLabel.CENTER);          image label
26
27    /** Construct ListCellRenderer */
28    public ListCellRendererDemo() {
29      // Load small and large image icons
30      for (int i = 0; i < NUMBER_OF_NATIONS; i++) {
31        icons[i] = new ImageIcon(getClass().getResource(             load image icons
32          "image/flagIcon" + i + ".gif"));
33        listModel.addElement(new Object[]{icons[i], nations[i]});     add elements
34
35        bigIcons[i] = new ImageIcon(getClass().getResource(          load image icons
36          "image/flag" + i + ".gif"));
37      }
38
39      // Set list cell renderer
40      jlstNations.setCellRenderer(renderer);                          set renderer
41      jlstNations.setPreferredSize(new Dimension(200, 200));
42      jSplitPane1.setLeftComponent(new JScrollPane(jlstNations));
43      jSplitPane1.setRightComponent(jlblImage);
44      jlstNations.setSelectedIndex(0);
45      jlblImage.setIcon(bigIcons[0]);
46      add(jSplitPane1, BorderLayout.CENTER);
47
48      // Register listener
49      jlstNations.addListSelectionListener(new ListSelectionListener() {   list listener
50        public void valueChanged(ListSelectionEvent e) {
51          jlblImage.setIcon(bigIcons[jlstNations.getSelectedIndex()]);
52        }
53      });
54    }
55 }
                                                                        main omitted
```

Two types of icons are used in this program. The small icons are created from files `flagIcon0.gif`, ..., `flagIcon6.gif` (lines 31–32). These image files are the flags for Denmark, Germany, China, India, Norway, UK, and US. The small icons are rendered inside the list. The large icons for the same countries are created from files `flag0.gif`, ..., `flag6.gif` (lines 35–36) and are displayed on a label on the right side of the split pane.

The `ListCellRendererDemo` class creates a list model (line 13) and adds the items to the model (line 33). Each item is an array of two elements (image icon and string). The list is created using the list model (line 16). The list cell renderer is created (line 19) and associated with the list (line 40).

The `ListCellRendererDemo` class creates a split pane (line 22) and places the list on the left (line 42) and a label on the right (line 43).

When you choose a country in the list, the list-selection event handler is invoked (lines 49–53) to set a new image to the label in the right side of the split pane (line 51).

30.10 JComboBox

The basic features of `JComboBox` were introduced in §15.8, "Combo Boxes," without using combo box models. This section introduces combo models and discusses the use of `JComboBox` in some detail.

A combo box is similar to a list. Combo boxes and lists are both used for selecting items from a list. A combo box allows the user to select one item at a time, whereas a list permits multiple selections. A combo box displays a drop-down list contained in a popup menu when the combo box is selected. The selected item can be edited in the cell as if it were a text field. Figure 30.25 shows the properties and constructors of `JComboBox`. The data for a combo box

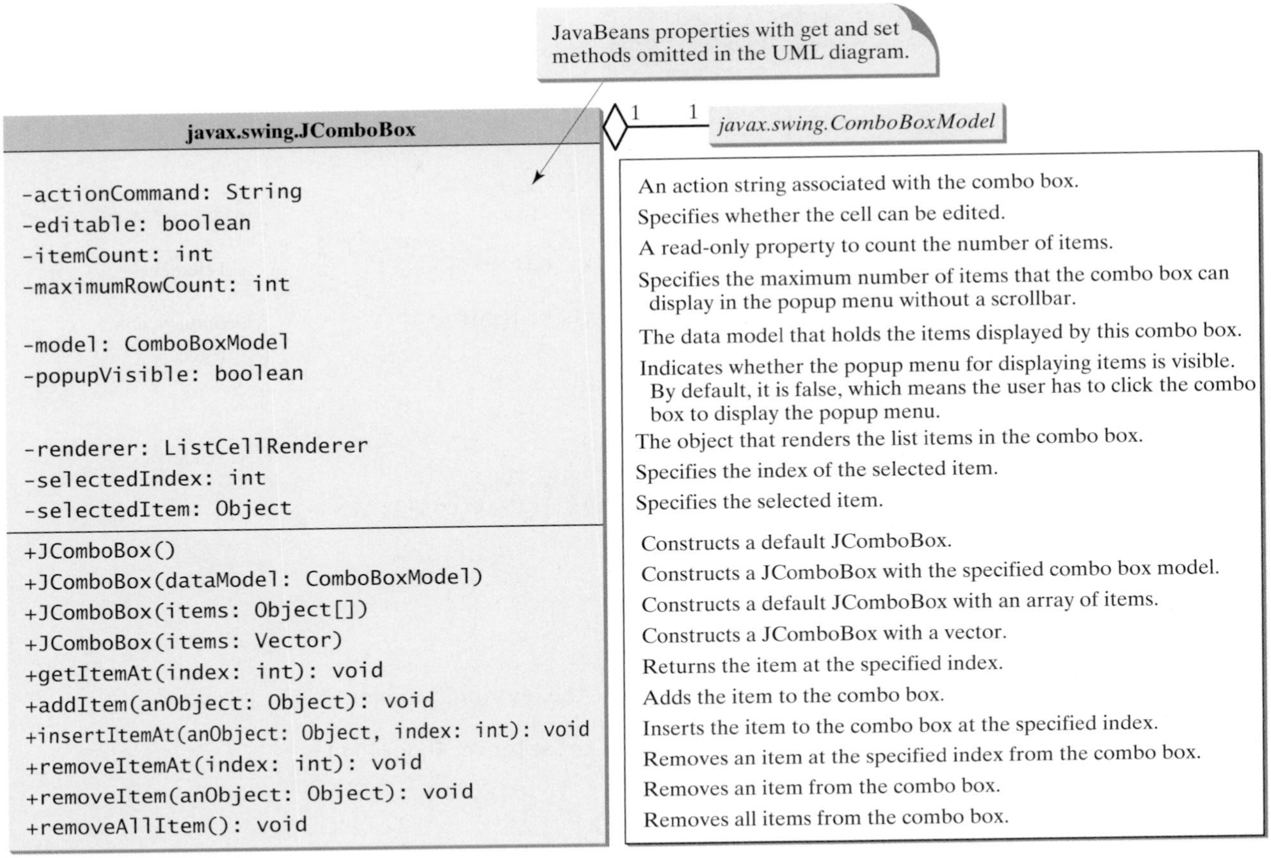

JavaBeans properties with get and set methods omitted in the UML diagram.

javax.swing.JComboBox	1 1	javax.swing.ComboBoxModel

```
-actionCommand: String
-editable: boolean
-itemCount: int
-maximumRowCount: int

-model: ComboBoxModel
-popupVisible: boolean


-renderer: ListCellRenderer
-selectedIndex: int
-selectedItem: Object
```

An action string associated with the combo box.

Specifies whether the cell can be edited.

A read-only property to count the number of items.

Specifies the maximum number of items that the combo box can display in the popup menu without a scrollbar.

The data model that holds the items displayed by this combo box.

Indicates whether the popup menu for displaying items is visible. By default, it is false, which means the user has to click the combo box to display the popup menu.

The object that renders the list items in the combo box.

Specifies the index of the selected item.

Specifies the selected item.

```
+JComboBox()
+JComboBox(dataModel: ComboBoxModel)
+JComboBox(items: Object[])
+JComboBox(items: Vector)
+getItemAt(index: int): void
+addItem(anObject: Object): void
+insertItemAt(anObject: Object, index: int): void
+removeItemAt(index: int): void
+removeItem(anObject: Object): void
+removeAllItem(): void
```

Constructs a default JComboBox.

Constructs a JComboBox with the specified combo box model.

Constructs a default JComboBox with an array of items.

Constructs a JComboBox with a vector.

Returns the item at the specified index.

Adds the item to the combo box.

Inserts the item to the combo box at the specified index.

Removes an item at the specified index from the combo box.

Removes an item from the combo box.

Removes all items from the combo box.

FIGURE 30.25 JComboBox displays elements in a list.

is stored in ComboBoxModel. You can create a combo box from a combo box model, an array of objects, or a vector.

JComboBox delegates the responsibilities of storing and maintaining data to its data model. All combo box models implement the ComboBoxModel interface, which extends the ListModel interface and defines the getSelectedItem and setSelectedItem methods for retrieving and setting a selected item. The methods for adding and removing items are defined in the MutableComboBoxModel interface, which extends ComboBoxModel. When an instance of JComboBox is created without explicitly specifying a model, an instance of DefaultComboBoxModel is used. The DefaultComboBoxModel class extends AbstractListModel and implements MutableComboBoxModel, as shown in Figure 30.26.

Usually you don't need to use combo box models explicitly, because JComboBox contains the methods for retrieving (getItemAt, getSelectedItem, and getSelectedIndex), adding (addItem and insertItemAt), and removing (removeItem, removeItemAt, and removeAllItems) items from the list.

JComboBox can generate ActionEvent and ItemEvent, among many other events. Whenever a new item is selected, JComboBox generates ItemEvent twice, once for deselecting the previously selected item, and the other for selecting the currently selected item. JComboBox generates an ActionEvent after generating an ItemEvent.

Combo boxes render cells exactly like lists, because the combo box items are displayed in a list contained in a popup menu. Therefore, a combo box cell renderer can be created exactly like a list cell renderer by implementing the ListCellRenderer interface. Like JList, JComboBox has a default cell renderer that displays a string or an icon, but not both at the same time. To display a combination of a string and an icon, you need to create a custom

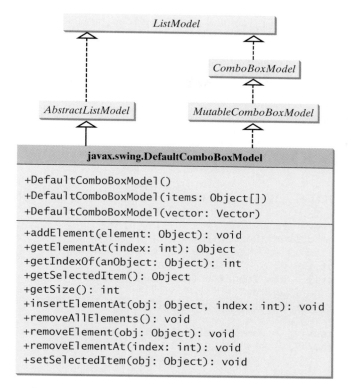

FIGURE 30.26 ComboBoxModel stores and manages data in a combo box.

renderer. The custom list cell renderer **MyListCellRenderer** in Listing 30.9 can be used as a combo box cell renderer without any modification.

Listing 30.11 gives an example that creates a combo box to display the flag image and name for each country as one item in the list, as shown in Figure 30.27. When a country is selected in the list, its flag is displayed in a panel below the combo box.

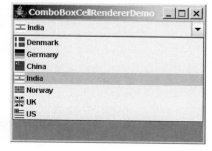

FIGURE 30.27 The image and the text are displayed in the list cell of a combo box.

LISTING 30.11 ComboBoxCellRendererDemo.java

```
1 import java.awt.*;
2 import java.awt.event.*;
3 import javax.swing.*;
4
5 public class ComboBoxCellRendererDemo extends JApplet {
6   private final static int NUMBER_OF_NATIONS = 7;
7   private String[] nations = new String[] {"Denmark",
8     "Germany", "China", "India", "Norway", "UK", "US"};
```

nation strings

small icons
big icons

combo box model

combo box

list cell renderer

image label

load image icons

add elements

load image icons

set renderer

action listener

main omitted

```java
 9    private ImageIcon[] icons = new ImageIcon[NUMBER_OF_NATIONS];
10    private ImageIcon[] bigIcons = new ImageIcon[NUMBER_OF_NATIONS];
11
12    // Create a combo box model
13    private DefaultComboBoxModel model = new DefaultComboBoxModel();
14
15    // Create a combo box with the specified model
16    private JComboBox jcboCountries = new JComboBox(model);
17
18    // Create a list cell renderer
19    private MyListCellRenderer renderer = new MyListCellRenderer();
20
21    // Create a label for displaying image
22    private JLabel jlblImage = new JLabel("", JLabel.CENTER);
23
24    /** Construct the applet */
25    public ComboBoxCellRendererDemo() {
26      // Load small and large image icons
27      for (int i = 0; i < NUMBER_OF_NATIONS; i++) {
28        icons[i] = new ImageIcon(getClass().getResource(
29          "image/flagIcon" + i + ".gif"));
30        model.addElement(new Object[]{icons[i], nations[i]});
31
32        bigIcons[i] = new ImageIcon(getClass().getResource(
33          "image/flag" + i + ".gif"));
34      }
35
36      // Set list cell renderer for the combo box
37      jcboCountries.setRenderer(renderer);
38      jlblImage.setIcon(bigIcons[0]);
39      add(jcboCountries, java.awt.BorderLayout.NORTH);
40      add(jlblImage, java.awt.BorderLayout.CENTER);
41
42      // Register listener
43      jcboCountries.addActionListener(new ActionListener() {
44        public void actionPerformed(java.awt.event.ActionEvent e) {
45          jlblImage.setIcon(bigIcons[jcboCountries.getSelectedIndex()]);
46        }
47      });
48    }
49  }
```

The program is very similar to the preceding example in Listing 30.10. Two types of image icons are loaded for each country and stored in the arrays **icons** and **bigIcons** (lines 27–34). Each item in the combo box is an array that consists of an icon and a string (line 30).

MyListCellRenderer, defined in the preceding example, is used to create a cell renderer in line 19. The cell renderer is plugged into the combo box in line 37.

When you choose a country from the combo box, the action event handler is invoked (lines 44–46). This handler sets a new image on the label (line 45).

KEY TERMS

CHAPTER SUMMARY

■ The fundamental issue in the model-view approach is to ensure consistency between the views and the model. Any change in the model should be notified to the dependent views, and all the views should display the same data consistently. The model can be implemented as a source with appropriate event and event listener registration methods. The view can be implemented as a listener. Thus, if data are changed in the model, the view will be notified.

■ Every Swing user interface component (e.g., `JButton`, `JTextField`, `JList`, and `JComboBox`) has a property named *model* that refers to its data model. The data model is defined in an interface whose name ends with `Model` (e.g., `SpinnerModel`, `ListModel`, `ComboBoxModel`, `TableModel`, and `TreeModel`).

■ Most simple Swing components (e.g., `JButton`, `JTextField`, `JTextArea`) contain some properties of their models, and these properties can be accessed and modified directly from the component without knowing the existence of the model.

■ A `JSpinner` is displayed as a text field with a pair of tiny arrow buttons on its right side that enable the user to select numbers, dates, or values from an ordered sequence. A `JSpinner`'s sequence value is defined by the `SpinnerModel` interface. `AbstractSpinnerModel` is a convenient abstract class that implements `SpinnerModel` and provides the implementation for its registration/deregistration methods. `SpinnerListModel`, `SpinnerNumberModel`, and `SpinnerDateModel` are concrete implementations of `SpinnerModel`. `SpinnerNumberModel` represents a sequence of numbers with properties `maximum`, `minimum`, and `stepSize`. `Spinner-DateModel` represents a sequence of dates. `SpinnerListModel` can store a list of any object values.

■ A `JSpinner` has a single child component, called the *editor*, which is responsible for displaying the current element or value of the model. Four editors are defined as static inner classes inside `JSpinner`: `JSpinner.DefaultEditor`, `JSpinner.NumberEditor`, `JSpinner.DateEditor`, and `JSpinner.ListEditor`.

■ `JList` has two supporting models: a list model and a list-selection model. The *list model* is for storing and processing data. The *list-selection model* is for selecting items. By default, items are rendered as strings or icons. You can also create a custom renderer implementing the `ListCellRenderer` interface.

■ `JComboBox` delegates the responsibilities of storing and maintaining data to its data model. All combo box models implement the `ComboBoxModel` interface, which extends the `ListModel` interface and defines the `getSelectedItem` and `setSelectedItem` methods for retrieving and setting a selected item. The methods for adding and removing items are defined in the `MutableComboBoxModel` interface, which extends `ComboBoxModel`. When an instance of `JComboBox` is created without explicitly specifying a model, an instance of `DefaultComboBoxModel` is used. The `DefaultComboBoxModel` class extends `AbstractListModel` and implements `MutableComboBoxModel`.

■ Combo boxes render cells exactly like lists, because the combo box items are displayed in a list contained in a popup menu. Therefore, a combo box cell renderer can be created exactly like a list cell renderer by implementing the `ListCellRenderer` interface.

REVIEW QUESTIONS

Sections 30.2–30.3

30.1 What is model-view-controller architecture?

30.2 How do you do implement models, views, and controllers?

30.3 What are the variations of MVC architecture?

Section 30.4 Swing Model-View-Controller Architecture

30.4 Does each Swing GUI component (except containers such as `JPanel`) have a property named `model`? Is the type of `model` the same for all the components?

30.5 Does each model interface have a default implementation class? If so, does a Swing component use the default model class if no model is specified?

Sections 30.5–30.6

30.6 If you create a `JSpinner` without specifying a data model, what is the default model?

30.7 What is the internal data structure for storing data in `SpinnerListModel`? How do you convert an array to a list?

Sections 30.7–30.9

30.8 Does `JList` have a method, such as `addItem`, for adding an item to a list? How do you add items to a list? Can `JList` display icons and custom GUI objects in a list? Can a list item be edited? How do you initialize data in a list? How do you specify the maximum number of visible rows in a list without scrolling? How do you specify the height of a list cell? How do you specify the horizontal margin of list cells?

30.9 How do you create a list model? How do you add items to a list model? How do you remove items from a list model?

30.10 What are the three list-selection modes? Can you set the selection modes directly in an instance of `JList`? How do you obtain the selected item(s)?

30.11 How do you create a custom list cell renderer?

30.12 What is the handler for handling the `ListSelectionEvent`?

Section 30.10 JComboBox

30.13 Can multiple items be selected from a combo box? Can a combo box item be edited? How do you specify the maximum number of visible rows in a combo box without scrolling? Can you specify the height of a combo box cell using a method in `JComboBox`? How do you obtain the selected item in a combo box?

30.14 How do you add or remove items from a combo box?

30.15 Why is the cell renderer for a combo box the same as the renderer for a list?

PROGRAMMING EXERCISES

Section 30.2 MVC

30.1****(Creating MVC components) Create a model, named `ChartModel`, which holds data in an array of double elements named `data`, and the names for the data in an array of strings named `dataName`. For example, the enrollment data {200, 40, 50, 100, 40} stored in the array `data` are for {"CS", "Math", "Chem", "Biol", "Phys"} in the array `dataName`. These two properties have their respective get methods, but not individual set methods. Both properties are set together in the `setChartData(String[] newDataName, double[] newData)` method so that they can be displayed properly. Create a view named `PieChart` to present the data in a pie chart, and create a view named `BarChart` to present the data in a bar chart, as shown in Figure 30.28.

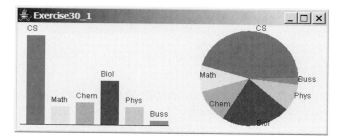

FIGURE 30.28 The two views, `PieChart` and `BarChart`, receive data from the `ChartModel`.

Hint

Each pie represents a percentage of the total data. Color the pie using the colors from an array named colors, which is {`Color.red`, `Color.yellow`, `Color.green`, `Color.blue`, `Color.cyan`, `Color.magenta`, `Color.orange`, `Color.pink`, `Color.darkGray`}. Use `colors[i % colors.length]` for the ith pie. Use black color to display the data names.

30.2* (*Revising Listing 30.3 CircleController.java*) `CircleController` uses a text field to obtain a new radius and a combo box to obtain a Boolean value to specify whether the circle is filled. Add a new row in `CircleController` to let the user choose color using the `JColorChooser` component, as shown in Figure 30.29. The new row consists of a label with text Color, a label to display color, and an eclipse button. The user can click the eclipse button to display a `JColorChooser` dialog box. Once the user selects a color, the color is displayed as the background for the label on the left of the eclipse button.

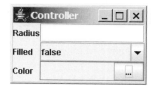 

FIGURE 30.29 Clicking the eclipse button displays the color chooser dialog box for specifying a color.

Sections 30.5–30.6

30.3** (*Synchronizing spinners*) The date spinner is synchronized with the day, month, and year spinners in Listing 30.6, SpinnerModelEditorDemo.java. Improve it to synchronize the day, month, and year spinners with the date spinner. In other words, when a new value is selected in the date spinner, the values in the day, month, and year spinners are updated accordingly.

30.4* (*Custom spinner model*) Develop a custom spinner model that represents a sequence of numbers of power 2, that is, 1, 2, 4, 8, 16, 32, and so on. Your model should implement `AbstractSpinnerModel`. The registration/deregistration methods for `ChangeListener` have already been implemented in `AbstractSpinnerModel`. You need to implement `getNextValue()`, `getPreviousValue()`, `getValue()`, and `setValue(Object)` methods.

30.5* (*Reversing the numbers displayed in a spinner*) The numbers displayed in a spinner increase when the up-arrow button is clicked and decrease when the down-arrow button is clicked. You can reverse the sequence by creating a new model that extends `SpinnerNumberModel` and overrides the `getNextValue` and `getPreviousValue` methods.

Sections 30.7–30.9

30.6* (*Removing selected items in a list*) Modify Listing 30.8, ListModelDemo.java, to meet the following requirements:

- Remove all the selected items from the list when the *Remove selected item* button is clicked.
- Enable the items to be deleted using the DELETE key.

30.7* (*Custom list cell renderer*) Listing 30.10, ListCellRendererDemo.java, has two types of images for each country. The small images are used for display in the list, and the large ones are used for display outside the list. Assume that only the large images are available. Rewrite the custom cell renderer to use a `JPanel` instead of a `JLabel` for rendering a cell. Each cell consists of an image and a string. Display the image in an `ImageViewer` and the string in a label. The `ImageViewer` component was introduced in Listing 13.15, ImageViewer.java. The image can be stretched in an `ImageViewer`. Set the size of an image viewer to 32 × 32, as shown in Figure 30.30. Revise Listing 30.10 to test the new custom cell renderer.

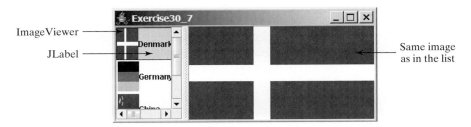

FIGURE 30.30 `ImageViewer` is used to render the image in the list.

30.8* (*Deleting selected items in a list using the DELETE key*) Modify Listing 30.10, ListCellRendererDemo.java, to delete selected items from the list using the DELETE key. After some items are deleted from the list, the index of a selected item in the list does not match the index of the item in the `bigIcons` array. As a result, you cannot use the image icon in the bigIcons array to display the image to the right side of the split pane. Revise the program to retrieve the icon from the selected item in the list and display it, as shown in Figure 30.31.

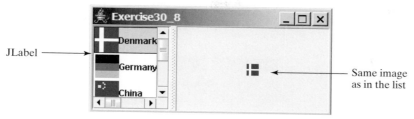

JLabel

Same image
as in the list

FIGURE 30.31 Images in the list are also used for display in the label placed in the right side of a split pane.

30.9* *(Rendering figures)* Create a program that shows a list of geometrical shapes along with a label in an instance of `JList`, as shown in Figure 30.32. Display the selected figure in a panel when selecting a figure from the list. The figures can be drawn using the `FigurePanel` class in Listing 13.5, FigurePanel.java.

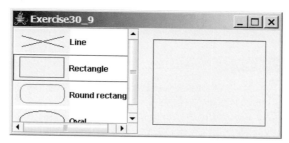

FIGURE 30.32 The list displays geometrical shapes and their names.

30.10* *(List of clocks)* Write a program that displays a list of cities and their local times in a clock, as shown in Figure 30.33. When a city is selected in the list, its clock is displayed in a large picture on the right.

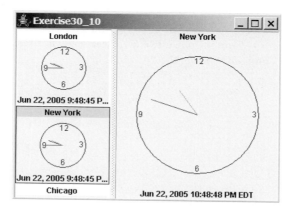

FIGURE 30.33 The list displays cities and clocks.

Section 30.10 JComboBox

30.11**(*Creating custom cell renderer in a combo box*) Create a program that shows a list of geometrical shapes along with a label in a combo box, as shown in Figure 30.34. This exercise may share the list cell renderer with the preceding exercise.

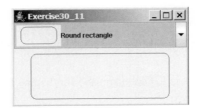

FIGURE 30.34   The combo box contains a list of geometrical shapes and the shape names.

30.12**(*Rendering colored text*) Write a program that enables the user to choose the foreground colors for a label, as shown in Figure 30.35. The combo box contains thirteen standard colors (BLACK, BLUE, CYAN, DARK_GRAY, GRAY, GREEN, LIGHT_GRAY, MAGENTA, ORANGE, PINK, RED, WHITE, YELLOW). Each color name in the combo box uses its own color for its foreground.

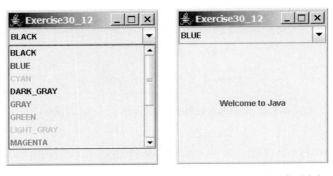

FIGURE 30.35   The combo box contains a list of color names, each of which uses its own color for its foreground.

30.13*(*Deleting a selected item in a combo box using the DELETE key*) Modify Listing 30.11, ComboBoxCellRendererDemo.java, to delete the selected item from the combo box using the DELETE key.

CHAPTER 31

JTABLE AND JTREE

Objectives

- To display tables using `JTable` (§31.2).
- To process rows and columns using `TableModel`, `DefaultTableModel`, `TableColumnModel`, `DefaultTableColumnModel`, and `ListSelectionModel` (§§31.3–31.4).
- To render and edit table cells using the default renderers and editors (§31.5).
- To render and edit table cells using the custom renderers and editors (§31.6).
- To handle table model events (§31.7).
- To display data in a tree hierarchy using `JTree` (§31.8).
- To model the structure of a tree using using `TreeModel` and `DefaultTreeModel` (§31.9).
- To add, remove, and process tree nodes using `TreeNode`, `DefaultMutableTreeNode`, and `TreePath` (§31.10).
- To select tree nodes and paths using `TreeSelection-Model` and `DefaultTreeSelectionModel` (§31.11).
- To render and edit tree nodes using the default and custom renderers and editors (§31.13).

31.1 Introduction

The preceding chapter introduced the model-view architecture, Swing MVC, and the models in **JSpinner**, **JList**, and **JComboBox**. This chapter introduces **JTable** and **JTree**, and how to use the models to process data in **JTable** and **JTree**.

31.2 **JTable**

JTable is a Swing component that displays data in rows and columns in a two-dimensional grid, as shown in Figure 31.1.

Country	Capital	Population in Millions	Democracy
USA	Washington DC	280	true
Canada	Ottawa	32	true
United Kingdom	London	60	true
Germany	Berlin	83	true
France	Paris	60	true
Norway	Oslo	4.5	true

FIGURE 31.1   **JTable** displays data in a table.

JTable doesn't directly support scrolling. To create a scrollable table, you need to create a **JScrollPane** and add an instance of **JTable** to the scroll pane. If a table is not placed in a scroll pane, its column header will not be visible, because the column header is placed in the header of the view port of a scroll pane.

JTable has three supporting models: a table model, a column model, and a list-selection model. The *table model* is for storing and processing data. The *column model* represents all the columns in the table. The *list-selection model* is the same as the one used by **JList** for selecting rows, columns, and cells in a table. **JTable** also has two useful supporting classes, **TableColumn** and **JTableHeader**. **TableColumn** contains the information on a particular column. **JTableHeader** contains the information on the header of a **JTable**. Each column has a default editor and renderer. You can also create a custom editor by implementing the **TableCellEditor** interface, and create a custom renderer by implementing the **TableCellRenderer** interface. The relationship of these interfaces and classes is shown in Figure 31.2.

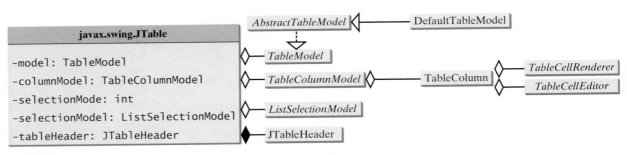

FIGURE 31.2   **JTable** contains many supporting interfaces and classes.

 Note

All the supporting interfaces and classes for **JTable** are grouped in the `javax.swing.table` package.

Figure 31.3 shows the constructors, properties, and methods of **JTable**.

The **JTable** class contains seven constructors for creating tables. You can create a table using its no-arg constructor, its models, row data in a two-dimensional array, and column header names in an array, or row data and column header names in vectors. Listing 31.1

javax.swing.JTable	JavaBeans properties with get and set methods omitted in the UML diagram.
-autoCreateColumnsFromModel: boolean	Indicates whether the columns are created in the table (default: true).
-autoResizeMode: int	Specifies how columns are resized (default: SUBSEQUENT_COLUMNS).
-cellEditor: TableCellEditor	Specifies a cell editor.
-columnModel: TableColumnModel	Maintains the table column data.
-columnSelectionAllowed: boolean	Specifies whether the rows can be selected (default: false).
-editingColumn: int	Specifies the column of the cell that is currently being edited.
-editingRow: int	Specifies the row of the cell that is currently being edited.
-gridColor: java.awt.Color	The color used to draw grid lines (default: GRAY).
-intercellSpacing: Dimension	Specifies the horizontal and vertical margins between cells (default: 1, 1).
-model: TableModel	Maintains the table model.
-rowCount: int	Read-only property that counts the number of rows in the table.
-rowHeight: int	Specifies the row height of the table (default: 16 pixels).
-rowMargin: int	Specifies the vertical margin between rows (default: 1 pixel).
-rowSelectionAllowed: boolean	Specifies whether the rows can be selected (default: true).
-selectionBackground: java.awt.Color	The background color of selected cells.
-selectionForeground: java.awt.Color	The foreground color of selected cells.
-showGrid: boolean	Specify whether the grid lines are displayed (write-only, default: true).
-selectionMode: int	Specifies a selection mode (write-only).
-selectionModel: ListSelectionModel	Specifies a selection model.
-showHorizontalLines: boolean	Specifies whether the horizontal grid lines are displayed (default: true).
-showVerticalLines: boolean	Specifies whether the vertical grid lines are displayed (default: true).
-tableHeader: JTableHeader	Specifies a table header.
+JTable()	Creates a default JTable with all the default models.
+JTable(numRows: int, numColumns: int)	Creates a JTable with the specified number of empty rows and columns.
+JTable(rowData: Object[][], columnData: Object[])	Creates a JTable with the specified row data and column header names.
+JTable(dm: TableModel)	Creates a JTable with the specified table model.
+JTable(dm: TableModel, cm: TableColumnModel)	Creates a JTable with the specified table model and table column model.
+JTable(dm: TableModel, cm: TableColumnModel, sm: ListSelectionModel)	Creates a JTable with the specified table model, table column model, and selection model.
+JTable(rowData: Vector, columnNames: Vector)	Creates a JTable with the specified row data and column data in vectors.
+addColumn(aColumn: TableColumn): void	Adds a new column to the table.
+clearSelection(): void	Deselects all selected columns and rows.
+editCellAt(row: int, column: int): void	Edits the cell if it is editable.
+getDefaultEditor(column: Class): TableCellEditor	Returns the default editor for the column.
+getDefaultRenderer(col: Class): TableCellRenderer	Returns the default renderer for the column.
+setDefaultEditor(column: Class, editor: TableCellEditor): void	Sets the default editor for the column.
+setDefaultRenderer(column: Class, editor: TableCellRenderer): void	Sets the default renderer for the column.

FIGURE 31.3 The **JTable** class is for creating, customizing, and manipulating tables.

creates a table with the row data and column names (line 20) and places it in a scroll pane (line 24). The table is displayed in Figure 31.1.

LISTING 31.1 TestTable.java

```
1 import javax.swing.*;
2
3 public class TestTable extends JApplet {
4    // Create table column names
5    String[] columnNames =                                    column names
6      {"Country", "Capital", "Population in Millions", "Democracy"};
7
```

row data

```
 8    // Create table data
 9    Object[][] data = {
10      {"USA", "Washington DC", 280, true},
11      {"Canada", "Ottawa", 32, true},
12      {"United Kingdom", "London", 60, true},
13      {"Germany", "Berlin", 83, true},
14      {"France", "Paris", 60, true},
15      {"Norway", "Oslo", 4.5, true},
16      {"India", "New Deli", 1046, true}
17    };
18
19    // Create a table
```

create table

```
20    JTable jTable1 = new JTable(data, columnNames);
21
22    public TestTable() {
```

scroll pane

```
23      add(new JScrollPane(jTable1));
24    }
```

main method omitted

```
25 }
```

Note

autoboxing

Primitive type values such as 280 and true in line 10 are autoboxed into new Integer(280) and new Boolean(true).

JTable is a powerful control with a variety of properties that provide many ways to customize tables. All the frequently used properties are documented in Figure 31.3. The **autoResizeMode** property specifies how columns are resized (you can resize table columns but not rows). Possible values are:

```
JTable.AUTO_RESIZE_OFF
JTable.AUTO_RESIZE_LAST_COLUMN
JTable.AUTO_RESIZE_SUBSEQUENT_COLUMNS
JTable.AUTO_RESIZE_NEXT_COLUMN
JTable.AUTO_RESIZE_ALL_COLUMNS
```

The default mode is **JTable.AUTO_RESIZE_SUBSEQUENT_COLUMNS**. Initially, each column in the table occupies the same width (75 pixels). With **AUTO_RESIZE_OFF**, resizing a column does not affect the widths of the other columns. With **AUTO_RESIZE_LAST_COLUMN**, resizing a column affects the width of the last column. With **AUTO_RESIZE_SUBSEQUENT_COLUMNS**, resizing a column affects the widths of all the subsequent columns. With **AUTO_RESIZE_NEXT_COLUMN**, resizing a column affects the widths of the next columns. With **AUTO_RESIZE_ALL_COLUMNS**, resizing a column affects the widths of all the columns.

Listing 31.2 gives an example that demonstrates the use of several **JTable** properties. The example creates a table and allows the user to choose an Auto Resize Mode, specify the row height and margin, and indicate whether the grid is shown. A sample run of the program is shown in Figure 31.4.

LISTING 31.2 TablePropertiesDemo.java

```
 1 import java.awt.*;
 2 import java.awt.event.*;
 3 import javax.swing.*;
 4 import javax.swing.event.*;
 5
 6 public class TablePropertiesDemo extends JApplet {
 7   // Create table column names
```

column names

```
 8   private String[] columnNames =
 9     {"Country", "Capital", "Population in Millions", "Democracy"};
10
```

```
11   // Create table data
12   private Object[][] rowData = {                                    table data
13     {"USA", "Washington DC", 280, true},
14     {"Canada", "Ottawa", 32, true},
15     {"United Kingdom", "London", 60, true},
16     {"Germany", "Berlin", 83, true},
17     {"France", "Paris", 60, true},
18     {"Norway", "Oslo", 4.5, true},
19     {"India", "New Deli", 1046, true}
20   };
21
22   // Create a table
23   private JTable jTable1 = new JTable(rowData, columnNames);        table
24
25   // Create two spinners
26   private JSpinner jspiRowHeight =
27     new JSpinner(new SpinnerNumberModel(16, 1, 50, 1));             spinners
28   private JSpinner jspiRowMargin =
29     new JSpinner(new SpinnerNumberModel(1, 1, 50, 1));
30
31   // Create a checkbox
32   private JCheckBox jchkShowGrid = new JCheckBox("showGrid", true);
33
34   // Create a combo box
35   private JComboBox jcboAutoResizeMode = new JComboBox(new String[]{
36     "AUTO_RESIZE_OFF", "AUTO_RESIZE_LAST_COLUMN",                   combo box
37     "AUTO_RESIZE_SUBSEQUENT_COLUMNS", "AUTO_RESIZE_NEXT_COLUMN",
38     "AUTO_RESIZE_ALL_COLUMNS"});
39
40   public TablePropertiesDemo() {
41     JPanel panel1 = new JPanel();
42     panel1.add(new JLabel("rowHeight"));                           create UI
43     panel1.add(jspiRowHeight);
44     panel1.add(new JLabel("rowMargin"));
45     panel1.add(jspiRowMargin);
46     panel1.add(jchkShowGrid);
47
48     JPanel panel2 = new JPanel();
49     panel2.add(new JLabel("autoResizeMode"));
50     panel2.add(jcboAutoResizeMode);
51
52     add(panel1, BorderLayout.SOUTH);
53     add(panel2, BorderLayout.NORTH);
54     add(new JScrollPane(jTable1));
55
56     // Initialize jTable1
57     jTable1.setAutoResizeMode(JTable.AUTO_RESIZE_OFF);             table properties
58     jTable1.setGridColor(Color.BLUE);
59     jTable1.setSelectionMode(ListSelectionModel.SINGLE_SELECTION);
60     jTable1.setSelectionBackground(Color.RED);
61     jTable1.setSelectionForeground(Color.WHITE);
62
63     // Register and create a listener for jspiRowHeight
64     jspiRowHeight.addChangeListener(new ChangeListener() {         spinner listener
65       public void stateChanged(ChangeEvent e) {
66         jTable1.setRowHeight(
67           ((Integer)(jspiRowHeight.getValue())).intValue());
68       }
69     });
70
```

spinner listener

check box listener

combo box listener

main omitted

```
71      // Register and create a listener for jspiRowMargin
72      jspiRowMargin.addChangeListener(new ChangeListener() {
73        public void stateChanged(ChangeEvent e) {
74          jTable1.setRowMargin (
75            ((Integer)(jspiRowMargin.getValue())).intValue());
76        }
77      });
78
79      // Register and create a listener for jchkShowGrid
80      jchkShowGrid.addActionListener(new ActionListener() {
81        public void actionPerformed(ActionEvent e) {
82          jTable1.setShowGrid (jchkShowGrid.isSelected());
83        }
84      });
85
86      // Register and create a listener for jcboAutoResizeMode
87      jcboAutoResizeMode.addActionListener(new ActionListener() {
88        public void actionPerformed(ActionEvent e) {
89          String selectedItem =
90            (String)jcboAutoResizeMode.getSelectedItem();
91
92          if (selectedItem.equals("AUTO_RESIZE_OFF"))
93            jTable1.setAutoResizeMode (JTable.AUTO_RESIZE_OFF);
94          else if (selectedItem.equals("AUTO_RESIZE_LAST_COLUMN"))
95            jTable1.setAutoResizeMode(JTable.AUTO_RESIZE_LAST_COLUMN);
96          else if (selectedItem.equals
97                    ("AUTO_RESIZE_SUBSEQUENT_COLUMNS"))
98            jTable1.setAutoResizeMode(
99              JTable.AUTO_RESIZE_SUBSEQUENT_COLUMNS);
100         else if (selectedItem.equals("AUTO_RESIZE_NEXT_COLUMN"))
101           jTable1.setAutoResizeMode(JTable.AUTO_RESIZE_NEXT_COLUMN);
102         else if (selectedItem.equals("AUTO_RESIZE_ALL_COLUMNS"))
103           jTable1.setAutoResizeMode(JTable.AUTO_RESIZE_ALL_COLUMNS);
104       }
105     });
106   }
107 }
```

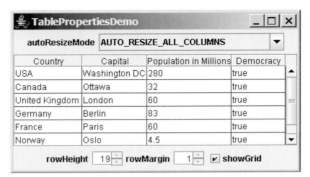

FIGURE 31.4 You can specify an auto-resizing mode, the table's row height and row margin, and whether to show the grid in the table.

If you know the row data in advance, creating a table using the constructor **JTable(Object[][] rowData, Object[] columnNames)** is convenient. As shown in line 23, a **JTable** is created using this constructor.

Two **JSpinner** objects (**jspiRowHeight**, **jspiRowMargin**) for selecting row height and row margin are created in lines 26–29. The initial value for **jspiRowHeight** is set to **16**, which is the default property value for `rowHeight`. The initial value for `jspiRowMargin` is set to 1, which is the default property value for `rowMargin`. A check box (`jchkShowGrid`) is created with label showGrid and initially selected in line 32. A combo box for selecting `autoResizeMode` is created in lines 35–38.

The values of the `JTable` properties (`autoResizeMode`, `gridColor`, `selectionMode`, `selectionBackground`, and `selectionForeground`) are set in lines 57–61.

The code for processing spinners, check boxes, and combo boxes is given in lines 64–105.

31.3 Table Models and Table Column Models

`JTable` delegates data storing and processing to its table data model. A table data model must implement the `TableModel` interface, which defines the methods for registering table model listeners, manipulating cells, and obtaining row count, column count, column class, and column name.   **TableModel**

The `AbstractTableModel` class provides partial implementations for most of the methods in `TableModel`. It takes care of the management of listeners and provides some conveniences for generating `TableModelEvents` and dispatching them to the listeners. To create a concrete `TableModel`, you simply extend `AbstractTableModel` and implement at least the following three methods: **AbstractTableModel**

- **public int** getRowCount()
- **public int** getColumnCount()
- **public** Object getValueAt(**int** row, **int** column)

The `DefaultTableModel` class extends `AbstractTableModel` and implements these three methods. Additionally, `DefaultTableModel` provides concrete storage for data. The data is stored in a vector. The elements in the vector are arrays of objects, each of which represents an individual cell value. The methods in `DefaultTableModel` for accessing and modifying data are shown in Figure 31.5.   **DefaultTableModel**

Listing 31.3 gives an example that demonstrates table models. The example creates a table model (line 16), plugs the model to the table (line 20), appends a row to the table (line 25), inserts a row before the first row (line 26), removes a row with index 1 (line 28), adds a new column (line 29), and sets new values at specified cells (lines 30–32). Figure 31.6 shows the output of the program.

LISTING 31.3 TestTableModel.java

```
1 import javax.swing.*;
2 import javax.swing.table.*;
3
4 public class TestTableModel extends JApplet {
5   // Create table column names
6   String[] columnNames =                                      column names
7     {"Country", "Capital", "Population in Millions", "Democracy"};
8
9   // Create table data
10  Object[][] data = {                                         row data
11    {"USA", "Washington DC", 280, true},
12    {"Canada", "Ottawa", 32, true}
13  };
14
15  // Create a model
16  DefaultTableModel tableModel =                              create table model
17    new DefaultTableModel(data, columnNames);
18
19  // Create a table
20  JTable jTable1 = new JTable(tableModel);                    create table
21
```

```
22   public TestTableModel() {
23     add(new JScrollPane(jTable1));
24
25     tableModel.addRow(new Object[]{"France", "Paris", 60, true});
26     tableModel.insertRow(0, new Object[]
27       {"India", "New Delhi", 1046, true});
28     tableModel.removeRow(1);
29     tableModel.addColumn("Area");
30     tableModel.setValueAt(10, 0, 4);
31     tableModel.setValueAt(20, 1, 4);
32     tableModel.setValueAt(30, 2, 4);
33   }
34 }
```

scroll pane

add row
insert row

remove row
add column
set value

main method omitted

«interface»
javax.swing.table.TableModel

+*getColumnClass(columnIndex: int): Class*
+*getColumnName(columnIndex: int): String*
+*getColumnCount(): int*
+*getRowCount(): int*
+*getValueAt(rowIndex: int, columnIndex: int): Object*
+*setValueAt(aValue: Object, rowIndex: int, columnIndex: int): void*
+*isCellEditable(rowIndex: int, columnIndex: int): boolean*
+*addTableModelListener(l: TableModelListener): void*
+*removeTableModelListener(l: TableModelListener): void*

javax.swing.table.AbstractTableModel

javax.swing.table.DefaultTableModel

+DefaultTableModel()
+DefaultTableModel(rowCount: int, columnCount: int)
+DefaultTableModel(columnNames: Object[], rowCount: int)
+DefaultTableModel(data: Object[][], columnNames: Object[])
+DefaultTableModel(columnNames: Vector, rowCount: int)
+DefaultTableModel(data: Vector, columnNames: Vector)
+DefaultTableModel(rowData: Vector, columnNames: Vector)
+addColumn(columnName: Object): void
+addColumn(columnName: Object, columnData: Vector)
+addRow(rowData: Object[]): void
+addRow(rowData: Vector): void
+getColumnCount(): int
+getDataVector(): Vector
+getRowCount(): int
+insertRow(row: int, rowData: Object[]): void
+insertRow(row: int, rowData: Vector): void
+removeRow(row: int): void
+setColumnCount(columnCount: int): void
+setColumnIdentifiers(newIdentifiers: Object[]): void
+setColumnIdentifiers(columnIdentifiers: Vector): void
+setDataVector(dataVector: Object[][], columnIdentifiers: Object[]): void
+setDataVector(dataVector: Vector, columnIdentifiers: Vector): void
+setRowCount(rowCount: int): void

FIGURE 31.5 TableModel stores and manages data in a table.

TestTableModel				
Country	Capital	Population in Millions	Democracy	Area
India	New Deli	1046	true	10
Canada	Ottawa	32	true	20
France	Paris	60	true	30

FIGURE 31.6 TableModel and DefaultTableModel contain the methods for adding, updating, and removing table data.

TableModel manages table data. You can add and remove rows through a TableModel. You can also add a column through a TableModel. However, you cannot remove a column through a TableModel. To remove a column from a JTable, you have to use a table column model.

Table column models manage columns in a table. They can be used to select, add, move, and remove table columns. A table column model must implement the TableColumnModel interface, which defines the methods for registering table column model listeners, and for accessing and manipulating columns, as shown in Figure 31.7.

TableColumnModel

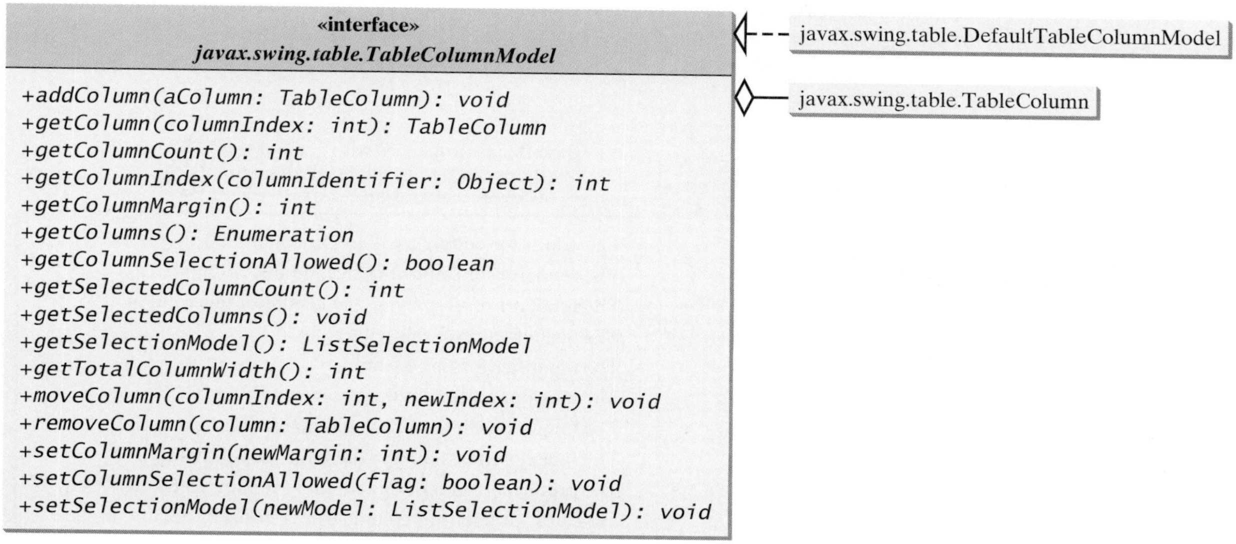

<table>
<tr><td colspan="1">«interface»
javax.swing.table.TableColumnModel</td></tr>
<tr><td>+addColumn(aColumn: TableColumn): void
+getColumn(columnIndex: int): TableColumn
+getColumnCount(): int
+getColumnIndex(columnIdentifier: Object): int
+getColumnMargin(): int
+getColumns(): Enumeration
+getColumnSelectionAllowed(): boolean
+getSelectedColumnCount(): int
+getSelectedColumns(): void
+getSelectionModel(): ListSelectionModel
+getTotalColumnWidth(): int
+moveColumn(columnIndex: int, newIndex: int): void
+removeColumn(column: TableColumn): void
+setColumnMargin(newMargin: int): void
+setColumnSelectionAllowed(flag: boolean): void
+setSelectionModel(newModel: ListSelectionModel): void</td></tr>
</table>

javax.swing.table.DefaultTableColumnModel

javax.swing.table.TableColumn

FIGURE 31.7 TableColumnModel manages columns in a table.

DefaultTableColumnModel is a concrete class that implements TableColumnModel and PropertyChangeListener. The DefaultTableColumnModel class stores its columns in a vector and contains an instance of ListSelectionModel for selecting columns.

DefaultTable-
ColumnModel

The column model deals with all the columns in a table. The TableColumn class is used to model an individual column in the table. An instance of TableColumn for a specified column can be obtained using the getColumn(index) method in TableColumnModel or the getColumn(columnIdentifier) method in JTable.

TableColumn

Figure 31.8 shows the properties, constructors, and methods in TableColumn for manipulating column width and specifying the cell renderer, cell editor, and header renderer.

Listing 31.4 gives an example that demonstrates table column models. The example obtains the table column model from the table (line 21), moves the first column to the second (line 22), and removes the last column (lines 23). Figure 31.9 shows the output of the program.

LISTING 31.4 TestTableColumnModel.java

```java
1  import javax.swing.*;
2  import javax.swing.table.*;
3
4  public class TestTableColumnModel extends JApplet {
5    // Create table column names
6    String[] columnNames =
7      {"Country", "Capital", "Population in Millions", "Democracy"};
8
9    // Create table data
10   Object[][] data = {
11     {"USA", "Washington DC", 280, true},
12     {"Canada", "Ottawa", 32, true}
13   };
```

column names

row data

create table model

main method omitted

```
14
15   // Create a table
16   JTable jTable1 = new JTable(data, columnNames);
17
18   public TestTableColumnModel() {
19     add(new JScrollPane(jTable1));
20
21     TableColumnModel columnModel = jTable1.getColumnModel();
22     columnModel.moveColumn(0, 1);
23     columnModel.removeColumn(columnModel.getColumn(3));
24   }
25 }
```

> JavaBeans properties with get and set methods omitted in the UML diagram.

javax.swing.table.TableColumn	
#cellEditor: TableCellEditor	The editor for editing a cell in this column.
#cellRenderer: TableCellRenderer	The renderer for displaying a cell in this column.
#headerRenderer: TableCellRenderer	The renderer for displaying the header of this column.
#headerValue: Object	The header value of this column.
#identifier: Object	The identifier for this column.
#maxWidth: int	The maximum width of this column.
#minWidth: int	The minimum width of this column (default: 15 pixels).
#modelIndex: int	The index of the column in the table model (default: 0).
#preferredWidth: int	The preferred width of this column (default: 75 pixels).
#resizable: boolean	Indicates whether this column can be resized (default: true).
#width: int	Specifies the width of this column (default: 75 pixels).
+TableColumn()	Constructs a default table column.
+TableColumn(modelIndex: int)	Constructs a table column for the specified column.
+TableColumn(modelIndex: int, width: int)	Constructs a table column with the specified column and width.
+TableColumn(modelIndex: int, width: int, cellRenderer: TableCellRenderer)	Constructs a table column with the specified column, width, and cell renderer.
+sizeWidthToFit(): void	Resizes the column to fit the width of its header cell.

FIGURE 31.8   The `TableColumn` class models a single column.

TestTableColumnModel		_ □ ×
Capital	Country	Population in Millions
Washington DC	USA	280
Ottawa	Canada	32

FIGURE 31.9   `TableColumnModel` contains the methods for moving and removing columns.

 Note

Some of the methods defined in the table model and the table column model are also defined in the `JTable` class for convenience. For instance, the `getColumnCount()` method is defined in `JTable`, `TableModel`, and `TableColumnModel`, the `addColumn` method defined in the column model is also defined in the table model, and the `getColumn()` method defined in the column model is also defined in the `JTable` class.

`JTableHeader` is a GUI component that manages the header of the `JTable` (see Figure 31.10). When you create a `JTable`, an instance of `JTableHeader` is automatically created and stored in the `tableHeader` property. By default, you can reorder the columns by dragging the header **TableHeader** of the column. To disable it, set the `reorderingAllowed` property to `false`.

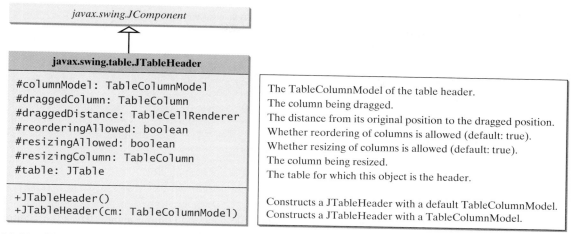

FIGURE 31.10 The `JTableHeader` class manages the header of the `JTable`.

31.4 Case Study: Modifying Rows and Columns

This case study demonstrates the use of table models, table column models, list-selection models, and the `TableColumn` class. The program allows the user to choose selection mode and selection type, the add or remove rows and columns, and save, clear, or restore the table, as shown in Figure 31.11(a).

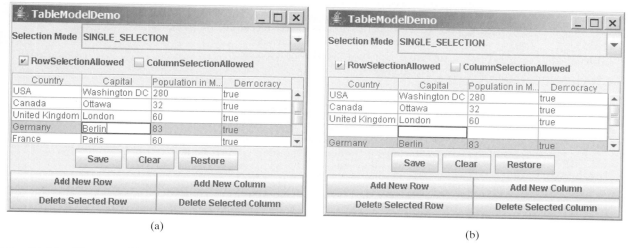

FIGURE 31.11 You can add, remove, and modify rows and columns in a table interactively.

The *Add New Row* button adds a new empty row before the currently selected row, as shown in Figure 31.11(b). If no row is currently selected, a new empty row is appended to the end of the table.

When you click the *Add New Column* button, an input dialog box is displayed to receive the title of the column, as shown in Figure 31.12(a). The new column is appended in the table, as shown in Figure 31.12(b).

The *Delete Selected Row* button deletes the first selected row. The *Delete Selected Column* button deletes the first selected column.

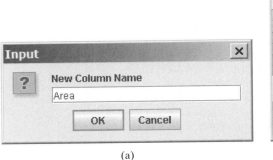

FIGURE 31.12   You can add a new column in a table.

The *Save* button saves the current table data and column names. The *Clear* button clears the row data in the table. The *Restore* button restores the save table.

Listing 31.5 gives the program.

LISTING 31.5   TableModelDemo.java

```
1  import java.awt.*;
2  import java.awt.event.*;
3  import javax.swing.*;
4  import javax.swing.table.*;
5  import java.io.*;
6  import java.util.Vector;
7
8  public class TableModelDemo extends JApplet {
9    // Create table column names
10   private String[] columnNames =
11     {"Country", "Capital", "Population in Millions", "Democracy"};
12
13   // Create table data
14   private Object[][] rowData = {
15     {"USA", "Washington DC", 280, true},
16     {"Canada", "Ottawa", 32, true},
17     {"United Kingdom", "London", 60, true},
18     {"Germany", "Berlin", 83, true},
19     {"France", "Paris", 60, true},
20     {"Norway", "Oslo", 4.5, true},
21     {"India", "New Deli", 1046, true}
22   };
23
24   // Create a table model
25   private DefaultTableModel tableModel = new DefaultTableModel(
26     rowData, columnNames);
27
28   // Create a table
29   private JTable jTable1 = new JTable(tableModel);
30
31   // Create buttons
32   private JButton jbtAddRow = new JButton("Add New Row");
33   private JButton jbtAddColumn = new JButton("Add New Column");
34   private JButton jbtDeleteRow = new JButton("Delete Selected Row");
35   private JButton jbtDeleteColumn = new JButton(
36     "Delete Selected Column");
```

column names

table data

table model

table

buttons

```
37   private JButton jbtSave = new JButton("Save");
38   private JButton jbtClear = new JButton("Clear");
39   private JButton jbtRestore = new JButton("Restore");
40
41   // Create a combo box for selection modes
42   private JComboBox jcboSelectionMode =                             combo box
43     new JComboBox(new String[] {"SINGLE_SELECTION",
44       "SINGLE_INTERVAL_SELECTION", "MULTIPLE_INTERVAL_SELECTION"});
45
46   // Create check boxes
47   private JCheckBox jchkRowSelectionAllowed =                       check boxes
48     new JCheckBox("RowSelectionAllowed", true);
49   private JCheckBox jchkColumnSelectionAllowed =
50     new JCheckBox("ColumnSelectionAllowed", false);
51
52   public TableModelDemo() {                                         create UI
53     JPanel panel1 = new JPanel();
54     panel1.setLayout(new GridLayout(2, 2));
55     panel1.add(jbtAddRow);
56     panel1.add(jbtAddColumn);
57     panel1.add(jbtDeleteRow);
58     panel1.add(jbtDeleteColumn);
59
60     JPanel panel2 = new JPanel();
61     panel2.add(jbtSave);
62     panel2.add(jbtClear);
63     panel2.add(jbtRestore);
64
65     JPanel panel3 = new JPanel();
66     panel3.setLayout(new BorderLayout(5, 0));
67     panel3.add(new JLabel("Selection Mode"), BorderLayout.WEST);
68     panel3.add(jcboSelectionMode, BorderLayout.CENTER);
69
70     JPanel panel4 = new JPanel();
71     panel4.setLayout(new FlowLayout(FlowLayout.LEFT));
72     panel4.add(jchkRowSelectionAllowed);
73     panel4.add(jchkColumnSelectionAllowed);
74
75     JPanel panel5 = new JPanel();
76     panel5.setLayout(new GridLayout(2, 1));
77     panel5.add(panel3);
78     panel5.add(panel4);
79
80     JPanel panel6 = new JPanel();
81     panel6.setLayout(new BorderLayout());
82     panel6.add(panel1, BorderLayout.SOUTH);
83     panel6.add(panel2, BorderLayout.CENTER);
84
85     add(panel5, BorderLayout.NORTH);
86     add(new JScrollPane(jTable1),
87       BorderLayout.CENTER);
88     add(panel6, BorderLayout.SOUTH);
89
90     // Initialize table selection mode
91     jTable1.setSelectionMode(ListSelectionModel.SINGLE_SELECTION);
92
93     jbtAddRow.addActionListener(new ActionListener() {              add row
94       public void actionPerformed(ActionEvent e) {
95         if (jTable1.getSelectedRow() >= 0)
96           tableModel.insertRow (jTable1.getSelectedRow(),
```

```
 97                 new java.util.Vector());
 98             else
 99                 tableModel.addRow(new java.util.Vector());
100         }
101     });
102
```

add column
```
103     jbtAddColumn.addActionListener(new ActionListener() {
104       public void actionPerformed(ActionEvent e) {
105         String name = JOptionPane.showInputDialog("New Column Name");
106         tableModel.addColumn(name, new java.util.Vector());
107       }
108     });
109
```

delete row
```
110     jbtDeleteRow.addActionListener(new ActionListener() {
111       public void actionPerformed(ActionEvent e) {
112         if (jTable1.getSelectedRow() >= 0)
113           tableModel.removeRow(jTable1.getSelectedRow());
114       }
115     });
116
```

delete column
```
117     jbtDeleteColumn.addActionListener(new ActionListener() {
118       public void actionPerformed(ActionEvent e) {
119         if (jTable1.getSelectedColumn() >= 0) {
120           TableColumnModel columnModel = jTable1.getColumnModel();
121           TableColumn tableColumn =
122               columnModel.getColumn(jTable1.getSelectedColumn());
123           columnModel.removeColumn(tableColumn);
124         }
125       }
126     });
127
```

save table
```
128     jbtSave.addActionListener(new ActionListener() {
129       public void actionPerformed(ActionEvent e) {
130         try {
131           ObjectOutputStream out = new ObjectOutputStream(
132             new FileOutputStream("tablemodel.dat"));
133           out.writeObject(tableModel.getDataVector());
134           out.writeObject(getColumnNames());
135           out.close();
136         }
137         catch (Exception ex) {
138           ex.printStackTrace();
139         }
140       }
141     });
142
```

clear table
```
143     jbtClear.addActionListener(new ActionListener() {
144       public void actionPerformed(ActionEvent e) {
145         tableModel.setRowCount(0);
146       }
147     });
148
```

restore table
```
149     jbtRestore.addActionListener(new ActionListener() {
150       public void actionPerformed(ActionEvent e) {
151         try {
152           ObjectInputStream in = new ObjectInputStream(
153             new FileInputStream("tablemodel.dat"));
154           Vector rowData = (Vector)in.readObject();
155           Vector columnNames = (Vector)in.readObject();
156           tableModel.setDataVector(rowData, columnNames);
157           in.close();
```

```
158          }
159        catch (Exception ex) {
160          ex.printStackTrace();
161        }
162      }
163    });
164
165    jchkRowSelectionAllowed.addActionListener(new ActionListener() {      row selection allowed
166      public void actionPerformed(ActionEvent e) {
167        jTable1.setRowSelectionAllowed (
168          jchkRowSelectionAllowed.isSelected());
169      }
170    });
171
172    jchkColumnSelectionAllowed.addActionListener(
173      new ActionListener() {                                              column selection allowed
174      public void actionPerformed(ActionEvent e) {
175        jTable1.setColumnSelectionAllowed (
176          jchkColumnSelectionAllowed.isSelected());
177      }
178    });
179
180    jcboSelectionMode.addActionListener(new ActionListener() {            choose selection mode
181      public void actionPerformed(ActionEvent e) {
182        String selectedItem =
183          (String) jcboSelectionMode.getSelectedItem();
184
185        if (selectedItem.equals("SINGLE_SELECTION"))
186          jTable1.setSelectionMode(
187            ListSelectionModel.SINGLE_SELECTION);
188        else if (selectedItem.equals("SINGLE_INTERVAL_SELECTION"))
189          jTable1.setSelectionMode(
190            ListSelectionModel.SINGLE_INTERVAL_SELECTION);
191        else if (selectedItem.equals("MULTIPLE_INTERVAL_SELECTION"))
192          jTable1.setSelectionMode(
193            ListSelectionModel.MULTIPLE_INTERVAL_SELECTION);
194      }
195    });
196  }
197
198  private Vector getColumnNames() {
199    Vector<String> columnNames = new Vector<String>();                    get column names
200
201    for (int i = 0; i < jTable1.getColumnCount(); i++)
202      columnNames.add(jTable1.getColumnName(i) );
203
204    return columnNames;
205  }
206 }
```

main omitted

A table model is created using `DefaultTableModel` with row data and column names (lines 25–26). This model is used to create a `JTable` (line 29).

The GUI objects (buttons, combo box, check boxes) are created in lines 32–50 and are placed in the UI in lines 53–88.

The table-selection mode is the same as the list-selection mode. By default, the selection mode is `MULTIPLE_INTERVAL_SELECTION`. To match the initial value in the selection combo box (`jcboSelectionMode`), the table's selection mode is set to `SINGLE_SELECTION`.

The *Add New Row* button action is processed in lines 93–101. The `insertRow` method inserts a new row before the selected row (lines 95–96). If no row is currently selected, the `addRow` method appends a new row into the table model (line 99).

The *Add New Column* button action is processed in lines 103–108. The `addColumn` method appends a new column into the table model (line 106).

The *Delete Selected Row* button action is processed in lines 110–115. The `removeRow(rowIndex)` method removes the selected row from the table model (line 113).

The *Delete Selected Column* button action is processed in lines 117–126. To remove a column, you have to use the `removeColumn` method in `TableColumnModel` (line 123).

The *Save* button action is processed in lines 128–141. It writes row data and column names to an output file using object stream (lines 133–134). The column names are obtained using the `getColumnNames()` method (lines 198–205). You may attempt to save `tableModel`, because `tableModel` is an instance of `DefaultTableModel` (lines 25–26) and `DefaultTableModel` is serializable. However, `tableModel` may contain non-serializable listeners for `TableModel` event.

The *Clear* button action is processed in lines 143–147. It clears the table by setting the row count to 0 (line 145).

The *Restore* button action is processed in lines 149–163. It reads row data and column names from the file using object stream (lines 154–155), and sets the new data and column names to the table model (line 156).

31.5 Table Renderers and Editors

Table cells are painted by cell renderers. By default, a cell object's string representation (`toString()`) is displayed and the string can be edited as it was in a text field. `JTable` maintains a set of predefined renderers and editors, listed in Table 31.1, which can be specified to replace default string renderers and editors.

TABLE 31.1 Predefined Renderers and Editors for Tables

Class	Renderer	Editor
`Object`	`JLabel` (left aligned)	`JTextField`
`Date`	`JLabel` (right aligned)	`JTextField`
`Number`	`JLabel` (right aligned)	`JTextField`
`ImageIcon`	`JLabel` (center aligned)	
`Boolean`	`JCheckBox` (center aligned)	`JCheckBox` (center aligned)

The predefined renderers and editors are automatically located and loaded to match the class returned from the `getColumnClass()` method in the table model. To use a predefined renderer or editor for a class other than `String`, you need to create your own table model by extending a subclass of `TableModel`. In your table model class, you need to override the `getColumnClass()` method to return the class of the column, as follows:

```java
public Class getColumnClass(int column) {
  return getValueAt(0, column).getClass();
}
```

By default, all cells are editable. To prohibit a cell from being edited, override the `isCellEditable(int rowIndex, int columnIndx)` method in `TableModel` to return `false`. By default, this method returns `true` in `AbstractTableModel`.

To demonstrate predefined table renderers and editors, let us write a program that displays a table for books. The table consists of three rows with the column names Title, Copies Needed, Publisher, Date Published, In-Stock, and Book Photo, as shown in Figure 31.13. Assume that dates and icons are not editable; prohibit users from editing these two columns.

Listing 31.6 gives a custom table model named `MyTableModel` that overrides the `getColumnClass` method (lines 15–17) to enable predefined renderers for Boolean and

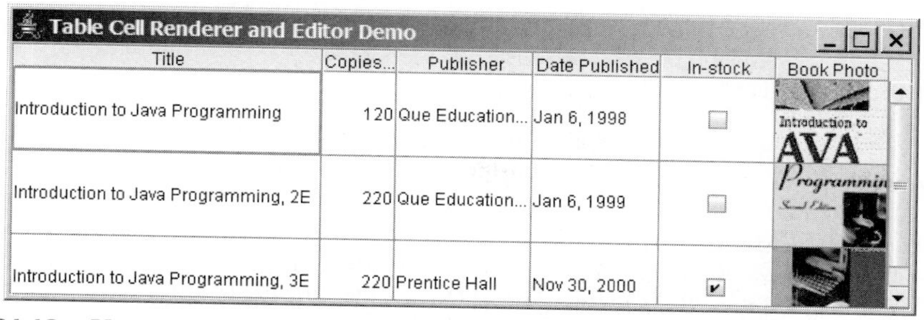

FIGURE 31.13   You need to use a custom table model to enable predefined renderers for Boolean and image cells.

image cells. MyTableModel also overrides the isCellEditable() method (lines 20–24). By default, isCellEditable() returns true. The example does not allow the user to edit image icons and dates, so this method is overridden to return false to disable editing of date and image columns. For a cell to be editable, both isCellEditable() in the table model and isEditing in JTable class must be true.

LISTING 31.6   MyTableModel.java

```
1  import javax.swing.*;
2  import javax.swing.table.*;
3  import java.util.*;
4
5  public class MyTableModel extends DefaultTableModel {
6    public MyTableModel() {
7    }
8
9    /** Construct a table model with specified data and columnNames */
10   public MyTableModel(Object[][] data, Object[] columnNames) {
11     super(data, columnNames);
12   }
13
14   /** Override this method to return a class for the column */
15   public Class getColumnClass(int column) {            // column class
16     return getValueAt(0, column).getClass();
17   }
18
19   /** Override this method to return true if cell is editable */
20   public boolean isCellEditable(int row, int column) {  // cell editable?
21     Class columnClass = getColumnClass(column);
22     return columnClass != ImageIcon.class &&
23       columnClass != Date.class;
24   }
25 }
```

If you create a JTable using a table model created from MyTableModel, the default renderers and editors for numbers, Boolean values, dates, and icons are used to display and edit these columns. Listing 31.7 gives a test program. The program creates a table model using MyTableModel (line 36). JTable assigns a predefined cell renderer and a predefined editor to the cell, whose class is specified in the getColumnClass() method in MyTableModel.

LISTING 31.7   TableCellRendererEditorDemo.java

```
1  import java.awt.*;
2  import javax.swing.*;
3  import java.util.*;
4
```

```
 5  public class TableCellRendererEditorDemo extends JApplet {
 6    // Create table column names
 7    private String[] columnNames =
 8      {"Title", "Copies Needed", "Publisher", "Date Published",
 9       "In-stock", "Book Photo"};
10
11    // Create image icons
12    private ImageIcon intro1eImageIcon = new ImageIcon(
13      getClass().getResource("image/intro1e.gif"));
14    private ImageIcon intro2eImageIcon = new ImageIcon(
15      getClass().getResource("image/intro2e.gif"));
16    private ImageIcon intro3eImageIcon = new ImageIcon(
17      getClass().getResource("image/intro3e.jpg"));
18
19    // Create table data
20    private Object[][] rowData = {
21      {"Introduction to Java Programming", 120,
22       "Que Education & Training",
23       new GregorianCalendar(1998, 1-1, 6).getTime(),
24       false, intro1eImageIcon},
25      {"Introduction to Java Programming, 2E", 220,
26       "Que Education & Training",
27       new GregorianCalendar(1999, 1-1, 6).getTime(),
28       false, intro2eImageIcon},
29      {"Introduction to Java Programming, 3E", 220,
30       "Prentice Hall",
31       new GregorianCalendar(2000, 12-1, 0).getTime(),
32       true, intro3eImageIcon},
33    };
34
35    // Create a table model
36    private MyTableModel tableModel = new MyTableModel(
37      rowData, columnNames);
38
39    // Create a table
40    private JTable jTable1 = new JTable(tableModel);
41
42    public TableCellRendererEditorDemo() {
43      jTable1.setRowHeight(60);
44      add(new JScrollPane(jTable1),
45        BorderLayout.CENTER);
46    }
47  }
```

The margin notes read: *column names*, *image icons*, *row data*, *table model*, *table*, *main omitted*.

The example creates two classes: `MyTableModel` and `TableCellRendererEditorDemo`. `MyTableModel` is an extension of `DefaultTableModel`. The purpose of `MyTableModel` is to override the default implementation of the `getColumnClass()` method to return the class of the column, so that an appropriate predefined `JTable` can be used for the column. By default, `getColumnClass()` returns `Object.class`.

31.6 Custom Table Renderers and Editors

Predefined renderers and editors are convenient and easy to use, but their functions are limited. The predefined image icon renderer displays the image icon in a label. The image icon cannot be scaled. If you want the whole image to fit in a cell, you need to create a custom renderer.

A custom renderer can be created by extending `DefaultTableCellRenderer`, which is a default implementation for the `TableCellRenderer` interface. The custom renderer must override the `getTableCellRendererComponent` method to return a component for rendering the table cell. The `getTableCellRendererComponent` method is defined as follows:

```
public Component getTableCellRendererComponent
    (JTable table, Object value, boolean isSelected,
     boolean isFocused, int row, int column)
```

This method signature is very similar to the `getListCellRendererComponent` method used to create custom list cell renderers.

This method is passed with a `JTable`, the value associated with the cell, information regarding whether the value is selected and the cell has the focus, and the row and column indices of the value. The component returned from the method is painted on the cell in the table. The class in Listing 31.8, `MyImageCellRenderer`, creates a renderer for displaying image icons in a panel.

LISTING 31.8 MyImageCellRenderer.java

```
1  import javax.swing.*;
2  import javax.swing.table.*;
3  import java.awt.*;
4
5  public class MyImageCellRenderer extends DefaultTableCellRenderer {
6    /** Override this method in DefaultTableCellRenderer */
7    public Component getTableCellRendererComponent
8        (JTable table, Object value, boolean isSelected,
9         boolean isFocused, int row, int column) {
10     Image image = ((ImageIcon)value).getImage();
11     ImageViewer imageViewer = new ImageViewer(image);
12     return imageViewer;
13   }
14 }
```

main omitted

You can also create a custom editor. `JTable` provides the `DefaultCellEditor` class, which can be used to edit a cell in a text field, a check box, or a combo box. To use it, simply create a text field, a check box, or a combo box, and pass it to `DefaultCellEditor`'s constructor to create an editor.

Using a custom renderer and editor, the preceding example can be revised to display scaled images and to use a custom combo editor to edit the cells in the Publisher column, as shown in Figure 31.14. The program is given in Listing 31.9.

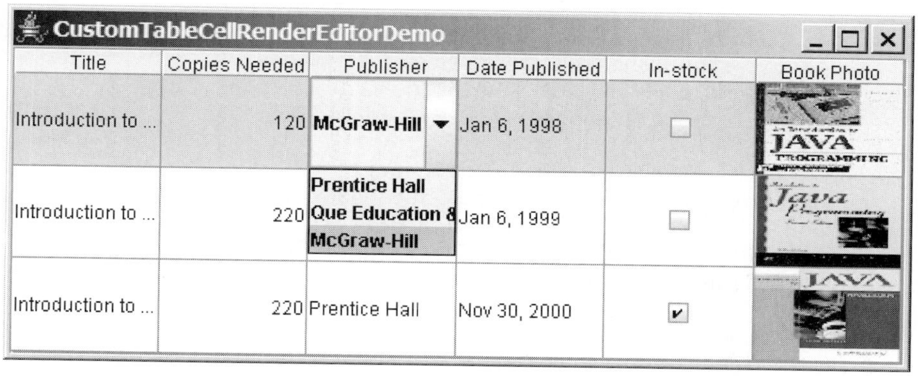

FIGURE 31.14 A custom renderer displays a scaled image, and a custom editor edits the Publisher column using a combo box.

LISTING 31.9 CustomTableCellRenderEditorDemo.java

```
1  import java.awt.*;
2  import javax.swing.*;
3  import javax.swing.table.*;
4  import java.util.*;
5
6  public class CustomTableCellRenderEditorDemo extends JApplet {
7    // Create table column names
8    private String[] columnNames =
9      {"Title", "Copies Needed", "Publisher", "Date Published",
10     "In-stock", "Book Photo"};
11
12   // Create image icons
13   private ImageIcon intro1eImageIcon =
14     new ImageIcon(getClass().getResource("image/intro1e.gif"));
15   private ImageIcon intro2eImageIcon =
16     new ImageIcon(getClass().getResource("image/intro2e.gif"));
17   private ImageIcon intro3eImageIcon =
18     new ImageIcon(getClass().getResource("image/intro3e.jpg"));
19
20   // Create table data
21   private Object[][] rowData = {
22     {"Introduction to Java Programming", 120,
23      "Que Education & Training",
24      new GregorianCalendar(1998, 1-1, 6).getTime(),
25      false, intro1eImageIcon},
26     {"Introduction to Java Programming, 2E", 220,
27      "Que Education & Training",
28      new GregorianCalendar(1999, 1-1, 6).getTime(),
29      false, intro2eImageIcon},
30     {"Introduction to Java Programming, 3E", 220,
31      "Prentice Hall",
32      new GregorianCalendar(2000, 12-1, 0).getTime(),
33      true, intro3eImageIcon},
34   };
35
36   // Create a table model
37   private MyTableModel tableModel = new MyTableModel(
38     rowData, columnNames);
39
40   // Create a table
41   private JTable jTable1 = new JTable(tableModel);
42
43   public CustomTableCellRenderEditorDemo() {
44     // Set custom renderer for displaying images
45     TableColumn bookCover = jTable1.getColumn("Book Photo");
46     bookCover.setCellRenderer(new MyImageCellRenderer());
47
48     // Create a combo box for publishers
49     JComboBox jcboPublishers = new JComboBox();
50     jcboPublishers.addItem("Prentice Hall");
51     jcboPublishers.addItem("Que Education & Training");
52     jcboPublishers.addItem("McGraw-Hill");
53
54     // Set combo box as the editor for the publisher column
55     TableColumn publisherColumn = jTable1.getColumn("Publisher");
56     publisherColumn.setCellEditor(
57         new DefaultCellEditor(jcboPublishers));
58
```

column names

image icons

row data

table model

table

set renderer

combo box

set editor

```
59      jTable1.setRowHeight(60);
60      add(new JScrollPane(jTable1),
61          BorderLayout.CENTER);
62   }
63 }
```

main omitted

This example uses the same table model (`MyTableModel`) that was created in the preceding example (lines 37–38). By default, image icons are displayed using the predefined image icon renderer. To use `MyImageCellRenderer` to display the image, you have to explicitly specify the `MyImageCellRenderer` renderer for the Book Photo column (line 46). Likewise, you have to explicitly specify the combo box editor for the Publisher column (lines 56–57); otherwise the default editor would be used.

When you edit a cell in the Publisher column, a combo box of three items is displayed. When you select an item from the box, it is displayed in the cell. You did not write the code for handling selections. The selections are handled by the `DefaultCellEditor` class.

When you resize the Book Photo column, the image is resized to fit into the whole cell. With the predefined image renderer, you can only see part of the image if the cell is smaller than the image.

31.7 Table Model Events

`JTable` does not fire table events. It fires events like `MouseEvent`, `KeyEvent`, and `ComponentEvent` that are inherited from its superclass, `JComponent`. Table events are fired by table models, table column models, and table-selection models whenever changes are made to these models. Table models fire `TableModelEvent` when table data is changed. Table column models fire `TableColumnModelEvent` when columns are added, removed, or moved, or when the column selection changes. Table-selection models fire `ListSelectionEvent` when the selection changes.

To listen for these events, a listener must be registered with an appropriate model and implement the correct listener interface. Listing 31.10 gives an example that demonstrates how to use these events. The program displays messages on a text area when a row or a column is selected, when a cell is edited, or when a column is removed. Figure 31.15 is a sample run of the program.

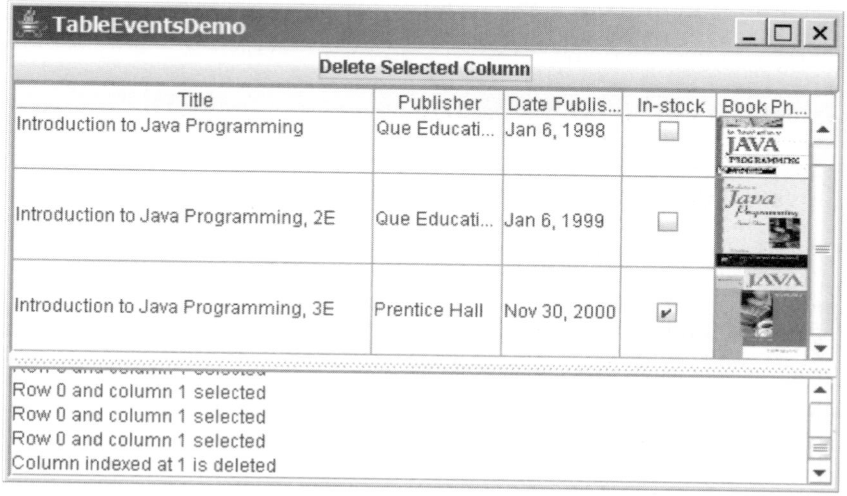

FIGURE 31.15 Table event handlers display table events on a text area.

LISTING 31.10 TableEventsDemo.java

```
1  import java.awt.*;
2  import java.awt.event.*;
3  import javax.swing.*;
4  import javax.swing.event.*;
5  import javax.swing.table.*;
6  import java.util.*;
7
8  public class TableEventsDemo extends JApplet {
9    // Create table column names
10   private String[] columnNames =
11     {"Title", "Copies Needed", "Publisher", "Date Published",
12      "In-stock", "Book Photo"};
13
14   // Create image icons
15   private ImageIcon intro1eImageIcon =
16     new ImageIcon(getClass().getResource("image/intro1e.gif"));
17   private ImageIcon intro2eImageIcon =
18     new ImageIcon(getClass().getResource("image/intro2e.gif"));
19   private ImageIcon intro3eImageIcon =
20     new ImageIcon(getClass().getResource("image/intro3e.jpg"));
21
22   // Create table data
23   private Object[][] rowData = {
24     {"Introduction to Java Programming", 120,
25      "Que Education & Training",
26      new GregorianCalendar(1998, 1-1, 6).getTime(),
27      false, intro1eImageIcon},
28     {"Introduction to Java Programming, 2E", 220,
29      "Que Education & Training",
30      new GregorianCalendar(1999, 1-1, 6).getTime(),
31      false, intro2eImageIcon},
32     {"Introduction to Java Programming, 3E", 220,
33      "Prentice Hall",
34      new GregorianCalendar(2000, 12-1, 0).getTime(),
35      true, intro3eImageIcon},
36   };
37
38   // Create a table model
39   private MyTableModel tableModel = new MyTableModel(
40     rowData, columnNames);
41
42   // Create a table
43   private JTable jTable1 = new JTable(tableModel);
44
45   // Get table column model
46   private TableColumnModel tableColumnModel =
47     jTable1.getColumnModel();
48
49   // Get table selection model
50   private ListSelectionModel selectionModel =
51     jTable1.getSelectionModel();
52
53   // Create a text area
54   private JTextArea jtaMessage = new JTextArea();
55
56   // Create a button
57   private JButton jbtDeleteColumn =
58     new JButton("Delete Selected Column");
59
```

Margin labels:
- column names (line 10)
- image icons (line 15)
- table data (line 23)
- table model (line 39)
- table (line 43)
- column model (line 46)
- selection model (line 50)

```java
60   public TableEventsDemo() {
61     // Set custom renderer for displaying images
62     TableColumn bookCover = jTable1.getColumn("Book Photo");
63     bookCover.setCellRenderer(new MyImageCellRenderer());
64
65     // Create a combo box for publishers
66     JComboBox jcboPublishers = new JComboBox();
67     jcboPublishers.addItem("Prentice Hall");
68     jcboPublishers.addItem("Que Education & Training");
69     jcboPublishers.addItem("McGraw-Hill");
70
71     // Set combo box as the editor for the publisher column
72     TableColumn publisherColumn = jTable1.getColumn("Publisher");
73     publisherColumn.setCellEditor(
74       new DefaultCellEditor(jcboPublishers));
75
76     jTable1.setRowHeight(60);
77     jTable1.setColumnSelectionAllowed(true);
78
79     JSplitPane jSplitPane1 = new JSplitPane(
80       JSplitPane.VERTICAL_SPLIT);
81     jSplitPane1.add(new JScrollPane(jTable1), JSplitPane.LEFT);
82     jSplitPane1.add(new JScrollPane(jtaMessage), JSplitPane.RIGHT);
83     add(jbtDeleteColumn, BorderLayout.NORTH);
84     add(jSplitPane1, BorderLayout.CENTER);
85
86     tableModel.addTableModelListener(new TableModelListener() {        table model listener
87       public void tableChanged(TableModelEvent e) {
88         jtaMessage.append("Table changed at row " +
89           e.getFirstRow() + " and column " + e.getColumn() + "\n");
90       }
91     });
92
93     tableColumnModel.addColumnModelListener(                           column model listener
94       new TableColumnModelListener() {
95       public void columnRemoved(TableColumnModelEvent e) {
96         jtaMessage.append("Column indexed at " + e.getFromIndex() +
97           " is deleted \n");
98       }
99       public void columnAdded(TableColumnModelEvent e) {
100      }
101      public void columnMoved(TableColumnModelEvent e) {
102      }
103      public void columnMarginChanged(ChangeEvent e) {
104      }
105      public void columnSelectionChanged(ListSelectionEvent e) {
106      }
107    });
108
109    jbtDeleteColumn.addActionListener(new ActionListener() {
110      public void actionPerformed(ActionEvent e) {
111        if (jTable1.getSelectedColumn() >= 0) {
112          TableColumnModel columnModel = jTable1.getColumnModel();
113          TableColumn tableColumn =
114              columnModel.getColumn(jTable1.getSelectedColumn());
115          columnModel.removeColumn(tableColumn);
116        }
117      }
118    });
119
```

selection model listener

```
120   selectionModel.addListSelectionListener(
121     new ListSelectionListener() {
122     public void valueChanged(ListSelectionEvent e) {
123       jtaMessage.append("Row " + jTable1.getSelectedRow() +
124         " and column " + jTable1.getSelectedColumn() +
125         " selected\n");
126     }
127   });
128   }
129 }
```

main omitted

To respond to the row and column selection events, you need to implement the **valueChanged** method in **ListSelectionListener**. To respond to the cell-editing event, you need to implement the **tableChanged** method in **TableModelListener**. To respond to the column-deletion event, you need to implement the **columnRemoved** method in **TableColumnModelListener**. Let's use the same table from the preceding example, but with a button added for deleting the selected column and a text area for displaying the messages.

A table model is created using **MyTableModel** (lines 39–40), which was given in Listing 31.6. When a table is created (line 43), its default column model and selection model are also created. Therefore, you can obtain the table column model and selection model from the table (lines 46–51).

When a row or a column is selected, a **ListSelectionEvent** is fired by **selectionModel**, which invokes the handler to display the selected row and column in the text area (lines 120–127). When the content or structure of the table is changed, a **TableModelEvent** is fired by **tableModel**, which invokes the handler to display the last row and last column of the changed data in the text area (lines 86–91). When a column is deleted by clicking the *Delete Selected Column* button, a **ColumnModelEvent** is fired by **tableColumnModel**, which invokes the handler to display the index of the deleted column (lines 93–107).

31.8 JTree

JTree is a Swing component that displays data in a treelike hierarchy, as shown in Figure 31.16.

FIGURE 31.16   **JTree** displays data in a treelike hierarchy.

All the nodes displayed in the tree are in the form of a hierarchical indexed list. The tree can be used to navigate structured data with hierarchical relationships. A node can have child nodes. A node is called a *leaf* if it has no children; a node with no parent is called the *root* of its tree. A tree may consist of many subtrees, each node acting as the root for its own subtree.

A nonleaf node can be expanded or collapsed by double-clicking on the node or on the node's handle in front of the node. The handle usually has a visible sign to indicate whether the node is expanded or collapsed. For example, on Windows, the + symbol indicates that the node can be expanded, and the − symbol, that it can be collapsed.

Like `JTable`, `JTree` is a very complex component with many supporting interfaces and classes. `JTree` is in the `javax.swing` package, but its supporting interfaces and classes are all included in the `javax.swing.tree` package. The supporting interfaces are `TreeModel`, `TreeSelectionModel`, `TreeNode`, and `MutableTreeNode`, and the supported classes are `DefaultTreeModel`, `DefaultMutableTreeNode`, `DefaultTreeCellEditor`, `DefaultTreeCellRenderer`, and `TreePath`.

While `JTree` displays the tree, the data representation of the tree is handled by `TreeModel`, `TreeNode`, and `TreePath`. `TreeModel` represents the entire tree, `TreeNode` represents a node, and `TreePath` represents a path to a node. Unlike the `ListModel` or `TableModel`, `TreeModel` does not directly store or manage tree data. Tree data is stored and managed in `TreeNode` and `TreePath`. `DefaultTreeModel` is a concrete implementation of `TreeModel`. `MutableTreeNode` is a subinterface of `TreeNode`, which represents a tree node that can be mutated by adding or removing child nodes, or by changing the contents of a user object stored in the node.

The `TreeSelectionModel` interface handles tree node selection. The `DefaultTreeCellRenderer` class provides a default tree node renderer that can display a label and/or an icon in a node. The `DefaultTreeCellEditor` can be used to edit the cells in a text field.

A `TreePath` is an array of `Object`s that are vended from a `TreeModel`. The elements of the array are ordered such that the root is always the first element (index 0) of the array. Figure 31.17 shows how these interfaces and classes are interrelated.

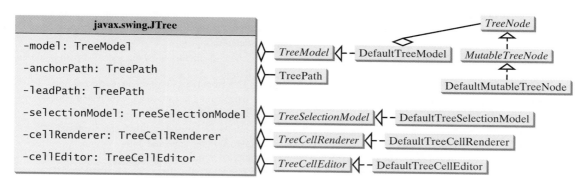

FIGURE 31.17 `JTree` contains many supporting interfaces and classes.

Figure 31.18 shows the constructors, frequently used properties, and methods of `JTree`.

The `JTree` class contains seven constructors for creating trees. You can create a tree using its no-arg constructor, a tree model, a tree node, a `Hashtable`, an array, or a vector. Using the no-arg constructor, a sample tree is created as shown in Figure 31.16. Using a `Hashtable`, an array, or a vector, a root is created but not displayed. All the keys in a `Hashtable`, all the objects in an array, and all the elements in a vector are added into the tree as children of the root. If you wish the root to be displayed, set the `rootVisible` property to `true`.

All the methods related to path selection are also defined in the `TreeSelectionModel` interface, which will be covered in §31.11, "`TreePath` and `TreeSelectionModel`."

> JavaBeans properties with get and set methods omitted in the UML diagram.

javax.swing.JTree	
#cellEditor: TreeCellEditor	Specifies a cell editor used to edit entries in the tree.
#cellRenderer: TreeCellRenderer	Specifies a cell renderer.
#editable: boolean	Specifies whether the cells are editable (default: false).
#model: TreeModel	Maintains the tree model.
#rootVisible: boolean	Specifies whether the root is displayed (depending on the constructor).
#rowHeight: int	Specifies the height of the row for the node displayed in the tree (default: 16 pixels).
#scrollsOnExpand: boolean	If true, when a node is expanded, as many of the descendants are scrolled to be visible (default: 16 pixels).
#selectionModel: TreeSelectionModel	Models the set of selected nodes in this tree.
#showsRootHandles: boolean	Specifies whether the root handles are displayed (default: true).
#toggleClickCount: int	Number of mouse clicks before a node is expanded (default: 2).
-anchorSelectionPath: TreePath	The path identified as the anchor.
-expandsSelectedPaths: boolean	True if paths in the selection should be expanded (default: true).
-leadSelectionPaths: TreePath	The path identified as the lead.
+JTree()	Creates a JTree with a sample tree model, as shown in Figure 31.16.
+JTree(value: java.util.Hashtable)	Creates a JTree with an invisible root and the keys in the Hashtable key/value pairs as its children.
+JTree(value: Object[])	Creates a JTree with an invisible root and the elements in the array as its children.
+JTree(newModel: TreeModel)	Creates a JTree with the specified tree model.
+JTree(root: TreeNode)	Creates a JTree with the specified tree node as its root.
+JTree(root: TreeNode, asksAllowsChildren: boolean)	Creates a JTree with the specified tree node as its root and decides whether a node is a leaf node in the specified manner.
+JTree(value: Vector)	Creates a JTree with an invisible root and the elements in the vector as its children.
+addSelectionPath(path: TreePath): void	Adds the specified TreePath to the current selection.
+addSelectionPaths(paths: TreePath[]): void	Adds the specified TreePaths to the current selection.
+addSelectionRow(row: int): void	Adds the path at the specified row to the current selection.
+addSelectionRows(rows: int[]): void	Adds the path at the specified rows to the current selection.
+clearSelection(): void	Clears the selection.
+collapsePath(path: TreePath): void	Ensures that the node identified by the specified path is collapsed and viewable.
+getSelectionPath(): TreePath	Returns the path from the root to the first selected node.
+getSelectionPaths(): TreePath[]	Returns the paths from the root to all the selected nodes.
+getLastSelectedPathComponent()	Returns the last node in the first selected TreePath.
+getRowCount():int	Returns the number of rows currently being displayed.
+removeSelectionPath(path: TreePath): void	Removes the node in the specified path.
+removeSelectionPaths(paths: TreePath[]): void	Removes the node in the specified paths.

FIGURE 31.18 The **JTree** class is for creating, customizing, and manipulating trees.

Listing 31.11 gives an example that creates four trees: a default tree using the no-arg constructor, a tree created from an array of objects, a tree created from a vector, and a tree created from a hash table, as shown in Figure 31.19. Enable the user to dynamically set the properties for **rootVisible**, **rowHeight**, and **showsRootHandles**.

LISTING 31.11 SimpleTreeDemo.java

```java
1 import java.awt.*;
2 import java.awt.event.*;
3 import javax.swing.*;
4 import javax.swing.event.*;
5 import java.util.*;
```

```
6
7   public class SimpleTreeDemo extends JApplet {
8     // Create a default tree
9     private JTree jTree1 = new JTree();                                    tree 1
10
11    // Create a tree with an array of Objects.
12    private JTree jTree2 = new JTree(new String[]                           tree 2
13      {"dog", "cow", "cat", "pig", "rabbit"});
14
15    // Create a tree with a Hashtable
16    private Vector vector = new Vector(Arrays.asList(                       tree 3
17      new Object[]{"red", "green", "black", "white", "purple"}));
18    private JTree jTree3 = new JTree(vector);
19
20    private Hashtable<Integer, String> hashtable =
21      new Hashtable<Integer, String>();
22    private JTree jTree4;                                                   tree 4
23
24    // Create a combo box for selecting rootVisible
25    private JComboBox jcboRootVisible = new JComboBox(
26      new String[]{"false", "true"});
27
28    // Create a combo box for selecting showRootHandles
29    private JComboBox jcboShowsRootHandles = new JComboBox(
30      new String[] {"false", "true"});
31
32    // Create a spinner for selecting row height
33    private JSpinner jSpinnerRowHeight = new JSpinner(
34      new SpinnerNumberModel(16, 1, 50, 1));
35
36    public SimpleTreeDemo() {
37      jTree1.setRootVisible(false);
38
39      hashtable.put(1, "red");
40      hashtable.put(2, "green");
41      hashtable.put(3, "blue");
42      hashtable.put(4, "yellow");
43      jTree4 = new JTree(hashtable);
44
45      JPanel panel1 = new JPanel(new GridLayout(1, 4));                     tree
46      panel1.add(new JScrollPane(jTree1));
47      panel1.add(new JScrollPane(jTree2));
48      panel1.add(new JScrollPane(jTree3));
49      panel1.add(new JScrollPane(jTree4));
50
51      JPanel panel2 = new JPanel();
52      panel2.add(new JLabel("rootVisible"));
53      panel2.add(jcboRootVisible);
54      panel2.add(new JLabel("rowHeight"));
55      panel2.add(jSpinnerRowHeight);
56      panel2.add(new JLabel("showsRootHandles"));
57      panel2.add(jcboShowsRootHandles);
58
59      add(panel1, BorderLayout.CENTER);
60      add(panel2, BorderLayout.SOUTH);
61
62      // Register listeners
63      jcboRootVisible.addActionListener(new ActionListener() {             combo box listener
64        public void actionPerformed(ActionEvent e) {
65          boolean rootVisible =
66            jcboRootVisible.getSelectedItem().equals("true");
```

```
67        jTree1.setRootVisible(rootVisible);
68        jTree2.setRootVisible(rootVisible);
69        jTree3.setRootVisible(rootVisible);
70        jTree4.setRootVisible(rootVisible);
71      }
72    });
73
74    jcboShowsRootHandles.addActionListener(new ActionListener() {
75      public void actionPerformed(ActionEvent e) {
76        boolean showsRootHandles =
77          jcboShowsRootHandles.getSelectedItem().equals("true");
78        jTree1.setShowsRootHandles(showsRootHandles);
79        jTree2.setShowsRootHandles(showsRootHandles);
80        jTree3.setShowsRootHandles(showsRootHandles);
81        jTree4.setShowsRootHandles(showsRootHandles);
82      }
83    });
84
```

spinner listener

```
85    jSpinnerRowHeight.addChangeListener(new ChangeListener() {
86      public void stateChanged(ChangeEvent e) {
87        int height =
88          ((Integer)(jSpinnerRowHeight.getValue())).intValue();
89        jTree1.setRowHeight(height);
90        jTree2.setRowHeight(height);
91        jTree3.setRowHeight(height);
92        jTree4.setRowHeight(height);
93      }
94    });
95  }
```

main omitted

```
96 }
```

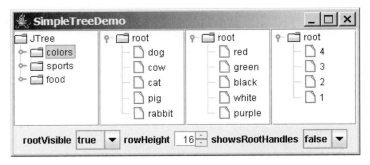

FIGURE 31.19   You can dynamically set the properties for **rootVisible**, **rowHeight**, and **showRootHandles** in a tree.

Four trees are created in this example. The first is created using the no-arg constructor (line 9) with a sample tree. The second is created using an array of objects (lines 12–13). All the objects in the array become the children of the root. The third is created using a vector (lines 16–18). All the elements in the vector become the children of the root. The fourth is created using a hash table (lines 39–43). A **Hashtable** is like a **Map**. **Hashtable** was introduced earlier than Java 2 and has since been replaced by **Map**. It is used in the Java API (e.g., **JTree**), which was developed before Java 2. The keys of the hash table become the children of the root.

JTree doesn't directly support scrolling. To create a scrollable tree, create a **JScrollPane** and add an instance of **JTree** to the scroll pane (lines 46–49).

The example enables you to specify whether the root is visible and whether the root handles are visible from two combo boxes (lines 63–83). It also lets you specify the row height of the node in a spinner (lines 85–94).

31.9 TreeModel and DefaultTreeModel

The TreeModel interface represents the entire tree. Unlike ListModel or TableModel, TreeModel does not directly store or manage tree data. TreeModel contains the structural information about the tree, and tree data is stored and managed by TreeNode.

DefaultTreeModel is a concrete implementation for TreeModel that uses TreeNodes. Figure 31.20 shows TreeModel and DefaultTreeModel.

«interface» javax.swing.tree.TreeModel	
+getChild(parent: Object, index: int): Object	Returns the child of the parent at the index in the parent's child array.
+getChildCount(parent: Object): int	Returns the number of children of the specified parent in the tree model.
+getIndexOfChild(parent: Object, child: Object): int	Returns the index of the child in the parent. If the parent or child is null, returns –1.
+getRoot(): Object	Returns the root of the tree. Returns null if the tree is empty.
+isLeaf(node: Object): boolean	Returns true if the specified node is a leaf.
+addTreeModelListener(listener: TreeModelListener): void	Adds a listener for the TreeModelEvent posted after the tree changes.
+removeTreeModelListener(listener: TreeModelListener): void	Removes a listener previously added with addTreeModelListener.
+valueForPathChanged(path: TreePath, newValue: Object): void	Messaged when the user has altered the value for the item identified by path to newValue.

javax.swing.tree.DefaultTreeModel	
#asksAllowsChildren: boolean	Tells how leaf nodes are determined. True if only nodes that do not allow children are leaf nodes, false if nodes that have no children are leaf nodes.
#root: TreeNode	The root of the tree.
+DefaultTreeModel(root: TreeNode)	Creates a DefaultTreeModel with the specified root.
+DefaultTreeModel(root: TreeNode, asksAllowsChildren: boolean)	Creates a DefaultTreeModel with the specified root and decides whether a node is a leaf node in the specified manner.
+asksAllowsChildren(): boolean	Returns asksAllowsChildren.
+getPathToRoot(aNode: TreeNode): TreeNode[]	Returns the nodes in an array from root to the specified node.
+insertNodeInto(newChild: MutableTreeNode, parent: MutableTreeNode, index: int): void	Inserts newChild at location index in parent's children.
+reload(): void	Reloads the model (invoke this method if the tree has been modified).
+removeNodeFromParent(node: MutableTreeNode): void	Removes the node from its parent.

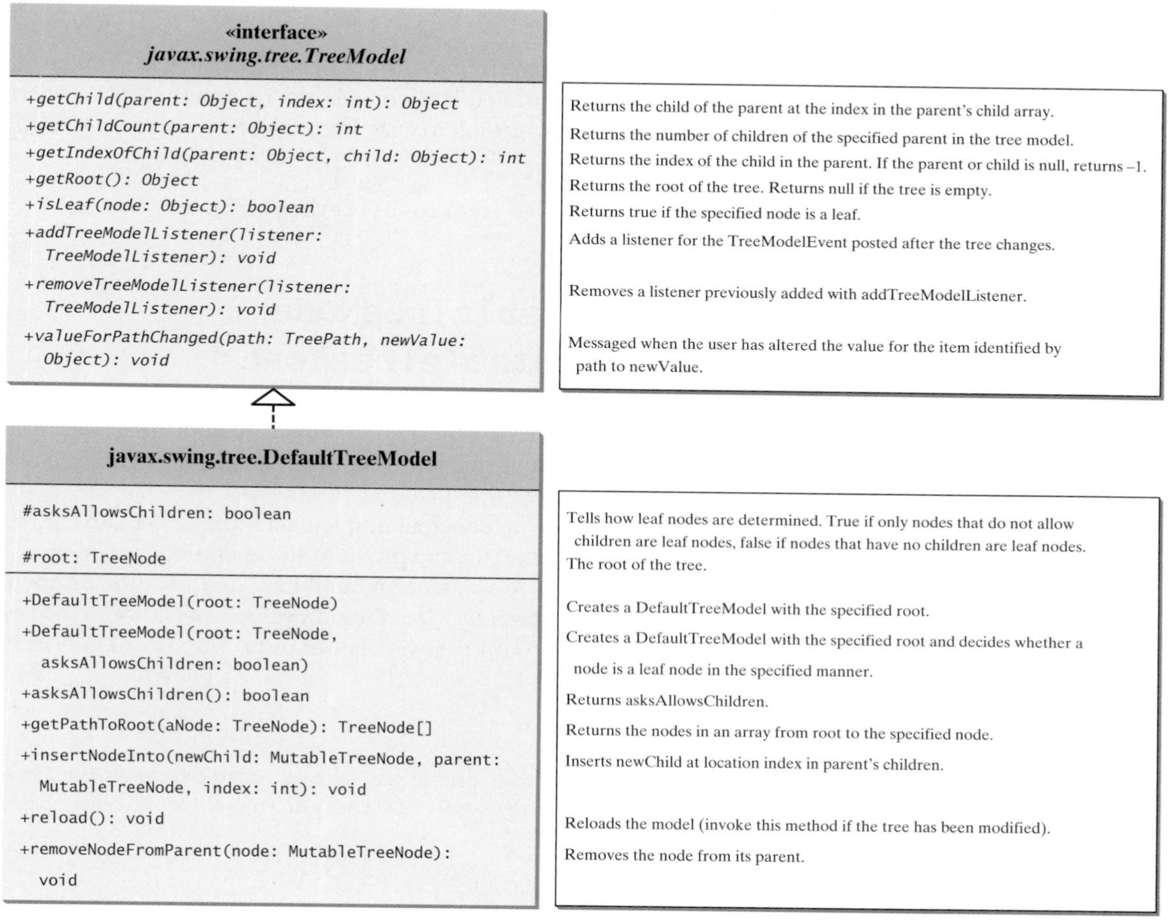

FIGURE 31.20 TreeModel represents an entire tree.

Once a tree is created, you can obtain its tree model using the getModel method. Listing 31.12 gives an example that traverses all the nodes in a tree using the tree model. Line 3 creates a tree using JTree's no-arg constructor with the default sample nodes, as shown in Figure 31.16. The tree model for the tree is obtained in line 4. Line 5 invokes the traversal method to traverse the nodes in the tree.

LISTING 31.12 TestTreeModel.java

```
1 public class TestTreeModel {
2   public static void main(String[] args) {
3     javax.swing.JTree jTree1 = new javax.swing.JTree();          default tree
4     javax.swing.tree.TreeModel model = jTree1.getModel();        tree model
5     traversal(model, model.getRoot());                           getRoot
6   }
```

```
7
8    private static void traversal
9        (javax.swing.tree.TreeModel model, Object root) {
10       System.out.print(root + " ");
11       if ( model.isLeaf(root)) return;
12       for (int i = 0; i < model.getChildCount(model.getRoot()); i++) {
13           traversal(model, model.getChild(root, i));
14       }
15   }
16 }
```

is leaf?
getChildCount
getChild

The `traversal` method starts from the root of the tree. The root is obtained by invoking the `getRoot` method (line 5). If the root is a leaf, the method returns (line 11). Otherwise, it recursively invokes the `traversal` method to start from the children of the root (line 13). The output of the program is

```
JTree colors blue violet red sports basketball soccer football
food hot dogs pizza ravioli
```

31.10 **TreeNode**, **MutableTreeNode**, and **DefaultMutableTreeNode**

While `TreeModel` represents the entire tree, `TreeNode` stores a single node of the tree. `MutableTreeNode` defines a subinterface of `TreeNode` with additional methods for changing the content of the node, for inserting and removing a child node, for setting a new parent, and for removing the node itself.

`DefaultMutableTreeNode` is a concrete implementation of `MutableTreeNode` that maintains a list of children in a vector and provides the operations for creating nodes, for examining and modifying a node's parent and children, and also for examining the tree to which the node belongs. Normally, you should use `DefaultMutableTreeNode` to create a tree node. Figure 31.21 shows `TreeNode`, `MutableTreeNode`, and `DefaultMutableTreeNode`.

Note

depth-first traversal

In graph theory, *depth-first traversal* is defined the same as preorder traversal, but in the `depthFirstEnumeration()` method in `DefaultMutableTreeNode`, it is the same as postorder traversal.

Note

You can create a **JTree** from a root using **new JTree(TreeNode)** or from a model using new JTree(TreeModel). To create a tree model, you first create an instance of **TreeNode** to represent the root of the tree, and then create an instance of **DefaultTreeModel** fitted with the root.

creating trees

Listing 31.13 gives an example that creates two trees to display world, continents, countries, and states. The two trees share the same nodes and thus display identical contents. The program also displays the properties of the tree in a text area, as shown in Figure 31.22.

LISTING 31.13 TreeNodeDemo.java

```
1 import java.awt.*;
2 import javax.swing.*;
3 import javax.swing.tree.*;
4 import java.util.*;
5
```

```
 6 public class TreeNodeDemo extends JApplet {
 7   public TreeNodeDemo() {
 8     // Create the first tree
 9     DefaultMutableTreeNode root, europe, northAmerica, us;            add children
10
11     europe = new DefaultMutableTreeNode("Europe");
12     europe.add(new DefaultMutableTreeNode("UK"));                    tree nodes
13     europe.add(new DefaultMutableTreeNode("Germany"));
14     europe.add(new DefaultMutableTreeNode("France"));
15     europe.add(new DefaultMutableTreeNode("Norway"));
16
17     northAmerica = new DefaultMutableTreeNode("North America");
18     us = new DefaultMutableTreeNode("US");
19     us.add(new DefaultMutableTreeNode("California"));               add children
20     us.add(new DefaultMutableTreeNode("Texas"));
21     us.add(new DefaultMutableTreeNode("New York"));
22     us.add(new DefaultMutableTreeNode("Florida"));
23     us.add(new DefaultMutableTreeNode("Illinois"));
24     northAmerica.add(us);
25     northAmerica.add(new DefaultMutableTreeNode("Canada"));
26
27     root = new DefaultMutableTreeNode("World");
28     root.add(europe);
29     root.add(northAmerica);
30
31     JPanel panel = new JPanel();
32     panel.setLayout(new GridLayout(1, 2));
33     panel.add(new JScrollPane(new JTree(root)));
34     panel.add(new JScrollPane(new JTree(new DefaultTreeModel(root))));
35
36     JTextArea jtaMessage = new JTextArea();
37     jtaMessage.setWrapStyleWord(true);
38     jtaMessage.setLineWrap(true);
39     add(new JSplitPane(JSplitPane.VERTICAL_SPLIT,
40       panel, new JScrollPane(jtaMessage)), BorderLayout.CENTER);
41
42     // Get tree information
43     jtaMessage.append("Depth of the node US is " + us.getDepth());
44     jtaMessage.append("\nLevel of the node US is " + us.getLevel());
45     jtaMessage.append("\nFirst child of the root is " +
46       root.getFirstChild());
47     jtaMessage.append("\nFirst leaf of the root is " +
48       root.getFirstLeaf());
49     jtaMessage.append("\nNumber of the children of the root is " +
50       root.getChildCount());
51     jtaMessage.append("\nNumber of leaves in the tree is " +
52       root.getLeafCount());
53     String breadthFirstSearchResult = "";
54
55     // Breadth-first traversal
56     Enumeration bf = root.breadthFirstEnumeration();
57     while (bf.hasMoreElements())
58       breadthFirstSearchResult += bf.nextElement().toString() + " ";
59     jtaMessage.append("\nBreath-first traversal from the root is "
60       + breadthFirstSearchResult);
61   }
62 }
```
main omitted

«interface» *javax.swing.tree.TreeNode*	
+children(): java.util.Enumeration	Returns the children of this node.
+getAllowsChildren(): boolean	Returns true if this node can have children.
+getChildAt(childIndex: int): TreeNode	Returns the child TreeNode at index childIndex.
+getChildCount(): int	Returns the number of children under this node.
+getIndex(node: TreeNode): int	Returns the index of the specified node in the current node's children.
+getParent(): TreeNode	Returns the parent of this node.
+isLeaf(): boolean	Returns true if this node is a leaf.

«interface» *javax.swing.tree.MutableTreeNode*	
+insert(child: MutableTreeNode, index: int): void	Adds the specified child under this node at the specified index.
+remove(index: int): void	Removes the child at the specified index from this node's child list.
+remove(node: MutableTreeNode): void	Removes the specified node from this node's child list.
+removeFromParent(): void	Removes this node from its parent.
+setParent(newParent: MutableTreeNode): void	Sets the parent of this node to the specified newParent.
+setUserObject(object: Object): void	Resets the user object of this node to the specified object.

javax.swing.tree.DefaultMutableTreeNode	
#allowsChildren: boolean	True if the node is able to have children.
#parent: MutableTreeNode	Stores the parent of this node.
#userObject: Object	Stores the content of this node.
+DefaultMutableTreeNode()	Creates a tree node without user object, and allows children.
+DefaultMutableTreeNode(userObject: Object)	Creates a tree node with the specified user object, and allows children.
+DefaultMutableTreeNode(userObject: Object, allowsChildren: boolean)	Creates a tree node with the specified user object and the specified mode to indicate whether children are allowed.
+add(newChild: MutableTreeNode)	Adds the specified node to the end of this node's child vector.
+getChildAfter(aChild: TreeNode): TreeNode +getChildBefore(aChild: TreeNode): TreeNode	These two methods return the next (previous) sibling of the specified child in this node's child vector.
+getFirstChild(): TreeNode +getLastChild(): TreeNode	These two methods return this node's first (last) child in the child's vector of this node.
+getFirstLeaf(): DefaultMutableTreeNode +getLastLeaf(): DefaultMutableTreeNode +getNextLeaf(): DefaultMutableTreeNode +getPreviousLeaf(): DefaultMutableTreeNode	These four methods return the first (last, next, and previous) leaf that is a descendant of this node. The first (last, next, and previous) leaf is recursively defined as the first (last, next, and previous) child's first (last, next, and previous) leaf.
+getLeafCount(): int	Returns the total number of leaves that are descendants of this node.
+getDepth(): int	Returns the depth of the tree rooted at this node.
+getLevel(): int	Returns the distance from the root to this node.
+getNextNode(): DefaultMutableTreeNode +getPreviousNode(): DefaultMutableTreeNode	Returns the node that follows (precedes) this node in a preorder traversal of this node.
+getSiblingCount(): int	Returns the number of siblings of this node.
+getNextSibling(): DefaultMutableTreeNode	Returns the next sibling of this node in the parent's child vector.
+getPath(): TreeNode[]	Returns the path from the root to this node.
+getRoot(): TreeNode	Returns the root of the tree that contains this node.
+isRoot(): boolean	Returns true if this node is the root of the tree.
+breadthFirstEnumeration(): Enumeration +depthFirstEnumeration(): Enumeration +postorderEnumeration(): Enumeration +preorderEnumeration(): Enumeration	These four methods create and return an enumeration that traverses the subtree rooted at this node in breadth-first order (depth-first order, postorder, preorder). These traversals were discussed in §20.4.3, "Tree Traversal."

FIGURE 31.21 TreeNode represents a node.

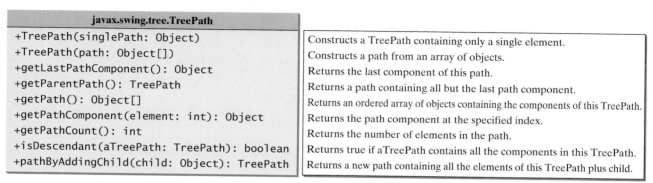

FIGURE 31.22   The two trees have the same data because their roots are the same.

You can create a JTree using a TreeNode root (line 33) or a TreeModel (line 34), whichever is convenient. A TreeModel is actually created using a TreeNode root (line 34). The two trees have the same contents because the root is the same. However, it is important to note that the two JTree objects are different, and so are their TreeModel objects, although both trees have the same root.

A tree is created by adding the nodes to the tree (lines 9–29). Each node is created using the DefaultMutableTreeNode class. This class provides many methods to manipulate the tree (e.g., adding a child, removing a child) and obtaining information about the tree (e.g., level, depth, number of children, number of leaves, traversals). Some examples of using these methods are given in lines 43–60.

As shown in this example, often you don't have to directly use TreeModel. Using DefaultMutableTreeNode is sufficient, since the tree data is stored in DefaultMutableTreeNode, and DefaultMutableTreeNode contains all the methods for modifying the tree and obtaining tree information.

31.11 TreePath and TreeSelectionModel

The JTree class contains the methods for selecting tree paths. The TreePath class represents a path from an ancestor to a descendant in a tree. Figure 31.23 shows TreePath.

javax.swing.tree.TreePath	
+TreePath(singlePath: Object)	Constructs a TreePath containing only a single element.
+TreePath(path: Object[])	Constructs a path from an array of objects.
+getLastPathComponent(): Object	Returns the last component of this path.
+getParentPath(): TreePath	Returns a path containing all but the last path component.
+getPath(): Object[]	Returns an ordered array of objects containing the components of this TreePath.
+getPathComponent(element: int): Object	Returns the path component at the specified index.
+getPathCount(): int	Returns the number of elements in the path.
+isDescendant(aTreePath: TreePath): boolean	Returns true if aTreePath contains all the components in this TreePath.
+pathByAddingChild(child: Object): TreePath	Returns a new path containing all the elements of this TreePath plus child.

FIGURE 31.23   TreePath represents a path from an ancestor to a descendant in a tree.

You can construct a TreePath from a single object or an array of objects, but often instances of TreePath are returned from the methods in JTree and TreeSelectionModel.

obtain tree paths

For instance, the `getLeadSelectionPath()` method in **JTree** returns the path from the root to the selected node. There are many ways to extract the nodes from a tree path. Often you use the `getLastPathComponent()` method to obtain the last node in the path, and then the `getParent()` method to get all the nodes in the path upward through the link.

The selection of tree nodes is defined in the **TreeSelectionModel** interface, as shown in Figure 31.24. The **DefaultTreeSelectionModel** class is a concrete implementation of the **TreeSelectionModel** that maintains an array of **TreePath** objects representing the current selection. The last **TreePath** selected, called the *lead path*, can be obtained using the `getLeadSelectionPath()` method. To obtain all the selection paths, use the `getSelectionPaths()` method, which returns an array of tree paths.

«interface» *javax.swing.tree.TreeSelectionModel*	
+addSelectionPath(path: TreePath): void	Adds the specified TreePath to the current selection.
+addSelectionPaths(paths: TreePath[]): void	Adds the specified TreePaths to the current selection.
+clearSelection(): void	Clears the selection.
+getLeadSelectionPath(): TreePath	Returns the last path in the selection.
+getSelectionCount(): int	Returns the number of paths in the selection.
+getSelectionPath(): TreePath	Returns the first path in the selection.
+getSelectionPaths(): TreePath[]	Returns all the paths in the selection.
+getSelectionMode(): int	Returns the current selection mode.
+removeSelectionPath(path: TreePath): void	Removes path from the selection.
+removeSelectionPaths(paths: TreePath[]): void	Removes paths from the selection.
+setSelectionMode(mode: int): void	Sets the selection mode.
+setSelectionPath(path: TreePath): void	Sets the selection to path.
+setSelectionPaths(paths: TreePath[]): void	Sets the selection to paths.
+addTreeSelectionListener(x: TreeSelectionListener): void	Register a TreeSelectionListener.
+removeTreeSelectionListener(x: TreeSelectionListener): void	Remove a TreeSelectionListener.

javax.swing.tree.DefaultTreeSelectionModel

FIGURE 31.24 The `TreeSelectionModel` handles selection in a tree.

tree selection modes

`TreeSelectionModel` supports three selection modes: contiguous selection, discontiguous selection, and single selection. *Single selection* allows only one item to be selected. *Contiguous selection* allows multiple selections, but the selected items must be contiguous. *Discontiguous selection* is the most flexible; it allows any item to be selected at a given time. The default tree selection mode is discontiguous. To set a selection mode, use the `setSelectionMode(int mode)` method in `TreeSelectionModel`. The constants for the three modes are:

- `CONTIGUOUS_TREE_SELECTION`

- `DISCONTIGUOUS_TREE_SELECTION`

- `SINGLE_TREE_SELECTION`

Note

bypass
TreeSelectionModel

When you create a `JTree`, a `DefaultTreeSelectionModel` is automatically created, and thus you rarely need to create an instance of `TreeSelectionModel` explicitly. Since most of the methods in `TreeSelectionModel` are also in `JTree`, you can get selection paths and process the selection without directly dealing with `TreeSelectionModel`.

Listing 31.14 gives an example that displays a selected path or selected paths in tree. The user may select a node or multiple nodes and click the *Show Path* button to display the properties of the first selected path or the *Show Paths* button to display all the selected paths in a text area, as shown in Figure 31.25. The Show Path button displays a path from the last node up to the root.

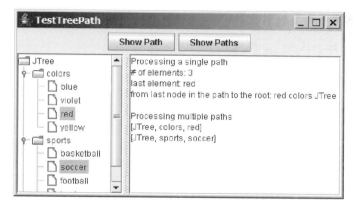

FIGURE 31.25   The selected path(s) are processed.

LISTING 31.14   TestTreePath.java

```java
1 import java.awt.*;
2 import java.awt.event.*;
3 import javax.swing.*;
4 import javax.swing.tree.*;
5
6 public class TestTreePath extends JApplet {
7   private JTree jTree = new JTree();                              // default tree
8   private JTextArea jtaOutput = new JTextArea();                  // text area
9   private JButton jbtShowPath = new JButton("Show Path");         // Show Path button
10  private JButton jbtShowPaths = new JButton("Show Paths");       // Show Paths button
11
12  public TestTreePath() {
13    JSplitPane splitPane = new JSplitPane(JSplitPane.HORIZONTAL_SPLIT,  // split pane
14      new JScrollPane(jTree), new JScrollPane(jtaOutput));
15
16    JPanel panel = new JPanel();
17    panel.add(jbtShowPath);
18    panel.add(jbtShowPaths);
19
20    add(splitPane, BorderLayout.CENTER);
21    add(panel, BorderLayout.NORTH);
22
23    jbtShowPath.addActionListener(new ActionListener() {          // Show Path button
24      public void actionPerformed(ActionEvent e) {
25        TreePath path = jTree.getSelectionPath();                 // selected path
26        jtaOutput.append("\nProcessing a single path\n");
27        jtaOutput.append("# of elements: " + path.getPathCount());  // path count
28        jtaOutput.append("\nlast element: "
29          + path.getLastPathComponent());
30        jtaOutput.append("\nfrom last node in the path to the root: ");
31        TreeNode node = (TreeNode)path.getLastPathComponent();    // last node
32        while (node != null) {
33          jtaOutput.append(node.toString() + " ");
```

get parent

```
34              node = node.getParent();
35            }
36        }});
37
```

Show Paths button
```
38        jbtShowPaths.addActionListener(new ActionListener() {
39          public void actionPerformed(ActionEvent e) {
40            jtaOutput.append("\nProcessing multiple paths\n");
```

selected paths
```
41            javax.swing.tree.TreePath[] paths = jTree.getSelectionPaths();
42            for (int i = 0; i < paths.length; i++)
```

display a path
```
43              jtaOutput.append(paths[i].toString() + "\n");
44          }});
45      }
```

main omitted
```
46 }
```

The `getSelectionPath()` method invoked from a **JTree** returns a **TreePath** in line 25. The first node in the path is always the root of the tree. The `getPathCount()` invoked from a **TreePath** returns the number of nodes in the path (line 27). The `getLastPathComponent()` invoked from a **TreePath** returns the last node in the path (line 29). The return node type is **Object**. You need to cast it to a **TreeNode** (line 31) in order to invoke the `getParent()` method from a **TreeNode** (line 34).

While the `getSelectionPath()` method (line 25) returns the first selected path, the `getSelectionPaths()` method (line 41) returns all the selected paths in an array of paths.

31.12 Case Study: Modifying Trees

Write a program to create two trees that display the same contents: world, continents, countries, and states, as shown in Figure 31.26. For the tree on the left, enable the user to choose a selection mode, specify whether it can be edited, add a new child under the first selected node, and remove all the selected nodes.

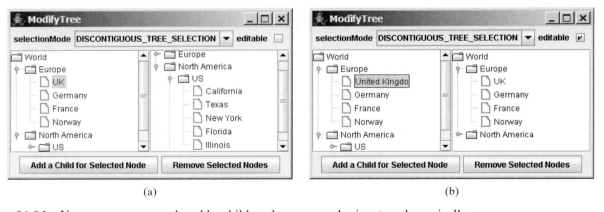

(a)   (b)

FIGURE 31.26   You can rename a node, add a child, and remove nodes in a tree dynamically.

You can choose a selection mode from the selectionMode combo box. You can specify whether the left tree nodes can be edited from the editable check box.

When you click a button, if there are no nodes currently selected in the left tree, a message dialog box is displayed, as shown in Figure 31.27(a). When you click the *Add a Child for Selected Node* button, an input dialog box is displayed to prompt the user to enter a child name for the selected node, as shown in Figure 31.27(b). The new node becomes a child of the first selected node. When you click the *Remove Selected Nodes* button, all the selected nodes in the left tree are removed.

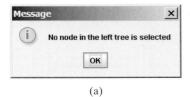

(a)   (b)

FIGURE 31.27   You can add a new node to the tree.

Listing 31.15 gives the program.

LISTING 31.15 ModifyTree.java

```
1 import java.awt.*;
2 import java.awt.event.*;
3 import javax.swing.*;
4 import javax.swing.tree.*;
5
6 public class ModifyTree extends JApplet {
7   // Create a combo box for choosing selection modes
8   private JComboBox jcboSelectionMode = new JComboBox(new String[]{          combo box
9     "CONTIGUOUS_TREE_SELECTION", "DISCONTIGUOUS_TREE_SELECTION",
10    "SINGLE_TREE_SELECTION"});
11
12  // Create a check box for specifying editable
13  private JCheckBox jchkEditable = new JCheckBox();                          check box
14
15  // Create two buttons
16  private JButton jbtAdd =                                                   buttons
17    new JButton("Add a Child for Selected Node");
18  private JButton jbtRemove = new JButton("Remove Selected Nodes");
19
20  // Declare two trees
21  private JTree jTree1, jTree2;                                              trees
22
23  public ModifyTree() {
24    // Create the first tree
25    DefaultMutableTreeNode root, europe, northAmerica, us;                  tree nodes
26
27    europe = new DefaultMutableTreeNode("Europe");                          fill nodes
28    europe.add(new DefaultMutableTreeNode("UK"));
29    europe.add(new DefaultMutableTreeNode("Germany"));
30    europe.add(new DefaultMutableTreeNode("France"));
31    europe.add(new DefaultMutableTreeNode("Norway"));
32
33    northAmerica = new DefaultMutableTreeNode("North America");
34    us = new DefaultMutableTreeNode("US");
35    us.add(new DefaultMutableTreeNode("California"));
36    us.add(new DefaultMutableTreeNode("Texas"));
37    us.add(new DefaultMutableTreeNode("New York"));
38    us.add(new DefaultMutableTreeNode("Florida"));
39    us.add(new DefaultMutableTreeNode("Illinois"));
40    northAmerica.add(us);
41    northAmerica.add(new DefaultMutableTreeNode("Canada"));
42
43    root = new DefaultMutableTreeNode("World");
44    root.add(europe);
45    root.add(northAmerica);
46
47    jcboSelectionMode.setSelectedIndex(1);
```

```
48
49        JPanel p1 = new JPanel();
50        p1.add(new JLabel("selectionMode"));
51        p1.add(jcboSelectionMode);
52        p1.add(new JLabel("editable"));
53        p1.add(jchkEditable);
54
55        JPanel p2 = new JPanel(new GridLayout(1, 2));
56        p2.add(new JScrollPane(jTree1 = new JTree(root)));
57        p2.add(new JScrollPane(jTree2 =
58          new JTree(new DefaultTreeModel(root)))); // Same root as jTree1
59
60        JPanel p3 = new JPanel();
61        p3.add(jbtAdd);
62        p3.add(jbtRemove);
63
64        add(p1, BorderLayout.NORTH);
65        add(p2, BorderLayout.CENTER);
66        add(p3, BorderLayout.SOUTH);
67
68        // Register listeners
69        jcboSelectionMode.addActionListener(new ActionListener() {
70          public void actionPerformed(ActionEvent e) {
71            if (jcboSelectionMode.getSelectedItem().
72              equals("CONTIGUOUS_TREE_SELECTION"))
73            jTree1.getSelectionModel().setSelectionMode(
74              TreeSelectionModel.CONTIGUOUS_TREE_SELECTION);
75            else if (jcboSelectionMode.getSelectedItem().
76              equals("DISCONTIGUOUS_TREE_SELECTION"))
77            jTree1.getSelectionModel().setSelectionMode(
78              TreeSelectionModel.DISCONTIGUOUS_TREE_SELECTION);
79            else
80            jTree1.getSelectionModel().setSelectionMode(
81              TreeSelectionModel.SINGLE_TREE_SELECTION);
82          }
83        });
84
85        jchkEditable.addActionListener(new ActionListener() {
86          public void actionPerformed(ActionEvent e) {
87            jTree1.setEditable(jchkEditable.isSelected());
88          }
89        });
90
91        jbtAdd.addActionListener(new ActionListener() {
92          public void actionPerformed(ActionEvent e) {
93            DefaultMutableTreeNode parent = (DefaultMutableTreeNode)
94              jTree1.getLastSelectedPathComponent();
95
96            if (parent == null) {
97              JOptionPane.showMessageDialog(null,
98                "No node in the left tree is selected");
99              return;
100           }
101
102           // Enter a new node
103           String nodeName = JOptionPane.showInputDialog(
104             null, "Enter a child node for " + parent, "Add a Child",
105             JOptionPane.QUESTION_MESSAGE);
106
107           // Insert the new node as a child of treeNode
108           parent.add(new DefaultMutableTreeNode(nodeName));
```

Margin notes (left column, aligned to line numbers):
- create **jTree1** (line 56)
- create **jTree2** (line 57)
- choose selection mode (line 69)
- set selection mode (line 73)
- choose editable (line 85)
- set editable (line 87)
- add child (line 91)
- get selected node (line 93)
- add new node (line 108)

```
109
110         // Reload the model since a new tree node is added
111         ((DefaultTreeModel)(jTree1.getModel())).reload();        reload tree model
112         ((DefaultTreeModel)(jTree2.getModel())).reload();
113       }
114     });
115
116     jbtRemove.addActionListener(new ActionListener() {            remove node
117       public void actionPerformed(ActionEvent e) {
118         // Get all selected paths
119         TreePath[] paths = jTree1.getSelectionPaths();            get selected paths
120
121         if (paths == null) {
122           JOptionPane.showMessageDialog(null,
123             "No node in the left tree is selected");
124           return;
125         }
126
127         // Remove all selected nodes
128         for (int i = 0; i < paths.length; i++) {
129           DefaultMutableTreeNode node = (DefaultMutableTreeNode)
130             (paths[i].getLastPathComponent());
131
132           if (node.isRoot()) {
133             JOptionPane.showMessageDialog(null,
134               "Cannot remove the root");
135           }
136           else
137             node.removeFromParent();                              remove node
138         }
139
140         // Reload the model since a new tree node is added
141         ((DefaultTreeModel)(jTree1.getModel())).reload();        reload tree model
142         ((DefaultTreeModel)(jTree2.getModel())).reload();
143       }
144     });
145   }
146 }
```

main omitted

Two **JTree** objects (**jTree1** and **jTree2**) are created with the same root (lines 56–58), but each has its own **TreeSelectionModel**. When you choose a selection mode in the combo box, the new selection mode is set in **jTree1**'s selection model (line 69–83). The selection mode for **jTree2** is not affected.

When the editable check box is checked or unchecked, the **editable** property in **jTree1** is set accordingly. If **editable** is true, you can edit a node in the left tree.

When you click the *Add a Child for Selected Node* button, the first selected node is returned as **parent** (lines 93–94). Suppose you selected Europe, UK, and US in this order, **parent** is Europe. If **parent** is **null**, no node is selected in the left tree (lines 96–100). Otherwise, prompt the user to enter a new node from an input dialog box (lines 103–105) and add this node as a child of **parent** (line 124). Since the tree has been modified, you need to invoke the **reload()** method to notify that the models for both trees have been changed (lines 111–112). Otherwise, the new node may not be displayed in **jTree1** and **jTree2**.

When you click the *Remove Selected Nodes* button, all the tree paths for each selected node are obtained in **paths** (line 119). Suppose you selected Europe, UK, and US in this order, three tree paths are obtained. Each path starts from the root to a selected node. If no node is selected, **paths** is **null**. To delete a selected node is to delete the last node in each selected tree path (128–138). The last node in a path is obtained using **getLast-PathComponent()**. If the node is the root, it cannot be removed (lines 132–134). The **removeFromParent()** method removes a node (line 137).

31.13 Tree Node Rendering and Editing

JTree delegates node rendering to a renderer. All renderers are instances of the **TreeCellRenderer** interface, which defines a single method, **getTreeCellRenderer-Component**, as follows:

```
public Component getTreeCellRendererComponent
   (JTree tree, Object value, boolean selected, boolean expanded,
    boolean leaf, int row, boolean hasFocus);
```

You can create a custom tree cell renderer by implementing the **TreeCellRenderer** interface, or use the **DefaultTreeCellRenderer** class, which provides a default implementation for **TreeCellRenderer**. When a new **JTree** is created, an instance of **DefaultTreeCellRenderer** is assigned to the tree renderer. The **DefaultTreeCell-Renderer** class maintains three icon properties named **leafIcon**, **openIcon**, and **closedIcon** for leaf nodes, expanded nodes, and collapsed nodes. It also provides colors for text and background. The following code sets new leaf, open and closed icons, and new background selection color in the tree:

```
DefaultTreeCellRenderer renderer =
   (DefaultTreeCellRenderer)jTree1.getCellRenderer();
renderer.setLeafIcon(yourCustomLeafImageIcon);
renderer.setOpenIcon(yourCustomOpenImageIcon);
renderer.setClosedIcon(yourCustomClosedImageIcon);
renderer.setBackgroundSelectionColor(Color.red);
```

 Note

The default leaf, open icon, and closed icon are dependent on the look-and-feel. For instance, on Windows look-and-feel, the open icon is −, and the closed icon is +.

JTree comes with a default cell editor. If **JTree**'s **editable** property is **true**, the default editor activates a text field for editing when the node is clicked three times. By default, this property is set to **false**. To create a custom editor, you need to extend the **DefaultCellEditor** class, which is the same class you used in table cell editing. You can use a text field, a check box, or a combo box, and pass it to **DefaultCellEditor**'s constructor to create an editor. The following code uses a combo box for editing colors. The combo box editor is shown in Figure 31.28(a).

```
// Customize editor
JComboBox jcboColor = new JComboBox();
jcboColor.addItem("red");
jcboColor.addItem("green");
jcboColor.addItem("blue");
jcboColor.addItem("yellow");
jcboColor.addItem("orange");

jTree1.setCellEditor(new javax.swing.DefaultCellEditor(jcboColor));
jTree1.setEditable(true);
```

There are two annoying problems with the editor created in the preceding code. First, it is activated with just one mouse click. Second, it overlaps the node's icon, as shown in Figure 31.28(a). These two problems can be fixed by using the **DefaultTreeCellEditor**, as shown in the following code:

```
jTree1.setCellEditor
   (new javax.swing.tree.DefaultTreeCellEditor(jTree1,
    new javax.swing.tree.DefaultTreeCellRenderer(),
    new javax.swing.DefaultCellEditor(jcboColor)));
```

The new editor is shown in Figure 31.28(b). Editing using **DefaultTreeCellEditor** starts on a triple mouse click. The combo box does not overlap the node's icon.

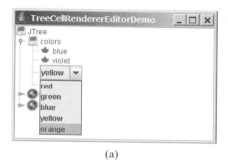 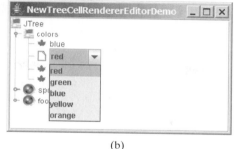

(a)   (b)

FIGURE 31.28   You can supply a custom editor for editing tree nodes.

31.14 Tree Events

JTree can fire TreeSelectionEvent and TreeExpansionEvent, among many other events. Whenever a new node is selected, JTree fires a TreeSelectionEvent. Whenever a node is expanded or collapsed, JTree fires a TreeExpansionEvent. To handle the tree selection event, a listener must implement the TreeSelectionListener interface, which contains a single handler named valueChanged method. TreeExpansionListener contains two handlers named treeCollapsed and treeExpanded for handling node expansion or node closing.

The following code displays a selected node:

```
void valueChanged(TreeSelectionEvent e) {
  TreePath path = e.getNewLeadSelectionPath();
  TreeNode treeNode = (TreeNode)path.getLastPathComponent();
  System.out.println("The selected node is " + treeNode.toString());
}
```

CHAPTER SUMMARY

- JTable has three supporting models: a table model, a column model, and a list-selection model. The *table model* is for storing and processing data. The *column model* represents all the columns in the table. The *list-selection model* is the same as the one used by JList for selecting rows, columns, and cells in a table. JTable also has two useful supporting classes, TableColumn and JTableHeader. TableColumn contains the information on a particular column. JTableHeader contains the information on the header of a JTable. Each column has a default editor and renderer. You can also create a custom editor by implementing the TableCellEditor interface, and you can create a custom renderer by implementing the TableCellRenderer interface.

- Like JTable, JTree is a very complex component with many supporting interfaces and classes. While JTree displays the tree, the data representation of the tree is handled by TreeModel, TreeNode, and TreePath. TreeModel represents the entire tree, TreeNode represents a node, and TreePath represents a path to a node. Unlike the ListModel or TableModel, the tree model does not directly store or manage tree data. Tree data is stored and managed in TreeNode and TreePath. A TreePath is an array of Objects that are vended from a TreeModel. The elements of the array are ordered such that the root is always the first element (index 0) of the array. The TreeSelectionModel interface handles tree node selection. The Default-TreeCellRenderer class provides a default tree node renderer that can display a label and/or an icon in a node. The `DefaultTreeCellEditor` can be used to edit the cells in a text field. The `TreePath` class is a support class that represents a set of nodes in a path.

■ `JTable` and `JTree` are in the `javax.swing` package, but their supporting interfaces and classes are all included in the `javax.swing.tree` and `javax.swing.table` packages, respectively.

REVIEW QUESTIONS

Sections 31.2–31.7

31.1 How do you initialize a table? Can you specify the maximum number of visible rows in a table without scrolling? How do you specify the height of a table cell? How do you specify the horizontal margin of table cells?

31.2 How do you modify table contents? How do you add or remove a row? How do you add or remove a column?

31.3 What is auto-resizing of a table column? How many types of auto-resizing are available?

31.4 What are the properties that show grids, horizontal grids, and vertical grids? What are the properties that specify the table row height, vertical margin, and horizontal margin?

31.5 What are the default table renderers and editors? How do you create a custom table cell renderer and editor?

31.6 What are the default tree renderers and editors? How do you create a custom tree cell renderer and editor?

31.7 How do you disable table cell editing?

Sections 31.8–31.14

31.8 How do you create a tree? How do you specify the row height of a tree node? How do you obtain the default tree model and tree selection model from an instance of `JTree`?

31.9 How do you initialize data in a tree using `TreeModel`? How do you add a child to an instance of `DefaultMutableTreeNode`?

31.10 How do you enable tree node editing?

31.11 How do you add or remove a node from a tree?

31.12 How do you obtain a selected tree node?

PROGRAMMING EXERCISES

Sections 31.2–31.7

31.1* (*Creating a table for a loan schedule*) Exercise 26.5 displays an amortization schedule in a text area. Write a program that enables the user to enter or choose the loan amount, number of years, and interest rate from spinners and displays the schedule in a table, as shown in Figure 31.29.

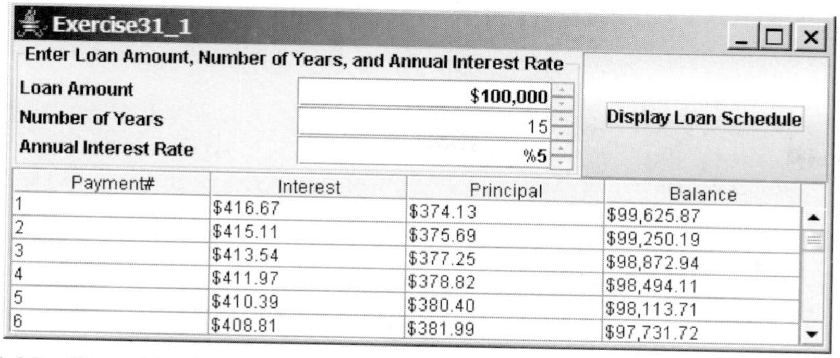

FIGURE 31.29 The table shows the loan schedule.

31.2* (*Deleting rows and columns*) Listing 31.5, TableModelDemo.java, allows you to delete only the first selected row or column. Enable the program to delete all the selected rows or columns. Also enable the program to delete a row or a column by pressing the DELETE key.

31.3** (*Creating a student table*) Create a table for student records. Each record consists of name, birthday, class status, in-state, and a photo, as shown in Figure 31.30. The name is of the **String** type; birthday is of the **Date** type; class status is one of the following five values: Freshman, Sophomore, Junior, Senior, or Graduate; in-state is a **boolean** value indicating whether the student is a resident of the state; and photo is an image icon. Use the default editors for name, birthday, and in-state. Supply a combo box as custom editor for class status.

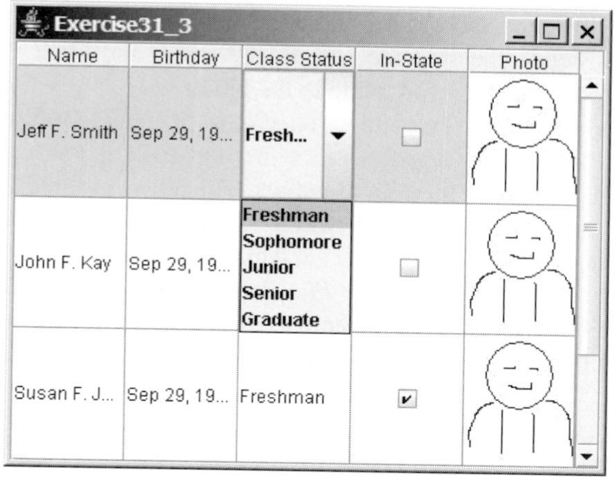

FIGURE 31.30 The table displays student records and supports add, remove, and edit operations.

31.4* (*Displaying a table for data from a text file*) Suppose that a table named Exercise31_4Table.txt is stored in a text file. The first line in the file is the header, and the remaining lines correspond to rows in the table. The elements are separated by commas. Write a program to display the table using the **JTable** component. For example, the following text file is displayed in a table, as shown in Figure 31.31:

```
Country, Capitol, Population, Democracy
USA, Washington DC, 280, true
Canada, Ottawa, 32, true
United Kingdom, London, 60, true
Germany, Berlin, 83, true
France, Paris, 60, true
Norway, Oslo, 4.5, true
India, New Deli, 1046, true
```

Country	Capitol	Population	Democracy
USA	Washington ...	280	true
Canada	Ottawa	32	true
United Kingdo...	London	60	true
Germany	Berlin	83	true
France	Paris	60	true
Norway	Oslo	4.5	true

FIGURE 31.31 The data in the file is displayed in a **JTable**.

31.5* (*Creating a controller using JTable*) In Exercise 30.1, you created a chart model (**ChartModel**) and two views (**PieChart** and **BarChart**). Create a controller that enables the user to modify the data, as shown in Figure 31.32. You will see the changes take effect in the pie chart view and the bar chart view. Your exercise consists of the following classes:

■ The controller named **Exercise31_5ChartController**. This class uses a table to display data. You can modify the data in the table. Click the *Insert* button to insert a new row above the selected row in the table, click the *Delete* button to delete the selected row in the table, and click the *Update* button to update the changes you made in the table.

■ The class **MyTableModel**. This class extends **DefaultTableModel** to override the **getColumnClass** method so that you can use the **JTable**'s default editor for numerical values. This class is same as in Listing 31.5.

■ The classes **ChartModel**, **PieChart**, and **BarChart** from Exercise 28.1.

■ The main class **Exercise31_5**. This class creates a user interface with a controller and two buttons, *View Pie Chart* and *View Bar Chart*. Click the *View Pie Chart* button to pop up a frame to display a pie chart, and click the *View Bar Chart* button to pop up a frame to display a bar chart.

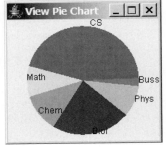
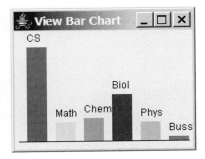

FIGURE 31.32 You can modify the data in the controller. The views are synchronized with the controller.

Sections 31.8–31.14

31.6* (*Creating a tree for book chapters*) Create a tree to display the table of contents for a book. When a node is selected in the tree, display a paragraph to describe the selected node, as shown in Figure 31.33.

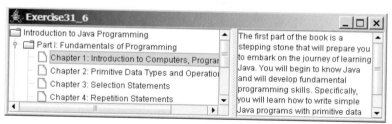

FIGURE 31.33 The content of the node is displayed in a text area when the node is clicked.

31.7** (*Adding and deleting tree nodes using the INSERT and DELETE keys*) Modify Listing 31.15, ModifyTree.java, to add a new child node by pressing the INSERT key, and delete a node by pressing the DELETE key.

31.8* (*Traversing trees*) Create a tree using the default **JTree** constructor and traverse the nodes in breadth-first, depth-first, preorder, and postorder.

31.9* (*Storing and restoring trees*) Modify Listing 31.15, ModifyTree.java, to add two buttons, as shown in Figure 31.34 to store and restore trees. Use the object I/O to store the tree model.

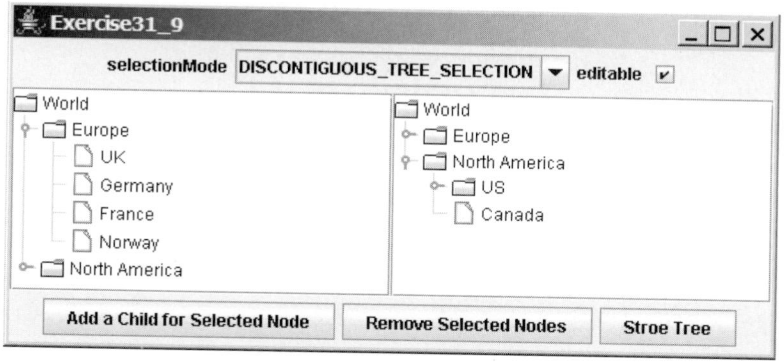

FIGURE 31.34 You can store tree data to a file and restore it later.

PART 8

WEB PROGRAMMING

This part is devoted to the development of Web applications using Java. Chapter 32 introduces the use of Java to develop database projects, Chapter 33 introduces advanced features of Java database programming, and Chapters 34 and 35 introduce how to use Java servlets and JSP to generate dynamic contents from Web servers. Chapter 36 introduces high-level network programming using remote method invocation.

Prerequisites for Part 8

You can cover Chapter 32 after Chapter 16, "Applets and Multimedia," and then cover Chapters 34 and 35. Chapter 33 is an optional chapter, which can be skipped completely. Chapter 36 can be covered after Chapter 16, "Applets and Multimedia."

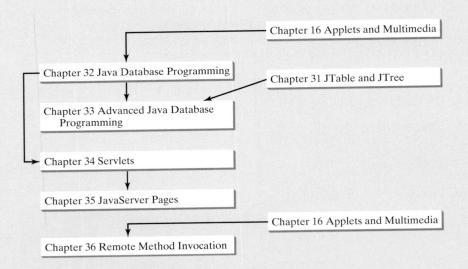

JAVA DATABASE PROGRAMMING

Objectives

- To understand the concept of database and database management systems (§32.2).
- To understand the relational data model: relational data structures, constraints, and languages (§32.2).
- To use SQL to create and drop tables, and to retrieve and modify data (§32.3).
- To learn how to load a driver, connect to a database, execute statements, and process result sets using JDBC (§32.4).
- To use prepared statements to execute precompiled SQL statements (§32.5).
- To handle transactions in the `Connection` interface (§32.6).
- To explore database metadata using the `DatabaseMetaData` and `ResultSetMetaData` interfaces.

32.1 Introduction

You may have heard a lot about database systems. Database systems are everywhere. Your social security information is stored in a database by the government. If you shop online, your purchase information is stored in a database by the company. If you attend a university, your academic information is stored in a database by the university. Database systems not only store data, they also provide means of accessing, updating, manipulating, and analyzing data. Your social security information is updated periodically, and you can register in courses online. Database systems play an important role in society and in commerce.

This chapter introduces database systems, SQL, and how to develop database applications using Java. If you already know SQL, you may skip §§32.2 and 32.3.

32.2 Relational Database Systems

database system

A *database system* consists of a database, the software that stores and manages data in the database, and the application programs that present data and enable the user to interact with the database system, as shown in Figure 32.1.

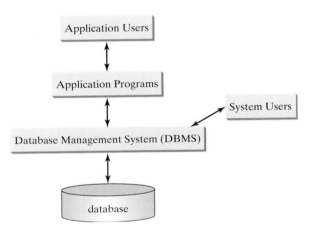

FIGURE 32.1 A database system consists of data, database management software, and application programs.

A database is a repository of data that together constitute information. When you purchase a database system from a software vendor, such as MySQL, Oracle, IBM, Microsoft, or Sybase, you actually purchase the software comprising a *database management system* (DBMS) from the vendor. Database management systems are designed for use by professional programmers and are not suitable for ordinary customers. Application programs are built on top of the DBMS for customers to access and update the database. Thus application programs can be viewed as the interfaces between the database system and its users. Application programs may be standalone GUI applications or Web applications, and may access several different database systems in the network, as shown in Figure 32.2.

DBMS

Most of today's database systems are *relational database systems*, based on the relational data model. A relational data model has three key components: structure, integrity, and language. *Structure* defines the representation of the data. *Integrity* imposes constraints on the data. *Language* provides the means for accessing and manipulating data.

32.2.1 Relational Structures

relational model

The relational model is built around a simple and natural structure. A relation is actually a table that consists of non-duplicate rows. Tables are easy to understand and easy to use. The relational model provides a simple yet powerful way to represent data.

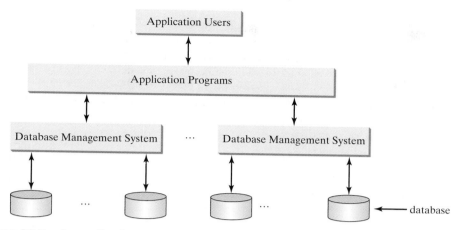

FIGURE 32.2   An application program may access multiple database systems.

A row of a table represents a record, and a column of a table represents the value of a single attribute of the record. In relational database theory, a row is called a *tuple* and a column is called an *attribute*. Figure 32.3 shows a sample table that stores information about the courses offered by a university. The table has eight tuples, and each tuple has five attributes.

tuple

attribute

courseId	subjectId	courseNumber	title	numOfCredits
11111	CSCI	1301	Introduction to Java I	4
11112	CSCI	1302	Introduction to Java II	3
11113	CSCI	3720	Database Systems	3
11114	CSCI	4750	Rapid Java Application	3
11115	MATH	2750	Calculus I	5
11116	MATH	3750	Calculus II	5
11117	EDUC	1111	Reading	3
11118	ITEC	1344	Database Administration	3

Relation/Table Name · Columns/Attributes · Course Table · Tuples/Rows

FIGURE 32.3   A table has a table name, column names, and rows.

Tables describe the relationship among data. Each row in a table represents a record of related data. For example, "11111", "CSCI", "1301", "Introduction to Java I", and "4" are related to form a record (the first row in Figure 32.3) in the `Course` table. Just as data in the same row are related, so too data in different tables may be related through common attributes. Suppose the database has two other tables named `Student` and `Enrollment`, as shown in Figures 32.4 and 32.5. The `Course` table and the `Enrollment` table are related through their common attribute `courseId`, and the `Enrollment` table and the `Student` table are related through `ssn`.

32.2.2   Integrity Constraints

An *integrity constraint* imposes a condition that all the legal values in a table must satisfy. Figure 32.6 shows an example of some integrity constraints in the `Subject` and `Course` tables.

integrity constraint

Student Table

ssn	firstName	mi	lastName	phone	birthDate		street	zipCode	deptID
444111110	Jacob	R	Smith	9129219434	1985-04-09	99	Kingston Street	31435	BIOL
444111111	John	K	Stevenson	9129219434	null	100	Main Street	31411	BIOL
444111112	George	K	Smith	9129213454	1974-10-10	1200	Abercorn St.	31419	CS
444111113	Frank	E	Jones	9125919434	1970-09-09	100	Main Street	31411	BIOL
444111114	Jean	K	Smith	9129219434	1970-02-09	100	Main Street	31411	CHEM
444111115	Josh	R	Woo	7075989434	1970-02-09	555	Franklin St.	31411	CHEM
444111116	Josh	R	Smith	9129219434	1973-02-09	100	Main Street	31411	BIOL
444111117	Joy	P	Kennedy	9129229434	1974-03-19	103	Bay Street	31412	CS
444111118	Toni	R	Peterson	9129229434	1964-04-29	103	Bay Street	31412	MATH
444111119	Patrick	R	Stoneman	9129229434	1969-04-29	101	Washington St.	31435	MATH
444111120	Rick	R	Carter	9125919434	1986-04-09	19	West Ford St.	31411	BIOL

FIGURE 32.4 A `Student` table stores student information.

Enrollment Table

ssn	courseId	dateRegistered	grade
444111110	11111	2004-03-19	A
444111110	11112	2004-03-19	B
444111110	11113	2004-03-19	C
444111111	11111	2004-03-19	D
444111111	11112	2004-03-19	F
444111111	11113	2004-03-19	A
444111112	11114	2004-03-19	B
444111112	11115	2004-03-19	C
444111112	11116	2004-03-19	D
444111113	11111	2004-03-19	A
444111113	11113	2004-03-19	A
444111114	11115	2004-03-19	B
444111115	11115	2004-03-19	F
444111115	11116	2004-03-19	F
444111116	11111	2004-03-19	D
444111117	11111	2004-03-19	D
444111118	11111	2004-03-19	A
444111118	11112	2004-03-19	D
444111118	11113	2004-03-19	B

FIGURE 32.5 An `Enrollment` table stores student enrollment information.

In general, there are three types of constraints: domain constraints, primary key constraints, and foreign key constraints. *Domain constraints* and *primary key constraints* are known as *intra-relational constraints*, meaning that a constraint involves only one relation. The *foreign key constraint* is *inter-relational*, meaning that a constraint involves more than one relation.

Domain Constraints

domain constraint

Domain constraints specify the permissible values for an attribute. Domains can be specified using standard data types, such as integers, floating-point numbers, fixed-length strings, and variant-length strings. The standard data type specifies a broad range of values. Additional constraints can be specified to narrow the ranges. For example, you can specify that the `numOfCredits` attribute (in the `Course` table) must be greater than `0` and less than `5`. You can also specify whether an attribute can be `null`, which is a special value in a database meaning unknown or not applicable. As shown in the `Student` table, `birthDate` may be `null`.

Primary Key Constraints

primary key
superkey

To understand primary keys, it is helpful to know superkeys, keys, and candidate keys. A *superkey* is an attribute or a set of attributes that uniquely identifies the relation. That is, no two tuples have the same values on a superkey. For example, `courseId` and `subjectId` together form a superkey, because no two tuples in the course table have the same value on courseId and subjectId. By definition, a relation consists of a set of distinct tuples. The set of all attributes in the relation forms a superkey.

A *key* K is a minimal superkey, meaning that any proper subset of K is not a superkey. A relation can have several keys. In this case, each of the keys is called a *candidate key*. The *primary* key is one of the candidate keys designated by the database designer. The primary key is often used to identify tuples in a relation. As shown in Figure 32.6, `courseId` is the primary key in the `Course` table.

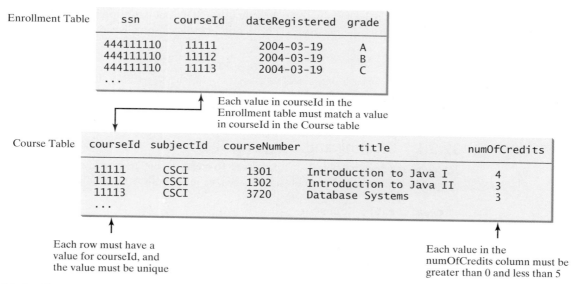

FIGURE 32.6 The `Enrollment` table and the `Course` table have integrity constraints.

Foreign Key Constraints

In a relational database, data are related. Tuples in a relation are related, and tuples in different relations are related through their common attributes. Informally speaking, the common attributes are foreign keys. The *foreign key constraints* define the relationships among relations. *foreign key*

Formally, a set of attributes *FK* is a *foreign key* in a relation *R* that references relation *T* if it satisfies the following two rules:

- The attributes in *FK* have the same domain as the primary key in *T*.

- A non-null value on *FK* in *R* must match a primary key value in *T*.

As shown in Figure 32.6, `courseId` is the foreign key in `Enrollment` that references the primary key `courseId` in `Course`. Every `courseId` value must match a `courseId` value in `Course`.

Enforcing Integrity Constraints

The database management system enforces integrity constraints and rejects operations that would violate them. For example, if you attempt to insert a new record (`'11113'`, `'3272'`, `'Database Systems'`, 0) into the `Course` table, it would fail because the credit hours must be greater than or equal to 0; if you attempt to insert a record with the same primary key as an existing record in the table, the DBMS would report an error and reject the operation, because the primary key values are unique; if you attempt to delete a record from the `Course` table whose primary key value is referenced by the records in the `Enrollment` table, the DBMS would reject this operation because it would violate the foreign key constraint.

Note
All relational database systems support primary key constraints and foreign key constraints. Not all database systems support domain constraints. For example, you cannot specify the constraint that numOfCredits is greater than 0 and less than 5 on the Microsoft Access database.

32.3 SQL

Structured Query Language (SQL) is the language for defining tables and integrity constraints and for accessing and manipulating data. SQL (pronounced "S-Q-L" or "sequel") is the universal language for accessing relational database systems. Application programs may allow users to access a database without directly using SQL, but these applications themselves must use SQL to access the database. This section introduces some basic SQL commands.

Note
There are hundreds of relational database management systems. They share the common SQL language but do not all support every feature of SQL. Some systems have their own extensions to SQL. This section introduces standard SQL supported by all systems.

32.3.1 Creating and Dropping Tables

Tables are the essential objects in a database. To create a table, use the `create table` statement to specify a table name, attributes, and types, as in the following example:

```
create table Course (
  courseId char(5),
  subjectId char(4) not null,
  courseNumber integer,
  title varchar(50) not null,
  numOfCredits integer,
  primary key (courseId)
);
```

This statement creates the `Course` table with attributes `courseId`, `subjectId`, `courseNumber`, `title`, and `numOfCredits`. Each attribute has a data type that specifies the type of data stored in the attribute. `char(5)` specifies that `courseId` consists of five characters. `varchar(50)` specifies that `title` is a variant-length string with a maximum of fifty characters. `integer` specifies that `courseNumber` is an integer. The primary key is `courseId`.

The tables `Student` and `Enrollment` can be created as follows:

```
create table Student (                create table Enrollment (
  ssn char(9),                          ssn char(9),
  firstName varchar(25),                courseId char(5),
  mi char(1),                           dateRegistered date,
  lastName varchar(25),                 grade char(1),
  birthDate date,                       primary key (ssn, courseId),
  street varchar(25),                   foreign key (ssn) references Student,
  phone char(11),                       foreign key (courseId) references Course
  zipCode char(5),                    );
  deptId char(4),
  primary key (ssn)
);
```

Note

naming convention

SQL keywords are not case-sensitive. This book adopts the following naming conventions: Tables are named in the same way as Java classes, and attributes are named in the same way as Java variables. SQL keywords are named in the same way as Java keywords.

If a table is no longer needed, it can be dropped permanently using the **drop table** command. For example, the following statement drops the **Course** table:

```
drop table Course;
```

If a table to be dropped is referenced by other tables, you have to drop the other tables first. For example, if you have created the tables **Course**, **Student**, and **Enrollment** and want to drop **Course**, you have to first drop **Enrollment**, because **Course** is referenced by **Enrollment**.

32.3.2 Using SQL on a Relational Database

SQL can be used on MySQL, Oracle, Sybase, IBM DB2, IBM Informix, Borland Interbase, MS Access, or any other relational database system. This chapter uses MySQL to demonstrate SQL and uses MySQL, Access, and Oracle to demonstrate JDBC programming. The Companion Website (www.prenhall.com/liang/intro6e.html) contains the following supplements on how to install and use SQL on three popular databases, MySQL, Oracle, and Access:

- Supplement IV.B: Tutorial for MySQL   MySQL Tutorial

- Supplement IV.C: Tutorial for Oracle   Oracle Tutorial

- Supplement IV.D: Tutorial for Microsoft Access   Access Tutorial

Assume that you have installed MySQL with the default configuration; you can access MySQL from the DOS command prompt using the command **mysql** from the **c:\mysql\bin** directory, as shown in Figure 32.7.

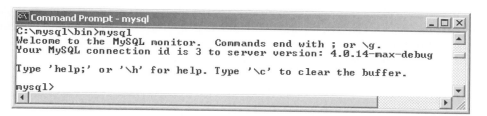

FIGURE 32.7   You can access a MySQL database server from the command window.

 Note

On Windows, your MySQL database server starts every time your computer starts. You can stop it by typing the command **net stop mysql** and restart it by typing the command **net start mysql**.

start mysql
stop mysql

By default, the server contains two databases named mysql and test. You can see these two databases displayed named mysql and test in Figure 32.8(a) using the command **show databases**.

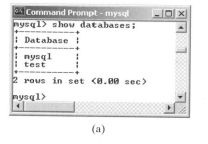   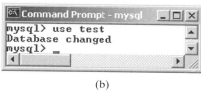

(a)   (b)

FIGURE 32.8   (a) The **show databases** command displays all available databases in the MySQL database server. (b) The **use test** command selects the test database.

The mysql database contains the tables that store information about the server and its users. This database is intended for the server administrator to use. For example, the administrator can use it to create users and grant or revoke user privileges. Since you are the owner of the server installed on your system, you have full access to the mysql database. However, you should not create user tables in the mysql database. You can use the test database to store data or create new databases. You can also create a new database using the command **create database** *databasename* or drop an existing database using the command **drop database** *databasename*.

To select a database for use, type the **use databasename** command. Since the test database is created by default in every MySQL database, let us use it to demonstrate SQL commands. As shown in Figure 32.8(b), the test database is selected. Enter the statement to create the **Course** table, as shown in Figure 32.9.

```
Command Prompt - mysql                            _ □ ×
mysql> create table Course (
    ->     courseId char(5),
    ->     subjectId char(4) not null,
    ->     courseNumber integer,
    ->     title varchar(50) not null,
    ->     numOfCredits integer,
    ->     primary key (courseId)
    -> );
Query OK, 0 rows affected (0.74 sec)

mysql>
```

FIGURE 32.9 The execution result of the SQL statements is displayed in the MySQL monitor.

If you make typing errors, you have to retype the whole command. To avoid retyping the whole command, you can save the command in a file, and then run the command from the file. To do so, create a text file to contain commands, named, for example, test.sql. You can create the text file using any text editor, such as NotePad, as shown in Figure 32.10. To comment a line, precede it with two dashes. You can now run the script file by typing **source test.sql** from the SQL command prompt, as shown in Figure 32.11.

```
Test - Notepad                                    _ □ ×
File  Edit  Format  Help
create table Course (
   courseId char(5),
   subjectId char(4) not null,
   courseNumber integer,
   title varchar(50) not null,
   numOfCredits integer,
   primary key (courseId)
);
```

FIGURE 32.10 You can use Notepad to create a text file for SQL commands.

```
Command Prompt - mysql                            _ □ ×
mysql> drop table Course;
Query OK, 0 rows affected (0.00 sec)

mysql> source c:\book\Test.sql   ◄──────── no semicolon (;) here
Query OK, 0 rows affected (0.00 sec)

mysql>
```

FIGURE 32.11 You can run the SQL commands in a script file from MySQL.

32.3.3 Simple Insert, Update, and Delete

Once a table is created, you can insert data into it. You can also update and delete records. This section introduces simple insert, update, and delete statements.

The general syntax to insert a record into a table is:

```
insert into tableName [(column1, column2, ..., column]]
values (value1, value2, ..., valuen);
```

insert

For example, the following statement inserts a record into the Course table. The new record has the courseId '11113', subjectId 'CSCI', courseNumber 3720, title 'Database Systems', and creditHours 3.

```
insert into Course (courseId, subjectId, courseNumber, title, numOfCredits)
values ('11113', 'CSCI', '3720', 'Database Systems', 3);
```

The column names are optional. If the column names are omitted, all the column values for the record must be entered even though the columns have default values. String values are case-sensitive and enclosed inside single quotation marks in SQL.

The general syntax to update a table is:

```
update tableName
set column1 = newValue1 [, column2 = newValue2, ...]
[where condition];
```

update

For example, the following statement changes the numOfCredits for the course whose title is Database Systems to 4:

```
update Course
set numOfCredits = 4
where title = 'Database Systems';
```

The general syntax to delete records from a table is:

```
delete [from] tableName
[where condition];
```

delete

For example, the following statement deletes the Database Systems course from the Course table:

```
delete Course
where title = 'Database System';
```

The following statement deletes all the records from the Course table:

```
delete Course;
```

32.3.4 Simple Queries

To retrieve information from tables, use a select statement with the following syntax:

```
select column-list
from table-list
[where condition];
```

select

The select clause lists the columns to be selected. The from clause refers to the tables involved in the query. The optional where clause specifies the conditions for the selected rows.

Query 1: Select all the students in the CS department, as shown in Figure 32.12.

```
select firstName, mi, lastName
from Student
where deptId = 'CS';
```

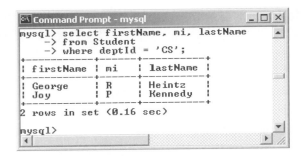

FIGURE 32.12 The result of the select statement is displayed in a window.

32.3.5 Comparison and Boolean Operators

SQL has six comparison operators, as shown in Table 32.1, and three Boolean operators, as shown in Table 32.2.

TABLE 32.1 Comparison Operators	
Operator	*Description*
=	Equal to
<> or !=	Not equal to
<	Less than
<=	Less or equal to
>	Greater than
>=	Greater than

TABLE 32.2 Boolean Operators	
Operator	*Description*
not	logical negation
and	logical conjunction
or	logical disjunction

Note

The comparison and Boolean operators in SQL have the same meaning as in Java. In SQL the `equal to` operator is =, but it is == in Java. In SQL the `not equal to` operator is <> or !=, but it is != in Java. The `not`, `and`, and `or` operators are !, && (&), and || (|) in Java.

Query 2: Get the names of the students who are in the CS dept and live in the zip code 31411.

```
select firstName, mi, lastName
from Student
where deptId = 'CS' and zipCode = '31411';
```

Note

To select all the attributes from a table, you don't have to list all the attribute names in the select clause. Instead you can just specify an *asterisk* (*), which stands for all the attributes. For example, the following query displays all the attributes of the students who are in the CS dept and live in the zip code 31411:

```
select *
from Student
where deptId = 'CS' and zipCode = '31411';
```

32.3.6 The `like`, `between-and`, and `is null` Operators

SQL has a `like` operator that can be used for pattern matching. The syntax to check whether a string `s` has a pattern `p` is

```
s like p or s not like p
```

You can use the wild card characters % (percent symbol) and _ (underline symbol) in the pattern p. % matches zero or more characters, and _ matches any single character in s. For example, lastName like '_mi%' matches any string whose second and third letters are m and i. lastName not like '_mi%' excludes any string whose second and third letters are m and i.

Note

On the earlier version of MS Access, the wild card character is *, and the character ? matches any single character.

The between-and operator checks whether a value v is between two other values, v1 and v2, using the following syntax:

    v between v1 and v2 or v not between v1 and v2

    v between v1 and v2 is equivalent to v >= v1 and v <= v2, and v not between v1 and v2 is equivalent to v < v1 and v > v2.

The is null operator checks whether a value v is null using the following syntax:

    v is null or v is not null

Query 3: Get the social security numbers of the students whose grades are between 'C' and 'A.'

```
select ssn
from Enrollment
where grade between 'C' and 'A';
```

32.3.7   Column Alias

When a query result is displayed, SQL uses the column names as column headings. Usually the user gives abbreviated names for the columns, and the columns cannot have spaces when the table is created. Sometimes it is desirable to give more descriptive names in the result heading. You can use the column aliases with the following syntax:

```
select columnName [as] alias
```

Query 4: Get the last name and zip code of the students in the CS department. Display the column headings as Last Name for lastName and Zip Code for zipCode. The query result is shown in Figure 32.13.

```
select lastName as "Last Name", zipCode as "Zip Code"
from Student
where deptId = 'CS';
```

Note

The as keyword is optional in MySQL and Oracle but is required in MS Access.

```
Command Prompt - mysql                                      _ □ ×
mysql> select lastName as "Last Name", zipCode as "Zip Code"
    -> from Student
    -> where deptId = 'CS';
+------------+----------+
| Last Name  | Zip Code |
+------------+----------+
| Heintz     | 31419    |
| Kennedy    | 31412    |
+------------+----------+
2 rows in set <0.00 sec>

mysql>
```

FIGURE 32.13   You can use a column alias in the display.

32.3.8 The Arithmetic Operators

You can use the arithmetic operators * (multiplication), / (division), + (addition), and – (subtraction) in SQL.

Query 5: Assume that a credit hour is fifty minutes of lectures; get the total minutes for each course with the subject CSCI. The query result is shown in Figure 32.14.

```
select title, 50 * numOfCredits as "Lecture Minutes Per Week"
from Course
where subjectId = 'CSCI';
```

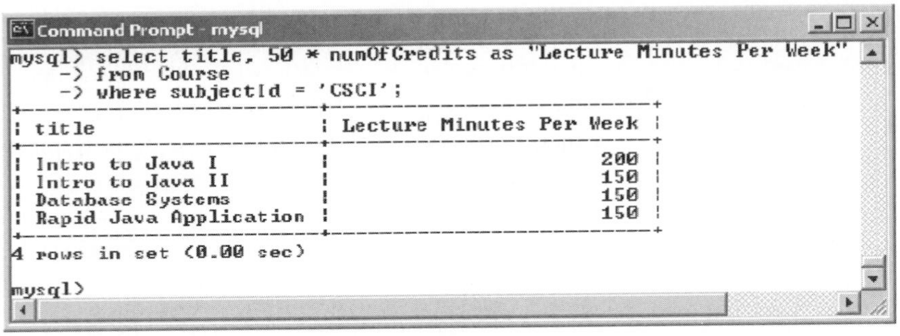

FIGURE 32.14 You can use arithmetic operators in SQL.

32.3.9 Displaying Distinct Tuples

SQL provides the **distinct** keyword, which can be used to suppress duplicate tuples in the output. For example, the following statement displays all the subject IDs used by the courses:

```
select subjectId as "Subject ID"
from Course;
```

This statement displays all the subject IDs. To display distinct tuples, add the **distinct** keyword in the **select** clause, as follows:

```
select distinct subjectId as "Subject ID"
from Course;
```

When there is more than one item in the **select** clause, the **distinct** keyword applies to all the items that find distinct tuples.

32.3.10 Displaying Sorted Tuples

SQL provides the **order by** clause to sort the output using the following general syntax:

```
select column-list
from table-list
[where condition]
[order by columns-to-be-sorted];
```

order by

In the syntax, `columns-to-be-sorted` specifies a column or a list of columns to be sorted. By default, the order is ascending. To sort in descending order, append the **desc** keyword. You could also append the **asc** keyword, but it is not necessary. When multiple columns are specified, the rows are sorted based on the first column, then the rows with the same values on the second column are sorted based on the second column, and so on.

```
Command Prompt - mysql                               _ □ ×
mysql> select lastName, firstName, deptId
    -> from Student
    -> where deptId = 'CS'
    -> order by lastName desc, firstName asc;
+----------+-----------+--------+
| lastName | firstName | deptId |
+----------+-----------+--------+
| Kennedy  | Joy       | CS     |
| Heintz   | George    | CS     |
+----------+-----------+--------+
2 rows in set (0.02 sec)

mysql> _
```

FIGURE 32.15   You can sort results using the order by clause.

Query 6: List the full names of the students in the CS department, ordered primarily on their last names in descending order and secondarily on their first names in ascending order. The query result is shown in Figure 32.15.

```
select lastName, firstName, deptId
from Student
where deptId = 'CS'
order by lastName desc, firstName asc;
```

32.3.11 Joining Tables

Often you need to get information from multiple tables, as demonstrated in the next query.

Query 7: List the courses taken by student Jacob Smith. To solve this query, you need to join tables **Student** and **Enrollment**, as shown in Figure 32.16.

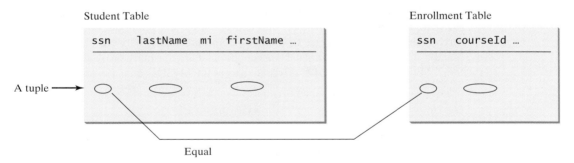

FIGURE 32.16   Student and Enrollment are joined on ssn.

You can write the query in SQL:

```
select distinct lastName, firstName, courseId
from Student, Enrollment
where Student.ssn = Enrollment.ssn and
   lastName = 'Smith' and firstName = 'Jacob';
```

The tables **Student** and **Enrollment** are listed in the **from** clause. The query examines every pair of rows, each made of one item from **Student** and another from **Enrollment**, and selects the pairs that satisfy the condition in the **where** clause. The rows in **Student** have the last name, Smith, and the first name, Jacob, and both rows from **Student** and **Enrollment** have the same **ssn** values. For each pair selected, **lastName** and **firstName** from `Student` and `courseId` from `Enrollment` are used to produce the result, as shown in Figure 32.17. `Student` and `Enrollment` have the same attribute `ssn`. To distinguish them in a query, use `Student.ssn` and `Enrollment.ssn`.

```
Command Prompt - mysql                                    _ □ X
mysql> select distinct lastName, firstName, courseId
    -> from Student, Enrollment
    -> where Student.ssn = Enrollment.ssn and
    ->    lastName = 'Smith' and firstName = 'Jacob';
+----------+-----------+----------+
| lastName | firstName | courseId |
+----------+-----------+----------+
| Smith    | Jacob     | 11111    |
| Smith    | Jacob     | 11112    |
| Smith    | Jacob     | 11113    |
+----------+-----------+----------+
3 rows in set (0.06 sec)

mysql>
```

FIGURE 32.17 Query 7 demonstrates queries involving multiple tables.

32.4 JDBC

The Java API for developing Java database applications is called *JDBC*. JDBC is the trademarked name of a Java API that supports Java programs that access relational databases. JDBC is not an acronym, but it is often thought to stand for Java Database Connectivity.

JDBC provides Java programmers with a uniform interface for accessing and manipulating a wide range of relational databases. Using the JDBC API, applications written in the Java programming language can execute SQL statements, retrieve results, present data in a user-friendly interface, and propagate changes back to the database. The JDBC API can also be used to interact with multiple data sources in a distributed, heterogeneous environment.

The relationships between Java programs, JDBC API, JDBC drivers, and relational databases are shown in Figure 32.18. The JDBC API is a set of Java interfaces and classes used to write Java programs for accessing and manipulating relational databases. Since a JDBC driver serves as the interface to facilitate communications between JDBC and a proprietary database, JDBC drivers are database-specific and are normally provided by the database vendors. You need MySQL JDBC drivers to access the MySQL database, and Oracle JDBC drivers

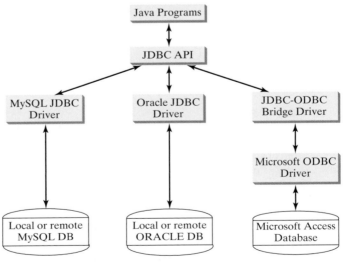

FIGURE 32.18 Java programs access and manipulate databases through JDBC drivers.

to access the Oracle database. For the Access database, use the JDBC-ODBC bridge driver included in JDK. ODBC is a technology developed by Microsoft for accessing databases on the Windows platform. An ODBC driver is preinstalled on Windows. The JDBC-ODBC bridge driver allows a Java program to access any ODBC data source.

32.4.1 Developing Database Applications Using JDBC

The JDBC API is a Java application program interface to generic SQL databases that enables Java developers to develop DBMS-independent Java applications using a uniform interface.

The JDBC API consists of classes and interfaces for establishing connections with databases, sending SQL statements to databases, processing the results of the SQL statements, and obtaining database metadata. Four key interfaces are needed to develop any database application using Java: `Driver`, `Connection`, `Statement`, and `ResultSet`. These interfaces define a framework for generic SQL database access. The JDBC API defines these interfaces. The JDBC driver vendors provide implementation for them. Programmers use the interfaces.

The relationship of these interfaces is shown in Figure 32.19. A JDBC application loads an appropriate driver using the `Driver` interface, connects to the database using the `Connection` interface, creates and executes SQL statements using the `Statement` interface, and processes the result using the `ResultSet` interface if the statements return results. Note that some statements, such as SQL data definition statements and SQL data modification statements, do not return results.

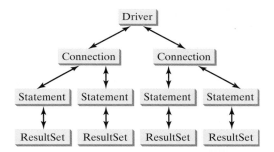

FIGURE 32.19   JDBC classes enable Java programs to connect to the database, send SQL statements, and process results.

The JDBC interfaces and classes are the building blocks in the development of Java database programs. A typical Java program takes the steps outlined below to access the database.

1. Loading drivers.

An appropriate driver must be loaded using the statement shown below before connecting to a database.

```
Class.forName("JDBCDriverClass");
```

A driver is a concrete class that implements the `java.sql.Driver` interface. The drivers for Access, MySQL, and Oracle are listed in Table 32.3.

The JDBC-ODBC driver for Access is bundled in JDK. The MySQL JDBC driver is contained in `mysqljdbc.jar` (downloadable from www.cs.armstrong.edu/liang/intro6e/book/ mysqljdbc.jar). The Oracle JDBC driver is contained in `classes12.jar` (downloadable from www.cs.armstrong.edu/liang/intro6e/book/classes12.jar). To use the MySQL and Oracle

`mysqljdbc.jar`
`classes12.jar`

TABLE 32.3 JDBC Drivers

Database	Driver Class	Source
Access	`sun.jdbc.odbc.JdbcOdbcDriver`	Already in JDK
MySQL	`com.mysql.jdbc.Driver`	Companion Website
Oracle	`oracle.jdbc.driver.OracleDriver`	Companion Website

drivers, you have to add mysqljdbc.jar and classes12.jar in the classpath using the following DOS command on Windows:

```
set classpath=%classpath%;c:\book\mysqljdbc.jar;c:\book\classes12.jar
```

If your program accesses several different databases, all their respective drivers must be loaded.

 Note

why load a driver?

`com.mysql.jdbc.Driver` is a class in `mysqljdbc.jar`, and `oracle.jdbc.driver.OracleDriver` is a class in `classes12.jar`. `mysqljdbc.jar` and `classes12.jar` contain many classes to support the driver. These classes are used by JDBC, but not directly by JDBC programmers. When you use a class explicitly in the program, it is automatically loaded by the JVM. The driver classes, however, are not used explicitly in the program, so you have to write the code to tell the JVM to load them.

2. Establishing connections.

To connect to a database, use the static method `getConnection(databaseURL)` in the `DriverManager` class, as follows:

```
Connection connection = DriverManager.getConnection(databaseURL);
```

where `databaseURL` is the unique identifier of the database on the Internet. Table 32.4 lists the URLs for the MySQL, Oracle, and Access databases.

TABLE 32.4 JDBC URLs

Database	URL Pattern
Access	`jdbc:odbc:dataSource`
MySQL	`jdbc:mysql://hostname/dbname`
Oracle	`jdbc:oracle:thin:@hostname:port#:oracleDBSID`

connect Access DB

For an ODBC data source, the `databaseURL` is `jdbc:odbc:dataSource`. An ODBC data source can be created using the ODBC Data Source Administrator on Windows. See Supplement IV.D, "Tutorial for Microsoft Access," on how to create an ODBC data source for an Access database. Suppose a data source named ExampleMDBDataSource has been created for an Access database. The following statement creates a `Connection` object:

```
Connection connection = DriverManager.getConnection
    ("jdbc:odbc:ExampleMDBDataSource");
```

The `databaseURL` for a MySQL database specifies the host name and database name to locate a database. For example, the following statement creates a `Connection` object for the local MySQL database test:

```
Connection connection = DriverManager.getConnection
    ("jdbc:mysql://localhost/test");
```

Recall that by default MySQL contains two databases named *mysql* and *test*. You can create a custom database using the MySQL SQL command `create database databasename`. connect MySQL DB

The `databaseURL` for an Oracle database specifies the *hostname*, the *port#* where the database listens for incoming connection requests, and the *oracleDBSID* database name to locate a database. For example, the following statement creates a `Connection` object for the Oracle database on liang.armstrong.edu with username scott and password tiger: connect Oracle DB

```
Connection connection = DriverManager.getConnection
  ("jdbc:oracle:thin:@liang.armstrong.edu:1521:orcl",
   "scott", "tiger");
```

3. Creating statements.

If a `Connection` object can be envisioned as a cable linking your program to a database, an object of `Statement` or its subclass can be viewed as a cart that delivers SQL statements for execution by the database and brings the result back to the program. Once a `Connection` object is created, you can create statements for executing SQL statements as follows:

```
Statement statement = connection.createStatement();
```

4. Executing statements.

An SQL DDL or update statement can be executed using `executeUpdate(String sql)`, and an SQL query statement can be executed using `executeQuery(String sql)`. The result of the query is returned in `ResultSet`. For example, the following code executes the SQL statement *create table Temp (col1 char(5), col2 char(5))*:

```
statement.executeUpdate
  ("create table Temp (col1 char(5), col2 char(5))");
```

The next code executes the SQL query `select firstName, mi, lastName from Student where lastName = 'Smith'`:

```
// Select the columns from the Student table
ResultSet resultSet = statement.executeQuery
  ("select firstName, mi, lastName from Student where lastName "
    + " = 'Smith'");
```

5. Processing `ResultSet`.

The `ResultSet` maintains a table whose current row can be retrieved. The initial row position is `null`. You can use the `next` method to move to the next row and the various get methods to retrieve values from a current row. For example, the code given below displays all the results from the preceding SQL query.

```
// Iterate through the result and print the student names
while (resultSet.next())
  System.out.println(resultSet.getString(1) + " "
    + resultSet.getString(2) + ". " + resultSet.getString(3));
```

The `getString(1)`, `getString(2)`, and `getString(3)` methods retrieve the column values for `firstName`, `mi`, and `lastName`, respectively. Alternatively, you can use `getString("firstName")`, `getString("mi")`, and `getString("lastName")` to retrieve the same three column values. The first execution of the `next()` method sets the current row to the first row in the result set, and subsequent invocations of the `next()` method set the current row to the second row, third row, and so on, to the last row.

Listing 32.1 is a complete example that demonstrates connecting to a database, executing a simple query, and processing the query result with JDBC. The program connects to a local MySQL database and displays the students whose last name is Smith.

LISTING 32.1 SimpleJDBC.java

```
1 import java.sql.*;
2
3 public class SimpleJdbc {
4   public static void main(String[] args)
5       throws SQLException, ClassNotFoundException {
6     // Load the JDBC driver
7     Class.forName("com.mysql.jdbc.Driver");
8     System.out.println("Driver loaded");
9
10    // Establish a connection
11    Connection connection = DriverManager.getConnection
12      ("jdbc:mysql://localhost/test");
13    System.out.println("Database connected");
14
15    // Create a statement
16    Statement statement = connection.createStatement();
17
18    // Execute a statement
19    ResultSet resultSet = statement.executeQuery
20      ("select firstName, mi, lastName from Student where lastName "
21      + " = 'Smith'");
22
23    // Iterate through the result and print the student names
24    while (resultSet.next())
25      System.out.println(resultSet.getString(1) + "\t" +
26        resultSet.getString(2) + "\t" + resultSet.getString(3));
27
28    // Close the connection
29    connection.close();
30  }
31 }
```

- load driver (line 7)
- connect database (line 11)
- create statement (line 16)
- execute statement (line 19)
- get result (line 24)
- close connection (line 29)

The statement in line 7 loads a JDBC driver for MySQL, and the statement in lines 11–12 connects to a local MySQL database. You may change them to connect to an Access or Oracle database. The last statement (line 29) closes the connection and releases resource related to the connection.

Note
Do not use a semicolon (;) to end the Oracle SQL command in a Java program. The semicolon does not work with the Oracle JDBC drivers. It does work, however, with the other drivers used in the book.

Note
The **Connection** interface handles transactions and specifies how they are processed. By default, a new connection is in auto-commit mode, and all its SQL statements are executed and committed as individual transactions. The commit occurs when the statement completes or the next execute occurs, whichever comes first. In the case of statements returning a result set, the statement completes when the last row of the result set has been retrieved or the result set has been closed. If a single statement returns multiple results, the commit occurs when all the results have been retrieved. You can use the **setAutoCommit(false)** method to disable auto-commit, so that all SQL statements are grouped into one transaction that is terminated by a call to either the **commit()** or the **rollback()** method. The **rollback()** method undoes all the changes made by the transaction.

32.4.2 Accessing a Database from a Java Applet

Using the JDBC-ODBC bridge driver, your program cannot run as an applet from a Web browser because the ODBC driver contains non-Java native code. The JDBC drivers for MySQL and Oracle are written in Java and can run from the JVM in a Web browser. This section gives an example that demonstrates connecting to a database from a Java applet. The applet lets the user enter the SSN and the course ID to find a student's grade, as shown in Figure 32.20. The code in Listing 32.2 uses the MySQL database on the host liang.armstrong.edu.

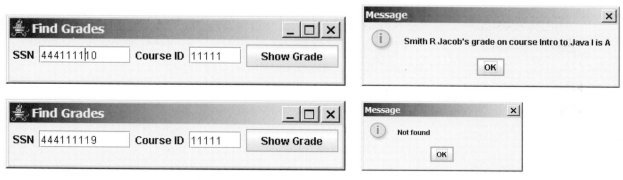

FIGURE 32.20   A Java applet can access the database on the server.

LISTING 32.2   FindGrade.java

```
1  import javax.swing.*;
2  import java.sql.*;
3  import java.awt.*;
4  import java.awt.event.*;
5
6  public class FindGrade extends JApplet {
7    private JTextField jtfSSN = new JTextField(9);
8    private JTextField jtfCourseId = new JTextField(5);
9    private JButton jbtShowGrade = new JButton("Show Grade");
10
11   // Statement for executing queries
12   private Statement stmt;
13
14   /** Initialize the applet */
15   public void init() {
16     // Initialize database connection and create a Statement object
17     initializeDB();
18
19     jbtShowGrade.addActionListener(
20       new java.awt.event.ActionListener() {
21       public void actionPerformed(ActionEvent e) {
22         jbtShowGrade_actionPerformed(e);
23       }
24     });
25
26     JPanel jPanel1 = new JPanel();
27     jPanel1.add(new JLabel("SSN"));
28     jPanel1.add(jtfSSN);
29     jPanel1.add(new JLabel("Course ID"));
30     jPanel1.add(jtfCourseId);
31     jPanel1.add(jbtShowGrade);
32
```

button listener

```
33        add(jPanel1, BorderLayout.NORTH);
34      }
35
36      private void initializeDB() {
37        try {
38          // Load the JDBC driver
39          Class.forName("com.mysql.jdbc.Driver");
40  //         Class.forName("oracle.jdbc.driver.OracleDriver");
41          System.out.println("Driver loaded");
42
43          // Establish a connection
44          Connection connection = DriverManager.getConnection
45            ("jdbc:mysql://liang.armstrong.edu/test");
46  //        ("jdbc:oracle:thin:@liang.armstrong.edu:1521:orcl",
47  //         "scott", "tiger");
48          System.out.println("Database connected");
49
50          // Create a statement
51          stmt = connection.createStatement();
52        }
53        catch (Exception ex) {
54          ex.printStackTrace();
55        }
56      }
57
58      private void jbtShowGrade_actionPerformed(ActionEvent e) {
59        String ssn = jtfSSN.getText();
60        String courseId = jtfCourseId.getText();
61        try {
62          String queryString = "select firstName, mi, " +
63            "lastName, title, grade from Student, Enrollment, Course " +
64            "where Student.ssn = '" + ssn + "' and Enrollment.courseId "
65            + "= '" + courseId +
66            "' and Enrollment.courseId = Course.courseId " +
67            " and Enrollment.ssn = Student.ssn";
68
69          ResultSet rset = stmt.executeQuery(queryString);
70
71          if (rset.next()) {
72            String lastName = rset.getString(1);
73            String mi = rset.getString(2);
74            String firstName = rset.getString(3);
75            String title = rset.getString(4);
76            String grade = rset.getString(5);
77
78            // Display result in a dialog box
79            JOptionPane.showMessageDialog(null, firstName + " " + mi +
80              " " + lastName + "'s grade on course " + title + " is " +
81              grade);
82          } else {
83            // Display result in a dialog box
84            JOptionPane.showMessageDialog(null, "Not found");
85          }
86        }
87        catch (SQLException ex) {
88          ex.printStackTrace();
89        }
90      }
91    }
```

load driver

Oracle drive commented

connect database

connect to Oracle
commented

create statement

execute statement

show result

main omitted

The `initializeDB()` method (lines 36–56) loads the MySQL driver (line 39), connects to the MySQL database on host liang.armstrong.edu (lines 44–45), and creates a statement (line 51).

You can run the applet standalone from the *main* method (note that the listing for the *main* method is omitted for all the applets in the book for brevity) or test the applet using the appletviewer utility, as shown in Figure 32.20. If this applet is deployed on the server where the database is located, any client on the Internet can run it from a Web browser. Since the client may not have a MySQL driver, you should make the driver available along with the applet in one archive file. This archive file can be created as follows:

1. Copy c:\book\mysqljdbc.jar to a new file named FindGrade.zip.

2. Add FindGrade.class into FindGrade.zip using the WinZip utility.

3. Add FindGrade$1.class into FindGrade.zip using the WinZip utility. FindGrade$1.class is for the anonymous inner event adapter class for listening to the button action.

You need to deploy FindGrade.zip and FindGrade.html on the server. FindGrade.html should use the applet tag with a reference to the Zip file, as follows:

```
<applet
  code = "FindGrade"
  archive = "FindGrade.zip"
  width = 380
  height = 80
>
</applet>
```

 Note
To access the database from an applet, security restrictions make it necessary for the applet to be downloaded from the server where the database is located. Therefore, you have to deploy the applet on the server.

32.5 **PreparedStatement**

Once a connection to a particular database is established, it can be used to send SQL statements from your program to the database. The `Statement` interface is used to execute static SQL statements that contain no parameters. The `PreparedStatement` interface, extending `Statement`, is used to execute a precompiled SQL statement with or without parameters. Since the SQL statements are precompiled, they are efficient for repeated executions.

A `PreparedStatement` object is created using the `preparedStatement` method in the `Connection` interface. For example, the following code creates a `PreparedStatement` `pstmt` on a particular `Connection connection` for an SQL `insert` statement:

```
Statement pstmt = connection.prepareStatement
  ("insert into Student (firstName, mi, lastName) " +
  "values (?, ?, ?)");
```

This `insert` statement has three question marks as placeholders for parameters representing values for `firstName`, `mi`, and `lastName` in a record of the `Student` table.

As a subinterface of `Statement`, the `PreparedStatement` interface inherits all the methods defined in `Statement`. It also provides the methods for setting parameters in the object of `PreparedStatement`. These methods are used to set the values for the parameters before executing statements or procedures. In general, the set methods have the following name and signature:

```
setX(int parameterIndex, X value);
```

where *X* is the type of the parameter, and `parameterIndex` is the index of the parameter in the statement. The index starts from 1. For example, the method `setString(int parameterIndex, String value)` sets a `String` value to the specified parameter.

The following statements pass the parameters `"Jack"`, `"A"`, `"Ryan"` to the placeholders for firstName, mi, and lastName in `PreparedStatement pstmt`:

```
pstmt.setString(1, "Jack");
pstmt.setString(2, "A");
pstmt.setString(3, "Ryan");
```

After setting the parameters, you can execute the prepared statement by invoking `executeQuery()` for a SELECT statement and `executeUpdate()` for a DDL or update statement.

The `executeQuery()` and `executeUpdate()` methods are similar to the ones defined in the `Statement` interface except that they have no parameters, because the SQL statements are already specified in the `preparedStatement` method when the object of `PreparedStatement` is created.

Using a prepared SQL statement, Listing 32.2 can be improved in Listing 32.3.

LISTING 32.3 FindGradeUsingPreparedStatement.java

```
 1 import javax.swing.*;
 2 import java.sql.*;
 3 import java.awt.*;
 4 import java.awt.event.*;
 5
 6 public class FindGradeUsingPreparedStatement extends JApplet {
 7   private JTextField jtfSSN = new JTextField(9);
 8   private JTextField jtfCourseId = new JTextField(5);
 9   private JButton jbtShowGrade = new JButton("Show Grade");
10
11   // PreparedStatement for executing queries
12   private PreparedStatement pstmt;
13
14   /** Initialize the applet */
15   public void init() {
16     // Initialize database connection and create a Statement object
17     initializeDB();
18
19     jbtShowGrade.addActionListener(
20       new java.awt.event.ActionListener() {
21       public void actionPerformed(ActionEvent e) {
22         jbtShowGrade_actionPerformed(e);
23       }
24     });
25
26     JPanel jPanel1 = new JPanel();
27     jPanel1.add(new JLabel("SSN"));
28     jPanel1.add(jtfSSN);
29     jPanel1.add(new JLabel("Course ID"));
30     jPanel1.add(jtfCourseId);
31     jPanel1.add(jbtShowGrade);
32
33     add(jPanel1, BorderLayout.NORTH);
34   }
35
```

```
36    private void initializeDB() {
37      try {
38        // Load the JDBC driver
39        Class.forName("com.mysql.jdbc.Driver");                          load driver
40 //       Class.forName("oracle.jdbc.driver.OracleDriver");
41        System.out.println("Driver loaded");
42
43        // Establish a connection
44        Connection connection = DriverManager.getConnection            connect database
45          ("jdbc:mysql://liang.armstrong.edu/test");
46 //       ("jdbc:oracle:thin:@liang.armstrong.edu:1521:orcl",
47 //        "scott", "tiger");
48        System.out.println("Database connected");
49
50        String queryString = "select firstName, mi, " +
51          "lastName, title, grade from Student, Enrollment, Course " +
52          "where Student.ssn = ? and Enrollment.courseId = ? " +       placeholder
53          "and Enrollment.courseId = Course.courseId";
54
55        // Create a statement
56        pstmt = connection.prepareStatement(queryString);              prepare statement
57      }
58      catch (Exception ex) {
59        ex.printStackTrace();
60      }
61    }
62
63    private void jbtShowGrade_actionPerformed(ActionEvent e) {
64      String ssn = jtfSSN.getText();
65      String courseId = jtfCourseId.getText();
66      try {
67        pstmt.setString(1, ssn);
68        pstmt.setString(2, courseId);
69        ResultSet rset = pstmt.executeQuery();                         execute statement
70
71        if (rset.next()) {                                             show result
72          String lastName = rset.getString(1);
73          String mi = rset.getString(2);
74          String firstName = rset.getString(3);
75          String title = rset.getString(4);
76          String grade = rset.getString(5);
77
78          // Display result in a dialog box
79          JOptionPane.showMessageDialog(null, firstName + " " + mi +
80            " " + lastName + "'s grade on course " + title + " is " +
81            grade);
82        }
83        else {
84          // Display result in a dialog box
85          JOptionPane.showMessageDialog(null, "Not found");
86        }
87      }
88      catch (SQLException ex) {
89        ex.printStackTrace();
90      }
91    }
92 }                                                                     main omitted
```

This example does exactly the same thing as Listing 32.2 except that it uses the prepared statement to dynamically set the parameters. The code in this example is almost the same as in the preceding example. The new code is highlighted.

A prepared query string is defined in lines 50–53 with **ssn** and **courseId** as parameters. An SQL prepared statement is obtained in line 56. Before executing the query, the actual values of **ssn** and **courseId** are set to the parameters in lines 67–68. Line 69 executes the prepared statement.

32.6 Retrieving Metadata

database metadata

JDBC provides the **DatabaseMetaData** interface for obtaining database-wide information and the **ResultSetMetaData** interface for obtaining information on the specific **ResultSet**, such as column count and column names.

32.6.1 Database Metadata

The **Connection** interface establishes a connection to a database. It is within the context of a connection that SQL statements are executed and results are returned. A connection also provides access to database metadata information that describes the capabilities of the database, supported SQL grammar, stored procedures, and so on. To obtain an instance of **Database-MetaData** for a database, use the **getMetaData** method on a **connection** object like this:

```
DatabaseMetaData dbMetaData = connection.getMetaData();
```

If your program connects to a local MySQL database, the following statements display the database information, as shown in Figure 32.21:

LISTING 32.4 TestDatabaseMetaData.java

```
 1  import java.sql.*;
 2
 3  public class TestDatabaseMetaData {
 4    public static void main(String[] args)
 5      throws SQLException, ClassNotFoundException {
 6      // Load the JDBC driver
 7      Class.forName("com.mysql.jdbc.Driver");
 8      System.out.println("Driver loaded");
 9
10      // Establish a connection
11      Connection connection = DriverManager.getConnection
12        ("jdbc:mysql://localhost/test");
13      System.out.println("Database connected");
14
15      DatabaseMetaData dbMetaData = connection.getMetaData();
16      System.out.println("database URL: " + dbMetaData.getURL());
17      System.out.println("database username: " +
18        dbMetaData.getUserName());
19      System.out.println("database product name: " +
20        dbMetaData.getDatabaseProductName());
21      System.out.println("database product version: " +
22        dbMetaData.getDatabaseProductVersion());
23      System.out.println("JDBC driver name: " +
24        dbMetaData.getDriverName());
25      System.out.println("JDBC driver version: " +
26        dbMetaData.getDriverVersion());
27      System.out.println("JDBC driver major version: " +
28        dbMetaData.getDriverMajorVersion());
29      System.out.println("JDBC driver minor version: " +
30        dbMetaData.getDriverMinorVersion());
```

load driver

connect database

database metadata
get metadata

```
31        System.out.println("Max number of connections: " +
32          dbMetaData.getMaxConnections());
33        System.out.println("MaxTableNameLength: " +
34          dbMetaData.getMaxTableNameLength());
35        System.out.println("MaxColumnsInTable: " +
36          dbMetaData.getMaxColumnsInTable());
37
38        // Close the connection
39        connection.close();
40      }
41 }
```

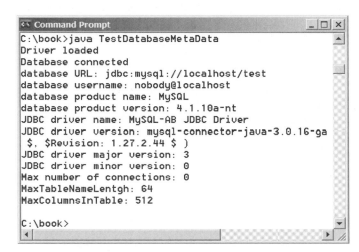

FIGURE 32.21   The `DatabaseMetaData` interface enables you to obtain database information.

32.6.2   Obtaining Database Tables

You can find all the tables in the database through database metadata using the `getTables` method. Listing 32.5 displays all the user tables in the test database on a local MySQL. Figure 32.22 shows a sample output of the program.

FIGURE 32.22   You can find all the tables in the database.

LISTING 32.5   FindUserTables.java

```
1 import java.sql.*;
2
3 public class FindUserTables {
4   public static void main(String[] args)
5       throws SQLException, ClassNotFoundException {
6     // Load the JDBC driver
7     Class.forName("com.mysql.jdbc.Driver");                          load driver
8     System.out.println("Driver loaded");
9
```

connect database

```
10      // Establish a connection
11      Connection connection = DriverManager.getConnection
12        ("jdbc:mysql://localhost/test");
13      System.out.println("Database connected");
14
```

database metadata

```
15      DatabaseMetaData dbMetaData = connection.getMetaData();
16
```

obtain tables

```
17      ResultSet rsTables = dbMetaData.getTables(null, null, null,
18        new String[] {"TABLE"});
19      System.out.print("User tables: ");
20      while (rsTables.next())
```

get table names

```
21        System.out.print(rsTables.getString("TABLE_NAME") + " ");
22
23      // Close the connection
24      connection.close();
25    }
26 }
```

Line 17 obtains table information in a result set using the getTables method. One of the columns in the result set is TABLE_NAME. Line 21 retrieves the table name from this result set column.

32.6.3   Result Set Metadata

The ResultSetMetaData interface describes information pertaining to the result set. A ResultSetMetaData object can be used to find the types and properties of the columns in a ResultSet. To obtain an instance of ResultSetMetaData, use the getMetaData method on a result set like this:

```
    ResultSetMetaData rsMetaData = resultSet.getMetaData();
```

You can use the getColumnCount() method to find the number of columns in the result and the getColumnName(int) method to get the column names. For example, Listing 32.6 displays all the column names and contents resulting from the SQL SELECT statement *select * from Enrollment*. The output is shown in Figure 32.23.

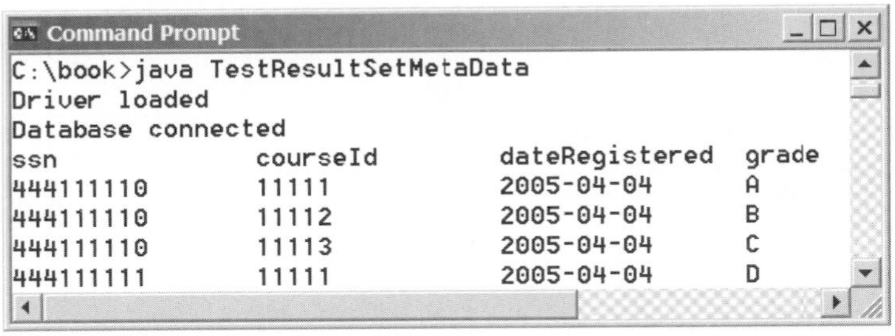

FIGURE 32.23   The ResultSetMetaData interface enables you to obtain resultset information.

LISTING 32.6   TestResultSetMetaData.java

```
1 import java.sql.*;
2
3 public class TestResultSetMetaData {
4   public static void main(String[] args)
5       throws SQLException, ClassNotFoundException {
6     // Load the JDBC driver
7     Class.forName("com.mysql.jdbc.Driver");
8     System.out.println("Driver loaded");
9
```

load driver

```
10       // Establish a connection
11       Connection connection = DriverManager.getConnection        connect database
12         ("jdbc:mysql://localhost/test");
13       System.out.println("Database connected");
14
15       // Create a statement
16       Statement statement = connection.createStatement();        create statement
17
18       // Execute a statement
19       ResultSet resultSet = statement.executeQuery               create resultset
20         ("select * from Enrollment");
21
22       ResultSetMetaData rsMetaData = resultSet.getMetaData();     resultset metadata
23       for (int i = 1; i <= rsMetaData.getColumnCount(); i++)      column count
24         System.out.printf("%-12s\t", rsMetaData.getColumnName(i)); column name
25       System.out.println();
26
27       // Iterate through the result and print the student names
28       while (resultSet.next()) {
29         for (int i = 1; i <= rsMetaData.getColumnCount(); i++)
30           System.out.printf("%-12s\t", resultSet.getObject(i));
31         System.out.println();
32       }
33
34       // Close the connection
35       connection.close();
36     }
37 }
```

KEY TERMS

attribute 1095	integrity constraint 1095
database management system 1094	primary key constraint 1096
database system 1094	relational database 1094
domain constraint 1096	Structured Query Language (SQL) 1098
foreign key constraint 1097	tuples 1095

CHAPTER SUMMARY

■ This chapter introduced the concepts of database systems, relational databases, relational data models, data integrity, and SQL. You learned how to develop database applications using Java.

■ The Java API for developing Java database applications is called *JDBC*. JDBC provides Java programmers with a uniform interface for accessing and manipulating a wide range of relational databases.

■ The JDBC API consists of classes and interfaces for establishing connections with databases, sending SQL statements to databases, processing the results of SQL statements, and obtaining database metadata.

■ Since a JDBC driver serves as the interface to facilitate communications between JDBC and a proprietary database, JDBC drivers are database-specific. A JDBC-ODBC bridge driver is included in JDK to support Java programs that access databases through ODBC drivers. If you use a driver other than the JDBC–ODBC bridge driver, make sure it is on the classpath before running the program.

■ Four key interfaces are needed to develop any database application using Java: `Driver`, `Connection`, `Statement`, and `ResultSet`. These interfaces define a framework for generic SQL database access. The JDBC driver vendors provide implementation for them.

■ A JDBC application loads an appropriate driver using the `Driver` interface, connects to the database using the `Connection` interface, creates and executes SQL statements using the `Statement` interface, and processes the result using the `ResultSet` interface if the statements return results.

■ The `PreparedStatement` interface is designed to execute dynamic SQL statements with parameters. These SQL statements are precompiled for efficient use when repeatedly executed.

■ Database *metadata* is information that describes the database itself. JDBC provides the `DatabaseMetaData` interface for obtaining database-wide information and the `ResultSetMetaData` interface for obtaining information on the specific `ResultSet`.

REVIEW QUESTIONS

Section 32.2 Relational Database Systems

32.1 What are superkeys, candidate keys, and primary keys? How do you create a table with a primary key?

32.2 What is a foreign key? How do you create a table with a foreign key?

32.3 Can a relation have more than one primary key or foreign key?

32.4 Does a foreign key need to be a primary key in the same relation?

32.5 Does a foreign key need to have the same name as its referenced primary key?

32.6 Can a foreign key value be null?

Section 32.3 SQL

32.7 Create the tables `Course`, `Student`, and `Enrollment` using the `create table` statements in Section 32.3.1, "Creating and Dropping Tables." Insert rows into `Course`, `Student`, and `Enrollment` using the data in Figures 32.3, 32.4, and 32.5.

32.8 List all CSCI courses with at least four credit hours.

32.9 List all students whose last names contain the letter *e* two times.

32.10 List all students whose birthdays are null.

32.11 List all students who take Math courses.

32.12 List the number of courses in each subject.

32.13 Assume that each credit hour is fifty minutes of lectures. Get the total minutes for the courses that each student takes.

Section 32.4 JDBC

32.14 What are the advantages of developing database applications using Java?

32.15 Describe the following JDBC interfaces: `Driver`, `Connection`, `Statement`, and `ResultSet`.

32.16 How do you load a JDBC driver? What are the driver classes for MySQL, Access, and Oracle?

32.17 How do you create a database connection? What are the URLs for MySQL, Access, and Oracle?

32.18 How do you create a `Statement` and execute an SQL statement?

32.19 How do you retrieve values in a `ResultSet`?

32.20 Does JDBC automatically commit a transaction? How do you set auto-commit to `false`?

Section 32.5 PreparedStatement

32.21 Describe prepared statements. How do you create instances of `Prepared-Statement`? How do you execute a `PreparedStatement`? How do you set parameter values in a `PreparedStatement`?

32.22 What are the benefits of using prepared statements?

Section 32.6 Retrieving Metadata

32.23 What is `DatabaseMetaData` for? Describe the methods in `DatabaseMetaData`. How do you get an instance of `DatabaseMetaData`?

32.24 What is `ResultSetMetaData` for? Describe the methods in `Result-SetMetaData`. How do you get an instance of `ResultSetMetaData`?

32.25 How do you find the number of columns in a result set? How do you find the column names in a result set?

Programming Exercises

32.1* (*Accessing and updating a Staff table*) Write a Java applet that views, inserts, and updates staff information stored in a database, as shown in Figure 32.24. The view button displays a record with a specified ID. The `Staff` table is created as follows:

```
create table Staff (
  id char(9) not null,
  lastName varchar(15),
  firstName varchar(15),
  mi char(1),
  address varchar(20),
  city varchar(20),
  state char(2),
  telephone char(10),
  email varchar(40),
  primary key (id)
);
```

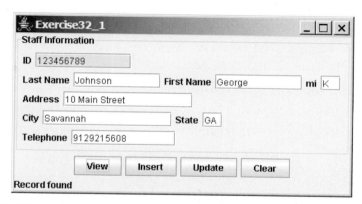

Figure 32.24   The applet lets you view, insert, and update staff information.

32.2** (*Displaying data*) Write a program that displays the number of students in each department in a pie chart and a bar chart, as shown in Figure 32.25. The number of students for each department can be obtained from the **Student** table (see Figure 32.4) using the following SQL statement:

```
select deptId, count(*)
from Student
group by deptId;
```

Use the **PieChart** component and the **BarChart** component created in Programming Exercise 30.1 to display the data.

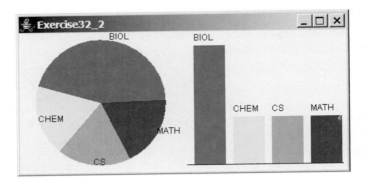

FIGURE 32.25 The **PieChart** and **BarChart** components display the query data obtained from the data module.

32.3* (*Connection dialog*) Develop a JavaBeans component named **DBConnectionPanel** that enables the user to select or enter a JDBC driver and a URL and to enter a username and password, as shown in Figure 32.26. When the OK button is clicked, a **Connection** object for the database is stored in the **connection** property. You can then use the **getConnection()** method to return the connection.

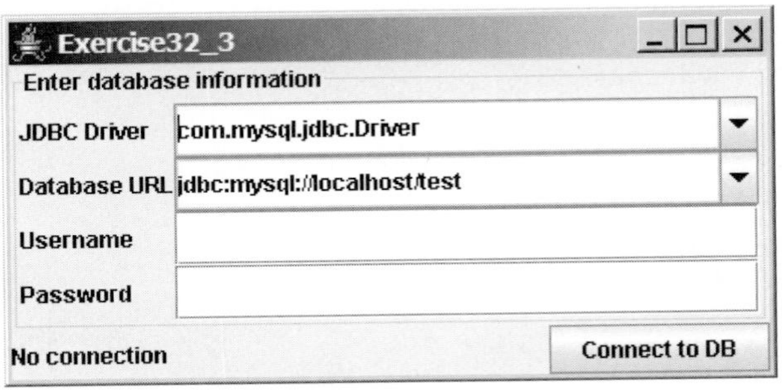

FIGURE 32.26 The **DBConnectionPanel** component enables the user to enter database information.

32.4* (*Finding grades*) Listing 32.2, FindGrade.java, presented an applet that finds a student's grade for a specified course. Rewrite the program to find all the grades for a specified student, as shown in Figure 32.27.

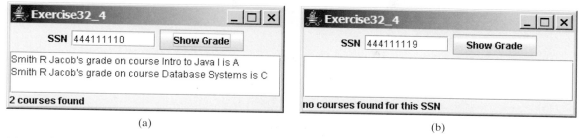

(a)   (b)

FIGURE 32.27   The applet displays the grades for the courses for a specified student.

32.5* (*Displaying table contents*) Write a program that displays the content for a given table. As shown in Figure 32.28(a), you enter a table and click the *Show Contents* button to display the table contents in the text area.

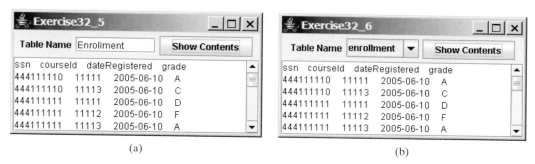

(a)   (b)

FIGURE 32.28   (a) Enter a table name to display the table contents. (b) Select a table name from the combo box to display its contents.

32.6* (*Finding tables and show their contents*) Write a program that fills in table names in a combo box, as shown in Figure 32.28(b). You can select a table from the combo box to display its contents in the text area.

ADVANCED JAVA DATABASE PROGRAMMING

Objectives

- To create a universal SQL client for accessing local or remote databases (§33.2).
- To execute SQL statements in a batch mode (§33.3).
- To process updateable and scrollable result sets (§33.4).
- To simplify Java database programming using RowSet (§33.5).
- To store and retrieve images in JDBC (§33.6).

33.1 Introduction

JDBC 2
JDBC 3

The preceding chapter introduced the basic features of JDBC. This chapter covers the advanced features of JDBC. Many of the advanced features are introduced in *JDBC 2* or *JDBC 3*, which are new standards for JDBC. You will learn how to develop a universal SQL client for accessing any local or remote relational database, learn how to execute statements in a batch mode to improve performance, learn scrollable result sets and how to update a database through result sets, learn how to use **RowSet** to simplify database access, and learn how to store and retrieve images.

33.2 A Universal SQL Client

In the preceding chapter, you used various drivers to connect to the database, created statements for executing SQL statements, and processed the results from SQL queries. This section presents a universal SQL client that enables you to connect to any relational database and execute SQL commands interactively, as shown in Figure 33.1. The client can connect to any JDBC data source, and can submit SQL SELECT commands and non-SELECT commands for execution. The execution result is displayed for the SELECT queries, and the execution status is displayed for the non-SELECT commands. Listing 33.1 gives the solution to the problem.

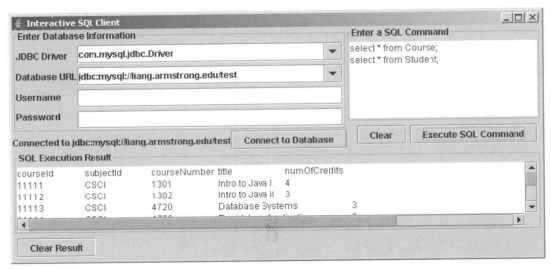

FIGURE 33.1 You can connect to any JDBC data source and execute SQL commands interactively.

LISTING 33.1 SQLClient.java

```
1 import java.awt.*;
2 import java.awt.event.*;
3 import javax.swing.*;
4 import javax.swing.border.*;
5 import java.sql.*;
6 import java.util.*;
7
8 public class SQLClient extends JApplet {
9   // Connection to the database
10   private Connection connection;
11
12   // Statement to execute SQL commands
13   private Statement statement;
14
```

connection

statement

```java
15    // Text area to enter SQL commands
16    private JTextArea jtasqlCommand = new JTextArea();
17
18    // Text area to display results from SQL commands
19    private JTextArea jtaSQLResult = new JTextArea();
20
21    // JDBC info for a database connection
22    JTextField jtfUsername = new JTextField();
23    JPasswordField jpfPassword = new JPasswordField();
24    JComboBox jcboURL = new JComboBox(new String[] {
25      "jdbc:mysql://liang.armstrong.edu/test",
26      "jdbc:odbc:exampleMDBDataSource",
27      "jdbc:oracle:thin:@liang.armstrong.edu:1521:orcl"});
28    JComboBox jcboDriver = new JComboBox(new String[] {
29      "com.mysql.jdbc.Driver", "sun.jdbc.odbc.JdbcOdbcDriver",
30      "oracle.jdbc.driver.OracleDriver"});
31
32    JButton jbtExecuteSQL = new JButton("Execute SQL Command");
33    JButton jbtClearSQLCommand = new JButton("Clear");
34    JButton jbtConnectDB1 = new JButton("Connect to Database");
35    JButton jbtClearSQLResult = new JButton("Clear Result");
36
37    // Create titled borders
38    Border titledBorder1 = new TitledBorder("Enter an SQL Command");
39    Border titledBorder2 = new TitledBorder("SQL Execution Result");
40    Border titledBorder3 = new TitledBorder(
41      "Enter Database Information");
42
43    JLabel jlblConnectionStatus = new JLabel("No connection now");
44
45    /** Initialize the applet */
46    public void init() {
47      JScrollPane jScrollPane1 = new JScrollPane(jtasqlCommand);
48      jScrollPane1.setBorder(titledBorder1);
49      JScrollPane jScrollPane2 = new JScrollPane(jtaSQLResult);
50      jScrollPane2.setBorder(titledBorder2);
51
52      JPanel jPanel1 = new JPanel(new FlowLayout(FlowLayout.RIGHT));
53      jPanel1.add(jbtClearSQLCommand);
54      jPanel1.add(jbtExecuteSQL);
55
56      JPanel jPanel2 = new JPanel();
57      jPanel2.setLayout(new BorderLayout());
58      jPanel2.add(jScrollPane1, BorderLayout.CENTER);
59      jPanel2.add(jPanel1, BorderLayout.SOUTH);
60      jPanel2.setPreferredSize(new Dimension(100, 100));
61
62      JPanel jPanel3 = new JPanel();
63      jPanel3.setLayout(new BorderLayout());
64      jPanel3.add(jlblConnectionStatus, BorderLayout.CENTER);
65      jPanel3.add(jbtConnectDB1, BorderLayout.EAST);
66
67      JPanel jPanel4 = new JPanel();
68      jPanel4.setLayout(new GridLayout(4, 1, 10, 5));
69      jPanel4.add(jcboDriver);
70      jPanel4.add(jcboURL);
71      jPanel4.add(jtfUsername);
72      jPanel4.add(jpfPassword);
73
74      JPanel jPanel5 = new JPanel();
```

URLs

drivers

create UI

```
 75       jPanel5.setLayout(new GridLayout(4, 1));
 76       jPanel5.add(new JLabel("JDBC Driver"));
 77       jPanel5.add(new JLabel("Database URL"));
 78       jPanel5.add(new JLabel("Username"));
 79       jPanel5.add(new JLabel("Password"));
 80
 81       JPanel jPanel6 = new JPanel();
 82       jPanel6.setLayout(new BorderLayout());
 83       jPanel6.setBorder(titledBorder3);
 84       jPanel6.add(jPanel4, BorderLayout.CENTER);
 85       jPanel6.add(jPanel5, BorderLayout.WEST);
 86
 87       JPanel jPanel7 = new JPanel();
 88       jPanel7.setLayout(new BorderLayout());
 89       jPanel7.add(jPanel3, BorderLayout.SOUTH);
 90       jPanel7.add(jPanel6, BorderLayout.CENTER);
 91
 92       JPanel jPanel8 = new JPanel();
 93       jPanel8.setLayout(new BorderLayout());
 94       jPanel8.add(jPanel2, BorderLayout.CENTER);
 95       jPanel8.add(jPanel7, BorderLayout.WEST);
 96
 97       JPanel jPanel9 = new JPanel(new FlowLayout(FlowLayout.LEFT));
 98       jPanel9.add(jbtClearSQLResult);
 99
100       jcboURL.setEditable(true);
101       jcboDriver.setEditable(true);
102
103       add(jPanel8, BorderLayout.NORTH);
104       add(jScrollPane2, BorderLayout.CENTER);
105       add(jPanel9, BorderLayout.SOUTH);
106
107       jbtExecuteSQL.addActionListener(new ActionListener() {
108         public void actionPerformed(ActionEvent e) {
109           executeSQL();
110         }
111       });
112       jbtConnectDB1.addActionListener(new ActionListener() {
113         public void actionPerformed(ActionEvent e) {
114           connectToDB();
115         }
116       });
117       jbtClearSQLCommand.addActionListener(new ActionListener() {
118         public void actionPerformed(ActionEvent e) {
119           jtasqlCommand.setText(null);
120         }
121       });
122       jbtClearSQLResult.addActionListener(new ActionListener() {
123         public void actionPerformed(ActionEvent e) {
124           jtaSQLResult.setText(null);
125         }
126       });
127     }
128
129     /** Connect to DB */
130     private void connectToDB() {
131       // Get database information from the user input
132       String driver = (String)jcboDriver.getSelectedItem();
133       String url = (String)jcboURL.getSelectedItem();
134       String username = jtfUsername.getText().trim();
```

execute SQL

connect database

clear command

clear result

```
135        String password = new String(jpfPassword.getPassword());
136
137        // Connection to the database
138        try {
139          Class.forName(driver);
140          connection = DriverManager.getConnection(
141            url, username, password);
142          jlblConnectionStatus.setText("Connected to " + url);
143        }
144        catch (java.lang.Exception ex) {
145          ex.printStackTrace();
146        }
147      }
148
149      /** Execute SQL commands */
150      private void executeSQL() {
151        if (connection == null) {
152          jtaSQLResult.setText("Please connect to a database first");
153          return;
154        }
155        else {
156          String sqlCommands = jtasqlCommand.getText().trim();
157          String[] commands = sqlCommands.replace('\n', ' ').split(";");
158
159          for (String aCommand: commands) {
160            if (aCommand.trim().toUpperCase().startsWith("SELECT")) {
161              processSQLSelect(aCommand);
162            }
163            else {
164              processSQLNonSelect(aCommand);
165            }
166          }
167        }
168      }
169
170      /** Execute SQL SELECT commands */
171      private void processSQLSelect(String sqlCommand) {
172        try {
173          // Get a new statement for the current connection
174          statement = connection.createStatement();
175
176          // Execute a SELECT SQL command
177          ResultSet resultSet = statement.executeQuery(sqlCommand);
178
179          // Find the number of columns in the result set
180          int columnCount = resultSet.getMetaData().getColumnCount();
181          String row = " ";
182
183          // Display column names
184          for (int i = 1; i <= columnCount; i++) {
185            row += resultSet.getMetaData().getColumnName(i) + "\t";
186          }
187
188          jtaSQLResult.append(row + '\n');
189
190          while (resultSet.next()) {
191            // Reset row to empty
192            row = " ";
193
194            for (int i = 1; i <= columnCount; i++) {
```

load driver
connect database

process select

process non-select

```
195              // A non-String column is converted to a string
196              row += resultSet.getString(i) + "\t";
197            }
198
199            jtaSQLResult.append(row + '\n');
200          }
201        }
202      catch (SQLException ex) {
203        jtaSQLResult.setText(ex.toString());
204      }
205    }
206
207    /** Execute SQL DDL, and modification commands */
208    private void processSQLNonSelect(String sqlCommand) {
209      try {
210        // Get a new statement for the current connection
211        statement = connection.createStatement();
212
213        // Execute a non-SELECT SQL command
214        statement.executeUpdate(sqlCommand);
215
216        jtaSQLResult.setText("SQL command executed");
217      }
218      catch (SQLException ex) {
219        jtaSQLResult.setText(ex.toString());
220      }
221    }
222  }
```

main omitted

The user selects or enters the JDBC driver, database URL, username, and password, and clicks the *Connect to Database* button to connect to the specified database using the `connectToDB()` method (lines 130–147).

When the user clicks the *Execute SQL Command* button, the `executeSQL()` method is invoked (lines 150–168) to get the SQL commands from the text area (`jtaSQLCommand`) and extract each command separated by a semicolon (;). It then determines whether the command is a SELECT query or a DDL or data modification statement (lines 160–165). If the command is a SELECT query, the `processSQLSelect` method is invoked (lines 171–205). This method uses the `executeQuery` method (line 177) to obtain the query result. The result is displayed in the text area (`jtaSQLResult`). If the command is a non-SELECT query, the `processSQLNonSelect()` method is invoked (lines 208–221). This method uses the `executeUpdate` method (line 214) to execute the SQL command.

The `getMetaData` method (lines 180, 185) in the `ResultSet` interface is used to obtain an instance of `ResultSetMetaData`. The `getColumnCount` method (line 180) returns the number of columns in the result set, and the `getColumnName(i)` method (line 185) returns the column name for the *i*th column.

33.3 Batch Processing

In all the preceding examples, SQL commands are submitted to the database for execution one at a time. This is inefficient for processing a large number of updates. For example, suppose you wanted to insert a thousand rows into a table. Submitting one INSERT command at a time would take nearly a thousand times longer than submitting all the INSERT commands in a batch at once. To improve performance, JDBC 2 introduced the batch update for processing nonselect SQL commands. A batch update consists of a sequence of nonselect SQL commands. These commands are collected in a batch and submitted to the database all together.

To use the batch update, you add nonselect commands to a batch using the **addBatch** method in the **Statement** interface. After all the SQL commands are added to the batch, use the **executeBatch** method to submit the batch to the database for execution.

For example, the following code adds a create table command, two insert statements in a batch, and executes the batch:

```
Statement statement = connection.createStatement();

// Add SQL commands to the batch
statement.addBatch("create table T (C1 integer, C2 varchar(15))");
statement.addBatch("insert into T values (100, 'Smith')");
statement.addBatch("insert into T values (200, 'Jones')");

// Execute the batch
int count[] = statement.executeBatch();
```

The **executeBatch()** method returns an array of counts, each of which counts the number of rows affected by the SQL command. The first count returns **0** because it is a DDL command. The other counts return **1** because only one row is affected.

Note

To find out whether a driver supports batch updates, invoke **supportsBatchUpdates()** on a **DatabaseMetaData** instance. If the driver supports batch updates, it will return **true**. The JDBC drivers for MySQL, Access, and Oracle all support batch updates.

To demonstrate batch processing, consider writing a program that gets data from a text file and copies the data from the text file to a table, as shown in Figure 33.2. The text file consists of lines that each corresponds to a row in the table. The fields in a row are separated by commas. The string values in a row are enclosed in single quotes. You can view the text file by clicking the *View File* button and copy the text to the table by clicking the *Copy* button. The table must already be defined in the database. Figure 33.2 shows the text file table.txt copied to table **Person**. **Person** is created using the following statement:

```
create table Person (
  firstName varchar(20),
  mi char(1),
  lastName varchar(20)
)
```

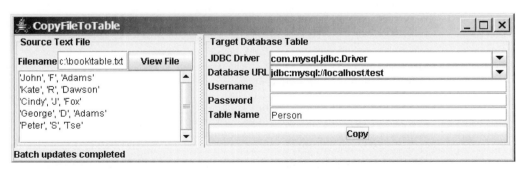

FIGURE 33.2 The `CopyFileToTable` utility copies text files to database tables.

Listing 33.2 gives the solution to the problem.

LISTING 33.2 CopyFileToTable.java

```
1 import javax.swing.*;
2 import javax.swing.border.*;
```

```
3  import java.awt.*;
4  import java.awt.event.*;
5  import java.io.*;
6  import java.sql.*;
7  import java.util.*;
8
9  public class CopyFileToTable extends JFrame {
10   // Text file info
11   private JTextField jtfFilename = new JTextField();
12   private JTextArea jtaFile = new JTextArea();
13
14   // JDBC and table info
15   private JComboBox jcboDriver = new JComboBox(new String[] {
16     "com.mysql.jdbc.Driver", "sun.jdbc.odbc.JdbcOdbcDriver",
17     "oracle.jdbc.driver.OracleDriver"});
18   private JComboBox jcboURL = new JComboBox(new String[] {
19     "jdbc:mysql://localhost/test", "jdbc:odbc:exampleMDBDataSource",
20     "jdbc:oracle:thin:@liang.armstrong.edu: 1521:orcl"});
21   private JTextField jtfUsername = new JTextField();
22   private JPasswordField jtfPassword = new JPasswordField();
23   private JTextField jtfTableName = new JTextField();
24
25   private JButton jbtViewFile = new JButton("View File");
26   private JButton jbtCopy = new JButton("Copy");
27   private JLabel jlblStatus = new JLabel();
28
29   public CopyFileToTable() {
30     JPanel jPane1 = new JPanel();
31     jPane1.setLayout(new BorderLayout());
32     jPane1.add(new JLabel("Filename"), BorderLayout.WEST);
33     jPane1.add(jbtViewFile, BorderLayout.EAST);
34     jPane1.add(jtfFilename, BorderLayout.CENTER);
35
36     JPanel jPane2 = new JPanel();
37     jPane2.setLayout(new BorderLayout());
38     jPane2.setBorder(new TitledBorder("Source Text File"));
39     jPane2.add(jPane1, BorderLayout.NORTH);
40     jPane2.add(new JScrollPane(jtaFile), BorderLayout.CENTER);
41
42     JPanel jPane3 = new JPanel();
43     jPane3.setLayout(new GridLayout(5, 0));
44     jPane3.add(new JLabel("JDBC Driver"));
45     jPane3.add(new JLabel("Database URL"));
46     jPane3.add(new JLabel("Username"));
47     jPane3.add(new JLabel("Password"));
48     jPane3.add(new JLabel("Table Name"));
49
50     JPanel jPane4 = new JPanel();
51     jPane4.setLayout(new GridLayout(5, 0));
52     jcboDriver.setEditable(true);
53     jPane4.add(jcboDriver);
54     jcboURL.setEditable(true);
55     jPane4.add(jcboURL);
56     jPane4.add(jtfUsername);
57     jPane4.add(jtfPassword);
58     jPane4.add(jtfTableName);
59
60     JPanel jPane5 = new JPanel();
61     jPane5.setLayout(new BorderLayout());
62     jPane5.setBorder(new TitledBorder("Target Database Table"));
```

Margin notes:
- drivers (line 15)
- URLs (line 18)
- create UI (line 29)

```
63        jPane5.add(jbtCopy, BorderLayout.SOUTH);
64        jPane5.add(jPane3, BorderLayout.WEST);
65        jPane5.add(jPane4, BorderLayout.CENTER);
66
67        add(jlblStatus, BorderLayout.SOUTH);
68        add(new JSplitPane(JSplitPane.HORIZONTAL_SPLIT,
69          jPane2, jPane5), BorderLayout.CENTER);
70
71        jbtViewFile.addActionListener(new ActionListener() {
72          public void actionPerformed(ActionEvent evt) {
73            showFile();                                              view file
74          }
75        });
76
77        jbtCopy.addActionListener(new ActionListener() {
78          public void actionPerformed(ActionEvent evt) {
79            try {
80              copyFile();                                           to table
81            }
82            catch (Exception ex) {
83              jlblStatus.setText(ex.toString());
84            }
85          }
86        });
87    }
88
89    /** Display the file in the text area */
90    private void showFile() {
91      Scanner input = null;
92      try {
93        // Use a Scanner to read text from the file
94        input = new Scanner(new File(jtfFilename.getText().trim()));
95
96        // Read a line and append the line to the text area
97        while (input.hasNext())
98          jtaFile.append(input.nextLine() + '\n');
99      }
100     catch (FileNotFoundException ex) {
101       System.out.println("File not found: " + jtfFilename.getText());
102     }
103     catch (IOException ex) {
104       ex.printStackTrace();
105     }
106     finally {
107       if (input != null) input.close();
108     }
109   }
110
111   private void copyFile() throws Exception {
112     // Load the JDBC driver
113     Class.forName(((String)jcboDriver.getSelectedItem()).trim());   load driver
114     System.out.println("Driver loaded");
115
116     // Establish a connection
117     Connection conn = DriverManager.getConnection               connect database
118       (((String)jcboURL.getSelectedItem()).trim(),
119       jtfUsername.getText().trim(),
120       String.valueOf(jtfPassword.getPassword()).trim());
121     System.out.println("Database connected");
122
```

```
insert row

123     // Read each line from the text file and insert it to the table
124     insertRows(conn);
125   }
126
127   private void insertRows(Connection connection) {
128     // Build the SQL INSERT statement
129     String sqlInsert = "insert into " + jtfTableName.getText()
130       + " values (";
131
132     // Use a Scanner to read text from the file
133     Scanner input = null;
134
135     // Get file name from the text field
136     String filename = jtfFilename.getText().trim();
137
138     try {
139       // Create a scanner
140       input = new Scanner(new File(filename));
141
142       // Create a statement
statement
143       Statement statement = connection.createStatement();
144
145       System.out.println("Driver major version? " +
146         connection.getMetaData().getDriverMajorVersion());
147
148       // Determine if batchUpdatesSupported is supported
149       boolean batchUpdatesSupported = false;
150
151       try {
152         if (connection.getMetaData().supportsBatchUpdates()) {
batch
153           batchUpdatesSupported = true;
154           System.out.println("batch updates supported");
155         }
156         else {
157           System.out.println("The driver is of JDBC 2 type, but " +
158             "does not support batch updates");
159         }
160       }
161       catch (UnsupportedOperationException ex) {
162         System.out.println("The driver does not support JDBC 2");
163       }
164
165       // Determine if the driver is capable of batch updates
166       if (batchUpdatesSupported) {
167         // Read a line and add the insert table command to the batch
168         while (input.hasNext()) {
169           statement.addBatch(sqlInsert + input.nextLine() + ")");
170         }
171
172         statement.executeBatch();
173
174         jlblStatus.setText("Batch updates completed");
175       }
176       else {
177         // Read a line and execute insert table command
178         while (input.hasNext()) {
execute batch
179           statement.executeUpdate(sqlInsert + input.nextLine() + ")");
180         }
181
182         jlblStatus.setText("Single row update completed");
183       }
184     }
```

```
185        catch (SQLException ex) {
186          System.out.println(ex);
187        }
188        catch (FileNotFoundException ex) {
189          System.out.println("File not found: " + filename);
190        }
191        catch (IOException ex) {
192          ex.printStackTrace();
193        }
194        finally {
195          if (input != null) input.close();
196        }
197      }
198 }
```

main omitted

The `insertRows` method (lines 127–197) uses the batch updates to submit SQL INSERT commands to the database for execution, if the driver supports batch updates. Lines 168–175 check whether the driver supports batch updates. If the driver is not JDBC 2 compatible, an `UnsupportedOperationException` exception will be thrown (line 152) when the `supportsBatchUpdates()` method is invoked.

The tables must already be created in the database. The file format and contents must match the database table specification. Otherwise, the SQL INSERT command will fail.

In Exercise 33.1, you will write a program to insert a thousand records to a database and compare the performance with and without batch updates.

33.4 Scrollable and Updateable Result Set

The result sets used in the preceding examples are read sequentially. A result set maintains a cursor pointing to its current row of data. Initially the cursor is positioned before the first row. The `next()` method moves the cursor forward to the next row. This is known as *sequential forward reading*. It is the only way of processing the rows in a result set that is supported by JDBC 1.

With JDBC 2, you can scroll the rows both forward and backward and move the cursor to a desired location using the `first`, `last`, `next`, `previous`, `absolute`, or `relative` method. Additionally, you can insert, delete, or update a row in the result set and have the changes automatically reflected in the database.

To obtain a scrollable or updateable result set, you must first create a statement with an appropriate type and concurrency mode. For a static statement, use

```
Statement statement = connection.createStatement
  (int resultSetType, int resultSetConcurrency);
```

For a prepared statement, use

```
PreparedStatement statement = connection.prepareStatement
  (String sql, int resultSetType, int resultSetConcurrency);
```

The possible values of `resultSetType` are the constants defined in the `ResultSet`:

scrollable?

- **TYPE_FORWARD_ONLY**: The result set is accessed forward sequentially.
- **TYPE_SCROLL_INSENSITIVE**: The result set is *scrollable*, but not sensitive to changes in the database.
- **TYPE_SCROLL_SENSITIVE**: The result set is scrollable and sensitive to changes made by others. Use this type if you want the result set to be scrollable and updateable.

The possible values of `resultSetConcurrency` are the constants defined in the `ResultSet`:

- **CONCUR_READ_ONLY**: The result set cannot be used to update the database.
- **CONCUR_UPDATEABLE**: The result set can be used to update the database.

updateable?

For example, if you want the result set to be scrollable and *updateable*, you can create a statement, as follows:

```
Statement statement = connection.createStatement
    (ResultSet.TYPE_SCROLL_SENSITIVE, ResultSet.CONCUR_UPDATEABLE)
```

You use the `executeQuery` method in a `Statement` object to execute an SQL query that returns a result set, as follows:

```
ResultSet resultSet = statement.executeQuery(query);
```

You can now use the methods `first()`, `next()`, `previous()`, and `last()` to move the cursor to the first row, next row, previous row, and last row. The `absolute(int row)` method moves the cursor to the specified row; and the `getXxx(int columnIndex)` or `getXxx(String columnName)` method is used to retrieve the value of a specified field at the current row. The methods `insertRow()`, `deleteRow()`, and `updateRow()` can also be used to insert, delete, and update the current row. Before applying `insertRow` or `updateRow`, you need to use the method `updateXxx(int columnIndex, Xxx value)` or `update(String columnName, Xxx value)` to write a new value to the field at the current row. The `cancelRowUpdates()` method cancels the updates made to a row. The `close()` method closes the result set and releases its resource. The `boolean wasNull()` method indicates whether the last column read had a value of SQL NULL.

`ResultSet` methods

update row

For example, the following code updates the phone number of the second row in the `ResultSet` to `"912921111"`:

```
resultSet.absolute(2); // moves the cursor to the 2nd row
resultSet.updateString("phone", "912921111"); // updates the column
resultSet.updateRow(); // updates the row in the data source
```

insert row

An updatable `ResultSet` object has a special row associated with it that serves as a staging area for building a row to be inserted. This special row is called the *insert row*. To insert a row, first invoke the `moveToInsertRow()` method to move the cursor to the insert row, then update the columns using the `updateXxx` method, and finally insert the row using the `insertRow()` method. For example, the following code inserts a new row with `lastName` "Yao" and firstName "An":

```
resultSet.moveToInsertRow(); // Move cursor to the insert row
resultSet.updateString("lastName", "Yao"); // Update the lastName
resultSet.updateString("firstName", "An"); // Update the firstName
resultSet.insertRow(); // Insert the row
resultSet.moveToCurrentRow(); // Move the cursor to the current row
```

Now let us turn our attention to developing a useful utility that displays all the rows of a database table in a `JTable` and uses a scrollable and updateable result set to navigate the table and modify its contents.

As shown in Figure 33.3, you enter or select a JDBC driver and database, enter a username and a password, and specify a table name to connect the database and display the table contents in the `JTable`. You can then use the buttons *First*, *Next*, *Prior*, and *Last* to move the cursor to the first row, next row, previous row, and last row in the table, and use the buttons *Insert*, *Delete*, and *Update* to modify the table contents. When you click the *Insert* button, a dialog box is displayed to receive input, as shown in Figure 33.4.

The status bar at the bottom of the window shows the current row in the result set and the `JTable`. The cursor in the result set and the row in the `JTable` are synchronized. You can move the cursor by using the navigation buttons or by selecting a row in the `JTable`.

Create three classes: `TestTableEditor` (Listing 33.3), `TableEditor` (Listing 33.4), and `NewRecordDialog` (Listing 33.5). `TestTableEditor` is the main class that enables the user to enter the database connection information and a table name. Once the database is connected,

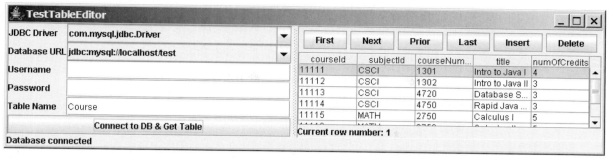

FIGURE 33.3 The program enables you to navigate and modify the table.

courseId	subjectId	courseNumb...	title	numOfCredits
12345	CSCI	3454	New Concept	3

Insert a New Record OK Cancel

FIGURE 33.4 The Insert a New Record dialog box lets the user enter a new record.

the table contents are displayed in an instance of `TableEditor`. The `TableEditor` class can be used to browse a table and modify a table. An instance of `NewRecordDialog` is displayed to let you enter a new record when you click the *Insert* button in `TableEditor`.

LISTING 33.3 TestTableEditor.java

```java
 1 import javax.swing.*;
 2 import java.awt.*;
 3 import java.awt.event.*;
 4 import java.sql.*;
 5
 6 public class TestTableEditor extends JApplet {
 7   private JComboBox jcboDriver = new JComboBox(new String[] {          drivers
 8     "com.mysql.jdbc.Driver", "oracle.jdbc.driver.OracleDriver",
 9     "sun.jdbc.odbc.JdbcOdbcDriver"});
10   private JComboBox jcboURL = new JComboBox(new String[] {             URLs
11     "jdbc:mysql://localhost/test", "jdbc:odbc:exampleMDBDataSource",
12     "jdbc:oracle:thin:@liang.armstrong.edu:1521:orcl"});
13
14   private JButton jbtConnect =
15     new JButton("Connect to DB & Get Table");
16   private JTextField jtfUserName = new JTextField();
17   private JPasswordField jpfPassword = new JPasswordField();
18   private JTextField jtfTableName = new JTextField();
19   private TableEditor tableEditor1 = new TableEditor();
20   private JLabel jlblStatus = new JLabel();
21
22   /** Creates new form TestTableEditor */
23   public TestTableEditor() {
24     JPanel jPanel = new JPanel();
25     jPanel.setLayout(new GridLayout(5, 0));                          create UI
26     jPanel.add(jcboDriver);
27     jPanel.add(jcboURL);
28     jPanel.add(jtfUserName);
29     jPanel.add(jpfPassword);
30     jPanel.add(jtfTableName);
31
```

```
32        JPanel jPanel2 = new JPanel();
33        jPanel2.setLayout(new GridLayout(5, 0));
34        jPanel2.add(new JLabel("JDBC Driver"));
35        jPanel2.add(new JLabel("Database URL"));
36        jPanel2.add(new JLabel("Username"));
37        jPanel2.add(new JLabel("Password"));
38        jPanel2.add(new JLabel("Table Name"));
39
40        JPanel jPane3 = new JPanel();
41        jPane3.setLayout(new BorderLayout());
42        jPane3.add(jbtConnect, BorderLayout.SOUTH);
43        jPane3.add(jPanel2, BorderLayout.WEST);
44        jPane3.add(jPanel, BorderLayout.CENTER);
45        tableEditor1.setPreferredSize(new Dimension(400, 200));
46
47        add(new JSplitPane(JSplitPane.HORIZONTAL_SPLIT,
48          jPane3, tableEditor1), BorderLayout.CENTER);
49        add(jlblStatus, BorderLayout.SOUTH);
50
51        jbtConnect.addActionListener(new ActionListener() {
52          public void actionPerformed(ActionEvent evt) {
53            try {
54              // Connect to the database
55              Connection connection = getConnection();
56              tableEditor1.setConnectionAndTable(connection,
57                jtfTableName.getText().trim());
58            }
59            catch (Exception ex) {
60              jlblStatus.setText(ex.toString());
61            }
62          }
63        });
64      }
65
66      /** Connect to a database */
67      private Connection getConnection() throws Exception {
68        // Load the JDBC driver
69        System.out.println((String)jcboDriver.getSelectedItem());
70        Class.forName(((String)jcboDriver.getSelectedItem()).trim());
71        System.out.println("Driver loaded");
72
73        // Establish a connection
74        Connection connection = DriverManager.getConnection
75          (((String)jcboURL.getSelectedItem()).trim(),
76          jtfUserName.getText().trim(),
77          new String(jpfPassword.getPassword()));
78        jlblStatus.setText("Database connected");
79
80        return connection;
81      }
82    }
```

연 connect database — line 51
load driver — line 70
connect database — line 74
main omitted — line 81

LISTING 33.4 TableEditor.java

```
1 import java.util.*;
2 import java.sql.*;
3 import javax.swing.table.*;
4 import javax.swing.event.*;
5 import javax.swing.*;
6 import java.awt.*;
```

```
 7  import java.awt.event.*;
 8
 9  public class TableEditor extends JPanel {
10    // Dialog box for inserting a new record
11    private NewRecordDialog newRecordDialog = new NewRecordDialog();
12
13    // JDBC Connection
14    private Connection connection;
15
16    // Table name
17    private String tableName;
18
19    // JDBC Statement
20    private Statement statement;
21
22    // Result set for the table
23    private ResultSet resultSet;
24
25    // Table model
26    private DefaultTableModel tableModel = new DefaultTableModel();         table model
27
28    // Table selection model
29    private DefaultListSelectionModel listSelectionModel =
30      new DefaultListSelectionModel();
31
32    // New row vector
33    private Vector rowVectors = new Vector();                               row data
34
35    // columnHeaderVector to hold column names
36    private Vector columnHeaderVector = new Vector();                       column names
37
38    // Column count
39    private int columnCount;                                                column count
40
41    private JButton jbtFirst = new JButton("First");                       buttons
42    private JButton jbtNext = new JButton("Next");
43    private JButton jbtPrior = new JButton("Prior");
44    private JButton jbtLast = new JButton("Last");
45    private JButton jbtInsert = new JButton("Insert");
46    private JButton jbtDelete = new JButton("Delete");
47    private JButton jbtUpdate = new JButton("Update");
48
49    private JLabel jlblStatus = new JLabel();
50    private JTable jTable1 = new JTable();
51
52    /** Creates new form TableEditor */
53    public TableEditor() {
54      jTable1.setModel(tableModel);                                        table model
55      jTable1.setSelectionModel(listSelectionModel);                       selection model
56
57      JPanel jPanel1 = new JPanel();
58      setLayout(new BorderLayout());
59      jPanel1.add(jbtFirst);
60      jPanel1.add(jbtNext);
61      jPanel1.add(jbtPrior);
62      jPanel1.add(jbtLast);
63      jPanel1.add(jbtInsert);
64      jPanel1.add(jbtDelete);
65      jPanel1.add(jbtUpdate);
66
67      add(jPanel1, BorderLayout.NORTH);
```

```
68      add(new JScrollPane(jTable1), BorderLayout.CENTER);
69      add(jlblStatus, BorderLayout.SOUTH);
70
```

button listeners
```
71      jbtFirst.addActionListener(new ActionListener() {
72        public void actionPerformed(ActionEvent evt) {
73          moveCursor("first");
74        }
75      });
76      jbtNext.addActionListener(new ActionListener() {
77        public void actionPerformed(ActionEvent evt) {
78          moveCursor("next");
79        }
80      });
81      jbtPrior.addActionListener(new ActionListener() {
82        public void actionPerformed(ActionEvent evt) {
83          moveCursor("previous");
84        }
85      });
86      jbtLast.addActionListener(new ActionListener() {
87        public void actionPerformed(ActionEvent evt) {
88          moveCursor("last");
89        }
90      });
91      jbtInsert.addActionListener(new ActionListener() {
92        public void actionPerformed(ActionEvent evt) {
93          insert();
94        }
95      });
96      jbtDelete.addActionListener(new ActionListener() {
97        public void actionPerformed(ActionEvent evt) {
98          delete();
99        }
100     });
101     jbtUpdate.addActionListener(new ActionListener() {
102       public void actionPerformed(ActionEvent evt) {
103         update();
104       }
105     });
106     listSelectionModel.addListSelectionListener(
107       new ListSelectionListener() {
108         public void valueChanged(ListSelectionEvent e) {
109           listSelectionModel_valueChanged(e);
110         }
111       });
112   }
113
114   private void delete() {
115     try {
116       // Delete the record from the database
```
db row
```
117       resultSet.deleteRow();
118       refreshResultSet();
119
120       // Remove the row in the table
```
JTable row
```
121       tableModel.removeRow(
122         listSelectionModel.getLeadSelectionIndex());
123     }
124     catch (Exception ex) {
125       jlblStatus.setText(ex.toString());
126     }
127   }
```

```
128
129    private void insert() {
130      // Display the dialog box
131      newRecordDialog.displayTable(columnHeaderVector);               new row
132      Vector newRecord = newRecordDialog.getNewRecord();
133
134      if (newRecord == null) return;
135
136      // Insert the record to the Swing table
137      tableModel.addRow(newRecord);                                   JTable row
138
139      // Insert the record to the database table
140      try {
141        for (int i = 1; i <= columnCount; i++) {
142          resultSet.updateObject(i, newRecord.elementAt(i - 1));
143        }
144
145        resultSet.insertRow();                                       db row
146        refreshResultSet();
147      }
148      catch (Exception ex) {
149        jlblStatus.setText(ex.toString());
150      }
151    }
152
153    /** Set cursor in the table and set the row number in the status */
154    private void setTableCursor() throws Exception {
155      int row = resultSet.getRow();                                  db row
156      listSelectionModel.setSelectionInterval(row - 1, row - 1);     JTable row
157      jlblStatus.setText("Current row number: " + row);
158    }
159
160    private void update() {
161      try {
162        // Get the current row
163        int row = jTable1.getSelectedRow();                          JTable row
164
165        // Gather data from the UI and update the database fields
166        for (int i = 1;
167          i <= resultSet.getMetaData().getColumnCount(); i++) {
168          resultSet.updateObject(i, tableModel.getValueAt(row, i - 1));
169        }
170
171        // Invoke the update method in the result set
172        resultSet.updateRow();                                       db row
173        refreshResultSet();
174      }
175      catch (Exception ex) {
176        jlblStatus.setText(ex.toString());
177      }
178    }
179
180    /** Move cursor to the next record */
181    private void moveCursor(String whereToMove) {
182      try {
183        if (whereToMove.equals("first"))
184          resultSet.first();
185        else if (whereToMove.equals("next"))
186          resultSet.next();
187        else if (whereToMove.equals("previous"))
```

```
188          resultSet.previous();
189        else if (whereToMove.equals("last"))
190          resultSet.last();
191        setTableCursor();
192      }
193      catch (Exception ex) {
194        jlblStatus.setText(ex.toString());
195      }
196    }
197
198    /** Refresh the result set */
199    private void refreshResultSet() {
200      try {
201        resultSet = statement.executeQuery(
202          "SELECT * FROM " + tableName);
203        // Set the cursor to the first record in the table
204        moveCursor("first");
205      }
206      catch (SQLException ex) {
207        ex.printStackTrace();
208      }
209    }
210
211    /** Set database connection and table name in the TableEditor */
212    public void setConnectionAndTable(Connection newConnection,
213        String newTableName) {
214      connection = newConnection;
215      tableName = newTableName;
216      try {
217        statement = connection.createStatement(ResultSet.
218          TYPE_SCROLL_SENSITIVE, ResultSet.CONCUR_UPDATEABLE);
219        showTable();
220        moveCursor("first");
221      }
222      catch (SQLException ex) {
223        ex.printStackTrace();
224      }
225    }
226
227    /** Display database table to a Swing table */
228    private void showTable() throws SQLException {
229      // Clear vectors to store data for a new table
230      rowVectors.clear();
231      columnHeaderVector.clear();
232
233      // Obtain table contents
234      resultSet = statement.executeQuery(
235        "select * from " + tableName + ";");
236
237      // Get column count
238      columnCount = resultSet.getMetaData().getColumnCount();
239
240      // Store rows to rowVectors
241      while (resultSet.next()) {
242        Vector singleRow = new Vector();
243        for (int i = 0; i < columnCount; i++)
244          // Store cells to a row
245          singleRow.addElement(resultSet.getObject(i + 1));
246        rowVectors.addElement(singleRow);
247      }
248
```

db to **JTable**

```
249      // Get column name and add to columnHeaderVector
250      for (int i = 1; i <= columnCount; i++)
251        columnHeaderVector.addElement(
252          resultSet.getMetaData().getColumnName(i));
253
254      // Set new data to the table model
255      tableModel.setDataVector(rowVectors, columnHeaderVector);
256    }
257
258    /** Handle the selection in the table */
259    void listSelectionModel_valueChanged(ListSelectionEvent e) {
260      int selectedRow = jTable1.getSelectedRow();
261
262      try {
263        resultSet.absolute(selectedRow + 1);
264        setTableCursor();
265      }
266      catch (Exception ex) {
267        jlblStatus.setText(ex.toString());
268      }
269    }
270 }
```

LISTING 33.5 NewRecordDialog.java

```
1 import java.util.*;
2 import java.awt.*;
3 import java.awt.event.*;
4 import javax.swing.*;
5 import javax.swing.table.*;
6
7 public class NewRecordDialog extends JDialog {
8   private JButton jbtOK = new JButton("OK");
9   private JButton jbtCancel = new JButton("Cancel");
10
11  private DefaultTableModel tableModel = new DefaultTableModel();    table model
12  private JTable jTable1 = new JTable(tableModel);                   table
13  private Vector newRecord;                                          row
14
15  /** Creates new form NewRecordDialog */
16  public NewRecordDialog(Frame parent, boolean modal) {
17    super(parent, modal);
18    setTitle("Insert a New Record");
19    setModal(true);
20
21    JPanel jPanel1 = new JPanel();
22    jPanel1.add(jbtOK);
23    jPanel1.add(jbtCancel);
24
25    jbtOK.addActionListener(new ActionListener() {
26      public void actionPerformed(ActionEvent evt) {
27        setVisible(false);
28      }
29    });
30    jbtCancel.addActionListener(new ActionListener() {
31      public void actionPerformed(ActionEvent evt) {
32        newRecord = null;
33        setVisible(false);
34      }
35    });
36
```

```
37        add(jPanel1, BorderLayout.SOUTH);
38        add(new JScrollPane(jTable1), BorderLayout.CENTER);
39    }
40
41    public NewRecordDialog() {
42        this(null, true);
43    }
44
45    public Vector getNewRecord() {
46        return newRecord;
47    }
48
49    /** Display the table */
50    void displayTable(Vector columnHeaderVector) {
51        this.setSize(new Dimension(400, 100));
52
53        tableModel.setColumnIdentifiers(columnHeaderVector);
54
55        // Must create a new vector for a new record
56        tableModel.addRow(newRecord = new Vector());
57        setVisible(true);
58    }
59 }
```

one row

The key class in this example is `TableEditor`, which can be used to navigate and modify the table contents. To use it, simply create an instance of `TableEditor` (line 19 in TestTableEditor.java), set the database connection and the table name in the instance, and place it in a graphical user interface. The `setConnectionAndTableName` method (lines 56–57 in TestTableEditor.java) involves creating a statement, obtaining a result set, and displaying the result set in the Swing table. The statement is created with the arguments `TYPE_SCROLL_SENSITIVE` and `CONCUR_UPDATEABLE` for obtaining scrollable and update-able result sets (lines 217–218 in TableEditor.java).

The `showTable()` method (lines 228–256 in TableEditor.java) is responsible for transferring data from the database table to the Swing table. The column names and column count are obtained using the `ResultSetMetaData` interface. An instance of the `ResultSetMetaData` interface is obtained using the `getMetaData` method for the result set. Each record from the result set is copied to a row vector. The row vector is added to another vector that stores all the rows for the table model (`tableModel`) for the `JTable`.

The handling of the navigation buttons *First*, *Next*, *Prior*, and *Last* is simply to invoke the methods `first()`, `next()`, `previous()`, and `last()` to move the cursor in the result set and, at the same time, set the selected row in the Swing table.

The handling of the *Insert* button involves displaying the "Insert a New Record" dialog box (`newRecordDialog1`) for receiving the new record. Once the record is entered, clicking the *OK* button dismisses the dialog box. The new record is obtained by invoking the `newRecordDialog1.getNewRecord()` method. To insert the new record into the database, use the `updateObject` method (line 142 in TableEditor.java) to update the fields, and then use the `insertRow` method to insert the record to the database table. Finally, you need to refresh the result set by re-executing the query. Theoretically, you should not have to refresh the result set (line 146 in TableEditor.java). The driver should automatically reflect the changes in the database to the result set. However, none of the drivers I have tested supports this. So it is safe to refresh the result set.

To implement the *Delete* button, invoke the `deleteRow()` method (line 117 in TableEditor.java) in the result set to remove the record from the database, and use the `removeRow` method in `TableModel` to remove a row from `JTable`.

To implement the *Update* button, invoke the `updateObject` method (line 168 in TableEditor.java) in the result set, and then invoke the `updateRow` method (line 172 in TableEditor.java) to update the result set.

To implement the handler for list-selection events on `jTable1`, set the cursor in the result set to match the row selected in `jTable1` (lines 259–269 in TableEditor.java).

Note

The `TableEditor` class in this example uses only the `updateObject(columnIndex, object)` method. This updates a string column. To update a column of **double** type, you have to use `updateDouble(columnIndex, doubleValue)`. See Programming Exercise 33.3 to revise the program to handle all types of columns.

Tip

To ensure the effect of editing a field in the table, you need to press the Enter key or move the cursor to other fields.

Note

Many JDBC drivers, including the MySQL and Oracle drivers, support the read-only scrollable result set but not the updateable scrollable result set. Thus you cannot modify the result set. You can use **supportsResultSetType(int type)** and **supportsResultSetConcurrency(int type, int concurrency)** in the **DatabaseMetaData** interface to find out which result type and currency modes are supported by the JDBC driver. But even if a driver supports the scrollable and updateable result set, a result set for a complex query might not be able to perform an update. For example, the result set for a query that involves several tables is likely not to support update operations.

33.5 **RowSet**, **JdbcRowSet**, and **CachedRowSet**

JDBC 2 introduced a new **RowSet** interface that can be used to simplify database programming. The **RowSet** interface extends `java.sql.ResultSet` with additional capabilities that allow a **RowSet** instance to be configured to connect to a JDBC url, username, password, set a SQL command, execute the command, and retrieve the execution result. In essence, it combines **Connection**, **Statement**, and **ResultSet** into one interface. A concrete **RowSet** class can be used as a JavaBeans component in a visual GUI development environment such as JBuilder and NetBeans.

extends **ResultSet**

Note

Not all JDBC drivers support **RowSet**. Currently, the JDBC-ODBC driver does not support all features of **RowSet**.

supported?

33.5.1 **RowSet** Basics

There are two types of **RowSet** objects: connected and disconnected. A *connected* **RowSet** object makes a connection with a data source and maintains that connection throughout its life cycle. A *disconnected* **RowSet** object makes a connection with a data source, executes a query to get data from the data source, and then closes the connection. A disconnected rowset may make changes to its data while it is disconnected and then send the changes back to the original source of the data, but it must reestablish a connection to do so.

connected vs. disconnected

There are several versions of **RowSet**. Two frequently used are **JdbcRowSet** and **CachedRowSet**. Both are subinterfaces of **RowSet**. **JdbcRowSet** is connected, while **CachedRowSet** is disconnected. Also, **JdbcRowSet** is neither serializable nor cloneable, while **CachedRowSet** is serializable and cloneable. The database vendors are free to provide concrete implementations for these interfaces. Sun has provided the reference implementation **JdbcRowSetImpl** for **JdbcRowSet** and **CachedRowSetImpl** for **CachedRowSet**. Figure 33.5 shows the relationship of these components.

The **RowSet** interface contains the JavaBeans properties with get and set methods. You can use the set methods to set a new url, username, password, and command for an SQL statement. Using a **RowSet**, Listing 32.1 can be simplified, as shown in Listing 33.6.

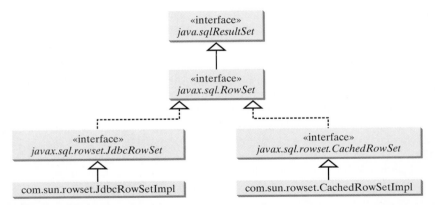

FIGURE 33.5 The `JdbcRowSetImpl` and `CachedRowSetImpl` are concrete implementations of `RowSet`.

LISTING 33.6 SimpleRowSet.java

```java
 1 import java.sql.SQLException;
 2 import javax.sql.RowSet;
 3 import com.sun.rowset.*;
 4
 5 public class SimpleRowSet {
 6   public static void main(String[] args)
 7       throws SQLException, ClassNotFoundException {
 8     // Load the JDBC driver
 9     Class.forName("com.mysql.jdbc.Driver");
10     System.out.println("Driver loaded");
11
12     // Create a row set
13     RowSet rowSet = new JdbcRowSetImpl();
14
15     // Set RowSet properties
16     rowSet.setUrl("jdbc:mysql://localhost/test");
17     rowSet.setCommand("select firstName, mi, lastName " +
18       "from Student where lastName = 'Smith'");
19     rowSet.execute();
20
21     // Iterate through the result and print the student names
22     while (rowSet.next() )
23       System.out.println(rowSet.getString(1) + "\t" +
24         rowSet.getString(2) + "\t" + rowSet.getString(3));
25
26     // Close the connection
27     rowSet.close();
28   }
29 }
```

load driver

create **RowSet**

set url
set command

execute command

get result

close connection

Line 13 creates a **RowSet** object using **JdbcRowSetImpl**. The program uses the **RowSet**'s **set** method to set a URL (line 16) and a command for a query statement (line 17). Line 19 executes the command in the **RowSet**. The methods **next()** are **getString(int)** for processing the query result (lines 22–24) are inherited from **ResultSet**.

using **CachedRowSet**

If you replace **JdbcRowSet** with **CachedRowSet** in line 13, the program will work just fine.

Tip

Since **RowSet** is a subinterface of **ResultSet**, all the methods in **ResultSet** can be used in **RowSet**. For example, you can obtain **ResultSetMetaData** from a **RowSet** using the get-MetaData() method.

obtain metadata

33.5.2 RowSet for PreparedStatement

The discussion in §32.5, "PreparedStatement," introduced processing parameterized SQL statements using the **PreparedStatement** interface. **RowSet** has the capability to support parameterized SQL statements. The set methods for setting parameter values in **PreparedStatement** are implemented in **RowSet**. You can use these methods to set parameter values for a parameterized SQL command. Listing 33.7 demonstrates how to use a parameterized statement in **RowSet**. Line 17 sets an SQL query statement with two parameters for lastName and mi in a **RowSet**. Since these two parameters are strings, the setString method is used to set actual values in lines 19–20.

connected vs. disconnected

LISTING 33.7   RowSetPreparedStatement.java

```
 1  import java.sql.*;
 2  import javax.sql.RowSet;
 3  import com.sun.rowset.*;
 4
 5  public class RowSetPreparedStatement {
 6    public static void main(String[] args)
 7        throws SQLException, ClassNotFoundException {
 8      // Load the JDBC driver
 9      Class.forName("com.mysql.jdbc.Driver");
10      System.out.println("Driver loaded");
11
12      // Create a row set
13      RowSet rowSet = new JdbcRowSetImpl();
14
15      // Set RowSet properties
16      rowSet.setUrl("jdbc:mysql://localhost/test");
17      rowSet.setCommand("select * from Student where lastName = ? " +
18        "and mi = ?");
19      rowSet.setString(1, "Smith");
20      rowSet.setString(2, "R");
21      rowSet.execute();
22
23      ResultSetMetaData rsMetaData = rowSet.getMetaData();
24      for (int i = 1; i <= rsMetaData.getColumnCount(); i++)
25        System.out.printf("%-12s\t", rsMetaData.getColumnName(i));
26      System.out.println();
27
28      // Iterate through the result and print the student names
29      while (rowSet.next()) {
30        for (int i = 1; i <= rsMetaData.getColumnCount(); i++)
31          System.out.printf("%-12s\t", rowSet.getObject(i));
32        System.out.println();
33      }
34
35      // Close the connection
36      rowSet.close();
37    }
38  }
```

load driver

create **RowSet**

set url
SQL with parameters

set parameter
set parameter
execute

metadata

close connection

33.5.3 Scrolling and Updating RowSet

By default, a ResultSet object is not scrollable and updateable. However, a RowSet object is scrollable and updatable. It is easier to scroll and update a database through a RowSet than a ResultSet. Listing 33.8 gives an example that scrolls and updates a database through a RowSet. You can use the methods (e.g., absolute(int)) to move the cursor and update the database using such methods as delete(), updateRow(), and insertRow().

LISTING 33.8 ScrollUpdateRowSet.java

```
 1 import java.sql.*;
 2 import javax.sql.RowSet;
 3 import com.sun.rowset.JdbcRowSetImpl;
 4
 5 public class ScrollUpdateRowSet {
 6   public static void main(String[] args)
 7       throws SQLException, ClassNotFoundException {
 8     // Load the JDBC driver
 9     Class.forName("com.mysql.jdbc.Driver");
10     System.out.println("Driver loaded");
11
12     // Create a row set
13     RowSet rowSet = new JdbcRowSetImpl();
14
15     // Set RowSet properties
16     rowSet.setUrl("jdbc:mysql://localhost/test");
17     rowSet.setCommand("select * from Student");
18     rowSet.execute();
19
20     // Iterate through the result and print the student names
21     System.out.println("Before update ");
22     ResultSetMetaData rsMetaData = rowSet.getMetaData();
23     while (rowSet.next()) {
24       for (int i = 1; i <= rsMetaData.getColumnCount(); i++)
25         System.out.printf("%-12s\t", rowSet.getObject(i));
26       System.out.println();
27     }
28
29     rowSet.absolute(2); // Move cursor to the 2nd row
30     rowSet.deleteRow(); // Delete the second row
31
32     rowSet.absolute(5); // Move cursor to the 5th row
33     rowSet.updateString("phone", "912921111"); // updates the column
34     rowSet.updateRow(); // updates the row in the data source
35
36     rowSet.moveToInsertRow(); // Move cursor to the insert row
37     rowSet.updateString("ssn", "1111111111"); // Update the lastName
38     rowSet.updateString("lastName", "Yao"); // Update the lastName
39     rowSet.updateString("firstName", "An"); // Update the firstName
40     rowSet.insertRow(); // Insert the row
41     rowSet.moveToCurrentRow(); // Move the cursor to the current row
42
43     System.out.println("After update ");
44     rowSet.first();
45     while (rowSet.next()) {
46       for (int i = 1; i <= rsMetaData.getColumnCount(); i++)
47         System.out.printf("%-12s\t", rowSet.getObject(i));
48       System.out.println();
49     }
50
```

load driver

create **RowSet**

set url
set SQL command
execute

before update

move cursor
delete row

update column
update row

prepare insert

insert row

after update

```
51      // Close the connection
52      rowSet.close();
53   }
54 }
```

If you replace JdbcRowSet with CachedRowSet in line 13, the database is not changed. To make the changes on the CachedRowSet effective in the database, you must invoke the acceptChanges() method after you make all the changes, as follows:

using **CachedRowSet**

```
rowSet.acceptChanges(); // Write changes back to the database
```

This method automatically reconnects to the database and writes all the changes back to the database.

33.5.4   RowSetEvent

A RowSet object fires a RowSetEvent whenever the object's cursor has moved, a row has changed, or the entire row set has changed. This event can be used to synchronize a RowSet with the components that rely on the RowSet. For example, a visual component that displays the contents of a RowSet should be synchronized with the RowSet. The RowSetEvent can be used to achieve synchronization. The handlers in RowSetListener are cursorMoved(RowSetEvent), rowChanged(RowSetEvent), and cursorSet-Changed(RowSetEvent).

Listing 33.9 gives an example that demonstrates RowSetEvent. A listener for RowSetEvent is registered in lines 14–26. When rowSet.execute() (line 31) is executed, the entire row set is changed, so the listener's rowSetChanged handler is invoked. When rowSet.last() (line 33) is executed, the cursor is moved, so the listener's cursorMoved handler is invoked. When rowSet.updateRow() (line 35) is executed, the row is updated, so the listener's rowChanged handler is invoked.

LISTING 33.9   TestRowSetEvent.java

```
1  import java.sql.*;
2  import javax.sql.*;
3  import com.sun.rowset.*;
4
5  public class TestRowSetEvent {
6    public static void main(String[] args)
7        throws SQLException, ClassNotFoundException {
8      // Load the JDBC driver
9      Class.forName("com.mysql.jdbc.Driver");
10     System.out.println("Driver loaded");
11
12     // Create a row set
13     RowSet rowSet = new CachedRowSetImpl();
14     rowSet.addRowSetListener(new RowSetListener() {
15       public void cursorMoved(RowSetEvent e) {
16         System.out.println("Cursor moved");
17       }
18
19       public void rowChanged(RowSetEvent e) {
20         System.out.println("Row changed");
21       }
22
23       public void rowSetChanged(RowSetEvent e) {
24         System.out.println("row set changed");
25       }
26     });
27
```

load driver

create **RowSet**

register listener

```
28        // Set RowSet properties
29        rowSet.setUrl("jdbc:mysql://localhost/test");
30        rowSet.setCommand("select * from Student");
31        rowSet.execute();
32
33        rowSet.last(); // Cursor moved
34        rowSet.updateString("lastName", "Yao"); // Update column
35        rowSet.updateRow(); // Row updated
36
37        // Close the connection
38        rowSet.close();
39      }
40  }
```

new row set

cursor moved

row updated

33.6 Storing and Retrieving Images in JDBC

A database can store not only numbers and strings, but also images. SQL3 introduced a new data type called BLOB (*B*inary *L*arge *OB*ject) for storing binary data, which can be used to store images. Another new SQL3 type is CLOB (*C*haracter *L*arge *OB*ject), for storing a large text in the character format. JDBC 2 introduced the interfaces `java.sql.Blob` and `java.sql.Clob` to support mapping for these new SQL types. JBDC 2 also added new methods in the interfaces `ResultSet` and `PreparedStatement`, such as `getBlob`, `setBinaryStream`, `getClob`, `setBlob` and `setClob`, to access SQL BLOB, and CLOB values.

To store an image into a cell in a table, the corresponding column for the cell must be of the BLOB type. For example, the following SQL statement creates a table whose type for the flag column is BLOB:

```
create table Country(name varchar(30), flag blob,
    description varchar(255));
```

In the preceding statement, the `description` column is limited to 255 characters, which is the upper limit for MySQL. For Oracle, the upper limit is 32,672 bytes. For a large character field, you can use the CLOB type for Oracle, which can store up to two GB characters. MySQL does not support CLOB. However, you can use BLOB to store a long string and convert binary data into characters.

supported?

 Note
Access does not support the BLOB and CLOB types.

To insert a record with images to a table, define a prepared statement like this one:

```
PreparedStatement pstmt = connection.prepareStatement(
    "insert into Country values(?, ?, ?)");
```

store image

Images are usually stored in files. You may first get an instance of `InputStream` for an image file and then use the `setBinaryStream` method to associate the input stream with a cell in the table, as follows:

```
// Store image to the table cell
File file = new File(imageFilename);
InputStream inputImage = new FileInputStream(file);
pstmt.setBinaryStream(2, inputImage, (int)(file.length()));
```

retrieve image

To retrieve an image from a table, use the `getBlob` method, as shown below:

```
// Retrieve image from the table cell
Blob blob = rs.getBlob(1);
ImageIcon imageIcon = new ImageIcon(
    blob.getBytes(1, (int)blob.length()));
```

To demonstrate how to store and retrieve images in JDBC, let us create a table, populate it with data, including images, and retrieve and display images. The table is named Country and can be created using the following SQL statement:

```
create table Country(name varchar(30), flag blob,
    description varchar(255));
```

Each record in the table consists of three fields: name, flag, and description. Flag is an image field. The program first creates the table and stores data to it. Then the program retrieves the country names from the table and adds them to a combo box. When the user selects a name from the combo box, the country's flag and description are displayed, as shown in Figure 33.6. Listing 33.10 gives the program.

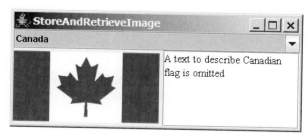

FIGURE 33.6 The program enables you to retrieve data, including images, from a table and displays them.

LISTING 33.10 StoreAndRetrieveImage.java

```
1 import java.sql.*;
2 import java.io.*;
3 import javax.swing.*;
4 import java.awt.*;
5 import java.awt.event.*;
6
7 public class StoreAndRetrieveImage extends JApplet {
8   // Connection to the database
9   private Connection connection;
10
11  // Statement for static SQL statements
12  private Statement stmt;
13
14  // Prepared statement
15  private PreparedStatement pstmt = null;
16  private DescriptionPanel descriptionPanel1 = new DescriptionPanel();
17
18  private JComboBox jcboCountry = new JComboBox();
19
20  /** Creates new form StoreAndRetrieveImage */
21  public StoreAndRetrieveImage() {
22    try {
23      connectDB(); // Connect to DB
24      storeDataToTable(); //Store data to the table (including image)
25      fillDataInComboBox(); // Fill in combo box
26      retrieveFlagInfo((String)(jcboCountry.getSelectedItem()));
27    }
28    catch (Exception ex) {
29      ex.printStackTrace();
30    }
31
32    jcboCountry.addItemListener(new ItemListener() {
33      public void itemStateChanged(ItemEvent evt) {
```

```
34              retrieveFlagInfo((String)(evt.getItem()));
35          }
36      });
37
38      add(jcboCountry, BorderLayout.NORTH);
39      add(descriptionPanel1, BorderLayout.CENTER);
40  }
41
42  private void connectDB() throws Exception {
43      // Load the driver
44      Class.forName("com.mysql.jdbc.Driver");
45      System.out.println("Driver loaded");
46
47      // Establish connection
48      connection = DriverManager.getConnection
49          ("jdbc:mysql://localhost/test");
50      System.out.println("Database connected");
51
52      // Create a statement for static SQL
53      stmt = connection.createStatement();
54
55      // Create a prepared statement to retrieve flag and description
56      pstmt = connection.prepareStatement("select flag, description " +
57          "from Country where name = ?");
58  }
59
60  private void storeDataToTable() {
61      String[] countries = {"Canada", "UK", "USA", "Germany",
62          "India", "China"};
63
64      String[] imageFilenames = {"image/ca.gif", "image/uk.gif",
65          "image/us.gif", "image/germany.gif", "image/india.gif",
66          "image/china.gif"};
67
68      String[] descriptions = {"A text to describe Canadian " +
69          "flag is omitted", "British flag ...", "American flag ...",
70          "German flag ...", "Indian flag ...", "Chinese flag ..."};
71
72      try {
73          // Create a prepared statement to insert records
74          PreparedStatement pstmt = connection.prepareStatement(
75              "insert into Country values(?, ?, ?)");
76
77          // Store all predefined records
78          for (int i = 0; i < countries.length; i++) {
79              pstmt.setString(1, countries[i]);
80
81              // Store image to the table cell
82              java.net.URL url =
83                  this.getClass().getResource(imageFilenames[i]);
84              InputStream inputImage = url.openStream();
85              pstmt.setBinaryStream(2, inputImage,
86                  (int)(inputImage.available()));
87
88              pstmt.setString(3, descriptions[i]);
89              pstmt.executeUpdate();
90          }
91
92          System.out.println("Table Country populated");
93      }
```

load driver

connect database

create statement

prepare statement

data to database

insert

get image URL

binary stream

```
 94        catch (Exception ex) {
 95          ex.printStackTrace();
 96        }
 97      }
 98
 99      private void fillDataInComboBox() throws Exception {
100        ResultSet rs = stmt.executeQuery("select name from Country");
101        while (rs.next()) {
102          jcboCountry.addItem(rs.getString(1));                          fill combo box
103        }
104      }
105
106      private void retrieveFlagInfo(String name) {
107        try {
108          pstmt.setString(1, name);                                      set name
109          ResultSet rs = pstmt.executeQuery();                           set name
110          if (rs.next()) {
111            Blob blob = rs.getBlob(1);
112            ImageIcon imageIcon = new ImageIcon(
113              blob.getBytes(1, (int)blob.length()));                     get image icon
114            descriptionPanel.setImageIcon(imageIcon);
115            descriptionPanel.setName(name);
116            String description = rs.getString(2);
117            descriptionPanel.setDescription(description);
118          }                                                              set description
119        }
120        catch (Exception ex) {
121          System.err.println(ex);
122        }
123      }
124 }
                                                                          main omitted
```

DescriptionPanel (line 16) is a component for displaying a country (name, flag, and description). This component was presented in Listing15.6, TextAreaDemo.java.

The storeDataToTable method (lines 60–97) populates the table with data. The fillDataInComboBox method (lines 99–104) retrieves the country names and adds them to the combo box. The retrieveFlagInfo(name) method (lines 106–123) retrieves the flag and description for the specified country name.

KEY TERMS

batch mode	1126	scrollable result set	1135
BLOB type	1150	updateable result set	1135
CLOB type	1150		

CHAPTER SUMMARY

- This chapter developed a universal SQL client that can be used to access any local or remote relational database.

- You can use the addBatch(SQLString) method to add SQL statements to a statement for batch processing.

- You can create a statement to specify that the result set be scrollable and updateable. By default, the result set is neither scrollable nor updateable.

■ The RowSet can be used to simplify Java database programming. A RowSet object is scrollable and updateable. A RowSet can fire a RowSetEvent. A concrete RowSet class can be used as a JavaBeans component in a visual GUI development environment such as JBuilder and NetBeans.

■ You can store and retrieve image data in JDBC using the SQL BLOB type.

REVIEW QUESTIONS

Section 33.3 Batch Processing

33.1 What is batch processing in JDBC? What are the benefits of using batch processing?

33.2 How do you add an SQL statement to a batch? How do you execute a batch?

33.3 Can you execute a SELECT statement in a batch?

33.4 How do you know whether a JDBC driver supports batch updates?

Section 33.4 Scrollable and Updateable Result Set

33.5 What is a scrollable result set? What is an updateable result set?

33.6 How do you create a scrollable and updateable ResultSet?

33.7 How do you know whether a JDBC driver supports a scrollable and updateable ResultSet?

Section 33.5 RowSet, JdbcRowSet, and CachedRowSetImpl

33.8 What are the advantages of RowSet?

33.9 What are JdbcRowSet and CachedRowSet? What are the differences between them?

33.10 How do you create a JdbcRowSet and a CachedRowSet?

33.11 Can you scroll and update a RowSet? What method must be invoked to write the changes in a CachedRowSet to the database?

33.12 Describe the handlers in RowSetListener.

Section 33.6 Storing and Retrieving Images in JDBC

33.13 How do you store images into a database?

33.14 How do you retrieve images from a database?

33.15 Does Oracle support the SQL3 BLOB type and CLOB type? How about MySQL and Access?

PROGRAMMING EXERCISES

33.1* (*Batch update*) Write a program that inserts a thousand records to a database, and compare the performance with and without batch updates, as shown in Figure 33.7(a). Suppose the table is defined as follows:

```
create table Temp(num1 double, num2 double, num3 double)
```

Use the Math.random() method to generate random numbers for each record. Create a dialog box that contains DBConnectionPanel, discussed in Programming Exercise 32.3. Use this dialog box to connect to the database. When you click the *Connect to Database* button in Figure 33.7(a), the dialog box in Figure 33.7(b) is displayed.

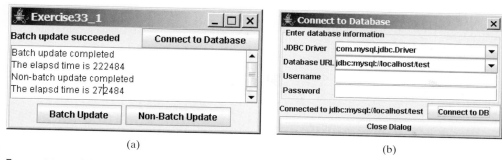

FIGURE 33.7 The program demonstrates the performance improvements that result from using batch updates.

33.2**(*Scrollable result set*) Write a program that uses the buttons *First*, *Next*, *Prior*, *Last*, *Insert*, *Delete*, and *Update* display, and modify a single record in the Address table, as shown in Figure 33.8.

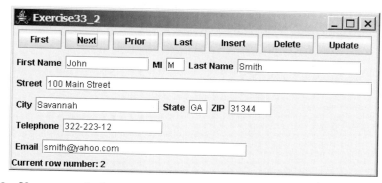

FIGURE 33.8 You can use the buttons to display and modify a single record in the Address table.

33.3**(*Handling all types of columns*) Rewrite the example in Listings 33.3, 33.4, and 33.5 (TestTableEditor.java, TableEditor.java, and NewRecordDialog.java) to enable it to insert all types of columns (not just strings).

33.4**(*Editing table using RowSet*) Rewrite the example in Listings 33.3, 33.4, and 33.5 (TestTableEditor.java, TableEditor.java, and NewRecordDialog.java) using RowSet.

33.5**(*Storing and retrieving images using RowSet*) Rewrite the example in Listing 33.10 (StoreAndRetrieveImage.java) using RowSet.

33.6* (*Displaying images from database*) Write a program that uses JTable to display the Country table created in Listing 33.10 (StoreAndRetrieveImage.java), as shown in Figure 33.9.

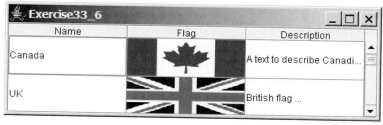

FIGURE 33.9 The Country table is displayed in a JTable instance.

SERVLETS

Objectives

- To understand the concept of servlets (§34.2).
- To run servlets with Tomcat (§34.3).
- To know the servlets API (§34.4).
- To create simple servlets (§34.5).
- To create and process HTML forms (§34.6).
- To develop servlets to access databases (§34.7).
- To use hidden fields, cookies, and `HttpSession` to track sessions (§34.8).
- To send images from servlets (§34.9).

34.1 Introduction

servlet

Servlet technology is primarily designed for use with the HTTP protocol of the Web. *Servlets* are Java programs that run on a Web server. Java servlets can be used to process client requests or produce dynamic Web pages. For example, you can write servlets to generate dynamic Web pages that display stock quotes or process client registration forms and store registration data in a database. This chapter introduces the concept of Java servlets. You will learn how to write Java servlets and run them from Tomcat. Tomcat is a Web server that supports Java servlets and JSP. It can be downloaded free.

34.2 HTML and Common Gateway Interface

Java servlets run in the Web environment. To understand Java servlets, let us review HTML and the Common Gateway Interface (CGI).

34.2.1 Static Web Contents

You create Web pages using HTML. Your Web pages are stored as files on the Web server. The files are usually stored in the /htdocs directory on Unix, as shown in Figure 34.1. A user types a URL for the file from a Web browser. The browser contacts the Web server and requests the file. The server finds the file and returns it to the browser. The browser then displays the file to the user. This works fine for static information that does not change regardless of who requests it or when it is requested. Static information is stored in HTML files. The information in the files can be updated, but at any given time every request for the same document returns exactly the same result.

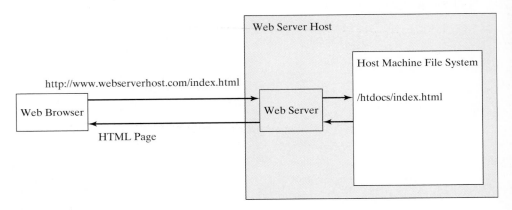

FIGURE 34.1 A Web browser requests a static HTML page from a Web server.

34.2.2 Dynamic Web Contents and Common Gateway Interface

Not all information, however, is static in nature. Stock quotes are updated every minute. Election vote counts are updated constantly on Election Day. Weather reports are frequently updated. The balance in a customer's bank account is updated whenever a transaction takes place. To view up-to-date information on the Web, the HTML pages for displaying this information must be generated dynamically. Dynamic Web pages are generated by Web servers. The Web server needs to run certain programs to process user requests from Web browsers in order to produce a customized response.

CGI

The *Common Gateway Interface*, or *CGI*, was proposed to generate dynamic Web content. The interface provides a standard framework for Web servers to interact with external programs, known as *CGI programs*. As shown in Figure 34.2, the Web server receives a request from a Web browser and passes it to the CGI program. The CGI program processes the request and generates a response at runtime. CGI programs can be written in any language, but the *Perl* language is the most popular choice. CGI programs are typically stored in the /cgi-bin directory. Here is a pseudocode example of a CGI program for displaying a customer's bank account balance:

1. Obtain account ID and password.

2. Verify account ID and password. If it fails, generate an HTML page to report incorrect account ID and password, and exit.

3. Retrieve account balance from the database; generate an HTML page to display the account ID and balance.

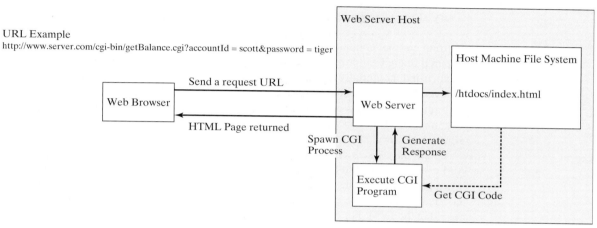

FIGURE 34.2 A Web browser requests a dynamic HTML page from a Web server.

34.2.3 The GET and POST Methods

The two most common HTTP requests, also known as *methods*, are GET and POST. The Web browser issues a request using a URL or an HTML form to trigger the Web server to execute a CGI program. HTML forms will be introduced in §34.6, "HTML Forms." When issuing a CGI request directly from a URL, the GET method is used. This URL is known as a *query string*. The URL query string consists of the location of the CGI program, parameters, and their values. For example, the following URL causes the CGI program **getBalance** to be invoked on the server side:

query string

```
http://www.webserverhost.com/cgi-bin/
    getBalance.cgi?accountId=scott+smith&password=tiger
```

The ? symbol separates the program from the parameters. The parameter name and value are associated using the = symbol. Parameter pairs are separated using the & symbol. The + symbol denotes a space character.

When issuing a request from an HTML form, either a GET method or a POST method can be used. The form explicitly specifies which of the two is used. If the GET method is used, the data in the form is appended to the request string as if it were submitted using a URL. If the POST method is used, the data in the form is packaged as part of the request file. The server program obtains the data by reading the file. The POST method is more secure than the GET method.

Note

The GET and POST methods both send requests to the Web server. The POST method always triggers the execution of the corresponding CGI program. The GET method may not cause the

GET vs. POST

CGI program to be executed if the previous same request is cached in the Web browser. Web browsers often cache Web pages so that the same request can be quickly responded to without contacting the Web server. The browser checks the request sent through the GET method as a URL query string. If the results for the exact same URL are cached on a disk, then the previous Web pages for the URL may be displayed. To ensure that a new Web page is always displayed, use the POST method. For example, use a POST method if the request will actually update the database. If your request is not time-sensitive, such as finding the address of a student in the database, use the GET method to speed up the performance.

34.2.4 From CGI to Java Servlets

CGI provides a relatively simple approach for creating dynamic Web applications that accept a user request, process it on the server side, and return responses to the Web browser. But CGI is very slow when handling a large number of requests simultaneously, because the Web server spawns a process for executing each CGI program. Each process has its own runtime environment that contains and runs the CGI program. It is not difficult to imagine what will happen if many CGI programs are executed simultaneously. System resource would be quickly exhausted, potentially causing the server to crash.

Several new approaches have been developed to remedy the performance problem of CGI programs. Java servlets are one successful technology for this purpose. Java servlets are Java programs that function like CGI programs. They are executed upon request from a Web browser. All servlets run inside a *servlet container*, also referred to as a *servlet server* or a *servlet engine*. A servlet container is a single process that runs a Java Virtual Machine. The JVM creates a thread to handle each servlet. Java threads have much less overhead than full-blown processes. All the threads share the same memory allocated to the JVM. Since the JVM persists beyond the life cycle of a single servlet execution, servlets can share objects already created in the JVM. For example, if multiple servlets access the same database, they can share the connection object. Servlets are much more efficient than CGI.

Servlets have other benefits that are inherent in Java. As Java programs, they are object-oriented, portable, and platform-independent. Since you know Java, you can develop servlets immediately with the support of Java API for accessing databases and network resources.

34.3 Creating and Running Servlets

To run Java servlets, you need a servlet container. Many servlet containers are available. *Tomcat*, developed by Apache (www.apache.org), is a standard reference implementation for Java servlets and JavaServer Pages. It can be used standalone as a Web server or be plugged into a Web server like Apache, Netscape Enterprise Server, or Microsoft Internet Information Server. Several versions of Tomcat are available. You should use Tomcat 5 or higher to take advantage of new specifications for servlets and JSP. This book uses Tomcat 5.5.9. You can download Tomcat in one zip file named jakarta-tomcat-5.5.9.zip from http://jakarta.apache.org/site/downloads/downloads_tomcat-5.cgi.

 Note

For more information on obtaining and installing Tomcat 5.5.9, see Supplement VII.E, "*Tomcat Tutorial.*"

34.3.1 Creating a Servlet

Before introducing the servlet API, it is helpful to use a simple example to demonstrate how servlets work. A servlet resembles an applet to some extent. Every Java applet is a subclass of the **Applet** class. You need to override appropriate methods in the **Applet** class to implement the applet. Every servlet is a subclass of the **HttpServlet** class. You need to override appropriate methods in the **HttpServlet** class to implement the servlet. Listing 34.1 is a servlet that generates a response in HTML using the **doGet** method.

LISTING 34.1 FirstServlet.java

```
1 import javax.servlet.*;
2 import javax.servlet.http.*;
3
4 public class FirstServlet extends HttpServlet {
5   /** Handle the HTTP GET method.
6    * @param request servlet request
7    * @param response servlet response
8    */
9   protected void doGet(HttpServletRequest request,                    process GET
10      HttpServletResponse response)
11      throws ServletException, java.io.IOException {
12     response.setContentType("text/html");                            content type
13     java.io.PrintWriter out = response.getWriter();                  output to browser
14     // output your page here
15     out.println("<html>");
16     out.println("<head>");
17     out.println("<title>Servlet</title>");
18     out.println("</head>");
19     out.println("<body>");
20     out.println("Hello, Java Servlets");
21     out.println("</body>");
22     out.println("</html>");
23     out.close();                                                     close stream
24   }
25 }
```

The doGet method (line 9) is invoked when the Web browser issues a request using the GET method. The doGet method has two parameters, request and response. request is for obtaining data from the Web browser, and response is for sending data back to the browser. Line 12 indicates that data sent back to the browser is text/html. Line 13 obtains an instance of PrintWriter for actually sending data to the browser.

request
response

PrintWriter

34.3.2 Creating the Context Root Directory

Suppose you have installed Tomcat 5.5.9 or higher in c:\jakarta-tomcat-5.5.9. To run servlets from Tomcat, you have to create a *context root* and place the servlets and other supporting files under the context root directory. The context root directory must be placed under the Tomcat webapps directory, as shown in Figure 34.3.

The *webapps* directory is automatically created when you install Tomcat. This book creates a context root directory named *liangweb*. You have to create a folder named *WEB-INF* under the root directory, then a folder named *classes* under WEB-INF to hold servlet classes and other supporting classes. If the class uses packages (e.g., package chapter34), you need to place the class file in the appropriate folders.

34.3.3 Compiling Servlets

To compile FirstServlet.java, you need to add c:\jakarta-tomcat-5.5.9\common\lib\servlet-api.jar to the classpath from the DOS prompt, as shown below:

```
set classpath=%classpath%;c:\jakarta-tomcat-5.5.9                     classpath
  \common\lib\servlet-api.jar
```

servlet-api.jar contains the classes and interfaces to support servlets. Use the following command to compile the servlet:

```
javac FirstServlet.java
```

Copy the resultant .class file into c:\jakarta-tomcat-5.5.9\webapps\liangweb\WEB-INF\classes so that it can be found at runtime.

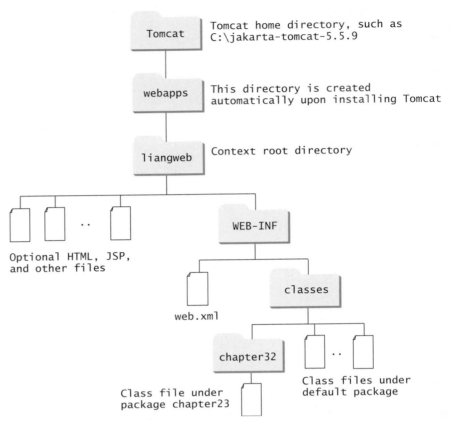

FIGURE 34.3 You have to create directories and files for Web applications in this pattern.

 Tip
You can compile FirstServlet directly into the target directory by using the −d option in the javac command:

```
javac FirstServlet.java –d targetdirectory
```

34.3.4 Mapping a Servlet to a URL

Before you can run a servlet in Tomcat 5.5.9, you have to first create the **web.xml** file with a servlet entry and a mapping entry. This file is located in **c:\jakarta-tomcat-5.5.9\ webapps\liangweb\WEB-INF\web.xml**. If the file already exists, insert a servlet entry and a mapping entry into web.xml for the servlet.

The servlet entry declares an internal servlet name for a servlet class using the following syntax:

```
<servlet>
  <servlet-name>Internal Name </servlet-name>
  <servlet-class>servlet class name </servlet-class>
</servlet>
```

The map entry maps an internal servlet name with a URL using the following syntax:

```
<servlet-mapping>
  <servlet-name>Internal Name</servlet-name>
  <url-pattern>URL </url-pattern>
</servlet-mapping>
```

For example, before running FirstServlet.class, you may insert the following lines to the web.xml file:

```
<web-app>
  <servlet>
      <servlet-name>FirstServlet</servlet-name>
      <servlet-class>FirstServlet</servlet-class>
  </servlet>

  <servlet-mapping>
      <servlet-name>FirstServlet</servlet-name>
      <url-pattern>/FirstServlet</url-pattern>
  </servlet-mapping>
</web-app>
```

Note

For your convenience, I have created the web.xml that contains the descriptions for running all the servlets in this chapter. You can download it from www.cs.armstrong.edu/liang/intro6e/supplement/web.xml.

download web.xml

Tip

You can use an IDE such as NetBeans, Eclipse, or JBuilder to simplify the development of Web applications. The tool can automatically create the directories and files. For more information, see the tutorials on NetBeans, Eclipse, and JBuilder on the Companion Website.

Web development tools

Tip

You can deploy a Web application using a Web archive file (WAR). For more information, see Supplement VII.E, *"Tomcat Tutorial."*

WAR file

34.3.5 Starting and Stopping Tomcat

Before running the servlet, you need to start the Tomcat servlet engine. To start Tomcat, you have to first set the JAVA_HOME environment variable to the JDK home directory using the command given below. Please note that there is no space before or after the = sign in the following line:

```
set JAVA_HOME=c:\Program Files\java\jdk1.5.0
```

The JDK home directory is where your JDK is stored. On my computer, it is c:\ProgramFiles\jdk1.5.0. You may have a different directory. You can now start Tomcat using the command **startup** from c:\jakarta-tomcat-5.5.9\bin, as follows:

```
c:\jakarta-tomcat-5.5.9\bin>startup
```

start Tomcat

Note

By default, Tomcat runs on port 8080. An error occurs if this port is currently being used. You can change the port number in c:\jakarta-tomcat-5.5.9\conf\server.xml.

Note

To terminate Tomcat, use the **shutdown** command from c:\jakarta-tomcat-5.5.9\bin.

shut down Tomcat

To prove that Tomcat is running, type the URL http://localhost:8080 from a Web browser, as shown in Figure 34.4.

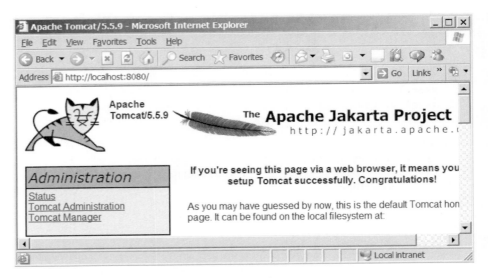

FIGURE 34.4 The default Tomcat page is displayed.

34.3.6 Running Servlets

To run the servlet, start a Web browser and type http://localhost:8080/liangweb/FirstServlet in the URL, as shown in Figure 34.5.

FIGURE 34.5 You can request a servlet from a Web browser.

Note

You can use the servlet from anywhere on the Internet if your Tomcat is running on a host machine on the Internet. Suppose the host name is liang.armstrong.edu; use the URL http://liang.armstrong.edu:8080/liangweb/FirstServlet to test the servlet.

Note

If you have modified the servlet, you need to shut down and restart Tomcat.

34.4 The Servlet API

You have to know the servlet API in order to understand the source code in FirstServlet.java. The servlet API provides the interfaces and classes that support servlets. These interfaces and classes are grouped into two packages, `javax.servlet` and `javax.servlet.http`, as shown in Figure 34.6. The `javax.servlet` package provides basic interfaces, and the `javax.servlet.http` package provides classes and interfaces derived from them, which provide specific means for servicing HTTP requests.

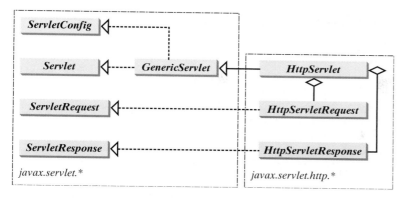

FIGURE 34.6   The servlet API contains interfaces and classes that you use to develop and run servlets.

34.4.1   The `Servlet` Interface

The `javax.servlet.Servlet` interface defines the methods that all servlets must implement. The methods are listed below:

```
/** Invoked for every servlet constructed */
public void init() throws ServletException;

/** Invoked to respond to incoming requests */
public void service(ServletRequest request, ServletResponse response)
   throws ServletException, IOException;

/** Invoked to release resource by the servlet */
public void destroy();
```

The `init`, `service`, and `destroy` methods are known as *life-cycle methods* and are called in the following sequence (see Figure 34.7):

    servlet life-cycle

1. The `init` method is called when the servlet is first created, and is not called again as long as the servlet is not destroyed. This resembles an applet's `init` method, which is invoked after the applet is created, and is not invoked again as long as the applet is not destroyed.

2. The `service` method is invoked each time the server receives a request for the servlet. The server spawns a new thread and invokes `service`.

3. The `destroy` method is invoked after a timeout period has passed or the Web server is being terminated. This method releases resources for the servlet.

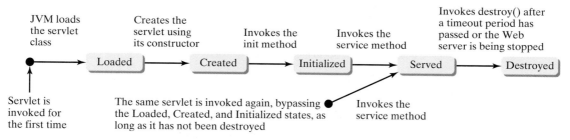

FIGURE 34.7   The JVM uses the `init`, `service`, and `destroy` methods to control the servlet.

34.4.2   The GenericServlet Class, ServletConfig Interface, and HttpServlet Class

The javax.servlet.GenericServlet class defines a generic, protocol-independent servlet. It implements javax.servlet.Servlet and javax.servlet.ServletConfig. ServletConfig is an interface that defines four methods (getInitParameter, getInitParameterNames, getServletContext, and getServletName) for obtaining information from a Web server during initialization. All the methods in Servlet and ServletConfig are implemented in GenericServlet except service. Therefore, GenericServlet is an abstract class.

The javax.servlet.http.HttpServlet class defines a servlet for the HTTP protocol. It extends GenericServlet and implements the service method. The service method is implemented as a dispatcher of HTTP requests. The HTTP requests are processed in the following methods:

- doGet is invoked to respond to a GET request.
- doPost is invoked to respond to a POST request.
- doDelete is invoked to respond to a DELETE request. Such a request is normally used to delete a file on the server.
- doPut is invoked to respond to a PUT request. Such a request is normally used to send a file to the server.
- doOptions is invoked to respond to an OPTIONS request. This returns information about the server, such as which HTTP methods it supports.
- doTrace is invoked to respond to a TRACE request. Such a request is normally used for debugging. This method returns an HTML page that contains appropriate trace information.

All these methods have the same signature:

```
protected void doXxx(HttpServletRequest req, HttpServletResponse resp)
    throws ServletException, java.io.IOException
```

The HttpServlet class provides default implementation for these methods. You need to override doGet, doPost, doDelete, and doPut if you want the servlet to process a GET, POST, DELETE, or PUT request. By default, nothing will be done. Normally, you should not override the doOptions method unless the servlet implements new HTTP methods beyond those implemented by HTTP 1.1. Nor is there any need to override the doTrace method.

Note
GET and POST requests are often used, whereas DELETE, PUT, OPTIONS, and TRACE are not. For more information about these requests, please refer to the HTTP 1.1 specification from www.cis.ohio-state.edu/htbin/rfc/rfc2068.html.

Note
Although the methods in HttpServlet are all nonabstract, HttpServlet is defined as an abstract class. Thus you cannot create a servlet directly from HttpServlet. Instead you have to define your servlet by extending HttpServlet.

The relationship of these interfaces and classes is shown in Figure 34.8.

34.4.3   The ServletRequest Interface and HttpServlet Request Interface

Every doXxx method in the HttpServlet class has a parameter of the HttpServletRequest type, which is an object that contains HTTP request information, including parameter name

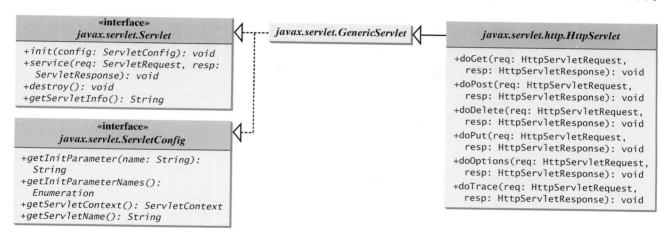

FIGURE 34.8 `HttpServlet` inherits abstract class `GenericServlet`, which implements interfaces `Servlet` and `ServletConfig`.

and values, attributes, and an input stream. `HttpServletRequest` is a subinterface of `ServletRequest`. `ServletRequest` defines a more general interface to provide information for all kinds of clients. The frequently used methods in these two interfaces are shown in Figure 34.9.

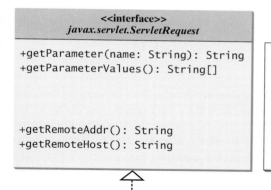

<<interface>> *javax.servlet.ServletRequest*	
+getParameter(name: String): String +getParameterValues(): String[]	Returns the value of a request parameter as a String, or null if the parameter does not exist. Request parameters are extra information sent with the request. For HTTP servlets, parameters are contained in the query string or posted from data. Only use this method when you are sure that the parameter has only one value. If it has more than one value, use getParameterValues.
+getRemoteAddr(): String	Returns the Internet Protocol (IP) address of the client that sent the request.
+getRemoteHost(): String	Returns the fully qualified name of the client that sent the request, or the IP address of the client if the name cannot be determined.

<<interface>> *javax.servlet.http.HttpServletRequest*	
+getHeader(name: String): String	Returns the value of the specified request header as a String. If the request did not include a header of the specified name, this method returns null. Since the header name is case-insensitive, you can use this method with any request header.
+getMethod(): String	Returns the name of the HTTP method with which this request was made; for example, GET, POST, DELETE, PUT, OPTIONS, or TRACE.
+getQueryString(): String	Returns the query string that is contained in the request URL after the path. This method returns null if the URL does not have a query string.
+getCookies(): javax.servlet.http.Cookies[]	Returns an array containing all of the cookie objects the client sent with the request. This method returns null if no cookies were sent. Using cookies is introduced in Sec. 34.8.2, "Session Tracking Using Cookies."
+getSession(create: boolean): HttpSession	getSession(true) returns the current session associated with this request. If the request does not have a session, it creates one. getSession(false) returns the current session associated with the request. If the request does not have a session, it returns null. The getSession method is used in session tracking, which is introduced in Sec. 34.8.3, "Session Tracking Using the Servlet API."

FIGURE 34.9 `HttpServletRequest` is a subinterface of `ServletRequest`.

34.4.4 The `ServletResponse` Interface and `HttpServletResponse` Interface

Every **do*Xxx*** method in the **HttpServlet** class has a parameter of the **HttpServletResponse** type, which is an object that assists a servlet in sending a response to the client. **HttpServletResponse** is a subinterface of **ServletResponse**. **ServletResponse** defines a more general interface for sending output to the client.

The frequently used methods in these two interfaces are shown in Figure 34.10.

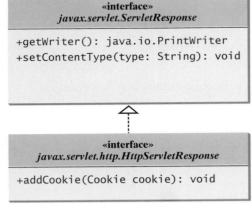

«interface» *javax.servlet.ServletResponse*
+getWriter(): java.io.PrintWriter
+setContentType(type: String): void

Returns a `PrintWriter` object that can send character text to the client.

Sets the content type of the response being sent to the client before writing the response to the client. When you are writing HTML to the client, the type should be set to "text/html." For plain text, use "text/plain." For sending a gif image to the browser, use "image/gif."

«interface» *javax.servlet.http.HttpServletResponse*
+addCookie(Cookie cookie): void

Adds the specified cookie to the response. This method can be called multiple times to set more than one cookie.

FIGURE 34.10 `HttpServletResponse` is a subinterface of `ServletResponse`.

34.5 Creating Servlets

Servlets are the opposite of Java applets. Java applets run from a Web browser on the client side. To write Java programs, you define classes. To write a Java applet, you define a class that extends the **Applet** class. The Web browser runs and controls the execution of the applet through the methods defined in the **Applet** class. Similarly, to write a Java servlet, you define a class that extends the **HttpServlet** class. The servlet container runs and controls the execution of the servlet through the methods defined in the **HttpServlet** class. Like a Java applet, a servlet does not have a **main** method. A servlet depends on the servlet server to call the methods. Every servlet has a structure like the one shown below:

```java
import javax.servlet.*;
import javax.servlet.http.*;
import java.io.*;

public class MyServlet extends HttpServlet {
  /** Called by the servlet engine to initialize servlet */
  public void init() throws ServletException {
    ...
  }

  /** Process the HTTP Get request */
  public void doGet(HttpServletRequest request, HttpServletResponse
    response) throws ServletException, IOException {
    ...
  }

  /** Process the HTTP Post request */
  public void doPost(HttpServletRequest request, HttpServletResponse
    response) throws ServletException, IOException {
    ...
  }
```

```
/** Called by the servlet engine to release resource */
public void destroy() {
  ...
}
// Other methods if necessary
}
```

The servlet engine controls the servlets using **init**, **doGet**, **doPost**, **destroy**, and other methods. By default, the **doGet** and **doPost** methods do nothing. To handle a GET request, you need to override the **doGet** method; to handle a POST request, you need to override the **doPost** method.

Listing 34.2 gives a simple Java servlet that generates a dynamic Web page for displaying the current time, as shown in Figure 34.11. The servlet is named **CurrentTime**. Compile it into `c:\jakarta-tomcat-5.5.9\webapps\liangweb\WEB-INF\classes`. Run the servlet using the URL

```
http://localhost:8080/liangweb/CurrentTime
```

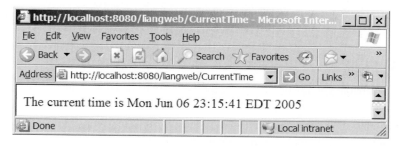

FIGURE 34.11   Servlet `CurrentTime` displays the current time.

Tip

The destination directory for CurrentTime.class is `c:\jakarta-tomcat-5.5.9\webapps\liangweb\WEB-INF\classes`. You can compile `CurrentTime.java` to generate `CurrentTime.class` and then move it into the destination directory. Or you can use the following command to compile and save the `.class` directly into the destination directory:

javac –d <destination directory> CurrentTime.java

Note

For every servlet example in this chapter, you have to insert a serlvet entry and a mapping entry into the web.xml file. For simplicity, this book uses /ServletClassName as the URL for the servlet.

LISTING 34.2   CurrentTime.java

```
1 import javax.servlet.*;
2 import javax.servlet.http.*;
3 import java.io.*;
4
5 public class CurrentTime extends HttpServlet {
6   /** Process the HTTP Get request */
7   public void doGet(HttpServletRequest request, HttpServletResponse
8       response) throws ServletException, IOException {                    process GET
9     response.setContentType("text/html");
10    PrintWriter out = response.getWriter();                               content type
11    out.println("<p>The current time is " + new java.util.Date());       output to browser
12    out.close(); // Close stream
13  }                                                                       close stream
14 }
```

The `HttpServlet` class has a `doGet` method. The `doGet` method is invoked when the browser issues a request to the servlet using the GET method. Your servlet class should override the `doGet` method to respond to the GET request. In this case, you write the code to display the current time.

Servlets return responses to the browser through an `HttpServletResponse` object. Since the `setContentType("text/html")` method sets the MIME type to "text/html," the browser will display the response in HTML. The `getWriter` method returns a `PrintWriter` stream (`out`) for sending HTML back to the client.

Note
The URL query string uses the GET method to issue a request to the servlet. The current time may not be current if the Web page for displaying the current time is cached. To ensure that a new current time is displayed, refresh the page in the browser. In the next example, you will write a new servlet that uses the POST method to obtain the current time.

Note

restart Tomcat

If you experience problems after Tomcat is successfully started, you may have to shut down and *restart Tomcat* after new servlet class files are added to the `c:\jakarta-tomcat-5.5.9\ webapps\liangweb\WEB-INF\classes` directory.

34.6 HTML Forms

HTML forms enable you to submit data to the Web server in a convenient form. As shown in Figure 34.12, the form can contain text fields, text area, check boxes, combo boxes, lists, radio buttons, and buttons.

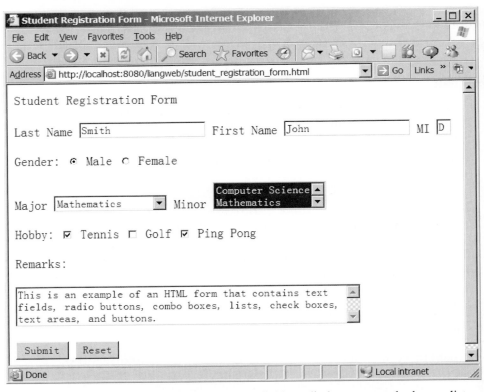

FIGURE 34.12   An HTML form may contain text fields, radio buttons, combo boxes, lists, check boxes, text areas, and buttons.

The HTML code for creating the form in Figure 34.12 is given in Listing 34.3. (If you are

HTML/XHTML Tutorial

unfamiliar with HTML, please see Supplement VII.A, "*HTML and XHTML Tutorial*.")

LISTING **34.3** Student_Registration_Form.html

```
1  <!--An HTML Form Demo -->
2  <html>
3    <head>
4      <title>Student Registration Form</title>
5    </head>
6    <body>
7      <h3>Student Registration Form</h3>
8
9      <form action = "http://localhost:8080/liangweb/GetParameters"         form tag
10        method = "get">
11        <!-- Name text fields -->
12        <p><label>Last Name</label>                                         label
13        <input type = "text" name = "lastName" size = "20" />               text field
14        <label>First Name</label>
15        <input type = "text" name = "firstName" size = "20" />
16        <label>MI</label>
17        <input type = "text" name = "mi" size = "1" /></p>
18
19        <!-- Gender radio buttons -->
20        <p><label>Gender:</label>
21        <input type = "radio" name = "gender" value = "M" checked /> Male   radio button
22        <input type = "radio" name = "gender" value = "F" /> Female</p>
23
24        <!-- Major combo box -->
25        <p><label>Major</label>
26          <select name = "major" size = "1">
27            <option value = "CS"> Computer Science</option>                 combo box
28            <option value = "Math">Mathematics</option>
29            <option>English</option>
30            <option>Chinese</option>
31          </select>
32
33        <!-- Minor list -->
34        <label>Minor</label>
35          <select name = "minor" size = "2" multiple>                       list
36            <option>Computer Science </option>
37            <option>Mathematics</option>
38            <option>English</option>
39            <option>Chinese</option>
40          </select></p>
41
42        <!-- Hobby check boxes -->
43        <p><label>Hobby:</label>
44          <input type = "checkbox" name = "tennis" /> Tennis                check box
45          <input type = "checkbox" name = "golf" /> Golf
46          <input type = "checkbox" name = "pingPong" checked />Ping Pong
47        </p>
48
49        <!-- Remark text area -->
50        <p>Remarks:</p>
51        <p><textarea name = "remarks" rows = "3" cols = "56"></textarea> </p>  text area
52
53        <!-- Submit and Reset buttons -->
54        <p><input type = "submit" value = "Submit" />                      submit button
55        <input type = "reset" value = "Reset" /></p>                       reset button
56      </form>
57    </body>
58  </html>
```

The following HTML tags are used to construct HTML forms:

`<from>`
action
method

- `<form>` ... `</form>` defines a form body. The attributes for the `<form>` tag are `action` and `method`. The `action` attribute specifies the server program to be executed on the Web server when the form is submitted. The `method` attribute is either `get` or `post`.

`<label>`

- `<label>` ... `</label>` simply defines a label.

`<input>`

- `<input>` defines an input field. The attributes for this tag are `type`, `name`, `value`, `checked`, `size`, and `maxlength`. The type attribute specifies the input type. Possible types are `text` for a one-line text field, `radio` for a radio button, and `checkbox` for a check box. The name attribute gives a formal name for the attribute. This `name` attribute is used by the servlet program to retrieve its associated value. The names of the radio buttons in a group must be identical. The value attribute specifies a default value for a text field and text area. The `checked` attribute indicates whether a radio button or a check box is initially checked. The `size` attribute specifies the size of a text field, and the `maxlength` attribute specifies the maximum length of a text field.

`<select>`

- `<select>` ... `</select>` defines a combo box or a list. The attributes for this tag are `name`, `size`, and `multiple`. The `size` attribute specifies the number of rows visible in the list. The `multiple` attribute specifies that multiple values can be selected from a list. Set `size` to 1 and do not use a `multiple` for a combo box.

`<option>`

- `<option>` ... `</option>` defines a selection list within a `<select>` ... `</select>` tag. This tag may be used with the value attribute to specify a value for the selected option (e.g., `<option value = "CS">Computer Science`). If no value is specified, the selected option is the value.

`<textarea>`

- `<textarea>` ... `</textarea>` defines a text area. The attributes are `name`, `rows`, and `cols`. The `rows` and `cols` attributes specify the number of rows and columns in a text area.

place .html files

Note
It is convenient to place all .html files under the context root directory (e.g., liangweb). Suppose you have placed student_registration_form.html into c:\jakarta-tomcat-5.5.9\webapps\liangweb. You can display it using the URL

`http://localhost:8080/liangweb/student_registration_form.html`

using relative URL

Tip
If you placed student_registration_form.html into `c:\jakarta-tomcat-5.5.9\webapps\liangweb`, you can replace

`http://localhost:8080/liangweb/GetParameters`

in line 9 in the HTML file with

`/liangweb/GetParameters`

This is better because it does not reference the port number. If you change the port number, you don't have to modify the HTML file.

34.6.1 Obtaining Parameter Values from HTML Forms

To demonstrate how to obtain parameter values from an HTML form, Listing 34.4 creates a servlet to obtain all the parameter values from the preceding student registration form in Figure 34.12 and display their values, as shown in Figure 34.13. The servlet is named

GetParameters and compiled into `c:\jakarta-tomcat-5.5.9\webapps\liangweb\`
`WEB-INF\classes`. Insert an appropriate servlet entry and a mapping entry into web.xml
for the GetParameters servlet.

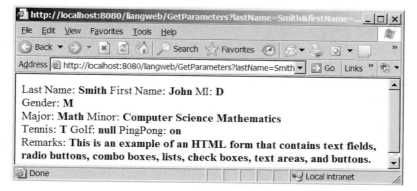

FIGURE 34.13 The servlet displays the parameter values entered in Figure 34.12.

LISTING 34.4 GetParameters.java

```java
1  import javax.servlet.*;
2  import javax.servlet.http.*;
3  import java.io.*;
4
5  public class GetParameters extends HttpServlet {
6    /** Process the HTTP Post request */
7    public void doGet (HttpServletRequest request, HttpServletResponse
8        response) throws ServletException, IOException {
9      response.setContentType("text/html");
10     PrintWriter out = response.getWriter();
11
12     // Obtain parameters from the client
13     String lastName = request.getParameter("lastName");
14     String firstName = request.getParameter("firstName");
15     String mi = request.getParameter("mi");
16     String gender = request.getParameter("gender");
17     String major = request.getParameter("major");
18     String[] minors = request.getParameterValues("minor");
19     String tennis = request.getParameter("tennis");
20     String golf = request.getParameter("golf");
21     String pingPong = request.getParameter("pingPong");
22     String remarks = request.getParameter("remarks");
23
24     out.println("Last Name: <b>" + lastName + "</b> First Name: <b>"
25       + firstName + "</b> MI: <b>" + mi + "</b><br>");
26     out.println("Gender: <b>" + gender + "</b><br>");
27     out.println("Major: <b>" + major + "</b> Minor: <b>");
28
29     if (minors != null)
30       for (int i = 0; i < minors.length; i++)
31         out.println(minors[i] + " ");
32
33     out.println("</b><br> Tennis: <b>" + tennis + "</b> Golf: <b>" +
34       golf + "</b> PingPong: <b>" + pingPong + "</b><br>");
35     out.println("Remarks: <b>" + remarks + "</b>");
36     out.close(); // Close stream
37   }
38 }
```

process **GET**

content type
output to browser

get parameters

close stream

The HTML form is already created in `student_registration_form.html` and displayed in Figure 34.12. Since the action for the form is http://localhost:8080/liangweb/GetParameters, clicking the *Submit* button invokes the `GetParameters` servlet.

Each GUI component in the form has a name attribute. The servlet uses the name attribute in the `getParameter(attributeName)` method to obtain the parameter value as a string. In case of a list with multiple values, use the `getParameterValues(attributeName)` method to return the parameter values in an array of strings (e.g., `getParameterValues("minor")` in line 18).

You may optionally specify the `value` attribute in a text field, text area, combo box, list, check box, or radio button in an HTML form. For text field and text area, the `value` attribute specifies a default value to be displayed in the text field and text area. The user can type in new values to replace it. For combo box, list, check box, and radio button, the `value` attribute specifies the parameter value to be returned from the `getParameter` and `getParameterValues` methods. If the `value` attribute is not specified for a combo box or a list, it returns the selected string from the combo box or the list. If the `value` attribute is not specified for a radio button or a check box, it returns string `on` for a checked radio button or a checked check box, and returns `null` for an unchecked check box.

Note

If an attribute does not exist, the `getParameter(attributeName)` method returns `null`. If an empty value of the parameter is passed to the servlet, the `getParameter(attributeName)` method returns a string with an empty value. In this case, the length of the string is 0.

34.6.2   Obtaining Current Time Based on Locale and Time Zone

This example creates a servlet that processes the GET and POST requests. The GET request generates a form that contains a combo box for locale and a combo box for time zone, as shown in Figure 34.14(a). The user can choose a locale and a time zone from this form to submit a POST request to obtain the current time based on the locale and time zone, as shown in Figure 34.14(b).

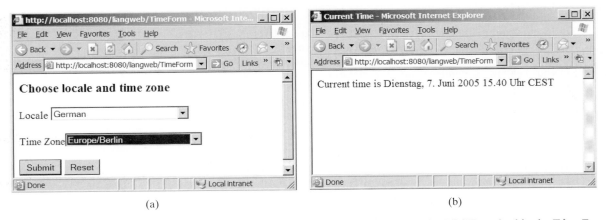

(a)   (b)

FIGURE 34.14   The GET method in the `TimeForm` servlet displays a form in (a), and the POST method in the `TimeForm` servlet displays the time based on locale and time zone in (b).

Create the servlet named `TimeForm` in Listing 34.5 and compile it into `c:\jakarta-tomcat-5.5.9\webapps\liangweb\WEB-INF\classes`. Run the servlet using the URL

```
http://localhost:8080/liangweb/TimeForm
```

LISTING 34.5 TimeForm.java

```
 1  import javax.servlet.*;
 2  import javax.servlet.http.*;
 3  import java.io.*;
 4  import java.util.*;
 5  import java.text.*;
 6
 7  public class TimeForm extends HttpServlet {
 8    private static final String CONTENT_TYPE = "text/html";
 9    private Locale[] allLocale = Locale.getAvailableLocales();
10    private String[] allTimeZone = TimeZone.getAvailableIDs();
11
12    /** Process the HTTP Get request */
13    public void doGet(HttpServletRequest request, HttpServletResponse
14        response) throws ServletException, IOException {
15      response.setContentType(CONTENT_TYPE);
16      PrintWriter out = response.getWriter();
17      out.println("<h3>Choose locale and time zone</h3>");
18      out.println("<form method=\"post\" action=" +
19        "/liangweb/TimeForm>");
20      out.println("Locale <select size=\"1\" name=\"locale\">");
21
22      // Fill in all locales
23      for (int i = 0; i < allLocale.length; i++) {
24        out.println("<option value=\"" + i +"\">" +
25          allLocale[i].getDisplayName() + "</option>");
26      }
27      out.println("</select>");
28
29      // Fill in all time zones
30      out.println("<p>Time Zone<select size=\"1\" name=\"timezone\">");
31      for (int i = 0; i < allTimeZone.length; i++) {
32        out.println("<option value=\"" + allTimeZone[i] +"\">" +
33          allTimeZone[i] + "</option>");
34      }
35      out.println("</select>");
36
37      out.println("<p><input type=\"submit\" value=\"Submit\" >");
38      out.println("<input type=\"reset\" value=\"Reset\"></p>");
39      out.println("</form>");
40      out.close(); // Close stream
41    }
42
43    /** Process the HTTP Post request */
44    public void doPost(HttpServletRequest request, HttpServletResponse
45        response) throws ServletException, IOException {
46      response.setContentType(CONTENT_TYPE);
47      PrintWriter out = response.getWriter();
48      out.println("<html>");
49      int localeIndex = Integer.parseInt(
50        request.getParameter("locale"));
51      String timeZoneID = request.getParameter("timezone");
52      out.println("<head><title>Current Time</title></head>");
53      out.println("<body>");
54      Calendar calendar =
55        new GregorianCalendar(allLocale[localeIndex]);
56      TimeZone timeZone = TimeZone.getTimeZone(timeZoneID);
57      DateFormat dateFormat = DateFormat.getDateTimeInstance(
58        DateFormat.FULL, DateFormat.FULL, allLocale[localeIndex]);
59      dateFormat.setTimeZone(timeZone);
```

process **GET**

content type
output to browser

create form

close stream

process **POST**

content type
output to browser

get locale

get time zone

create calendar

close stream

```
60    out.println("Current time is " +
61      dateFormat.format(calendar.getTime()) + "</p>");
62    out.println("</body></html>");
63    out.close(); // Close stream
64  }
65 }
```

When you use the URL http://localhost:8080/liangweb/TimeForm, the servlet `TimeForm`'s `doGet` method is invoked to generate the time form dynamically. The method of the form is POST, and the action invokes the same servlet, `TimeForm`. When the form is submitted to the server, the `doPost` method is invoked to process the request.

The variables `allLocale` and `allTimeZone` (lines 9–10), respectively, hold all the available locales and time zone IDs. The names of the locales are displayed in the locale list. The values for the locales are the indexes of the locales in the array `allLocale`. The time zone IDs are strings. They are displayed in the time zone list. They are also the values for the list. The indexes of the locale and the time zone are passed to the servlet as parameters. The `doPost` method obtains the values of the parameters (lines 49–51) and finds the current time based on the locale and time zone.

 Note

If you choose an Asian locale (e.g., Chinese, Korean, or Japanese), the time will not be displayed properly because the default character encoding is UTF-8. To fix this problem, add the following statement in line 48 to set an international character encoding:

set character encoding

```
response.setCharacterEncoding("GB18030");
```

For information on encoding, see §26.6, "Character Encoding."

34.7 Database Programming in Servlets

Many dynamic Web applications use databases to store and manage data. Servlets can connect to any relational database via JDBC. In Chapter 33, "Advanced Java Database Programming," you learned how to create Java programs to access and manipulate relational databases via JDBC. Connecting a servlet to a database is no different from connecting a Java application or applet to a database. If you know Java servlets and JDBC, you can combine them to develop interesting and practical Web-based interactive projects.

To demonstrate connecting to a database from a servlet, let us create a servlet that processes a registration form. The client enters data in an HTML form and submits it to the server, as shown in Figure 34.15. The result of the submission is shown in Figure 34.16. The server collects the data from the form and stores it in a database.

The registration data is stored in an `Address` table consisting of the following fields: `firstName`, `mi`, `lastName`, `street`, `city`, `state`, `zip`, `telephone`, and `email`, defined in the following statement:

```
create table Address (
  firstname varchar(25),
  mi char(1),
  lastname varchar(25),
  street varchar(40),
  city varchar(20),
  state varchar(2),
  zip varchar(5),
  telephone varchar(10),
  email varchar(30)
)
```

MySQL, Oracle, and Access were used in Chapter 32. You can use any relational database. An ODBC data source ExampleMDBDataSource was used in Chapter 32. This example

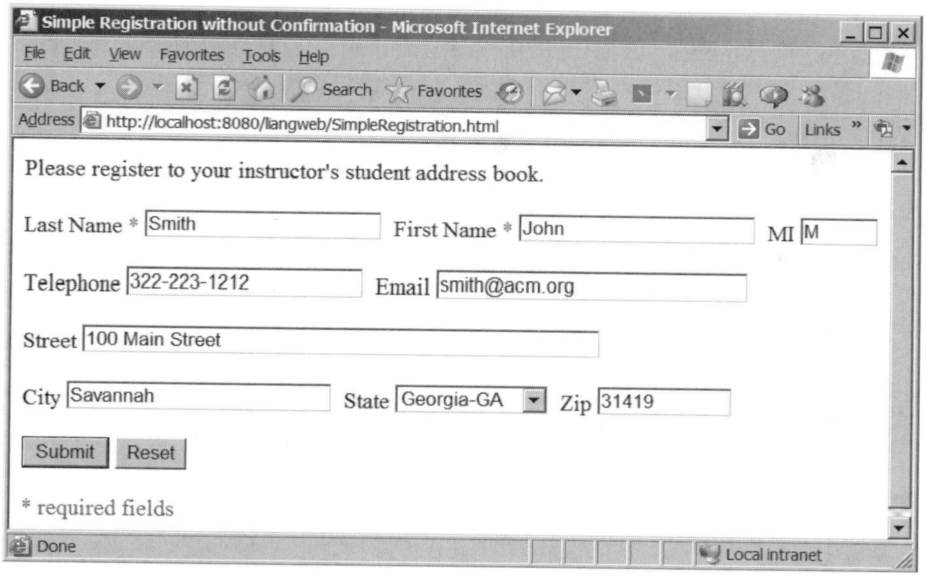

FIGURE 34.15 The HTML form enables the user to enter student information.

FIGURE 34.16 The servlet processes the form and stores data in a database.

assumes that the table is stored in this data source. If the servlet uses a database driver other than the JDBC-ODBC driver (e.g., the MySQL JDBC driver and the Oracle JDBC driver), you need to place the JDBC driver (e.g., `mysqljdbc.jar` for MySQL and `classes12.jar` for Oracle) into `c:\jakarta-tomcat-5.5.9\common\lib`.

mysqljdbc.jar
classes12.jar

Create an HTML file named SimpleRegistration.html in Listing 34.6 for collecting the data and sending it to the database using the post method. This file is almost identical to Listing 34.3, Student_Registration_Form.html. You should place this file under `c:\jakarta-tomcat-5.5.9\webapps\liangweb`.

place .html file

LISTING 34.6 SimpleRegistration.html

```
1  <!-- SimpleRegistration.html -->
2  <html>
3    <head>
4      <title>Simple Registration without Confirmation</title>
5    </head>
6    <body>
7      Please register to your instructor's student address book.
8
9      <form method = "post" action = "/liangweb/SimpleRegistration">
10       <p>Last Name <font color = "#FF0000">*</font>
```

action

```
11        <input type = "text" name = "lastName">
12        First Name <font color = "#FF0000">*</font>
13        <input type = "text" name = "firstName">
14        MI <input type = "text" name = "mi" size = "3">
15     </p>
16     <p>Telephone
17        <input type = "text" name = "telephone" size = "20">
18        Email
19        <input type = "text" name = "email" size = "28">
20     </p>
21     <p>Street <input type = "text" name = "street" size = "50">
22     </p>
23     <p>City <input type = "text" name = "city" size = "23">
24        State
25        <select size = "1" name = "state">
26          <option value = "GA">Georgia-GA</option>
27          <option value = "OK">Oklahoma-OK</option>
28          <option value = "IN">Indiana-IN</option>
29        </select>
30        Zip <input type = "text" name = "zip" size = "9">
31     </p>
32     <p><input type = "submit" name = "Submit" value = "Submit">
33        <input type = "reset" value = "Reset">
34     </p>
35   </form>
36   <p><font color = "#FF0000">* required fields</font></p>
37   </body>
38 </html>
```

submit form

Create the servlet named **SimpleRegistration** in Listing 34.7 and compile it into
c:\jakarta-tomcat-5.5.9\webapps\liangweb\WEB-INF\classes.

LISTING 34.7 SimpleRegistration.java

```
1  import javax.servlet.*;
2  import javax.servlet.http.*;
3  import java.io.*;
4  import java.sql.*;
5
6  public class SimpleRegistration extends HttpServlet {
7    // Use a prepared statement to store a student into the database
8    private PreparedStatement pstmt;
9
10   /** Initialize variables */
11   public void init() throws ServletException {
12     initializeJdbc();
13   }
14
15   /** Process the HTTP Post request */
16   public void doPost(HttpServletRequest request, HttpServletResponse
17       response) throws ServletException, IOException {
18     response.setContentType("text/html");
19     PrintWriter out = response.getWriter();
20
21     // Obtain parameters from the client
22     String lastName = request.getParameter("lastName");
23     String firstName = request.getParameter("firstName");
24     String mi = request.getParameter("mi");
25     String phone = request.getParameter("telephone");
26     String email = request.getParameter("email");
```

place .class file

initialize db

process **POST**

content type
output to browser

get parameters

```
27        String address = request.getParameter("street");
28        String city = request.getParameter("city");
29        String state = request.getParameter("state");
30        String zip = request.getParameter("zip");
31
32        try {
33          if (lastName.length() == 0 || firstName.length() == 0) {
34            out.println("Last Name and First Name are required");
35            return; // End the method
36          }
37
38          storeStudent(lastName, firstName, mi, phone, email, address,       store record
39            city, state, zip);
40
41          out.println(firstName + " " + lastName +
42            " is now registered in the database");
43        }
44        catch(Exception ex) {
45          out.println("Error: " + ex.getMessage());
46        }
47        finally {
48          out.close(); // Close stream                                        close stream
49        }
50      }
51
52      /** Initialize database connection */
53      private void initializeJdbc() {
54        try {
55          // Declare driver and connection string
56          String driver = "sun.jdbc.odbc.JdbcOdbcDriver";                     load driver
57          String connectionString = "jdbc:odbc:exampleMDBDataSource";
58          // For MySQL                                                        MySQL driver commented
59          // String driver = "com.mysql.jdbc.Driver";
60          // String connectionString = "jdbc:mysql://localhost/test";
61          // For Oracle                                                       Oracle driver commented
62          // String driver = "oracle.jdbc.driver.OracleDriver";
63          // String connectionString = "jdbc:oracle:" +
64          //   "thin:scott/tiger@liang.armstrong.edu:1521:orcl";
65
66          // Load the driver                                                  load driver
67          Class.forName(driver);
68
69          // Connect to the sample database                                   connect db
70          Connection conn = DriverManager.getConnection
71            (connectionString);
72
73          // Create a Statement
74          pstmt = conn.prepareStatement("insert into Address " +             prepare statement
75            "(lastName, firstName, mi, telephone, email, street, city, "
76            + "state, zip) values (?, ?, ?, ?, ?, ?, ?, ?, ?)");
77        }
78        catch (Exception ex) {
79          ex.printStackTrace();
80        }
81      }
82
83      /** Store a student record to the database */
84      private void storeStudent(String lastName, String firstName,
85        String mi, String phone, String email, String address,
86        String city, String state, String zip) throws SQLException {
87        pstmt.setString(1, lastName);                                         set values
```

```
88        pstmt.setString(2, firstName);
89        pstmt.setString(3, mi);
90        pstmt.setString(4, phone);
91        pstmt.setString(5, email);
92        pstmt.setString(6, address);
93        pstmt.setString(7, city);
94        pstmt.setString(8, state);
95        pstmt.setString(9, zip);
96        pstmt.executeUpdate();
97      }
98 }
```

execute SQL

The `init` method (line 11) is executed once when the servlet starts. After the servlet has started, the servlet can be invoked many times as long as it is alive in the servlet container. Load the driver, and connect to the database from the servlet's `init` method. If a prepared statement or a callable statement is used, it should also be created in the `init` method. In this example, a prepared statement is desirable, because the servlet always uses the same insert statement with different values.

A servlet can connect to any relational database via JDBC. The `initializeJdbc` method in this example loads a JDBC-ODBC bridge driver (line 56). Use of the other driver is commented in the code (line 58–64). Once connected, it creates a prepared statement for inserting a student record into the database. The Access database and the Oracle database are the same as were used in Chapter 32, "Java Database Programming." To use the MS Access database, the ODBC data source `exampleMDBDataSource` must be created. To use the Oracle database, you must have the Oracle JDBC Thin driver in the library of the project.

Last name and first name are required fields. If either of them is empty, the servlet sends an error message to the client (lines 33–36). Otherwise, the servlet stores the data in the database using the prepared statement.

34.8 Session Tracking

Web servers use the Hyper-Text Transport Protocol (HTTP). HTTP is a stateless protocol. An HTTP Web server cannot associate requests from a client, and therefore treats each request independently. This protocol works fine for simple Web browsing, where each request typically results in an HTML file or a text file being sent back to the client. Such simple requests are isolated. However, the requests in interactive Web applications are often related. Consider the two requests in the following scenario:

- Request 1: A client sends registration data to the server; the server then returns the data to the user for confirmation.

- Request 2: The client confirms the data by resubmitting it.

In Request 2, the data submitted in Request 1 is sent back to the server. These two requests are related in a session. A *session* can be defined as a series of related interactions between a single client and the Web server over a period of time. Tracking data among requests in a session is known as *session tracking*.

This section introduces three techniques for session tracking: *using hidden values, using cookies,* and *using the session tracking tools from servlet API.*

34.8.1 Session Tracking Using Hidden Values

You can track a session by passing data from the servlet to the client as hidden values in a dynamically generated HTML form by including a field like this one:

```
<input type = "hidden" name = "lastName" value = "Smith">
```

The next request will submit the data back to the servlet. The servlet retrieves this hidden value just like any other parameter value, using the `getParameter` method.

Let us use an example to demonstrate using hidden values in a form. The example creates a servlet that processes a registration form. The client submits the form using the GET method, as shown in Figure 34.17. The server collects the data in the form, displays it to the client, and asks the client for confirmation, as shown in Figure 34.18. The client confirms the data by submitting the request with the hidden values using the POST method. Finally, the servlet writes the data to a database.

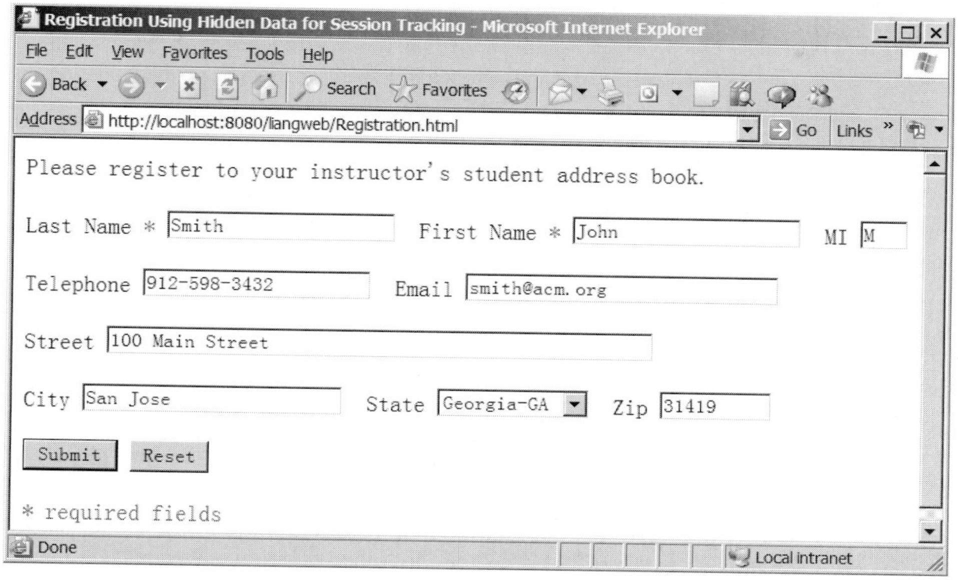

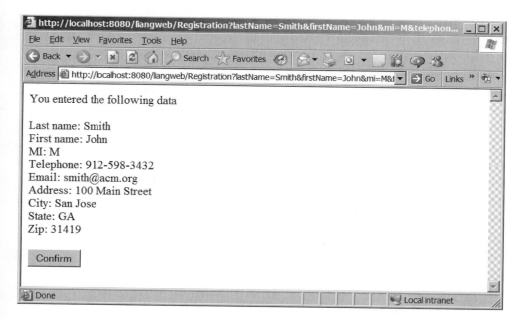

FIGURE 34.17   The registration form collects user information.

FIGURE 34.18   The servlet asks the client for confirmation of the input.

Create an HTML form named Registration.html in Listing 34.8 for collecting the data and sending it to the database using the GET method for confirmation. This file is almost identical to Listing 34.3, Student_Registration_Form.html. Place this file under `c:\jakarta-tomcat-5.5.9\webapps\liangweb`.

LISTING 34.8 Registration.html

```
 1  <!-- Registration.html -->
 2  <html>
 3    <head>
 4      <title>Using Hidden Data for Session Tracking</title>
 5    </head>
 6    <body>
 7      Please register to your instructor's student address book.
 8
 9      <form method = "get" action = "/liangweb/Registration">
10        <p>Last Name <font color = "#FF0000">*</font>
11          <input type = "text" name = "lastName">
12          First Name <font color = "#FF0000">*</font>
13          <input type = "text" name = "firstName">
14          MI <input type = "text" name = "mi" size = "3">
15        </p>
16        <p>Telephone
17          <input type = "text" name = "telephone" size = "20">
18          Email
19          <input type = "text" name = "email" size = "28">
20        </p>
21        <p>Street <input type = "text" name = "street" size = "50">
22        </p>
23        <p>City <input type = "text" name = "city" size = "23">
24          State
25          <select size = "1" name = "state">
26            <option value = "GA">Georgia-GA</option>
27            <option value = "OK">Oklahoma-OK</option>
28            <option value = "IN">Indiana-IN</option>
29          </select>
30          Zip <input type = "text" name = "zip" size = "9">
31        </p>
32        <p><input type = "submit" name = "Submit" value = "Submit">
33          <input type = "reset" value = "Reset">
34        </p>
35      </form>
36      <p><font color = "#FF0000">* required fields</font></p>
37    </body>
38  </html>
```

action (line 9)

submit form (line 32)

Create the servlet named Registration in Listing 34.9 and compile it into
`c:\jakarta-tomcat-5.5.9\webapps\liangweb\WEB-INF\classes`.

LISTING 34.9 Registration.java

```
 1  import javax.servlet.*;
 2  import javax.servlet.http.*;
 3  import java.io.*;
 4  import java.sql.*;
 5
 6  public class Registration extends HttpServlet {
 7    // Use a prepared statement to store a student into the database
 8    private PreparedStatement pstmt;
 9
10    /** Initialize variables */
11    public void init() throws ServletException {
12      initializeJdbc();
13    }
14
```

initialize db (line 12)

```
15   /** Process the HTTP Get request */
16   public void doGet(HttpServletRequest request, HttpServletResponse       process GET
17     response) throws ServletException, IOException {
18     response.setContentType("text/html");                                 content type
19     PrintWriter out = response.getWriter();                               output to browser
20
21     // Obtain data from the form
22     String lastName = request.getParameter("lastName");                   get parameters
23     String firstName = request.getParameter("firstName");
24     String mi = request.getParameter("mi");
25     String telephone = request.getParameter("telephone");
26     String email = request.getParameter("email");
27     String street = request.getParameter("street");
28     String city = request.getParameter("city");
29     String state = request.getParameter("state");
30     String zip = request.getParameter("zip");
31
32     if (lastName.length() == 0 || firstName.length() == 0) {
33       out.println("Last Name and First Name are required");
34       return; // End the method
35     }
36
37     // Ask for confirmation
38     out.println("You entered the following data");
39     out.println("<p>Last name: " + lastName);
40     out.println("<br>First name: " + firstName);
41     out.println("<br>MI: " + mi);
42     out.println("<br>Telephone: " + telephone);
43     out.println("<br>Email: " + email);
44     out.println("<br>Address: " + street);
45     out.println("<br>City: " + city);
46     out.println("<br>State: " + state);
47     out.println("<br>Zip: " + zip);
48
49     // Set the action for processing the answers
50     out.println("<p><form method=\"post\" action=" +                      client verification
51       "/liangweb/Registration>");
52     // Set hidden values
53     out.println("<p><input type=\"hidden\" " +
54       "value=" + lastName + " name=\"lastName\">");
55     out.println("<p><input type=\"hidden\" " +
56       "value=" + firstName + " name=\"firstName\">");
57     out.println("<p><input type=\"hidden\" " +
58       "value=" + mi + " name=\"mi\">");
59     out.println("<p><input type=\"hidden\" " +
60       "value=" + telephone + " name=\"telephone\">");
61     out.println("<p><input type=\"hidden\" " +
62       "value=" + email + " name=\"email\">");
63     out.println("<p><input type=\"hidden\" " +
64       "value=" + street + " name=\"street\">");
65     out.println("<p><input type=\"hidden\" " +
66       "value=" + city + " name=\"city\">");
67     out.println("<p><input type=\"hidden\" " +
68       "value=" + state + " name=\"state\">");
69     out.println("<p><input type=\"hidden\" " +
70       "value=" + zip + " name=\"zip\">");
71     out.println("<p><input type=\"submit\" value=\"Confirm\" >");
72     out.println("</form>");
73
74     out.close(); // Close stream
75   }
```

```
76
77    /** Process the HTTP Post request */
78    public void doPost(HttpServletRequest request, HttpServletResponse
79      response) throws ServletException, IOException {
80      response.setContentType("text/html");
81      PrintWriter out = response.getWriter();
82
83      try {
84        String lastName = request.getParameter("lastName");
85        String firstName = request.getParameter("firstName");
86        String mi = request.getParameter("mi");
87        String telephone = request.getParameter("telephone");
88        String email = request.getParameter("email");
89        String street = request.getParameter("street");
90        String city = request.getParameter("city");
91        String state = request.getParameter("state");
92        String zip = request.getParameter("zip");
93
94        storeStudent(lastName, firstName, mi, telephone, email,
95          street, city, state, zip);
96
97        out.println(firstName + " " + lastName +
98          " is now registered in the database");
99      }
100     catch(Exception ex) {
101       out.println("Error: " + ex.getMessage());
102       return; // End the method
103     }
104   }
105
106   /** Initialize database connection */
107   private void initializeJdbc() {
108     try {
109       // Declare driver and connection string
110       String driver = "sun.jdbc.odbc.JdbcOdbcDriver";
111       String connectionString = "jdbc:odbc:exampleMDBDataSource";
112       /* For Oracle
113       String driver = "oracle.jdbc.driver.OracleDriver";
114       String connectionString = "jdbc:oracle:" +
115         "thin:scott/tiger@liang.armstrong.edu:1521:orcl";
116       */
117       // Load the Oracle JDBC Thin driver
118       Class.forName(driver);
119
120       // Connect to the sample database
121       Connection conn = DriverManager.getConnection
122         (connectionString);
123
124       // Create a Statement
125       pstmt = conn.prepareStatement("insert into Address " +
126         "(lastName, firstName, mi, telephone, email, street, city, "
127         + "state, zip) values (?, ?, ?, ?, ?, ?, ?, ?, ?)");
128     }
129     catch (Exception ex) {
130       System.out.println(ex);
131     }
132   }
133
```

process **POST**

content type
output to browser

get parameters

store record

```
134   /** Store a student record to the database */
135   private void storeStudent(String lastName, String firstName,
136      String mi, String phone, String email, String address,
137      String city, String state, String zip) throws SQLException {
138      pstmt.setString(1, lastName);
139      pstmt.setString(2, firstName);
140      pstmt.setString(3, mi);
141      pstmt.setString(4, phone);
142      pstmt.setString(5, email);
143      pstmt.setString(6, address);
144      pstmt.setString(7, city);
145      pstmt.setString(8, state);
146      pstmt.setString(9, zip);
147      pstmt.executeUpdate();
148   }
149 }
```

The servlet processes the GET request by generating an HTML page that displays the client's input and asks for the client's confirmation. The input data consists of hidden values in the newly generated forms, so it will be sent back in the confirmation request. The confirmation request uses the POST method. The servlet retrieves the hidden values and stores them in the database.

Since the first request does not write anything to the database, it is appropriate to use the GET method. Since the second request results in an update to the database, the POST method must be used.

 Note

The hidden values could also be sent from the URL query string if the request uses the GET method.

34.8.2   Session Tracking Using Cookies

You can track sessions using cookies, which are small text files that store sets of name-value pairs on the disk in the client's computer. Cookies are sent from the server through the instructions in the header of the HTTP response. The instructions tell the browser to create a cookie with a given name and its associated value. If the browser already has a cookie with the key name, the value will be updated. The browser will then send the cookie with any request submitted to the same server. Cookies can have expiration dates set, after which they will not be sent to the server. The `javax.servlet.http.Cookie` is used to create and manipulate cookies, as shown in Figure 34.19.

To send a cookie to the browser, use the `addCookie` method in the `HttpServletResponse` class, as shown below:

```
response.addCookie(cookie);
```

where `response` is an instance of `HttpServletResponse`.

To obtain cookies from a browser, use

```
request.getCookies();
```

where `request` is an instance of `HttpServletRequest`.

To demonstrate the use of cookies, let us create an example that accomplishes the same task as Listing 34.9, Registration.java. Instead of using hidden values for session tracking, it uses cookies.

javax.servlet.http.Cookie	
+Cookie(name: String, value: String)	Creates a cookie with the specified name-value pair.
+getName(): String	Returns the name of the cookie.
+getValue(): String	Returns the value of the cookie.
+setValue(newValue: String): void	Assigns a new value to a cookie after the cookie is created.
+getMaxAge(): int	Returns the maximum age of the cookie, specified in seconds.
+setMaxAge(expiration: int): void	Specifies the maximum age of the cookie. By default, this value is –1, which implies that the cookie persists until the browser exits. If you set this value to 0, the cookie is deleted.
+getSecure(): boolean	Returns true if the browser is sending cookies only over a secure protocol.
+setSecure(flag: boolean): void	Indicates to the browser whether the cookie should only be sent using a secure protocol, such as HTTPS or SSL.
+getComment(): String	Returns the comment describing the purpose of this cookie, or null if the cookie has no comment.
+setComment(purpose: String): void	Sets the comment for this cookie.

FIGURE 34.19   Cookie stores a name-value pair and other information about the cookie.

Create the servlet named RegistrationWithHttpCookie in Listing 34.10. Compile it into
`c:\jakarta-tomcat-5.5.9\webapps\liangweb\WEB-INF\classes`.

Create an HTML file named RegistrationWithCookie.html that is identical to Registration.
html except that the action is replaced by

`http://localhost:8080/liangweb/RegistrationWithCookie`

LISTING 34.10   RegistrationWithCookie.java

```
1 import javax.servlet.*;
2 import javax.servlet.http.*;
3 import java.io.*;
4 import java.sql.*;
5
6 public class RegistrationWithCookie extends HttpServlet {
7   private static final String CONTENT_TYPE = "text/html";
8   // Use a prepared statement to store a student into the database
9   private PreparedStatement pstmt;
10
11  /** Initialize variables */
12  public void init() throws ServletException {
13    initializeJdbc();
14  }
15
16  /** Process the HTTP Get request */
17  public void doGet(HttpServletRequest request, HttpServletResponse
18      response) throws ServletException, IOException {
19    response.setContentType("text/html");
20    PrintWriter out = response.getWriter();
21
22    // Obtain data from the form
23    String lastName = request.getParameter("lastName");
24    String firstName = request.getParameter("firstName");
25    String mi = request.getParameter("mi");
26    String telephone = request.getParameter("telephone");
```

process GET

get parameters

```
27        String email = request.getParameter("email");
28        String street = request.getParameter("street");
29        String city = request.getParameter("city");
30        String state = request.getParameter("state");
31        String zip = request.getParameter("zip");
32
33        // Create cookies and send cookies to browsers
34        Cookie cookieLastName = new Cookie("lastName", lastName);          create cookies
35        // cookieLastName.setMaxAge(1000);
36        response.addCookie(cookieLastName);                                send cookies
37        Cookie cookieFirstName = new Cookie("firstName", firstName);
38        response.addCookie(cookieFirstName);
39        // cookieFirstName.setMaxAge(0);
40        Cookie cookieMi = new Cookie("mi", mi);
41        response.addCookie(cookieMi);
42        Cookie cookieTelephone = new Cookie("telephone", telephone);
43        response.addCookie(cookieTelephone);
44        Cookie cookieEmail = new Cookie("email", email);
45        response.addCookie(cookieEmail);
46        Cookie cookieStreet = new Cookie("street", street);
47        response.addCookie(cookieStreet);
48        Cookie cookieCity = new Cookie("city", city);
49        response.addCookie(cookieCity);
50        Cookie cookieState = new Cookie("state", state);
51        response.addCookie(cookieState);
52        Cookie cookieZip = new Cookie("zip", zip);
53        response.addCookie(cookieZip);
54
55        System.out.println("MaxAge? " + cookieLastName.getMaxAge());
56        System.out.println("MaxAge fir? " + cookieFirstName.getMaxAge());
57
58        if (lastName.length() == 0 || firstName.length() == 0) {
59          out.println("Last Name and First Name are required");
60          return; // End the method
61        }
62
63        // Ask for confirmation                                            client verification
64        out.println("You entered the following data");
65        out.println("<p>Last name: " + lastName);
66        out.println("<br>First name: " + firstName);
67        out.println("<br>MI: " + mi);
68        out.println("<br>Telephone: " + telephone);
69        out.println("<br>Email: " + email);
70        out.println("<br>Street: " + street);
71        out.println("<br>City: " + city);
72        out.println("<br>State: " + state);
73        out.println("<br>Zip: " + zip);
74
75        // Set the action for processing the answers
76        out.println("<p><form method=\"post\" action=" +
77          "/liangweb/RegistrationWithCookie>");
78        out.println("<p><input type=\"submit\" value=\"Confirm\" >");
79        out.println("</form>");
80        out.close(); // Close stream
81      }
82
83    /** Process the HTTP Post request */                                  process POST
84    public void doPost(HttpServletRequest request, HttpServletResponse
85        response) throws ServletException, IOException {
```

```
86        response.setContentType(CONTENT_TYPE);
87        PrintWriter out = response.getWriter();
88
89        String lastName = "";
90        String firstName = "";
91        String mi = "";
92        String telephone = "";
93        String email = "";
94        String street = "";
95        String city = "";
96        String state = "";
97        String zip = "";
98
99        // Read the cookies
100       Cookie[] cookies = request.getCookies();
101
102       // Get cookie values
103       for (int i = 0; i < cookies.length; i++) {
104         if (cookies[i].getName().equals("lastName"))
105           lastName = cookies[i].getValue();
106         else if (cookies[i].getName().equals("firstName"))
107           firstName = cookies[i].getValue();
108         else if (cookies[i].getName().equals("mi"))
109           mi = cookies[i].getValue();
110         else if (cookies[i].getName().equals("telephone"))
111           telephone = cookies[i].getValue();
112         else if (cookies[i].getName().equals("email"))
113           email = cookies[i].getValue();
114         else if (cookies[i].getName().equals("street"))
115           street = cookies[i].getValue();
116         else if (cookies[i].getName().equals("city"))
117           city = cookies[i].getValue();
118         else if (cookies[i].getName().equals("state"))
119           state = cookies[i].getValue();
120         else if (cookies[i].getName().equals("zip"))
121           zip = cookies[i].getValue();
122       }
123
124       try {
125         storeStudent(lastName, firstName, mi, telephone, email, street,
126           city, state, zip);
127
128         out.println(firstName + " " + lastName +
129           " is now registered in the database");
130
131         out.close(); // Close stream
132       }
133       catch(Exception ex) {
134         out.println("Error: " + ex.getMessage());
135         return; // End the method
136       }
137     }
138
139     /** Initialize database connection */
140     private void initializeJdbc() {
141       try {
142         // Declare driver and connection string
143         String driver = "sun.jdbc.odbc.JdbcOdbcDriver";
144         String connectionString = "jdbc:odbc:exampleMDBDataSource";
```

get cookies

store record

```
145        // For Oracle
146        // String driver = "oracle.jdbc.driver.OracleDriver";
147        // String connectionString = "jdbc:oracle:" +
148        //   "thin:scott/tiger@liang.armstrong.edu:1521:orcl";
149
150        // Load the Oracle JDBC Thin driver
151        Class.forName(driver);
152        System.out.println("Driver " + driver + " loaded");
153
154        // Connect to the sample database
155        Connection conn = DriverManager.getConnection
156          (connectionString);
157        System.out.println("Database " + connectionString +
158          " connected");
159
160        // Create a Statement
161        pstmt = conn.prepareStatement("insert into Address " +
162          "(lastName, firstName, mi, telephone, email, street, city, "
163          + "state, zip) values (?, ?, ?, ?, ?, ?, ?, ?, ?)");
164      }
165      catch (Exception ex) {
166        System.out.println(ex);
167      }
168    }
169
170    /** Store a student record to the database */
171    private void storeStudent(String lastName, String firstName,
172      String mi, String telephone, String email, String street,
173      String city, String state, String zip) throws SQLException {
174      pstmt.setString(1, lastName);
175      pstmt.setString(2, firstName);
176      pstmt.setString(3, mi);
177      pstmt.setString(4, telephone);
178      pstmt.setString(5, email);
179      pstmt.setString(6, street);
180      pstmt.setString(7, city);
181      pstmt.setString(8, state);
182      pstmt.setString(9, zip);
183      pstmt.executeUpdate();
184    }
185 }
```

You have to create a cookie for each value you want to track, using the Cookie class's only constructor, which defines a cookie's name and value as shown below (line 34):

```
Cookie cookieLastName = new Cookie("lastName", lastName);
```

To send the cookie to the browser, use a statement like this one (line 36):

```
response.addCookie(cookieLastName);
```

If a cookie with the same name already exists in the browser, its value is updated; otherwise, a new cookie is created.

Cookies are automatically sent to the Web server with each request from the client. The servlet retrieves all the cookies into an array using the getCookies method (line 100):

```
Cookie[] cookies = request.getCookies();
```

To obtain the name of the cookie, use the getName method (line 104):

```
String name = cookies[i].getName();
```

The cookie's value can be obtained using the `getValue` method:

```
String value = cookies[i].getValue();
```

Cookies are stored as strings just like form parameters and hidden values. If a cookie represents a numeric value, you have to convert it into an integer or a double, using the `parseInt` method in the `Integer` class or the `parseDouble` method in the `Double` class.

By default, a newly created cookie persists until the browser exits. However, you can set an expiration date, using the `setMaxAge` method, to allow a cookie to stay in the browser for up to 2,147,483,647 seconds (approximately 24,855 days).

34.8.3 Session Tracking Using the Servlet API

You have now learned both session tracking using hidden values and session tracking using cookies. These two session-tracking methods have problems. They send data to the browser either as hidden values or as cookies. The data is not secure, and anybody with knowledge of computers can obtain it. The hidden data is in HTML form, which can be viewed from the browser. Cookies are stored in the Cache directory of the browser. Because of security concerns, some browsers do not accept cookies. The client can turn the cookies off and limit their number. Another problem is that hidden data and cookies pass data as strings. You cannot pass objects using these two methods.

To address these problems, Java servlet API provides the `javax.servlet. http.HttpSession` interface, which provides a way to identify a user across more than one page request or visit to a Web site and to store information about that user. The servlet container uses this interface to create a session between an HTTP client and an HTTP server. The session persists for a specified time period, across more than one connection or page request from the user. A session usually corresponds to one user, who may visit a site many times. The session enables tracking of a large set of data. The data can be stored as objects and is secure because they are kept on the server side.

To use the Java servlet API for session tracking, first create a session object using the `getSession()` method in the `HttpServletRequest` interface:

```
HttpSession session = request.getSession();
```

This obtains the session or creates a new session if the client does not have a session on the server.

The `HttpSession` interface provides the methods for reading and storing data to the session, and for manipulating the session, as shown in Figure 34.20.

Note
HTTP is stateless. So how does the server associate a session with multiple requests from the same client? This is handled behind the scenes by the servlet container and is transparent to the servlet programmer.

To demonstrate using `HttpSession`, let us rewrite Listing 34.9, Registration.java, and Listing 34.10, RegistrationWithCookie.java. Instead of using hidden values or cookies for session tracking, it uses servlet `HttpSession`.

Create the servlet named `RegistrationWithHttpSession` in Listing 34.11. Compile it into `c:\jakarta-tomcat-5.5.9\webapps\liangweb\WEB-INF\classes`. Note that this servlet contains two class files, `RegistrationWithHttpSession.class` and `RegistrationWithHttpSession$Student.class`.

Create an HTML file named `RegistrationWithHttpSession.html` that is identical to `Registration.html` except that the action is replaced by

```
http://localhost:8080/liangweb/RegistrationWithHttpSession
```

«interface» *javax.servlet.http.HttpSession*	
+getAttribute(name: String): Object	Returns the object bound with the specified name in this session, or null if no object is bound under the name.
+setAttribute(name: String, value: Object): void	Binds an object to this session, using the specified name. If an object of the same name is already bound to the session, the object is replaced.
+getId(): String	Returns a string containing the unique identifier assigned to this session. The identifier is assigned by the servlet container and is implementation dependent.
+getLastAccessedTime(): long	Returns the last time the client sent a request associated with this session, as the number of milliseconds since midnight January 1, 1970 GMT, and marked by the time the container received the request.
+invalidate(): void	Invalidates this session, then unbinds any objects bound to it.
+isNew(): boolean	Returns true if the session was just created in the current request.
+removeAttribute(name: String): void	Removes the object bound with the specified name from this session. If the session does not have an object bound with the specified name, this method does nothing.
+getMaxInactiveInterval(): int +setMaxInactiveInterval(interval: int): void	Returns the time, in seconds, between client requests before the servlet container will invalidate this session. A negative time indicates that the session will never time-out. Use setMaxInactiveInterval to specify this value.

FIGURE 34.20 `HttpSession` establishes a persistent session between a client with multiple requests and the server.

LISTING 34.11 RegistrationWithHttpSession.java

```java
1  import javax.servlet.*;
2  import javax.servlet.http.*;
3  import java.io.*;
4  import java.sql.*;
5
6  public class RegistrationWithHttpSession extends HttpServlet {
7    // Use a prepared statement to store a student into the database
8    private PreparedStatement pstmt;
9
10   /** Initialize variables */
11   public void init() throws ServletException {
12     initializeJdbc();
13   }
14
15   /** Process the HTTP Get request */
16   public void doGet(HttpServletRequest request, HttpServletResponse
17       response) throws ServletException, IOException {
18     // Set response type and output stream to the browser
19     response.setContentType("text/html");
20     PrintWriter out = response.getWriter();
21
22     // Obtain data from the form
23     String lastName = request.getParameter("lastName");
24     String firstName = request.getParameter("firstName");
25     String mi = request.getParameter("mi");
26     String telephone = request.getParameter("telephone");
27     String email = request.getParameter("email");
28     String street = request.getParameter("street");
29     String city = request.getParameter("city");
```

process **GET**

get parameters

```
30        String state = request.getParameter("state");
31        String zip = request.getParameter("zip");
32
33        if (lastName.length() == 0 || firstName.length() == 0) {
34          out.println("Last Name and First Name are required");
35          return; // End the method
36        }
37
38        // Create a Student object
39        Student student = new Student(lastName, firstName,
40          mi, telephone, email, street, city, state, zip);
41
42        // Get an HttpSession or create one if it does not exist
43        HttpSession httpSession = request.getSession();
44
45        // Store student object to the session
46        httpSession.setAttribute("student", student);
47
48        // Ask for confirmation
49        out.println("You entered the following data");
50        out.println("<p>Last name: " + lastName);
51        out.println("<p>First name: " + firstName);
52        out.println("<p>MI: " + mi);
53        out.println("<p>Telephone: " + telephone);
54        out.println("<p>Email: " + email);
55        out.println("<p>Address: " + street);
56        out.println("<p>City: " + city);
57        out.println("<p>State: " + state);
58        out.println("<p>Zip: " + zip);
59
60        // Set the action for processing the answers
61        out.println("<p><form method=\"post\" action=" +
62          "/liangweb/RegistrationWithHttpSession>");
63        out.println("<p><input type=\"submit\" value=\"Confirm\" >");
64        out.println("</form>");
65
66        out.close(); // Close stream
67      }
68
69      /** Process the HTTP Post request */
70      public void doPost(HttpServletRequest request, HttpServletResponse
71          response) throws ServletException, IOException {
72        // Set response type and output stream to the browser
73        response.setContentType("text/html");
74        PrintWriter out = response.getWriter();
75
76        // Obtain the HttpSession
77        HttpSession httpSession = request.getSession();
78
79        // Get the Student object in the HttpSession
80        Student student = (Student)(httpSession.getAttribute("student"));
81
82        try {
83          storeStudent(student);
84
85          out.println(student.firstName + " " + student.lastName +
86            " is now registered in the database");
87          out.close(); // Close stream
88        }
89        catch(Exception ex) {
```

Margin notes:
create student (line 39)
create session (line 43)
set attribute (line 46)
process **POST** (line 70)
get session (line 77)
get student (line 80)
store student (line 83)

```
 90        out.println("Error: " + ex.getMessage());
 91        return; // End the method
 92      }
 93    }
 94
 95    /** Initialize database connection */
 96    private void initializeJdbc() {
 97      try {
 98        // Declare driver and connection string
 99        String driver = "sun.jdbc.odbc.JdbcOdbcDriver";
100        String connectionString = "jdbc:odbc:exampleMDBDataSource";
101
102        // Load the Oracle JDBC Thin driver
103        Class.forName(driver);
104        System.out.println("Driver " + driver + " loaded");
105
106        // Connect to the sample database
107        Connection conn = DriverManager.getConnection
108          (connectionString);
109        System.out.println("Database " + connectionString +
110          " connected");
111
112        // Create a Statement
113        pstmt = conn.prepareStatement("insert into Address " +
114          "(lastName, firstName, mi, telephone, email, street, city, "
115          + "state, zip) values (?, ?, ?, ?, ?, ?, ?, ?, ?)");
116      }
117      catch (Exception ex) {
118        System.out.println(ex);
119      }
120    }
121
122    /** Store a student record to the database */
123    private void storeStudent(Student student) throws SQLException {
124      pstmt.setString(1, student.getLastName());
125      pstmt.setString(2, student.getFirstName());
126      pstmt.setString(3, student.getMi());
127      pstmt.setString(4, student.getTelephone());
128      pstmt.setString(5, student.getEmail());
129      pstmt.setString(6, student.getStreet());
130      pstmt.setString(7, student.getCity());
131      pstmt.setString(8, student.getState());
132      pstmt.setString(9, student.getZip());
133      pstmt.executeUpdate();
134    }
135
136    class Student {                                            inner class
137      private String lastName = "";
138      private String firstName = "";
139      private String mi = "";
140      private String telephone = "";
141      private String email = "";
142      private String street = "";
143      private String city = "";
144      private String state = "";
145      private String zip = "";
146
147      Student(String lastName, String firstName,
148        String mi, String telephone, String email, String street,
149        String city, String state, String zip) {
150        this.lastName = lastName;
```

```
151        this.firstName = firstName;
152        this.mi = mi;
153        this.telephone = telephone;
154        this.email = email;
155        this.street = street;
156        this.city = city;
157        this.state = state;
158        this.zip = zip;
159     }
160
161     public String getLastName() {
162        return lastName;
163     }
164
165     public String getFirstName() {
166        return firstName;
167     }
168
169     public String getMi() {
170        return mi;
171     }
172
173     public String getTelephone() {
174        return telephone;
175     }
176
177     public String getEmail() {
178        return email;
179     }
180
181     public String getStreet() {
182        return street;
183     }
184
185     public String getCity() {
186        return city;
187     }
188
189     public String getState() {
190        return state;
191     }
192
193     public String getZip() {
194        return zip;
195     }
196   }
197 }
```

The statement (line 43)

```
HttpSession httpSession = request.getSession();
```

obtains a session, or creates a new session if the session does not exist.

Since objects can be stored in **HttpSession**, this program defines a **Student** class. A **Student** object is created and is stored in the session using the **setAttribute** method, which binds the object with a name like the one shown below (line 46):

```
httpSession.setAttribute("student", student);
```

To retrieve the object, use the following statement (line 80):

```
Student student = (Student)(httpSession.getAttribute("student"));
```

There is only one session between a client and a servlet. You can store any number of objects in a session. By default, a session stays alive as long as the servlet is not destroyed. You can explicitly set the session active time using the `setMaxInactiveInterval` method.

34.9 Sending Images from Servlets

So far you have learned how to write Java servlets that generate dynamic HTML text. Java servlets are not limited to sending text to a browser. They can return images on demand. The images can be stored in files or created from programs.

34.9.1 Sending Image from Files

You can use the HTML `<img>` tag to send images from files. The syntax for the tag is:

```
<img src = URL alt = text align = [top | middle | bottom | texttop]>
```

The attribute `src` specifies the source of the image. The attribute `alt` specifies an alternative text to be displayed in case the image cannot be displayed on the browser. The attribute `align` tells the browser where to place the image.

To demonstrate getting images from a file in a servlet, let us create a servlet that dynamically generates the flag of a country and a text that describes the flag, as shown in Figure 34.21. The flag is stored in an image file, and the text that describes the flag is stored in a text file.

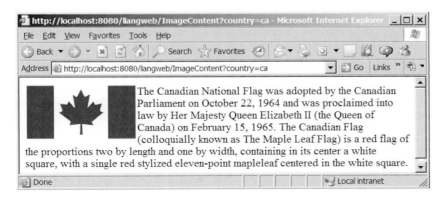

FIGURE 34.21   The servlet returns an image along with the text.

Create the servlet named `ImageContent` in Listing 34.12. Compile it into `c:\jakarta-tomcat-5.5.9\webapps\liangweb\WEB-INF\classes`. Run the servlet using the URL

```
http://localhost:8080/liangweb/ImageContent?country=ca
```

LISTING 34.12   ImageContent.java

```
1 import javax.servlet.*;
2 import javax.servlet.http.*;
3 import java.io.*;
4
5 public class ImageContent extends HttpServlet {
```

```
 6   /** Process the HTTP Get request */
 7   public void doGet(HttpServletRequest request, HttpServletResponse
 8       response) throws ServletException, IOException {
 9     response.setContentType("text/html");
10     PrintWriter out = response.getWriter();
11
12     String country = request.getParameter("country");
13
14     out.println("<img src = \"/liangweb/images/" + country + ".gif"
15       + "\" align=left>");
16
17     // Read description from a file and send it to the browser
18     java.util.Scanner in = new java.util.Scanner(
19             new File("c:\\book\\" + country + ".txt"));
20
21     // Text line from the text file for flag description
22     String line;
23
24     // Read a line from the text file and send it to the browser
25     while (in.hasNext()) {
26       out.println(in.nextLine());
27     }
28
29     out.close();
30   }
31 }
```

image tag is referenced at lines 14–15.

read file is referenced at lines 18–19.

You should store the image files in `c:\jakarta-tomcat-5.5.9\webapps\liangweb\`
`images`.

The `country` parameter determines which image file and text file are displayed. The servlet sends the HTML contents to the browser. The contents contain an `<img>` tag (lines 14–15) that references to the image file.

The servlet reads the characters from the text file and sends them to the browser (lines 18–27).

34.9.2   Sending Images from the `Image` Object

The preceding example displays an image stored in an image file. You can also send an image dynamically created in the program.

Before the image is sent to a browser, it must be encoded into a format acceptable to the browser. Image encoders are not part of Java API, but several free encoders are available. One of them is the `GifEncoder` class (http://www.acme.com/java/software/Acme.JPM.Encoders.GifEncoder.html), which is included in `\book\acme.jar`. Use the following statement to encode and send the image to the browser:

```
new GifEncoder(image, out, true).encode();
```

where `out` is a binary output stream from the servlet to the browser, which can be obtained using the following statement:

```
OutputStream out = response.getOutputStream();
```

To demonstrate dynamically generating images from a servlet, let us create a servlet that displays a clock to show the current time, as shown in Figure 34.22.

acme.jar

Create the servlet named `ImageContentWithDrawing` in Listing 34.13. Place `acme.jar` in `c:\jarkata-tomcat-5.5.9\common\lib` directory to ensure that `GifEncoder` and its supporting classes are available at runtime for the server. You also need to add `acme.jar` to the classpath to be able to compile the servlet. Compile `ImageContentWithDrawing` into `c:\jakarta-tomcat-5.5.9\webapps\liangweb\WEB-INF\classes`. Run the servlet using the URL

```
http://localhost:8080/liangweb/ImageContentWithDrawing
```

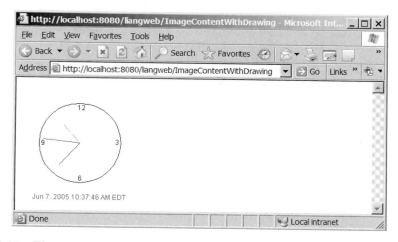

FIGURE 34.22   The servlet returns a clock that displays the current time.

LISTING 34.13   ImageContentWithDrawing.java

```java
 1 import javax.servlet.*;
 2 import javax.servlet.http.*;
 3 import java.io.*;
 4 import java.util.*;
 5 import java.text.*;
 6 import java.awt.*;
 7 import java.awt.image.BufferedImage;
 8 import Acme.JPM.Encoders.GifEncoder;                              import GifEncoder
 9
10 public class ImageContentWithDrawing extends HttpServlet {
11   /** Initialize variables */
12   private final static int width = 300;
13   private final static int height = 300;
14
15   /** Process the HTTP Get request */
16   public void doGet(HttpServletRequest request, HttpServletResponse    process GET
17     response) throws ServletException, IOException {
18     response.setContentType("image/gif");                          gif type
19     OutputStream out = response.getOutputStream();
20
21     // Create image
22     Image image = new BufferedImage(width, height,                 image
23       BufferedImage.TYPE_INT_ARGB);
24
25     // Get Graphics context of the image
26     Graphics g = image.getGraphics();                              graphics
27
28     drawClock(g); // Draw a clock on graphics                      draw graphics
29
30     // Encode the image and send to the output stream
31     new GifEncoder(image, out, true).encode();
32
33     out.close(); // Close stream                                   close stream
34   }
35
36   private void drawClock(Graphics g) {                            draw clock
37     // Initialize clock parameters
38     int clockRadius =
39       (int)(Math.min(width, height) * 0.7 * 0.5);
40     int xCenter = (width) / 2;
```

```
41      int yCenter = (height) / 2;
42
43      // Draw circle
44      g.setColor(Color.black);
45      g.drawOval(xCenter - clockRadius, yCenter - clockRadius,
46        2 * clockRadius, 2 * clockRadius);
47      g.drawString("12", xCenter - 5, yCenter - clockRadius + 12);
48      g.drawString("9", xCenter - clockRadius + 3, yCenter + 5);
49      g.drawString("3", xCenter + clockRadius - 10, yCenter + 3);
50      g.drawString("6", xCenter - 3, yCenter + clockRadius - 3);
51
52      // Get current time using GregorianCalendar
53      TimeZone timeZone = TimeZone.getDefault();
54      GregorianCalendar cal = new GregorianCalendar(timeZone);
55
56      // Draw second hand
57      int second = (int)cal.get(GregorianCalendar.SECOND);
58      int sLength = (int)(clockRadius * 0.9);
59      int xSecond = (int)(xCenter + sLength * Math.sin(second *
60        (2 * Math.PI / 60)));
61      int ySecond = (int)(yCenter - sLength * Math.cos(second *
62        (2 * Math.PI / 60)));
63      g.setColor(Color.red);
64      g.drawLine(xCenter, yCenter, xSecond, ySecond);
65
66      // Draw minute hand
67      int minute = (int)cal.get(GregorianCalendar.MINUTE);
68      int mLength = (int)(clockRadius * 0.75);
69      int xMinute = (int)(xCenter + mLength * Math.sin(minute *
70        (2 * Math.PI / 60)));
71      int yMinute = (int)(yCenter - mLength * Math.cos(minute *
72        (2 * Math.PI / 60)));
73      g.setColor(Color.blue);
74      g.drawLine(xCenter, yCenter, xMinute, yMinute);
75
76      // Draw hour hand
77      int hour = (int)cal.get(GregorianCalendar.HOUR_OF_DAY);
78      int hLength = (int)(clockRadius * 0.6);
79      int xHour = (int)(xCenter + hLength * Math.sin((hour + minute
80        / 60.0) * (2 * Math.PI / 12)));
81      int yHour = (int)(yCenter - hLength * Math.cos((hour + minute
82        / 60.0) * (2 * Math.PI / 12)));
83      g.setColor(Color.green);
84      g.drawLine(xCenter, yCenter, xHour, yHour);
85
86      // Set display format in specified style, locale and timezone
87      DateFormat formatter = DateFormat.getDateTimeInstance
88        (DateFormat.MEDIUM, DateFormat.LONG);
89
90      // Display current date
91      g.setColor(Color.red);
92      String today = formatter.format(cal.getTime());
93      FontMetrics fm = g.getFontMetrics();
94      g.drawString(today, (width -
95        fm.stringWidth(today)) / 2, yCenter + clockRadius + 30);
96    }
97 }
```

Since the image is sent to the browser as binary data, the content type of the response is set to image/gif (line 18). The **GifEncoder** class is used to encode the image into content understood by the browser (line 31). The content is sent to the **OutputStream** object **out**.

The program creates an image with the specified width, height, and image type, using the `BufferedImage` class (lines 22–23):

```
Image image = new BufferedImage(width, height,
    BufferedImage.TYPE_INT_ARGB);
```

To draw things on the image, you need to get its graphics context using the `getGraphics` method (line 26):

```
Graphics g = image.getGraphics();
```

You can use various drawing methods in the `Graphics` class to draw simple shapes, or you can use Java 2D to draw more sophisticated graphics. This example uses simple drawing methods to draw a clock that displays the current time.

34.9.3   Sending Images and Text Together

The servlets in the preceding example return images. Often images are mixed with other contents. In this case, you have to set the content type to "image/gif" before sending images, and set the content type to "text/html" before sending the text. However, the content type cannot be changed in one request. To circumvent this restriction, you may embed a GET request for displaying the image in an `<img>` tag in the HTML content. When the HTML content is displayed, a separate GET request for retrieving the image is then sent to the server. Thus text and image are obtained through two separate GET requests.

To demonstrate mixing images and texts, let us create a servlet that mixes the clock image created in the preceding example with some text, as shown in Figure 34.23.

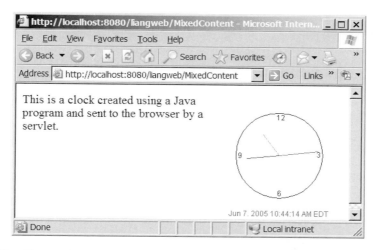

FIGURE 34.23   The servlet returns an image along with the text.

Create the servlet named `MixedContent` in Listing 34.14 and compile it into `c:\jakarta-tomcat-5.5.9\webapps\liangweb\WEB-INF\classes`. Run the servlet using the URL

```
http://localhost:8080/liangweb/MixedContent
```

LISTING 34.14   MixedContent.java

```
1 import javax.servlet.*;
2 import javax.servlet.http.*;
3 import java.io.*;
4
5 public class MixedContent extends HttpServlet {
```

process **GET**

content type

get parameter

image tag

close stream

```
 6   /** Process the HTTP Get request */
 7   public void doGet(HttpServletRequest request, HttpServletResponse
 8       response) throws ServletException, IOException {
 9     response.setContentType("text/html");
10     PrintWriter out = response.getWriter();
11
12     String country = request.getParameter("country");
13
14     out.println("<img src = \"/liangweb/" +
15       "ImageContentWithDrawing\" align=right>");
16
17     out.println("This is a clock created using a Java program " +
18       "and sent to the browser by a servlet.");
19
20     out.close();
21   }
22 }
```

The servlet generates an HTML file with the image tag

```
<img src = "/liangweb/ImageContentWithDrawing" align = "right">
```

The HTML file is rendered by the browser. When the browser sees the image tag, it sends the request to the server. `ImageContentWithDrawing`, created in Listing 34.13, is invoked to send the image to the browser.

KEY TERMS

CGI programs 1160	life-cycle methods 1165
Common Gateway Interface 1158	URL query string 1159
Cookie 1185	servlet 1158
GET and POST methods 1159	servlet container (servlet engine) 1160
HTML form 1170	Tomcat 1160

CHAPTER SUMMARY

■ A servlet is a special kind of program that runs from a Web server that supports servlets. Tomcat is a Web server that can run servlets. You start Tomcat using the **startup** command and stop Tomcat using the **shutdown** command from the Tomcat bin directory.

■ A servlet URL is specified by the hostname, port, and request string (e.g., http://localhost:8080/liangweb/ServletClass). There are several ways to invoke a servlet: (1) by typing a servlet URL from a Web browser, (2) by placing a hyper reference link in an HTML page, and (3) by embedding a servlet URL in an HTML form. All the requests trigger the GET method except that you explicitly specify the POST method in the HTML form.

■ You develop a servlet by defining a class that extends the `HttpServlet` class, implements the `doGet(HttpServletRequest, HttpServletResponse)` method to respond to the GET method, and implements the `doPost(HttpServletRequest, HttpServletResponse)` method to respond to the POST method.

■ The request information passed from a client to the servlet is contained in an object of `HttpServletRequest`. You can use the methods `getParameter`, `getParameterValues`, `getRemoteAddr`, `getRemoteHost`, `getHeader`, `getQueryString`, `getCookies`, and `getSession` to obtain the information from the request.

■ The content sent back to the client is contained in an object of `HttpServletResponse`. To send content to the client, first set the type of the content (e.g., html/plain) using the `setContentType(contentType)` method, then output the content through an I/O stream on the `HttpServletResponse` object. You can obtain a character `PrintWriter` stream using the `getWriter()` method and obtain a binary `OutputStream` using the `getOutputStream()` method.

■ `HttpServletResponse` extends the `ServletResponse` interface to provide HTTP-specific functionality in sending a response. You can use the `getWriter` method to get an instance of `PrintWriter` to send a response to the client and the `setContentType` method to set the type of the content, such as html.

■ There are three ways to track a session. You can track a session by passing data from the servlet to the client as a hidden value in a dynamically generated HTML form by including a field such as `<input type="hidden" name="lastName" value="Smith">`. The next request will submit the data back to the servlet. The servlet retrieves this hidden value just like any other parameter value using the `getParameter` method.

■ You can track sessions using cookies. A cookie is created using the constructor `new Cookie(String name, String value)`. Cookies are sent from the server through the object of `HttpServletResponse` using the `addCookie(aCookie)` method to tell the browser to add a cookie with a given name and its associated value. If the browser already has a cookie with the key name, the value will be updated. The browser will then send the cookie with any request submitted to the same server. Cookies can have expiration dates set, after which they will not be sent to the server.

■ Java servlet API provides a session-tracking tool that enables tracking of a large set of data. A session can be obtained using the `getSession()` method through an `HttpServletRequest` object. The data can be stored as objects and are secure because they are kept on the server side using the `setAttribute(String name, Object value)` method.

■ Java servlets are not limited to sending text to a browser. They can return images in GIF, JPEG, or PNG format.

REVIEW QUESTIONS

Sections 34.1–34.2

34.1 What is the common gateway interface?

34.2 What are the differences between the GET and POST methods in an HTML form?

34.3 Can you submit a GET request directly from a URL? Can you submit a POST request directly from a URL?

34.4 What is wrong in the following URL for submitting a GET request to the servlet FindScore on host liang at port 8080 with parameter `name`?

`http://liang:8080/FindScore?name="P Yates"`

34.5 What are the differences between CGI and servlets?

Section 34.3 Creating and Running Servlets

34.6 Can you display an HTML file (e.g., `c:\test.html`) by typing the complete file name in the Address field of Internet Explorer? Can you run a servlet by simply typing the servlet class file name?

34.7 Before you start Tomcat, what value should be set to the environment variable `JAVA_HOME`?

34.8 How do you start Tomcat? How do you stop Tomcat?

34.9 How do you test whether Tomcat is running?

34.10 To compile a servlet program, what library file has to be included in the classpath?

34.11 When you run Tomcat, which port does it use? What happens if the port is already in use?

Section 34.4 The Servlet API

34.12 Describe the life cycle of a servlet.

34.13 Suppose that you started Tomcat, ran the following servlet twice by issuing an appropriate URL from a Web browser, and finally stopped Tomcat. What was displayed on the console when the servlet was first invoked? What was displayed on the console when the servlet was invoked for the second time? What was displayed on the console when Tomcat was shut down?

```java
import javax.servlet.*;
import javax.servlet.http.*;
import java.io.*;

public class Test extends HttpServlet {
  public Test() {
    System.out.println("Constructor called");
  }

  /** Initialize variables */
  public void init() throws ServletException {
    System.out.println("init called");
  }

  /** Process the HTTP Get request */
  public void doGet(HttpServletRequest request,
      HttpServletResponse
      response) throws ServletException, IOException {
    System.out.println("doGet called");
  }

  /** Clean up resources */
  public void destroy() {
    System.out.println("destroy called");
  }
}
```

Sections 34.5–34.7

34.14 What would be displayed if you changed the content type to `"html/plain"` in Listing 34.2, CurrentTime.java?

34.15 The statement `out.close()` is used to close the output stream to response. Why isn't this statement enclosed in a `try-catch` block?

34.16 What happens when you invoke `request.getParameter(paramName)` if `paramName` does not exist?

34.17 How do you write a text field, combo box, check box, and text area in an HTML form?

34.18 How do you retrieve the parameter values for a text field, combo box, list, check box, radio button, and text area from an HTML form?

34.19 If the servlet uses a database driver other than the JDBC-ODBC driver, where should the driver be placed?

Section 34.8 Session Tracking

34.20 What is session tracking? What are three techniques for session tracking?

34.21 How do you create a cookie, send a cookie to a browser, get cookies from a browser, get the name of a cookie, set a new value in the cookie, and set cookie expiration time?

34.22 How do you get a session, set object value for the session, and get object value from the session?

Section 34.9 Sending Images from Servlets

34.23 What output stream should you use to send images to the browser? What content type do you have to set for the response?

34.24 How do you deal with dynamic contents with images and text?

PROGRAMMING EXERCISES

Section 34.5 Creating Servlets

34.1* (*Factorial table*) Write a servlet to display a table that contains factorials for the numbers from 0 to 10, as shown in Figure 34.24.

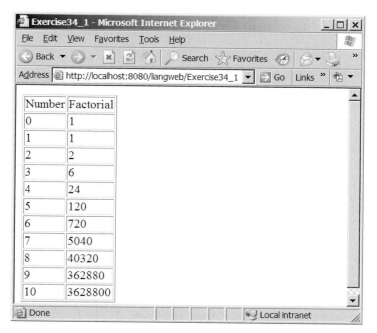

FIGURE 34.24 The servlet displays factorials for the numbers from 0 to 10 in a table.

34.2* (*Multiplication table*) Write a servlet to display a multiplication table, as shown in Figure 34.25.

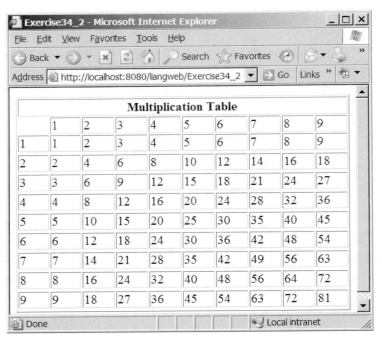

FIGURE 34.25   The servlet displays the multiplication table.

34.3*   (*Visit count*) Develop a servlet that displays the number of visits on the servlet. Also display the client's host name and IP address, as shown in Figure 34.26.

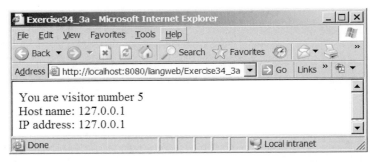

FIGURE 34.26   The servlet displays the number of visits and the client's host name, IP address, and request URL.

Implement this program in three different ways:

1. Use an instance variable to store `count`. When the servlet is created for the first time, `count` is 0. `count` is incremented every time the servlet's `doGet` method is invoked. When the Web server stops, `count` is lost.

2. Store the count in a file named Exercise34_3.dat, and use `RandomAccessFile` to read the count in the servlet's `init` method. The count is incremented every time the servlet's `doGet` method is invoked. When the Web server stops, store the count back to the file.

3. Instead of counting total visits from all clients, count the visits by each client identified by the client's IP address. Use `Map` to store a pair of IP addresses and visit counts. For the first visit, an entry is created in the map. For subsequent visits, the visit count is updated.

Section 34.6 HTML Forms

34.4* (*Calculating tax*) Write an HTML form to prompt the user to enter taxable income and filing status, as shown in Figure 34.27(a). Clicking the *Compute Tax* button invokes a servlet to compute and display the tax, as shown in Figure 34.27(b). Use the `computeTax` method in the `ComputeTax` class introduced in Listing 6.11, ComputingTax.java, to compute personal income tax for year 2002.

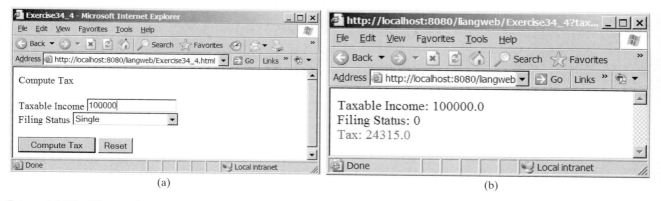

(a)   (b)

FIGURE 34.27   The servlet computes the tax.

34.5* (*Calculating loan*) Write an HTML form that prompts the user to enter loan amount, interest rate, and number of years, as shown in Figure 34.28(a). Clicking the *Compute Loan Payment* button invokes a servlet to compute and display the monthly and total loan payments, as shown in Figure 34.28(b). Use the **Loan** class introduced in §7.15, "Case Study: The **Loan** Class," to compute the monthly and total payments.

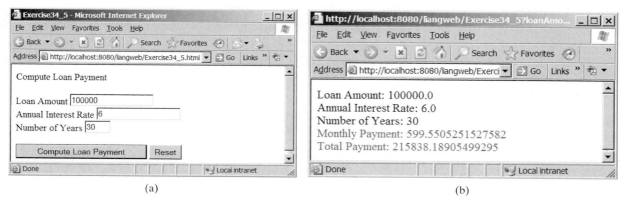

(a)   (b)

FIGURE 34.28   The servlet computes the loan payment.

34.6** (*Finding scores from text files*) Write a servlet that displays the student name and the current score, given the SSN and class ID. For each class, a text file is used to store the student name, SSN, and current score. The file is named after the class ID with the .txt extension. For instance, if the class ID were csci1301, the file name would be `csci1301.txt`. Suppose each line consists of student name, SSN, and score. These three items are separated by the # sign. Create an HTML form that enables the user to enter the SSN and class ID, as shown in Figure 34.29(a). Upon clicking the *Submit* button, the result is displayed, as shown in Figure 34.29(b). If the SSN or the class ID does not match, report an error. Assume there are three courses available: CSCI1301, CSCI1302, and CSCI3720.

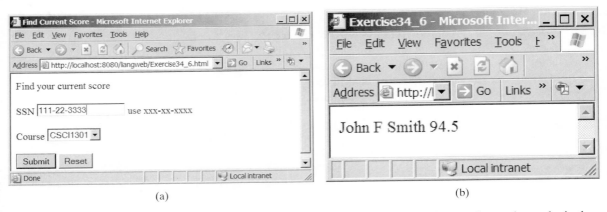

(a)   (b)

FIGURE 34.29 The HTML form accepts the SSN and class ID from the user and sends them to the servlet to obtain the score.

Section 34.7 Database Programming in Servlets

34.7** (*Finding scores from database tables*) Rewrite the preceding servlet. Assume that for each class, a table is used to store the student name, ssn, and score. The table name is the same as the class ID. For instance, if the class ID were csci1301, the table name would be csci1301.

34.8* (*Changing the password*) Write a servlet that enables the user to change the password from an HTML form, as shown in Figure 34.30(a). Suppose that the user information is stored in a database table named Account with three columns, username, password, and name, where name is the real name of the user. The servlet performs the following tasks:

  a. Verify that the username and old password are in the table. If not, report the error and redisplay the HTML form.

  b. Verify that the new password and the confirmed password are the same. If not, report this error and redisplay the HTML form.

  c. If the user information is entered correctly, update the password and report the status of the update to the user, as shown in Figure 34.30(b).

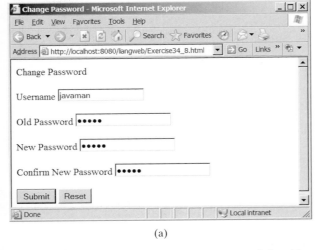
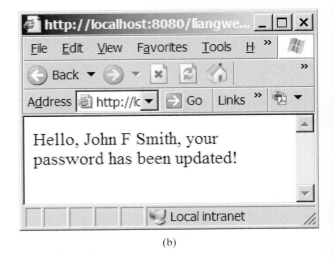

(a)   (b)

FIGURE 34.30 The user enters the username and the old password and sets a new password. The servlet reports the status of the update to the user.

34.9** *(Displaying database tables)* Write an HTML form that prompts the user to enter or select a JDBC driver, database URL, username, password, and table name, as shown in Figure 34.31(a). Clicking the *Submit* button displays the table content, as shown in Figure 34.31(b).

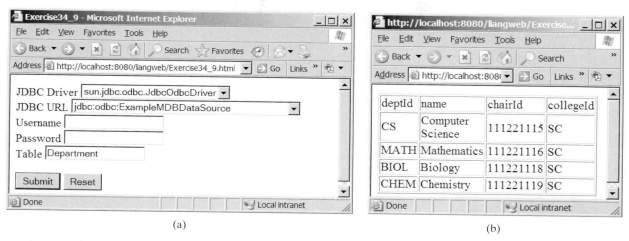

(a)   (b)

FIGURE 34.31 The user enters database information and specifies a table to display its content.

Section 34.8 Session Tracking

34.10* *(Storing cookies)* Write a servlet that stores the following cookies in a browser, and set their max age for two days:

> Cookie 1: name is "color" and value is red.
>
> Cookie 2: name is "radius" and value is 5.5.
>
> Cookie 3: name is "count" and value is 2.

34.11* *(Retrieving cookies)* Write a servlet that displays all the cookies on the client. The client types the URL of the servlet from the browser to display all the cookies stored on the browser. See Figure 34.32.

FIGURE 34.32 All the cookies on the client are displayed in the browser.

Comprehensive

34.12** *(Syntax highlighting)* Create an HTML form that prompts the user to enter a Java program in a text area, as shown in Figure 34.33(a). The form invokes a servlet that displays the Java source code in a syntax-highlighted HTML format, as shown in Figure 34.33(b). The keywords, comments, and literals are displayed in bold navy, green, and blue, respectively.

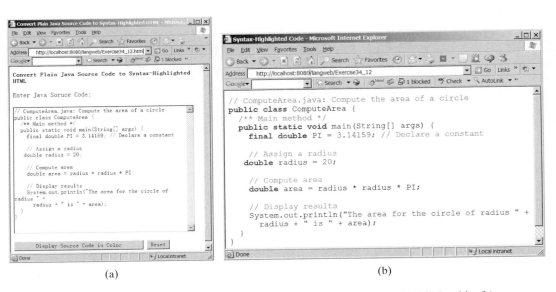

(a)   (b)

FIGURE 34.33 The Java code in plain text in (a) is displayed in HTML with syntax highlighted in (b).

34.13***(*Opinion poll*) Create an HTML form that prompts the user to answer the question "Do you support the Iraq war?", as shown in Figure 34.34(a). Upon clicking the *Submit* button, the servlet increases the Yes or No count in a database and displays the current Yes and No counts, as shown in Figure 34.34(b).

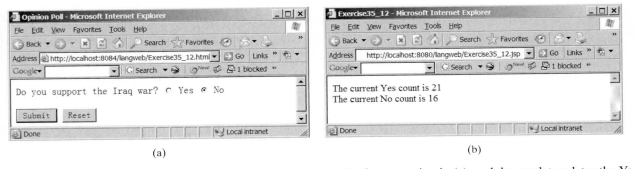

(a)   (b)

FIGURE 34.34 The HTML form prompts the user to enter Yes or No for a question in (a), and the servlet updates the Yes or No counts in (b).

Create a table named **Poll**, as follows:

```
create table Poll (
    question varchar(40) primary key,
    yesCount int,
    noCount int);
```

Insert one row into the table, as follows:

```
insert into Poll values ('Do you support the Iraq war? ', 0, 0);
```

CHAPTER 35

JavaServer Pages

Objectives

- To know what JSP is (§35.2).
- To comprehend how a JSP page is processed (§35.3).
- To learn how to use JSP constructs (§35.4).
- To become familiar with JSP predefined variables and JSP directives (§§35.5–35.6).
- To use JavaBeans components in JSP (§35.7–35.9).
- To develop database applications using JSP (§35.7–35.9).
- To know how to forward requests from JSP (§35.10).

35.1 Introduction

Servlets can be used to generate dynamic Web content. One drawback, however, is that you have to embed HTML tags and text inside the Java source code. Using servlets, you have to modify the Java source code and recompile it if changes are made to the HTML text. If you have a lot of HTML script in a servlet, the program is difficult to read and maintain, since the HTML text is part of the Java program. JavaServer Pages (JSP) technology was introduced to remedy this drawback. JSP enables you to write regular HTML script in the normal way and embed Java code to produce dynamic content.

35.2 A Simple JSP Page

JSP provides an easy way to create dynamic Web pages and simplify the task of building Web applications. A JavaServer page is like a regular HTML page with special tags, known as *JSP tags*, which enable the Web server to generate dynamic content. You can create a Web page with HTML script and enclose the Java code for generating dynamic content in the JSP tags. Here is an example of a simple JSP page.

JSP tag

```
<!-- CurrentTime.jsp -->
<html>
  <head>
    <title>
      CurrentTime
    </title>
  </head>
  <body>
    Current time is <%= new java.util.Date() %>
  </body>
</html>
```

JSP tag

The dynamic content is enclosed in the tag that begins with `<%=` and ends with `%>`. The current time is returned as a string by invoking the `toString` method of an object of the `java.util.Date` class.

To display the JSP page, you need to create a text file for the page, name the file CurrentTime.jsp, and store the file in `c:\jakarta-tomcat-5.5.9\webapps\liangweb`. Assume you have started Tomcat. You can run it from a Web browser using the URL http://localhost:8080/liangweb/CurrentTime.jsp, as shown in Figure 35.1.

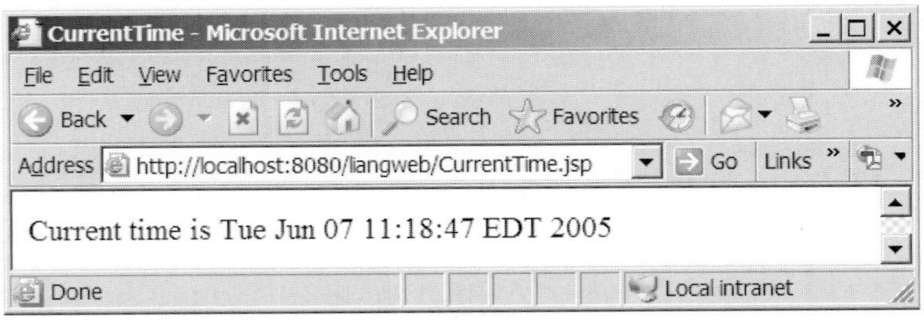

store JSP files

FIGURE 35.1 A JSP page is displayed in a Web browser.

Note

You created the context root directory *liangweb* under the Tomcat webapps directory in the preceding chapter. The easiest way to run JSP for new JSP programmers is to store all the JSP files in `c:\jakarta-tomcat-5.5.9\webapps\liangweb`. You can also place JSP files elsewhere. For more information, see Supplement VII.E, "*Tomcat Tutorial.*"

35.3 How Is a JSP Page Processed?

A JSP page must first be processed by a Web server before it can be displayed in a Web browser. The Web server must support JSP, and the JSP page must be stored in a file with a .jsp extension. The Web server translates the .jsp file into a Java servlet, compiles the servlet, and executes it. The result of the execution is sent to the browser for display. Figure 35.2 shows how a JSP page is processed by a Web server. CurrentTime.jsp in Figure 35.1 is translated into a servlet named CurrentTime_jsp.java in `c:\jakarta-tomcat-5.5.9\work\standalone\localhost\liangweb`. Viewing the file will help you to better understand that JSP is based on the servlet.

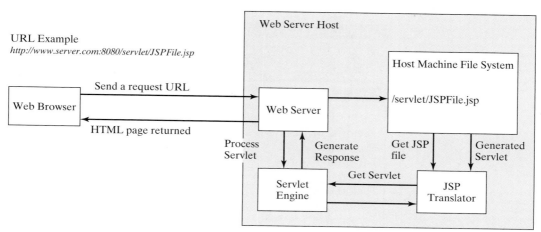

FIGURE 35.2   A JSP page is translated into a servlet.

 Note

A JSP page is translated into a servlet when the page is requested for the first time. It is not retranslated if the page is not modified. To ensure that the first-time real user does not get a delay, JSP developers may test the page after it is installed.

35.4 JSP Scripting Constructs

There are three main types of JSP constructs: scripting constructs, directives, and actions. *Scripting elements* enable you to specify Java code that will become part of the resultant servlet. *Directives* enable you to control the overall structure of the resultant servlet. *Actions* enable you to control the behavior of the JSP engine. This section introduces scripting constructs.

scripting element
directive
action

There are three types of JSP scripting constructs that can be used to insert Java code into a resultant servlet: expressions, scriptlets, and declarations.

A *JSP expression* is used to insert a Java expression directly into the output. It has the following form:

JSP expression

```
<%= Java expression %>
```

The expression is evaluated, converted into a string, and sent to the output stream of the servlet.

A *JSP scriptlet* enables you to insert a Java statement into the servlet's `jspService` method, which is invoked by the `service` method. A JSP scriptlet has the following form:

JSP scriptlet

```
<% Java statement %>
```

A *JSP declaration* is for declaring methods or fields into the servlet. It has the following form:

JSP declaration

```
<%! Java declaration %>
```

HTML comments have the following form:

```
<!-- HTML Comment -->
```

JSP comment

If you don't want the comment to appear in the resultant HTML file, use the following comment in JSP:

```
<%-- JSP Comment --%>
```

Listing 35.1 creates a JavaServer page that displays factorials for numbers from 0 to 10. The program is named Factorial.jsp and saved in `c:\jakarta-tomcat-5.5.9\webapps\liangweb`. You run it from the URL http://localhost:8080/liangweb/Factorial.jsp, as shown in Figure 35.3.

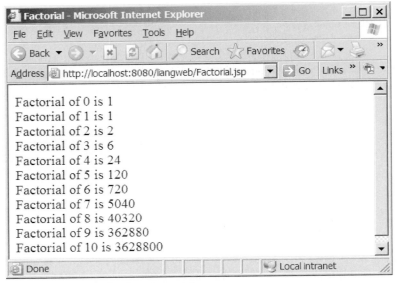

FIGURE 35.3 The JSP page displays factorials.

LISTING 35.1 Factorial.jsp

```
 1 <html>
 2   <head>
 3     <title>
 4       Factorial
 5     </title>
 6   </head>
 7   <body>
 8
 9   <% for (int i = 0; i <= 10; i++) { %>
10       Factorial of <%= i %> is
11         <%= computeFactorial(i) %> <br />
12   <% } %>
13
14   <%! private long computeFactorial(int n) {
15         if (n == 0)
16           return 1;
17         else
18           return n * computeFactorial(n - 1);
19     }
20   %>
21
22   </body>
23 </html>
```

JSP scriptlet
JSP expression

JSP declaration

JSP scriptlets are enclosed between <% and %>. Thus

```
for (int i = 0; i <= 10; i++) {,        (line 9)
```

is a scriptlet and as such is inserted directly into the servlet's `jspService` method.
JSP expressions are enclosed between <%= and %>. Thus

```
<%= i %>,    (line 10)
```

is an expression and is inserted into the output stream of the servlet.
JSP declarations are enclosed between <%! and %>. Thus

```
<%! private long computeFactorial(int n) {
      ...
    }
%>
```

is a declaration that defines methods or fields in the servlet.

What would be different if line 9 is replaced by the two alternatives shown below? Both work fine, but there is an important difference. In (a), `i` is a local variable in the servlet, whereas in (b) `i` is an instance variable when translated to the servlet.

```
<% int i = 0; %>
<% for ( ; i <= 10; i++) { %>
```

(a)

```
<%! int i; %>
<% for (i = 0; i <= 10; i++) { %>
```

(b)

Caution

For JSP, the loop body must be placed inside braces even though the body contains a single statement. It would be wrong to delete the opening brace ({) in line 9 and the closing brace (<% } %>) in line 12.

Caution

There is no semicolon at the end of a JSP expression. For example, <%= i; %> is incorrect. But there must be a semicolon for each Java statement in a JSP scriptlet. For example, <% int i = 0 %> is incorrect.

Caution

JSP and Java elements are case-sensitive, but HTML is not case-sensitive.

35.5 Predefined Variables

You can use variables in JSP. For convenience, JSP provides eight predefined variables from the servlet environment that can be used with JSP expressions and scriptlets. These variables are also known as *JSP implicit objects*.

JSP implicit object

- **request** represents the client's request, which is an instance of `HttpServlet-Request`. You can use it to access request parameters and HTTP headers, such as cookies and hostname.

  request

- **response** represents the servlet's response, which is an instance of `HttpServlet-Response`. You can use it to set response type and send output to the client.

  response

- **out** represents the character output stream, which is an instance of `PrintWriter` obtained from `response.getWriter()`. You can use it to send character content to the client.

  out

- **session** represents the `HttpSession` object associated with the request, obtained from `request.getSession()`.

  session

application

- **application** represents the ServletContext object for storing persistent data for all clients. The difference between session and application is that session is tied to one client, but application is for all clients to share persistent data.

config

- **config** represents the ServletConfig object for the page.

pageContext

- **pageContext** represents the PageContext object. PageContext is a new class introduced in JSP to give a central point of access to many page attributes.

page

- **page** is an alternative to this.

As an example, let us write an HTML page that prompts the user to enter loan amount, annual interest rate, and number of years, as shown in Figure 35.4(a). Clicking the *Compute Loan Payment* button invokes a JSP to compute and display the monthly and total loan payments, as shown in Figure 35.4(b).

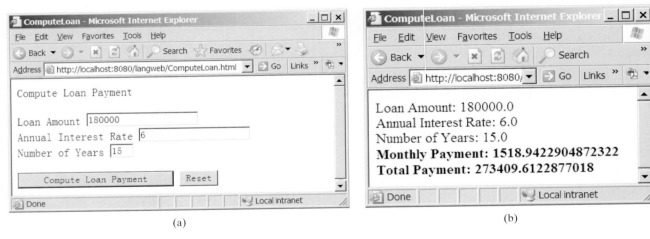

(a)   (b)

FIGURE 35.4 The JSP computes the loan payments.

The HTML file is named ComputeLoan.html (Listing 35.2). The JSP file is named ComputeLoan.jsp (Listing 35.3). Store both files in c:\jakarta-tomcat-5.5.9\ webapps\liangweb.

LISTING 35.2 ComputeLoan.html

```
1  <!-- ComputeLoan.html -->
2  <html>
3    <head>
4      <title>ComputeLoan</title>
5    </head>
6    <body>
7      <form method = "get" action = "/liangweb/ComputeLoan.jsp">
8      Compute Loan Payment<br />
9      Loan Amount
10     <input type = "text" name = "loanAmount" /><br />
11     Annual Interest Rate
12     <input type = "text" name = "annualInterestRate" /><br />
13     Number of Years
14     <input type = "text" name = "numberOfYears" size = "3" /><br />
15     <p><input type = "submit" name = "Submit"
16         value = "Compute Loan Payment" />
17     <input type = "reset" value = "Reset" /></p>
18     </form>
19   </body>
20 </html>
```

form action

text field

submit

LISTING 35.3   ComputeLoan.jsp

```
1  <!-- ComputeLoan.jsp -->
2  <html>
3    <head>
4      <title>ComputeLoan</title>
5    </head>
6    <body>
7  <% double loanAmount = Double.parseDouble(
8        request.getParameter("loanAmount"));
9      double annualInterestRate = Double.parseDouble(
10       request.getParameter("annualInterestRate"));
11     double numberOfYears = Integer.parseInt(
12       request.getParameter("numberOfYears"));
13     double monthlyInterestRate = annualInterestRate / 1200;
14     double monthlyPayment = loanAmount * monthlyInterestRate /
15       (1 - 1 / Math.pow(1 + monthlyInterestRate, numberOfYears * 12));
16     double totalPayment = monthlyPayment * numberOfYears * 12; %>
17   Loan Amount: <%= loanAmount %><br />
18   Annual Interest Rate: <%= annualInterestRate %><br />
19   Number of Years: <%= numberOfYears %><br />
20   <b>Monthly Payment: <%= monthlyPayment %><br />
21   Total Payment: <%= totalPayment %><br /></b>
22   </body>
23 </html>
```

JSP scriptlet
get parameters

JSP expression

ComputeLoan.html is displayed first to prompt the user to enter the loan amount, annual interest rate, and number of years. Since this file does not contain any JSP elements, it is named with an .html extension as a regular HTML file.

http://localhost:8080/liangweb/ComputeLoan.jsp is invoked upon clicking the *Compute Loan Payment* button in the HTML form. The JSP page obtains the parameter values using the predefined variable **request** in lines 7–12 and computes monthly payment and total payment in lines 13–16. The formula for computing monthly payment is given in §2.12.1, "Example: Computing Loan Payments."

What is wrong if the JSP scriptlet **<%** in line 7 is replaced by the JSP declaration **<%!**? The predefined variables (e.g., **request**, **response**, **out**) correspond to local variables defined in the servlet methods **doGet** and **doPost**. They must appear in JSP scriptlets, not in JSP declarations.

Tip

ComputeLoan.jsp can also be invoked using the following query string: http://localhost:8080/liangweb/ComputeLoan.jsp?loanAmount=10000&annualInterestRate=6&numberOfYears=15.

35.6 JSP Directives

A JSP directive is a statement that gives the JSP engine information about the JSP page. For example, if your JSP page uses a Java class from a package other than the `java.lang` package, you have to use a directive to import this package. The general syntax for a JSP directive is shown below:

```
<%@ directive attribute = "value" %>, or
<%@ directive attribute1 = "value1"
              attribute2 = "value2"
              ...
              attributen = "valuen" %>
```

The possible directives are:

- **page** lets you provide information for the page, such as importing classes and setting up content type. The page directive can appear anywhere in the JSP file.

- **include** lets you insert a file to the servlet when the page is translated to a servlet. The **include** directive must be placed where you want the file to be inserted.

- **tablib** lets you define custom tags.

The following are useful attributes for the **page** directive:

- **import** specifies one or more packages to be imported for this page. For example, the directive `<%@ page import="java.util.*, java.text.*" %>` imports `java.util.*` and `java.text.*`.

- **contentType** specifies the content type for the resultant JSP page. By default, the content type is `text/html` for JSP. The default content type for servlets is `text/plain`.

- **session** specifies a `boolean` value to indicate whether the page is part of the session. By default, `session` is `true`.

- **buffer** specifies the output stream buffer size. By default, it is 8KB. For example, the directive `<%@ page buffer="10KB" %>` specifies that the output buffer size is 10KB. The directive `<%@ page buffer="none" %>` specifies that a buffer is not used.

- **autoFlush** specifies a `boolean` value to indicate whether the output buffer should be automatically flushed when it is full or whether an exception should be raised when the buffer overflows. By default, this attribute is `true`. In this case, the buffer attribute cannot be `none`.

- **isThreadSafe** specifies a `boolean` value to indicate whether the page can be accessed simultaneously without data corruption. By default, it is `true`. If it is set to `false`, the JSP page will be translated to a servlet that implements the `SingleThreadModel` interface.

- **errorPage** specifies a JSP page that is processed when an exception occurs in the current page. For example, the directive `<%@ page errorPage="HandleError.jsp" %>` specifies that HandleError.jsp is processed when an exception occurs.

- **isErrorPage** specifies a `boolean` value to indicate whether the page can be used as an error page. By default, this attribute is `false`.

35.6.1 Example: Importing Classes

This example shows how to use the page directive to import a class. The example uses the Loan class created in §7.15, "Case Study: The Loan Class," to simplify Listing 35.3, ComputeLoan.jsp. You can create an object of the Loan class and use its `getMonthlyPayment()` and `getTotalPayment()` methods to compute the monthly payment and total payment. The new ComputeLoan.jsp is shown in Listing 35.4.

LISTING 35.4 ComputeLoan1.jsp

```
1 <!-- ComputeLoan1.jsp -->
2 <html>
3   <head>
4     <title>ComputeLoan Using the Loan Class</title>
5   </head>
```

```
 6   <body>
 7     <%@ page import = "chapter35.Loan" %>                          JSP directive
 8     <% double loanAmount = Double.parseDouble(
 9         request.getParameter("loanAmount"));
10       double annualInterestRate = Double.parseDouble(
11         request.getParameter("annualInterestRate"));
12       int numberOfYears = Integer.parseInt(
13         request.getParameter("numberOfYears"));
14       Loan loan =
15         new Loan(annualInterestRate, numberOfYears, loanAmount);     create object
16     %>
17     Loan Amount: <%= loanAmount %><br />
18     Annual Interest Rate: <%= annualInterestRate %><br />
19     Number of Years: <%= numberOfYears %><br />
20     <b>Monthly Payment: <%= loan.getMonthlyPayment() %><br />
21     Total Payment: <%= loan.getTotalPayment() %><br /></b>
22   </body>
23 </html>
```

To import a class, the class must be placed in a package explicitly. Create a new **Loan** class in package chapter35 as follows:

```
package chapter35;

public class Loan {
  // Same as Listing 7.9, Loan.java, so omitted
}
```

Compile it into `c:\jakarta-tomcat-5.5.9\webapps\liangweb\WEB-INF\classes\chapter35`.

Tip
The destination directory for Loan.class is `c:\jakarta-tomcat-5.5.9\webapps\liangweb\WEB-INF\classes`. You may create a subdirectory named chapter35 under the destination directory and then move Loan.class into it. As an alternative, you can use the following command to compile and save the .class directly into the destination directory:

```
javac -d chapter35 Loan.java
```

This command automatically creates the subdirectory chapter35, since it is in the package statement of the **Loan** class.

The directive `<%@ page import ="chapter35.Loan" %>` imports the **Loan** class in line 7. Line 14 creates an object of **Loan** for the given loan amount, annual interest rate, and number of years. Lines 20–21 invokes the **Loan** object's **getMonthlyPayment()** and **getTotalPayment()** methods to display monthly payment and total payment.

35.6.2   Example: Using Error Pages

This example prompts the user to enter an integer (see Figure 35.5(a)) and displays the factorial for the integer (see Figure 35.5(b)). If a noninteger value is entered by mistake, an error page is displayed, as shown in Figure 35.5(c).

Create three files named FactorialInput.html (Listing 35.5), ComputeFactorial.jsp (Listing 35.6), FactorialInputError.jsp (Listing 35.7), and save the files into `c:\jakarta-tomcat-5.5.9\webapps\liangweb`. Display FactorialInput.html first, as shown in Figure 35.5(a).

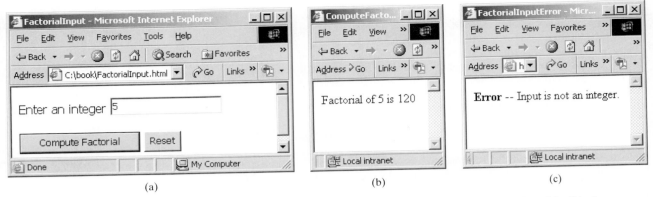

FIGURE 35.5 You enter an integer to obtain its factorial in (a). The factorial of the integer is displayed in (b). An error page is displayed in (c) when an exception occurs.

LISTING 35.5 FactorialInput.html

```
1  <!-- FactorialInput.html -->
2  <html>
3    <head>
4      <title>
5        FactorialInput
6      </title>
7    </head>
8    <body>
9      <form method = "post" action = "/liangweb/ComputeFactorial.jsp">
10       Enter an integer <input name = "number" /><br /><br />
11       <input type = "submit" name = "Submit"
12         value = "Compute Factorial" />
13       <input type = "reset" value = "Reset" />
14     </form>
15   </body>
16 </html>
```

form action — line 9

LISTING 35.6 ComputeFactorial.jsp

```
1  <!-- ComputeFactorial.jsp -->
2  <html>
3    <head>
4      <title>
5        ComputeFactorial
6      </title>
7    </head>
8    <body>
9      <%@ page import = "java.text.*" %>
10     <%@ page errorPage = "FactorialInputError.jsp" %>
11
12     <% NumberFormat format = NumberFormat.getNumberInstance();
13       int number =
14         Integer.parseInt(request.getParameter("number")); %>
15       Factorial of <%= number %> is
16     <%= format.format(computeFactorial(number)) %>
17
18     <%! private long computeFactorial(int n) {
19         if (n == 0)
20           return 1;
```

import directive — line 9
error page directive — line 10
create object — line 12
JSP declaration — line 18

```
21              else
22                 return n * computeFactorial(n - 1);
23          }
24       %>
25    </body>
26 </html>
```

LISTING 35.7 `FactorialInputError.jsp`

```
1  <!-- FactorialInputError.jsp -->
2  <html>
3    <head>
4      <title>
5        FactorialInputError
6      </title>
7    </head>
8    <body>
9      <%@ page isErrorPage = "true" %>
10
11     <b>Error</b> -- Input is not an integer.
12
13   </body>
14 </html>
```

JSP directive

FactorialInput.html is displayed first to prompt the user to enter an integer. Upon clicking the *Compute Factorial* button, the JSP page ComputeFactorial.jsp is invoked to compute the factorial for the number. If the user enters an integer, its factorial is displayed; otherwise, the error page is displayed.

In ComputeFactorial.jsp, the directive `<%@ page import = "java.text.*" %>` (line 9) imports the `java.text` package because the `NumberFormat` class is in this package. The directive `<%@ page errorPage = "FactorialInputError.jsp" %>` (line 10) specifies that FactorialInputError.jsp is processed when an exception in ComputeFactorial.jsp occurs. The directive `<%@  page isErrorPage = "true" %>` (line 9 in FactorialInputError.jsp) denotes that FactorialInputError.jsp can be used as an error page.

35.7 Using JavaBeans in JSP

You used the `computeFactorial` method to compute the factorial in Listings 35.1 and 35.6, Factorial.jsp and ComputeFactorial.jsp. You defined the method in both examples. You could have defined the method in a class and shared it in both examples. Normally you create an instance of a class in each program and use it in that program. This method is for sharing the class, not the object. JSP allows you to share the object of a class among different pages.To enable an object to be shared, its class must be a JavaBeans component. Recall that a class is a JavaBeans component if it has the following three features:

■ The class is public.

■ The class has a public constructor with no arguments.

■ The class is serializable. (This requirement is not necessary in JSP.)

To create an instance for a JavaBeans component, use the following syntax:

```
<jsp:useBean id = "objectName" scope = "scopeAttribute"
   class = "ClassName" />
```

This syntax is equivalent to

```
<% ClassName objectName = new ClassName() %>
```

except that the scope attribute specifies the scope of the object, and the object is not recreated if it is already within the scope. Listed below are four possible values for the scope attribute:

- **application** specifies that the object is bound to the application. The object can be shared by all sessions of the application.
- **session** specifies that the object is bound to the client's session. Recall that a client's session is automatically created between a Web browser and a Web server. When a client from the same browser accesses two servlets or two JSP pages on the same server, the session is the same.
- **page** is the default scope, which specifies that the object is bound to the page.
- **request** specifies that the object is bound to the client's request.

When `<jsp:useBean id="objectName" scope="scopeAttribute" class="ClassName" />` is processed, the JSP engine first searches for an object of the class with the same id and scope. If found, the preexisting bean is used; otherwise, a new bean is created.

Here is another syntax for creating a bean:

```
<jsp:useBean id = "objectName" scope = "scopeAttribute"
  class = "ClassName" >
    statements
</jsp:useBean>
```

The statements are executed when the bean is created. If a bean with the same ID and class name already exists in the scope, the statements are not executed.

Listing 35.8 creates a JavaBeans component named **Count** and uses it to count the number of visits to a JSP page, as shown in Figure 35.6.

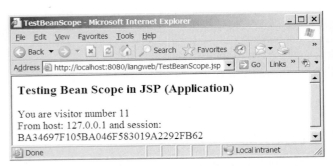 

FIGURE 35.6 The number of visits to the page is increased when the page is visited.

The JavaBeans component is named Count.java (Listing 35.8) and compiled into `c:\jakarta-tomcat-5.5.9\webapps\liangweb\WEB-INF\classes\chapter35`.

LISTING 35.8 Count.java

package statement

```
 1  package chapter35;
 2
 3  public class Count {
 4    private int count = 0;
 5
 6    /** Return count property */
 7    public int getCount() {
 8      return count;
 9    }
10
```

```
11    /** Increase count */
12    public void increaseCount() {
13        count++;
14    }
15 }
```

The JSP page is named TestBeanScope.jsp (Listing 35.9) and saved in `c:\jakarta-tomcat-5.5.9\webapps\liangweb`. Run it from the URL http://localhost:8080/liangweb/TestBeanScope.jsp, as shown in Figure 35.6.

LISTING 35.9 TestBeanScope.jsp

```
1  <!-- TestBeanScope.jsp -->
2  <%@ page import = "chapter35.Count" %>                    ← import directive
3  <jsp:useBean id = "count" scope = "application"          ← create bean
4      class = "chapter35.Count">
5  </jsp:useBean>
6  <html>
7    <head>
8      <title>TestBeanScope</title>
9    </head>
10   <body>
11     <h3>Testing Bean Scope in JSP (Application)</h3>
12     <% count.increaseCount(); %>                          ← use bean
13     You are visitor number <%= count.getCount() %><br />
14     From host: <%= request.getRemoteHost() %>             ← request
15     and session: <%= session.getId() %>                   ← session
16   </body>
17 </html>
```

The **scope** attribute specifies the scope of the bean. **scope="application"** (line 3) specifies that the bean is alive in the JSP engine and available for all clients to access. The bean can be shared by any client with the directive **<jsp:useBean** id="count" *scope="application"* class="Count" >** (lines 3–4). Every client accessing TestBeanScope.jsp causes the count to increase by 1. The first client causes **count** object to be created, and subsequent access to **TestBeanScope** uses the same object.

If **scope="application"** is changed to **scope="session"**, the scope of the bean is limited to the session from the same browser. The count will increase only if the page is requested from the same browser. If **scope="application"** is changed to **scope="page"**, the scope of the bean is limited to the page, and any other page cannot access this bean. The page will always display count 1. If **scope="application"** is changed to **scope="request"**, the scope of the bean is limited to the client's request, and any other request on the page will always display count 1.

If the page is destroyed, the count restarts from 0. You can fix the problem by storing the count in a random access file or in a database table. Assume that you store the count in the **Count** table in a database. The **Count** table contains an attribute named **countValue**. The **Count** class can be modified in Listing 35.10.

LISTING 35.10 Count.java

```
1  package chapter35;                                        ← package statement
2
3  import java.sql.*;
4
5  public class Count {
6      private int count = 0;
7      private Statement statement = null;
8
```

```
 9   public Count() {
10     initializeJdbc();
11   }
12
13   /** Return count property */
14   public int getCount() {
15     try {
16       ResultSet rset = statement.executeQuery
17         ("select countValue from Count");
18       rset.next();
19       count = rset.getInt(1);
20     }
21     catch (Exception ex) {
22       ex.printStackTrace();
23     }
24
25     return count;
26   }
27
28   /** Increase count */
29   public void increaseCount() {
30     count++;
31     try {
32       statement.executeUpdate(
33         "update Count set countValue = " + count);
34     }
35     catch (Exception ex) {
36       ex.printStackTrace();
37     }
38   }
39
40   /** Initialize database connection */
41   public void initializeJdbc() {
42     try {
43       Class.forName("sun.jdbc.odbc.JdbcOdbcDriver");
44
45       // Connect to the sample database
46       Connection connection = DriverManager.getConnection(
47         "jdbc:odbc:exampleMDBDataSource");
48
49       statement = connection.createStatement();
50     }
51     catch (Exception ex) {
52       ex.printStackTrace();
53     }
54   }
55 }
```

(margin notes: execute SQL; load driver; connection; statement)

35.8 Getting and Setting Properties

By convention, a JavaBeans component provides the get and set methods for reading and modifying its private properties. You can get the property in JSP using the syntax shown below:

```
<jsp:getProperty name = "beanId" property = "sample" />
```

This is equivalent to

```
<%= beanId.getSample() %>
```

You can set the property in JSP using the following syntax:

```
<jsp:setProperty name = "beanId"
  property = "sample" value = "test1" />
```

This is equivalent to

```
<% beanId.setSample("test1"); %>
```

35.9 Associating Properties with Input Parameters

Often properties are associated with input parameters. Suppose you want to get the value of the input parameter named **score** and set it to the JavaBeans property named **score**. You could write the following code:

```
<% double score = Double.parseDouble(
      request.getParameter("score")); %>
<jsp:setProperty name = "beanId" property = "score"
   value = "<%= score %>" />
```

This is cumbersome. JSP provides a convenient syntax that can be used to simplify it:

```
<jsp:setProperty name = "beanId" property = "score"
   param = "score" />
```

Instead of using the **value** attribute, you use the **param** attribute to name an input parameter. The value of this parameter is set to the property.

> **Note**
>
> Simple type conversion is performed automatically when a bean property is associated with an input parameter. A string input parameter is converted to an appropriate primitive data type or a wrapper class for a primitive type. For example, if the bean property is of the **int** type, the value of the parameter will be converted to the **int** type. If the bean property is of the **Integer** type, the value of the parameter will be converted to the **Integer** type.

Often the bean property and the parameter have the same name. You can use the following convenient statement to associate all the bean properties in **beanId** with the parameters that match the property names:

```
<jsp:setProperty name = "beanId" property = "*" />
```

35.9.1 Example: Computing Loan Payments Using JavaBeans

This example uses JavaBeans to simplify Listing 35.4, ComputeLoan1.jsp, by associating the bean properties with the input parameters. The new ComputeLoan.jsp is given in Listing 35.11.

LISTING 35.11 ComputeLoan2.jsp

```
 1  <!-- ComputeLoan2.jsp -->
 2  <html>
 3    <head>
 4      <title>ComputeLoan Using the Loan Class</title>
 5    </head>
 6    <body>
 7      <%@ page import = "chapter35.Loan" %>                              import
 8      <jsp:useBean id = "loan" class = "chapter35.Loan"                  create bean
 9        scope = "page" ></jsp:useBean>
10      <jsp:setProperty name = "loan" property = "*" />
11      Loan Amount: <%= loan.getLoanAmount() %>  <br />                   use bean
12      Annual Interest Rate: <%= loan.getAnnualInterestRate() %><br />
13      Number of Years: <%= loan.getNumberOfYears() %><br />
14      <b>Monthly Payment: <%= loan.getMonthlyPayment() %><br />
15      Total Payment: <%= loan.getTotalPayment() %> <br /></b>
16    </body>
17  </html>
```

Line 8

```
<jsp:useBean id = "loan" class = "chapter35.Loan" scope = "page">
    </jsp:useBean>
```

creates a bean named loan for the Loan class. Line 10

```
<jsp:setProperty name = "loan" property = "*" />
```

associates the bean properties `loanAmount`, `annualInteresteRate`, and `numberOfYears` with the input parameter values and performs type conversion automatically.

Lines 11–13 use the accessor methods of the loan bean to get the loan amount, annual interest rate, and number of years.

This program acts the same as in Listing 35.3 and 35.4, ComputeLoan.jsp and ComputeLoan1.jsp, but the coding is much simplified.

35.9.2 Example: Computing Factorials Using JavaBeans

This example creates a JavaBeans component named `FactorialBean` and uses it to compute the factorial of an input number in a JSP page named FactorialBean.jsp, as shown in Figure 35.7.

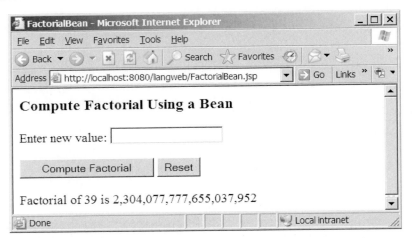

FIGURE 35.7 The factorial of an input integer is computed using a method in `FactorialBean`.

Create a JavaBeans component named FactorialBean.java (Listing 35.12) and compile it into `c:\jakarta-tomcat-5.5.9\webapps\liangweb\WEB-INF\classes\chapter35`.

LISTING 35.12 FactorialBean.java

package statement

get

set

```
 1 package chapter35;
 2
 3 public class FactorialBean {
 4   private int number;
 5
 6   /** Return number property */
 7   public int getNumber() {
 8     return number;
 9   }
10
11   /** Set number property */
12   public void setNumber(int newValue) {
13     number = newValue;
14   }
15
```

```
16    /** Obtain factorial */
17    public long getFactorial() {
18      long factorial = 1;
19      for (int i = 1; i <= number; i++)
20        factorial *= i;
21      return factorial;
22    }
23 }
```

Create FactorialBean.jsp (Listing 35.13) and save it into `c:\jakarta-tomcat-5.5.9\webapps\liangweb`. Run it from the URL http://localhost:8080/liangweb/FactorialBean.jsp, as shown in Figure 35.7.

LISTING 35.13 FactorialBean.jsp

```
1  <!-- FactorialBean.jsp -->
2  <%@ page import = "chapter35.FactorialBean" %>                       import
3  <jsp:useBean id = "factorialBeanId"                                 create bean
4    class = "chapter35.FactorialBean" scope = "page" >
5  </jsp:useBean>
6  <jsp:setProperty name = "factorialBeanId" property = "*" />
7  <html>
8    <head>
9      <title>
10       FactorialBean
11     </title>
12   </head>
13   <body>
14   <h3>Compute Factorial Using a Bean</h3>
15   <form method = "post">                                            form
16     Enter new value: <input name = "number" /><br /><br />
17     <input type = "submit" name = "Submit"
18       value = "Compute Factorial" />
19     <input type = "reset" value = "Reset" /><br /><br />
20     Factorial of
21       <jsp:getProperty name = "factorialBeanId"                     get property
22         property = "number" /> is
23     <%@ page import = "java.text.*" %>
24     <% NumberFormat format = NumberFormat.getNumberInstance(); %>
25     <%= format.format(factorialBeanId.getFactorial()) %>
26   </form>
27   </body>
28 </html>
```

The `jsp:useBean` tag (lines 3–5) creates a bean `factorialBeanId` of the `FactorialBean` class. Line 6 `<jsp:setProperty name="factorialBeanId" property="*" />` associates all the bean properties with the input parameters that have the same name. In this case, the bean property `number` is associated with the input parameter `number`. When you click the *Compute Factorial* button, JSP automatically converts the input value for `number` from string into `int` and sets it to `factorialBean` before other statements are executed.

Lines 21–22 `<jsp:getProperty name="factorialBeanId" property="number" />` is equivalent to `<%= factorialBeanId.getNumber() %>`. The method `factorialBeanId.getFactorial()` (line 25) returns the factorial for the number in `factorialBeanId`.

35.9.3 Example: Displaying International Time

Listing 34.5, TimeForm.java, gives a Java servlet that uses the `doGet` method to generate an HTML form for the user to specify a locale and time zone (Figure 34.14(a)), and uses the `doPost` method to display the current time for the specified time zone in the specified locale

(Figure 34.14(b)). This section rewrites the servlet using JSP. You have to create two JSP pages, one for displaying the form and the other for displaying the current time.

In the TimeForm.java servlet, arrays **allLocale** and **allTimeZone** are the data fields. The **doGet** and **doPost** methods both use the arrays. Since the available locales and time zones are used in both pages, it is better to create an object that contains all available locales and time zones. This object can be shared by both pages.

Let us create a JavaBeans component named TimeBean.java (Listing 35.14) and compile it into c:\jakarta-tomcat-5.5.9\webapps\liangweb\WEB-INF\classes\chapter35. This class simply obtains all the available locales.

LISTING 35.14 TimeBean.java

<table>
<tr><td>package statement</td><td>

```
1 package chapter35;
2
3 import java.util.*;
4
5 public class TimeBean {
```
</td></tr>
<tr><td>all locales
all time zones</td><td>

```
6   private Locale[] allLocale = Locale.getAvailableLocales();
7   private String[] allTimeZone = TimeZone.getAvailableIDs();
8
```
</td></tr>
<tr><td>return all locales</td><td>

```
9   public Locale[] getAllLocale() {
10    return allLocale;
11  }
12
```
</td></tr>
<tr><td>return all time
zones</td><td>

```
13  public String[] getAllTimeZone() {
14    return allTimeZone;
15  }
16 }
```
</td></tr>
</table>

Create DisplayTimeForm.jsp (Listing 35.15) and save it into c:\jakarta-tomcat-5.5.9\webapps\liangweb. This page displays a form just like the one shown in Figure 34.14(a). Line 2 imports the **TimeBean** class. A bean is created in lines 3–5 and is used in lines 17, 19, 24, and 26 to return all locales and time zones. The scope of the bean is application (line 4), so the bean can be shared by all sessions of the application.

LISTING 35.15 DisplayTimeForm.jsp

<table>
<tr><td></td><td>

```
1 <!-- DisplayTimeForm.jsp -->
```
</td></tr>
<tr><td>import class
timeBeanId</td><td>

```
2 <%@ page import = "chapter35.TimeBean" %>
3 <jsp:useBean id = "timeBeanId"
4   class = "chapter35.TimeBean" scope = "application" >
5 </jsp:useBean>
6
7 <html>
8   <head>
9     <title>
10      Display Time Form
11    </title>
12  </head>
13  <body>
14  <h3>Choose locale and time zone</h3>
```
</td></tr>
<tr><td>action</td><td>

```
15  <form method = "post" action = "DisplayTime.jsp">
16    Locale <select size = "1" name = "locale">
17    <% for (int i = 0; i < timeBeanId.getAllLocale().length; i++) {%>
18          <option value = "<%= i %>">
```
</td></tr>
<tr><td>all locales</td><td>

```
19          <%= timeBeanId.getAllLocale()[i] %>
20        </option>
21    <%}%>
22      </select><br />
```
</td></tr>
</table>

```
23     Time Zone <select size = "1" name = "timezone">
24     <% for (int i = 0; i < timeBeanId.getAllTimeZone().length; i++) {%>
25          <option value= "<%= i %>">
26          <%= timeBeanId.getAllTimeZone()[i] %>                      all time zones
27          </option>
28       <%}%>
29       </select><br />
30     <input type = "submit" name = "Submit"
31       value = "Get Time" />
32     <input type = "reset" value = "Reset" />
33     </form>
34   </body>
35 </html>
```

Create DisplayTime.jsp (Listing 35.16) and save it into c:\jakarta-tomcat-5.5.9\
webapps\liangweb. This page is invoked from DisplayTimeForm.jsp to display the time
with the specified locale and time zone, just as in Figure 34.14(b).

LISTING 35.16 DisplayTime.jsp

```
 1 <!-- DisplayTime.jsp -->
 2 <%@page pageEncoding = "GB18030"%>                                page encoding
 3 <%@ page import = "java.util.*" %>                               import
 4 <%@ page import = "java.text.*" %>
 5 <%@ page import = "chapter35.TimeBean" %>
 6 <jsp:useBean id = "timeBeanId"                                    timeBeanId
 7   class = "chapter35.TimeBean" scope = "application" >
 8 </jsp:useBean>
 9
10 <html>
11   <head>
12     <title>
13       Display Time
14     </title>
15   </head>
16   <body>
17   <h3>Choose locale and time zone</h3>
18     <%
19     out.println("<html>");
20     int localeIndex = Integer.parseInt(
21       request.getParameter("locale"));                            get parameter
22     String timeZoneID = request.getParameter("timezone");         get parameter
23     out.println("<head><title>Current Time</title></head>");
24     out.println("<body>");
25     Calendar calendar =
26       new GregorianCalendar(timeBeanId.getAllLocale()[localeIndex]);  use object
27     TimeZone timeZone = TimeZone.getTimeZone(timeZoneID);
28     DateFormat dateFormat = DateFormat.getDateTimeInstance(
29       DateFormat.FULL, DateFormat.FULL,
30       timeBeanId.getAllLocale()[localeIndex]);                    use object
31     dateFormat.setTimeZone(timeZone);
32     out.println("Current time is " +
33       dateFormat.format(calendar.getTime()) + "</p>");
34     out.println("</body></html>");
35     %>
36   </body>
37 <html>
```

Line 2 sets the character encoding for the page to GB18030 for displaying international characters. By default, it is UTF-8.

Since this page uses the `TimeZone` class from the `java.util` package and the `DateFormat` class from the `java.text` package, these two packages are imported in lines 3–4.

Line 5 imports `chapter35.TimeBean` and creates a bean using the same id as in the preceding page. Since the object is already created in the preceding page, the `beanFormId` in this page (lines 6–8) and in the preceding page point to the same object.

35.9.4 Example: Registering Students

Listing 34.11, RegistrationWithHttpSession.java, gives a Java servlet that obtains student information from an HTML form (see Figure 34.17) and displays the information for user confirmation (see Figure 34.18). Once the user confirms it, the servlet stores the data into the database. This section rewrites the servlet using JSP. You will create two JSP pages, one named GetRegistrationData.jsp for displaying the data for user confirmation and the other named StoreData.jsp for storing the data into the database.

Since every session needs to connect to the same database, you should declare a class for connecting to the database and for storing a student to the database. This class named `StoreData` is given in Listing 35.17. The `initializeJdbc` method (lines 14–38) connects to the database and creates a prepared statement for storing a record to the `Address` table. The `storeStudent` method (lines 41–52) executes the prepared statement to store a student record. A `Student` class that contains the data fields and their get and set methods is shown in Listing 35.18.

LISTING 35.17 StoreData.java

```java
1  package chapter35;
2
3  import java.sql.*;
4
5  public class StoreData {
6    // Use a prepared statement to store a student into the database
7    private PreparedStatement pstmt;
8
9    public StoreData() {
10     initializeJdbc();
11   }
12
13   /** Initialize database connection */
14   private void initializeJdbc() {
15     try {
16       // Declare driver and connection string
17       String driver = "sun.jdbc.odbc.JdbcOdbcDriver";
18       String connectionString = "jdbc:odbc:exampleMDBDataSource";
19
20       // Load the Oracle JDBC Thin driver
21       Class.forName(driver);
22       System.out.println("Driver " + driver + " loaded");
23
24       // Connect to the sample database
25       Connection conn = DriverManager.getConnection
26         (connectionString);
27       System.out.println("Database " + connectionString +
28         " connected");
29
30       // Create a Statement
31       pstmt = conn.prepareStatement("insert into Address " +
32         "(lastName, firstName, mi, telephone, email, street, city, "
33         + "state, zip) values (?, ?, ?, ?, ?, ?, ?, ?, ?)");
34     }
```

initialize **DB**

```
35      catch (Exception ex) {
36        System.out.println(ex);
37      }
38    }
39
40    /** Store a student record to the database */
41    public void storeStudent(Student student) throws SQLException {          store student
42      pstmt.setString(1, student.getLastName());
43      pstmt.setString(2, student.getFirstName());
44      pstmt.setString(3, student.getMi());
45      pstmt.setString(4, student.getTelephone());
46      pstmt.setString(5, student.getEmail());
47      pstmt.setString(6, student.getStreet());
48      pstmt.setString(7, student.getCity());
49      pstmt.setString(8, student.getState());
50      pstmt.setString(9, student.getZip());
51      pstmt.executeUpdate();
52    }
53  }
```

LISTING 35.18 Student.java

```
1  package chapter35;                                                          package chapter35
2
3  public class Student {
4    private String firstName;
5    private String mi;
6    private String lastName;
7    private String telephone;
8    private String street;
9    private String city;
10   private String state;
11   private String email;
12   private String zip;
13
14   public String getFirstName() {
15     return this.firstName;
16   }
17
18   public void setFirstName(String firstName) {
19     this.firstName = firstName;
20   }
21
22   public String getMi() {
23     return this.mi;
24   }
25
26   public void setMi(String mi) {
27     this.mi = mi;
28   }
29
30   public String getLastName() {
31     return this.lastName;
32   }
33
34   public void setLastName(String lastName) {
35     this.lastName = lastName;
36   }
37
```

```
38    public String getTelephone() {
39        return this.telephone;
40    }
41
42    public void setTelephone(String telephone) {
43        this.telephone = telephone;
44    }
45
46    public String getEmail() {
47        return this.email;
48    }
49
50    public void setEmail(String email) {
51        this.email = email;
52    }
53
54    public String getStreet()  {
55        return this.street;
56    }
57
58    public void setStreet(String street)  {
59        this.street = street;
60    }
61
62    public String getCity() {
63        return this.city;
64    }
65
66    public void setCity(String city) {
67        this.city = city;
68    }
69
70    public String getState() {
71        return this.state;
72    }
73
74    public void setState(String state) {
75        this.state = state;
76    }
77
78    public String getZip() {
79        return this.zip;
80    }
81
82    public void setZip(String zip) {
83        this.zip = zip;
84    }
85 }
```

The HTML file that displays the form is identical to `Registration.html` in Listing 34.8 except that the action is replaced by

`http://localhost:8080/liangweb/GetRegistrationData.jsp`

GetRegistrationData.jsp, which obtains the data from the form, is shown in Listing 35.19. A bean is created in lines 3–4. Line 5 obtains the property values from the form. This is a short-hand notation. Note that the parameter names and the property names must be the same to use this notation.

LISTING 35.19 GetRegistrationData.jsp

```
1  <!-- GetRegistrationData.jsp -->
2  <%@ page import = "chapter35.Student" %>                          import
3  <jsp:useBean id = "studentId"                                     studentId
4    class = "chapter35.Student" scope = "session"></jsp:useBean>
5  <jsp:setProperty name = "studentId" property = "*" />             get property values
6
7  <html>
8    <body>
9      <h1>Registration Using JSP</h1>
10
11     <%
12     if (studentId.getLastName() == null ||
13             studentId.getFirstName() == null) {
14       out.println("Last Name and First Name are required");
15       return; // End the method
16     }
17     %>
18
19     <p>You entered the following data</p>
20     <p>Last name: <%= studentId.getLastName() %></p>
21     <p>First name: <%= studentId.getFirstName() %></p>
22     <p>MI: <%= studentId.getMi() %></p>
23     <p>Telephone: <%= studentId.getTelephone() %></p>
24     <p>Email:  <%= studentId.getEmail() %></p>
25     <p>Address: <%= studentId.getStreet() %></p>
26     <p>City: <%= studentId.getCity() %></p>
27     <p>State: <%= studentId.getState() %></p>
28     <p>Zip: <%= studentId.getZip() %></p>
29
30     <!-- Set the action for processing the answers -->
31     <form method = "post" action = "/liangweb/StoreStudent.jsp">
32       <input type = "submit" value = "Confirm">
33     </form>
34   </body>
35 </html>
```

GetRegistrationData.jsp invokes StoreStudent.jsp (Listing 35.20) when the user clicks the *Confirm* button. The same **studentId** is shared with the preceding page within the scope of the same session in lines 3–4. A bean for **StoreData** is created in lines 5–6 with the scope of application.

LISTING 35.20 StoreStudent.jsp

```
1  <!-- StoreStudent.jsp -->                                         import
2  <%@ page import = "chapter35.Student" %>                          studentId
3  <jsp:useBean id = "studentId" class = "chapter35.Student"
4    scope = "session"></jsp:useBean>
5  <jsp:useBean id = "storeDataId" class = "chapter35.StoreData"     storeDataId
6    scope = "application" ></jsp:useBean>
7
8  <html>
9    <body>
10     <%
11       storeDataId.storeStudent(studentId);
12
```

```
13        out.println(studentId.getFirstName() + " " +
14              studentId.getLastName() +
15          " is now registered in the database");
16        out.close(); // Close stream
17      %>
18    </body>
19  </html>
```

Note

appropriate scopes

The scope for `studentId` is *session*, but the scope for `storeDataId` is *application*. Why? GetRegistrationData.jsp obtains student information, and StoreData.jsp stores the information in the same session. So the *session* scope is appropriate for `studentId`. All the sessions access the same database and use the same prepared statement to store data. With the *application* scope for `storeDataId`, the bean for `StoreData` needs to be created just once.

Note

exceptions

The `storeStudent` method in line 11 may throw a `java.sql.SQLException`. In JSP, you can omit the `try-block` for checked *exceptions*. In case of an exception, JSP displays an error page.

35.10 Forwarding Requests from JavaServer Pages

Web applications developed using JSP generally consist of many pages linked together. JSP provides a forwarding tag in the following syntax that can be used to forward a page to another page:

```
<jsp:forward page = "destination" />
```

35.11 Case Study: Browsing Database Tables

This section presents a very useful JSP application for browsing tables. When you start the application, the first page prompts the user to enter the JDBC driver, URL, username, and password for a database, as shown in Figure 35.8. After you log in to the database, you can select a table to browse, as shown in Figure 35.9. Upon clicking the *Browse Table Content* button, the table content is displayed, as shown in Figure 35.10.

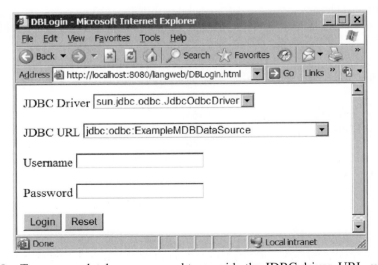

FIGURE 35.8 To access a database, you need to provide the JDBC driver, URL, username, and password.

FIGURE 35.9   You can select a table to browse from this page.

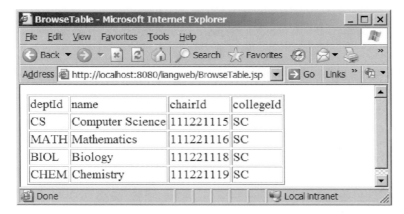

FIGURE 35.10   The contents of the selected table are displayed.

Create a JavaBeans component named `DBBean.java` (Listing 35.21) and compile it into
`c:\jakarta-tomcat-5.5.9\webapps\liangweb\WEB-INF\classes\chapter35`.

LISTING 35.21   DBBean.java

```java
1 package chapter35;
2
3 import java.sql.*;
4
5 .public class DBBean {
6    private Connection connection = null;
7    private String username;
8    private String password;
9    private String driver;
10   private String url;
11
12   /** Initialize database connection */
13   public void initializeJdbc() {
14     try {
15       System.out.println("Driver is " + driver);
16       Class.forName(driver);
17
18       // Connect to the sample database
19       connection = DriverManager.getConnection(url, username,
20         password);
21     }
```

load driver

connect db

```
22      catch (Exception ex) {
23        ex.printStackTrace();
24      }
25    }
26
27    /** Get tables in the database */
28    public String[] getTables() {
29      String[] tables = null;
30
31      try {
32        DatabaseMetaData dbMetaData = connection.getMetaData();
33        ResultSet rsTables = dbMetaData.getTables(null, null, null,
34          new String[] {"TABLE"});
35
36        int size = 0;
37        while (rsTables.next()) size++;
38
39        rsTables = dbMetaData.getTables(null, null, null,
40          new String[] {"TABLE"});
41
42        tables = new String[size];
43        int i = 0;
44        while (rsTables.next())
45          tables[i++] = rsTables.getString("TABLE_NAME");
46      }
47      catch (Exception ex) {
48        ex.printStackTrace();
49      }
50
51      return tables;
52    }
53
54    /** Return connection property */
55    public Connection getConnection() {
56      return connection;
57    }
58
59    public void setUsername(String newUsername) {
60      username = newUsername;
61    }
62
63    public String getUsername() {
64      return username;
65    }
66
67    public void setPassword(String newPassword) {
68      password = newPassword;
69    }
70
71    public String getPassword() {
72      return password;
73    }
74
75    public void setDriver(String newDriver) {
76      driver = newDriver;
77    }
78
79    public String getDriver() {
80      return driver;
81    }
```

get tables

return table names

```
82
83    public void setUrl(String newUrl) {
84      url = newUrl;
85    }
86
87    public String getUrl() {
88      return url;
89    }
90  }
```

Create an HTML file named DBLogin.html (Listing 35.22) that prompts the user to enter database information and three JSP files named DBLoginInitialization.jsp (Listing 35.23), Table.jsp (Listing 35.24), and BrowseTable.jsp (Listing 35.25) to process and obtain database information. All the files are stored in c:\jakarta-tomcat5.5.9\webapps\liangweb.

LISTING 35.22 DBLogin.html

```
1  <!-- DBLogin.html -->
2  <html>
3    <head>
4      <title>
5        DBLogin
6      </title>
7    </head>
8    <body>
9      <form method = "post"                                          form action
10       action = "/liangweb/DBLoginInitialization.jsp">
11     JDBC Driver
12     <select name = "driver" size = "1">                           combo box
13       <option>sun.jdbc.odbc.JdbcOdbcDriver</option>
14       <option>oracle.jdbc.driver.OracleDriver</option>
15     </select><br /><br />
16     JDBC URL
17     <select name = "url" size = "1">                              combo box
18       <option>jdbc:odbc:ExampleMDBDataSource</option>
19       <option>jdbc:oracle:thin:@liang.armstrong.edu:1521:orcl</option>
20       <option>jdbc:oracle:thin:@localhost:1521:test</option>
21     </select><br /><br />
22     Username <input name = "username" /><br /><br />
23     Password <input name = "password" /><br /><br />
24     <input type = "submit" name = "Submit" value = "Login" />     submit
25     <input type = "reset" value = "Reset" />
26     </form>
27   </body>
28 </html>
```

LISTING 35.23 DBLoginInitialization.jsp

```
1  <!-- DBLoginInitialization.jsp -->
2  <%@ page import = "chapter35.DBBean" %>                          import
3  <jsp:useBean id = "dBBeanId" scope = "session"                  create bean
4    class = "chapter35.DBBean">
5  </jsp:useBean>
6  <jsp:setProperty name = "dBBeanId" property = "*" />
7  <html>
8    <head>
9      <title>DBLoginInitialization</title>
10   </head>
11   <body>
```

```
12
13   <%-- Connect to the database --%>
14    <% dBBeanId.initializeJdbc(); %>
15
16    <% if (dBBeanId.getConnection() == null) { %>
17      Error: Login failed. Try again.
18    <% }
19      else {%>
20        <jsp:forward page = "Table.jsp" />
21    <% } %>
22    </body>
23  </html>
```

connect db — line 14
report error — line 17
get tables — line 20

LISTING 35.24   Table.jsp

```
1  <!-- Table.jsp -->
2  <%@ page import = "chapter35.DBBean" %>
3  <jsp:useBean id = "dBBeanId" scope = "session"
4    class = "chapter35.DBBean">
5  </jsp:useBean>
6  <html>
7    <head>
8      <title>Table</title>
9    </head>
10   <body>
11   <% String[] tables = dBBeanId.getTables();
12     if (tables == null) { %>
13       No tables
14   <% }
15     else { %>
16       <form method = "post" action = "BrowseTable.jsp">
17         Select a table
18         <select name = "tablename" size = "1">
19       <% for (int i = 0; i < tables.length; i++) { %>
20           <option><%= tables[i] %></option>
21       <% }
22     } %>
23         </select><br /><br /><br />
24     <input type = "submit" name = "Submit"
25       value = "Browse Table Content">
26     <input type = "reset" value = "Reset">
27     </form>
28   </body>
29 </html>
```

import — line 2
get bean — line 3
get tables — line 11
create form — line 16

LISTING 35.25   BrowseTable.jsp

```
1  <!-- BrowseTable.jsp -->
2  <%@ page import = "chapter35.DBBean" %>
3  <jsp:useBean id = "dBBeanId" scope = "session"
4    class = "chapter35.DBBean" >
5  </jsp:useBean>
6  <%@ page import = "java.sql.*" %>
7  <html>
8    <head>
9      <title>BrowseTable</title>
10   </head>
11   <body>
```

import — line 2
get bean — line 3

```
12
13   <% String tableName = request.getParameter("tablename");          get table name
14
15      ResultSet rsColumns = dBBeanId.getConnection().getMetaData().   table column
16        getColumns(null, null, tableName, null);
17   %>
18   <table border = "1">
19     <tr>
20       <% // Add column names to the table
21       while (rsColumns.next()) { %>                                  column names
22         <td><%= rsColumns.getString("COLUMN_NAME") %></td>
23     <% } %>
24     </tr>
25
26     <% Statement statement =
27         dBBeanId.getConnection().createStatement();
28       ResultSet rs = statement.executeQuery(                         table content
29         "select * from " + tableName);
30
31       // Get column count
32       int columnCount = rs.getMetaData().getColumnCount();
33
34       // Store rows to rowData
35       while (rs.next()) {                                            display content
36         out.println("<tr>");
37         for (int i = 0; i < columnCount; i++) { %>
38           <td><%= rs.getObject(i + 1) %></td>
39     <% }
40         out.println("</tr>");
41       } %>
42   </table>
43   </body>
44 </html>
```

You start the application from DBLogin.html. This page prompts the user to enter a JDBC driver, URL, username, and password to log into a database. A list of accessible drivers and URLs is provided in the selection list. You must make sure that these databases are accessible from the JSP server and that their drivers are installed in `c:\jakarta-tomcat-5.5.9\ common\lib`.

When you click the *Login* button, DBLoginInitialization.jsp is invoked. When this page is processed for the first time, an instance of **DBBean** named **dBBeanId** is created. The input parameters **driver**, **url**, **username**, and **password** are passed to the bean properties. The **initializeJdbc** method loads the driver and establishes a connection to the database. If login fails, the **connection** property is **null**. In this case, an error message is displayed. If login succeeds, control is forwarded to Table.jsp.

Table.jsp shares **dBBeanId** with DBLoginInitialization.jsp in the same session, so it can access **connection** through **dBBeanId** and obtain tables in the database using the database metadata. The table names are displayed in a selection box in a form. When the user selects a table name and clicks the *Browse Table Content* button, BrowseTable.jsp is processed.

BrowseTable.jsp shares **dBBeanId** with Table.jsp and DBLoginInitialization.jsp in the same session. It retrieves the table contents for the selected table from Table.jsp.

JSP Scripting Constructs Syntax

- **<%= Java expression %>** The expression is evaluated and inserted into the page.

- **<% Java statement %>** Java statements inserted in the **jspService** method.

- **<%! Java declaration %>** Defines data fields and methods.

- `<%-- JSP comment %>` The JSP comments do not appear in the resultant HTML file.

- `<%@ directive attribute="value" %>` The JSP directives give the JSP engine information about the JSP page. For example, `<%@ page import="java.util.*, java.text.*" %>` imports `java.util.*` and `java.text.*`.

- `<jsp:useBean id="objectName" scope="scopeAttribute" class="Class-Name" />` Creates a bean if new. If a bean is already created, associates the id with the bean in the same scope.

- `<jsp:useBean id="objectName" scope="scopeAttribute" class="Class-Name"> statements </jsp:useBean>` The statements are executed when the bean is created. If a bean with the same id and class name already exists, the statements are not executed.

- `<jsp:getProperty name="beanId" property="sample" />` Gets the property value from the bean, which is the same as `<%= beanId.getSample() %>`.

- `<jsp:setProperty name="beanId" property="sample" value="test1" />` Sets the property value for the bean, which is the same as `<% beanId.setSample("test1"); %>`.

- `<jsp:setProperty name="beanId" property="score" param="score" />` Sets the property with an input parameter.

- `<jsp:setProperty name="beanId" property="*" />` Associates and sets all the bean properties in `beanId` with the input parameters that match the property names.

- `<jsp:forward page="destination" />` Forwards this page to a new page.

JSP Predefined Variables

- **application** represents the `ServletContext` object for storing persistent data for all clients.

- **config** represents the `ServletConfig` object for the page.

- **out** represents the character output stream, which is an instance of `PrintWriter`, obtained from `response.getWriter()`.

- **page** is alternative to `this`.

- **request** represents the client's request, which is an instance of `HttpServletRequest` in the servlet's `service` method.

- **response** represents the client's response, which is an instance of `HttpServletResponse` in the servlet's `service` method.

- **session** represents the `HttpSession` object associated with the request, obtained from `request.getSession()`.

CHAPTER SUMMARY

- A JavaServer page is like a regular HTML page with special tags, known as *JSP tags*, which enable the Web server to generate dynamic content. You can create a Web page with static HTML and enclose the code for generating dynamic content in the JSP tags.

- A JSP page must be stored in a file with a .jsp extension. The Web server translates the .jsp file into a Java servlet, compiles the servlet, and executes it. The result of the execution is sent to the browser for display.

- A JSP page is translated into a servlet when the page is requested for the first time. It is not retranslated if the page is not modified. To ensure that the first-time real user does not get a delay, JSP developers may test the page after it is installed.

- In order to display a JSP page, the page must be placed in a designated directory (e.g., `c:\jakarta-tomcat-5.5.9\webapps\liangweb`) and must be accessed from a JSP-enabled Web server with an appropriate URL (e.g., http://localhost:8080/liangweb/CurrentTime.jsp).

- There are three main types of JSP constructs: scripting constructs, directives, and actions. *Scripting* elements enable you to specify Java code that will become part of the resultant servlet. *Directives* enable you to control the overall structure of the resultant servlet. *Actions* enable you to control the behaviors of the JSP engine.

- There are three types of scripting constructs that can be used to insert Java code into the resultant servlet: expressions, scriptlets, and declarations.

- The scope attribute (application, session, page, and request) specifies the scope of a JavaBeans object. Application specifies that the object be bound to the application. Session specifies that the object be bound to the client's session. Page is the default scope, which specifies that the object be bound to the page. Request specifies that the object be bound to the client's request.

- Web applications developed using JSP generally consist of many pages linked together. JSP provides a forwarding tag in the following syntax that can be used to forward a page to another page: `<jsp:forward page="destination" />`.

REVIEW QUESTIONS

Sections 35.1–35.3

35.1 What is the file name extension of a JavaServer page? How is a JSP page processed?

35.2 Where should a JSP file be placed for it to run from Tomcat?

35.3 You can display an HTML file (e.g., `c:\test.html`) by typing the complete file name in the Address field of Internet Explorer. Why can't you display a JSP file by simply typing the file name?

Section 35.4 JSP Scripting Constructs

35.4 What are a JSP expression, a JSP scriptlet, and a JSP declaration? How do you write these constructs in JSP?

35.5 Find three syntax errors in the following JSP code:

```
<%! int k %>
<% for (int j = 1; j <= 9; j++) %>
   <%= j; %> <br />
```

35.6 In the following JSP, which variables are instance variables and which are local variables when it is translated in the servlet?

```
<%! int k; %>
<%! int i; %>
<% for (int j = 1; j <= 9; j++) k += 1;%>
<%= k<br /> <%= i<br /> <%= getTime()<br />
<% private long getTime() {
     long time = System.currentTimeMillis();
     return time;
   } %>
```

Section 35.5 Predefined Variables

35.7   Describe the predefined variables in JSP.

35.8   What is wrong if the JSP scriptlet **<%** in line 7 in ComputeLoan.jsp (Listing 35.3) is replaced by JSP declaration **<%!**?

35.9   Can you use predefined variables (e.g., `request`, `response`, `out`) in JSP declarations?

Section 35.6 JSP Directives

35.10   Describe the JSP directives and attributes for the `page` directive.

35.11   If a class does not have a package statement, can you import it?

35.12   If you use a custom class from a JSP, where should the class be placed?

Section 35.7 Using JavaBeans in JSP

35.13   You can create an object in a JSP scriptlet. What is the difference between an object created using the `new` operator and a bean created using the `<jsp:useBean ... >` tag?

35.14   What is the `scope` attribute for? Describe four scope attributes.

35.15   Describe how a `<jsp:useBean ... >` statement is processed by the JSP engine.

Sections 35.8–35.10

35.16   How do you associate bean properties with input parameters?

35.17   How do you write a statement to forward requests to another JSP page?

PROGRAMMING EXERCISES

Section 35.4 JSP Scripting Constructs

35.1   (*Factorial table in JSP*) Rewrite Exercise 34.1 using JSP.

35.2   (*Multiplication table in JSP*) Rewrite Exercise 34.2 using JSP.

Section 35.5 Predefined Variables

35.3*   (*Obtaining parameters in JSP*) Rewrite the servlet in Listing 34.4, GetParameters.java, using JSP. Create an HTML form that is identical to student_registration_form.html in Listing 34.3 except that the action is replaced by /liangweb/Exercise35_3.jsp for obtaining parameter values.

Section 35.6 JSP Directives

35.4   (*Calculating tax in JSP*) Rewrite Exercise 34.4 using JSP. You need to import ComputeTax in the JSP. Create a new ComputeTax.java in package chapter35 and compile it into `c:\jakarta-tomcat-5.5.9\webapps\liangweb\WEB-INF\classes\chapter35`.

35.5*   (*Finding scores from text files*) Rewrite Exercise 34.6 using servlets.

35.6**   (*Finding scores from database tables*) Rewrite Exercise 34.7 using servlets.

Section 35.7 Using JavaBeans in JSP

35.7**   (*Changing the password*) Rewrite Exercise 34.8 using servlets.

Comprehensive

35.8*   (*Storing cookies in JSP*) Rewrite Exercise 34.10 using JSP. Use `response.addCookie(Cookie)` to add a cookie.

35.9* (*Retrieving cookies in JSP*) Rewrite Exercise 34.11 using JSP. Use `Cookie[]`
`cookies = request.getCookies()` to add all cookies. ·

35.10 (*Drawing images*) Rewrite Listing 34.12, ImageContent.java, using JSP.

35.11***(*Syntax highlighting*) Rewrite Exercise 34.12 using JSP.

35.12**(*Opinion poll*) Rewrite Exercise 34.13 using JSP.

35.13***(*Multiple-question opinion poll*) The `Poll` table in Exercise 34.13 contains
only one question. Suppose the table contains multiple questions. Write a JSP
that reads all the questions from the table and displays them in a form, as shown
in Figure 35.11(a). When the user clicks the *Submit* button, another JSP page is
invoked. This page updates the Yes or No counts for each question and displays
the current Yes and No counts for each question in the `Poll` table, as shown in
Figure 35.11(b). Note that the table may contain many questions. The three
questions in the figure are just examples. Sort the questions in alphabetical order.

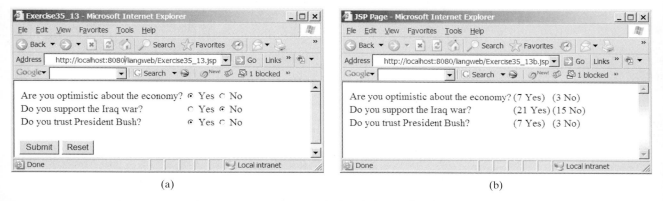

(a)   (b)

FIGURE 35.11   The form prompts the user to enter Yes or No for each question in (a), and the updated Yes or No counts
are displayed in (b).

REMOTE METHOD INVOCATIONS

Objectives

- To know how RMI works (§36.2).
- To learn the process of developing RMI applications (§36.3).
- To know the differences between RMI and socket-level programming (§36.4).
- To develop three-tier applications using RMI (§36.5).
- To use callbacks to develop interactive applications (§36.6).

36.1 Introduction

Remote Method Invocation (RMI) technology provides a framework for building distributed Java systems. Using RMI, a Java object on one system can invoke a method in an object on another system on the network. A *distributed Java system* can be defined as a collection of cooperative distributed objects on the network. This chapter introduces RMI basics. You will learn how to use RMI to create useful distributed applications.

36.2 RMI Basics

RMI is the Java Distributed Object Model for facilitating communications among distributed objects. RMI is a higher-level API built on top of sockets. Socket-level programming allows you to pass data through sockets among computers. RMI enables you not only to pass data among objects on different systems, but also to invoke methods in a remote object. Remote objects can be manipulated as if they were residing on the local host. The transmission of data among different machines is handled by the JVM transparently.

client
server

In many ways, RMI is an evolution of the client/server architecture. A *client* is a component that issues requests for services, and a *server* is a component that delivers the requested services. Like the client/server architecture, RMI maintains the notion of clients and servers, but the RMI approach is more flexible than the client/server paradigm.

- An RMI component can act as both a client and a server, depending on the scenario in question.

- An RMI system can pass functionality from a server to a client, and vice versa. A client/server system typically only passes data back and forth between server and client.

36.2.1 How Does RMI Work?

local object

remote object

All the objects you have used before this chapter are called *local objects*. *Local objects* are accessible only within the local host. Objects that are accessible from a remote host are called *remote objects*. For an object to be invoked remotely, it must be defined in a Java interface accessible to both the server and the client. Furthermore, the interface must extend the `java.rmi.Remote` interface. Like the `java.io.Serializable` interface, `java.rmi.Remote` is a marker interface that contains no constants or methods. It is only used to identify remote objects.

The key components of the RMI architecture are listed below (see Figure 36.1):

- **Server object interface:** A subinterface of `java.rmi.Remote` that defines the methods for the server object.

- **Server implementation:** A class that implements the remote object interface.

- **Server object:** An instance of the server implementation.

- **RMI registry:** A utility that registers remote objects and provides naming services for locating objects.

- **Client program:** A program that invokes the methods in the remote server object.

- **Server stub:** An object that resides on the client host and serves as a surrogate for the remote server object.

- **Server skeleton:** An object that resides on the server host, and communicates with the stub and the actual server object.

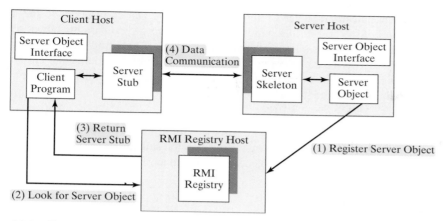

FIGURE 36.1   Java RMI uses a registry to provide naming services for remote objects, and uses the stub and the skeleton to facilitate communications between client and server.

RMI works as follows:

1. A server object is registered with the RMI registry.

2. A client looks through the RMI registry for the remote object.

3. Once the remote object is located, its stub is returned in the client.

4. The remote object can be used in the same way as a local object. Communication between the client and the server is handled through the stub and the skeleton.

The implementation of the RMI architecture is complex, but the good news is that RMI provides a mechanism that liberates you from writing the tedious code for handling parameter passing and invoking remote methods. The basic idea is to use two helper classes known as the *stub* and the *skeleton* for handling communications between client and server.

stub
skeleton

The stub and the skeleton are automatically generated in JDK 1.5. The *stub* resides on the client machine. It contains all the reference information the client needs to know about the server object. When a client invokes a method on a server object, it actually invokes a method that is encapsulated in the stub. The stub is responsible for sending parameters to the server, and for receiving the result from the server and returning it to the client.

The *skeleton* communicates with the stub on the server side. The skeleton receives parameters from the client, passes them to the server for execution, and returns the result to the stub.

Note

JDK 1.5 has simplified RMI development and deployment. Please use JDK 1.5 for this chapter.

JDK 1.5 RMI

36.2.2   Passing Parameters

When a client invokes a remote method with parameters, passing the parameters is handled by the stub and the skeleton. Obviously, invoking methods in a remote object on a server is very different from invoking methods in a local object on a client, since the remote object is in a different address space on a separate machine. Let us consider three types of parameters:

- **Primitive data types**, such as `char`, `int`, `double`, or `boolean`, are passed-by-value like a local call.

primitive type

- **Local object types**, such as `java.lang.String`, are also passed-by-value, but this is completely different from passing an object parameter in a local call. In a local

local object

call, an object parameter's reference is passed, which corresponds to the memory address of the object. In a remote call, there is no way to pass the object reference because the address on one machine is meaningless to a different JVM. Any object can be used as a parameter in a remote call as long as it is serializable. The stub serializes the object parameter and sends it in a stream across the network. The skeleton deserializes the stream into an object.

remote object

■ **Remote object types** are passed differently from local objects. When a client invokes a remote method with a parameter of a *remote object* type, the stub of the remote object is passed. The server receives the stub and manipulates the parameter through it. Passing remote objects is discussed in §36.6, "RMI Callbacks."

36.2.3 RMI Registry

How does a client locate the remote object? The RMI registry provides the registry services for the server to register the object and for the client to locate the object.

You can use several overloaded static `getRegistry()` methods in the `LocateRegistry` class to return a reference to a `Registry`, as shown in Figure 36.2. Once a `Registry` is obtained, you can bind an object with a unique name in the registry using the `bind` or `rebind` method or locate an object using the lookup method, as shown in Figure 36.3.

java.rmi.registry.LocateRegistry	
+getRegistry(): Registry	Returns a reference to the remote object Registry for the local host on the default registry port of 1099.
+getRegistry(port: int): Registry	Returns a reference to the remote object Registry for the local host on the specified port.
+getRegistry(host: String): Registry	Returns a reference to the remote object Registry on the specified host on the default registry port of 1099.
+getRegistry(host:String, port: int): Registry	Returns a reference to the remote object Registry on the specified host and port.

FIGURE 36.2 The `LocateRegistry` class provides the methods for obtaining a registry on a host.

java.rmi.registry.Registry	
+bind(name: String, obj: Remote): void	Binds the specified name with the remote object.
+rebind(name: String, obj: Remote): void	Binds the specified name with the remote object. Any existing binding for the name is replaced.
+unbind(name: String): void	Destroys the binding for the specified name that is associated with a remote object.
+list(name: String): String[]	Returns an array of the names bound in the registry.
+lookup(name: String): Remote	Returns a reference, a stub, for the remote object associated with the specified name.

FIGURE 36.3 The `Registry` class provides the methods for binding and obtaining references to remote objects in a remote object registry.

36.3 Developing RMI Applications

Now that you have a basic understanding of RMI, you are ready to write simple RMI applications. The steps in developing an RMI application are shown in Figure 36.4.

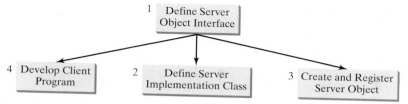

FIGURE 36.4 The steps in developing RMI applications.

1. *Define a server object interface* that serves as the contract between the server and its clients, as shown in the following outline:

```
public interface ServerInterface extends Remote {
    public void service1(...) throws RemoteException;
    // Other methods
}
```

A server object interface must extend the `java.rmi.Remote` interface.

2. Define a class that implements the server object interface, as shown in the following outline:

```
public class ServerInterfaceImpl extends UnicastRemoteObject
        implements ServerInterface {
    public void service1(...) throws RemoteException {
        // Implement it
    }
    // Implement other methods
}
```

The server implementation class must extend the `java.rmi.server.UnicastRemoteObject` class. The `UnicastRemoteObject` class provides support for point-to-point active object references using TCP streams.

3. *Create a server object* from the server implementation class and register it with an RMI registry:

```
ServerInterface server = new ServerInterfaceImpl(...);
Registry registry = LocateRegistry.getRegistry();
registry.rebind("RemoteObjectName", obj);
```

4. *Develop a client* that locates a remote object and invokes its methods, as shown in the following outline:

```
Registry registry = LocateRegistry.getRegistry(host);
ServerInterface server = (ServerInterfaceImpl)
    registry.lookup("RemoteObjectName");
server.service1(...);
```

The example that follows demonstrates the development of an RMI application through these steps.

36.3.1 Example: Retrieving Student Scores from an RMI Server

This example creates a client that retrieves student scores from an RMI server. The client, shown in Figure 36.5, displays the score for the specified name.

1. Create a server interface named **StudentServerInterface** in Listing 36.1. The interface tells the client how to invoke the server's **findScore** method to retrieve a student score.

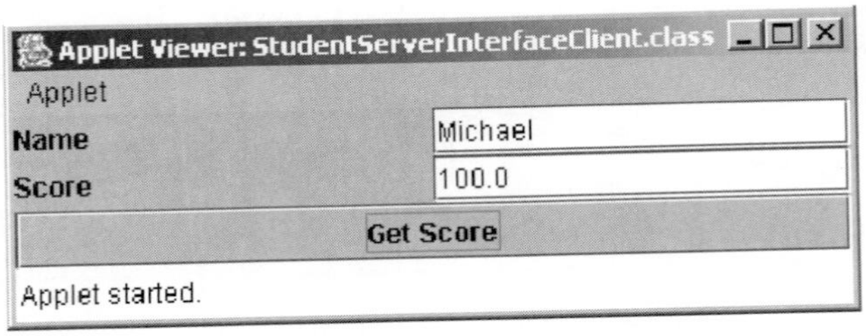

FIGURE 36.5 You can get the score by entering a student name and clicking the *Get Score* button.

LISTING 36.1 StudentServerInterface.java

subinterface

```
1 import java.rmi.*;
2
3 public interface StudentServerInterface extends Remote {
4   /**
5    * Return the score for the specified name
6    * @param  name    the student name
7    * @return an double score or  -1 if the student is not found
8    */
```

server method

```
9   public double findScore(String name) throws RemoteException;
10 }
```

Any object that can be used remotely must be defined in an interface that extends the `java.rmi.Remote` interface (line 3). `StudentServerInterface`, extending `Remote`, defines the `findScore` method that can be remotely invoked by a client to find a student's score. Each method in this interface must declare that it may throw a `java.rmi.RemoteException` (line 9). Therefore your client code that invokes this method must be prepared to catch this exception in a `try-catch` block.

2. Create a server implementation named `StudentServerInterfaceImpl` (Listing 36.2) that implements `StudentServerInterface`. The `findScore` method returns the score for a specified student. It returns −1 if the score is not found.

LISTING 36.2 StudentServerInterfaceImpl.java

```
1 import java.rmi.*;
2 import java.rmi.server.*;
3 import java.util.*;
4
5 public class StudentServerInterfaceImpl extends UnicastRemoteObject
6     implements StudentServerInterface  {
7   // Stores scores in a map indexed by name
```

hash map

```
8   private HashMap scores = new HashMap();
9
10   public StudentServerInterfaceImpl() throws RemoteException {
11     initializeStudent();
12   }
13
14   /** Initialize student information */
15   protected void initializeStudent() {
```

store score

```
16     scores.put("John", new Double(90.5));
17     scores.put("Michael", new Double(100));
18     scores.put("Michelle", new Double(98.5));
19   }
20
```

```
21    /** Implement the findScore method from the Student interface */
22    public double findScore(String name) throws RemoteException {
23      Double d = (Double)scores.get(name);                                    get score
24
25      if (d == null) {
26        System.out.println("Student " + name + " is not found ");
27        return -1;
28      }
29      else {
30        System.out.println("Student " + name + "\'s score is "
31          + d.doubleValue());
32        return d.doubleValue();
33      }
34    }
35  }
```

The `StudentServerInterfaceImpl` class implements `StudentServerInterface`. This class must also extend the `java.rmi.server.RemoteServer` class or its subclass. `RemoteServer` is an abstract class that defines the methods needed to create and export remote objects. Often its subclass `java.rmi.server.UnicastRemoteObject` is used (line 5). This subclass implements all the abstract methods defined in `RemoteServer`.

`StudentServerInterfaceImpl` implements the `findScore` method (lines 22–34) defined in `StudentServerInterface`. For simplicity, three students, John, Michael, and Michelle, and their corresponding scores are stored in an instance of `java.util.HashMap` named `scores`. `HashMap` is a concrete class of the `Map` interface in the Java Collections Framework, which makes it possible to search and retrieve a value using a key. Both values and keys are of `Object` type. The `findScore` method returns the score if the name is in the hash map, and returns `-1` if the name is not found (line 27).

3. Create a server object from the server implementation and register it with the RMI server (Listing 36.3).

LISTING 36.3   RegisterWithRMIServer.java

```
1  import java.rmi.registry.*;
2
3  public class RegisterWithRMIServer {
4    /** Main method */
5    public static void main(String[] args) {
6      try {
7        StudentServerInterface obj = new StudentServerInterfaceImpl();       server object
8        Registry registry = LocateRegistry.getRegistry();                    registry reference
9        registry.rebind("StudentServerInterfaceImpl", obj);                  register
10       System.out.println("Student server " + obj + " registered");
11     }
12     catch (Exception ex) {
13       ex.printStackTrace();
14     }
15   }
16 }
```

`RegisterWithRMIServer` contains a `main` method, which is responsible for starting the server. It performs the following tasks: (1) create a server object (line 7); (2) obtain a reference to the RMI registry (line 8), and (3) register the object in the registry (line 9).

4. Create a client as an applet named `StudentServerInterfaceClient` in Listing 36.4. The client locates the server object from the RMI registry and uses it to find the scores.

LISTING 36.4 StudentServerInterfaceClient.java

```java
1  import java.rmi.*;
2  import javax.swing.*;
3  import java.awt.*;
4  import java.awt.event.*;
5  import java.rmi.registry.LocateRegistry;
6  import java.rmi.registry.Registry;
7
8  public class StudentServerInterfaceClient extends JApplet {
9    // Declare a Student instance
10   private StudentServerInterface student;
11
12   private boolean isStandalone; // Is applet or application
13
14   private JButton jbtGetScore = new JButton("Get Score");
15   private JTextField jtfName = new JTextField();
16   private JTextField jtfScore = new JTextField();
17
18   public void init() {
19     // Initialize RMI
20     initializeRMI();
21
22     JPanel jPanel1 = new JPanel();
23     jPanel1.setLayout(new GridLayout(2, 2));
24     jPanel1.add(new JLabel("Name"));
25     jPanel1.add(jtfName);
26     jPanel1.add(new JLabel("Score"));
27     jPanel1.add(jtfScore);
28
29     add(jbtGetScore, BorderLayout.SOUTH);
30     add(jPanel1, BorderLayout.CENTER);
31
32     jbtGetScore.addActionListener(new ActionListener() {
33       public void actionPerformed(ActionEvent evt) {
34         getScore();
35       }
36     });
37   }
38
39   private void getScore() {
40     try {
41       // Get student score
42       double score = student.findScore(jtfName.getText().trim());
43
44       // Display the result
45       if (score < 0)
46         jtfScore.setText("Not found");
47       else
48         jtfScore.setText(new Double(score).toString());
49     }
50     catch(Exception ex) {
51       ex.printStackTrace();
52     }
53   }
54
55   /** Initialize RMI */
56   protected void initializeRMI() {
57     String host = " ";
58     if (!isStandalone) host = getCodeBase().getHost();
59
```

(margin notes:)
remote object
standalone?
initialize RMI
register listener
get score

```
60      try {
61        Registry registry = LocateRegistry.getRegistry(host);
62        student = (StudentServerInterface)                            locate student
63          registry.lookup("StudentServerInterfaceImpl");
64        System.out.println("Server object " + student + " found");
65      }
66      catch(Exception ex) {
67        System.out.println(ex);
68      }
69    }
70
71    /** Main method */
72    public static void main(String[] args) {
73      StudentServerInterfaceClient applet =                            main method
74        new StudentServerInterfaceClient();
75      applet.isStandalone = true;                                      standalone
76      JFrame frame = new JFrame();
77      frame.setTitle("StudentServerInterfaceClient");
78      frame.add(applet, BorderLayout.CENTER);
79      frame.setSize(250, 150);
80      applet.init();
81      frame.setLocationRelativeTo(null);
82      frame.setVisible(true);
83      frame.setDefaultCloseOperation(3);
84    }
85  }
```

StudentServerInterfaceClient invokes the findScore method on the server to find the score for a specified student. The key method in StudentServerInterfaceClient is the initializeRMI method (lines 56–69), which is responsible for locating the server stub.

The initializeRMI() method treats standalone applications differently from applets. The host name should be the name where the applet is downloaded. It can be obtained using the Applet's getCodeBase().getHost(). For standalone applications, the host name should be specified explicitly.

The lookup(String name) method (line 63) returns the remote object with the specified name. Once a remote object is found, it can be used just like a local object. The stub and the skeleton are used behind the scenes to make the remote method invocation work.

5. Follow the steps below to run this example.

5.1. Start the RMI Registry by typing "**start rmiregistry**" at a DOS prompt from the c:\book directory. By default, the port number 1099 is used by rmiregistry. To use a different port number, simply type the command "**start rmiregistry** *portnumber*" at a DOS prompt.

5.2. Start the server RegisterWithRMIServer using the following command at c:\book directory:

C:\book>**java RegisterWithRMIServer**

5.3. Run the client StudentServerInterfaceClient as an application. A sample run of the application is shown in Figure 36.6.

5.4. Run the client StudentServerInterface.html from the appletviewer. A sample run is shown in Figure 36.5.

Note

You must start rmiregistry from the directory where you will run the RMI server. Otherwise, you will receive the error ClassNotFoundException on StudentServerInterfaceImpl_Stub.

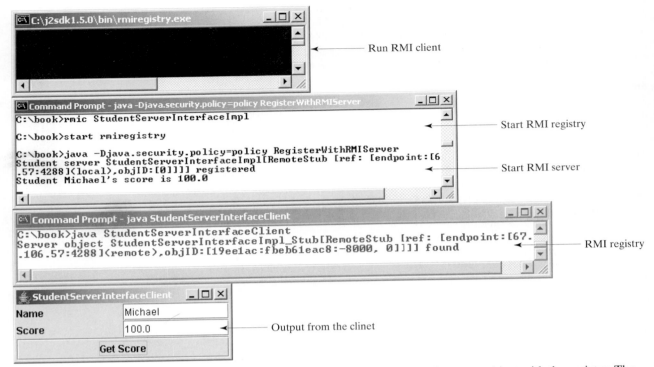

FIGURE 36.6 To run an RMI program, first start the RMIRegistry, then register the server object with the registry. The client locates it from the registry.

Note
Server, registry, and client can be on three different machines. If you run the client and the server on separate machines, you need to place **StudentServerInterface** on both machines. If you deploy the client as an applet, place all client files on the registry host.

Caution
If you modify the remote object implementation class, you need to restart the server class to reload the object to the RMI registry. In some old versions of rmiregistry, you may have to restart rmiregistry.

36.4 RMI vs. Socket-Level Programming

RMI enables you to program at a higher level of abstraction. It hides the details of socket server, socket, connection, and sending or receiving data. It even implements a multithreading server under the hood, whereas with socket-level programming you have to explicitly implement threads for handling multiple clients.

RMI applications are scalable and easy to maintain. You can change the RMI server or move it to another machine without modifying the client program except for resetting the URL to locate the server. (To avoid resetting the URL, you can modify the client to pass the URL as a command-line parameter.) In socket-level programming, a client operation to send data requires a server operation to read it. The implementation of client and server at the socket level is tightly synchronized.

RMI clients can directly invoke the server method, whereas socket-level programming is limited to passing values. Socket-level programming is very primitive. Avoid using it to develop client/server applications. As an analogy, socket-level programming is like programming in assembly language, while RMI programming is like programming in a high-level language.

36.5 Developing Three-Tier Applications Using RMI

Three-tier applications have gained considerable attention in recent years, largely because of the demand for more scalable and load-balanced systems to replace traditional two-tier client/server database systems. A centralized database system does not just handle data access, it also processes the business rules on data. Thus, a centralized database is usually heavily loaded because it requires extensive data manipulation and processing. In some situations, data processing is handled by the client and business rules are stored on the client side. It is preferable to use a middle tier as a buffer between client and database. The middle tier can be used to apply business logic and rules, and to process data to reduce the load on the database.

A three-tier architecture does more than just reduce the processing load on the server. It also provides access to multiple network sites. This is especially useful to Java applets that need to access multiple databases on different servers, since an applet can only connect with the server from which it is downloaded.

To demonstrate, let us rewrite the example in §36.3.1, "Example: Retrieving Student Scores from an RMI Server," to find scores stored in a database rather than a hash map. In addition, the system is capable of blocking a client from accessing a student who has not given the university permission to publish his/her score. An RMI component is developed to serve as a middle tier between client and database; it sends a search request to the database, processes the result, and returns an appropriate value to the client.

For simplicity, this example reuses the `StudentServerInterface` interface and `StudentServerInterfaceClient` class from §36.3.1 with no modifications. All you have to do is to provide a new implementation for the server interface and create a program to register the server with the RMI. Here are the steps to complete the program:

1. Store the scores in a database table named `Score` that contains three columns: `name`, `score`, and `permission`. The permission value is 1 or 0, which indicates whether the student has given the university permission to release his/her grade. The following is the statement to create the table and insert three records:

```
create table Scores (name varchar(20),
  score number, permission number);

insert into Scores values ('John', 90.5, 1);
insert into Scores values ('Michael', 100, 1);
insert into Scores values ('Michelle', 100, 0);
```

2. Create a new server implementation named `Student3TierImpl` in Listing 36.5. The server retrieves a record from the `Scores` table, processes the retrieved information, and sends the result back to the client.

LISTING 36.5 `Student3TierImpl.java`

```java
1  import java.rmi.*;
2  import java.rmi.server.*;
3  import java.sql.*;
4
5  public class Student3TierImpl extends UnicastRemoteObject
6      implements StudentServerInterface {
7    // Use prepared statement for querying DB
8    private PreparedStatement pstmt;
9
10   /** Constructs Student3TierImpl object and exports it on
11    * default port.
12    */
```

initialize db

```java
13    public Student3TierImpl() throws RemoteException {
14      initializeDB();
15    }
16
17    /** Constructs Student3TierImpl object and exports it on
18     * specified port.
19     * @param port The port for exporting
20     */
21    public Student3TierImpl(int port) throws RemoteException {
22      super(port);
23      initializeDB();
24    }
25
26    /** Load JDBC driver, establish connection and create statement */
27    protected void initializeDB() {
28      try {
29        // Load the JDBC driver
30        // Class.forName("oracle.jdbc.driver.OracleDriver");
31        Class.forName("sun.jdbc.odbc.JdbcOdbcDriver");
32        System.out.println("Driver registered");
33
34        // Establish connection
35        /*Connection conn = DriverManager.getConnection
36          ("jdbc:oracle:thin:@drake.armstrong.edu:1521:orcl",
37            "scott", "tiger");  */
38        Connection conn = DriverManager.getConnection
39          ("jdbc:odbc:exampleMDBDataSource", " ", " " );
40        System.out.println("Database connected");
41
42        // Create a prepared statement for querying DB
43        pstmt = conn.prepareStatement(
44          "select * from Scores where name = ?");
45      }
46      catch (Exception ex) {
47        System.out.println(ex);
48      }
49    }
50
51    /** Return the score for specified the name
52     * Return -1 if score is not found.
53     */
54    public double findScore(String name) throws RemoteException  {
55      double score = -1;
56      try {
57        // Set the specified name in the prepared statement
58        pstmt.setString(1, name);
59
60        // Execute the prepared statement
61        ResultSet rs = pstmt.executeQuery();
62
63        // Retrieve the score
64        if (rs.next()) {
65          if (rs.getBoolean(3))
66            score = rs.getDouble(2) ;
67        }
68      }
69      catch (SQLException ex) {
70        System.out.println(ex);
71      }
72
```

load driver

connect db

prepare statement

set name

execute SQL

get score

```
73      System.out.println(name + "\'s score is " + score);
74      return score;
75    }
76  }
```

`Student3TierImpl` is similar to StudentServerInterfaceImpl in §36.3.1 except that the `Student3TierImpl` class finds the score from a JDBC data source instead from a hash map.

The table named `Scores` consists of three columns, `name`, `score`, and `permission`, where permission indicates whether the student has given permission to show his/her score. Since SQL does not support a `boolean` type, permission is defined as a number whose value of `1` indicates `true` and `0` indicates `false`.

The `initializeDB()` method (lines 27–49) loads the appropriate JDBC driver, establishes connections with the database, and creates a prepared statement for processing the query.

The `findScore` method (lines 54–75) sets the name in the prepared statement, executes the statement, processes the result, and returns the score for a student whose permission is `true`.

3. Write a `main` method in the class `RegisterStudent3TierServer` (Listing 36.6) that registers the server object using `StudentServerInterfaceImpl`, the same name as in Listing 36.2, so that you can use StudentServerInterfaceClient, created in §36.3.1, to test the server.

LISTING 36.6   `RegisterStudent3TierServer.java`

```
1  import java.rmi.registry.*;
2
3  public class RegisterStudent3TierServer {
4    public static void main(String[] args) {
5      try {
6        StudentServerInterface obj = new Student3TierImpl();
7        Registry registry = LocateRegistry.getRegistry();
8        registry.rebind("StudentServerInterfaceImpl", obj);
9        System.out.println("Student server " + obj + " registered");
10     } catch (Exception ex) {
11       ex.printStackTrace();
12     }
13   }
14 }
```

4. Follow the steps below to run this example.

4.1. Start RMI Registry by typing "**start rmiregistry**" at a DOS prompt from the book directory.

4.2. Start the server `RegisterStudent3TierServer` using the following command at C:\book directory:

   C:\book>**java RegisterStudent3TierServer**

4.3. Run the client `StudentServerInterfaceClient` as an application or applet. A sample run is shown in Figure 36.6.

36.6 RMI Callbacks

In a traditional client/server system, a client sends a request to a server, and the server processes the request and returns the result to the client. The server cannot invoke the methods on a client. One of the important benefits of RMI is that it supports *callbacks*, which enable the server to invoke methods on the client. With the RMI callback feature, you can develop interactive distributed applications.

In §25.9, "Case Studies: Distributed TicTacToe Games," you developed a distributed TicTacToe game using stream socket programming. The following example demonstrates the use of the RMI callback feature to develop an interactive TicTacToe game.

All the examples you have seen so far in this chapter have simple behaviors that are easy to model with classes. The behavior of the TicTacToe game is somewhat complex. To create the classes to model the game, you need to study and understand it and distribute the process appropriately between client and server.

Clearly the client should be responsible for handling user interactions, and the server should coordinate with the client. Specifically, the client should register with the server, and the server can take two and only two players. Once a client makes a move, it should notify the server; the server then notifies the move to the other player. The server should determine the status of the game, that is, whether the game has been won or drawn, and should notify the players. The server should also coordinate the turns, that is, which client has the turn at a given time. The ideal approach for notifying a player is to invoke a method in the client that sets appropriate properties in the client or sends messages to a player. Figure 36.7 illustrates the relationship between clients and server.

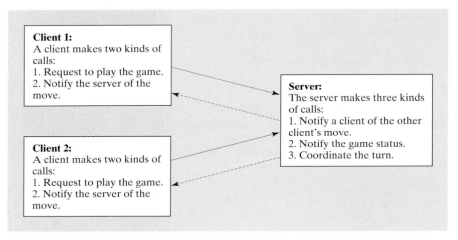

FIGURE 36.7 The server coordinates the activities with the clients.

All the calls a client makes can be encapsulated in one remote interface named **TicTacToe** (Listing 36.7), and all the calls the server invokes can be defined in another interface named **CallBack** (Listing 36.8).

LISTING 36.7 TicTacToeInterface.java

```
 1  import java.rmi.*;
 2
 3  public interface TicTacToeInterface extends Remote {
 4    /**
 5     * Connect to the TicTacToe server and return the token.
 6     * If the returned token is ' ', the client is not connected to
 7     * the server
 8     */
 9    public char connect(CallBack client) throws RemoteException;
10
```

subinterface

server method

```
11   /** A client invokes this method to notify the server of its move*/
12   public void myMove(int row, int column, char token)                      server method
13       throws RemoteException;
14 }
```

LISTING 36.8 CallBack.java

```
1 import java.rmi.*;
2
3 public interface CallBack extends Remote {                                   subinterface
4   /** The server notifies the client for taking a turn */
5   public void takeTurn(boolean turn) throws RemoteException;                 server method
6
7   /** The server sends a message to be displayed by the client */
8   public void notify(java.lang.String message)
9     throws RemoteException;                                                  server method
10
11   /** The server notifies a client of the other player's move */
12   public void mark(int row, int column, char token)
13     throws RemoteException;                                                 server method
14 }
```

What does a client need to do? The client interacts with the player. Assume that all the cells are initially empty, and that the first player takes the X token and the second player takes the O token. To mark a cell, the player points the mouse to the cell and clicks it. If the cell is empty, the token (X or O) is displayed. If the cell is already filled, the player's action is ignored.

From the preceding description, it is obvious that a cell is a GUI object that handles mouse-click events and displays tokens. The candidate for such an object could be a button or a panel. Panels are more flexible than buttons. The token (X or O) can be drawn on a panel in any size, but it only can be displayed as a text on a button.

Let Cell be a subclass of JPanel. You can declare a 3 × 3 grid to be an array Cell[][] cell = new Cell[3][3] for modeling the game. How do you know the state of a cell (marked or not)? You can use a property named marked of the boolean type in the Cell class. How do you know whether the player has a turn? You can use a property named myTurn of boolean. This property (initially false) can be set by the server through a callback.

The Cell class is responsible for drawing the token when an empty cell is clicked, so you need to write the code for listening to the MouseEvent and for painting the shape for tokens X and O. To determine which shape to draw, introduce a variable named marker of the char type. Since this variable is shared by all the cells in a client, it is preferable to declare it in the client and to declare the Cell class as an inner class of the client so that this variable will be accessible to all the cells.

Now let us turn our attention to the server side. What does the server need to do? The server needs to implement TicTacToeInterface and notify the clients of the game status. The server has to record the moves in the cells and check the status every time a player makes a move. The status information can be kept in a 3 × 3 array of char. You can implement a method named isFull() to check whether the board is full and a method named isWon(token) to check whether a specific player has won.

Once a client is connected to the server, the server notifies the client which token to use; that is, X for the first client, and O for the second. Once a client notifies the server of its move, the server checks the game status and notifies the clients.

Now the most critical question is how the server notifies a client. You know that a client invokes a server method by creating a server stub on the client side. A server cannot directly invoke a client, because the client is not declared as a remote object. The CallBack interface was created to facilitate the server's callback to the client. In the implementation of CallBack, an instance of the client is passed as a parameter in the constructor of CallBack.

The client creates an instance of **CallBack** and passes its stub to the server, using a remote method named **connect()** defined in the server. The server then invokes the client's method through a **CallBack** instance. The triangular relationship of client, **CallBack** implementation, and server is shown in Figure 36.8.

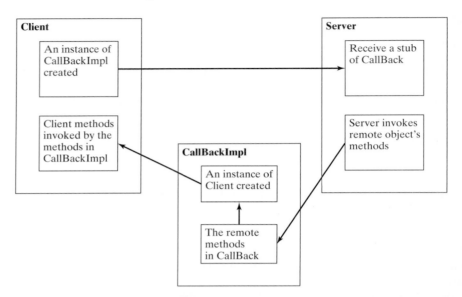

FIGURE 36.8 The server receives a **CallBack** stub from the client and invokes the remote methods defined in the **CallBack** interface, which can invoke the methods defined in the client.

Here are the steps to complete the example.

1. Create TicTacToeImpl.java (Listing 36.9) to implement **TicTacToeInterface**. Add a **main** method in the program to register the server with the RMI.

LISTING 36.9 TicTacToeImpl.java

```
1  import java.rmi.*;
2  import java.rmi.server.*;
3  import java.rmi.registry.*;
4  import java.rmi.registry.*;
5
6  public class TicTacToeImpl extends UnicastRemoteObject
7      implements TicTacToeInterface {
8    // Declare two players, used to call players back
9    private CallBack player1 = null;
10   private CallBack player2 = null;
11
12   // board records players' moves
13   private char[][] board = new char[3][3];
14
15   /** Constructs TicTacToeImpl object and exports it on default port.
16    */
17   public TicTacToeImpl() throws RemoteException {
18     super();
19   }
20
21   /** Constructs TicTacToeImpl object and exports it on specified
22    * port.
23    * @param port The port for exporting
24    */
```

call back objects

```
25    public TicTacToeImpl(int port) throws RemoteException {
26      super(port);
27    }
28
29    /**
30     * Connect to the TicTacToe server and return the token.
31     * If the returned token is ' ', the client is not connected to
32     * the server
33     */
34    public char connect(CallBack client) throws RemoteException {          implement connect
35      if (player1 == null) {
36        // player1 (first player) registered
37        player1 = client;
38        player1.notify("Wait for a second player to join");
39        return 'X';
40      }
41      else if (player2 == null) {
42        // player2 (second player) registered
43        player2 = client;
44        player2.notify("Wait for the first player to move");
45        player2.takeTurn(false);
46        player1.notify("It is my turn (X token)");
47        player1.takeTurn(true);
48        return '0';
49      }
50      else {
51        // Already two players
52        client.notify("Two players are already in the game");
53        return ' ';
54      }
55    }
56
57    /** A client invokes this method to notify the server of its move*/
58    public void myMove(int row, int column, char token)                    implement myMove
59        throws RemoteException  {
60      // Set token to the specified cell
61      board[row][column] = token;
62
63      // Notify the other player of the move
64      if (token == 'X')
65        player2.mark(row, column, 'X');
66      else
67        player1.mark(row, column, '0');
68
69      // Check if the player with this token wins
70      if (isWon(token)) {
71        if (token == 'X') {
72          player1.notify("I won!");
73          player2.notify("I lost!");
74          player1.takeTurn(false);
75        }
76        else {
77          player2.notify("I won!");
78          player1.notify("I lost!");
79          player2.takeTurn(false);
80        }
81      }
82      else if (isFull()) {
83        player1.notify("Draw!");
84        player2.notify("Draw!");
85      }
```

```
86      else if (token == 'X') {
87        player1.notify("Wait for the second player to move");
88        player1.takeTurn(false);
89        player2.notify("It is my turn, (0 token)");
90        player2.takeTurn(true);
91      }
92      else if (token == '0') {
93        player2.notify("Wait for the first player to move");
94        player2.takeTurn(false);
95        player1.notify("It is my turn, (X token)");
96        player1.takeTurn(true);
97      }
98    }
99
100   /** Check if a player with the specified token wins */
101   public boolean isWon(char token) {
102     for (int i = 0; i < 3; i++)
103       if ((board[i][0] == token) && (board[i][1] == token)
104         && (board[i][2] == token))
105         return true;
106
107     for (int j = 0; j < 3; j++)
108       if ((board[0][j] == token) && (board[1][j] == token)
109         && (board[2][j] == token))
110         return true;
111
112     if ((board[0][0] == token) && (board[1][1] == token)
113       && (board[2][2] == token))
114       return true;
115
116     if ((board[0][2] == token) && (board[1][1] == token)
117       && (board[2][0] == token))
118       return true;
119
120     return false;
121   }
122
123   /** Check if the board is full */
124   public boolean isFull() {
125     for (int i = 0; i < 3; i++)
126       for (int j = 0; j < 3; j++)
127         if (board[i][j] == '\u0000')
128           return false;
129
130     return true;
131   }
132
133   public static void main(String[] args) {
134     try {
135       TicTacToeInterface obj = new TicTacToeImpl();
136       Registry registry = LocateRegistry.getRegistry();
137       registry.rebind("TicTacToeImpl", obj);
138       System.out.println("Server " + obj + " registered");
139     }
140     catch (Exception ex) {
141       ex.printStackTrace();
142     }
143   }
144 }
```

isWon

isFull

register object

2. Create CallBackImpl.java (Listing 36.10) to implement the **CallBack** interface.

LISTING 36.10 CallBackImpl.java

```
 1 import java.rmi.*;
 2 import java.rmi.server.*;
 3
 4 public class CallBackImpl extends UnicastRemoteObject
 5     implements CallBack {
 6   // The client will be called by the server through callback
 7   private TicTacToeClientRMI thisClient;
 8
 9   /** Constructor */
10   public CallBackImpl(Object client) throws RemoteException {
11     thisClient = (TicTacToeClientRMI)client;
12   }
13
14   /** The server notifies the client for taking a turn */
15   public void takeTurn(boolean turn) throws RemoteException {
16     thisClient.setMyTurn(turn);
17   }
18
19   /** The server sends a message to be displayed by the client */
20   public void notify(String message) throws RemoteException {
21     thisClient.setMessage(message);
22   }
23
24   /** The server notifies a client of the other player's move */
25   public void mark(int row, int column, char token)
26     throws RemoteException {
27     thisClient.mark(row, column, token);
28   }
29 }
```

implement (line 15)

implement (line 20)

implement (line 25)

3. Create an applet **TicTacToeClientRMI** (Listing 36.11) for interacting with a player and communicating with the server. Enable it to run standalone.

LISTING 36.11 TicTacToeClientRMI.java

```
 1 import java.rmi.*;
 2 import java.awt.*;
 3 import java.awt.event.*;
 4 import javax.swing.*;
 5 import javax.swing.border.*;
 6 import java.rmi.registry.Registry;
 7 import java.rmi.registry.LocateRegistry;
 8
 9 public class TicTacToeClientRMI extends JApplet {
10   // marker is used to indicate the token type
11   private char marker;
12
13   // myTurn indicates whether the player can move now
14   private boolean myTurn = false;
15
16   // Each cell can be empty or marked as 'O' or 'X'
17   private Cell[][] cell;
18
19   // ticTacToe is the game server for coordinating with the players
20   private TicTacToeInterface ticTacToe;
21
22   // Border for cells and panel
23   private Border lineBorder =
24     BorderFactory.createLineBorder(Color.yellow, 1);
```

server object (line 20)

create UI

registry host

server object

call back

```
25
26    private JLabel jlblStatus = new JLabel("jLabel1");
27    private JLabel jlblIdentification = new JLabel();
28
29    boolean isStandalone = false;
30
31    /** Initialize the applet */
32    public void init() {
33      JPanel jPanel1 = new JPanel();
34      jPanel1.setBorder(lineBorder);
35      jPanel1.setLayout(new GridLayout(3, 3, 1, 1));
36
37      add(jlblStatus, BorderLayout.SOUTH);
38      add(jPanel1, BorderLayout.CENTER);
39      add(jlblIdentification, BorderLayout.NORTH);
40
41      // Create cells and place cells in the panel
42      cell = new Cell[3][3];
43      for (int i = 0; i < 3; i++)
44        for (int j = 0; j < 3; j++)
45          jPanel1.add(cell[i][j] = new Cell(i, j));
46
47      try {
48        initializeRMI();
49      }
50      catch (Exception ex) {
51        ex.printStackTrace();
52      }
53    }
54
55    /** Initialize RMI */
56    protected boolean initializeRMI() throws Exception {
57      String host = "";
58      if (!isStandalone) host = getCodeBase().getHost();
59
60      try {
61        Registry registry = LocateRegistry.getRegistry(host);
62        ticTacToe = (TicTacToeInterface) registry.lookup("TicTacToeImpl");
63        System.out.println("Server object " + ticTacToe + " found");
64      }
65      catch (Exception ex) {
66        System.out.println(ex);
67      }
68
69      // Create callback for use by the server to control the client
70      CallBackImpl callBackControl = new CallBackImpl(this);
71
72      if (
73        (marker = ticTacToe.connect((CallBack)callBackControl)) != ' ')
74      {
75        System.out.println("connected as " + marker + " player.");
76        jlblIdentification.setText("You are player " + marker);
77        return true;
78      }
79      else {
80        System.out.println("already two players connected as ");
81        return false;
82      }
83    }
84
```

```
85      /** Set variable myTurn to true or false */
86      public void setMyTurn(boolean myTurn) {
87        this.myTurn = myTurn;
88      }
89
90      /** Set message on the status label */
91      public void setMessage(String message) {
92        jlblStatus.setText(message);
93      }
94
95      /** Mark the specified cell using the token */
96      public void mark(int row, int column, char token) {
97        cell[row][column].setToken(token);
98      }
99
100     /** Inner class Cell for modeling a cell on the TicTacToe board */
101     private class Cell extends JPanel {
102       // marked indicates whether the cell has been used
103       private boolean marked = false;
104
105       // row and column indicate where the cell appears on the board
106       int row, column;
107
108       // The token for the cell
109       private char token;
110
111       /** Construct a cell */
112       public Cell(final int row, final int column) {
113         this.row = row;
114         this.column = column;
115         addMouseListener(new MouseAdapter() {                        register listener
116           public void mouseClicked(MouseEvent e) {
117             if (myTurn && !marked) {
118               // Mark the cell
119               setToken(marker);
120
121               // Notify the server of the move
122               try {
123                 ticTacToe.myMove(row, column, marker);
124               }
125               catch (RemoteException ex) {
126                 System.out.println(ex);
127               }
128             }
129           }
130         });
131
132         setBorder(lineBorder);
133       }
134
135       /** Set token on a cell (mark a cell) */
136       public void setToken(char c) {
137         token = c;
138         marked = true;
139         repaint();
140       }
141
142       /** Paint the cell to draw a shape for the token */
143       protected void paintComponent(Graphics g) {
144         super.paintComponent(g);
```

```
145
146       // Draw the border
147       g.drawRect(0, 0, getSize().width, getSize().height);
148
149       if (token == 'X') {
150         g.drawLine(10, 10, getSize().width - 10,
151           getSize().height - 10);
152         g.drawLine(getSize().width - 10, 10, 10,
153           getSize().height - 10);
154       }
155       else if (token == '0') {
156         g.drawOval(10, 10, getSize().width - 20,
157           getSize().height - 20);
158       }
159     }
160   }
161
162   /** Main method */
163   public static void main(String[] args) {
164     TicTacToeClientRMI applet = new TicTacToeClientRMI();
165     applet.isStandalone = true;
166     applet.init();
167     applet.start();
168     JFrame frame = new JFrame();
169     frame.setDefaultCloseOperation(JFrame.EXIT_ON_CLOSE);
170     frame.setTitle("TicTacToeClientRMI");
171     frame.add(applet, BorderLayout.CENTER);
172     frame.setSize(400, 320);
173     frame.setVisible(true);
174   }
175 }
```

standalone

4. Follow the steps below to run this example.

    4.1. Start RMI Registry by typing "**start rmiregistry**" at a DOS prompt from the book directory.

    4.2. Start the server `TicTacToeImpl` using the following command at C:\book directory:

        C:\book>java TicTacToeImpl

    4.3. Run the client `TicTacToeClientRMI` as an application or an applet. A sample run is shown in Figure 36.9.

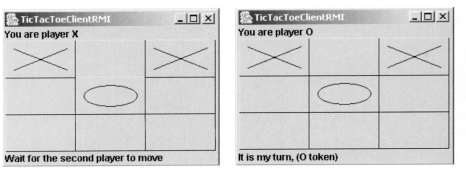

FIGURE 36.9 Two players play each other through the RMI server.

`TicTacToeInterface` defines two remote methods, `connect(CallBack client)` and `myMove(int row, int column, char token)`. The `connect` method plays two roles: one is to pass a `CallBack` stub to the server, and the other is to let the server assign a token for the player. The `myMove` method notifies the server that the player has made a specific move.

The `CallBack` interface defines three remote methods, `takeTurn(boolean turn)`, `notify(String message)`, and `mark(int row, int column, char token)`. The `takeTurn` method sets the client's `myTurn` property to `true` or `false`. The `notify` method displays a message on the client's status label. The `mark` method marks the client's cell with the token at the specified location.

`TicTacToeImpl` is a server implementation for coordinating with the clients and managing the game. The variables `player1` and `player2` are instances of `CallBack`, each of which corresponds to a client, passed from a client when the client invokes the `connect` method. The variable `board` records the moves by the two players. This information is needed to determine the game status. When a client invokes the `connect` method, the server assigns a token X for the first player and O for the second player, and only two players are accepted by the server. You can modify the program to accept additional clients as observers. See Exercise 36.7 for more details.

Once two players are in the game, the server coordinates the turns between them. When a client invokes the `myMove` method, the server records the move and notifies the other player by marking the other player's cell. It then checks to see whether the player wins or whether the board is full. If neither conditions applies and therefore the game continues, the server gives a turn to the other player.

The `CallBackImpl` implements the `CallBack` interface. It creates an instance of `TicTacToeClientRMI` through its constructor. The `CallBackImpl` relays the server request to the client by invoking the client's methods. When the server invokes the `takeTurn` method, `CallBackImpl` invokes the client's `setMyTurn()` method to set the property `myTurn` in the client. When the server invokes the `notify()` method, `CallBackImpl` invokes the client's `setMessage()` method to set the message on the client's status label. When the server invokes the `mark` method, `CallBackImpl` invokes the client's `mark` method to mark the specified cell.

`TicTacToeClientRMI` can run as a standalone application or as an applet. The `initializeRMI` method is responsible for creating the URL for running as a standalone application or as an applet, for locating the `TicTacToeImpl` server stub, for creating the `CallBack` server object, and for connecting the client with the server.

Interestingly, obtaining the `TicTacToeImpl` stub for the client is different from obtaining the `CallBack` stub for the server. The `TicTacToeImpl` stub is obtained by invoking the `lookup()` method through the RMI registry, and the `CallBack` stub is passed to the server through the `connect` method in the `TicTacToeImpl` stub. It is a common practice to obtain the first stub with the `lookup` method, but to pass the subsequent stubs as parameters through remote method invocations.

Since the variables `myTurn` and `marker` are defined in `TicTacToeClientRMI`, the `Cell` class is defined as an inner class within `TicTacToeClientRMI` in order to enable all the cells in the client to access them. Exercise 36.7 suggests alternative approaches that implement the `Cell` as a non-inner class.

KEY TERMS

callback 1255	skeleton 1245
RMI registry 1246	stub 1245

CHAPTER SUMMARY

- RMI is a high-level Java API for building distributed applications using distributed objects.

- The key idea of RMI is its use of stubs and skeletons to facilitate communications between objects. The stub and skeleton are automatically generated, which relieves programmers of tedious socket-level network programming.

- For an object to be used remotely, it must be defined in an interface that extends the `java.rmi.Remote` interface.

- In an RMI application, the initial remote object must be registered with the RMI registry on the server side and be obtained using the `lookup` method through the registry on the client side. Subsequent use of stubs of other remote objects may be passed as parameters through remote method invocations.

- RMI is especially useful for developing scalable and load-balanced multi-tier distributed applications.

REVIEW QUESTIONS

Sections 36.2–36.3

36.1 How do you define an interface for a remote object?

36.2 Describe the roles of the stub and the skeleton.

36.3 Are the stub and the skeleton generated automatically in JDK 1.5?

36.4 What is an RMI registry for? How do you create an RMI registry?

36.5 What is the command to start an RMI Registry?

36.6 How do you register a remote object with an RMI registry?

36.7 What is the command to start a custom RMI server?

36.8 How does a client locate a remote object stub through an RMI registry?

36.9 What can you do if you encounter a security violation?

Sections 36.4–36.6

36.10 What are the advantages of RMI over socket-level programming?

36.11 Describe how parameters are passed in RMI.

36.12 What is the problem if the `connect` method in the `TicTacToeInterface` is defined as

```
public boolean connect(CallBack client, char token)
  throws RemoteException;
```

or as

```
public boolean connect(CallBack client, Character token)
  throws RemoteException;
```

36.13 What is callback? How does callback work in RMI?

PROGRAMMING EXERCISES

Section 36.3 Developing RMI Applications

36.1* (*Limiting the number of clients*) Modify the example in §36.3.1, "Example: Retrieving Student Scores from an RMI Server," to limit the number of concurrent clients to ten.

36.2* (*Computing loan*) Rewrite Exercise 25.3 using RMI. You need to define a remote interface for computing monthly payment and total payment.

36.3** (*Web visit count*) Rewrite Exercise 25.4 using RMI. You need to define a remote interface for obtaining and increasing the count.

36.4**(*Displaying and adding addresses*) Rewrite Exercise 34.6 using RMI. You need to define a remote interface for adding addresses and retrieving address information.

Section 36.5 Developing Three-Tier Applications Using RMI

36.5** (*Address in a database table*) Rewrite Exercise 36.4. Assume that address is stored in a table.

36.6** (*Three-tier application*) Use the three-tier approach to modify Exercise 32.1, as follows:

- Create an applet client to manipulate student information, as shown in Figure 32.24.
- Create a remote object interface with methods for retrieving, inserting, and updating student information, and an object implementation for the interface.

Section 36.6 RMI Callbacks

36.7** (*Improving TicTacToe*) Modify the TicTacToe example in §36.6, "RMI Callbacks," as follows:

- Allow a client to connect to the server as an observer to watch the game.
- Rewrite the Cell class as a non-inner class.

36.8** (*Chat*) Rewrite Exercise 25.10 using RMI. You need to define a remote interface for sending and receiving a line.

APPENDIXES

Java Keywords

The following fifty keywords are reserved for use by the Java language:

abstract	double	int	super
assert	else	interface	switch
boolean	enum	long	synchronized
break	extends	native	this
byte	for	new	throw
case	final	package	throws
catch	finally	private	transient
char	float	protected	try
class	goto	public	void
const	if	return	volatile
continue	implements	short	while
default	import	static	
do	instanceof	strictfp*	

The keywords **goto** and **const** are C++ keywords reserved, but not currently used, in Java. This enables Java compilers to identify them and to produce better error messages if they appear in Java programs.

The literal values **true**, **false**, and **null** are not keywords, just like literal value **100**. However, you cannot use them as identifiers, just as you cannot use 100 as an identifier.

assert is a keyword added in JDK 1.4 and **enum** is a keyword added in JDK 1.5.

---

*The **strictfp** keyword is a modifier for method or class to use strict floating-point calculations. Floating-point arithmetic can be executed in one of two modes: *strict* or *nonstrict*. The strict mode guarantees that the evaluation result is the same on all Java Virtual Machine implementations. The nonstrict mode allows intermediate results from calculations to be stored in an extended format different from the standard IEEE floating-point number format. The extended format is machine-dependent and enables code to be executed faster. However, when you execute the code using the nonstrict mode on different JVMs, you may not always get precisely the same results. By default, the nonstrict mode is used for floating-point calculations. To use the strict mode in a method or a class, add the **strictfp** keyword in the method or the class declaration. Strict floating-point may give you slightly better precision than nonstrict floating-point, but the distinction will only affect some applications. Strictness is not inherited; that is, the presence of **strictfp** on a class or interface declaration does not cause extended classes or interfaces to be strict.

APPENDIX B

The ASCII Character Set

Tables B.1 and B.2 show ASCII characters and their respective decimal and hexadecimal codes. The decimal or hexadecimal code of a character is a combination of its row index and column index. For example, in Table B.1, the letter A is at row 6 and column 5, so its decimal equivalent is 65; in Table B.2, letter A is at row 4 and column 1, so its hexadecimal equivalent is 41.

TABLE B.1   ASCII Character Set in the Decimal Index

	0	1	2	3	4	5	6	7	8	9
0	nul	soh	stx	etx	eot	enq	ack	bel	bs	ht
1	nl	vt	ff	cr	so	si	dle	dc1	dc2	dc3
2	dc4	nak	syn	etb	can	em	sub	esc	fs	gs
3	rs	us	sp	!	"	#	$	%	&	'
4	(	)	*	+	,	-	.	/	0	1
5	2	3	4	5	6	7	8	9	:	;
6	<	=	>	?	@	A	B	C	D	E
7	F	G	H	I	J	K	L	M	N	O
8	P	Q	R	S	T	U	V	W	X	Y
9	Z	[	\	]	^	_	`	a	b	c
10	d	e	f	g	h	i	j	k	l	m
11	n	o	p	q	r	s	t	u	v	w
12	x	y	z	{	|	}	~	del		

TABLE B.2   ASCII Character Set in the Hexadecimal Index

	0	1	2	3	4	5	6	7	8	9	A	B	C	D	E	F
0	nul	soh	stx	etx	eot	enq	ack	bel	bs	ht	nl	vt	ff	cr	so	si
1	dle	dc1	dc2	dc3	dc4	nak	syn	etb	can	em	sub	esc	fs	gs	rs	us
2	sp	!	"	#	$	%	&	'	(	)	*	+	,	-	.	/
3	0	1	2	3	4	5	6	7	8	9	:	;	<	=	>	?
4	@	A	B	C	D	E	F	G	H	I	J	K	L	M	N	O
5	P	Q	R	S	T	U	V	W	X	Y	Z	[	\	]	^	_
6	`	a	b	c	d	e	f	g	h	i	j	k	l	m	n	o
7	p	q	r	s	t	u	v	w	x	y	z	{	|	}	~	del

1273

APPENDIX C

Operator Precedence Chart

The operators are shown in decreasing order of precedence from top to bottom. Operators in the same group have the same precedence, and their associativity is shown in the table.

Operator	Name	Associativity
()	Parentheses	Left to right
()	Function call	Left to right
[]	Array subscript	Left to right
.	Object member access	Left to right
++	Postincrement	Right to left
--	Postdecrement	Right to left
++	Preincrement	Right to left
--	Predecrement	Right to left
+	Unary plus	Right to left
-	Unary minus	Right to left
!	Unary logical negation	Right to left
(type)	Unary casting	Right to left
new	Creating object	Right to left
*	Multiplication	Left to right
/	Division	Left to right
%	Remainder	Left to right
+	Addition	Left to right
-	Subtraction	Left to right
<<	Left shift	Left to right
>>	Right shift with sign extension	Left to right
>>>	Right shift with zero extension	Left to right
<	Less than	Left to right
<=	Less than or equal to	Left to right
>	Greater than	Left to right
>=	Greater than or equal to	Left to right
instanceof	Checking object type	Left to right
==	Equal comparison	Left to right
!=	Not equal	Left to right

Operator	Name	Associativity
&	(Unconditional AND)	Left to right
^	(Exclusive OR)	Left to right
|	(Unconditional OR)	Left to right
&&	Conditional AND	Left to right
||	Conditional OR	Left to right
?:	Ternary condition	Right to left
=	Assignment	Right to left
+=	Addition assignment	Right to left
-=	Subtraction assignment	Right to left
*=	Multiplication assignment	Right to left
/=	Division assignment	Right to left
%=	Remainder assignment	Right to left

APPENDIX D

Java Modifiers

Modifiers are used on classes and class members (constructors, methods, data, and class-level blocks), but the final modifier can also be used on local variables in a method. A modifier that can be applied to a class is called a *class modifier*. A modifier that can be applied to a method is called a *method modifier*. A modifier that can be applied to a data field is called a *data modifier*. A modifier that can be applied to a class-level block is called a *block modifier*. The following table gives a summary of the Java modifiers.

Modifier	class	constructor	method	data	block	Explanation
`(default)*`	√	√	√	√	√	A class, constructor, method, or data field is visible in this package.
`public`	√	√	√	√		A class, constructor, method, or data field is visible to all the programs in any package.
`private`		√	√	√		A constructor, method or data field is only visible in this class.
`protected`		√	√	√		A constructor, method or data field is visible in this package and in subclasses of this class in any package.
`static`			√	√	√	Define a class method, or a class data field or a static initialization block.
`final`	√		√	√		A final class cannot be extended. A final method cannot be modified in a subclass. A final data field is a constant.
`abstract`	√		√			An abstract class must be extended. An abstract method must be implemented in a concrete subclass.

*Default access has no modifier associated with it. For example: `class Test {}`

Modifier	class	constructor	method	data	block	Explanation
native			√			A native method indicates that the method is implemented using a language other than Java.
synchronized			√		√	Only one thread at a time can execute this method.
strictfp	√	√				Use strict floating-point calculations to guarantee that the evaluation result is the same on all JVMs.
transient				√		Mark a nonserializable instance data field.

APPENDIX E

Special Floating-Point Values

Dividing an integer by zero is invalid and throws `ArithmeticException`, but dividing a floating-point value by zero does not cause an exception. Floating-point arithmetic can overflow to infinity if the result of the operation is too large for a `double` or a `float`, or underflow to zero if the result is too small for a double or a `float`. Java provides the special floating-point values `POSITIVE_INFINITY`, `NEGATIVE_INFINITY`, and `NaN` (Not a Number) to denote these results. These values are defined as special constants in the `Float` class and the `Double` class.

If a positive floating-point number is divided by zero, the result is `POSITIVE_INFINITY`. If a negative floating-point number is divided by zero, the result is `NEGATIVE_INFINITY`. If a floating-point zero is divided by zero, the result is `NaN`, which means that the result is undefined mathematically. The string representation of these three values are Infinity, -Infinity, and NaN. For example,

```
System.out.print(1.0 / 0); // Print Infinity
System.out.print(-1.0 / 0); // Print -Infinity
System.out.print(0.0 / 0); // Print NaN
```

These special values can also be used as operands in computations. For example, a number divided by `POSITIVE_INFINITY` yields a positive zero. Table E.1 summarizes various combinations of the /, *, %, +, and - operators.

TABLE E.1 Special Floating-Point Values

x	y	x/y	$x*y$	$x\%y$	$x + y$	$x - y$
Finite	± 0.0	± ∞	± 0.0	NaN	Finite	Finite
Finite	± ∞	± 0.0	± 0.0	x	± ∞	∞
± 0.0	± 0.0	NaN	± 0.0	NaN	± 0.0	± 0.0
± ∞	Finite	± ∞	± 0.0	NaN	± ∞	± ∞
± ∞	± ∞	NaN	± 0.0	NaN	± ∞	∞
± 0.0	± ∞	± 0.0	NaN	± 0.0	± ∞	± 0.0
NaN	Any	NaN	NaN	NaN	NaN	NaN
Any	NaN	NaN	NaN	NaN	NaN	NaN

Note

If one of the operands is NaN, the result is NaN.

APPENDIX F

Bit Operations

To write programs at the machine-level, often you need to deal with binary numbers directly and perform operations at the bit-level. Java provides the bitwise operators and shift operators defined in Table F.1.

The bit operators apply only to integer types (`byte`, `short`, `int`, and `long`). A character involved in a bit operation is converted to an integer. All bitwise operators can form bitwise assignment operators, such as =, |=, <<=, >>=, and >>>=.

TABLE F.1

Operator	Name	Example (using bytes in the example)	Description
&	Bitwise AND	10101110 **&** 10010010 yields 10000010	The AND of two corresponding bits yields a 1 if both bits are 1.
|	Bitwise inclusive OR	10101110 | 10010010 yields 10111110	The OR of two corresponding bits yields a 1 if either bit is 1.
^	Bitwise exclusive OR	10101110 ^ 10010010 yields 00111100	The XOR of two corresponding bits yields a 1 only if two bits are different.
~	One's complement	~10101110 yields 01010001	The operator toggles each bit from 0 to 1 and from 1 to 0
<<	Left shift	10101110 << 2 yields 10111000	Shift bits in the first operand left by the number of bits specified in the second operand, filling with 0s on the right.
>>	Right shift with sign extension	10101110 >> 2 yields 11101011 00101110 >> 2 yields 00001011	Shift bit in the first operand right by the number of bits specified in the second operand, filling with the highest (sign) bit on the left.
>>>	Right shift with zero extension	10101110 >>> 2 yields 00101011 00101110 >>> 2 yields 00001011	Shift bit in the first operand right by the number of bits specified in the second operand, filling with 0s on the left.

INDEX